Handbook of Industry Profiles 2009

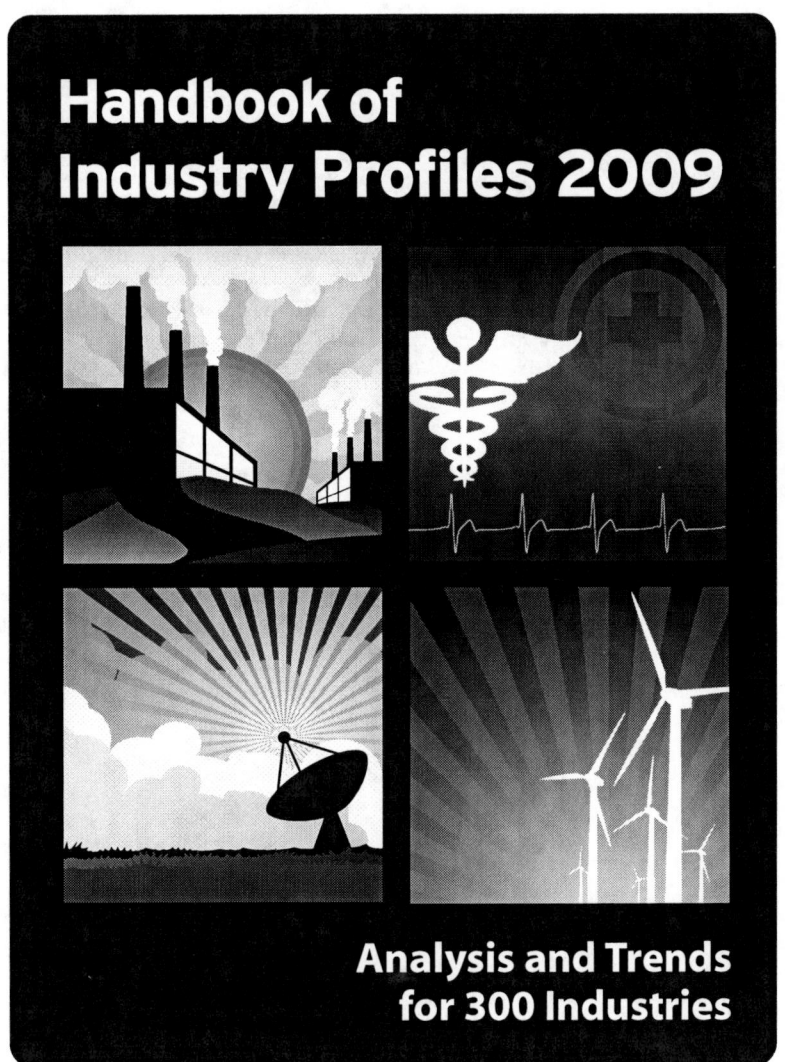

Analysis and Trends for 300 Industries

A D&B COMPANY

Austin, Texas

Handbook of Industry Profiles 2009 is intended to provide readers with information about the industries and enterprises covered in it. In many cases Hoover's has relied on third-party material that we believe to be trustworthy, but were unable to independently verify. Though Hoover's uses extensive procedures to promote data accuracy, the information will contain a degree of error. Readers should not rely on any information contained herein in instances where such reliance might cause loss or damage. Hoover's, the editors, and their third-party data and content suppliers specifically disclaim all warranties, including accuracy, completeness, currentness, and the implied warranties of merchantability and fitness for a specific purpose. This book is sold with the understanding that the publisher, the editors, or any third-party data or content suppliers are not engaged in providing investment, financial, accounting, legal, or other professional advice. Hoover's is a trademark of Hoover's, Inc.

10 9 8 7 6 5 4 3 2 1

Publishers Cataloging-in-Publication Data

Handbook of Industry Profiles 2009

    Includes indexes.

    ISBN 978-1-57311-133-1

    HD 2328.H74

    Industries — United States

First Research's industry profiles are available on the Internet at www.firstresearch.com. Hoover's Company Information is available on the Internet at www.hoovers.com. A catalog of Hoover's products is available on the Internet at www.hooversbooks.com.

The Handbook of Industry Profiles 2009 is produced for Hoover's Business Press by:

Sycamore Productions, Inc.
5808 Balcones Drive, Suite 205
Austin, Texas 78731
info@syprod.com

Cover design is by Cheri LeClear. Electronic prepress and printing are by Yurchak Printing, Landisville, PA.

U.S. AND WORLD BOOK SALES

Hoover's, Inc.
5800 Airport Blvd.
Austin, TX 78752
Phone: 512-374-4500
Fax: 512-374-4538
e-mail: orders@hoovers.com
Web: www.hooversbooks.com

EUROPEAN BOOK SALES

William Snyder Publishing Associates
5 Five Mile Drive
Oxford OX2 8HT
England
Phone & fax: +44-186-551-3186
e-mail: snyderpub@aol.com

Hoover's, Inc.

Founder: Gary Hoover
President: Hyune Hand
EVP Sales: Karen Kennedy
EVP Marketing and Business Development: Peter Poulin
VP Technology: Mamie Jones
VP Operations: Shannon Kovar
VP Business Development: Heidi Tucker
VP Advertising Sales and Operations: Mark Walters
Leader e-Commerce & Books: Dan Tharp
Leader New Business Acquisitions: Amy Bible
Leader Human Resources: Robin Pfahler

(For the latest updates on Hoover's, please visit: http://hoovers.com/global/corp)

First Research, Inc.

Founder: Bobby Martin
Director, Editorial: Margaret C. Lynch
VP Research Operations: Audrey Forrester
Manager Research Operations: Amy Short
Director of Information Systems: Hank McCauley
Director of Network Operations: Charles Short
Leader e-Commerce & Books: Dan Tharp
Senior Editor, Editorial: Barbara Redding
Associate Editor, Editorial: David Woodruff
Industry Specialists, Editorial: James Bryant, Linnea Kirgan, Rebecca Mallett, Patrice Sarath, Nikki Sein, Lee Simmons, Kathi Whitley, Randy Williams
Search Editors, Editorial: Paul Dubiansky, Rich Grogan, Kimberley McCauley
QA Editors, Editorial: Carrie Geis, Rosie Hatch, Diane Lee, John Willis
Customer Service: Leah Kirkwood

Hoover's Business Press

Senior Manager: Daniel Tharp
Distribution Manager: Rhonda Mitchell
Customer Support and Fulfillment Manager: Michael Febonio

ABOUT FIRST RESEARCH

First Research, a division of Hoover's (a D&B company), is the leading provider of Industry Intelligence tools that help sales and marketing teams perform faster and smarter, open doors, and close more deals. First Research analyzes hundreds of sources to create insightful and easy-to-digest Industry Intelligence to better understand a prospect's or client's business issues. Customers include leading companies in banking, accounting, insurance, technology, telecommunications, business process out-sourcing, and professional services such as ADP, Bank of America, Career Builder, and Sprint. Used by more than 95,000 business professionals, First Research can benefit any organization that has prospects in multiple industries. First Research industry information is also available through First Research (www.firstresearch.com), the company's premier online service. For more information call (866) 788-9389. The company is headquartered in Austin, Texas.

ABOUT HOOVER'S, INC.

Hoover's, a D&B company, provides its customers the fastest path to business with insight and actionable information about companies, industries and key decision makers, along with the powerful tools to find and connect to the right people to get business done. Hoover's provides this information for sales, marketing, business development, and other professionals who need intelligence on U.S. and global companies, industries, and the people who lead them. Hoover's unique combination of editorial expertise and one-of-a-kind data collection with user-generated and company-supplied content gives customers a 360-degree view and competitive edge. This information, along with powerful tools to search, sort, download and integrate the content, is available through Hoover's (http://www.hoovers.com), the company's premier online service. Hoover's is headquartered in Austin, Texas.

Contents

Industries Profiled

Industries Profiled (continued)

About the Handbook of Industry Profiles 2009

Hoover's Business Press, a leading provider of company information and publisher of the popular Hoover's Handbooks series, has teamed up once again with First Research, Inc., a leading industry intelligence resource, to bring you the second edition of the *Handbook of Industry Profiles 2009: Analysis and Trends for 300 Industries*.

Industry Intelligence Tools from First Research improve both your efficiency and effectiveness. Without adding hours to your workday, you can infuse sales calls, business meetings, presentations, proposals and outreach efforts with accurate, up-to-date industry information that demonstrates a thorough understanding of your potential and existing clients' business challenges and opportunities.

Industry Intelligence allows you to be strategic through every stage of the sales cycle. Instead of focusing on your products, you bring value to the table with industry insights that your prospects and clients can use to make more informed decisions and better meet their own goals. In doing so, it is easy to engage Business Decision Makers while positioning your products and services as solutions that address the industry and economic developments already impacting their business.

ABOUT FIRST RESEARCH

First Research was founded in 1998 by a sales professional in the financial industry who recognized a direct correlation between the amount of time he spent preparing for and learning about a client's business and industry conditions and the success of the sales call. Today, First Research is the leading Industry Intelligence company.

In addition to the information presented in the Handbook of Industry Profiles, First Research offers a number of other industry data points through its premier, subscription-based Web site at www.firstresearch.com. First Research updates each online Industry Profile quarterly and sends out email alerts to ensure content is both timely and top of mind.

Used by over 95,000 business professionals, First Research Industry Intelligence can benefit any organization that has prospects in multiple industries.

HOOVER'S TOP COMPANIES

To help readers understand the breadth of the 300 industries included in this book, we have supplemented First Research's industry analysis with lists of the largest and fastest-growing companies extracted from Hoover's extensive company information database. These lists vary in length and content, depending on the concentration of large, public companies within a given industry versus those industries with a preponderance of small, private companies.

HOOVER'S FOR BUSINESS NEEDS

In addition to Hoover's widely used MasterList and Handbooks series, comprehensive coverage of more than 40,000 business enterprises is available in electronic format on our Web site at www.hoovers.com. Our goal is to provide our customers the fastest path to business with insight and actionable information about companies, industries, and key decision makers, along with the powerful tools to find and connect to the right people to get business done. Hoover's has partnered with other prestigious business information and service providers to bring you all the right business information, services, and links in one place.

We believe that anyone who buys from, sells to, invests in, lends to, competes with, interviews with, or works for a company should know as much as possible about that enterprise. We believe our extensive print and online products represent the most complete source of corporate information readily available to the general public.

As always, we hope you find our books useful. We invite your comments via phone (512-374-4500), fax (512-374-4538), mail (5800 Airport Boulevard, Austin, Texas 78752), or e-mail (custsupport@hoovers.com).

The Editors,
Austin, Texas,
April 2009

Using the Handbook

First Research Industry Intelligence Profiles are broken down into sections so users can access the content they need quickly and efficiently.

The profiles feature:

Industry Overview — Provides a succinct summary of an industry so users can gain clarity and insight in just a few minutes.

Competitive Landscape — Offers an industry breakdown of key players and the competitive status of the industry.

Products, Operations and Technology — This section overviews the products, operations and technology currently used and the prevalence in the industry.

Sales and Marketing — Suggests ways to gain an advantage in every stage of the sales and marketing cycle. Use this section of Industry Intelligence to infuse marketing and communications efforts with meaningful, industry-specific information that speaks to your clients. Shorten pre-call planning, improve presentations and proposals and realize higher client retention rates.

Human Resources — Summarizes employment trends, growth and wages and the overall state of the industry from a human resources perspective.

Call Preparation Questions — Helps you to quickly prepare for appointments, build confidence and save time. These industry overviews allow you to tailor sales calls, initiate business-oriented conversations and refine sales messaging.

Web Links and Acronyms — Delivers news and industry associations along with clear definitions of the most frequently used industry acronyms, so you can speak a prospect's language from the start.

ADDITIONAL INFORMATION

Additionally, boxed features quickly provide a roundup of:

Business Challenges — Provides valuable awareness of your prospect's key vertical issues so you understand business pain points.

Fast Facts — Offers key highlights in an industry and enables you to quickly establish credibility without wasting hours searching for the information you need.

To round out the profile, where available we provide:

Industry Employment Growth — Based on Bureau of Labor Statistics (BLS) data, the graph shows industry employment growth over a 5-year period.

Average Hourly Earnings — Based on Bureau of Labor Statistics (BLS) data, the graph shows average hourly earnings and wage increases over a 5-year period.

HOOVER'S TOP COMPANIES

The companies in the lists that accompany each industry profile were chosen from the Hoover's database of company information. The lists were created to represent an overall snapshot of each industry, to give an idea of the major US participants and the size of the industry. A variety of company types are represented, including public, private, subsidiaries, and business units. Although there are certainly foreign companies that compete in many of the industries, we chose to focus the lists on US-based businesses.

In some cases, an industry's major players are subsidiaries or business units of larger conglomerates. If we felt the industry represented a significant portion of the parent company's operations, the parent company is listed, otherwise the specific subsidiary or business unit is listed. Also, in these cases, even if the parent is a foreign company, we listed its US subsidiary.

Companies are generally ranked by sales, but in some instances where sales numbers are incomplete, we have ranked companies by employees.

Two indexes complete the book. The first sorts the industry profiles by sector to allow you to compare related profiles within a larger sector — for instance, the Construction and Real Estate sector. The second sorts Hoover's Top Companies alphabetically.

Handbook of Industry Profiles 2009

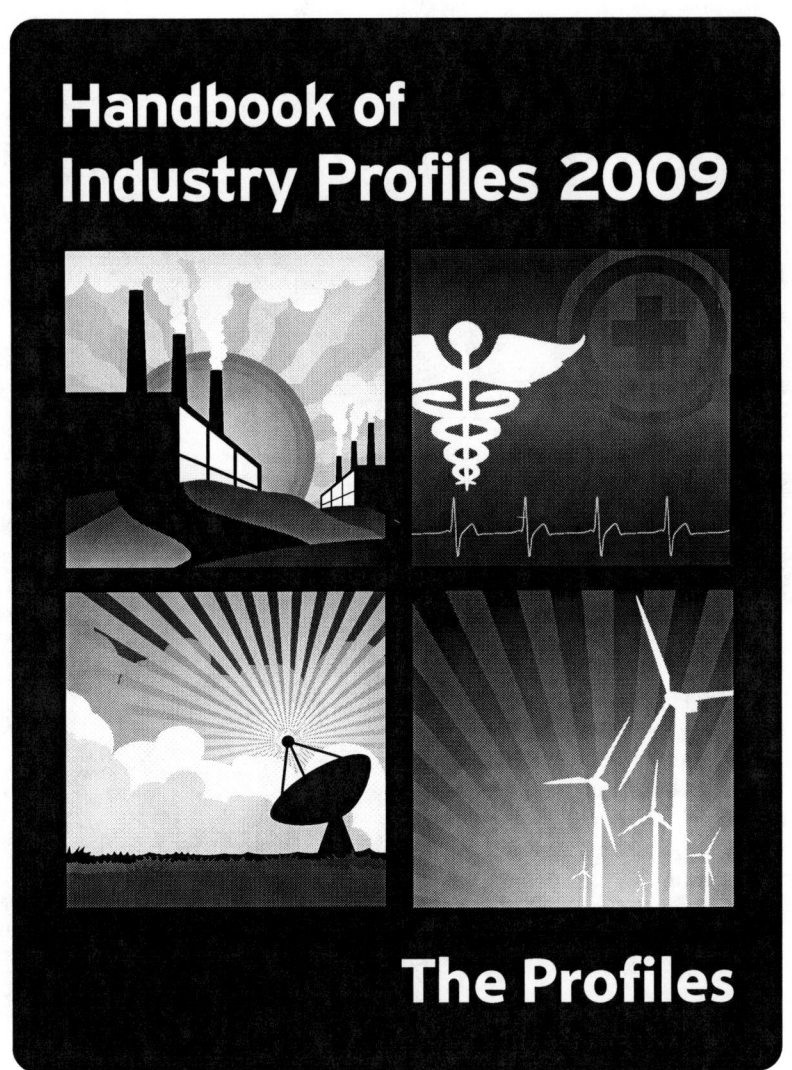

The Profiles

Accounting Services

The US accounting and tax preparation industry includes about 100,000 firms with combined annual revenue of $95 billion. Large companies include PricewaterhouseCoopers, KPMG, Deloitte Touche Tohmatsu, Ernst & Young, and H&R Block. The industry is fragmented: the 50 largest companies hold less than 50 percent of the market. Most firms are small, with annual revenue under $1 million; large local firms may have revenue of $5 to $10 million.

The industry includes firms that provide primarily accounting, tax preparation, auditing, bookkeeping, and related services, but doesn't include companies like law firms that may provide such services as a secondary line of business.

Competitive Landscape

Demand for accounting services depends on new business formations, the increasing complexity of corporate business, and higher personal income. The profitability of individual firms depends on the right mix of services and effective marketing. Large firms have advantages in providing a range of services to large corporate clients and having the resources to serve customers with many locations. Small firms can compete effectively by specializing and providing superior service. The industry's average annual revenue per worker is $100,000.

Products, Operations & Technology

Major services include tax preparation, payroll services, auditing, bookkeeping, tax consulting, and general accounting. Tax preparation accounts for 25 percent of industry revenue, payroll services for 25 percent, and auditing for 15 percent. Bookkeeping represents 10 percent of industry revenue, and tax consulting and general accounting, 5 percent each. Other services include computerized accounting systems, training, financial statement re-

BUSINESS CHALLENGES

» New Regulatory Restrictions

Congress can legislate changes in regulations that affect how accounting firms operate and how companies and other organizations report on their operations and pay taxes. The Sarbanes-Oxley Act (SOX) created more disclosures and greater federal scrutiny of the public accounting industry and increased accounting fraud penalties. SOX bans accounting firms from providing many services to audit clients and subjects foreign operations to new US rules.

» Dependence on Skilled Personnel

Accounting firms depend heavily on the reputation and expertise of senior partners and the competence of junior accountants, who often do most of the actual work. In large firms, turnover can be high, especially among entry-level personnel, due to the heavy work load. Experienced employees often find that their large firm experience is highly valued at smaller practices. The departure of a senior partner in a small firm can greatly impact revenue.

» Litigation Risk

Accounting firms are increasingly implicated in lawsuits regarding their clients' business reporting and operational results. Accounting practices that serve as consultants in shaping clients' business decisions are at high risk. Other factors that can lead to lawsuits against accounting firms include preparing financial statements that don't adequately disclose risks, and failure to detect corporate fraud.

view and procedures, and management consulting. Some accountants have branched into accounting-related information technology consulting, business consulting, and personal financial planning. Small business owners often rely heavily on their accounting firms for advice.

Operations focus on providing a set of accounting-related services to businesses, individuals, or both. Most activities involve preparing, analyzing, and verifying financial documents as a way to provide information to clients. Common activities include setting up and maintaining accounting procedures and books, developing budgets, auditing accounting records, preparing financial statements and tax returns, processing payrolls, and billing. Metrics include client retention and acquisition rates, billing recovery rates, and quality, as measured by percentage of results contested by government or lawsuits.

Bookkeeping and accounting work involves the classification of financial transactions into appropriate account categories in the double-entry accounting system used in the US. Accountants may handle tasks directly for a client or supervise the customer's own accounting practices, whether manual or computer-based. Successful bookkeeping and accounting work often leads to tax preparation and related consulting for the same clients.

Audit work typically involves investigating the accuracy of a client's accounting system and tracking sample financial transactions through it. Typically, a small team of accountants conducts an audit over a period of weeks or months. In large client corporations with complicated businesses, external auditors may have an ongoing onsite presence. Auditing is challenging: to audit properly, an accounting firm must ask hard questions of the client, but to retain the client's business, the auditor must present an acceptable audit. The government requires publicly traded companies to have their accounts audited annually, and forbids an external auditing firm from providing consulting and certain other services to audit clients.

Technology helps accounting firms operate more efficiently and accurately. Software tailored to the industry is common and typically has separate modules for specific functions, such as accounting, auditing, tax preparation, and payroll and billing services. Software producers update industry-specific products to reflect changes in accounting, tax, and auditing rules. An accounting firm's knowledge of a variety of commercially available accounting programs helps serve clients who use different software in their own businesses or personally. Accounting firms often use websites to project the firm's image and promote services.

Sales & Marketing

Typical customers are businesses, nonprofits, government, and individuals; some accounting practices specialize by segment or industry.

The major sales channel is the practice's partners, who maintain a wide range of professional and personal contacts. Customer referrals are an important source of new business.

Major types of industry marketing are direct mail, customer visits, seminars, and ads in Yellow Pages, newspapers, and magazines. Tax preparation firms often advertise heavily in local media. Corporate marketing may include PR like sponsoring sports events and participating in customer industry conferences and trade shows. Accounting firms that ally with other practices benefit from expanded marketing reach and sales capability. Customer service and account relationships are important for retention.

Typical prices vary greatly, from $50 to thousands hourly, depending on locale, specialty, and competition. Per-project fees depend on the complexity of the tasks or the number of transactions, such as in payroll or billing services. Small tax preparation firms serving individuals compete with walk-in facilities like those of H&R Block.

Human Resources

Most industry jobs require a bachelor's or advanced degree in accounting or a related subject. Accountants and auditors of public companies need to be a Certified Public Accountant (CPA). Average industry wages, including for CPAs, non-certified accountants, and support staff, are about 10 percent above the national average. Injury rates are negligible, due to the sedentary nature of office work.

Industry Employment Growth

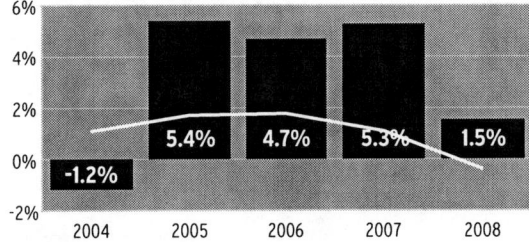

Average Hourly Earnings

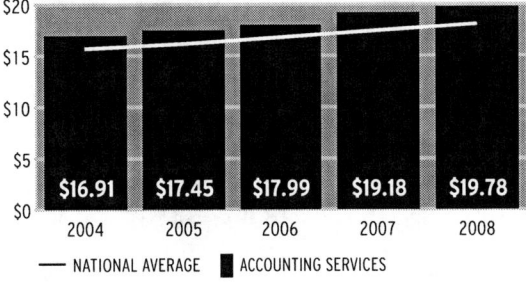

SOURCE: BUREAU OF LABOR STATISTICS

FAST FACTS

» The US accounting and tax preparation industry includes about 100,000 firms with combined annual revenue of $95 billion.

» Large companies include PricewaterhouseCoopers, KPMG, Deloitte Touche Tohmatsu, Ernst & Young, and H&R Block.

» Major services include tax preparation, payroll services, auditing, bookkeeping, tax consulting, and general accounting.

» Typical customers are businesses, nonprofits, government, and individuals; some accounting practices specialize by segment or industry.

» Cash flow is often seasonal, coinciding with the preparation of annual reports and tax returns.

Call Preparation Questions

How have new government regulations affected the firm's business in recent years?

Congress can legislate changes in regulations that affect how accounting firms operate and how companies and other organizations report on their operations and pay taxes.

What concerns does the firm have about litigation risks?

Accounting firms are increasingly implicated in lawsuits regarding their clients' business reporting and operational results.

What opportunities does the firm see in offering non-accounting business services?

Some accounting firms have added other business services to the usual tax and accounting work they do for clients.

How important are business startups to the practice?

The high number of newly formed businesses provides opportunities for accounting firms.

Web Links

Accounting Today

Industry news.
http://www.webcpa.com/current_issue.cfm?pub=ato

Accounting.com

List of CPA firms, news, and resources.
www.accounting.com

Financial Accounting Standards Board

Technical accounting issues.
www.fasb.org

Journal of Accountancy Online

Feature articles.
www.aicpa.org/pubs/jofa/joahome.htm

Securities and Exchange Commission

Regulator of public accounting industry.
www.sec.gov/about/offices/oca.htm

Glossary of Acronyms

AICPA — American Institute of Certified Public Accountants
FASB — Financial Accounting Standards Board
GAAP — Generally Accepted Accounting Practices
IASB — International Accounting Standards Board
IT — information technology
MDP — multidisciplinary partnership
PCAOB — Public Company Accounting Oversight Board
SOX — Sarbanes-Oxley Act

HOOVER'S TOP COMPANIES

Largest Companies by Sales	($ mil.)
PricewaterhouseCoopers International	28,185.0
Deloitte Touche Tohmatsu	27,400.0
Ernst & Young Global	24,500.0
KPMG International	19,810.0
H&R Block, Inc.	4,403.9
RGIS, LLC	1,249.6
Grant Thornton International	1,036.0
BDO Seidman, LLP	589.0
BKD, LLP	353.9
Jackson Hewitt Tax Service Inc.	278.5

Largest Employers	Employees
Deloitte Touche Tohmatsu	165,000
PricewaterhouseCoopers International	155,693
H&R Block, Inc.	137,200
Ernst & Young	135,000
KPMG	123,322
RGIS, LLC	41,000
Grant Thornton International	27,861
Jefferson Wells International, Inc.	2,500
BKD, LLP	1,900
Crowe Horwath LLP	1,800

Fastest Growing* by Five-Year Sales Growth	(%)
UHY Advisors, Inc.	16.3
Kaufman Rossin & Co., P.A.	14.5
PricewaterhouseCoopers International	13.9
Deloitte Touche Tohmatsu	12.7
Jackson Hewitt Tax Service Inc.	10.2
Accretive Solutions, Inc.	5.9
H&R Block, Inc.	3.1

Fastest Growing* by Five-Year Employee Growth	(%)
Kaufman Rossin & Co., P.A.	17.9
UHY Advisors, Inc.	8.8
Deloitte Touche Tohmatsu	6.7
Accretive Solutions, Inc.	5.4
PricewaterhouseCoopers International	4.9
H&R Block, Inc.	3.0

Top Public Companies by Market Value	($ mil.)
H&R Block, Inc.	7,129.9
Jackson Hewitt Tax Service Inc.	423.8
PRG-Schultz International, Inc.	184.5

* These rates are compounded annualized increases and may have resulted from acquisitions or one time gains. If less than 6 years of data are available, growth is for the years available.

SOURCE: HOOVER'S, INC., DATABASE

Advertising and Marketing

The advertising and marketing services industry in the US includes about 30,000 companies, with combined annual revenue of $60 billion. The industry includes large companies such as Interpublic, Omnicom, and WPP. The industry is fragmented: the top 50 companies have less than 40 percent of the market. A typical local agency has $5 million of annual revenue and 30 employees.

Competitive Landscape

Demand comes largely from corporations that sell consumer products, and telecommunications, entertainment, and financial services. The profitability of individual companies depends on creative skills and good marketing. Large companies are advantaged in being able to serve the varied needs of large customers, but small companies can be competitive through special talent or lower pricing or through special services. The industry is labor-intensive, but the high value of the product produces annual revenue per employee of about $150,000.

Products, Operations & Technology

The industry provides advertising creative services, direct mail advertising, and PR and media sales services. While large agencies provide a full range of services, smaller ones often specialize in market or product niches. The large advertising companies, like Omnicom, own dozens of small "brand name" agencies that provide the particular services that customers use.

The two major activities of advertising agencies are the creative development of TV, audio, print, and billboard ads, and the placement of ads with media outlet companies such as Viacom, Disney, and Fox that have a national audience, or with local TV and radio stations and cable companies, or with magazines, newspapers, and billboard companies.

BUSINESS CHALLENGES

» Dependence on Ad Spending

Demand for ad services is highly sensitive to the health of the economy, as spending depends heavily on retail sales and consumer confidence. During the early 2000s recession, magazine ad pages fell 10 percent; magazine ad revenues fell 5.

» Dependence on Large Customers

A majority of ad sales are attributable to only a handful of conglomerates with multiple brands. Manufacturer and financial and service companies' consolidation has created larger ad accounts that require larger ad agencies. Many ad agencies have just a few customers, and the loss of a single large account can consequently have huge adverse consequences. Agencies often specialize in an industry, but can't work for more than one client at a time in that industry.

» Dependence on Large Media Companies

Consolidation in the media industry has concentrated more advertising outlets in the hands of fewer companies. While this concentration makes it easier for agencies to buy advertising, it also gives media companies more pricing power.

Sales & Marketing

Customers are commercial businesses that want to advertise products or services. The larger agencies typically work with corporate customers with multimillion dollar advertising budgets. Because some accounts have very large budgets, even large agencies depend heavily on a few large clients; a small agency may depend on just a handful. Agencies usually aren't allowed to work for companies that compete with existing customers, but customers often hire several different agencies. Relationships with customers can typically be canceled with 90 days' notice. While agencies charge fees for a large number of services, the largest industry revenues are from commissions on "billings," the amounts customers spend actually buying advertising time on TV, etc. The standard commission on billings is 15 percent.

Customers are acquired through reputation and personal contacts. Large customers may ask advertising companies to compete for large accounts by creating the outlines of an ad campaign and mock ads.

Human Resources

Major resources of ad service companies are staff talent and expertise. Salaries are the largest expense for advertising companies, often amounting to between 50 and 70 percent of revenue. Recruiting and retaining staff are a major concern for individual companies. Except for senior managers, however, employment contracts are rare.

Industry Employment Growth

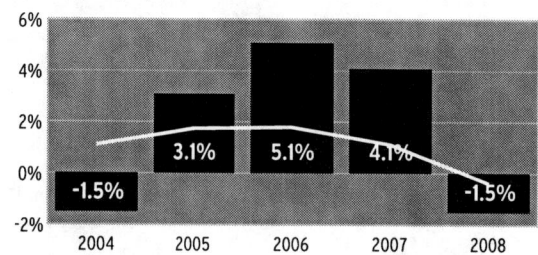

	2004	2005	2006	2007	2008
	-1.5%	3.1%	5.1%	4.1%	-1.5%

Average Hourly Earnings

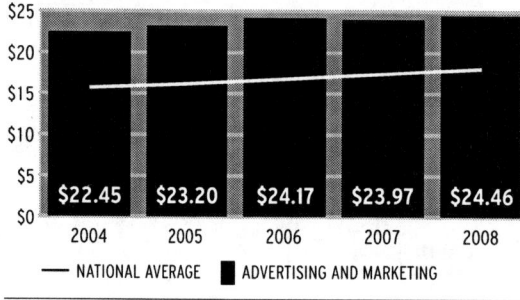

	2004	2005	2006	2007	2008
	$22.45	$23.20	$24.17	$23.97	$24.46

— NATIONAL AVERAGE ■ ADVERTISING AND MARKETING

SOURCE: BUREAU OF LABOR STATISTICS

Call Preparation Questions

How does the company cope with the cyclical nature of ad spending?

Demand for ad services is highly sensitive to the health of the economy, as spending depends heavily on retail sales and consumer confidence.

How reliant is the company on a few large customers?

A majority of ad sales are attributable to only a handful of conglomerates with multiple brands.

How is consolidation of media sources affecting the company?

Consolidation in the media industry has concentrated more advertising outlets in the hands of fewer companies.

What opportunities or challenges does the global market present for the company?

Advertising companies have grown to be able to serve customers in foreign, as well as US, markets.

How is the company taking advantage of expanding channels for ad and marketing income?

Consultancy, PR, brand management, health care, and specialist communication activities continue to grow faster than traditional media advertising, as clients seek more added value in marketing.

Web Links

Advertising Age

Industry news, statistics.
www.adage.com

American Advertising Federation

Government relations information and news.
www.aaf.org

American Association of Advertising Agencies

Links, research, resources.
www.aaaa.org

American Marketing Association (AMA)

Resources, publications, links.
www.marketingpower.com

Cabletelevision Advertising Bureau (CAB)

Network profiles, programming, information, news, links, events, and studies.
www.thecab.tv

Direct Marketing Association (DMA)

Library, events, individual services, professional development, and governmental affairs.
www.the-dma.org

Interactive Advertising Bureau (IAB)

News.
www.iab.net

International Advertising Association (IAA)

Global best practices, technology and the world, advertising and constitutional practices, advocacy and self-regulation.
www.iaaglobal.org

Radio Advertising Bureau

Industry statistics.
www.rab.com

Television Bureau of Advertising

Industry statistics.
www.tvb.org

The Ad Council

News, media calendars, events, and research reports.
www.adcouncil.org

Glossary of Acronyms

AMA — American Marketing Association
DMA — Direct Marketing Association

HOOVER'S TOP COMPANIES

Largest Companies by Sales	($ mil.)
Omnicom Group Inc.	13,359.9
Yahoo! Inc.	7,208.5
The Interpublic Group of Companies, Inc.	6,962.7
Clear Channel Outdoor Holdings, Inc.	3,289.3
Grey Group Inc. (WPP)	4,380.5
Advantage Sales and Marketing, LLC	4,379.5
Guthy-Renker Corporation	1,800.0
Vertis, Inc.	1,365.2

Largest Employers	Employees
Omnicom Group Inc.	70,000
The Interpublic Group of Companies, Inc.	43,000
Yahoo! Inc.	13,600
AHL Services, Inc.	13,000
Young & Rubicam Brands	12,700
Advantage Sales and Marketing, LLC	12,000
Euro RSCG Worldwide, Inc.	11,000
Grey Group Inc. (WPP)	10,500
SPAR Group, Inc.	8,800
Saatchi & Saatchi	7,000

Fastest Growing* by Five-Year Sales Growth	(%)
Affinity Solutions	86.2
Kowabunga! Inc.	78.2
ValueClick, Inc.	46.6
Sanna Mattson MacLeod, Inc.	46.0
Local.com Corporation	43.0
Travelzoo Inc.	35.2
Organic, Inc.	27.0
Adstar, Inc.	16.9
Rainmaker Systems, Inc.	13.3

Fastest Growing* by Five-Year Employee Growth	(%)
Rainmaker Systems, Inc.	71.8
Travelzoo Inc.	41.6
Organic, Inc.	24.1
ValueClick, Inc.	16.8
Omnicom Group Inc.	6.3
The Richards Group, Inc.	3.2

Top Public Companies by Market Value	($ mil.)
Yahoo! Inc.	16,977.0
Omnicom Group Inc.	8,272.5
Lamar Advertising Company	959.6
ValueClick, Inc.	593.3

* These rates are compounded annualized increases and may have resulted from acquisitions or one time gains. If less than 6 years of data are available, growth is for the years available.

SOURCE: HOOVER'S, INC., DATABASE

Aerospace Products and Parts Manufacture

The US aerospace industry includes about 1,500 companies with combined annual revenue of $125 billion. Large companies include Boeing, Northrop Grumman, Lockheed Martin, Raytheon, and General Dynamics. The industry is highly concentrated: the 20 largest companies account for more than 90 percent of industry revenue. Many companies work primarily as subcontractors to the five largest manufacturers.

Competitive Landscape

Demand is driven by the US military budget and the overall economic climate, which affects airline traffic and demand for new commercial aircraft. The profitability of individual companies depends on technical expertise and the ability to accurately price long-term contracts. Large companies enjoy economies of scale in design, manufacturing, and purchasing. Small companies can compete effectively by concentrating on selected components and parts manufacturing for particular prime contractors. Increasingly, small companies are developing system integration capabilities as large firms outsource more aspects of contracts. Production of aircraft and major aircraft components is highly automated: average revenue per employee is over $300,000.

Products, Operations & Technology

Major products are aircraft, including commercial, military, private and business planes; aircraft components, including engines, fuselages, interiors, and avionics; missiles and satellites; and space vehicles. Aircraft manufacturing accounts for over 50 percent of industry revenue, aircraft components for about 30 percent, missiles and satellites for about 10 percent, and space vehicles for less than 5 percent.

Boeing is the only US manufacturer for commercial aircraft, but outsources portions of its business to numerous subcontractors. Pri-

BUSINESS CHALLENGES

» Volatility of Government Spending

Dependent in large part on federal government spending, the aerospace industry is cyclical by nature and unpredictable, due to uncertainty of the annual government budgeting process, election cycles, and the ebb and flow of spending levels. In five of the last 15 years, annual production of aerospace products and parts fluctuated over 10 percent from the previous year.

» Dependence on Air Travel

Commercial aircraft and parts production, which is twice as large as military aircraft production, depends highly on worldwide air travel. Air travel, in turn, depends greatly on general economic activity and security issues. Consumers reduce pleasure travel as prices rise, and business travel falls as security measures lengthen how long it takes to get to destinations. Reduced air travel decreases the need for new aircraft and changes existing orders from developed planes to newer, more efficient aircraft.

» Access to Foreign Markets Depends on Government Policy

Sales outside the US are influenced by US government relationships and trade policies with specific foreign countries. Federal law prohibits US manufacturers from paying foreign officials to win contracts. Sales cycles can last many years, during which the domestic political environment can change, affecting US foreign relations and trade policies.

vate and business aircraft are made by companies such as General Dynamics, through its Gulfstream subsidiary, and Cessna. Subcontractors specialize in producing assemblies for various systems, such as engines, fuselages, interiors, rotors, electronic and hydraulic control systems, avionics, and guidance systems.

The manufacturing process involves forming, forging, metal fabricating, painting, and finishing activities. These activities require greater precision and higher grade materials such as aluminum, titanium, and special steel alloys, than in general manufacturing. Assemblies and systems are manufactured according to designs specified by the prime contractor, and often developed in tandem by the prime and subcontractor. Small contractors generally work for a specific prime contractor.

Manufacturing costs are dominated by the costs of materials and supplies, especially aluminum, titanium, and carbon and boron composites. Some materials are available from only a few suppliers. As such, the timing and pricing of some materials and commodities can fluctuate widely.

Technology is constantly changing in the industry. R&D expenses approximate 2 percent of company revenues. Systems development is especially important in the manufacture of guidance systems, communications, and space vehicles. Lockheed Martin and Raytheon both have business units devoted solely to electronic systems development. Aircraft are designed through CAD that allows companies to design an entire aircraft, including its components, by computer. Investment in computer-aided manufacturing (CAM) is common.

Sales & Marketing

The federal government, primarily the Department of Defense, is by far the largest customer. For example, 75 percent of Raytheon's revenue is from the federal government. Other end-customers include private airline and cargo transportation companies worldwide and telecommunication companies.

Commercial aircraft are generally sold fixed-price with indexed price escalation clauses. List prices for Boeing commercial aircraft can range from $50 to $200 million. Private jets list for $6 to $45 million depending on size.

Commercial airplanes are built and then modified by customer request. Airlines specify requirements for their needs including range, size, cargo, and seating arrangements, then invite manufacturers to submit bids. The winning bid is generally based on cost and favorable financing. The testing and prototype stages can take years. Once in production, the manufacturing line can be active for years, with modifications made depending on changing specifications.

Government contracts are fixed-price, fixed-price incentive, or cost reimbursement. In the fixed-price incentive contract, the manufacturer shares with the government any savings or additional costs from the original contract price. A cost reimbursement contract allows costs plus a fee.

Government contracts begin with an announced need for military aircraft, satellites, or missile systems, and specify various requirements. Aerospace companies submit bids detailing their solutions and designs as well as cost estimates. Firms may undergo substantial R&D to enhance their bid. Following negotiation, a contractor is selected and a prototype developed, built, and tested.

Once won, a government contract is conditional upon continuing availability of Congressional funding. Funds are appropriated on a fiscal year basis even though contract performance may extend over several years. If a contract is terminated due to lack of continued funding, the contractor is entitled to the purchase price for delivered items, reimbursement from the costs of work in progress, and a profit allowance.

Sales cycles can be long, so relationship building is important, as is having a voice on Capitol Hill. Though they're subcontractors, aircraft component manufactures may also sell directly to airlines and the military to have their products specified in orders for new planes. Marketing consists primarily of establishing and using personal contacts with the relatively small number of customers. Aerospace companies advertise in aviation and defense publications and journals.

Human Resources

Production workers are highly skilled and include a large number of unionized workers and many engineers and scientists. Average hourly earnings for production workers are about 50 percent higher than the national average. About 30 percent of all workers in the aircraft and parts sector are unionized.

Industry Employment Growth

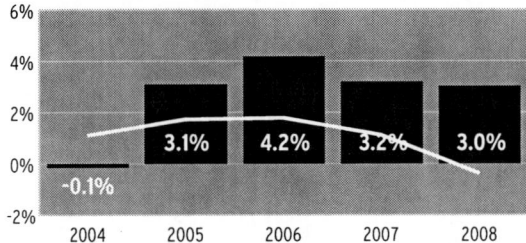

Average Hourly Earnings

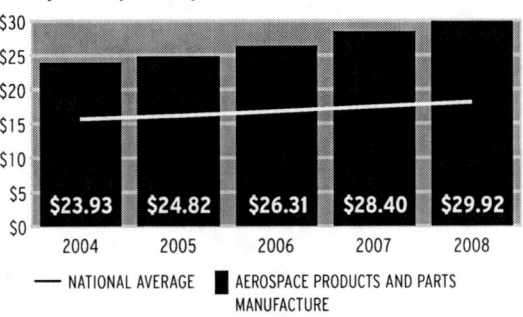

— NATIONAL AVERAGE ■ AEROSPACE PRODUCTS AND PARTS MANUFACTURE

SOURCE: BUREAU OF LABOR STATISTICS

Call Preparation Questions

How does the company manage the cyclical nature of government spending?

Dependent in large part on federal government spending, the aerospace industry is cyclical by nature and unpredictable, due to uncertainty of the annual government budgeting process, election cycles, and the ebb and flow of spending levels.

How is the level of commercial air travel affecting the company?

Commercial aircraft and parts production, which is twice as large as military aircraft production, depends highly on worldwide air travel.

What opportunities does the company see in unmanned combat aerial vehicles?

Future generations of fighter jets will be robotic and pilotless vehicles that transmit signals through satellite relays to ground stations and piloted aircraft.

What opportunities does the company anticipate in the after-market industry?

As existing fleets age, emphasis is on maintenance and modernization, which are increasingly being outsourced.

Web Links

Aerospace Industries Association

Industry news, links, events, press releases, government issues.
www.aia-aerospace.org

Assembly Magazine

Industry news, product news, links.
www.assemblymag.com

Aviation Week

Industry news, homeland security news and issues, links.
www.aviationweek.com/aw/awhome.jsp

General Aviation Manufacturers Association

Industry news.
www.gama.aero/home.php

The Manufacturer

Information about manufacturing in the US and UK.
www.themanufacturer.com

US Department of Defense

Military news.
www.defenselink.mil

Glossary of Acronyms

CAD — computer-aided design
CAM — computer-aided manufacturing
DOD — Department of Defense
UCAV — Unmanned Combat Aerial Vehicle

HOOVER'S TOP COMPANIES

Largest Companies by Sales	($ mil.)
The Boeing Company	60,909.0
Lockheed Martin Corporation	42,731.0
Honeywell International Inc.	36,556.0
Northrop Grumman Corporation	33,887.0
General Dynamics Corporation	29,300.0
Raytheon Company	23,174.0
L-3 Communications Holdings, Inc.	14,901.0
Textron Inc.	14,246.0
ITT Corporation	11,694.8
GE Aviation	—

Largest Employers	Employees
The Boeing Company	159,300
Lockheed Martin Corporation	140,000
Northrop Grumman Corporation	122,600
Honeywell International Inc.	122,000
General Dynamics Corporation	83,500
Raytheon Company	72,100
L-3 Communications Holdings, Inc.	64,600
Textron Inc.	44,000
ITT Corporation	39,700
Goodrich Corporation	23,400

Fastest Growing* by Five-Year Sales Growth	(%)
Aircastle Limited	773.7
Force Protection, Inc.	221.3
SpaceDev, Inc.	59.1
Arotech Corporation	55.2
Ceradyne, Inc.	46.3
Spirit AeroSystems Holdings, Inc.	46.1
AeroVironment, Inc.	45.8
Argon ST, Inc.	45.0
DRS Technologies, Inc.	37.3
Astronics Corporation	29.8

Fastest Growing* by Five-Year Employee Growth	(%)
Aircastle Limited	53.3
SpaceDev, Inc.	50.4
Ceradyne, Inc.	36.7
Argon ST, Inc.	35.1
National Presto Industries, Inc.	27.9
AAR CORP.	26.9
Kreisler Manufacturing Corporation	25.8
DRS Technologies, Inc.	22.2
Arotech Corporation	22.1
L-3 Communications Holdings, Inc.	10.9

Top Public Companies by Market Value	($ mil.)
Lockheed Martin Corporation	33,234.4
The Boeing Company	31,004.0
Honeywell International Inc.	24,116.5
General Dynamics Corporation	22,270.7
Northrop Grumman Corporation	14,728.7

* These rates are compounded annualized increases and may have resulted from acquisitions or one time gains. If less than 6 years of data are available, growth is for the years available.

SOURCE: HOOVER'S, INC., DATABASE

Agriculture Crop Production

The agricultural crop industry includes around 1.3 million farms with harvested cropland operating on 300 million harvested acres, with combined annual revenue of $175 billion. Major companies include produce farms owned by Dole Food Company and Fresh Del Monte Produce, and grain farms owned by Monsanto, Syngenta, and DuPont. As a whole, the industry is fragmented: 10 percent of companies account for one-third of revenue. Vegetable and melon farms are more concentrated, with the top 10 percent of companies representing two-thirds of industry revenue.

Crop farming is the growing and harvesting of field crops like grain, oilseed, tobacco, dry beans, and potatoes; vegetables and melons; fruits and nuts; and floriculture.

Competitive Landscape

Demand is driven by federal agricultural policy programs, food consumption trends, and the grain and oilseed export market. The profitability of individual companies depends on maximizing crop yield and minimizing disease risk. Large companies have advantages in highly automated technologies and access to the latest in seed and crop technologies. Small operations can compete effectively by harvesting heirloom, non-genetically modified (GM), or specialty products. The industry is highly labor-intensive: average annual revenue per employee (operator and hired laborers) is $100,000.

Products, Operations & Technology

Major products are corn for grain (30 percent of industry revenue); soybeans (15 percent); fruits and nuts (10 percent); and hay (10 percent). Other major crops include wheat, vegetables and melons, cotton, and potatoes. Of all farms, 15 percent are grain or oilseed, accounting for two-thirds of all cropland revenue and 40 percent of all US farm earnings.

BUSINESS CHALLENGES

» Highly Volatile Crop Prices

Crop prices can vary sharply due to demand, number of acres planted, resulting yield, and inventory levels. The price of corn, soybeans, and many vegetables has fluctuated considerably in recent years, sometimes swinging 10 percent or more in a single month. To reduce exposure to price volatility, many farms rely on futures contracts.

» Dependence on Government Regulations

The federal government supports crop production through numerous pricing, conservation, marketing, credit, development, and research programs. Government subsidy programs total around $15 billion annually, with $5 billion in direct payments to farmers. The top 10 percent of crop subsidy recipients accounts for two-thirds of total government payouts. Every five years, the federal Farm Bill determines any revisions, updates, or renewals in financial support to farmers; major changes can significantly impact operations.

» Highly Seasonal Cash Flow

Cash flow from farming operations is highly seasonal, as farmers typically don't get paid for crops until after harvest. Farm expenses are often highest during harvesting when crop inventories are at a peak and prices are low. Many farms operate with seasonal debt.

Crop farming operations consist of soil preparation; planting; application of fertilizer, pesticides, and water; and harvesting. Most farmers concentrate on one or a few crops, depending on local soil, weather, and water conditions. Many farms harvest multiple crops multiple times during the year. Corn for grain is planted in spring after the danger of frost has passed, while wheat is planted in fall to allow its root system to develop over the winter.

Grain and oilseed farmers commonly practice crop rotation, typically alternating between plantings of grain corn and soybeans. Planting these two crops in succession improves weed control, lowers pest and disease risk, and requires less fertilizer.

Farmers must accurately measure the number of seeds per acre: crowded seeds can delay maturity and stunt growth, while low plant populations result in poor yields. Farmers closely monitor crop yield per acre, which is affected by weather, fertilizer, and pesticide applications and proper crop and seed selection. Yields can fluctuate yearly. For most crops, plants are harvested when moisture content drops to a certain level.

Most crop farms are highly mechanized for activities like tilling, planting, and applying fertilizer. Harvesting is often done using specialized machinery, but also may require large amounts of manual labor, depending on the crop. One-third of all grain and oilseed farms require farm labor beyond the operator's own contribution.

The average grain or oilseed farm is 700 acres. Vegetable and melon farms average 325 acres; fruit and nut farms, 120.

Common inputs include seed, fertilizer, chemicals for weed control, fuel, electricity, machinery, and repairs.

Recent technological advances include new strains of hybridized and GM seed and improved fertilizers and chemicals for controlling weeds, pests, and disease. Farm machine innovations have improved seed planting, threshing, and the transfer of grains and oilseeds to silos and elevators. New GPS guidance and autosteer technologies can improve crop yield.

Sales & Marketing

Typical customers include grain elevator operators and cooperatives, oilseed processors, food distributors, food processors, livestock ranches and feedlots, and ethanol plants.

To increase leverage when selling products or buying supplies, many farms are members of cooperatives. Around 1,500 marketing cooperatives sell over 40 percent of all agricultural products; over 1,000 supply sell raw materials, seed, and supply to farm operators.

Larger companies and cooperatives advertise through TV, radio, national newspapers, and magazines. Small farms limit marketing to word-of-mouth, magazine, or newspaper advertising. Farms that sell directly to consumers may advertise in local publications or tourism brochures.

Internet sales are rare, though the USDA posted county price (PCP) and open market rates are readily available online. Two-thirds of

all crop farmers have computer access; 40 percent use a computer for their business.

Prevailing market prices almost always exceed the federal subsidy rate. Prices depend on a wide variety of factors, including local supply and demand, product quality, exports and imports, world prices, and government actions. About 20 percent of cropland is grown under production contracts. The extreme volatility of prices for many crops limits the number of fixed-price production contracts.

Some crops can be stored during periods of low demand. For grain oilseed farms owning their own elevator warehouses or sitting on unsold inventory, storage costs can total 5 to 10 cents per bushel.

Human Resources

Grain and oilseed farmers are highly automated, requiring minimal labor beyond the operator's own contribution. Vegetable and fruit farming depends on low-skilled manual labor for most daily operational needs, particularly at harvest. Qualified labor can be in short supply during harvest. To guarantee that plants and fruits are harvested at an optimal time, farmers sometimes turn to licensed Farm Labor Contractors (FLCs) to provide guaranteed labor.

Total wages average around $10 an hour, nearly half the national average. Wages are highest in the Northeast ($12 an hour) and lowest in the Southeast and Southern Plains ($8.50). Field workers earn around $7 an hour; supervisory personnel typically earn twice that. Workers operating special equipment (irrigation systems, industrial farm equipment) often require product-specific training and skills. Farm managers may require specialized horticultural knowledge and often have college degrees from agricultural universities.

The injury rate for grain and oilseed farms is 40 percent lower than the national average. The labor-intensity of vegetable and melon, fruit and nut, and greenhouse farming results in an injury rate 50 percent higher than the national average, mostly due to sprains, falls, and overexertion.

Call Preparation Questions

How does the farm hedge against volatile crop prices?

Crop prices can vary sharply due to demand, number of acres planted, resulting yield, and inventory levels.

How do government regulations affect the company's operations?

The federal government supports crop production through numerous pricing, conservation, marketing, credit, development, and research programs.

How does the farm manage highly seasonal cash flow?

Cash flow from farming operations is highly seasonal, as farmers typically don't get paid for crops until after harvest.

How is new seed technology benefiting the farm?

New seed varieties are improving crop quality for better yield, pest resistance, and drought tolerance.

How has the growth of the alternative fuels industry impacted farm operations?

Concerns about the environment and dependence on foreign oil are leading to growing interest in the production of alternative fuels from crops.

Web Links

Agriculture Online

Agriculture news, polls, weather, markets, discussions and information.
www.agriculture.com

AgWeb.com

News, analysis and market information.
www.agweb.com

American Corn Growers Association

Information about cotton, wheat, rice, corn, soybeans and hay — price support loan rate, export and domestic use, and gross income per acre.
www.acga.org

American Farm Bureau

Excellent industry issues.
www.fb.org

American Soybean Association

Information and news from a national not-for-profit commodity organization representing soybean growers.
www.soygrowers.com

National Association of Wheat Growers

News, market reports, and legislative information.
www.wheatworld.org

USDA Agricultural Outlook

Monthly statistical reports on a variety of crops.
www.ers.usda.gov/publications/outlook

USDA Economic Research Service

Farm and market reports, news, links and data.
www.ers.usda.gov

USDA National Agricultural Statistics Service

Statistics and analysis on US agriculture.
www.nass.usda.gov

Glossary of Acronyms

CCC — Commodity Credit Corporation
FLC — farm labor contractors
GM — genetically modified
LDP — Loan Deficiency Payment
PCP — posted county price
TMDL — total maximum daily load

HOOVER'S TOP COMPANIES

Largest Companies by Sales	($ mil.)
Murdock Holding Company	7,900.0
Dole Food Company, Inc.	6,931.0
Chiquita Brands International, Inc.	4,662.8
Roll International Corporation	1,980.0
Wm. Bolthouse Farms, Inc.	600.0
A. Duda & Sons, Inc.	494.5
Village Farms, L.P.	164.6
Sun World International, LLC	159.7
Bionova Produce, Inc.	3.9
Well-Pict Berries, Inc.	2.3

Largest Employers	Employees
Murdock Holding Company	90,204
Dole Food Company, Inc.	45,000
Chiquita Brands International, Inc.	24,000
Roll International Corporation	3,714
Sun World International, LLC	2,500
Wm. Bolthouse Farms, Inc.	2,300
J.G. Boswell Company	2,000
A. Duda & Sons, Inc.	1,600
BBI Produce Inc.	1,200
D'Arrigo Bros. Company	935

Fastest Growing* by Five-Year Sales Growth	(%)
US Farms, Inc.	2,275.0
Alico, Inc.	19.2
Chiquita Brands International, Inc.	18.6
Roll International Corporation	15.7
Dole Food Company, Inc.	9.8
Murdock Holding Company	6.3

Fastest Growing* by Five-Year Employee Growth	(%)
Alico, Inc.	21.3
Roll International Corporation	17.6
Murdock Holding Company	9.7

Top Public Companies by Market Value	($ mil.)
Chiquita Brands International, Inc.	786.0
Alico, Inc.	349.7
US Farms, Inc.	346.3
Maui Land & Pineapple Company, Inc.	235.9

* These rates are compounded annualized increases and may have resulted from acquisitions or one time gains. If less than 6 years of data are available, growth is for the years available.

SOURCE: HOOVER'S, INC., DATABASE

Agriculture Livestock Production

The US livestock and poultry industry includes more than 1 million farms with combined annual revenue of about $125 billion. Major companies include Cargill, Smithfield Foods, Pilgrim's Pride, Tyson, and Dean Foods. Hog farming, poultry and egg production, and dairy operations are all concentrated industries: the top 10 percent of companies in each of these three industries holds 90 percent or more of the total market. Cattle ranching and feedlot operations are much more fragmented, with the top 10 percent of companies controlling only 30 percent of the market.

This industry includes feedlot farms that prepare livestock for slaughter, but doesn't include slaughter, processing, or packing operations. The industry includes farm fishing operations (aquaculture), but not commercial fishing.

Competitive Landscape

Demand for meat, poultry, and dairy products is driven by domestic food consumption trends. The profitability of individual farms depends on efficient operations. Large companies have advantages in vertically integrated operations and economies of scale. Small operations can compete effectively by supplying local markets, specializing in heritage breeds, or raising humanely treated or hormone-free animals. Average annual revenue per worker for all US livestock and poultry farmers is $100,000.

Products, Operations & Technology

Major products are live cattle and beef (40 percent of industry revenue); dairy products (30 percent); chicken (15 percent); and live hogs and pork (10 percent). Other products include sheep, eggs, turkey, and farmed fish.

Livestock and poultry operators breed animals, supply feed, maintain animal health, provide shelter, and dispose of animal wastes. Feed (typically corn or soybean meal) is the largest

BUSINESS CHALLENGES

» Volatile Market Prices

Livestock market prices can fluctuate considerably monthly and yearly. Futures prices for hog bellies can vary 100 percent in 12 months; for cattle, 30 percent. Chicken prices are less volatile, but often vary 10 percent during the year; the costs of animal feed, principally corn, can vary 30 percent.

» Risk of Catastrophic Animal Diseases

Despite advances in medicine, the risk of infection is always present, and disease can wipe out an entire herd. Animals that are undetected carriers of foot-and-mouth disease (FMD); bovine spongiform encephalopathy (BSE); or swine flu can enter the country in spite of border checks. A recurrence of BSE could halt all US meat exports and decimate the industry. Farms have increased biosecurity measures (hand sanitizers, sanitary foot baths) to limit the spread of disease.

» Customer Consolidation

Consolidation in feedlot and meatpacking industries often means fewer buyers for animals, with only two or three bidders at many animal auctions. The top five companies in beef packing, pork packing, and chicken processing account for more than 50 percent of US meat production. With fewer buyers, farmers have less leverage on prices, especially when packers are also raising animals.

direct cost of raising animals. Farmers must balance the cost of feed against its nutritional value. The feed efficiency rate measures how many pounds of feed are needed to increase the weight of the animal by one pound. Typical rates are six pounds of feed for beef cattle, 2.5 for hogs, and two for chickens. Cattle and sheep farmers can use grassland as feed. Average monthly grazing fees on leased private land ranges from $8 per head in Oklahoma to $20 in Nebraska.

More than 750,000 cattle operations maintain 97 million head of cattle. Three-quarters of this inventory is intended for beef production and one-quarter for dairy. Beef is produced from cows (females that have borne at least one calf); steers (castrated males); heifers (females that have never given birth); and bulls under two years old. Major breeds include Angus, Hereford, and Limousin.

Cattle operations are divided into two main operations: cow-calf and livestock feedlots. Cow/calf operations are typically located on land unsuitable for crop production. Most cattle are maintained on pasture and subsist on grassland. Each cow requires two to five acres of land for sufficient grazing, although arid areas may require much more acreage per head. The average beef cow herd is 40 head. The 10 percent of cow/calf operations that manage 100 or more head account for half of the total beef cow inventory.

Feeder calves gain four or more pounds each day in livestock feedlots, with a typical finishing weight of 1,100 to 1,400 pounds. More than 30 million cattle are slaughtered annually, around one-third of total inventory. On average, 14 million head of cattle are "on feed" in preparation for marketing.

Around 75,000 milk cow farms manage a total of 9 million cows; 75 percent of farms have fewer than 100 cows. Only 3,000 farms have more than 500, but account for 40 percent of the industry's milk. The average cow produces over 20,000 pounds of milk, double the rate in the 1970s.

The number of hog operations has declined in recent years to 66,000 farms as large, highly efficient operations absorb or displace smaller farms. The national hog herd consists of about 65 million animals. The nation's hog kill totals 10 million head a year. Of US hog farms, 60 percent have fewer than 100 sows but represent just 20 percent of industry revenue. Farms are increasingly specializing in a specific stage of the hog life cycle.

Poultry is raised for egg production or as meat, on either traditional or commercial farms. The bulk of chickens are raised on specialized commercial farms that produce 9 billion broilers annually. Egg hatcheries produce 90 billion eggs annually.

Major inputs common to most livestock and poultry farms include feed, fencing, vaccines, animal branding and identification tools, and transport vehicles. Although larger producers have automated many processes, such as for milking cows or feeding animals, most farms still depend heavily on low-paid manual labor.

New advances in technology include improved genetics and breeding, radio frequency identification (RFID) tags that monitor and trace livestock, improved ultrasound monitoring in cows, and antibiotics to reduce illness and disease outbreaks.

Sales & Marketing

Typical customers are feedlot operators and slaughterhouses (packers). The sale of livestock depends on the type of animal and the size of the farm. Small farms typically sell by auction, on contract, and through cooperatives, brokers, or dealers. Many large farming operations contract directly with packers, basing prices on the expected quantity, weight, and quality of the animal. Some ranchers are members of cooperatives that collectively sell herds to the large packers.

Increasingly, farmers market on a contract basis to large buyers, setting prices according to formulas that only partly reflect market demand. Prices have stabilized over the past decade due to advances in inventory and distribution systems for cold and frozen meat. These systems help ensure a ready supply of meat regardless of where or when it's slaughtered. The cattle industry goes through a regular eight- to 12-year cattle cycle due to price changes, demand, and the biological constraints that prevent operators from instantly responding to price changes.

Checkoff marketing programs are a per-head tax on livestock sold: $1 per head on cattle and 0.45 percent of the market value of hogs (just under $1). Managed by the National Beef Board and the National Pork Board, the programs use funds to promote the industry and advance animal research and education. Participation is mandatory, although some producers have challenged it in court.

Farmers generally concentrate on selling, not marketing. Producers may market through trade shows, local magazines, or trade publications. Small "ag tourism" farms often advertise in travel publications and within the local community. Internet sales are generally limited to small and specialty farms that process their own meat. Most market and trading prices are readily available online. Around half of all livestock and poultry farmers have access to the Internet and use the computer for farm business.

Prices are usually quoted in dollars per hundredweight ($/cwt) and can vary substantially from year to year. Typical prices are around $80 to $90/cwt for cattle, $40 to $50/cwt for hogs, and 40 to 45 cents per pound for chickens. Milk is also measured by cwt; typical prices range from $15 to $20/cwt. Wholesale egg prices range from $1 to $1.50 per dozen.

Human Resources

Livestock production wages average $13 per hour, about 30 percent lower than the national average. Livestock production managers are typically paid $25 per hour; livestock breeders earn an average $16 per hour. Livestock farmworkers receive an average $10 per hour, but pay can be as low as $7 at some operations.

Livestock breeders and farm field managers require technical and scientific skills with a detailed knowledge of the specific breeds that they care for. Livestock labor requires physical strength to brand, castrate, weigh, and load animals onto transport vehicles.

The annual injury rate in livestock production is nearly 90 percent higher than the national average. Most injuries involve sprains, strains, fractures, bruises, and soreness from handling containers, falling, driving, and overexertion. Injuries resulting from animal encounters are 50 times higher than the national average.

Call Preparation Questions

How does the farm manage fluctuating prices for its products?

Livestock market prices can fluctuate considerably monthly and yearly.

How does the farm reduce risk of losses due to livestock disease?

Despite advances in medicine, the risk of infection is always present, and disease can wipe out an entire herd.

How have feedlot operator and meatpacker consolidation affected the farm?

Consolidation in feedlot and meatpacking industries often means fewer buyers for animals, with only two or three bidders at many animal auctions.

How will the operation benefit or be challenged by selling directly to consumers, bypassing processors?

Livestock producers are adding value to their products by selling directly to consumers, often within their local communities.

Has the company explored converting manure into renewable energy?

Manure management is moving beyond traditional fertilizer use to systems that can convert animal waste into biofuel.

Web Links

AgWeb.com

Agricultural news and analysis.
www.agweb.com

American Meat Institute

Fact sheets, background, and industry data.
www.meatami.com

Farms.com

Links to farm and livestock resources.
www.farms.com

Feed & Grain

Commercial feed, grain and allied processing industry news.
www.feedandgrain.com

Livestock Marketing Information Center – Current Situation and Analysis

Current prices, production, news and trends in the livestock industry.
www.lmic.info

Livestock, Dairy and Poultry Outlook – USDA

Full monthly data on production, slaughter, prices, and margins.
www.ers.usda.gov/Publications/LDP

Meat and Poultry Online

News and analysis, industry news, featured articles.
www.meatandpoultryonline.com

National Cattlemen's Beef Association

Online library, business information, news, and updated production indexes.
www.beef.org

National Farmers Union

News, issues, links, and publications.
www.nfu.org

National Milk Producers Federation

Market data and economic analysis, news and publications, government and industry issues, and FAQs.
www.nmpf.org

National Pork Board

Industry information, current news, and more.
www.porkboard.org

Pig Progress

Global pork information
www.pigprogress.net

The Beef Site

News for the global beef industry.
thebeefsite.com

The Poultry Science Association (PSA)

A professional organization with information on the
poultry industry.
www.poultryscience.org

US Meat Export Federation

Trade association statistics and figures on leading
markets for beef, pork, and lamb, also supplier
information, marketing tips, fact sheets, export
statistics and impacts, and links.
www.usmef.org

USDA – Agricultural Research Service

News, publications, data products, state fact sheets
and outlooks.
www.ars.usda.gov

USDA National Agriculture Statistics Service – Fact Finder Charts.

Livestock, economic, and research reports.
www.nass.usda.gov/Charts_and_Maps

Glossary of Acronyms

BSE — bovine spongiform encephalopathy (mad cow
disease)
CAFO — concentrated animal feeding operations
CRP — Conservation Resource Program
CWT — hundredweight
FSA — Farm Service Agency
FMD — foot-and-mouth disease
LDP — Loan Deficiency Payments

HOOVER'S TOP COMPANIES

Largest Companies by Sales	($ mil.)
Tyson Foods, Inc.	26,862.0
Smithfield Foods	11,351.2
Land O'Lakes, Inc.	8,924.9
Pilgrim's Pride Corporation	8,525.1
Foster Poultry Farms	1,890.0
Sanderson Farms, Inc.	1,723.6
Michael Foods, Inc.	1,467.8
O.K. Industries, Inc.	928.3
Cal-Maine Foods, Inc.	915.9

Largest Employers	Employees
Tyson Foods, Inc.	107,000
Smithfield Foods	58,100
Pilgrim's Pride Corporation	44,750
Sanderson Farms, Inc.	10,739
Foster Poultry Farms	10,000
Land O'Lakes, Inc.	8,700
Mountaire Corporation	6,000
O.K. Industries, Inc.	4,600
Michael Foods, Inc.	3,759
Cal-Maine Foods, Inc.	1,800

Fastest Growing* by Five-Year Sales Growth	(%)
Cal-Maine Foods, Inc.	18.8
Sanderson Farms, Inc.	14.6
Pilgrim's Pride Corporation	9.7
Land O'Lakes, Inc.	8.8
Foster Poultry Farms	5.7
Michael Foods, Inc.	4.7
Tyson Foods, Inc.	1.8

Fastest Growing* by Five-Year Employee Growth	(%)
Sanderson Farms, Inc.	7.5
Cal-Maine Foods, Inc.	3.2
Pilgrim's Pride Corporation	2.5
Land O'Lakes, Inc.	1.7

Top Public Companies by Market Value	($ mil.)
Tyson Foods, Inc.	3,895.8
Cal-Maine Foods, Inc.	665.1
Sanderson Farms, Inc.	633.4

* These rates are compounded annualized increases and may
have resulted from acquisitions or one time gains. If less
than 6 years of data are available, growth is for the years
available.

SOURCE: HOOVER'S, INC., DATABASE

Air Charter Services

THIS INDUSTRY INCLUDES:

SIC CODES
4522   Air Transportation, Nonscheduled

NAICS CODES
4812   Nonscheduled Air Transportation

The air charter services industry includes about 2,500 companies with combined annual revenue of $8 billion. Major companies include NetJets, Flexjet, Evergreen Aviation, and Global Aero Logistics. The industry is concentrated: the 50 largest companies account for 60 percent of industry revenue.

Air charter is the on-demand, nonscheduled transportation of passengers and cargo and is distinct from the $20 billion commercial airline industry.

Competitive Landscape

Demand is driven by corporate profits and the needs of the US military. The profitability of individual companies depends on effective marketing and customer service. Large companies have advantages in fleet size and name recognition. Smaller companies can compete effectively by serving small local markets and offering lower prices. The industry is capital-intensive: average annual revenue per worker is nearly $250,000.

Products, Operations & Technology

Major services include domestic passenger travel (50 percent of industry revenue); international passenger travel (15 percent); domestic air freight (10 percent); and international air freight (5 percent). Other services include surveying and photography, crop dusting, and aerial advertising.

Charter flights are used by wealthy individuals, large corporations, sports teams, the US military, and government agencies. In general, charter flight is more flexible, extensive, and efficient than traditional commercial air travel. Air charter planes have access to over 5,000 general aviation airports; scheduled commercial aircraft are restricted to the 700 US commercial airports.

Charter aircraft include small pistonprop planes; helicopters; turboprop aircraft; light,

BUSINESS CHALLENGES

» Demand Tied to Economic Cycles

Corporate profits and hiring trends strongly impact the use of air charter services for both business and leisure travel. Air charter services are typically a luxury item that can be cut during tough economic times. Operators face high carrying costs during economic slowdowns, as charter airplanes sit idle on runways and load factors fall.

» Competition from Alternative Products

Air charter competes directly with commercial airlines and auto transportation. A company looking to cut costs may require executives to fly commercial aircraft or rent a limo rather than charter an airplane. The air charter industry argues that charter flights can save time and money because general aviation airports provide access to a greater number of US cities. Rarely is air charter travel the only transportation available.

» Volatile Fuel Prices

Fuel prices are highly volatile and typically represent 15 to 25 percent of a charter airline's total expenses. Smaller operations that don't enter into fuel contracts or use jet fuel hedging strategies are particularly vulnerable to fuel price increases. Most charter operators and fractional ownership companies increase fuel surcharges to passengers and fractional owners to help recover the cost of higher fuel prices.

midweight, and heavy jets; and large, multi-engine jet airliners. Of the 12,000 charter aircraft in operation, around 85 percent are fixed-wing aircraft and 15 percent are helicopters. The smallest pistonprop charter plane accommodates one pilot and one to five passengers, has a non-pressurized aircraft cabin, and a range of several hundred miles. A typical turboprop is cabin-pressurized, accommodates one or two pilots and eight passengers, has a range of around 1,000 miles, and travels 200 miles per hour. Traveling up to 8,000 miles at 500 miles per hour, pressurized heavy jets are flown by two pilots, can accommodate 18, and include a full bathroom and flight attendant service. Depending on fuselage configuration, large charter jet airliners can transport cargo or accommodate up to 500 people. Jet airliners transporting more than 30 passengers must fly under the more restrictive FAA Part 121 guidelines governing scheduled commercial air transportation.

A charter aircraft typically departs from a military base or a small general aviation terminal known as a fixed base operation (FBO). US TSA employees verify passenger identification but don't screen passengers or luggage. On smaller charter aircraft, pilots may be responsible for nonflying tasks such as checking baggage, seating passengers, and performing minor aircraft maintenance or repairs. Upon arrival, charter flights and crew may wait for the passengers until the return flight to the home base. However, around 40 percent of charter travel is comprised of "empty leg" flights: return trips to a plane's home base with no passengers or cargo. Each chartered plane flies an average of 400 hours annually. Charter flights last an average of one hour, and the average aircraft consumes 25 gallons of fuel per hour.

Common metrics in the industry include revenue passenger miles (the total distance traveled by all paying customers); available seat miles (total number of seats available multiplied by miles flown); and load factor (the ratio of revenue passenger miles to available seat miles). The air charter industry's annual 20 billion available seat miles is about one-fifth the size of the commercial airline industry. The average industry load factor is 60 percent; the commercial airline industry has an average load factor of 80 percent.

Major technical aircraft innovations include incorporating GPS on charter planes; developing prototypes of low-cost very light jets (VLJ); and improving a plane's aerodynamic efficiency and load capacity. Third-party companies provide online software and marketplaces for charter airline booking, billing, and customer service operations.

Sales & Marketing

Typical customers are high net worth individuals, large corporations, sports teams, the US military, and government agencies. With an industry load factor around 60 percent, many planes are underused. Air charter brokers capitalize on this available capacity by connecting interested buyers with national networks of managed fleets and individual aircraft owners.

Some brokers specialize in chartering empty leg flights that might otherwise return to a home base without passengers or cargo. Long-term contracts may be awarded by the military for on-demand cargo and personnel transport.

Companies rely on positive word-of-mouth, advertise in industry publications and magazines, and take advantage of media relations to attract new clients. A few larger companies have had success through effective product placement on popular TV shows.

Some brokers and operators use the Internet to provide price estimates, showcase the company's fleet, and highlight the company's safety record. While customers can use the Internet to explore prices and plane options, most charter sales are ultimately over the phone.

Typical prices vary based on customer needs, the type of aircraft, local and federal tax rates, and fuel costs. Charter flights are charged per-hour. Hourly prices can range from $1,000 for a turboprop seating four to as much as $15,000 for a heavy jet. Additional fees such as fuel surcharges, empty leg fees, catering services, and pilot time can often double the quoted hourly rate.

New pricing models have lowered the cost of charter ownership. Around 20 percent of industry revenue comes from buying fractional ownership of a jet, usually sold in one-eighth or one-sixteenth fractions. A typical one-sixteenth fractional contract lasts five years, provides 50 annual flight hours, and costs $500,000 each year plus additional hourly usage and monthly management fees.

Jet card programs account for around 10 percent of charter air service sales. Jet cards require deposits from $100,000 to $250,000 for 20 to 25 hours of flying time. Flying hours, which cost from $5,000 to $10,000 for domestic travel, are then deducted from the initial deposit.

Human Resources

Wages are 50 percent higher than the national average. Pilots earn on average $100,000 annually. Charter pilots must hold a commercial pilot's license, an instrument rating, and a multi-engine rating. Before piloting a commercial aircraft, pilots must accumulate a minimum of 1,200 hours of pilot-in-command experience; however, insurance companies may require additional hours for more complex aircraft. Every six months, pilots must pass a three-day FAA pilot flight check to demonstrate competency. Regular physical examinations are mandatory, and pilots must abide by FAA requirements for rest in between flights.

The overall industry injury rate is 35 percent higher than the national average. Common injuries include sprains, strains, and bruises, typically resulting from overexertion.

FAST FACTS

» The air charter services industry includes about 2,500 companies with combined annual revenue of $8 billion.

» Major companies include NetJets, Flexjet, Evergreen Aviation, and Global Aero Logistics.

» Major services include domestic passenger travel (50 percent of industry revenue); international passenger travel (15 percent); domestic air freight (10 percent); and international air freight (5 percent).

» Typical customers are high net worth individuals, large corporations, sports teams, the US military, and government agencies.

» Cash flow is relatively steady, as summer tourism makes up for a slowdown in business-related charter travel.

Industry Employment Growth

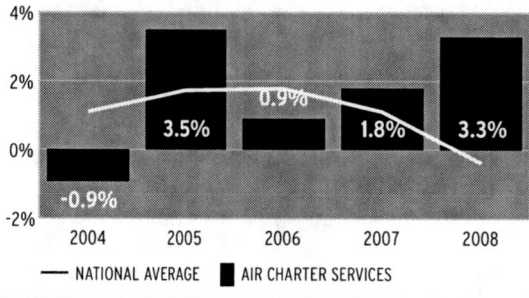

SOURCE: BUREAU OF LABOR STATISTICS

Call Preparation Questions

How do economic conditions, such as corporate profits, impact the company's profitability?

Corporate profits and hiring trends strongly impact the use of air charter services for both business and leisure travel.

Does the company compete directly with commercial, scheduled air travel, and ground transportation?

Air charter competes directly with commercial airlines and auto transportation.

How might the company benefit by adding very light jets (VLJs) to its fleet inventory?

Early versions of a new class of aircraft, very light jets (VLJ), show initial promise in lowering the cost of air charter.

Is the company incorporating GPS technology in its fleet?

By 2020, the FAA will replace current outdated radar systems with GPS-based air traffic control technology.

Web Links

AirCharterGuide.com: Aircraft Information

Descriptions of charter aircraft.
www.aircharterguide.com/ChooseAircraft.aspx

General Aviation Manufacturers Association

Industry association for small plane manufacturers.
www.gama.aero

Halogen Guides – Jets

Fractional jet ownership news.
jets.halogenguides.com

National Air Transportation Association

Industry association for general aviation.
www.nata.aero

National Business Aviation Administration

General aviation aircraft news.
web.nbaa.org/public/news/update

Thirty Thousand Feet: Aviation Directory

Air charter resources and service providers.
www.thirtythousandfeet.com/charter.htm

Glossary of Acronyms

ACS — air charter service
ADS-B — automatic dependent surveillance — broadcast
FAR — Federal Aviation Regulation
FBO — fixed base operation
FDSO — Flight Standards District Office
MEL — minimum equipment list

HOOVER'S TOP COMPANIES

Largest Companies by Sales	($ mil.)
Bristow Group Inc.	1,012.8
World Airways, Inc.	500.0
PHI, Inc.	486.5
Air Methods Corporation	396.4
NetJets Inc.	347.3
Bombardier Flexjet	159.8
Avantair Inc.	115.6
Flight Options LLC	89.8
Omni Air International, Inc.	74.3

Largest Employers	Employees
NetJets Inc.	4,467
Evergreen Holdings, Inc.	4,411
Bristow Group Inc.	3,644
Air Methods Corporation	3,133
PHI, Inc.	2,382
Flight Options LLC	1,800
World Airways, Inc.	1,400
Bombardier Flexjet	1,129
Omni Air International, Inc.	750
Express.Net Airlines, LLC	250

Fastest Growing* by Five-Year Sales Growth	(%)
Air Methods Corporation	24.8
Bristow Group Inc.	12.3
PHI, Inc.	11.2

Fastest Growing* by Five-Year Employee Growth	(%)
Pogo Jet, Inc.	20.0
Air Methods Corporation	15.7
PHI, Inc.	8.8
Bristow Group Inc.	2.5

Top Public Companies by Market Value	($ mil.)
Bristow Group Inc.	1,336.6
Air Methods Corporation	603.6
PHI, Inc.	90.1
Avantair Inc.	29.7

* These rates are compounded annualized increases and may have resulted from acquisitions or one time gains. If less than 6 years of data are available, growth is for the years available.

SOURCE: HOOVER'S, INC., DATABASE

Aircraft Parts Manufacture

In the US, 1,500 companies manufacture aircraft parts with combined annual revenue of about $45 billion. The engine sector is dominated by GE Aviation and Pratt & Whitney, which together account for about 80 percent of engine revenue. The remainder of the industry is highly fragmented. Aside from divisions of a few large companies like Honeywell and Northrop Grumman, few parts manufacturers have annual revenue in excess of $100 million. A typical parts company has 150 employees and revenue of $25 million.

Competitive Landscape

Demand for commercial, military, and private airplanes drives the aircraft parts industry. The profitability of individual companies depends on efficient operations and the ability to secure long-term contracts. Small companies can compete by specializing in high-end, low-volume, or hard-to-find parts, or in production of low-price commodity parts. Large companies have economies of scale in production and purchasing. Annual revenue per employee is about $200,000 at larger companies, $125,000 at smaller ones.

Products, Operations & Technology

Manufacturers usually specialize in producing parts for one of several major systems, including engine, fuselage, propellers and rotors, landing gear, electric and hydraulic control systems, and electronic systems (avionics). Primary subcontractors ("primes") that deliver major systems like engines or wings to the original equipment manufacturer (OEM), in turn subcontract much of the component manufacturing activity to smaller contractors.

Aircraft parts manufacture is generally high-precision and high-technology, where the performance of a part is often more important than its price. Much like the automobile industry, the aircraft industry consists of a few large

BUSINESS CHALLENGES

» Customer Concentration

Aircraft part producers depend on the few, large, remaining aircraft manufacturers, which hold enormous power over their subcontracted suppliers. The high dependence of many US part makers on major US airplane producer Boeing is a long-term business risk. Due to customer concentration, part makers have little leverage in negotiating contracts and have been forced to consolidate to compete, because airplane manufacturers favor larger subcontractors that can produce entire subassemblies.

» Strong Dependence on Air Travel, Military Spending

Demand for airplanes depends on the health of the US and international economies and military budgets. The end of the Cold War resulted in lower purchases of military aircraft during the next decade. US production of aircraft and parts dropped 30 percent during the last recession.

» Dependence on Regulators

The FAA plays a significant role in ensuring the quality and safety of aircraft and the parts that go into them. The FAA approves the manufacturing processes of aircraft, including parts and subassemblies used in the planes, plus it approves replacement parts. Companies that provide parts for military aircraft must abide by a large number of government regulations. Exports of some aircraft parts are regulated, and manufacturers can face severe penalties if they run afoul of regulations.

OEMs, like Boeing, that design, assemble, and sell aircraft, and a large number of subcontractors that manufacture the parts. OEMs supply the designs and specifications for many parts.

Most companies specialize in producing specific parts for a particular airplane ("platform") and often hold requirements contracts that commit buyers to purchasing from that supplier all their needs for a particular part. Such exclusive contracts compensate the supplier for the investment in capital equipment often needed to produce a specific part. Because of the many parts in the many different aircraft in service, even relatively small companies may manufacture a very large number of different parts or subassemblies.

The operations of most parts manufacturers are located in a single facility and involve forging, forming, fabricating, machining, finishing, painting, and similar types of manufacturing activities. The processes often require greater precision and use higher-grade materials, such as aluminum, titanium, and specialty steel alloys, than in other manufacturing processes.

Raw materials are usually readily available from a number of vendors. Parts are produced according to designs and specifications furnished by the OEM. The manufacturing process for most aircraft parts must be approved by the OEM, or by the FAA through a Parts Manufacturer Approval (PMA), and usually requires extensive testing and other control steps. Quality control is a major concern for manufacturers, requiring a large number of quality control personnel.

In addition to new plane production, there is a large aftermarket for replacement parts and special equipment such as avionics, which are electronic communications and sensing systems. The FAA mandates that certain kinds of parts be replaced after a specified number of takeoffs and landings. This requirement spurs the aftermarket segment, which can be significant for parts makers.

The FAA must approve all replacement parts. Parts are sometimes produced under license from the OEM or original manufacturer. The replacement part market is sizable because of the long useful life of many aircraft. The active US aircraft fleet includes about 8,000 commercial aircraft; 16,000 military aircraft (almost half of them helicopters); and 220,000 private planes.

Investment in expensive machinery, often with computerized controls, is common. CAD and computer-aided manufacture (CAM) are used throughout the industry.

Sales & Marketing

The market for new aircraft is divided into commercial, military, and general aviation (private) planes. Annual US production is about 500 commercial planes, 300 commercial helicopters, 400 military planes, and 2,500 general aviation planes. In dollar terms, the commercial sector is about 55 percent of the market; the military sector, 30 percent; and the general aviation sector, 15 percent.

Because the customer base is aircraft manufacturers, parts sales concentrate on these few, huge, powerful corporations. Boeing, which holds about 50 percent of the worldwide commercial aircraft market, is by far the largest OEM customer for aircraft parts; followed by defense contractors Lockheed Martin and Raytheon; and makers of private planes, like General Dynamics (Gulfstream); Raytheon (Beech); and Textron (Cessna). GE and Pratt & Whitney are the largest buyers of parts for engines.

Parts manufacturers usually get new work by submitting a bid in response to a request for quotation (RFQ) from an OEM or a prime contractor for a particular "program," which is a contract for quantities of a specific aircraft. Requirements contracts are often of the fixed-price variety, especially for government work, and usually cover several years of anticipated production, although actual quantities and delivery dates are frequently modified.

Sales to the aftermarket occur through distributors like AAR Corporation and certified repair stations operated by OEMs, airlines, and independent service companies.

Marketing consists largely of establishing and using personal contacts at the relatively small number of potential customer companies. A manufacturer's previous experience with a customer is often the basis for new business.

Human Resources

Because of the high level of training required, industry workers are paid 35 percent more than the average US worker. Manufacturing has a 30 percent annual personnel turnover rate. The annual injury rate of the industry is better than the national average.

Industry Employment Growth

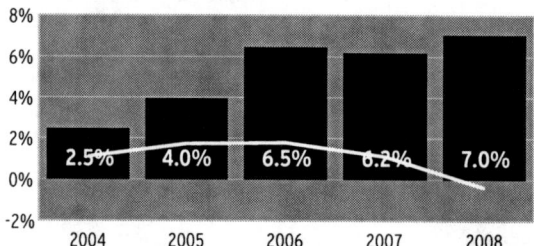

Average Hourly Earnings

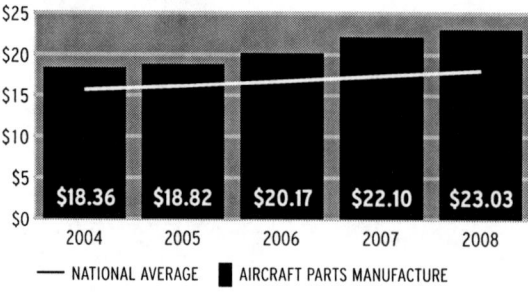

—— NATIONAL AVERAGE ■ AIRCRAFT PARTS MANUFACTURE

SOURCE: BUREAU OF LABOR STATISTICS

Call Preparation Questions

How has consolidation of aircraft manufacturers affected the company?

Aircraft part producers depend on the few, large, remaining aircraft manufacturers, which hold enormous power over their subcontracted suppliers.

What percentage of company products is sold to the commercial, military, or general aviation markets?

Demand for airplanes depends on the health of the US and international economies and military budgets.

What opportunities does the company see in developing and producing avionics?

Electronic sensing, communications, and control systems are becoming more important to the aircraft business, especially the military.

Web Links

Aerospace Industries Association (AIA)

Industry association. Statistics.
www.aia-aerospace.org

Aircraft Electronics Association (AEA)

General aviation.
www.aea.net

Aviation Distributors & Manufacturers Association (ADMA)

Industry news.
www.adma.org

Aviation Suppliers Association (ASA)

Excellent list of members.
www.aviationsuppliers.org

Aviation Week

Aviation Week industry news.
www.aviationweek.com/aw

General Aviation Manufacturers Association (GAMA)

Excellent industry news.
www.gama.aero/home.php

Glossary of Acronyms

ADMA — Aviation Distributors & Manufacturers Association

AEA — Aircraft Electronics Association

AIA — Aerospace Industry Association

ARAC — Aviation Rulemaking Advisory Committee (advises FAA on effect of rules)

ASA — Airline Suppliers Association

GAMA — General Aviation Manufacturers Association

ITC — International Trade Commission

PMA — Parts Manufacturer Approval (from the FAA)

UPN — Unapproved Parts Notification (from the FAA)

HOOVER'S TOP COMPANIES

Largest Companies by Sales	($ mil.)
General Electric Company	182,515.0
United Technologies Corporation	58,681.0
Lockheed Martin Corporation	42,731.0
Honeywell International Inc.	36,556.0
Textron Inc.	14,246.0
ITT Corporation	11,694.8
Goodrich Corporation	7,061.7
Northrop Grumman Aerospace Systems	5,067.0
Rockwell Collins, Inc.	4,769.0
Spirit AeroSystems Holdings, Inc.	3,771.8

Largest Employers	Employees
General Electric Company	327,000
United Technologies Corporation	225,600
Lockheed Martin Corporation	140,000
Honeywell International Inc.	122,000
Textron Inc.	44,000
ITT Corporation	39,700
Goodrich Corporation	23,400
Rockwell Collins, Inc.	20,300
Spirit AeroSystems Holdings, Inc.	13,089
Sequa Corporation	10,000

Fastest Growing* by Five-Year Sales Growth	(%)
Limco-Piedmont Inc.	50.1
Spirit AeroSystems Holdings, Inc.	46.1
AeroVironment, Inc.	45.8
Astronics Corporation	29.8
BE Aerospace, Inc.	27.6
HEICO Corporation	27.0
Moller International, Inc.	24.6
Butler National Corporation	22.8
Esterline Technologies Corporation	21.4
TransDigm Group Incorporated	19.5

Fastest Growing* by Five-Year Employee Growth	(%)
Kreisler Manufacturing Corporation	25.8
Astronics Corporation	18.6
HEICO Corporation	18.2
TransDigm Group Incorporated	17.3
Esterline Technologies Corporation	15.6
Triumph Group, Inc.	15.1
BE Aerospace, Inc.	14.5
Spirit AeroSystems Holdings, Inc.	11.6
LMI Aerospace, Inc.	10.5
AeroVironment, Inc.	9.7

Top Public Companies by Market Value	($ mil.)
General Electric Company	170,697.7
United Technologies Corporation	50,595.2
Lockheed Martin Corporation	33,234.4
Honeywell International Inc.	24,116.5
Textron Inc.	3,720.2

* These rates are compounded annualized increases and may have resulted from acquisitions or one time gains. If less than 6 years of data are available, growth is for the years available.

SOURCE: HOOVER'S, INC., DATABASE

Airlines

THIS INDUSTRY INCLUDES:

SIC CODES
4512   Air Transportation,
        Scheduled

NAICS CODES
4811   Scheduled Air
        Transportation

The US airline industry consists of about 3,000 companies, with combined annual revenue of $120 billion. Major airlines include American, United, and Delta, and the air operations of cargo and courier companies, such as FedEx and UPS. The industry is highly concentrated: almost 90 percent of revenue comes from the top 12 companies.

The government classifies airlines as "major," "national," "regional," and various others. About 40 national airlines have annual revenue between $100 million and $1 billion, and 90 regional airlines have annual revenue under $100 million. The remainder of the industry consists of small air companies that generally have annual revenue between $5 and $50 million.

Competitive Landscape

Airlines depend highly on the health of the US economy, which affects air travel by business and consumer passengers. Because many costs are fixed, the profitability of individual companies is determined by efficient operations and on favorable fuel and labor costs. Small airlines can compete by servicing local or regional routes. The industry is highly capital-intensive: average annual revenue per employee is about $200,000.

Products, Operations & Technology

Airlines carry passengers, cargo, and mail, or have specialized functions, such as medical air transport or oil platform servicing. Flights may be scheduled or nonscheduled (charter). About 70 percent of industry revenue comes from scheduled passenger traffic, 10 percent from carrying cargo and express mail, 4 percent from charter flights, and 1 percent from hauling US mail. Other revenue comes from providing maintenance, servicing, training, and reservations. Some airlines carry only cargo, using specially equipped planes. Some major airlines,

BUSINESS CHALLENGES

» Profitability Depends on Business, Consumer Travel
Both business and tourist travel are reduced when the economy slows. Global aviation traffic rises and falls at twice the pace of economic output, so a change in the economy doubles the impact for airlines. Because of relatively high fixed-costs of airplanes, airport facilities, and labor, airlines can't easily adjust to reduced passenger traffic.

» Fuel Costs can Vary Highly
Aviation fuel accounts for 15 to 20 percent of industry operating costs, relatively more for airlines with low labor costs. Fuel costs can change rapidly, making it difficult for airlines to adjust ticket prices. Some airlines use futures contracts to protect against cost increases. Newer planes have better fuel consumption.

» High Labor Costs
Labor costs for many large airlines have remained high, despite lower ticket prices and reduced passenger volume. Wages, salaries, and benefits accounted for 32 percent of American Airlines parent company AMR's operating costs in 2005. The financial success of discount airlines has depended heavily on lower labor costs.

including United, Northwest, and American, have large cargo operations that contribute 5 to 10 percent of revenue. For smaller passenger airlines, cargo may contribute more than 10 percent of revenue.

The basic operations of airlines include acquiring and maintaining airplanes, acquiring and operating airport facilities, acquiring passengers or freight, managing staff, and operating flights.

The flight equipment (airplanes) that an airline uses is crucial to efficient operations. The cost, capacity, and fuel efficiency of airplanes vary substantially. The major airlines operate about 20 types of aircraft with a total of about

4,700 planes; of these, around 600 were made by Airbus and around 4,000 by Boeing. Manufacturers of smaller aircraft for regional airlines, with seating capacities of 30 to 90, include Bombardier, Fokker, Embraer, and Saab. The largest aircraft can hold 360 passengers or 70 tons of cargo, and are used for long flights with a "stage length" of more than 3,000 miles, but the major carriers operate mainly planes that hold from 130 to 175 passengers.

A large plane like the Boeing 747 consumes 3,500 gallons of fuel per hour, while a midsize one like the Boeing 737 consumes about 800 gallons. Larger planes require a larger crew. The operating cost of an airplane is often expressed in cents per seat mile, with typical values between 3 and 7 cents. The list price for a new Boeing 737-700 is close to $50 million. A Boeing 747-400 lists for $200 million. The actual price airlines pay for new planes can be substantially lower than the list price, especially if they place big orders. A large market exists for used aircraft, which can have a useful life of 20 years or more.

Airlines lease terminals; ticket counters; gates (sometimes called "slots"); cargo facilities; and maintenance facilities from airports, which are usually owned by local government authorities. In some cases, airlines can sublease their facilities to other airlines. About 640 airports have regular airline service in the US; close to 220 are served by the large carriers. American and Delta have service to virtually all 220, while Southwest serves about 60. In addition to paying for airport facilities, airlines pay landing fees for each flight, which are $1 per 1,000 pounds of landing weight at a regional airport, or about $100 for a Boeing 737. Landing fees at major airports can be more than twice as high. Routine aircraft maintenance is done at local airports, but the big carriers typically have one or several large central maintenance facilities for major overhauls. Many smaller airlines contract maintenance out to the major carriers.

Because of the large number of flight departures — American, Delta, and Southwest each handle 1 million departures annually — scheduling staff and equipment is a major logistics problem. Southwest operates its million departures with 365 aircraft and 30,000 employees; 10,000 are flight crew and 15,000 ground crew. Airlines measure in terms of departures, rather than flights, because a single flight may have several stops. Each airplane makes an average of 2,700 departures, about eight per day.

Airlines measure their performance using a number of metrics. Southwest carried 78 million revenue passengers in a recent year, about 75 per flight, and flew 60 billion revenue passenger miles (RPM). The average flight segment stage length was 600 miles. The full capacity of its flights in a recent year was 85 billion available seat miles (ASM). The load factor of its flights was 71 percent; that is, the average flight was 71 percent full (divide RPM by ASM). Operating revenue per ASM was 9 cents, while operating expense per ASM was 8 cents. The average passenger fare was $94, which translates into average revenue of about $7,000 per flight for this discount carrier.

Sales & Marketing

Most ticket sales occur via computerized reservation systems (CRS) that show the various flight options between cities. Airlines pay fees to CRS operators for tickets bought through their system, such as Sabre, Worldspan, Amadeus, SystemOne, and Galileo, which are accessed by travel agents and online sites. Internet travel sites like Expedia, Travelocity, and Orbitz also feed reservations to the airlines. Airlines also operate their own reservation websites. Airline-operated sites are captive, in that they promote only one airline and its partners, and are an increasingly important source of passengers. Southwest, for example, receives the majority of its passengers through its own website, since it doesn't sell through other travel sites.

Major airlines use TV and magazine advertising, but smaller airlines often do no media advertising. Marketing alliances — for example, with other airlines, travel organizations, and destination sites —and code-sharing agreements have become common ways for airlines to effectively expand the number of markets they serve and passengers they can reach. Code-sharing allows a ticketing airline to use the operating airline's flight code to book flights on that airline's planes.

Pricing systems vary considerably among airlines. Small airlines typically have set prices, but some large airlines have complicated computerized pricing schemes that attempt to maximize the revenue for a particular flight by offering different prices at different times, depending on how quickly a flight is filling. In addition to selling tickets individually, airlines may sell blocks of discounted tickets to wholesalers, such as Hotwire, Priceline, and Travelweb. Many airlines run loyalty programs in the form of mileage or point accumulation systems (frequent flyer programs) that entitle passengers to free tickets or upgraded service.

Human Resources

Annual personnel turnover is around 40 percent, lower than the national average of 46 percent for all private industry. The industry injury rate is very high, more than three times the national average, mainly due to handling baggage and freight. A third of accidents are serious enough to result in more than 30 days away from work.

The employees of most airlines belong to unions that represent the various specialized functions in their company, including pilots, flight attendants, mechanics, and ground crew. Because labor is the largest single expense of airlines, wages and benefits are critical. Pilots and mechanics require special certification by the FAA. Pilots and other flight crew are limited, on average, to working no more than 20 hours per week.

Industry Employment Growth

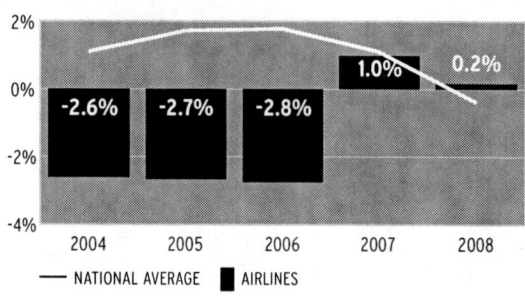

SOURCE: BUREAU OF LABOR STATISTICS

Call Preparation Questions

How has the company adapted to changes in business and leisure travel?

Both business and tourist travel are reduced when the economy slows.

How does the company protect itself against rising fuel prices?

Aviation fuel accounts for 15 to 20 percent of industry operating costs, relatively more for airlines with low labor costs.

Has the airline been able to lower labor costs?

Labor costs for many large airlines have remained high, despite lower ticket prices and reduced passenger volume.

Does the airline plan to acquire more fuel-efficient aircraft?

The fuel consumption of aircraft varies widely.

How is the Internet affecting ticket sales for the airline?

The convenience of buying airplane tickets over the Internet appeals to passengers and is an inexpensive source of customers for airlines.

Web Links

Air Transport Association

News, economics, government affairs, and publications.
www.airlines.org

Air Transport World

News. Other information by subscription.
www.atwonline.com

AirWise.com

International industry news.
news.airwise.com

Aviation Week

US industry news.
www.aviationweek.com/aw

Boeing — Aircraft List Prices

Current list prices for new aircraft.
www.boeing.com/commercial/prices

Boeing — Current Market Outlook

Boeing strategic airline market assessment.
www.boeing.com/commercial/cmo

Bureau of Transportation Statistics (BTS)

Industry operating and financial statistics.
www.bts.gov

DOT Office of the Assistant Secretary for Aviation and International Affairs

Quarterly financial and operating statistics for all major airlines. Policy and regulatory issues.
ostpxweb.dot.gov/aviation

EIA — Jet Fuel

Spot prices for jet fuel from the Energy Information Administration.
tonto.eia.doe.gov/dnav/pet/hist/rjetnyhM.htm

International Air Transport Association (IATA)

News, statistics, and articles on opening page.
www.iata.org

Regional Airline Association

Regional statistics.
www.raa.org

Glossary of Acronyms

ASM — available seat miles
BTS — Bureau of Travel Statistics
CRS — computerized reservation system
LCC — low-cost carrier
OEM — original equipment manufacturer
PMA — parts manufacturing authorities
RPM — revenue passenger miles

HOOVER'S TOP COMPANIES

Largest Companies by Sales	($ mil.)
AMR Corporation	23,766.0
Delta Air Lines, Inc.	22,697.0
UAL Corporation	20,194.0
Continental Airlines, Inc.	15,241.0
Northwest Airlines Corporation	12,528.0
US Airways Group, Inc.	12,118.0
Southwest Airlines Co.	11,023.0
Alaska Air Group, Inc.	3,662.6
SkyWest, Inc.	3,496.3
JetBlue Airways Corporation	3,388.0

Largest Employers	Employees
AMR Corporation	85,500
Delta Air Lines, Inc.	55,044
UAL Corporation	55,000
Continental Airlines, Inc.	45,610
US Airways Group, Inc.	39,600
Southwest Airlines Co.	34,378
Northwest Airlines Corporation	34,000
Alaska Air Group, Inc.	14,710
JetBlue Airways Corporation	11,632
SkyWest, Inc.	10,249

Fastest Growing* by Five-Year Sales Growth	(%)
Allegiant Travel Company	58.7
Hawaiian Holdings, Inc.	33.9
SkyWest, Inc.	31.5
Republic Airways Holdings Inc.	28.6
JetBlue Airways Corporation	27.7
Frontier Airlines Holdings, Inc.	24.4
AirTran Holdings, Inc.	22.7
Mesa Air Group, Inc.	17.2
Gulfstream International Group, Inc.	15.8
Pinnacle Airlines Corp.	13.6

Fastest Growing* by Five-Year Employee Growth	(%)
Allegiant Travel Company	48.3
Republic Airways Holdings Inc.	26.6
SkyWest, Inc.	19.9
Pinnacle Airlines Corp.	13.4
Frontier Airlines Holdings, Inc.	12.8
AirTran Holdings, Inc.	11.5
JetBlue Airways Corporation	8.6
Horizon Air Industries, Inc.	2.8

Top Public Companies by Market Value	($ mil.)
Delta Air Lines, Inc.	7,966.3
Southwest Airlines Co.	6,378.7
Northwest Airlines Corporation	3,430.6
AMR Corporation	2,976.4
UAL Corporation	1,543.2

* These rates are compounded annualized increases and may have resulted from acquisitions or one time gains. If less than 6 years of data are available, growth is for the years available.

SOURCE: HOOVER'S, INC., DATABASE

Ambulance Services

THIS INDUSTRY INCLUDES:

SIC CODES
4119   Local Passenger
         Transportation

NAICS CODES
621910 Ambulance
         Services

The US ambulance services industry includes about 3,000 firms with combined annual revenue over $7 billion. Major companies are American Medical Response and Rural/Metro Corporation. The industry is fragmented: the 50 largest companies represent 45 percent of revenue. Most ambulance companies are small and local with one location and fewer than 15 employees; only about 200 have revenue over $5 million.

This industry profile doesn't include public, fire department, and hospital-based ambulance services, or non-medical transportation services for the disabled or elderly.

Competitive Landscape

Emergency medical events and an aging population drive demand for ambulance services. The profitability of individual companies depends on quick and effective response and operational efficiency. Large companies have advantages of scale in contract negotiations, service capabilities, technology, and geographic coverage. Small companies can compete effectively by providing superior service in specific locales. The industry is labor intensive: average annual revenue per worker is a relatively low $54,000.

Products, Operations & Technology

The major service is medical transport of patients, which provides over 90 percent of industry revenue; sales of medical equipment, supplies, and other items provides 3 percent. Other services each provide less than 1 percent of industry revenue, and include patient care and rental or lease of goods and equipment. Medical transport services are for emergency and non-emergency patients; emergency calls often require medical assistance. Non-emergency services include transportation for medically unstable patients and medical transfers between health care facilities.

BUSINESS CHALLENGES

» Dependence on Healthcare, Insurance Industries
Ambulance service firms depend on the health care and insurance industries, which are highly regulated and have strict procedures, especially for awarding contracts and paying contractors. Ambulance firms with municipal or other government contracts must provide emergency service, regardless of a patient's ability to pay, and are subject to insurance companies' reimbursement rates. Non-reimbursable services can equal 20 percent of some ambulance firms' gross revenue. Consolidation of hospitals and other health care facilities limits opportunities for ambulance services contracts.

» Rapid Growth in Demand
As the US population ages and increases, demand for ambulance transport is rising dramatically. Ambulance service employment, an indicator of demand, grew 22 percent in a recent five-year period; national employment rose only 3.9 percent. The population 65 and over will increase 35 percent between 2010 and 2020, according to government projections. Continually rising demand affects preparedness planning and operations at ambulance services companies.

» High Risk, High Liability Exposure
Due to the high risk, life-or-death nature of emergency medical services and transport, ambulance firms have high liability exposure. Medical errors, inadequate response time, and vehicle accidents can lead to negligence, malpractice, or wrongful death lawsuits. Liability lawsuits can be complicated and costly. Increases in the number of patient lawsuits and the value of jury awards have been common in recent years, which contribute to the rising cost of general and professional liability insurance.

Ambulance service companies respond to emergency calls by dispatching vehicles and personnel to attend to patients at their location and en route to a hospital. A dispatched ambulance usually has a driver with some first aid skills and may have a non-medical attendant, an

Emergency Medical Technician, or a more highly trained paramedic, who can administer life-saving procedures and medicine. Ambulance firms generally receive emergency calls from the local 911 center, but some may operate the service. Firms use their own dispatch systems to communicate with their vehicles and other facilities in the public's Emergency Medical System, such as hospitals, police, and fire departments. Firms handle non-emergency calls by request or on a schedule.

Ambulance companies provide services to clients, such as medical facilities or towns, either on a master contract and/or on standby. Contracts generally range from one to five years with renewal options, and require the ambulance service provider to meet response time and other performance criteria. Contracts with public entities, including towns, counties, and fire departments, usually require a formal bidding process and response to a Request for Proposal. Ambulance firms may serve as subcontractors to other entities or may hire subcontractors, such as paramedics. Almost half of the 200 largest US cities outsourced ambulance services to private providers in 2005, according to the Journal of Emergency Medical Services. Private companies are the primary providers of non-emergency ambulance services.

The key industry metric is response level. For emergency ground ambulance service, the response level is the percentage of sites a company reaches within the industry standard of 10 minutes or less from the first call. Contracts for emergency ambulance services often specify meeting the response standard in over 90 percent of cases. For emergency aircraft, the response metric is the number of minutes from call receipt to liftoff. Quick response is crucial for patients with life-threatening conditions; many in the industry refer to the first 60 minutes from illness onset or injury as the "golden hour" within which to save lives. For non-emergencies, the response metric reflects reliability in picking up patients on time. Internal operational metrics include transport volume, amount collected per transport, and cost per transport.

Payment for services comes mainly from third-party payers, such as Medicare, Medicaid, and commercial insurance companies. Bills also go directly to self-pay patients, typically those who don't have insurance or government benefits. Third-party payers don't always pay the entire bill and self-pay patients have a high rate of non-payment; partial or non-payment results in write-offs. Accurate documentation of patients,

services, and processes is extremely important to comply with government, insurance, and financial requirements; to get paid; and to avoid or address complaints.

Equipment and supplies are generally bought through distributors. Emergency vehicles include ground, helicopter, and fixed-wing ambulances; critical care trucks; and supervisory vehicles. Medical equipment and supplies for emergency patient care include heart monitors, automatic blood pressure cuffs, head immobilizers, stretchers, and gurneys. Ambulance service companies maintain vehicles and equipment in-house or outsource it.

Technology is critical to operations. On-board medical equipment is highly technical and computerized. Computer-aided dispatch and deployment systems function 24/7 year-round using dedicated radio frequencies licensed by the FCC. GPS tracks vehicle locations, helping deploy the nearest ambulance to the emergency site. Communication systems enable ambulance personnel to describe patient status to the hospital emergency medical team, who advise en-route treatment. On-board monitors detect driver safety infractions and document activity. Post-call and while on-board, medics record and send patient data wirelessly to billing and backoffice systems. Status planning and management systems gather and analyze data for operations review. Compliance systems track adherence to government requirements, such as for health care operations, corporate reporting, and patient privacy.

Sales & Marketing

Typical customers are towns, counties, and other government entities; hospitals, nursing facilities, and other health care providers; and insurance companies. Government entities that provide local emergency 911 services are major customers. Consumers are the end-user recipients of ambulance service transport and medical care. Patients either have health insurance or are self-payers, a category that includes those unable or unwilling to pay for services.

In larger companies, selling is via a sales force and account managers, but in small firms the owners are the primary salespeople. Marketing is primarily via customer and prospect visits and by formally qualifying to participate in bidding opportunities. Often the only way to sell is by responding to Requests for Proposals, a common process in awarding ambulance services contracts. The main goals of sales and marketing teams are to renew and get new contracts.

Sales of emergency response contracts cover ad-hoc needs, but some ambulance firms allow regular customers to order non-emergency services via the Internet. Using the Internet, facilities can order medical transport of patients at prearranged pickup times. Doctor offices, hospitals, nursing homes, and case managers often initiate such requests.

Service prices per ambulance ride range from $500 to well over $1,000; the price for medicine and medical procedures can be at least as much. Customer contracts define prices that ambulance companies can charge. Third-party payers, including Medicare, Medicaid, and insurance companies, heavily influence prices by limiting reimbursements to ambulance service providers. Competition comes mainly from government entities, hospitals, other private providers, and local and volunteer groups. Local fire departments are often the major competitor, due to their role as first responder for emergencies and their expansion into emergency care.

Human Resources

Ambulance drivers and non-medical attendants usually need external and on-the-job skills training, including emergency driving, first aid, and safety. Paramedics and emergency medical technicians need specific medical training and, in most states, certification or licensing. Ongoing safety training addresses ambulance operation, medical protocols, equipment use, and patient-focused care.

Average pay at commercial ambulance services is more than 10 percent below the national average wage; ambulance jobs in private firms have lower pay and benefits than in the public sector. Many employees work part-time. Lower pay and irregular hours contribute to commercial ambulance services having higher than average personnel turnover. Industry injury rates are three times higher than the national average. Injuries result mainly from lifting patients. Many employees are members of unions.

Industry Employment Growth

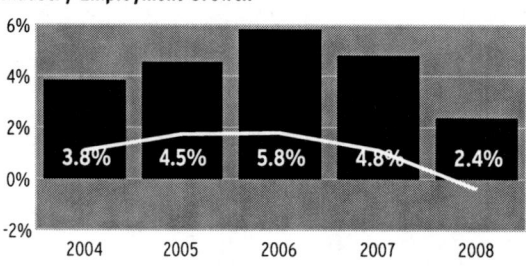

Average Hourly Earnings

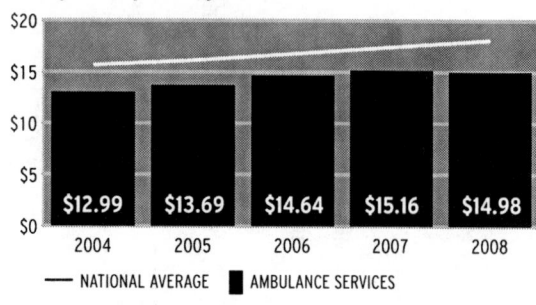

NATIONAL AVERAGE ■ AMBULANCE SERVICES

SOURCE: BUREAU OF LABOR STATISTICS

Call Preparation Questions

What health care and insurance requirements challenge the firm?

Ambulance service firms depend on the health care and insurance industries, which are highly regulated and have strict procedures, especially for awarding contracts and paying contractors.

How are demand changes affecting the company?

As the US population ages and increases, demand for ambulance transport is rising dramatically.

How does the company contain its liability exposure?

Due to the high risk, life-or-death nature of emergency medical services and transport, ambulance firms have high liability exposure.

What advantages or challenges does the company see in M&As?

Acquisitions and mergers among ambulance services firms enable efficiencies related to health care reimbursement, new technology purchases, and participation in managed care plans, which require larger provider networks.

What opportunities does the company have for geographic expansion?

Opportunities exist to expand commercial ambulance services to small towns and rural areas that depend on volunteer emergency teams.

Web Links

American Ambulance Association

Industry issues, initiatives, links.
www.the-aaa.org

Association of Air Medical Services

Features, survival stories.
www.aams.org//AM/Template.cfm?Section=Home

Best Practices in Emergency Services

News, articles.
www.emergencybestpractices.com

Commission on Accreditation of Ambulance Services

Standards, accreditation.
www.caas.org

EMS Responder.com

Industry, product news; success stories.
www.emsresponder.com

Journal of Emergency Medical Services (JEMS.com)

Daily news and articles, training and career information, resource links.
www.jems.com

MERGINET

Articles about operations, technology, management, products.
www.merginet.com

National Association of Emergency Medical Technicians

Industry and job issues, educational programs, research.
www.naemt.org

National Highway Transportation Safety Administration, EMS Division

www.nhtsa.dot.gov/portal/site/nhtsa/
menuitem.2a0771e91315babbbf30811060008a0c/

Glossary of Acronyms

AMR — American Medical Response, Inc.
GIS — geographic information system
HIPAA — Health Insurance Portability and Accountability Act
SSM — system status management

HOOVER'S TOP COMPANIES

Largest Companies by Sales	($ mil.)
Emergency Medical Services Corporation	2,409.9
Rural/Metro Corporation	487.5
Air Methods Corporation	396.4
Acadian Ambulance Service, Inc.	—

Largest Employers	Employees
Emergency Medical Services Corporation	18,015
Rural/Metro Corporation	7,869
Air Methods Corporation	3,133
Acadian Ambulance Service, Inc.	1,600

Fastest Growing* by Five-Year Sales Growth	(%)
Air Methods Corporation	24.8
Emergency Medical Services Corporation	13.3

Top Public Companies by Market Value	($ mil.)
Air Methods Corporation	603.6
Emergency Medical Services Corporation	351.7
Rural/Metro Corporation	50.1

* These rates are compounded annualized increases and may have resulted from acquisitions or one time gains. If less than 6 years of data are available, growth is for the years available.

SOURCE: HOOVER'S, INC., DATABASE

Amusement Parks and Arcades

THIS INDUSTRY INCLUDES:

SIC CODES
7993   Coin-Operated
       Amusement
       Devices
7996   Amusement Parks

NAICS CODES
7131   Amusement Parks
       and Arcades

The amusement parks and arcades industry includes approximately 2,500 companies with total annual revenue of $10 billion. Large companies include Walt Disney, Six Flags, Paramount Parks, Busch Entertainment, and arcade operators Namco Cybertainment and Dave & Busters. The industry is highly concentrated: the eight largest park operators hold about 75 percent of total industry revenue. The fragmented arcade segment accounts for about 15 percent of industry revenue.

About 600 amusement parks and 2,500 arcades operate in the US. A large amusement park has annual revenue of about $100 million, while a midsized park has $10 million of revenue and 75 employees. The annual revenue of a typical arcade is less than $1 million.

Competitive Landscape

Demand is closely linked to the health of the economy, especially consumer income. The profitability of individual companies depends on good marketing. Large companies can build expensive rides and have economies of scale in operations and advertising. Smaller companies can compete by serving smaller markets or offering special rides. The industry is labor-intensive: annual revenue per employee is about $90,000 for large parks, $50,000 for arcades.

Products, Operations & Technology

Amusement park operators offer various types of rides such as roller coasters, tower and "kiddie" rides, and water slides. They also produce entertainment, and sell food and merchandise; arcade operators offer mainly video games. Six Flags operates 30 to 40 rides in each of its amusement parks, including several roller coaster and other "thrill" rides. Rides, shows, shops, and food outlets are generally intermingled to encourage cross-selling. A typical park is spread over 100 to 200 acres.

BUSINESS CHALLENGES

» Highly Dependent on Consumer Spending
Because amusement parks are relatively expensive entertainment, the number of customers declines during economic downturns. With high fixed-costs, even a small drop in attendance can have major financial consequences. During the last recession, attendance at Six Flags parks dropped 12 percent.

» Liability Risks High
Injuries and fatalities can lead to lawsuits, with damages and trial costs in the millions. Injuries are also costly at the gate, as attendance drops after media coverage of accidents. Each year at amusement parks, 4,000 customers have accidents or are killed. The rate of accidents is actually low, but public attention to individual cases is high.

» Revenue Susceptible to Unpredictable Events
Poor weather, natural catastrophes, or terrorist threats can sharply affect industry revenue. The largest parks are in Florida, which is prone to hurricanes, and California, prone to earthquakes. In northern states, even short spells of bad weather have a heightened effect on revenue because of the relatively short operating season.

New rides may be developed internally (the norm for Disney) or bought from manufacturers like Premier Rides, Huss, S&S, and Verkoma. Some large rides are custom installations, but most can be disassembled and transported by truck. Many park operators regularly buy or develop new rides, or switch rides among several parks they own, to attract repeat customers. The market in used rides is active. Major rides may cost up to $20 million, but most rides cost less than $1 million and many kiddie rides cost under $100,000. Electricity is the major energy cost. Arcades typically have dozens, sometimes hundreds, of video games that may cost from $500 to $2,000 each.

Amusement parks get about 55 percent of their revenues from admissions, 15 percent from food sales, and 15 percent from merchandise sales. The remainder is made from a mix of parking fees, commission income from third-party exhibitors, advertising revenue, revenue from hosting parties, etc. Many parks operate only for a portion of the year because of weather. Half of amusement parks, including 70 percent of water parks, are closed during the cold months. Parks open year-round may also operate hotels, stores, condos, golf courses, or other operations in the vicinity.

Many rides are technically sophisticated and rely on computer controls. Computerized sensors have become important safety features of rides that feature high speeds or sudden turns. The larger park companies operate sophisticated Internet sites that encourage potential customers to buy tickets online. Large operators are also linked to computerized hotel reservation systems that allow customers to buy tickets as part of a travel package.

Sales & Marketing

Amusement parks try to attract families with children who prefer sedate rides and food, and young adults who prefer thrill rides. Parks typically attract customers who live within a two-hour driving radius and are prepared to spend many hours at the park. Companies site their parks to draw customers from a particular metropolitan area or areas. Only a few parks are large enough to attract customers from a wider area who are willing to spend several days at the park. There are about 320 million park admissions annually, according to the International Association of Amusement Parks and Attractions.

Amusement parks use a wide variety of regional advertising and promotion, including TV, newspaper, magazine and radio ads, billboards, and direct mail. Internet sites have become an important source of ticket sales. Companies sell tickets directly to individuals and groups, and indirectly through travel agents.

Amusement parks typically charge a flat admission fee and usually don't charge extra for individual rides. Typical gate prices for all-day admission are $15 to $50, but gate prices are usually discounted in a number of ways. In a recent year, Six Flags had 43 million visitors at 40 parks, who paid an average admission price of $15. Arcades don't charge admission but charge for individual games, sometimes with coins and sometimes with tokens (so that prices can easily be changed). Many parks encourage repeat

visits by selling season passes at prices equal to just a few regular admissions.

Human Resources

Most jobs in amusement parks and arcades require few skills and have low wages. Average hourly earnings are about 30 percent lower than for the average US worker. Many jobs are seasonal or part-time. Because of the low pay, personnel turnover can be high. Annual personnel turnover in the entertainment industry as a whole is a very high 75 percent. Because of the presence of moving machinery and heights, workers in the industry have an above-average risk of injury.

Industry Employment Growth

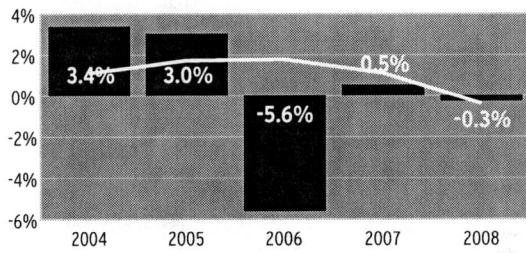

Average Hourly Earnings

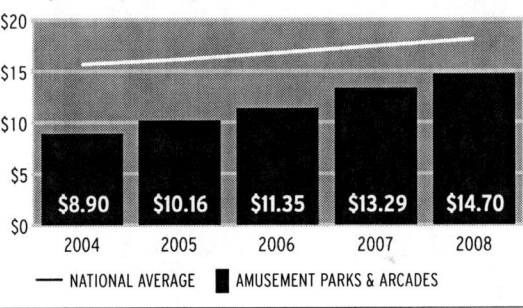

SOURCE: BUREAU OF LABOR STATISTICS

Call Preparation Questions

How much of a recovery has the company seen since the 2001 recession?

Because amusement parks are relatively expensive entertainment, the number of customers declines during economic downturns.

What programs does the company have to prevent accidents?

Injuries and fatalities can lead to lawsuits, with damages and trial costs in the millions.

How much has the company been affected by bad weather?

Poor weather, natural catastrophes, or terrorist threats can sharply affect industry revenue.

FAST FACTS

» The amusement parks and arcades industry includes approximately 2,500 companies with total annual revenue of $10 billion.

» Large companies include Walt Disney, Six Flags, Paramount Parks, Busch Entertainment, and arcade operators Namco Cybertainment and Dave & Busters.

» Amusement park operators offer various types of rides such as roller coasters, tower and "kiddie" rides, and water slides.

» Amusement parks try to attract families with children who prefer sedate rides and food, and young adults who prefer thrill rides.

» Revenue for most amusement parks varies widely during the year, with the bulk of revenue coming in the summer months.

How does the company plan to attract the growing number of older adults?

In contrast to no growth for amusement parks' current target audience, the number of Americans 45 to 64 will increase 30 percent between 2000 and 2010 and make up more than a quarter of the US population.

What investments is the company making in computer controls for rides?

To increase safety, parks can use sophisticated centralized computers to monitor amusement rides, adjust them while in operation, and if necessary, shut them down automatically.

Web Links

American Amusement Machine Association

Legislative news. Information about the Parental Advisory System.
www.coin-op.org

Amusement Today

Industry news.
www.amusementtoday.com

Consumer Product Safety Commission

Statistics about amusement park accidents.
www.cpsc.gov/library/data.html

International Association of Amusement Parks and Attractions

Revenue and attendance statistics.
www.iaapa.org

National Amusement Park Historical Association (NAPHA)

Industry news.
www.napha.org

Outdoor Amusement Business Association

Industry group primarily for carnivals, fairs and other mobile amusement businesses.
www.oaba.org

RideAccidents.com

News stories about amusement park ride accidents.
www.rideaccidents.com

Ultimate Rollercoaster

Industry news.
www.ultimaterollercoaster.com/news

World Waterpark Association

Water park industry news, marketing trends and operating strategies.
www.waterparks.com

Glossary of Acronyms

IAAPA — International Association of Amusement Parks and Attractions

HOOVER'S TOP COMPANIES

Largest Employers	Employees
Walt Disney	37,000
Six Flags, Inc.	29,594
Cedar Fair, L.P.	16,200
Palace Entertainment Holdings, Inc.	9,000
Hershey Entertainment & Resorts Company	7,500
Busch Entertainment Corporation	3,500
Santa Cruz Seaside Company	500
Ripley Entertainment, Inc.	225
Adventureland Park	150
Waterpark Management, Inc.	100

SOURCE: HOOVER'S, INC., DATABASE

Apparel Manufacture

THIS INDUSTRY INCLUDES:

SIC CODES

2253   Knit Outerwear Mills

2353   Hats, Caps, and Millinery

NAICS CODES

315   Apparel Manufacturing

About 15,000 companies manufacture clothing in the US, with combined annual revenue of about $30 billion. Large companies include VF, Levi Strauss, and Warnaco. The industry is highly fragmented: the 50 largest companies hold less than 40 percent of the market. Some plants in the industry have 500 workers and annual sales of $50 million, but most manufacturers operate a single plant with fewer than 50 employees and annual revenue under $5 million. The industry includes knitting mills, but most apparel is cut and sewn.

Competitive Landscape

Demand is largely determined by consumer tastes and the comparative costs of manufacture in the US and overseas. The profitability of individual companies depends on operation efficiency and the ability to secure contracts with clothing marketers. Small companies can compete effectively with large ones by specializing in a particular type of apparel manufacture. There are few economies of scale in manufacture, because of the high labor content of most apparel. The industry is labor-intensive: average annual revenue per production worker is about $125,000.

Products, Operations & Technology

Because of the different skills and equipment needed to produce different types of clothes, manufacturers usually specialize in one type. The largest product segments are men's pants (20 percent of industry revenue); women's skirts and pants (15 percent); women's tops (15 percent); men's tops (12 percent); dresses (10 percent); and women's underwear (9 percent).

Several types of manufacturers exist. Integrated manufacturers, like Levi Strauss, design and market their own clothing brands, and make products both in their own manufacturing plants and in those of independent contractors. Licensees like Warnaco operate their own

BUSINESS CHALLENGES

» Foreign Production Cheaper

More than 50 percent of apparel sold in the US is made abroad because of lower labor costs and the high labor content of most products. Imports come from foreign apparel makers, but also from the foreign plants of US and contract manufacturers. Many US clothing companies have transferred most production capacity abroad. Annual imports of apparel are close to $65 billion.

» Dependence on Large Retailers

Many apparel manufacturers depend on a few large customers for most revenue. Clothing chains with more than 100 stores account for about 50 percent of industry sales. The growth of large chains also cuts smaller manufacturers out of large orders because they're unable to supply the quantity of goods needed.

» Dependence on Trade Regulations

Textile and apparel trade regulations are major bargaining chips in international politics. Import protection is provided through a series of quotas and tariffs that limit the quantity of imports from specific countries. In pursuit of greater freedom in international trade, the US has lowered its protection of the US apparel industry, which is likely to continue, since textile and apparel exports are important to many nations that the US wishes to help.

manufacturing plants and market clothing under license from the brand owner. Many clothing designers market their own brands, but contract out the manufacturing. Contract manufacturers may have long-standing relationships (but not actual contracts) with designers and marketers, or may use brokers to get new business.

The operations of most apparel manufacturers are similar. Designs for a piece of clothing are converted into cloth patterns along with a plan for the sewing steps needed to produce the finished product. Cloth is cut in various sizes (typically six to eight sizes) in a cutting room (or cutting plant), and is then sewn (or "made-up") into finished items by individual workers at sewing stations, in a series of assembly-line steps that may require special sewing equipment. Finished goods are pressed, inspected, and packaged for delivery.

The large labor content of the finished product has encouraged manufacturers to use the lowest-cost labor available. The US apparel manufacturing industry has shrunk 50 percent in recent years, as clothing companies have either moved plants offshore or outsourced production to foreign manufacturers. Wages in many countries are much lower than in the US; consequently, more apparel is now imported than produced domestically.

Despite attempts at greater automation, most apparel is still sewn by hand, using specialized sewing machines. Equipment is bought from makers like Pfaff (made by VSM Group), Yamato, or Juki. Computer systems have had a limited effect on the industry, although computerized machines may be used to produce patterns and cut materials.

Sales & Marketing

Marketing activities depend on whether the manufacturing operation works under contract or is part of an integrated company. Contract manufacturers get business on their ability to produce goods at low cost and on time. Poor quality work is typically returned to the manufacturer for reworking or is discounted. The manufacturer placing the order typically owns and supplies the materials used by contractors.

The apparel marketing business is highly competitive, based on both price and fashion. Under many supply agreements, customers can cancel orders or return unwanted inventory. Small integrated manufacturers rely heavily on trade shows and personal contacts to market products to merchandise buyers. Larger companies have a sales force.

Human Resources

Production workers in apparel manufacture are semiskilled, but receive wages about 40 percent below the national average, due to shrinking employment opportunities. Fringe benefits are a low 14 percent of wages. The number of jobs in apparel manufacturing has dropped 35 percent in recent years. Paradoxically, the average level of wages has increased in recent years as more highly skilled specialty jobs have remained in US factories, while lower-skilled, lower-paying jobs have moved offshore.

Despite the continuing existence of sweatshops, working conditions in apparel manufacture are generally good. The industry injury rate is better than average.

Industry Employment Growth

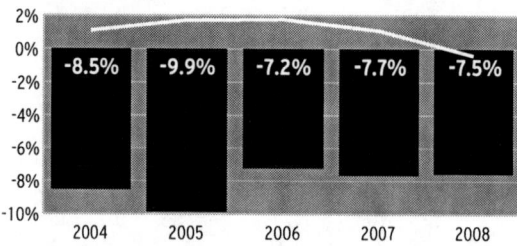

2004	2005	2006	2007	2008
-8.5%	-9.9%	-7.2%	-7.7%	-7.5%

Average Hourly Earnings

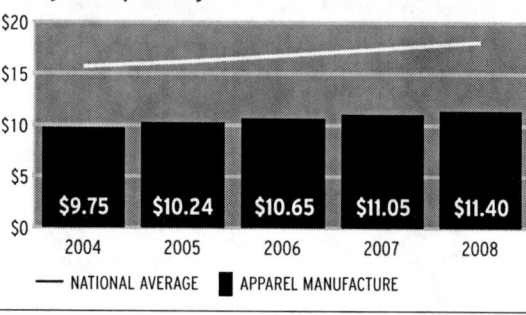

2004	2005	2006	2007	2008
$9.75	$10.24	$10.65	$11.05	$11.40

— NATIONAL AVERAGE   ■ APPAREL MANUFACTURE

SOURCE: BUREAU OF LABOR STATISTICS

Call Preparation Questions

How is the company managing competitive pressure from low-priced foreign imports?

More than 50 percent of apparel sold in the US is made abroad because of lower labor costs and the high labor content of most products.

What steps is the company taking to better compete for the business of large retailers?

Many apparel manufacturers depend on a few large customers for most revenue.

How has the decline in federal trade protection affected the company?

Textile and apparel trade regulations are major bargaining chips in international politics.

How is the company capitalizing on speed to market?

The apparel business is marked by rapid and continuous changes in fashion.

How is the company advantaged by producing expensive specialty apparel?

Much of the apparel business is price-sensitive, but the manufacturing cost of expensive garments is often a minor consideration; quality and reliability are more important.

Web Links

American Apparel & Footwear Association

Industry issues.
www.apparelandfootwear.org

American Apparel Producers' Network

Association of apparel contractors.
www.aapnetwork.net/content/127.htm

Apparel News

Industry news. Trade show calendar.
www.apparelnews.net

Daily News Record

Industry news.
www.dnrnews.com

Embroidery Trade Association

Links to trade shows and magazines.
www.embroiderytrade.org

Sewn Products Equipment & Suppliers of the Americas

Links to apparel equipment makers, by category.
www.spesa.org

US Office of Textiles and Apparel (OTEXA)

Statistics. Import quotas. International Agreements.
www.otexa.ita.doc.gov

Womens Wear Daily

Industry news.
www.wwd.com

World Trade Organization

International trade issues.
www.wto.org

Glossary of Acronyms

EAS — electronic article surveillance
FLSA — Fair Labor Standards Act
ITC — International Trade Commission
OTEXA — Office of Textiles and Apparel (of US Department of Commerce)
WTO — World Trade Organization

HOOVER'S TOP COMPANIES

Largest Companies by Sales	($ mil.)
V.F. Corporation	7,642.6
Polo Ralph Lauren Corporation	4,880.1
Levi Strauss & Co.	4,400.9
Hanesbrands Inc.	4,248.8
Liz Claiborne, Inc.	3,984.9
Jones Apparel Group, Inc.	3,616.4
Phillips-Van Heusen Corporation	2,425.2
Quiksilver, Inc.	2,264.6
Kellwood Company	1,961.8
The Warnaco Group, Inc.	1,860.1

Largest Employers	Employees
V.F. Corporation	54,200
Hanesbrands Inc.	47,600
Kellwood Company	30,000
Fruit of the Loom, Inc.	23,000
Liz Claiborne, Inc.	16,500
Polo Ralph Lauren Corporation	15,000
Russell Corporation	14,400
Phillips-Van Heusen Corporation	11,600
Levi Strauss & Co.	11,550
Guess?, Inc.	9,900

Fastest Growing* by Five-Year Sales Growth	(%)
True Religion Apparel Inc.	157.2
American Apparel, Inc.	141.7
Under Armour, Inc.	44.4
Volcom, Inc.	34.4
Cygne Designs, Inc.	31.9
Guess?, Inc.	24.6
Perry Ellis International, Inc.	23.1
Frederick's of Hollywood Group Inc.	22.9
G-III Apparel Group, Ltd.	20.7
Delta Apparel, Inc.	20.0

Fastest Growing* by Five-Year Employee Growth	(%)
True Religion Apparel Inc.	121.7
Frederick's of Hollywood Group Inc.	88.1
Under Armour, Inc.	53.4
Carter's, Inc.	36.7
Perry Ellis International, Inc.	27.8
Volcom, Inc.	25.1
Hampshire Group, Limited	15.2
Guess?, Inc.	15.1
G-III Apparel Group, Ltd.	13.7
Columbia Sportswear Company	6.2

Top Public Companies by Market Value	($ mil.)
V.F. Corporation	6,247.0
Guess?, Inc.	3,528.2
Polo Ralph Lauren Corporation	3,238.2
Phillips-Van Heusen Corporation	2,212.9
Hanesbrands Inc.	1,232.6

* These rates are compounded annualized increases and may have resulted from acquisitions or one time gains. If less than 6 years of data are available, growth is for the years available.

SOURCE: HOOVER'S, INC., DATABASE

Architects Offices

THIS INDUSTRY INCLUDES:

SIC CODES
0781   Landscape Counseling and Planning
8712   Architectural Services

NAICS CODES
54131   Architectural Services
54132   Landscape Architectural Services

The US architecture industry includes about 17,000 firms, with combined annual revenue of $20 billion. Large firms include Gensler; Hellmuth, Obata + Kassabaum (HOK); and Perkins + Will. The industry is highly fragmented: only about 100 firms have annual revenue of more than $100 million. The typical architecture firm has 10 employees and annual revenue of $1 million.

Competitive Landscape

Demand for architects' services depends heavily on the volume of residential and commercial construction. Because most costs are fixed, profitability depends on a constant inflow of work. Architectural firms are often small because there are few economies of scale in the industry: architectural design can be done as well, and for the same cost, by a small or large company.

Products, Operations & Technology

Architects prepare detailed plans that can be used by construction companies to build or modify various types of structures. Most architectural work has both an aesthetic and an engineering component. About 60 percent of typical firm billings are for basic architect design work; the rest comes from planning and pre-design work, expanded design, and construction phase services. For many projects, the architect's responsibility (and the work contract) extends from the initial design work through to the end of construction, a process that may span several years. On most projects, architects work closely with engineering and construction companies. A typical small firm has three licensed partners, four professional design assistants, and three administrative staff.

The broad categories of buildings that architects work on are schools and hospitals (48 percent of revenue); office, retail, and industrial buildings (33 percent); and residential buildings

BUSINESS CHALLENGES

» Dependence on Construction Activity

The industry greatly depends on the amount of building construction in the US, which often changes in multi-year cycles. The value of new nonresidential construction in the US increased 54 percent from 1995 to 2000, then fell 20 percent during the subsequent recession. Demand in specific segments, like schools or office buildings, can be even more volatile.

» Dependence on Skilled Labor

Many architectural firms depend heavily on the reputation of a single partner and on personnel trained to operate various CAD systems. Because design skills are also in demand in other industries, many firms have trouble finding and keeping technical and design staff. Because of the difficulty of finding skilled workers, firms often keep all workers even when business is slow.

» Increasing Design Complexity

Technology and security considerations have affected building design, and state and local building codes have become more complicated. Tracking and complying with all regulations can be difficult for architects, especially if they work on a project outside their usual territory.

(9 percent). Only 5 percent of industry revenue involves single-family homes, although single-family construction accounts for a third of all US construction. Because most firms are small, they often specialize in the design of one particular type of building.

Architect offices are heavy users of computer technology. CAD has profoundly affected the architecture business, enabling small firms to compete with large ones by eliminating the clerical drafting work that could most effectively be done by larger firms. Most architectural plans are now produced and delivered to the client electronically.

Sales & Marketing

The success of most architecture firms is closely linked to the reputation of the leading partners. Firms cultivate contacts with engineering and construction firms, developers and government officials, and commercial property owners and managers. Large and small firms spend very little money marketing; some advertise in trade publications. Firms may be invited by potential customers to submit plans for a competitive selection. The customer eventually selects a particular design based on total estimated design and construction costs, rather than on the architect's fee. Small firms typically get 50 percent of new work from repeat customers, 20 percent from new clients through non-competitive selections, and 30 percent through competitive selections. Large firms get about half their work from competitive selections. Large companies often work for large corporate customers with continuing design needs. Gensler, for example, grew rapidly by providing design work for 1,500 Gap stores. Large firms may have a sizable international business.

Human Resources

Workers in architect offices earn a high hourly wage, about 40 percent above the national average. Because demand for construction drives an architecture firm's business, junior architects' jobs can be at risk when business is slow. The personnel turnover rate for professional services approaches 60 percent, though architecture firms can avoid hiring and laying-off by contracting with independent architects on a per-project basis. Injury rates in the industry are negligible.

Industry Employment Growth

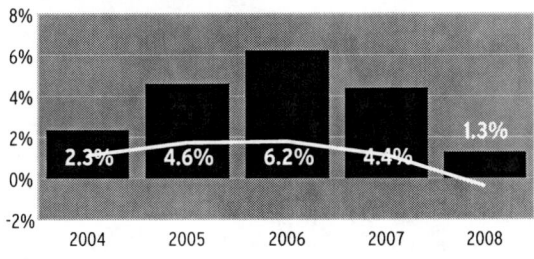

	2004	2005	2006	2007	2008
	2.3%	4.6%	6.2%	4.4%	1.3%

Average Hourly Earnings

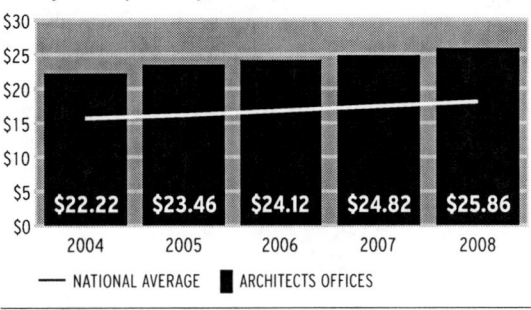

	2004	2005	2006	2007	2008
	$22.22	$23.46	$24.12	$24.82	$25.86

— NATIONAL AVERAGE ■ ARCHITECTS OFFICES

SOURCE: BUREAU OF LABOR STATISTICS

Call Preparation Questions

How do changes in design codes and trends affect the firm's work?

Technology and security considerations have affected building design, and state and local building codes have become more complicated.

What challenges has the company experienced from industry consolidation?

Since larger firms are better able to provide a constant work supply and offer a greater range of services than smaller firms, many firms have an active consolidation strategy.

What kind of buildings does the firm specialize in?

Spending to improve or replace public buildings, like schools and hospitals, is likely to continue at high levels in future years.

Web Links

American Architectural Foundation

Educational organization.
www.archfoundation.org/aaf/aaf

American Institute of Architects

Primary site for information, articles, and statistics.
www.aia.org

Architectural Record

Online magazine, design news.
www.archrecord.com

e-Architect

News from American Institute of Architects.
www.e-architect.com

Engineering News-Record

Design-build news and trends.
www.enr.com

Glossary of Acronyms

AAF — American Architect Foundation
AIA — American Institute of Architects
BSA — Business Software Alliance
GIS — geographic information systems
NAR — National Association of Realtors

Armored Vehicle Manufacturing

THIS INDUSTRY INCLUDES:

SIC CODES
3711 Motor Vehicles and Passenger Car Bodies
3795 Tanks and Tank Components

NAICS CODES
336992 Military Armored Vehicle, Tank, and Tank Component Manufacturing

The US armored vehicle industry includes about 10 companies with combined annual revenue of $10 billion, although revenues can fluctuate markedly depending on the level of global conflict. Major companies include BAE Systems, Textron, General Dynamics, Oshkosh Corporation, Force Protection, and AM General.

Competitive Landscape

Demand is driven by the US military budget, which typically changes with perceived threats to US national security. The profitability of individual companies depends on the effective management of subcontractors and raw materials costs and technological expertise. Large companies enjoy economies of scale in design, manufacturing, and purchasing. While small companies often introduce innovation, large companies are often able to adapt more quickly to the evolving demands of modern warfare. Small companies can compete by providing niche products to prime contractors, and by forming joint ventures with larger contractors. The industry's manufacturing processes are highly automated: average annual revenue per employee is about $350,000.

Products, Operations & Technology

Major products include wheeled, armored combat, and tactical vehicles; tracked main battle tanks; infantry fighting vehicles; heavy equipment transporters; and mobile bridge systems.

Like the auto industry, armored vehicle makers use assembly lines to maximize efficiency through increased automation. However, the industry demands greater manufacturing flexibility than auto makers do, as components are more often custom built and production runs are shorter. Armored vehicles are assembled in only a few dozen factories in the US, which tend to be about 100,000 square feet or larger.

BUSINESS CHALLENGES

» Dependence on Defense Spending

The Department of Defense is the major customer for armored vehicles. Demand depends both on the level of defense activity and need for specific weapons. Demand for armored vehicles increased because of the wars in Iraq and Afghanistan, and could drop when those conflicts wind down.

» Economy Affects Demand

Defense budgets are affected by the health of the US economy. During economic downturns, spending on some weapons systems may be delayed and the effectiveness of weapons examined more closely. Changing priorities, such as more spending on social programs as the population ages, also pressure defense spending.

» Increasing Foreign Competition

Only a handful of armored vehicle manufacturers remain after years of global industry consolidation. Much of the consolidation has crossed international boundaries with US manufacturers being bought by foreign competitors. Remaining US competitors must vie for global armored vehicle contracts with both domestic and foreign companies.

Raw materials include steel, bullet-resistant glass, electronics, and plastics and ceramics used in composite and other armor. Some components, including engines and drive-trains, are often bought from subcontractors. Components bought from subcontractors are added to armored vehicle chassis that are produced by skilled labor using machine tooling. Armored vehicles are delivered directly from manufacturing facilities to customers. Compared to the manufacture of other types of vehicles, there are relatively few significant inventories, warehousing, or shipping logistics.

The quantity of armored vehicles delivered in a given year depends largely on the contracts a specific company has with the US military and the strategic allies of the US government. Delivery quantity may be limited by production capacity, especially if battlefield conditions, such as shifting enemy weapons or tactics, require rush orders or alternative technologies.

Computer technology is used in the automated assembly process and in designing armored vehicles. Certain design technologies are protected with patents and licenses. R&D is crucial as vehicle designs are forced to adapt to ever-evolving enemy threats, weapons, and tactics. R&D often occurs under fixed-price or cost-plus contracts with the US government, but can also be self-funded.

Sales & Marketing

The federal government, through the Department of Defense, is by far the largest customer for armored vehicles. Other customers include governments of strategic allies of the US.

Armored vehicle makers' sales executives are primarily responsible for sales and marketing. Companies often participate in military shows and conferences, such as the US Army Annual Conference and Winter Symposium, to get their products before military decision-makers. Products are also promoted through company websites, brochures, and advertising aimed at the military community.

Maintaining relationships with various agencies inside the US government and actively lobbying legislators are important to sell and market armored vehicles.

Armored vehicles are generally sold to the US government through fixed-price contracts that aren't usually adjustable to account for manufacturing cost overruns, unless the cost increase is caused by changes ordered by the government. Costs vary depending on the type of vehicle, its specifications, and intended use.

An armored Humvee costs about $150,000; a heavier duty Mine Resistant Ambush Protected (MRAP) vehicle, from $700,000 to over $1 million; an M1 Abrams main battle tank, about $5.5 million.

Human Resources

Armored vehicles are highly advanced and technologically complex; their manufacture requires a highly skilled, qualified workforce. Although some workers at specific manufacturers may be represented by collective bargaining agreements, union representation is generally low. In some cases, employees of armored vehicle manufacturers may be required to maintain specified levels of Department of Defense security clearances.

Call Preparation Questions

How does the company manage the unpredictable nature of defense spending?

The Department of Defense is the major customer for armored vehicles.

What larger economic issues might impact the company?

Defense budgets are affected by the health of the US economy.

How has industry consolidation affected the company?

Only a handful of armored vehicle manufacturers remain after years of global industry consolidation.

Does the company have a strategy for the Future Combat Systems (FCS) program?

The FCS is an ambitious plan to produce a highly integrated future capability for the Army that will include various types of armored vehicles.

How important is the Joint Light Tactical Vehicle (JLTV) to the company's business?

A replacement for the Humvee, the JLTV, will come in several versions for the Army and Marines.

Web Links

Global Security

Information, news, and links for defense, space, intelligence, WMD, and Homeland Security issues.
www.globalsecurity.org

Manufacturing.gov

Information on issues facing US manufacturers.
www.manufacturing.gov

National Defense Industrial Association

Industry events, meetings, news, and links.
www.ndia.org

US Department of Defense

Military news.
www.defenselink.mil

Glossary of Acronyms

DOD — Department of Defense
FCS — Future Combat Systems
HMMWV — High Mobility Multi-Wheeled Vehicle
IED — improvised explosive device
MRAP — mine-resistant ambush protected
JLTV — Joint Light Tactical Vehicle
UGV — Unmanned Ground Vehicle

HOOVER'S TOP COMPANIES

Largest Companies by Sales	($ mil.)
Textron Inc.	14,246.0
Oshkosh Corporation	7,138.3
Force Protection, Inc.	890.7
General Dynamics Land Systems Inc.	730.0
BAE Systems Land and Armaments	513.0
Napco International LLC	23.0
AM General, LLC	—

Largest Employers	Employees
Textron Inc.	44,000
Oshkosh Corporation	14,000
General Dynamics Land Systems Inc.	7,300
BAE Systems Land and Armaments	5,130
AM General, LLC	1,559
Napco International LLC	65

Fastest Growing* by Five-Year Sales Growth	(%)
Force Protection, Inc.	221.3
Oshkosh Corporation	30.0

Top Public Companies by Market Value	($ mil.)
Textron Inc.	3,720.2
Oshkosh Corporation	979.5
Force Protection, Inc.	319.4

* These rates are compounded annualized increases and may have resulted from acquisitions or one time gains. If less than 6 years of data are available, growth is for the years available.

SOURCE: HOOVER'S, INC., DATABASE

Audio and Video Equipment Manufacturing

THIS INDUSTRY INCLUDES:

SIC CODES

3651   Household Audio and Video Equipment

NAICS CODES

334310   Audio and Video Equipment Manufacturing

The US audio and video equipment manufacturing industry includes about 550 companies with combined annual revenue of about $10 billion. Major companies include Harman International, Bose, and US divisions of foreign companies like Sony and Philips. The industry is highly concentrated: the 50 largest companies hold almost 90 percent market share.

Competitive Landscape

Demand is driven by consumer income and the rate of product innovation. The profitability of individual companies depends on manufacturing efficiency and effective marketing and distribution. Large companies have advantages in economies of scale in manufacturing, marketing, and distribution. Small companies can compete effectively by offering specialty products or components in system solutions, such as speakers in a home theatre system. Average annual revenue per worker is about $500,000 per year.

Audio and video equipment, primarily TV and radio, compete with PCs and game consoles in the consumer home entertainment market.

Products, Operations & Technology

Major products are TVs (about 40 percent of revenue); speakers, (about 25 percent); and auto and home radios (about 15 percent). Additional products include DVD players, CD players, camcorders, and other home stereo equipment.

Audio and video equipment manufacturers depend on product engineers to design new products that are high performance, low cost, and easy to use. Small companies tend to focus on being either first to market with premium-priced products offering higher functionality and performance, or being a "fast follower" with lower-priced products. Large manufacturers may follow both strategies by having multiple product lines. The industry is extremely competitive and new products are a major source of profits. Some companies spend 8 to 10 percent of revenue on R&D.

Production processes include installing circuit boards and relays, soldering, bending and drilling metal and plastics for casements, assembling, painting, inspecting, and packing and shipping products. Most manufacturing operations employ fewer than 100.

Raw materials include printed circuit boards (some manufacturers build their own); relay switches; sheet metal (steel and aluminum);

BUSINESS CHALLENGES

» Competition from Imports

The US market is the world's largest for audio and video products, and imports comprise about 90 percent of US sales. Audio and video product imports have grown over 50 percent during the past five years. China and Mexico are the largest import sources, accounting for roughly two-thirds of the total. Besides direct imports, foreign companies are also performing final assembly operations in US facilities to avoid high tariffs levied on some finished products.

» Competition from Other Electronic Products

TV and radio's domination of home entertainment is giving way to new electronic devices. PCs, video game consoles, and MP3 players compete as entertainment devices in the home and as portable audio and video sources. Most homes have multiple types of equipment, but time spent watching and listening to traditional TV and radio is shrinking as other electronic devices grow in popularity.

» Mature US Market for TVs

About 98 percent of US households have a TV. About 280 million TV sets, or an average of 2.4 per TV household, make TV the most pervasive electronic device in the US. Consequently, new TVs will be sold primarily to replace older sets that have failed or because of the enhanced features of new models.

plastics; and glass. Raw material costs represent about 60 percent of revenues. Some major components are controlled by a few large suppliers, who may also produce their own finished products in competition with their customers.

Digital technologies are replacing analog components in audio and video equipment. The majority of video products are digital; radio is still primarily analog, but the transition is underway. Rapid technological innovation is an industry trademark. Companies invest in information systems to support new product development, increase manufacturing efficiency, and manage product distribution. Given the short product life of many new products, manufacturing technologies and processes are designed to be flexible and easy to change.

Sales & Marketing

Typical customers are big box retailers, electronic superstores, and specialty audio and video stores. These retail outlets are serviced by direct sales forces, distributors, and, in some cases, manufacturer reps.

Marketing programs include newspaper, TV, and online advertising; instore promotions; and demonstrations. Retail sales personnel require technical knowledge of products and typically receive training from manufacturers. Manufacturers use the annual Consumer Electronics Show, the largest electronics product showcase in the world, to introduce products.

Manufacturers use the Internet extensively to promote and sell products. In addition to company-owned websites where customers can buy products directly, many support third-party retail websites. These include websites of both online-only retailers and brick-and-mortar retailers.

Typical product prices range from $19 for a simple AM/FM radio to $3,000 or more for HDTVs. Prices are highly competitive and major retailers are constantly pressuring manufacturers for lower prices. Professional products sold to concert arenas, performing bands, and mixing studios sell for much more.

Human Resources

Engineering talent is critical for companies that compete based on product innovation. Shop floor manufacturing skills include blueprint reading, metalworking, circuit board assembly, inspection, and quality assurance. Community colleges and trade schools offer

training in many of the required skills, but companies also train on the job. Production workers average about $20 per hour, roughly 25 percent higher than the overall manufacturing sector.

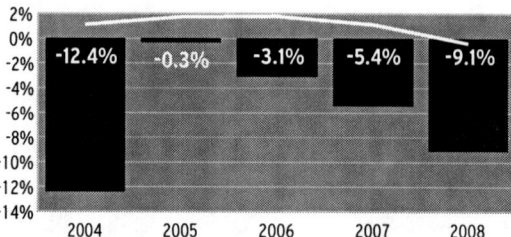

Industry Employment Growth

Year	Growth
2004	-12.4%
2005	-0.3%
2006	-3.1%
2007	-5.4%
2008	-9.1%

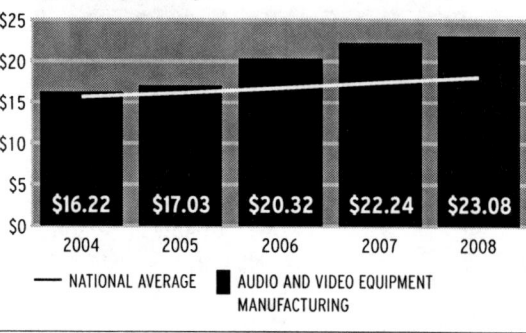

Average Hourly Earnings

Year	Earnings
2004	$16.22
2005	$17.03
2006	$20.32
2007	$22.24
2008	$23.08

—— NATIONAL AVERAGE ■ AUDIO AND VIDEO EQUIPMENT MANUFACTURING

SOURCE: BUREAU OF LABOR STATISTICS

Call Preparation Questions

How do imports affect the company's US sales?

The US market is the world's largest for audio and video products, and imports comprise about 90 percent of US sales.

What other electronic entertainment devices compete with the company's products?

TV and radio's domination of home entertainment is giving way to new electronic devices.

How mature is the market for the company's products?

About 98 percent of US households have a TV. About 280 million TV sets, or an average of 2.

Does the company manufacture products used in home theaters?

About one-third of US homes have some form of home theater, according to the Consumer Electronics Association (CEA).

What products does the company offer that are used in multi-room audio environments?

Consumers are expanding audio throughout the house, not confining it to just the den or a single room.

Web Links

Consumer Electronics Association

Source for regulatory and other industry issues.
www.ce.org

Consumer Electronics Show

Coverage and press releases from companies at the largest consumer electronics showcase.
www.cesweb.org/news/releases.asp

HomeMediaMagazine

Information of the home digital entertainment industry.
www.homemediamagazine.com

Leichtman Research Group

Provides industry coverage of media, entertainment and broadband industries.
www.leichtmanresearch.com/press.html

Sound and Vision Magazine Online

Product comparisons, industry articles, consumer issues.
www.soundandvisionmag.com

Glossary of Acronyms

CEA — Consumer Electronics Association
CES — Consumer Electronics Show
CPSC — Consumer Product Safety Commission
HD-DVD — high definition DVD
OLED — organic light emitting diode

HOOVER'S TOP COMPANIES

Largest Companies by Sales	($ mil.)
Harman International Industries, Incorporated	4,112.5
Sony Electronics, Inc.	2,949.7
Bose Corporation	2,180.0
VIZIO, Inc.	1,970.0
Audiovox Corporation	591.4
Universal Electronics Inc.	272.7
Philips Electronics North America	—
Panasonic Corporation of North America	—

Largest Employers	Employees
Philips Electronics North America Corporation	27,175
Sony Electronics, Inc.	26,000
Panasonic Corporation of North America	24,000
Bose Corporation	8,000
Mitsubishi Digital Electronics America, Inc.	2,400
Altec Lansing Technologies, Inc.	1,800
Pioneer Speakers, Inc.	1,500
Zenith Electronics Corporation	976
Monster Cable Products, Inc.	700

Fastest Growing* by Five-Year Sales Growth	(%)
ICOP Digital, Inc.	223.1
American Technology Corporation	53.8
TiVo Inc.	23.2
Universal Electronics Inc.	21.3
Soyo Group, Inc.	17.5
Harman International Industries, Incorporated	13.0
Koss Corporation	6.8
DTS, Inc.	3.1
LOUD Technologies Inc.	2.1

Fastest Growing* by Five-Year Employee Growth	(%)
DTS, Inc.	80.5
TiVo Inc.	14.8
Audiovox Corporation	12.0
Universal Electronics Inc.	2.3
Harman International Industries, Incorporated	2.1

Top Public Companies by Market Value	($ mil.)
Harman International Industries, Incorporated	2,422.1
TiVo Inc.	876.7
Universal Electronics Inc.	487.3
DTS, Inc.	317.3
Audiovox Corporation	185.3

* These rates are compounded annualized increases and may have resulted from acquisitions or one time gains. If less than 6 years of data are available, growth is for the years available.

SOURCE: HOOVER'S, INC., DATABASE

Automobile Dealerships

THIS INDUSTRY INCLUDES:

SIC CODES

5511   Motor Vehicle Dealers (New and Used)

5521   Motor Vehicle Dealers (Used Only)

NAICS CODES

4411   Automobile Dealers

The automobile dealer industry includes about 50,000 new and used vehicle dealers with combined annual revenue of $770 billion. Major companies include AutoNation, Penske Automotive Group, Sonic Automotive, and CarMax. The industry is highly fragmented: the top 50 companies have less than 15 percent of industry sales.

Competitive Landscape

Consumer spending and interest rates drive demand. The profitability of individual companies depends on the volume and mix of cars and services sold. Large companies can offer a wider selection of cars and have advantages in marketing, purchasing, and finance. Small companies can compete effectively by offering superior customer service or serving a local market. Annual revenue per worker averages $600,000 for new car dealerships and $700,000 for used.

For vehicle sales, auto dealers compete with private market sellers, who are increasingly using the Internet to bypass traditional retail channels. Companies compete with various retail outlets, such as oil change centers, tire stores, and independent service shops and chains, for service revenue.

Products, Operations & Technology

Products sold include new cars (60 percent of industry sales); used cars (30 percent); and services and parts (10 percent). Sales of financing plans, extended warranties, insurance, and accessories generate aftermarket income.

New car dealers have franchise agreements with car manufacturers, which give dealerships non-exclusive rights to sell certain brands of cars and offer related parts and services within a specified market area. Franchise agreements typically impose various requirements for operations, including inventory levels, working capital, sales practices, showrooms service

BUSINESS CHALLENGES

» Volatile Demand

Consumer demand for cars can vary significantly from year to year, due to a variety of factors, including changing economic conditions, consumer spending, inflation, and fuel prices. Sales for particular brands or styles are especially vulnerable to evolving consumer preferences. During a recent recessionary period, the number of autos sold declined, despite large financial incentives from car makers. As gas prices spiked between 2004 and 2007, sales volume for light duty trucks (which include low mileage SUVs) declined 10 percent.

» Interest Rates Affect Sales and Inventory Costs

Significant increases in interest rates can reduce consumer ability to buy cars and increase floor plan financing costs. Most customers buy vehicles with loans or leases. Dealer inventories are typically financed through variable interest rate loans. Increasing interest rates can reduce profits by affecting both sales volume and dealer costs.

» Dependence on Car Manufacturers

Dealers rely on car manufacturers for new vehicle inventory, financing, marketing, and warranty and service work. Companies have limited control over the colors and features of cars received, and often face the task of selling cars that may not be exactly what a customer wants. Financial distress can cause car manufacturers to cut marketing support or change floor plan or customer financing programs.

facilities, and monthly reporting. Multiple franchise agreements with different car manufacturers allow dealers to offer a broad range of vehicles. The average new car dealership generates $30 million and sells 775 new cars annually, according to the NADA.

Dealers acquire new vehicles from manufacturers through an allocation system based on historical sales, and typically have limited influence over the colors and features of cars received. Companies buy used vehicles from a variety of sources, including trade-ins, auctions, other dealers, leasing companies, and rental companies. To set a price for a trade-in, used dealers consider a car's age, mileage, and condition to develop an appraisal. Used vehicles may require reconditioning prior to sale; vehicles unfit for retail resale are generally sold through wholesale auctions. Some manufacturers allow dealers to sell certified pre-owned (CPO) vehicles with extended warranties.

Service and parts operations may offer repair, maintenance, body work, and warranty services. A typical service department has 18 service bays and handles over 12,000 repair orders annually at an average value of just over $200 per order. Car manufacturers may authorize dealers to perform warranty work.

Auto dealers rely on computerized information systems to store vehicle information, track vehicle movement, and process sales transactions. Inventory management systems help companies optimize the supply and mix of vehicles, and are especially useful for companies monitoring inventory across multiple dealerships. Customer databases store information on existing and potential customers and help dealerships develop marketing programs. Radio frequency identification (RFID) devices capture test drive information.

Sales & Marketing

Marketing and promotional vehicles include newspaper, TV, radio, and outdoor (billboard) advertising and direct mail. Dealers benefit from national advertising from car manufacturers, which are among the largest TV advertisers. Manufacturers may offer consumer incentives, such as cash rebates and low interest financing, to drive sales.

With intense competition among dealers, customer satisfaction has become an important differentiator and a key tool in developing repeat sales. While most auto dealers rely on a commissioned sales force, negative publicity about high-pressure sales tactics has made fixed-price selling, non-commissioned sales staff, and Internet sales more popular. Good customer experiences in service departments help dealers develop ongoing relationships with customers.

Internet sites allow dealers to reach customers beyond local markets. Auto manufacturer and syndicated websites, such as Autotrader.com or cars.com, help generate sales

leads and drive dealership traffic. Dealer websites may let customers search inventory, review pricing, compare vehicles, calculate payments, and estimate trade-in values. Companies may allow customers to apply for financing and finalize purchases via the Internet.

The average retail price for a new car is about $29,000, according to the NADA. Retail prices for used cars average $16,000. Manufacturers establish the manufacturer suggested retail price (MSRP) for vehicles, but dealers usually discount the list price.

Human Resources

Typical jobs include sales associates, technicians, service and parts workers, and administrative staff. Overall wages are roughly equal to the average for all US workers, although employees in new car dealers tend to earn more than workers in used car dealers. Turnover of experienced sales staff can be high. The industry injury rate is about 15 percent lower than the national average.

Industry Employment Growth

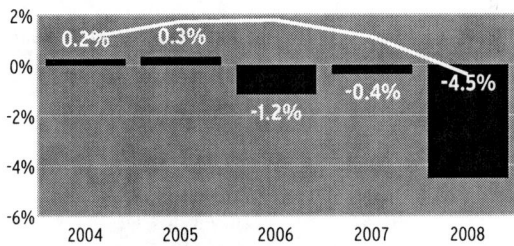

Average Hourly Earnings

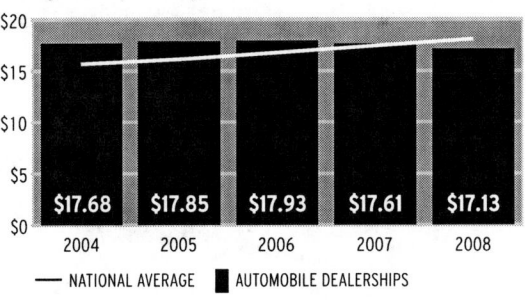

SOURCE: BUREAU OF LABOR STATISTICS

Call Preparation Questions

How does the company perform during adverse economic conditions or periods of weak consumer demand?

Consumer demand for cars can vary significantly from year to year, due to a variety of factors, including changing economic conditions, consumer spending, inflation, and fuel prices.

How do fluctuating interest rates affect the company's business?

Significant increases in interest rates can reduce consumer ability to buy cars and increase floor plan financing costs.

FAST FACTS

» The automobile dealer industry includes about 50,000 new and used vehicle dealers with combined annual revenue of $770 billion.

» Major companies include AutoNation, Penske Automotive Group, Sonic Automotive, and CarMax.

» Products sold include new cars (60 percent of industry sales); used cars (30 percent); and services and parts (10 percent).

» Marketing and promotional vehicles include newspaper, TV, radio, and outdoor (billboard) advertising and direct mail.

» Sales are seasonal, with peaks during spring and summer.

How does the company rate its relationship with manufacturers?

Dealers rely on car manufacturers for new vehicle inventory, financing, marketing, and warranty and service work.

How important are aftermarket sales to the company?

Dealers improve profitability by selling or installing high-margin aftermarket products, such as accessories, financing, insurance, and service contracts.

Web Links

American International Automobile Dealers Association

Advocates free trade and addresses industry issues and news affecting dealerships with foreign manufacturers.
www.aiada.org

AutoExec magazine

Dealer news.
www.autoexecmag.com

Automotive Service Association (ASA)

Magazine, news, events, and links.
www.asashop.org

JD Power and Associates

Consumer information and forecasting about the auto industry.
www.jdpower.com

National Association of Minority Automobile Dealers (NAMAD)

Schedules, directories, and legislative updates.
www.namad.org

National Automobile Dealers Association News

News, industry information, and more.
www.nada.org

National Highway Traffic Safety Administration

Recalls, crash tests.
www.nhtsa.gov

National Independent Automobile Dealers Association (NIADA)

State association information, government watch, events, and magazine.
www.niada.com

Ward's Dealer Business

Dealership news.
www.wardsdealer.com

Glossary of Acronyms

CPO — certified pre-owned
CRM — customer relationship management
RFID — radio frequency identification

HOOVER'S TOP COMPANIES

Largest Companies by Sales	($ mil.)
AutoNation, Inc.	14,131.9
JM Family Enterprises, Inc.	12,200.0
Penske Automotive Group, Inc.	11,646.3
Sonic Automotive, Inc.	8,336.9
CarMax, Inc.	8,285.4
Asbury Automotive Group, Inc.	5,713.0
Gulf States Toyota, Inc.	5,700.0
Group 1 Automotive, Inc.	5,654.1
Lithia Motors, Inc.	3,219.0
Penske Corporation	—

Largest Employers	Employees
AutoNation, Inc.	25,000
Penske Automotive Group, Inc.	15,800
CarMax, Inc.	15,637
Sonic Automotive, Inc.	11,400
Group 1 Automotive, Inc.	8,932
Asbury Automotive Group, Inc.	8,300
Rosenthal Automotive Organization	8,000
Larry H. Miller Group	5,700
JM Family Enterprises, Inc.	4,700
Hendrick Automotive Group	4,700

Fastest Growing* by Five-Year Sales Growth	(%)
CarBiz Inc.	156.2
CarMax, Inc.	15.3
Internet Brands, Inc.	14.2
JM Family Enterprises, Inc.	13.9
America's Car-Mart, Inc.	12.1
Gulf States Toyota, Inc.	9.0
Lithia Motors, Inc.	6.3
Asbury Automotive Group, Inc.	5.0
Group 1 Automotive, Inc.	4.6
Sonic Automotive, Inc.	3.3

Fastest Growing* by Five-Year Employee Growth	(%)
CarMax, Inc.	11.8
America's Car-Mart, Inc.	9.0
Lithia Motors, Inc.	6.4
JM Family Enterprises, Inc.	4.5
Group 1 Automotive, Inc.	3.1
Asbury Automotive Group, Inc.	1.0

Top Public Companies by Market Value	($ mil.)
CarMax, Inc.	4,013.8
AutoNation, Inc.	1,747.3
Penske Automotive Group, Inc.	702.2
Sonic Automotive, Inc.	567.2
Asbury Automotive Group, Inc.	475.3

* These rates are compounded annualized increases and may have resulted from acquisitions or one time gains. If less than 6 years of data are available, growth is for the years available.

SOURCE: HOOVER'S, INC., DATABASE

Automobile Manufacture

THIS INDUSTRY INCLUDES:

SIC CODES

3711   Motor Vehicles and Passenger Car Bodies

NAICS CODES

33611   Automobile and Light Duty Motor Vehicle Manufacturing

The US automobile manufacturing industry includes about 160 companies with combined annual revenue of about $250 billion. Major companies are Chrysler, Ford, and GM. The industry is highly concentrated: the eight largest companies account for more than 90 percent of revenue and the top 20 for 98 percent.

Competitive Landscape

The major drivers of US demand for autos are employment and interest rates. The profitability of individual companies depends on manufacturing efficiency, product quality, and effective marketing. Large companies manufacture multiple product lines, marketed under different brand names. Smaller companies manufacture a few or single product lines. Large companies have advantages of economy of scale; smaller companies compete by focusing on specialized markets. Due to highly automated manufacturing processes, the average annual revenue per employee is about $1.4 million.

Products, Operations & Technology

Major product categories are cars (45 percent of industry revenue) and light trucks (55 percent). Light trucks include SUVs.

The assembly line is an invention of the auto manufacturing industry of the early 1900s. Many refinements have made the assembly line more efficient, and it remains the primary method for automobile assembly. Robotics and other computer automation have reduced the number of workers on a line. Between 2002 and 2005, the number of auto production workers decreased 8.5 percent while shipments increased 5 percent. Assembly plants now require as little as 15 to 25 labor hours per vehicle.

A typical automobile plant has capacity to produce about 200,000 vehicles annually. Flexible manufacturing has enabled different car models to be manufactured on the same assem-

BUSINESS CHALLENGES

» Import Competition

Imports represent a rising percentage of total US auto sales. Between 1996 and 2006, US market share for Chrysler, Ford, and GM dropped from 73 to 54 percent. Rising fuel prices favor imports that generally are smaller and more fuel-efficient. Offshore manufacturers also enjoy the advantage of substantially lower wages and benefits for employees and lower costs for suppliers. The strength of the dollar against the yen and other foreign currencies can impact import prices.

» Dependence on Employment, Interest Rates

Auto sales are subject to the health of the US economy, especially employment and interest rates. A new car purchase is the second-largest investment most families make, next to a home. Consumers often delay buying new cars during times of job uncertainty. Most new vehicle purchases are financed, so costs are sensitive to interest rate changes.

» Corporate Average Fuel Economy (CAFE)

CAFE, administered by the National Highway Transportation Safety Board, requires car and light truck manufacturers to achieve certain average miles per gallon ratings across their total fleet. National concern over global warming and energy independence may lead to increases in the current average mileage requirements. Auto manufacturers fear that the increases will be so stringent that achievement will be technologically infeasible or cost too much.

bly line, saving hundreds of millions in setup and tooling costs. Tighter tolerance of parts enables greater consistency of product quality and reduces line stoppages. US manufacturers also operate facilities that make parts for their assembly plants. Foundries, powertrain facilities, and transmission plants deliver parts and subassemblies to final assembly locations.

Raw materials include steel, aluminum, glass, plastic, rubber, and coatings. As many as 15,000 parts are required on some vehicle assemblies, and material costs represent about 70 percent of total shipment value. Assembly plants require a high degree of supply chain management and coordination, as many parts and sub-assemblies are delivered to assembly plants for same day usage to minimize inventory storage and carrying costs. Many suppliers have established manufacturing or warehouse locations near assembly plants.

In addition to automated assembly processes and supply chain management, computer technology is used extensively for product design. Sophisticated computer modeling programs help with material, fuel efficiency, emissions, safety, and product quality design choices.

Sales & Marketing

Independent dealers are the primary sales and distribution channel for cars in the US. About 21,500 dealers serve the US market, and sold over 16 million new cars and trucks, including imports, in 2006. The Internet is gaining popularity as a shopping venue, but the dealership is still the primary sales outlet, even if the buyer shops online.

Dealers enter into multi-year sales agreements with manufacturers. Some dealers have exclusive agreements with a single manufacturer; other dealers represent multiple manufacturers. Manufacturers impose various operating requirements on the dealer for inventory, working capital, sales practices, showrooms, service facilities, and monthly reporting. Dealers also agree to offer warranty service, parts, general maintenance, and repair of the manufacturer's products. Most manufacturers require that certified technicians perform this work.

Manufacturers typically own multiple product lines, often marketed under different brands. Ford Motor Company offers Ford, Lincoln, and Mercury brands in North America and also owns all or significant percentages of Mazda, Volvo, Jaguar, and Land Rover. Brands are targeted to consumers by income, age, and sex by highlighting model characteristics, such as performance, economy, quality, and safety. Ads are delivered primarily by TV, radio, newspaper, and the Internet. Manufacturers advertise directly and also support cooperative dealer advertising programs.

The average price of a new car in 2006 was $27,800, according to Edmunds. Prices range from about $15,000 for economy models to over $100,000 for exotic luxury models.

Human Resources

The average hourly wage of an automotive production worker is about $30, over 75 percent above the average for US manufacturing overall. Labor unions represent production employees in virtually all automobile assembly plants in the US. A few foreign-owned plants, such as Honda, are non-union. Fringe benefits, including health care and retirement programs, average about 45 percent of the hourly wage.

Worker safety is a significant issue in auto manufacturing plants. While improving over the past several years, the industry still has an accident record about 50 percent higher than the average for all manufacturing industries.

Industry Employment Growth

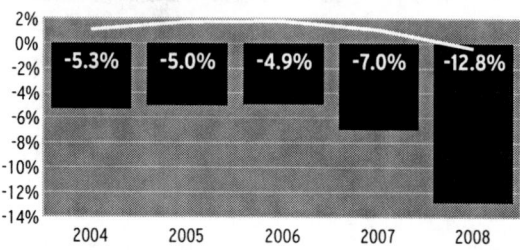

Average Hourly Earnings

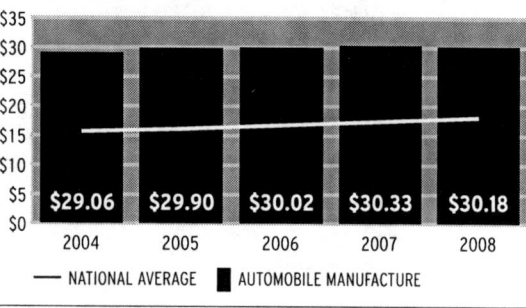

SOURCE: BUREAU OF LABOR STATISTICS

Call Preparation Questions

How is the company's business affected by imports?

Imports represent a rising percentage of total US auto sales.

How are current economic conditions affecting the company's sales?

Auto sales are subject to the health of the US economy, especially employment and interest rates.

What challenges does the company see in meeting stricter CAFE standards?

CAFE, administered by the National Highway Transportation Safety Board, requires car and light truck manufacturers to achieve certain average miles per gallon ratings across their total fleet.

How is the company improving fuel efficiency of its products?

Consumers and government want greater fuel efficiency.

What steps is the company taking to reduce parts and material costs?

US manufacturers are increasing offshore sources for parts and sub-assemblies in an attempt to reduce material costs.

Web Links

Alliance of Automobile Manufacturers

Industry news and updates.
www.autoalliance.org

Assembly Magazine

Industry news, product news, links.
www.assemblymag.com

Automotive News

Daily industry news.
www.autonews.com

Chrysler Motors

Worldwide car manufacturer.
www.chrysler.com/en

Ford Motor Company

One of Detroit Three.
www.ford.com

General Motors

One of Detroit Three.
www.gm.com

The Car Connection

Daily news site.
www.thecarconnection.com

Glossary of Acronyms

CAFE — Corporate Average Fuel Economy
CARB — California Air Resource Board
CUV — crossover utility vehicle
EIA — Energy Information Administration
ESC — electronic stability control
NHTSB — National Highway Transportation Safety Board
UAW — United Auto Workers
ZEV — zero-emission vehicles

HOOVER'S TOP COMPANIES

Largest Companies by Sales	($ mil.)
General Motors Corporation	148,979.0
Ford Motor Company	146,277.0
Chrysler LLC	59,700.0

Largest Employers	Employees
General Motors Corporation	266,000
Ford Motor Company	246,000
Chrysler LLC	66,409
Honda North America, Inc.	40,000
Nissan North America, Inc.	13,000
Toyota Motor North America, Inc.	8,950
New United Motor Manufacturing, Inc.	4,800
Mercedes-Benz U.S. International, Inc.	3,869
Mitsubishi Motors North America, Inc.	3,600
Subaru of Indiana Automotive, Inc.	2,300

Top Public Companies by Market Value	($ mil.)
Ford Motor Company	5,360.9
General Motors Corporation	1,953.5
Torvec, Inc.	98.1
ZAP	44.1

SOURCE: HOOVER'S, INC., DATABASE

Automobile Parts and Accessories Manufacture

The US auto parts manufacturing industry consists of about 4,500 companies and has annual revenue of about $225 billion. Large companies include Delphi, Lear, Visteon, Dana, and ArvinMeritor. Industry sales are concentrated among the largest suppliers, but 80 percent of firms employ fewer than 100.

Competitive Landscape

Demand for auto parts is driven by new car sales, which are strongly affected by interest rates, and by the replacement market. Company profitability industry depends partly on the difficulty of manufacturing products and partly on demand volume, since many costs are fixed. Small companies can compete successfully by focusing on a small number of products or some highly technical ones.

The structure of the industry is complex, with most smaller companies (referred to as "tier 2" and "tier 3" suppliers) selling parts to larger suppliers (referred to as "tier 1" suppliers), who in turn sell component assemblies or modules to car and truck assemblers such as GM and Ford — collectively called OEMs.

Products, Operations & Technology

Auto part suppliers make components that are assembled by the car companies. Major product categories are transmission and power train components (17 percent of revenue); engines and engine parts (16 percent); metal stamping of body parts and trim (13 percent); electrical and electronic equipment (11 percent); seating and interior trim (9 percent); and brake systems (6 percent). Other products include steering and suspension components and air conditioning systems. Parts manufacturing plants are often located close to the assembly plants of the car companies, usually within 100 miles.

Because car and truck companies (or VMs — vehicle manufacturers) focus increasingly on

BUSINESS CHALLENGES

» Customer Concentration

Consolidation of car companies and demand for larger and more complicated component assemblies have created larger, but fewer, auto part suppliers. To cut costs, auto manufacturers have been awarding a larger share of business to a smaller number of large tier 1 auto part suppliers. As large suppliers become the de facto manufacturing arms of car companies, they gain greater power over smaller suppliers. Many tier 2 and tier 3 suppliers depend financially on a few large contracts.

» International Competition

In recent years, the volume of car parts manufactured in low-cost countries like Mexico, China, and Taiwan has increased rapidly. The largest importers to the US are Canada, Mexico, and Japan; imported car parts now hold about 30 percent of the US market. Many US suppliers reduce costs by moving production to lower-cost countries or by investing capital in more efficient facilities and equipment.

» Cyclical Demand

The auto industry depends on a favorable economy, relying on personal income and employment levels. Amid the current economic slowdown, US annual vehicle sales have fallen by nearly 3 million units. Observers expect that US production will continue to slip during the next few years as US automakers retool to accommodate consumer demand for more fuel-efficient vehicles, overall demand eases, and more production moves to lower-cost regions.

design, assembly, and marketing operations (and less on actual manufacturing), the parts industry produces virtually everything that goes into a car or truck.

Tier 1 suppliers, of which there are roughly 1,000, usually concentrate in one or two distinct industry segments such as axles, power trains, brakes, exhaust systems, suspensions, electrical components, seating, engine parts, or accessories. OEMs still build most of their own engines.

The production process depends on the types of parts a manufacturer produces. Companies may buy components from suppliers or make products from scratch by working raw materials like metals and plastics. Companies may own one or several production plants and may have large inventories of raw and finished materials.

Companies often own the tooling needed to manufacture parts, but tooling may also be owned by the customer the product is being made for. Tooling used for simple production processes may be bought from other manufacturers; companies may also develop their own special tooling for making proprietary products or components.

Engineering and quality assurance are important in the manufacturing process, both for producing parts to the specifications required by the customer, and for achieving cost efficiencies. Industrial engineering technology is a rapidly evolving field. Computer systems are extensively used for designing parts and for process control and inventory management. Many suppliers are integrating supply chain systems with customers to support "just-in-time" (JIT) delivery of parts to assembly operations. Big car companies are requiring suppliers to upgrade their electronic data interchange (EDI) capabilities to increase supply chain efficiency.

Sales & Marketing

The operations of most parts manufacturers are determined by the production cycle of autos, which are often substantially redesigned every few years. As part of the product development process, tier 1 suppliers are consulted by the OEMs about the manufacturing feasibility and cost of individual components, and are given contracts to produce them. Tier 1 companies in turn award contracts to smaller suppliers based on their ability to produce a part and the cost. Once chosen as the component supplier for a particular car or truck platform, a parts manufacturer can count on a continuing flow of business from that line for several years, even producing replacement parts after the vehicle is no longer made. But because OEMs and big suppliers buy "as needed" from smaller ones, long-term contracts don't necessarily guarantee stable sales.

Sales and marketing is usually handled by senior managers, since relations with a few large customers are crucial to company revenues.

Many suppliers sell both to OEMs and the higher-margin aftermarket, which includes retail auto parts chains like AutoZone and Genuine Parts, auto and truck dealers, repair shops; and about 20,000 traditional parts distributors ("jobbers") like NAPA, which sell to installers. Although big chains concentrate mainly on the consumer market, some also have a large commercial business that competes with jobbers.

Human Resources

Production jobs in auto parts manufacture typically involve operating complex machinery and are generally well-paid: about 15 percent above the average for all US manufacturing. The high average hourly earnings reflect both the skilled nature of the work and that the labor content of many auto parts has decreased in the past decade, allowing companies to pay higher wages to fewer workers. Fringe benefits typically are a fairly high 25 to 30 percent of wages. The high pay and benefits keep turnover low.

Due to challenging market conditions including high fuel prices, consumer preferences shifting from large SUVs and trucks, and intense foreign competition, car makers and their suppliers have had to lay off employees and renegotiate labor agreements. Union labor costs for many large suppliers have dropped to about $30 from $50 per hour; union labor costs at smaller suppliers can be around $20 per hour.

The safety record of the industry has improved rapidly in the past decade, but injury rates are still about 10 percent higher than the national average.

Industry Employment Growth

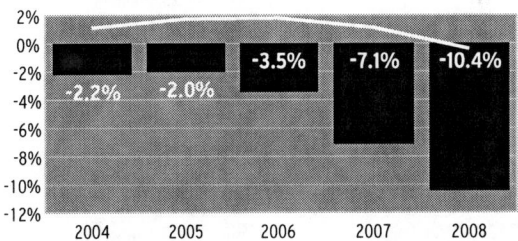

Average Hourly Earnings

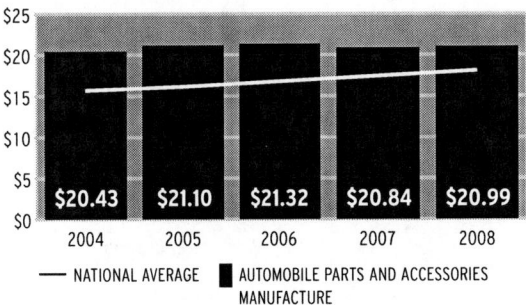

SOURCE: BUREAU OF LABOR STATISTICS

Call Preparation Questions

How is customer consolidation impacting the company's pricing strategies?

Consolidation of car companies and demand for larger and more complicated component assemblies have created larger, but fewer, auto part suppliers.

How is increased foreign competition in the US auto market affecting the company?

In recent years, the volume of car parts manufactured in low-cost countries like Mexico, China, and Taiwan has increased rapidly.

How is the company positioning itself to take advantage of growing demand for electronic technology in auto parts?

In the early 1990s electronic content in vehicles accounted for about 10 percent of a vehicle's cost; by 2010 experts predict that number will rise to about 40 percent.

Web Links

Alliance of Automobile Manufacturers

Industry public relations group, addressing public policy issues.
www.autoalliance.org

Assembly Magazine

Industry news, product news, links.
www.assemblymag.com

Automotive Aftermarket Industry Association (AAIA)

Segment news, facts, trade shows, news and events.
www.aftermarket.org

Automotive Body Parts Association

Technical information, industry description, publications, and conventions.
www.autobpa.com

Automotive News

News. Subscription required.
www.autonews.com

Motor & Equipment Manufacturers Association (MEMA)

Media news.
www.mema.org/news/news.php

The Auto Channel

Industry news.
www.theautochannel.com

Glossary of Acronyms

EDI — electronic data interchange

JIT — just-in-time

NADA — National Automobile Dealers Association

OEM — original equipment manufacturers

HOOVER'S TOP COMPANIES

Largest Companies by Sales	($ mil.)
Johnson Controls, Inc.	38,062.0
Delphi Corporation	18,060.0
Lear Corporation	15,995.0
TRW Automotive Holdings Corp.	14,995.0
Cummins, Inc.	14,342.0
Visteon Corporation	11,266.0
Robert Bosch LLC	9,500.0
Dana Holding Corporation	7,344.0
ArvinMeritor, Inc.	7,167.0
Federal-Mogul Corporation	6,865.6

Largest Employers	Employees
Delphi Corporation	169,500
Johnson Controls, Inc.	140,000
Lear Corporation	91,000
TRW Automotive Holdings Corp.	66,300
Federal-Mogul Corporation	50,000
Visteon Corporation	41,500
Cummins, Inc.	37,800
Dana Holding Corporation	35,000
Robert Bosch LLC	25,600
Cooper-Standard Automotive Inc.	21,123

Fastest Growing* by Five-Year Sales Growth	(%)
U.S. Auto Parts Network, Inc.	50.1
Noble International, Ltd.	47.4
MIRENCO, Inc.	43.1
LKQ Corporation	42.6
Fuel Systems Solutions, Inc.	38.6
Accuride Corporation	24.0
Commercial Vehicle Group, Inc.	21.6
J.B. Poindexter & Co., Inc.	19.1
Cummins, Inc.	17.9
Amerigon Incorporated	17.0

Fastest Growing* by Five-Year Employee Growth	(%)
U.S. Auto Parts Network, Inc.	65.9
Noble International, Ltd.	38.5
LKQ Corporation	38.3
Commercial Vehicle Group, Inc.	36.4
Fuel Systems Solutions, Inc.	28.0
Accuride Corporation	16.3
Cooper-Standard Automotive Inc.	15.8
Amerigon Incorporated	15.5
J.B. Poindexter & Co., Inc.	12.0
Federal-Mogul Corporation	0.3

Top Public Companies by Market Value	($ mil.)
Johnson Controls, Inc.	17,918.9
Cummins, Inc.	5,380.7
BorgWarner Inc.	2,515.1
LKQ Corporation	1,631.5
Federal-Mogul Corporation	420.7

* These rates are compounded annualized increases and may have resulted from acquisitions or one time gains. If less than 6 years of data are available, growth is for the years available.

SOURCE: HOOVER'S, INC., DATABASE

Automobile Parts — Wholesale and Retail

The wholesale and retail auto parts industry includes approximately 45,000 companies with combined annual revenue of $135 billion. Top companies include Genuine Parts, AutoZone, Advance Auto Parts, O'Reilly Automotive, and The Pep Boys. About 25 wholesalers and 40 retailers each have annual sales over $100 million. Many large firms operate both wholesale distribution centers and retail stores.

The industry is concentrated at the top: the 50 largest wholesalers hold over 50 percent of the wholesale segment. The retail segment is a bit less concentrated, with the top 50 companies holding about 40 percent of the segment. The used parts segment is highly fragmented.

Competitive Landscape

Demand for aftermarket parts is driven by the age and mileage of vehicles, generally increasing when fewer new cars are sold. The profitability of individual companies depends largely on inventory management and marketing. Small companies can compete effectively by carrying specialized parts or providing extra services such as machining or fast delivery. Average annual revenue per employee is about $700,000 for wholesalers, $100,000 for small retailers, and $175,000 for large retailers.

Products, Operations & Technology

The industry sells parts and other products used to maintain and repair cars and trucks in the so-called auto "aftermarket." Products are sold both to consumers who work on their own cars, the do-it-yourselfers (DIY); and to commercial installers like auto repair shops, gas stations, fleet operators, and car dealer service departments (do-it-for-me, DIFM market). The DIY segment accounts for about 30 percent of the market, the DIFM segment 70 percent.

Products include "hard parts" like brakes, mufflers, batteries, starters, alternator, and pumps; maintenance items like oil, oil filters,

BUSINESS CHALLENGES

» Auto Parts Spending Driven by Economy

Because auto parts sales depend on auto driving, demand decreases during recessions. During economic downturns, tourists and businesspeople travel less, and car owners delay maintenance and repairs. For example, sales of auto parts retail stores grew 4 percent in 2000, then fell 1 percent in the 2001 recession.

» Competition from Mass Merchants Pressures Prices

Retail auto parts stores face greater competition from large retailers such as Wal-Mart, Costco, Sears, and supermarket chains. These retailers are large enough to buy items directly from manufacturers, pressuring prices of auto supply stores. Mass merchants carry high-volume items such as oil, additives, lubricants, cleaners, mats, and wipers.

» Slow Industry Growth

Although the number of new autos in the US grows about 2 percent per year, because of better technology new cars need fewer repairs and less maintenance. Many car manufacturers now recommend oil changes only every 10,000 miles. The total number of auto and truck crashes dropped in recent years to about 6.2 million per year, which in turn has decreased demand for replacement parts.

lubricants, additives, spark plugs, fuel injectors, lights, wipers, paints, waxes, and hoses; tools like wrenches and diagnostic equipment; and accessories like trim, hub caps, and audio systems.

Most wholesalers and retailers operate a single location, but economies of scale in purchasing have encouraged the growth of large wholesale and retail networks. AutoZone, for example, operates 3,200 stores; Genuine Parts has 58 distribution centers and 900 retail stores. A typical distributor warehouse handles about $15 million in annual sales; a typical retail store $1 to $2 million.

In general, wholesalers sell to retail operators (stores and repair shops), who in turn serve car owners. But the similarity between wholesale and retail operations has drawn many wholesalers into the retail business and vice versa. Big retailers like AutoZone, Advance Auto Parts, Pep Boys, and O'Reilly Automotive operate their own distribution network. Some retailers sell both to consumers and local repair shops; some retailers operate their own repair department.

The traditional structure of the industry includes jobbers as intermediaries between wholesale distributors and retail operations, but the increasing efficiency of distribution operations is rapidly eliminating jobbers.

The operations of both wholesalers and retailers revolve around inventory management. A typical wholesale distribution center may carry 300,000 parts (stock-keeping units, SKUs). A retailer may carry 25,000 SKUs onsite in a 7,500 square foot store. Wholesalers must also operate an efficient delivery system so that orders can be filled the same day or by the next. Same-day service is essential for supplying repair shops. Wholesalers and many retailers operate their own delivery trucks.

Parts are bought from the large auto parts manufacturers like Delphi, Johnson Controls, and Visteon, from thousands of smaller manufacturers that make parts for the auto companies under new vehicle programs, and from manufacturers that make replacement parts specifically for the aftermarket. A wholesaler typically buys from 200 to 300 vendors. Production programs for new cars typically include 5 to 10 percent of production that goes to the aftermarket. Long-term supply contracts are rare, and in most cases, several suppliers are available for any particular product. Large repair assemblies like entire doors or fenders are usually available only from a single source or used parts suppliers.

Computer technology is essential to auto parts wholesalers and retailers because they deal with large inventories of many items, bought from many suppliers, and with numerous small orders from customers, many that buy on account. Computerized catalogs that allow customers to find the correct parts based on auto year and make are common, and some companies, like AutoZone.com, NAPAonline.com, Delphi.com, and Usedpartslive.com, allow customers to buy parts over the Internet using electronic catalogs.

Sales & Marketing

Sales and marketing initiatives center on the type of customer a company is trying to serve. Wholesalers rely heavily on a sales force, advertising in trade magazines, and on trade shows. Retailers use typical retail advertising such as newspapers and Yellow Pages. Large retailers also advertise on TV and radio.

Some wholesalers and retailers belong to Program Distribution Organizations (program groups), similar to franchise networks, that buy in bulk and provide marketing services for members. Among the largest are the National Automotive Parts Association (NAPA); Automotive Distribution Network; and CARQUEST.

Human Resources

The majority of employees in the industry are in the retail segment. Retail is also the lower paid portion of the industry: the average wage is $12 per hour, compared to parts distribution at $16, which is the same as the national average. Because of the relatively low wages, personnel turnover can be high. Special training about car parts and computerized catalogs is necessary, especially at the wholesale level. The injury rate for retail is slightly above four cases per 100 full-time workers, the same as the national average, but the wholesale segment's is one case higher.

Industry Employment Growth

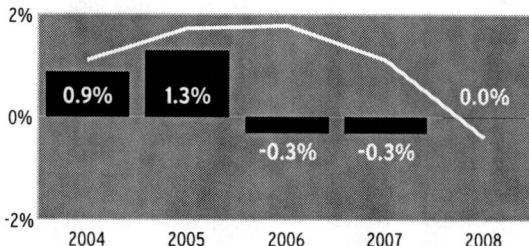

Average Hourly Earnings

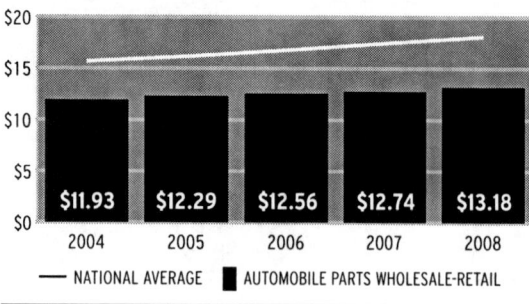

— NATIONAL AVERAGE ■ AUTOMOBILE PARTS WHOLESALE-RETAIL

SOURCE: BUREAU OF LABOR STATISTICS

Call Preparation Questions

How does the company adjust to lower demand?

Because auto parts sales depend on auto driving, demand decreases during recessions.

With cars requiring less maintenance, where does the company see future industry demand?

Although the number of new autos in the US grows about 2 percent per year, because of better technology new cars need fewer repairs and less maintenance.

How does the company plan to expand its service business?

The largest growth is coming from the do-it-for-me (DIFM) segment, which is the least price-sensitive because costs are passed to consumers.

Does the company plan to add various types of installation services?

More retailers combine store sales with installation services for such products as audio, video, and phone systems; exhaust pipes; rims and wheels; and trim.

Web Links

Aftermarket Business

Industry news. Top 100 distributors. Consumer surveys.
aftermarketbusiness.search-autoparts.com

Automotive Aftermarket Industry Association

Industry statistics, trends.
www.aftermarket.org

Automotive Parts Manufacturers' Association

Canadian association. Good industry links.
www.apma.ca

Automotive Recyclers Association

www.a-r-a.org

Detroit Free Press

Industry news.
www.freep.com/index/autos.htm

National Automotive Parts Association

www.napaonline.com

National Highway Traffic Safety Administration

Regulatory and safety information.
www.nhtsa.dot.gov

Specialty Equipment Market Association

Statistics for this segment of the industry.
www.sema.org

Wards Auto

News and auto industry statistics.
www.wardsauto.com

Glossary of Acronyms

DIFM — do-it-for-me
DIY — do-it-yourselfer
JIT — just-in-time
SKU — stock-keeping unit

HOOVER'S TOP COMPANIES

Largest Companies by Sales	($ mil.)
Genuine Parts Company	11,015.3
AutoZone, Inc.	6,522.7
Advance Auto Parts, Inc.	5,142.3
O'Reilly Automotive, Inc.	3,576.6
General Parts, Inc.	2,870.0
Discount Tire Co. Inc.	2,310.0
The Pep Boys — Manny, Moe & Jack	2,138.1
American Tire Distributors Holdings, Inc.	1,877.5
Interstate Battery System of America, Inc.	1,500.0
Les Schwab Tire Centers	1,480.0

Largest Employers	Employees
AutoZone, Inc.	55,000
Advance Auto Parts, Inc.	44,065
O'Reilly Automotive, Inc.	40,735
Genuine Parts Company	32,000
The Pep Boys — Manny, Moe & Jack	18,564
General Parts, Inc.	18,000
Discount Tire Co. Inc.	11,630
Les Schwab Tire Centers	7,900
American Tire Distributors Holdings, Inc.	2,400
FleetPride, Inc.	2,197

Fastest Growing* by Five-Year Sales Growth	(%)
U.S. Auto Parts Network, Inc.	50.1
O'Reilly Automotive, Inc.	18.8
Interstate Battery System of America, Inc.	17.1
American Tire Distributors Holdings, Inc.	12.1
General Parts, Inc.	11.7
Discount Tire Co. Inc.	10.3
Dorman Products, Inc.	9.0
Les Schwab Tire Centers	8.2
Advance Auto Parts, Inc.	8.0
Genuine Parts Company	5.4

Fastest Growing* by Five-Year Employee Growth	(%)
U.S. Auto Parts Network, Inc.	65.9
O'Reilly Automotive, Inc.	11.8
Interstate Battery System of America, Inc.	9.5
Advance Auto Parts, Inc.	6.4
Les Schwab Tire Centers	5.7
Discount Tire Co. Inc.	5.4
General Parts, Inc.	5.2
American Tire Distributors Holdings, Inc.	4.6
AutoZone, Inc.	2.8
Genuine Parts Company	0.5

Top Public Companies by Market Value	($ mil.)
AutoZone, Inc.	8,180.0
Genuine Parts Company	6,036.5
O'Reilly Automotive, Inc.	4,144.6
Advance Auto Parts, Inc.	3,238.2
The Pep Boys — Manny, Moe & Jack	628.0

* These rates are compounded annualized increases and may have resulted from acquisitions or one time gains. If less than 6 years of data are available, growth is for the years available.

SOURCE: HOOVER'S, INC., DATABASE

Automobile Rental and Leasing

The auto rental and leasing industry in the US includes 5,000 companies with combined annual revenue of about $50 billion. Large companies include Hertz, Enterprise Rent-A-Car, Vanguard Car Rental Group, Avis Budget Group, U-Haul International (a subsidiary of AMERCO), and Dollar Thrifty Automotive Group. The industry is highly concentrated: the 50 largest companies hold more than 80 percent of the market.

Competitive Landscape

The industry depends highly on the general state of the US economy because most customers are business or vacation/leisure travelers, whose numbers can rapidly fall during an economic slowdown.

The big companies have economies of scale in acquiring vehicles and customers. Small companies typically operate a single rental location, but can compete effectively with larger companies by providing better service, alternative products, or lower prices. Individual rental locations typically have annual revenue of about $1 million and eight employees, but may have revenue over $10 million and 200 employees. Revenue per employee ranges from $100,000 at a small location to $200,000 at a large one.

Products, Operations & Technology

Operations are similar for car, truck, or specialty vehicle rental operations. A typical car rental operation has to acquire, maintain, clean, fuel, and repair cars, and dispose of older cars, and must operate a reservation system to acquire customers. Efficient operations are crucial for profitability, because the value of the rental asset is high.

The difference between the acquisition price of cars and their residual value when disposed of is crucial in determining the profitability of rental companies. Large companies like Hertz and Avis buy new cars directly from car manu-

BUSINESS CHALLENGES

» Demand Depends Strongly on Air Travel

Car rental demand depends on air travel, which in turn is affected by the health of the national economy. During the last recession, car rental revenue dropped 8 percent as air passenger traffic dropped 8 percent. Car rental companies also see seasonal changes in business depending on their location and the type of traveler they serve.

» Profitability Depends on Auto Resale Values

The profitability of rental companies is sharply affected by the difference between new and used car and truck prices. Even companies that acquire cars through guaranteed residual value programs eventually see larger spreads between acquisition and residual values if used car prices are weak. Used car prices dropped 8 percent during the last recession.

» Inventory Management Important for Profitability

A small inventory of vehicles produces dissatisfied customers; a large inventory produces idle assets. To avoid disappointing customers, rental companies typically carry too large an inventory; however, those with multiple locations in a geographical area can use their inventory more efficiently than can one-location companies.

facturers under "repurchase" or "residual value" programs that guarantee a repurchase price at which cars are taken back by the manufacturer as long as mileage limits are not exceeded (typically 30,000 miles) and cars are in reasonable condition. Such cars are called "non-risk" or "program" cars. Companies with high annual car turnover may get a large share of their cars through such programs, more than 90 percent for Hertz and Avis.

National car rental companies typically operate cars for less than a year, with an average fleet age of four to six months. The average annual revenue per fleet car is around $12,000. Trucks and RVs aren't usually bought through manufacturer programs, because they remain in rental service longer than cars and their residual value is more difficult to forecast.

Smaller rental companies may be able to buy fleets directly from car manufacturers under manufacturer programs, but more typically acquire them from local dealers, financial leasing companies, other rental companies, or through leasing programs operated by the big car rental companies for their franchisees. Thirteen percent of Budget's revenue came from leasing cars to franchisees in 2005. Dollar Thrifty's was 4 percent, down from 50 percent three years earlier, the result of the company's conversion of franchises into corporate operations.

Used vehicles are returned to manufacturers or leasing operators, or are sold to used car dealers, wholesalers, other fleet operators or at auction. Some companies have their own retail sales operations.

Truck rental customers are either short-term users like home movers and businesses with seasonal needs, or corporations that engage in long-term contracts for trucks, maintenance services, truck supplies, and sometimes even drivers. Budget provided a fleet of 32,100 trucks through 2,700 locations in 2005. Contract services are marketed through a sales force; short-term rentals, through Yellow Pages' advertising.

Most of the large national car chains operate in local markets through franchisees. Hertz owns virtually all its local operations, but large portions of the Avis system are franchised. Thrifty has bought back many of its franchisees in key markets. Franchise operations are usually exclusive within a geographic area. Franchisees make some required payments and can also contract for other services with the parent chain, including car leasing and reservations systems. Basic fees are tied to gross annual revenue. Thrifty franchisees, for example, pay annual required fees of 3 percent of revenue for administrative support and 2.5 to 5 percent for advertising. Under car leasing programs, the parent acquires cars from manufacturers and leases them to the franchisees.

Sales & Marketing

The main customer markets for rental cars are the airport market (business or leisure travelers using the local airport); business travelers; vacation or leisure travelers; and the local or suburban market. The airport market is by far the largest source of customers. To serve airport customers, rental companies typically lease counter space and vehicle lots from airport authorities. Other business and leisure travelers rent cars to travel to locations when air travel is too expensive or complicated. The local or suburban market consists mainly of customers who need a replacement car because theirs is being repaired (with costs paid by car dealers or insurance companies) or who temporarily need an additional car.

Typical airport concession agreements call for fixed rent payments and a percentage of car rental revenue. Part of the airport market is also served by downtown locations near major hotels. Location isn't as important for companies in the local market because cars are often delivered to the customer. Location also isn't very important for truck and RV rental companies.

Most airport customers reserve a car beforehand, usually at the same time they book their air flight and hotel. To have access to these customers, rental companies may have agreements with the major global reservations systems such as Sabre, Galileo, Worldspan, and Amadeus, with Internet travel sites such as Expedia and Orbitz, with individual airline, hotel, and travel companies and with tour operators. Rental companies with many locations may also operate their own Internet rental site. For the local market, rental companies often have arrangements with local hotels, corporate customers, repair shops, car dealerships, and insurance agencies.

The national chains advertise heavily on TV, but local market advertising is often limited to telephone directories and billboards. In local markets, referrals are often more important than advertising. Pricing is highly competitive, varies from market to market, and can change rapidly in response to local market conditions. Daily rental prices for a full-size car from the same firm vary from $50 in Chicago to $30 in Birmingham. Prices are usually higher for walk-in customers.

Human Resources

Most jobs in the industry require relatively low skills, and wages are therefore modest, about 15 percent lower than for the average US worker. Personnel turnover can be high because of low wages. Most jobs are clerical or involve car care, and many are part-time because of uneven customer traffic during the week and year. The industry injury rate is about 50 percent higher than for all US workers.

Industry Employment Growth

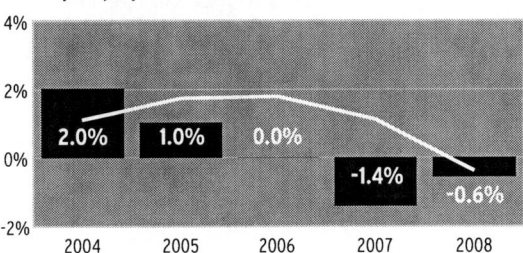

Average Hourly Earnings

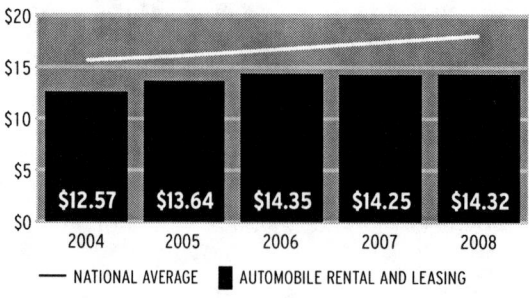

	2004	2005	2006	2007	2008
	$12.57	$13.64	$14.35	$14.25	$14.32

— NATIONAL AVERAGE ■ AUTOMOBILE RENTAL AND LEASING

SOURCE: BUREAU OF LABOR STATISTICS

Call Preparation Questions

How does the company protect itself from fluctuations in rental demand and in the economy?

Car rental demand depends on air travel, which in turn is affected by the health of the national economy.

What opportunities or benefits does the company see in providing corporate fleet management services?

The desire of many corporations to outsource transportation functions has presented opportunities for rental companies to provide logistics and maintenance services for corporate-owned fleets, or provide complete fleet management, including acquisition, ownership, and disposal of vehicles.

What other rental equipment has the company considered offering, and why?

In addition to renting just cars or trucks, many companies also rent related equipment such as baby seats, trailers, RVs, and construction equipment.

Web Links

American Car Rental Association

Limited information.
www.acraorg.com

Fleet-Central

Click on "Auto Rental News — more news" for news articles in recent months.
www.fleet-central.com/t_home.cfm

National Business Travel Association

Tracks business travel. Periodic reports on rental cars.
www.nbta.org

National Vehicle Leasing Association

Represents the vehicle leasing industry, provides educational opportunities, promotes responsible legislation and communicates with members regarding developments and trends in vehicle leasing.
www.nvla.org

RV America

Links to RV rental centers.
www.rvamerica.net

ServNet Auction Group

Association of wholesale auto auctions.
www.servnetauctions.com

Glossary of Acronyms

NAFA — National Association of Fleet Administrators

TIAA — Travel Industry Association of America

HOOVER'S TOP COMPANIES

Largest Companies by Sales	($ mil.)
Enterprise Rent-A-Car Company	9,500.0
Hertz Global Holdings, Inc.	8,685.6
Ryder System, Inc.	6,203.7
Avis Budget Group, Inc.	5,984.0
PHH Corporation	2,960.0
Vanguard Car Rental Group Inc.	1,304.2
AMERCO	2,049.2
Dollar Thrifty Automotive Group, Inc.	1,760.8

Largest Employers	Employees
Enterprise Rent-A-Car Company	66,700
Avis Budget Group, Inc.	30,000
Hertz Global Holdings, Inc.	29,350
Ryder System, Inc.	28,800
AMERCO	18,500
Vanguard Car Rental Group Inc.	12,600
Dollar Thrifty Automotive Group, Inc.	8,500
Alamo Rent A Car, LLC	7,000

Fastest Growing* by Five-Year Sales Growth	(%)
Hertz Global Holdings, Inc.	11.8
Dollar Thrifty Automotive Group, Inc.	9.2
Ryder System, Inc.	5.3

Fastest Growing* by Five-Year Employee Growth	(%)
Dollar Thrifty Automotive Group, Inc.	7.6
AMERCO	2.8
Hertz Global Holdings, Inc.	0.3
Ryder System, Inc.	0.2

Top Public Companies by Market Value	($ mil.)
Hertz Global Holdings, Inc.	5,114.4
Ryder System, Inc.	2,158.4
AMERCO	1,120.8
PHH Corporation	690.7
Avis Budget Group, Inc.	71.2

* These rates are compounded annualized increases and may have resulted from acquisitions or one time gains. If less than 6 years of data are available, growth is for the years available.

SOURCE: HOOVER'S, INC., DATABASE

Automotive Repair Shops

THIS INDUSTRY INCLUDES:

SIC CODES

7532   Top, Body, and Upholstery Repair Shops and Paint Shops

7536   Automotive Glass Replacement Shops

7538   General Automotive Repair Shops

NAICS CODES

8111   Automotive Repair and Maintenance

The US auto repair shop industry includes about 170,000 firms with combined annual revenue of $90 billion. Large companies include Midas, Monro Muffler Brake, and Belron US. The industry is extremely fragmented: the 50 largest companies hold less than 10 percent of the market. This industry generally includes quick oil change shops and car washes and excludes tire shops.

Competitive Landscape

Demand depends on car usage and the number of cars on the road. The profitability of individual companies depends on convenient location and good marketing. Large companies can maximize use of expensive diagnostic equipment and have advantages in purchasing, distribution, and marketing. Small companies can compete effectively by providing superior customer service or offering specialized services. The industry is labor-intensive: average annual revenue per worker is about $100,000.

Competition includes other venues that provide automotive services, including some gas stations, car dealerships, and branches of chain stores, like Sears and Kmart. Auto repair shops perform an estimated 70 percent of repairs for out-of-warranty vehicles, according to the Automotive Service Association (ASA).

Products, Operations & Technology

About 70 percent of industry revenue comes from mechanical repair and 30 percent from collision repair. Mechanical jobs include repairs to "undercar" systems, (mufflers and exhausts, transmissions, brakes, and shock absorbers) or in "underhood" systems (engines, electrical systems, radiators). Body work includes exterior and interior repair and glass replacement. Other services include oil changes and car washes. Companies may sell parts for do-it-yourselfers (DIY).

BUSINESS CHALLENGES

» Competition from Large Repair Shops and Chains

The greater operational and pricing efficiencies of large shops allow them to take business from smaller shops, despite some having less convenient locations. Franchise chains, dealerships, and large shops also have advantages in buying, managing inventory, and amortizing expensive equipment. Because of strong competition in local markets, repair shops have limited ability to raise prices.

» Public Mistrust

Because of the complexity of cars, consumers can't easily judge if a repair shop has treated them fairly. Polls consistently show that a high percentage of consumers believe that repair shops make unnecessary repairs, overcharge, or use inferior replacement parts. Press stories about repair shops engaged in unethical practices, including insurance fraud, are frequent.

» Body Shops Depend on Insurance

Revenue generated by insurance direct repair programs (DRP) can account for almost all of a shop's business, particularly large shops that gross over $1 million annually, according to Body Shop Business. Large companies, such as Allstate, State Farm, Farmers, Nationwide, and Progressive, dominate the insurance industry. To maintain their insurance business, body shops must conform to insurance company demands about billable rates, replacement parts, and warranties. Some shops feel forced to agree with insurance suggestions, like overlooking auto damage or installing cheaper aftermarket parts.

The industry includes national and regional chains, franchises, and independent operators. The majority of auto repair shops are independently owned, although many are franchises of large companies. Car repair shops may specialize in a particular field of repair, such as brake jobs or collision repair, because of the specialized knowledge and equipment required. Most companies in the mechanical field provide generalized services, such as regular maintenance, in addition to specialty services.

In auto repair shops, estimators review vehicles and give customers quotes on the approximate cost of a repair. Estimators may rely on car makers' recommendations or computer software to help develop an accurate estimate. Repairs sometimes uncover other problems, resulting in additional work and charges in excess of the estimate. Regardless of the cause of error, inaccurate estimates have resulted in unhappy customers and general mistrust of the industry.

Mechanical repair shops deal mainly with deterioration of parts due to normal wear. Common repairs involve air conditioning, brake, transmission, and electrical systems. Because of the increased technological complexity of newer cars, most shops have specialized diagnostic equipment to identify and fix problems. Shops typically keep an inventory of replacement parts or have arrangements with quick delivery parts suppliers. Experienced, well-trained auto technicians are critical to quality repair work. Companies may also employ apprentice or entry-level technicians.

Collision repair involves two distinct types of repair: body work and painting (or refinishing). In the body shop, technicians correct damaged car frames and panels. Each repair is unique and depends on the accident that caused damage. The painting process includes several standard steps and operates more like an assembly line. Paint preparation includes feathering (smoothing the surface) and priming. Paint application typically involves applying multiple coats. Finishing provides a protective clear coat. Collision repair jobs usually take four to eight days. Equipment includes welders, paint booths, frame machines, and plasma cutters. Key staff includes framers, technicians, and painters.

A typical mechanical repair shop has seven service bays and averages 5,300 square feet, according to the Automotive Service Association (ASA). The average number of repairs ranges from about 200 to 250 per month. A typical body shop has 17 service bays and averages 12,000 square feet. Body shops average about 85 repairs monthly. Fewer than 5 percent of auto repair shop customers return for additional work on the same problem ("comebacks"). The majority of comebacks are due to defective parts. The average body shop generates about $600,000 annually, according to Body Shop Business.

Auto repair shops may buy replacement parts and supplies from full-line vendors, such

as NAPA, or have supply arrangements with multiple distributors. Some large companies have purchasing contracts with specific suppliers. Chains of repair shops often maintain parts distribution centers to minimize the parts inventory needs at individual stores. With hundreds of parts needed for thousands of car models and production years, individual stores can't keep complete inventories. Shops may install OEM or aftermarket parts (rebuilt).

Many shops use computerized information systems to help manage point-of-sale, inventories, purchasing, accounting, and customer relations. Database programs give companies fast access to customer and vehicle information and repair histories. Electronic cataloging allows companies to research maintenance requirements and specific parts needed for a vehicle's particular make, model, and mileage. Diagnostic computer systems are essential equipment for mechanical repair shops because modern cars are filled with sensors and onboard diagnostics (OBD) — a vehicle's self-diagnostic system.

Sales & Marketing

Almost 80 percent of mechanical repair shop and 60 percent of collision repair shop customers are repeat, according to the Automotive Service Association (ASA). Auto repair shops typically draw customers from a 20- to 30-mile radius.

Marketing and promotional vehicles include phone directories; signage; local newspaper, TV, and radio ads; and direct mail. Because business related to insurance claims can be a large percentage of sales, relationships with insurance agents and companies are important for large body shops. Body shops that participate in insurance-sponsored "approved service provider" programs or direct repair programs (DRPs) can generate double the sales of a non-DRP shop, according to Body Shop Business.

Because companies depend on repeat business, customer satisfaction is key to generating loyalty. Shoddy or unnecessary repairs by some unscrupulous shops have resulted in general mistrust of the industry. Companies rely heavily on customer referrals. An honest reputation can generate positive word-of-mouth. Many shops offer warranties on repairs, in case problems arise.

Many shops have websites that communicate basic information, including hours of operation and basic services performed. Some companies allow customers to schedule appointments or obtain estimates online. Recommendations and links from consumer ratings websites, such as Angieslist.com, can help generate referrals.

Repair "tickets" range from $275 to $400 for mechanical repair shops, split about evenly between parts and labor. The average ticket is about $2,000 for body shops, split about evenly between parts and supplies and labor. Mechanical repair shops service the same car about three times annually.

Human Resources

Owners and managers of repair shops are usually experienced mechanics who directly oversee the technicians who do most of the actual repair work. Technicians can receive various grades of certification from professional groups like the American Institute for Automotive Service Excellence (ASE). To gain experience, many workers start as apprentice technicians. A mechanical repair shop employs about half a dozen technicians, while a collision repair shop employs about eight, according to the Automobile Service Association (ASA).

Because average hourly wages are about 15 percent below the national average, turnover, particularly among entry-level workers, can be high. The industry injury rate is about 20 percent lower than the national average.

Industry Employment Growth

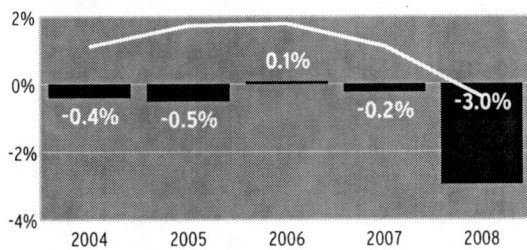

Average Hourly Earnings

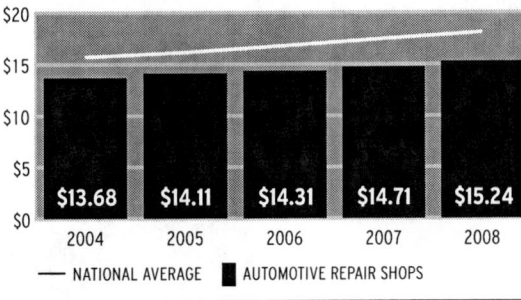

SOURCE: BUREAU OF LABOR STATISTICS

Call Preparation Questions

How does the company compete against large repair chains and car dealers?

The greater operational and pricing efficiencies of large shops allow them to take business from smaller shops, despite some having less convenient locations.

How does the company build trust with customers?

Because of the complexity of cars, consumers can't easily judge if a repair shop has treated them fairly.

What types of problems has the company experienced when dealing with insurance companies?

Revenue generated by insurance direct repair programs (DRP) can account for almost all of a shop's business, particularly large shops that gross over $1 million annually, according to Body Shop Business.

What specialized services does the company offer?

Auto repair shops can create a niche by developing expertise in nontraditional or specialized vehicles.

How does paintless dent repair fit into the company's service offerings?

By providing paintless dent repair (PDR), repair shops can fix small dings and dents at a reasonable cost to the customer.

Web Links

Automotive Body Repair News

Industry news.
www.abrn.com/abrn

Automotive Industries Association of Canada

News from Canadian trade association for the automotive aftermarket.
www.aiacanada.com

Automotive Service Association

Industry news, trends and statistics from trade association. Annual business survey in AutoInc Magazine.

www.asashop.org

BodyShop Business Magazine

Industry news, trends, and statistics. Annual business survey for body shops.

www.bodyshopbusiness.com

Bureau of Transportation Statistics

Statistics about car and truck registrations and driving trends.

www.bts.gov

Canadian Automotive Repair & Service Council

News from Canadian trade association for auto technicians.

www.cars-council.ca

CollisionWeek

Collision industry news.

www.collisionweek.com

INSIGHT

Collision industry repair news.

www.collision-insight.com

National Automobile Dealers Association

See "NADA Data" for details of parts and service department operations of car dealers.

www.nada.org

National Highway Traffic Safety Administration

Crash statistics and economics.

www.nhtsa.gov

National Institute for Automotive Service Excellence

National certification organization for auto technicians.

www.ase.com

Professional Tool & Equipment News

Auto repair tool and equipment market news.

www.pten.com

Glossary of Acronyms

ASA — Automotive Service Association
ASE — Automotive Service Excellence
DIY — do-it-yourself
DRP — direct repair program
OBD — on-board diagnostics
OEM — original equipment manufacturer
PDR — paintless dent repair
POS — point-of-sale
UST — underground storage tank

HOOVER'S TOP COMPANIES

Largest Companies by Sales	($ mil.)
Bridgestone Retail Operations	2,090.5
Pittsburgh Glass Works LLC	1,010.0
Monro Muffler Brake, Inc.	439.4
Midas, Inc.	180.0
Jiffy Lube International, Inc.	150.0

Largest Employers	Employees
Bridgestone Retail Operations	23,000
Pittsburgh Glass Works LLC	4,400
Jiffy Lube International, Inc.	3,000
United Road Services, Inc.	2,300
Lucor, Inc.	2,011
Caliber Holdings Corporation	1,500
Belle Tire Distributors	1,100
Peach Holding Co., Inc.	500
True2Form Collision Repair Centers, Inc.	450
Bauer Built, Inc.	450

Fastest Growing* by Five-Year Sales Growth	(%)
Monro Muffler Brake, Inc.	11.2
Tilden Associates, Inc.	8.4

Top Public Companies by Market Value	($ mil.)
Monro Muffler Brake, Inc.	300.4
Midas, Inc.	203.0
Mace Security International, Inc.	33.4

* These rates are compounded annualized increases and may have resulted from acquisitions or one time gains. If less than 6 years of data are available, growth is for the years available.

SOURCE: HOOVER'S, INC., DATABASE

Aviation Services

About 1,500 companies provide airport support services to the general aviation (private and business plane) market, with combined annual revenue of $3 billion. Most companies are either privately held, like Air Serv, or are divisions of larger corporations, such as TAC Air, owned by Truman Arnold Companies, and Signature Flight Support, owned by BBA Aviation. Most aviation services firms are single-facility operations with annual revenue less than $1 million. About 50 companies have annual revenue over $10 million and operate facilities at multiple airports.

This industry does not service commercial airlines or airports.

Competitive Landscape

Local and regional air travel, especially business travel, drives demand for aviation services to small and private aircraft. Profitability is based on sales volume, as prices fluctuate only periodically. Small companies can compete effectively in hometown markets. Big companies have more clout in negotiating with suppliers, which allows them better pricing options for their own services.

Products, Operations & Technology

Aviation services consist of refueling operations and fixed base operations (FBOs). Full-service FBOs usually include refueling. Over 4,000 FBOs operate in the US, often with several servicing the larger airports. (The US has 5,300 public airports.) The services provided are similar to the airport services that airline companies have for their commercial fleets: line operations, such as parking, refueling, de-icing, tie-down, hangar, and preheating; aircraft management services, such as maintenance, inspection, parts sales, aircraft sales, aircraft rental, chartering, and flight instruction; and personal services, such as food service, VIP terminals, car

BUSINESS CHALLENGES

» Dependence on Local Aviation Activity

National economic trends, like demand for general aviation (GA) planes and weather trends, may impact aviation services. However, most aviation service companies operate locally or regionally; as a result, they're especially vulnerable to local business demands. Service companies must be able to endure cyclical economic periods of lower business and recreational flying activity, when revenue from fuel sales and maintenance may be down sharply.

» Vulnerable to High Fuel Prices

Companies that carry large fuel inventories are exposed to considerable price risk. In recent years, the spot price of jet fuel has varied sharply from month to month. Because of intense competition, companies can't always pass higher costs to customers. High fuel costs also discourage recreational flyers.

» Regulatory Restrictions on General Aviation

Airspace and airport restrictions and security regulations may decrease the attractiveness of general aviation (GA) and reduce demand for aviation services. GA passengers and baggage may eventually have to be screened. Because many accidents are due to poor maintenance, FAA requires general aviation to adhere to strict maintenance procedures. For example, maintenance operations are required to send all tooling, including calibrated wrenches, to the FAA for inspection.

rentals, conference rooms, pilot lounges, flight planning, and business services.

Fuel sales are usually one of the most profitable services. Jet fuel is the predominant type of aviation fuel in commercial aviation, but aviation gasoline (avgas) is the primary fuel used by GA. Companies typically buy fuel from wholesalers. Fuel tanks, usually kept above ground, must comply with EPA regulations. Because aircraft can choose where to refuel during travel, companies go to great lengths to compete, as refueling revenue for a typical private jet may be as much as $2,000. Airplane owners lease hangar space at daily and monthly rates that depend on the size of the airplane. Hangar space for a small plane may cost $30 per day or $200 per month. Many locations consider long-term hangar rentals as loss-leaders. Companies, which usually lease their space and facilities from the host airport, provide low monthly hangar rates to make more-lucrative sales of fuel, maintenance, and other services.

Companies, particularly those with multiple locations, may use customer-oriented computer technology to support clients. Websites allow customers to plan trips, reserve services at various airports, and track maintenance and service records and reminders. Waiting rooms offer modem hook-ups and high-speed Internet connections. New computerized maintenance tools give maintenance personnel information about any part on a specific plane.

Sales & Marketing

While customers can be anyone from the hobby flyer to a corporation, business travel drives revenue for the typical service company. Sales representatives call on corporate accounts and individual aircraft owners. Marketing is through local advertising, telemarketing, and increasingly through the Internet. Competitive factors include turnaround time, safety, service quality, price, and personal knowledge. Recently, local operators have faced increased competition from national chains like Mercury Air Centers.

Human Resources

Aviation operations personnel earn an average wage slightly below that of the average US worker. The annual personnel turnover rate is 45 percent. The industry injury rate is slightly above average. Most jobs in the industry are maintenance- or service-oriented.

Industry Employment Growth

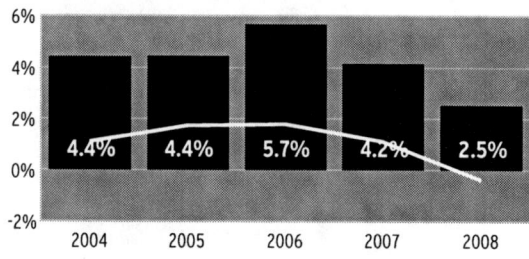

	2004	2005	2006	2007	2008
	4.4%	4.4%	5.7%	4.2%	2.5%

Average Hourly Earnings

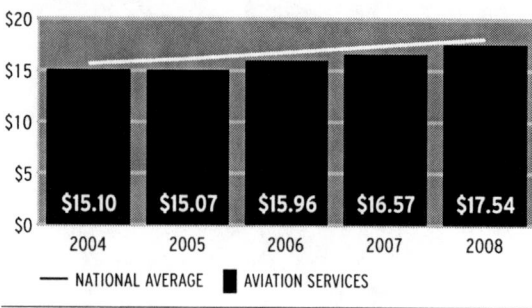

	2004	2005	2006	2007	2008
	$15.10	$15.07	$15.96	$16.57	$17.54

— NATIONAL AVERAGE ■ AVIATION SERVICES

SOURCE: BUREAU OF LABOR STATISTICS

Call Preparation Questions

How does the company lessen fluctuations in local demand and the economy?

National economic trends, like demand for general aviation (GA) planes and weather trends, may impact aviation services.

How vulnerable is the company to changes in fuel prices?

Companies that carry large fuel inventories are exposed to considerable price risk.

How might the company be impacted by more government regulation of the general aviation (GA) industry?

Airspace and airport restrictions and security regulations may decrease the attractiveness of general aviation (GA) and reduce demand for aviation services.

How have security issues at the major airlines impacted the company's business volume from corporate customers?

Because of scheduling and security problems at the major airlines, more corporate travel is expected to be through general aviation (GA).

How can technology help the company improve services?

With more sophisticated computerized equipment, fixed base operations (FBOs) can offer specialized and efficient services to smaller aircraft owners and airlines.

Web Links

Aircraft Maintenance Technology

Aviation news.
www.amtonline.com/article/article_news.jsp

Aircraft Owners and Pilots Association

Links, news, and more.
www.aopa.org

AirNav.com

Aviation fuel prices.

www.airnav.com/fuel

Airport Business

News articles.

www.airportbusiness.com

Aviation Week's Aviation Now

Aviation Week industry news.

www.aviationweek.com/aw/index.jsp

FAA – Office of Aviation Research & Development

Research from hundreds of sources by topic.

research.faa.gov/aar

FBOWeb.com

Airport information, flight training, aviation employment, business consultants, FBO directories, frequencies, file flight plans with the FAA, fuel price location map, and weather.

www.fboweb.com

National Air Transportation Association

Press releases, fact sheet, monthly reports, and links for GA business service providers.

www.nata.aero

National Business Aviation Association (NBAA)

Maintenance news.

www.nbaa.org

Professional Aviation Maintenance Association (PAMA)

Industry news, publications, trade shows, regulatory information, and links.

www.pama.org

Thirty Thousand Feet – Aviation Directory

Aviation news and FBO listings.

member.newsguy.com/~ericmax/fbo.htm

Glossary of Acronyms

AOPA — Aircraft Owners and Pilots Association

FBO — fixed base operations

GA — general aviation

GAMA — General Aviation Manufacturers Association

MRO — maintenance repair operations

NBAA — National Business Aviation Association

PAMA — Professional Aviation Maintenance Association

HOOVER'S TOP COMPANIES

Largest Employers	Employees
Air Serv Corporation	5,400
Signature Flight Support Corporation	4,000
Evergreen Aviation Ground Logistics Enterprise, Inc.	3,500
Macquarie Infrastructure Company LLC	2,700
Mercury Air Group, Inc.	1,049
Universal Weather and Aviation, Inc.	455
Aircraft Service International Group, Inc.	250
KaiserAir, Inc.	166
PrimeFlight Aviation Services, Inc.	135
Jet Source Inc.	106

SOURCE: HOOVER'S, INC., DATABASE

Bakeries

The US bakery industry has about 2,600 commercial bakeries, with combined annual revenue of $25 billion, and 7,000 small retail bakeries, with $2 billion total revenue. Large companies include Interstate Bakeries and Flowers Foods, plus divisions of companies such as Sara Lee and Nabisco. The commercial side of the industry is highly concentrated: the 50 largest commercial bakers hold more than 80 percent of the market. The retail side of the industry is fragmented: although big companies may operate dozens of bakeries, the typical baker operates just one facility.

Competitive Landscape

Demand is related to eating trends and to the changing structure of the grocery industry. Profitability for individual companies is determined by efficiency of operations. Large companies have scale advantages in procurement, production, and distribution. Small companies can compete by offering specialty goods or superior local distribution services. Despite high automation, the low value of the product produces a fairly modest $150,000 in annual revenue per employee for commercial bakers.

Products, Operations & Technology

Baking is a low technology business that produces low-priced products from commodity ingredients. Fifty percent of industry volume is from baked breads, mainly white, wheat and rye; 20 percent from rolls, buns, muffins, bagels and croissants; 11 percent from soft cakes; and the rest from pies, pastries, donuts and a variety of sweet goods. Annual US per capita consumption of bread is close to 60 pounds, according to the Wheat Foods Council.

Bread bakers buy wheat, high fructose corn syrup, yeast, and shortening (mainly soybean oil), mix them into various dough combinations, then bake, package, and distribute the goods. Other raw materials include fruits, eggs,

BUSINESS CHALLENGES

» Raw Material, Energy Costs Volatile

The costs of major raw materials, such as wheat, vegetable oils, fuel for delivery fleets, and natural gas for ovens, can change rapidly. Futures prices for wheat and vegetable oil can vary more than 50 percent during a year; natural gas futures by more than 100 percent. To protect against sharp increases in raw material costs, many bakers use futures contracts.

» Competition from Customers

Consolidation in the supermarket industry has produced large chains that can efficiently operate their own bakeries. Publix operates a central bakery to supply its stores in the Southeast. Grocery-owned bakeries typically supply "fresh-baked" goods, while longer-shelf-life products are bought from commercial bakers.

» Low Demand Growth

Consumption of bakery products is limited by the growth of the US population, about 1 percent per year. Because this is a mature industry, the growth of individual bakers comes only at the expense of others. As customers like supermarket chains (including Wal-Mart) get bigger and have greater leverage with suppliers, small bakers find themselves squeezed by bigger producers that can negotiate nationwide contracts.

sugar, oils, milk, and chocolate. The cost of ingredients constitutes from 15 to 30 percent of the wholesale selling price. Some bakers buy premixed dough from suppliers. Ovens burn natural gas or propane. Management in most commercial bakeries focuses on lowering production and distribution costs.

Large economies of scale occur in producing baked products, mainly because labor costs can be reduced dramatically in large bakery facilities. A big automated bakery can produce a million bread loaves a week with just 100 employees working two shifts. The size of production facilities is limited by the need to distribute a highly perishable product to a large number of customers. Usually a large baking facility can service an area within a 300-mile radius.

The most modern bakeries are highly automated. To track and help assure compliance with government regulations that affect bakeries, companies deploy software, such as the American Bakers Association's Environmental Quality Management program. Bakery firms may use computer systems to receive orders, track sales, and exchange other data with large customers.

Sales & Marketing

Commercial bakers sell to supermarkets, convenience stores, restaurants, hotels, fast food outlets, schools, and other institutions, using their own sales force. Competition is intense from other national and regional bakeries, and from supermarkets and grocery stores with their own bakeries.

Distribution is crucial, as customers — mainly supermarkets — expect distributors to restock shelves several times a day. Distribution costs are high. Some bakers invest heavily in computer technology to coordinate ordering and distribution systems. Delivery may be direct from the bakery, called direct-store-delivery (DSD), or via a distribution center. Bakeries may have their own distribution staff and fleet of delivery vehicles, or use independent distributors. Depending on the size of their distribution areas, bakers may have a network of distribution warehouses. Bakeries may have underground fuel storage tanks at distribution centers they own.

Human Resources

Bakery production personnel need minimal training for production facilities or in-store operations, and are paid accordingly. Average hourly wages for production bakers are $12.56, well below the national average of $16. Fringe benefits run about 20 percent of total compensation. The injury rate for retail bakeries is half that of the national average, but commercial bakeries have seven cases per 100 full-time workers, two cases higher than the national average. The personnel turnover rate for nondurable goods manufacturing, including bakeries, is 31 percent.

Industry Employment Growth

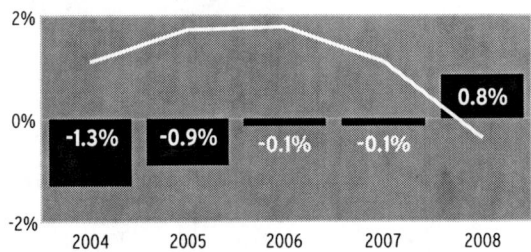

Average Hourly Earnings

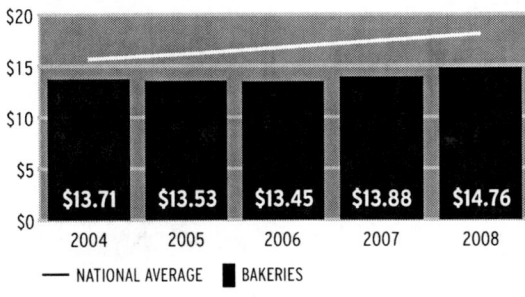

— NATIONAL AVERAGE ■ BAKERIES

SOURCE: BUREAU OF LABOR STATISTICS

Call Preparation Questions

How does the bakery protect against higher raw material costs?

The costs of major raw materials, such as wheat, vegetable oils, fuel for delivery fleets, and natural gas for ovens, can change rapidly.

How do supermarket bakeries challenge the company?

Consolidation in the supermarket industry has produced large chains that can efficiently operate their own bakeries.

What is the company's strategy to maintain market share in a competitive, slow-growth industry?

Consumption of bakery products is limited by the growth of the US population, about 1 percent per year.

What opportunities do high-quality, specialty products present the bakery?

Changing consumer tastes have given rise to "artisan" or gourmet breads.

Has demand for par-baked products increased for the baker?

Bakeries are marketing par-baked products to grocery stores and restaurants as a faster and more cost-effective alternative to baking from scratch.

Web Links

American Bakers Association

Industry lobbying organization.
www.americanbakers.org

American Society of Baking

Industry news, links, associations, events, and publications for wholesale or large-scale bakery production.
www.asbe.org

Bakery-Net Magazine

Industry news.
www.bakery-net.com

BakingBusiness.com

Newsletter and today's news.
www.bakingbusiness.com

BEMA

BEMA is an international, nonprofit trade association representing leading bakery and food equipment manufacturers and suppliers.
www.bema.org

International Dairy-Deli-Bakery Association

Industry information and links.
www.iddba.org

Retail Bakers of America

Events, legal watch, industry links, and resources.
www.rbanet.com

The Baking Association of Canada

Canadian industry issues.
www.bakingassoccanada.com

Wheat Foods Council

The Wheat Foods Council publishes From Wheat to Bread, used by the National Baking Center's basic bread course. Contains a grains nutrition newsletter, education resources and links to health-, nutrition- and grains-related sites.
www.wheatfoods.org

Glossary of Acronyms

ABA — American Bakers Association
DSD — direct-store-delivery
FALCPA — Food Allergen Labeling and Consumers Protection Act
IDDBA — International Dairy-Deli-Bakery Association
OTA — Organic Trade Association
SPCC — Spill Prevention, Control and Countermeasures

HOOVER'S TOP COMPANIES

Largest Companies by Sales	($ mil.)
Sara Lee Corporation	13,212.0
Interstate Bakeries Corporation	2,798.3
Flowers Foods, Inc.	2,414.9
Dawn Food Products, Inc.	1,370.0
McKee Foods Corporation	1,100.0

Largest Employers	Employees
Sara Lee Corporation	44,000
Interstate Bakeries Corporation	22,000
Flowers Foods, Inc.	7,800
Bimbo Bakeries USA	7,000
McKee Foods Corporation	6,000
Interbake Foods LLC	4,750
Dawn Food Products, Inc.	3,950
Lewis Brothers Bakeries Incorporated	2,500

Fastest Growing* by Five-Year Sales Growth	(%)
Dawn Food Products, Inc.	11.1
Flowers Foods, Inc.	10.7
McKee Foods Corporation	2.4
Tasty Baking Company	1.8

Fastest Growing* by Five-Year Employee Growth	(%)
Dawn Food Products, Inc.	1.3

Top Public Companies by Market Value	($ mil.)
Sara Lee Corporation	8,603.4
Flowers Foods, Inc.	2,212.0
Tasty Baking Company	27.0

* These rates are compounded annualized increases and may have resulted from acquisitions or one time gains. If less than 6 years of data are available, growth is for the years available.

SOURCE: HOOVER'S, INC., DATABASE

Banks and Credit Unions

The US banking system includes about 7,100 commercial banks, 1,200 savings banks, and 8,000 credit unions, with combined annual revenue of about $630 billion. Large commercial banks include JPMorgan Chase, Bank of America, Citibank, and Wells Fargo. ING Direct and Navy Federal Credit Union are among the largest savings banks and credit unions, respectively. The industry is concentrated: the 50 largest firms hold more than 60 percent of the market. Commercial banks account for 81 percent of industry revenue; savings banks, 13 percent; and credit unions, 6 percent.

Competitive Landscape

Demand for banking services is closely tied to economic activity and the level of interest rates. The profitability of individual banks depends on marketing skills, efficient operations, and good risk management. Large economies of scale exist in some segments of the industry, which has encouraged industry consolidation. Smaller banks can compete successfully in segments where customer service or knowledge of the local market is more important. The industry is capital-intensive and highly automated: annual revenue per employee is close to $300,000.

Many banks and thrifts aggressively offered adjustable rate and subprime mortgages during the housing boom of the early 2000s only to find themselves saddled with loan defaults and extensive losses when the housing bubble burst. Deep exposure to subprime mortgages and mortgage-backed securities caused bank failures, government takeovers, and involuntary mergers.

Products, Operations & Technology

Major products are bank loans, account services, brokerage services, credit card and leasing services, trust management, and investment services. Bank loans provide 54 per-

BUSINESS CHALLENGES

» Concentration of Real Estate Loans

Banks earn substantial fees from real estate loan transactions, and hold large portfolios of real estate loans and securities. Less demand for real estate credit would cut the fee income of banks, while decreased real estate loan quality would cut profits.

» Exposure to Interest Rate Changes

Because many banks make money mainly by lending funds at higher interest rates than they have to pay to acquire funds, their profits are sensitive to changes in interest rates. When the cost of funds rises, bankers may be unable to increase the interest rates on their outstanding loans by an equal amount. As interest rates rise, demand for loans typically falls. Some banks use elaborate hedging strategies to protect against rate changes.

» Competition from Non-Bank Lenders

Consumers now hold a greater share of their assets in brokerage accounts, mutual funds, and insurance company annuities than in bank deposits. Mortgage bankers originate the largest share of home mortgages. Finance companies and industrial corporations like GE provide equipment financing, credit cards, and consumer loans. Investment banks, REITs, and insurance companies are major loan competitors. Large corporations, formerly among the best customers of commercial banks, can borrow money directly from capital markets.

cent of industry revenue, account services provide 10 percent, the other major services each provide less than 5 percent. Following the Gramm-Leach-Bliley Act of 1999, some banks have used the financial services company structure to acquire large insurance or retail securities brokerage operations. Commercial banks, savings institutions, and credit unions provide many of the same products. However, commercial banks get a large percent of their revenue from services, while savings banks and credit unions get a majority of their revenue from loans.

Banks generate revenue mainly through interest income and service fees. Some banks also have significant revenue from investment activities. For commercial banks, interest income generates more than 55 percent of revenue. The level of interest rates is important to banks because much of their revenue comes from the "spread" between the rate at which they can lend money and the rate they must pay to acquire money. When interest rates are high, the spread is usually high, increasing revenue. On the other hand, when interest rates are high, demand for loans usually decreases.

The biggest operating concerns for most banks are service and loan production (sales); funds acquisition (deposits and borrowed funds); risk management (the quality of loans and investments); interest rate management (correctly pricing loans, deposits, and services); liquidity management (timing differences in the maturity of loans and deposits); and transactions processing.

Commercial banks and savings institutions often operate a network of branches. Large commercial banks have 40 branches, on average. Labor costs are the biggest single operating expense for banks. Heavy investment in computer technology in the past decade has allowed banks to cut labor costs and has encouraged bank mergers.

Computer systems are used extensively in banking because of the large number of transactions that are processed, like checking and credit card transactions, or interest credits, and because of internal and external demands for account information. Banks often use separate computer systems to run internal functions such as accounting; credit review; and customer relationship, cash, and investment management. Customer-operated functions like ATMs and Internet banking require additional sophisticated computer systems.

Commerical Banks

Commercial banks receive their revenue from both commercial customers and consumers. Revenue comes from the gathering and lending of deposits as well as from fees for providing a wide range of services. Banks are one of the largest sources of real estate lending, including home mortgages, land commercial construction loans, and commercial mortgages. On average, a commercial bank loan portfolio consists of about 55 percent real estate loans, 21 percent commercial and industrial loans, 14

percent consumer loans (credit cards and auto loans), 1 percent farm loans and 9 percent other loans.

The average size of commercial and industrial loans is less than $700,000. Commercial banks have fewer restrictions than savings institutions on the loans they can make and the securities they can invest in. Commercial banks have regulatory requirements from the Office of the Comptroller of the Currency, the Federal Reserve, and the Federal Deposit Insurance Corporation (FDIC).

Savings Institutions

Savings institutions, also known as thrifts, include savings banks and savings and loan associations. Typically larger than credit unions, their main purpose is to provide mortgage loans to home owners, funded by consumer deposits. Under tight oversight, savings institutions are largely restricted to investing in US treasury securities or mortgage-backed securities.

A typical thrift loan portfolio consists of about 66 percent mortgages, 9 percent nonresidential loans, 9 percent consumer loans, 7 percent commercial loans, 5 percent construction and land loans and 4 percent multifamily loans. A typical thrift loan portfolio is about 80 percent real estate-related; the remainder consists mainly of consumer loans and commercial loans. To raise new funds, mortgages are often sold to the Federal National Mortgage Association (FNMA or "Fannie Mae") and the Federal Home Loan Mortgage Corporation (FHLMC or "Freddie Mac"). Savings institutions are regulated by the Federal Reserve or the Office of Thrift Supervision and by the FDIC, which provides insurance through the Bank Insurance Fund (BIF) and the Savings Association Insurance Fund (SAIF). Most thrifts belong to the private Federal Home Loan Bank system, which extends credit to its members.

Credit Unions

Credit unions are tax-advantaged banking entities owned by their depositors. Like thrifts, credit unions' principal source of deposits is personal savings. Unlike thrifts, however, credit unions have traditionally made small consumer loans rather than mortgage loans. Most serve employee groups of midsized and large companies and are consequently small, with assets less than $50 million. Credit unions may also serve "affinity" groups or neighborhood associations. Credit unions generally have low expenses and officers often aren't paid. They specialize in making auto loans, small personal loans, home equity loans, and mortgage loans to their members, with payments frequently made through payroll deductions. Credit unions traditionally don't offer business accounts and business lending services, but some make small business loans.

Because direct investing of excess cash in financial instruments is impractical for small credit unions, many are members of federally-insured corporate credit unions ("wholesale corporates"), which pool the cash of their members. Corporate credit unions, in turn, are members of the US Central Credit Union. Typical investments of corporate credit unions are short-term US treasury securities; collateralized mortgage obligations (CMOs); and various types of asset-backed securities based on credit card, auto, and home equity loans. Credit unions may be chartered by the federal government or the states, and are regulated and insured by the National Credit Union Administration.

Sales & Marketing

Most banks must attract both depositors and borrowers and often use separate marketing approaches for the two, emphasizing low costs for loans and high returns on deposits. Marketing is through newspaper and billboard ads, TV and radio, direct mail, and telemarketing. Because many consumers simply choose a bank close to them, a network of branches or ATMs is often necessary to acquire deposits. Certificates of deposit (CDs) with high interest rates are a prime source of funds for some banks.

Many commercial customers care more about the availability and quality of services than about the precise cost of services and are usually approached through a sales force that attempts to maintain long-term relationships with customer executives. Larger banks may segment their sales force according to the size of potential customers.

Small banks often have "correspondent" relationships with bigger banks that effectively allow them to offer a wider range of services.

Human Resources

Many jobs in commercial banking are clerical, and hourly wages accordingly are 8 percent below the average for all US workers. The number of jobs in commercial banking has been relatively flat in the past decade, even though the volume of banking business increased substantially, as computer technology has allowed banks to eliminate many positions. The industry injury rate is very low, and personnel turnover is two-thirds the national average.

Industry Employment Growth

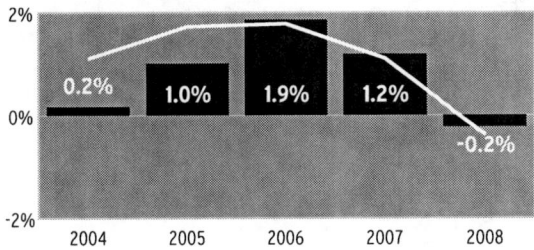

Average Hourly Earnings

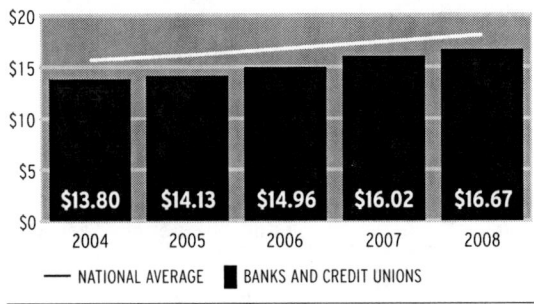

SOURCE: BUREAU OF LABOR STATISTICS

Call Preparation Questions

How is the current real estate market affecting the company?

Banks earn substantial fees from real estate loan transactions, and hold large portfolios of real estate loans and securities.

What changes does the bank expect in interest rates in the next year?

Because many banks make money mainly by lending funds at higher interest rates than they have to pay to acquire funds, their profits are sensitive to changes in interest rates.

How does the bank plan to increase consumer deposits?

Consumers now hold a greater share of their assets in brokerage accounts, mutual funds, and insurance company annuities than in bank deposits.

Does the bank plan to offer new services such as insurance or stock brokerage?

Through the financial holding company structure, banks are able to provide new services to consumers and businesses, including insurance, stock brokerage, and investment management.

Does the bank plan to expand online services for customers?

Online banking, by consumers and businesses, is becoming more common.

Web Links

American Banker

News and issues, by subscription only.
www.americanbanker.com

American Bankers Association

Excellent industry issues, news, statistics, studies.
www.aba.com

Bank Technology News

Industry news and issues.
www.banktechnews.com

Credit Union Journal

Industry news.
www.cujournal.com

Federal Deposit Insurance Corporation

News. Excellent banking statistics.
www.fdic.gov

Federal Financial Institutions Examination Council

Reports and press releases.
www.ffiec.gov

Federal Reserve

Statistics, issues, and regulations.
www.federalreserve.gov

Independent Community Bankers of America

Industry issues.
www.icba.org

National Credit Union Administration

News, links, and data.
www.ncua.gov

National Information Center (Federal Reserve)

Bank statistics. Top 50 banks.
www.ffiec.gov/nicpubweb/nicweb/nichome.aspx

National Mortgage News

Industry news.
www.nationalmortgagenews.com

Office of the Comptroller of the Currency

Regulatory information.
www.occ.treas.gov

Office of Thrift Supervision

Industry data, laws, regulations, and policies.
www.ots.treas.gov

US Banker

Industry news.
www.us-banker.com

Glossary of Acronyms

BIF — Bank Insurance Fund

C&I — commercial and industrial

CIP — customer identification program

CMO — collateralized mortgage obligation

CRM — customer relationship management

FFIEC — Federal Financial Institutions Examination Council

FHLMC — "Freddie Mac" — Federal Home Loan Mortgage Corporation

FNMA — "Fannie Mae" — Federal National Mortgage Association

OCC — Office of the Comptroller of the Currency

OTS — Office of Thrift Supervision

SAIF — Savings Association Insurance Fund

HOOVER'S TOP COMPANIES

Largest Companies by Sales	($ mil.)
Citigroup Inc.	130,005.0
Bank of America Corporation	124,132.0
JPMorgan Chase & Co.	112,190.0
Wachovia Corporation	56,662.0
Wells Fargo & Company	52,389.0
U.S. Bancorp	20,207.0
The Bank of New York Mellon Corporation	16,339.0
SunTrust Banks Inc.	13,012.7
HSBC USA Inc.	10,205.0
Regions Financial Corporation	9,636.6

Largest Employers	Employees
Citigroup Inc.	387,000
Bank of America Corporation	210,000
JPMorgan Chase & Co.	180,667
Wells Fargo & Company	159,800
Wachovia Corporation	120,000
U.S. Bancorp	54,000
The Bank of New York Mellon Corporation	42,100
Regions Financial Corporation	33,161
SunTrust Banks Inc.	32,323
BB&T Corporation	29,400

Fastest Growing* by Five-Year Sales Growth	(%)
Southern National Bancorp of Virginia, Inc.	120.4
The Bank Holdings	74.3
WSB Financial Group, Inc.	72.8
Pinnacle Financial Partners, Inc.	62.1
ING Bank, fsb	61.0
Southwest Corporate Federal Credit Union	59.9
Signature Bank	57.6
Tennessee Commerce Bancorp, Inc.	56.3
Bank of Florida Corporation	53.9
First Clover Leaf Financial Corp.	34.0

Fastest Growing* by Five-Year Employee Growth	(%)
Pinnacle Financial Partners, Inc.	547.7
Tidelands Bancshares, Inc.	146.0
United Bancorp, Inc.	82.8
Beach First National Bancshares, Inc.	56.6
The Bank Holdings	45.0
The Bancorp, Inc.	42.8
Kentucky First Federal Bancorp	38.3
Southern National Bancorp of Virginia, Inc.	28.0
Cathay General Bancorp	2.7

Top Public Companies by Market Value	($ mil.)
JPMorgan Chase & Co.	117,695.2
Bank of America Corporation	70,645.5
U.S. Bancorp	43,893.4
Citigroup Inc.	36,570.0
The Bank of New York Mellon Corporation	32,536.1

* These rates are compounded annualized increases and may have resulted from acquisitions or one time gains. If less than 6 years of data are available, growth is for the years available.

SOURCE: HOOVER'S, INC., DATABASE

Bars and Nightclubs

THIS INDUSTRY INCLUDES:

SIC CODES

5813   Drinking Places
        (Alcoholic
        Beverages)

NAICS CODES

722410 Drinking Places
        (Alcoholic
        Beverages)

The bar and nightclub industry includes about 50,000 locations with combined annual revenue of about $15 billion. No major companies dominate; varying state liquor laws complicate the ability to form large chains. The industry is highly fragmented: the 50 largest companies hold just over 5 percent of sales.

Competitive Landscape

Personal income and entertainment needs drive demand. The profitability of individual companies depends on the ability to drive traffic and develop a loyal clientele. Large companies can offer a wide variety of food, drinks, and entertainment, and have scale advantages in purchasing, financing, and marketing. Small companies can compete effectively by serving a local market, offering unique products or entertainment, or providing superior customer service. The industry is extremely labor-intensive: average annual revenue per worker is $45,000.

Bars and nightclubs compete with other venues that offer alcoholic drinks or entertainment, including restaurants, hotels, casinos, and consumer homes.

Products, Operations & Technology

Beer is about 40 percent of sales, distilled spirits or hard liquor 30 percent, food and non-alcoholic beverages 10 percent, and wine 7 percent. Customers consume the majority of bar drinks on-premise, and companies may specialize in certain beverages, like craft beers or martinis. Entertainment includes live music, DJs, dancing, and adult entertainment.

While most customers go to bars and nightclubs to socialize, bar activities tend to focus more on drinking, while nightclubs focus on entertainment and dancing. Types of bars include microbreweries, taverns, pubs, wine bars, and martini bars. Bars and nightclubs may have themes, like sports or country-western. The failure rate for nightclubs can be high due to

BUSINESS CHALLENGES

» Flat Category Demand

Growing sales can be difficult due to flat alcoholic beverage consumption. Per capita consumption of alcoholic beverages remained relatively constant, at about 25 gallons per person annually, between 1994 and 2004. Declining demand for beer (the majority of the market) offsets consumption gains for wine and hard liquor. Increased public focus on responsible drinking and stricter drunk driving and underage drinking laws have helped limit demand growth.

» Competition from Alternative Venues

Bars and nightclubs face competition from restaurants, hotel lounges, and customers who entertain at home. Restaurants, which offer better food options, value bar business because alcoholic drinks are especially profitable. Hotel lounges, which compete for the tourist market, may also offer entertainment and dancing. In addition, some consumers avoid the high retail markups on alcohol by drinking and entertaining at home.

» Impact of Government Regulations

Federal, state, and local government regulations can restrict a company's operations, and changes (like earlier closing times) can significantly affect sales. According to Nightclub and Bar magazine, sales can decrease 15 to 30 percent after a state enacts a smoking ban, a loss that struggling bars and nightclubs can't afford. Liquor law violations, particularly those involving underage drinking, can result in various penalties ranging from a stiff fine to permanent closure. In addition, excise tax increases can result in higher distributor prices, affecting profitability.

the trend-driven nature of the industry; an estimated eight of 10 nightclubs will fail during the first year of operation, according to Nightclub and Bar magazine.

To open a bar or nightclub, a location must have proper zoning from local government. Community resistance to new bars and nightclubs is common due to anticipated problems with drunken patrons and noise. Companies may need both a standard liquor license to sell alcohol, and a pouring license to serve alcohol for consumption on-premise. Multiple types of liquor licenses dictate what types of alcohol a bar can sell, and the availability and cost of licenses can vary greatly. Licenses to serve beer and wine tend to be less expensive than to serve hard liquor. Some communities issue a limited number of liquor licenses, and companies may have to buy one from an existing licensee. Local municipalities may also require an entertainment license to provide TV programming, live music, or dancing.

Local laws typically dictate days and hours of operation. A venue may announce a "last call," or last chance, to buy an alcoholic beverage, prior to the required closing time. The majority of business is during the weekend. Most nightclubs aren't open during the day, and many open only two to three nights per week.

Almost all companies consist of a single operation, although the industry includes some regional chains and franchises. Tourist destinations can be good locations, since vacationers tend to visit bars and nightclubs. Size varies greatly, from small corner taverns to warehouse-sized dance clubs. The majority of nightclubs range from 3,500 to 7,000 square feet, according to nightclubbiz.com. Experienced owners tend to run the largest nightclubs, which range from 10,000 to 30,000 square feet. A 3,000 square foot club can gross between $24,000 and $64,000 per month. A 15,000 square foot club can gross between $100,000 and $260,000 per month.

Bars that serve food may have an area for table seating. Nightclubs may have one or more bars, table seating, a stage, or a dance floor. Outdoor seating is popular in warm weather and many tourist locations. Most companies use lighting and decor to create a distinctive ambiance or image to attract specific clientele. For example, a sports bar may have numerous large screen TVs and sports memorabilia to draw sports fans, while a nightclub may have expensive lighting and sound systems to draw the dance crowd. In addition, a friendly bartender or a popular DJ can help develop a loyal customer base. Some nightclubs promote an image of exclusivity, and may be selective as to which patrons can enter.

Bartenders are responsible for mixing and serving drinks. How fast a bartender operates and how much a bartender pours can significantly affect sales and profitability. Companies may use special pour spouts to standardize liquor dispensation. In addition, secret audits monitor liquor consumption and can be used to identify "heavy-handed" bartenders. Some companies audit liquor inventory daily.

Companies typically buy alcoholic beverages from state-licensed liquor distributors. Federal and state laws prohibit direct sales from manufacturers. Large bars and nightclubs can hold sizable, expensive inventories of alcohol, especially if the company stocks high-end liquor. Inventory management and cost control can be difficult due to employee error, overpouring, and theft. Proper storage is important to minimize bottle breakage and prevent theft. Bars and nightclubs that serve food typically buy ingredients from food distributors.

Companies may use computerized point-of-sale (POS) systems to record orders, look up drink recipes, and manage bar tabs. Beverage monitoring systems use miniature sensors attached to liquor bottles to record individual drink servings and transmit data wirelessly to inventory management systems. Handheld scanners help track inventory. For nightclubs, technology plays an important role in providing entertainment and ambiance. Computer systems that integrate sound, light, special effects, and music videos help create a distinctive environment. In addition, some companies use digital surveillance systems to catch illegal activity by both customers and employees.

Sales & Marketing

While the core customer is between 21 and 35, most companies target by interest, with biker bars, sports bars, singles bars, and dance clubs attracting different types of individuals. Tourists are an important customer group, as many vacationers frequent bars and nightclubs.

Marketing vehicles include local radio, print, outdoor, newspaper, and TV advertising, and the Internet. Companies may receive marketing assistance from manufacturers through distributors. Word-of-mouth can be critical, especially for nightclubs where the social makeup of the crowd can be important. Referrals from hotel concierges are important in tourist markets. Celebrity customers can increase the popularity of a venue, and may cause huge increases in traffic.

Companies may use the Internet to communicate weekly drink promotions and special events. Text messaging and e-vites (electronic invitations) target technology-driven young adults. Some companies partner with social networking websites, like myspace.com, to reach specific demographics with highly targeted promotions.

In areas with a high concentration of bars, companies may hand out flyers on nearby streets. Happy hours offer discounted drinks or food and help drive traffic during slow periods, like weeknights. Ladies night promotions are important because the presence of women attracts male customers. To promote an image of exclusivity, nightclubs may offer VIP or members-only rooms to important patrons. While special events, like a performance by a popular music group, can help draw a one-time crowd, bars and nightclubs need a core group of regular customers to survive.

Hospitality is extremely important to develop a loyal clientele. Friendly bartenders and waitstaff help companies develop relationships with customers. Attractive waitresses also help companies target the male demographic. Large bars and nightclubs host corporate events and dedicate sales resources to targeting large groups.

While retail prices in bars and nightclubs vary greatly by market, most drinks cost between $4 and $10. The average price for a specialty cocktail made with high-end liquor in New York City is $16. Customers may spend anywhere from $10 to $50 a night. Many nightclubs have a cover charge to gain entry.

Human Resources

Wages are low, about half the average for all US workers, because most jobs require few skills. As a result of low wages and odd hours, bars and nightclubs rely on part-time help and turnover can be high. Many workers rely on tips to supplement wages. The industry injury rate is significantly below the national average, although workers in the kitchen tend to experience more burns.

Bartenders must have thorough drink knowledge and the ability to serve a crowd quickly. Some states allow bartenders as young as 18. Security guards or bouncers may check age identification, manage crowd control, and deal with intoxicated patrons. Industry experts recommend one security guard for every 100 patrons.

Industry Employment Growth

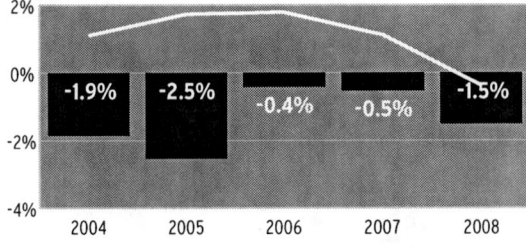

Average Hourly Earnings

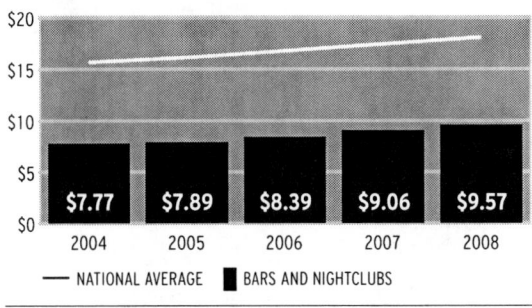

SOURCE: BUREAU OF LABOR STATISTICS

Call Preparation Questions

How has flat demand in the overall alcoholic beverage market affected the company?

Growing sales can be difficult due to flat alcoholic beverage consumption.

What are the company's biggest competitive threats, besides other bars and nightclubs?

Bars and nightclubs face competition from restaurants, hotel lounges, and customers who entertain at home.

What changes in laws or regulations affect the company the most?

Federal, state, and local government regulations can restrict a company's operations, and changes (like earlier closing times) can significantly affect sales.

What kind of customer experience does the company aim to deliver?

By focusing on providing a distinctive customer experience, bars and nightclubs can better compete with alternative venues that serve alcohol.

How has growth in the high-end drink category affected the company's product mix?

Bars and nightclubs can leverage growing demand for specialty drinks and super-premium liquor.

Web Links

Alcohol and Tobacco Tax and Trade Bureau

Excise taxes, federal regulations.
www.ttb.gov

American Beverage Licensees

Trade association for liquor retailers.
www.ablusa.org

Distilled Spirits Council of the United States

Trade association for distillers/hard liquor
manufacturer — good consumption data.
www.discus.org

Nightclub & Bar Magazine

American Beverage Licensee publication — great
source of news and trends.
www.nightclub.com

Nightclubbiz.com

Nightclub consulting website — good operational
information.
www.nightclubbiz.com

The Beverage Information Group

Industry research and consumption statistics used by
major manufacturers.
www.bevinfogroup.com

Glossary of Acronyms

ABL — American Beverage Licensees
ATF — Federal Bureau of Alcohol, Tobacco, Firearms,
and Explosives
DISCUS — Distilled Spirits Council of the USA
MADD — Mothers Against Drunk Driving
NRA — National Restaurant Association
POS — point-of-sale
TTB — Alcohol and Tobacco Tax and Trade Bureau

HOOVER'S TOP COMPANIES

Largest Employers	Employees
Fox & Hound Restaurant Group	4,800
Kahunaville Management, Inc.	3,300
McMenamins, Inc.	1,400
Ala Carte Entertainment, Inc.	1,300
Hospitality USA Investment Group, Inc.	1,200
Rick's Cabaret International, Inc.	1,100
Top Public Companies by Market Value	**($ mil.)**
Rick's Cabaret International, Inc.	86.2

SOURCE: HOOVER'S, INC., DATABASE

Battery Manufacture

The US battery manufacturing industry includes about 125 companies with combined annual revenue of about $6 billion. Major companies are Exide Technologies, Energizer Holdings, Procter & Gamble (Duracell), and Spectrum Brands (Rayovac). Divisions of large electronics companies such as Sony also manufacture batteries. The industry is highly concentrated: the largest eight companies have about 75 percent market share and the largest 50 have more than 98 percent.

Competitive Landscape

Demand depends primarily on the level of activity in the automotive and electronic sectors of the economy. Personal income drives new battery purchases in consumer goods, while consumer usage levels drive demand for replacement batteries. Large companies have advantages in efficiency of operations and economies of scale. Smaller producers compete by focusing on specialized product offerings and superior customer service. Annual revenue per employee is about $240,000.

Products, Operations & Technology

Major product categories are storage batteries (55 percent) and primary batteries (45 percent). Storage batteries are rechargeable, while primary batteries are discarded after the initial stored energy is consumed. Examples of storage batteries are automotive and laptop computer batteries. Primary batteries include standard dry cell batteries (AA, AAA, C, D, and 9-volt) used in flashlights, radios, remote controls, and a variety of specialty applications, such as hearing aids and implantable medical devices.

Raw materials include heavy metals such as lead, cadmium, nickel, and mercury. These materials are bought new or from battery recycling centers and other collection and processing centers. While the shape, size, and materials of batteries may vary, they all use the same basic

BUSINESS CHALLENGES

» Material Cost Increases

Raw material costs as a percentage of total revenue have risen steadily in recent years, and now are about 50 percent of revenue. For example, about 70 percent of lead consumption in the US is for batteries. Battery manufacturers use recycled battery materials for both cost and environmental purposes. Recycled battery material prices follow metals and commodity exchange prices, such as the London Metal Exchange.

» Competition from Imports

The number of production employees in US battery manufacturing facilities has decreased about 25 percent since 2000 due to competition from imports. Offshore manufacturers capitalize on low-cost labor sources to compete in the US market. To offset this disadvantage, many US manufacturers have acquired or started business operations in countries where low cost labor is available.

» Price Pressure from Large Customers

Manufacturers of primary batteries sell to large companies with significant purchasing power. Mass retailers, major drugstore chains, large manufacturers, and nationwide distributors combine to make both OEM and aftermarket pricing extremely competitive. Sales to Wal-Mart represent 18 percent of Spectrum Brands' revenue. The ability of battery manufacturers to raise prices to achieve adequate profit margins is challenged by these very large and powerful customers. This customer concentration, along with competition from imports, resulted in a 1.8 percent decline in producer prices for primary batteries from 2000 to 2005.

electrochemical process. Dissimilar metals act as negative and positive poles in the presence of an electrolyte, creating a reaction where electrons gather on the poles. These electrons are released in the form of electrical current when they contact an external conduit such as a wire.

Common battery types are lead-acid (automotive); alkaline (common dry cell); zinc-carbon (common AA, C, or D); nickel-cadmium (premium AA, C, or D); lithium-ion (laptops and cell phones); metal-chloride (electric vehicles such as golf carts and fork lifts); and nickel-metal hydride (hybrid autos). The terms "dry cell" or "wet cell" refer to whether the electrolyte is solid or liquid. Voltages and currents are controlled by the materials used and the configuration of individual cells within a battery.

Battery manufacturing is quite varied depending on the configuration, raw materials, and intended end use, but generally follows a similar process. One of the most popular batteries is the alkaline dry cell battery. To manufacture alkaline-manganese dry cell batteries, a steel can that functions as the cathode (positive electrode) is first cleaned and de-greased. A conductive film is then sprayed on the inside surface to ensure good electrical conductivity. Next, a mixture of manganese dioxide and carbon is inserted as a solid ring with a center opening into the can to complete the cathode. A cylindrical separator made of plastic is then inserted and the center opening filled with an electrolyte. A gel of zinc particles and an alkaline solution are inserted in the center as the material for the anode (negative electrode). A cap, known as the current collector, is put in place and functions as the anode terminal.

After assembly, the battery is sealed to prevent leakage and drying, then labeled and inspected for proper voltage, current, and appearance. Size of manufacturing facilities range from 40,000 to several hundred thousand square feet. Most batteries are standard products and are built to stock. However, some specialty applications, such as a power system for an urban rapid transit system, may be a one-of-a-kind design and can be very large and expensive.

Companies invest in research and development to provide longer life, lighter weight, and lower cost models. Product development is aided by computer simulations of new battery designs. Computers are also used in manufacturing for process control, production monitoring, and inventory management. The manufacturing process for standard size dry cell batteries is highly automated.

Sales & Marketing

Major customers are OEMs in the transportation, electronics, and consumer product sectors. OEM sales represent about 20 percent of battery consumption in the US. Aftermarket customers account for 80 percent of battery sales and include mass retailers, drug and grocery chains, automotive supply outlets, and general merchandise stores. These two distinct channels require substantially different sales and marketing approaches.

Selling to OEMs is through the company's sales force in direct negotiations with OEM purchasing personnel. Marketing is limited to product-specific presentation materials and tools. End-users are unlikely to buy based on the OEM's choice of batteries, so price, not brand awareness, is the primary buying criterion.

For aftermarket sales, consumer brand awareness becomes critical to securing retail shelf space and growing market share. National marketing campaigns, including print and TV advertising, are used to build consumer awareness. Sales to wholesalers and distributors that supply retail chains are common in the aftermarket.

Prices range from a few dollars for a household battery pack to thousands for batteries to power transportation systems.

Human Resources

Production employees in battery manufacturing earn about $34,000 annually, just slightly higher than the national average for all manufacturing employees. Fringe benefits average about 34 percent. Large companies may have some locations that are unionized; most small manufacturers are non-union.

Injury rates for production employees are comparable to the national average for the manufacturing sector. Major safety concerns revolve around the safe handling of lead and other heavy metals that are toxic and carcinogenic.

Industry Employment Growth

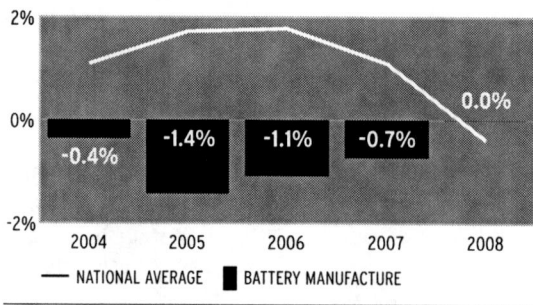

	2004	2005	2006	2007	2008
BATTERY MANUFACTURE	-0.4%	-1.4%	-1.1%	-0.7%	0.0%

— NATIONAL AVERAGE   ■ BATTERY MANUFACTURE

SOURCE: BUREAU OF LABOR STATISTICS

Call Preparation Questions

How does the company handle raw material price increases?

Raw material costs as a percentage of total revenue have risen steadily in recent years, and now are about 50 percent of revenue.

How do imports impact company revenues?

The number of production employees in US battery manufacturing facilities has decreased about 25 percent since 2000 due to competition from imports.

How concentrated is the company's customer base?

Manufacturers of primary batteries sell to large companies with significant purchasing power.

How important are export markets to the company's business?

US battery exports have increased every year since 2002.

What new battery applications is the company pursuing?

As companies develop new products and designs, opportunities for special battery applications increase.

Web Links

Alternative Energy Battery Technology

Alternative battery news.
www.alternative-energy-news.info/technology/battery-power

Batteries International

Magazine with latest industry news.
www.batteriesinternational.com

Battery Council International

Lead-acid battery industry trade association.
www.batterycouncil.org

Battery Power, Products & Technology

New products and industry news.
www.batterypoweronline.com

Energizer Holdings

A leading battery manufacturer.
www.energizer.com

Exide Technologies

Battery manufacturer focused on industrial applications.
www.exide.com

Spectrum Brands

Maker of Rayovac batteries.
www.spectrumbrands.com

Glossary of Acronyms

CERCLA — Comprehensive Environmental Responsibility, Compensation, and Liability Act
IPO — initial public offering
LME — London Metal Exchange
MTBF — mean time between failure
RBRC — Rechargeable Battery Recycling Corporation
IT — information technology
UPS — uninterruptible power supply

HOOVER'S TOP COMPANIES

Largest Companies by Sales	($ mil.)
Energizer Holdings, Inc.	4,331.0
Exide Technologies	3,696.7
Spectrum Brands, Inc.	2,688.0
EnerSys Inc.	2,026.6
Greatbatch, Inc.	546.6
Johnson Controls Power Solutions	400.0
C&D Technologies, Inc.	346.1
Ultralife Corporation	254.7
FuelCell Energy, Inc.	100.7
A123 Systems, Inc.	41.3

Largest Employers	Employees
Energizer Holdings, Inc.	16,410
Exide Technologies	13,027
EnerSys Inc.	8,600
Spectrum Brands, Inc.	7,000
Johnson Controls Power Solutions	4,000
Greatbatch, Inc.	2,445
C&D Technologies, Inc.	1,400
A123 Systems, Inc.	1,160
Ultralife Corporation	1,092
FuelCell Energy, Inc.	534

Fastest Growing* by Five-Year Sales Growth	(%)
A123 Systems, Inc.	668.1
Hoku Scientific, Inc.	137.8
Lithium Technology Corporation	91.9
ZBB Energy Corporation	63.0
Valence Technology, Inc.	51.6
Active Power, Inc.	37.0
Ultralife Corporation	26.3
FuelCell Energy, Inc.	24.4
Spectrum Brands, Inc.	23.9
Aura Systems, Inc.	20.5

Fastest Growing* by Five-Year Employee Growth	(%)
Ener1, Inc.	26.6
Medis Technologies Ltd.	21.3
Valence Technology, Inc.	21.2
ZBB Energy Corporation	15.5
Greatbatch, Inc.	14.3
Lithium Technology Corporation	8.7
FuelCell Energy, Inc.	7.5
EnerSys Inc.	7.2
Spectrum Brands, Inc.	7.0
Ultralife Corporation	4.0

Top Public Companies by Market Value	($ mil.)
Energizer Holdings, Inc.	4,686.6
Ener1, Inc.	3,652.4
EnerSys Inc.	1,173.5
Exide Technologies	986.1
Medis Technologies Ltd.	561.2

* These rates are compounded annualized increases and may have resulted from acquisitions or one time gains. If less than 6 years of data are available, growth is for the years available.

SOURCE: HOOVER'S, INC., DATABASE

Beef Cattle Ranching

THIS INDUSTRY INCLUDES:

SIC CODES

0211   Beef Cattle Feedlots

0212   Beef Cattle, Except Feedlots

NAICS CODES

11211   Beef Cattle Ranching and Farming, including Feedlots

The US beef ranching industry includes about 750,000 operators with combined annual revenue of $50 billion. Only about 5,000 operations have more than 500 head of cattle. The industry is highly fragmented: the 50 largest operators hold less than 2 percent of the market.

Competitive Landscape

Demand is driven by food prices, population growth, and global trade policies. The profitability of individual operations depends on production efficiency and anticipating market demand. Large operators have some advantages in volume purchasing and efficient use of labor. Small operators can compete successfully by producing special grades of beef cattle and by using "family" labor.

Products, Operations & Technology

Major products are beef cattle and calves ready to be slaughtered or ready for "finishing" in feedlots. Annual US sales of beef animals include about 45 million cattle and 10 million calves.

The operations of beef ranchers revolve around breeding cows, feeding cattle, and providing veterinary care. Beef cattle ranchers mainly breed their own animals, with a traditional calving season in the early spring. Cows can produce one calf per year and are either naturally bred by a bull or artificially inseminated by a technician. Beef cows have a nine month gestation period. From birth until weaning, calves depend on their mother's milk and forage resources. Calves are typically weaned when they weigh between 400 and 600 pounds and are either retained by the rancher or sold. Weaned calves either go directly to the feedlot for finishing or are fed a high forage diet. Generally calves enter the "feedlot" phase, where they're transitioned to a high grain ration, at around 800 pounds. Cattle are typically ready for slaughter when they weigh around 1,200

BUSINESS CHALLENGES

» Cattle Prices Can Vary Sharply

Variations in beef supply and demand can change prices for cattle sharply. Consumer demand for beef is affected by the relative prices of beef and chicken. Ranchers often all increase or decrease herds at the same time. Because of supply-demand imbalances, prices for cattle can vary more than 50 percent within three months.

» Vulnerability to Growing Conditions, Diseases

Beef ranchers are vulnerable to weather, disease, and other growing conditions. Drought can severely affect the quantity and quality of forage, and therefore the animal carrying capacity of grazing land. Harsh weather conditions can affect calf survival and winter feed costs. Infectious diseases can decrease performance or destroy entire herds. A few US cases of mad cow disease would shut down beef exports and affect US beef consumption.

» Vulnerability to Government Regulation

Federal and state governments are closely involved in the operations of the ranching industry. Low grazing fees on public lands are essential to some cattle ranchers. Health officials can prevent the movement and sale of animals. A national identification program for cattle is currently voluntary. The government requires open price reporting at various stages of the cattle processing chain. Threats to the safety of the beef food supply could quickly result in tighter regulation.

pounds and have been fed a grain-based ration for at least 120 days.

Because the quality of the forage on grazing land varies widely, the animal carrying capacity of land also varies. The actual stocking rate on land is the number of acres per animal unit (typically a cow-calf pair), or the number of 1,000-pound animal units per month (AUM) on a particular piece of land. Depending on the quality of the forage, a beef cow may need from three acres in high-rainfall areas to 40 in arid regions. A higher than recommended stocking rate may reduce the live-weight gain per animal per day, which is typically between 1 and 2 pounds. Ranches often rotate their animals through a number of pastures to prevent overgrazing and soil erosion in any one spot during grazing season. Ranchers may produce or buy harvested forage (typically hay) to feed their cattle during the winter months.

Veterinary services are needed to help in calving problems, treat illnesses, and provide routine vaccinations to prevent diseases, especially communicable ones. About 4 million cattle and calves are lost every year to injury or disease. Bovine spongiform encephalitis (BSE), otherwise known as mad cow disease, can be transmitted by eating meat or byproducts from an infected animal.

Although most ranchers raise cattle on their own land, some may lease private land or have permits to use federal lands. The federal grazing fee for a cow-calf AUM is determined annually by the Bureau of Land Management and the Forest Service, and has in recent years been just under $2 per month. Federal grazing permits are tied to a rancher's "deeded" land and are transferable upon the sale of deeded land. Often, deeded and federal lands are intermingled on a ranch: rarely is it possible for a rancher to operate entirely on federal lands.

Computer technology to identify animals from birth to slaughter has increased in recent years due to concerns about product traceability and for herd management. Radio frequency identification (RFID) ear tags attached at birth allow animals to be monitored remotely in the field and as they pass to feedlots or slaughterhouses. Most ranchers also use the Internet to monitor cattle prices and get production information.

Sales & Marketing

Customers are local feedlot operators, dealers, other ranchers, or slaughterhouses. Most cattle are sold locally, then trucked to feeding areas, either a pasture or feedlot. The majority of cattle are fed to finish in the Corn Belt (Iowa and Illinois) or high plains (Texas to Nebraska). In some cases, ranchers will retain ownership of

their animals in feedlots, eventually selling fed cattle directly to packers (slaughterhouses).

Cattle producers have a variety of methods to market cattle. Local auctions are among the oldest and useful for producers selling small numbers of calves and cows. Forward contracting with a buyer and video auctions allow producers to price the cattle several weeks to months before actual delivery, but these methods may require the producer to be able to deliver truckload quantities of similar weights, sex, and quality. Finished cattle sold to packers generally are priced for delivery within one to two weeks.

Prices are quoted in dollars per hundred pounds ($/cwt). The price per cwt is based on the weight, sex, and quality of the calf; location of cattle; and the projected costs to finish. Finished cattle sell for the lowest price per cwt and lightweight calves typically sell for the highest price per cwt. Bred cows and replacement heifers typically sell by the head and often sell for more (on a per head basis) than feeder cattle of the same weight.

Human Resources

Because of the relatively low education and skills required for most ranching work, pay is low, about 65 percent of the national average for all workers. Injury rates for ranch workers are high, about twice the average for all US workers, and twice the rate of serious injuries that result in 30 days or more away from work. Most injuries result from being hit by an animal.

Call Preparation Questions

How does the ranch adjust to variations in local cattle prices?

Variations in beef supply and demand can change prices for cattle sharply.

What measures does the ranch take to prevent cattle diseases?

Beef ranchers are vulnerable to weather, disease, and other growing conditions.

Does the ranch expect more government regulation of the industry?

Federal and state governments are closely involved in the operations of the ranching industry.

Does the ranch raise cattle specifically for free-range beef?

Demand for beef from cattle raised without antibiotics or growth hormones has increased steadily in recent years, along with "free-range" beef raised on grass and forage.

What opportunities does the ranch see for exporting beef?

Demand for US beef has grown in selected international markets.

Web Links

Centers for Disease Control and Prevention

News about cattle diseases.
www.cdc.gov

Farm Industry News

News about new products and technology for the farm.
www.farmindustrynews.com

National Cattlemen's Beef Association

News, issues, and statistics from trade association.
www.beefusa.org

TheCattleSite.com

News concerning beef industry.
www.thecattlesite.com

US Department of Agriculture

See especially the Animal Production section, the Briefing Rooms, and the National Agricultural Statistics Service.
www.usda.gov

Glossary of Acronyms

ADG — average daily gain
AUM — animal unit month
BSE — bovine spongiform encephalitis (mad cow disease)
CWT — hundredweight
FCR — feed conversion rate
NAIS — National Animal Identification System
RFID — radio frequency identification

HOOVER'S TOP COMPANIES

Largest Employers	Employees
Agri Beef Co.	1,000
King Ranch, Inc.	683
AzTx Cattle Co., Ltd.	175

SOURCE: HOOVER'S, INC., DATABASE

Beer, Wine, and Spirits Distributorships

THIS INDUSTRY INCLUDES:

SIC CODES

5181 Beer and Ale
5182 Wine and Distilled Alcoholic Beverages

NAICS CODES

4248 Beer, Wine, and Distilled Alcoholic Beverage Merchant Wholesalers

The beer, wine, and alcoholic beverage distribution industry includes about 5,000 companies with combined annual revenue of about $100 billion. Major companies include Southern Wine & Spirits of America, Glazer's Wholesale Drug, National Wine & Spirits, and The Charmer Sunbelt Group. The beer wholesale industry is fragmented: the top 50 companies account for about a third of industry revenue. The wine and distilled spirits wholesale industry is more concentrated: the top 50 companies account for more than 70 percent of industry revenue.

The beer, wine, and alcoholic beverage wholesale industry doesn't include alcohol beverage retailers or suppliers that manufacture beer, wine, or distilled spirits.

Competitive Landscape

Demand is driven by consumer preferences in alcohol consumption and demographic trends. The profitability of individual companies depends on effective sales operations and maintaining low operating costs. Large companies have advantages in exclusive distribution rights in large markets. Small operations can compete effectively by distributing rare and expensive products. Average annual revenue per employee is nearly $450,000 for beer wholesalers and $700,000 for wine and distilled spirits wholesalers.

Products, Operations & Technology

Major products are beer, wine, and distilled spirits (hard liquor). Distributors tend to specialize in either beer or wine and spirits. About half of industry revenue comes from the sale of beer, 30 percent from liquor, and 20 percent from wine.

Most alcoholic beverages sold in the US move through a federally mandated three-tier distribution system. Producers or importers must sell to distributors, who then sell the product to retailers. There are a few notable ex-

BUSINESS CHALLENGES

» Demand Tied to Quality, Selling

Consumer demand depends on suppliers making quality products and retailers effectively selling these products. When either of these two tiers falters, distributors often feel the pinch, yet they have limited ability to change the outcome. Consumers can be fickle about beer, wine, and spirits. A distributor's success or failure can often depend on domestic beverage trends that are out of their realm of influence.

» Legal Challenges to the Three-Tier System

Distributors must actively lobby to ensure the federal three-tier system remains in place. State and national challenges to the three-tier system can potentially have a major impact on the distribution business. Distributors worry that any erosion of the three-tier system will eventually lead to direct sales from producers to retailers. Some states now allow intrastate shipping of wine and beer directly to consumers, bypassing distributors and retailers. The Internet has greatly expanded consumer accessibility to small producers.

» Vulnerable to Government Regulation

The alcohol industry is closely regulated by states, localities, and the federal government. While some laws aid distributors, others are largely intended to control and reduce alcohol sales. New local, state, and federal restrictions on alcohol are a constant possibility. Beer, wine, and spirits distributors actively lobby state and federal legislators to limit taxes and government regulation.

ceptions: some states allow small brewpubs to distribute their own beer, and many states allow wineries to ship directly to consumers.

Thirty-two states are license states that allow private industry to manage the distribution and sale of distilled spirits. The remaining 18 are control states that solely manage the wholesaling of liquor as a state-run enterprise. Many of these control states also regulate the retail side of the spirits business, only selling alcohol in state-run stores.

The distributor industry buys from a variety of domestic suppliers: about 5,000 commercial wineries; 400 breweries; 1,400 microbreweries; and 80 liquor distillers. A few large producers dominate, such as Anheuser-Busch, Miller Brewing, Molson Coors, E&J Gallo, Constellation Brands, and The Wine Group. Many large producers have acquired or allied with international suppliers. Major importers include Anheuser-Busch, Diageo, Heineken USA, Miller Brewing, and Molson Coors.

For the last decade, annual per capita consumption of alcohol has remained flat at around 22 gallons of beer, 2 gallons of wine, and 1 gallon of hard liquor. Alcohol purchases account for 15 percent of an average American household's total food budget.

Beer and wine distributors generally have contracts with producers giving them exclusive distribution rights to certain products within a defined market area, if they don't carry competing brands. Exclusive territories are the dominant form of distribution, followed by a system of area of primary responsibility (APR). In many markets, for example, one distributor will carry Budweiser while another will carry Miller beer. Some distributor territories cover several states and overlap with those of other distributors; however, most are smaller, spanning several counties.

Major inputs include diesel fuel, electricity, pallets for receiving and storage, and vehicle repairs. A distributor typically owns one or several warehouses, a large inventory, and a truck fleet. Most beer wholesalers are independent, family-run companies operating from a single location with a fleet of 12 to 15 trucks. Some distributors maintain a truck service center with full-time mechanics.

Recent technological advances include wireless devices to track retail sales; integrated computer systems to order, track, and distribute hundreds of products to hundreds or thousands of retailers; and radio frequency identification (RFID) tags that follow cases or kegs as they travel through the supply chain.

Sales & Marketing

Typical customers are retailers such as private and state-run liquor stores; drug, convenience, and grocery stores; and bars and restaurants. Sales are sometimes classified as pre-sales (custom orders) or delivery/driver sales (drivers restocking customer inventory as needed). Sales and marketing is handled by an in-house sales force that often works in tandem with a supplier's sales team or network of brokers.

Major types of marketing include instore product samples, beverage tastings, "end-cap" promotions, consumer word-of-mouth, and retailer discounts. Some states don't allow instore product samples. Most states require distributors to offer the same discount to all retailers regardless of size or buying power, though enforcing this rule can vary. Large beverage suppliers often promote products through mass market advertising channels like TV, radio, magazines, and newspapers.

Distributors don't sell products on the Internet and typically oppose attempts by suppliers to direct-ship alcohol. Large wholesalers may require suppliers and retailers to place orders through a secure Intranet.

While the price of alcohol varies considerably, distributors typically mark up products 25 to 35 percent when selling to a retailer. High-volume products like domestic beer may have lower distributor markups.

Human Resources

Beer, wine, and alcoholic beverage wholesale industry wages average $19 per hour, about 5 percent higher than the national average. Truck drivers -responsible for beer, wine, and alcoholic beverage delivery — require special driver training, certification, and licensing.

The annual injury rate in beer, wine, and alcoholic beverage wholesaling is more than double the national average. Most injuries involve sprains, strains, bruises, and soreness from overexertion, lifting, and driving. Injuries involving containers are nearly eight times higher than the national average.

Industry Employment Growth

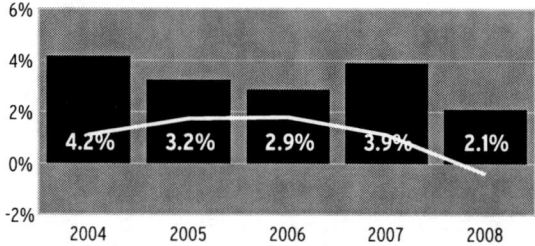

Average Hourly Earnings

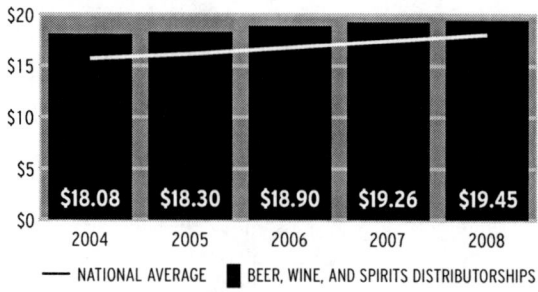

— NATIONAL AVERAGE ■ BEER, WINE, AND SPIRITS DISTRIBUTORSHIPS

SOURCE: BUREAU OF LABOR STATISTICS

Call Preparation Questions

What strategies does the company have to combat slow growth in consumption?

Consumer demand depends on suppliers making quality products and retailers effectively selling these products.

How worried is the company about direct sales to consumers?

Distributors must actively lobby to ensure the federal three-tier system remains in place.

What technology does the company use to increase efficiency and customer service? How adaptive is the technology?

Technological advances that help locate trucks, control temperature, and manage inventory are improving the industry.

Web Links

Alcohol and Tobacco Tax and Trade Bureau (TTB)

Production statistics, federal tax rates, and regulatory matters.
ttb.gov

Alcohol Policy Information System (APIS)

Statistics and resource for alcohol-related policies.
alcoholpolicy.niaaa.nih.gov

Beverage Industry

Trade magazine covering current trends and issues.
www.bevindustry.com

Beverage World

Trade magazine covering current beverage trends and issues.
www.beverageworld.com

Distilled Spirits Council of the United States (DISCUS)

Trade association with industry-related insight.
www.discus.org

Just-Drinks

Beverage industry magazine with news, features, conferences, legislation, and briefings.
www.just-drinks.com

The Beverage Information Group

Industry news and opinion.
www.beveragenet.net

Glossary of Acronyms

APIS — Alcohol Policy Information System
APR — area of primary responsibility
BAL — blood alcohol level
EDI — electronic data interchange

NABCA — National Alcohol Beverage Control Association
NBWA — National Beer Wholesalers Association
NTSB — National Transportation Safety Board
SKU — stock-keeping unit
TTB — Alcohol and Tobacco Tax and Trade Bureau

HOOVER'S TOP COMPANIES

Largest Companies by Sales	($ mil.)
Reyes Holdings LLC	10,100.0
Southern Wine & Spirits of America, Inc.	8,300.0
The Charmer Sunbelt Group	4,600.0
RNDC Texas, LLC	4,320.0
Glazer's Wholesale Drug Company, Inc.	3,150.0
Young's Market Company, LLC	2,200.0
Central European Distribution Corporation	2,136.6
Wirtz Corporation	1,400.0
Topa Equities, Ltd.	1,200.0
National Distributing Company, Inc.	—

Largest Employers	Employees
Southern Wine & Spirits of America, Inc.	10,300
Reyes Holdings LLC	8,700
The Charmer Sunbelt Group	7,000
RNDC Texas, LLC	6,000
Glazer's Wholesale Drug Company, Inc.	5,900
National Distributing Company, Inc.	3,000
Topa Equities, Ltd.	2,133
Young's Market Company, LLC	2,130
Wirtz Corporation	2,000
National Wine & Spirits, Inc.	1,725

Fastest Growing* by Five-Year Sales Growth	(%)
Central European Distribution Corporation	37.9
Drinks Americas Holdings, Ltd.	28.9
Reyes Holdings LLC	19.3
Southern Wine & Spirits of America, Inc.	13.5
Glazer's Wholesale Drug Company, Inc.	12.5
Topa Equities, Ltd.	4.0

Fastest Growing* by Five-Year Employee Growth	(%)
Reyes Holdings LLC	16.8
Glazer's Wholesale Drug Company, Inc.	8.6
Southern Wine & Spirits of America, Inc.	7.7
Drinks Americas Holdings, Ltd.	6.5
Central European Distribution Corporation	3.4
Topa Equities, Ltd.	1.0

Top Public Companies by Market Value	($ mil.)
Central European Distribution Corporation	927.8
Drinks Americas Holdings, Ltd.	20.3

* These rates are compounded annualized increases and may have resulted from acquisitions or one time gains. If less than 6 years of data are available, growth is for the years available.

SOURCE: HOOVER'S, INC., DATABASE

Beverage Manufacture and Bottling

The soda drink and bottled water industry in the US includes about 3,000 companies that manufacture and distribute beverages, with combined annual US revenue of $70 billion. Coca-Cola and PepsiCo hold more than 50 percent of the market, following strong consolidation in the past decade. Only a few other companies have annual revenue above $500 million. Most are local or regional manufacturing and bottling operations with annual revenue under $100 million.

Competitive Landscape

Demand for non-alcoholic beverages is driven by consumer tastes and demographics. The profitability of individual companies depends on effective marketing. Large manufacturers have economies of scale in production and distribution, with average annual revenue per production worker close to $1 million. Small companies can compete by producing new products, catering to local tastes, or selling at lower prices.

Products, Operations & Technology

Nonalcoholic beverages include sodas (carbonated soft drinks, or CSD), bottled waters, juices, and a large variety of mixtures. Sodas account for about 60 percent of the market. The manufacture and distribution of most national soda brands, including Coke and Pepsi, is a two-tiered process. The primary manufacturer produces a flavored syrup called concentrate that is sold to local bottlers who manufacture and distribute the finished product. In a typical bottling operation, the flavored syrup, corn syrup (sugar), and filtered water are mixed in appropriate proportions, carbon dioxide gas is injected, and the finished soda product is poured into bottles or cans, which are capped, labeled, and packaged.

The two-tiered structure is most efficient for national companies with large volume, because the manufacturing process is simple and because water, the main ingredient of sodas, is expensive to ship and is available locally. Smaller companies combine the syrup production and bottling operations in one plant. For soft drink bottlers, the major raw materials, aside from the flavored syrup, are corn syrup and containers — glass bottles, aluminum cans, or plastic bottles made from polyethylene terephthalate (PET).

Bottlers frequently operate sizable distribution systems, including warehouses and fleets of specialized delivery trucks. Production and distribution volume is usually measured in

BUSINESS CHALLENGES

» Dependence on National Manufacturers

To retain valuable relationships with national manufacturers, local bottlers and wholesalers have to meet certain financial and operating tests that restrict their ability to diversify, and force them to spend money on advertising and promotion. The consolidation of beverage brands into just a few national companies gives bottlers and wholesalers little option but to agree to whatever restrictions national companies place on them.

» Soda Health Concerns

The large amounts of sugar in many sodas are believed to contribute strongly to the obesity epidemic in US children. Sodas typically contain 150 calories per can, entirely from sugar, and have no other nutritional value. Also criticized are the relatively high levels of caffeine in diet sodas, like Pepsi One, that are heavily consumed by teenage girls. In response, many soda makers are creating new diet or decaffeinated product versions.

» Slow Demand Growth

Demand for beverages is limited by the growth of the US population, about 1 percent per year. In recent years, production of beverages has been flat. Large manufacturers look to international markets for better growth.

cases of 192 ounces, although actual cases of 12-ounce cans now contain 288 ounces. Coca-Cola produces more than 4 billion cases of soft drinks per year; PepsiCo, over 3 billion. In addition to producing canned and bottled soft drinks, large manufacturers sell sweetened syrups to restaurants and other retailers that produce the finished product at the point of sale by mixing the syrup with carbonated water to produce fountain products. About 35 percent of Coca-Cola's US product is in the form of fountain sales and 60 percent in bottled sales.

The manufacturing process for most non-soda beverages is usually more complicated than the mix-carbonate-and-bottle soda process and therefore isn't usually handled by local bottlers. In most cases, non-soda products are bottled by the manufacturer and distributed through the same types of channels--wholesalers, distributors, brokers--used by food manufacturers, although bottlers may also participate. Bottled waters, a rapidly growing category of beverage, are either bottled at specific springs or made locally from filtered tap water.

Manufacturers and bottlers typically operate under contracts, called Bottler Agreements, that specify the territory within which the bottler has an exclusive right to make, sell, and distribute the manufacturer's brand in bottles or cans. Fountain products are often sold separately through wholesalers, under Distributor Agreements. Bottle and fountain territories may overlap and bottlers may also be fountain distributors. Coca-Cola sells products through about 80 local bottlers and 500 fountain wholesalers.

Bottler Agreements usually require that container and packaging materials be bought from suppliers that are approved by the manufacturer, and that the bottlers not handle competing products. Agreements also specify the price that the bottler must pay for concentrate. The manufacturer has no control over the prices the bottler charges customers, and usually isn't obligated to spend money for marketing or promotions in the bottler's territory. Often, however, the manufacturer will provide marketing and promotion support. In one year, for example, Coca-Cola provided about $600 million in marketing support to Coca-Cola Enterprises, its largest bottler. Many Coke and Pepsi bottlers hold perpetual contracts that can be terminated only for breach of contract.

The industry depends on technology for developing new products in the labs and packaging product at the plants. Most bottling plants are highly automated with a combination of mechanical automation and computerized robotics.

Sales & Marketing

Beverage manufacturers, bottlers, and wholesalers sell products through a variety of channels, such as food and convenience stores, restaurants, vending machines, mass merchandisers, and institutions, including schools and colleges. Soda bottlers typically own local vending machines. The marketing approach to each of these channels is quite different and often includes promotional spending. Large manufacturers may also sell directly to national accounts and usually advertise on national or regional TV and in print.

Manufacturers typically produce a line of brands and often test and introduce new products into the market through their existing distribution channels.

Human Resources

Soft drink production workers earn on average $18 hourly, $2 more than the national wage. Manufacturing non-alcoholic beverages from concentrate and operating bottling lines are highly automated, requiring workers with some shop floor skills. Annual injury rates of beverage manufacturers are high: 10 cases per 100 full-time workers, four more than for the manufacturing sector as a whole. In this industry, fringe benefits can average an additional 26 percent of wages.

Industry Employment Growth

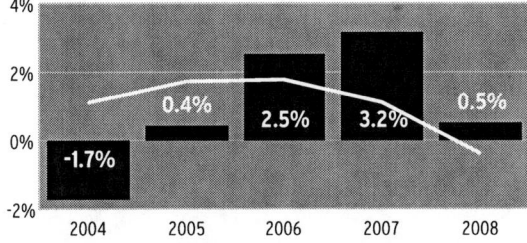

Average Hourly Earnings

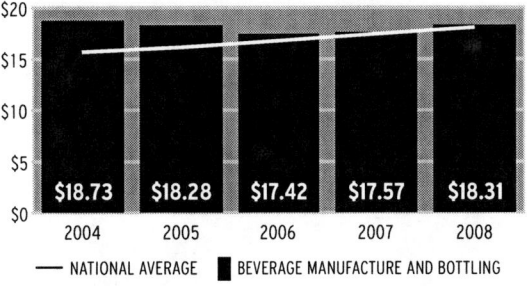

SOURCE: BUREAU OF LABOR STATISTICS

Call Preparation Questions

If a bottler or wholesaler, what demands do manufacturers place on the company?

To retain valuable relationships with national manufacturers, local bottlers and wholesalers have to meet certain financial and operating tests that restrict their ability to diversify, and force them to spend money on advertising and promotion.

How are health concerns about soft drink consumption affecting company sales and product mix?

The large amounts of sugar in many sodas are believed to contribute strongly to the obesity epidemic in US children.

What strategies does the company have to combat slow consumption growth?

Demand for beverages is limited by the growth of the US population, about 1 percent per year.

What opportunities does the company see in sports and energy drink sales?

The success of Gatorade launched the new category of performance enhancement drinks for sports and exercise and is selling well.

In which countries does the company have opportunities for growth?

While North America is the largest soft drinks market, the fastest growth is in markets in Asian countries.

Web Links

American Beverage Association

Good issues.
www.ameribev.org

Beverage Digest

Some data but mainly by subscription.
www.beverage-digest.com

Beverage World

News.
www.beverageworld.com

BevNET

News.
www.bevnet.com

BNP Media

News.
www.myfoodandpackaging.com

Food and Drug Administration

www.fda.gov

Glossary of Acronyms

CSD — carbonated soft drinks
PET — polyethylene terephthalate

HOOVER'S TOP COMPANIES

Largest Companies by Sales	($ mil.)
PepsiCo, Inc.	43,251.0
The Coca-Cola Company	31,944.0
Coca-Cola Enterprises Inc.	21,807.0
The Pepsi Bottling Group, Inc.	13,796.0
Reyes Holdings LLC	10,100.0
Dr Pepper Snapple Group, Inc.	5,700.0
PepsiAmericas, Inc.	4,937.2
Roll International Corporation	1,980.0
Cott Corporation	1,776.4
Nestlé Waters North America Inc.	—

Largest Employers	Employees
PepsiCo, Inc.	185,000
The Coca-Cola Company	90,500
Coca-Cola Enterprises Inc.	73,000
The Pepsi Bottling Group, Inc.	69,100
PepsiAmericas, Inc.	20,700
Dr Pepper Snapple Group, Inc.	20,000
Reyes Holdings LLC	8,700
Nestlé Waters North America Inc.	7,500
Coca-Cola Bottling Co. Consolidated	5,800
The Honickman Group	5,000

Fastest Growing* by Five-Year Sales Growth	(%)
Hansen Natural Corporation	56.4
XELR8 Holdings, Inc.	41.4
Central European Distribution Corporation	37.9
Drinks Americas Holdings, Ltd.	28.9
ForeverGreen Worldwide Corporation	23.8
Reyes Holdings LLC	19.3
Roll International Corporation	15.7
Jones Soda Co.	12.3
Reed's, Inc.	11.3
PepsiCo, Inc.	9.9

Fastest Growing* by Five-Year Employee Growth	(%)
Hansen Natural Corporation	42.5
The Coca-Cola Company	28.3
Jones Soda Co.	21.2
Roll International Corporation	17.6
Reyes Holdings LLC	16.8
PepsiAmericas, Inc.	13.7
Reed's, Inc.	11.1
Reddy Ice Holdings, Inc.	7.9
Drinks Americas Holdings, Ltd.	6.5
Central European Distribution Corporation	3.4

Top Public Companies by Market Value	($ mil.)
The Coca-Cola Company	104,664.2
PepsiCo, Inc.	84,731.7
Coca-Cola Enterprises Inc.	5,868.2
The Pepsi Bottling Group, Inc.	4,642.0
PepsiAmericas, Inc.	2,546.9

* These rates are compounded annualized increases and may have resulted from acquisitions or one time gains. If less than 6 years of data are available, growth is for the years available.

SOURCE: HOOVER'S, INC., DATABASE

Biofuels Production

**THIS INDUSTRY
INCLUDES:**

SIC CODES
2869   Industrial Organic
        Chemicals

NAICS CODES
325193 Ethyl Alcohol
        Manufacturing

The biofuels industry in the US includes about 200 companies with combined annual revenue of about $3 billion. Major companies include Archer Daniels Midland, Cargill, BP, and Chevron. Most companies in the industry are small (under $10 million in revenue). Biofuels is a young industry that has grown at a rate of 25 to 50 percent each year. New entrants enter the field constantly and new technology break-throughs are frequent. Federal and state government subsidies and loan guarantees keep barriers to entry relatively low.

Competitive Landscape

Demand is driven by federal legislation and regulations that establish a government-mandated market for biofuels. The profitability of biofuel production facilities depends on prices of gas and diesel, which fluctuate based on world petroleum demand and domestic refinery utilization. Economies of scale in ethanol production are limited due to the transportation costs associated with gathering feedstocks (corn and other biomasses) and transporting the ethanol to blending sites. As a result, large companies operate multiple production facilities. Small companies can compete effectively by developing business relations with distributors and being able to assure delivery consistently. Revenue per employee in ethanol production facilities is about $1 million per year.

Products, Operations & Technology

The major products of the biofuels industry are ethanol and biodiesel. Ethanol makes up over 90 percent of current US biofuels production of about 4 billion gallons per year.

Ethanol production requires corn or other high-starch grains, water, chemicals, enzymes and yeast, and denaturants such as unleaded gas. In the dry milling process (used for about 80 percent of production), corn or other high-

BUSINESS CHALLENGES

» Economic Viability Depends on Fuel Prices

Sustained high oil prices are encouraging the development of alternative fuels with increased R&D investment and capital outlays to build new production facilities. Ethanol's current production cost, and that it gets about 30 percent less mileage than gas, means that it's uneconomical unless gas retails for over $3 per gallon. Biofuels enjoy political and popular support and benefit from government mandates and subsidies; however, for long-term viability, they must become cost-competitive with petroleum-based fuels.

» Dependence on Government Support

Due to current economics, the biofuel industry depends on government support to establish itself and grow. Government regulations mandate the use of specific amounts of biofuels as blends of fuel, and the EPA will impose quotas on refiners and importers for biofuel use. In addition, the government is giving tax rebates for biofuel production and sale, equipping retail outlets to handle higher content fuels, and supporting R&D with grants. While the Energy Policy Act of 2005 was written with an eight-year horizon, its key tax and grant provisions must be funded annually.

» Limited Supply of Crop-based Feedstocks

USDA studies indicate that about 16 billion gallons of ethanol (about 10 percent of year 2030 requirements) can be produced from crop-based sugars and starches (primarily corn) before the food market is significantly impacted. This competition with food uses of crop-based feedstocks is a major drawback of current ethanol production methods. To become a viable replacement for petroleum-based fuels, the biofuel industry must develop the ability to use alternative feedstocks that don't have value as a food source.

starch grains are first ground into meal and then mixed with water and enzymes to form a mash. The mash is processed at a high temperature in cookers to liquefy the mixture and reduce bacteria levels prior to fermentation. Next, the mash is cooled and secondary enzymes added to convert the starches into glucose sugars. Yeast and ammonia are added to the mash and the mixture is passed through several fermenters, completing the process of converting the sugar to ethanol and carbon dioxide.

After fermentation, the fermented mash, which is about 10 percent alcohol, is transferred to distillation, where the ethanol is separated from the residual solids. The ethanol is concentrated to 190 proof using conventional distillation methods, and then dehydrated to approximately 200 proof (100 percent alcohol). The resulting ethanol is then blended with about 5 percent denaturant, usually gas, to prevent human consumption, and is then ready for shipment to a blending site. The residual solids are processed and sold as high-protein animal feed.

In the wet milling process (used for about 20 percent of ethanol production), the grain is first steeped in a dilute sulphuric acid to facilitate separation of the grain into its component parts. The mixture is then ground, the germ separated, and enzymes added to convert the starches to glucose. After fermentation and distillation of the ethanol, the remaining mash is recombined with fiber and sold as corn gluten, an animal feed.

Development is underway to enable production of cellulosic ethanol, ethanol made from cellulose found in wood and agricultural wastes. Cellulose materials are dissolved using acids and special engineered enzymes and bacteria to convert the residual starches and sugars into glucose. The ability to use cellulose materials as feed stocks will reduce dependence on food crops for ethanol production. Processes to produce cellulosic ethanol have been proven in the lab, but not in commercial production. Current ethanol facilities can be upgraded to produce cellulosic ethanol once the production process becomes commercially viable.

Ethanol cannot be transported through pipelines because it's highly corrosive and readily absorbs water; therefore, transporting it from the production facility to the blending facility is an issue. Most bulk transportation is by rail in specially equipped tanker cars. While many refineries are located in coastal areas, transporting ethanol by water (barge or tanker) presents a number of problems that make heavy use impractical.

Biodiesel is a clean-burning alternative fuel derived from vegetable oils or animal fats. Biodiesel contains no petroleum, but can be blended with petroleum diesel to create a biodiesel blend. Diesel engines require no major modifications to burn either biodiesel

blends such as B20 (a 20 percent biodiesel, 80 percent petroleum diesel blend) or B100 (100 percent biodiesel). Biodiesel production is fairly simple and requires no elaborate equipment: fat or oil is mixed with methyl alcohol and a catalyst such as sodium or potassium hydroxide, and heated to produce glycerin and biodiesel (methyl ester). The glycerin is then separated from the biodiesel, purified, and sold as a separate product.

The average ethanol production facility makes about 40 million gallons per year. The average commercial-scale biodiesel plant produces about 6 million gallons per year. The industry is composed of mostly small producers that operate a single facility. Archer Daniels Midland, the largest producer, has seven production facilities.

Sales & Marketing

The major customers of biofuel companies are motor vehicle users who buy biofuels blended with their regular petroleum products.

Ethanol is being substituted for other oxygenates, primarily Methyl Tertiary Butyl Ether (MTBE), in gasoline as a blend called E10 (10 percent ethanol, 90 percent gasoline) for use in most gas-powered vehicles. Oxygenates are additives to gas to reduce carbon monoxide emissions, and MTBE has been found to contaminate groundwater. About 6 million GM, Ford, and Daimler-Chrysler late model cars are equipped to burn fuel mixtures containing up to 85 percent ethanol (E85). While the number of gas stations dispensing ethanol mixtures is small, the numbers are increasing rapidly. Some stations are taking advantage of American concerns over fuel imports by advertising the availability of ethanol blends.

Biodiesel is having difficulty getting established, due to the smaller market of diesel vehicles and lack of incentive for widespread adoption, such as MTBE replacement. A common local sales strategy is to sell to operators of truck fleets that have their own fuel storage. These are usually municipalities or environmentally conscious companies looking to promote a "green" public image.

Human Resources

Technology and processing facilities, while highly automated, aren't highly sophisticated and can be operated by staff with moderate training and education. The high degree of automation allows revenue per worker of $500,000 to over $1 million per year. Technical professionals with bioengineering and chemical engineering backgrounds are needed to develop new conversion methods and optimize production processes.

Call Preparation Questions

How have fluctuating retail gas prices the past six months affected the company?

Sustained high oil prices are encouraging the development of alternative fuels with increased R&D investment and capital outlays to build new production facilities.

How dependent on government support is the company?

Due to current economics, the biofuel industry depends on government support to establish itself and grow.

What impact might the growing use of crops for ethanol production have on the company?

USDA studies indicate that about 16 billion gallons of ethanol (about 10 percent of year 2030 requirements) can be produced from crop-based sugars and starches (primarily corn) before the food market is significantly impacted.

Has the company established a market for the byproducts of production?

Many biofuel processes produce a waste that can be dried and used as a high-protein animal food supplement.

Web Links

Department of Energy

Government overview of biofuels programs.
www.doe.gov/energysources/renewables.htm

Ethanol Market

Market news updated daily.
www.ethanolmarket.com

Greenwire

Energy and environmental policy news.
www.eenews.net/gw

National Biodiesel Board

Trade association for the biodiesel industry.
www.nbb.org

Renewable Fuels Association

Trade association for the ethanol industry.
www.ethanolrfa.org

Glossary of Acronyms

B20 — blend of 20 percent biodiesel and 80 percent petroleum diesel

B100 — 100 percent biodiesel

E10 — blend of 10 percent ethanol and 90 percent gasoline

E85 — blend of 85 percent ethanol and 15 percent gasoline

ERP — enterprise resource planning

MTBE — methyl tertiary butyl ether

HOOVER'S TOP COMPANIES

Largest Companies by Sales	($ mil.)
Chevron Corporation	273,005.0
Cargill, Incorporated	120,439.0
Archer Daniels Midland Company	69,816.0
Aventine Renewable Energy Holdings, Inc.	1,571.6
VeraSun Energy Corporation	848.3
Pacific Ethanol, Inc.	461.5
Golden Grain Energy, LLC	278.7
Lake Area Corn Processors, LLC	103.7
Badger State Ethanol, LLC	—

Largest Employers	Employees
Cargill, Incorporated	160,000
Chevron Corporation	65,000
Archer Daniels Midland Company	27,600
Aventine Renewable Energy Holdings, Inc.	331
Pacific Ethanol, Inc.	220
Abengoa Bioenergy Corporation	165
Green Plains Renewable Energy, Inc.	50
Golden Grain Energy, LLC	43
United Wisconsin Grain Producers, LLC	40
Northern Growers, LLC	39

Fastest Growing* by Five-Year Sales Growth	(%)
VeraSun Energy Corporation	185.9
Pacific Ethanol, Inc.	129.5
Golden Grain Energy, LLC	57.4
Aventine Renewable Energy Holdings, Inc.	23.5
Archer Daniels Midland Company	17.9
Chevron Corporation	17.5
Cargill, Incorporated	17.2
Lake Area Corn Processors, LLC	9.6
Verenium Corporation	7.9

Fastest Growing* by Five-Year Employee Growth	(%)
Pacific Ethanol, Inc.	216.2
VeraSun Energy Corporation	34.5
Cargill, Incorporated	10.3
Golden Grain Energy, LLC	9.2
Aventine Renewable Energy Holdings, Inc.	3.1
Archer Daniels Midland Company	1.5
Chevron Corporation	1.4

Top Public Companies by Market Value	($ mil.)
Chevron Corporation	148,253.0
Archer Daniels Midland Company	21,735.0
Aventine Renewable Energy Holdings, Inc.	532.5
Pacific Ethanol, Inc.	333.4
Verenium Corporation	314.8

* These rates are compounded annualized increases and may have resulted from acquisitions or one time gains. If less than 6 years of data are available, growth is for the years available.

SOURCE: HOOVER'S, INC., DATABASE

Biotechnology Sector

THIS INDUSTRY INCLUDES:

SIC CODES

2836   Biological Products, Except Diagnostic Substances

NAICS CODES

325414   Biological Product (except Diagnostic) Manufacturing

541711   Research and Development in Biotechnology

The US biotechnology industry includes about 1,000 companies, with combined annual revenue close to $50 billion. Large companies include Amgen, Monsanto, Genentech, Applera, Genzyme, and Biogen. Because many drugs are now developed using biotechnology, the biotechnology and pharmaceutical industries overlap considerably. The industry consists of a few very large companies and many very small ones, and is fragmented by type of product. Most companies have annual sales under $50 million.

Competitive Landscape

Demand for biotechnology products and services is driven primarily by the willingness of insurers to pay for new medical treatments. The profitability of individual companies depends on the discovery and effective marketing of new products. Because the market for potential products is so large, small biotechnology companies can co-exist successfully with large ones if they have expertise in a particular line of research.

Products, Operations & Technology

The most successful uses of biotechnology so far have been the production of therapeutic drugs (biologics); genetically modified (GM) plants; and medical diagnostic tools such as DNA testing.

The biotechnology industry is characterized by the manipulation of living cells and their components to make new products. Some companies make only research tools that are sold to other biotechnology companies. Because they rely on advanced scientific knowledge, biotechnology companies frequently evolve from research departments at universities. Genentech, the first biotechnology company, evolved from studies of bacterial cells at Stanford and the University of California. Most biotechnology companies use a particular line of research

BUSINESS CHALLENGES

» Expensive Development of Products, Uncertain Approval

The FDA and other regulators can decline to approve a new drug, even after years of company tests and millions in costs. Biotech companies take, on average, eight to 10 years to ready a single drug for FDA approval. Since the success of many biotech companies hinges on development of a single product, lack of approval can be financially fatal. Many European countries have refused to approve genetically modified foods.

» Companies Depend Highly on Patent Protection

Specialized biotech methods and products can be protected through patents, but only for 20 years from the date of application. By the time a new product is available, many years of development and testing may already have passed. The multiple patents on various biotech methods also leave companies open to patent infringement lawsuits.

» Medical Insurers' Acceptance Key

Even after regulatory approval, a drug may not reach the market if insurance payers don't authorize its use. Payers, including managed care companies and Medicare, may decline to authorize the use of new drugs if they're too costly or only slightly more effective than cheaper drugs. Consequently, the commercial market for a new drug may be restricted even after it receives regulatory approval.

begun at a university, and are often run by scientists with an academic background.

Typically, the research at a biotechnology company involves developing a specific laboratory method (a "technology") to make a biological product and then applying the same technology to develop similar products. For example, Genentech first developed the technology of using modified bacterial cells to produce human insulin, then used the same method to produce other biological chemicals. Similarly, Abgenix developed a technology to produce a human antibody against cancers using altered mouse cells, then used the same method to produce antibodies with other functions. Research costs are usually high, equal to 20 to 25 percent of revenue at large companies and often much more at small companies that don't yet have a commercial product.

While some companies develop their own technology, many license technology from another company or a university that "owns" the technology (through patents), usually paying a royalty on subsequent product sales. Technology licensing arrangements are a common way for large companies to acquire new research avenues, and for small companies to get revenue without having to commercialize a product.

The actual manufacture of products is often by third-party contract manufacturers. Typically, a small company will use a contract manufacturer in the initial stages of producing a new product, and will build its own manufacturing facility if the product is financially successful. Manufacturing costs are usually smaller than research and sales costs.

Sales & Marketing

Commercialization of a product includes patent protection, regulatory approval, sales, marketing, and distribution. Patents can be received for a basic biotechnology laboratory process (like the polymerase chain reaction, PCR), or for a process used to make a specific product, and for a product itself. A patent gives the owner exclusive rights for 20 years from the date of application. In the biotechnology industry, patents on processes are more numerous and important than patents on individual products, because a good process can lead to many new products. The large number of patents on processes results in frequent litigation for patent infringement. Most large biotechnology companies are constantly involved in patent litigation.

Sales and marketing efforts for a new biotechnology drug are usually aimed at individual doctors, large medical centers, and managed-care companies, and may include sales representatives, advertising in medical journals, direct mailings, and promotional events such as medical meetings. Actual sales are usually made to wholesale distributors who supply hospitals and drugstores. Sales and marketing costs are typically the largest single expense item for a biotechnology company, equaling 30 to 40 percent of revenue. Small companies with an approved drug often turn to large pharmaceutical companies for sales and

marketing help. Marketing and distribution agreements are common.

Human Resources

Employees of biotech companies are chiefly scientists and laboratory technicians, although the larger companies also have a sales staff. Technicians are usually skilled in a particular area of research and are well-paid: they earn an average hourly wage of $30, double the national average. Fringe benefits can add at least 20 percent to total compensation. Senior scientists with expertise in a specific technology are vital to small biotechnology companies and usually have employment contracts and an equity interest in their company. The industry's injury rate is below the national average.

Industry Employment Growth

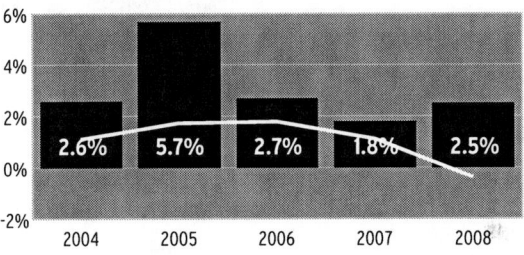

Average Hourly Earnings

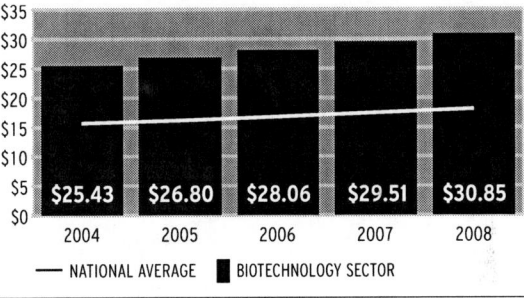

— NATIONAL AVERAGE ■ BIOTECHNOLOGY SECTOR

SOURCE: BUREAU OF LABOR STATISTICS

Call Preparation Questions

How have government regulations impacted the company?

The FDA and other regulators can decline to approve a new drug, even after years of company tests and millions in costs.

What benefits and obstacles does patent protection create for the company?

Specialized biotech methods and products can be protected through patents, but only for 20 years from the date of application.

What strategies does the company use to ensure that medical insurance companies accept new products?

Even after regulatory approval, a drug may not reach the market if insurance payers don't authorize its use.

How is the use of DNA chips benefiting the company's product development?

DNA chips enable identification of gene activity and potentially their interaction.

What opportunities do individualized drug therapy present for the company?

By accounting for the differences in each individual's DNA, researchers hope to be able to tailor drugs for a particular person.

Web Links

AgBioForum

Agricultural biotechnology economics and issues.
www.agbioforum.missouri.edu

BiolinkDirect

Excellent company list and links.
www.biolinkdirect.com

BioSpace

News on biotechnology.
biospace.com

Biotechnology Industry Organization

Good issues, some statistics, company news.
www.bio.org

BioWorld

Industry news. Industry reports for sale.
www.bioworld.com

National Center for Biotechnology Information

Research information in various biotechnology fields.
www.ncbi.nlm.nih.gov

North Carolina Biotechnology Center

Good introduction to biotechnology, glossary.
www.ncbiotech.org

Recombinant Capital

Information about biotechnology alliances, agreements, etc.
www.recap.com

US Patent and Trademark Office

Information on patents.
www.uspto.gov

USDA – Biotechnology Regulatory Services

www.aphis.usda.gov/biotechnology/brs_main.shtml

Glossary of Acronyms

BLA — Biologics License Application
GM — genetically modified
IVD — in vitro diagnostic device
NDA — New Drug Application
PCR — polymerase chain reaction
RNAI — RNA interference

HOOVER'S TOP COMPANIES

Largest Companies by Sales	($ mil.)
Amgen Inc.	15,003.0
Genentech, Inc.	13,418.0
Baxter International Inc.	12,348.0
Monsanto Company	11,365.0
Quest Diagnostics Incorporated	7,249.5
Gilead Sciences, Inc.	5,335.8
Genzyme Corporation	4,605.0
Biogen Idec Inc.	4,097.5
Quintiles Transnational Corp.	2,700.0
Celgene Corporation	2,254.8

Largest Employers	Employees
Baxter International Inc.	46,000
Quest Diagnostics Incorporated	43,500
Monsanto Company	26,400
Quintiles Transnational Corp.	21,000
Amgen Inc.	17,500
Genentech, Inc.	11,174
Genzyme Corporation	10,000
Charles River Laboratories International, Inc.	8,500
Life Technologies Corporation	4,300
Biogen Idec Inc.	4,300

Fastest Growing* by Five-Year Sales Growth	(%)
Tercica, Inc.	1,966.7
Halozyme Therapeutics, Inc.	344.8
Samaritan Pharmaceuticals, Inc.	295.8
NovaBay Pharmaceuticals, Inc.	293.3
Genoptix, Inc.	258.9
Alnylam Pharmaceuticals, Inc.	243.9
Affymax, Inc.	233.7
Replidyne, Inc.	202.5
Pain Therapeutics, Inc.	132.0
Osiris Therapeutics, Inc.	115.4

Fastest Growing* by Five-Year Employee Growth	(%)
CV Therapeutics, Inc.	136.6
Sucampo Pharmaceuticals, Inc.	72.4
CytRx Corporation	69.9
Illumina, Inc.	66.6
Insmed Incorporated	54.6
Micromet, Inc.	51.9
DOV Pharmaceutical, Inc.	51.4
Dynavax Technologies Corporation	49.9
Genoptix, Inc.	37.2
Biogen Idec Inc.	13.5

Top Public Companies by Market Value	($ mil.)
Genentech, Inc.	87,304.2
Monsanto Company	62,676.7
Amgen Inc.	60,464.3
Gilead Sciences, Inc.	46,528.1
Baxter International Inc.	33,011.1

* These rates are compounded annualized increases and may have resulted from acquisitions or one time gains. If less than 6 years of data are available, growth is for the years available.

SOURCE: HOOVER'S, INC., DATABASE

Boat Building

THIS INDUSTRY INCLUDES:

SIC CODES
3732   Boat Building and Repairing

NAICS CODES
336612   Boat Building

The boat building industry includes about 1,000 companies with combined annual revenue of about $10 billion. Large companies include Brunswick, which makes about 25 brands, Genmar, and Century. The industry is concentrated: the largest 50 companies hold about 75 percent market share. A typical company has 10 employees and less than $2 million in annual sales.

Competitive Landscape

Demand depends on growth in consumer income. The profitability of individual companies is linked to manufacturing efficiencies. Large companies have advantages in name recognition and product distribution. Small companies compete by focusing on a market niche in a local or regional area. Because of automation and high product prices, annual revenue per employee is a fairly high $180,000.

Products, Operations & Technology

Major product segments are outboard motorboats (40 percent of revenues); inboard motorboats (35 percent); and inboard-outdrive boats (20 percent). Other product types include sailboats and canoes. Some boat builders also do repair work, operate marinas, and sell auxiliary equipment and supplies on premises.

Boat building facilities vary from a few thousand square feet to more than 100,000, and outside storage areas may extend to several acres. Most manufacturing locations for larger boats are on navigable waterways, as the finished product can't be shipped over road. Other boat manufacturers locate as close to primary markets as possible to minimize transportation costs.

Manufacturing facilities are set up with custom-built molds, jigs, and fixtures designed for the particular makes and models. Most boats are made of fiberglass requiring carefully controlled use of resins, epoxies, and coatings.

BUSINESS CHALLENGES

» Demand Tied to Income Growth, Interest Rates

The industry depends greatly on income growth because boats are a luxury, and on interest rates because many sales are financed. Sales of lower-priced boats tend to be hardest hit by economic downturns: the total number of boats sold in the US dropped 9 percent in the last recession, and sales of inboard ski boats fell 18 percent.

» Slow Growth in Boating

The number of participants in the recreational boating industry, estimated to be about 70 million, has been relatively flat the last 15 years, despite population growth in coastal areas. The typical first-time boat buyer is a male in his late 30s; however, the number of males 20 to 44 is projected to grow only 5 percent in the US from 2000 to 2020. Boat manufacturers and dealers are collaborating to promote greater participation in boating.

» Unreliable Dealer Service

Independent dealers are the face of manufacturers to the buying public, so brand images are tarnished and sales suffer if dealer customer service and support is lacking. In a survey of recent boat buyers, service was the number one area cited needing improvement at boat dealerships. Almost one-third of recent buyers rate their last boat repair experience as "fair or poor." To improve customer service, some manufacturers provide monetary incentives to dealer technicians for training and certification on their products.

Basic construction consists of the multiple layering of fiberglass mesh over molds. Strength and flexibility characteristics are achieved by the specific combination of fiberglass with resins and epoxies, which are generally sprayed on. Custom builders perform this process by hand; high-volume manufacturers use robotics.

Smaller, less expensive boats are frequently made of aluminum. Structural components are made from extrusions while exterior coverings are made from formed sheet.

The largest single material cost is the engine. Large boat builders, such as Brunswick and Century, typically use engines (Mercury and Yamaha) made by operating divisions of the same parent company.

In larger facilities, computers are used extensively in design and manufacturing. Companies compete through new design offerings that provide improved performance, passenger comfort, fuel efficiency, and cost-effectiveness. Many small boat builders still rely on "craftsmen" to produce custom-built boats.

Sales & Marketing

The primary sales outlet for boats are retail dealerships; some 5,000 retail dealers sell boats in the US. Dealers typically handle more than one brand, and some are exclusive dealers of a single manufacturer that offers multiple brands.

About 300,000 new power boats and 400,000 canoes and kayaks are sold annually in the US. Boats cost anywhere from a few hundred dollars for canoes and kayaks to several million for large luxury cruisers. The average price is about $25,000, according to MarineMax.

Marketing is targeted for particular uses such as fishing, cruising, sailing and general recreation (primarily skiing and wakeboarding). Trade shows, dealer-distributed brochures, demos, and websites are the most popular forms of marketing. Advertising in newspapers and boating magazines is common.

Human Resources

A skilled boat building workforce is of paramount importance to manufacturers. The average production worker makes about $15 per hour. Fringe benefits average about 23 percent of payroll. On-the-job training is the most common form of employee development.

Industry Employment Growth

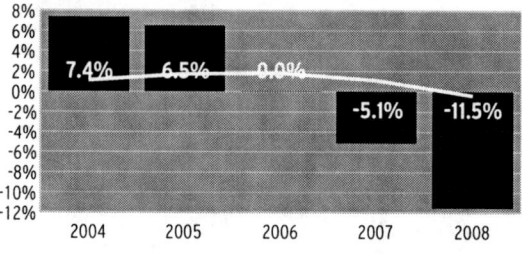

Average Hourly Earnings

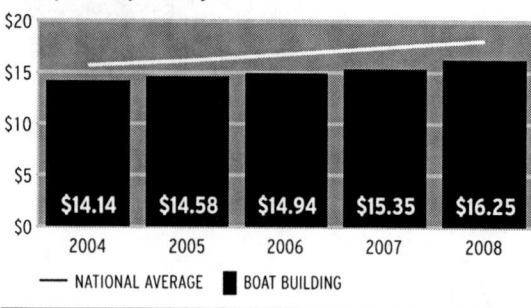

SOURCE: BUREAU OF LABOR STATISTICS

Call Preparation Questions

How might the current economic outlook affect the company's business?

The industry depends greatly on income growth because boats are a luxury, and on interest rates because many sales are financed.

How is the company increasing participation in boating?

The number of participants in the recreational boating industry, estimated to be about 70 million, has been relatively flat the last 15 years, despite population growth in coastal areas.

How is the company improving customer service by its dealers?

Independent dealers are the face of manufacturers to the buying public, so brand images are tarnished and sales suffer if dealer customer service and support is lacking.

How has average pricing for the company's products changed over the past few years?

Consumers are buying higher-priced boats that include more options and upgrades.

How has the range of products the company offers changed the past few years?

Manufacturers examine buyer behaviors and determine where to add complementary products to round out product lines.

Web Links

American Boat & Yacht Council

Non-profit dedicated to developing industry standards and training.
www.abyc.com

American Boat Builders & Repairers Association

Press releases and legislation updates.
www.abbra.org

American Boatbuilders Association, Inc.

Collective purchasing group with raw material pricing information.
www.ababoats.com

Boating Industry

Industry articles and information.
www.boating-industry.com

Boating News

Daily news updates on the boating market.
www.boatingnews.com

BoatUS

News releases and updates.
www.boatus.com/news

Marine Retailers Association of America

Trade association for boat dealers, news and links.
www.mraa.com

National Marine Manufacturers Association

Largest association of boat manufacturers.
www.nmma.org

Recreational Boat Building Industry

Statistics and historical data on the industry.
www.rbbi.com

Glossary of Acronyms

ABA — American Boatbuilders Association
ABYC — American Boat & Yacht Council
ISO — International Standards Organization
MRAA — Marine Retailers Association of America
NMMA — National Marine Manufacturers Association
PWC — personal watercraft
VOC — volatile organic compounds

HOOVER'S TOP COMPANIES

Largest Companies by Sales	($ mil.)
Brunswick Corporation	4,708.7
Genmar Holdings, Inc.	1,000.0
Yamaha Motor Corporation, U.S.A. (Century Boats)	521.5
Viking Yacht Company	176.4
Marine Products Corporation	175.6
Carver Boat Corporation, LLC	89.4
Fountain Powerboat Industries, Inc.	68.2
Mastercraft Boat Company, LLC	46.5

Largest Employers	Employees
Brunswick Corporation	29,920
Genmar Holdings, Inc.	5,000
Viking Yacht Company	1,400
Marine Products Corporation	1,100
Carver Boat Corporation, LLC	950
Mastercraft Boat Company, LLC	499
Yamaha Motor Corporation, U.S.A. (Century Boats)	400
Fountain Powerboat Industries, Inc.	322
Sea Fox Boat Company, Inc.	135
Jupiter Marine International Holdings, Inc.	120
Cigarette Racing Team, LLC.	99

Fastest Growing* by Five-Year Sales Growth	(%)
Fountain Powerboat Industries, Inc.	3.6
Brunswick Corporation	2.7

Fastest Growing* by Five-Year Employee Growth	(%)
Brunswick Corporation	6.5
Marine Products Corporation	3.1

Top Public Companies by Market Value	($ mil.)
Brunswick Corporation	369.4
Marine Products Corporation	204.7

* These rates are compounded annualized increases and may have resulted from acquisitions or one time gains. If less than 6 years of data are available, growth is for the years available.

SOURCE: HOOVER'S, INC., DATABASE

Boat Dealers

THIS INDUSTRY INCLUDES:

SIC CODES
5551   Boat Dealers

NAICS CODES
441222   Boat Dealers

About 5,000 retail dealers sell boats and related products and services in the US, with combined annual revenue of about $12 billion. MarineMax, the largest retailer, has only a 2 percent market share in this highly fragmented industry: the 50 largest dealers hold less than 30 percent of the market. Most dealers operate a single location, are privately owned, and have less than $3 million in annual sales. Larger dealers can have more than $10 million in annual sales.

Competitive Landscape

Demand for boats is closely linked to personal income and the general economy. The profitability of individual companies depends on good marketing. Large companies may have economies of scale in advertising and purchasing. Small companies compete by specializing in a certain category of boats, such as fishing boats, or by focusing on a specific customer segment, such as sailing enthusiasts. Because of the high value of the product, average sales per employee are a high $300,000.

Products, Operations & Technology

Dealers sell new and used boats, engines, parts, and a large variety of associated products. Dealers also provide maintenance and repair services, and may operate marinas and winter storage services; sell service contracts, especially for boats with expired warranties; and provide financing, insurance, and boat brokerage services.

Most dealers sell only powerboats or only sailboats. Powerboats are categorized by intended use as motor yachts, pleasure, fishing or high-performance boats, and by their configuration as outboard, inboard, sterndrive, or jetboats. Outboard boats account for the bulk of sales, with the motor usually sold separately. There are many hundreds of boat models, and fiberglass is the material used most often for

BUSINESS CHALLENGES

» Demand Closely Tied to National Economy

New boat sales are highly cyclical and depend on the economy, disposable personal income, and consumption. A strong economy, low interest rates, and demographic trends drive boating popularity. Improved yacht sales reflect consumer increased spending on high-end luxury products. In a slower economy, boat dealers experience more repossessions and fewer high-priced sales. During the last recession, unit sales of outboard boats, the biggest category, dropped 12 percent.

» Manufacturer Concentration

Brunswick, the world's largest manufacturer of boats and marine engines, yields great leverage over dealers. Although dozens of other boat manufacturers operate in the US, dealers compete to distribute the popular Brunswick products, and therefore have little ability to negotiate prices or other terms. Brunswick's well-known brands include Sea Ray, Bayliner, Boston Whaler, Hatteras, and Mercury Marine.

» Dependence on Credit Access

Like cars, most new boats are sold on credit, with financing usually supplied by a third-party lender. Since the characteristics of marine lending are specialized, not all banks make boat loans.

construction. Smaller fishing boats are often made from aluminum, and high-priced handmade boats may be made from wood.

Boat dealer operations are similar to those of auto dealers. Dealers typically stock several brands of boats and motors, but often distribute a line from only one manufacturer. Brunswick, the manufacturer of Hatteras, Sea Ray, and Boston Whaler boats, and maker of Mercury Marine engines, is the largest supplier. Other major suppliers include Century (a Yamaha boat company); MB Sports; Sea Hunt; Yamaha; Honda; and Suzuki (marine engines). Dealers may have exclusive distribution rights within a particular area.

Dealers use computer systems to link electronically to manufacturers for sales, service, and parts information, to help them serve customers and prospects.

Sales & Marketing

Dealers typically promote through print advertising, referrals from local marinas, sponsored events, and boat shows. Dealers are using websites more for product and company information. Customer service is an important component of sales, since many buyers are unfamiliar with their boat and may be new to boating. Rather than a product, dealers are selling the boating lifestyle. Salespeople often work on commission.

Customer segments vary by personal income and type of boat purchase. The average boat owner is about 48, married, either a professional or retired, with an annual income of $71,000. Buyers of cruisers are slightly older and have higher incomes than buyers of runabouts, fishing boats, or personal watercraft (PWC). Aluminum boat buyers have the lowest average income. Over 12 million boats are registered in the US: Michigan has the largest number, followed by California, Florida, Minnesota, and Texas.

Typically, retail prices for new boats are discounted from manufacturer suggested retail prices. Prices for new boats range from several hundred dollars to several million. The average industry sales price is close to $25,000, according to MarineMax.

Human Resources

Personnel management is an important concern for dealers, who must recruit and retain workers with different skills to work in sales, finance, maintenance, and customer service. Average hourly wages are slightly below the average for all US workers. Boat dealers have a better safety record than most industries.

Call Preparation Questions

How does the company deal with cyclical demand?

New boat sales are highly cyclical and depend on the economy, disposable personal income, and consumption.

How has boat manufacturer consolidation impacted the company?

Brunswick, the world's largest manufacturer of boats and marine engines, yields great leverage over dealers.

How does lending company scrutiny of customers affect company sales?

Like cars, most new boats are sold on credit, with financing usually supplied by a third-party lender.

What marketing strategies does the company use to provide boat product information to consumers?

Boat shows have long been the main source of information for consumers and members of the boating industry, but the Internet is a growing resource for boat information.

What opportunities does the dealer see in selling associated services such as maintenance?

Service and maintenance are becoming a greater and more stable source of revenue for dealers.

Web Links

American Boat & Yacht Council (ABYC)

Publications, links, education and certification programs.
www.abycinc.org

Boat Owners World

Thousands of links to manufacturers, dealers, boating, sailing, fishing, and PWCs.
www.boatowners.com

Boating Industry

International articles and news on marine finance, regulatory reviews, trends, retail updates, and market outlooks.
www.boating-industry.com

BoatTrader.com

Large listing of boats for sale.
www.boattraderonline.com

Marine Retailers Association of America

News and links.
www.mraa.com

National Marine Manufacturers Association

Schedule of boat shows, industry statistics, marketing advice, news, and links.
www.nmma.org

Personal Watercraft Industry Association

Boating education, model legislation, law enforcement, sound reduction, environmental protection, hot issues, and links.
www.pwia.org

Population Estimates

People Participating in Recreational Boating (1989 – 2005) by NMMA.
www.nmma.org/facts/boatingstats/2005/files/populationstats1.asp

Recreational Boats in Use

All registered and non-registered boats in use by NMMA.

www.nmma.org/facts/boatingstats/2005/files/populationstats3.asp

Retail Boating Market

Retail unit and dollar sales for outboard boats, inboard boats, sterndrive boats, jet boats, personal watercraft, sailboats, canoes, inflatable boats, sailboards, total all boats, boat trailers, outboard motors, and sterndrive and inboard engines, by NMMA.

www.nmma.org/facts/boatingstats/2005/files/market1.asp

Glossary of Acronyms

DPI — disposable personal income
ITC — International Trade Commission
MSD — Marine Sanitation Device
MBIA — Michigan Boating Industries Association
MBLO — Marine Business Leaders Outlook
NMMA — National Marine Manufacturers Association
PWC — personal watercraft
RMRC — Recreational Marine Research Center

HOOVER'S TOP COMPANIES

Largest Companies by Sales	($ mil.)
MarineMax, Inc.	885.4
West Marine, Inc.	679.6

Largest Employers	Employees
West Marine, Inc.	4,941
MarineMax, Inc.	1,759

Top Public Companies by Market Value	($ mil.)
West Marine, Inc.	197.5
MarineMax, Inc.	133.2

SOURCE: HOOVER'S, INC., DATABASE

Book Publishers

THIS INDUSTRY INCLUDES:

SIC CODES
2731   Books: Publishing, or Publishing and Printing

NAICS CODES
51113   Book Publishers

The US book publishing industry consists of about 2,600 companies with combined annual revenue of $30 billion. Large US publishers include McGraw-Hill, Pearson, John Wiley & Sons, and Scholastic. Some of the biggest publishers are units of large media companies, including HarperCollins (News Corp.); Random House (Bertelsmann); and Simon & Schuster (CBS). The industry is highly concentrated: the top 50 companies hold 80 percent of the market.

Competitive Landscape

Demand for books is driven by demographics and is largely resistant to economic cycles. The profitability of individual companies depends on product development and marketing. Large publishers have an advantage in bidding for new manuscripts or authors. Small and mid-sized publishers can succeed if they focus on a specific subject or market. Because of the high value of the product, average annual revenue per employee is a high $300,000.

Products, Operations & Technology

Publishers produce books for general reading (adult "trade" books); text, professional, technical, children's, and reference books. Trade books account for 30 percent of the market, textbooks 25 percent, and professional books 15 percent.

About 150,000 new books are published in the US every year; however, most are low-volume products. The number of books produced by major trade publishers and university presses is closer to 40,000.

Operations include acquiring content, managing relationships with authors, editing, designing books, manufacturing, and marketing. Publishers acquire content by contracting with authors to produce new work, buying finished manuscripts offered for sale, or acquiring the rights to existing content through licensing

BUSINESS CHALLENGES

» Low Growth in Some Segments

Although the industry's total revenue has grown an average 3 percent annually, demand in some segments has been weak in recent years. Sales of adult fiction, which compete with other sources of entertainment, have been flat. A study by the National Endowment for the Arts shows that fewer than half of adults read literature for entertainment.

» Industry Consolidation

Taking advantage of economies of scale in production and marketing, a handful of large book publishers have grown rapidly by acquiring smaller publishers. Larger publishers can more easily sell a full line of books to big booksellers like Barnes & Noble, Borders, and Amazon. Smaller publishers have less marketing leverage. Just eight large publishers hold more than 50 percent of the US book market.

» Unfavorable Textbook Demographics

The market for school and college textbooks will be depressed by flat enrollments during the next decade. Although the amount of educational material used per pupil is expected to rise due to efforts to improve performance, the number of students in school won't change. The US population five to 19 will increase just 1 percent from 2000 to 2010, and will fall in some states.

agreements. Publishers often have contracts with authors for multi-book deals. The editorial staff usually specializes in a particular area. A large publisher may own several "imprints" (brand names such as Penguin or Viking) or branded book series such as CliffsNotes, each with its own editorial staff.

Editorial work on a book includes proofing and editing, acquiring illustrations, choosing fonts and paper, and design work such as layout and cover art. Most publishers outsource printing and book binding to commercial printers, with the cost of paper borne by the publisher.

Large publishers operate their own warehouses from which they ship books as needed.

Publishers or their parent companies often produce complementary products such as magazines, TV programs, films, DVDs and videos, audiobooks, and toys.

Computer technology is essential in book publishing for creating and editing content and book design, printing, managing inventory and distribution, and creating new electronic or other products. Publishers can use the same digital sources in print, online, and for new products, such as on-demand publishing and customized books made-to-order. For example, a college can select specific chapters for its own version of a textbook.

Electronic availability of the information from traditional books has so far been successful mainly with professional and technical material, such as legal texts and subscriptions. Publishers offer this material both on the Internet and through CDs or DVDs. Industry revenue from such electronic products is about $1 billion annually.

Sales & Marketing

Book publishers sell mainly to wholesalers, retailers, school districts, colleges, libraries, businesses, and book clubs. Publishers produce and sell newly-created books (the "frontlist") and books that are reissued (the "backlist"). Publishers usually have a field sales force and a website for marketing and inquiries. Trade shows are an important source of sales. Most large book publishers don't sell directly to consumers but conduct consumer advertising campaigns. Major distributors are Baker & Taylor and Ingram International.

Multi-faceted promotion and publicity campaigns are key marketing strategies for adult and children's trade books. Tactics include in-store advertising, author readings, book signings, and posting a sample chapter online for free access. High-profile or best-selling authors appear on national television shows.

In the children's market, sales hinge primarily on price and quality, while brand name marketing and licensing are important. Marketing tie-ins that complement book sales include branded merchandise such as toys (Harry Potter dolls) and video games. Despite higher prices, interactive and audio books are popular.

Professional and technical books are advertised in industry trade magazines, industry or professional associations, and direct mail.

In the public education market, publishers compete to win contracts with state and local school systems. About 20 states buy textbooks through large contracts, on a statewide basis, each according to its own "adoption" cycle, which can span five to seven years. In other states ("open territories"), school districts buy books independently. Publishers sell with a direct sales force and by sending sample copies to teachers and government reviewers.

Because book stores have limited shelf space and constantly make way for new books, many books have only a short sales period, which Internet retailers like Amazon that don't have inventory constraints can extend.

A major concern for publishers is determining how many copies of a book to print. Technical books may have just a few thousand copies printed, while mass-market books are printed in the hundreds of thousands. Rarely, (like the Harry Potter series) books sell in the millions. Books a retailer can't sell are usually returned to the publisher for full credit. Returned books may be re-sold at highly discounted prices, or destroyed.

Publishers sell books with a suggested retail price that may be twice as high as their wholesale price but that is typically discounted by retailers. Large retail book chains like Barnes & Noble routinely sell books at a 30 to 40 percent discount from the list price. In recent years, list prices for adult trade hardcover books have been just under $30, while paperback versions list for about $15. Mass market paperbacks sell at retail for less than $10. Prices for professional books and college textbooks, on the other hand, are often over $50.

Human Resources

Though highly educated, the professional staff at book publishers earn a relatively modest wage, about 10 percent more than the average US worker. Fringe benefits are a fairly low 16 percent of total compensation. The industry historically has a high percentage of female workers. The industry's injury rate is negligible.

Industry Employment Growth

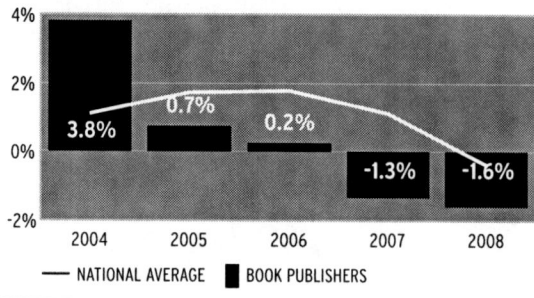

— NATIONAL AVERAGE ▪ BOOK PUBLISHERS

SOURCE: BUREAU OF LABOR STATISTICS

Call Preparation Questions

How does the company mitigate changes in readership trends?

Although the industry's total revenue has grown an average 3 percent annually, demand in some segments has been weak in recent years.

What age demographic does the company primarily sell to?

The market for school and college textbooks will be depressed by flat enrollments during the next decade.

Has the company considered alternative publishing formats, like CD-ROMs or audiobooks?

Audiobooks on CD-ROM and tape are a growing part of the market, despite higher product prices; and professional, technical, and reference books on CD are a major part.

Are the company's products suitable for reading on the Internet?

Publishers make a large number of books available on the Internet through subscription services; legal, scientific and other technical books are the most popular, with college textbooks a growing market.

Web Links

American Booksellers Association

Industry news.
news.bookweb.org

Association of American Publishers

Posts weekly news.
www.publishers.org

Association of American University Presses

Information about electronic publishing initiatives.
aaupnet.org

Book Industry Study Group

A non-profit membership organization for the book industry and its supply chain.
www.bisg.org

BookWire

Annual industry volume and price statistics.
www.bookwire.com/bookwire

Publishers Weekly

Industry news.
www.publishersweekly.com

The American Booksellers Foundation for Free Expression

Posts news about efforts for First Amendment protection.
www.abffe.com

Glossary of Acronyms

AAP — Association of American Publishers
BISG — Book Industry Study Group
NEA — National Endowment for the Arts
NRF — National Retail Federation

HOOVER'S TOP COMPANIES

Largest Companies by Sales	($ mil.)
The McGraw-Hill Companies, Inc.	6,355.1
Random House, Inc.	2,649.4
Scholastic Corporation	2,205.6
John Wiley & Sons, Inc.	1,673.7
Thomson West	935.5
Pearson Education, Inc.	878.4
Houghton Mifflin Company	413.2
Thomas Nelson, Inc.	250.0
Hachette Book Group USA	—
Simon & Schuster, Inc.	—

Largest Employers	Employees
The McGraw-Hill Companies, Inc.	21,171
Scholastic Corporation	10,200
Thomson West	8,025
Pearson Education, Inc.	7,742
Random House, Inc.	5,764
John Wiley & Sons, Inc.	4,800
Houghton Mifflin Company	3,113
HarperCollins Publishers, Inc.	1,425
Cengage Gale	1,232
W.W. Norton & Company, Inc.	1,000

Top Public Companies by Market Value	($ mil.)
The McGraw-Hill Companies, Inc.	7,291.1
John Wiley & Sons, Inc.	2,255.5
Scholastic Corporation	1,133.4
Educational Development Corporation	21.1

SOURCE: HOOVER'S, INC., DATABASE

Bookstores

THIS INDUSTRY INCLUDES:

SIC CODES
5942   Book Stores

NAICS CODES
451211   Book Stores

The US bookstore industry includes almost 11,000 stores with combined annual revenue of about $15 billion. Major companies include Barnes & Noble, Borders Group, and Books-A-Million. The industry is concentrated: the 50 largest companies hold about 75 percent of sales.

Competitive Landscape

Demand is driven by demographics and consumer income. The profitability of individual companies depends on merchandising and marketing. Large companies can provide broader selections and lower prices. Small companies can compete by offering specialized products or serving a local market. The industry is labor-intensive: sales per employee are about $120,000. Sales per employee tend to be lower for smaller, independent bookstores. Major competitors include mass merchandisers, warehouse clubs, Internet retailers, and mail order catalogs.

Products, Operations & Technology

The industry is segmented into general, college, and specialty bookstores. General bookstores account for over 60 percent of sales and college bookstores for 30 percent. General bookstores sell mostly "trade" books (fiction, non-fiction, adult, children's); college bookstores, mostly textbooks; and specialty bookstores, mostly religious books. Bookstores may also sell music, DVDs, magazines, and gifts.

Bookstore retailing includes national and regional chains, and independent local bookstores. The dominant chains have "superstores" that can exceed 20,000 square feet, and usually anchor large strip malls in high traffic areas. Chains also have bookstores located in indoor shopping malls, which average 4,000 square feet. Most independent bookstores don't exceed 5,000 square feet, and occupy smaller strip malls or shopping centers. The failure rate of

BUSINESS CHALLENGES

» Chronic Drop in Adult Readership

The declining number of adults who regularly read books will have long-term effects on the bookstore industry. In the last 10 years, the population of adults who read literature decreased 4 million, according to the National Endowment of the Arts. The percentage of young adults who read regularly declined even faster, as TV and Internet use increased.

» Flat Prices Squeeze Margins

Trade book (fiction, non-fiction, adult, children's) pricing has basically been flat the last 10 years. Publishers indirectly set maximum retail prices, so retailers must rely on increased volume or decreased discounts to sustain profitability. Flat pricing makes maintaining margins especially difficult for independent bookstores, as they lack the volume to realize economies of scale.

» Competition from the Internet

Book sales represent over $4 billion in sales for Internet and mail order retailers, cutting into sales growth for bookstores. Since Amazon's introduction, bookstore sales went from growing faster than total retail to growing slower.

independent bookstores has historically exceeded that of all US businesses.

Book superstores carry large inventories and often stock over 100,000 titles in a single location. Mall bookstores average 20,000 titles, and focus on bestsellers. The number of titles an independent bookstore carries varies by the store size and subject matter. Independent bookstores may carry many titles for a limited number of subjects, or specialize in a particular genre like children's books.

Chains buy large quantities of books directly from publishers and get substantial discounts. Most independent bookstores buy from distributors or wholesalers that stock products from multiple publishers. Ingram Book Group and

Baker & Taylor are major distributors. In general, wholesalers can deliver books faster than publishers.

Trade shows and publisher's sales representatives are important sources of information when deciding what to buy. Companies may preorder major releases, depending how strong publishers think demand will be. Wholesale prices allow for a 30 to 50 percent margin based on the suggested retail price set by publishers. Unlike most retail industries, bookstores are able to return almost all unsold books for full credit.

A book superstore typically has a manager, two assistant managers, and 50 full and part-time employees. A mall bookstore has a manager, an assistant manager, and seven full- and part-time employees. In many independent bookstores, the owner serves as manager. Variable peak selling hours, extended hours of operation, and seasonality increase the need for part-time help. Bookstore employees generally have low skill requirements.

Book superstores can generate over $5 million annually; mall bookstores average about $1 million, and most independent bookstores average $1 million or less. Book superstore sales average about $240 per square foot; mall bookstores, $280; and independent bookstores, $300.

Many bookstores use electronic data interchange (EDI) or Web-based technology to streamline order processing. Pubnet allows over 3,000 bookstores to place and track orders with over 150 publishers, wholesalers, and distributors. In addition, bookstores may use electronic databases, like Books-in-Print, which hold data on millions of subjects and titles, and allow stores to search for information and customize inventory accordingly. Barnes & Noble's proprietary inventory management system links retail locations with distribution centers and wholesalers, providing rapid replenishment of books.

Sales & Marketing

The typical bookstore customer is a highly educated, relatively affluent, married woman.

Marketing and promotion are mainly through print, radio, direct mail, and in-store advertising. Special events like author appearances, book clubs, and children’s storytelling can increase store traffic. Publishers may reimburse a retailer for supporting an in-store event. Comfortable environments and in-store cafes encourage browsing, and frequent buyer programs are used to reward loyal customers with special discounts. National chains allow stores to individualize their inventory and promotions. Independent bookstores often mar-

ket cooperatively with other retailers to save on costs. The American Booksellers Association (ABA) offers Book Sense, a national marketing program that can be tailored for independent bookstores.

Internet operations allow bookstores to offer customers an even larger selection and access to hard-to-find books. Barnes & Noble operates its own website, and pays referral fees to other sites that link to Barnes&Noble.com. Independent bookstores can use third parties like Booksite.com to provide Internet retail operations. Some independent bookstores have successfully sold specialty products through the Internet. Internet pricing is usually lower than in-store to compensate for shipping charges.

By printing a price on books, publishers set a maximum price, which many retailers discount. Chains offer discounts of up to 30 percent on bestsellers to narrow the Internet pricing gap. The retail price of an adult trade hardback book is just under $30, while paperback versions retail for about $15. Mass market paperbacks retail for less than $10; college textbooks for over $50.

Human Resources

Wages are low, averaging $10 per hour in 2004 versus $16 per hour for all US workers, reflecting the low level of skill required. Personnel turnover for retailing is high, averaging about 50 percent per year. Bookstores rely greatly on part-time employees. Seasonality increases the need for part-time help during the back-to-school and holiday buying months.

Industry Employment Growth

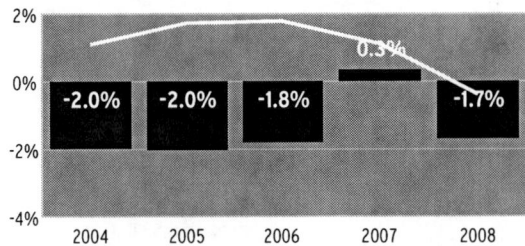

Average Hourly Earnings

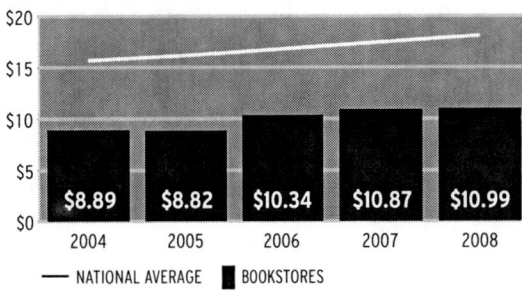

SOURCE: BUREAU OF LABOR STATISTICS

Call Preparation Questions

How has the declining number of adult readers affected the company?

The declining number of adults who regularly read books will have long-term effects on the bookstore industry.

How does the company plan to grow revenue when pricing has remained flat?

Trade book (fiction, non-fiction, adult, children's) pricing has basically been flat the last 10 years.

How has Internet retailing affected the company's performance?

Book sales represent over $4 billion in sales for Internet and mail order retailers, cutting into sales growth for bookstores.

How successful are the non-book segments of the company's business?

Music, movies, gifts, and coffee represent opportunities for incremental revenue.

How is the company capitalizing on rapid growth in the higher education market?

Full-time college enrollment is projected to rise 19 percent between 2000 and 2010.

Web Links

American Booksellers Association

Association for independent bookstores — publishes ABACUS, a yearly survey of performance statistics for independent bookstores.
www.bookweb.org

Book Industry Study Group

Trade association for organizations involved in print or electronic media.
www.bisg.org

BookWire

Book industry production and pricing statistics, bestseller statistics.
www.bookwire.com/bookwire

National Association of College Stores

Good source for information on college bookstores.
www.nacs.org

Glossary of Acronyms

ABA — American Booksellers Association

EDI/EC — electronic data interchange/electronic commerce

POP — point of purchase

HOOVER'S TOP COMPANIES

Largest Companies by Sales	($ mil.)
Amazon.com, Inc.	19,166.0
Barnes & Noble, Inc.	5,410.8
Borders Group, Inc.	3,820.9
Follett Corporation	2,520.0
Nebraska Book Company, Inc.	581.2
Books-A-Million, Inc.	535.1
Bookspan	401.9
Family Christian Stores, Inc.	360.3
Half Price Books, Records, Magazines	136.1
Powell's Books, Inc.	64.8

Largest Employers	Employees
Barnes & Noble, Inc.	40,000
Borders Group, Inc.	29,500
Amazon.com, Inc.	17,000
Follett Corporation	8,000
Books-A-Million, Inc.	5,300
Family Christian Stores, Inc.	4,600
Nebraska Book Company, Inc.	3,400
Bookspan	2,300
Half Price Books, Records, Magazines	1,740
Powell's Books, Inc.	482

Fastest Growing* by Five-Year Sales Growth	(%)
Amazon.com, Inc.	29.5
Nebraska Book Company, Inc.	9.4
Books-A-Million, Inc.	3.9
Borders Group, Inc.	1.7
Barnes & Noble, Inc.	0.5

Fastest Growing* by Five-Year Employee Growth	(%)
Amazon.com, Inc.	19.0
Nebraska Book Company, Inc.	3.2
Books-A-Million, Inc.	0.8
Barnes & Noble, Inc.	0.5

Top Public Companies by Market Value	($ mil.)
Amazon.com, Inc.	21,947.8
Barnes & Noble, Inc.	2,051.8
Borders Group, Inc.	656.7
Books-A-Million, Inc.	168.1

* These rates are compounded annualized increases and may have resulted from acquisitions or one time gains. If less than 6 years of data are available, growth is for the years available.

SOURCE: HOOVER'S, INC., DATABASE

Bowling Centers

The bowling center industry includes about 5,000 centers with combined annual revenue of about $3 billion. Major companies include Brunswick Corporation and AMF Bowling Worldwide. The industry is highly fragmented: the top 50 companies hold about 30 percent of sales.

Competitive Landscape

Demographics, personal income, and leisure time drive demand. The profitability of individual companies depends on the ability to drive traffic and provide a superior customer experience. Large companies have advantages in purchasing, finance, and marketing. Small companies can compete effectively by serving a local market or offering a unique experience. The industry is very labor-intensive: average annual revenue per worker is just under $40,000.

Bowling is both a competitive sport and recreational entertainment. As such, bowling competes with other leisure time activities, like sports, hobbies, and electronic media (movies and TV).

Products, Operations & Technology

Bowling centers generate 60 percent of revenue from lane usage fees and 30 percent from food and beverage sales. Other sources of revenue include equipment rental, bowling merchandise, and receipts from video games, slot machines, and billiard tables. Bowling centers may have on-site snack bars, restaurants, or cocktail lounges. Larger centers may provide child-care, as well as meeting and party rooms. Most centers offer organized competitive bowling through leagues as well as recreational bowling or open play.

Specialty forms of bowling include sport bowling, cosmic bowling, and bumper bowling. In sport bowling, carefully controlled lane conditions emphasize a bowler's specific skills. For recreational bowlers, cosmic bowling may in-

BUSINESS CHALLENGES

» Dependence on Personal Income

Bowling is a recreational activity, and participation and spending depend on personal income. During the last recession, the number of bowling participants remained flat, according to the National Sporting Goods Association. While bowling is generally less expensive than many sports, decreased consumer spending can detrimentally affect even the most economical leisure activities.

» Sensitivity to Energy Costs

Because bowling centers are generally large, the energy required for day-to-day operations can be significant. Energy needed for heating and cooling to maintain a comfortable environment can be costly. Changes in the price of electricity required to operate equipment can also affect operating margins.

» Decreases in League Play

Between 1996 and 2005, the number of league bowlers in the US and Canada declined almost 35 percent, according to the United States Bowling Congress. Bowling centers depend on league play as a primary source for steady revenue. The largest decline was among women league bowlers; the smallest from youth bowlers. To encourage participation, some centers offer leagues with shorter schedules and better lane times.

clude glow-in-the-dark effects, special lighting, and themed music. Children may play bumper bowling, where bumpers prevent gutter balls.

The vast majority of companies have a single bowling center, although the industry also includes small and large chains (100 plus locations). The number of lanes dictates the number of lines, or games bowled. Most large bowling centers have 40 lanes. Less than half of small chains and single locations have 24 lanes or more. A 24-lane center requires 2.5 acres of land; a 40-lane center requires 4. A center typically needs a population within a five-mile radius of 2,000 to 3,000 per lane to support business, according to bowlingmarketing.com.

A well-run center can achieve between 12,000 and 15,000 games bowled per lane per year. A lane that averages 11,000 games per year generates about $37,000 annually. The average bowling center has about $700,000 to $800,000 in annual sales, though larger bowling centers can generate over $1 million.

FAST FACTS

- The bowling center industry includes about 5,000 centers with combined annual revenue of about $3 billion.
- Major companies include Brunswick Corporation and AMF Bowling Worldwide.
- Bowling centers generate 60 percent of revenue from lane usage fees and 30 percent from food and beverage sales.
- While bowling appeals to a wide demographic, the typical customer is a 30 year-old adult with at least a high school education.
- Cash flow is seasonal, and typically peaks in the winter due to the bowling league season, which runs late summer to mid-spring.

Lane scheduling is important. Centers may allow customers to call ahead and reserve lanes or check wait times. Some centers set aside lanes during open play to accommodate walk-in customers. Improper lane scheduling can cause long waits or empty lanes, both of which hurt business.

Good lane conditions are important, especially for centers that rely on league play. Older centers may have wood lanes. New centers tend to have synthetic lanes, which are easier to maintain and create more consistent playing conditions. Lane conditioning machines clean and spread oil in distinct patterns to protect lanes from ball friction. Automated pinspotters, credited with revolutionizing play in the 1950s, reset pins. Most centers have automated ball returns and electronic scoring systems. Centers may replace pins annually.

Bowling equipment costs range from $18,000 to $45,000 per lane, depending on whether the equipment is used or new. Equipment can last more than 30 years with proper maintenance. Centers buy supplies and equipment from manufacturers, distributors, dealers, and retailers. Brunswick is the leading supplier of bowling products. Because bowling centers are relatively large buildings, heating and air conditioning expenses can be high.

Microprocessors control automated pinspotters, and computerized electronic scoring speeds play to allow more games bowled. To manage maintenance schedules, centers may use software integrated with lane conditioning equipment. Many centers use automated lane scheduling software to maximize lane use.

Sales & Marketing

While bowling appeals to a wide demographic, the typical customer is a 30 year-old adult with at least a high school education. Bowlers are slightly more likely to be men. Children 6 to 17 represent about 35 percent of bowlers, and are a growing segment. Bowling is one of the largest indoor sports in the US, and allows entire families to participate.

Marketing includes direct mail and local print, TV, or newspaper advertising. Hosting and promoting league play is extremely important because leagues generate dependable revenue versus recreational play, which can vary greatly. The Bowling Proprietor's Association of America (BPAA) offers national promotional programs to individual centers through third parties. Many centers dedicate sales resources to sell corporate events or birthday parties to attract groups. Centers may run promotions targeting children and seniors to attract play during non-peak times — primarily weekday mornings and afternoons.

A clean, modern facility is important to providing a good customer experience. Many older bowling centers have upgraded lighting, interior decor, and bathrooms to stay competitive. Large centers may add other forms of entertainment, like bumper cars or laser tag, to broaden appeal. Customer service is also important in generating repeat visits. AMF uses a secret shopper program to identify service and cleanliness issues.

Bowling centers may use the Internet to communicate events, activities, and league schedules. Some websites offer information on group events, tournaments, and lessons.

Bowling is a relatively low cost sport, and lane usage fees are typically less than $5. Centers may rent lanes by the game or hour. Discounting to promote daytime (non-peak) play is common. While most centers rent bowling shoes, many provide balls for free.

Human Resources

Bowling centers depend on part-time employees, and most workers require few skills. As a result, wages are extremely low compared to the average for all US workers. Many centers have pro shop operators to manage bowling equipment sales and instructional programs. The industry injury rate is significantly below the US average, with most injuries related to contact with equipment. Most bowling centers employ 20 to 50.

Industry Employment Growth

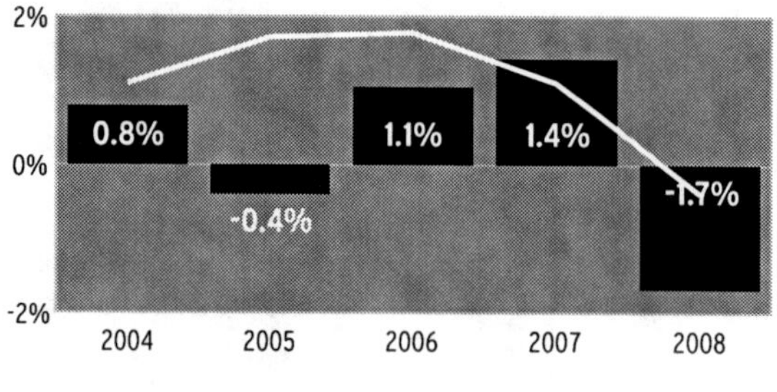

Average Hourly Earnings

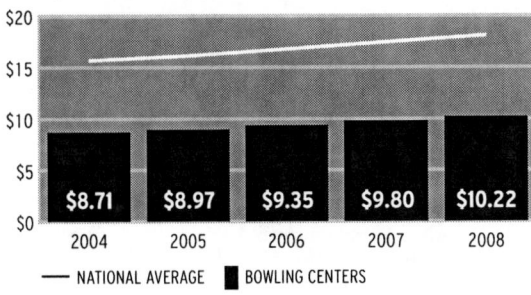

	2004	2005	2006	2007	2008
BOWLING CENTERS	$8.71	$8.97	$9.35	$9.80	$10.22

— NATIONAL AVERAGE ■ BOWLING CENTERS

SOURCE: BUREAU OF LABOR STATISTICS

Call Preparation Questions

How do trends in the local economy affect the company's sales?

Bowling is a recreational activity, and participation and spending depend on personal income.

How sensitive are the company's operating margins to changes in energy costs?

Because bowling centers are generally large, the energy required for day-to-day operations can be significant.

What changes has the company seen in league participation?

Between 1996 and 2005, the number of league bowlers in the US and Canada declined almost 35 percent, according to the United States Bowling Congress.

What types of entertainment does the company provide in addition to bowling?

Providing entertainment in addition to bowling helps attract a broader target and encourages customers to spend more money.

How important are sales from areas other than lane fees?

While most revenue comes from lane fees, centers also realize sales through food and beverage services, pro shops, and lessons.

Web Links

AMF

Bowling center operator.
www.amf.com

Bowling Center Management

Trade journal for BPAA — good statistics on operations.
www.bcmmag.com

Bowling Proprietor's Association of America

Trade association for bowling center owners — regulatory issues, trends.
www.bpaa.com

BowlingMarketing.com

Provides marketing support for bowling centers — good source for operational information.
www.bowlingmarketing.com

Brunswick

Bowling center operator and bowling equipment manufacturer.
www.brunswick.com

National Sporting Goods Association

Trade association for sporting goods industry — good research and trends on participation, demographics.
www.nsga.org

United States Bowling Congress

Amateur and youth bowling organization — bowling statistics, league membership, state information.
www.bowl.com

Glossary of Acronyms

BPAA — Bowling Proprietors Association of America
IBPSIA — International Bowling Pro Shop and Instructors Association
NSGA — National Sporting Goods Association
PBA — Professional Bowlers Association
USBC — United States Bowling Congress

HOOVER'S TOP COMPANIES

Largest Companies by Sales	($ mil.)
Brunswick Corporation	4,708.7
AMF Bowling Worldwide, Inc.	499.1
Bowl America Incorporated	30.1

Largest Employers	Employees
Brunswick Corporation	29,920
AMF Bowling Worldwide, Inc.	9,362
Bowl America Incorporated	750

Fastest Growing* by Five-Year Sales Growth	(%)
Brunswick Corporation	2.7
Bowl America Incorporated	0.5

Fastest Growing* by Five-Year Employee Growth	(%)
Brunswick Corporation	6.5
Bowl America Incorporated	3.5

Top Public Companies by Market Value	($ mil.)
Brunswick Corporation	369.4
Bowl America Incorporated	50.4

* These rates are compounded annualized increases and may have resulted from acquisitions or one time gains. If less than 6 years of data are available, growth is for the years available.

SOURCE: HOOVER'S, INC., DATABASE

Breakfast Cereal Manufacturing

THIS INDUSTRY INCLUDES:

SIC CODES
2043   Cereal Breakfast
        Foods

NAICS CODES
31123   Breakfast Cereal
        Manufacturing

The breakfast cereals manufacturing industry includes about 50 companies with combined annual revenue of $9 billion. Major companies include Kellogg; General Mills; Post (part of Ralcorp Holdings); and PepsiCo's Quaker Food and Beverage subsidiary. The industry is highly concentrated: the top four companies account for 80 percent of industry revenue.

Breakfast cereal manufacturing includes companies that make ready-to-serve packaged cereal and cereals like oatmeal and farina that must be cooked prior to eating. It doesn't include the manufacturing of granola bars, breakfast bars, or packaged cereal snacks.

Competitive Landscape

Demand is driven by demographics and health considerations, particularly the attitudes of busy families and working professionals toward the first meal of the day. The profitability of individual companies depends on managing raw material costs, operating efficiently, and maximizing retail shelf space. Large companies have advantages in purchasing, distribution, and marketing. Small operations can compete effectively by manufacturing cereals that emphasize organic or healthful ingredients. The industry is capital-intensive: average annual revenue per employee is $600,000.

Breakfast cereals compete against other popular breakfast items prepared at home, including eggs, yogurt, bacon, donuts, muffins, toaster pastries, bread, coffee, and fruit. Breakfast cereals also compete with restaurants and food kiosks that sell breakfast food items. Cereal also competes against the trend to skip breakfast entirely.

Products, Operations & Technology

The industry's major product is ready-to-eat (RTE) cereal, which represents 90 percent of total industry revenue. The most popular cereals are made with corn flakes, wheat, oats,

BUSINESS CHALLENGES

» Competition from Breakfast Alternatives
Cereal manufacturers depend highly on a single type of product (cold, ready-to-eat cereal) that's overwhelmingly consumed at a single time of day. Because cereal can't be consumed on-the-go, busy families and professionals may be inclined to select more convenient breakfast foods like toaster pastries, bagels, and yogurt. Quickserve restaurants also compete with cereal, expanding menus to include so-called "grab-and-go" and "dashboard dining" breakfast products.

» Volatile Commodity Prices
The price and availability of cereal grains can fluctuate sharply due to farm yield, weather patterns, and government farm subsidies. Wheat, corn, and oat prices routinely swing 10 percent or more from year-to-year. Price and supply instability isn't limited to grains: cocoa, soybean oil, and sugar are key ingredients that can experience supply shortages.

» Shifting Demographics
Cereal manufacturers must pay close attention to shifting demographics of the US population. Children 6 to 17 are the biggest consumers of cereal, yet the following age bracket (young adults 18 to 35) consume the least amount. These two groups are projected to grow much slower than all other age groups over the next 50 years. Demographic considerations go beyond overall cereal demand: an aging population will affect demand for individual cereal brands and attributes, such as fiber-rich cereal.

mixed grains, or puffed rice. Other products include instant hot cereal, rolled oats, farina, and infant cereal.

To make breakfast cereal, grain is received, inspected, and cleaned at the cereal factory, then crushed by large metal rollers. Whole-grain cereals retain all three parts of the grain: the endosperm, bran, and germ. For flour-based cereals, crushers remove the germ and bran and finely process the remaining endosperm.

Whole grain, flaked cereals are steam-cooked using a rotating pressure cooker. Workers (or, in some cases, automated dispensers) add flavoring agents, sweeteners, salt, and water. Once cooked, the grain mixture exits the cooker onto a conveyor belt and passes through a drying oven in a process known as tempering. The cooked grains retain around 30 percent water moisture so that they can be flattened by large metal rollers, shaped, and cut into flakes. The flakes are conveyed to ovens and tossed into a blast of very hot air.

Puffed and shaped cereals are often cooked by large corkscrew extruders. A flour-based mix passes through the extruder, retaining around 20 percent moisture as it cooks. A rotating knife cuts the dough into distinct shapes as a dye machine adds colors. The cereal is then dried in a large gas-powered oven. For puffed cereal, a process called gun-puffing uses steam pressure and high heat to puff and dry the cereal.

Cooked cereal moves from the drying ovens by conveyor belt, and is typically coated with flavorings, frosting, preservatives, and fortifying vitamins and minerals. It then enters a cooling tower, where a heat exchanger cools the cereal and removes almost all moisture before loading it into a hopper for packaging. An automated packaging machine can pack cereal at about 80 to 100 boxes per minute. Cereal boxes are held in company warehouses on pallets until shipped by truck by the company or a food distributor.

A large cereal processing plant can process 50 to 80 tons of grain in a single 10-hour shift and around 30,000 tons of grain a year. To reduce shipping costs, companies typically operate multiple manufacturing plants across the US. Most plants are capable of manufacturing a wide range of cereal brands, though each plant typically specializes in one or two cooking processes.

Common inputs include the grains themselves (corn, oats, wheat, and rice in roughly equal amounts); sweeteners like brown, beet, and cane sugar; cocoa; fats and oils; vitamins, minerals, and chemical preservatives; and plastic and cardboard for packaging. Key manufacturing and energy inputs include water, electricity, and natural gas.

Recent technological advances include the twin-screw cooking extruder, which increases the flow of the dough and can lower cooking time from several hours to 20 minutes. Other important advances include computer-controlled temperature gauges, automation improvements, highly precise quality control

metrics, and a rapid ability to prototype and develop new products.

Sales & Marketing

Next to coffee, cereal is the most popular breakfast item in the US. The typical customer is anyone who eats breakfast. According to data from ACNielsen and NPD Group, 95 percent of US households buys cereal at least once a year and the average American consumes 150 bowls a year. On any given day, 40 percent of all Americans eating breakfast are eating cereal. An NPD study shows that the largest consumers of cereal are children 6 to 17; single adults under 35 eat the least amount.

Major marketing includes advertising on TV and radio; coupons in newspapers, magazines, and on the Internet; co-promotions with major movie studios, TV networks, retail stores, and technology companies; in-store discounts and end-cap promotions; sweepstakes; and product-specific websites. Advertising can reach up to 25 percent of total sales, sometimes a dollar a box. Customers redeem more cereal coupons than any other grocery offering: cereal's 5 percent redemption rate is twice the retail average. Cereal makers repay retailers for manufacturer coupons and loyalty card discounts. Private-label manufacturers don't advertise and can offer comparable products at a 20 to 40 percent discount.

Product placement on store shelves is critical to a brand's success. Conventional wisdom holds true: kids' cereals are intentionally placed at a child's eye level. Esoteric and slow-selling brands are often in the top corner away from the end-cap. Manufacturers pay a premium to place cereals at the end-cap, around the corner from the end-cap, and in the middle of the cereal aisle.

Sales teams are often organized by product or key retail account. Many companies rely on a network of third-party brokers to supplement an inside sales force. Cereal companies invest heavily in customer service operations in an effort to retain customers, many of whom "cherry pick" brands based on price and lack product loyalty. Companies manage toll-free help lines and Web-based e-mail submission forms to address product questions and concerns.

Cereal companies don't sell products on the Internet, but invest heavily in the web for product promotions and advertising. Sites like cheerios.com and specialk.com emphasize health benefits; youth-oriented websites like Cocoa Puffs' cuckooshow.com focus more on entertainment and less on product benefits. Most large processors manage restricted-access Intranets or electronic data interchange (EDI) systems to facilitate e-commerce transactions and manage inventory.

Typical product prices are $3.50 to $4.50 for a 15-ounce box. Private-labels typically cost

$1.50 less than branded cereal. Organic cereals generally command a dollar premium. Cereals marketed to kids are less price elastic than traditional cereals and can often command a slightly higher price.

Human Resources

Wages average $18 per hour, around 5 percent higher than the national average. Breakfast cereal manufacturing requires mechanical, scientific, and technical skills. Production workers must be physically able to operate machinery and lift heavy objects. A few Midwestern universities offer advanced degrees in cereal grain science.

The annual injury rate in breakfast cereal manufacturing is nearly 5 percent higher than the national average. Most injuries involve sprains, strains, fractures, and cuts from handling containers and operating machinery.

Call Preparation Questions

How dependent is the company on the success of ready-to-eat cereal?

Cereal manufacturers depend highly on a single type of product (cold, ready-to-eat cereal) that's overwhelmingly consumed at a single time of day.

How will demographic trends in the US population affect the company's business?

Cereal manufacturers must pay close attention to shifting demographics of the US population.

How can the company use packaging to increase consumer convenience and product differentiation?

Cereal packaging hasn't changed much in nearly 50 years, and some manufacturers are exploring new ways to modernize the look of the cereal box.

How is the company extending its cereal products beyond breakfast?

Breakfast cereal manufacturers are capitalizing on the USDA's recommendation to increase daily grain consumption by expanding cereal beyond breakfast.

Web Links

American Association of Cereal Chemists

Organization focused on the use of cereal grains in foods.

www.aaccnet.org

Cereal Foods World

Assortment of articles about cereals and other grain-based products, a publication of the American Association of Cereal Chemists.

www.aaccnet.org/cerealfoodsworld/tablescontents.asp

Progressive Grocer

Search for cereal or RTE cereal for the latest news.

progressivegrocer.com

Glossary of Acronyms

DVR — digital video recorder
EDI — electronic data interchange
GM — genetically modified
PCM — price-cost margin
QSR — quickservice restaurant
RTE — ready-to-eat

HOOVER'S TOP COMPANIES

Largest Companies by Sales	($ mil.)
PepsiCo, Inc.	43,251.0
General Mills, Inc.	13,652.1
Kellogg Company	12,822.0
Ralcorp Holdings, Inc.	2,824.4

Largest Employers	Employees
PepsiCo, Inc.	185,000
General Mills, Inc.	29,500
Kellogg Company	26,000
Ralcorp Holdings, Inc.	9,000
Gilster-Mary Lee Corporation	4,000
Malt-O-Meal Company	1,100
Organic Milling Corporation	210
Barbara's Bakery Inc.	175
Homestat Farm, Ltd.	20

Fastest Growing* by Five-Year Sales Growth	(%)
Ralcorp Holdings, Inc.	16.7
PepsiCo, Inc.	9.9
Kellogg Company	7.8
General Mills, Inc.	5.4

Fastest Growing* by Five-Year Employee Growth	(%)
Ralcorp Holdings, Inc.	17.7
PepsiCo, Inc.	8.6
General Mills, Inc.	1.6
Kellogg Company	0.8

Top Public Companies by Market Value	($ mil.)
PepsiCo, Inc.	84,731.7
General Mills, Inc.	20,617.9
Kellogg Company	17,202.8
Ralcorp Holdings, Inc.	3,793.9

* These rates are compounded annualized increases and may have resulted from acquisitions or one time gains. If less than 6 years of data are available, growth is for the years available.

SOURCE: HOOVER'S, INC., DATABASE

Breweries

THIS INDUSTRY INCLUDES:

SIC CODES
2082   Malt Beverages

NAICS CODES
312120   Breweries

The US brewery industry includes about 1,400 breweries with combined annual revenue of about $18 billion. Major companies are Anheuser-Busch InBev, MillerCoors, and Pabst. The industry is highly concentrated: the top two breweries account for 90 percent of revenue, and the top 50 for 98 percent. Most breweries are small, with a single location and fewer than five employees.

Competitive Landscape

The major driver of demand is consumer leisure activity. The profitability of individual companies depends on marketing, distribution, and operational efficiency. Large companies have advantages in marketing and sales, production economies of scale, and influence with distributors. Small companies can compete effectively by developing specialty products and serving a local or regional market. Average annual revenue per worker is $625,000, but is typically around $140,000 in small companies.

Competition among beers is with national, regional, and local brands, and imported brews. Competition also comes from other alcoholic beverages, especially lower-priced wine, and from non-alcoholic drinks.

Products, Operations & Technology

Major brewery products are malt beverages, primarily beer and ale, packaged in cans, bottles, barrels (31 US gallons), or kegs (half-barrels). Canned beer and ale case goods account for about 50 percent of industry revenue; bottled beer and ale case goods, for about 40 percent; and beer and ale in barrels and kegs, for 6 percent. Additional products include other malt beverages, such as porter, stout, and non-alcoholic beer, and brewing materials, such as brewers grains and malt extracts.

The brewing process takes two or three weeks, depending on the product. Breweries crack purchased malts by milling and then add

BUSINESS CHALLENGES

» Dependence on Changing Consumer Demand
Brewery production depends on consumer demand, which reflects current tastes, social trends, and demographic shifts. Domestic demand for US beer has been declining for a decade, decreasing US brewery industry revenue 30 percent. Brewery production fell 10 percent over the same period and per capita consumption was flat. Growth in the population of US males between 20 and 44, the heaviest consumers of beer, is projected to be flat from 2000 to 2010.

» Competition from Imports
Imports constitute a growing share of the market for brewery products. US imports of malt and beer more than doubled in a decade and grew over 30 percent in only five years. Imports now account for 15 percent of the national market for malt and beer, up from 8 percent a decade ago.

» Competition for Distributors
Competition for distributors can challenge smaller and midsize breweries, due to the difficulty of getting and maintaining accounts. The distributor channel is fragmented, making sales coverage more difficult for small breweries. Of the approximately 1,000 beer distributors, the 50 largest ones represent only about a third of the US beer market. Many distributors limit the number of brands they handle. Large breweries often award exclusive geographical contracts to distributors, monopolizing their sales efforts.

water to form a mash, a mixture of hot water and crushed grain. The mash is heated and stirred in a mash tun, a large cask for liquids, to convert the mixture into fermentable sugars. The mixture is then strained and rinsed in a lauter tun to produce wort, a liquid with high levels of fermentable sugars. The wort flows from the wort receiver into a brew kettle that boils and concentrates the liquid. The resulting flavor of the wort depends on the hops additives, temperature, and length of brewing.

The next steps include straining, cooling, and storing in a fermentation cellar. Brewers add yeast to jumpstart fermentation, which converts sugars into alcohol and carbon dioxide, the source of carbonation. The fermented beer cools for about a week until it clarifies and develops the desired flavor. Filtration, if used, removes extra yeast, after which the brew is ready to package for delivery to distributors. Breweries package beverages in bottles or cans, typically in 6- or 12-packs, for delivery in cases for eventual retail sale, and in barrels or kegs for on-premise draft (draught) sales.

Large breweries strategically locate plants near major distribution centers to minimize shipping costs. The largest brewery has 12 production facilities and over 550 independent wholesalers. Most producers have a single brewery and from one to dozens of wholesalers. Breweries have contracts (equity agreements) with each wholesaler that specify the distributor's rights and responsibilities, including geographical sales territory, brands they can sell, sales performance standards, and warehousing requirements that ensure freshness. Some breweries also have contracts to sell beer from international producers.

The key industry production metric is volume, measured in number of barrels a brewery produces per year. The largest US brewery ships over 100 million barrels a year domestically. Small breweries produce less than 2 million barrels annually. Regional breweries produce between 15,000 and 2 million barrels a year, whereas microbreweries produce less than 15,000. A brewpub is a restaurant-brewery that sells at least 25 percent of its beer onsite, sometimes directly from its storage tanks.

Craft breweries are small (under 2 million barrels annually); independent (less than 25 percent ownership or control by a big beer company); and traditional, which have a predominantly malt flagship (the brewer's highest volume brand) and use additives to enhance, not lighten, flavor. Regional craft breweries are independents that meet the craft definitions of small and traditional.

Breweries obtain raw materials through contractual agreements and on the open (spot) market. Grain crops are subject to adverse weather, so companies have secondary sources as alternatives, especially for barley. In addition to barley, corn, and other grains, breweries buy malt and sweeteners, including dextrose, corn syrup, cane and beet sugar, and sugar substitutes. Packaging materials include paperboard, aluminum cans, bottles, barrels, and kegs. The

cost of aluminum cansheet can be volatile. Long-term contracts and hedging help manage supply and costs. Larger breweries typically own or have an equity investment in multiple supplier companies.

The brewery business is highly automated. Advanced process equipment and filtration systems monitor each batch to flag quality control and mechanical problems. Environmental management systems control temperatures and minimize the amount of oxygen that enters the beer. Quality control labs are important: some brewers have over 125 tests, tastings, and evaluations per batch to ensure that each conforms to company standards. Breweries use automated bottling and keg lines. Radio frequency identification (RFID) and other electronic codes identify products and shipping pallets. Production data feeds into back-office systems for analysis and inventory management, order fulfillment, and to monitor distributor sales commitments. Companies also use electronic data exchange with suppliers and distributors, and electronic funds transfers to receive payments.

Sales & Marketing

Breweries collectively sell to about 1,000 independent distributors, who in turn sell to on-premise customers, such as restaurants and bars, and off-premise retail outlets, such as liquor stores, supermarkets, and food concession contractors. This three-tier distribution system — from producer or importer, to distributor, to retailer — is typical in the US. Depending on the state, breweries may own distributors and distributors may own retailers, but most states prohibit breweries from owning retailers.

Major types of marketing include TV, radio, print, and billboard advertisements, and sponsorships of sports and music events. Beer makers are one of the largest advertisers on TV. Brewers also build their images through public service programs against drinking and driving. Discount promotions and coupons are common when price competition at the consumer level intensifies.

Breweries use a sales force to recruit distributors, maintain relationships, and provide marketing support. Breweries often grant distributors exclusive distribution rights to specific products within a certain market area, if the wholesaler won't carry competing brands. Through cooperative advertising, breweries share costs with distributors for regional or local ads. Breweries also provide point-of-sale displays for distributors to use at commercial locations. Some breweries may own branches that handle sales, merchandising, and delivery services in select areas. Alliances and joint ventures are common, mainly with overseas producers for distribution in the US or abroad. Some breweries produce beverages for other companies under private label ("contract brewing").

Typical producer beer prices are between $100 and $200 per barrel. The industry generally prices according to three main categories: above-premium (also called "super-premium"); premium; and value ("budget"). Above-premium beer accounts for about 5 percent of industry sales; premium, for about 20 percent. Companies typically have multiple brands and price points in their product portfolios. Breweries often use sales promotions and discounts to attract consumers, while keeping their regular or frontline prices constant.

Human Resources

Advanced technical skills are pivotal to the success of a brewery, whose staff typically have graduate degrees in subjects such as biochemistry, food science, and quality control. Accordingly, average pay at US breweries is about 25 percent above the national average wage. Fringe benefits account for almost 30 percent of total compensation. Labor unions, mainly the Teamsters, are active at a number of breweries.

The brewery industry has a relatively good safety record, with half the rate of injuries as the US average. Sprains and strains are the most common injuries, most often from contact with equipment or falling. The industry has improved its safety record in recent years, although long-term absences are a third higher than the national average.

Industry Employment Growth

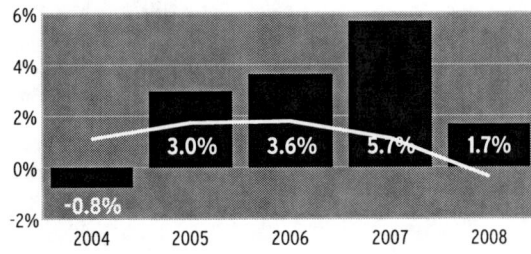

Average Hourly Earnings

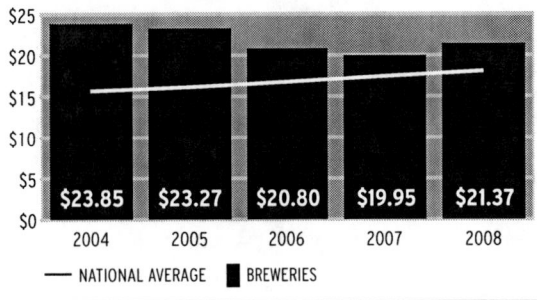

SOURCE: BUREAU OF LABOR STATISTICS

Call Preparation Questions

What trends is the company seeing in consumer preferences?

Brewery production depends on consumer demand, which reflects current tastes, social trends, and demographic shifts.

How are imports affecting the company's business?

Imports constitute a growing share of the market for brewery products.

What challenges does the company see in the distribution channel?

Competition for distributors can challenge smaller and midsize breweries, due to the difficulty of getting and maintaining accounts.

How does the company determine how to innovate products, packaging, or marketing?

Innovation in products, packaging, and marketing are important to attract today's consumers, who are more willing to try new products.

What plans does the company have to gain distribution rights for imports?

US breweries are contracting for distribution rights to bring international brands to the domestic market.

Web Links

Beer & Brewing Terminology

Common beer and brewing terms.
beeradvocate.com/beer/101/terms.php

Beer Institute

Industry regulatory issues, statistics, recent presentations, responsibility programs.
www.beerinstitute.org

Beer Mapping Project

Map of US breweries and brew-pubs by region.
beermapping.com/us-brewery-map

Beer Online Profit Guide

Industry and company news, prepared by Anheuser-Busch.
www.beerprofitguide.com

Beer Styles

Guide to beer styles.
beeradvocate.com/beer/style

BeerNet

Daily brewery and retail news; monthly distributor news.
www.beernet.com

Beertown.org

Craft beer news.
www.beertown.org

National Beer Wholesalers Association

Industry news, highlighted by state.
www.nbwa.org

Glossary of Acronyms

A-B — Anheuser-Busch
ABV — alcohol by volume
NBWA — National Beer Wholesalers Association
TTB — Alcohol and Tobacco Tax and Trade Bureau

HOOVER'S TOP COMPANIES

Largest Companies by Sales	($ mil.)
Anheuser-Busch Companies, Inc.	16,685.7
Molson Coors Brewing Company	4,774.3
The Boston Beer Company, Inc.	398.4
High Falls Brewing Company, Inc.	92.0
The Gambrinus Company	41.9
Craft Brewers Alliance, Inc.	41.5
Mendocino Brewing Company, Inc.	36.8
City Brewing Company, LLC	34.0
Deschutes Brewery, Inc.	32.9
Pabst Brewing Company	—

Largest Employers	Employees
Anheuser-Busch Companies, Inc.	30,849
Molson Coors Brewing Company	9,700
The Boston Beer Company, Inc.	775
Pabst Brewing Company	700
City Brewing Company, LLC	400
High Falls Brewing Company, Inc.	362
The Gambrinus Company	300
New Belgium Brewing Company Inc.	210
Breckenridge Brewery	200
Craft Brewers Alliance, Inc.	196

Fastest Growing* by Five-Year Sales Growth	(%)
The Boston Beer Company, Inc.	13.9
Mendocino Brewing Company, Inc.	7.1
Anheuser-Busch Companies, Inc.	4.2
Molson Coors Brewing Company	3.6
Craft Brewers Alliance, Inc.	2.0

Fastest Growing* by Five-Year Employee Growth	(%)
The Boston Beer Company, Inc.	16.1
Anheuser-Busch Companies, Inc.	5.9
Craft Brewers Alliance, Inc.	0.3

Top Public Companies by Market Value	($ mil.)
Molson Coors Brewing Company	7,390.0
The Boston Beer Company, Inc.	269.4
Craft Brewers Alliance, Inc.	55.6
Mendocino Brewing Company, Inc.	3.6

* These rates are compounded annualized increases and may have resulted from acquisitions or one time gains. If less than 6 years of data are available, growth is for the years available.

SOURCE: HOOVER'S, INC., DATABASE

Building Material Supply

The building material supply industry in the US includes 50,000 companies with combined annual sales of $250 billion. Large companies include The Home Depot and Lowe's Companies. Some independently owned stores belong to wholesale cooperatives like Ace Hardware and True Value Company, that buy materials in bulk, and resell them to members. Despite consolidation at the top, the industry remains fragmented. A large individual store has annual revenue of $10 million.

Competitive Landscape

The industry is driven mainly by residential real estate construction and renovation. Large chains have expanded rapidly in recent years by focusing on the home improvement market, with contractor sales as a sideline. Smaller companies, often family-owned lumberyards, can compete effectively by catering to contractors (for whom price is less important than other services), through a wider range of specialty products and services, and by serving areas unattractive to the big-box stores because of limited customer concentration.

Products, Operations & Technology

Building materials are sold primarily through two distribution channels: wholesale supply outlets and retail outlets like home stores, hardware stores, and lumberyards. The two major types of customers are the do-it-yourselfers (DIY), and the small or midsized construction contractor. (Large contractors often buy directly from manufacturers.)

Products include everything involved in building a house: lumber, hardware, paint, plumbing and electrical products, tools, floor coverings, wallpaper, and lawn and garden products. In addition to selling products, many companies sell installation services (so-called "installed sales") using their own or outside contractors.

BUSINESS CHALLENGES

» Volatile Supply Prices

Although raw material price increases can often be passed to consumers, suppliers that maintain large inventories can be hurt if prices move sharply. Lumber prices, especially, can be volatile, affected by changing demand, domestic supply, and imports from Canada. Lumber prices can change 40 or 50 percent in a couple of months. Import disputes between the US and Canada increase the uncertainty of supply.

» Cyclical Industry

The building material supplier industry is highly cyclical, depending on the level of new home construction, improvements, and repairs, and the volume of home sales. Homeowners and contractors are more likely to buy material supplies when housing starts and home sales are increasing. Repair and remodeling are somewhat less cyclical than new construction.

» Competition from Big Retailers

The expansion of large chains like Home Depot and Lowe's has driven many smaller stores out of business and forced others to adopt business strategies that don't rely on low prices. Big chain expansion draws do-it-yourselfers (DIY) from small suppliers, especially in larger metropolitan areas, forcing smaller companies to concentrate on the lower-margin contractor.

The items sold in largest volume by most companies are lumber and plywood panels--commodity products with relatively low margins. Some companies sell only lumber, but most also carry an assortment of higher-margin goods. Inventory management is a major operating concern for most retailers, including stocking the right products, pricing, re-ordering, and tracking sales. A typical Home Depot store carries 40,000 items. Big chains buy many products directly from large suppliers like Georgia-Pacific and Louisiana-Pacific, while smaller companies buy from a large number of regional distributors. Lowe's buys products from 7,000 vendors. Chains with many retail outlets often operate their own distribution centers. Some big homebuilders, like Centex and Pulte, are large enough to have their own supply operations.

Sales & Marketing

Consumer-oriented merchants use typical retail marketing such as TV, radio, and print ads, direct mail campaigns, and special sales events. Contractor-oriented companies establish and maintain long-term relationships with local builders and contractors. Credit availability is important for contractors, who typically aren't paid until a job is completed. Up to 80 percent of contractor business is based on credit. Because small suppliers develop close ties with contractors who often are building only one or a few homes at a time, they can extend credit based on prior experience. Credit losses are typically low, although risk for loss is greater for smaller suppliers. Companies that cater to contractors often can maintain low inventories because they custom-order the supplies needed at a construction site from regional distributors.

Human Resources

Jobs at building supply wholesalers require fairly detailed technical knowledge of numerous products in order to sell to construction businesses, a skill reflected in the fairly high hourly wage of $17. Average hourly wages at building supply retailers are $13, a dollar higher than most retail jobs. Due to uneven demand during the day, week, and year, many stores employ part-time workers, who generally receive lower benefits, but require more training. Injury rates are 70 percent higher than the national average.

Industry Employment Growth

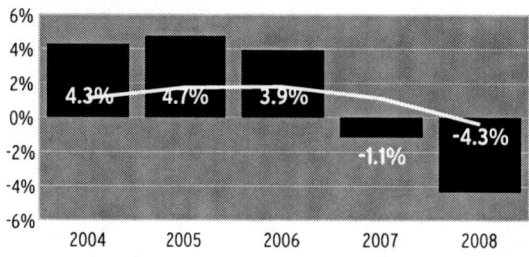

	2004	2005	2006	2007	2008
	4.3%	4.7%	3.9%	-1.1%	-4.3%

Average Hourly Earnings

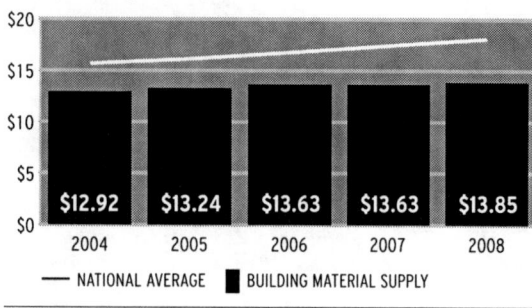

	2004	2005	2006	2007	2008
BUILDING MATERIAL SUPPLY	$12.92	$13.24	$13.63	$13.63	$13.85

— NATIONAL AVERAGE ■ BUILDING MATERIAL SUPPLY

SOURCE: BUREAU OF LABOR STATISTICS

Call Preparation Questions

How does the company mitigate volatile material costs?

Although raw material price increases can often be passed to consumers, suppliers that maintain large inventories can be hurt if prices move sharply.

How does the company manage cyclical variation in residential construction demand?

The building material supplier industry is highly cyclical, depending on the level of new home construction, improvements, and repairs, and the volume of home sales.

How does the company compete with the big retailers?

The expansion of large chains like Home Depot and Lowe's has driven many smaller stores out of business and forced others to adopt business strategies that don't rely on low prices.

How useful are expanded services in improving company revenue and customer retention?

Rather than just resell products bought from manufacturers and distributors, more retailers and suppliers are adding services such as equipment rental, training and education, custom-assembly of items like roof trusses and precut lumber, specialty ordering, and contacts with other contractors such as cement mixers and roofers.

How reliant is the company on the residential remodeling market?

As house prices rise and the economy recovers, remodeling projects are expected to increase.

Web Links

Builder Online

Industry news and useful links to manufacturers, distributors, and suppliers.
www.builderonline.com

Building Material

Information on and prices of building materials from NAHB.

www.nahb.org/reference_list.aspx?sectionID=133

Engineering News-Record

News and construction pricing information; most recent cost trends for key construction materials.

www.enr.construction.com

Home Channel News

Online version of the National Home Center News magazine, links to national associations, industry calendar of trade shows and meetings.

www.homechannelnews.com

National Association of Homebuilders

Hot topics and news reports on the industry.

www.nahb.org

National Lumber & Building Material Dealers Association

Resources, links, publications, and governmental affairs.

www.dealer.org

North American Retail Hardware Association

Industry news. Annual Market Measure report.

www.nrha.org

The Merchant Magazine & Building Products Digest

Subscriptions to two magazines about the building material product industry.

www.building-products.com

United States Census Bureau – Construction Statistics

Useful statistics on various segments of construction.

www.census.gov/const/www/newresconstindex.html

Glossary of Acronyms

BCI — Building Cost Index
CCI — Construction Cost Index
CPI — Consumer Price Index
DIY — do-it-yourselfer
ENR — Engineering News-Record
MCI — Material Cost Index
NAR — National Association of Realtors
NAHB — National Association of Home Builders
PPI — Producer Product Index
RMI — Remodeling Market Index

HOOVER'S TOP COMPANIES

Largest Companies by Sales	($ mil.)
The Home Depot, Inc.	77,349.0
Lowe's Companies, Inc.	48,283.0
Menard, Inc.	7,800.0
Boise Cascade Holdings, L.L.C.	5,413.5
Pro-Build Holdings Inc.	5,000.0
Ace Hardware Corporation	3,970.6
84 Lumber Company	3,100.0
Tractor Supply Company	3,007.9
BlueLinx Holdings Inc.	2,779.7

Largest Employers	Employees
The Home Depot, Inc.	331,000
Lowe's Companies, Inc.	216,000
Menard, Inc.	40,000
Pro-Build Holdings Inc.	17,000
Tractor Supply Company	12,800
Fastenal Company	12,013
Stock Building Supply Inc.	10,936
Boise Cascade Holdings, L.L.C.	10,042
84 Lumber Company	7,000
American Builders & Contractors Supply Co., Inc.	5,243

Fastest Growing* by Five-Year Sales Growth	(%)
Orgill, Inc.	68.3
Beacon Roofing Supply, Inc.	26.1
Fastenal Company	18.7
Colonial Commercial Corp.	17.4
Tractor Supply Company	15.4
Bradco Supply Corp.	14.9
Associated Materials Incorporated	13.8
American Builders & Contractors Supply Co., Inc.	13.0
Lowe's Companies, Inc.	12.8
Interline Brands, Inc.	12.6

Fastest Growing* by Five-Year Employee Growth	(%)
Interline Brands, Inc.	37.8
Pro-Build Holdings Inc.	15.3
Tractor Supply Company	14.9
Fastenal Company	13.6
Beacon Roofing Supply, Inc.	12.0
Five Star Products, Inc.	8.2
Bradco Supply Corp.	8.0
Associated Materials Incorporated	7.3
American Builders & Contractors Supply Co., Inc.	7.2
Lowe's Companies, Inc.	7.1

Top Public Companies by Market Value	($ mil.)
The Home Depot, Inc.	51,460.5
Lowe's Companies, Inc.	37,251.9
Fastenal Company	5,176.3
Tractor Supply Company	1,244.8
Beacon Roofing Supply, Inc.	700.1

* These rates are compounded annualized increases and may have resulted from acquisitions or one time gains. If less than 6 years of data are available, growth is for the years available.

SOURCE: HOOVER'S, INC., DATABASE

Business and Professional Associations

The business and professional associations industry includes about 25,000 organizations with combined annual revenue of $55 billion. Major organizations include the US Chamber of Commerce, the National Retail Federation, the American Association for the Advancement of Science, and the American Bar Association. The industry is highly fragmented: the top 50 organizations have about one-quarter of industry revenue.

Associations promote the business and professional interests of members. These groups may include chambers of commerce and generally exclude social advocacy groups and civic organizations.

Competitive Landscape

Business and job growth drive demand. The profitability of individual organizations depends on the ability to grow membership and solicit contributions. Large organizations have advantages in marketing and finance. Small organizations can appeal to businesses in niche industries or serve local markets. The industry is labor-intensive: average annual revenue per worker is $150,000.

Products, Operations & Technology

Major sources of revenue include membership dues (50 percent of revenues); convention and seminar fees (20 percent); contributions (10 percent); and publications (5 percent). Contributions may include government or private donations, grants, or gifts. Associations may also generate revenue through ad sales, merchandise sales, or investment income.

Business, or trade, associations, represent groups of businesses within an industry, whose members are typically individual companies. Professional associations represent groups of individuals within a specific field, such as law, medicine, or science. By representing large numbers of companies and professionals, both

BUSINESS CHALLENGES

» Revenue Tied to Industry Health

An association's performance is directly tied to the health of the industry it represents. The majority of business associations operate regionally or locally and depend on small to midsized businesses for funding. During industry downturns, smaller businesses can be driven out of business, affecting membership and contributions; large businesses may decrease contributions or cut convention and trade show participation.

» Membership Depends on Job Growth

Job growth is critical to drive total membership and cash flow from membership fees for professional associations. Membership fees are over half of industry revenue. A weak job market in a particular industry can result in hiring freezes and career changes, eventually affecting new memberships and renewals. Manufacturing-based associations may struggle to maintain membership as more US jobs shift to the service sector.

» Competition from Private Sector

Associations face increasing competition for many member services from organizations within the private sector. Industry conferences organized by private companies compete with association meetings and trade shows. For example, law and public relations firms provide advocacy functions, such as lobbying; private training companies and consulting firms offer industry training and education; and syndicated data providers produce and publish industry research and statistics.

types can collectively promote group interests more effectively than can individual members. While 85 percent of all associations operate at regional, state, or local levels, they may have national or international chapters. Total membership can vary greatly, depending on the industry and markets served. Some of the largest associations, such as the US Chamber of Commerce and the National Retail Federation, claim several million members.

Associations spend almost 20 percent of their budgets providing member education, according to the American Society for Association Executives. An organization may offer members certification to ensure proper qualifications or to designate level of expertise. Educational forums include conferences, seminars, and web- or computer-based training. Many associations develop industry and ethical standards, which include environmental and safety regulations. The American National Standards Institute (ANSI) encourages and coordinates voluntary industry standard and guideline development.

As advocates for members, associations actively monitor government regulations and lobby for favorable legislation. While political involvement can be controversial, associations spend almost 15 percent of their budgets on lobbying. Some associations have political action committees (PACs) that raise and donate money to political groups to further industry interests. Associations also conduct industry research and gather statistics to provide information for members, government groups, and the general public.

Three-quarters of all associations hold annual conventions, according to Meetings & Conventions. Within a convention, organizations may have trade shows with exhibits that showcase products and services. A typical convention costs $465,000, uses 56,000 square feet of exhibit space, and spans two to four days. Large conventions can attract thousands. Organizations may use association management software to manage membership, event planning, communication, educational programming, dues collection, and financial systems. Database management programs track member information and help monitor retention. Electronic payment makes membership renewals easier. Teleconferencing, webcasts, and virtual meetings allow associations to communicate with members interactively without travel costs.

Sales & Marketing

Association membership consists primarily of businesses and professional individuals, and can include any group related to an industry. For example, a manufacturing association may include suppliers, distributors, and retailers. Within an association, membership can vary and include both small and large businesses. Professional association members may have different skill levels.

Internet sites have become an increasingly important marketing tool by serving as a central location for industry information and distributing important news to members quickly. Association websites may have chatrooms, message boards, or blogs to foster communication among members. Internet sites can also serve as social and professional networks for members. Effective content management is critical to delivering timely, relevant information. Associations may also use websites to survey members and gather industry data.

Other marketing and promotional vehicles include trade shows, industry publications, direct mail, e-mail, and brochures. Trade shows allow members to introduce products and provide a forum for sharing research and discussing relevant issues. An association may publish "white papers" to highlight a particular industry topic or technology. Press releases communicate critical information, such as product recalls or safety warnings, to the public.

In general, association dues can range from $15 to $1,000 or more, according to the American Society for Association Executives. Associations may have tiered membership levels and offer discounts to students or spouses of members.

Human Resources

To provide member services, associations seek out workers with in-depth industry knowledge or experience in an industry's for-profit sector. Many association jobs are professional and require legal, public relations, market research, or training experience. Wages are 30 to 45 percent higher than the average for all US workers, although most associations pay less than private sector employers. The American Society for Association Executives (ASAE) offers programs for workers with management potential to become a Certified Association Executive (CAE). To help manage payroll costs, associations may use volunteers to supplement the paid workforce.

Most associations report to a governing advisory board, which typically consists of prominent industry executives. Association boards average 13 to 18 members with an executive committee of five to seven. Board positions may have terms of two to three years and many associations have term limits.

Industry Employment Growth

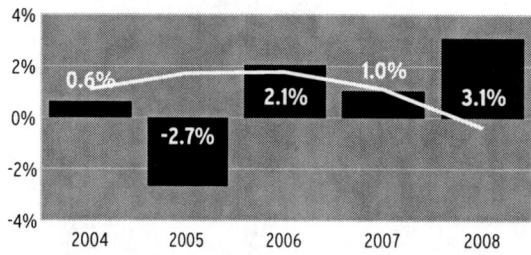

Average Hourly Earnings

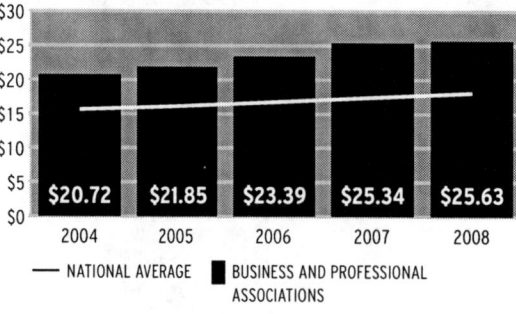

— NATIONAL AVERAGE ■ BUSINESS AND PROFESSIONAL ASSOCIATIONS

SOURCE: BUREAU OF LABOR STATISTICS

Call Preparation Questions

How does the industry's economic health affect the organization's performance?

An association's performance is directly tied to the health of the industry it represents.

How does industry employment affect the organization's financial health?

Job growth is critical to drive total membership and cash flow from membership fees for professional associations.

What is the organization's biggest competitive threat?

Associations face increasing competition for many member services from organizations within the private sector.

What are some of the organization's most successful partnerships?

By collaborating with other organizations with similar interests and complementary skills, associations can further industry goals more effectively.

What are the organization's biggest growth opportunities?

Associations can reduce reliance on membership dues by offering new services that target industry growth sectors.

Web Links

American Society for Association Executives

News, trends, statistics, operating ratio study from trade association.
www.asaecenter.org

Association Meetings

News and trends for association meetings.
meetingsnet.com/associationmeetings

Association News

News and trends for state and local associations.
www.associationnews.com

Association Trends

News and trends.
www.associationtrends.com

Center for Exhibition Industry Research

News, trends, and statistics on conventions, exhibitions, and trade shows.
www.ceir.org

Convention Industry Council

News and trends about association conventions.
www.conventionindustry.org

Meetings & Conventions Online

News, trends, statistics, annual surveys on conventions.
www.mcmag.com

Glossary of Acronyms

AAAS — American Association for the Advancement of Science
ABA — American Bar Association
AHA — American Hospital Association
AMA — American Medical Association
ANSI — American National Standards Institute
ASAE — American Society for Association Executives
CAE — Certified Association Executive
CEIR — Center for Exhibition Industry Research
CHA — Craft and Hobby Association
NACDS — National Association for Chain Drug Stores
NRF — National Retail Federation
PAC — political action committee
VCA — Vision Council of America

Candy Manufacturing

The US candy manufacturing industry includes about 1,600 companies with combined annual revenue of $17 billion. Major companies include Mars, Nestlé, Cadbury, and The Hershey Company. The total candy industry is fragmented: the largest 50 companies hold less than 40 percent of the market. However, consolidation is occurring and each major market has dominant companies: Hershey and Mars in chocolates, Wrigley in chewing/bubble gum, and Jelly Belly in jelly beans.

The industry includes three major segments: companies that make chocolate from beans, companies that use purchased chocolate to make candies, and companies that make non-chocolate candy.

Competitive Landscape

Demand is driven by consumer tastes and population growth. The profitability of individual companies depends on manufacturing efficiency, supply chain efficiency, and marketing. Large companies have advantages in economies of scale in manufacturing and purchasing. Small companies can compete effectively by offering premium and specialty products. The industry is highly automated: average annual revenue per worker for a typical company is about $300,000.

Products, Operations & Technology

Major industry products are chocolates, candy made from purchased chocolate, and non-chocolate candy. Candy made from purchased chocolate accounts for about half of industry revenue, non-chocolate candy for 30 percent, and chocolate for 20 percent. Non-chocolate candies include a wide variety of products: jellybeans, chewing/bubble gum, marshmallows, mints, and hard candies.

Chocolate is made from dried beans of the cacao tree. The beans are roasted and the inner meat is ground and refined to produce a warm non-alcoholic cacao liquor, from which cacao butter, powder, and chocolate can be made, depending on the quality of the liquor. Further mechanical processing, such as conching and tempering, affect the chocolate's texture. The type of chocolate made depends on the various amounts of cacao butter, high-quality cacao liquor, and other ingredients. Sugar, other sweeteners, flavorings, nuts, fruits, and potassium carbonate may be added before the chocolate is poured into molds, cooled, and packaged. "Cacao" and "cocoa" are often interchangeably in the industry.

BUSINESS CHALLENGES

» Vulnerable to Raw Material Prices

Prices of key raw materials such as cocoa beans, dairy products, and sugar, or sugar substitute, can change without warning. Cocoa bean prices can be volatile due to civil unrest in the key producing region of West Africa. US dairy producers may increase prices over 20 percent in a year. High sugar prices can cause manufacturers to switch to alternative sweeteners.

» Competition from Imports

US candy imports grew 50 percent in the last four years to take 20 percent of the market. Imports from low-cost countries, such as Mexico and China, increase price competition. Pressure to maintain retail shelf space increases as imports and new products expand. Imports of higher-end products from Belgium, Switzerland, and France are also important.

» Energy Price Sensitivity

Purchased chocolate depends highly on energy to melt, conch, temper, mix, and cool the product. Conching, continuously turning and grinding the product in a large vat, can last from three hours to three days. The longer the product is conched, the higher the quality of chocolate produced. Chocolate is cooled very slowly in a highly controlled environment. All these processes require a regulated and reliable source of heat.

Candy made from purchased chocolate, such as candy bars, typically use chocolate as an outer layer over a variety of ingredients like nuts, fruits, sugars, flavorings, and various stabilizers that may be ground, mixed, cooked, or baked together. Production lines are typically made up of individual machines that specialize in a particular step, along with tanks for ingredients and packaging machinery.

Non-chocolate confectionery products are made in various ways. Jelly beans use two steps: the centers are molded from cooked sugar and corn syrup, then the outer shell is added in a rotating drum, or engrossing pan. Chewing and bubble gums are made from natural or synthetic gums that are ground, cooked, mixed with various flavorings, then rolled, cut, and packaged. Hard candies are mixtures of sugars and flavorings, boiled and poured into molds to harden.

Important raw materials like sugar and corn syrup are readily available from many sources. Cacao beans may be bought through import brokers or on commodity exchanges like the New York Board of Trade. The quality, availability, and price of cacao beans vary according to conditions in the major growing countries of West Africa and South America. Energy is an important input for most candy manufacture, required for roasting, liquefying, or cooking. Companies try to minimize the impact of price fluctuations in raw materials and energy costs by forward purchasing and hedging.

IT is used extensively in supply chain management. Comprehensive information systems help candy manufacturers synchronize plans between customers and suppliers. Good supply chain management helps improve forecasting, reduce inventory, and increase overall efficiency.

Sales & Marketing

Customers are wholesalers and large retail chains. Grocery and convenience stores together account for about 30 percent of retail candy sales; Wal-Mart for another 10 percent. At the retail level, chocolate and non-chocolate candies (including gum) each take about half the market.

Large companies typically use an in-house sales force to reach customers; smaller companies may use independent food brokers. Manufacturers typically produce a line of brands, and often test and introduce products into the market through existing distribution channels.

Since candies are largely impulse shopping items, strong, frequent marketing and merchandising programs directed at consumers are critical. Extensive marketing, including TV, print, and radio advertising, coupons, direct mail, and sampling, are used. Special marketing efforts are made for seasonal sales, mainly around Halloween, Easter, Valentine's Day, and Christmas, which together account for about 10 percent of annual sales.

Because most candies are low-cost, under $1 for a candy bar or pack of gum, price isn't a major factor in consumer decisions. Retailers typically price all candy bars the same. Consumer prices for candy and chewing gum increased a moderate 10 percent over the last five years. The average retail markup from the manufacturer price is close to 50 percent.

Competing products include other snack and impulse purchases. Key marketplace metrics provided to the industry are consumer takeaway and market share.

Human Resources

Average hourly earnings are slightly below the US average, as production requires few special skills. Injury rates in the industry are about 30 percent higher than the national average due to contact with equipment and machinery, especially because equipment is often hot.

Industry Employment Growth

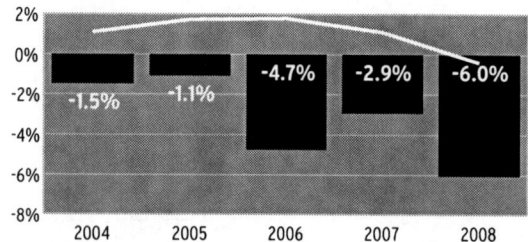

Average Hourly Earnings

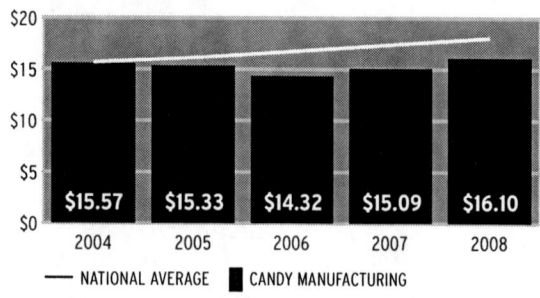

— NATIONAL AVERAGE ■ CANDY MANUFACTURING

SOURCE: BUREAU OF LABOR STATISTICS

Call Preparation Questions

What raw materials pose the greatest cost problems for the company?

Prices of key raw materials such as cocoa beans, dairy products, and sugar, or sugar substitute, can change without warning.

How much is the company affected by import competition?

US candy imports grew 50 percent in the last four years to take 20 percent of the market.

How is the company reducing energy costs?

Purchased chocolate depends highly on energy to melt, conch, temper, mix, and cool the product.

What type of new products is the company exploring?

Consumers continue to look for healthier snack options such as chocolate with nuts, granola, or grains.

Is the company planning organic products?

Organic candy products are rapidly growing market share.

Web Links

Chocolate Manufacturers Association

Science and nutrition information from the Chocolate Manufacturers Association.
www.chocolateusa.org/Science-and-Nutrition

Chocolate Manufacturers Association (CMA)

General candy facts, information, news.
www.candyusa.org

Global Magazine of Chocolate and Confectionery

Candy industry articles and news items.
www.candyindustry.com

National Confectioners Association (NCA)

Public policy, industry issues, industry performance.
www.ecandy.com

World Cocoa Foundation

Information about growing cocoa. Encouraging sustainable, responsible growing practices and programs.
www.worldcocoafoundation.org

Glossary of Acronyms

CMA — Chocolate Manufacturers Association
GDS — global data synchronization

HOOVER'S TOP COMPANIES

Largest Companies by Sales	($ mil.)
Mars, Incorporated	25,000.0
Wm. Wrigley Jr. Company	5,389.1
The Hershey Company	5,132.8
Russell Stover Candies Inc.	610.0
Tootsie Roll Industries, Inc.	496.0
See's Candies, Inc.	229.8
Godiva Chocolatier, Inc.	121.0
Nestlé USA, Inc.	—

Largest Employers	Employees
Mars, Incorporated	48,000
Wm. Wrigley Jr. Company	16,400
Nestlé USA, Inc.	15,500
The Hershey Company	14,400
Russell Stover Candies Inc.	6,000
See's Candies, Inc.	2,300
Tootsie Roll Industries, Inc.	2,200
Godiva Chocolatier, Inc.	2,200
The New England Confectionery Company, Inc.	1,400
Ferrara Pan Candy Company	1,250

Fastest Growing* by Five-Year Sales Growth	(%)
Wm. Wrigley Jr. Company	14.4
Rocky Mountain Chocolate Factory, Inc.	10.3
Mars, Incorporated	9.1
Chase General Corporation	7.3
Tootsie Roll Industries, Inc.	4.8
The Hershey Company	4.2

Fastest Growing* by Five-Year Employee Growth	(%)
Mars, Incorporated	9.9
Wm. Wrigley Jr. Company	7.8
The Hershey Company	1.6

Top Public Companies by Market Value	($ mil.)
The Hershey Company	5,778.1
Tootsie Roll Industries, Inc.	885.0
Rocky Mountain Chocolate Factory, Inc.	76.0

* These rates are compounded annualized increases and may have resulted from acquisitions or one time gains. If less than 6 years of data are available, growth is for the years available.

SOURCE: HOOVER'S, INC., DATABASE

Car Washes

THIS INDUSTRY INCLUDES:

SIC CODES
7542   Carwashes

NAICS CODES
811192   Car Washes

The car wash industry in the US includes 14,000 full-service car washes with combined annual revenue of about $5 billion. Large chains include Wash Depot, Oasis Car Wash, and Autobell Car Wash. The industry is highly fragmented: the 50 largest chains hold just 15 percent of the market. Chains are local or regional. A typical firm has one location. A large location has 35 employees and $1.5 million of annual revenue.

Competitive Landscape

Demand is driven by favorable weather, new car sales, and growth in consumer income. The profitability of individual firms depends on favorable location and efficient operations. There are few economies of scale. Chains have advantages in advertising and customer recognition. Small firms can compete successfully by good location. The industry is highly labor-intensive: annual revenue per employee is just $40,000.

Products, Operations & Technology

Major services are exterior wash, exterior and interior cleaning, waxing, underside cleaning, vacuuming, and premium "detailing." Ancillary products and services such as pick-up/drop-off services, fast food, greeting cards, and automotive products are also offered at some locations. "Detailing" services consist of intensive interior and exterior cleaning, and waxing and polishing by hand.

There are three types of car washes: a conveyor or "tunnel" wash system, where the car is pulled through a tunnel lined with washing equipment; an in-bay automatic or "rollover" wash system, where the car is parked in a bay and the washing equipment moves over the car; and a self-service or "wand" wash system, where the car is parked in a bay and the customer manually washes the car with provided equipment. Self-service and roll-over locations typi-

BUSINESS CHALLENGES

» Consumer Income Affects Revenue
Because car washes aren't a necessity, consumers use them less during periods of economic difficulty. Consumers don't stop using car washes altogether, but gravitate toward lower-cost services. Car washes typically respond to slower demand by restricting hours to cut labor costs.

» Revenue Affected by High Gas Prices
When gas prices are high, many customers compensate by not using car wash services, which are considered a luxury. Many consumers must budget how much they can spend on total auto expenses, including loan payments, taxes, insurance, gas, and maintenance. The link between gas prices and car wash services is especially strong, as many car washes are located at or near gas stations.

» Higher Water, Sewer Costs
Rates for water and sewer services have increased sharply in many municipalities in recent years, raising operating costs for car washes. Especially affected are towns with older systems that need extensive upgrading. Typical recent charges in California are $3 per hundred cubic feet for water and $2 for sewer. Sewer charges now exceed water charges in many towns.

cally have several bays, while one-conveyor tunnel locations are very common.

In-bay automatic and self-serve car wash systems require only minimal supervision, but conveyor systems require from one to five attendants. The maximum throughput for conveyor systems is about 50 cars per hour, versus 12 cars per hour for in-bay systems and even fewer for self-serve. Large locations may serve over 1,000 cars per day. Demand is typically highest on weekends.

A conveyor system requires a building of about 4,000 square feet. Typical equipment includes sprayers, pumps, mitters, dryers, detection devices, and conveyors. Equipment for conveyor and in-bay automatic systems costs up to $50,000 per installation. Equipment for a self-service bay costs about $10,000. Water is the primary raw material; detergents and waxes are also used. Automatic equipment uses about 32 gallons of water per car. Car washes must have a waste water collection and treatment system to avoid the flow of detergents, road salts, oils, and other contaminants directly into municipal sewers. "Reclaimed" water is increasingly used in regions of the country with tight water supplies.

Industry technological improvements are directed at efficiently using water and energy. Equipment has evolved to increase the power of water sprays and reduce the amount of water needed. Efficient blowers can reduce energy used for drying.

Sales & Marketing

Individuals are the major type of customer, but auto dealers and businesses with car fleets may also have contracts with car wash firms. Local advertising — newspaper, radio, coupons, and the Yellow Pages — is the primary marketing tool. Direct mail and local/cable TV advertising are used selectively. Companies may use charity car wash events as a promotional tool. Coupon books or other customer loyalty programs that give price discounts to frequent users are common. Prices typically range from about $10 for an exterior wash, to more than $25 for a package of premium services. "Detailing" services can cost over $100.

Human Resources

Car wash attendants are largely unskilled and consequently have low pay, about 40 percent lower than the average for all US workers. Many employees work part-time, as demand is highly uneven throughout the day and week. Low pay causes high personnel turnover.

Industry Employment Growth

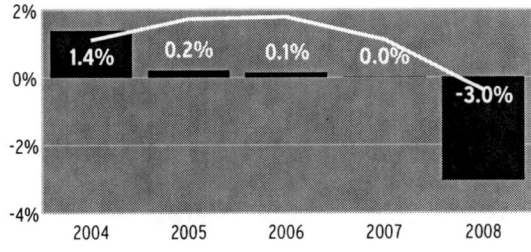

Average Hourly Earnings

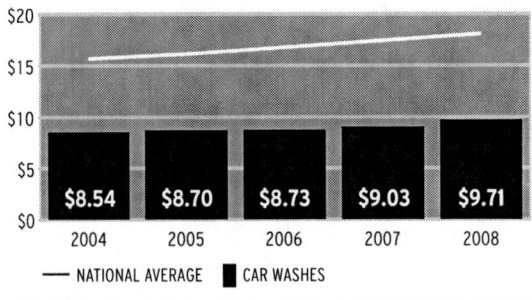

SOURCE: BUREAU OF LABOR STATISTICS

Call Preparation Questions

How vulnerable is the local economy to sudden changes in employment?

Because car washes aren't a necessity, consumers use them less during periods of economic difficulty.

How do higher gas prices affect the company's business?

When gas prices are high, many customers compensate by not using car wash services, which are considered a luxury.

How does the company control water and sewer costs?

Rates for water and sewer services have increased sharply in many municipalities in recent years, raising operating costs for car washes.

Does the firm advertise itself as a time-saving convenience?

The number of consumers who use commercial car washes regularly is expected to increase as consumer "free time" decreases.

How is the company establishing additional sources of revenue?

Because their customers are likely to buy on impulse, car washes can offer them additional products.

Web Links

Auto Laundry News

Industry news, events, issues.
www.carwashmag.com

Canadian Carwash Association

News for members and industry information.
www.canadiancarwash.ca

Car-Wash-Equipment

Information regarding equipment, system resources, associations, trade shows.
www.car-wash-equipment.net

How Car Washes Work

Detailed description of how a car wash works.
auto.howstuffworks.com/car-wash.htm

International Carwash Association

Research and weekly news.
www.carcarecentral.com

Midwest Carwash Association

News and resources.
www.midwestcarwash.com

Modern Car Care

Industry news, ranking of companies.
moderncarcare.com

National Association of Convenience Stores

News on related items like product, gasoline, and
auto travel issues.
www.nacsonline.com

Northeast Carwasher

Articles.
www.northeastcarwasher.com

Professional Carwashing & Detailing

Industry news, monographs, industry studies
supplier.
www.carwash.com

Southwest Car Wash Association

News and links.
www.swcarwash.org

Western Carwash Association

News and events.
www.wcwa.org

Glossary of Acronyms

UIC WELL — underground injection control well
EIA — Energy Information Administration

HOOVER'S TOP COMPANIES

Largest Employers	Employees
Blue Beacon International, Inc.	3,800
Wash Depot Holdings, Inc.	1,400
Waterway Gas & Wash	800

SOURCE: HOOVER'S, INC., DATABASE

Catering Services

The catering industry includes 10,000 companies with combined annual revenue of $5 billion. Large companies include Centerplate, Compass Group USA, and Wolfgang Puck Catering, but no major companies dominate. The catering industry is very highly fragmented: the top 50 companies account for less than 15 percent of industry revenue.

While many hotels, facilities management companies, restaurants, and food service contractors also cater events, these businesses aren't included in this industry.

Competitive Landscape

Demand is driven by corporate profits and consumer income. The profitability of individual companies depends on cost controls and effective marketing. Large companies have advantages in offering expanded services such as facilities management, room rental, and entertainment. Small companies can compete effectively by serving small groups and offering personalized service. The industry is labor-intensive: average annual revenue per worker for a typical company is just over $40,000.

Products, Operations & Technology

Major services include off-premises catering (food prepared away from the premises where it's served) and on-premises catering (meals prepared and served at the same location). Off-premises catering represents 45 percent of the market; on-premises, 40 percent. Other services include alcohol sales and facility rentals.

A typical catering event starts with a consultation with a potential client to assess the type of event, guest count, venue, and special food requests. The client may want the caterer to also coordinate facility rental, flowers, entertainment, and photography. The caterer produces a detailed proposal that includes the menu, beverages, a list of rental needs, special requirements, and a detailed price quote. After

BUSINESS CHALLENGES

» Demand Driven by Economic Cycles
Economic slowdowns reduce the number and size of catered events. During downturns in the economy, corporations limit spending on catered events to only essential functions. Individuals usually continue to host celebrations, but the size and scale tend to be more modest.

» Competition from Fullservice Restaurants, Hotels
Many fullservice restaurants, hotels, and food service contractors provide catering services and compete directly with independent caterers. Competition goes beyond onsite events: many restaurants and contractors have the resources and staff to work offsite catering functions. Companies that operate regular breakfast, lunch, or dinner service can better leverage staffing, kitchen, and cash resources.

» High Personnel Turnover
The majority of catering kitchen and waitstaff work part-time, without benefits, for a low hourly wage. The industry attracts people just getting started with their career, and high employee turnover is common. Two-thirds of all food service employees are under 34, compared to one-third for all US industries.

the client accepts a proposal, frequent communications are maintained with the client until the event takes place.

Major operations on the day of the event include cooking, setting up, serving food and drinks, and cleaning up. On-premises catered meals are typically served buffet-style or as seated functions. Off-premises catering includes boxed lunches, buffets, "finger food," barbecues, clambakes, and seated meals. Large off-premises functions may require a portable kitchen. The optimal server-to-guest ratio for a sit-down dinner is one waiter per 10 to 15 guests; for buffets and standing receptions, the ratio can be as high as 1:50. If the event includes alcohol, caterers typically supply one bartender per 100 guests.

A caterer's waitstaff is critical to a successful catering event. Servers typically help set up the event, serve food, and break down tables once the event is complete. Since waitstaff work is irregular and pay is low, finding dependable waitstaff can be a challenge. The seasonal demand for catering makes it even more difficult, as servers are often unavailable at a caterer's busiest time of year: summertime and just before Christmas.

Cooks and chefs are important to the success of a catered event. As with servers, work is generally part-time, irregular, seasonal, and often stressful. Work includes preparing, transporting, and cooking food before the event; serving food at carving tables and chef stations; and cleaning the kitchen. Food can be pre-prepared and pre-proportioned, but many catering chefs still make meals from scratch. Caterers plan for around 10 percent "overage" to avoid leaving people hungry or dissatisfied.

Kitchen facilities may be large or small, depending on the types of events a caterer services. While a caterer will prepare standard food items, specialty items like wedding cakes may be subcontracted out.

Many caterers use event management software to help with deliveries, logistics, and inventory management. New CAD software can help caterers draw up floor plans to maximize the use of floor space.

Sales & Marketing

Typical customers are individuals celebrating milestone events such as weddings, birthdays, graduations, and reunions; organizations hosting fundraisers; and corporations.

Most caterers have a small marketing budget and limit advertising to a local region. Major types of marketing include the Yellow Pages, newspapers, and radio. Word-of-mouth is typically considered the most effective form of advertising. Some companies partner with rental companies, event coordinators, and entertainment companies to share leads and recommend each other's services to their customer base.

The Internet plays a limited role in the catering business. Company websites typically highlight the owner and chef's experience, the caterer's client list, customer recommendations, and a food menu.

Prices vary widely. Catered box lunches may be priced at $10 each. Catered meals at weddings typically cost around $60 per person. A full sit-down dinner with open bar can cost

around $100 a person. Food extravaganzas led by high-profile caterers can reach up to $750 a head. Small events with a limited menu may be priced as low as $500 in total, while a high-profile caterer can charge up to $1 million for a single event. A typical wedding costs around $30,000, of which half is for the catered reception. The average caterer organizes around 200 events per year, typically scheduled between Wednesday and Saturday.

Catering contracts typically include a guaranteed number of guests. If fewer people show than expected, the client is still charged based on this guaranteed number. Additional guests are charged on a per-person basis. Contracts typically include a 15 to 20 percent overhead fee to cover fixed and variable operational costs such as transportation, utilities, and supplies. Caterers may tip the waitstaff using a portion of this overhead fee. Competition comes from hotels, restaurants, food service contractors, and entertainment facilities, many of which offer on- and off-premises catering.

Human Resources

Servers require minimal training and education and are typically paid on an hourly basis without benefits. Wages are about 30 percent lower than the US average. Employment is somewhat seasonal, peaking in June and December. Hiring needs can drop as much as 15 percent from December to January. A chef from a culinary arts school or well-known restaurant can bring knowledge of nutritional guidelines, food safety, and health compliance in addition to creative cooking skills.

The injury rate for special food services is 50 percent higher than the US average, due primarily to cuts and hand injuries in food preparation.

Industry Employment Growth

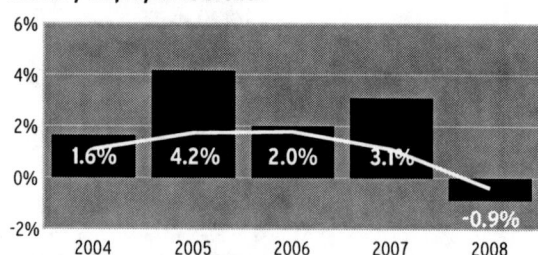

Average Hourly Earnings

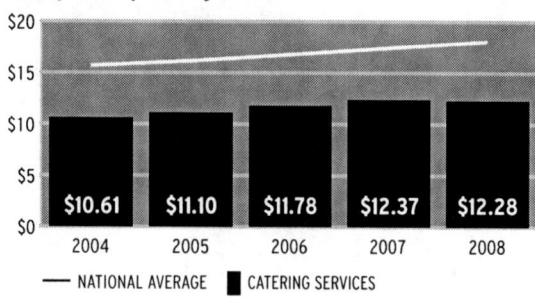

— NATIONAL AVERAGE   ■ CATERING SERVICES

SOURCE: BUREAU OF LABOR STATISTICS

Call Preparation Questions

How do changes in the economy affect the caterer's business?

Economic slowdowns reduce the number and size of catered events.

Does the company compete with restaurants or hotels for catered events?

Many fullservice restaurants, hotels, and food service contractors provide catering services and compete directly with independent caterers.

Does the company employ full-time service staff?

The majority of catering kitchen and waitstaff work part-time, without benefits, for a low hourly wage.

Is the company seeing an increase in high-ticket events celebrating milestones?

Many groups celebrating milestones are spending large amounts to make the event memorable.

Does the company offer services beyond catering, such as event management?

Caterers can grow their business beyond food to include event management.

Web Links

CatererSearch

Hospitality news and job opportunities.
www.caterersearch.com

catersource

Education, products, and news for caterers.
catersource.com

International Caterers Association

Non-profit emphasizing education and mentoring for caterers.
www.icacater.org

National Association of Catering Executives

Education, networking, and resources for catering professionals.
nace.net

Special Events Magazine

International resource for event professionals and caterers.
specialevents.com/caterers

The Free Library – Catering

Catering industry articles and news.
www.thefreelibrary.com/Caterers+and+catering-s18232

Glossary of Acronyms

CPCE — Certified Professional Catering Executive
IFCA — International Flight Catering Association
NACE — National Association of Catering Executives
OHC — out-of-home catering
WPCE — Wolfgang Puck Catering and Events

HOOVER'S TOP COMPANIES

Largest Employers	Employees
Flying Food Group, LLC	2,606
Universal Sodexho USA	1,100
Wolfgang Puck Catering Inc.	500
Hospitality, Inc.	250
Along Came Mary, Inc.	250
Grandview Management, Inc.	160
Someone's in the Kitchen	120
Waters Catering, Inc.	115
The French Gourmet, Inc.	75
Dagar's of Austin Caterers, Inc.	40

SOURCE: HOOVER'S, INC., DATABASE

Cement, Concrete and Construction Material

The US mineral construction materials industry makes bulk construction products with combined annual revenue of about $75 billion, of which 60 percent is due to cement and concrete products. Foreign companies own a majority of US cement capacity, including Holcim (Switzerland); CEMEX (Mexico); Buzzi Unicem (Italy); and Lafarge (France). The industry includes about 120 cement manufacturers, hundreds of local sand and gravel quarries, and thousands of ready-mix concrete operators. About 130 companies operate brick plants, 500 produce asphalt, 200 make gypsum products, and about 1,000 make concrete blocks and pipes.

Competitive Landscape

Because cement is a commodity product, manufacturers compete chiefly based on price. Production economies of scale are important, but are limited by the cost of transporting the finished product. The efficiencies that can be achieved with new energy-efficient (but capital-intensive) "dry" production technology are a major source of competition. Small manufacturers may not have the financial resources or production volume to justify investing in the most efficient technology, putting them at a competitive cost disadvantage. Cement imports from Canada are an important competitor in northern states.

Products, Operations & Technology

Cement and other mineral construction materials are used mainly to construct buildings, roads, bridges, sewers, and other types of infrastructure. Because of the limited processing required to produce these materials, most companies that mine the raw material also make and distribute the finished product. Raw materials, like sand, gravel, shale, gypsum, and limestone, are quarried from open pits or mined in capital-intensive operations using drills, explosives, and heavy machinery. Kilns

BUSINESS CHALLENGES

» High Dependence on Cyclical Construction Industry

Demand for sand, stone, bricks, gravel, cement, and gypsum is highly cyclical, depending on the level of new construction. Local construction markets, which can be very volatile, are affected by weather, interest rates, population migration, business spending, and government revenues.

» Pricing Pressures

Because basic construction materials are commodity products, manufacturers compete largely based on price. With excess capacity in the US, industry returns were low in the past decade, a big reason why the majority of capacity has passed into foreign ownership.

» Cost Advantages for Big Producers

Technological improvements can reduce energy costs for cement manufacturers that can afford to invest in new production plants; however, generally only high-volume producers can afford or justify the investment. Because cement and similar products are commodities, with no branding potential, cost-cutting is the only avenue to higher profitability.

for making cement and plaster are fired with oil, gas, or coal dust; energy amounts to 25 percent or more of the cost of making cement.

Cement is made from limestone that is crushed, finely ground, mixed with clays, and heated to 3,000 degrees in large (up to 500 feet long) rotary kilns. The heat-treated material, called "clinker," is ground to powder and mixed with a small amount of gypsum. Cement of various qualities can be made by adding other ingredients. The most common type of cement produced is called portland cement.

Concrete is made by mixing cement with sand and rock (called "aggregate"), and water. The proportions of these ingredients, and the types of aggregate, determine the concrete's physical characteristics. Concrete begins to set within a few hours after being mixed, although total curing takes many days. Over 70 percent of cement is sold to "ready-mix" operators who custom-mix and deliver batches of liquid concrete to construction sites.

Bricks are made from shale rock that is crushed, mixed with various additives for color and other characteristics, and fired in kilns at 2,000 degrees.

Gypsum is quarried, crushed, and heated in rotary kilns to form plaster, which is mixed with water and other additives and sandwiched between layers of paperboard to make gypsum board.

Asphalt is made by mixing bitumen, a waste product of crude oil refining, with crushed stone ("aggregate").

Sales & Marketing

The relatively low value of bulk construction materials compared to their weight makes them expensive to transport large distances. Most cement and concrete producers have a network of regional plants and distribution centers, usually located within a 400-mile radius of customers, to keep transportation costs low. Sand and stone are usually quarried locally and shipped no more than 100 miles. Bitumen can economically be shipped over a somewhat wider area.

Manufacturers use a sales force to keep in touch with customers, mainly ready-mix cement companies, producers of concrete products, building materials suppliers, and large construction companies. Cement is bought mainly based on price and consistent customer supply. Long-term contracts are rare. Most distribution is in bulk in a two-tiered distribution system of rail-to-terminal, and then truck-to-customer.

Construction material use is seasonal, with nearly two-thirds of US cement consumption between May and October. This seasonality results in large swings of cement and clinker (unfinished raw material) inventories at cement plants or distribution facilities over the course of a year. Cement producers typically build inventories during winter, and draw them down during summer.

Human Resources

Average pay in the cement industry is almost $17 hourly, slightly low for the manufacturing sector, but above the national wage. Injury rates are high, at eight cases per 100 full-time workers, two cases more than most manufacturing industries. Manufacturers typically have about a 30 percent annual personnel turnover rate.

Industry Employment Growth

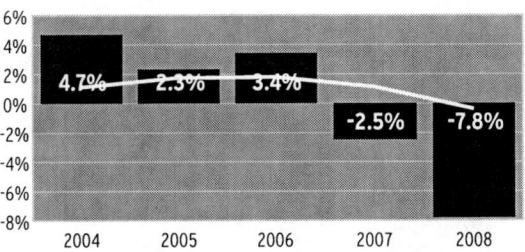

Average Hourly Earnings

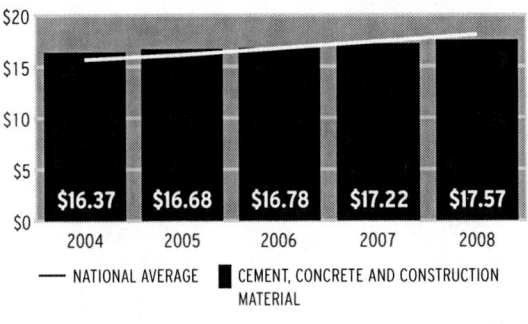

SOURCE: BUREAU OF LABOR STATISTICS

Call Preparation Questions

How does the company mitigate the seasonality of the business?

Demand for sand, stone, bricks, gravel, cement, and gypsum is highly cyclical, depending on the level of new construction.

How does the company compete in a commodity business where sales are based mostly on price?

Because basic construction materials are commodity products, manufacturers compete largely based on price.

What are the company's planned annual capital investments and how will they be funded?

Technological improvements can reduce energy costs for cement manufacturers that can afford to invest in new production plants; however, generally only high-volume producers can afford or justify the investment.

How do recent trends in government highway spending affect the company?

The national highway system includes the nearly 45,000 mile interstate system, and carries 40 percent of the nation's total traffic.

How is the company adapting its products to capitalize on security needs of public buildings?

Owners of high-rises and government office centers have recently stepped up interior and exterior security measures, including using more precast concrete median barriers.

Web Links

American Concrete Institute

Concrete and building specifications.
www.aci-int.org/general/home.asp

American Concrete Pavement Association

Industry news, publications, legislation, and
technical news.
www.pavement.com

Asphalt Institute

Hot topics, news, research, and publications.
www.asphaltinstitute.org

Asphalt Pavement Alliance

Industry coalition including Asphalt Institute,
National Asphalt Pavement Association, and the
State Asphalt Pavement Associations; includes
publications, outreach through industry meetings
and conferences, and targeted communications to
public officials.
www.asphaltalliance.com

Concrete Products

Industry news, trade show schedules, and links.
www.concreteproducts.com

National Concrete Masonry Association

Uses and applications, resources and materials, and
list of state associations.
www.ncma.org

National Ready Mixed Concrete Association

Concrete basics, consumer uses, government links,
safety and environmental issues.
www.nrmca.org

National Stone, Sand & Gravel Association

Industry issues.
www.nssga.org

Portland Cement Association

Excellent industry and market data.
www.cement.org

Rock Products

Industry news.
www.rockproducts.com

Tilt-Up Concrete Association

Information about this type of construction.
www.tilt-up.org

World of Concrete

Portal to Concrete Construction, Concrete Producer,
Masonry Construction and other magazines.
Excellent articles archive.
www.worldofconcrete.com

Glossary of Acronyms

ARTBA — American Road & Transportation Builders
Association
BIA — Brick Industry Association
EMS — Environmental Management Systems
ENR — Engineering News-Record
FHWA — Federal Highway Administration
MMS — Minerals Management Service
MMT — million metric tons
MSHA — Mine Safety and Health Administration
PCA — Portland Cement Association

HOOVER'S TOP COMPANIES

Largest Companies by Sales	($ mil.)
CEMEX Inc.	4,170.4
Vulcan Materials, Inc.	3,651.4
Lafarge North America Inc.	3,318.4
Ash Grove Cement Company	1,270.0
Texas Industries, Inc.	1,028.8
Headwaters Incorporated	886.4
U.S. Concrete, Inc.	803.8
Lehigh Cement Company	—
Rinker Materials Corporation	—

Largest Employers	Employees
Oldcastle, Inc.	38,150
Lafarge North America Inc.	16,400
CEMEX Inc.	11,050
Vulcan Materials, Inc.	10,522
Rinker Materials Corporation	10,085
Lehigh Cement Company	6,000
Headwaters Incorporated	3,400
Ash Grove Cement Company	2,800
Texas Industries, Inc.	2,680
Ameron International Corporation	2,600

Fastest Growing* by Five-Year Sales Growth	(%)
Headwaters Incorporated	18.0
U.S. Concrete, Inc.	9.8
Smith-Midland Corporation	6.9
Ash Grove Cement Company	6.7
Ready Mix, Inc.	6.6
Continental Materials Corporation	5.6
Ameron International Corporation	2.1
The Monarch Cement Company	1.8

Top Public Companies by Market Value	($ mil.)
Vulcan Materials, Inc.	7,672.6
Texas Industries, Inc.	2,004.2
Headwaters Incorporated	553.6
Ameron International Corporation	495.1
U.S. Concrete, Inc.	131.1

* These rates are compounded annualized increases and may
have resulted from acquisitions or one time gains. If less
than 6 years of data are available, growth is for the years
available.

SOURCE: HOOVER'S, INC., DATABASE

Chemical Manufacturing — Agricultural

In the US, about 700 companies are involved in the manufacture of agricultural chemicals, with combined annual revenue of $30 billion. Large companies include divisions of Dow and DuPont, and specialized producers like FMC, Mosaic, and Terra Industries. Many smaller companies are involved in mixing purchased raw materials to produce customized fertilizer compounds with special characteristics.

The industry is highly concentrated because of economies of scale in marketing and distribution. The eight largest producers of phosphate fertilizers control 90 percent of the market. The eight largest producers of nitrogen fertilizers control almost 80 percent of the market. Concentration is also high in the pesticide segment, where the eight largest producers control 70 percent of the market.

Competitive Landscape

Demand for agricultural chemicals depends mainly on demand for various crops, which in turn depends on crop prices. The profitability of individual companies is linked to efficient operations and marketing. Big producers have large economies of scale in production. Smaller companies can compete effectively by making specialty chemicals or fertilizer mixtures for local markets. Operations are capital-intensive and highly automated: annual revenue per employee at a large plant is close to $700,000.

Products, Operations & Technology

Companies manufacture fertilizers, herbicides and insecticides, or produce fertilizer or pesticide mixtures. Fertilizers and pesticides each account for about 50 percent of industry revenue. Fertilizers are a handful of commodity chemicals that contain nitrogen, phosphorous, or potassium. Pesticides are a broader group of chemicals, but many of the biggest sellers are also commodity products.

BUSINESS CHALLENGES

» Volatile Raw Material Prices

Producing nitrogen fertilizer requires access to large supplies of ammonia, which is made from natural gas, a commodity with high price volatility. The cost of natural gas represents as much as 80 percent of the cost of ammonia. In recent years, the market price of natural gas has varied between $2 and $10 per thousand cubic feet (mcf), and availability has sometimes been restricted.

» Government Regulation

Due to environmental, safety, or health issues, both federal and state governments restrict the production, distribution, application, and disposal of pesticides, fertilizers, and other agricultural chemicals. The EPA regulates the use of most pesticides because of their negative impact on water sources and animal life. Ongoing chemical testing could lead to a ban on some agricultural products if toxicity levels for humans are found to be unacceptable.

» Chemicals Used More Sparingly

Because fertilizer and pesticide costs can be more than 40 percent of operating costs, farmers have a strong incentive to use chemicals sparingly. New methods, such as direct injection into the ground, slow-release pellets, and better soil analysis, have already cut per-acre consumption of agricultural chemicals. The concentration of more farming acreage in large industrial farms will accelerate the more efficient use of fertilizers and pesticides.

Nitrogen fertilizers include products like ammonia; urea; ammonium nitrate (AN); and urea-ammonium nitrate (UAN). Phosphorous fertilizers include phosphoric acid; mono-ammonium phosphate (MAP); di-ammonium phosphate (DAP); and superphosphates like tri-sodium phosphate (TSP). Potassium fertilizers (potash) are common salts of potassium such as potassium chloride (muriate of potash) and potassium sulphate (sulphate of potash). Nitrogen is the most important fertilizer. In a typical year, US farmers use 12 million tons of nitrogen, 5 million tons of potash, and 4 million tons of phosphorous fertilizer. The largest volume fertilizer products are UAN, DAP, and muriate of potash.

Nitrogen fertilizers are based on ammonia, which is made from the nitrogen in the air, using natural gas as a source of hydrogen and heat. Nitrogen fertilizer plants are often located near sources of natural gas. Phosphate fertilizers are produced from phosphate rock that is mined, crushed, and treated with sulfuric acid. The largest deposits of phosphate rock in the US are located in Florida. Potash is mined from salt deposits and purified into different grades of fertilizer by various solution and crystallization techniques. Potash and phosphate manufacturing plants are often located near potash and phosphate mines.

Pesticides include herbicides (mainly used to control weeds), insecticides, fungicides, rodenticides, and biological agents. About 1,000 different pesticides are used in the US, including atrazine, metolachor, metam sodium, and various organochlorates, organophosphates, carbamates, and pyrethroids. Herbicides account for the largest dollar volume of pesticide production (50 percent), followed by insecticides (30 percent). Most pesticides are synthesized from basic industrial chemicals.

Fertilizer mixtures contain various concentrations of nitrogen (N); phosphorous (P); and potassium (K); with the phosphorous and potassium concentrations often specified as equivalents of phosphorous pentoxide (P2O5) and potassium oxide (K20). Fertilizer mixtures are often made in local plants from basic fertilizer bought from large producers. Local soil and crop conditions typically require custom mixtures of the three main fertilizer products.

The chemical technology used to manufacture most agricultural chemicals is basic and well-understood. Mixing operations use fairly simple technology and are often small, but most bulk fertilizer plants are large because of the economies of scale in production, and are expensive to build. The goal in most production plants is to achieve the highest possible yield of finished product from the raw materials, and the lowest volume of by-products and waste. Large manufacturing plants use sophisticated computerized process control systems.

Sales & Marketing

Manufacturers of both fertilizers and pesticides sell their products mainly to dealers and distributors, although some products may be sold directly to farm cooperatives and large farms. Manufacturers also sell bulk quantities to local fertilizer and pesticide mixers, who use various dry and wet mixing techniques to produce a large variety of chemicals suitable for different soil, crop, and weather characteristics. Sales are handled by an internal sales force and are mainly based on delivered price.

Fertilizers are commodities available in large supply, whose prices depend on the cost of raw materials. Prices for nitrogen fertilizers fluctuate most sharply because of the heavy use of natural gas. Ammonia prices can fluctuate as much as 50 percent within a year. Phosphate prices are more stable, but have declined steadily in the past decade.

Human Resources

Major fertilizer and pesticide production plants are highly automated, requiring relatively few workers. A large number of plant workers are engineers. Due to requirements for a relatively high level of expertise and low number of workers, pay is high: around $21 hourly, compared to an average $17 for the manufacturing sector. Fringe benefits average a fairly low 20 percent addition to payroll in fertilizer plants, but a fairly high 28 percent in pesticide plants. To retain experienced workers, who often know the important operating quirks of a chemical plant, companies may provide a high level of retirement benefits. Annual injury rates are low, four cases per 100 full-time workers, two less than for the manufacturing sector as a whole.

Industry Employment Growth

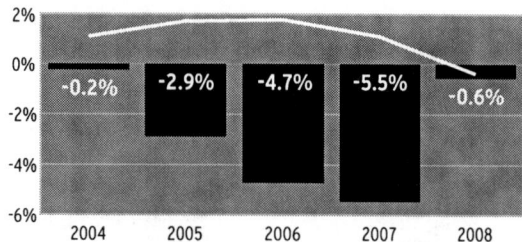

Year	Growth
2004	-0.2%
2005	-2.9%
2006	-4.7%
2007	-5.5%
2008	-0.6%

Average Hourly Earnings

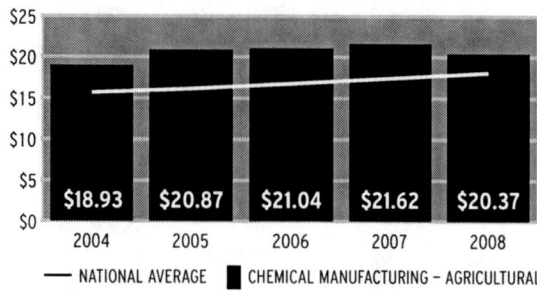

2004	$18.93
2005	$20.87
2006	$21.04
2007	$21.62
2008	$20.37

— NATIONAL AVERAGE ■ CHEMICAL MANUFACTURING – AGRICULTURAL

SOURCE: BUREAU OF LABOR STATISTICS

Call Preparation Questions

How does the company protect against volatile raw material prices?

Producing nitrogen fertilizer requires access to large supplies of ammonia, which is made from natural gas, a commodity with high price volatility.

How is the company managing increased government regulation?

Due to environmental, safety, or health issues, both federal and state governments restrict the production, distribution, application, and disposal of pesticides, fertilizers, and other agricultural chemicals.

How is the company mitigating farmers' declining use of chemicals?

Because fertilizer and pesticide costs can be more than 40 percent of operating costs, farmers have a strong incentive to use chemicals sparingly.

What opportunities or challenges does the company see in biological pesticides?

Growth in organic farming and farmers' desire to use less-expensive ways to manage crop pests have increased demand for biological control methods; basically, using bugs to combat other bugs.

How is rising export competition affecting company sales?

World fertilizer consumption, which grew very rapidly in the 1970s and 1980s but was flat during the 1990s, might see a recovery in growth in the current decade.

Web Links

American Chemical Society

News and information.
portal.acs.org/portal/acs/corg/content

American Chemistry Council

Focuses on the basic (or commodity) chemical industry, and safety, health, and legal concerns for members.
www.americanchemistry.com

Association of American Plant Food Control Officials

State fertilizer control officials.
www.aapfco.org

Canadian Fertilizer Institute

News and facts.
www.cfi.ca

Chem Industry.com

Search engine.
www.chemindustry.com

ChemAlliance

Regulatory information for the chemical process industry. News on regulatory tools, EPA, safety, and websites on environmental compliance.
www.chemalliance.org

Chemical Producers and Distributors Association

Pesticide industry lobbying organization. Issues.
www.cpda.com

Chemical Week Magazine

Publications, articles, indexes, news, and numerous links to related sites.
www.chemweek.com

Chemistry & Industry

Online magazine that includes searchable news archives.
www.chemind.org

CropLife America

Pesticide industry association.
www.croplifeamerica.org

EPA Pesticide Home Page

Federal regulations and programs.
www.epa.gov/pesticides

ICIS Search

Database of chemicals suppliers and products. www.icis.com/Search

International Fertilizer Industry Association

International production and consumption statistics. www.fertilizer.org/ifa

Pesticide and Toxic Chemical News

News about the pesticide segment of the industry. www.foodregulation.com/aius/home.jsp? pagetitle=aiusfp&pubId=ag100

The Fertilizer Institute

US fertilizer association. Statistics. Issues. www.tfi.org

USDA Newsroom — Latest Crop Reports

Calendar and reports of US and world crop estimates. www.usda.gov/news/releases/rptcal/calindex.htm

Glossary of Acronyms

AN — ammonium nitrate
DAP — di-ammonium phosphate
ESA — Endangered Species Act
FIFRA — Federal Insecticide, Fungicide and Rodenticide Act
IFDC — International Fertilizer Development Center
IRED — Interim Registration Eligibility Decision
ISAAA — International Services for the Acquisitions of Agri-biotech Applications
K2O — potassium oxide
GM — genetically modified
MAP — mono-ammonium phosphate
MCF — thousand cubic feet
P2O5 — phosphorous pentoxide
TMDL — total maximum daily load
TSP — tri-sodium phosphate
UAN — urea-ammonium nitrate

HOOVER'S TOP COMPANIES

Largest Companies by Sales	($ mil.)
The Mosaic Company	9,812.6
CF Industries Holdings, Inc.	3,921.1
FMC Corporation	3,115.3
The Scotts Miracle-Gro Company	2,981.8
Terra Industries Inc.	2,891.5
Agrium U.S. Inc.	3,294.0
Central Garden & Pet Company	1,705.4
Syngenta Corporation	1,063.4
Dow AgroSciences LLC	—
DuPont Agriculture & Nutrition	—

Largest Employers	Employees
The Mosaic Company	7,400
The Scotts Miracle-Gro Company	6,378
Dow AgroSciences LLC	5,500
FMC Corporation	5,000
Syngenta Corporation	5,134
Central Garden & Pet Company	4,600
Agrium U.S. Inc.	2,500
LSB Industries, Inc.	1,788
CF Industries Holdings, Inc.	1,500
Terra Industries Inc.	871

Fastest Growing* by Five-Year Sales Growth	(%)
Phosphate Holdings, Inc.	48.6
American Soil Technologies, Inc.	43.1
Intrepid Potash, Inc.	38.1
The Mosaic Company	30.7
CF Industries Holdings, Inc.	23.4
American Vanguard Corporation	16.6
Terra Industries Inc.	16.4
LSB Industries, Inc.	15.6
Terra Nitrogen Company, L.P.	14.2
Itronics, Inc.	12.1

Fastest Growing* by Five-Year Employee Growth	(%)
American Vanguard Corporation	8.3
The Scotts Miracle-Gro Company	6.4
LSB Industries, Inc.	3.8
Intrepid Potash, Inc.	3.4

Top Public Companies by Market Value	($ mil.)
The Mosaic Company	55,632.7
Terra Nitrogen Company, L.P.	2,766.6
CF Industries Holdings, Inc.	2,378.9
Terra Industries Inc.	1,655.8
Intrepid Potash, Inc.	1,554.6

* These rates are compounded annualized increases and may have resulted from acquisitions or one time gains. If less than 6 years of data are available, growth is for the years available.

SOURCE: HOOVER'S, INC., DATABASE

Chemical Manufacturing — Industrial

In the US, about 1,200 companies produce basic industrial chemicals, with combined annual revenue of $120 billion. Large companies include divisions of multibillion dollar companies like Dow, DuPont, and Occidental. The overall concentration of the industry is high: the 50 largest companies hold close to 70 percent of the market. Specific market segments are often dominated by just a handful of competitors. For example, eight companies control 85 percent of industrial gas production, eight control 95 percent of alkali production, and only six companies manufacture soda ash.

Competitive Landscape

Demand depends on the overall strength of the US economy, because most industrial chemicals are used in the manufacture of more-complicated products like fibers, plastics, paints, and paper. The profitability of individual companies is closely linked to efficient operations, because most products are commodities. Big producers have large economies of scale in production, which is why some chemicals are made by just a handful of companies. Small companies can compete effectively by making specialized or highly-purified products. The industry is highly automated: average annual revenue per employee is over $600,000.

Products, Operations & Technology

Industrial chemicals include gases like oxygen and nitrogen, dyes and pigments, chlorine and caustic soda, sulfuric and nitric acids, and thousands of organic chemicals. Unlike advanced chemicals that are manufactured through complicated chemical reactions, most industrial chemicals are made by extraction and purification from natural substances, including minerals, natural gas, petroleum, plants, air, and water. Oxygen and nitrogen gas are made by freezing air, phosphates from marine deposits, ethanol by fermenting corn, chlorine

from salt water, and a large number of chemicals are made by boiling petroleum.

Manufacturing facilities are often located close to raw materials. Because production facilities often consist of equipment that is specialized for the product being made, and because of economies of scale, most companies operate a single large production plant and produce only a handful of related products. Manufacturing operations focus on obtaining the highest possible yield of finished product from the raw materials. Access to high-quality raw materials is a primary consideration. Many companies either own their raw material supply or acquire it under long-term leases. Most producers of soda ash, for example, obtain raw material under long-term leases from mining operations in the Green River area of Wyoming.

Extracting basic chemicals from raw materials typically requires large amounts of energy. For many products, the cost of energy can be 30 percent or more of the total manufacturing cost. In many industrial processes, energy is used in the form of steam, which often is generated from coal. Energy-intensive chemical plants are often located where the cost of energy is low, such as near hydroelectric plants or coal mining areas.

Because producing industrial chemicals is usually a purification process, many producers (especially those that use minerals as a raw material) must dispose of large quantities of waste materials, of which there may be many pounds for each pound of finished product. Some wastes, like the mash that remains after corn has been fermented to ethanol, can be sold as animal feed or fertilizer, but many have no economic value.

The technology used to produce most industrial chemicals is well known and relatively simple, involving basic chemical reactions. Phosphates, for example, are made by dissolving phosphate rock in sulfuric acid; chlorine is made by passing an electric current through salt water. Many plants are highly automated with computerized process control systems because the control of chemical reactions is critical.

Sales & Marketing

The major customers for industrial chemicals are other chemical and manufacturing companies that use them in their own manufacturing processes, consumer products companies that use them directly to formulate products like detergents and toothpaste, and wholesale dealers that resell them in smaller quantities to a variety of small customers. Companies often have large, long-term contracts with a few large customers. In some cases, a producer with a long-term contract will build a plant next to the manufacturing facility of a major customer. Many products, however, are sold to a wide variety of customers through a sales force that may consist largely of chemists or chemical engineers who can explain product properties and understand technical requirements.

The more basic the product, the more sales depend purely on pricing. For bulky products, like soda ash or phosphates, transportation costs to a customer's location can be a significant factor. Prices for many products are linked to the cost of energy.

Human Resources

Production jobs in industrial chemical manufacture typically involve operating and maintaining complex process machinery, and are accordingly well-paid. Many workers have technical training or an engineering degree. Average hourly wages are about 50 percent above the national average. Fringe benefits typically are 27 percent of wages.

The safety record of the industry is very good. The annual injury rate per 100 full-time workers is slightly over two cases, compared to an average of six cases for all manufacturers.

To retain experienced workers who often know the important operating quirks of a chemicals plant, companies may provide a high level of retirement benefits.

Industry Employment Growth

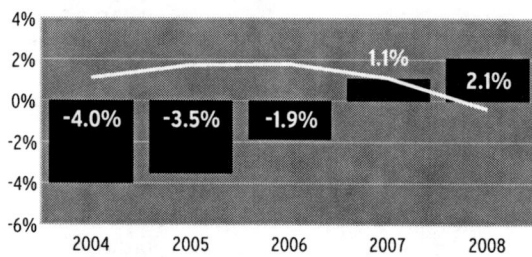

Average Hourly Earnings

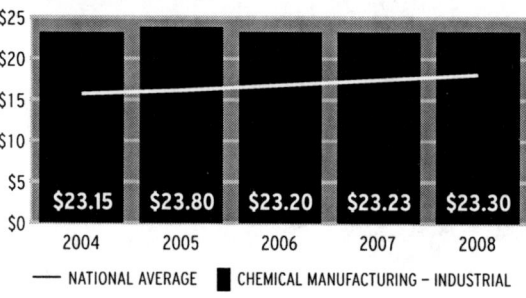

— NATIONAL AVERAGE   ■ CHEMICAL MANUFACTURING – INDUSTRIAL

SOURCE: BUREAU OF LABOR STATISTICS

Call Preparation Questions

How does the company mitigate cyclical demand?

Demand for industrial chemicals is more volatile than for the rest of the US economy.

How does the company finance capital projects and inventories?

Many producers of industrial chemicals can't afford to make the large investments required to obtain newer technology, processes, or equipment.

What opportunities do methanol fuel cells present the company?

Although production models aren't yet on the road, cars powered by fuel cells using methanol will be more energy-efficient than gasoline-powered cars, and will emit no pollutants.

What steps is the company taking to capitalize on projected demand for ethanol?

Produced from grains such as corn, ethanol is a source of oxygen used to enhance the burning characteristics of gasoline.

Web Links

American Chemical Society

Focuses on the basic (or commodity) chemical industry, and safety, health, and legal concerns for members.

portal.acs.org/portal/acs/corg/content

Canadian Chemical Producers' Association

Canadian industry news.

www.ccpa.ca

Chem Alliance

Regulatory information for the chemical process industry. News on regulatory tools, EPA, safety, and websites on environmental compliance.

www.chemalliance.org

Chem Industry.com

Search engine.

www.chemindustry.com

Chemical Buyers Directory

News, chemical prices and much more.

www.icis.com/Search

Chemical Online

News on business trends, products, and technology for the chemical process industries.

www.chemicalonline.com/content/hubs/dir.asp?hub=News

Chemical Week Magazine

Publications, articles, indexes, news, and numerous links to related sites.

www.chemweek.com

Chemistry & Industry

Online magazine that includes searchable news archives.

www.chemind.org/CI

Glossary of Acronyms

ACC — American Chemistry Council
EIA — Energy Information Agency
FERC — Federal Energy Regulatory Commission
HPV — high production volume
MTBE — methyl tert-butyl ether
PFCAS — perfluorocarboxylates
PFOA — perfluorooctanoic acid
PPI — Producer Price Index
TAEP — Texas Alliance of Energy Producers

HOOVER'S TOP COMPANIES

Largest Companies by Sales	($ mil.)
The Dow Chemical Company	57,514.0
E. I. du Pont de Nemours and Company	31,836.0
3M Company	25,269.0
Equistar Chemicals, LP	13,037.0
Praxair, Inc.	10,796.0
Air Products and Chemicals, Inc.	10,414.5
Union Carbide Corporation	7,493.0
Celanese Corporation	6,823.0
BASF Corporation	—
ExxonMobil Chemical Company	—

Largest Employers	Employees
3M Company	79,183
E. I. du Pont de Nemours and Company	60,000
The Dow Chemical Company	45,856
Praxair, Inc.	27,992
Ecolab Inc.	26,050
Air Products and Chemicals, Inc.	21,100
The InterTech Group, Inc.	16,000
Nalco Holding Company	11,560
Eastman Chemical Company	10,800
BASF Corporation	9,826

Fastest Growing* by Five-Year Sales Growth	(%)
Allegro Biodiesel Corporation	311.1
VeraSun Energy Corporation	185.9
Changing World Technologies, Inc.	144.9
Pacific Ethanol, Inc.	129.5
Altair Nanotechnologies Inc.	97.9
Flotek Industries, Inc.	72.5
Clean Diesel Technologies, Inc.	65.1
Golden Grain Energy, LLC	57.4
Hexion Specialty Chemicals, Inc.	51.0
Sterling Chemicals, Inc.	48.5

Fastest Growing* by Five-Year Employee Growth	(%)
Pacific Ethanol, Inc.	216.2
Flotek Industries, Inc.	68.9
Altair Nanotechnologies Inc.	37.2
VeraSun Energy Corporation	34.5
ADA-ES, Inc.	31.3
American Pacific Corporation	21.5
Synthetech, Inc.	19.4
OM Group, Inc.	13.7
Charles & Colvard, Ltd.	13.5
Senomyx, Inc.	11.5

Top Public Companies by Market Value	($ mil.)
3M Company	39,906.5
E. I. du Pont de Nemours and Company	22,830.1
Praxair, Inc.	18,215.3
Air Products and Chemicals, Inc.	14,337.3
The Dow Chemical Company	13,948.4

* These rates are compounded annualized increases and may have resulted from acquisitions or one time gains. If less than 6 years of data are available, growth is for the years available.

SOURCE: HOOVER'S, INC., DATABASE

Chemicals

About 10,000 companies produce chemicals in the US, with combined annual revenues of $500 billion. Although large companies like Dow and DuPont produce hundreds of chemicals, most companies specialize in one or two product lines. The typical chemical company has annual revenue under $10 million. While the industry as a whole is fragmented, the concentration in many segments is very high: just a handful of manufacturers hold 80 percent or more of the segment.

Competitive Landscape

Demand is driven by the health of the US economy because chemicals are used to make a wide variety of industrial and consumer products. The profitability of individual companies is closely tied to efficient operations. Big companies have large economies of scale in production. Small companies can compete effectively by producing specialty products, of which there are a large number, or by operating a single plant highly efficiently. The industry is highly automated: average annual revenue per employee is over $500,000.

Products, Operations & Technology

Basic chemicals include petrochemicals, industrial gases, dyes and pigments, alkalies and chlorine, alcohols, and various other organic (based on the chemistry of carbon and oxygen) and inorganic chemicals. These basic chemicals are made from mined materials like crude oil, natural gas, and minerals, or from crops and other natural substances. The raw materials are called feedstocks. Chemicals companies use basic chemicals to produce intermediate products like polyethylene; polyethylene oxide (PO); ethylene oxide (EO); and ethylene glycol, or final products like phosphate and nitrogen agricultural fertilizers.

Basic and intermediate chemicals are collectively referred to as commodity chemicals.

BUSINESS CHALLENGES

» Sensitivity to Energy Prices

Because of the high energy content of many chemicals, higher energy prices can greatly affect production costs. For many products, energy accounts for 30 percent or more of total costs. Many manufacturers use natural gas as a source of heat, or natural gas or petroleum as feedstock. In recent years, energy costs have been volatile.

» Health, Environmental Regulations

Despite large investments to prevent air, water, and ground pollution, chemical companies have ongoing exposure to environmental and health issues, because regulations continue to tighten and past practices continue to result in large cleanup costs or litigation. Many chemical companies have been cited for liability at Superfund sites or for illnesses caused by their chemicals.

» Customer Concentration

Chemical manufacturers often sell large quantities of product to a few customers, or to customers all in the same industry. The fortunes of some chemical manufacturers are therefore closely tied to the success of their large customers or to an entire end-use industry. For example, a large portion of soda ash production is used to manufacture glass containers.

Commodity chemicals are produced mainly by large companies, often as byproducts of petroleum refining, using widely-known manufacturing processes. Margins on commodity chemicals are usually low because the chemicals are so widely produced. Commodity chemicals account for about 45 percent of industry revenue.

Commodity chemicals are used to produce more complicated chemicals, known as specialty chemicals, which include resins, plastics, synthetic fibers, pesticides, lubricants, paints, coatings, adhesives, soaps and cleaners, pharmaceuticals, and a huge number of other products with special applications. Margins are generally higher on these products, which account for 55 percent of industry revenue.

The manufacturing process usually involves mixing various raw materials and adding heat to produce a series of chemical reactions, then using various physical techniques to isolate the finished product. Production may involve dozens of intermediate steps. Many specialty chemicals are produced in batches, while commodity chemicals are often produced in continuous-flow operations. Special reaction vessels, valves, piping, and control instruments are used to produce different chemicals. Companies generally employ a large number of engineers to manage the manufacturing process. There are usually waste products to be disposed of, and energy inputs are often high. Large amounts of energy are typically used to drive chemical reactions, and natural gas or petroleum is used as feedstock for many chemicals.

Manufacturing process technology is important in securing a high product yield from the raw materials. For the production of complex chemicals in particular, precise control of chemical reactions is required. Most manufacturing plants are highly automated. The design of esoteric chemicals such as drugs may be done with sophisticated computer systems.

Sales & Marketing

Chemical companies sell their products to a large variety of customers in the industrial, agricultural, construction, textile, health care, and consumer products sectors. In many product segments, however, companies may do most of their business with just a few large customers. Most chemicals are sold as intermediate products to other chemical manufacturers.

Sales representatives and trade shows are the chief means of marketing. Many salespeople are chemists and chemical engineers because technical specifications of products are extremely important. Pricing for commodity chemicals is often set by a price leader, usually one of the large companies. Prices for commodity chemicals depend largely on raw material and energy prices. Pricing for specialty chemicals depends more on demand in end-use markets.

Human Resources

Production jobs in chemicals manufacture typically involve operating and maintaining complex process machinery, and are accordingly well-paid. Many workers have technical training or an engineering degree. Hourly wages are 25 percent above the national average. Fringe benefits typically are 25 to 30 percent of wages. Companies can afford to pay workers fairly well because their productivity is high. The worker safety record of the industry is better than average.

To retain experienced workers, who often know the important operating quirks of a chemicals plant, companies may provide a high level of retirement benefits.

Industry Employment Growth

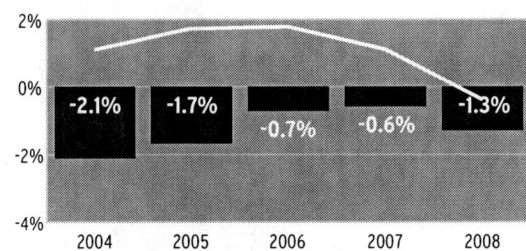

Average Hourly Earnings

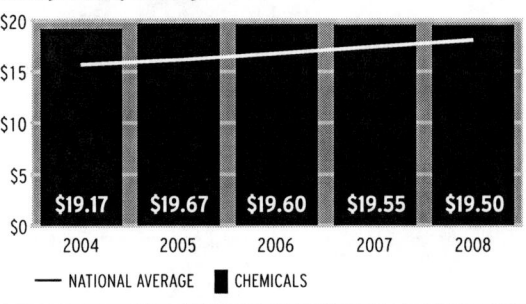

SOURCE: BUREAU OF LABOR STATISTICS

Call Preparation Questions

How has the company been affected by recent changes in energy and raw material costs?

Because of the high energy content of many chemicals, higher energy prices can greatly affect production costs.

How does the company track compliance with federal regulations?

Despite large investments to prevent air, water, and ground pollution, chemical companies have ongoing exposure to environmental and health issues, because regulations continue to tighten and past practices continue to result in large cleanup costs or litigation.

How reliant is the company on its top customers?

Chemical manufacturers often sell large quantities of product to a few customers, or to customers all in the same industry.

How might the company benefit by supplying specialty chemicals to the computer industry?

Some industries that use large amounts of chemicals, like electronics, have grown rapidly in recent years, creating good opportunities for specialty chemicals.

How are technological developments changing the company's production processes and costs?

Until recently, many chemicals were produced through processes that had changed little in the past 50 years.

Web Links

American Chemical Society

News and information.

portal.acs.org/portal/acs/corg/content

American Chemistry Council

Focuses on the basic (or commodity) chemical industry, and safety, health, and legal concerns for members.

www.accnewsmedia.com

ChemAlliance

Excellent regulatory information.

www.chemalliance.org

Chemical Online

News on business trends, products, and technology for the chemical process industries.

www.chemicalonline.com/content/hubs/dir.asp?hub= News

Chemical Week Magazine

Publications, articles, indexes, news, and numerous links to related sites.

www.chemweek.com

ChemIndustry.com

Search engine.

www.chemindustry.com

Commercial Development and Marketing Association

Chemical Management and Resources Association (CMRA) and Commercial Development Association (CDA) combined in 1999 to form this professional association dedicated to fostering, promoting, and sharing business processes for the chemical industry.

www.cdmaonline.org

National Association of Chemical Distributors

US association providing news bites, publications, calendars, press releases, and congressional links.

www.nacd.com

Glossary of Acronyms

ACC — American Chemical Council

CSB — US Chemical Safety and Hazard Investigation Board

EIA — Energy Information Association

mcf — thousand cubic feet

PFCAs — perfluorocarboxylates

PFOA — perfluorooctanoic acid

POP — persistent organic pollutant

TAEP — Texas Alliance of Energy Producers

HOOVER'S TOP COMPANIES

Largest Companies by Sales	($ mil.)
The Dow Chemical Company	57,514.0
E. I. du Pont de Nemours and Company	31,836.0
Chevron Phillips Chemical Company LLC	12,986.0
Praxair, Inc.	10,796.0
Air Products and Chemicals, Inc.	10,414.5
Union Carbide Corporation	7,493.0
Westlake Chemical Corporation	3,692.4
BASF Corporation	—
Equistar Chemicals, LP	
ExxonMobil Chemical Company	—

Largest Employers	Employees
E. I. du Pont de Nemours and Company	60,000
The Dow Chemical Company	45,856
Praxair, Inc.	27,992
Air Products and Chemicals, Inc.	21,100
BASF Corporation	9,826
W. R. Grace & Co.	6,500
Chevron Phillips Chemical Company LLC	5,500
FMC Corporation	5,000
J.M. Huber Corporation	4,500
Union Carbide Corporation	3,800

Fastest Growing* by Five-Year Sales Growth	(%)
Allegro Biodiesel Corporation	311.1
VeraSun Energy Corporation	185.9
Changing World Technologies, Inc.	144.9
Pacific Ethanol, Inc.	129.5
Altair Nanotechnologies Inc.	97.9
Rentech, Inc.	90.1
Clean Diesel Technologies, Inc.	65.1
Sterling Chemicals, Inc.	48.5
KMG Chemicals, Inc.	34.2
Aventine Renewable Energy Holdings, Inc.	23.5

Fastest Growing* by Five-Year Employee Growth	(%)
Pacific Ethanol, Inc.	216.2
Altair Nanotechnologies Inc.	37.2
VeraSun Energy Corporation	34.5
KMG Chemicals, Inc.	29.6
Rentech, Inc.	27.0
TOR Minerals International, Inc.	9.2
J.M. Huber Corporation	6.5
NewMarket Corporation	4.0
The Dow Chemical Company	4.0
Aventine Renewable Energy Holdings, Inc.	3.1

Top Public Companies by Market Value	($ mil.)
E. I. du Pont de Nemours and Company	22,830.1
Praxair, Inc.	18,215.3
Air Products and Chemicals, Inc.	14,337.3
The Dow Chemical Company	13,948.4
FMC Corporation	3,243.4

* These rates are compounded annualized increases and may have resulted from acquisitions or one time gains. If less than 6 years of data are available, growth is for the years available.

SOURCE: HOOVER'S, INC., DATABASE

Chemicals Distributors

The chemicals distribution industry in the US includes about 10,000 companies with combined annual revenue of $70 billion. Major companies include Univar, Ashland Distribution, and Brenntag. The industry is fairly fragmented: the largest 50 companies hold only about 40 percent of the market.

Competitive Landscape

Chemical distribution is a cyclical business dependent on industrial demand. The profitability of individual companies depends on an efficient distribution system. Larger companies can offer more products and services. Local and regional distributors can compete effectively through superior service. The industry is highly automated: annual industry revenue per employee is about $800,000.

Products, Operations & Technology

Major products are plastics materials, alkalis and chlorine, detergents and soaps, adhesives, and industrial gases. Plastics account for almost 25 percent of industry revenue.

In addition to selling and transporting chemicals, distributors offer other services including blending, packaging, technical training, and managing customer inventories. Waste removal is a particularly common service to offer. Many suppliers specialize in certain types of chemicals.

Products are bought from manufacturers of industrial chemicals, including petroleum refiners. Multiple suppliers exist for almost all chemical products. A large distributor typically buys from several dozen chemical manufacturers, such as DuPont, Dow, and BASF. Distributors may have long-term distribution agreements with suppliers that specify quantities and price formulas. Such agreements typically renew automatically each year.

Large wholesalers have multiple facilities around the country. Brenntag has over 100 lo-

BUSINESS CHALLENGES

» Uneven Demand

End-user demand for industrial chemicals can vary sharply from year to year, heavily depending on the economy and manufacturing activity. For example, during the last recession, US production of basic chemicals dropped almost 15 percent, with only a slow recovery in subsequent years. Production of plastic resins can vary from year to year by more than 5 percent, and can be very uneven throughout the year. Because of low gross margins and high fixed-costs, a drop in sales volume sharply affects distribution profitability.

» Vulnerable to Higher Energy Costs

Energy costs can affect chemical distributors by impacting both product and distribution costs. Many basic chemicals, such as plastic resins, are derived from crude oil or natural gas, and distributors are large consumers of diesel fuel for truck fleets. While some energy cost increases can be passed to consumers, strong competition may prevent complete cost recovery.

» Significant Legal Liability

Handling, storing, and transporting hazardous materials create a large safety and health risk for chemical distributors. Chemical distribution is subject to numerous regulations and substantial fines for property damage, environmental pollution, chemical spills, or explosions.

cations, Univar has about 85, and Ashland Distribution has 70. Facilities include warehouses, tank farms, and custom blending facilities, and are usually located close to major industrial areas. A typical distributor has 3 million gallons of bulk storage capacity and 350,000 square feet of warehouse space. Distributors that offer waste removal and disposal services typically operate a centralized processing facility. Chemical waste is incinerated, blended into fuels, or recycled.

Products are distributed chiefly by truck, often in mixed truckload or less-than-truckload (LTL) quantities. A typical distributor has a fleet of 50 trucks and may operate a central maintenance and fueling site.

Computer technology plays an important role in improving the efficiency of inventory and distribution operations. Computer programs and truck GPS are used to minimize truck routes. Sensing systems at customer locations can be used for automatic replenishment programs.

Sales & Marketing

Major customers are local manufacturers of plastics, paints, adhesives, soaps, cosmetics, and pharmaceuticals. Customers are mainly small and midsized manufacturers or repackagers who don't have a high enough production volume to buy raw materials directly from bulk chemical manufacturers.

Distributors use mainly an internal sales force to find new and provide service to existing customers. Trade shows are commonly used as an important marketing channel. Large distributors may have many customers — JLM has 1,400 — but local distributors may depend highly on a specific local industry for a large percentage of revenue. Pricing generally consists of a percentage markup on supplier costs.

Human Resources

Employment payrolls of chemicals distributors include salespeople, administrative staff, and transportation personnel, some of whom are unionized by the Teamsters or Oil, Chemical, and Atomic Workers Union. Production workers' wages, including transportation personnel, average about $19 an hour, above the $16 national average. The industry's annual injury rate is low: slightly more than two cases per 100 full-time employees, which is about half the US average.

Industry Employment Growth

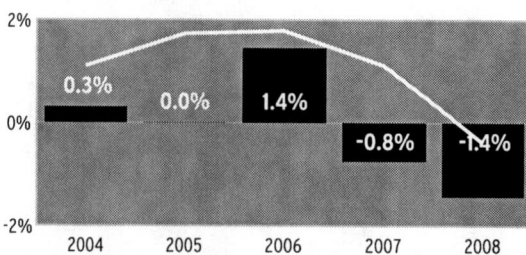

Average Hourly Earnings

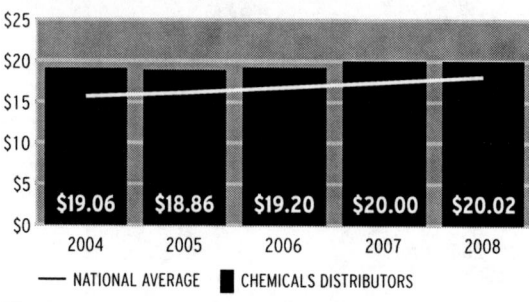

SOURCE: BUREAU OF LABOR STATISTICS

Call Preparation Questions

How does the company plan for changes in demand?

End-user demand for industrial chemicals can vary sharply from year to year, heavily depending on the economy and manufacturing activity.

How have changes in energy costs affected the company?

Energy costs can affect chemical distributors by impacting both product and distribution costs.

How does the company minimize the risks of dealing with hazardous materials?

Handling, storing, and transporting hazardous materials create a large safety and health risk for chemical distributors.

Does the company provide inventory management services for customers?

Distributors may actively manage the chemical inventories of their customers.

Does the company have reciprocal arrangements with other distributors?

Distributor alliances provide a greater marketing area for individual companies.

Web Links

American Chemical Society

Chemical industry basics; member site with safety and legal issues.
portal.acs.org/portal/acs/corg/content

Brenntag North America

Company web site with insights affecting the industry.
www.brenntagnorthamerica.com

ChemAlliance

Focuses on regulatory matters for producers.
www.chemalliance.org

Harcros Chemicals

Small company web site.
www.harcroschem.com

National Association of Chemical Distributors

Industry and regulatory news and updates.
www.nacd.com

Purchasing

Company rankings, news, trade show highlights, industry trends.
www.purchasing.com

Scorecard

Site of a pollution information and watch guard group.
www.scorecard.org/chemical-profiles

US Department of Transportation, Office of Hazardous Materials Safety

Regulations and data.
hazmat.dot.gov

Glossary of Acronyms

JIT — just-in-time
LTL — less-than-truckload
PFOA — perfluorooctanoic acid
WTI — West Texas Intermediate

HOOVER'S TOP COMPANIES

Largest Companies by Sales	($ mil.)
Ashland Inc.	8,381.0
Transammonia, Inc.	8,339.4
Univar USA Inc.	4,300.0
Airgas, Inc.	4,017.0
Brenntag North America, Inc.	2,900.0
Helena Chemical Company	2,632.5
Sigma-Aldrich Corporation	2,200.7
ICC Industries Inc.	1,800.0
Praxair Distribution, Inc.	1,400.0

Largest Employers	Employees
Airgas, Inc.	14,500
Ashland Inc.	11,700
Sigma-Aldrich Corporation	7,862
Praxair Distribution, Inc.	5,000
Univar USA Inc.	4,400
Brenntag North America, Inc.	3,000
FinishMaster, Inc.	1,910
ICC Industries Inc.	1,700
Helena Chemical Company	1,000
Composites One LLC	600

Fastest Growing* by Five-Year Sales Growth	(%)
Transammonia, Inc.	29.3
Airgas, Inc.	17.6
ICC Industries Inc.	15.8
Hawkins, Inc.	13.6
JCI Jones Chemicals, Inc.	12.3
Sigma-Aldrich Corporation	11.1
FinishMaster, Inc.	6.4
Aceto Corporation	5.8
Ashland Inc.	1.3

Fastest Growing* by Five-Year Employee Growth	(%)
Airgas, Inc.	9.6
Sigma-Aldrich Corporation	7.1
FinishMaster, Inc.	5.5
Transammonia, Inc.	4.2
Hawkins, Inc.	3.4

Top Public Companies by Market Value	($ mil.)
Sigma-Aldrich Corporation	5,157.5
Airgas, Inc.	3,741.6
Ashland Inc.	1,842.1
Aceto Corporation	186.8
Hawkins, Inc.	156.2

* These rates are compounded annualized increases and may have resulted from acquisitions or one time gains. If less than 6 years of data are available, growth is for the years available.

SOURCE: HOOVER'S, INC., DATABASE

Child-care Facilities

THIS INDUSTRY INCLUDES:

SIC CODES
8351   Child Day Care
        Services

NAICS CODES
6244   Child Day Care
        Services

The US child-care industry includes about 40,000 commercial companies with combined annual revenue of $22 billion, and 25,000 non-profit organizations, with combined annual revenue of $10 billion. Large firms include Knowledge Learning, Bright Horizons Family Solutions, and Learning Care Group. The industry is highly fragmented: the top 50 companies hold less than 20 percent of the market. The average facility of one of the larger companies has $700,000 in annual revenue and employs 120.

Competitive Landscape

Job and income growth drive demand for child-care centers. The profitability of individual companies depends on good marketing and efficient operations. Large companies have economies of scale in advertising and administration. Smaller companies can compete effectively in local markets by owning convenient locations. The industry is highly labor-intensive: annual revenue per worker is only about $30,000.

Products, Operations & Technology

Child-care centers provide supervision and educational programs for pre-school and school-age children. The type of care varies according to a child's age, which may range from 6 weeks to 16 years. Most commercial companies operate child-care centers that are open to the public, but some operate corporate-sponsored centers for employees' children. Most commercial facilities concentrate on a small age range, since each age group requires a different program.

A typical facility of a national operator occupies 12,000 square feet, with kitchen and bathrooms, and accommodates 150 children. Hours may be from 6:00 am to 6:00 pm. Educational programs, usually age-specific learning curricula, have the goal of advancing emotional,

BUSINESS CHALLENGES

» Regulators Can Increase Operating Costs

Due to the sensitive nature of the services child-care centers provide, state regulation is detailed. Regulations can result in large cost increases for centers, particularly for certification, licensing, caregiver training, and compliance with government-required paperwork. Though regulations vary from state to state, they can specify the amount of space required per child; types of facilities, food, and care; hours of operation; types of personnel who must be available, such as nurses; personnel background checks; and the ratio of personnel to children.

» Accident Liability

Centers face lawsuits and bad publicity if a child is injured while under their care, onsite, or during company-run transport to and from the center. Playground injuries and inadequate supervision generate the most losses, according to insurers. A study of 1,916 cases of sudden infant death syndrome (SIDS) finds that about 20 percent occur in day care centers.

» High Workforce Turnover

Personnel turnover in a center can reach 50 percent a year, primarily due to employee dissatisfaction with low wages. Many states mandate high staff-to-child ratios, creating a cost-control issue that centers address by paying low wages. Only half of the states require child development training for caregivers.

physical, social, and intellectual skills. Some care centers transport children to and from schools and homes, but most require parents to provide their own transportation.

The general ratio of children-to-staff at child-care centers is 5:1, but varies according to the children's ages. The ratio is lower for infants, higher for school-age children. State regulations may mandate the ratio. Low children-to-staff ratios are a primary selling point for facilities. Labor costs are the major operating expense.

Occupancy and tuition are the common operating measures. Typical occupancies range from 60 to 90 percent of licensed capacity. Occupancy may vary during the day, depending on the number of part-time (not full-day) children. Some facilities may be full even though their occupancy rate is only 60 percent. Tuition is usually collected weekly and varies greatly from market to market and firm to firm. Hourly rates for part-time children generally are higher than fees for full-time children. Average weekly tuition may be close to $150. In contrast, day care with an unregulated home provider may cost $50 per week. Convenient location is more important to many parents than cost.

Child-care by nature is a low-technology business, with the exception of computerized back office systems that large firms use. Educational tools, however, are increasingly computer-based, especially in those centers that cater to upscale families. Some centers use security cameras that parents can gain access to from the Internet.

Sales & Marketing

Marketing often includes newspaper, magazine, and Yellow Pages' advertising. Referrals from existing customers are an important source of new business and are encouraged through financial incentives. One important marketing tool for a child-care facility is accreditation. The National Association for the Education of Young Children is one of several associations that establish standards for facilities and staff.

A growing number of centers call themselves "early childhood education" facilities. Some companies target wealthier customers by offering facilities with elaborate options such as tennis courts, foreign language classes, exercise rooms, and computer training. About 7 million preschool children and 2 million school-age children attend child-care programs, with another 3 million in home care.

Human Resources

Staff turnover is high, sometimes as much as 50 percent per year, because workers are paid low wages. Average annual pay for employees is less than $15,000. Personnel recruiting and training are constant management concerns, especially in regard to appropriate conduct of employees and child safety.

Industry Employment Growth

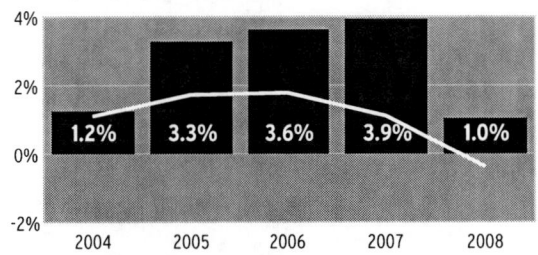

2004	2005	2006	2007	2008
1.2%	3.3%	3.6%	3.9%	1.0%

Average Hourly Earnings

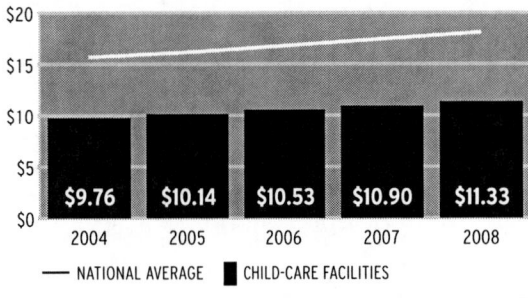

2004	2005	2006	2007	2008
$9.76	$10.14	$10.53	$10.90	$11.33

— NATIONAL AVERAGE ■ CHILD-CARE FACILITIES

SOURCE: BUREAU OF LABOR STATISTICS

Call Preparation Questions

What compliance issues do state regulations create for the company?

Due to the sensitive nature of the services child-care centers provide, state regulation is detailed.

How does the company mitigate the possibility or threat of litigation?

Centers face lawsuits and bad publicity if a child is injured while under their care, onsite, or during company-run transport to and from the center.

How does the company find staff and manage turnover?

Personnel turnover in a center can reach 50 percent a year, primarily due to employee dissatisfaction with low wages.

What opportunities do employer-sponsored child-care offer the company?

Employer-sponsored programs encourage child-care, provide a steady stream of revenue for centers under contract, and are one of the fastest-growing segments in child-care.

How does, or would, the company benefit from providing extra or "deluxe" services?

A growing number of "early childhood education" facilities offer expensive extras for the wealthiest of the nation's 13 million preschool children in day care.

Web Links

Center for the Child Care Workforce

Articles and research on early care and child education.

www.ccw.org/press_news.html

Child Welfare League of America, Inc. (CWLA)

News.

www.cwla.org/newsevents

Child-Care Information Exchange

Information and resources on child-care center environment and design.

www.ccie.com

National Association for Child-Care Professionals

Useful information on accreditation and more.

www.naccp.org

National Association for the Education of Young Children (NAEYC)

Resource catalog listing brochures, books, and videos; several publications available that provide background information and detail on resources for early childhood facilities' planning and design.

www.naeyc.org

National Child-Care Association (NCCA)

Legislative news.

www.nccanet.org

National Child-Care Information Center

Links, education, and other information.

www.nccic.org

National Institute for Early Education Research

Provides objective, nonpartisan information on early childhood education.

nieer.org/news

The Child Care Bureau

News and research from the US Department of Health and Human Services.

www.acf.hhs.gov/programs/ccb

Glossary of Acronyms

ASP — Application Service Provider
CDC — Centers for Disease Control and Prevention
CPSC — Consumer Product Safety Commission
NAEYC — National Association for the Education of Young Children
NCCA — National Child Care Association
SIDS — Sudden Infant Death Syndrome

HOOVER'S TOP COMPANIES

Largest Companies by Sales	($ mil.)
Knowledge Learning Corporation	1,620.0
Bright Horizons Family Solutions, Inc.	774.6
Learning Care Group, Inc.	522.0
Nobel Learning Communities, Inc.	206.2
Child Development Schools, Inc.	47.4
New Horizon Kids Quest, Inc.	20.4

Largest Employers	Employees
Knowledge Learning Corporation	42,000
Learning Care Group, Inc.	23,000
Bright Horizons Family Solutions, Inc.	18,400
Nobel Learning Communities, Inc.	4,700
Child Development Schools, Inc.	2,500
New Horizon Kids Quest, Inc.	600

Fastest Growing* by Five-Year Sales Growth	(%)
Bright Horizons Family Solutions, Inc.	13.7
Nobel Learning Communities, Inc.	6.6

Fastest Growing* by Five-Year Employee Growth	(%)
Nobel Learning Communities, Inc.	12.9
Bright Horizons Family Solutions, Inc.	4.2
Knowledge Learning Corporation	1.2

Top Public Companies by Market Value	($ mil.)
Bright Horizons Family Solutions, Inc.	907.7
Nobel Learning Communities, Inc.	144.7

* These rates are compounded annualized increases and may have resulted from acquisitions or one time gains. If less than 6 years of data are available, growth is for the years available.

SOURCE: HOOVER'S, INC., DATABASE

Churches & Religious Groups

THIS INDUSTRY INCLUDES:

SIC CODES
8661   Religious
       Organizations

NAICS CODES
8131   Religious
       Organizations

Churches and religious groups in the US include about 360,000 congregations that have combined annual revenue of about $95 billion. Some 60 percent of Americans say they're members of a congregation, and slightly more than 40 percent say they attend services weekly or almost every week.

In terms of membership, the largest faiths in the US are Catholic (about 23 percent of the population), Baptist (17 percent), Methodist (6 percent), and Lutheran (5 percent). The size of individual congregations varies. The median US congregation has 75 regular, weekly participants. The top 10 percent of US congregations by membership account for about 50 percent of all weekly worshipers.

Competitive Landscape

Demand is driven by consumers' desire for spiritual growth, guidance, and inspiration and by demographics — older Americans are more likely to attend church than younger ones. The profitability of a church depends primarily on the congregation's ability to attract members who can provide financial support. Large congregations have advantages in their ability to offer more programs and activities. Small congregations can compete effectively by maintaining stronger connections with members.

Products, Operations & Technology

Religious congregations are similar to charitable organizations, in that they solicit money in various ways to fund charitable and educational programs, often called missions or ministries. These programs most often benefit congregation members or members of the community in which the church is located. Some churches may also have programs aimed at communities elsewhere in the US or overseas.

Most programs funded by churches are labor- rather than materials-intensive. Personnel costs for clergy, educational staff, and cleri-

BUSINESS CHALLENGES

» Revenues Depend Strongly on Economy
Church member contributions are strongly influenced by economic circumstances. Church income from contributions may decline during difficult economic periods, just as demand for church programs increases. Employment levels and personal income growth can affect the amount contributed to churches. Church membership growth tends to be strongest in communities with rapid economic growth.

» Declining Membership, Attendance
Although church membership remains higher in the US than in many other countries, individual congregations may face declines because of changing local demographics or inability to recruit new members. Kindling the interest of teenagers and young adults, who often see religion as irrelevant, is especially difficult for many churches. Overall, some 60 percent of Americans say they are members of a congregation. That figure was closer to 70 percent as recently as the late 1990s.

» Dependence on Large Contributors
Many churches rely on contributions from a relatively small number of wealthy members for a significant portion of income. About 5 percent of US Christians provide 60 percent of the money that their churches and religious groups use to operate. The loss of a major contributor can be difficult for a church to overcome.

cal employees are the largest expense for most churches. Programs are primarily educational (religious study for children and adults); charitable (soup kitchens, aid to the elderly); or spiritual (bereavement and marriage counseling). A major program for some churches is private education at the primary, secondary, and higher education levels. The Catholic Church operates 8,000 schools in the US, mostly elementary and secondary. A number of large church groups operate universities, divinity schools, and hospitals.

Organizational hierarchy within religious groups varies significantly. All Catholic congregations in the US belong to the Catholic Church. But Baptist congregations, for example, may belong to the Southern Baptist Convention, the National Baptist Convention, the American Baptist Churches, or to smaller organizations, or they may be totally independent. Many religious groups have hierarchical structures, but a large number of churches operate independently.

Churches use computers to prepare budgets; account for donations, grants, and bequests; maintain membership rolls; perform stewardship analysis; produce materials such as bulletins and newsletters; keep asset inventories; and communicate with members, other religious organizations, and the community at large.

Sales & Marketing

Many programs of religious groups are aimed at the congregants themselves and at nonmembers who might join. Some congregations sponsor programs that encourage participation by nonmembers, partly for the purpose of bringing in new members. Some faiths encourage or require congregants to recruit new members.

Marketing is usually informational. Many churches maintain websites as part of their marketing and outreach strategies and to enhance members' participation. Larger congregations or national groups may produce radio or TV programming.

Human Resources

Salaries for religious workers are generally lower than salaries in the private sector and even those in the rest of the nonprofit sector. Pay for clergy varies widely based on congregation size and geographic location. The average senior pastor receives about $80,000 a year in wages and benefits. Most jobs in local congregations, aside from clergy, are clerical. Most congregations rely heavily on volunteers to conduct their activities.

Call Preparation Questions

How do the demographics and economic situation of the local community impact the church?

Church member contributions are strongly influenced by economic circumstances.

What is the church doing to increase its membership?

Although church membership remains higher in the US than in many other countries, individual congregations may face declines because of changing local demographics or inability to recruit new members.

How financially dependent is the church on one or several large donors?

Many churches rely on contributions from a relatively small number of wealthy members for a significant portion of income.

What programs does the church offer for older members?

Although attendance and membership dynamics vary significantly for different churches and regions, older Americans are more likely than younger ones to regularly attend church.

How involved is the church in creating or sponsoring TV or radio programs?

The multiplicity of cable channels and satellite radio stations makes producing programs on TV and radio easier for religious groups.

Web Links

Adherents

Statistics on US religious affiliation.
www.adherents.com

Association of Statisticians of American Religious Bodies

Statistics on church membership.
www.asarb.org

Association of Theological Schools

Catholic, Protestant and Jewish schools.
www.ats.edu

Christianity Today Magazine

Articles on Christian church issues.
www.christianitytoday.com

National Council of Churches

News.
www.ncccusa.org

National Religious Broadcasters

Religious radio news.
www.nrb.org

Religion News Service

News.
www.religionnews.com

The Association of Religious Data Archives

Data on church membership in 1980 and 1990 and 2000.
www.thearda.com

The Interfaith Broadcasting Commission

Provides religious news to media sources.
www.interfaithbroadcasting.com

The Pew Forum on Religion & Public Life

Research and news.
pewforum.org

Wabash Center

Links to official religious body websites.
www.wabashcenter.wabash.edu

Yearbook of American and Canadian Churches

www.electronicchurch.org

Glossary of Acronyms

ABCUSA — American Baptist Churches USA
IBC — Interfaith Broadcasting Commission
NCC — National Council of Churches
SBC — Southern Baptist Convention
UMC — United Methodist Church
USCCB — United States Conference of Catholic Bishops
VBS — Vacation Bible School

Clothing Stores

The US retail clothing industry includes 100,000 stores with combined annual revenue of more than $150 billion. Large companies include TJX Companies (TJ Maxx, Marshalls); Gap; Limited Brands; Ross; and Abercrombie & Fitch. The industry is concentrated: the 50 largest companies account for 65 percent of industry revenue.

The industry generally includes clothing accessory stores, but not shoe stores or jewelry stores.

Competitive Landscape

Personal income and fashion trends drive demand for clothing. The profitability of individual companies depends heavily on effective merchandising and marketing. Large companies can offer wide selections of clothing and have advantages in purchasing, distribution, and marketing. Small stores can compete by offering unique merchandise, targeting a specific demographic, providing superior customer service, or serving a local market. The industry is labor-intensive: annual revenue per worker is about $130,000.

Competition includes department stores, mass merchandisers, and Internet and catalog retailers.

Products, Operations & Technology

The clothing retail industry includes stores specializing in family clothing (50 percent of industry sales); women's clothing (25 percent); or men's clothing (6 percent). Stores may also specialize in children's clothing or accessories. Children's clothing stores include infant wear. Accessory stores may specialize in hats or caps, costume jewelry, gloves, handbags, ties, wigs, or belts. Within their specialty, stores typically sell a full range of items including clothing, outerwear, and underwear. Many clothing stores also sell shoes, accessories, makeup, and perfumes.

BUSINESS CHALLENGES

» Demand Depends on the Economy

Consumers buy more clothing when they have more disposable income and the economy is healthy. Under recessionary conditions, clothing stores sales can slow significantly. Economic factors that drive consumer spending, including personal income, consumer confidence, and credit availability, affect demand. When money is tight, consumers often cut discretionary purchases, including clothing and accessories.

» Competition from Mass Merchants

The rapid expansion of mass merchants like Wal-Mart and Target has pressured clothing retailers at the lower and middle segments of the market. By selling stylish clothes and accessories at low prices, mass merchants attract consumers looking for fashion and value. Many industry experts credit mass merchants for creating the "cheap chic" clothing category. These stores also offer one-stop shopping by selling other products besides clothes.

» Dependence on Imports

The large majority of clothes sold in US stores is made abroad by low-cost manufacturers. Tariffs, quotas, foreign exchange risk, and other import restrictions can affect the supply and cost of clothing. Purchasing typically requires long lead times, limiting a company's ability to react quickly to fashion trends. In addition, poor working conditions in factories by some foreign suppliers have generated negative publicity and resulted in limited protests.

The industry includes national and regional chains and independent retailers. While family clothing stores represent half of industry sales, women's clothing stores dominate the retail landscape, accounting for over 35 percent of all clothing stores. Store sizes vary greatly. Boutique stores may be smaller than 2,000 square feet; a typical mall-based store is about 7,000; large off-price retailers are about 30,000. Major companies may have large flagship stores in well-known shopping areas. Most clothing stores are located in retail centers, such as shopping or strip malls, and benefit from customer traffic drawn by larger anchor retailers. Large companies may have outlet stores in more remote locations. Companies measure how effectively they use space by monitoring annual sales per square foot.

Most companies have a staff of buyers who make merchandising (product selection) decisions. Products are introduced by brand representatives or at seasonal meetings with major vendors. Trade shows and fashion weeks, where designers showcase upcoming collections, are an important source of information about new fashions. Apparel buyers need thorough knowledge of consumer and fashion trends to make good buying decisions.

Clothing stores buy from independent manufacturers, although a few chains have a manufacturing arm to produce their own brands. Depending on the depth of merchandise selection, companies can deal with hundreds (some, even thousands) of vendors. Large companies may use buying agents to manage vendor relationships. Some chains, such as Gap, may have significant private-label sales. To produce private-label merchandise, companies design their own clothes and outsource production. Because a large percentage of the apparel sold in the US is imported, the supply chain can be long and complicated. Reacting quickly to fashion trends is challenging, particularly for small retailers with limited influence over their supply chain.

The two major clothes selling seasons are spring and fall. Retailers place orders with manufacturers well ahead of time, build inventory in anticipation of these seasons, and replenish inventory as product is sold. Chains usually receive merchandise at a central distribution facility and deliver goods to individual retail stores with their own fleet of trucks or outside carriers.

Clothing market segments include various styles (casual, contemporary, professional, formal); occasions (resort, special occasion, athletic); and price tiers that target a specific type of buyer. Major apparel brand names, such as Calvin Klein, Ralph Lauren, or DKNY, represent a certain lifestyle and appeal to a distinct customer. Designers often have multiple lines, each representing a particular style within a price tier to appeal to different customer types. Clothing stores select the designer line that best represents their target demographic. Companies must also buy the appropriate mix of sizes and colors to satisfy demand.

An effective store layout positions merchandise to maximize sales. Companies may have flexible floor plans that allow them to reposition products as needed. Clothing stores often display merchandise as coordinated outfits to help customers visualize combinations and drive complementary sales. Many clothing stores aim to deliver a distinct shopping experience or image, through unique decor, merchandise displays, a particular type of background music, or customer service.

Most stores use bar-coded tags on clothing and point-of-sale (POS) registers to track sales. Companies that sell expensive apparel typically use electronic merchandise tags to deter theft. Inventory management programs help companies identify slow- and fast-moving items and can sometimes automatically replenish inventory when levels are low. Real-time access to inventory information is especially important when larger companies need to balance merchandise across multiple stores and warehouses. Many companies use electronic data interchange (EDI) to facilitate purchasing with vendors.

Sales & Marketing

Customer demographics vary according to an individual company's strategy; for example, Gap sells men's, women's, and children's clothing. Gap also operates Old Navy (targeting value-oriented consumers) and Banana Republic (targeting sophisticated consumers). Companies also consider customer lifestyle (casual, working professional, etc.) when developing marketing plans.

Marketing and promotional vehicles include TV, print, and newspaper advertising; direct mail; catalogs; and in-store events. Large chains may run extensive national TV and print campaigns. In-store events include fashion and trunk shows. Locally, clothing stores often use window displays to attract store traffic. Companies may use a signature decor to define store image. For example, Abercrombie stores feature an entertaining but comfortable environment to appeal to college students: TJ Maxx and Marshall's discount stores purposely have a bare-bones look to appeal to value-oriented shoppers. Companies offer loyalty programs, which offer special discounts for frequent or large purchases. Loyalty programs may be linked to proprietary credit cards.

Price markdowns or discounts are a common marketing strategy and often warrant direct mail or advertising campaigns. Clearance sales help drive store traffic and sell excess merchandise. Large companies may perform sophisticated pricing analysis to determine the timing and amount of discounting needed to maximize profitability.

Customer service is especially important in high-end or designer clothing stores, where garments can cost thousands. High-end companies may have an established clientele and rely heavily on repeat business. Sales associates often have personal relationships with loyal customers and contact them when new merchandise arrives. Even mid-price chains may offer personal shopper services to help busy customers and promote related item sales.

Many chains sell merchandise through catalogs and Internet sites. While still a small percentage of total retail clothing sales, apparel is one of the top-selling online categories, according to Forrester Research. Clothing retailers may offer colors, styles, or sizes not available in stores through websites or catalogs. Some companies advertise in-store promotions on Internet sites or run exclusive web-only sales. Emails to website customers are a quick, inexpensive way to communicate promotions.

US consumers buy an average of 67 items of clothing and eight pairs of shoes annually, according to the American Apparel and Footwear Association (AAFA). Designer brand apparel is typically the most expensive. Bridge wear features designer or brand names at moderate prices. Off-price clothing stores typically offer a wide assortment of brands and styles at 20 to 60 percent below standard retail prices.

Human Resources

Most jobs in clothing stores require few skills and are low paid. Wages are almost 40 percent lower than the average for all US workers. Annual personnel turnover in retail is high, over 50 percent, requiring constant hiring and training of new employees. Because of uneven demand during the day, week, and year, many companies use part-time employees. The annual injury rate is 40 percent lower than the US average.

Industry Employment Growth

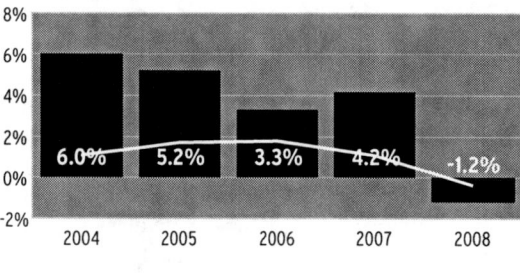

Average Hourly Earnings

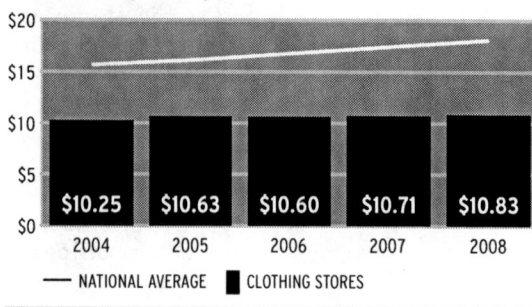

SOURCE: BUREAU OF LABOR STATISTICS

Call Preparation Questions

How does the company protect itself from drops in consumer spending?

Consumers buy more clothing when they have more disposable income and the economy is healthy.

How does the company address competition from mass merchants, such as Target and Wal-Mart?

The rapid expansion of mass merchants like Wal-Mart and Target has pressured clothing retailers at the lower and middle segments of the market.

How does import dominance in the US clothing market affect the company's operations?

The large majority of clothes sold in US stores is made abroad by low-cost manufacturers.

How has growing demand for plus-size clothing influenced the company's merchandising plans?

Demand for plus-size apparel is growing, driven by the American consumer's ongoing struggle with weight.

How beneficial is the company's "frequent shopper" or "loyalty" program?

To improve the loyalty of notoriously fickle shoppers, many clothing stores reward frequent shoppers, typically through discounts or free merchandise.

Web Links

Accessories Magazine

Industry news, trends, and statistics on the fashion accessory segment.
www.accessoriesmagazine.com

American Apparel & Footwear Association

Lobbying association.
www.apparelandfootwear.org

Apparel Magazine

Industry news, trends, and statistics.
www.apparelmag.com

Dept. of Commerce – Office of Textiles and Apparel

Trade statistics and policy.
otexa.ita.doc.gov

National Retail Federation

Legislative issues.
www.nrf.com

NPD

Market research on the fashion industry.
www.npd.com

Retail Council of Canada

News and periodic statistics.
www.retailcouncil.org

Women's Wear Daily

Industry news.
www.wwd.com

Glossary of Acronyms

AAFA — American Apparel and Footwear Association
DPI — disposable personal income
EDI — electronic data interchange
ICSC — International Council of Shopping Centers
ITC — US International Trade Commission
POS — point-of-sale
RFID — radio frequency identification
WTO — World Trade Organization

HOOVER'S TOP COMPANIES

Largest Companies by Sales	($ mil.)
The TJX Companies, Inc.	18,647.1
The Gap Inc.	15,763.0
Limited Brands, Inc.	10,134.0
Nordstrom, Inc.	8,828.0
Ross Stores, Inc.	5,975.2
Abercrombie & Fitch Co.	3,749.9
Burlington Coat Factory Warehouse Corporation	3,424.0
American Eagle Outfitters, Inc.	3,055.4
Charming Shoppes, Inc.	3,009.9
AnnTaylor Stores Corporation	2,396.5

Largest Employers	Employees
The Gap Inc.	150,000
The TJX Companies, Inc.	129,000
Abercrombie & Fitch Co.	99,000
Limited Brands, Inc.	97,500
Nordstrom, Inc.	55,000
Ross Stores, Inc.	39,100
American Eagle Outfitters, Inc.	38,700
Charming Shoppes, Inc.	30,200
Burlington Coat Factory Warehouse Corporation	26,580
The Children's Place Retail Stores, Inc.	23,800

Fastest Growing* by Five-Year Sales Growth	(%)
Metropark USA, Inc.	149.5
Urban Outfitters, Inc.	29.0
Citi Trends, Inc.	28.5
Zumiez Inc.	28.2
Chico's FAS, Inc.	26.4
The Children's Place Retail Stores, Inc.	26.4
Bluefly, Inc.	24.5
Forever 21, Inc.	23.8
Aéropostale, Inc.	23.6
Jos. A. Bank Clothiers, Inc.	19.9

Fastest Growing* by Five-Year Employee Growth	(%)
Aéropostale, Inc.	52.1
Abercrombie & Fitch Co.	35.1
Coldwater Creek, Inc.	27.0
Urban Outfitters, Inc.	25.6
Chico's FAS, Inc.	25.5
Citi Trends, Inc.	24.8
Jos. A. Bank Clothiers, Inc.	21.4
Zumiez Inc.	20.5
American Eagle Outfitters, Inc.	19.7
The Children's Place Retail Stores, Inc.	18.5

Top Public Companies by Market Value	($ mil.)
The Gap Inc.	14,195.6
The TJX Companies, Inc.	12,932.6
Nordstrom, Inc.	8,782.5
Abercrombie & Fitch Co.	7,070.2
Limited Brands, Inc.	6,688.2

* These rates are compounded annualized increases and may have resulted from acquisitions or one time gains. If less than 6 years of data are available, growth is for the years available.

SOURCE: HOOVER'S, INC., DATABASE

Coal Mining

The US coal mining industry includes about 1,000 companies that operate 1,500 mines, with combined annual revenue of $25 billion. Large producers include Peabody Energy, Arch Coal, CONSOL Energy, and Massey Energy. The industry is concentrated: the 10 largest companies hold about 65 percent of the market.

Competitive Landscape

Demand comes mainly from generators of electricity. Profitability depends on efficient operations, as the product is a commodity sold on the basis of price. Small companies can compete if they hold long-term contracts or if they supply local customers. Big companies have large economies of scale in production and distribution. The industry is capital-intensive and highly automated: average annual revenue per employee is almost $300,000.

Products, Operations & Technology

Bituminous coal is the major product but comes in many grades of heat value and with different impurities like sulfur. Low-grade coals, like peat and lignite, have a low heat value, a high moisture content, and high residual ash when burned. Anthracite is the highest-grade coal, with a 95 percent carbon content, but is found in only a few areas in the US. Bituminous coal is the most plentiful, with a moisture content less than 20 percent, and heat values that range from 8,000 to 14,000 BTUs per pound. Coal usually contains various contaminating materials, the most important of which are sulfur and various metals. When coal is burned, any contaminants end up either in the air (sulfur and mercury) or in the ash (heavy metals).

Coal is produced either from underground or surface mines. The Powder River Basin in Wyoming contains the largest surface mines. In underground mines, coal is removed using either room-and-pillar or longwall mining techniques. Surface mines use large machines

BUSINESS CHALLENGES

» Demand Closely Tied to Electricity Generation

Demand for coal depends on demand for electricity, which depends on the health of the US economy. For example, during much of the 1990s, US electricity generation grew at an annual rate of 2 percent, but dropped 20 percent during the last recession. Many new electric plants are built to use natural gas instead of coal.

» Prices Linked to Alternative Energy Costs

Coal prices are linked to prices for alternative energy sources, including oil and natural gas. Coal prices are generally more stable than other prices, but can change 10 percent in a year. To be competitive, coal must be priced less than natural gas, which burns more cleanly.

» Vulnerability to Electrical Industry Regulations

When costly compliance to regulations forces electricity utilities to close plants, their coal suppliers feel the impact. Some older electricity plants function too uneconomically to support the cost of major upgrades in pollution-control technology. If strict air emissions' standards are imposed on older electricity plants, they'd be closed by owners, putting local coal suppliers out of business. The regulation of sulfur dioxide emissions by coal-burning utilities is largely responsible for the greater use of low-sulfur coals. Tighter regulation of other utility pollutants such as mercury, carbon dioxide, and fly ash could severely affect the coal industry.

called draglines to remove the earth and rock (the "overburden") that covers a coal seam, after which giant excavators, shovels, and loaders remove the coal. Many mining operations include preparation plants where the coal is crushed to the proper size for customers, so that the delivered product can be used directly.

Surface mining is cheaper and safer than underground mining. Excavating costs at surface mines are about 30 percent less on a per-ton basis, but yield coal that sells for about half the price of coal from underground mines. Large surface mines can produce up to 100,000 tons of coal per year per employee. Operators sometimes own the land they mine, but most often hold leases that allow them to remove the coal in exchange for royalty payments. Some operators mine coal under contract to the owners. The value of a mine depends on the amount of recoverable reserves it contains.

Because coal is bulky and costly to ship, transportation from mine to customer is an important consideration, as customers usually pay those costs. Since it is cheaper to move electricity than coal, utility companies, the primary coal customer, often locate generation facilities close to mining areas. About 50 percent of coal is moved by rail, while barges, trucks, slurry pipelines, and conveyor belts move the rest. Coal that will be shipped by rail is fed into giant silos, which can precisely load a constantly moving train of 100 hopper cars in less than an hour.

Sales & Marketing

Electric utilities are the primary customer of the US coal industry. Utilities use 85 percent of US coal production to generate electricity. Coal companies also sell coal to industrial customers to produce steam for various manufacturing processes, and a small amount of coal is exported. Coal producers sell a very small portion, about 2 percent, to the steel industry to make coke for steelmaking. Such metallurgical coal has tighter grade specifications than ordinary steam coal. Because about half of all electricity generated in the US is produced using coal, coal producers are greatly concerned about the issues facing the electricity industry, including air pollution and the disposal of coal ash (fly ash).

Most coal is sold directly to end-users through long-term supply contracts, although 20 percent is sold in the spot market and some through brokers. The terms of long-term contracts vary significantly among customers and usually include provisions for price adjustments, coal quality and quantity, and a variety of renegotiation and termination conditions. Mining operators depend highly on their customers, as many sell to just a few large customers, and small operations may sell to just one.

Coal prices are determined largely by the grade of the coal, including its sulfur content and heat value. Although prices are usually quoted free on board (FOB) at the mine, the delivered price to their generation facilities is of greatest concern to electric utility customers. Utilities pay less for high-sulfur coal, because they must incur extra costs to remove the sul-

fur, in the form of sulfur dioxide, from the airstream when the coal is burned. Prices are often quoted in dollars per million BTU because the heat content of coal varies from mine to mine, and even within the same mine. Prices are also quoted in dollars per ton. In 2006, typical FOB spot prices were $60 per ton in Appalachia, $35 per ton in the Illinois Basin, and $10 per ton in the Powder River Basin.

Human Resources

Jobs in traditional underground coal mines require special skills to operate complex mining and extraction machinery. Jobs in surface mines involve operating large pieces of earthmoving equipment. Due to the specialized nature of both types of work, employees are well-paid. The average wage is 40 percent higher than the national average. Many miners, both underground and surface, are members of the United Mine Workers of America (UMWA) union. Mines with nonunion workers generally pay the same hourly wages as union mines. The cost of fringe benefits differs for underground and surface workers: underground mines pay an extra 40 percent of payroll for fringe benefits; surface mines pay 30 percent.

The number of miners has been steadily decreasing for several decades because of more efficient machinery and because a greater proportion of coal is produced from surface mines, which are less labor-intensive.

As more coal mining has moved above ground, the rate of accidents has declined, but safety is still a major issue. The industry injury rate is still almost three times as high as the national average. More than half of accidents are serious, resulting in more than 30 days away from work.

Industry Employment Growth

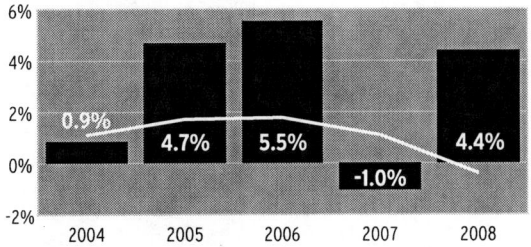

Average Hourly Earnings

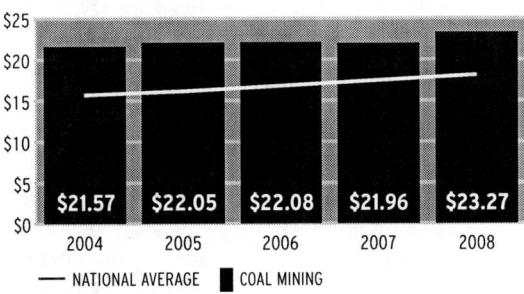

SOURCE: BUREAU OF LABOR STATISTICS

Call Preparation Questions

How does the company protect itself from price volatility?

Coal prices are linked to prices for alternative energy sources, including oil and natural gas.

How does regulation of electrical energy utilities impact the company?

When costly compliance to regulations forces electricity utilities to close plants, their coal suppliers feel the impact.

How is the company advantaged if it cleans coal for electrical customers?

Electricity-generating plants work most efficiently if they burn coal that previously has been precisely crushed and cleaned.

What are the pros and cons of the company expanding into coal gasification and liquefaction?

Although still uneconomical, several demonstration plants are refining the technology of processing coal into cleaner-burning liquid and gas products.

Web Links

National Mining Association

News, issues, statistics.
www.nma.org

Office of Fossil Energy

US Department of Energy site that deals with clean coal technology.
www.fe.doe.gov

Office of Surface Mining Reclamation and Enforcement

US Department of Interior land reclamation information.
www.osmre.gov

US Department of Energy – Coal

Extensive statistics, descriptions, forecasts and price information.
www.eia.doe.gov/fuelcoal.html

Glossary of Acronyms

BTU — British thermal unit
DOE — Department of Energy
EIA — Energy Information Association
ETS — Emergency Temporary Standard
MSHA — Mine Safety and Health Administration
OSM — Office of Surface Mining
PPI — Producer Price Index
PRB — Powder River Basin
PUC — public utility commission
SRF — state revolving fund
SDWA — Safe Drinking Water Act
UMWA — United Mine Workers of America

HOOVER'S TOP COMPANIES

Largest Companies by Sales	($ mil.)
Peabody Energy Corporation	6,593.4
CONSOL Energy Inc.	4,652.4
Massey Energy Company	2,989.8
Arch Coal, Inc.	2,983.8
Alpha Natural Resources, Inc.	2,554.1
Drummond Company, Inc.	1,890.0
Foundation Coal Holdings, Inc.	1,690.1
Patriot Coal Corporation	1,654.6
Cloud Peak Energy Inc.	1,558.7
Walter Industries, Inc.	1,487.1

Largest Employers	Employees
CONSOL Energy Inc.	7,728
Peabody Energy Corporation	7,200
Drummond Company, Inc.	5,600
Massey Energy Company	5,407
Arch Coal, Inc.	4,030
Alpha Natural Resources, Inc.	3,546
Foundation Coal Holdings, Inc.	3,000
Walter Industries, Inc.	2,700
Alliance Resource Partners, L.P.	2,500
Alliance Holdings GP, L.P.	2,500

Fastest Growing* by Five-Year Sales Growth	(%)
National Coal Corp.	196.5
Rhino Resources, Inc.	68.5
Evergreen Energy Inc.	56.4
Hallador Petroleum Company	30.7
Natural Resource Partners L.P.	27.8
Alpha Natural Resources, Inc.	26.4
Patriot Coal Corporation	19.2
International Coal Group, Inc.	19.2
Peabody Energy Corporation	18.4
Alliance Resource Partners, L.P.	16.3

Fastest Growing* by Five-Year Employee Growth	(%)
International Coal Group, Inc.	43.6
Evergreen Energy Inc.	18.7
James River Coal Company	18.5
National Coal Corp.	14.3
Alpha Natural Resources, Inc.	12.4
Cloud Peak Energy Inc.	9.8
Alliance Resource Partners, L.P.	8.7
Westmoreland Coal Company	6.1
Drummond Company, Inc.	4.8
Arch Coal, Inc.	4.4

Top Public Companies by Market Value	($ mil.)
Peabody Energy Corporation	6,066.2
CONSOL Energy Inc.	5,160.1
Arch Coal, Inc.	2,326.7
Massey Energy Company	1,178.3
Alpha Natural Resources, Inc.	1,141.6

* These rates are compounded annualized increases and may have resulted from acquisitions or one time gains. If less than 6 years of data are available, growth is for the years available.

SOURCE: HOOVER'S, INC., DATABASE

Coastal and Great Lakes Shipping

The coastal and Great Lakes shipping industry includes about 850 companies with combined annual revenue of $7 billion. Major companies include Horizon Lines, Alexander and Baldwin, and American Steamship. The industry is highly concentrated: the 50 largest companies account for 85 percent of industry revenue.

Coastal ("coastwise") shipping involves the freight transport of cargo within 20 miles of the Atlantic, Pacific, and Gulf Coasts; between the US mainland and Puerto Rico, Alaska, Hawaii, and other US Pacific Islands; and between US coasts by way of the Panama Canal. Great Lakes ("lakewise") shipping is the transport of freight among the five US Great Lakes and along the Saint Lawrence Seaway System.

Deep-sea shipping to foreign ports and inland transport along US rivers aren't included in this industry.

Competitive Landscape

Demand is driven primarily by the level of petroleum refining, coal use, and need for scrap metal and iron ore. The profitability of individual companies depends on efficient operations and a good safety record. Large companies have advantages in handling a broad range of cargo and diversifying freight and logistics operations. Small companies can compete effectively by transporting unusual cargo and offering excellent customer service. Average annual revenue per worker is nearly $250,000.

Coastal and Great Lakes shipping competes directly against railroads, pipelines, and trucks to transport cargo and bulk commodities.

Products, Operations & Technology

Major services include self-propelled coastal freight shipping (70 percent of industry revenue); barge freight transport along the coasts and on the Great Lakes (15 percent); and self-propelled Great Lakes freight shipping (10 percent).

Major products shipped along US coasts include petroleum products, crude oil, and coal. A fleet of 8,000 US-built and -owned coastal vessels annually ships around 200 million tons of

BUSINESS CHALLENGES

» Coastal Dependence on Petroleum

Although petroleum is nearly 75 percent of all domestic coastal shipping, coastwise petroleum shipments have dropped steadily the past 10 years. Domestic crude oil production peaked in the mid-1980s and fell 20 percent in the past decade. Petroleum companies off the Gulf Coast struggle to compete against Middle East oil. New oil pipelines from Alaska have reduced demand for Pacific Coast petroleum shipping. Hurricanes Rita and Katrina raised new concerns about the long-term health of offshore petroleum shipping. The number of domestic tankers has dropped from 230 in 1985 to around 100 today.

» Great Lakes Shipping Depends on Steel

Coal, iron ore, and limestone, three key commodities in steel manufacture, are around 85 percent of the total traffic transported on the Great Lakes. The Great Lakes shipping industry depends on three industries, steel, utilities, and construction, which account for 90 percent of the total value of shipments, and which depend heavily on the health of the US economy. Economic slowdowns or competition from foreign steel manufacturers could greatly impact industry profitability.

» Vulnerable to Fuel Costs

A 2005 US Maritime Administration (MARAD) survey of Great Lakes carriers ranked fuel costs as the most critical operational concern, well above labor issues, regulatory concerns, and vessel maintenance costs. Residual fuel, the fuel class commonly used to power vessels, has doubled in price since 2004. In the survey, carriers said that higher fuel prices would likely impact future investment decisions.

cargo along the Gulf, Atlantic, and Pacific Coasts. Around 75 percent of all ton-mile trade is bulk petroleum. Common carriers include dry cargo barges, towboats, roll-on/roll-off vessels for unloading wheeled cargo, and liquid tanker barges. Transport modes are evenly split between barge traffic and self-propelled vessels.

Major products shipped among the Great Lakes include iron ore, coal, limestone, cement, scrap metal, and exported agricultural products. Around 85 percent of all bulk cargo shipped is used in steel manufacture. Nearly 500 vessels transport 100 million tons of cargo via the Great Lakes and Saint Lawrence Seaway. The Great Lakes fleet is comprised primarily of self-unloading dry bulk carriers, dry cargo barges, tankers and tank barges, and towboats. Self-propelled vessels transport 80 percent of the total volume of shipments. Cold weather shuts down Great Lakes transportation January through March.

Container ships moving general cargo represent only 5 percent of all coastwise traffic, around 2 million 20-foot equivalent units (TEUs) annually. Container shipping is nearly nonexistent within the Great Lakes: most container ships are too big to pass through the Saint Lawrence lock system.

Dry cargo barges are capable of carrying 1,500 tons of cargo; a typical tow of 15 barges carries as much cargo as 900 trucks or 225 railcars. The average barge trip is 1,250 miles for a coastal route and just over 500 on the Great Lakes, traveling around 10 to 20 knots (12 to 25 miles per hour). Crew size ranges from 20 to 25. Most barges are around 25 years old. Towboats range from 500 to 9,000 engine horsepower; the average towboat has a 2,000 horsepower engine and is 30 years old.

Ships typically travel upbound or downbound in established shipping lanes to avoid collisions. Locks, almost all owned and operated by the US Army Corps of Engineers, raise and lower vessels between waterways of different levels. Vessels are docked, moored, or serviced at commercial facilities classified as either deep draft or shallow. Draft refers to the distance between the waterline and the bottom of the hull. Deep draft waterways are greater than 12 feet deep. Deep draft facilities account for two-thirds of the 6,500 coastal commercial facilities and 600 of the 750 Great Lakes facilities.

Large carriers use logistics systems and software to schedule and route shipments and improve operational efficiencies. GPS provides navigational information to pilots, and radio frequency identification (RFID) tags track shipments. Many companies also provide Web-based access for customers to track shipments and expected delivery times.

Sales & Marketing

Major customers are steel producers and energy, chemical, and industrial companies. Sales are by an internal sales force; ship brokers (intermediaries between carriers and shippers); and freight forwarders (booking agents for shippers).

Major types of marketing include trade publications, public relations, and trade shows. Larger companies use the Internet to post charter schedules and prices. Customer service is available by phone and e-mail. Most contracts are secured over the phone or in person. Large contracts are often a significant portion of a carrier's business, and account managers typically focus significantly on maintaining key client relationships.

Shipping prices vary based upon the time of year, demand, and vessel direction. Fixed-rate contracts range from one to 15 years, with adjustments for fuel surcharges. On the Great Lakes, 80 percent of all cargo is shipped under long-term contracts.

Charter carriers are typically paid daily charter rates based on cargo classification and volume. During peak periods, coastal and Great Lakes carriers schedule daily and weekly trips among major ports. Typical prices for contract and on-demand charter shipping is around 50 cents to $1 per ton-mile. Daily charter rates for tug-tank barges range from $10,000 to $30,000.

Coastal and Great Lakes carriers compete with trucks, railroads, and pipelines. For many large shipments, barges are the most economical form of transportation. On a cost per ton-mile basis, rail can be three times and trucks 30 times more expensive than a 15-barge lakewise tow. However, coastal and Great Lakes vessels can take anywhere from three to 10 days to complete a voyage.

Human Resources

Coastal and Great Lakes shipping wages are over 50 percent higher than the national average. A Great Lakes sailor makes about 25 percent more than the national average. Coastal earn less than Great Lakes sailors, but wages are still nearly 10 percent higher than the national average. Captains typically earn over $50,000 a year and must be licensed by the US Coast Guard (USCG) with accumulated experience or maritime education. Any crew member of a US Merchant Marine vessel over 100 Gross Register Tons must have a Merchant Mariner's document from the USCG. Unlicensed merchant mariners are unionized through the Seafarer's International Union.

Injuries in the Coastal and Great Lakes shipping industry involve primarily sprains, fractures, and physical strains due to overexertion and cargo or equipment mishandling. The injury rate is about 30 percent higher than the national average.

Great Lakes crews work for 60 days straight followed by 30 days off. Crew members generally don't work during winter when lakes are frozen. To compensate for long stretches away from home, carriers offer attractive benefits and retirement packages.

Call Preparation Questions

What trend has the company experienced in petroleum shipping revenues?

Although petroleum is nearly 75 percent of all domestic coastal shipping, coastwise petroleum shipments have dropped steadily the past 10 years.

How dependent is the company on the strength of the steel industry?

Coal, iron ore, and limestone, three key commodities in steel manufacture, are around 85 percent of the total traffic transported on the Great Lakes.

How have rising fuel costs impacted the company?

A 2005 US Maritime Administration (MARAD) survey of Great Lakes carriers ranked fuel costs as the most critical operational concern, well above labor issues, regulatory concerns, and vessel maintenance costs.

Is the company investing in articulated tug and barges?

Articulated tug and barges (ATBs) are more efficient, cheaper, and safer to transport dry cargo.

What opportunities does the company see in using secondary ports to avoid overcrowded large ports?

The nation's largest coastal ports are becoming overcrowded with large international containerships, making smaller ports a more attractive and underused resource for midsized shippers.

Web Links

American Association of Port Authorities

Shipping trade association.
www.aapa-ports.org

Great Lakes Saint Lawrence Seaway System

Nonprofit US and Canadian waterway agencies.
www.greatlakes-seaway.com/en

Gulf Shipper

Trade publication.
www.gulfshipper.com

Lake Carriers' Association

Information about US-flag Great Lakes Shipping.
www.lcaships.com

US Army Corps of Engineers, Navigation Data Center

Data on domestic waterborne commerce and vessels.
www.iwr.usace.army.mil/ndc

US Army Corps of Engineers, Navigation Information Connection

Tracks lock conditions and vessel locations.
www2.mvr.usace.army.mil/NIC2

US Maritime Administration

Oversees US maritime transportation system.
www.marad.dot.gov

Glossary of Acronyms

ATB — articulated tug and barges
MARAD — Department of Transportation, Maritime Administration
MTSA — Maritime Transportation Security Act of 2002
RFID — radio frequency identification
TEU — 20-foot equivalent unit
USCG — United States Coast Guard

HOOVER'S TOP COMPANIES

Largest Companies by Sales	($ mil.)
Alexander & Baldwin, Inc.	1,898.0
Crowley Maritime Corporation	1,620.0
Horizon Lines, Inc.	1,304.3
Tidewater Inc.	1,270.2
K-Sea Transportation Partners L.P.	326.3
Foss Maritime Company	300.0
American Steamship Company	233.0
Rand Logistics, Inc.	94.8
Alaska Tanker Company, LLC	66.7

Largest Employers	Employees
Tidewater Inc.	8,400
Crowley Maritime Corporation	4,171
Alexander & Baldwin, Inc.	2,197
Horizon Lines, Inc.	2,151
Foss Maritime Company	1,200
K-Sea Transportation Partners L.P.	1,044
Moran Towing Corporation	900
Alaska Tanker Company, LLC	400
Rand Logistics, Inc.	281
Crosby Tugs, LLC	250

Fastest Growing* by Five-Year Sales Growth	(%)
Rand Logistics, Inc.	454.9
K-Sea Transportation Partners L.P.	35.9
Tidewater Inc.	14.8
Crowley Maritime Corporation	10.6
Alexander & Baldwin, Inc.	9.0
Horizon Lines, Inc.	8.0

Fastest Growing* by Five-Year Employee Growth	(%)
K-Sea Transportation Partners L.P.	25.6
Horizon Lines, Inc.	3.9
Tidewater Inc.	3.9
Crowley Maritime Corporation	1.3
Alexander & Baldwin, Inc.	0.9

Top Public Companies by Market Value	($ mil.)
Tidewater Inc.	2,883.3
Alexander & Baldwin, Inc.	1,027.5
K-Sea Transportation Partners L.P.	369.6
Horizon Lines, Inc.	108.9
Rand Logistics, Inc.	65.1

* These rates are compounded annualized increases and may have resulted from acquisitions or one time gains. If less than 6 years of data are available, growth is for the years available.

SOURCE: HOOVER'S, INC., DATABASE

Coffee and Tea Manufacture

The coffee and tea manufacturing industry includes about 250 companies with combined annual revenue of almost $6 billion. Major companies include divisions of Proctor & Gamble, Kraft Foods, Nestlé, and Sara Lee. The industry is highly concentrated: the top 50 companies hold over 90 percent of the market.

Competitive Landscape

Consumer taste and population growth drive demand in the consumer sector, while economic growth of businesses, like restaurants and hotels, drives demand in the commercial sector. The profitability of individual companies depends on effectively managing raw ingredient costs, efficient operations, and effective marketing. Large companies have scale advantages in purchasing, distribution, manufacturing, and marketing. Small companies can compete effectively by offering specialized products or serving a local market. The industry is capital-intensive: average annual revenue per worker is about $500,000.

Coffee and tea manufacturers face intense competition from other beverage companies, especially soft drink, bottled water, and juice manufacturers. Although the US coffee market is in long-term decline, the US is the largest coffee consumer in the world.

Products, Operations & Technology

Major products include roasted coffee (70 percent of the market); tea (15 percent); and coffee concentrates (10 percent). Roasted coffee includes whole beans and ground-roasted beans. Tea includes tea bags, and loose and instant tea. Coffee concentrates include freeze-dried, frozen, or liquid concentrates, along with coffee substitutes. Companies in the commercial sector may provide wholesale customers coffee brewing and grinding equipment to maintain product quality, and some own and operate retail coffee shops. Specialty coffees and

BUSINESS CHALLENGES

» Highly Volatile Raw Ingredient Costs

The cost of green coffee beans, the primary ingredient in coffee, can fluctuate greatly, depending on the country of origin and the actions of grower organizations. Green coffee prices can change more than 100 percent in a single year. Trade organizations, like the International Coffee Organization, try to manage supply and control pricing to protect growers. Bad weather, political unrest, and economic issues can affect the price of green coffee.

» Shrinking US Coffee Market

The coffee market has been in long-term decline since the 1940s, due to increasing consumption of soft drinks, bottled water, and other beverages. Per capita coffee consumption in 2004 was less than half the 16 pounds per person consumed in 1946. Production, which declined 35 percent between 1990 and 2005, can be volatile, due to changing consumer tastes and variable demand in the commercial segment.

» Dependence on Economy

Coffee and tea manufacturers depend on a healthy economy and strong consumer spending to drive sales, as consumer spending drives demand for higher-priced specialty products. Companies in the commercial segment depend on the economic health of businesses, like restaurants and hotels, to drive out-of-home consumption. Economic downturns affect both segments, as consumers dine out less frequently and limit spending on pricier goods during tough times.

teas are generally high-quality, premium-priced products.

Coffee production starts with the harvest of coffee cherries, either by hand or machine. Suppliers remove the coffee bean from the cherry and dry the beans to produce green coffee. To produce decaffeinated coffee, companies or processors use water, chemicals, or carbon dioxide to extract caffeine. Swiss Water decaffeination is a chemical-free patented process.

Blending multiple types of green coffee results in different flavors. Roasting machines heat beans through a process known as pyrolysis, producing the coffee's flavor and aroma, and air or water is used to cool the roasted beans. During roasting, the caffeol (oil inside the beans) emerges and the beans turn brown. Roasted beans fall into color categories — light, medium, medium-dark, and dark.

To produce ground coffee, roasted beans go through grinders. To produce instant coffee, extraction equipment converts specially ground-roasted coffee into a coffee concentrate. Next, dehydration through freeze- or spray-drying removes moisture from the concentrate to produce dry instant coffee granules. Manufacturers must add back aroma, as instant coffee loses much aroma during processing.

Packaging uses bags (paper, plastic, or foil) or cans (plastic or metal), and in some cases, single-serving pods meant for use with proprietary brewing appliances. Packaging is about 15 percent of product cost. Companies in the commercial segment may provide private label products for businesses, and offer custom packaging bearing the institution's name. Companies typically have a network of distribution centers or warehouses to store products prior to delivery. Many specialty products require fast delivery to maintain flavor and freshness.

Types of tea include green, oolong, and black. Most Americans drink iced tea brewed from black tea. Herbal teas aren't actually tea, but a combination of leaves, bark, roots, and flowers of other plants. Processing defines different types of tea, as all tea originates from the same plant. After harvest, withering removes moisture from tea leaves, then roller machines break leaves and release key enzymes. Oxidation exposes tea to air to produce different flavors and colors. Screens sort leaves by size. Orange pekoe is the classification for the largest leaves, followed by pekoe, and pekoe souchong.

After processing, manufacturers blend tea to produce a desired flavor and may add or spray on additional flavors, like cinnamon or vanilla. Automated bagging machines produce tea bags for individual servings. Companies sell loose tea for multiple servings. Institutions, like restaurants and food service vendors, use tea concentrates and extracts to produce mass servings. Instant sweet tea typically consists of sugar, additives, and a very small amount of tea.

Companies typically establish contracts to buy tea from foreign manufacturers, importers, and growers; most teas are imports from the

Far East and Argentina. Large companies, like Lipton (Unilever), own foreign tea estates.

Green coffee beans are agricultural commodities. Most beans are imports from countries with tropical climates conducive to growing coffee trees. Companies may use brokers to buy coffee on the open market. Manufacturers may also have direct agreements with farms, estates, exporters, and cooperative groups, especially if the company produces specialty coffee. Companies may hold futures contracts and options to protect against price changes.

The two main varieties of green coffee are arabica and robusta. Manufacturers typically use high-quality arabica beans in specialty coffees, and robusta beans in commercial or instant coffee. Arabica beans generally command a premium price, although blending allows companies to mix in less expensive robusta beans and still produce high-quality coffee.

Electronic sorters remove defective or discolored coffee beans by scanning for particular colors. Coffee roasters, which may be retrofitted with computers to control temperature, may use infrared technology to generate heat. Because fast delivery and product freshness are important, many companies have computerized ordering and inventory management systems.

Sales & Marketing

Typical customers in the consumer segment include grocery stores, grocery wholesalers, mass merchandisers, warehouse clubs, drugstores, and specialty food stores. Customers in the commercial segment include food distributors, institutional food service operators, office coffee services, hotels, restaurants, hospitals, and convenience stores.

Marketing and promotional vehicles in the consumer segment include TV, print, and radio advertising, coupons, direct mail, and sampling. Brand names, like Maxwell House, Folgers, Lipton, and Starbucks, are very important. Trade promotions, through in-store ads or price reductions, are common. Companies may offer products through multiple retail channels to maximize brand awareness.

Large companies use an in-house sales force. Medium and small companies may rely on food brokers, who, because they typically represent many other products, are incentivized using commissions. In the commercial segment, trade shows are especially important, as is superior service, since commercial customers view coffee as a commodity.

Some companies, especially specialty product manufacturers, sell products through mail order or Internet operations to reach consumers beyond a local market area. Websites also allow companies to sell higher priced premium products that don't meet volume requirements for large retailers. Some websites offer automatic reordering and ship products to consumers on a fixed schedule.

The average retail price for a pound of coffee in 2005 was $3.27, according to the International Coffee Organization (ICO). Specialty coffee is generally more expensive than traditional; commercial blend is the least expensive. Retail prices can be unstable due to volatile pricing of green coffee beans. Manufacturers may raise and lower wholesale prices as ingredient costs change, resulting in comparable retail price fluctuations.

Human Resources

Coffee production is highly automated, and most jobs require expertise in roasting and operating machinery. Companies may employ master roasters due to the complexities of the roasting process. Tasters or cuppers evaluate beans and brewed coffee throughout the manufacturing process to ensure a proper roast. Wages are about 25 percent higher than the US average, and fringe benefits about 20 percent of total compensation. The industry injury rate is significantly below the US average.

Call Preparation Questions

How does the company deal with major changes in raw ingredient costs?

The cost of green coffee beans, the primary ingredient in coffee, can fluctuate greatly, depending on the country of origin and the actions of grower organizations.

How has the long-term decline of the coffee market affected the company?

The coffee market has been in long-term decline since the 1940s, due to increasing consumption of soft drinks, bottled water, and other beverages.

How do changes in personal spending and the economy affect the company?

Coffee and tea manufacturers depend on a healthy economy and strong consumer spending to drive sales, as consumer spending drives demand for higher-priced specialty products.

How important are specialty products to the company?

Specialty coffee volume grew over 40 percent between 2000 and 2005, according to the Specialty Coffee Association of American (SCAA).

What is the company's opinion of Fair Trade Certified products?

Fair Trade Certified coffees are a small but fast-growing segment of the coffee market.

Web Links

International Coffee Organization

Governing trade association for worldwide coffee trade — global trade and pricing statistics. www.ico.org

National Coffee Association of USA

Manufacturers Trade Association — industry statistics, historical information.

www.ncausa.org

Specialty Coffee Association of America

Trade association for the specialty coffee industry — statistics for specialty categories.

www.scaa.org

Tea & Coffee Trade Journal

Trade journal — trends, interviews with industry experts.

www.teaandcoffee.net

Tea Association of the USA

Trade association for tea industry — background and statistics on tea.

www.teausa.org

Glossary of Acronyms

ICO — International Coffee Organization
NCA — National Coffee Association
NOSB — National Organic Standards Board
SCAA — Specialty Coffee Association of America

HOOVER'S TOP COMPANIES

Largest Companies by Sales	($ mil.)
The Procter & Gamble Company	83,503.0
Kraft Foods Inc.	42,201.0
Starbucks Corporation	10,383.0
The J. M. Smucker Company	2,524.8
Green Mountain Coffee Roasters, Inc.	500.3
Farmer Bros. Co.	266.5
Nestlé USA, Inc.	—
Sara Lee Food & Beverage	—

Largest Employers	Employees
Starbucks Corporation	176,000
The Procter & Gamble Company	138,000
Kraft Foods Inc.	98,000
Nestlé USA, Inc.	15,500
The J. M. Smucker Company	3,250
Reily Foods Company	1,454
Farmer Bros. Co.	1,233
Green Mountain Coffee Roasters, Inc.	1,220
Community Coffee Company L.L.C.	1,000
S&D Coffee, Inc.	850

Fastest Growing* by Five-Year Sales Growth	(%)
Javo Beverage Company, Inc.	83.8
Green Mountain Coffee Roasters, Inc.	33.8
Coffee Holding Co., Inc.	28.7
Starbucks Corporation	20.6
The Procter & Gamble Company	14.0
The J. M. Smucker Company	14.0
Kraft Foods Inc.	6.4
Farmer Bros. Co.	5.7

Fastest Growing* by Five-Year Employee Growth	(%)
Green Mountain Coffee Roasters, Inc.	16.3
Starbucks Corporation	15.2
The Procter & Gamble Company	7.1
Farmer Bros. Co.	6.7
Coffee Holding Co., Inc.	5.9
The J. M. Smucker Company	3.2
Kraft Foods Inc.	1.4

Top Public Companies by Market Value	($ mil.)
The Procter & Gamble Company	184,419.5
Kraft Foods Inc.	39,450.7
Starbucks Corporation	11,003.1
The J. M. Smucker Company	2,724.6
Green Mountain Coffee Roasters, Inc.	943.7

* These rates are compounded annualized increases and may have resulted from acquisitions or one time gains. If less than 6 years of data are available, growth is for the years available.

SOURCE: HOOVER'S, INC., DATABASE

Coffee Shops

THIS INDUSTRY INCLUDES:

SIC CODES
5812   Eating Places

NAICS CODES
722213   Snack and
          Nonalcoholic
          Beverage Bars

The coffee shop industry includes 20,000 stores with combined annual revenue of about $11 billion. Major companies include Starbucks, Caribou, Coffee Bean and Tea Leaf, and Diedrich (Gloria Jean's). The industry is highly concentrated at the top and fragmented at the bottom: the top 50 companies have over 70 percent of industry sales.

Competitive Landscape

Consumer taste and personal income drive demand. The profitability of individual companies depends on the ability to secure prime locations, drive store traffic, and deliver high quality products. Large companies have advantages in purchasing, finance, and marketing. Small companies can compete effectively by offering specialized products, serving a local market, or providing a personal level of customer service. The industry is extremely labor-intensive: average annual revenue per worker is $40,000.

Starbucks dominates with over 10,000 stores worldwide. Caribou Coffee is a distant second with almost 400 locations. Besides other coffee shops, companies compete with convenience stores, gas stations, quick service and fast food restaurants, gourmet food shops, and donut shops.

Products, Operations & Technology

Major products include beverages and food. Beverages include brewed coffee and tea; espresso drinks (cappuccinos, lattes); cold blended beverages; bottled water; soft drinks; and juices. Food includes pastries, bakery items, desserts, sandwiches, and candy. Many coffee shops sell whole or ground coffee beans for home consumption. Some coffee shops sell coffee or espresso-making equipment, grinders, mugs, and other accessories. Most coffee shops serve high-quality, premium coffee known as specialty coffee.

BUSINESS CHALLENGES

» Volatile Raw Ingredient Costs

The cost and supply of green coffee depends on the weather, political and economic conditions of grower countries, and the influence of groups like the International Coffee Organization. Companies may rely on just a single estate for a particular type of coffee. Coffee shops depend particularly on the supply of higher-priced arabica beans required to produce premium coffee. The cost of dairy products used for specialty drinks is also volatile and can affect profits.

» Competition from Other Outlets

Coffee shops face stiff competition from gas stations; convenience stores (c-stores); fast food and quickservice restaurants; and donut shops. Consumers bought coffee from gas stations and c-stores more than any other outlet, according to a 2004 National Omnibus survey. More gas stations and c-stores are featuring gourmet coffee stations. Fast food restaurants, like McDonald's, have added premium coffee at lower prices. By offering specialty coffee and espresso drinks, Dunkin' Donuts realizes over 60 percent of sales from beverages.

» Dependence on Healthy Economy

Specialty coffee sales depend on personal income and a strong economy. During the last recession, growth of specialty coffee retail sales and the number of coffee shops slowed considerably. Consumers consider specialty coffee and espresso drinks affordable luxuries due to premium pricing. Personal finance experts often recommend cutting back on expensive coffee to save money during tough economic times.

Companies may blend and roast green coffee to produce unique flavors, though some coffee shops use pre-roasted coffee. Grinders reduce roasted coffee beans to particles, and most coffee shops grind roasted beans immediately prior to brewing to ensure freshness. Grind level is matched to brewing time. Brewing equipment controls water temperature and brewing and mixing time. Companies may use water filtration systems to screen out minerals that affect taste. High-quality coffee filters are also important to extract the right amount of flavor from ground coffee. Baristas (or trained coffeemakers) operate espresso machines, which use pressurized hot water and specially ground coffee to produce espresso. Combining espresso with other beverages (like milk) produces specialty beverages like cappuccinos. Companies typically limit how long ground coffee can sit before being served.

Starbucks is the only national chain. Other companies include regional chains, franchises, licensed stores, and independent stores. Franchises allow third parties to leverage a recognizable store name and benefit from economies and efficiencies of the franchiser. Companies may issue licenses to other businesses to gain access to highly desirable retail locations with tenant restrictions, like airports. Some large companies are expanding internationally through licensing agreements.

Coffee shops depend greatly on customer traffic and are most often located in areas with convenient access for pedestrians or drivers. Typical locations include downtown or suburban retail centers, shopping malls, office buildings, and university campuses. Store format and size vary by site, as some locations offer more space than others. Caribou Coffeehouses range from 200 to 3,000 square feet, with an average store 1,200 to 1,600. Some chains offer a kiosk format, without seating, for small spaces like airports and grocery stores. A drive-thru window offers customers convenience and increases off-premise consumption. A comfortable environment is important to provide a positive customer experience and increase store traffic, since many customers consume beverages on premise.

Starbucks and Peet's generate about $1 million annually per store, while other regional chain stores generate about $500,000. Independent coffee shops generate about $200,000 in coffee beverage and bean sales, according to the 2005 Specialty Coffee Association/Gourmet Retailer Specialty Coffee Survey.

Companies may use contracts to buy green coffee (unroasted coffee) from brokers, farms, estates, exporters, or cooperative groups. Coffee shops may also purchase roasted coffee from independent roasters. The vast majority of green coffee is imported from countries with tropical climates. Most companies use high-grade arabica beans, which trade for a premium above commodity prices. Pricing and supply can be volatile due to changing weather conditions, the political and economic climate of grower countries, and the actions of trade or-

ganizations. Coffee shops also buy significant amounts of dairy products from regional suppliers. The price of dairy products is also volatile, and most companies use contracts to lock in pricing.

Companies tend to keep higher levels of inventory for green coffee, because roasted coffee is more perishable. Since coffee quality starts to deteriorate after roasting, shops may discard old beans. Coffee shops must also monitor supplies of dairy products due to limited shelf life. Chains often vary their product mix, depending on store size and location.

Computer systems manage point-of-sale (POS) transactions; credit card processing; and customer loyalty card purchases. Information systems also record employee hours and generate sales reports. Computerized warehouse management systems track inventory of coffee and other products. Some companies use Internet-based systems to link stores and warehouses to ensure rapid replenishment of roasted coffee.

Sales & Marketing

The typical customer for a coffee shop is 25 to 45, affluent, and educated. While baby boomers have driven the success of coffee shops, specialty coffee appeals to a diverse adult demographic, including college students and young adults. Larger companies may also sell coffee beans wholesale to commercial customers, such as grocery stores and restaurants.

Marketing and promotional vehicles include print, radio, outdoor, and T V advertising; direct mail or e-mail; point-of-purchase displays; and customer purchase cards. Brand names, like Starbucks and Gloria Jean's, are extremely important. Community programs, like fundraisers for local charities and schools, help independent coffee shops establish local relationships. Special products available for a limited time, like Starbuck's Pumpkin Spice Latte or Caribou's Amy's Blend (supporting the National Breast Cancer Foundation), increase consumer interest.

Outstanding service and an inviting store environment are extremely important. Coffee shops depend on friendly, knowledgeable employees to develop customer loyalty. Some companies use "mystery shoppers" to evaluate customer service. In addition, companies in shopping malls must offer fast service, since many customers are in a hurry. Comfortable seating and children's play areas encourage longer store visits. Coffee shops may provide wireless Internet access or entertainment to drive store traffic. Positive word-of-mouth is especially important for independent coffee shops with small marketing budgets.

Through the Internet, some companies offer products for retail sale to customers living outside local markets. Information on out-of-market sales can help companies spot areas of strong demand and identify new locations. Companies may also partner with prominent Internet retailers: Tully's Coffee sells products through Amazon's gourmet food site and Starbucks links to Cooking.com. Websites may allow consumers to buy and reload customer purchase cards or offer automatic coffee re-ordering. The Internet allows independent coffee shops with highly specialized blends to reach a broader audience.

Retail prices for coffee shop beverages vary. The retail price for an espresso-based drink can exceed $4. Due to the cost volatility of green coffee and dairy, retail prices often fluctuate. A pound of roasted coffee beans may retail for between $10 and $20. A pound of high-end or "reserve" coffee, like some Peet's coffees, can retail for between $50 and $80 per pound.

Human Resources

Coffee shops depend highly on part-time employees, and most workers require few skills. Many employees make just above the minimum wage, and pay can be significantly below the average for all US workers. Starting wages for Starbucks' employees are about $8 an hour. Some Starbucks' employees are forming unions to negotiate better wages, hours, and benefits.

A typical chain coffee shop may have one manager and 10 to 15 workers; independents have six to seven. New employees may go through training courses and receive in-store training to ensure superior customer service and product consistency. Master roasters oversee coffee roasting to develop trademark blends and flavors. Baristas receive training to operate commercial grade espresso machines used to make specialty drinks.

Call Preparation Questions

How does the company manage fluctuations in raw ingredient costs?

The cost and supply of green coffee depends on the weather, political and economic conditions of grower countries, and the influence of groups like the International Coffee Organization.

What is the company's competitive advantage versus other retailers, like gas stations and c-stores?

Coffee shops face stiff competition from gas stations; convenience stores (c-stores); fast food and quickservice restaurants; and donut shops.

How do economic conditions and personal spending affect the company?

Specialty coffee sales depend on personal income and a strong economy.

What unique drinks or products does the company offer?

Nontraditional drinks can generate customer excitement and seasonal offerings can help boost sales.

How important are sales of products other than coffee?

Coffee shops can drive incremental sales by offering complementary foods, alternative beverages, and related merchandise.

Web Links

Fresh Cup

Trade magazine for specialty coffee retailers.
www.freshcup.com

Gourmet Retailer

Specialty retailer magazine — periodic surveys on specialty coffee retail.
www.gourmetretailer.com

National Coffee Association

Trade association for coffee manufacturers.
www.ncausa.org

Specialty Coffee Association of America

Trade association for specialty coffee companies.
www.scaa.org

Specialty-Coffee Retailer

Trade magazine for specialty coffee retailers — good articles on industry forecasts.
www.specialty-coffee.com

Glossary of Acronyms

FLSA — Federal Fair Labor Standards Act
ICO — International Coffee Organization
NCA — National Coffee Association
NOSB — National Organic Standards Board
POS — point-of-sale
SCA — Specialty Coffee Association

HOOVER'S TOP COMPANIES

Largest Companies by Sales	($ mil.)
Starbucks Corporation	10,383.0
Krispy Kreme Doughnuts, Inc.	429.3
International Coffee & Tea (The Coffee Bean & Tea Leaf)	299.0
Peet's Coffee & Tea, Inc.	284.8
Caribou Coffee Company, Inc.	253.9
Tully's Coffee Corporation	69.1
Diedrich Coffee, Inc.	46.3
Dunkin' Brands, Inc.	—

Largest Employers	Employees
Starbucks Corporation	176,000
Caribou Coffee Company, Inc.	6,616
International Coffee & Tea (The Coffee Bean & Tea Leaf)	4,400
Krispy Kreme Doughnuts, Inc.	4,033
Peet's Coffee & Tea, Inc.	3,678
It's A Grind Coffee, Inc.	3,000
Tully's Coffee Corporation	975
Dunkin' Brands, Inc.	953
Port City Java, Inc.	900
Diedrich Coffee, Inc.	220

Fastest Growing* by Five-Year Sales Growth	(%)
Starbucks Corporation	20.6
Peet's Coffee & Tea, Inc.	18.9
Caribou Coffee Company, Inc.	15.5
Tully's Coffee Corporation	6.3

Fastest Growing* by Five-Year Employee Growth	(%)
Peet's Coffee & Tea, Inc.	20.4
Starbucks Corporation	15.2
Caribou Coffee Company, Inc.	7.3
Tully's Coffee Corporation	0.7
Krispy Kreme Doughnuts, Inc.	0.6

Top Public Companies by Market Value	($ mil.)
Starbucks Corporation	11,003.1
Peet's Coffee & Tea, Inc.	303.5
Krispy Kreme Doughnuts, Inc.	188.9
Caribou Coffee Company, Inc.	29.1

* These rates are compounded annualized increases and may have resulted from acquisitions or one time gains. If less than 6 years of data are available, growth is for the years available.

SOURCE: HOOVER'S, INC., DATABASE

Colleges and Universities

THIS INDUSTRY INCLUDES:

SIC CODES

8221   Colleges, Universities, and Professional Schools

NAICS CODES

6113   Colleges, Universities, and Professional Schools

In the US, nearly 4,000 degree-granting colleges and universities receive combined annual revenue over $200 billion. Sixty percent of industry revenue goes to state-operated public schools, 40 percent to private schools. While some large public universities have more than 100,000 students and budgets over $1 billion, 40 percent have fewer than 1,000 students and annual revenue below $20 million.

About 1,700 schools are publicly funded, another 1,700 are private nonprofit institutions, and 600 are operated on a for-profit basis. Close to 80 percent of students are enrolled in public schools. Mainly because of big state universities, the industry is highly concentrated: 50 percent of all students are enrolled in the 400 largest schools. About 60 percent of students (including graduate students) are enrolled in four-year schools, 40 percent are in two-year (junior or community) colleges.

Competitive Landscape

Demand for higher education services is largely driven by population dynamics, but also by employer requirements. The financial success of schools is closely related to the number of students enrolled, because many costs are fixed. Public schools have the advantage of public funding and are typically larger than private schools. Small schools can compete effectively by providing a superior education.

Products, Operations & Technology

Colleges and universities provide educational instruction leading to the granting of a degree that testifies to the student's competence. Many also provide room and board for students and a variety of other services. Some schools also operate hospitals and research facilities. About 16 million students are enrolled in colleges and universities, many on a part-time basis. US schools annually award 600,000 associates degrees (two-year colleges); 1.3 mil-

BUSINESS CHALLENGES

» Growing Expenses, Government Mandates

After adjusting for inflation, college spending per student rose almost 40 percent in the last 10 years, with the biggest increase in administrative costs. Colleges are spending more partly because of a greater responsibility (legal liability) for students, and partly because of increases in state and federal mandates and programs. Annual spending per student at public colleges is about $20,000.

» Slow Enrollment Pressures Revenue

Total college enrollment in the US is projected to grow only 1 percent annually during the next 10 years; for many colleges, enrollment will be flat or lower. Because enrollment at many colleges won't grow as fast as expenses, revenues from tuition charges, government support, or other sources must rise or financial difficulties will result.

» Public Universities Depend on Government Budgets

Government financial support for public universities depends on government revenues, which can change from year to year. On average, 45 percent of public university revenue comes from government grants, mainly from the states. During the 2001 recession, when state revenues declined, many states cut their support for universities.

lion bachelor's degrees; 500,000 master's degrees; and 120,000 professional degrees.

The operations of colleges and universities involve both instruction and administration. Instruction includes hiring and managing teachers, establishing academic programs of study, and providing necessary educational equipment. Administration includes providing classroom facilities, managing support staff, providing student services such as room and board, and maintaining facilities. In general, costs for instruction are about 60 percent of total costs, but the percent can vary substantially, depending on the services a school provides. To manage expenses, schools pay close attention to the student-teacher ratio — nationally about 15:1 for all colleges (private, public, two-year, and four-year) and the total student-staff ratio — nationally about 5:1.

Colleges and universities have been among the leaders in using computer technology for administrative management functions, instruction, and communications. Many colleges have built campus-wide wired or wireless networks that allow students to sign up for courses, communicate with teachers, get classroom materials, see taped lectures, and communicate with administrative offices and other students. A growing number of schools offer distance learning via the Internet. Schools also use Internet sites for admissions, alumni, and fundraising functions.

Sales & Marketing

Aside from about 200 colleges that draw students from around the country, colleges recruit students mainly from a local or regional area, with much of the recruiting based on reputation. Independently published college handbooks are an important source of information for prospective students, and an important marketing tool for colleges. Measures of academic quality used to compare colleges include incoming freshman grade point average (GPA) and average verbal and mathematics SAT scores. Non-academic programs, such as sports, and financial aid are important marketing tools for many schools. Many schools selectively use scholarship funds to "buy down" tuition for desirable students.

Administrators (except those at 200 elite schools that have more applications than admissions) must attract enough students to cover college costs, which are mainly fixed. Schools closely monitor the number of admission applications; the acceptance rate (how many applicants are accepted); the enrollment rate (how many of those who are accepted actually enroll); the retention rate (how many freshmen return as sophomores); and the graduation rate (how many freshmen graduate). Schools can, and do, work to increase the various rates, both out of concern for students and to keep revenue high.

Human Resources

Faculty are the largest single cost for most schools, even though only 45 percent of staff, on average, are teachers: 65 percent of faculty are full-time teachers, and 50 percent of those have tenure (basically, a lifetime employment contract). Two-year colleges use a much higher proportion of part-time teachers, about 65 percent. The average full-time faculty salary is close to $60,000 (full professors $75,000; instructors $40,000). Colleges' annual injury rate is very low, half the national average.

Industry Employment Growth

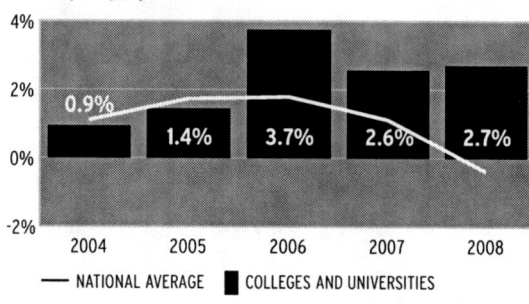

	2004	2005	2006	2007	2008
Colleges and Universities	0.9%	1.4%	3.7%	2.6%	2.7%

— NATIONAL AVERAGE ■ COLLEGES AND UNIVERSITIES

SOURCE: BUREAU OF LABOR STATISTICS

Call Preparation Questions

How does the school manage salary and costs increases?

After adjusting for inflation, college spending per student rose almost 40 percent in the last 10 years, with the biggest increase in administrative costs.

How does the school cope with changing levels of government financial support?

Government financial support for public universities depends on government revenues, which can change from year to year.

What advantages or obstacles do distance learning programs create for the school?

Distance education allows students to attend classes over a computer network without physically going to a campus.

What auxiliary services does the school offer, and with what success?

Because of their reputation and store of expertise, private colleges have opportunities to engage in commercial activities like publishing or consulting to increase revenue, even though there are regulatory constraints on activities funded with public money.

Web Links

American Federation of Teachers

Teacher perspective on higher education issues.
www.aft.org/higher_ed

Association of American Colleges and Universities

Concerned with quality of education.
www.aacu.org

Association of Governing Boards of Universities and Colleges

Management issues.
www.agb.org

Canadian Education Association

News and information.
www.cea-ace.ca/home.cfm

College Board

Administers the SATs. Statistics.
www.collegeboard.com

National Association of Independent Colleges and Universities

News.
www.naicu.edu

National Center for Education Statistics

Voluminous statistics on higher education.
www.nces.ed.gov

US Department of Education

Government announcements, events, and news.
www.ed.gov

Glossary of Acronyms

AFT — American Federation of Teachers
FTE — full-time equivalents
IIE — Institute of International Education
IPEDS — Integrated Postsecondary Education Data System
NACUBO — National Association of College and University Business Officers
NCES — National Center for Education Statistics
NCPPHE — National Center for Public Policy and Higher Education
NEA — National Education Association
SLS — supplemental loans to students

HOOVER'S TOP COMPANIES

Largest Employers	Employees
University of California	127,368
The State University of New York	83,547
The University of Texas System	73,329
The Ohio State University	39,120
The University of Michigan	37,925
Apollo Group, Inc.	36,418
The City University of New York	33,460
The University of Wisconsin System	28,345
University of Washington	28,198
University System of Maryland	28,000

Top Public Companies by Market Value	($ mil.)
Apollo Group, Inc.	10,091.4
DeVry Inc.	3,827.2
Strayer Education, Inc.	3,020.9
Corinthian Colleges, Inc.	989.4
Capella Education Company	979.3

SOURCE: HOOVER'S, INC., DATABASE

Commercial and Industrial Equipment Rental

The commercial and industrial equipment rental industry includes over 8,000 companies with combined annual revenue of about $42 billion. Major companies include United Rentals, Sunbelt Rentals, and Hertz. The top 50 companies account for over 55 percent of industry revenue. About 40 companies have annual sales of more than $100 million.

The industry rents or leases capital equipment to businesses.

Competitive Landscape

Demand is driven by economic growth, particularly in nonresidential construction. The profitability of individual companies depends on the merchandising mix and cost of financing rental inventory. Large companies have economies of scale advantages in buying equipment and having multiple outlets to share equipment. Small companies can compete effectively by providing specialty products for a local market and superior customer service. The industry is capital intensive. Average revenue per worker is about $300,000.

Products, Operations & Technology

Major rental product categories are heavy construction equipment (26 percent of revenue); aircraft (11 percent); computers and peripheral equipment (11 percent); medical equipment (8 percent); and railroad cars (8 percent). Other rental product categories include audio/visual and motion picture and theatrical equipment.

Businesses rent rather than buy equipment due to the equipment's high cost or to meet a temporary business need. Commercial rental companies typically don't operate store-front facilities and are located in industrial zones. Company sites are generally about three acres and have a storage yard for the equipment, a maintenance center, offices, and, sometimes, a showroom. Companies can stock hundreds of

BUSINESS CHALLENGES

» Dependence on Economic Growth

The industrial rental industry depends heavily on the growth of the US GDP, particularly nonresidential construction, which can be cyclical. Rental revenue rises and falls relative to overall economic activity. The late 2000s recession stalled nonresidential construction which led to a slowdown in the commercial rental industry. Because the industrial rental industry has high inventory acquisition costs, decreases in equipment use rates affect profitability.

» Volatile Raw Material, Energy Prices

The commercial equipment rental industry is affected by price increases in raw materials and energy, which drive up prices from equipment manufacturers. Having new equipment for rental customers is important, so as equipment prices rise, costs are either absorbed by lower profits or passed on to customers. Increasing energy costs can also increase equipment transportation costs, which the rental company bears.

» Sensitivity to Interest Rates

Commercial rental companies have substantial interest expense, as they finance the majority of their inventory. Most companies finance equipment through leasing companies, banks, or equipment manufacturers. As interest rates rise, inventory financing costs also rise. Higher interest costs may be difficult to recover, as rental rates are typically fixed over the duration of the contract.

items or specialize in a niche and provide just a few dozen items. Companies use full service leases where they maintain ownership of equipment and service it. Rental companies often deliver their equipment to customer sites and retrieve it at the rental conclusion. Some companies also provide maintenance and supplies for tools and equipment their customers own.

Rental equipment companies buy equipment from a variety of manufacturers. Because commercial and industrial equipment is expensive, companies generally finance inventory with financial service companies. Rental equipment is recorded at cost and depreciated over the estimated useful life, generally one to 10 years. Salvage values are generally only about 10 percent of the purchase price. Some companies have relationships with used equipment dealers to dispose of depreciated equipment, or have their own used equipment business.

Computer systems support inventory management, ordering, bill processing, and equipment sharing among locations. Companies have created websites that both showcase inventory and allow online rentals. GPS is increasingly being used to track large pieces of equipment between customer sites to better schedule service and maintenance.

Sales & Marketing

Typical customers are construction companies, transportation companies, government agencies, and medical facilities. Rental companies have direct sales forces and inside sales teams to generate sales and telemarket.

Major types of marketing include trade publications, telephone books, and online directories. New equipment or rental programs are often introduced at trade shows and industry conferences. Companies sponsor local events where they demonstrate equipment and provide training on how to use the equipment. Many commercial rental companies maintain websites to showcase product inventory. The Internet serves primarily as an advertising medium for the industry, although an increasing number of rental companies offer online rentals.

Commercial equipment costs range from less than $100 for tools to over $250,000 for heavy construction equipment. Rental leases are generally by the week or month, and include insurance and maintenance.

Companies compete with national rental chains, as well as other local competitors. A larger company may have greater purchasing power, enabling the company to offer more competitive pricing than a smaller company. The cyclical nature of nonresidential activity and the seasonality of the equipment rental industry cause demand to be cyclical, as well. During times when demand for rental equipment is low, rental rates become more competitive.

Human Resources

Commercial equipment rental salespeople require training and product knowledge, due to the complexity of commercial equipment and its applications. Other jobs are primarily clerical and transportation positions with no special skills required. Industry wages average slightly higher than the national norm. Total employment has grown the past few years as more companies choose to rent, rather than buy, equipment. Personnel turnover is similar to the national average. Total industry injuries are one third below the national average.

Industry Employment Growth

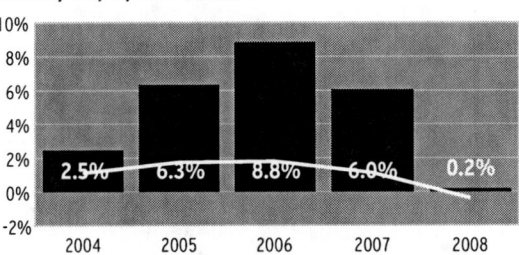

Average Hourly Earnings

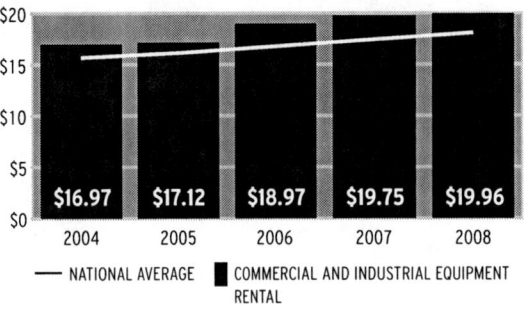

SOURCE: BUREAU OF LABOR STATISTICS

Call Preparation Questions

How is the company impacted by changes in the US economy?

The industrial rental industry depends heavily on the growth of the US GDP, particularly nonresidential construction, which can be cyclical.

To what extent is the company affected by energy price fluctuations?

The commercial equipment rental industry is affected by price increases in raw materials and energy, which drive up prices from equipment manufacturers.

How sensitive is the company to changes in interest rates?

Commercial rental companies have substantial interest expense, as they finance the majority of their inventory.

How important are medical equipment rentals to the company?

Medical equipment prices have increased over the past several years; hospitals and medical offices may be able to save money by renting expensive, high-tech equipment rather than buying it.

Does the company use GPS to track equipment?

Some equipment manufacturers install GPS on large construction equipment that moves to various construction sites, enabling inventory tracking and helping schedule maintenance and service.

Web Links

American Rental Association

Industry news, events.
www.ararental.org

Equipment Leasing and Finance Association

Industry news and information; legislative issues.
www.elfaonline.org

Equipment Rental

Links to manufacturers, distributors, and rental centers.
www.equipmentrental.com

Rental Equipment Register

Industry publication.
rermag.com

Rental Product News

News and articles about the construction industry and equipment.
www.forconstructionpros.com/cover/Rental-Product-News/6FCP

Sunbelt Rentals

Construction and industrial equipment rental company; subsidiary of Ashed Group (UK).
www.sunbeltrentals.com

United Rentals

Construction equipment rental company.
www.ur.com

Glossary of Acronyms

ARA — American Rental Association
ELFA — Equipment Leasing and Finance Association

HOOVER'S TOP COMPANIES

Largest Companies by Sales	($ mil.)
Hertz Global Holdings, Inc.	8,685.6
United Rentals, Inc.	3,267.0
RSC Holdings Inc.	1,765.2
GATX Corporation	1,443.1
TTX Company	1,118.1
ePlus inc.	849.3
Boeing Capital Corporation	815.0
Aircastle Limited	582.6
TAL International Group, Inc.	420.0

Largest Employers	Employees
Hertz Global Holdings, Inc.	29,350
United Rentals, Inc.	10,900
RSC Holdings Inc.	5,014
Sunbelt Rentals, Inc.	3,730
GATX Corporation	2,119
Mobile Mini, Inc.	2,095
TTX Company	1,800
Universal Hospital Services, Inc.	1,318
Southworth-Milton, Inc.	1,300
Aggreko USA LLC	828

Fastest Growing* by Five-Year Sales Growth	(%)
Aircastle Limited	773.7
ePlus inc.	23.2
Mobile Mini, Inc.	23.2
AeroCentury Corp.	22.1
McGrath RentCorp	18.4
CAI International, Inc.	17.0
Aggreko USA LLC	16.1
Willis Lease Finance Corporation	15.2
Popular Equipment Finance, Inc.	14.8
Marlin Business Services Corp.	13.9

Fastest Growing* by Five-Year Employee Growth	(%)
Aircastle Limited	53.3
CAI International, Inc.	15.4
Popular Equipment Finance, Inc.	10.9
Universal Hospital Services, Inc.	9.8
Mobile Mini, Inc.	9.5
Aggreko USA LLC	9.4
Electro Rent Corporation	6.0
Willis Lease Finance Corporation	4.4
McGrath RentCorp	4.1
TTX Company	3.8

Top Public Companies by Market Value	($ mil.)
Hertz Global Holdings, Inc.	5,114.4
GATX Corporation	1,509.0
RSC Holdings Inc.	880.7
Financial Federal Corporation	591.8
United Rentals, Inc.	546.2

* These rates are compounded annualized increases and may have resulted from acquisitions or one time gains. If less than 6 years of data are available, growth is for the years available.

SOURCE: HOOVER'S, INC., DATABASE

Commercial Construction Contractors

The US commercial construction industry includes about 90,000 firms with combined annual revenue around $465 billion. Large companies include Bechtel, Fluor, and Turner Construction. The industry is highly fragmented, with many small companies working as subcontractors on larger projects.

Commercial construction includes apartments, office and retail buildings, hotels, schools, public buildings, industrial and manufacturing buildings, highways and bridges, sewers, pipelines, power lines, power plants, and other civil engineering projects.

Competitive Landscape

Demand depends heavily on the health of the US economy, including corporate profits and local government budgets. The profitability of individual companies depends on accurate project bids and efficient operations. Large companies have advantages in their ability to engage in multiple projects simultaneously and in many types of construction. Small companies can compete effectively by specializing, working in a limited geography, or serving as subcontractors on larger projects. Average annual revenue per industry worker is $290,000.

Products, Operations & Technology

Major industry services are constructing nonresidential buildings, including for industrial, commercial, and institutional use, and heavy and civil engineering projects. Commercial and institutional building construction accounts for 50 percent of industry revenue; heavy and civil engineering construction, for over 40 percent; and industrial building construction, about 5 percent.

Operations focus on bidding for projects and managing project plans, labor, equipment, and construction materials. Larger companies may own much of their equipment and retain full-time construction crews, while smaller firms

BUSINESS CHALLENGES

» Highly Cyclical Demand

Commercial construction depends highly on the health of the US economy, which can be cyclical. Construction of nonresidential buildings declined 25 percent during a recent recession. Demand in specific construction segments, like schools, office buildings, or power plants, can be even more volatile. Many companies try to protect against volatility by working on different types of construction projects or in both the public and private sectors.

» Uneven Revenue, Expenses

Although commercial contractors incur a steady stream of expenses, payments from customers are periodic, including amounts retained until after a project is complete. Bad weather can significantly delay construction schedules, creating uneven cash flow. Prices and availability of major raw materials like lumber, structural steel, and concrete can change rapidly. On large projects, prime contractors handle more complicated cash flows, including progress payments to subcontractors.

» Dependence on Skilled Personnel

Companies often have difficulty hiring enough skilled workers for projects. The complexity of many commercial construction projects requires contractors to use skilled personnel for job cost estimation, project design and management, and actual implementation. Due to the cyclical nature of demand, many companies can't afford to keep a complete full-time workforce and must hire additional workers for each project. Even large construction companies have a relatively small management staff, so the loss of a few individuals can significantly affect projects.

typically lease equipment for a particular project and hire much of their labor on a project basis. Industry metrics include proposal accuracy and project performance-to-plan, including planned labor, time, and budget.

Larger companies typically negotiate an overall contract with a project owner and function as the prime contractor, acquiring equipment and materials, managing the construction schedule, and hiring specialist subcontractors for much of the actual construction work. Any one project can have from a dozen to hundreds of subcontractors who specialize in "ground up" work (foundation, floors, walls, roof) or in more profitable "finish out" work (interior walls, electrical, painting, plumbing, HVAC). Prime contractors and many subcontractors have general contractor licenses. General contractors need special managerial skills or staff to interact with project owners, architects, engineers, consultants, suppliers, accountants, the government, attorneys, insurance carriers, and unions.

On private sector projects, customers typically invite well-reputed contractor firms to respond to a Request for Proposal (RFP). Public projects are usually open to pre-qualified bidders. Three types of contracts are common: guaranteed maximum cost, fixed-price, and cost-plus-fee. Guaranteed maximum price contracts require the project owner to pay for costs, materials, and other incidentals up to a maximum amount, after which the contractor is responsible for additional costs. If the total project cost is less than the estimate, the owner and contractor often split the savings. With fixed-price contracts, the contractor keeps any cost savings and is responsible for cost overruns. In cost-plus-fee contracts, the owner pays all costs, including the contractor's negotiated fee. Most contracts contain penalties for late completion.

Because construction projects are increasingly complex, many project owners prefer to use the same firm to design and build the project, so that accountability lies with one company. The growing popularity of design-build contracts has encouraged many construction companies to develop a design capability or acquire a design firm. In addition to exterior facade and interior layout, the design plan specifies materials, which contractors buy from building supply distributors. Building material prices and availability can fluctuate greatly, making supply contracts an important way to manage costs. Steel prices can be volatile and copper is particularly costly, leading to increased job-site theft.

Commercial construction contractors use technology throughout operations. Industry-specific software supports proposal development, project plans, labor and material allocation, and project performance monitoring. Computerized management reports enable firms, especially large ones, to monitor performance-to-plan daily. Construction machinery and equipment have computerized controls that enable precise functions, such as where to dig or lift and place material. Large firms have extensive, interconnected computer systems that enable employees to collaborate and communicate on projects; in-field handheld devices also communicate with in-office systems. Small firms generally have a PC-based or small, multi-user system.

Sales & Marketing

Typical customers are property developers, other corporations, institutions, and government. Major sales channels are senior executives and sales forces. Contacts with business leaders, architects, engineers, developers, and other construction companies are important sources of leads and upcoming projects.

Major types of marketing include customer visits, ads in magazines and trade publications, and attendance at customer industries' trade shows. Property developers often mention their major contractors in sales and marketing materials for specific developments.

Commercial construction firms use websites for marketing and promotion and supplier portals, but not for sales. Responses to RFPs, however, can be submitted online, as long as both parties use compatible software.

Typical prices for commercial construction projects run in the upper thousands to multi-millions, depending on the scale and scope of the contract. Contractors determine prices based on the type of contract, inherent risks, and costs, including labor, materials, fees, permits, and licenses. The going rates in a locale depend highly on the local economy and the presence of competition.

Human Resources

Nonresidential construction jobs often require special training or experience and, accordingly, pay relatively high wages. Architects and engineers need special degrees and an understanding of steel, concrete, and other commercial building materials. Field workers need to operate large machines like cranes, backhoes, graders, and concrete pumpers. Average hourly wages are about 25 percent above the national wage.

Field work in the industry is relatively dangerous: injury rates are about 40 percent higher than the national average. Fatalities numbered over 450 in a recent year, with about half in building construction and half in heavy and civil engineering construction. Unions are active in many geographies.

Construction work is mostly seasonal, so many companies keep a core of full-time employees and hire extra workers for each project. Workers employed only on a project basis receive no long-term fringe benefits. On average, industry fringe benefits add less than 25 percent to wages.

Industry Employment Growth

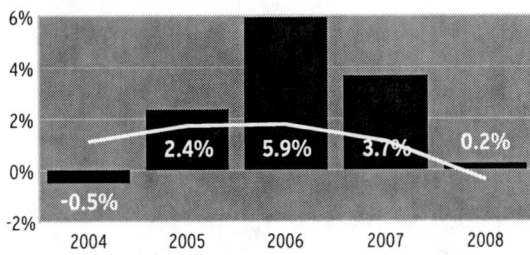

Average Hourly Earnings

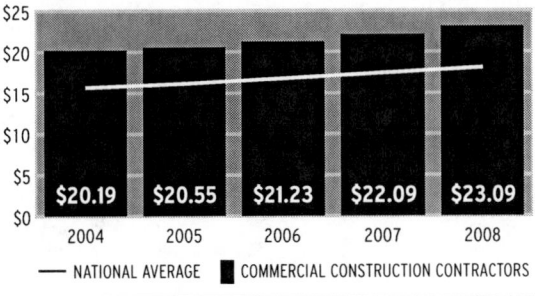

— NATIONAL AVERAGE ■ COMMERCIAL CONSTRUCTION CONTRACTORS

SOURCE: BUREAU OF LABOR STATISTICS

Call Preparation Questions

What strategies does the firm use to protect against changes in construction spending?

Commercial construction depends highly on the health of the US economy, which can be cyclical.

How seasonal or erratic is the company's cash flow?

Although commercial contractors incur a steady stream of expenses, payments from customers are periodic, including amounts retained until after a project is complete.

What challenges does the company have finding qualified workers?

Companies often have difficulty hiring enough skilled workers for projects.

How dependent is the company on projects related to high-growth population segments?

Growth in certain population segments will present opportunities for the commercial construction industry.

Which market segments tend to be most resilient for the company, even when the economy or other construction declines?

Nonresidential construction spending often is positive, even when residential construction spending is negative.

Web Links

Associated Builders and Contractors (ABC)

Legislative issues, PACs, up-to-date news by region.
www.abc.org

Canadian Construction Association

Canadian construction trends, issues.
www.cca-acc.com

Commercial Property News

Commercial real estate news.
www.cpnonline.com/cpn/print

Construction Financial Management Association (CFMA)

Tax and legislative news.
www.cfma.org

Construction Management Association of America (CMAA)

Certification, publications, project leads and referrals, awards.
cmaanet.org

Engineering News-Record (ENR)

News.
www.enr.com

McGraw-Hill Construction

News, forecasts, links.
www.construction.com/NewsCenter

McGraw-Hill Construction Dodge

Statistics, forecasts, news, publications, job project pipeline for members.
www.fwdodge.com

ONCOR International

Office market statistics.
www.oncorintl.com

The Associated General Contractors of America

News.
www.agc.org/index.ww

Glossary of Acronyms

ABC — Associated Builders and Contractors

AGCA — Associated General Contractors of America

CFMA — Construction Financial Management Association

CMAA — Construction Management Association of America

D-B OR D/B — Design-Build

GC — general contractor

RFP — Request for Proposal

HOOVER'S TOP COMPANIES

Largest Companies by Sales	($ mil.)
Bechtel Group, Inc.	27,000.0
Fluor Corporation	22,325.9
KBR, Inc.	11,581.0
Jacobs Engineering Group Inc.	11,252.2
The Shaw Group Inc.	6,998.0
Foster Wheeler AG	6,854.3
McDermott International, Inc.	6,572.4
Peter Kiewit Sons', Inc.	6,200.0
Perini Corporation	5,660.3
Clark Enterprises, Inc.	4,220.0

Largest Employers	Employees
KBR, Inc.	52,000
Jacobs Engineering Group Inc.	43,700
Bechtel Group, Inc.	42,500
Fluor Corporation	41,260
McDermott International, Inc.	28,400
The Shaw Group Inc.	26,000
Turner Industries Group, L.L.C.	15,000
Peter Kiewit Sons', Inc.	15,000
Foster Wheeler AG	13,859
Zachry Group	11,500

Fastest Growing* by Five-Year Sales Growth	(%)
Argan, Inc.	98.0
Perini Corporation	32.7
TIC Holdings, Inc.	27.8
McDermott International, Inc.	23.0
Fluor Corporation	20.5
Sterling Construction Company, Inc.	19.5
Jacobs Engineering Group Inc.	19.5
Parsons Corporation	18.6
Bechtel Group, Inc.	18.4
The Whiting-Turner Contracting Company	16.2

Fastest Growing* by Five-Year Employee Growth	(%)
The Shaw Group Inc.	139.2
McDermott International, Inc.	41.4
Sterling Construction Company, Inc.	28.1
Meadow Valley Corporation	28.0
The Walsh Group	23.3
Foster Wheeler AG	20.1
The Weitz Company, LLC	14.3
Dycom Industries, Inc.	13.7
The Whiting-Turner Contracting Company	10.5
Fluor Corporation	8.8

Top Public Companies by Market Value	($ mil.)
Fluor Corporation	8,146.4
Jacobs Engineering Group Inc.	6,663.9
The Shaw Group Inc.	4,138.3
Toll Brothers, Inc.	3,707.7
Foster Wheeler AG	2,957.6

* These rates are compounded annualized increases and may have resulted from acquisitions or one time gains. If less than 6 years of data are available, growth is for the years available.

SOURCE: HOOVER'S, INC., DATABASE

Commercial Printing

The US commercial printing industry includes about 35,000 companies with over $100 billion annual revenue. Large companies include RR Donnelley and Canadian printer Quebecor World. The majority of commercial printers are small or midsized local businesses that operate one production plant, employ fewer than 20, and have annual revenue under $5 million. Despite continuing consolidation, the industry is highly fragmented: the largest 50 companies account for about 30 percent of the market.

The commercial printing industry includes printing on apparel and textile products, paper, metal, glass, and plastics; it also includes typesetting, platemaking, and book binding. The industry doesn't include book or newspaper publishing.

Competitive Landscape

Demand is driven by advertising and product needs of business customers. The profitability of individual companies is closely linked to effective sales operations. Large companies have scale advantages in buying materials like paper and ink, serving large customers with regional or national needs, and making efficient use of expensive presses. Small companies can compete effectively by offering better local service in a specific product category. Annual revenue per employee averages about $160,000.

Digital technology has changed the competitive landscape of the commercial printing market. Prices for digital color pages are falling below offset printing prices and companies that fall behind in the shift to digital printing are at risk, especially in the pre-media portion of printing.

Products, Operations & Technology

Commercial printers produce magazines, phone books, labels, advertising brochures, catalogs, newspaper inserts, direct mail marketing

BUSINESS CHALLENGES

» Dependence on Business Activity

The volume of commercial printing is closely tied to the health of the US economy, particularly advertising and consumer spending. While advertising is the mainstay of commercial printing, financial printing has also grown rapidly in the past decade. Both advertising and financial activity are sharply affected by the economy and stock market.

» Fluctuating Paper, Ink Costs

Printers feel the impact of cost fluctuations of paper and ink prices, as paper accounts for about 25 percent of printing costs. Paper price increases don't directly affect profits for many printers because they pass paper costs to customers, but lower prices encourage more volume. Environmental issues in paper manufacture may raise paper prices. Ink prices are affected by fluctuations in oil and resin prices.

» Reduced Use of Printed Material

Information distribution via electronic means, such as the Internet and especially e-mail, is reducing demand for printed materials. Company annual reports and prospectuses are now available electronically over the Internet, electronic catalogs are replacing print catalogs for orders placed over the Internet or via phone, and electronic versions of documents that can be stored and viewed on portable devices are becoming more popular.

pieces, corporate reports and other financial printing, training manuals, promotional materials, and business forms. Most commercial printers offer four distinct services: design and other prepress services; actual printing; finishing (including folding, cutting, and binding); and fulfillment, which includes packing, storing, and shipping (often on a "just-in-time" basis). Other services can include packaging, database management, Web design, CD services, training, and consulting.

A typical commercial printer has different presses and binding equipment available to work on various types of jobs. The main printing process used is offset lithography, using either individual sheets (sheet-fed presses) or continuous rolls of paper (web presses). Sheet-fed presses print up to 16 pages of letter-sized product (a 16 page "signature") at a time, at speeds up to 15,000 impressions per hour. Web presses print 32 pages at a time at speeds over 40,000 impressions per hour, and are usually used for production runs of more than 50,000 copies.

Presses usually print in one, two, four, or six colors; some presses can print eight. Digital presses are increasing in use, especially for print runs under 5,000 pieces. Digital technology is also becoming the norm in pre-media services and design.

Paper is the biggest individual manufacturing cost, often amounting to 25 percent of revenues. Printing papers are often coated, and are bought in sheets or rolls from distributors. Many customers provide their own paper. Paper prices can vary significantly from year to year. Commercial printers generally don't keep large inventories of paper as requirements change from job to job; instead, they rely on regional distributors to provide the many varieties and grades. Inks, films, printing plates, and cleaning solvents are other major material costs. The solvents used to clean inks off the presses can be an air quality issue.

Major press manufacturers include Heidelberg and Komori for conventional presses; and Xerox, Hewlett-Packard's Indigo, Kodak's Nexpress, and Punch Graphix's Xeikon for digital. Large ink manufacturers include Sun Chemical and Flint Group.

Printing technology is evolving rapidly. Virtually all prepress work is now done with computers. Digital presses are still expensive, but falling in price and used mainly for smaller runs, but movement to an all-digital printing environment is rapid. Small printers that delayed transforming to digital technology are beginning to do so as the price falls. Digital presses also have the benefit of added labor productivity, reducing the man-hours required for press setup.

Sales & Marketing

The largest single market for printing services is advertising for newspaper inserts, magazines, and direct mail materials. Although some work may be done regularly for large customers under long-term contracts (magazines, product catalogs, and phone books), most is on a project basis, often after a bidding process. Work may be episodic and many printers keep extra presses to meet anticipated peak demands. Marketing is usually by a traditional sales force calling on potential customers.

Commercial printing is a local business. Small printers can compete effectively because the small size and high variability of most printing jobs means that few economies are achieved by having larger presses. The high degree of personal attention that most print jobs require, such as client approvals of proofs and "press checks" during actual printing, means that customers prefer to use a local printer. Price is often a secondary consideration to quality and timeliness. Some types of printing, such as magazines and catalogs with large print runs, are more effectively handled by large printers.

Human Resources

Production personnel in commercial printing plants includes employees with special skills in operating complicated machines, and lower-paid, relatively unskilled workers. Average hourly wages are near the national average. Fringe benefits are about 20 percent of wages. Large commercial printers can have a large number of unionized employees. Although some printing jobs are directly concerned with presses, an increasing number are in prepress design and layout that make greater use of computer skills.

The number of employees in commercial printing has declined in the last five years, as more work is automated. The industry's annual injury rate is comparable to the national average for all industries.

Industry Employment Growth

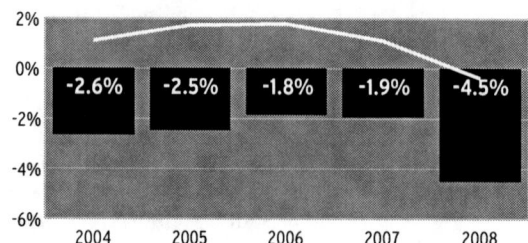

Average Hourly Earnings

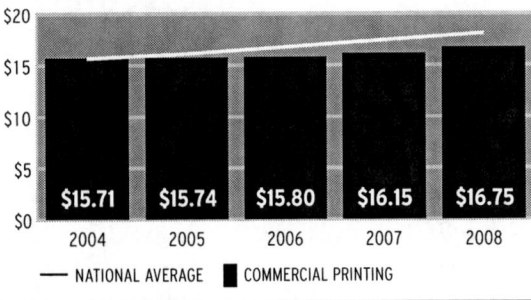

	2004	2005	2006	2007	2008
	$15.71	$15.74	$15.80	$16.15	$16.75

— NATIONAL AVERAGE ■ COMMERCIAL PRINTING

SOURCE: BUREAU OF LABOR STATISTICS

Call Preparation Questions

How does the company respond to fluctuating demand?

The volume of commercial printing is closely tied to the health of the US economy, particularly advertising and consumer spending.

How does the company mitigate increases in ink and paper costs?

Printers feel the impact of cost fluctuations of paper and ink prices, as paper accounts for about 25 percent of printing costs.

How does increased use of digital media affect the company's production volume and sales?

Information distribution via electronic means, such as the Internet and especially e-mail, is reducing demand for printed materials.

What plans does the company have to add new computer or digital technology to improve production and services?

Increased use of digital files and low-cost courier services, and the increased ability of modern presses to accurately reproduce digitally prescribed colors, allow printers to solicit and fulfill orders from distant customers using the Internet.

What non-printing value-added services does the company offer, and to what benefit?

Front-end design services and back-end inventory and distribution services are often as valuable as press operations.

Web Links

Graphic Arts Online

Business magazine for the printing industry.
www.graphicartsonline.com

Ink World

Articles on printing ink and coating industry.
www.inkworldmagazine.com

National Association for Printing Leadership (NAPL)

Newsletters, publications, discussion forums, events, an online marketplace, and advice on sales, marketing, human relations, operations, technology, and financial management.
www.napl.org

National Association of Printing Ink Manufacturers

Convention and general information; publications; issues concerning health, safety, and the environment; two magazines.
www.napim.org

Print Solutions Magazine

Top distributors, news, links, stock watches, archives, and FAQs for form printing entrepreneurs written by the Document Manufacturers Industries Association.
www.printsolutionsmag.com

Printing Industries of America

Industry news.

gain.org

Printing News

News.

www.printingnews.com

Specialty Graphic Imaging Association (SGIA)

Industry news and weekly updates on the advances and interests of digital and specialty imaging and printing.

www.sgia.org

The Association for Suppliers of Printing, Publishing, and Converting Technologies

Conferences, trade shows, education, government affairs, international trade, market data, market research, product safety, standards, publications, and legal issues.

www.npes.org

WhatTheyThink

"Competitive intelligence for printing executives." members.whattheythink.com/results.cfm

Glossary of Acronyms

CAD — computer-aided design

CTP — computer-to-plate

EDI — electronic document interchange

EDSF — Electronic Document Systems Foundation

NPES — The Association for Suppliers of Printing, Publishing, and Converting Technologies

PIA — Printing Industries of America, Inc.

HOOVER'S TOP COMPANIES

Largest Companies by Sales	($ mil.)
R.R. Donnelley & Sons Company	11,587.1
Quad/Graphics, Inc.	2,050.0
Cenveo, Inc.	2,046.7
M & F Worldwide Corp.	1,906.2
Taylor Corporation	1,700.0
Deluxe Corporation	1,468.7
Consolidated Graphics, Inc.	1,095.4
The Standard Register Company	865.4
Bowne & Co., Inc.	850.6
American Reprographics Company	701.0

Largest Employers	Employees
R.R. Donnelley & Sons Company	65,000
Taylor Corporation	12,500
Quad/Graphics, Inc.	12,000
Cenveo, Inc.	10,700
Deluxe Corporation	7,991
Ennis, Inc.	6,256
Merrill Corporation	5,644
Consolidated Graphics, Inc.	5,550
American Reprographics Company	4,400
Bowne & Co., Inc.	3,600

Fastest Growing* by Five-Year Sales Growth	(%)
InnerWorkings, Inc.	91.7
M & F Worldwide Corp.	81.9
Document Security Systems, Inc.	53.7
Schawk, Inc.	23.9
Merisel, Inc.	21.6
Ennis, Inc.	20.5
R.R. Donnelley & Sons Company	19.5
Multi-Color Corporation	16.1
American Reprographics Company	11.0
Consolidated Graphics, Inc.	9.1

Fastest Growing* by Five-Year Employee Growth	(%)
M & F Worldwide Corp.	1,572.5
InnerWorkings, Inc.	90.6
Schawk, Inc.	25.7
Ennis, Inc.	22.2
R.R. Donnelley & Sons Company	16.7
American Reprographics Company	15.8
Courier Corporation	7.3
Champion Industries, Inc.	5.9
Consolidated Graphics, Inc.	4.8
Cenveo, Inc.	1.0

Top Public Companies by Market Value	($ mil.)
R.R. Donnelley & Sons Company	8,148.1
Cenveo, Inc.	938.1
Deluxe Corporation	764.9
Bowne & Co., Inc.	750.7
Consolidated Graphics, Inc.	621.0

* These rates are compounded annualized increases and may have resulted from acquisitions or one time gains. If less than 6 years of data are available, growth is for the years available.

SOURCE: HOOVER'S, INC., DATABASE

Commercial Real Estate Brokerage and Management

THIS INDUSTRY INCLUDES:

SIC CODES

6512 Operators of Nonresidential Buildings

6531 Real Estate Agents and Managers

NAICS CODES

531312 Nonresidential Property Managers

The US commercial real estate service industry includes about 25,000 companies with combined annual revenue of about $30 billion. Major companies include CB Richard Ellis, Jones Lang LaSalle, and Cushman & Wakefield. The industry is fragmented: the 50 largest companies account for one-third of industry revenue.

The industry includes sales and leasing brokers and agents for commercial property — including apartment buildings — and property managers. Many companies combine these functions. Many owners of commercial property perform their own leasing and property management, and aren't included in this industry. Commercial real estate financing is not included in this industry.

Competitive Landscape

Demand, which is driven by the volume of commercial real estate transactions, is heavily influenced by real estate vacancy rates. The profitability of individual companies depends on efficient operations. Large companies have advantages in performing a full range of services in multiple markets. Small companies can compete effectively by specializing in local markets. Average annual revenue per worker is over $200,000 for brokers and agents, but under $100,000 for property managers, reflecting the more labor-intensive nature of the work.

Products, Operations & Technology

Commercial real estate brokers and agents buy and sell commercial real estate property and lease space within commercial buildings. Most owners of commercial real estate property, including individuals, companies, and REITs, don't occupy their property but instead lease space to others.

Property managers are typically involved in the day-to-day operations of a commercial property, such as rent collection, maintenance and

BUSINESS CHALLENGES

» Demand for Services Cyclical

Demand for commercial real estate services can vary sharply from year to year. The volume of brokered transactions and the amount of space under management can fall more than 10 percent per year. Demand for commercial real estate is closely tied to the economy.

» Demand Depends on Local Conditions

Lease and vacancy rates and rents can vary in different markets. Office space may lease for $20 per square foot in Omaha and $90 in New York. Local vacancy rates can double or triple in a year, depending on the strength of the local economy.

» Brokerage Depends on Key Employees

Commercial brokerage depends on the contacts and efforts of individual brokers. Top brokers largely work independently and often take clients with them if they join a different company. Brokerage management consists mainly of recruiting new brokers and keeping top brokers happy.

repair, security, cleaning, trash disposal, providing activities for tenants in common areas, and providing special items such as telecommunications, Internet access, cable, office and food services, and landscaping. The services depend on the type of property being managed. While some services are performed by the property manager's employees, many are contracted out to specialists.

Brokerage, leasing, and property management operations vary according to the type of property. Major types of commercial property are apartment buildings, office buildings, retail space and shopping centers, and warehouses and industrial buildings. Buildings that mix apartments, offices, and retail space are typically more difficult to manage.

Brokers and agents are typically paid a commission that's a percentage of the sales price of a property or of the leasing amount. Property managers are paid a fee that depends on the level of service they provide, but is also related to the amount of space they manage. A large company may have 50 million square feet under management.

Computer technology is used to list available properties and commercial space on the Internet, and is used by property managers to monitor individual leases and manage services.

Sales & Marketing

Typical customers are owners and buyers of commercial real estate, companies that want to lease commercial space, and individuals who want to rent an apartment.

Apartment rental depends highly on direct-to-consumer advertising in newspapers and on the Internet. Leasing commercial space may involve a broker or agent at either end of the transaction, advertising in trade magazines, and using Internet databases similar to residential multiple listing services (MLS).

Buying and selling large properties and getting contracts for managing large properties depend heavily on personal relationships and referrals.

Broker commissions for leasing commercial space are around 5 percent of the entire lease amount, which may cover several years. Lease rates are quoted in annual dollars per square foot of space ($/sq ft).

Human Resources

The brokerage segment of the industry depends heavily on the skills and connections of individuals. Individual brokers and agents are usually paid on a commission structure, which may pay them the majority of the commissions they bring into the company. Wages in commercial property management are slightly higher than the national average.

Industry Employment Growth

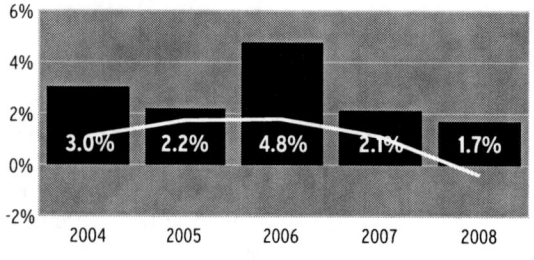

2004	2005	2006	2007	2008
3.0%	2.2%	4.8%	2.1%	1.7%

Average Hourly Earnings

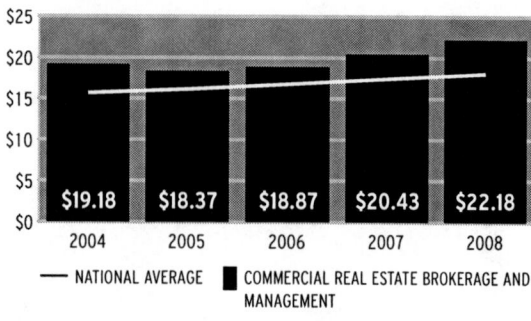

2004	2005	2006	2007	2008
$19.18	$18.37	$18.87	$20.43	$22.18

— NATIONAL AVERAGE   ■ COMMERCIAL REAL ESTATE BROKERAGE AND MANAGEMENT

SOURCE: BUREAU OF LABOR STATISTICS

Call Preparation Questions

How does the company respond to real estate cycles?

Demand for commercial real estate services can vary sharply from year to year.

How quickly can local rents or vacancies change in the company's market?

Lease and vacancy rates and rents can vary in different markets.

How dependent is the company on key employees?

Commercial brokerage depends on the contacts and efforts of individual brokers.

How much does the company spend on Internet advertising?

To reach more customers, commercial brokers use the Internet, which allows potential customers to look at a wide variety of properties.

What new services does the company plan to offer?

Many companies have expanded the services they offer to include brokerage and property management, analytical services, and access to financing sources.

Web Links

Commercial Property News

Commercial real estate news.
www.cpnonline.com/cpn/print

Commercial Property Price Index

Developed by the MIT Center for Real Estate, for apartment, industrial, office, and retail properties.
web.mit.edu/cre/research/credl/rca.html

Construction Spending

New spending on residential and commercial construction.
www.census.gov/const/www/c30index.html

Grubb & Ellis

Quarterly statistics about national and local office markets and other commercial real estate.
www.grubb-ellis.com

MPF YieldStar

News and reports on multi-family housing.
www.realpage.com/yieldstar/news

National Association of Realtors

Legislative issues. Industry statistics.
www.realtor.org

National Real Estate Investor

News, industry rankings.
nreionline.com

Real Property Association of Canada

News.
www.cipprec.ca

Society of Industrial and Office Realtors

Industrial and office market reports.
www.sior.com

Glossary of Acronyms

CBD — central business district
MLS — multiple listing service

HOOVER'S TOP COMPANIES

Largest Companies by Sales	($ mil.)
Realogy Corporation	5,967.0
CB Richard Ellis Group, Inc.	5,128.8
Tishman Realty & Construction	3,560.0
Jones Lange LaSalle	2697.6
Colliers International Property Consultants, Inc.	1,600.0
Cushman & Wakefield, Inc.	242.7
The Inland Real Estate Group of Companies, Inc.	—

Largest Employers	Employees
Jones Lange LaSalle	32,700
CB Richard Ellis Group, Inc.	29,000
Cushman & Wakefield, Inc.	11,000
Colliers International Property Consultants, Inc.	10,092
Realogy Corporation	7,500
Binswanger Corporation	5,200
Newmark Knight Frank	4,500
The Inland Real Estate Group of Companies, Inc.	1,289
Marcus & Millichap Real Estate Investment	550
Studley, Inc.	401

Top Public Companies by Market Value	($ mil.)
CB Richard Ellis Group, Inc.	1,133.3
Grubb & Ellis Company	415.5
ZipRealty, Inc.	53.7

SOURCE: HOOVER'S, INC., DATABASE

Community Colleges

About 1,100 community colleges in the US receive combined annual revenue of $25 billion. Ninety percent of community colleges are publicly operated and 10 percent are operated by private, nonprofit institutions. Slightly less than half of all undergraduate students in the US are enrolled in community colleges. The typical college has 4,000 students and 400 employees, roughly 60 percent of whom are faculty.

Competitive Landscape

Demand for services depends on the demographic composition of the communities that surround a school. Because they are state-mandated institutions, community colleges have some leeway in balancing their budgets. There is no competition among schools, because admission is usually restricted to residents of surrounding communities. A large proportion of students (75 percent in California and Arizona) are part-time.

Products, Operations & Technology

Community colleges offer mainly two-year programs of study that prepare students either for transfer to a four-year college or university, or for direct entry into the workforce; they also offer continuing education for workers. Graduates earn an associates degree or various industry/trade certificates. They are public institutions under state or local control and generally must admit any state resident with a high school diploma. Community colleges usually serve a particular district within a state (California operates 108 colleges in 72 districts), and most of their students live within the district. Some community colleges offer specialized education and some provide training especially for the types of work available in their district. Community colleges differ from four-year colleges in academic quality, program offerings, and finances.

BUSINESS CHALLENGES

» Trouble Funding Budgets

Because community colleges are funded primarily by the states, their budgets can shrink during periods of declining state revenues. Many states struggle with budget deficits, along with political demands to increase funding for community colleges.

» Growing Expenses, Government Mandates

Adjusted for inflation, spending per student at community colleges increased 20 percent in the past decade; the biggest increase has been in administrative costs. Colleges are spending more to manage the same number of students partly because of a greater responsibility (legal liability) for students, partly because of increases in state and federal mandates and programs.

» Faculty Turnover

The average age of American professors is rising, and in the next few years, campuses may experience a surge in faculty retirement. With instructor salaries low, community colleges struggle to attract and keep qualified teachers, which may lead to problems as schools lose experienced senior faculty leaders.

Like other colleges, community colleges hire and manage faculty and support staff, design teaching programs, manage buildings, and may provide non-academic services such as sports. Most don't provide room and board because students typically live at home, near the school. Operations focus on classroom instruction: 45 percent of total expenses are related to direct instruction, versus less than 30 percent at four-year colleges. To minimize expenses, community colleges hire many part-time teachers, typically 65 percent of the faculty. The student/teacher ratio is about 18:1, versus 11:1 at private four-year colleges.

Community colleges provide both academic and occupational courses of study. The leading occupational programs are bookkeeping/accounting, administrative assistant, electronics/computer technician, and nursing. Occupational programs are often designed with the help of skill competencies, lists of the skills that the programs need to teach. To ensure that these skills are actually useful in local business or industry, many colleges get input from industry advisory boards.

Sales & Marketing

Since community colleges must be non-selective about admissions and depend on local political support, they try to enroll the largest possible number of students. Community colleges advertise on radio and TV, and use direct mail and telemarketing. Some use a sales force to offer employers continuing education courses for their workers. Community groups and organizations frequently help enlist new students. PR is an ongoing effort for community college presidents.

To justify their state funding, community colleges need to show accountability in fulfilling their mission. Consequently, they track retention rates (the percentage of students, particularly new students, who re-enroll in the subsequent semester or year); transfer rates (the percentage of students who transfer to four-year colleges); the number of degrees and certificates awarded; occupational success (the percentage of employed graduates); and community service (the success of remedial English and math programs, enrolling minority students equal to their representation in the surrounding community, etc.). Retention rates for freshmen in the California community college system are less than 50 percent.

Human Resources

Salaries vary by state, from a high of $75,000 for a professor in New Jersey to a low of $35,000 in New Mexico. Instructors are generally paid about half as much as professors. Because of the large percentage of part-time employees, the cost of providing fringe benefits is relatively low. Fringe benefits in the California community college system are equal to 20 percent of salaries. As an industry, community colleges' annual injury rates, not surprisingly, are well below the national average.

Call Preparation Questions

What steps is the college taking to control operating costs?

Adjusted for inflation, spending per student at community colleges increased 20 percent in the past decade; the biggest increase has been in administrative costs.

How does the college retain faculty and prevent turnover?

The average age of American professors is rising, and in the next few years, campuses may experience a surge in faculty retirement.

How responsive is the college to the changing needs of local businesses and the community?

States see public two-year colleges as more adept than universities at tailoring themselves to the immediate needs of community businesses and industries, and at adapting quickly to changing priorities.

How does the college market itself?

Collaborating with communities and local businesses can benefit community colleges, especially with state budgets tightening.

Web Links

American Association of Community Colleges

Headlines and legislative news.
www.aacc.nche.edu

American Federation of Teachers

Teacher perspective on higher education issues.
www.aft.org

Association of Community College Trustees

Press releases.
www.acct.org

Community College Week

News.
www.ccweek.com

National Center for Education Statistics

Voluminous statistics on Community Colleges.
www.nces.ed.gov

Glossary of Acronyms

AACC — American Association of Community Colleges

AFT — American Federation of Teachers

CCSSE — Community College Survey of Student Engagement

FTES — full-time equivalent student

IPEDS — Integrated Postsecondary Education Data System

NCES — National Center for Education Statistics

NTS — National Testing Service

Computer and Office Equipment Distributors

THIS INDUSTRY INCLUDES:

SIC CODES

5044 Office Equipment

5045 Computers and Computer Peripheral Equipment and Software

NAICS CODES

423420 Office Equipment Merchant Wholesalers

423430 Computer and Computer Peripheral Equipment and Software Merchant Wholesalers

The US computer and office equipment distribution industry includes about 10,000 companies with combined annual revenues of $180 billion. Large companies include Ingram Micro, Tech Data, SYNNEX, Avnet, and Arrow Electronics. The industry is concentrated: the top 50 companies account for almost 60 percent of industry revenue.

Competitive Landscape

Demand is strongly affected by the level of business activity. The profitability of individual companies depends on merchandising and efficient operations. Large companies have economies of scale in purchasing. Smaller companies can compete effectively by offering specialty products or superior service. The industry is highly automated: annual revenue per employee is about $600,000.

Products, Operations & Technology

Major products include computers, packaged software, copiers, data drives, and printers. Computers account for 25 percent of industry revenue, packaged software for 10 percent, copiers for 10 percent, data drives for 10 percent, and printers for 5 percent. Other products include a large number of peripheral computer devices and supplies, such as networking equipment, scanners, and ink cartridges.

Distributors buy products from equipment manufacturers or importers and resell them to local customers. Distributors are especially important for small manufacturers that can't directly reach end-users. Most distributors operate one or more warehouses, but in some cases merely process orders shipped directly to customers from a manufacturer. Large warehouses exceed 100,000 square feet. Orders may be taken over the phone by a product specialist with technical knowledge, or received electronically over a website or by electronic data exchange (EDI). Companies monitor performance

BUSINESS CHALLENGES

» Revenue Tied to Business Activity

Sales of office and computer equipment depend on a growing economy and rising corporate profits. During the latest recession, industry revenue fell almost 20 percent, after increasing 10 percent in previous years. During economic downturns, customers can delay buying new computer and office equipment.

» Risk of Declining Inventory Value

The value of computer and office equipment distributor inventories can rapidly decrease. Because of innovation, manufacturers frequently improve products and cut prices. Distributors may have price protection agreements with some suppliers, but try mainly to protect themselves by rapidly moving inventory. The monthly inventory/sales ratio for the industry is low. Despite these protections, distributors face a high risk of inventory write-downs as retail prices fall.

» Competition from Manufacturers

Many large manufacturers bypass distributors and sell products directly to resellers or end-users. Only about two-thirds of US office and computer equipment pass through distributors; the other third is sold directly by manufacturers. In general, manufacturers sell to large customers who don't need immediate delivery. Developing Internet sales systems and improving shipping capabilities allow even small manufacturers to sell products directly to users.

measures such as "fill rate" (the percentage of orders filled in a period of time, such as 24 hours) and "stock-outs" (how often ordered products are out of stock). Products typically are shipped using independent shipping companies.

To minimize inventories, purchases are made according to recent sales mix or only when requested by customers. Major suppliers include Hewlett-Packard, IBM, Xerox, Cisco, Seagate, and Microsoft. Trade shows are a major source of information about new products and suppliers. Large distributors may buy from several hundred suppliers and sell to thousands of customers, but many small distributors specialize in the products of just a few suppliers. Contracts with suppliers may designate a distributor as an "authorized distributor" and specify a sales territory, but contracts are often non-exclusive and can easily be canceled. Authorized distributors may provide services such as installation, maintenance, repair, and training for the products they sell.

Computer systems are heavily used. Radio and bar code scanning allows real-time inventory tracking and improves the accuracy of order fulfillment. Information systems also enter documents to streamline accounts payable and accounts receivable processing.

Sales & Marketing

Major customers are retailers, corporate end-users, and value-added resellers (VAR). Large retailers include CompUSA, Office Depot, Amazon.com, and CDW. Resellers include companies that customize standard computers with special components or software. Even large customers, which could buy directly from manufacturers, often prefer to buy from distributors because of the large number of highly technical products they stock, the need for frequent replacement with newer versions, and the efficiency of delivery from a local distributor.

Sales are typically handled by a sales force and may be supplemented by telemarketing. Internet sites are an increasing source of sales and many distributors have websites with both product information and order entry capabilities.

Prices for computers and peripheral equipment decrease steadily and price competition is widespread. Discounts are used frequently to move older merchandise. The price of a typical home computer system has fallen below $1,000.

Human Resources

Because of very large increases in productivity due to sophisticated logistics systems and consolidation in both the retail and supplier segments, employment in the industry has steadily decreased in recent years. Labor productivity doubled in the last five years. Companies generally have about a third of their workforce in each of three functions: sales, administration, and warehouse management and shipping. Wages are well above the national average because of the highly technical skills required to sell and service electronic products. Industry wages are 60 percent higher than the average US wage. The wholesale industry has a good safety record with only two injuries per 100 full-time workers annually.

Industry Employment Growth

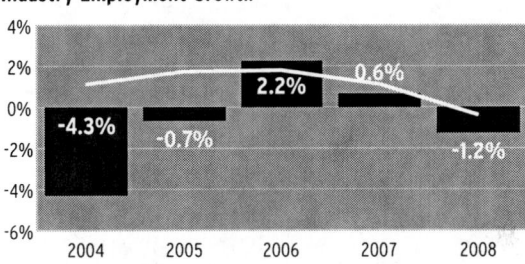

Average Hourly Earnings

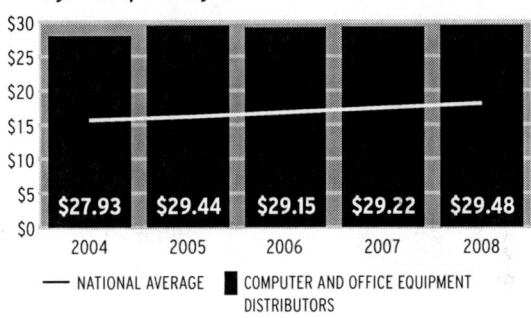

— NATIONAL AVERAGE   ■ COMPUTER AND OFFICE EQUIPMENT DISTRIBUTORS

SOURCE: BUREAU OF LABOR STATISTICS

Call Preparation Questions

How are anticipated changes in the US economy expected to impact the company?

Sales of office and computer equipment depend on a growing economy and rising corporate profits.

How does the company protect itself from falling prices?

The value of computer and office equipment distributor inventories can rapidly decrease.

How much does the company compete with manufacturers for large customers?

Many large manufacturers bypass distributors and sell products directly to resellers or end-users.

What percentage of revenue does the company get from services?

As profit margins for commodity-like computer products narrow, distributors can offer higher-margin logistics and leasing services.

Does the company help customers install computer systems?

For complicated products such as computer networks, some distributors offer technical installation services.

Web Links

ChannelWeb

Industry and company news, trade show news, executive interviews.
www.crn.com

eWeek Channel Insider

Industry news, technical analysis, company updates.
www.thechannelinsider.com

Information Week

Computer industry news and links.
www.informationweek.com

National Association of Wholesaler-Distributors

Common issues facing distributors.
www.naw.org

Glossary of Acronyms

EAR — Export Administration Regulations
SMB — small to medium business
VAR — value-added reseller

HOOVER'S TOP COMPANIES

Largest Companies by Sales	($ mil.)
Ingram Micro Inc.	34,362.1
Tech Data Corporation	23,423.1
Avnet, Inc.	17,952.7
Arrow Electronics, Inc.	16,761.0
SYNNEX Corporation	7,768.2
IKON Office Solutions, Inc.	4,168.3
Software House International	2,330.0
ScanSource, Inc.	2,175.5
MA Laboratories, Inc.	2,000.0
Newegg Inc.	1,900.0

Largest Employers	Employees
Ingram Micro Inc.	15,000
IKON Office Solutions, Inc.	15,000
Avnet, Inc.	12,800
Arrow Electronics, Inc.	12,700
Tech Data Corporation	8,300
CompuCom Systems, Inc.	7,700
SYNNEX Corporation	7,672
Black Box Corporation	5,000
Pomeroy IT Solutions, Inc.	2,212
Newegg Inc.	1,500

Fastest Growing* by Five-Year Sales Growth	(%)
Incentra Solutions, Inc.	97.1
IceWEB, Inc.	57.2
PFSweb, Inc.	36.8
Quest Solution Inc.	36.2
MTM Technologies, Inc.	34.3
MA Laboratories, Inc.	29.1
Newegg Inc.	23.9
ePlus inc.	23.2
ScanSource, Inc.	17.0
Avatech Solutions, Inc.	16.6

Fastest Growing* by Five-Year Employee Growth	(%)
Incentra Solutions, Inc.	78.7
MA Laboratories, Inc.	41.4
SYNNEX Corporation	35.8
Black Box Corporation	23.1
PFSweb, Inc.	18.8
TransNet Corporation	16.7
Newegg Inc.	11.8
Media Sciences International, Inc.	11.8
ASI Computer Technologies, Inc.	8.6
Pomeroy IT Solutions, Inc.	8.6

Top Public Companies by Market Value	($ mil.)
Avnet, Inc.	4,143.5
Ingram Micro Inc.	2,255.4
Arrow Electronics, Inc.	2,247.8
Tech Data Corporation	1,815.0
ScanSource, Inc.	705.1

* These rates are compounded annualized increases and may have resulted from acquisitions or one time gains. If less than 6 years of data are available, growth is for the years available.

SOURCE: HOOVER'S, INC., DATABASE

Computer and Software Stores

THIS INDUSTRY INCLUDES:

SIC CODES
5734   Computer and
        Computer
        Software Stores

NAICS CODES
443120 Computer and
        Software Stores

The computer and software store (computer store) industry includes about 10,000 stores with combined annual revenue of almost $20 billion. Major companies include CDW Corporation and GameStop. Computer manufacturers, such as Apple and Dell, also have retail operations. The industry is concentrated: the top 50 companies have 70 percent of industry revenue.

The computer store industry includes video game stores.

Competitive Landscape

Business growth, personal income, and technological innovation drive demand. The profitability of individual companies depends on effective merchandising, competitive pricing, and reliable service. Large companies have advantages in purchasing, distribution, and marketing. Small companies can compete effectively by serving a local market, offering unique products, or providing superior customer service. Average annual revenue per worker is about $230,000.

The primary competitors for computer stores are consumer electronics stores and Internet and catalog retailers. Computer stores also compete with office supply stores, computer and peripheral manufacturers and distributors, value-added resellers, mass merchandisers, and warehouse clubs.

Products, Operations & Technology

Major products sold by computer stores are computers and peripherals (65 percent of revenue); software (20 percent); parts, repair, and installation services (7 percent); and video recorders, cameras, and electronic game devices (5 percent). Other products include audio equipment, office equipment, and used or refurbished equipment. Companies may also offer technical support and training classes. Some retailers custom build PC systems.

BUSINESS CHALLENGES

» Falling Retail Prices

Rapidly declining retail prices for computers, peripherals, and software can squeeze margins, even when companies account for decreasing manufacturer prices. Intense competition and consumer demand for affordability have resulted in falling price points. In a recent five-year period, retail prices for computers and peripherals decreased over 50 percent, 25 percent for software and accessories. Low retail prices have driven industry growth by making computers and peripherals more accessible to consumers and small businesses.

» Competition from Alternative Channels

Computer stores face intense competition from a variety of sources, including consumer electronic stores, Internet retailers, computer and peripheral manufacturers, and office supply stores. As the general population becomes more computer-literate, customers require less help in making buying decisions, allowing a broader range of retailers to compete. Consumer electronics and Internet retailers are among the top sellers of computers and related products. Manufacturers like Apple and Dell can offer a wider selection of brand-specific products with the latest technology, and typically have highly trained sales staff and strong technical support.

» Keeping Pace with Technology

New product proliferation and short product life cycles challenge the operations of computer stores. The computer market changes constantly due to rapidly advancing technology and evolving industry standards. Companies may have to stock multiple versions of products to maintain compatibility. Multiple product introductions can strain marketing and operational resources.

The industry consists mainly of national and regional chains, along with independent retailers. Both chains and independent retailers may offer a "superstore" format, which can exceed 25,000 square feet. Specialized computer retailers, like video game stores, can range between 1,200 and 1,600 square feet. Computer stores are typically located in high traffic areas within strip malls or indoor shopping malls. As an alternative approach to retailing, Dell Direct stores allow customers to try products and place orders online with the help of a technical salesperson.

Companies may display demonstration merchandise that allows customers to experience products before purchase. Video game stores typically have interactive game stations that feature the latest hardware and games.

While large companies may buy directly from manufacturers, small companies typically rely on distributors. Computer retailers may use distributors, like Ingram Micro or Techdata, to ship products directly to customers. Some retailers are authorized dealers for certain products, and may perform repair or warranty work on behalf of manufacturers.

Inventory size and selection can vary greatly. A computer superstore can offer a wide variety of products and may have as many as 20,000 stock-keeping units (SKUs) in-store, with even more items available through catalogs or online. A video game store may offer between 3,000 and 5,000 products, including a selection of used products. Large retailers may offer private-label products, like computers or accessories. To reduce the risk of inventory obsolescence due to advancing technology and price changes, most large retailers protect themselves by carefully monitoring product movement and taking advantage of limited price protection and return policies offered by manufacturers.

In the video game segment, demand for new titles or hardware systems can exceed supply. New products generate the greatest percentage of sales in the first few days or weeks of release. As a result, video game retailers strive to be first-to-market with new releases. Large retailers typically have highly efficient distribution systems to coordinate product introductions, and tend to receive a disproportionate share of allocations for new items. Retailers may allow customers to place advance orders for big releases to better gauge demand and ensure adequate supply.

Many companies use integrated computer systems to link point of sale (POS); inventory; distribution; and financial systems. Large retailers may have proprietary inventory management systems. Integrating POS and inventory allows for automatic replenishment. Traffic-counting technology helps compare store performance to store traffic.

Sales & Marketing

The typical customer is an adult between 30 and 59; commercial customers include small businesses, state and local governments, and schools. Video game store customers tend to be men between 18 and 34. An increasing number of customers across all industry outlets are women.

Marketing and promotional vehicles include newspaper, print, radio, TV, in-store, and Internet advertising; catalogs; and direct mail. Companies may use cooperative allowances from suppliers to fund marketing programs. Due to the competitive nature of the industry, companies frequently offer rebates and price promotions. Some companies offer customer loyalty programs that discount frequent or large purchases.

Sales associates require proper training, and need to stay abreast of new products and features due to rapidly changing technology. Companies may dedicate sales resources to corporate, government, or education customers. The complexities of computers and related networks make customer service, technical support, and installation extremely important. Companies may offer help through onsite technicians, emergency response teams, call centers, or the Internet.

Many companies have Internet sites that offer product, rebate, and store information. Companies may offer special web-only pricing or products not available at retail locations. Customers may use the Internet to research products and compare pricing. Through websites, video game stores may advertise release dates for new titles and allow customers to place advance orders. Some video stores are exploring online game distribution as an alternative delivery method and a way to compete with Web-based games.

The average retail price for a computer has fallen below $1,000; inkjet and laser printers sell for just over $200. Rebates, price reductions, and package deals can reduce the effective price of computers and related products. Retail prices have fallen steadily and should continue to fall, as electronic components become faster and less expensive.

Human Resources

Workers in computer stores require technical expertise, and wages are almost 40 percent higher than the US average. Many companies employ part-time staff, especially during peak periods. Computer stores typically require employees to attend training classes to fully understand product features and new introductions. Manufacturers may provide education for technical support staff. The industry injury rate is significantly below the US average.

Video game stores typically try to hire gaming enthusiasts and may allow workers to take home and try new games to better assist customers.

Industry Employment Growth

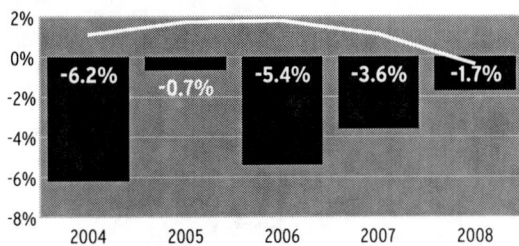

	2004	2005	2006	2007	2008
	-6.2%	-0.7%	-5.4%	-3.6%	-1.7%

Average Hourly Earnings

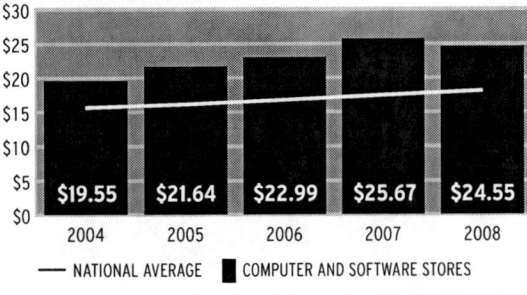

	2004	2005	2006	2007	2008
	$19.55	$21.64	$22.99	$25.67	$24.55

— NATIONAL AVERAGE ■ COMPUTER AND SOFTWARE STORES

SOURCE: BUREAU OF LABOR STATISTICS

Call Preparation Questions

How have retail price trends affected the company?

Rapidly declining retail prices for computers, peripherals, and software can squeeze margins, even when companies account for decreasing manufacturer prices.

How does the company develop a competitive strategy that addresses multiple types of alternative retailers?

Computer stores face intense competition from a variety of sources, including consumer electronic stores, Internet retailers, computer and peripheral manufacturers, and office supply stores.

How does rapid change in product technology affect the company's operations?

New product proliferation and short product life cycles challenge the operations of computer stores.

How has demand for the company's technical services changed in the past few years?

Computer stores can leverage growing demand for technical services, as computers become a more integral part of household and business operations.

What types of end-user education does the company offer?

Offering training classes for beginners and experts can help computer stores provide added value and develop customer loyalty.

Web Links

ComputerWorld

Product news and trends.
www.computerworld.com

Consumer Electronics Association

Industry news, statistics, and research.
www.ce.org

Entertainment Software Association

Trade association for video and computer game
developers — trends and statistics.
www.theesa.com

PC World

Product news and trends.
www.pcworld.com

TWICE (This Week in Consumer Electronics)

News and statistics for computer and consumer
electronics industries.
www.twice.com

Glossary of Acronyms

CEA — Consumer Electronics Association
ESA — Entertainment Software Association
GSA — Federal General Services Administration
POS — point-of-sale
SKU — stock-keeping unit
TWICE — This Week In Consumer Electronics

HOOVER'S TOP COMPANIES

Largest Companies by Sales	($ mil.)
Dell Inc.	61,133.0
Apple Inc.	32,479.0
CDW Corporation	8,100.0
GameStop Corp.	7,094.0
Insight Enterprises, Inc.	4,800.4
Systemax Inc.	2,779.9
Fry's Electronics, Inc.	2,350.0
Newegg Inc.	1,900.0
PC Connection, Inc.	1,785.4
Micro Electronics, Inc.	1,400.0

Largest Employers	Employees
Dell Inc.	88,200
GameStop Corp.	43,000
Apple Inc.	35,100
Fry's Electronics, Inc.	14,000
CDW Corporation	6,900
Insight Enterprises, Inc.	4,763
Systemax Inc.	3,535
Handleman Company	2,600
Micro Electronics, Inc.	2,300
PC Connection, Inc.	1,616

Fastest Growing* by Five-Year Sales Growth	(%)
Apple Inc.	39.2
Newegg Inc.	23.9
Wayside Technology Group, Inc.	22.5
CDW Corporation	13.7
Systemax Inc.	12.4
Dell Inc.	11.5
Insight Enterprises, Inc.	10.7
Zones, Inc.	10.4
PC Connection, Inc.	8.4
PC Mall, Inc.	6.4

Fastest Growing* by Five-Year Employee Growth	(%)
Apple Inc.	27.2
Fry's Electronics, Inc.	19.9
CDW Corporation	18.9
Dell Inc.	17.7
PC Mall, Inc.	13.6
Newegg Inc.	11.8
Zones, Inc.	6.3
PC Connection, Inc.	3.8
Wayside Technology Group, Inc.	3.6
Insight Enterprises, Inc.	1.5

Top Public Companies by Market Value	($ mil.)
Apple Inc.	113,918.9
Dell Inc.	41,921.0
GameStop Corp.	8,456.1
Insight Enterprises, Inc.	883.9
Systemax Inc.	733.4

* These rates are compounded annualized increases and may
have resulted from acquisitions or one time gains. If less
than 6 years of data are available, growth is for the years
available.

SOURCE: HOOVER'S, INC., DATABASE

Computer Manufacture

The computer manufacturing industry in the US includes about 1,500 companies with combined annual revenue of $75 billion. Major companies include IBM, Hewlett-Packard, Sun Microsystems, and Dell. The industry is highly concentrated: the top 50 companies hold more than 85 percent of the market.

Competitive Landscape

Demand is tied to consumer and business income. The profitability of individual computer companies depends on purchasing and production efficiencies, and on technological expertise. Large companies have economies of scale in purchasing and production. Small companies can compete successfully by specializing in certain products or by developing superior technology. The industry is capital-intensive and highly automated: annual revenue per employee is about $500,000.

Products, Operations & Technology

Major products include PCs, printers, monitors, mainframes, servers, and disk drives. PCs, including desktop, laptops, and workstations, account for almost 50 percent of industry revenue. Input-output devices such as printers, monitors, keyboards, and mice account for 20 percent of revenue, mainframes and servers for 15 percent, and disk drives for 12 percent.

The manufacturing process for PCs consists of integrating circuit boards, disk drives, and input/output devices into a final product. Companies typically assemble PCs from components bought from other manufacturers. Key components like "motherboards" are specially made for a particular product, while disk drives and other components may be off-the-shelf parts. Despite automation gains, some assembly work is still labor-intensive. Manufacturers of specialized devices like printers, monitors, and disk drives may also buy some components from outside

BUSINESS CHALLENGES

» Industry Revenue Closely Tied to Economic Growth

Sales of computer equipment depend on rising consumer income and corporate profits. For example, during the last recession, US production of computers fell about 5 percent, compared to 30 percent annual growth during the 1990s. Although consumers and businesses typically replace computers every few years, they can easily delay doing so if finances are weak.

» Customers Expect Lower Prices

Demand for computers and peripheral equipment is related to steadily lower prices; without these continuing price declines, the market would probably shrink. In a recent five-year period, manufacturer prices dropped 35 percent overall, an average 7 percent per year; laptop prices dropped 75 percent.

» Rapid Technological Innovation

The life cycle of computer products is relatively short; better and cheaper machines are introduced frequently, making current models obsolete. Without access to new technology and lower costs, companies quickly are overtaken by competitors. As demand for hardware products shifts or declines, companies can be left with obsolete inventory.

vendors. The manufacture of some products requires highly sophisticated machinery.

Although components and other materials can usually be bought from a variety of vendors, some components are available from just a few suppliers. For example, Intel is the major supplier of processor chips for PCs. Many components are bought from foreign vendors and many US manufacturers have foreign manufacturing operations, mainly in Asia.

Computer manufacturers rely heavily on technology to produce better products and lower costs. R&D spending at large manufacturers generally varies between 5 and 15 percent of product revenue, and can be higher for smaller companies or low for pure assemblers, like Dell. Patent licensing is common and patent disputes frequent. Technological advances can rapidly make products obsolete. The life cycle for a product is often less than 18 months, which is based on a common industry concept called Moore's Law, which states the capacity of a computer chip must double every 18 months to keep up with evolving technology. Moore's Law has held true for several decades.

Sales & Marketing

Major end-use customers are consumers and businesses. Manufacturers sell to consumers mainly through large retailers like Best Buy and Circuit City, or directly through websites. Large business customers are reached mainly through an in-house sales force. Partnerships with software companies, IT consultants, and other vendors can be important to reach smaller business customers. Manufacturers of components rely heavily on a sales force and trade shows.

Advertising is widely used in the industry, especially to reach consumers and business IT managers. Magazine advertising is common. Internet advertising has also become important.

For many years, the industry has been characterized by steadily falling prices. Advances in technology have made many devices cheaper to manufacture even as their performance improves. In the past decade, wholesale industry prices dropped 60 percent.

Human Resources

Production workers account for a relatively small proportion of US computer manufacturing personnel, about 30 percent of total employment. Due to rapid innovation and technological advancement, another 30 percent are engineers, technicians, and other skilled workers. Average hourly earnings of production workers are relatively high, around $23, compared to the average national wage of $16.

Industry consolidation, productivity improvements, and off-shoring have resulted in a 30 percent decline in US employment in computer manufacture in recent years. The industry maintains a very safe work environment, with less than one injury per 100 full-time workers per year.

Industry Employment Growth

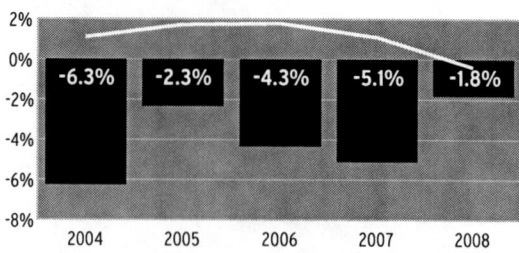

Average Hourly Earnings

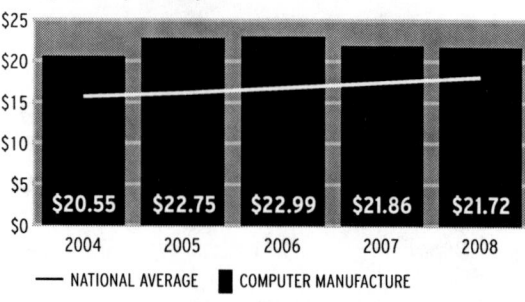

— NATIONAL AVERAGE   ■ COMPUTER MANUFACTURE

SOURCE: BUREAU OF LABOR STATISTICS

Call Preparation Questions

Does the company expect strong US and global demand for its products in the next year?

Sales of computer equipment depend on rising consumer income and corporate profits.

What product price changes does the company expect in the next year?

Demand for computers and peripheral equipment is related to steadily lower prices; without these continuing price declines, the market would probably shrink.

What products does the company expect to introduce in the coming year?

The life cycle of computer products is relatively short; better and cheaper machines are introduced frequently, making current models obsolete.

How do more image-intensive computer applications impact the company's product designs?

Because processor costs are low, designers are producing machines with multiple processors to handle simultaneous tasks such as image processing.

How much of company revenue comes from non-hardware products or services?

As computers become a commodity business with low margins, some manufacturers have expanded into related businesses such as sales of software or consulting services.

Web Links

American Electronics Association

News, governmental affairs, legislative updates.
www.aeanet.org

Computer Business Review

Issues facing the computer and technology industries.
www.cbronline.com

Computerworld

Industry news and information.
www.computerworld.com

Electronics Industries Alliance

Industry and company news.
www.eia.org

InformationWeek

Industry and company news, legislative issues, links, company financial updates.
www.informationweek.com

Institute of Electrical and Electronics Engineers

Industry news and trends.
www.computer.org

PC Magazine

Consumer product developments.
www.pcmag.com

PC World

Trends in personal computing.
www.pcworld.com

TechWeb

Industry and company news.
www.techweb.com

The Computer Information Center

List of sources.
www.compinfo-center.com

Glossary of Acronyms

IT — information technology
OEM — original equipment manufacturer
SSD — solid state drive

HOOVER'S TOP COMPANIES

Largest Companies by Sales	($ mil.)
Hewlett-Packard Company	118,364.0
International Business Machines Corporation	103,630.0
Dell Inc.	61,133.0
Apple Inc.	32,479.0
Xerox Corporation	17,608.0
Lenovo Group Limited	16,352.0
EMC Corporation	14,876.2
Sun Microsystems, Inc.	13,880.0
Seagate Technology LLC	12,708.0
Western Digital Corporation	8,074.0

Largest Employers	Employees
International Business Machines Corporation	426,969
Hewlett-Packard Company	321,000
Dell Inc.	88,200
Xerox Corporation	57,400
Seagate Technology LLC	54,000
EMC Corporation	37,700
Apple Inc.	35,100
Sun Microsystems, Inc.	34,900
Western Digital Corporation	29,572
NCR Corporation	23,200

Fastest Growing* by Five-Year Sales Growth	(%)
Franklin Wireless Corp.	387.2
Data Domain, Inc.	330.2
MPC Corporation	249.5
Isilon Systems, Inc.	144.8
Compellent Technologies, Inc.	119.7
3PAR Inc.	70.5
InPlay Technologies, Inc.	69.8
Protocall Technologies Incorporated	65.1
Sierra Nevada Corporation	62.6
CopyTele, Inc.	60.0

Fastest Growing* by Five-Year Employee Growth	(%)
Data Domain, Inc.	121.0
Avocent Corporation	80.2
Brocade Communications Systems, Inc.	64.4
Rackable Systems, Inc.	64.4
Network Engines, Inc.	62.1
Blue Coat Systems, Inc.	39.6
SanDisk Corporation	34.7
Alanco Technologies, Inc.	33.6
Super Micro Computer, Inc.	32.6
eMagin Corporation	32.1

Top Public Companies by Market Value	($ mil.)
Apple Inc.	113,918.9
International Business Machines Corporation	112,698.3
Hewlett-Packard Company	92,446.2
Dell Inc.	41,921.0
EMC Corporation	21,075.5

* These rates are compounded annualized increases and may have resulted from acquisitions or one time gains. If less than 6 years of data are available, growth is for the years available.

SOURCE: HOOVER'S, INC., DATABASE

Computer Networking Equipment Manufacturing

THIS INDUSTRY INCLUDES:

SIC CODES
3661   Telephone and Telegraph Apparatus

NAICS CODES
334210   Telephone Apparatus Manufacturing

The computer networking equipment industry includes about 1,000 companies with combined annual revenue of $60 billion. Major US companies include Cisco Systems, Juniper Networks, Extreme Networks, and Foundry Networks. Large foreign competitors in the US market include Nortel, Fujitsu, NEC, Alcatel-Lucent, and Siemens. The industry is concentrated: the 10 largest companies hold 50 percent of the market.

Competitive Landscape

Demand is driven by economic growth as enterprises and service providers expand networks to meet increasing user needs, and by the superior performance of new equipment, which encourages replacement of existing equipment. Profitability of individual companies depends on timely development and delivery of products in high volumes for large customers. Small companies can successfully compete by designing and developing products that meet highly specialized needs. The industry is capital-intensive: average annual revenue per employee is about $500,000.

The US telecommunication industry is in transition: the current telephone backbone network is being converted from circuit-switched to multimedia networks combining voice, data, and video over high-speed links. This transition will require replacing a substantial portion of equipment, presenting an opportunity for all equipment vendors.

Products, Operations & Technology

Major products of networking equipment manufacturers are switches, routers, and network control equipment interconnected using fiber optic and high-speed wiring. Major services of equipment suppliers include system and network design, software development, installation, monitoring, and maintenance. Other hardware and software products include intru-

BUSINESS CHALLENGES

» Growth Raising Internet Architectural Issues

As potentially billions of new entities are added to the Internet, architectural and topological issues are becoming more of a concern. Older routers connecting sub-networks are approaching their table limits on the number of entities, and current growth rates could press even the most technologically advanced routers. While the Internet Engineering Task Force (IETF) is searching for architectural solutions, large customers are reluctant to invest in new equipment that may have to be replaced near-term.

» Competition from Foreign Suppliers

Because telecom services are being standardized throughout the world, equipment makers for foreign markets can also sell their products to US service providers. Many of the largest equipment competitors in the US market are foreign, including Nortel, Alcatel, Nokia, NEC, and Siemens. Many foreign companies target the US because it's the largest telecom market in the world.

» Availability of Engineering Talent

Domestically, qualified design engineers, particularly those with advanced degrees, are in short supply. Many companies try to get a sufficient number of H1-B visas for foreign technology professionals to live and work domestically. The annual quota of 65,000 H1-B visas was reached four months before the start of fiscal year 2007. While Congress debates increasing the number of visas, companies are relocating design facilities offshore to take advantage of available foreign engineers.

sion prevention devices, remote termination equipment, firewalls, and network appliances.

Most major computer networking equipment companies have outsourced volume production of standard products to contract manufacturers. Equipment companies specialize in system design and software development; they maintain limited production facilities to produce the initial versions of new products for in-house testing and development. Initial versions are built using standard components to verify design. During final development, some product functions may be converted to application specific integrated circuits (ASICs) to improve performance. Design and quality-control teams from the networking equipment company, located at the contract manufacturer's facilities, resolve manufacturing issues, ensure integration of design changes, and oversee testing and acceptance prior to shipment.

Since components, such as ASICs and circuit boards, may be manufactured in one location and shipped to the final assembly plant, manufacturing locations are chosen to minimize transportation and labor costs. Volume manufacture is highly automated, but requires skilled labor for final assembly, testing, and quality assurance. To minimize equipment failures at initial installation and operation, large complex equipment is operated at higher temperatures during final test to eliminate marginal components.

Computer networking equipment companies use CAD systems extensively, and most use enterprise resource planning (ERP) systems. Companies also have high-speed, high-capacity communication systems to connect design, manufacturing, sales, and administrative facilities. These systems allow designers to communicate changes directly to the manufacturer's computer automated manufacturing systems (CAM). Many companies also have logistics and supply chain management systems.

Sales & Marketing

Typical customers are business enterprises; communication service providers (including common carriers); and federal, state, and local governments. Computer networking companies use a direct sales force to reach large customers and value-added resellers to reach small and medium. Some companies also sell through other equipment vendors or wholesale and retail outlets.

Marketing to businesses consists primarily of advertising in trade magazines and participating in industry trade shows. Larger companies build brand identities by acquiring stadium naming rights, sponsoring golf tournaments, and advertising on TV.

Equipment is sold based on performance, standards compliance, reliability, maintainability, and price. Since customers depend highly on their networks, stringent availability requirements are written into most contracts. If a system fails, it must be repaired or replaced within a defined interval. To meet customer needs for network availability, most equipment vendors maintain large customer service forces and multiple supply depots. Vendors also offer maintenance certification training for resellers and customer personnel.

Depending on configuration, switches cost from $1,000 to more than $20,000, and routers from $25,000 to over $100,000. Generally, a new network for a large enterprise will cost in the millions, including hardware, software, installation testing, and warranty.

Human Resources

Networking equipment manufacturers depend heavily on a workforce of highly educated and well-paid engineers to design products, manage manufacturing, and help with sales. Technicians who assemble complicated products like telephone switches also require special training and have high earnings. Overall, industry wages are 15 percent above the national average. Except for some equipment installers, the industry isn't unionized.

Overall employment in the industry has been declining as manufacturing is offshored and design and support facilities relocated. Domestically, design engineers, particularly at the masters and doctoral levels, are in short supply, leading companies to hire foreign nationals.

Call Preparation Questions

How do potential architectural limits of the Internet affect the company's growth outlook?

As potentially billions of new entities are added to the Internet, architectural and topological issues are becoming more of a concern.

How do foreign competitors threaten the company's US business?

Because telecom services are being standardized throughout the world, equipment makers for foreign markets can also sell their products to US service providers.

How is the company challenged by hiring qualified engineers?

Domestically, qualified design engineers, particularly those with advanced degrees, are in short supply.

What opportunities does the company see in special products to facilitate network protocol transitions?

As communication networks transition from current technologies and protocols to Ethernet and then to the next generation of networks, network operators will require transition products to help interconnect users on both old and new networks.

Web Links

ComputerWorld

News from an IT viewpoint, including networking.
www.computerworld.com

eWeek

News from an Internet perspective.
www.eweek.com

Federal Communications Commission FCC

Regulatory actions and policy.
www.fcc.gov

National Cable & Telecommunications Association

Good industry overview, industry issues.
www.ncta.com

NetworkWorld.com

News and events in the industry.
www.networkworld.com

Telecommunications Industry Association

Industry statistics, policy issues.
www.tiaonline.org

Telephony Online

Industry news.
telephonyonline.com

Glossary of Acronyms

ASIC — application specific integrated circuit
BGP — border gateway protocol
CAM — computer automated manufacturing
ERP — enterprise resource planning
FMC — fixed mobile convergence
ICANN — Internet Corporation for Assigned Names and Numbers
IMS — IP multimedia systems
IP — Internet protocol
MPLS — multi-protocol label switching
NEBS — network equipment building standards
NGN — new generation network
PBT — provider backbone transport
VoIP — voice over Internet protocol
WAN — wide area network

HOOVER'S TOP COMPANIES

Largest Companies by Sales	($ mil.)
Cisco Systems, Inc.	39,540.0
Juniper Networks, Inc.	3,572.4
ADC Telecommunications, Inc.	1,456.4
3Com Corporation	1,294.9
ARRIS Group, Inc.	1,144.6
Ciena Corporation	902.5
Avocent Corporation	657.1
Infinera Corporation	519.2
ADTRAN, Inc.	500.7

Largest Employers	Employees
Cisco Systems, Inc.	66,129
ADC Telecommunications, Inc.	9,050
Juniper Networks, Inc.	5,879
3Com Corporation	5,572
Oplink Communications, Inc.	2,828
Ciena Corporation	2,203
ARRIS Group, Inc.	1,992
Avocent Corporation	1,797
ADTRAN, Inc.	1,611
Fujitsu Network Communications, Inc.	1,450

Fastest Growing* by Five-Year Sales Growth	(%)
Infinera Corporation	442.4
Franklin Wireless Corp.	387.2
Acme Packet, Inc.	103.9
InPlay Technologies, Inc.	69.8
Occam Networks, Inc.	65.5
ShoreTel, Inc.	61.8
Oplink Communications, Inc.	50.8
Blue Coat Systems, Inc.	46.2
Juniper Networks, Inc.	38.5
Soapstone Networks Inc.	30.3

Fastest Growing* by Five-Year Employee Growth	(%)
3Com Corporation	201.2
Avocent Corporation	80.2
ShoreTel, Inc.	45.7
ARRIS Group, Inc.	39.9
Blue Coat Systems, Inc.	39.6
Oplink Communications, Inc.	33.1
Acme Packet, Inc.	30.4
Infinera Corporation	24.4
Sycamore Networks, Inc.	21.3
Cisco Systems, Inc.	19.8

Top Public Companies by Market Value	($ mil.)
Cisco Systems, Inc.	132,180.0
Juniper Networks, Inc.	9,223.4
3Com Corporation	1,022.3
Sycamore Networks, Inc.	987.8
ARRIS Group, Inc.	978.6

* These rates are compounded annualized increases and may have resulted from acquisitions or one time gains. If less than 6 years of data are available, growth is for the years available.

SOURCE: HOOVER'S, INC., DATABASE

Computer Software Development

Computer software production in the US involves about 50,000 companies with combined annual revenue of about $180 billion, more than half from sales of packaged products and the rest from custom programming. Large companies include Microsoft, Oracle, CA, and Electronic Arts. The packaged products segment is concentrated: the 50 largest companies hold about 70 percent of the market. The custom programming segment is highly fragmented.

Competitive Landscape

The US economy heavily influences business spending for software products. The success of programming companies depends heavily on strong technical expertise. The success of packaged-software companies depends on technical expertise and good marketing. Small software companies compete mainly by developing packaged products in small niches or producing custom products for individuals. Many small companies form alliances with larger ones to market their products.

Products, Operations & Technology

Packaged software products are generally small programs that can be installed and operated by the customer without assistance. Business-oriented packaged products may cost up to $10,000, but most consumer-oriented products cost less than $500. Custom programming either creates a new software product from scratch, or, more typically, customizes an existing software product for customer use. Custom program products can be very large, costing millions, and may require special training and technical support.

Software is of three major types: operating systems, like Windows, UNIX and Linux, that allow computers to perform basic functions; user applications, like word processing, spreadsheets, and games that run on individual com-

BUSINESS CHALLENGES

» Demand Tied to Computer Sales

Demand for different types of software depends on different end-user trends, but overall demand is heavily influenced by corporate profitability, consumer spending, and total computer sales. Software sales grew very rapidly during the 1990s, as consumers and businesses bought PCs and automated many business functions. But growth in demand has been slower in the past five years, as computers are replaced less frequently.

» Rapid Technology Innovation

The shelf-life of software products is short and growing shorter every year, as technology spending continues to boom. Because of the rapid development of new products, software has a shelf-life of only a few years (at most) before it's superseded by superior products. Although software may be in general use for many years, the effective sales period is short.

» Large Competitors Dominate Market Segments

The domination of several large companies in specific market segments, such as spreadsheet products, database products, and Web browsers, makes it extremely difficult for smaller companies to develop competing products in those areas. Quite aside from the programming expertise of the dominant companies, the marketing costs required to sell a competing product are beyond the capability of most small software companies.

puters; and network applications, like e-mail, Internet Web browsers, and sophisticated signal switching programs that allow computers to communicate with each other. About 100 operating systems are in common use, most of which are proprietary products of computer manufacturers like IBM. User applications, of which there are tens of thousands, form the largest segment of the market, but the network software segment is growing most rapidly, due to the popularity of the Internet.

Computer programs are a series of instructions to a computer, written as sentences in a variety of computer languages. Each sentence is called a "line of code." A complicated software application may contain hundreds of thousands (even millions) of lines of code, usually produced in chunks (modules or subroutines) that work together. Inevitably, such complicated, lengthy programs contain errors, or "bugs."

Both packaged software products and custom programming are typically produced by teams of programmers who design the structure of a product and write the individual lines of code. The rough draft of a new program is called the alpha version. The beta version is an almost-final version that is tested by actual users to find and correct additional bugs. The release version of most software still contains bugs that aren't apparent until the software is used by many people. Typically, programmers begin work on a new version of a product as soon as the current version is released for sale. The complexity of most software requires that software companies provide technical assistance to users, often an expensive operation for small companies.

Software is written in various languages like COBOL, C++, Visual Basic, SQL, Java, HTML, XML, and many others, that translate complicated human concepts like a sentence, a picture, or a mathematical operation into machine code, a succession of 1s and 0s that is the actual language of computers. Different software languages are most effective for different types of applications. For example, SQL is a language suitable for manipulating large databases. Software producers often create products to run on a particular "platform," a combination of operating system and computer configuration.

Sales & Marketing

Software is created for four types of users: business; consumers; IT professionals (to operate and maintain computer systems); and software developers (developer tools).

Software companies usually concentrate on developing an expertise in a relatively narrow market, hoping to dominate and then expand their niche. Microsoft dominates the market for consumer operating systems and productivity software (word processing, spreadsheets, and slide presentations); Computer Associates for customized business software (accounting, finance, inventory, manufacturing operations); Oracle for database software, now a rapidly growing market as large database systems are essential to Internet commerce.

Many software companies spend heavily on R&D to develop new products and improve existing ones, but sales and marketing costs are the largest single expense item for most, usually running more than 30 percent of revenues. The type of sales effort depends on the market the company is selling to. Consumer sales require heavy advertising in computer and consumer magazines, while business sales require heavy participation in industry trade shows and a large sales force.

Custom programming is often priced at a specified rate per hour, up to a maximum price. Costs for installing large business software systems are typically fixed, and packaged products are sold at a fixed price. While custom programming is sold directly to end-users, packaged software is sold to distributors, retailers, or computer manufacturers. Technically, most packaged software isn't sold as a product but as a license to use the product.

Human Resources

Producing computer software requires special skills and is accordingly very well paid. Average hourly wages are almost $40, more than double the national wage. Companies go to great lengths to retain senior programmers, who often represent a large amount of the company's expertise. Because much computer programming development is still by small companies, key employees often hold significant amounts of company stock.

The shortage of qualified computer programmers in the US has prompted many companies to hire software engineers from other English-speaking countries, notably India. Foreign engineers are often brought temporarily to the US through visas under the H-1B program.

Industry Employment Growth

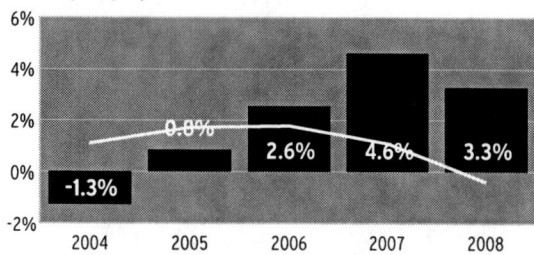

	2004	2005	2006	2007	2008
	-1.3%	0.8%	2.6%	4.6%	3.3%

Average Hourly Earnings

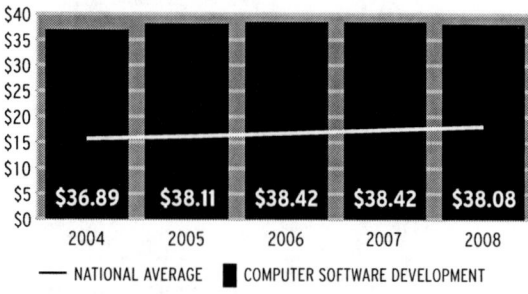

	2004	2005	2006	2007	2008
	$36.89	$38.11	$38.42	$38.42	$38.08

— NATIONAL AVERAGE   ■ COMPUTER SOFTWARE DEVELOPMENT

SOURCE: BUREAU OF LABOR STATISTICS

Call Preparation Questions

How does the company manage shifts in customer technology spending?

Demand for different types of software depends on different end-user trends, but overall demand is heavily influenced by corporate profitability, consumer spending, and total computer sales.

How is the company addressing the shortened shelf-life of products?

The shelf-life of software products is short and growing shorter every year, as technology spending continues to boom.

How is growing demand for networking and online software impacting the company's product development?

Network software development is currently at the forefront of the industry, as demand for Internet products grows.

Web Links

Business Software Alliance

Represents the interests of software companies with government and legislative policy initiatives. Mainly an anti-piracy group.
www.bsa.org

Computerworld

News, features, and opinions of IT, software, and computers.
www.computerworld.com

E-Commerce Times

Computer industry news.
www.ecommercetimes.com

Forrester Research

Research, news, and more related to computer and information technology.
www.forrester.com

Information Technology Association of America

News and policy discussion of IT issues.
www.itaa.org

PC Magazine

Personal technology magazine.
www.pcmag.com

Software & Information Industry Association

Industry association with articles on current policy issues, statistics for the packaged software industry.
www.siia.net

Glossary of Acronyms

CRM — customer relationship management

HOOVER'S TOP COMPANIES

Largest Companies by Sales	($ mil.)
International Business Machines Corporation	103,630.0
Microsoft Corporation	60,420.0
Oracle Corporation	22,430.0
Symantec Corporation	5,874.4
SunGard Data Systems Inc.	4,901.0
CA, Inc.	4,277.0
Electronic Arts Inc.	3,665.0
Adobe Systems Incorporated	3,579.9
Lender Processing Services, Inc.	3,446.0
Fidelity National Information Services, Inc.	3,446.0

Largest Employers	Employees
International Business Machines Corporation	426,969
Microsoft Corporation	91,000
Oracle Corporation	84,233
Fidelity National Information Services, Inc.	31,000
SunGard Data Systems Inc.	17,900
Symantec Corporation	17,600
CA, Inc.	13,700
DST Systems, Inc.	11,000
SAS Institute Inc.	10,737
Infor Global Solutions, Inc.	9,000

Fastest Growing* by Five-Year Sales Growth	(%)
Solera Holdings, Inc.	1,292.3
Collexis Holdings, Inc.	355.6
MPC Corporation	249.5
Lyris, Inc.	169.8
NewMarket Technology Inc.	147.6
Accordent Technologies, Inc.	122.9
Glu Mobile Inc.	118.6
Medidata Solutions, Inc.	108.8
Omniture, Inc.	102.4
SXC Health Solutions Corp.	97.5

Fastest Growing* by Five-Year Employee Growth	(%)
InfoLogix, Inc.	800.0
Silverstar Holdings, Ltd.	131.7
eGain Communications Corporation	121.2
Etelos, Inc.	112.5
Nimsoft	93.7
Riverbed Technology, Inc.	91.7
Incentra Solutions, Inc.	78.7
Nuance Communications, Inc.	76.4
Omniture, Inc.	75.6
Collexis Holdings, Inc.	68.6

Top Public Companies by Market Value	($ mil.)
Microsoft Corporation	251,744.0
Oracle Corporation	117,626.0
International Business Machines Corporation	112,698.3
Electronic Arts Inc.	15,874.6
Symantec Corporation	14,118.5

* These rates are compounded annualized increases and may have resulted from acquisitions or one time gains. If less than 6 years of data are available, growth is for the years available.

SOURCE: HOOVER'S, INC., DATABASE

Concrete and Masonry Contractors

Concrete and masonry contractors in the US have combined annual revenue of about $40 billion, a figure that fluctuates with the amount of annual construction activity. This highly fragmented, local industry has no large publicly traded companies. Most of the approximately 40,000 contractors specialize in either concrete or masonry, although many also do asphalt work. While a few hundred companies have more than 50 employees and revenues up to $20 million, the average contractor has between five and 20 workers and annual revenues less than $1 million.

Competitive Landscape

Except in specialized applications such as high-rise work, large bridges, or marine work, concrete work is considered virtually a commodity business, with contracts awarded largely based on low price. In most markets, competition is intense. Large companies do not necessarily have an advantage over smaller ones. The ability to perform work on schedule is important, as most work is done for general contractors as one part of a larger project.

Products, Operations & Technology

Concrete contractors primarily mix and pour concrete into prepared forms and molds, which often contain reinforcing steel bars ("rebar"). About two-thirds of business is real estate construction (about one-quarter in single family construction where the contractor pours the foundation and basement walls) and one-third is non-real estate: driveways and parking areas, highways, streets, sidewalks, bridges, tunnels, sewers, and specialty architectural applications. About 60 percent of the interstate highway system is concrete, especially in urban areas with heavy traffic.

Masonry contractors use primarily concrete blocks and other pre-formed elements to build walls. Virtually all this business relates to real

BUSINESS CHALLENGES

» High Dependence on Cyclical Construction Industry
Demand for concrete and masonry services depends on activity in the construction industry, which can vary highly. Concrete contractors depend heavily on nonresidential construction like streets and highways, office buildings, industrial construction, and schools. Masonry contractors depend mainly on residential projects. Local real estate markets, which can be very volatile, are affected by economic factors out of a concrete contractor's control.

» Limited Market Area
Contractors are usually limited to business that can be found in a fairly small market. Penetrating new markets is difficult due to the personal relationships often involved in securing business.

» Dependence on Large Customers
Many smaller contractors get a large portion of business from a few large customers, such as developers or municipalities. The loss of a large customer can have a major impact on revenue.

estate; about one-third to single family construction. Most masonry projects specify a particular type of concrete block, which the contractor usually buys from wholesalers. Masonry walls may contain reinforcing elements. The mortar that binds the blocks is mixed at the construction site.

Concrete is a highly versatile material. Its characteristics depend on the types and proportions of the various materials mixed to create it. Concrete contains portland cement (the binding material made from limestone); sand; gravel (or other kinds of crushed rock, all called "aggregate"); and water. Some concretes also contain coloring agents, sealants, and other additives to provide special physical properties. On construction projects, the type of concrete needed is usually specified very precisely and may be tested periodically to ensure good quality. Contractors usually mix ingredients at a central yard just before delivery to a construction site, where the concrete must be poured within a few hours before it begins to harden.

Most concrete contractors erect their own forms or molds and place patterns of reinforcing rods — which can be quite complicated — before pouring (both form and "rebar" work is sometimes subcontracted as a specialty trade). Various devices used during the pouring process ensure that air pockets do not form and that the concrete is well compacted. In addition to the familiar rotating cement trucks, contractors may use lift buckets and concrete pumps.

Sales & Marketing

Marketing is mainly through personal contacts and by reputation for efficient work. Long-term relationships with developers and construction companies provide most business. Bidding is required for government work. Contractors must often bid for large private projects and must have detailed knowledge of local building codes.

Human Resources

Due to special skills and the risky nature of the work, concrete and masonry workers' wages and injury rates are above the national average. Hourly wages are about 20 percent higher than the average for all US workers. Injury rates for construction workers are about 70 percent higher than the US average.

Industry Employment Growth

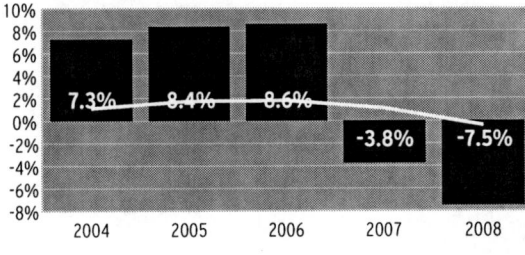

	2004	2005	2006	2007	2008
	7.3%	8.4%	8.6%	-3.8%	-7.5%

Average Hourly Earnings

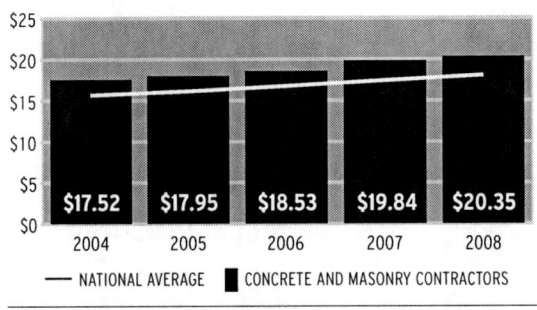

	2004	2005	2006	2007	2008
	$17.52	$17.95	$18.53	$19.84	$20.35

— NATIONAL AVERAGE ■ CONCRETE AND MASONRY CONTRACTORS

SOURCE: BUREAU OF LABOR STATISTICS

Call Preparation Questions

What are the company's contingency plans for downturns or sudden surges in demand?

Demand for concrete and masonry services depends on activity in the construction industry, which can vary highly.

How is the company challenged by expanding its geographic coverage?

Contractors are usually limited to business that can be found in a fairly small market.

How reliant is the company on a few large customers?

Many smaller contractors get a large portion of business from a few large customers, such as developers or municipalities.

How is the company capitalizing on new concrete or masonry construction methods or trends?

New formulations have increased the use of concrete for architectural applications such as countertops, driveways, and decorative floors and walls.

What opportunities does the company have in highway maintenance?

National focus has shifted from building new highways to maintaining and repairing the existing network.

Web Links

American Concrete Institute

Concrete and building specifications.
www.aci-int.org/general/home.asp

American Concrete Pavement Association

Industry news, publications, legislation, and technical news.
www.pavement.com

American Road & Transportation Builders Association

Industry lobbying association with government affairs, industry links, and news.
www.artba.org

American Society of Concrete Contractors

Hotline questions and event information.
www.ascconline.org/home.asp

Cement Americas

Industry magazine.
cementamericas.com

CONCRETE CONSTRUCTION Online

Industry news.
www.concreteconstruction.net

Concrete Contractor

Industry news, trade show schedules, and links.
www.concreteconceptsmag.com/cc

Concrete Products

Industry news.
concreteproducts.com

CONCRETE.com

News.
www.concrete.com

Construction Financial Management Association (CFMA)

The Construction Financial Management Association is the only professional association dedicated to meeting the information needs of construction financial managers.
www.cfma.org

Masonry Construction

Industry news.
www.masonryconstruction.com

National Concrete Masonry Association

Uses and applications, resources and materials, and list of state associations.
www.ncma.org

National Ready Mixed Concrete Association

Concrete basics, consumer uses, government links, safety and environmental issues.
www.nrmca.org

Portland Cement Association

Represents cement companies in the US and Canada and provides news and information.
www.cement.org

Tilt-Up Concrete Association

Information about this type of construction.
www.tilt-up.org

TranStats

Statistics relating to highway transportation.
www.transtats.bts.gov

World of Concrete

Portal to Concrete Construction, Masonry Construction and other magazines. Excellent articles archive.
www.worldofconcrete.com

Glossary of Acronyms

ACPA — American Concrete Pavement Association
AHP — Association Health Plans
ARTBA — American Road & Transportation Builders Association
FHWA — Federal Highway Administration
NAHB — National Association of Home Builders
NRMCA — National Ready Mixed Concrete Association
PCA — Portland Cement Association

HOOVER'S TOP COMPANIES

Largest Employers	Employees
Hirschfeld Holdings LP	2,000
Baker Concrete Construction, Inc.	2,000
Ceco Concrete Construction, LLC	1,800
Schuff International, Inc.	1,700
United Forming, Inc.	1,500
Structural Group	1,500
Stewart Builders, Ltd.	1,400
Western Construction Group	1,224
Suncoast Post-Tension, LP.	500
Williams Industries, Incorporated	333

SOURCE: HOOVER'S, INC., DATABASE

Construction Machinery Manufacturing

THIS INDUSTRY INCLUDES:

SIC CODES

3531 Construction Machinery and Equipment

NAICS CODES

33312 Construction Machinery Manufacturing

The US construction machinery manufacturing industry consists of more than 700 companies that have combined annual revenue of $25 billion. Large manufacturers include Caterpillar, Terex, Komatsu, and Hitachi, and the construction divisions of heavy equipment manufacturers CNH, Deere, and Volvo. The industry is highly concentrated: the 50 largest companies hold more than 80 percent of the market.

Competitive Landscape

Demand is highly dependent on the cyclical construction industry. During the last recession, production dropped 30 percent. The profitability of individual companies depends on efficient manufacturing operations, since customers are very sensitive to price. Because of the large capital investment required to produce heavy construction machinery, this segment of the market is served mainly by the large manufacturers. Smaller companies can compete effectively by producing equipment that has specialized applications, or that is relatively simple to make. The industry is capital-intensive: annual revenue per worker is more than $300,000.

Products, Operations & Technology

Major products are bulldozers, loaders, backhoes, power cranes, excavators, graders and rollers, crushers, mixers, pavers, concrete pumps, various types of off-road trucks and trailers, and a wide variety of specialized machinery. Such equipment is used for three major activities: earthmoving, paving, and lifting.

Like auto manufacturers, construction equipment manufacturers typically buy key components like engines and gears, hydraulic pumps and hosing, and structural steel and castings from parts suppliers, perform various finishing operations, and assemble the components. Materials represent 60 percent of fin-

BUSINESS CHALLENGES

» High Dependence on Cyclical Construction Industry

Demand for construction equipment is even more volatile than demand in the highly variable and cyclical construction industry. Machinery production expands rapidly when construction activity increases, but buyers defer new purchases when construction activity slows. During the last recession, production fell 30 percent.

» Competition from Imports

Imports of construction machinery have grown rapidly and now account for about 50 percent of the US market. The high value of machinery makes worldwide trade possible, despite transportation costs. US imports of construction machinery almost doubled in the last five years. Japan, Canada, and Germany are the biggest source of imports. Imports from China, though smaller, increased 75 percent in 2005.

» Customer Concentration in Rental

A large portion of sales are to the equipment rental industry, which consolidated rapidly in the last decade. JLG, the largest manufacturer of aerial platforms, gets more than 50 percent of revenue from just 10 customers, all rental companies.

ished product costs. Much equipment is large and expensive: a 175 ton truck-mounted crane can cost more than $1 million; off-road trucks cost almost $200,000; and even small loaders cost more than $50,000. High prices create incentives for significant import competition for crawler tractors and excavators, and for commodity-type items like concrete mixers, pumps, and winches. The effective life for most equipment is no more than 10 years, and often shorter.

Sales & Marketing

Large machinery buyers include equipment rental companies, homebuilders, construction companies, surface mining companies, the US

Army Corps of Engineers, and the equipment leasing arms of financial service companies like GE and Citibank. The high cost of much equipment, combined with only sporadic need, means that end-users frequently prefer to lease (long-term) or rent (short-term, for days or hours) equipment from large rental firms like United Rentals, Hertz Equipment Rental, and NationsRent.

Manufacturers sell directly to large customers, such as rental firms, and through networks of independent distributors that have exclusive rights within their territory but often also carry competitors' products. A manufacturer may use several different distributor networks to sell different product lines.

Distributors are usually supported by manufacturer sales managers, advertising, and participation at trade shows. Product prices are usually negotiable. There is a large market for replacement parts and a secondary market in used equipment, fed by regular turnover at lease and rental firms. Customer service, replacement parts, maintenance, training, and used equipment reconditioning are important features in generating new sales.

Human Resources

Manufacturing components and assembling construction equipment require skilled labor that is accordingly well-paid. To retain skilled workers, companies provide a fairly high level of benefits, an average addition of 32 percent to payroll costs.

Call Preparation Questions

What are the company's contingency plans to cope with large swings in demand?

Demand for construction equipment is even more volatile than demand in the highly variable and cyclical construction industry.

How much competition does the company face from imports?

Imports of construction machinery have grown rapidly and now account for about 50 percent of the US market.

How has consolidation in the rental market affected company sales?

A large portion of sales are to the equipment rental industry, which consolidated rapidly in the last decade.

Does the company expect public construction spending to increase in its market?

Public infrastructure spending has remained at high levels in recent years.

What advantages, if any, has the company gained from adding new electronics to its products?

New design technologies to monitor equipment in use mean that machinery requires fewer major repairs, a primary concern of equipment fleet managers.

Web Links

American Rental Association

Industry association.
www.ararental.org

Association of Equipment Manufacturers

Industry news, issues.
www.aem.org

Caterpillar

Construction equipment manufacturer.
http://www.cat.com/cda/layout?m=8703&x=7

Construction Distribution

Industry news, issues.
www.constructiondist.com

Construction Equipment

Construction indicators.
www.constructionequipment.com/community/862/Economic+Outlook/23395.html

Equipment Rental

Links to manufacturers, distributors, rental centers.
www.equipmentrental.com

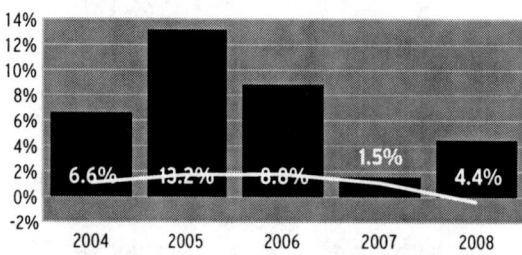

Industry Employment Growth

6.6%   13.2%   8.8%   1.5%   4.4%
2004   2005   2006   2007   2008

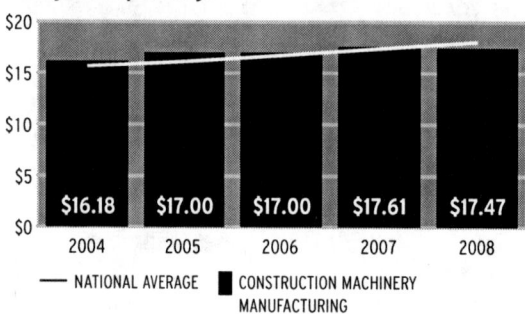

Average Hourly Earnings

$16.18 $17.00 $17.00 $17.61 $17.47
2004   2005   2006   2007   2008

— NATIONAL AVERAGE   ■ CONSTRUCTION MACHINERY MANUFACTURING

SOURCE: BUREAU OF LABOR STATISTICS

Equipment Today

News.
www.forconstructionpros.com/cover/Equipment-Today/5FCP

EquipmentWorld.com

Industry news.
www.equipmentworld.com

IronPlanet

Online construction equipment auctioneer.
www.ironplanet.com

Komatsu

Construction equipment manufacturer.
www.komatsuamerica.com

OEM Off-Highway

Manufacturers of off-highway construction
equipment news.
www.oemoffhighway.com

Reed Construction Data

National, regional, and local construction data.
www.reedconstructiondata.com

Rental Management Magazine

Industry news.
www.rentalmanagementmag.com

Glossary of Acronyms

AEM — Association of Equipment Manufacturers
BLS — Bureau of Labor Statistics
CE — construction equipment
CPC — collaborative product commerce
NAM — National Association of Manufacturers
TEA-21 — 1998 Transportation Equity Act of the 21st
Century

HOOVER'S TOP COMPANIES

Largest Companies by Sales	($ mil.)
Caterpillar Inc.	51,324.0
Terex Corporation	9,889.6
The Manitowoc Company, Inc.	4,503.0
Astec Industries, Inc.	973.7
Blount International, Inc.	597.0
JLG Industries, Inc.	473.2
Gehl Company	457.6

Largest Employers	Employees
Caterpillar Inc.	112,887
Terex Corporation	21,000
The Manitowoc Company, Inc.	10,500
Astec Industries, Inc.	8,875
Atlas Copco North America Inc.	5,114
JLG Industries, Inc.	4,088
Blount International, Inc.	3,200
Vermeer Corporation	2,062
The Charles Machine Works, Inc.	1,315
Besser Company	1,000

Fastest Growing* by Five-Year Sales Growth	(%)
Manitex International, Inc.	138.3
The Manitowoc Company, Inc.	23.4
Terex Corporation	20.5
Astec Industries, Inc.	17.9
Caterpillar Inc.	17.7
Gehl Company	14.5
Gencor Industries, Inc.	9.6
Blount International, Inc.	1.3

Fastest Growing* by Five-Year Employee Growth	(%)
Astec Industries, Inc.	974.5
The Manitowoc Company, Inc.	14.6
Caterpillar Inc.	10.3
Gencor Industries, Inc.	7.8
Terex Corporation	5.3
Gehl Company	3.4

Top Public Companies by Market Value	($ mil.)
Caterpillar Inc.	26,870.2
Terex Corporation	1,628.1
The Manitowoc Company, Inc.	1,128.9
Astec Industries, Inc.	705.2
Blount International, Inc.	451.4

* These rates are compounded annualized increases and may
have resulted from acquisitions or one time gains. If less
than 6 years of data are available, growth is for the years
available.

SOURCE: HOOVER'S, INC., DATABASE

Consulting Services

The US consulting services industry includes just over 250,000 companies with combined annual revenue of nearly $400 billion. Major companies include IBM, Accenture, Deloitte, McKinsey, Electronic Data Systems (EDS), and Affiliated Computer Services (ACS). The industry is highly fragmented: the top 50 companies account for around 25 percent of total industry revenue. The average consulting firm has fewer than 10 employees and annual revenue under $1 million; 75 percent of consulting firms are one- or two-person operations.

Consulting services includes IT consulting, management consulting, and outsourced payroll services. The industry doesn't include companies that provide labor or staffing solutions to other companies, nor does it include corporations with an internal consulting division.

Competitive Landscape

Demand is driven by corporate profitability and the overall health of the US economy. The profitability of individual companies depends largely on the special expertise the firm provides to clients. Large firms have advantages in the range of services offered, which often span across all three major consulting disciplines. Small firms can compete effectively by specializing in new technologies or niche industries. The industry is labor-intensive, particularly for payroll services. Average annual revenue per employee is around $100,000 ($40,000 in the payroll services industry).

Products, Operations & Technology

Major services include computer systems consulting (20 percent of industry revenue); custom computer programming (15 percent); general management consulting (15 percent); and professional payroll services (10 percent). Other services include computer facilities management, executive recruiting, and marketing consulting.

BUSINESS CHALLENGES

» Dependence on Economic Growth

Consulting revenue depends on economic growth, and especially on corporate profits. Consultants are considered an expendable (or at least, delayable) cost when companies face an economic slowdown. During recessions, corporate profits may fall 10 percent.

» Employee Attrition

Consulting firms depend heavily on the intellectual capital of employees, yet most companies face high levels of voluntary attrition. The typical employee tenure at a major consulting firm is around two years; companies regularly face annual attrition rates of 20 to 40 percent. Work conditions are difficult, as long hours and extensive travel are the norm. Companies spend significant resources recruiting new employees and providing incentives to retain them.

» Competition from Offshoring

India and China's rapid development of technology capabilities creates both a risk and an opportunity for US-based consulting firms. Consulting companies are losing out to offshore agencies that develop IT solutions at cheaper rates. However, consulting companies with a global network may be able to integrate and market offshore solutions to prospective clients.

Most consulting firms specialize in only one area of expertise or in a particular industry. Many of the largest IT consulting firms are offshoots of big accounting firms. About half of IT consulting revenue comes from the design and delivery of integrated "turnkey" computer systems for a client; the other half is from producing computer system design specifications, custom programming, computer system testing and maintenance, and sales of computer hardware and software.

General management consulting provides advice to senior and middle corporate managers about the operations or strategic direction of various functions in the client organization, including finance, marketing, HR, production, logistics, etc. Technical consultants provide expert assessments in environmental, legal, scientific, and other areas. Professional payroll services provide outsourced HR, payroll, and accounting services.

Most consulting jobs are project-oriented assignments, also called "engagements." Clients usually send a request for proposal (RFP) to several potential consultants; consulting firms respond with a proposal that specifies the approach the firm would take to address the task, the resources it would use, a timetable, the "deliverables" it would provide, and an estimated cost. In management and technical consulting, the major deliverable is usually a report or action plan. In IT consulting, the deliverable may be a complete computer system.

The work of consulting firms is highly labor-intensive. Although cost is a major factor for clients in deciding which consulting firm to choose, reputation and experience can be more important. Most consulting assignments involve a period of study or research, formulation of possible solutions, and the production of a report.

Technology plays an increasingly important role in consulting services. Annual revenue from computer consulting services is nearly twice that of management and scientific consulting. Firms often pitch and develop complex software solutions, including enterprise resource planning (ERP); customer relationship management (CRM); or sales force automation (SFA). Many general management consulting firms have a division or sister company that specializes in technological consulting; often, the two work off of one another to present an "end-to-end" solution for clients.

Sales & Marketing

Typical customers are Fortune 500 companies, banking institutions, consumer packaged goods companies, retailers, logistics providers, and government agencies.

Marketing is most often indirect, and includes hosting seminars or participating in industry conferences and trade shows, and mailing materials to prospective customers. Senior members may spend most of their time in activities where they can make personal contacts with prospective clients. Partners at most firms are expected to bring in new business and work on assignments. Some firms have business development managers whose major function is to find new business. For small firms,

especially, a majority of work may be repeat business from customers or referrals.

Internet sales are generally in the form of capturing leads through white papers, case studies, and testimonials.

Pricing can vary depending on the firm's reputation and the size of the project. Most consulting contracts specify a maximum cost based on estimated days of work multiplied by the billing rates of those who will work on the assignment. Administrative and other expenses are often priced at a "cost-plus" premium. Senior consultants may be billed to clients at rates in excess of $2,000 per day, while junior consultants are billed at $1,000 per day or less, depending on the field of work. Partners in well-known firms may be billed at rates up to $10,000 per day. Fixed-price contracts are common in government work.

Human Resources

Consulting wages vary based on the services offered. Average wages for IT consultants are $35 per hour, twice the national average. Management consultants receive an average of $25 per hour, nearly 50 percent higher than the private sector. HR consultants receive the lowest wages in the industry: $18 per hour, comparable to the national average.

Consulting services require advanced education and high-level technical training. IT consultants typically have degrees in computer science and technology; management consultants often have degrees in business or finance. Top-tier firms require an MBA or an advanced masters degree to be on the track to partner.

Injuries are minimal. IT consulting and management consulting injury rates are 70 percent lower than the national average.

Industry Employment Growth

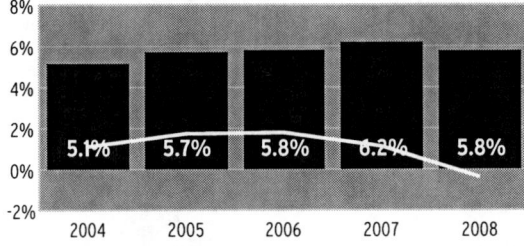

Average Hourly Earnings

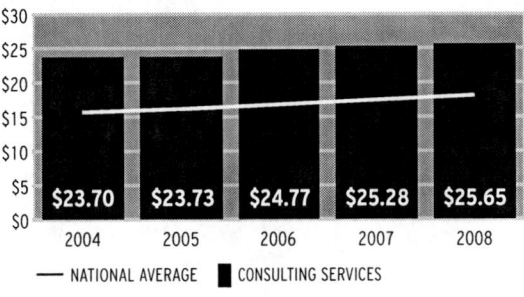

— NATIONAL AVERAGE ■ CONSULTING SERVICES

SOURCE: BUREAU OF LABOR STATISTICS

Call Preparation Questions

Is the shift to offshoring and outsourcing a competitive threat or an opportunity?

India and China's rapid development of technology capabilities creates both a risk and an opportunity for US-based consulting firms.

Does the company partner with technology firms? If so, to what benefit?

Many larger IT consulting firms are partnering with technology firms that provide computer hardware or software.

How dependent is the company on consulting with government agencies?

Federal demand for consulting services remains high post-9/11, and the federal mandate to improve departments like FEMA and Homeland Security provide new opportunities for consulting firms.

Web Links

American Association of Healthcare Consultants

News and directories.
www.aahc.net

Association of Management Consulting Firms

Publishes annual operating ratios for consulting firms.
www.amcf.org

Harvard Business Review

Frequent articles about consultants.
www.hbsp.harvard.edu/products/hbr

Information Technology Services Marketing Association (ITSMA)

News articles about IT consulting.
www.itsma.com

Institute of Management Consultants

Certifications and programs for consulting professionals.
imcusa.org

Vault

Rankings of top 50 management consulting companies.
www.vault.com/nr/consulting_rankings/
consulting_rankings.jsp

Glossary of Acronyms

CRM — customer relationship management
ERP — enterprise resource planning
ITSMA — Information Technology Services Marketing Association
KM SYSTEMS — Knowledge Management Systems
RFP — request for proposal
ROI — return on investment
SFA — sales force automation

HOOVER'S TOP COMPANIES

Largest Companies by Sales	($ mil.)
International Business Machines Corporation	103,630.0
Electronic Data Systems, LLC	22,134.0
Computer Sciences Corporation	16,499.5
Affiliated Computer Services, Inc.	6,160.5
McKinsey & Company	5,330.0
Unisys Corporation	5,233.2
Booz Allen Hamilton Inc.	4,100.0
BearingPoint, Inc.	3,455.6
Hewitt Associates, Inc.	3,227.6
Deloitte Consulting LLP	—

Largest Employers	Employees
International Business Machines Corporation	426,969
Electronic Data Systems, LLC	139,500
Computer Sciences Corporation	89,000
Affiliated Computer Services, Inc.	65,000
Deloitte Consulting LLP	33,000
Unisys Corporation	30,000
Hewitt Associates, Inc.	23,000
Booz Allen Hamilton Inc.	19,000
BearingPoint, Inc.	17,100
McKinsey & Company	15,600

Fastest Growing* by Five-Year Sales Growth	(%)
Democracy Data & Communications, L.L.C.	162.0
Huron Consulting Group Inc.	43.5
Local.com Corporation	43.0
MedAssets, Inc.	38.8
ICF International, Inc.	36.8
Turnaround Partners, Inc.	35.4
FTI Consulting, Inc.	34.9
HireRight, Inc.	34.7
Hill International, Inc.	30.8
The Boston Consulting Group Inc.	24.7

Fastest Growing* by Five-Year Employee Growth	(%)
Watson Wyatt Worldwide, Inc.	60.9
Huron Consulting Group Inc.	37.8
ICF International, Inc.	31.6
Democracy Data & Communications, L.L.C.	30.9
FTI Consulting, Inc.	27.1
HireRight, Inc.	23.5
The Corporate Executive Board Company	18.9
Bain & Company, Inc.	13.0
The Advisory Board Company	11.3
Thomas Group, Inc.	10.6

Top Public Companies by Market Value	($ mil.)
International Business Machines Corporation	112,698.3
Computer Sciences Corporation	6,165.6
Affiliated Computer Services, Inc.	4,865.0
Hewitt Associates, Inc.	3,433.6
FTI Consulting, Inc.	3,019.1

* These rates are compounded annualized increases and may have resulted from acquisitions or one time gains. If less than 6 years of data are available, growth is for the years available.

SOURCE: HOOVER'S, INC., DATABASE

Consumer Electronics Stores

THIS INDUSTRY INCLUDES:

SIC CODES

5731   Radio, Television, and Consumer Electronics Stores

NAICS CODES

443112   Radio, Television, and Other Electronics Stores

The US consumer electronics store industry includes 24,000 stores with combined annual revenue of $50 billion. Major companies include Best Buy, RadioShack, and GameStop. The industry is highly concentrated: the 50 largest companies have 80 percent of sales.

Competitive Landscape

Technological innovation and the need to replace or upgrade products drive demand. Profitability for individual companies depends on the ability to generate store traffic and repeat business, and effective merchandising. Large companies can offer wide selections of products and low prices. Small companies can compete effectively by offering specialized products, technological expertise, or superior customer service. Average annual revenue per employee is about $200,000. Competitors include mass merchandisers, warehouse clubs, department stores, Internet and mail order retailers, specialty office and computer retailers, and some manufacturers.

Products, Operations & Technology

Major product segments include computer equipment, TVs, audio equipment, video equipment, phones, and electronic games. Computer hardware and software account for almost 20 percent of sales; TVs, audio equipment and video equipment each account for about 15 percent. Audio equipment includes stereo components, MP3 players, CD players, car stereos, home theatre audio systems, and accessories. Video equipment includes video recorders, video cameras, videotapes, digital cameras, DVDs, and electronic game devices. Stores may offer installation and repair or maintenance agreements, and third party wireless phone service, broadband Internet service, or satellite TV or radio subscriptions.

Consumer electronics retailers include national and regional chains and independent re-

BUSINESS CHALLENGES

» Significant Declines in Retail Prices

Retail prices for many major segments of consumer electronics products have been steadily declining. Between 1996 and 2005, retail prices for TVs declined almost 60 percent; 80 percent for computers and peripherals. While electronics retailers have historically relied on increased volume to compensate for price declines, market saturation levels of products may limit growth and affect profitability.

» Competition from Alternative Channels

Consumer electronics stores face heavy competition from numerous other channels, including warehouse clubs, mass merchandisers, department stores, and Internet and mail order retailers. Internet and mail order retailers sell over $20 billion in computer hardware annually. Alternative channels will continue to threaten electronics stores, as entry-level electronic products become less complex and easier to sell.

» Rapid Advances in Technology

Consumer electronics retailers struggle to predict product life cycles to reduce or eliminate excess inventory, as manufacturers constantly leverage new technology to develop electronic products. Consumers will sometimes delay purchases in anticipation of new models. Before manufacturers introduce product upgrades, retailers will often offer deep discounts on current year models to minimize risk.

tailers. Major chains and some regional chains may offer a "superstore" format, which can exceed 30,000 square feet. Superstores are most often located in large strip malls in high traffic areas. Other chains may have smaller retail locations ranging from 1,500 to 10,000 square feet, located in indoor shopping or smaller strip malls. Chains may also offer a limited selection of products through kiosks (about 90 square feet) located in other retailers. Independent stores vary widely in size, from a few thousand square feet to larger than a typical superstore.

A typical superstore generates $15 to $40 million annually, and averages $500 to $900 per square foot. A store that specializes in high-end products can generate $7 million annually and averages $700 per square foot. A small, mall-based store generates $1 million annually and averages $400 per square foot.

Many stores carry high levels of inventory for expensive items like plasma screen TVs and personal computer systems to avoid out-of-stocks. Inventory management and sales forecasting are critical to profitability, as rapid advances in technology can significantly decrease demand for older products. In contrast, during the winter holiday, demand for "hot" products like new video game systems and portable music systems can exceed supply. Many large chains offer private-label products to fill gaps in existing product offerings.

Most large retailers buy directly from large manufacturers like Sony, Panasonic, Hewlett Packard, and Toshiba. Independent retailers buy through established buying groups like Nationwide and Metropolitan Appliance Radio and Television Association (MARTA) to increase individual buying power. In most product segments of the consumer electronics industry, suppliers are highly concentrated: Best Buy and Circuit City rely on just five suppliers for 30 to 50 percent of total merchandise. For highly anticipated new products like game systems or video games, retailers may place advance orders to guarantee supply.

Large retailers use integrated computer systems to manage point-of-sale transactions and inventory management, which allow for automatic replenishment at the store level. Some systems integrate online orders, and allow for in-store pickup or direct shipment.

Advances in technology drive sales of new electronic products. For example, digital technology created the market for products like MP3 players and HDTVs. Increased microprocessor power drives demand for newer computers and gaming systems with better graphics and higher performance.

Sales & Marketing

The traditional demographic for the consumer electronics store customer varies depending on product specialization, but is typically an affluent, professional man. Families with children, professional women, and small

businesses also are important customer segments for categories like digital cameras, video recorders, and computers.

Marketing and promotional vehicles include TV, newspaper, radio, and Internet advertising, direct mail, and in-store events. Retailers frequently use discounts, rebates, and other promotions to generate store traffic and establish competitive pricing with mass merchandisers and Internet retailers. Major chains may have loyalty programs that reward repeat customers and collect information on buying trends.

The technical nature of many electronic products requires professional installation services and trained sales associates able to explain complicated features to customers. Superior customer service generates repeat business and allows higher-priced independent stores to compete effectively against major chains.

Most major chains have retail Internet operations, and may link to other websites, like Amazon, to drive online sales. Many customers use store websites to research products and compare prices. Customers may have the option of having purchases shipped directly or picked up at the nearest retail location. Over half of Circuit City's online purchases are picked up at stores. Specialized retailers have leveraged the Internet by selling products like used video games and refurbished computers, which have limited availability.

Human Resources

Seasonal sales make stores reliant on part-time labor, especially during the winter holiday. At over $16 per hour, employees earn higher wages than the $12 per hour average for all US retail employees, but lower wages than the US average for all industries. Some store sales staff are on commission. Sales staff training is important due to the technical nature and high cost of most electronics.

A typical superstore has a manager; several assistant managers (including a sales manager); and up to 100 full and part-time employees, who cover sales, sales support, and technical service functions. Smaller stores may have a manager, up to two assistant managers, up to 30 full- and part-time sales associates, and up to 15 technical and administrative support staff.

Industry Employment Growth

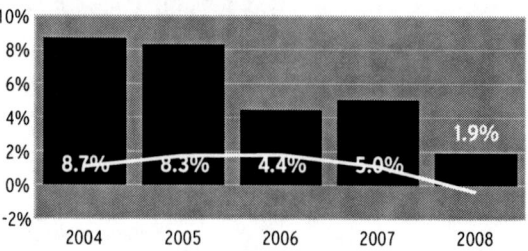

	2004	2005	2006	2007	2008
	8.7%	8.3%	4.4%	5.0%	1.9%

Average Hourly Earnings

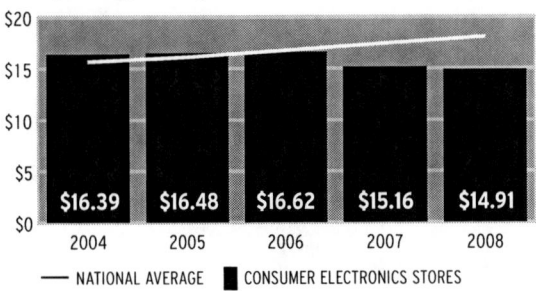

	2004	2005	2006	2007	2008
CONSUMER ELECTRONICS STORES	$16.39	$16.48	$16.62	$15.16	$14.91

— NATIONAL AVERAGE ■ CONSUMER ELECTRONICS STORES

SOURCE: BUREAU OF LABOR STATISTICS

Call Preparation Questions

How have declining retail prices affected the company?

Retail prices for many major segments of consumer electronics products have been steadily declining.

How does the company deal with increasing competition from alternative channels?

Consumer electronics stores face heavy competition from numerous other channels, including warehouse clubs, mass merchandisers, department stores, and Internet and mail order retailers.

How does rapidly changing product technology affect the company's operations?

Consumer electronics retailers struggle to predict product life cycles to reduce or eliminate excess inventory, as manufacturers constantly leverage new technology to develop electronic products.

How successful has the company been in the digital TV market?

Demand for digital TVs and associated accessories should increase significantly, due to regulations requiring the conversion of all analog TV signal transmissions to digital by 2009.

Web Links

Consumer Electronics Association

Trade organization — good source for statistics and trends.
www.ce.org

National Retail Federation

Retail trade organization — general retail trends and statistics.
www.nrf.com

North American Retail Dealers Association

Trade organization for independent consumer electronics retailers.
www.narda.com

This Week in Consumer Electronics (TWICE)

Industry publication — statistics, trends, news.
www.twice.com

Glossary of Acronyms

CEA — Consumer Electronics Association
MARTA — Metropolitan Appliance Radio and Television Association
NARDA — North American Retail Dealers Association
POS — point-of-sale

HOOVER'S TOP COMPANIES

Largest Companies by Sales	($ mil.)
Best Buy Co., Inc.	40,023.0
RadioShack Corporation	4,224.5
Fry's Electronics, Inc.	2,350.0
P.C. Richard & Son	1,290.0
hhgregg, Inc.	1,256.7
Interbond Corporation of America	1,030.0
Conn's, Inc.	824.1
Brookstone, Inc.	562.8

Largest Employers	Employees
Best Buy Co., Inc.	150,000
RadioShack Corporation	35,800
Fry's Electronics, Inc.	14,000
Brookstone, Inc.	3,504
Tweeter Home Entertainment Group, Inc.	3,200
hhgregg, Inc.	3,171
Conn's, Inc.	2,950
P.C. Richard & Son	2,700
Interbond Corporation of America	2,600
ABC Appliance, Inc.	1,750

Fastest Growing* by Five-Year Sales Growth	(%)
Appliance Recycling Centers of America, Inc.	17.1
Best Buy Co., Inc.	13.8
hhgregg, Inc.	13.7
Conn's, Inc.	13.1
Brookstone, Inc.	8.4
Fry's Electronics, Inc.	3.3

Fastest Growing* by Five-Year Employee Growth	(%)
Fry's Electronics, Inc.	19.9
Best Buy Co., Inc.	11.2
Conn's, Inc.	5.4
hhgregg, Inc.	4.6
Brookstone, Inc.	3.2

Top Public Companies by Market Value	($ mil.)
Best Buy Co., Inc.	17,659.0
RadioShack Corporation	1,493.5
Conn's, Inc.	431.8
hhgregg, Inc.	363.2
REX Stores Corporation	198.7

* These rates are compounded annualized increases and may have resulted from acquisitions or one time gains. If less than 6 years of data are available, growth is for the years available.

SOURCE: HOOVER'S, INC., DATABASE

Consumer Finance

About 5,000 companies in the US engage primarily in making personal loans to consumers, with combined annual revenue of about $40 billion, although industry size is uncertain. Large companies include HSBC, American General Finance, and divisions of large financial companies. Certain segments of the industry, such as unsecured cash loans, are highly fragmented, while others, like credit card lending, have become concentrated in a few large lenders.

Competitive Landscape

Demand is driven by consumer income and demographics. The profitability of individual companies depends on the correct assessment of repayment likelihood and effective collections activities. Large companies have an advantage in using computers to serve large portfolios of mortgage and credit card loans, and also have access to cheaper sources of funds, but small companies can compete effectively in the cash lending or sales finance segments, where personal contact is more important.

Products, Operations & Technology

Consumer finance companies offer the same kinds of loans to consumers that banks and credit unions do, but operate in the "subprime" portion of the market. Subprime borrowers may have a history of delinquent loan payments or no credit history, and often have low income and a higher debt-to-income ratio. Several broad subprime product segments exist, and companies may participate in a number of them or specialize in only one: automobile financing; credit card lending (revolving credit); sales financing (typically for furniture, jewelry, or appliances); and unsecured cash loans.

Consumer finance revenue comes mainly from the difference between the "yield" on loans (the finance charge) and the cost to fund

BUSINESS CHALLENGES

» Predatory Lending Regulations

Consumer finance companies need to be wary of state regulations against subprime "predatory" lending practices (high interest rates and fees, deceptive advertising, and contracts that confuse borrowers) because they often make credit available to consumers with poor or thin credit who may have limited financial sophistication. The industry is vulnerable to punitive damages in class action lawsuits from claims of predatory lending or deceptive marketing. The industry may be subject to increased state and federal regulations, especially about allowable interest rate spreads and add-on products.

» Vulnerability to Economic Slowdowns

Consumer finance companies are more vulnerable to financial losses during economic slowdowns, when delinquencies, bankruptcies, and foreclosures are disproportionately higher for subprime borrowers. Lower-income consumers, the primary customers of finance companies, are most likely to have financial difficulties during a recession or periods of high inflation.

» Competition from Banks

The strong profitability of the industry has prompted many banks to increase their subprime lending. Federal regulators established new examination guidelines for banks with more than 25 percent of their loans in the subprime category.

the loans. Various fees may also be charged to originate, insure, or collect loans. Consumer finance companies generally charge higher interest rates than prime lenders, expect to take larger loan losses, and service their loans more intensively to avoid losses. Differences exist between car or sales loans, where the asset being financed can be repossessed relatively easily, and credit card or cash loans, where the value of the loan depends entirely on payments from the borrower. Unlike banks and credit unions, finance companies don't take deposits and therefore are not subject to deposit regulations, deposit insurance, or deposit reserve requirements.

Finance companies control credit risk by assessing the borrower's credit worthiness when extending credit, and by vigorously managing delinquent loans. Sophisticated computer systems are used to "score" potential borrowers at the time of application, and to process and manage loans. To minimize loan losses, companies may use special collections teams that contact delinquent borrowers as soon as one day after a loan payment is past due to work out a payment plan, and that maintain frequent contact through phone, mail, and personal visits. A credit collector handles about 100 delinquent accounts and is compensated partly based on amounts recovered. This work is labor-intensive, especially considering the small average size of subprime loans. Delinquent loans are usually "cured" quickly or become a loss.

Sales & Marketing

Direct issuers of subprime credit cards, home equity, and unsecured loans market through direct mail, local advertising, and telemarketing. Auto lenders typically work through auto dealerships, selling their services via a direct sales force. Issuers of private-label credit cards and companies that market sales financing services directly to commercial customers.

Human Resources

The average hourly wage for consumer finance workers is around $19, three dollars above the national wage. Because credit offices usually have only a small staff, and due to the need for good quality control and tight supervision, 48 percent of workers are in supervisory or management positions, higher than the average of 30 percent for other industries. Most collections work is after-hours and on weekends. Personnel turnover in entry-level positions is high, as many workers find themselves unsuited to credit interviews and loan collections.

FAST FACTS

» About 5,000 companies in the US engage primarily in making personal loans to consumers, with combined annual revenue of about $40 billion, although industry size is uncertain.

» Large companies include HSBC, American General Finance, and divisions of large financial companies.

» Consumer finance companies offer the same kinds of loans to consumers that banks and credit unions do, but operate in the "subprime" portion of the market.

» Direct issuers of subprime credit cards, home equity, and unsecured loans market through direct mail, local advertising, and telemarketing.

» Consumer finance companies essentially are managers of receivables.

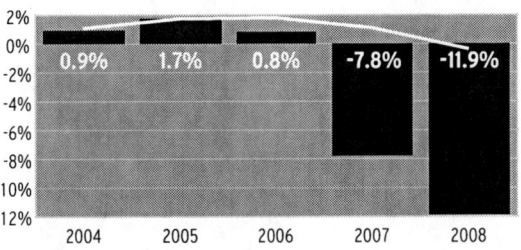

Industry Employment Growth

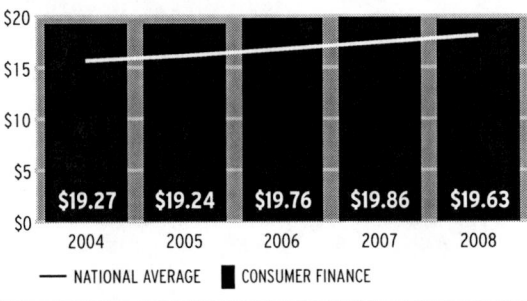

Average Hourly Earnings

NATIONAL AVERAGE ■ CONSUMER FINANCE

SOURCE: BUREAU OF LABOR STATISTICS

Call Preparation Questions

What programs does the company have to ensure compliance with predatory lending regulations?

Consumer finance companies need to be wary of state regulations against subprime "predatory" lending practices (high interest rates and fees, deceptive advertising, and contracts that confuse borrowers) because they often make credit available to consumers with poor or thin credit who may have limited financial sophistication.

How does the company protect itself from losses during economic downturns?

Consumer finance companies are more vulnerable to financial losses during economic slowdowns, when delinquencies, bankruptcies, and foreclosures are disproportionately higher for subprime borrowers.

How has rising competition from banks impacted the company?

The strong profitability of the industry has prompted many banks to increase their subprime lending.

How successfully has the company sold other products or services, like insurance or tax preparation?

Many finance companies sell additional services to customers.

What revenue opportunities does the company see in wholesale portfolio servicing?

In addition to managing their own receivables, some finance companies manage the receivables of others on a wholesale basis for a fee.

Web Links

American Financial Services Association (AFSA)

Industry operations, issues, news.
www.afsaonline.org

Association of Community Organizations for Reform Now (ACORN)

Consumer group critical of consumer lending practices.
www.acorn.org

Consumer Bankers Association

Reports and press releases.
www.cbanet.org

Consumer Credit Insurance Association

News and views.
www.cciaonline.com

Federal Trade Commission

News releases.
www.ftc.gov

Glossary of Acronyms

ACORN — Association of Community Organizations for Reform Now

AFSA — American Financial Services Association

AMR — average managed receivables

ARM — adjustable rate mortgage

CFSA — Consumer Financial Services Association

FHA — Federal Housing Administration

MBA — Mortgage Bankers Association

NHEMA — National Home Equity Mortgage Association

NAMB — National Association of Mortgage Brokers

HOOVER'S TOP COMPANIES

Largest Companies by Sales	($ mil.)
GMAC LLC	37,735.0
American Express Company	31,920.0
HSBC Finance Corporation	22,156.0
Capital One Financial Corporation	17,856.0
American International Group, Inc.	11,104.0
SLM Corporation	8,385.0
Synovus Mortgage Corp.	4,150.0
AmeriCredit Corp.	2,543.1

Largest Employers	Employees
American International Group, Inc.	116,000
American Express Company	66,000
HSBC North America Holdings Inc.	53,000
GMAC LLC	26,700
HSBC Finance Corporation	19,020
Capital One Financial Corporation	17,800
Residential Capital, LLC	13,700
SLM Corporation	11,000
GMAC Mortgage, LLC	7,500
Advance America, Cash Advance Centers, Inc.	7,000

Fastest Growing* by Five-Year Sales Growth	(%)
ASI Technology Corporation	63.3
American Mortgage Acceptance Company	41.8
The First Marblehead Corporation	41.7
Centerline Holding Company	37.5
Consumer Portfolio Services, Inc.	33.8
First Cash Financial Services, Inc.	26.7
Nelnet, Inc.	26.3
United PanAm Financial Corp.	25.9
AmeriCredit Corp.	21.0
Cash America International, Inc.	18.7

Fastest Growing* by Five-Year Employee Growth	(%)
United PanAm Financial Corp.	23.0
First Cash Financial Services, Inc.	21.3
Nelnet, Inc.	21.2
Centerline Holding Company	17.8
AmeriCredit Corp.	15.0
Security National Financial Corporation	13.0
World Acceptance Corporation	12.9
Federal Agricultural Mortgage Corporation	11.7
SLM Corporation	10.0
Cash America International, Inc.	9.5

Top Public Companies by Market Value	($ mil.)
American Express Company	21,518.0
Capital One Financial Corporation	12,494.4
SLM Corporation	10,050.2
American International Group, Inc.	4,222.8
AmeriCredit Corp.	1,002.6

* These rates are compounded annualized increases and may have resulted from acquisitions or one time gains. If less than 6 years of data are available, growth is for the years available.

SOURCE: HOOVER'S, INC., DATABASE

Consumer Product Rental

The consumer product rental industry includes about 15,000 companies with combined annual revenue of $22 billion. Major companies include Blockbuster, Movie Gallery, Aaron Rents, and Rent-A-Center. The industry is concentrated: the largest 50 companies account for about 60 percent of industry revenue. Video tape and disc rental account for half of industry revenue.

The industry includes companies that rent personal and household goods for short periods.

Competitive Landscape

Demand is driven by personal income and the timing and popularity of new movie releases. The profitability of individual companies depends on the right merchandise mix and inventory financing costs. Large companies have advantages in economies of scale in purchasing, distribution, and advertising. Small companies compete effectively by providing superior customer service and catering to local demographics. The industry is labor intensive: average revenue per worker for a typical company is less than $100,000.

Products, Operations & Technology

Major services include renting video tape and discs (51 percent of revenue); home health equipment (15 percent); and consumer electronics and appliances (12 percent). Other services include renting furniture, formal wear and costumes, and party supplies.

Most video rental companies are small, although close to half are franchises of large retail chains. Videos are the most important revenue source for the movie industry. Movie studios generally release a movie as a video during an exclusive "distribution window" of 30 to 60 days, during which the film isn't available on TV, cable, or pay-per-view. Some movies are released as "sell-through" where consumers can buy the movie at relatively low prices at the

BUSINESS CHALLENGES

» Dependence on Consumer Spending

Consumer spending on entertainment like video rentals is discretionary, and therefore driven by personal income. Personal income also drives spending on rental of consumer goods like furniture and appliances. During difficult economic times, many consumers eliminate or delay spending on these discretionary items.

» Sensitivity to Interest Rates

Most rental companies finance inventory. Companies finance from local banks, furniture manufacturers, and leasing companies. Interest expense can be a significant cost item for rental companies, and changes in interest rates impact the rental prices customers are charged.

» Reliance on Movie Distribution Window

Video rental companies rely heavily on new movie releases for revenue. Historically, the exclusive distribution window for home video rentals has been the first distribution channel after the box office, and lasts from 30 to 60 days. Some studios are testing different distribution schemes, such as bringing a film to pay-per-view sooner than normal. Any change in the distribution window for video rentals would significantly impact rental companies.

same time the movie is released to rental stores.

Rental of consumer electronics, furniture, and some home health care equipment is on a contract basis, usually week-to-week, where the consumer, such as a student or temporary worker, either wants the item for a short period, or prefers to pay week-to-week on a rent-to-own basis. The rental company retains title to the merchandise during the rental term. Only about 25 percent of initial rental agreements are taken to full term. To cover relatively high operating expenses, rental purchase agreements generally charge higher amounts than purchase plans. Tools, formal wear, and party supplies are generally rented for only a short period; frequent turnover on such items is necessary to be profitable.

Video stores are typically open 365 days a year and stock hundreds of titles. Household goods rental companies usually have several thousand items in their stores, which can approach 9,000 square feet. Video and rent-to-own companies have large automated distribution facilities that store merchandise before delivery to local stores. Video companies generally use a third-party delivery agent, such as UPS. Furniture and appliance rental companies usually have their own truck fleets to deliver merchandise, both to stores and to customers.

Rental companies have computerized inventory systems to efficiently track merchandise. Video companies use customer relationship management (CRM) systems to track consumer purchases and create a transaction database to formulate and adjust marketing plans. Increasingly, companies are using radio frequency identification (RFID) tags on inventory to help tracking and reduce losses.

Sales & Marketing

Video rental customers include almost the entire US population: over 80 percent of US households own a DVD player. Consumer product rental customers are generally consumers earning a weekly paycheck who may not have credit. Consumer product rental companies often operate a store-front; many also sell via the Internet.

Major types of marketing include national and local TV advertising, direct mail, and promotional materials. Some companies have sports marketing initiatives, including sponsoring major sports events. Companies are attuned to customer service, as big ticket item customers have the option of returning rented merchandise at any time. Returned items are serviced and then evaluated for additional rental. Non-video rental companies generally have training facilities to teach employees store operations and customer service.

Internet sales have changed the video rental market. The large rental stores also include online rentals, a growing segment. The emergence of movie downloads to home computers is competitively pressuring the rental business.

Prices for video rental are generally $3 to $5. Large appliances, electronics, and furniture rental prices are a function of the contract length, usually up to 18 months. Formal wear rental is generally $50 to $100 for a tuxedo and accessories.

Human Resources

Most jobs in consumer goods rental companies require no special skills. The vast majority of jobs are clerical, retail, or warehousing, and pay less than the US average. Low wages often result in high employee turnover. Video rental stores generally have about 10 employees; appliance and furniture rental stores can average several dozen. Total industry employment has decreased over the past several years as automation has reduced the number of employees required in distribution centers and the back office. Total industry injury rates are well below the national norm.

Industry Employment Growth

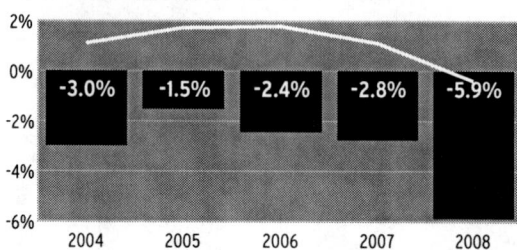

Average Hourly Earnings

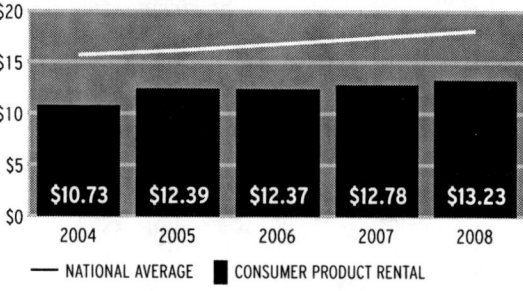

— NATIONAL AVERAGE ■ CONSUMER PRODUCT RENTAL

SOURCE: BUREAU OF LABOR STATISTICS

Call Preparation Questions

How does the general economy affect the company's sales?

Consumer spending on entertainment like video rentals is discretionary, and therefore driven by personal income.

How does the company acquire inventory?

Most rental companies finance inventory. Companies finance from local banks, furniture manufacturers, and leasing companies.

How might the company be threatened if movie studios changed their distribution window?

Video rental companies rely heavily on new movie releases for revenue.

How large a portion of company revenue is medical equipment?

The aging US population, combined with a desire to keep seniors in their homes longer, should increase demand for home medical equipment.

What role does the Internet play in the company's business?

The video market has changed with online renting.

Web Links

Association of Progressive Rental Organizations (APRO)

News of state organizations, legislation.
www.rtohq.org

HomeCare

News of homecare equipment rental.
www.homecaremag.com

Rental Management

Industry news.
www.rentalmanagementmag.com

Rental Site

Directory of rental providers.
www.rentalsite.com

The Entertainment Merchant Association

Industry and technology news.
www.vsda.org

Glossary of Acronyms

CRM — customer relationship management
EMA — Entertainment Merchant Association
RFID — radio frequency identification
RTO — rent-to-own
VSDA — Video Software Dealers Association

HOOVER'S TOP COMPANIES

Largest Companies by Sales	($ mil.)
Blockbuster Inc.	5,542.4
Rent-A-Center, Inc.	2,884.2
Movie Gallery, Inc.	2,452.4
Aaron Rents, Inc.	1,494.9
Netflix, Inc.	1,364.7
Rotech Healthcare Inc.	559.3

Largest Employers	Employees
Blockbuster Inc.	59,643
Movie Gallery, Inc.	41,400
Rent-A-Center, Inc.	18,600
Aaron Rents, Inc.	9,600
Rotech Healthcare Inc.	4,800
David's Bridal, Inc.	3,000
Netflix, Inc.	2,670
Progressive Medical, Inc.	105

Fastest Growing* by Five-Year Sales Growth	(%)
Netflix, Inc.	38.0
Movie Gallery, Inc.	35.9
Aaron Rents, Inc.	18.5
Rent-A-Center, Inc.	5.3

Fastest Growing* by Five-Year Employee Growth	(%)
Netflix, Inc.	64.6
Movie Gallery, Inc.	30.0
Aaron Rents, Inc.	14.9
Rent-A-Center, Inc.	9.6

Top Public Companies by Market Value	($ mil.)
Netflix, Inc.	1,759.4
Rent-A-Center, Inc.	1,164.6
Aaron Rents, Inc.	871.4
Blockbuster Inc.	414.5
Rotech Healthcare Inc.	9.7

* These rates are compounded annualized increases and may have resulted from acquisitions or one time gains. If less than 6 years of data are available, growth is for the years available.

SOURCE: HOOVER'S, INC., DATABASE

Convenience Stores

THIS INDUSTRY INCLUDES:

SIC CODES

5411   Grocery Stores

NAICS CODES

44512   Convenience Stores

447110   Gasoline Stations with Convenience Stores

The convenience store (c-store) industry includes about 120,000 stores with combined annual revenue of an estimated $400 billion. Major companies include 7-Eleven; Circle K (a division of Alimentation Couche-Tard); and The Pantry. Large oil companies own and operate some c-stores. The industry is fragmented: the top 50 companies hold about 35 percent of industry sales. The industry generally includes establishments that are gas station/c-store combinations.

Competitive Landscape

Consumer and commercial driving trends drive demand. The profitability of individual stores depends on competitive pricing, effective merchandising, and the ability to secure high-traffic locations. Large companies have advantages in purchasing and finance. Small companies can compete effectively by acquiring superior locations or offering specialized merchandise or services. Average annual revenue per worker is about $500,000 for gas station/c-store combinations and $150,000 for c-stores without gas.

Because c-stores sell gas, food, and other types of merchandise, companies compete with a wide range of retailers, including gas stations, grocery stores, mass merchandisers, and warehouse clubs. C-stores that sell prepared meals also compete with restaurants.

Products, Operations & Technology

Major products sold include fuel (60 to 70 percent of sales); groceries and cigarettes (15 percent each); and beer (5 percent). Fuel includes regular, mid-grade, and premium unleaded gas; and diesel fuel. Groceries include soft drinks, candy, snacks, and dairy products. Stores may also sell meals or lottery tickets. Services include money orders and check cashing.

The industry includes national chains, franchises, and independent retailers. The majority

BUSINESS CHALLENGES

» Narrow Margins on Gas

While c-stores rely on fuel sales to drive store traffic, gas carries extremely low margins and fluctuating wholesale prices can drastically reduce profits. Driven by highly volatile commodity prices for crude oil, manufacturer prices for gas can change up to 45 percent in a single year. Competition and price sensitivity limit companies' ability to raise retail gas prices to cover increased costs. When wholesale gas prices increase suddenly, stores may make just pennies per gallon. With thin margins on gas, c-stores must depend on non-fuel merchandise sales to generate profits.

» Competition from Alternative Retailers

C-stores face competition from various alternative retailers for both gas and non-fuel merchandise sales. As more retailers capitalize on the traffic-generating benefits of selling gas, more outlets are adding gas pumps. Grocery stores, mass merchandisers, and warehouse clubs have added gas stations and generally offer lower prices on comparable non-fuel items. Many large retailers stock a wide variety of merchandise and can provide customers a different type of convenience with one-stop shopping. Even large home improvement centers, such as Home Depot, have experimented with c-store prototypes.

» Price-Based Competition

The retail gas market is extremely price-competitive, so c-stores can lose profitable non-fuel sales by pricing gas too high. Many consumers are willing to drive to alternate locations to save a few pennies per gallon, especially during periods of rising retail gas prices. Store operators that fail to address competitive pricing action can lose business quickly.

of c-stores are small and independently owned. Almost 80 percent sell motor fuel, according to the National Association of Convenience Stores (NACS). Some independent retailers have dealer relationships with large oil companies.

Store size can range from about 800 square feet (for a kiosk) to 5,000. A traditional c-store averages 2,000 to 3,000 square feet, has eight to nine fuel pumps, and offers six to 12 parking spaces. Most modern gas pumps have digital displays and allow customers to pay at the pump using a variety of methods, including credit and debit cards. Underground storage tanks (UST) store fuel; average monthly gas volume is just over 100,000 gallons. The average c-store generates about $4 million annually.

While location types can vary, most companies target high-traffic sites. C-stores off major interstates and highways tend to attract travelers and truckers. Stores at high-traffic intersections and in densely populated areas may depend on local customers. The shopping radius for many c-stores is two to six miles. Many stores operate 24/7. Store layouts can vary, but may include fountain drink stations, hot beverage centers, or food preparation areas.

C-stores sell more than 80 percent of gas sold in the US. Companies may sell branded or unbranded gas; the most common type of fuel sold is regular unleaded gas. Fuel suppliers include oil companies, refineries, or distributors (also known as "jobbers"). Companies may have supply agreements, which typically require minimum annual purchases and may offer volume-based allowances. The purchase price may be a Dealer Tank Wagon (DTW) price set by the supplier or a fixed markup over the "rack," or market, price. While motor fuels are the majority of c-store sales, gas generates low margins; thus, getting the lowest possible wholesale cost is critical to profitability.

Typical non-fuel merchandise includes high volume goods (beverages and cigarettes); impulse items (snacks and candy); and staples (milk). Prepared foods include sandwiches, pizzas, and/or hot dogs, and some chains offer nationally branded products from restaurant franchises. Many items are immediately consumable and some are perishable and require refrigeration. Depending on merchandise offerings, companies may buy non-fuel goods from a variety of sources, including manufacturers, grocery wholesalers, or distributors. Large chains may have long-term contracts with suppliers; some offer private-label brands. Non-fuel merchandise carries higher margins than fuel and typically generates the majority of store profits.

Many c-stores have computerized information systems linking point-of-sale (POS); gas pump; inventory; accounting; and finance operations. Scanners track individual items by Universal Product Code (UPC). Inventory management systems identify slow- and fast-moving products. Most c-stores with gas pumps offer cashless, pay-at-the-pump systems. Gas tank monitoring systems detect leaks, monitor tank levels, and may trigger purchase orders when gas levels are low. Innovation in payment technology includes using radio frequency identification (RFID) tags or biometric identification (fingerprints) to pay. Database systems manage customer loyalty programs.

Sales & Marketing

While the historical demographic for c-stores is low to middle income men, customer profiles can vary and depend on the surrounding market. A typical c-store that sells fuel serves about 1,000 customers per day, according to the National Association for Convenience Stores (NACS).

Because price and location are the primary factors driving store traffic, marketing and promotions are generally limited. C-stores often rely on outdoor signage to generate awareness and attract customers. Window and in-store signage communicates featured items. Companies may receive marketing allowances from suppliers to promote certain products. Large chains may use traditional marketing vehicles, including TV, newspaper, and radio ads. Proprietary products, such as 7-Eleven's Slurpee, can help companies differentiate from competition.

Developing customer loyalty can be difficult due to price-driven competition in the retail gas market. Companies offer discounts, rebates, or free items to encourage frequent store visits. Stores with oil company affiliations may run promotions for purchases made with company-issued credit cards. Fast service can also help differentiate c-stores from other retailers. The average transaction time, including time spent walking to and from a car, is three to four minutes.

While Internet sales are limited, about 60 percent of c-stores have websites. Most c-store websites provide basic company information, although some use the Internet to recruit workers, communicate in-store promotions, or solicit customer feedback.

Convenience commands price premiums and retail prices for most non-fuel items in c-stores are higher than prices in other retailers, such as grocery stores and mass merchandisers. Because gas sales drive store traffic, companies tend to price gas competitively. Stores may change retail gas prices as often as daily, due to rapidly changing market conditions.

Human Resources

C-store workers require few skills; consequently, wages are about half the average for all US workers. A typical store employs 10 workers weekly, according to the National Association of Convenience Stores (NACS), and many c-stores operate 24/7. Most rely on part-time help, particularly to fill night shifts. Many companies mandate employee training to prevent the sale of alcohol or tobacco products to underage customers. Employee theft can be problematic since workers typically have minimal supervision and access to cash.

The industry injury rate is significantly lower than the average for all US workers. However, c-stores workers have a high mortality rate because low staffing during late night hours puts employees at increased risk for crimes.

Industry Employment Growth

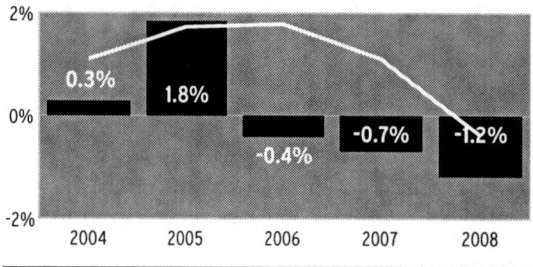

SOURCE: BUREAU OF LABOR STATISTICS

Call Preparation Questions

How does the company maintain profitability on gas sales?

While c-stores rely on fuel sales to drive store traffic, gas carries extremely low margins and fluctuating wholesale prices can drastically reduce profits.

What is the company's biggest competitive threat?

C-stores face competition from various alternative retailers for both gas and non-fuel merchandise sales.

What does the company consider when setting retail gas prices?

The retail gas market is extremely price-competitive, so c-stores can lose profitable non-fuel sales by pricing gas too high.

What types of services does the company offer?

To reduce dependence on gas sales to drive traffic, c-stores are providing a growing number of services, including banking, dry cleaning, and pharmacies.

How important are food items to the company's sales?

C-stores can expand their customer base and take advantage of "on-the-go" eating by selling a wider range of food products.

Web Links

Convenience Store News

Industry, company, and state-specific news and trends. Research available for purchase.
www.csnews.com

Convenience Stores Decisions

Industry news and trends.
www.csdecisions.com

National Association of Convenience Stores

Industry news, trends, statistics, state of the industry survey from trade association.
www.nacsonline.com/NACS/Pages

National Petroleum News

Industry news, trends, and statistics.
npnweb.com

Glossary of Acronyms

DTW — Dealer Tank Wagon
NACS — National Association of Convenience Stores
NCHS — National Center for Health Statistics
POS — point-of-sale
RFID — radio frequency identification
UPC — Universal Product Code
UST — underground storage tank

HOOVER'S TOP COMPANIES

Largest Companies by Sales	($ mil.)
The Kroger Co. (Quik Stop, Kwik Shop)	70,235.0
Flying J Inc.	16,200.0
The Pantry, Inc.	8,995.6
QuikTrip Corporation	8,300.0
Cumberland Farms, Inc.	8,100.0
TravelCenters of America LLC	7,658.4
Love's Travel Stops & Country Stores, Inc.	7,000.0
RaceTrac Petroleum, Inc.	5,520.0
7-Eleven, Inc.	—
Alimentation Couche-Tard (Circle K)	—

Largest Employers	Employees
The Kroger Co. (Quik Stop, Kwik Shop)	323,000
Alimentation Couche-Tard (Circle K)	37,000
7-Eleven, Inc.	31,000
Speedway SuperAmerica LLC	18,265
Casey's General Stores, Inc.	17,983
Wawa, Inc.	16,426
Flying J Inc.	16,000
The Pantry, Inc.	14,221
Pilot Travel Centers LLC	13,000
QuikTrip Corporation	10,500

Fastest Growing* by Five-Year Sales Growth	(%)
Love's Travel Stops & Country Stores, Inc.	40.0
Susser Holdings Corporation	29.8
Flying J Inc.	28.4
The Pantry, Inc.	26.7
TravelCenters of America LLC	24.2
Casey's General Stores, Inc.	17.5
Wawa, Inc.	13.7
Holiday Companies	9.9
Kum & Go, L.C.	9.7
The Kroger Co.	6.3

Fastest Growing* by Five-Year Employee Growth	(%)
The Pantry, Inc.	9.6
Love's Travel Stops & Country Stores, Inc.	9.6
Casey's General Stores, Inc.	7.6
Susser Holdings Corporation	6.7
Flying J Inc.	6.4
The Kroger Co.	2.2
Wawa, Inc.	1.3
Kum & Go, L.C.	0.2

Top Public Companies by Market Value	($ mil.)
The Kroger Co. (Quik Stop, Kwik Shop)	17,224.7
Casey's General Stores, Inc.	1,122.7
The Pantry, Inc.	414.7
Susser Holdings Corporation	225.6
TravelCenters of America LLC	39.9

* These rates are compounded annualized increases and may have resulted from acquisitions or one time gains. If less than 6 years of data are available, growth is for the years available.

Cookie and Cracker Manufacturing

THIS INDUSTRY INCLUDES:

SIC CODES

2052   Cookies and Crackers

NAICS CODES

311821   Cookie and Cracker Manufacturing

The cookie and cracker manufacturing industry includes about 300 companies with combined annual revenue of $10 billion. Major companies include Kraft's Nabisco subsidiary, Kellogg's US Snacks Division, and Interbake Foods. The industry is highly concentrated: the top 50 companies account for 90 percent of industry revenue.

The cookie and cracker manufacturing industry doesn't include companies that make tortilla, potato, or corn chips; fresh-baked cookies, pies, or breads; hard or soft pretzels; or refrigerated flour or dough mixes.

Competitive Landscape

Demand is driven by population growth, consumer tastes, and health considerations. The profitability of individual companies depends on efficient operations, effective marketing, and a strong sales force. Large companies have advantages in purchasing, distribution, and marketing. Small operations can compete effectively by manufacturing allergen- and sugar-free products, high-end cookies and crackers, or products containing unusual ingredients. Average annual revenue per employee is $325,000.

Cookie and cracker manufacturing competes against other "impulse" food providers, including bakeries, fast food restaurants, and manufacturers of snack items like candy and potato chips.

Products, Operations & Technology

The industry's major products are crackers (50 percent) and cookies (50 percent). Major types of crackers include saltine, cracker sandwiches, and graham crackers. Other cracker products include melba toast, cracker meal and crumbs, and taco shells. Popular cookies include chocolate chip, oatmeal, creme-filled, and sandwich cookies. Other products in the cookie

BUSINESS CHALLENGES

» Highly Competitive Industry

The cookie and cracker industry competes with a number of other impulse purchases and snacking options, including potato chips, nuts, energy bars, in-store bakery items, fast food, and baking at home. Cookies and crackers are indulgence items that are among the first foods eliminated or restricted for those trying to lose weight. Cookie and cracker manufacturers compete against one another, bidding for space on store shelves of major retailers and battling for consumer mindshare.

» Volatile Ingredient Prices

The price of critical commodity inputs such as wheat flour, shortening, soybean oil, corn sweetener, and chocolate can increase significantly due to poor farm yields, unpredictable weather patterns, high import tariffs, and government farm subsidies. Ingredient prices typically represent 50 percent of a cookie and cracker manufacturer's total cost of goods sold. Because of the large number of competitive substitutes and that cookies and crackers are discretionary purchases, manufacturers are often unable to pass higher costs to consumers.

» Vulnerability to Litigation, Regulation

Increased awareness of obesity in the US has made cookie and cracker manufacturers more vulnerable to litigation and federal regulation. Leading companies are often sued; recent litigation surrounded the use of trans fats, accusations of marketing unhealthy products to children, and weight-loss claims. Companies emphasize the importance of industry self-regulation, trying to stay one step ahead of potential lawsuits and federal clampdowns on advertising, ingredients, and labeling claims.

domain include toaster pastries, ice cream cones, and wafers for ice cream sandwiches.

Cookie and cracker making typically begins by blending starter ingredients like granulated sugar, shortening and oils, leavening, and flavorings in industrial mixers. If the food uses yeast or requires fermentation, the initial mix may need to rest for several hours. Following the initial blend and waiting period, workers mix in water and bonding agents like oats, gluten, and wheat flour. Blenders can quickly process 2,000 pounds of dough per batch.

After mixing, dough is lifted into a hopper. Crackers are spread onto a sheet and layered (laminated) by a series of metal gauging rolls. If the machine makes shaped crackers (animal or round), rotary cutting machines slice the dough into shapes. Excess dough is lifted and mixed with fresh dough in the hopper. Round cookie dough is forced through inch-long openings at the end of the hopper cylinder, which cuts pieces off with a sharp blade or wire.

The cut cookie or cracker dough moves by conveyor belt to a series of natural gas ovens, which can be up to 300 feet long. Crackers and cookies typically take five minutes to bake and 15 to cool down. The cooled product moves to a finishing station. For sandwich cookies, a stenciling machine squirts a shortening-and-sugar mix onto alternating rows of cookies. Air suction brings the two cookies together to complete the sandwich. In some cases, machines spray flavoring agents like cinnamon, icing, or chocolate. Crackers often receive a final application of spices, herbs, and salt.

The packaging stage varies depending on the product and where it's sold. Cookies and crackers can be individually plastic-wrapped or sold in snack packs or boxes. Finished products are put into cartons and warehoused for shipping. To reduce shipping costs, companies typically operate multiple manufacturing plants across the US. Most plants can manufacture a range of products, though each plant typically specializes in one or two popular brands.

Common inputs include wheat flour; soybean and cottonseed oil; sweeteners like cane and beet sugar, high-fructose corn syrup (HFCS), molasses, and honey; cocoa powder and chocolate syrup; and flavorings like herbs, salt, and spices. Key energy inputs include water, electricity, and natural gas. Commodities can be in short supply due to unpredictable weather patterns and government farm subsidies for competing products. Imported ingredients like chocolate and cinnamon can be in short supply and sometimes of inferior quality, depending on the conditions of major producers in Africa and South America. Manufacturers increasingly rely on HFCS in place of sugar, which is expensive due to federal price supports.

Recent technological advances include the ability to quickly prototype and launch new products, automated quality control instrumentation, more uniformity in product shapes, and fully integrated networks to automate baking and packaging. Most large companies track sales in real time using a network of handheld wireless devices and centralized enterprise resource planning (ERP) systems.

Sales & Marketing

Typical customers are grocery wholesalers, warehouse clubs, restaurant chains, food service distributors, vending machine distributors, and convenience stores (c-stores). Sales channels include third-party brokers, internal sales forces, food distributors, and direct store delivery (DSD), where products are stocked and pulled by the company's distribution arm. Many companies rely on a combination of these.

For most cookie and cracker manufacturers, Wal-Mart accounts for 10 to 20 percent of total sales. Several companies specialize in producing private-label brands for grocery and c-stores. As an aggregate category, the private-label segment is typically among the top five revenue-generating cookie and cracker brands.

Major marketing includes TV and radio advertising, coupons, celebrity tie-ins, in-store discounts and end-cap promotions, sweepstakes, and product-specific websites. Companies latch on to emerging food trends by publishing recipes that incorporate the product into a meal or snack (Ritz "bruschetta"). Cookie and cracker makers often co-promote with other food manufacturers to further extend a brand (Domino's Oreo dessert pizza, Honey Maid graham cracker pie crust).

Customer service operations can be extensive, as bad publicity can severely damage a brand. Most companies manage toll-free help lines and Web-based e-mail submission forms to address product questions and concerns. Companies invest heavily in Internet promotions, developing extensive, highly interactive websites to promote brand awareness. Most large processors manage restricted-access Intranets or electronic data interchange (EDI) systems to facilitate e-commerce transactions and manage inventory. A few small specialty cookie companies sell directly to consumers on the Internet.

Typical product prices are $3 to $4 for a 16-ounce box. Individually wrapped items cost around $0.50 to $1. Private-label brands cost 20 to 40 percent less than name brand. Distributors typically mark up prices 20 to 30 percent from the manufacturer's price; retailers add another 10 to 20 percent.

Human Resources

Cookie and cracker manufacturing wages for production workers average nearly 30 percent less than the US national average. Cookie and cracker manufacturing requires mechanical, scientific, and technical skills. Production workers must be physically able to operate machinery and lift heavy objects. A number of schools and institutes offer programs in baking science. Several baking institutes lease manufacturing equipment, providing startup businesses a chance to test and prototype cookies and crackers prior to launch.

The annual injury rate in cookie and cracker manufacturing is about 15 percent higher than the national average. Most injuries involve sprains, strains, fractures, and bruises from handling containers, operating machinery, and falling. Amputations are eight times higher than the national average.

Industry Employment Growth

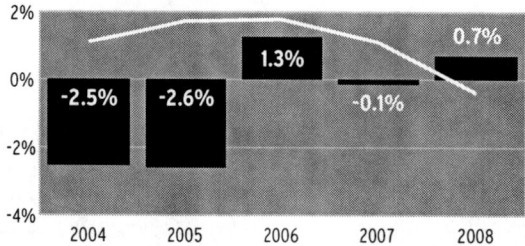

Average Hourly Earnings

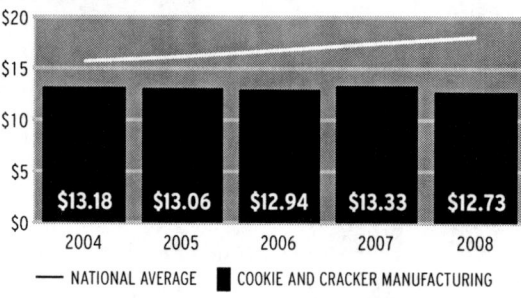

— NATIONAL AVERAGE ▪ COOKIE AND CRACKER MANUFACTURING

SOURCE: BUREAU OF LABOR STATISTICS

Call Preparation Questions

Who are the company's primary competitors?

The cookie and cracker industry competes with a number of other impulse purchases and snacking options, including potato chips, nuts, energy bars, in-store bakery items, fast food, and baking at home.

How do volatile ingredient prices affect the company?

The price of critical commodity inputs such as wheat flour, shortening, soybean oil, corn sweetener, and chocolate can increase significantly due to poor farm yields, unpredictable weather patterns, high import tariffs, and government farm subsidies.

How has the rise in obesity rates affected the company's strategy?

Increased awareness of obesity in the US has made cookie and cracker manufacturers more vulnerable to litigation and federal regulation.

Does the company make allergen- or gluten-free products?

Demand for gluten-free cookies and crackers is growing, fueled by more diagnoses of celiac disease.

What is the company's convenience store sales strategy?

As the grocery segment continues to consolidate and flex its buying power, cookie and cracker makers are revisiting their convenience store (c-store) sales strategy.

Web Links

American Bakers Association (ABA)

Trade association for bakeries, including cookie and cracker manufacturers.
www.americanbakers.org

American Institute of Baking (AIB)

Broad industry association that includes packaging companies and food suppliers.
www.aibonline.org

Baking Management Magazine

Baking industry news, tips.
www.bakingbusiness.com

Food Timeline: Cookies, Crackers, and Biscuits

Historical snapshots for a wide range of cookies, crackers, and biscuits.
www.foodtimeline.org/foodcookies.html

Milling & Baking News

Grain-based foods information site.
www.bakingbusiness.com

Private Label Magazine

News and insights into private label manufacturing.
www.privatelabelmag.com

Snack Food and Wholesale Bakery

News, interviews, new products, and feature stories covering cookies, crackers, and other snack foods.
snackandbakery.com

The Biscuit and Cracker Manufacturers Association

Trade association for cracker manufacturers.
www.thebcma.org

Glossary of Acronyms

ABA — American Bakers Association
AIB — American Institute of Baking
DSD — direct store delivery
EDI — electronic data interchange
ERP — enterprise resource planning
FOB — freight on board
HFCS — high fructose corn syrup

HOOVER'S TOP COMPANIES

Largest Companies by Sales	($ mil.)
PepsiCo, Inc.	43,251.0
Kraft Foods Inc.	42,201.0
Kellogg Company	12,822.0
Lance, Inc.	852.5
Interbake Foods LLC	532.3

Largest Employers	Employees
PepsiCo, Inc.	185,000
Kraft Foods Inc.	98,000
Kellogg Company	26,000
Interbake Foods LLC	4,750
Lance, Inc.	4,700
D.F. Stauffer Biscuit Company	850
Joy Cone Co.	500
Otis Spunkmeyer, Inc.	481
Horizon Food Group, Inc.	350
Silver Lake Cookie Company Inc.	250

Fastest Growing* by Five-Year Sales Growth	(%)
PepsiCo, Inc.	9.9
Lance, Inc.	8.7
Kellogg Company	7.8
Kraft Foods Inc.	6.4

Fastest Growing* by Five-Year Employee Growth	(%)
PepsiCo, Inc.	8.6
Kraft Foods Inc.	1.4
Kellogg Company	0.8

Top Public Companies by Market Value	($ mil.)
PepsiCo, Inc.	84,731.7
Kraft Foods Inc.	39,450.7
Kellogg Company	17,202.8
Lance, Inc.	694.1

* These rates are compounded annualized increases and may have resulted from acquisitions or one time gains. If less than 6 years of data are available, growth is for the years available.

SOURCE: HOOVER'S, INC., DATABASE

Cosmetics, Beauty Supply, and Perfume Stores

THIS INDUSTRY INCLUDES:

SIC CODES

5999 Miscellaneous Retail Stores

NAICS CODES

446120 Cosmetics, Beauty Supplies, and Perfume Stores

The cosmetic, beauty supply, and perfume store (beauty store) industry includes about 10,000 stores with combined annual revenue of almost $7 billion. Major companies include Sally Beauty Supply, Ulta, Sephora, and divisions of Limited Brands (Bath & Body Works) and L'Oreal (The Body Shop International). The industry is concentrated: the top 50 companies have almost 75 percent of industry revenue.

Companies specializing in professional beauty products may restrict sales to salons and salon professionals, due to manufacturer policies. Salons may resell products to the public or use products for customer treatments.

Competitive Landscape

Demographics, consumer spending, and fashion trends drive demand. The profitability of individual stores depends on the ability to generate store traffic and effective merchandising. Large companies can offer a wide selection of products, and have advantages in purchasing, distribution, and marketing. Small companies can compete effectively by selling specialty products, providing superior customer service, or serving a local market. The industry is labor-intensive: average annual revenue per worker is about $85,000.

Major competitors include department stores, mass merchandisers, drug stores, TV shopping networks, Internet retailers, distributors, supermarkets, manufacturers, and salons. In addition, some beauty stores compete with dermatologists and plastic surgeons in the high-end market for cosmetics and skin care.

Products, Operations & Technology

Major products sold in beauty stores include hair and shaving, deodorant, hand, oral, and baby hygiene products (65 percent of sales), and makeup, facial care, and fragrance products (30 percent). The hair care category includes shampoo, conditioner, and color. Makeup categories

BUSINESS CHALLENGES

» Competition from Alternative Retailers

Beauty stores face a wide range of competitors across all price segments, including department stores, mass merchandisers, TV shopping networks, and Internet retailers. Department stores are the top channel for beauty products, driven by dominance in the prestige market. By stocking a wide range of products, mass merchandisers benefit from heavy customer traffic. Both TV shopping networks and Internet retailers have had strong growth in beauty products sales.

» Dependence on Consumer Spending

Sales of beauty products, particularly high-end, are susceptible to decreased consumer spending. Consumers consider many beauty products luxuries, and segments of the industry are vulnerable to economic downturns. During the last recession, sales of prestige brands were flat and sales of prestige fragrances declined almost 4 percent, according to NPD Group. Consumers tend to reduce discretionary purchases and may switch to less expensive beauty products during tough economic times.

» Supplier Concentration

Large multinational companies dominate the beauty products manufacturing industry and typically favor big retailers. Major manufacturers, such as L'Oréal, Estée Lauder, and Procter & Gamble, control a wide array of brands across multiple market segments, and continue to grow by acquiring smaller brands and distributors. Large retailers often receive favorable treatment through volume discounts and priority access to new products. Continued consolidation at the top of the beauty industry reduces the negotiating power of small retailers.

include eyes, lips, and face (foundations and concealers). Facial care includes moisturizers, cleansers, and exfoliators. Some beauty stores sell personal care appliances, such as hair dryers and curling irons. Companies may provide salon services, including hair styling, manicures, pedicures, or facials.

While open-line stores sell to both traditional retail customers and salon professionals, professional customers typically receive a special discount. Full-service stores sell only to salons and salon professionals, and carry professional use only products for resale and use in salons. Beauty retailers offering services may rent booth space to salon professionals.

Beauty stores include national and regional chains, franchises, and independent retailers. Many independent retailers have a single location ranging between 1,000 and 2,500 square feet, according to Beauty Store Business. Beauty superstores can range between 5,000 and 10,000 square feet. Typical locations include strip malls, indoor shopping malls, and floor space within larger retailers. Companies consider demographics, neighboring tenants, store visibility, and traffic accessibility when selecting locations.

Retailers offering both beauty products and salon services can generate more than $400,000 annually and between $100 and $500 per square foot, according to Beauty Store Business. Stores selling only beauty products average less than $300,000 annually and less than $250 per square foot. Stores specializing in high-end beauty products can generate over $1,000 per square foot.

Most companies arrange store layouts by product category. Strategic product placement encourages cross-selling. New products and promotional items at the front of the store, and testers for sampling, promote impulse buying. Some companies, particularly those with strong ethnic customer bases, use localized merchandising strategies to match market demographics.

Major inventory categories include hair care, skin care, cosmetics (makeup), and fragrance. Inventory mix varies depending on a company's target market. Prestige brands, such as Estée Lauder, Lancôme, and Clinique, are premium-priced products traditionally found in department stores. Mass market brands, such as L'Oréal, Revlon, and Clairol, tend to be lower priced, and found in mass merchandisers and drugstores. Beauty stores may carry private-label products or controlled label products (products for which a company has exclusive distribution rights). Professional or salon-only brands include Matrix, Redken, and Paul Mitchell.

The majority of beauty stores buy directly from manufacturers or manufacturer representatives, although some companies use distributors. To meet manufacturer requirements to sell salon-only products, a retailer may install a single stylist chair anywhere in the store. Agreements with suppliers may have minimum purchase requirements, particularly for relationships involving exclusive distribution rights. Some manufacturers accept product returns according to strict guidelines. Beauty supply buyers typically attend trade shows to identify the latest trends and select merchandise.

Computer systems and scanners track point of sale (POS) data and inventory movement, and may replenish merchandise automatically. Analysis of store sales data helps buyers make purchasing decisions. Some companies use radio frequency technology for security. In addition, computer systems can track and analyze information from customer databases to help companies develop targeted marketing programs.

Sales & Marketing

Typical customers include women 25 to 55, salon professionals, and salons. Demographics differ depending on product segment. For example, women 18 to 24 are the heaviest users of fragrance products, while older women tend to buy more prestige beauty products.

Marketing and promotional vehicles include instore flyers and displays; newspaper, print, and TV advertising; and direct mail. Manufacturer-provided samples, testers, and gifts with purchase promotions are especially helpful with more expensive goods. A distinctive store environment and instore demonstrations help companies create unique shopping experiences. Word-of-mouth is important to develop a customer base. Some beauty stores have loyalty programs encouraging volume purchases.

Customer service can be particularly important for stores specializing in high-end beauty products. Experienced sales associates typically recommend products to match a customer's physical characteristics, such as hair color or skin type. For beauty retailers with instore salons, a popular hair stylist or aesthetician can help create a loyal customer following.

Companies may have Internet sites listing store information and offering products for retail sale. Store websites may offer special discounts for online or instore purchases. Websites may also allow customers to participate in loyalty programs and redeem rewards.

Beauty stores may provide special discounts for salon professionals. The average customer sale ranges between $15 and $50 for stores without salons and exceeds $25 in stores with salons, according to Beauty Store magazine.

Human Resources

Beauty retailers, especially high-end stores selling expensive skin care or makeup systems, may employ sales staff with cosmetology backgrounds. Stores with salons require licensed professionals for various services, including haircuts, nail care, or facials. Some companies use commissions as incentives for sales associates to promote high margin products. Other companies avoid commissions to differentiate themselves from department store sales forces.

On average, a beauty store has seven full-time and two part-time employees, according to Beauty Store Business. Companies may add part-time workers during peak periods, such as the winter holidays. The industry injury rate is significantly below the national average.

Industry Employment Growth

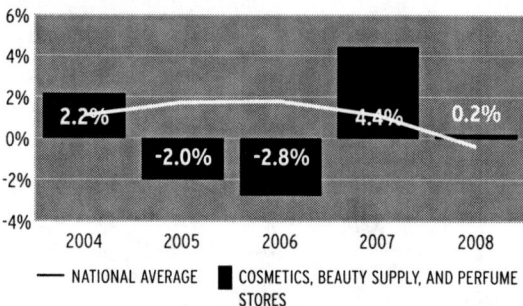

SOURCE: BUREAU OF LABOR STATISTICS

Call Preparation Questions

What is the company's most significant competitive threat?

Beauty stores face a wide range of competitors across all price segments, including department stores, mass merchandisers, TV shopping networks, and Internet retailers.

How vulnerable is the company's product mix to changes in consumer spending?

Sales of beauty products, particularly high-end, are susceptible to decreased consumer spending.

How does the company maximize relationships with large suppliers?

Large multinational companies dominate the beauty products manufacturing industry and typically favor big retailers.

How is the company capitalizing on the growing population of older consumers?

Favorable demographics should allow beauty stores to leverage growing demand for beauty products suited for aging consumers.

How important is the ethnic market to the company?

While the ethnic market can be important to beauty retailers, companies need to recognize disparities in purchase habits among different groups to effectively target unique customer segments.

Web Links

Beauty Store Business

US industry news and trends, company profiles, annual store survey.

www.beautystorebusiness.com

Cosmetics Business

Global news, some reports available for purchase.

www.cosmeticsbusiness.com

Global Cosmetic Industry

Global industry news, trends, and statistics.

www.gcimagazine.com

NPD Group

Statistics, trends, and news from market research firm NPD Beauty Group.

www.npd.com

Personal Care Products Council

Regulatory and legal issues from trade association for personal care products.

www.personalcarecouncil.org

Professional Beauty Association

Industry issues from trade association for the professional beauty industry.

www.probeauty.org

Glossary of Acronyms

CPSC — Consumer Products Safety Commission
CTFA — Cosmetic, Toiletry, and Fragrance Association
PBA — Professional Beauty Association
POS — point-of-sale

HOOVER'S TOP COMPANIES

Largest Companies by Sales	($ mil.)
Limited Brands, Inc.	10,134.0
The Estée Lauder Companies Inc.	7,910.8
Sally Beauty Holdings, Inc.	2,648.2
Mary Kay Inc.	2,400.0
Ulta Salon, Cosmetics & Fragrance, Inc.	912.1
Bare Escentuals, Inc.	556.2
Perfumania Holdings, Inc.	301.8
L'Oréal USA, Inc.	—
Sephora USA, Inc.	—

Largest Employers	Employees
Limited Brands, Inc.	97,500
The Estée Lauder Companies Inc.	32,000
Sally Beauty Holdings, Inc.	21,140
L'Oréal USA, Inc.	8,300
Ulta Salon, Cosmetics & Fragrance, Inc.	7,900
Mary Kay Inc.	5,000
Sephora USA, Inc.	5,000
Perfumania Holdings, Inc.	1,794
Bare Escentuals, Inc.	1,571

Fastest Growing* by Five-Year Sales Growth	(%)
Bare Escentuals, Inc.	42.5
Ulta Salon, Cosmetics & Fragrance, Inc.	22.9
The Estée Lauder Companies Inc.	9.1
Mary Kay Inc.	9.0
Perfumania Holdings, Inc.	8.4
Sally Beauty Holdings, Inc.	7.7
Limited Brands, Inc.	3.7

Fastest Growing* by Five-Year Employee Growth	(%)
Bare Escentuals, Inc.	65.1
Sally Beauty Holdings, Inc.	15.7
The Estée Lauder Companies Inc.	10.5
Mary Kay Inc.	6.8
Ulta Salon, Cosmetics & Fragrance, Inc.	5.5
Perfumania Holdings, Inc.	2.8

Top Public Companies by Market Value	($ mil.)
Limited Brands, Inc.	6,688.2
The Estée Lauder Companies Inc.	5,427.2
Sally Beauty Holdings, Inc.	1,561.0
Ulta Salon, Cosmetics & Fragrance, Inc.	839.4
Bare Escentuals, Inc.	422.3

* These rates are compounded annualized increases and may have resulted from acquisitions or one time gains. If less than 6 years of data are available, growth is for the years available.

SOURCE: HOOVER'S, INC., DATABASE

Credit Card Processing

The US credit card processing industry includes fewer than 500 companies with combined annual revenue under $10 billion. Major companies include First Data Corporation, Total System Services, Global Payments, and Bank of America's BA Merchant Services. The industry is highly concentrated: the top four companies account for 40 percent of industry revenues.

Competitive Landscape

Demand is driven by consumer spending. The profitability of individual companies depends on efficient operations, as services are sold largely based on cost. Large companies have big economies of scale in processing and can provide more services; small companies can compete by specializing in industries and providing custom services. The business is highly automated and capital-intensive: average annual revenue per employee is about $225,000.

Products, Operations & Technology

Processors provide transaction services to banks that issue credit cards and to merchants that accept credit card payments. Merchant products include authorizing, capturing, and settling merchants' credit and debit card transactions, and handling chargebacks. Chargebacks occur when a consumer disputes a charge and charges it back to the merchant. Processors also sell or lease point-of-sale (POS) terminals. Card issuer products include transaction authorization and posting, statement generation and printing, and card embossing.

Large processors such as First Data Corporation and Total System Services provide services to both sides of the transaction. Small processors typically offer either merchant or card issuing services, and may specialize in particular vertical markets such as credit unions or retail cards. For every merchant transaction there is a card issuing transaction.

BUSINESS CHALLENGES

» Revenues Affected by Consumer Spending
Industry revenues are closely tied to the number of credit card transactions, which depend on consumer spending. For example, during the 2001 recession, transaction revenues for major industry player First Data were flat, versus 20 percent increases in other years. Over a third of all consumer retail purchases are made using credit cards.

» Financial Consolidation Pushes Industry Consolidation
Bank consolidations often result in lost business for a specific processor. An acquiring bank will usually transfer the credit card portfolio of the acquired bank to its own processor. As consolidation continues, the processing industry will become more concentrated.

» Competition from Credit Card Networks
Substantial investment in data communications and transmission technology is required for credit card processing. Visa and First Data have sued and counter-sued each other over Visa's attempt to prohibit its member institutions from using some of First Data's services.

A credit card transaction occurs when a cardholder makes a purchase using a credit card. The merchant swipes the card through a POS terminal, which transmits the card number, amount, and merchant identification number over the processor's electronic network. The information is transmitted to the credit or debit card network, which relays the data to the bank that issued the card. For example, the data goes to Visa or MasterCard for credit transactions; and to STAR, NYCE, or PULSE EFT for debit transactions. The bank then verifies that the cardholder has sufficient funds/credit for the purchase, and sends the merchant an authorization via these same networks. At the end of the day the merchant sends the day's charges in batch to its processor, which sends the information to individual banks for settlement through the Federal Reserve Bank's Automated Clearinghouse (ACH).

The industry handles a high volume of transactions. First Data processes around 20 billion merchant transactions yearly; Total System Services, about 10 billion. First Data had 400 million card accounts from 1,400 credit card issuers in a recent year, and accounts with 4 million merchants. Processors have multiple processing and telecommunications centers across the country. First Data has 95 merchant servicing centers and 10 card issuing centers in the US. Major processing costs include telecommunications expense, personnel, and computer network maintenance.

The industry is technology-based. Transactions occur electronically over the processors' data and communications networks. Constant investment is required in computer and telecommunications equipment to stay abreast of customer demands.

Sales & Marketing

Customers who pay for processing services are financial institutions and retailers that issue their own credit cards and the merchants that accept them as payment. Major end-use customers are consumers and businesses that use credit and debit cards to pay for goods and services.

Sales channels on the merchant side of the business are mostly through Independent Sales Organizations (ISOs) and through strategic alliances. ISOs include small processors and companies that sell POS terminals and other equipment and services to merchants. Alliances include such organizations as the Credit Union Association, which acts on behalf of its members and negotiates a processing agreement for the members as a unit. The card issuer sales channel is primarily via direct sales. Processors market directly to both merchants and financial institutions through print and direct mail advertising and major industry trade shows and publicity events.

Revenues are derived from discount fees charged to the merchant, either a percentage of the credit card transaction — 2 percent is typical — or a fixed dollar amount per transaction. Long-term contracts are negotiated between the processor and the merchant or financial institution for a minimum annual processing fee; these contracts average about six years. Other fees include application fees, equipment rental, voice verification charges, and monthly statement fees.

Human Resources

While some jobs in the industry require technical expertise in computer and communications systems, many involve customer service, a lower-paying function. Accordingly, industry pay is average, just slightly higher than the national wage of $16. Annual personnel turnover exceeds 20 percent. Occupational injuries are low, at one case per 100 full-time workers annually.

Industry Employment Growth

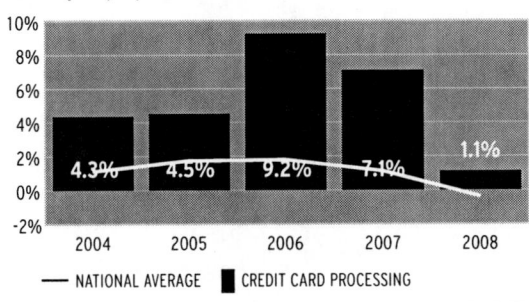

SOURCE: BUREAU OF LABOR STATISTICS

Call Preparation Questions

How have recent trends in credit card transactions impacted the company?

Industry revenues are closely tied to the number of credit card transactions, which depend on consumer spending.

How concentrated is the company's customer base?

Bank consolidations often result in lost business for a specific processor.

How much spending on technology does the company plan in the next few years?

Substantial investment in data communications and transmission technology is required for credit card processing.

What opportunities exist for the company to expand overseas?

As credit cards increase as a means of payment abroad, the potential business for processing increases.

How does the company expect increased Internet shopping to impact the industry?

With the Internet being more accepted as a shopping channel, the use of credit cards will only grow, increasing the number of transactions that need to be processed.

Web Links

Card Forum

Credit card news from multiple sources. Free registration required.

www.cardforum.com

CardTechnology.com

News about smart cards.

www.cardtechnology.com

Elavon

News about this processor.

www.elavon.com/acquiring

Entrepreneur

Articles about how small business use credit cards; fraud prevention.

www.entrepreneur.com

First Data Corporation

News about the largest card processor.

www.firstdata.com

MasterCard

Credit card issuer association.

www.mastercard.com/us/gateway.html

Payments News

MasterCard and VISA news, new product news.

www.paymentsnews.com

The Nilson Report

A leading publication for the payments industry; news, articles statistics.

www.nilsonreport.com

Total System Services

News about this major processor.

www.tsys.com

Visa

Credit card issuer association.

www.usa.visa.com/?country=us&ep=v_gg_new

Glossary of Acronyms

ACH — Automated Clearinghouse
ISO — Independent Sales Organizations
POS — point-of-sale

HOOVER'S TOP COMPANIES

Largest Companies by Sales	($ mil.)
First Data Corporation	8,051.4
Visa Inc.	6,263.0
The Western Union Company	5,282.0
MasterCard Incorporated	4,991.6
Fiserv, Inc.	4,739.0
Lender Processing Services, Inc.	3,446.0
U.S. Central Federal Credit Union	2,599.1
DST Systems, Inc.	2,285.4
Alliance Data Systems Corporation	2,025.3
Total System Services, Inc.	1,938.6

Largest Employers	Employees
First Data Corporation	27,000
Fiserv, Inc.	25,000
DST Systems, Inc.	11,000
Alliance Data Systems Corporation	7,400
Total System Services, Inc.	6,921
The Western Union Company	6,100
Metavante Technologies, Inc.	5,900
Visa Inc.	5,479
MasterCard Incorporated	5,000
Global Payments Inc.	4,899

Fastest Growing* by Five-Year Sales Growth	(%)
Money Centers of America, Inc.	144.3
Pipeline Data Inc.	114.5
ASI Technology Corporation	63.3
Southwest Corporate Federal Credit Union	59.9
Visa Inc.	55.2
Euronet Worldwide, Inc.	38.6
Western Corporate Federal Credit Union	36.0
Cardtronics, Inc.	34.9
Liquidity Services, Inc.	34.2
Online Resources Corporation	31.6

Fastest Growing* by Five-Year Employee Growth	(%)
Euronet Worldwide, Inc.	64.3
Cardtronics, Inc.	38.7
MoneyGram International, Inc.	32.1
Liquidity Services, Inc.	26.9
Heartland Payment Systems, Inc.	23.1
Online Resources Corporation	21.9
Ocwen Financial Corporation	15.3
Global Cash Access Holdings, Inc.	12.6
Viad Corp	10.1
TNS, Inc.	9.5

Top Public Companies by Market Value	($ mil.)
Visa Inc.	27,487.1
MasterCard Incorporated	14,062.3
The Western Union Company	10,175.7
Fiserv, Inc.	5,670.1
Global Payments Inc.	3,760.4

* These rates are compounded annualized increases and may have resulted from acquisitions or one time gains. If less than 6 years of data are available, growth is for the years available.

SOURCE: HOOVER'S, INC., DATABASE

Credit Collections and Services

In the US, about 1,600 credit reporting agencies and 5,000 credit collections agencies generate annual revenues of $14 billion. Large collection agencies include Asset Acceptance Capital and NCO Group; big reporting agencies include Dun & Bradstreet, TransUnion, Equifax, and Experian. The collections segment of the industry is fairly fragmented: the 50 largest companies hold less then 50 percent of the market. The credit reporting segment is highly concentrated: the 50 largest companies hold 90 percent of the market.

Competitive Landscape

Demand for credit reporting and for collections services are driven by the volume of financial transactions, and by the health of the economy. The profitability of individual companies depends largely on efficiency of operations. The profitability of collections companies that buy receivables portfolios depends on their ability to assess recovery potential. Large credit reporting companies have significant economies of scale in operations. Small companies can compete successfully in the collections segment because of the labor-intensive nature of the work.

Products, Operations & Technology

Credit reporting agencies help businesses decide whether to extend credit to customers, while collections agencies help businesses recover funds that had been loaned. Credit reports are used by businesses to determine the creditworthiness of individuals and businesses that want to buy goods and services on credit, including credit cards, auto and bank loans, mortgages, and business accounts. Collections agencies attempt to recover loans from individuals and businesses that are delinquent in making payments. Some large companies like Equifax do both credit reporting and collections, but most companies participate in only one segment.

BUSINESS CHALLENGES

» **Economy Affects Receivables Recovery Rates, Credit Reporting Volume**

Collection agencies benefit from downturns in the economy because of more business, but they have a greater risk of paying too much for receivables if the economy is deteriorating. Credit reporting is driven by the need for credit and financing, which are stronger when the economy is healthy.

» **Faulty Information, Identity Theft**

As consumer information is more widely used to make credit decisions, credit companies face greater risk that their data is faulty or will be stolen or misused. Inappropriate disclosure of consumer information is a PR problem, may result in lawsuits, and may run afoul of privacy laws. More government regulation in this area is likely.

» **Competition from Customers**

In some cases, potential customers are doing more of their own collections because the size of their operations makes it profitable to do the work internally. Consolidation in the banking, utilities, telecom, and health care industries in recent years means that there are fewer, but larger, customers for collection agencies. In other cases, customers outsource collections only to large companies that can handle national accounts, cutting smaller agencies out of the business.

The credit reporting side of the industry consists of Dun & Bradstreet (the main source of commercial credit information), three "national repositories" of consumer credit information (TransUnion, Equifax, and Experian, each of which maintains 190 million credit files), about 1,300 consumer reporting agencies, and 300 commercial reporting agencies. Dun & Bradstreet and the three national consumer credit companies collect credit information from sources like commercial companies, banks, credit card companies, mortgage bankers, and finance companies. Reporting agencies are affiliated with one or more of the national reporting companies. About 1 billion credit reports are generated every year. A typical consumer credit report shows current and historical status of credit card and auto loan accounts, bank loans, mortgages, public information about relevant court proceedings, and recent credit inquiries. In addition to listing information, reporting agencies use proprietary formulas to produce a credit "score" that allows customers to rate credit risks.

The collections side (also called "receivables management") deals mainly with the 2 percent of mortgage debt and 4.5 percent of credit card debt that is typically delinquent at any one time, as well as collections for child support, bounced checks, student loans, and uninsured health care costs. Collections consist largely of writing letters and making phone calls, and finding the addresses and phone numbers of debtors who have moved, called "skiptracing." Companies find debtors by using the US Post Office National Change of Address service, electronic phone directories, voter registration records, and motor vehicle registrations.

The three main types of collection services agencies offer are contingency fee collections, portfolio purchasing, and receivables outsourcing. Contingency fee collections, the mainstay of the industry, pay agencies a percentage of all funds recovered. The typical range is 15 to 35 percent but goes as high as 50 percent for old loans or those that have already been extensively serviced. The average fee for the health care industry is 15 percent. Some agencies have sufficient capital resources to engage in portfolio purchasing, which entails buying an entire portfolio of nonperforming loans and keeping all of the collected funds. Because collections agencies are in the receivables business already, many companies use them for complete receivables outsourcing, and pay a fee to have all their receivables functions handled.

Collection agencies are strictly limited in terms of the methods they can use to persuade debtors to pay on their loans. One of the most powerful tools is the threat of reporting the bad debt to the national credit bureaus, where it will remain for up to seven years. Quick response is important in debt collection. The probability of collecting a delinquent account drops with the length of delinquency. Experts estimate that after only three months, the probability of collection drops to around 75 percent;

after six months, to only 45 percent; and after a year, to around 25 percent.

To track the large stream of credit information, reporting agencies rely heavily on computer technology. Consolidation in the industry has been driven by the large economies of scale allowed by the operation of efficient electronic systems for receiving, sorting, and reporting information. The collections segment is also becoming more computerized, as companies get access to databases of external information that allow them to find debtors.

Sales & Marketing

The national reporting companies sell information directly to large users like Fortune 500 companies and big financial institutions, while small reporting agencies act essentially as middlemen, buying information from the national companies and reselling it to small users. Eighty percent of collections business comes from the banking, utilities, telecommunications, and health care industries. Because customers are mainly businesses, direct sales with a sales force is common, as are trade advertising and direct mail to small businesses.

Human Resources

Many workers in the credit reporting segment have special skills working with computer and communications systems, and receive pay that is above the average national wage of $16. Workers in the collections segment, however, need no special skills and are relatively low-paid, more than a dollar less than the national average. Personnel turnover in collections is high.

Industry Employment Growth

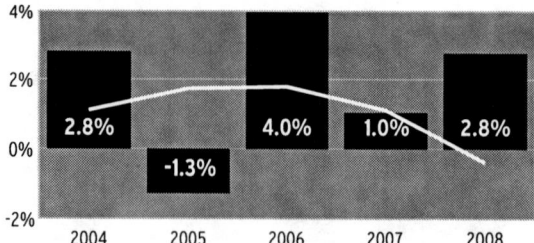

Average Hourly Earnings

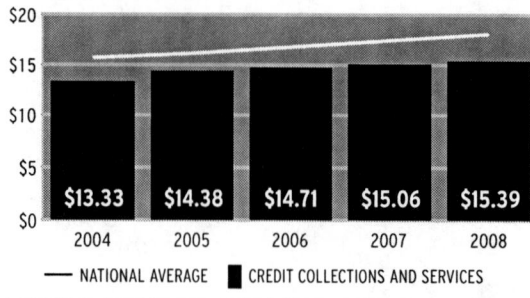

— NATIONAL AVERAGE ■ CREDIT COLLECTIONS AND SERVICES

SOURCE: BUREAU OF LABOR STATISTICS

Call Preparation Questions

How much is the company's business affected by economic forces?

Collection agencies benefit from downturns in the economy because of more business, but they have a greater risk of paying too much for receivables if the economy is deteriorating.

What actions has the company taken to protect against data theft?

As consumer information is more widely used to make credit decisions, credit companies face greater risk that their data is faulty or will be stolen or misused.

Has the company seen large customers take more of their collection work in-house?

In some cases, potential customers are doing more of their own collections because the size of their operations makes it profitable to do the work internally.

Does the company expect demand for collection and reporting services to keep growing?

A sharp increase in consumer and other debt in recent years has increased opportunities in the credit and collections business.

Web Links

ACA International

Industry information and statistics.
www.acainternational.org

Commercial Collection Agency Association

Code of ethics, profiles, links, free literature, news and surveys.
www.ccaacollect.com

Consumer Data Industry Association

Credit information.
www.cdiaonline.org

Credit Research Foundation

Surveys and publications.
www.crfonline.org

insideARM

News about accounts receivable management.
www.insidearm.com

National Foundation for Credit Counseling

News.
www.nfcc.org/Newsroom/newsroom.cfm

Glossary of Acronyms

ABI — American Bankruptcy Institute
ACA — American Collectors Association
CCAA — Commercial Collection Agency Association
NFCC — National Federation of Credit Counselors

HOOVER'S TOP COMPANIES

Largest Companies by Sales	($ mil.)
Equifax Inc.	1,935.7
Moody's Corporation	1,755.4
The Dun & Bradstreet Corporation	1,726.3
NCO Group, Inc.	1,290.0
TransUnion LLC	1,200.0
Fair Isaac Corporation	744.8
Intersections Inc.	361.6
Experian Americas	284.7
Portfolio Recovery Associates, Inc.	263.3

Largest Employers	Employees
NCO Group, Inc.	29,000
Equifax Inc.	7,000
Experian Americas	6,765
The Dun & Bradstreet Corporation	4,900
TransUnion LLC	4,000
Moody's Corporation	3,600
Fair Isaac Corporation	2,737
Asset Acceptance Capital Corp.	1,708
Fitch Ratings Inc.	1,700
Portfolio Recovery Associates, Inc.	1,240

Fastest Growing* by Five-Year Sales Growth	(%)
Portfolio Recovery Associates, Inc.	25.4
Intersections Inc.	19.7
Encore Capital Group, Inc.	16.8
NCO Group, Inc.	12.9
CreditRiskMonitor.com, Inc.	10.0
Equifax Inc.	9.6
Lamont, Hanley & Associates, Inc.	9.1
Asset Acceptance Capital Corp.	7.9
Moody's Corporation	7.1
TransUnion LLC	6.3

Fastest Growing* by Five-Year Employee Growth	(%)
NCO Group, Inc.	25.5
Equifax Inc.	23.4
Intersections Inc.	19.7
Moody's Corporation	11.4
Portfolio Recovery Associates, Inc.	5.7
Encore Capital Group, Inc.	5.1
The Dun & Bradstreet Corporation	4.0

Top Public Companies by Market Value	($ mil.)
Moody's Corporation	4,724.1
The Dun & Bradstreet Corporation	4,114.8
Equifax Inc.	3,349.5
Fair Isaac Corporation	1,117.3
Portfolio Recovery Associates, Inc.	517.3

* These rates are compounded annualized increases and may have resulted from acquisitions or one time gains. If less than 6 years of data are available, growth is for the years available.

SOURCE: HOOVER'S, INC., DATABASE

Dairy Products Manufacture

The US dairy products manufacturing industry consists of about 1,200 companies that have combined annual revenue of $60 billion. Large industry participants include Dean Foods, cooperatives like Dairy Farmers of America and Land O'Lakes, and the US subsidiaries of foreign companies like Danone. The industry is rapidly consolidating: the 50 largest companies hold 75 percent of the market. Although most companies in the industry are small, a few large companies have been built through acquisitions.

Competitive Landscape

Changes in consumer income drive demand for various types of dairy foods. The profitability of individual companies depends on efficient operations and marketing, as milk is a commodity product. There are few economies of scale in the manufacturing process, which is why small companies can effectively compete with the large ones in local markets.

Products, Operations & Technology

The four major product segments are fluid milk and milk products ($30 billion); cheese ($20 billion); frozen desserts ($10 billion); and butter ($1 billion). Most companies specialize in only one product segment, although large companies may participate in several. Because of the perishable nature of much of the products, especially fluid milk, local production is the norm. Companies receive raw milk from local producers, process it, and distribute the products to local customers. Large companies own many local plants; Dean Foods (formerly Suiza Foods) owns about 77 local production plants.

Nearly all milk sold in the US is pasteurized and homogenized. The basic steps in a milk processing plant are separating milk fat from milk; adjusting the fat content; heating the milk to kill bacteria (pasteurization); pressure-treating to disperse fat droplets throughout the

BUSINESS CHALLENGES

» Consumer Milk Consumption Flat

Total consumption of fluid milk in the US has been flat for the past 10 years. Milk consumption per person decreased 20 percent, while consumption of some other dairy products increased. Each year, the average American consumer drinks 23 gallons of milk, compared to 50 gallons of soft drinks and 26 gallons of coffee.

» Government Controls Raw Milk Prices

Because of state and federal support of dairy farmers, the price of raw milk is regulated, though not fixed. Regulation raises prices for consumers and reduces the incentive for dairy product manufacturers to control their major raw material cost by, for example, entering into fixed-price supply contracts. Manufacturers can't always pass along price increases.

» Competition from Big Customers

Large grocery chains use a large enough volume of dairy products to justify their own manufacturing facilities, buying raw milk directly from farmers. Kroger, one of the largest US grocery chains, operates dairies, ice cream plants, and cheese plants. While large customers may not get all their needs supplied from captive manufacturing operations, they often take a large share of the market in major cities.

liquid (homogenization); and bottling in cartons or plastic containers. Milk designated as raw hasn't been pasteurized or homogenized. Butter is produced by solidifying milk fat.

Cheese, yogurt, cottage cheese, and sour cream are made from milk by adding various cultures of bacteria that coagulate the proteins in the milk. Ice cream is made by chilling a mixture of milk fat and sugar. Manufacturing processes are usually standardized and highly automated. Testing for product safety and quality is done at numerous steps in the production process. The number of products within each major segment is large, with differences in fat content, additives, flavors, and textures.

Milk, the major raw ingredient, is usually bought from individual local farms or farm cooperatives, which can be very large, with hundreds or thousands of members. Dairy Farmers of America, the largest cooperative, has almost 20,000 members in 45 states. Long-term supply contracts are rare, mainly because milk production has been abundant in the US. Supply contracts typically extend for a year and specify quantities, but not prices. Minimum prices for raw milk are set by states and the federal government.

Advances in dairy farming technology, including computerized, automated milking systems, and technology-based feeding systems, have created excess milk production capacity in the US. In ten years, annual milk yield per cow increased 15 percent to 19,200 pounds. As a consequence, total milk production increased to 171 billion pounds, even though the number of milk cows decreased to 9 million.

Sales & Marketing

Dairy products are sold to retailers like grocery, convenience, and club stores; food service customers like schools, hospitals, restaurants, and hotels; and food manufacturers. Because of the perishable nature of many dairy products, most manufacturers provide direct-to-store delivery (DSD), using their own or third-party refrigerated trucks. The success of large companies like Dean Foods in what is essentially a commodity business has resulted largely from their development of an extensive and dependable distribution system. In fact, some smaller dairy producers piggyback on the distribution systems of the large ones.

Customer consolidation, especially among grocery chains, has advantaged large manufacturers that can provide DSD to all customer stores. Companies usually use an in-house sales force to get new customers, and companies with several dairies may use a local sales force at each dairy to serve the local market. Products are often sold under a variety of local brand names or under the customer's private label. The growth in the size of customers has produced competition from customers, especially in the milk segment, as large grocery chains have entered the production business. Kroger, a grocery chain, is also one of the largest dairy products manufacturers in the country.

Human Resources

Some jobs in dairy product manufacture are technical, involving specialized machine operations and product testing, but many jobs are highly manual, such as handling products in warehouses and during distribution. Average hourly pay is around $17, about a dollar more than the average national wage. Manufacturing processes are highly automated, with very high revenue per production worker of $750,000. To retain workers, employers provide benefits that total an additional 30 percent of wages. The operation of machinery, and extremes of heat and cold in some processes, leads to a higher than average number of injuries. The industry's annual injury rate is over eight cases per 100 full-time workers, almost double the national average.

Industry Employment Growth

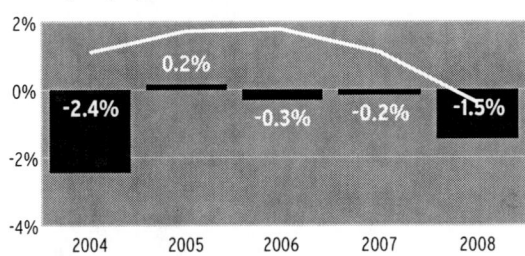

Average Hourly Earnings

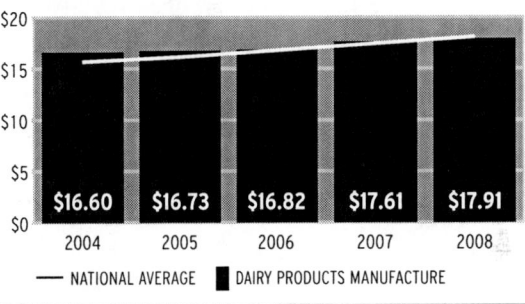

SOURCE: BUREAU OF LABOR STATISTICS

Call Preparation Questions

How has the low US milk consumption rate affected the company's business?

Total consumption of fluid milk in the US has been flat for the past 10 years.

How is the company positioning itself to compete against large grocers entering the dairy production industry?

Large grocery chains use a large enough volume of dairy products to justify their own manufacturing facilities, buying raw milk directly from farmers.

What strategies does the company have to improve profitability and margins?

Profitability can be increased by more efficient production and distribution operations, or by creating products with higher profit margins.

Web Links

Agriculture and Agri-Food Canada

Canadian dairy industry statistics.
www.agr.ca

Dairy Farmers of America

Largest farmers cooperative. Market information, good industry links.
www.dfamilk.com

Dairy Foods

News. Industry statistics. Top 100 dairy companies.
www.dairyfoods.com

Dairy Management Inc.

Industry promotion information. Links to dairy associations.
www.dairyinfo.com

Dairy Product Processing Descriptions

Description of various dairy products processing steps from the University of Guelph, Canada.
www.foodsci.uoguelph.ca/dairyedu/fluid.html

Dairy.com

News.
www.dairy.com

International Dairy Foods Association

News. Industry statistics. Prices.
www.idfa.org

Livestock, Dairy, and Poultry Outlook

Annual dairy statistics.
www.ers.usda.gov/publications/ldp/LDPTables.htm

National Milk Producers Federation

Lobbying organization. Milk production and price statistics. Legislative update.
www.nmpf.org

US Dairy Export Council (USDEC)

Export reports and issues
www.usdec.org

USDA Dairy Programs

Programs operated by the Department of Agriculture.
www.ams.usda.gov/dairy

Glossary of Acronyms

CME — Chicago Mercantile Exchange
CWT — Cooperative Working Together
DEIP — Dairy Export Incentive Program
DSD — direct-to-store delivery
IDFA — International Dairy Foods Association
MILC — Milk Income Loss Contract
MREA — Milk Regulatory Equity Act

HOOVER'S TOP COMPANIES

Largest Companies by Sales	($ mil.)
Kraft Foods Inc.	42,201.0
Dean Foods Company	12,454.6
Dairy Farmers of America, Inc.	11,100.0
Land O'Lakes, Inc.	8,924.9
Leprino Foods Company	2,620.0
HP Hood LLC	2,300.0
Great Lakes Cheese Company, Inc.	1,700.0
Foremost Farms USA, Cooperative	1,600.0
Schreiber Foods Inc.	1,264.0
Nestlé USA, Inc.	—

Largest Employers	Employees
Kraft Foods Inc.	98,000
Dean Foods Company	25,585
Nestlé USA, Inc.	15,500
Land O'Lakes, Inc.	8,700
Schreiber Foods Inc.	4,800
HP Hood LLC	4,500
Dairy Farmers of America, Inc.	4,000
Michael Foods, Inc.	3,759
Leprino Foods Company	3,000
Wells' Dairy, Inc.	2,500

Fastest Growing* by Five-Year Sales Growth	(%)
Emerald Dairy, Inc.	57.4
American Home Food Products, Inc.	38.0
Lifeway Foods, Inc.	26.0
HP Hood LLC	18.1
Great Lakes Cheese Company, Inc.	14.8
Dairy Farmers of America, Inc.	11.5
Tillamook County Creamery Association	9.1
Land O'Lakes, Inc.	8.8
Kraft Foods Inc.	6.4
Dean Foods Company	6.3

Fastest Growing* by Five-Year Employee Growth	(%)
HP Hood LLC	21.5
Lifeway Foods, Inc.	19.1
Tillamook County Creamery Association	8.4
Great Lakes Cheese Company, Inc.	5.5
Land O'Lakes, Inc.	1.7
Kraft Foods Inc.	1.4

Top Public Companies by Market Value	($ mil.)
Kraft Foods Inc.	39,450.7
Dean Foods Company	2,768.0
Emerald Dairy, Inc.	374.9
Lifeway Foods, Inc.	199.1
American Home Food Products, Inc.	2.2

* These rates are compounded annualized increases and may have resulted from acquisitions or one time gains. If less than 6 years of data are available, growth is for the years available.

SOURCE: HOOVER'S, INC., DATABASE

Deep Sea Shipping

THIS INDUSTRY INCLUDES:

SIC CODES

4424   Deep Sea Domestic Transportation of Freight

NAICS CODES

483111   Deep Sea Freight Transportation

The deep sea shipping industry includes about 500 companies with combined annual revenue of nearly $9 billion. Major carriers include Crowley, Horizon Lines, APL, and Overseas Shipholding Group. The industry is highly concentrated: the 50 largest companies account for nearly 95 percent of industry revenue.

Deep sea shipping is the transport of cargo to and from foreign ports. Ships that travel within the US or that transport passengers aren't included in this industry.

Competitive Landscape

Demand is driven by macroeconomic trends in global imports and exports. The profitability of individual companies depends on efficient operations and a good safety record. Large companies have advantages in fleet size and port access. Small companies can compete effectively by chartering services out of smaller ports and transporting unusual cargo. Average annual revenue per worker for a typical company is nearly $500,000.

The global shipping industry transports over 90 percent of the world's total commerce, according to the International Shipping Federation (ISF). Deep sea shipping is a highly competitive industry; however, competition from other forms of transportation is limited.

Products, Operations & Technology

Deep sea shipping services include international freight transportation (95 percent of industry revenue) and cargo loading and unloading, known in the industry as stevedoring (4 percent).

The US is the world's largest importer and exporter, shipping 1.2 billion metric tons of cargo annually. Worldwide, over 30,000 large, privately owned vessels transport merchandise across oceans. Less than 500 (2 percent) of these ships are registered in the US. An additional 700 ships are owned by American compa-

BUSINESS CHALLENGES

» Dependence on International Trade Policies

Cabotage laws, disputes over American protectionist policies, and trade boycotts significantly shape the health and outlook of the US deep sea shipping industry. Major modifications or a repeal of international trade polices could have major impact on a carrier's profitability. Changes to international flags of convenience standards could increase labor costs. A repeal of the Jones Act would allow foreign-flag vessel operators to transport goods between US ports and compete directly against US ships. The shipping industry actively promotes the retention of current trade policies.

» Vulnerability to Fuel Costs

Bunker fuel represents up to 60 percent of total vessel operating expenses, or about 15 percent of revenues. Prices for bunker fuel have doubled over the past five years. A dollar increase in the price of bunker fuel can add several million in additional operating expenses for a large shipping company. Carriers can offset fuel price increases through a Bunker Adjustment Factor (BAF), a surcharge passed to shippers that covers price fluctuations in bunker fuel, however, BAF hikes may be difficult to collect.

» Criticism of "Flags of Convenience"

Of US-operated ships, 60 percent are registered in foreign countries. The Bahamas, Liberia, the Marshall Islands, and Panama account for nearly two-thirds of all US ships registered under a foreign flag. Carriers register in so-called "flags of convenience" to employ lower-wage crew members, avoid higher US excise taxes, and bypass tough US environmental regulations. The International Transport Workers Federation (ITF) has vigorously criticized foreign ship registry.

nies but registered in so-called "flags of convenience," primarily the Bahamas, Liberia, the Marshall Islands, and Panama.

Vessels include dry bulk carriers, which transport commodities such as iron ore, coal, and food; liquid bulk carriers such as tankers that ship crude oil, chemicals, and petroleum products; diesel-powered container ships; general cargo ships; and roll on-roll off (RORO) vessels that transport wheeled cargo such as cars, trucks, and trains.

Service takes three different forms: liner, charter, and tanker service. Liner service is regular, scheduled stops at ports along a fixed route. Liner routes are dominated by container ships transporting manufactured goods. Charter service, also known as tramping, is an "as-needed" mode of shipping that moves between ports based on cargo availability. Tramps inexpensively transport a single form of dry bulk cargo (grain, coal, ore, sugar) for a single shipper. Tanker service transports crude oil, petroleum, and other liquid products. Tankers can be chartered, but most are owned and operated by major oil companies.

Container-based liner service represents only 30 percent of global ton-miles (cargo weight times distance traveled) yet accounts for 80 percent of the total value of shipments. Liquid and dry bulk cargo represents the other 70 percent of ton-miles shipped but only 20 percent of the total value of shipments.

A ship's capacity is measured by several formulas. Dead weight tonnage (DWT) is the total weight of cargo, supplies, and crew that can be loaded on an "empty" ship. Gross register tonnage (GRT) measures the total internal capacity of a vessel. One GRT is equal to a volume of 100 cubic feet. The average tanker is between 250,000 and 350,000 DWT; dry bulk carriers average 100,000 to 150,000. Twenty-foot equivalent units (TEUs) refer to a container ship's total cargo-carrying capacity. The average container ship has a capacity of around 5,000 TEUs and can carry around 3,000 40-foot containers.

The average deep sea ship travels around 15 to 20 miles per hour (12 to 15 knots). An average excursion across the Atlantic covers 4,000 miles and takes about 12 days. On average, 20 crew members sail with the ship. The average age of the US privately owned fleet is around 15 years; 40 percent of the fleet has been built within the past 10 years. Most ships are rebuilt two or three times in their lifetime, lasting 25 to 40 years before being scrapped.

Ships depend highly on complex information systems to maintain vessel schedules and efficiently manage terminal operations. Deep sea shippers manage ship routing through real-time, Web-based tracking systems. Some shippers outsource route optimization to technology companies that track weather and wind patterns. Radio frequency identification (RFID) tagging allows customers to track containers and cargo throughout the entire voyage. A mandatory international safety protocol, the Global Maritime Distress & Safety System (GMDSS), replaces Morse Code by automating distress signaling and locating.

Sales & Marketing

Typical deep sea shipping customers include energy, chemical, industrial, auto, retail, and consumer product companies. Some carriers work directly with the US government to transport military goods and international mail. Sales are by an internal sales force; ship brokers (intermediaries between carriers and shippers); freight forwarders (booking agents for shippers); and non-vessel-operating common carriers (NVOCCs, resellers of carrier space). These intermediaries are broadly known as ocean transportation intermediaries (OTIs).

Major types of marketing include trade publications, public relations, and trade shows. Account managers focus significant attention on maintaining key client relationships. Carriers often partner with container companies and develop relationships with US and foreign ports, particularly ports that are efficiently run with limited congestion. Customer service is available by phone, e-mail, and Web-based chat.

Prior to deregulation under the Ocean Shipping Reform Act of 1998 (OSRA, or the Shipping Act), carriers were exempt from anti-trust laws and met at conferences to collectively agree on shipping rates. Now, around 80 percent of ocean carriers sign private service contracts with shippers (the industry term for customers transporting goods overseas). Carriers are under no obligation to post rates. By law, intermediaries (OTIs) must charge a set rate based on the cargo and route. OTIs publish price quotes on the Internet and typically charge a monthly or per-use fee to access tariff information. Many carriers and OTIs provide online ordering of shipping services.

Shipping prices vary based on demand and direction (December freight rates from China to the US are much higher than westbound rates).

Charter carriers are typically paid daily charter rates based on cargo classification and volume. A six-month charter rate for a 4,000 twenty-foot equivalent unit (TEU) container ship is around $20,000 a day. An average liner service rate for a trans-Pacific voyage is around $2,000 per TEU (westbound) and $1,000 per TEU (eastbound). Rates can increase due to hazardous cargo, less than full containers, or unusual sizes.

Human Resources

Wages in the deep sea shipping industry are over 40 percent higher than the national average. A typical captain earns an average of $60,000 annually. Captains and pilots must be licensed by the US Coast Guard (USCG) and must either accumulate sea time or graduate from a maritime academy. Sailors and marine oilers must have USCG documentation and a USCG license if they work on liquid bulk carriers. Wages for US sailors are about 10 percent lower than the national average.

Flags of convenience (FOC) ships have lower working standards and regulations than US flagships. Wages are much lower, and low-skilled crew workers (also known as "rates") earn as little as $6,000 a year. Some carriers don't pay any wages to these workers, only offering room and board.

Deep sea shipping injuries are typically due to overexertion and mishandling cargo or equipment at land or port. The injury rate is about 30 percent higher than the national average.

Crew retention is a challenge due to extended time at sea. Crews work seven days a week and typically follow a cyclical schedule of four hours on and eight off. Voyages last several months, which can be difficult for workers with families. Large companies have tried to retain workers with more comfortable accommodations and wireless communications, but 30 percent of officer trainees quit before training is complete.

Call Preparation Questions

Is the company concerned about possible shifts in international trade policies or the US position on shipping?

Cabotage laws, disputes over American protectionist policies, and trade boycotts significantly shape the health and outlook of the US deep sea shipping industry.

How does the company manage increases in the cost of bunker fuel?

Bunker fuel represents up to 60 percent of total vessel operating expenses, or about 15 percent of revenues.

How many of the company's ships are registered outside the US?

Of US-operated ships, 60 percent are registered in foreign countries.

What opportunities does the company see in using Arctic routes?

Due to melting sea ice, the Arctic's Northwest Passage has become a more navigable route between Europe and Asia.

Are any of the company's vessels equipped to mix bulk and break-bulk cargo?

Carriers are increasingly mixing bulk and break-bulk cargo (palletized items too large to be placed into containers) in a single shipment.

Web Links

Chamber of Shipping of America

Trade association for 30 US-based carriers.
www.knowships.org

Equasis

Search safety records of individual ships.
www.equasis.org

International Association of Dry Cargo Shipowners (INTERCARGO)

Trade association for cargo shipowners.
www.intercargo.org

International Association of Independent Tanker Owners (INTERTANKO)

Trade association for international oil and chemical tankers.
www.intertanko.com

International Chamber of Shipping (ICS)

International trade association for merchant ship operators.
www.marisec.org/ics

International Maritime Organization (IMO)

UN agency charged with setting international shipping standards and regulations.
www.imo.org

International Shipping Federation (ISF)

International labor organization for ship operators.
www.marisec.org/isf

US Department of Transportation, Maritime Administration

Insightful data on the US shipping industry.
www.marad.dot.gov

Glossary of Acronyms

DWT — dead weight tons
FMC — Federal Maritime Commission
FOC — flags of convenience
GMDSS — Global Maritime Distress and Safety System
GRT — gross register tonnage
ICS — International Chamber of Shipping
ISF — International Shipping Federation
INTERTANKO — International Association of Independent Tanker Owners
IMO — International Maritime Organization
ITF — International Transport Workers Federation
MARISEC — Maritime International Secretariat Services Limited
MARPOL — International Convention for the Prevention of Pollution by Ships
OTI — ocean transportation intermediaries
TEU — twenty-foot equivalent units
VLCC — very large crude carriers

HOOVER'S TOP COMPANIES

Largest Companies by Sales	($ mil.)
The Washington Companies	4,300.0
Alexander & Baldwin, Inc.	1,898.0
SEACOR Holdings Inc.	1,656.0
Crowley Maritime Corporation	1,620.0
Horizon Lines, Inc.	1,304.3
APL Limited	1,195.5
Overseas Shipholding Group, Inc.	1,129.3
Hornbeck Offshore Services, Inc.	432.1
Genco Shipping & Trading Limited	405.4
K-Sea Transportation Partners L.P.	326.3

Largest Employers	Employees
SEACOR Holdings Inc.	5,268
APL Limited	4,782
Crowley Maritime Corporation	4,171
Overseas Shipholding Group, Inc.	3,754
Alexander & Baldwin, Inc.	2,197
Horizon Lines, Inc.	2,151
The Washington Companies	1,900
Hornbeck Offshore Services, Inc.	1,092
K-Sea Transportation Partners L.P.	1,044
OSG America L.P.	665

Fastest Growing* by Five-Year Sales Growth	(%)
Genco Shipping & Trading Limited	282.2
The Washington Companies	81.9
OSG America L.P.	73.2
K-Sea Transportation Partners L.P.	35.9
Overseas Shipholding Group, Inc.	33.5
SEACOR Holdings Inc.	32.5
Hornbeck Offshore Services, Inc.	31.3
U.S. Shipping Partners L.P.	22.3
Crowley Maritime Corporation	10.6
Trailer Bridge, Inc.	9.5

Fastest Growing* by Five-Year Employee Growth	(%)
Eagle Bulk Shipping Inc.	359.1
Genco Shipping & Trading Limited	64.0
General Maritime Corporation	33.4
K-Sea Transportation Partners L.P.	25.6
Hornbeck Offshore Services, Inc.	18.4
Overseas Shipholding Group, Inc.	16.7
U.S. Shipping Partners L.P.	8.3
Horizon Lines, Inc.	3.9
International Shipholding Corporation	2.7
SEACOR Holdings Inc.	2.3

Top Public Companies by Market Value	($ mil.)
Overseas Shipholding Group, Inc.	2,314.3
SEACOR Holdings Inc.	1,334.2
Alexander & Baldwin, Inc.	1,027.5
General Maritime Corporation	783.1
Genco Shipping & Trading Limited	469.3

* These rates are compounded annualized increases and may have resulted from acquisitions or one time gains. If less than 6 years of data are available, growth is for the years available.

SOURCE: HOOVER'S, INC., DATABASE

Dentists Offices and Clinics

About 120,000 dentists offices and clinics operate in the US, generating annual revenue of over $80 billion. The large majority of dentists are sole practitioners and practice general dentistry; the rest specialize in oral surgery, periodontics, pediatric dentistry, oral pathology, or orthodontics. Average annual revenue per office is about $600,000. The industry is highly fragmented.

Competitive Landscape

Demand for dental services is driven largely by demographics. While the growth in the number of children 5 to 19 (who require prophylactic and orthodontic work) is increasing only slightly, aging Americans are increasing the number of adults over 55 who may need more specialized dental work. Large practices have advantages in marketing and possible specialties within the office. Small practices are successful due to the personality and competence of the dentist. Dentists typically have several direct competitors in the same geographical area. The industry is labor-intensive.

Products, Operations & Technology

Dentists practicing general dentistry provide amalgam and composite fillings, regular teeth cleanings, cosmetic dentistry, root canals, sealants, oral surgery, gum disease treatment, TMJ therapy, tobacco cessation and nutrition counseling, crowns and bridges, dentures, and dental implants.

Most dentists offices include dental hygienists and office staff. The average office has one dentist and three employees (usually a receptionist and two hygienists). Insurance paperwork, bill collection, scheduling, and restocking supplies are the main concerns of the office staff. Typical equipment includes X-ray machines; chair-mounted systems such as drills,

BUSINESS CHALLENGES

» Reduced Demand for Traditional Services

Americans' teeth are much healthier than 30 years ago, reducing demand for traditional dental services. Because demand is limited by the growth of the US population, about 1 percent per year, more dentists are looking for new ways to expand revenue, like more preventive and cosmetic care, dental implants, and specialized treatments for disorders like TMJ.

» Growing Importance of Dental Insurance Providers

Several years of double-digit increases in the cost of health insurance have made quality health care, especially dental care, unaffordable for growing numbers of Americans. Dentists who contract with dental insurance plans have to accept the fees dictated by the insurer, which are often lower than fees charged to other customers. As more Americans are covered by managed care plans that include dental care, dentists will have less control over fees and will be pushed to contain costs.

» Heavy Local Competition

In many urban and suburban markets, consumers have convenient access to several dentist offices and can easily switch. In many cases, price is less important than individual preference. Specialists typically have less patient-switching than do general dentists.

suction, spray, etc.; and computer imaging systems.

The typical office sees around 4,000 patients annually. Most visits are routine cleanings, which are done by dental hygienists with the dentist reviewing the hygienists' work. Increasingly, hygienists are doing more routine dental procedures allowing dentists to conduct complex procedures and consult with patients on their oral health.

Rapid technological changes in the last decade, including ultra-high-speed drills; sand blasting; better analgesics; new filling, bonding, and implant compounds; and computer imaging and laser bleaching systems, have changed dental practices considerably. Intra-oral TV and t-scan devices are used to educate patients about their teeth and the prescribed treatment.

Computerized management systems have become the norm in most dentist offices. While dentists were slower than physicians to adopt information systems, dentists now use them for patient scheduling, to refer patients to other specialists, and for insurance billing. The number of Americans with dental insurance plans has increased steadily over the past 20 years, increasing the need for insurance-processing capabilities.

Sales & Marketing

Americans with dental insurance typically visit the dentist every six months, as most insurance plans cover biannual dental checkups and cleanings. Per capita spending on dental care is about $275 annually.

Most dentists get new customers primarily through referrals from existing patients and from inclusion on approved company insurance lists. The industry has historically taken a non-aggressive approach to advertising since most patients are due to referrals. TV, radio, or newspaper advertising are rare because most people use a dentist located in their immediate geographic area. Direct mailings and billboard advertising are sometimes used. Specialized dentists may get referrals from doctors and hospitals. Dentists generally spend less than 1 percent of income for marketing.

Prices for dental procedures vary from around $100 for a normal checkup and cleaning, to $1,500 to $3,000 for an implant, and $400 to $600 per tooth for a root canal. Teeth whitening treatments at dental offices are about $500 per treatment.

Human Resources

Because of the special training that dental hygienists and other office assistants must have, industry pay is relatively high; average hourly earnings are above the national average. Dentists offices have low injury rates, about one-third the national average.

Industry Employment Growth

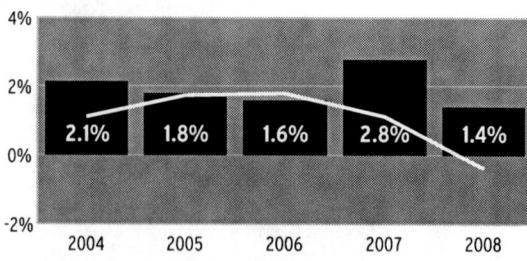

2004	2005	2006	2007	2008
2.1%	1.8%	1.6%	2.8%	1.4%

Average Hourly Earnings

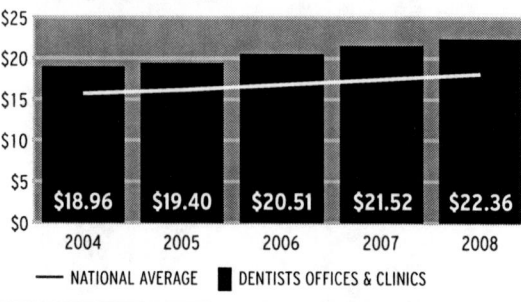

2004	2005	2006	2007	2008
$18.96	$19.40	$20.51	$21.52	$22.36

— NATIONAL AVERAGE ■ DENTISTS OFFICES & CLINICS

SOURCE: BUREAU OF LABOR STATISTICS

Call Preparation Questions

What strategies does the practice use to expand its customer base and revenues?

Americans' teeth are much healthier than 30 years ago, reducing demand for traditional dental services.

How is the lack of dental insurance impacting the practice?

Several years of double-digit increases in the cost of health insurance have made quality health care, especially dental care, unaffordable for growing numbers of Americans.

How much local competition does the practice face?

In many urban and suburban markets, consumers have convenient access to several dentist offices and can easily switch.

What opportunities does the aging population present for the practice?

Aging baby boomers, the largest segment of the US population, are expected to want and need more dental care than any previous generation.

What portion of visits is for cosmetic reasons? Is that number changing?

Cosmetic dentistry has risen in importance as the primary activity of dentists.

Web Links

Academy of General Dentistry

News, publications, hot issues, conventions, consumer information, and links.

www.agd.org

American Dental Association

General information and news on issues facing dentists.

www.ada.org/prof

American Dental Hygienists' Association

Articles and news on oral health, industry issues, FAQs, and a newsletter.

www.adha.org

Dental Globe

Worldwide directory of dentists, glossary of dental terms, guide to dental organizations.

dentalglobe.com

Dental Icon

Reference library, product and dealer guides, insurance information, dental journals and organizations.

www.dentalicon.com

Dental-Related Internet Resources

Latest dental online websites.

www.dental-resources.com

National Association of Dental Laboratories

News, calendars, directories and information on technician and laboratory certification.

nadl.org

Glossary of Acronyms

DMSO — Dental Management Service Organization

HIPAA — Health Insurance Portability and Accountability Act

LEAT — least expensive alternative treatment

NADL — National Association of Dental Laboratories

TMJ — temporomandibular joint

HOOVER'S TOP COMPANIES

Largest Employers	Employees
Bright Now! Dental, Inc.	4,100
OrthoSynetics, Inc.	3,296
American Dental Partners, Inc.	2,197
Coast Dental Services, Inc.	700

SOURCE: HOOVER'S, INC., DATABASE

Department Stores

THIS INDUSTRY
INCLUDES:

SIC CODES
5311   Department Stores

NAICS CODES
452111 Department Stores
        (except Discount
        Department
        Stores)

The department store industry includes about 3,300 stores with a combined annual revenue of $90 billion. Major companies include Sears; JCPenney; Macy's (includes Bloomingdales); and Dillard's. The industry is highly concentrated: the top 50 companies are almost 100 percent of industry sales.

Department stores are different from discount department stores because most department stores have checkout registers within individual merchandise departments as opposed to having a central checkout area.

Competitive Landscape

Consumer spending and fashion trends drive demand. The profitability of individual companies depends on effective merchandising and marketing. Large companies have advantages in purchasing, distribution, and marketing. Small companies can compete effectively by offering unique merchandise, providing superior customer service, or delivering a distinctive store experience. The industry is labor-intensive: average annual revenue per worker is $130,000.

Department stores compete with discount department stores and mass merchandisers, specialty stores, off-price and outlet stores, Internet and mail-order retailers, and home shopping networks.

Products, Operations & Technology

Major products sold include apparel (50 percent of sales); cosmetics and appliances (10 percent each); and footwear (7 percent). Apparel includes women's, men's, and children's clothing. Cosmetics include makeup, skin care, hair care, and fragrances. Appliances include refrigerators, stoves, washers, dryers, and dishwashers. Companies may also sell kitchenware, bedding, towels, and sheets. Services include gift wrapping, delivery, appliance installation, and personal shopping.

BUSINESS CHALLENGES

» Competition from Alternative Retailers

Companies face intense competition from a wide variety of retailers, including discount department stores, warehouse clubs, and specialty stores. Department store sales declined over 10 percent between 1999 and 2005 while total retail sales grew. Discount department stores, such as Target, have upgraded apparel selection and offer quality merchandise at low prices. Warehouse clubs sell basic items at rock-bottom prices. Specialty retailers provide better selections and service within a particular category. Private-label apparel from all types of retailers has also hurt department stores.

» Dependence on Consumer Spending

Consumer spending drives department store sales. During the last recession, sales declined 10 percent and employment declined 8 percent. Many products sold in department stores, particularly apparel and cosmetics, are considered discretionary. During tough economic periods, consumers may cut back or shop at less expensive retailers, such as discount department stores and mass merchandisers. Sales were basically flat between 2002 and 2005, as the industry has yet to recover from the last recession.

» Demand Dependent on Trends

Trends and fads drive demand for apparel and other fashion-oriented categories, which represent the majority of sales in department stores. Fashion trends can change quickly, leaving companies with inventory problems. Inability to predict trends and react quickly can result in unplanned markdowns or lost sales due to underforecasting. Stocking dated merchandise can also affect a company's reputation, since most companies try to be as fashion-forward as possible.

National and regional chains dominate the department store industry. Store format and merchandise selection depends on a company's target market. For example, Neiman Marcus targets affluent shoppers, sells high-end designer apparel, and offers an elegant shopping environment. Kohl's targets family-oriented shoppers, sells moderately priced merchandise, and offers a convenience-based store design. Some companies lease space to independent companies to sell products requiring sales expertise (furs, designer handbags, high-end cosmetics). Effective store layouts and eye-catching merchandise displays can generate complementary sales and impulse purchases. Companies may have outlets to help sell excess inventory.

Most department stores are anchor tenants in large malls and a store's presence is used to drive traffic. Companies consider demographics, population density, and lifestyle when selecting locations. Store size averages about 80,000 square feet, according to Chain Store Age. Some companies have flagship stores that can exceed 250,000 square feet. A single department store typically generates between $10 to $20 million and averages $150 to $270 per square foot, although high-end stores can sell between $380 to $625 per square foot.

Because department stores deal with tens of thousands of stock keeping units (SKUs), effective supply chain management is critical to keeping costs low and supporting timely merchandise flow. Companies have extensive networks of warehouses and distribution centers to route products from suppliers to stores. Cross-docking facilities allow companies to unload and reallocate products in a single operation, minimizing storage costs. Dedicated distribution centers and call centers often support Internet or catalog sales.

Department stores buy inventory from manufacturers, importers, and distributors, and may work with thousands of suppliers. While long-term supplier relationships are common, few companies have long-term contracts. Lead times can be long: buyers may place orders six to nine months in advance for apparel and shoes and three to six months for handbags and jewelry. Buyers make purchasing decisions based on trends and historical sales, and may take local preferences and climate into account. Companies may receive allowances from suppliers for markdowns and advertising.

Inventory changes seasonally, with apparel driven by fall and spring selling periods. Private-label brands allow companies to offer their own designs and help develop customer loyalty. Some department stores have exclusive rights to sell certain brands. "Soft goods" include clothing, bedding, and sheets. "Hard goods" include appliances, furniture, and tools. Most companies have either eliminated hard goods or reduced selling space for hard goods due to the proliferation of specialty retailers in those segments.

Department stores rely highly on information systems to manage functional areas, including sales, merchandising, purchasing, inventory control, distribution, finance, and accounting. Point-of-sale (POS) systems record sales transactions and process credit card orders. Merchandise planning systems help companies forecast demand and allocate merchandise across stores. Inventory management systems monitor inventory levels and trigger replenishment orders. Electronic data interchange (EDI) allows companies to process purchase orders more efficiently. While most department stores use bar codes to identify and track products through the supply chain, some companies are testing radio frequency identification (RFID) to monitor merchandise movement.

Sales & Marketing

The typical department store customer is an educated woman between 25 and 54. Income can very greatly depending on a company's target market. For example, income for Neiman Marcus customers averages $125,0000, while income for Belk customers ranges from $45,000 to $100,000.

Marketing and promotional vehicles include TV, print, newspaper, and radio advertising; direct mail (catalogs, flyers); instore displays and events; and sponsorships. While brand name products are important, private-label goods are a growing segment of the industry's merchandise mix. Special events, such as promotional sales and trunk shows, drive store traffic. Loyalty programs reward frequent customers with special discounts and free merchandise, encourage repeat purchases, and help companies develop targeted marketing programs. Loyalty club members generate about half of sales at Neiman Marcus.

To maintain superior customer service, high-end department stores may require sales associates to maintain frequent, personal contact with key customers. Sales staff often personally inform customers of special promotions or new merchandise arrivals. Associates may keep detailed records of customer purchases and preferences and handwrite "thank you" notes. Offering personal shopping services help companies establish long-term customer relationships and maximize selling opportunities.

Most companies offer retail Internet sites to complement store offerings, build store awareness, and generate customer traffic. Companies may hold web-only promotions or advertise store events on Internet sites. Most companies let customers return merchandise purchased on websites to store locations. Internet sites allow department stores to offer products not found in stores and reach consumers beyond local markets. Web sales growth for department stores has resulted in some companies reducing catalog circulation.

Retail pricing depends on a company's target market and merchandising mix. Due to increasing competition, department stores are relying more on sales and promotional pricing to sell slow-moving or end-of-season merchandise. Consumers buy over 60 percent of department store merchandise on sale, according to NPD Group.

Human Resources

Most jobs in department stores involve sales or inventory-stocking and require few skills. Wages are about 40 percent lower than the average for all US workers; as a result, turnover is high and most companies rely on part-time workers. Some department stores, especially those specializing in high-end merchandise, use commissions to motivate sales staff. Companies may also receive compensation from suppliers to pay for dedicated employees who work in leased departments. A small percentage of department store workers belong to unions.

The industry injury rate is over 30 percent higher than the average for all US workers, primarily due to a higher incidence of strains, sprains, and bruising due to lifting required to load/unload and restock merchandise.

Industry Employment Growth

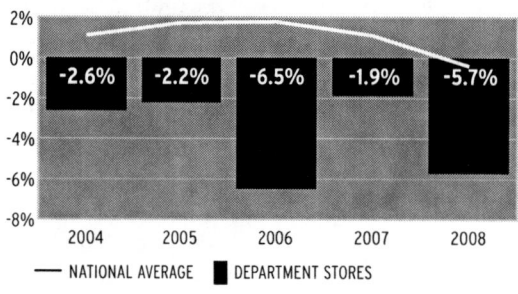

SOURCE: BUREAU OF LABOR STATISTICS

Call Preparation Questions

What is the company's biggest competitive threat?

Companies face intense competition from a wide variety of retailers, including discount department stores, warehouse clubs, and specialty stores.

How do changes in consumer spending affect the company?

Consumer spending drives department store sales.

What are the most significant fashion trends affecting the company?

Trends and fads drive demand for apparel and other fashion-oriented categories, which represent the majority of sales in department stores.

How important are private-label brands to the company's merchandising mix?

Private-label and exclusive brands allow department stores to differentiate from competition and develop customer loyalty.

What type of store experience does the company try to deliver?

By delivering a superior store experience, companies make shopping entertaining.

Web Links

Advance Monthly Retail Sales

Sales data by retail category from Census Bureau. www.census.gov/mrts/www/mrts.html

Chain Store Age

News, trends, statistics, operational and competitive information. www.chainstoreage.com

International Council of Shopping Centers

Global retail news and trends.
www.icsc.org

National Association for Retail Marketing Services

Weekly and quarterly news and trends.
www.narms.com

National Retail Federation

News, consumer trends, seasonal trends, legislative issues.
www.nrf.com

Private Label Magazine

News and trends for private label/store brand market.
www.privatelabelmag.com

Retail Industry Leaders Association

Legislative news.
www.retail-leaders.org/latest

Glossary of Acronyms

EDI — electronic data interchange

ICSC — International Council of Shopping Centers

NARMS — National Association for Retail Merchandising Services

NRF — National Retail Federation

POS — point-of-sale

RFID — radio frequency identification

RILA — Retail Industry Leaders Association

SKU — stock-keeping unit

HOOVER'S TOP COMPANIES

Largest Companies by Sales	($ mil.)
Sears Holdings Corporation	46,770.0
Macy's, Inc.	26,313.0
J. C. Penney Company, Inc.	19,860.0
Kohl's Corporation	16,473.7
Dillard's, Inc.	7,370.8
The Neiman Marcus Group, Inc.	4,600.5
Belk, Inc.	3,824.8
The Bon-Ton Stores, Inc.	3,467.7
Saks Incorporated	3,282.6
Stage Stores, Inc.	1,545.6

Largest Employers	Employees
Sears Holdings Corporation	337,000
Macy's, Inc.	182,000
J. C. Penney Company, Inc.	155,000
Kohl's Corporation	125,000
Dillard's, Inc.	49,938
The Bon-Ton Stores, Inc.	32,700
Belk, Inc.	26,375
The Neiman Marcus Group, Inc.	18,000
Saks Incorporated	16,700
Stage Stores, Inc.	14,608

Fastest Growing* by Five-Year Sales Growth	(%)
The Bon-Ton Stores, Inc.	37.1
Sears Holdings Corporation	15.0
Kohl's Corporation	12.6
Stage Stores, Inc.	12.0
Belk, Inc.	11.3
Macy's, Inc.	11.3
The Neiman Marcus Group, Inc.	5.9
J. C. Penney Company, Inc.	2.2

Fastest Growing* by Five-Year Employee Growth	(%)
The Bon-Ton Stores, Inc.	30.6
Kohl's Corporation	10.8
Stage Stores, Inc.	10.4
Macy's, Inc.	10.0
Belk, Inc.	8.2
The Neiman Marcus Group, Inc.	2.3
J. C. Penney Company, Inc.	0.9

Top Public Companies by Market Value	($ mil.)
Kohl's Corporation	14,259.8
Macy's, Inc.	11,751.6
J. C. Penney Company, Inc.	10,767.0
Sears Holdings Corporation	4,992.2
Saks Incorporated	2,600.3

* These rates are compounded annualized increases and may have resulted from acquisitions or one time gains. If less than 6 years of data are available, growth is for the years available.

SOURCE: HOOVER'S, INC., DATABASE

Direct Marketing Services

THIS INDUSTRY INCLUDES:

SIC CODES

7331   Direct Mail
       Advertising
       Services

NAICS CODES

541860   Direct Mail
         Advertising

The direct marketing services industry includes about 3,700 companies with combined annual revenue of over $11 billion. Major companies include Harte-Hanks, infoUSA Services Group, R.R. Donnelley & Sons, and Acxiom. The industry is relatively fragmented: the 50 largest firms account for 46 percent of industry revenue.

Competitive Landscape

Demand is driven by economic activity and corporate profits. The profitability of individual companies depends on their targeting services, creative skills, and marketing ability. Large companies have advantages in economies of scale in database analytics, marketing, and automated operations, which allow them to compete more aggressively on price. Small companies can compete effectively by specializing in a particular industry, geographic market, or service type. The direct marketing services industry is labor-intensive: average annual revenue per employee is less than $150,000.

Products, Operations & Technology

Major services are letter shop services (preparing and sorting mail pieces); printing; mailing list services; concept development; and full direct mail services, which include all of the above. Full direct mail services accounts for almost two-thirds of industry revenue. Companies providing only letter shop services account for about 15 percent of industry revenue, and companies providing only print services account for about 8 percent. Other offerings include fulfillment, sales promotion, and distribution services.

Historically, direct marketing referred to direct mail and telemarketing. Direct marketing can use any medium to reach specific customers, including mail, TV, print, e-mail, banner ads, and billboards. The direct marketing industry is changing as organizations allocate

BUSINESS CHALLENGES

» Dependence on US Economy

Spending on direct marketing is highly sensitive to the financial health of the US economy. Marketing spending is often viewed as a discretionary expense that can be cut when corporate profits fall. Increased demand for direct marketing services often lags an economic recovery as firms remain cautious in setting marketing budgets.

» Shift to Electronic Correspondence

The shift from letter correspondence to e-mail may force the US Postal Service (USPS) to increase rates on standard mail to cover costs. While standard mail volume has grown over the past five years, first class mail volume has declined. Higher postal rates increase the cost of direct mail advertising.

» Identity Theft, Personal Privacy

Direct marketers have a responsibility to protect mailing lists and marketing databases containing personal information about consumers. Negative publicity from cases of identity theft has increased consumer concern and attracted government attention. Privacy legislation with increased penalties for identity theft has been introduced in Congress and many states. Direct marketers must work with legislators to ensure that new privacy laws don't restrict their right to gather and use marketing information.

more of their advertising budgets to online marketing.

The most commonly used medium for direct marketing remains direct mail, where marketing pieces are sent to prospects using the USPS. Direct mail typically uses standard mail rates (previously known as bulk or third class mail), which are less expensive than first class mail. Marketers use customer databases to target those most likely to buy a product or service. Mailing lists are bought or rented from list compilers to reach prospective customers. The communication piece — a catalog, postcard, or mailer — is developed and then printed, packaged, sorted, and mailed. Responses are tracked to measure the effectiveness of the campaign, and changes may be made to improve response rates. Response rates for direct mail are typically 1 to 3 percent.

Direct mail marketing uses large amounts of paper, which is bought in bulk under long-term contracts. Postage is a major cost and firms depend on prices and mailing rules set by the USPS. Standard mail accounts for nearly half of the mail volume handled by the USPS, so rates are raised periodically as labor costs rise.

Many organizations have invested in customer relationship management (CRM) software, which allows them to collect more information about customers. Direct marketing firms use client CRM information to target prospects. List compilers invest in software to analyze their databases and develop segmentation strategies. Some large firms have invested in data warehousing and database management solutions for clients. Letter shop companies have special machinery to prepare, sort, and bundle mail.

Sales & Marketing

Customers are commercial businesses that want to advertise their products and services to a specific target audience. Direct mail is used frequently by the financial services, technology, telecommunications, packaged goods, and travel and tourism industries.

Small direct marketers may have just a few clients and rely on company executives to develop client relationships. Large companies have direct sales forces that sell their services and manage key accounts.

Direct marketing companies are very active at marketing trade shows and conferences and shows specific to their customers' industries. These events are a major source of new customer contacts.

Direct marketers generally have long-term customer contracts, with initial terms of two years. Direct marketing services are priced either on a program or campaign basis for a period, or project-by-project.

Human Resources

The major resource of direct marketing firms is their professional staff. Full-service firms require technical staff with expertise in data analytics and database management, and creative talent for advertising concept development and design. Firms focused on printing or

mailing services employ relatively low-skilled production workers and equipment operators. Wages have historically lagged the national norm, but have been rising as automation replaces low-skilled positions. The industry injury rate is minimal.

Industry Employment Growth

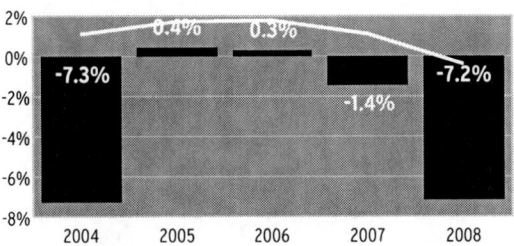

Average Hourly Earnings

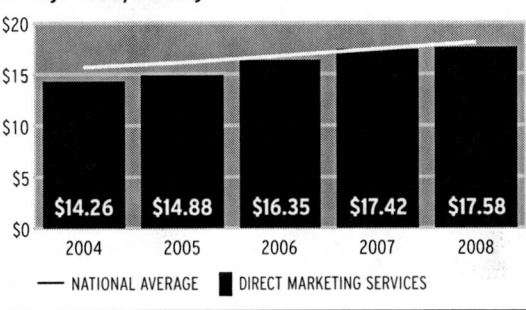

SOURCE: BUREAU OF LABOR STATISTICS

Call Preparation Questions

What trend is the company seeing in demand for its services?

Spending on direct marketing is highly sensitive to the financial health of the US economy.

How has the growth of e-mail affected the company's business?

The shift from letter correspondence to e-mail may force the US Postal Service (USPS) to increase rates on standard mail to cover costs.

How is the company protecting consumer privacy?

Direct marketers have a responsibility to protect mailing lists and marketing databases containing personal information about consumers.

What are the company's most promising new channels for reaching target audiences?

While direct mail remains the largest channel for direct marketing, marketers search for new ways to effectively reach target audiences.

How does spam affect the company's ability to use e-mail marketing?

The biggest challenge for e-marketers to improve online direct marketing is eliminating spam.

Web Links

American Marketing Association

News and events.
www.marketingpower.com

Direct

News and legal issues.
directmag.com

Direct Marketing Association

Regulatory items and industry news.
www.the-dma.org

DMNews

News on all aspects of direct marketing.
www.dmnews.com

Harte-Hanks

Major direct marketer.
www.harte-hanks.com

Glossary of Acronyms

AMA — American Marketing Association
CDI — customer data integration
CRM — customer relationship management
DMA — Direct Marketing Association
PRC — Postal Regulatory Commission
USPS — US Postal Service

HOOVER'S TOP COMPANIES

Largest Companies by Sales	($ mil.)
R.R. Donnelley & Sons Company	11,587.1
Convergys Corporation	2,785.8
Valassis Communications, Inc.	2,381.9
West Corporation	2,099.5
Guthy-Renker Corporation	1,800.0
Sitel Corporation	1,700.0
TeleTech Holdings, Inc.	1,400.2
Acxiom Corporation	1,384.1
Vertis, Inc.	1,365.2
inVentiv Health, Inc.	1,119.8

Largest Employers	Employees
Convergys Corporation	75,000
Sitel Corporation	66,000
R.R. Donnelley & Sons Company	65,000
TeleTech Holdings, Inc.	47,000
West Corporation	42,000
Sykes Enterprises, Incorporated	29,560
ICT Group, Inc.	19,006
APAC Customer Services Inc.	9,500
Aegis PeopleSupport, Inc.	8,550
StarTek, Inc.	8,200

Fastest Growing* by Five-Year Sales Growth	(%)
Red Ventures	205.0
Selling Source, LLC	76.9
Aegis PeopleSupport, Inc.	48.0
Vertical Branding, Inc.	46.9
inVentiv Health, Inc.	37.9
Sitel Corporation	33.6
Onvia, Inc.	23.8
Valassis Communications, Inc.	21.0
West Corporation	20.7
R.R. Donnelley & Sons Company	19.5

Fastest Growing* by Five-Year Employee Growth	(%)
Red Ventures	192.2
Selling Source, LLC	49.8
Aegis PeopleSupport, Inc.	42.7
Sitel Corporation	42.1
inVentiv Health, Inc.	24.2
Onvia, Inc.	21.7
infoGROUP Inc.	19.2
Valassis Communications, Inc.	17.0
R.R. Donnelley & Sons Company	16.7
Convergys Corporation	14.2

Top Public Companies by Market Value	($ mil.)
R.R. Donnelley & Sons Company	8,148.1
Convergys Corporation	1,171.7
Acxiom Corporation	917.6
Sykes Enterprises, Incorporated	787.3
TeleTech Holdings, Inc.	532.9

* These rates are compounded annualized increases and may have resulted from acquisitions or one time gains. If less than 6 years of data are available, growth is for the years available.

SOURCE: HOOVER'S, INC., DATABASE

Directory and Mailing List Publishers

The directory and mailing list publishing industry includes about 1,100 companies with combined annual revenue of about $20 billion. Major companies include R.H. Donnelley, Idearc, Acxiom, and infoUSA. The industry is highly concentrated: the 50 largest companies account for over 90 percent of industry revenue; the four largest account for over 60 percent.

The industry includes companies that publish phone directories and mailing lists used for marketing. While directories are primarily print, lists are generally delivered online.

Competitive Landscape

Demand for directories is driven by local population growth and local ad spending; demand for mailing lists is driven by corporate profits and spending on marketing. The profitability of individual companies depends on efficient operations and new customers. Large companies have advantages in supplier negotiations and servicing large geographies; small companies compete by targeting niche or specialized markets. Average revenue per worker for a typical company is about $300,000.

Products, Operations & Technology

Major products include printed directories (80 percent of industry revenue) and mailing lists (6 percent). Other products include database subscriptions, both via print and the Internet. While online directory use is growing, 87 percent of consumers still use print phone directories.

Directory companies publish printed white and Yellow Page listings, generally in one directory; in large markets, separate white and Yellow Page directories are published. State public utility commissions require local exchange carriers (LECs) to produce white page directories for all consumers and businesses, called incumbent markets. Companies also provide directories in expansion markets, markets where

another publisher has the incumbent relationship with the local phone company.

Directory companies establish long-term contracts with local carriers to provide white page service and with printing vendors. Directories are published on a 12-month cycle; publication dates for different markets are staggered throughout the year to optimize production capacity. Major directory inputs include paper and ink. Most companies have annual contracts with multiple paper and ink suppliers. Directories are generally delivered by hand or through the US Postal Service (USPS); distribution time generally ranges from three to eight weeks.

Yellow Pages provide ad revenue in a variety of ways. Advertisers can pay for additional, highlighted, or bolded listings; better listing placement; an ad column; or a display ad. Display ads can range from a quarter page to two full pages and may include photos, illustrations, and company logos.

Mailing list companies create information databases that can include names, addresses, business information, news, liens, and judgments, and that can be filtered by selected criteria to create a specific list. Database information is compiled and verified from thousands of sources: mailing list databases can include up to 200 million consumer records and 100 million business records. About 65 percent of the content of databases can change each year.

Technological change characterizes the industry. Electronic document distribution and Internet technologies have changed how directories and mailing lists are compiled and distributed. The Internet has become the mailing list delivery mechanism of choice, replacing disks, magnetic tape, and paper.

Sales & Marketing

Typical directory customers are small to midsized local businesses and national advertisers such as rental car, auto repair, and pizza delivery businesses. Directory publishers generally have large local sales forces, as 85 percent of their ad revenue is from local businesses. Directory companies also use independent Certified Marketing Representatives (CMRs) who design ad placements for national advertisers and sell to Yellow Page directories nationwide.

Typical mailing list customers are commercial businesses and organizations that use lists to generate sales leads and for direct marketing. Mailing list companies use sales reps to call on national accounts and service major customers.

Major types of marketing for directory publishers include TV, radio, newspaper, and billboard ads. Major types of marketing for mailing list companies include direct mail, outbound telemarketing, banner advertising, and e-mail ads.

Directories are free in local calling areas. Yellow Page ads are sold based on size and placement. Mailing list prices vary by the number of selection items in the search, and the number of names desired. Subscription prices vary by number of data elements searched,

number of lists generated, and the length of the contract.

Human Resources

The major resource of directory and mailing list publishers is their staff. Increasingly, a larger portion of the mailing list staff have technical skills, including expertise in data analytics and database management. Firms focused on publishing directories and mailing services have a greater portion of lower-skilled production workers, a large portion of whom may be unionized. The average industry wage is higher than the national average wage. The industry injury rate is minimal.

Industry Employment Growth

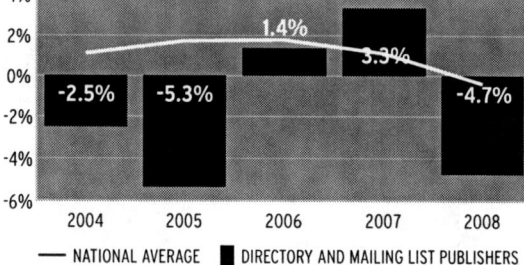

SOURCE: BUREAU OF LABOR STATISTICS

Call Preparation Questions

What trend is the company seeing in Yellow Pages' ad spending?

Yellow Page advertising is a function of local business ad expenditures.

How does the company manage changes in paper prices?

Paper is still the predominant medium to deliver phone directories.

What is the company's position on potential regulations restricting delivery of phone books?

As part of "going green," some states are considering legislation that would restrict publishers to deliver phone books to only those customers who choose to receive them.

How much of the company's business is print versus online directories?

Searching for local business information is shifting from printed directories to online tools.

How much of the company's business is online Internet subscriptions?

Traditional direct mail services are declining, replaced by online Internet subscription services.

Web Links

Advertising Age

General advertising news, statistics.
adage.com

American Marketing Association

News and events.
www.marketingpower.com

Association of Directory Publishers

News, links.
www.adp.org

Direct

News and legal issues.
directmag.com

Direct Marketing Association

News (for members), events, lists information.
www.the-dma.org

Yellow Pages Association

News, public policy, regulations.
www.ypassociation.org

Glossary of Acronyms

DMA — Direct Marketing Association
LEC — local exchange carrier
PRC — Postal Regulatory Commission
USPS — US Postal Service
YPA — Yellow Pages Association

HOOVER'S TOP COMPANIES

Largest Companies by Sales	($ mil.)
Idearc Inc.	3,189.0
R.H. Donnelley Corporation	2,680.3
Yellow Book USA	1,931.6
Acxiom Corporation	1,384.1
infoGROUP Inc. (infoUSA Services Group)	688.8
The Bureau of National Affairs, Inc.	352.2
Franklin Electronic Publishers, Incorporated	60.6
ZAGAT Survey, LLC	7.9

Largest Employers	Employees
Yellow Book USA	8,000
Idearc Inc.	7,200
Acxiom Corporation	6,610
infoGROUP Inc. (infoUSA Services Group)	4,815
R.H. Donnelley Corporation	4,700
The Bureau of National Affairs, Inc.	1,719
Franklin Electronic Publishers, Incorporated	185
ZAGAT Survey, LLC	120
Local Insight Media, LLC	13

Fastest Growing* by Five-Year Sales Growth	(%)
R.H. Donnelley Corporation	57.9
infoGROUP Inc. (infoUSA Services Group)	17.9
Acxiom Corporation	7.6
The Bureau of National Affairs, Inc.	2.6

Fastest Growing* by Five-Year Employee Growth	(%)
R.H. Donnelley Corporation	49.6
infoGROUP Inc. (infoUSA Services Group)	19.2
Acxiom Corporation	0.1

Top Public Companies by Market Value	($ mil.)
Acxiom Corporation	917.6
infoGROUP Inc. (infoUSA Services Group)	504.6
Franklin Electronic Publishers, Incorporated	17.4
SportsNuts, Inc.	0.4

* These rates are compounded annualized increases and may have resulted from acquisitions or one time gains. If less than 6 years of data are available, growth is for the years available.

SOURCE: HOOVER'S, INC., DATABASE

Discount Stores

The discount department store industry includes about 5,000 stores with combined annual revenue of $130 billion. Major companies include Kohl's, Wal-Mart Stores (excluding supercenters), Target, and Kmart (a subsidiary of Sears Holdings). The industry is highly concentrated: the top eight companies hold 100 percent of industry sales.

Unlike most traditional department stores, discount department stores have a central checkout versus checkout registers within individual departments.

Competitive Landscape

Population growth and consumer spending drive demand. The profitability of individual companies depends on efficient supply chain management, effective merchandising, and competitive pricing. Large companies dominate the industry, and enjoy advantages in purchasing, distribution, and marketing. Average annual revenue per worker is $175,000.

Discount department stores carry a wide range of merchandise and compete with a diverse set of retailers, including department, drug, grocery, off-price, outlet, and specialty stores; warehouse clubs; and Internet and catalog retailers.

Products, Operations & Technology

Major products sold include apparel (20 percent of sales); personal care products (15 percent); electronics and groceries (7 percent each); and toys (6 percent). Apparel includes women's, men's, and children's. Personal care includes cosmetics and health and beauty products. Electronics include video and audio equipment (TVs, DVD players, stereo systems). Companies may also sell kitchenware, sporting goods, towels and sheets, and footwear. Discount department stores may have instore pharmacies, photo processing services, or restaurants.

BUSINESS CHALLENGES

» Competition from Alternative Retailers

Because discount department stores carry diverse merchandise, companies compete with a wide variety of retailers. Department and specialty stores periodically mark down merchandise, resulting in comparable or better pricing. By offering deep discounts on a limited assortment of goods, outlets, off-price stores, and warehouse clubs attract price-conscious consumers and bargain hunters. Internet retailers can offer extremely competitive pricing due to low overhead. For groceries, supermarkets are typically more convenient and provide better selections.

» Dependence on Consumer Spending

Consumer spending drives sales of many key categories in discount department stores. While sales of consumables, such as toothpaste, shampoo, and paper towels, are fairly recession-proof, discount department stores depend on other more economy-sensitive categories, such as apparel and toys, to increase a customer's total purchase. When money is tight, consumers make fewer impulse buys. During the last recession, discount department store sales decreased almost 2 percent, while total retail sales grew.

» Dependence on High Volume

Because discount department stores carry low margins, companies depend on high volume sales to generate profits and create economies of scale. Volume discounts from suppliers are key to maintaining profitability. Slow store traffic can significantly affect sales and upset the low margin/high volume business model. Gross margins in discount department stores can be between 10 to 20 percent lower than margins in traditional department stores. Margin differences versus specialty retailers can be even greater.

Large chains dominate. Companies aim to provide "one-stop shopping" for price-conscious consumers by providing a wide range of merchandise at low prices. By leveraging low operating and purchasing costs, companies are generally able to offer everyday retail prices lower than those in most other retailers. Some discount department stores are open 24 hours a day. Centralized checkout areas, typically in the front of stores, allow companies to process large numbers of customers efficiently.

Discount department stores occupy a big footprint and require large amounts of real estate: average size is about 100,000 square feet. Most stores are either stand-alone or anchors in large strip malls. Some companies select locations near population centers, other retail centers, or major highways. Wal-Mart has been successful by targeting small towns and rural locations, where few retail options exist. Most companies also have a supercenter format, which averages 180,000 square feet and offers a more extensive merchandise selection and a complete grocery section. A typical discount department store can generate between $40 and $50 million annually. Sales per square foot may range from $300 to $450.

Large volume purchases allow companies to buy most merchandise directly from manufacturers and enjoy volume discounts. Because discount department stores represent significant volume opportunity for suppliers, companies negotiate hard and typically receive favorable purchasing terms. Companies may forgo advertising allowances and vendor-supplied transportation in favor of lower purchase prices. Effective purchasing helps companies offer retail discounts while maintaining margins.

The discount department store industry has pioneered effective supply chain management. Efficiencies within networks of warehouses and distribution centers reduce replenishment time and shipping costs. Deliveries from suppliers come in large shipments in pallet quantities by truckload. Within distribution centers, workers may manage sorting equipment to assemble orders for individual stores. Dispatchers coordinate truck scheduling, and stores may receive shipments several times a week. To reduce costs and transit time, companies occasionally use cross-docking, allowing suppliers to ship products directly to stores. Companies may dedicate distribution centers to certain categories, such as grocery products, apparel, online sales, or imports.

Inventory includes many major consumer retail categories with a broad selection of products within each category. Companies offer both brand name and private-label products. "Hard goods" include tools, furniture, home accessories, and kitchenware; "soft goods" include apparel, footwear, and bedding. Because many customers rely on discount department stores for household staples, such as toothpaste and soap, maintaining high in-stock levels are important. To maximize product availability, Wal-Mart allows some suppliers to monitor their own inventory levels and generate replenishment orders.

Technology, including point-of-sale (POS) systems, automated distribution centers, and computerized inventory management systems, has been crucial in keeping operating costs low. Companies use hand held scanners, bar codes, and radio frequency identification (RFID) tags to track merchandise movement electronically. Because monitoring sales and inventory across the nation is so important, Wal-Mart has a dedicated satellite communication system linking all facilities.

Sales & Marketing

Because discount department stores carry a wide variety of merchandise, customers span a broad demographic. An important customer group is value-oriented women 25 and 54, particularly those with children. Income can vary: Wal-Mart customers tend to have lower incomes, while Target customers tend to be more affluent. Over 80 percent of US households have shopped at Wal-Mart or Target, according to Scarborough Research, and Wal-Mart's most frequent shoppers make 50 to 60 visits annually.

Marketing and promotional vehicles include TV, print, and newspaper advertising; newspaper inserts; and direct mail. Companies may receive advertising allowances from suppliers for product-specific promotions. During themed merchandising events, such as Super Bowl or Valentine's Day promotions, stores may build elaborate product displays to create excitement and drive sales. By offering special rewards and discounts to proprietary credit card holders, Target encourages customer loyalty and frequent purchases. In line with keeping costs low, most discount department stores provide very basic levels of customer service.

» The discount department store industry includes about 5,000 stores with combined annual revenue of $130 billion.

» Major companies include Kohl's, Wal-Mart Stores (excluding supercenters), Target, and Kmart (a subsidiary of Sears Holdings).

» Major products sold include apparel (20 percent of sales); personal care products (15 percent); electronics and groceries (7 percent each); and toys (6 percent).

» Because discount department stores carry a wide variety of merchandise, customers span a broad demographic.

» Sales are seasonal, with the main peak during the winter holiday.

While discount department stores were slow to embrace the Internet, companies now operate retail websites that complement instore merchandise, advertise promotions, and help drive traffic. Most companies offer an even greater selection of goods through Internet sites, including additional sizes and colors not found in stores. Discount department store sites may offer web-only promotions, allow customers to check product availability or pick up or return Internet purchases in stores. Some companies have used Internet sites to identify sales trends in advance of when merchandise hits retail.

In general, merchandise in discount department stores is less expensive than the same products in other retailers. As part of a value-based strategy, Wal-Mart uses everyday low pricing (EDLP), with discounts of about 20 percent. Wal-Mart also passes costs savings to customers through "price rollbacks."

Human Resources

Most jobs in discount department stores require few skills and wages are almost 40 percent lower than the average for all US workers. The majority of workers are employed in checkout areas, warehouses, and distribution centers. Turnover is high and companies rely on part-time workers. Discount department stores are prime targets for union involvement because of their large labor forces.

The industry injury rate is over 30 percent higher than the US average. Jobs involving lifting and moving heavy merchandise account for a higher incidence of strains, sprains, and bruises.

Industry Employment Growth

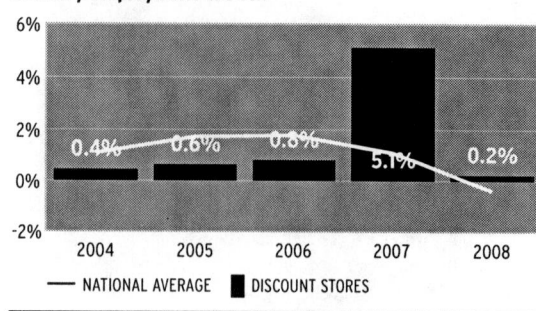

SOURCE: BUREAU OF LABOR STATISTICS

Call Preparation Questions

What is the company's biggest competitive threat?

Because discount department stores carry diverse merchandise, companies compete with a wide variety of retailers.

How does the economy affect the company's financial performance?

Consumer spending drives sales of many key categories in discount department stores.

How much does the company rely on economies of scale to maintain profitability?

Because discount department stores carry low margins, companies depend on high volume sales to generate profits and create economies of scale.

How important are private-label products to the company's merchandising mix?

By offering private-label products, companies can provide consumers better value and generate higher margins.

What benefits does the company see in Internet marketing?

Through the Internet, companies can offer more merchandise than selections in stores and test market new products.

Web Links

Chain Store Age

News, trends, statistics, and special reports.
www.chainstoreage.com

National Association for Retail Marketing Services

News, trends, and statistics.
www.narms.com

National Retail Federation

News, trends, and statistics from trade organization.
www.nrf.com

Retailing Today

News and trends by category.
www.retailingtoday.com

Target

Major discount department retailer.
www.target.com

Wal-Mart

Website of largest discount department retailer.
www.walmart.com

Glossary of Acronyms

EDLP — every day low price
NRF — National Retail Federation
POS — point-of-sale
RFID — radio frequency identification

HOOVER'S TOP COMPANIES

Largest Companies by Sales	($ mil.)
Wal-Mart Stores, Inc.	378,799.0
Target Corporation	63,367.0
Sears Holdings Corporation	46,770.0
J. C. Penney	19,860.0
Kmart Corporation	17,256.0
Kohl's Corporation	16,473.7
Dollar General Corporation	9,495.3
Family Dollar Stores, Inc.	6,983.6
Big Lots, Inc.	4,656.3

Largest Employers	Employees
Wal-Mart Stores, Inc.	2,100,000
Target Corporation	366,000
Sears Holdings Corporation	337,000
J. C. Penney	155,000
Kohl's Corporation	125,000
Dollar General Corporation	71,500
Family Dollar Stores, Inc.	44,000
Dollar Tree, Inc.	42,600
Big Lots, Inc.	38,153

Fastest Growing* by Five-Year Sales Growth	(%)
Sears Holdings Corporation	15.0
Dollar Tree, Inc.	12.7
Kohl's Corporation	12.6
99 Cents Only Stores	10.9
Fred's, Inc.	10.0
Dollar General Corporation	9.3
Wal-Mart Stores, Inc.	9.0
Cost Plus, Inc.	8.1
Family Dollar Stores, Inc.	8.0
Target Corporation	7.6

Fastest Growing* by Five-Year Employee Growth	(%)
99 Cents Only Stores	13.7
Kohl's Corporation	10.8
Dollar Tree, Inc.	9.2
Wal-Mart Stores, Inc.	8.4
Cost Plus, Inc.	7.8
Dollar General Corporation	6.0
Fred's, Inc.	5.3
Target Corporation	3.6
Tuesday Morning Corporation	2.8
Family Dollar Stores, Inc.	2.4

Top Public Companies by Market Value	($ mil.)
Wal-Mart Stores, Inc.	201,590.0
Target Corporation	46,709.0
Kohl's Corporation	14,259.8
J. C. Penney	10,767.0
Sears Holdings Corporation	4,992.2

* These rates are compounded annualized increases and may have resulted from acquisitions or one time gains. If less than 6 years of data are available, growth is for the years available.

SOURCE: HOOVER'S, INC., DATABASE

Distillers

The distillery industry includes about 80 companies with combined annual revenue of $6 billion. Major US companies include Brown-Foreman, Beam Global Spirits & Wine, and Heaven Hill Distilleries. The industry is concentrated: the top 25 companies account for 90 percent of industry revenue.

The industry includes businesses that distill, blend, or mix liquors. Some businesses distill alcohol onsite; others take neutral spirits and infuse alcohol with flavoring agents. Businesses not included in this industry include brandy or non-potable alcohol manufacturers, companies that market bottled liquors made elsewhere, and US subsidiaries of multinational corporations.

Competitive Landscape

Demand is driven primarily by trends in alcohol consumption and personal income. The profitability of individual companies depends on efficient operations and strong distribution channels. Large companies have advantages in brand recognition and economies of scale. Small operations can compete effectively by specializing in high-end or unusual spirits. Average annual revenue per employee is about $1 million.

US distilleries compete against wine and beer producers for share of consumer alcohol spending, and with global spirits companies such as Diageo, Bacardi, and Pernod Ricard.

Products, Operations & Technology

Major products include whiskey and bourbon (30 percent of industry revenues); vodka (10 percent); cordials and liqueurs (10 percent); bottled cocktails (10 percent); gin (5 percent); and distillers dried grains used for animal feed (5 percent). Other products include unflavored (neutral) spirits and unclassified or specialty liquors.

Making liquor involves six steps: mashing, fermenting, distilling, maturing, filtering, and

BUSINESS CHALLENGES

» Dependence on Consumer Tastes

US liquor companies compete directly with wine, beer, and international spirits manufacturers. Consumer alcohol preferences can shift quickly based on news articles, entertainment and celebrity trends, and health concerns. Spirits and wine have gained over beer in recent years, but beer sales still account for 50 percent of the total market. Liquor's market share, currently one-third of the total US alcohol market, is below its historical peak of 40 percent in the early 1970s.

» Compliance with Government Regulations

The liquor industry is one of the most regulated industries in the US. Distilleries must abide by the three-tier distribution system, which puts the success of their product largely in the hands of a wholesaler that is likely carrying and representing competing products. Some states maintain a monopoly on distributing and retailing distilled spirits, yet all 18 of these states permit wine and beer to be sold by private retail outlets for off-premises consumption. The Alcohol and Tobacco Tax and Trade Bureau (TTB) regulates the production, marketing, and transport of distilled products.

» High Taxes

Distilled spirits are one of the most heavily taxed consumer products in the US. More than half the price of a typical bottle of distilled spirits goes to excise or income taxes. Based on alcohol content, the federal excise tax burden for liquor is around $14 per proof gallon. The federal tax burden per proof gallon is around $6 for beer and $5 for wine. Liquor is the only alcohol beverage that pays a greater share of public revenues than its total market share: the liquor industry's market share is around 33 percent, but its share of taxes is about 45 percent.

bottling. A distiller first cooks (mashes) sweet or starchy raw materials to convert starch to sugar. With whiskey, the mash is corn with a blend of barley, rye, or wheat. The mash is strained and the resulting sweet liquid (wort) is cooled and transferred to fermenting tanks. Leftover wet grains are dried and sold as animal feed.

The cooled wort is inoculated with yeast in fermentation tanks at around 85°F. Yeast converts the grain sugars into water, alcohol, and carbon dioxide. The yeast also produces congeners — flavor and aroma compounds such as higher alcohols, esters, and tannins that impart unique characteristics on the final product. Fermentation typically lasts three to 10 days. The final fermented grain alcohol mixture, called "beer," is transferred to a beer well until it's distilled.

Distillation separates and concentrates alcohol from the fermented beer mash. Water, alcohol, and fuel oils have different boiling points that separate when heated. As the beer is heated, alcohol vapors rise into a condenser, where circulating cool water causes the vapors to return to liquid form, falling into a flask. The distiller removes undesirable runoffs. "Heads" are lighter, often poisonous alcohols; "tails" are low-boiling-point compounds below the minimum acceptable proof level. The number of rounds of distilling depends on the taste the distiller desires. Additional rounds of distilling produce a smoother, purer product.

Maturation is the storing and aging of distilled alcohol in barrels. By law, whiskey and bourbon are aged for at least two years in new oak barrels that have been first charred on the inside. Aging imparts distinct aroma, flavor, and color; unaged, or "green," whiskey is as clear as a grain neutral spirit like vodka. Seasonal temperature changes cause the whiskey to expand and contract, creating a chemical reaction and extraction between whiskey and wood, and turns the clear alcohol a golden hue. Hotter and more extreme temperatures allow Tennessee and Kentucky whiskeys to mature much more rapidly than those distilled in Canada, Ireland, or Scotland. The longer a whiskey or bourbon is aged, the more flavor it takes from the wood. Several dozen whiskeys and bourbons are aged more than 20 years.

After aging in the warehouse, the distilled liquor is emptied into tanks, filtered, and bottled. Tennessee whiskey is simply bourbon that has been filtered through 10 feet of charcoal made from sugar maple. A distiller may add demineralized water to lower the proof to acceptable or legal standards. Some companies don't distill onsite, but infuse spirits from other ethanol companies and then age and bottle the final product. Such companies are still considered distilleries.

Most distilleries produce liquor at a single facility. A distillery is often owned by a holding company that has controlling interest in several other distilleries and liquor manufacturers. A small-batch distiller typically produces around 1,250 to 2,500 barrels (250,000 to 500,000 liters) of liquor annually; the largest distillers annually produce 40,000 to 50,000 barrels (8 to 10 million liters).

Common inputs include water, natural gas, malted grains, glass, and cartons. A whiskey producer needs around 100 kilograms of grain to produce 600 liters of liquor. High-proof, fruit-infused gins require around 90 kilograms of fruit to produce 600 liters.

Major food inputs depend on the final product. Vodka is a neutral spirit made from rye, wheat, corn, beets, or potatoes; gin is vodka flavored with botanicals; and cordials can be made from coffee beans, fruit, or herbs. Federal regulations can also drive inputs: by law, bourbon mash must be at least 51 percent corn and the final liquid must be aged in charred new oak barrels.

Technological advances include increased bottling and packaging efficiencies. The industry has reduced the weight of glass bottles and is expanding the use of containers made from polyethylene terephthalate (PET), a thermoplastic polymer. The distillation process hasn't changed much over the years, though improved yeast strains have helped create more consistent and efficient fermented mash. Distilleries aren't being converted from potable alcohol manufacturing to fuel ethanol plants, in spite of growing demand for ethanol fuel. Fuel ethanol plants are much bigger than most distilleries, and a converted distillery simply wouldn't have the size or scale to compete against large fuel manufacturing plants.

Sales & Marketing

A distillery's primary customer is a wholesaler (distributor). Under the federally mandated three-tier system, in place since Prohibition was lifted, alcohol companies can't sell directly to US retailers. Distilleries establish regionally exclusive relationships with distributors to represent and market the distillery's brands. In 18 "control" states, these distributors are the states themselves, which maintain a monopoly on liquor distribution and retail sales. In the remaining 32 states, liquor wholesalers sell to privately run stores. Companies employ product representatives to oversee a wholesaler's promotional programs. Distilleries selling internationally can sell directly to retailers or work through a third-party wholesaler.

Indirect customers are retailers, restaurants, and bars that carry the distillery's product, as well as consumers of spirits. Whiskey drinkers tend to be middle-to-upper class white males. Vodka, gin, and rum drinkers tend to mix the alcohol into fruit-based cocktails, which generally appeal to women and entry-level drinkers.

» The distillery industry includes about 80 companies with combined annual revenue of $6 billion.

» Major US companies include Brown-Foreman, Beam Global Spirits & Wine, and Heaven Hill Distilleries.

» Major products include whiskey and bourbon (30 percent of industry revenues); vodka (10 percent); cordials and liqueurs (10 percent); bottled cocktails (10 percent); gin (5 percent); and distillers dried grains used for animal feed (5 percent).

» A distillery's primary customer is a wholesaler (distributor).

» Cash flow is seasonal, with two peaks: summer and the winter gift-giving season.

Major types of marketing include TV, Internet, radio, and magazine advertising. The US liquor industry spends around $500 million annually to advertise spirits. In the mid-1990s, the Distilled Spirits Council (DISCUS) and most major TV and cable networks rescinded a voluntary ban on liquor advertising on TV. On-premise promotions include bartender incentives, free glassware, and themed parties. Liquor companies experiment with a wide range of co-marketing programs, including product placement in movies, sponsoring adult-oriented TV shows, and co-branding with food and drink products as diverse as barbecue sauce, colas, sunflower seeds, and cheesecake.

While the three-tier system forbids liquor companies and distributors from selling via the Internet, online alcohol retailers can sell and ship liquor to states that permit it. Many liquor wholesalers claim that online sales make illegal buying and consumption of alcohol easy for teenagers. A 2006 Teenage Research Unlimited study shows that 2 percent of Americans 14 to 20 buy alcohol online.

Typical product prices are around $12 for a 750 ml bottle of "premium" (mid-range) whiskey, vodka, or gin. The industry classifies brands into four categories: value, premium, high-end, and super-premium. Value brands can be as low as $10 a 1.75 liter. Super-premium brands can cost up to $200 per 750ml. Nearly 60 percent of the cost of a bottle of liquor is taxes, split evenly among federal, state, and indirect taxes, such as personal and corporate income, payroll, and property taxes. US distilleries compete on price with international spirits manufacturers, and with beer and wine producers.

Human Resources

Average wages for distillery workers are slightly higher than the national average for all workers. Most companies require distillers to have a strong science background to understand the precise technical, and potentially dangerous, process of distillation. Head distiller and management positions typically require advanced degrees in brewing and distillation. Several schools offer onsite and distance learning programs, which can range from one-day workshops to a distance learning MBA program in brewing and distilling.

The annual injury rate in distilleries is about 10 percent higher than the national average. Most injuries involve sprains, strains, cuts, and lacerations as a result of moving containers and equipment.

Industry Employment Growth

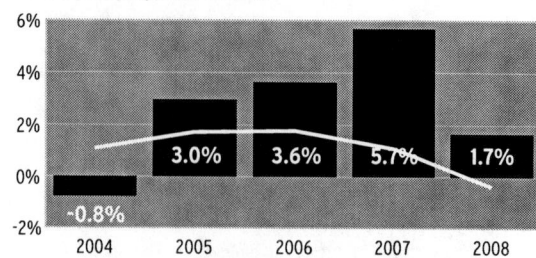

Average Hourly Earnings

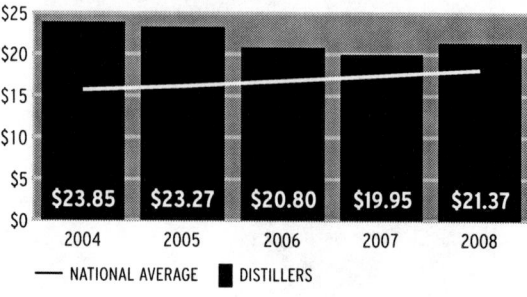

NATIONAL AVERAGE   DISTILLERS

SOURCE: BUREAU OF LABOR STATISTICS

Call Preparation Questions

Who are the company's key competitors?

US liquor companies compete directly with wine, beer, and international spirits manufacturers.

How does the company ensure compliance with local, state, and federal regulations?

The liquor industry is one of the most regulated industries in the US.

How does taxation impact company profits?

Distilled spirits are one of the most heavily taxed consumer products in the US.

How is the company impacted by the micro-distillery trend?

A new generation of small distillers is trying to replicate the explosive growth in the craft beer industry.

How important are exports to the company's sales growth?

Liquor exports have been rising, but China remains a large, relatively untapped, opportunity.

Web Links

American Distiller

Industry association focused on the micro-distillery industry.
www.distilling.com

BevMo – Beverages and more!

Great resource for real-world prices of spirits. Sells online.
www.bevmo.com

DISCUS News and Press Releases

News from the Distilled Spirits Council of the United States.
www.discus.org/media/press

Distillers Grains Quarterly

Information on distillers grains prices and trends.
www.distillersgrainsquarterly.com

Just Drinks

News and information for the beverage industry.
www.just-drinks.com

Online Distillery Network

News for spirits and fuel ethanol manufacturers.
www.distill.com

ProBrewer.com: Distilling

Provides an overview of how different products are distilled.
probrewer.com/resources/distilling

Glossary of Acronyms

ABV — alcohol by volume
AWOL — alcohol without liquid
CSPI — Center for Science in the Public Interest
DDGS — dried distillers grains with solubles
DISCUS — Distilled Spirits Council of the United States
FMB — flavored malt beverage
GNS — grain-neutral spirit
GMO — genetically modified organism
MADD — Mothers Against Drunk Driving
PET — polyethylene terephthalate
RTD — ready-to-drink
SFA — sales force automation
TTB — Alcohol and Tobacco Tax and Trade Bureau

HOOVER'S TOP COMPANIES

Largest Employers	Employees
Brown-Forman Corporation	4,466
Beam Global Spirits & Wine, Inc.	3,682
Pernod Ricard USA	1,985
Heaven Hill Distilleries, Inc.	485
A. Smith Bowman Distillery, Inc.	350
Paramount Distillers, Inc.	337
Bacardi U.S.A., Inc.	325
Future Brands LLC	300
McCormick Distilling Co., Inc.	152
Skyy Spirits, LLC	80

Top Public Companies by Market Value	($ mil.)
Brown-Forman Corporation	3,764.9
Castle Brands Inc.	16.1

* These rates are compounded annualized increases and may have resulted from acquisitions or one time gains. If less than 6 years of data are available, growth is for the years available.

SOURCE: HOOVER'S, INC., DATABASE

Drugstores

THIS INDUSTRY INCLUDES:

SIC CODES
5912   Drug Stores and
        Proprietary Stores

NAICS CODES
44611   Pharmacies and
        Drug Stores

In the US, about 40,000 drugstores have combined annual revenues of about $160 billion. Large companies include Walgreen, CVS Caremark, and Rite Aid. The industry has become more concentrated: the 50 largest companies hold close to 70 percent of the market. A typical drugstore has 30 employees and $6 million of annual revenue.

Competitive Landscape

Demand is driven by the aging of the US population and advances in medical treatment. The profitability of individual companies depends on access to medical insurance groups. Large companies have economies of scale in purchasing and in access to large groups of customers. Small companies can compete effectively through convenient location or special merchandising. Average annual revenue per employee is close to $200,000.

Products, Operations & Technology

Drugstores sell two types of products: prescription drugs, and "front-store" products, including over-the-counter (OTC) drugs, health and beauty aids, greeting cards, photo-finishing services, and general merchandise. Prescription drugs draw customers to the store, and stores focus their efforts on the number of new prescriptions they fill. The average store fills around 1,000 prescriptions per week. However, higher margin front-store merchandise sales often account for more than half of sales and an even larger percentage of profits.

The operations of drugstores focus on merchandising (which items to stock), advertising, inventory management, billing, and personnel management. Many are freestanding, about 12,000 square feet, and have a drive-through window to more easily accommodate elderly customers. Because older, and often sicker, customers buy most prescription drugs, many drugstores offer free home delivery. To use (ex-

BUSINESS CHALLENGES

» Lower Margins for Prescription Drugs

The share of prescriptions paid for by insurance or other third parties has grown, resulting in lower profit margins. Low margins on prescription drugs may push drugstores to expand front-store merchandise sales, where they compete with discount stores, or into related businesses such as pharmacy benefit management (PBM).

» Regulatory Pressure to Contain Drug Prices

The continuing rise in prescription drug costs has encouraged proposals to control drug prices, either through legislation or the formation of large public buyer groups that can negotiate lower prices with drug suppliers. Controls on drug prices cut drugstore margins.

» Insurers Negotiate Lower Prices

Managed care companies and other health insurers, because they control access to large numbers of patients, are able to negotiate lower prices with drug manufacturers and drugstore chains. The share of prescriptions paid for by insurance or other third parties has grown.

pensive) pharmacists more efficiently, drugstores use various aids in medicine dispensing.

Drugstore chains generally buy drugs and other products directly from manufacturers or large wholesalers like AmerisourceBergen, Cardinal Health, and McKesson, and distribute them to their stores through a warehouse system. Independent stores usually buy from a local distributor or may participate in buying co-ops that purchase from manufacturers.

Computer and other technology is becoming more important in dispensing prescription drugs, driven by demands of large third-party payers and the greater likelihood of errors or drug interactions as the number of drugs increases. Computer systems point out potential drug side effects or drug interactions and aid in billing; pill-counting machines are more accurate than humans; and 24-hour telephone lines allow customers to refill prescriptions automatically. Electronic prescriptions eliminate problems with reading doctors' handwriting, allow pharmacies to search databases for drug interactions, and let them bill third-party payers electronically.

Sales & Marketing

Major customers of drugstores are the third-party payers that account for 80 percent of prescription sales. Pharmacies contract with third-party payers like insurance companies, HMOs, or other managed care plans to provide prescription drugs to group members at reduced prices. The margins on this business are lower than on cash sales, but volume can be high, increasing sales of front-store products, so drugstores compete vigorously for this business. Independent drugstores often can't bid for this business because of a lack of locations.

Marketing and advertising often focus on services provided, such as drive-through service or home delivery. Convenient location is often the most important factor that draws customers. Advertising is mainly through newspapers, although large chains also use TV. Since drugstores usually get most of their prescription drug sales from repeat customers, they typically emphasize friendly, helpful, and discrete service.

Human Resources

Although pharmacists have advanced degrees and very good salaries, most drugstore employees are minimally skilled retail workers with relatively low pay and high turnover. Accordingly, the average hourly pay is about $14, a couple of dollars below the national wage. The industry's annual injury rate is low, at two per 100 full-time workers, which is about half the national average.

Industry Employment Growth

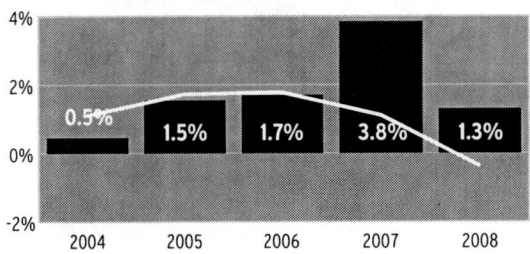

Average Hourly Earnings

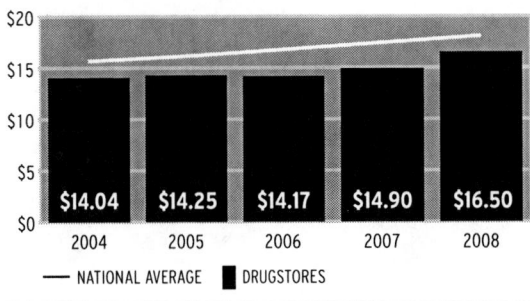

SOURCE: BUREAU OF LABOR STATISTICS

Call Preparation Questions

What steps is the company taking to improve profit margins?

The share of prescriptions paid for by insurance or other third parties has grown, resulting in lower profit margins.

How is regulatory pressure to reduce drug prices affecting company sales?

The continuing rise in prescription drug costs has encouraged proposals to control drug prices, either through legislation or the formation of large public buyer groups that can negotiate lower prices with drug suppliers.

What incentives does the company get from MCOs and insurers to increase sales of less expensive generic drugs?

Managed care companies and other health insurers, because they control access to large numbers of patients, are able to negotiate lower prices with drug manufacturers and drugstore chains.

How is the company positioning itself for the forecast continued rise in drug prescribing?

Prescription drug sales are expected to rise 75 percent in the next five years.

How is the company benefiting from the growing availability of OTC drugs?

The OTC share of the pharmaceutical market is expected to climb as high as one-fourth of the pharmaceutical industry within five years.

Web Links

American Pharmacists Association

Consumer information, publications, government affairs, and public relations.
www.pharmacist.com/am/template.cfm?Section=Home2

Canadian Association of Chain Drug Stores

Organization that represents Canadian retail chain pharmacies.
www.cacds.com

Drug Store News

Comprehensive industry news.
www.drugstorenews.com

Food and Drug Administration

Press releases, news, regulations.
www.fda.gov

National Association of Chain Drug Stores

Industry facts, news, and resources.
www.nacds.org

National Community Pharmacists Association

Industry news posted twice a week under Rx Headlines on home page.
www.ncpanet.org

Glossary of Acronyms

CMS — Centers for Medicare and Medicaid Services
EPC — electronic product code
NACDS — National Association of Chain Drug Stores
NCPA — National Community Pharmacists Association
PBM — pharmacy benefit managers
PHRMA — Pharmaceutical Research and Manufacturers of America

HOOVER'S TOP COMPANIES

Largest Companies by Sales	($ mil.)
CVS Caremark Corporation	87,471.9
Walgreen Co.	59,034.0
Rite Aid Corporation	24,326.8
Duane Reade Inc.	1,686.8
Marc Glassman, Inc.	1,130.0
VS Holdings, Inc.	537.9
drugstore.com, inc.	445.7

Largest Employers	Employees
Walgreen Co.	237,000
CVS Caremark Corporation	200,000
Rite Aid Corporation	112,800
Marc Glassman, Inc.	6,850
Duane Reade Inc.	6,700
VS Holdings, Inc.	2,880
Discount Drug Mart Inc.	2,700
Kinney Drugs, Inc.	2,000
The Bartell Drug Company	1,600
Snyder's Drug Stores Inc.	1,400

Fastest Growing* by Five-Year Sales Growth	(%)
CVS Caremark Corporation	26.9
drugstore.com, inc.	18.1
Walgreen Co.	12.7
VS Holdings, Inc.	11.6
Rite Aid Corporation	9.0
Marc Glassman, Inc.	6.6
Nyer Medical Group, Inc.	3.5
Duane Reade Inc.	1.8

Fastest Growing* by Five-Year Employee Growth	(%)
Nyer Medical Group, Inc.	18.5
drugstore.com, inc.	16.6
CVS Caremark Corporation	16.2
VS Holdings, Inc.	10.3
Walgreen Co.	9.8
Rite Aid Corporation	9.4
Duane Reade Inc.	2.1

Top Public Companies by Market Value	($ mil.)
CVS Caremark Corporation	41,350.1
Walgreen Co.	36,035.7
Rite Aid Corporation	2,216.7
drugstore.com, inc.	310.2
Nyer Medical Group, Inc.	5.8

* These rates are compounded annualized increases and may have resulted from acquisitions or one time gains. If less than 6 years of data are available, growth is for the years available.

SOURCE: HOOVER'S, INC., DATABASE

Dry Cleaning and Laundry Facilities

THIS INDUSTRY INCLUDES:

SIC CODES

7211   Power Laundries, Family and Commercial

7215   Coin-Operated Laundries and Drycleaning

7216   Drycleaning Plants, Except Rug Cleaning

7219   Laundry and Garment Services

NAICS CODES

81231   Coin-Operated Laundries and Drycleaners

81232   Drycleaning and Laundry Services (except Coin-Operated)

Laundry and dry cleaning services in the US are provided by 30,000 companies with combined annual revenue of $20 billion. Large companies include Coinmach Service and Martin Franchises. The industry includes 20,000 companies that provide retail laundry and dry cleaning services, 9,000 that provide services through coin-operated laundromats, and about 1,000 that provide commercial/industrial laundry services. The industry is highly fragmented: the 50 largest firms hold only about 40 percent of the market.

Competitive Landscape

Demand is related to growth in consumer income. The profitability of individual companies depends on efficient operations and favorable store locations. Large companies have efficiencies of scale in centralized cleaning operations. Small companies can compete successfully by owning favorable locations or providing special services. The industry is labor-intensive: average annual revenue per employee is just $60,000.

Products, Operations & Technology

Major products are consumer dry cleaning services, commercial laundry services, and coin-operated laundry services. Retail dry cleaning stores account for 40 percent of industry revenue, commercial launderers for 30 percent, and coin-operated laundromats for 15 percent. The additional remaining 15 percent of industry revenue consists of shoe and clothing repair services and washing machine "route" operators who service machines in apartments.

Retail dry cleaning operations consist of collecting and tagging clothing, operating the actual dry cleaning machinery either on the retail premises or at central facilities that serve a number of stores, and pressing, bagging, and returning clothing to customers. Average annual revenue for large retail locations is about

BUSINESS CHALLENGES

» Vulnerability to Government Regulations

Dry cleaners, subject to strict regulations from EPA, OSHA, and state and local agencies, must control water, groundwater, and air emissions, and properly dispose of hazardous waste. Due to the high flammability of some cleaning solvents, worker safety is a primary regulatory issue, as are plant layout, employee safety gear, and fire protection systems. Some dry cleaning chemicals, like perc, are considered hazardous.

» Vulnerability to Higher Energy Costs

Dry cleaners and commercial laundries use fairly large amounts of energy in the form of electricity to power motors or dryers, or natural gas and fuel oil to heat water. Some commercial washing machines work on a continuous batch system that conserves hot water, or recycles the final rinse water to use as the first wash water for the next batch.

» Lower Demand as Dress Styles, Fabrics Change

Changes in the business, school, and social world toward less formal dress have decreased demand for cleaning services. Newer fabrics also resist wrinkling and stains. More clothes can be washed at home and don't need to be pressed or ironed.

$500,000. Commercial dry cleaners service hospitals, hotels, and restaurants. Commercial dry cleaners may provide specialized services, such as "clean room" laundry facilities that serve chemicals, semiconductor, and pharmaceutical markets. Commercial laundry companies often also manufacture and lease uniforms. Average annual revenue for commercial launderers is about $5 million.

Coin-operated laundries (laundromats) provide washers and dryers for people who don't have laundry facilities in their own home. Most are single-location companies, with annual revenue under $300,000. In addition to operating retail locations, companies install and service laundromats in private buildings such as apartment complexes or college dorms under long-term contracts (so-called "laundry routes"). Mac-Gray services 30,000 laundry rooms. Operations mainly consist of money collection and maintenance.

Equipment is the largest investment for both dry cleaners and laundromats, and includes washer-extractors, finishing and ironing machines, folders, equipment computer systems, and dryers. Usually leased or financed from manufacturers or distributors, equipment is less expensive if rebuilt rather than new, and several equipment companies specialize in rebuilding machines for resale. Typical laundromat washers and dryers cost $700 to $2,500 each, depending on capacity.

Sales & Marketing

Retail dry cleaners depend heavily on store location to attract customers. Dry cleaners estimate that businesspeople may spend between $500 and $1,500 annually, but the average annual dry cleaning bill for a typical family is under $150. Repeat business and customer retention are crucial to success. Owners of coin-operated machines in apartment buildings either pay the landlord a fixed monthly fee or a percentage of revenue.

Human Resources

Most jobs in the dry cleaning and laundry industry require few skills and pay low wages; accordingly, personnel turnover is high. Pay is about 40 percent lower than the average for all US workers. The industry's annual injury rate is slightly higher than the national average.

Industry Employment Growth

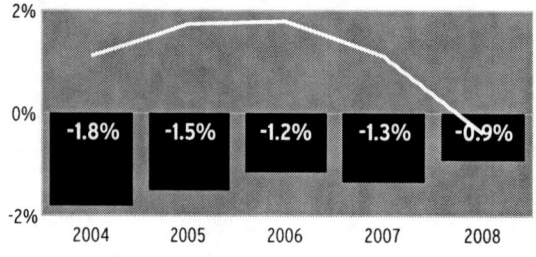

Average Hourly Earnings

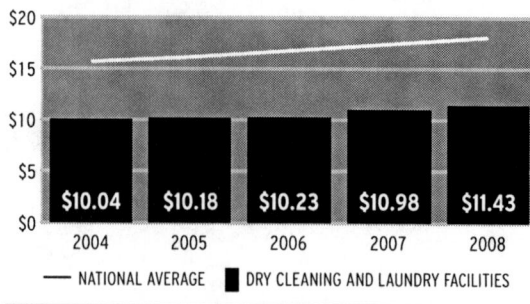

SOURCE: BUREAU OF LABOR STATISTICS

Call Preparation Questions

What actions has the company taken to reduce its perc demand and liability risk?

Dry cleaners, subject to strict regulations from EPA, OSHA, and state and local agencies, must control water, groundwater, and air emissions, and properly dispose of hazardous waste.

How can the company cut energy costs?

Dry cleaners and commercial laundries use fairly large amounts of energy in the form of electricity to power motors or dryers, or natural gas and fuel oil to heat water.

Does the company expect good growth in demand in its market?

Changes in the business, school, and social world toward less formal dress have decreased demand for cleaning services.

How might the company benefit from using wet cleaning methods?

A new process being used in the US for cleaning in water, wet cleaning, uses special technology, detergents, and additives to minimize adverse effects on fabrics.

What types of ancillary services is the company selling to customers, and to what benefit?

Increased discretionary incomes and lifestyle changes have created new lucrative markets for dry cleaners, such as wash-and-fold services that charge per pound, and pickup and delivery services.

Web Links

Cleaners Online

Issues, allied trades, news, views, links, associations, and consumer information.
www.cleanersonline.com

Coin Laundry Association

Operating statistics and surveys.
www.coinlaundry.org

Dry Cleaner News

News, links, and other useful information.
www.dcn-online.com

Drycleaning & Laundry Institute International

News, directories, industry information and more.
www.ifi.org

Laundry Today

News for the dry cleaning industry.
www.laundrytoday.com

National Cleaners Association

News, links, information.
www.nca-i.com

National Clothesline

Monthly newsletter on issues, news, people, and events in the cleaner industry.
www.natclo.com

OSHA Dry Cleaning Links

Links to OSHA regulations, training and control procedures related to the dry cleaning industry.
www.osha.gov/SLTC/drycleaning

Textile Care Allied Trades Association (TCATA)

Textile-related news.
www.tcata.org

The State Coalition for Remediation of Drycleaners (SCRD)

Provides news and information related to established state dry cleaner programs.
www.drycleancoalition.org/news.cfm

Glossary of Acronyms

EIA — Energy Information Association
IFI — International Fabricare Institute
TCATA — Textile Care Allied Trades Association

HOOVER'S TOP COMPANIES

Largest Employers	Employees
Coinmach Service Corp.	1,950
Zoots Corporation	850
Mac-Gray Corporation	737
PWS, Inc.	100
DRYCLEAN USA, Inc.	33

Fastest Growing* by Five-Year Sales Growth	(%)
Mac-Gray Corporation	14.5
DRYCLEAN USA, Inc.	9.7

Top Public Companies by Market Value	($ mil.)
Mac-Gray Corporation	149.5
DRYCLEAN USA, Inc.	6.3

* These rates are compounded annualized increases and may have resulted from acquisitions or one time gains. If less than 6 years of data are available, growth is for the years available.

SOURCE: HOOVER'S, INC., DATABASE

Drywall, Plaster, Acoustic and Insulation Contractors

THIS INDUSTRY INCLUDES:

SIC CODES

1742   Plastering, Drywall, Acoustical, and Insulation Work

NAICS CODES

23831   Drywall and Insulation Contractors

The drywall contractor industry in the US includes about 20,000 businesses with combined annual revenue of $25 billion. Large companies include Performance Contracting Group, KHS&S, and Acousti Engineering. Half of the companies in the industry are small with fewer than five employees. The average company has less than $500,000 of annual revenue.

New construction accounts for 80 percent of total industry revenue, the rest is from renovations. Commercial construction accounts for 65 percent of revenues, especially construction of office buildings, commercial space, schools, apartments, hospitals, and hotels; single family residential construction accounts for the rest.

Competitive Landscape

Demand is driven heavily by new building construction. The profitability of individual companies depends on a steady volume of work, accurate job estimating, and good cost controls. Large companies have an advantage in bidding on large jobs. Companies usually specialize in either residential or commercial work. Residential contractors have competition from a large number of independent workers.

Products, Operations & Technology

Commercial contractors install the metal framing that underlies walls in commercial buildings and the gypsum wallboard that covers it. They also install other types of walls (such as movable partitions or stone veneer), acoustic and specialty ceilings, and various types of insulation and fireproofing. Many commercial contractors are sales representatives for manufacturers of floor, wall or ceiling products, from companies such as USG, Armstrong, Johns Manville, and Sound Concepts.

Residential contractors install heat and sound insulation, ceilings, and interior walls in single-family homes. Walls and ceilings are typically made from various types of gypsum pan-

BUSINESS CHALLENGES

» Revenue Depends Highly on Construction Activity
Residential, and especially commercial, construction levels can vary sharply from year to year. For example, from 2001 to 2003, total US commercial construction was down 25 percent due to the recession; office construction dropped 40 percent on average and much more in some local markets.

» Dependence on Local Economy
Despite national trends, demand for housing can be volatile in local markets. Even in a large market such as Atlanta, demand for new single family homes can change 50 percent in just two years; in smaller markets the change can be 100 percent. Demand volatility is due mainly to population shifts.

» Customer Concentration
Small contractors may have only a few or just one customer that provides the bulk of revenue, which is especially likely in the residential market if a company works for a major developer. Such a high concentration is often bad for profitability and increases the risk of uneven cash flow and default.

els nailed into place over wood framing installed by the builder. Various finishing work hides joints and prepares the surfaces for painting. Insulation materials typically are fiberglass pads and foam panels, but may also be sprayed or loose materials like cellulose.

Both commercial and residential contractors may also do related work, like installing floors and painting.

Commercial contractors may have an Internet site that allows potential customers to view projects and see samples of the types of materials they've worked with. Computer technology may be used in project cost estimating, materials ordering, and project coordination with the primary contractor.

Sales & Marketing

Most drywall contractors work as subcontractors on construction projects. They try to develop and maintain close relationships with local homebuilders, developers, and construction companies. In the residential segment, contractors often get repeat business from homebuilders. In the commercial segment, contractors frequently have to bid on projects. On private projects, bidding may be by invitation; on public projects bidding is usually open to any contractor who meets certain technical and financial criteria.

Human Resources

Labor is the largest cost for contractors. Drywall work requires skilled labor that may be in short supply during peak construction months. Average wages are high, around $21 per hour, about six dollars more than the average national wage. Because the work is often seasonal, employers may keep a core permanent workforce and hire extras when needed. Annual injury rates average seven cases per 100 full-time workers, higher than the national average of just over four cases.

Industry Employment Growth

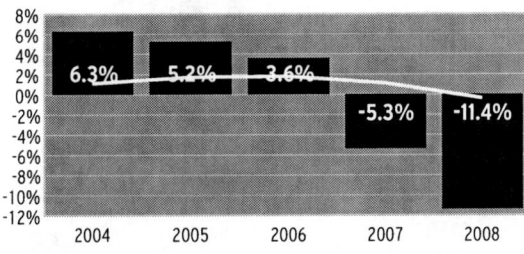

	2004	2005	2006	2007	2008
	6.3%	5.2%	3.6%	-5.3%	-11.4%

Average Hourly Earnings

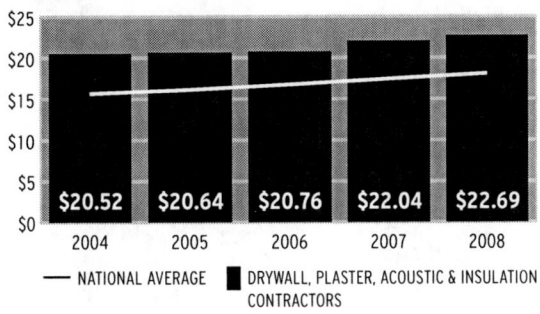

	2004	2005	2006	2007	2008
	$20.52	$20.64	$20.76	$22.04	$22.69

— NATIONAL AVERAGE ■ DRYWALL, PLASTER, ACOUSTIC & INSULATION CONTRACTORS

SOURCE: BUREAU OF LABOR STATISTICS

Call Preparation Questions

How does the company adjust to cyclical demand?

Residential, and especially commercial, construction levels can vary sharply from year to year.

How difficult is shifting work to other markets if the local market is flat?

Despite national trends, demand for housing can be volatile in local markets.

How successful is the company at diversifying its customer base?

Small contractors may have only a few or just one customer that provides the bulk of revenue, which is especially likely in the residential market if a company works for a major developer.

Can the company expand its remodeling work when new construction is flat?

According to the National Association of Home Builders, the remodeling market grew nearly 50 percent in the past decade, and continues to grow.

Web Links

American Subcontractors Association

General subcontractor issues.
www.asaonline.com

Association of the Wall and Ceiling Industry

Construction Dimensions magazine.
www.awci.org

Gypsum Today

Industry news.
www.gypsumtoday.com

National Association of Home Builders

Industry news.
www.nahb.org

Walls & Ceilings Magazine

Industry news.
www.wconline.com

Glossary of Acronyms

ASA — American Subcontractors Association
NAHB — National Association of Home Builders

HOOVER'S TOP COMPANIES

Largest Employers	Employees
Performance Contracting Group, Inc.	5,700
KHS&S Contractors	3,500
Irex Contracting Group	2,500
United Subcontractors, Inc.	1,900
Acousti Engineering Company of Florida	1,500
Baker Triangle	1,115
Component Assembly Systems, Inc.	750
Petrin Corporation	670
Industrial Acoustics Company, Inc.	500
W. G. Valenzuela Drywall, Inc.	300

SOURCE: HOOVER'S, INC., DATABASE

Edible Oils Manufacturing

The edible oils manufacturing industry includes about 200 companies with combined annual revenue of $38 billion. Major companies include Archer Daniels Midland, ConAgra, Cargill Foods, and CHS. The industry is highly concentrated: the 50 largest companies account for about 70 percent of industry revenue.

Edible oils manufacturing includes wet-milling corn (separating corn into its basic components); processing soybeans, tree nuts, and vegetables into oil; refining vegetable fats; and blending vegetable fats with purchased animal fats. This industry doesn't include companies that render or refine animal fats, wet-mill corn into ethyl alcohol, or mill-dry corn for flour.

Competitive Landscape

Demand is driven by consumer trends in consuming sweeteners, fats, and food oils, and in eating meat, since soybean meal is used primarily to feed poultry, swine, and cattle. The profitability of individual companies depends on managing raw material costs, leveraging federal farm subsidies, and operating efficiently. Large companies have advantages in purchasing, distribution, and marketing. Small operations can compete effectively by serving a local market or offering specialized products. The industry is capital-intensive: average annual revenue per employee is $1.5 million.

Products, Operations & Technology

Major products include soybean cake and meal (40 percent of the market); shortening and cooking oils (20 percent); and corn sweeteners (20 percent). Other products include margarine, butter blends, butter substitutes, and soybean oil.

To produce soybean meal and oil, beans are transported by truck or rail to a soybean processing facility. The beans are inspected, cleaned, and cracked to remove the hull.

BUSINESS CHALLENGES

» Dependence on Government Support

Corn processors actively lobby the federal government to support corn and sugar subsidies, which can directly and indirectly result in windfall profits. Over a recent 10-year period, the federal government paid farmers $50 billion in corn subsidies, 25 percent of total revenue; CHS, a leading soybean and corn processor, received $50 million in government subsidies. Price supports for sugar dissuade food manufacturers from buying refined sugar, often turning instead to high fructose corn syrup for sweetener needs.

» Dependence on Livestock Industry

Of all domestically processed soybean meal, 75 percent is used to feed livestock; poultry and swine account for 80 percent of all soybean meal consumption. Changing patterns in domestic chicken and pork consumption could lower demand for soybean meal. An outbreak of disease, such as avian influenza, could cause demand to plummet.

» Dependence on Ethanol

The corn processing industry has nearly tripled its total output of corn in the past 10 years, but 98 percent of this growth is from secondary ethanol production. All other corn and industrial uses have remained steady or declined. Ethanol manufacturers benefit from a federal mandate to double current levels of ethanol production by 2022, and from subsidies for ethanol of almost $1.50 per gallon produced. The wet corn processing industry could be negatively impacted by changes in federal price supports, a glut in ethanol, or increased efficiencies from ethanol made with switchgrass or wood chips. Price supports for ethanol result in higher prices for soybean meal, as farmers switch from planting soybeans to highly profitable grain corn.

Rolling machines disrupt the oil cells, facilitating oil extraction. Oil is typically solvent-extracted using hexane, a highly flammable liquid agent. Solvent extraction removes all but 1 percent of the oil from the meal. The defatted soy flakes enter a rotary dryer, are cooled, then ground to the preferred level of fineness. Around 95 percent of defatted soy flakes are processed as soybean meal for animal feed, although some flakes are ground into soy flour, soy grits, soy protein concentrates, or textured vegetable protein (TVP). The remaining soybean oil is further refined and processed for food or industrial use.

US soybean processors crush 2 billion bushels of soybeans each year (a bushel of soybeans is 60 pounds). The average soybean processing facility can process 65,000 bushels of beans a day. Each bushel yields 44 pounds of meal and 11 pounds of oil; 75 percent of all edible fats and oils consumed in the US are derived from soybeans.

To produce corn-based oils and sweeteners, #2 yellow dent corn is shipped by truck or rail to a wet corn mill. The corn is inspected and cleaned twice to remove the cob, chaff, and dust. Cleaned corn enters steep tanks in a continuous batch process, where the grain is steeped in a rotating water solution containing 0.1 percent sulfuric acid. This 24- to 48-hour process softens the kernel for milling and helps break down proteins. After steeping, the corn flows in a water slurry to a germ separator, where cyclone separators spin the corn germ out of the slurry. Further refining of the germ produces corn oil for cooking. Corn germ contains 85 percent of corn's total oil content.

The remaining slurry of fiber, starch, and protein is ground, screened, and separated. Corn starch is washed up to 15 times to remove all traces of proteins. Processors use various acids or enzymes to convert the liquid starch into dextrose, maltose, or high-fructose corn syrup (HFCS). Dextrose is typically fermented and distilled to produce fuel ethanol.

The corn milling industry processes 3.5 billion bushels of corn annually (a bushel of corn is 56 pounds). A bushel of wet-milled corn produces about 33 pounds of HFCS (dry weight); 15 pounds of gluten feed; and 2 pounds of crude corn oil. Each year, processors manufacture 15 million tons of HFCS, representing nearly 60 percent of the US nutritive sweeter market. The industry also processes 5 million tons of corn oil meal for livestock and 500,000 tons of corn oil annually. The largest wet corn mills have a daily grind capacity of 2 million bushels.

Common inputs in the edible oils industry include electricity, water, chemicals to extract oils, and equipment repairs. Buying the grains or oilseed is, by far, the largest material cost.

Recent technological advances often involve uncovering new uses for processed soybean or corn. New products include dextrose-based biodegradable plastic, soy- and corn-based lubricants and chemicals, and food oils that are free of unhealthy trans fats. Large processors with advanced research capabilities genetically modify soybean and corn strains to create new hybrids and improve the viability of existing seed.

Sales & Marketing

Customers range widely, depending on the type of product produced and at what stage of processing the product is sold. Typical customers include animal feed mills, poultry confinement operators, commercial feedlots that hold swine and cattle prior to slaughter, edible oil refiners, and food manufacturers. Processors that manufacture value-added products also sell to food distributors and restaurants.

Major types of marketing include trade publications, promotional events, trade shows, on-site demonstrations, and customer visits. Large processors may advertise nationally on TV, radio, or in newspapers. Sales teams are often organized by geographic territory, selling a wide range of commodities and products within a multi-county or multi-state region. Many companies rely on a network of third-party brokers to supplement an inside sales force. Other companies use technical service teams to seek out customer needs and develop long-term custom solutions.

Processors are typically highly diversified, so companies commonly joint venture with a retailer or food manufacturer to develop co-branded products. Processors with a consumer product focus maintain Web-based and toll-free customer service operations to address inquiries, publish recipes, and provide advice on how to cook with oils and fats.

Since most products are sold to refiners, manufacturers, and mills, Internet sales tend to have a business-to-business focus. Large companies manage restricted-access Intranets for customers to review and place orders. Vertically integrated processors rely on complex electronic data interchange (EDI) programs to facilitate e-commerce transactions and manage inventory. Companies generally don't use the Internet to sell products directly to consumers.

Typical product prices are $200 per ton of soybean meal; $0.30 a pound for soybean and corn oil; and $0.25 to $0.30 a pound for HFCS, depending on its sugar concentration. Prices are susceptible to commodity shortages due to weather-related problems. Food oils and fats derived from oilseed compete against peanut oil, coconut oil, palm oil, and lard. HFCS competes directly with refined sugar and sugar substitutes. Federal price supports for sugar have made HFCS a much cheaper sweetener than sugar. HFCS and hydrogenated oils are shelf-stable, providing a competitive edge against refined sugar, animal fat, and butter.

Human Resources

Edible oils manufacturing wages average $19 per hour, about 5 percent higher than the national average. Productivity has steadily increased in recent years, rising nearly 40 percent in the 10 years ending 2005. Edible oils manufacturing requires mechanical, scientific, and technical skills. Some universities offer advanced degrees in food science with an emphasis in oilseed chemistry. The annual injury rate in edible oils manufacturing is 25 percent lower than the national average. Most injuries involve sprains, strains, fractures, and bruises resulting from operating machinery and falling. Amputations are eight times higher than the national average.

Industry Employment Growth

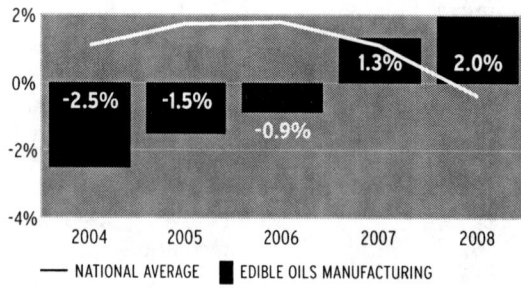

Bar values: -2.5% (2004), -1.5% (2005), -0.9% (2006), 1.3% (2007), 2.0% (2008)

— NATIONAL AVERAGE ■ EDIBLE OILS MANUFACTURING

SOURCE: BUREAU OF LABOR STATISTICS

Call Preparation Questions

How important is lobbying the government to the company's bottom line?

Corn processors actively lobby the federal government to support corn and sugar subsidies, which can directly and indirectly result in windfall profits.

How critical is the livestock feed industry to the company's success?

Of all domestically processed soybean meal, 75 percent is used to feed livestock; poultry and swine account for 80 percent of all soybean meal consumption.

How dependent is the company on ethanol production?

The corn processing industry has nearly tripled its total output of corn in the past 10 years, but 98 percent of this growth is from secondary ethanol production.

Is the consumer shift from trans fatty acids a liability or an opportunity for the company?

Edible oil manufacturers are developing new trademarked brands of fats and oil blends containing minimal to no trans fats.

How important are finished or value-added products to the company's overall profitability?

Edible oil processors are expanding product development capabilities, manufacturing more finished food products for retail sale.

Web Links

Archer Daniels Midland (ADM)

Nation's largest oilseed and corn processor.
www.admworld.com/naen

Corn Refiners Association

Industry association of wet corn mills.
www.corn.org

HFCS Facts

HFCS promotion and defense by the Corn Refiners Association.
www.hfcsfacts.com

National Oilseed Processors Association

Association of oilseed processors and vegetable oil and oilseed meal manufacturers.
www.nopa.org

Soyatech

News and facts about oilseeds, meal, and corn.
www.soyatech.com

Soystats

Soybean facts and figures.
www.soystats.com

USDA Soybean Briefing Room

Facts and data on soybeans, including cake, meal, and oil.
www.ers.usda.gov/Briefing/SoybeansOilCrops

USDA Sugar Briefing Room

Facts and data on sweeteners, including HFCS.
www.ers.usda.gov/Briefing/Sugar/Data.htm

Glossary of Acronyms

ADM — Archer Daniels Midland
EDI — electronic data interchange
FSA — Farm Service Agency
GM — genetically modified
GMO — genetically modified organism
HFCS — high fructose corn syrup
HVO — hydrogenated vegetable oil
PHVO — partially hydrogenated vegetable oil
TVP — texturized vegetable protein

HOOVER'S TOP COMPANIES

Largest Companies by Sales	($ mil.)
Cargill, Incorporated	120,439.0
Archer Daniels Midland Company	69,816.0
Bunge Limited	52,574.0
CHS Inc.	32,167.5
ConAgra Foods, Inc.	11,605.7
Corn Products International, Inc.	3,944.0
Solae, LLC	1,000.0

Largest Employers	Employees
Cargill, Incorporated	160,000
Archer Daniels Midland Company	27,600
ConAgra Foods, Inc.	25,000
Bunge Limited	23,889
Corn Products International, Inc.	7,100
CHS Inc.	6,885
Solae, LLC	3,500
Tate & Lyle Ingredients Americas, Inc.	2,098
Ventura Foods, LLC	1,840
PYCO Industries, Inc.	251

Fastest Growing* by Five-Year Sales Growth	(%)
CHS Inc.	27.9
Bunge Limited	18.9
Archer Daniels Midland Company	17.9
Cargill, Incorporated	17.2
Corn Products International, Inc.	13.4
Solae, LLC	7.7

Fastest Growing* by Five-Year Employee Growth	(%)
Cargill, Incorporated	10.3
Solae, LLC	5.3
Archer Daniels Midland Company	1.5
Bunge Limited	0.8
Corn Products International, Inc.	0.7
CHS Inc.	0.2

Top Public Companies by Market Value	($ mil.)
Archer Daniels Midland Company	21,735.0
ConAgra Foods, Inc.	11,324.6
Bunge Limited	6,296.9
Corn Products International, Inc.	2,136.1
CHS Inc.	232.1

* These rates are compounded annualized increases and may have resulted from acquisitions or one time gains. If less than 6 years of data are available, growth is for the years available.

SOURCE: HOOVER'S, INC., DATABASE

Education and Training Services

THIS INDUSTRY INCLUDES:

SIC CODES

8244   Business and Secretarial Schools

NAICS CODES

6114   Business Schools and Computer and Management Training

6115   Technical and Trade Schools

6116   Other Schools and Instruction

The education and training services industry includes about 45,000 companies and 300,000 self-employed individuals with combined annual revenue of nearly $30 billion. Major companies include Kaplan; Career Education Corporation (CEC); ITT Educational Services; and Sylvan Learning. The industry is highly fragmented: depending on the segment, the 50 largest companies represent only 15 to 40 percent of total revenue.

Education and training services is a broad category that encompasses job-specific certification; professional training; and classes emphasizing self-fulfillment, leisure, and hobbies. Many of the industry's programs, classes, and training services fall under the category of career and technical education (CTE), historically known as vocational education, or "vo-tech." High schools, community colleges, universities, and educational support services aren't included in this industry.

Competitive Landscape

Demand for certification classes is driven by employment trends in the medical, high technology, and manufacturing industries. Demand for classes emphasizing self-fulfillment is driven by personal income. The profitability of individual companies depends on maintaining low operating costs and recruiting enough students. Large companies have advantages in marketing and offering a wide range of classes and services. Small companies can compete effectively through personalized service and customized instruction. The industry is highly labor-intensive: average annual revenue per worker is around $80,000.

Products, Operations & Technology

Major services include management development and training (16 percent of industry revenue); technical and trade schools (15 percent); and computer training (13 percent). Other services include fine arts schools, sports and recreation instruction, exam preparation and tutoring, and flight training.

Education and training services cater to a broad demographic, ranging from a teenager taking a driving class to a CEO on a leadership retreat. Around 15 million Americans are enrolled in an educational and training services program. According to the Association for Career and Technical Education (ACTE), nearly all US high school students take at least one career

BUSINESS CHALLENGES

» Compliance with Government Policies

Educational and training services, particularly certificate-granting programs, are heavily regulated by the US government. Educational policies addressing financial aid programs, classroom funding, accreditation status, and standardized testing can change considerably based on the political climate and philosophy of the legislative and executive branches. Establishing a track record of success can be difficult for career and technical programs in light of this ever-changing regulatory climate.

» Dependence on Personal Income

Leisure studies is a $7 billion annual industry that relies on individual desire for self-expression and self-fulfillment. Non-certificate classes such as yoga, calligraphy, and fly fishing depend highly on consumer spending patterns. A recession or period of high unemployment would likely impact hobby, arts, and sports instruction.

» Vulnerability to Federal Funding Cutbacks

While government funding represents only 5 percent of overall industry revenues, a number of CTE institutions rely heavily on federal loan programs to support enrollment. Cutbacks or changes to federal programs could have a major effect on the profitability of educational and training institutions. For example, 60 percent of ITT Technical Institute's revenues come from federal student financial aid programs.

and technical class, and 25 percent take three or more courses in a single discipline. One-third of college students are involved in CTE programs, and 40 million adults have taken short-term occupational training.

Coursework can take place in an individual's home, an educational institution, office, online, or in the field. The goal of the class can be as varied as the subject matter, ranging from certification requirements to become employed or advance in a specific field, to leisure and hobby classes purely for self-fulfillment. Certificate programs are offered both online and in university campus settings and typically take 12 months to complete.

Operations involve both instruction and administration. Instruction expenses include faculty salaries, course materials, bad debt expense, lease and occupancy costs, and educational equipment. Administration expenses include direct marketing, finance and accounting, admission expenses, and legal fees. Instruction costs are about 60 percent of total costs and administrative costs around 20 percent, though this can vary considerably based on the type of program.

In addition to teaching technical skills, most educational and training services are heavily invested in Internet-based distance learning. Synchronous courses are "virtual classrooms" in which students view streaming media and converse with the teacher and other students through instant messaging. Non-synchronous classes allow students to learn whenever convenient, with minimum weekly login requirements.

Sales & Marketing

Typical customers are individuals who choose (or are required to by law or an employer) to take a class for career advancement or self-fulfillment.

Technical, business, and computer schools often invest in high school recruitment programs using videos, presentations, and referral incentive programs to attract students. Other marketing programs include career fairs, open houses, print marketing in local newspapers, and brochures.

Educational and training services recruit heavily on the Internet. In addition to traditional banner advertisements, many larger CTE schools have a presence on social networking sites.

Typical product prices for educational and training services vary based on the type of in-

struction. Typically, the cost difference between an online or classroom course is minimal. Schools offering certification programs generally require individual tuition; average tuition for a year-long CTE certificate program is around $4,000. Professional and management classes typically charge a corporate group rate. Self-fulfillment classes usually charge monthly, hourly, or per-session program fees.

Depending on the type of instruction, competition can come from a number of sources: free self-education on the Internet, entrance into the workforce directly instead of pursuing career and technical instruction, or the option to choose a liberal arts program instead of a CTE education.

Human Resources

Employment has risen considerably in the educational and training services sector, particularly in management training, technical and trade schools, fine arts schools, and sports and recreation instruction. Overall employment is nearly 15 percent higher than 10 years ago. The two notable exceptions are computer training classes and secretarial schools, where industry employment has fallen 15 percent over the past five years.

Wages in the educational and technical service industry are equal to the national average, with one exception: salaries in the business schools and computer and management training segment are nearly 30 percent higher than the national average. Not surprisingly, the injury rate in the educational and training services sector is much lower than the national average.

Industry Employment Growth

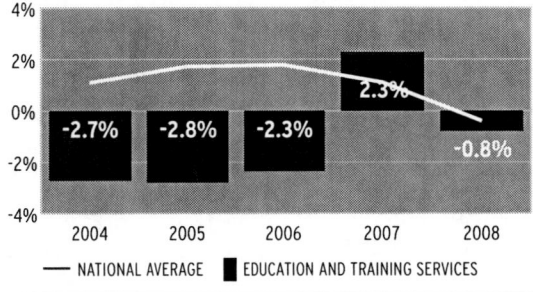

SOURCE: BUREAU OF LABOR STATISTICS

Call Preparation Questions

How challenging is the regulatory climate in CTE education?

Educational and training services, particularly certificate-granting programs, are heavily regulated by the US government.

How dependent is the company on consumer demand for leisure studies?

Leisure studies is a $7 billion annual industry that relies on individual desire for self-expression and self-fulfillment.

How dependent is the company on federal funding?

While government funding represents only 5 percent of overall industry revenues, a number of CTE institutions rely heavily on federal loan programs to support enrollment.

How important is online education to the company?

Over 3 million Americans are enrolled in at least one online course, according to the Alfred P Sloan foundation.

Web Links

American Association for Adult and Continuing Education (AAACE)

Organization for Adult Learning.
www.aaace.org

Career/Technical Education Statistics

Statistics from the Institute of Education Sciences.
nces.ed.gov/surveys/ctes/tables

Council for Higher Education Accreditation – Directory

Directory of specialized and professional accrediting agencies.
www.chea.org/Directories/special.asp

International Association for Continuing Education & Training (IACET)

Administrator of Continuing Education Units.
www.iacet.org/content/about-iacet.html

National Association of State Directors of Career Technical Education Consortium

Professional society of state leaders responsible for career technical education.
www.careertech.org

Office of Vocational and Adult Education

Federal administrator of Perkins Fund.
www.ed.gov/about/offices/list/ovae

Glossary of Acronyms

CEU — continuing education unit
CTE — career and technical education
HEA — Higher Education Act of 1965
NCLB — No Child Left Behind
NCES — National Center for Education Statistics
OVAE — Office of Vocational and Adult Education
SEA — state education authorities
STEM — Science, Technical, Education, and Math

HOOVER'S TOP COMPANIES

Largest Companies by Sales	($ mil.)
Kaplan, Inc.	2,331.6
Career Education Corporation	1,705.3
Laureate Education, Inc.	1,420.0
ITT Educational Services, Inc.	1,015.3
Lincoln Educational Services Corporation	376.9
Universal Technical Institute, Inc.	343.5
SkillSoft Public Limited Company	281.2
Whitney Information Network, Inc.	207.6
Educate, Inc. (Sylvan Learning Center)	—

Largest Employers	Employees
Laureate Education, Inc.	28,500
Career Education Corporation	14,479
Educate, Inc. (Sylvan Learning Center)	10,161
Kaplan, Inc.	7,600
ITT Educational Services, Inc.	7,200
Management & Training Corporation	7,000
The Princeton Review, Inc.	3,511
Lincoln Educational Services Corporation	2,671
Universal Technical Institute, Inc.	2,360
SkillSoft Public Limited Company	1,133

Fastest Growing* by Five-Year Sales Growth	(%)
Whitney Information Network, Inc.	27.3
HealthStream, Inc.	22.7
SkillSoft Public Limited Company	22.6
Laureate Education, Inc.	18.6
SmartPros Ltd.	14.6
ITT Educational Services, Inc.	14.2
Lincoln Educational Services Corporation	13.6
Universal Technical Institute, Inc.	11.8
Peoples Educational Holdings, Inc.	9.5
Career Education Corporation	7.5

Fastest Growing* by Five-Year Employee Growth	(%)
HealthStream, Inc.	19.1
SkillSoft Public Limited Company	13.4
SmartPros Ltd.	13.3
Laureate Education, Inc.	12.0
ITT Educational Services, Inc.	9.5
Lincoln Educational Services Corporation	8.5
Learning Tree International, Inc.	5.4
Universal Technical Institute, Inc.	2.6

Top Public Companies by Market Value	($ mil.)
ITT Educational Services, Inc.	3,677.3
Career Education Corporation	1,610.1
SkillSoft Public Limited Company	1,000.2
Universal Technical Institute, Inc.	428.0
Lincoln Educational Services Corporation	345.7

* These rates are compounded annualized increases and may have resulted from acquisitions or one time gains. If less than 6 years of data are available, growth is for the years available.

SOURCE: HOOVER'S, INC., DATABASE

Electric Energy Distribution

THIS INDUSTRY INCLUDES:

SIC CODES

4911   Electric Services

NAICS CODES

22112   Electric Power
        Transmission,
        Control, and
        Distribution

Over 6,000 companies in the US are involved in the wholesale trade and retail distribution of electricity, with combined annual revenue of more than $220 billion. Companies include owners of high-voltage transmission lines and retail distribution systems, and intermediaries like energy dealers and brokers. The US consumes close to 4 billion megawatt hours (MWh) of electricity per year, about 50 percent of which is bought and sold on the wholesale market.

Competitive Landscape

The electric energy industry in the US is currently in a state- and federally-sponsored transition, or Electric Restructuring. The traditional electricity industry consists of large investor-owned utilities (IOUs); municipal utilities; rural cooperatives; and government entities, like the Tennessee Valley Authority (TVA), that own the generation, transmission, and retail distribution facilities within a limited area, and serve all customers within that area as tightly regulated "natural monopolies." Under restructuring, the generation, transmission, and distribution operations are carried out by separate companies, and the owners of local distribution lines make their lines available to competitors. About half the states have adopted restructuring legislation, but only a third are actively engaged in restructuring.

The intended purpose of moving toward a less regulated electricity market is to decrease the cost of electricity by fostering competition among producers. The practical effect of federal and state legislation has been the divestment of generation facilities by local utilities. Despite restructuring, many local electricity distributors are owned by utility holding companies that also own power generation facilities, wholesale transmission lines, and wholesale power trading companies.

BUSINESS CHALLENGES

» Electricity Demand Varies with Economy

Although some portions of electricity demand, such as for residential and commercial use, increase steadily, US industrial use varies with the level of economic activity. Residential electricity use grew 6 percent from 2000 to 2002, but industrial use declined 9 percent, due to the recession.

» Dependence on Regulators

The rates electricity distributors can charge are regulated by state Public Utility Commissions (PUCs). Rates are usually set to enable the distributor to earn an appropriate ROI, but politics can prevent distributors from passing on higher costs. The first step toward deregulation of the electricity market was 1978 in the US, when the Public Utility Regulatory Polices Act was enacted, opening wholesale power markets to non-utility producers of electricity. Utilities in California went bankrupt when they were unable to pass on higher wholesale prices, causing many states to rethink deregulation. The California electricity crisis of 2000, and subsequent market manipulations by large energy trading companies like Enron and Dynegy, have prompted calls for re-regulation.

» Uncertain Power Availability

The margin between available electricity supply and demand was in decline for more than a decade before rebounding, making electrical energy shortages more likely during down years. In a deregulated environment, power generators can't be sure how many customers they will have, and may delay new generating capacity until demand is proven.

Products, Operations & Technology

The actual operations of retail electricity distributors consist of generating or acquiring wholesale power (often under long-term supply contracts), maintaining and extending a line network, and billing and collections.

Retail distributors generate their own power or buy power in the wholesale market. If local utilities can't meet demand through their own generation facilities, extra electricity may be bought from another utility with spare capacity. While such trading was done informally, the wholesale market has evolved rapidly since 1996, when the Federal Energy Regulatory Commission (FERC) required utilities to open transmission facilities and establish electronic information systems to share capacity information.

Power marketing companies are intermediaries in the wholesale market, buying power from generators and selling to distributors through short- or long-term contracts.

The two basic wholesale forward contracts are the Day-Ahead and the Block Forward. The Day-Ahead spot contract is for electricity to be delivered at a specified hour and transmission point during the next day. The Block Forward contract specifies that a block of electricity be delivered daily for a month at some time in the future. Forward contracts are expressed in dollars per megawatt hour ($/MWh); typical prices range from $15/MWh to $50/MWh, although much higher prices are sometimes paid. Day-Ahead contracts are established on local power exchanges. Futures contracts are traded on the Chicago Board of Trade (CBOT) and the New York Mercantile Exchange (NYMEX).

Sales & Marketing

In states that have adopted restructuring, local distributors may compete with alternative retail electric suppliers (ARES). Because electricity is a commodity, competition is based solely on price and availability.

Marketing efforts are usually limited to low-cost advertising that lists the advantages of electricity over competing sources of heating energy such as oil or natural gas.

The three major types of customer for electricity are residential, commercial, and industrial; each account for about a third of US electricity demand. Because of economies of scale in delivering power, industrial customers pay the lowest prices while residential customers pay the highest. In 2004, residential and commercial customers paid an average of 8 cents per KWh; industrial customers paid about 5 cents.

Human Resources

Many jobs in electrical distribution require highly technical skills and accordingly pay very well. Average hourly wages of $26 are $10 higher than the national average. Workers often are members of unions and generally receive a high level of benefits. The industry's average annual injury rate per 100 full-time workers is around five cases, about one more than the national average.

Industry Employment Growth

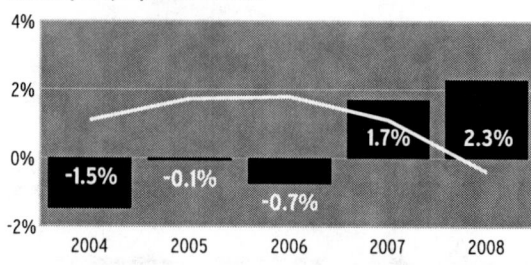

Average Hourly Earnings

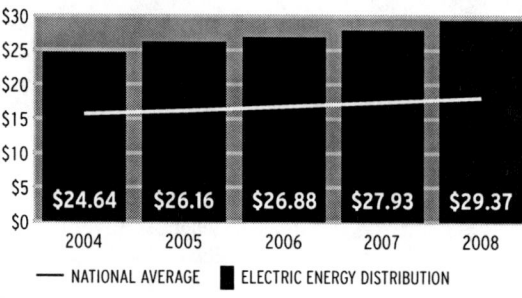

— NATIONAL AVERAGE ■ ELECTRIC ENERGY DISTRIBUTION

SOURCE: BUREAU OF LABOR STATISTICS

Call Preparation Questions

How do recent economic shifts in the company's service area impact energy demand?

Although some portions of electricity demand, such as for residential and commercial use, increase steadily, US industrial use varies with the level of economic activity.

How are changes in federal regulation impacting the company?

The rates electricity distributors can charge are regulated by state Public Utility Commissions (PUCs).

What concerns does the company have about the stability and reliability of the electrical power grid?

The margin between available electricity supply and demand was in decline for more than a decade before rebounding, making electrical energy shortages more likely during down years.

What expansion or construction plans does the company have for the next few years?

Electricity demand in the US has generally grown at twice the rate of population in the past decade, making slow but steadily increasing demand a long-term trend in the industry.

Besides distribution, what other services are profitable for the company?

In a deregulated environment, operators can more easily offer other services to customers, such as energy management, engineering, and communications services.

Web Links

American Public Power Association

Association of municipal utilities. List of mergers and acquisitions.
www.appanet.org

Electric Power Supply Association

Press releases.
www.epsa.org

Electricity Distributors Association

Canadian industry issues.
www.eda-on.ca

Energy Information Administration

Part of the Department of Energy. Excellent industry statistics.
www.eia.doe.gov

Federal Energy Regulatory Commission (FERC)

Federal regulator. Policy issues and orders.
www.ferc.gov/industries/electric.asp

Platts

Global energy industry publication, news.
www.platts.com

Power Marketing Association

News, pricing information for wholesale electricity, spot, and futures.
www.powermarketers.com

The Society of Energy Professionals

Canadian labor issues.
www.thesociety.ca

Glossary of Acronyms

ARES — alternative retail electric supplier
BPL — broadband over power line
EIA — Energy Information Administration
EPSA — Electric Power Supply Association
FERC — Federal Electric Regulatory Commission
IOU — investor-owned utility
ISO — Independent System Operator
KWH — Kilowatt hour
MWH — Megawatt hour
NERC — North American Electric Reliability Councils
PUC — Public Utility Commission
ROE — return on equity

HOOVER'S TOP COMPANIES

Largest Companies by Sales	($ mil.)
Constellation Energy Group, Inc.	21,193.2
Exelon Corporation	18,859.0
Southern Company	17,127.0
FPL Group, Inc.	16,410.0
Dominion Resources, Inc.	16,290.0
The AES Corporation	16,070.0
American Electric Power Company, Inc.	14,440.0
Edison International	14,112.0
FirstEnergy Corp.	13,627.0
Consolidated Edison, Inc.	13,583.0

Largest Employers	Employees
The AES Corporation	28,000
Alabama Power Company	27,276
Southern Company	26,742
American Electric Power Company, Inc.	20,861
PG&E Corporation	20,050
Exelon Corporation	17,800
Duke Energy Corporation	17,800
Edison International	17,275
Dominion Resources, Inc.	17,000
Consolidated Edison, Inc.	15,214

Fastest Growing* by Five-Year Sales Growth	(%)
First Wind Holdings, Inc.	1,442.7
Entech Solar, Inc.	98.5
Akeena Solar, Inc.	78.3
AMEN Properties, Inc.	67.0
ITC Holdings Corp.	48.7
Constellation Energy Group, Inc.	35.1
NRG Energy, Inc.	28.9
Denton County Electric Cooperative, Inc.	23.6
Commerce Energy Group, Inc.	22.7
Covanta Holding Corporation	21.9

Fastest Growing* by Five-Year Employee Growth	(%)
The Connecticut Light and Power Company	131.3
ITC Holdings Corp.	48.5
CH Energy Group, Inc.	29.0
Wisconsin Power and Light Company	27.4
AMEN Properties, Inc.	22.0
Avista Corporation	21.5
Environmental Power Corporation	16.9
Dynegy Inc.	14.6
Otter Tail Corporation	13.7
Union Electric Company	10.2

Top Public Companies by Market Value	($ mil.)
Exelon Corporation	36,604.9
Southern Company	28,771.2
Dominion Resources, Inc.	20,894.7
FPL Group, Inc.	20,580.7
Duke Energy Corporation	19,092.7

* These rates are compounded annualized increases and may have resulted from acquisitions or one time gains. If less than 6 years of data are available, growth is for the years available.

SOURCE: HOOVER'S, INC., DATABASE

Electric Power Generation

The electric power generation industry consists of 2,200 power generating plants with combined revenue of $80 billion. Major companies include Duke Energy, Exelon, American Electric Power, and Consolidated Edison. The industry is highly concentrated: the 50 largest firms operate more than 50 percent of the generating facilities and earn over 85 percent of industry revenue. In addition to investor-owned utilities, there are about 2,000 government-owned electric power companies at the federal, state, and municipal level, and another 900 user-owned electric cooperatives.

Competitive Landscape

Demand is driven by commercial, government, and residential needs for electrical power, which depend on population growth, economic activity, and electricity prices. Profitability is determined by government regulations and fuel costs. Large companies have an advantage in negotiating fuel contracts and being able to pass the costs of implementing government regulations directly to consumers. Small companies can compete effectively by exploiting market niches, such as offering "green power" in regulated markets. The industry is capital-intensive: average annual revenue per employee is $642,000.

The electric power industry has been moving to deregulation for many years. Federal laws have been modified to remove many of the structural constraints, and state laws are changing to encourage competitive provision of electric power. Structurally, deregulation policies are separating transmitting and delivering electric power from power generation, and companies are either divesting their generation facilities or putting them in an independent corporate entity.

BUSINESS CHALLENGES

» Industry Consolidation

Between 2003 and 2006, 271 power plants representing about 12 percent of domestic power capacity changed ownership in the US. Analysts see a likelihood of similar deals, although they caution that the volatility of fuel prices and the involvement of newly invigorated regulators will stymie some plans. The hunt for acquisitions is being driven by the huge capital demands power companies face over the next quarter century. A common premise in the industry is that for every dollar in operating and maintenance expense that can be reduced in a merger, up to five can be invested in infrastructure upgrades.

» Declining Power Capacity Margins

Additional power plants beyond those currently planned are required to meet growth of electrical demand. Electric utilities forecast US demand to increase 19 percent over the next 10 years, while generating capacity will increase only 6 percent. This gap will erode capacity margins and could result in regional curtailments of power availability (brownouts and rolling blackouts) during peak demand. Addressing the gap will require large investments by utilities.

» Regulatory Uncertainty

Power utilities are subject to regulation by multiple federal and state regulatory agencies, which can greatly influence operating environments and ability to recover costs from utility customers. Utilities that operate in several states face the added complexity of dealing with multiple state utility commissions and environmental control agencies. The agencies of different states rarely coordinate their regulatory activities. Changes in the regulations of any state or the federal government can adversely impact a company's operations.

Products, Operations & Technology

The primary product of the industry is alternating current (AC) electrical power (95 percent of revenue). Byproducts of generation that are also sold include natural gas and steam.

Electricity is produced by generators that convert mechanical energy into electrical energy when large coils are rotated in a powerful magnetic field. About 80 percent of commercial power comes from turbine engines powered by steam produced by burning fossil fuels (coal, petroleum, and natural gas); about 9 percent is produced using steam from nuclear reactors; about 6 percent from conventional hydroelectric conversion; and about 5 percent from renewable sources (solar, wind, and geothermal). Power plants typically produce between 500 and 900 megawatts of power, or enough to supply the needs of 500,000 to 1 million households. Larger plants require special metals and fabrication and require more downtime for maintenance, while smaller units aren't as economical to operate.

The output of the generation plant is stepped up to a high voltage (typically 155,000 to 765,000 volts) at the transmission substation for connection to the power distribution grid. The grid transports power from multiple power stations to local distribution systems for delivery to homes and businesses.

Selecting the method of powering an electric generator is key to its long-term efficiency, since fuel costs are 80 to 90 percent of plant operations and maintenance costs. The cost of environmental pollution controls are also a major consideration in selecting a power source. Petroleum and natural gas emissions can be controlled at reasonable costs, but prices for these fuels are often volatile. Coal prices are the most stable of potential fuels, but emission controls can be expensive and some of the control technology is untested. Challenges to designs, extensive environmental studies, and lack of a long-term solution for nuclear waste drove the costs of nuclear power plants to five times that of conventional plants and the approval process to more than 12 years. Hydroelectric plants are the most thermally efficient and least polluting generation method, but the number of suitable locations for dams is limited and long-term downstream effects are a growing concern.

Some consideration is being given to having multiple power sources for generators, but that raises power plant costs considerably. A number of state initiatives, particularly in the western US, are aimed at increasing power from renewable sources to about 15 percent of commercial electric power.

Power plants are highly automated with monitoring equipment sensing and measuring all operations, from burning fuel to controlling plant output voltage, frequency, and amperage. Monitoring equipment senses load changes in milliseconds and adjusts output accordingly. In nuclear power plants, monitoring is highly sophisticated and includes reactor performance and radiation monitoring. The control systems at nuclear power plants can sense dangerous conditions and automatically shut down the reactor.

Sales & Marketing

Typical customers of electrical power plants are wholesale and retail power distributors and brokers. In deregulated states, owners of power generation sites may market directly to end consumers (residential and commercial) and bill for usage through the local electric power distributor.

In deregulated states where markets are highly competitive, power suppliers usually market intensively through newspaper, radio, and TV advertising. Marketing emphasizes the uniqueness of the supplier — either price, as compared to the dominant supplier, or the environmental friendliness of the power generation. Competitive suppliers also offer discount packages based on volume of usage, length of contract, etc. In regulated markets, the dominant supplier usually uses print and broadcast advertising to promote its service and dependability.

Traditionally, pricing has been based on capital and operations and maintenance costs. Prices are generally proposed by the company and set by a state regulatory commission. Regulatory commissions have generally not allowed investment in new power plants to be factored into rate bases until the facilities were in service, which discourages investment in new nuclear power plants due to their long approval cycles. During transition to competitive markets, utility commissions retain regulatory approval of the prices charged (base rate) by the dominant supplier and establish that rate as the "rate to beat." This allows consumers to compare competitive rates and determine potential savings.

Electricity rates vary greatly throughout the US, depending on the availability of natural resources and the stringency of environmental controls. Washington state, with its available hydro-power, has residential rates of about 6 cents per kilowatt-hour (kwh); New York, which must import all its fuel, has rates of 15 cents per kwh; California's stringent environmental controls result in rates of 13 cents.

Human Resources

About 120,000 workers are employed in electric power generation facilities. Wages, at $26 per hour, are about 40 percent above the national average. The industry employs large numbers of degreed engineers — electrical, civil, mechanical, and nuclear — many of whom receive special certification training from the National Electricity Reliability Council as qualified systems operators.

Injury and illness rates in the industry are slightly under the national average for all industries.

Industry Employment Growth

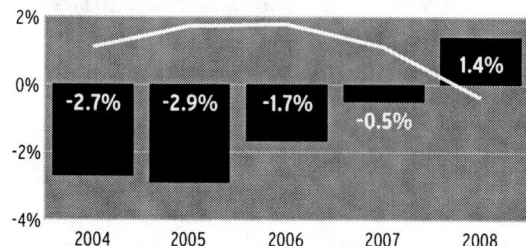

Average Hourly Earnings

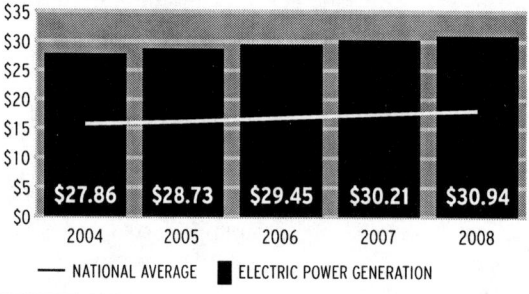

— NATIONAL AVERAGE ▮ ELECTRIC POWER GENERATION

SOURCE: BUREAU OF LABOR STATISTICS

Call Preparation Questions

Is the company actively buying or selling power plants?

Between 2003 and 2006, 271 power plants representing about 12 percent of domestic power capacity changed ownership in the US.

Is the company planning additional generation facilities?

Additional power plants beyond those currently planned are required to meet growth of electrical demand.

How has the company been challenged in dealing with multiple regulatory commissions and agencies?

Power utilities are subject to regulation by multiple federal and state regulatory agencies, which can greatly influence operating environments and ability to recover costs from utility customers.

Does the utility have a "green" marketing program?

In several states with deregulation, companies are successfully marketing power produced exclusively from renewable, non-polluting sources.

Is the utility promoting electric vehicles that can be recharged using ordinary power?

States are pressing auto manufacturers to introduce electric cars with enough capacity to be used in daily commutes to work.

Web Links

American Public Power Association

Association of municipal utilities. List of mergers and acquisitions.

www.appanet.org

Edison Electric Institute

Association of Investor Owned Utilities.

www.eei.org

Electric Power Supply Association

Industry news.

www.epsa.org

Energy Information Administration

Part of the Department of Energy. Excellent industry statistics.

www.eia.doe.gov

Federal Energy Regulatory Commission

Federal regulator. Policy issues and orders.

www.ferc.gov

Platt's Global Energy

Industry news.

www.platts.com

Glossary of Acronyms

EIA — Energy Information Administration
FERC — Federal Electric Regulatory Commission
KWH — Kilowatt hour
MWH — Megawatt hour
NERC — North American Electric Reliability Councils
NRC — Nuclear Regulatory Commission
PUC — Public Utility Commission

HOOVER'S TOP COMPANIES

Largest Companies by Sales	($ mil.)
Constellation Energy Group, Inc.	21,193.2
FPL Group, Inc.	16,410.0
The AES Corporation	16,070.0
Edison International	14,112.0
Public Service Enterprise Group Incorporated	13,322.0
Tenaska, Inc.	11,600.0
Calpine Corporation	9,937.0
Progress Energy, Inc.	9,167.0
NRG Energy, Inc.	6,885.0
Northeast Utilities	5,800.1

Largest Employers	Employees
The AES Corporation	28,000
Edison International	17,275
Progress Energy, Inc.	11,000
FPL Group, Inc.	10,500
Constellation Energy Group, Inc.	10,200
PacifiCorp	6,470
Energy East Corporation	5,884
Northeast Utilities	5,869
Alliant Energy Corporation	5,151
Carolina Power & Light Company	5,000

Fastest Growing* by Five-Year Sales Growth	(%)
First Wind Holdings, Inc.	1,442.7
Entech Solar, Inc.	98.5
Akeena Solar, Inc.	78.3
Tenaska, Inc.	39.1
Constellation Energy Group, Inc.	35.1
NRG Energy, Inc.	28.9
Ormat Technologies, Inc.	23.6
Covanta Holding Corporation	21.9
Old Dominion Electric Cooperative	14.3
The AES Corporation	13.8

Fastest Growing* by Five-Year Employee Growth	(%)
Avista Corporation	21.5
Environmental Power Corporation	16.9
Dynegy Inc.	14.6
Tenaska, Inc.	6.3
Old Dominion Electric Cooperative	5.3
Edison International	4.4
Black Hills Corporation	3.5
Constellation Energy Group, Inc.	3.2
Great Plains Energy Incorporated	2.5
IDACORP, Inc.	1.8

Top Public Companies by Market Value	($ mil.)
FPL Group, Inc.	20,580.7
Constellation Energy Group, Inc.	18,242.5
Public Service Enterprise Group Incorporated	14,760.5
Progress Energy, Inc.	10,520.4
Edison International	10,465.1

* These rates are compounded annualized increases and may have resulted from acquisitions or one time gains. If less than 6 years of data are available, growth is for the years available.

SOURCE: HOOVER'S, INC., DATABASE

Electrical Contractors

THIS INDUSTRY
INCLUDES:

SIC CODES
1731   Electrical Work

NAICS CODES
23821   Electrical
        Contractors and
        Other Wiring
        Installation
        Contractors

The very fragmented electrical contracting industry includes about 60,000 companies with combined annual revenue of $70 billion. Large firms include EMCOR Group, Quanta Services, Integrated Electrical Services, and the electrical divisions of large construction firms. Most firms have less than $500,000 in annual revenue, fewer than 10 employees, and work in a single market.

Competitive Landscape

Much electrical work is driven by new residential and nonresidential construction. Maintenance and repair work (sometimes called "facilities services") is less sensitive to real estate cycles. Larger companies have an advantage in getting contracts because of the increasing complexity of electrical projects and systems, and due to consolidation in the real estate management industry. Building managers prefer to deal with contractors who can provide service in multiple markets.

Products, Operations & Technology

Electrical contracting involves installing and maintaining electrical power systems, conduits, cables, control panels, generators, lighting systems, video and data systems, and low voltage systems (fire alarms). The three major categories of contracting work are new construction; electrical systems replacement in existing buildings ("retrofitting"); and maintenance, repair, and replacement work, also called "MRR" work.

Electrical contractors often work as subcontractors on larger projects. Sources of work are industrial buildings (27 percent) including plants, factories, airports, and warehouses; commercial buildings (28 percent) including hotels, restaurants, and office buildings; residential buildings (12 percent) such as single family houses and multifamily apartments; and infrastructure work for local governments and

BUSINESS CHALLENGES

» High Dependence on Cyclical Construction Industry
Industry revenue is closely tied to new industrial, commercial, and residential construction, which can be highly cyclical and volatile. Changes in individual regional construction markets can be even more severe. Retrofitting and maintenance are somewhat more stable sources of revenue.

» Dependence on Skilled Labor
Because electricians must be licensed and certified, skilled electricians can be hard to find during periods of high construction activity. Training new electricians costs time and money: it takes four to five years to train a journeyman. Many electrical contractors are reluctant to invest in apprentices during difficult financial times.

» Competition from Utilities
Electrical contractors could face increased competition from deregulated utilities, especially for industrial and commercial work. Electrical contractors are also concerned about competition from large non-utility energy companies.

utilities (33 percent). Electrical work accounts for 10 percent of the value of new industrial and commercial buildings and 5 to 10 percent of new residential projects. Industrial and commercial contracts most often involve modernization and retrofit work, while residential contracts involve mainly new construction and maintenance.

Sales & Marketing

Electrical contractors negotiate various types of contracts with customers. Contracts result from open competitive bids (28 percent); prequalified bids (15 percent); negotiated contracts with established customers (44 percent); and new customers (13 percent). Due to the more favorable gross margins, most electrical contractors prefer contracts with established customers, where design engineering is often included. Once negotiated, most contracts are fixed-price, with the contractor bearing the risk of changes in material and labor costs. Copper wire, for instance, is an important commodity product, whose price can change rapidly. About a third of a contractor's costs are for materials and equipment; two-thirds involve labor.

Referrals are an important source of business. Most public-sector construction projects are open for bidding by any contractor. Private-sector projects often restrict bidding to a small number of invited participants. Management experience and skills are important to successful bidding, due to the difficulty of "costing out" a contract — forecasting labor, equipment, and material costs. Success in getting contracts also depends on the availability of licensed electricians, good customer relationships, reputation of the company, safety record, bonding capacity, and experience in specialized fields.

In addition to estimating costs for contracts, operations involve reviewing engineers' plans and specifications, scheduling crews, managing inventory, and scheduling equipment to ensure that a contract is fulfilled according to schedule.

Human Resources

Jobs in electrical contracting require special education and training and state licensing, and are accordingly well-paid. Strong demand from new construction and the installation of computer and telecommunications wiring in existing buildings increased the number of jobs by 27 percent between 1995 and 2005.

Electricians are often the most highly paid trade workers at construction sites, earning an average of about $22 hourly. Apprenticeship training is required in most states, and, depending on experience, apprentices usually start at between 30 and 50 percent of the rate paid to experienced electricians. Many employers also provide training for experienced electricians to improve skills. Safety is an issue, as the industry's annual injury rate is around six cases per 100 full-time workers, about one case more than the national average.

Although most electricians are permanent employees, a large portion of this workforce takes temporary positions, especially in the residential construction sector. Because of strong demand for workers in recent years, employers have had to provide incentives to recruit new workers and retain their workforce. Histori-

cally, fringe benefits have averaged a 24 percent addition to payroll.

Industry Employment Growth

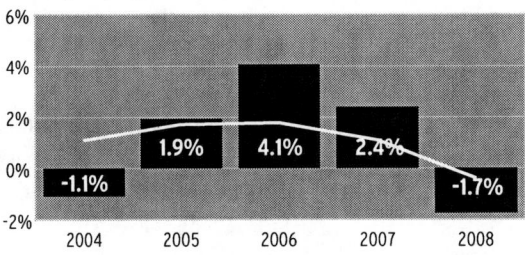

Average Hourly Earnings

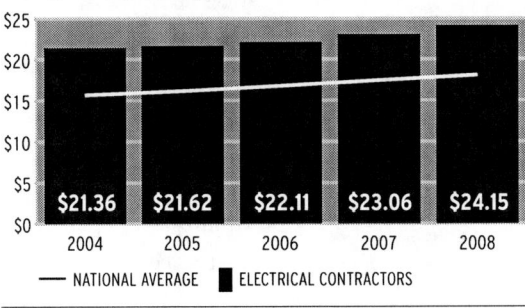

— NATIONAL AVERAGE ▪ ELECTRICAL CONTRACTORS

SOURCE: BUREAU OF LABOR STATISTICS

Call Preparation Questions

How does the company protect itself from economic or industry volatility?

Industry revenue is closely tied to new industrial, commercial, and residential construction, which can be highly cyclical and volatile.

What strategies does the company use to retain a core of skilled employees?

Because electricians must be licensed and certified, skilled electricians can be hard to find during periods of high construction activity.

How is competition from electric utilities impacting the company?

Electrical contractors could face increased competition from deregulated utilities, especially for industrial and commercial work.

What opportunities does the company see in diversifying?

The trend toward a more "value-added" approach — where contractors solve customer problems and therefore generate improved gross margins — is particularly true of commercial and industrial demand, where high-tech capability and modernization projects are common.

How is the company capitalizing on strong consumer demand for home networking?

Electrical contractors are benefiting from the growth of home automation.

Web Links

American Subcontractors Association (ASA)

Construction subcontractor's online portal to advocacy, leadership, networking, and education.
www.asaonline.com

Associated Builders and Contractors

Legislative issues affecting contractors, PACs, up-to-date news by region, and more.
www.abc.org

Construction Financial Management Association (CFMA)

A professional association dedicated to meeting the information needs of construction financial managers. CFMA focuses exclusively on the full range of responsibilities faced by today's construction financial manager.
www.cfma.org

EC Online

Electrical contracting articles, trends, products, resources, and links.
www.econline.com

Electrical Contractor Magazine

Excellent news, industry information, and feature articles.
www.ecmag.com

Federal Energy Regulatory Commission (FERC)

Federal regulator. Policy issues and orders.
www.ferc.gov

Independent Electrical Contractors

Government affairs, news, and events.
www.ieci.org

International Brotherhood of Electrical Workers

Congressional actions, library, and journals.
www.ibew.org

National Association of Electrical Distributors

Short segments on industry trends, events.
www.naed.org

National Electrical Contractors Association

Industry information.
www.necanet.org

The Electrical Distributor Magazine

Contractor and industry news.
www.tedmag.com/common/home.asp?ShowType=ted

The Institute of Electrical and Electronics Engineers

Resources, publications, news, products, services, and events.
www.ieee.org/portal

Glossary of Acronyms

ECA — Electrical Contractors Association
FERC — Federal Energy Regulatory Commission
MRR — maintenance, repair and replacement
NECA — National Electrical Contractors Association
NFPA — National Fire Protection Association

HOOVER'S TOP COMPANIES

Largest Companies by Sales	($ mil.)
EMCOR Group, Inc.	6,785.2
Quanta Services, Inc.	2,656.0
Integrated Electrical Services, Inc.	818.3
MYR Group Inc.	610.3

Largest Employers	Employees
EMCOR Group, Inc.	29,000
Quanta Services, Inc.	15,261
Integrated Electrical Services, Inc.	4,938
MYR Group Inc.	2,900
Fisk Corporation	2,300
Bergelectric Corporation	2,200
Rosendin Electric, Inc.	1,800
Florida Technical Services, LLC	1,800
Cupertino Electric, Inc.	1,608
Industrial Specialty Contractors, L.L.C.	1,550

Fastest Growing* by Five-Year Sales Growth	(%)
Lime Energy Co.	65.5
MISCOR Group, Ltd.	20.6
MYR Group Inc.	9.5
Quanta Services, Inc.	8.7
EMCOR Group, Inc.	8.4
Edd Helms Group, Inc.	5.2
The Goldfield Corporation	4.1

Fastest Growing* by Five-Year Employee Growth	(%)
MISCOR Group, Ltd.	48.2
The Goldfield Corporation	5.7
EMCOR Group, Inc.	5.6
Quanta Services, Inc.	5.4

Top Public Companies by Market Value	($ mil.)
Quanta Services, Inc.	4,467.5
EMCOR Group, Inc.	1,469.6
Integrated Electrical Services, Inc.	259.1
MISCOR Group, Ltd.	186.4
Lime Energy Co.	44.4

* These rates are compounded annualized increases and may have resulted from acquisitions or one time gains. If less than 6 years of data are available, growth is for the years available.

SOURCE: HOOVER'S, INC., DATABASE

Electrical, Plumbing, and Hardware Distributors

The wholesale distribution of hardware, plumbing, heating, and electrical supplies is a $200 billion industry with about 30,000 outlets. Big distributors include Graybar Electric, True Value, and WESCO International. The industry is fragmented: the 50 largest companies hold less than 40 percent of the market.

Competitive Landscape

Sales are driven by demand from the construction, electrical distribution, telecommunications, and hardware retailing industries. Profitability depends largely on merchandising and efficient inventory management. Small operators can compete successfully by stocking specialty products, stocking all the parts their particular customers need, or delivering superior service. The industry is highly automated: average annual revenue per employee is around $450,000.

Products, Operations & Technology

Distributors are middlemen between manufacturers and end-users. The companies in this industry buy large quantities from hundreds of manufacturers, then "break bulk" and resell them to thousands of customers, thereby allowing customers to buy small quantities of products from many different manufacturers. In addition to selling products, many distributors provide technical knowledge and support and some provide maintenance and repair. A specialty distributor of fasteners (screws, nuts, bolts) may buy some 100,000 stock-keeping units (SKUs) from 1,000 manufacturers and sell to around 6,000 customers. Electrical supplier WESCO buys some 200,000 items from around 6,000 suppliers and sells to about 130,000 customers.

Small distributors usually operate out of a single location. Tracking inventory and sales and restocking are major activities. A national distributor might operate numerous small distribution centers of 20,000 to 50,000 square feet throughout the country, or might maintain a hierarchical system of zone and area warehouses and district distribution centers. A regional distributor might service mainly from a large central 500,000 square feet distribution center.

Companies take orders over the phone, by fax, and increasingly by electronic data interchange (EDI) or over the Internet. Large deliveries may be made via a fleet of owned trucks or by third parties. Small orders are usually picked up by the customer.

Fast service and a wide selection are key, as firms act as the inventory warehouse for customers. Distributors closely monitor "fill-rate,"

BUSINESS CHALLENGES

» Heavy Dependence on Construction Industry

A large portion of sales goes to contractors in the construction industry, especially residential, which tends to be cyclical and seasonal. While construction has been very strong in recent years, it can also fall rapidly, especially when interest rates rise.

» More Customers Move Overseas

During the past decade, more US manufacturing has moved to countries with lower labor costs, leaving behind US distributors that supply them with small industrial parts. Distributors that supply only US manufacturing companies face a market with limited growth.

» Big Users Bypass Distributors

Consolidation among customers in some industry segments makes bypassing distributors attractive for manufacturers. Home Depot, Lowe's, and a handful of other large chains now control 50 percent of the home improvement market and can buy in bulk directly from manufacturers. The same phenomenon occurs in the electric utilities, communications, manufacturing, and construction industries.

the percentage of items shipped to customers within 24 or 48 hours; a good rate is above 95 percent. Many distributors provide free same- or next-day delivery, extend credit, and offer product advice and training.

Sales & Marketing

Typical industry customers include construction contractors; retail home centers; hardware stores; building material dealers; mass merchandisers; industrial companies; utilities; and installation, maintenance, and repair (IMR) businesses.

Most distributors have a sales force that visits customers regularly and has detailed technical knowledge of customer business needs. Companies also advertise in specialty magazines and attend trade shows. Internet sites and Internet advertising are rapidly becoming important sales tools. To build customer loyalty, wholesalers provide value-added services such as training seminars, new product kickoff lunches, and counter days.

Human Resources

Industry wages vary by segment, with wholesalers of electrical equipment making more than their counterparts who sell plumbing and hardware equipment. Salespeople require training on product specifications and computerized sales systems, and need to be familiar with customers' use of equipment. Accordingly, salespeople are well paid, but many employees work in warehouse and delivery jobs and earn less. On average, wages are slightly higher than the national wage. The industry's annual safety record is good, with fewer injuries than the national average.

Industry Employment Growth

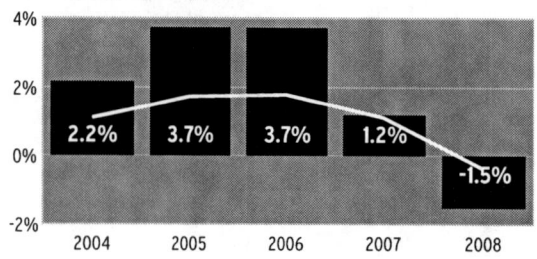

Average Hourly Earnings

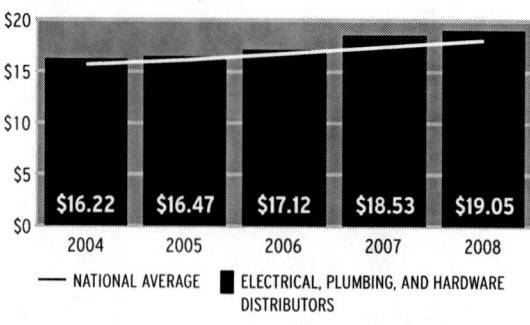

— NATIONAL AVERAGE   ■ ELECTRICAL, PLUMBING, AND HARDWARE DISTRIBUTORS

SOURCE: BUREAU OF LABOR STATISTICS

Call Preparation Questions

What risk management does the company use to protect against swings in demand?

A large portion of sales goes to contractors in the construction industry, especially residential, which tends to be cyclical and seasonal.

What expansion or construction plans does the company have for the next few years?

During the past decade, more US manufacturing has moved to countries with lower labor costs, leaving behind US distributors that supply them with small industrial parts.

What concerns does the company have about manufacturers assuming distributor responsibilities?

Consolidation among customers in some industry segments makes bypassing distributors attractive for manufacturers.

How could managing customer inventories lead to greater revenues for the company?

Rather than just selling customers the parts they need, some distributors manage their inventories for them, leveraging their knowledge of sophisticated computer systems and purchasing services.

What Internet capabilities could improve the company's market areas?

Internet ordering can serve existing customers and expand the reach of a distributor to other market areas.

Web Links

American Hardware Manufacturers Association

Industry news, online industry services, online products, conventions and events, and library.
www.ahma.org

American Supply Association

Information and articles about plumbing, heating, cooling, and piping wholesalers.
www.asa.net

Electrical Wholesaling

Useful articles about issues facing the industry.
www.ewweb.com

Industrial Supply Association

World's largest trade association of distributors to industry, offering literature, statistical analysis, resource links, events, and small distributor information.
www.isapartners.org

National Association of Wholesaler-Distributors

Government issues.
www.naw.org

Supply House Times

Online magazine that ranks plumbing wholesalers by category.
www.supplyht.com

The Electrical Distributor Magazine

Industry news.
www.tedmag.com

Glossary of Acronyms

ASA — American Supply Association
EDI — electronic data interchange
ISM — Institute for Supply Management
IMR — installation, repair and maintenance
NAED — National Association of Electrical Distributors
RF — radio frequency
SKU — stock-keeping units

HOOVER'S TOP COMPANIES

Largest Companies by Sales	($ mil.)
W.W. Grainger, Inc.	6,850.0
Anixter International Inc.	6,136.6
WESCO International, Inc.	6,110.8
Graybar Electric Company, Inc.	5,258.3
Consolidated Electrical Distributors, Inc.	3,900.0
Snap-on Incorporated	2,934.7
Fastenal Company	2,340.4
Watsco, Inc.	1,700.2
Interline Brands, Inc.	1,195.7
Ferguson Enterprises, Inc.	—

Largest Employers	Employees
Ferguson Enterprises, Inc.	23,000
W.W. Grainger, Inc.	18,036
Fastenal Company	12,013
Snap-on Incorporated	11,600
Graybar Electric Company, Inc.	8,600
Anixter International Inc.	8,000
WESCO International, Inc.	7,300
Consolidated Electrical Distributors, Inc.	6,160
Rexel, Inc.	4,700
Interline Brands, Inc.	3,763

Fastest Growing* by Five-Year Sales Growth	(%)
ICx Technologies, Inc.	252.9
PepperBall Technologies, Inc.	86.1
Orgill, Inc.	68.3
American Electric Technologies, Inc.	62.6
WFI Industries Ltd.	20.1
Houston Wire & Cable Company	19.3
Fastenal Company	18.7
Anixter International Inc.	18.5
Colonial Commercial Corp.	17.4
Universal Power Group, Inc.	16.6

Fastest Growing* by Five-Year Employee Growth	(%)
American Electric Technologies, Inc.	138.5
Interline Brands, Inc.	37.8
Universal Power Group, Inc.	15.2
Fastenal Company	13.6
Anixter International Inc.	12.5
WFI Industries Ltd.	9.8
WESCO International, Inc.	8.9
Mayer Electric Supply Company Inc.	5.4
Consolidated Electrical Distributors, Inc.	4.3
W.W. Grainger, Inc.	3.8

Top Public Companies by Market Value	($ mil.)
W.W. Grainger, Inc.	5,895.7
Fastenal Company	5,176.3
Snap-on Incorporated	2,360.9
Anixter International Inc.	1,136.3
Watsco, Inc.	941.3

* These rates are compounded annualized increases and may have resulted from acquisitions or one time gains. If less than 6 years of data are available, growth is for the years available.

SOURCE: HOOVER'S, INC., DATABASE

Electronic Components and Semiconductor Manufacture

THIS INDUSTRY INCLUDES:

SIC CODES

3671   Electron Tubes

3672   Printed Circuit Boards

3674   Semiconductors and Related Devices

3675   Electronic Capacitors

3676   Electronic Resistors

3677   Electronic Coils, Transformers, and Other Inductors

3678   Electronic Connectors

3679   Electronic Components

NAICS CODES

3344   Semiconductor and Other Electronic Component Manufacturing

The US semiconductor and electronic components manufacturing industry consists of about 5,000 companies with combined annual revenue of about $150 billion. Large companies include Intel, Texas Instruments, Micron Technology, and Advanced Micro Devices (AMD). The industry is highly concentrated: the 50 largest companies hold about 70 percent of the market.

Competitive Landscape

The industry depends highly on demand from the computer industry and makers of telecommunications products such as cell phones, which can vary sharply from year to year. Companies can be successful producing standard parts at low cost or by producing highly specialized components. Small companies can compete effectively with large ones by producing specialized products or developing new applications. Technological expertise is extremely important. The industry is highly automated: average annual revenue per employee is about $300,000.

Products, Operations & Technology

Major products include semiconductors (computer chips); printed circuit boards; and various components like electron tubes and electronic connectors. Semiconductors account for almost 60 percent of industry revenue, circuit boards for 25 percent.

The manufacture of computer chips starts with long cylinders of pure silicon (or other semi-conducting materials, such as gallium arsenide) cut into thin "wafers." In photolithography, various layers of conducting and insulating materials are deposited on a wafer and etched away after exposure to light or other beams in patterns that trace the various elements of the integrated circuits. Hundreds of chips can be produced on one wafer. The thickness of the integrated circuit lines determines how many ele-

BUSINESS CHALLENGES

» Demand Linked to Cyclical Computer Manufacture

Demand for electronic components depends directly on demand for computers and similar electronic devices. For example, US production of computers and video and audio equipment on average grew more than 30 percent yearly in the 1990s, but averaged less than half that annual growth rate between 2003 and 2007.

» Foreign Competition

Much production of nonspecialized electronic components (including standard memory chips) has moved abroad to lower-cost manufacturers in Asia. US imports of semiconductors and other electronic components have recently been nearly $70 billion per year.

» Rapid Product Obsolescence

Many electronics manufacturers specialize in a small number of product lines that depend on a particular technology application. Specialization increases the risk of obsolete product technology due to the increasingly short life cycle of many electronic products. As more electronic functions are crammed into computer chips, freestanding resistors, transistors, and capacitors will become obsolete, just as radio tubes have.

ments can be packed into one chip. After fabrication, chips are extensively tested to weed out those with defects. The yield is the percentage of chips that pass the testing process.

Microprocessors, memory, and image sensors are the three main types of computer chips. Major memory chips are dynamic random access memory (DRAM) and flash memory, which doesn't lose information if power is turned off. Image sensors currently used in digital cameras are charge-coupled devices (CCD) or complementary metal-oxide semiconductors (CMOS). Chipsets are groups of chips designed to work together for a particular application.

Even big chip makers specialize: Intel is the leading manufacturer of microprocessors, the brains of computers, while Texas Instruments concentrates on chips that translate analog signals, such as light, touch, and voice, into digital signals, and chips for digital signal processing. Micron is a large producer of memory chips. Most chip design companies are fabless, meaning they don't manufacture their own products because of the huge cost associated with advanced facilities. Fabless companies instead farm the process out to contract manufacturers (chip-making "foundries"). A chip manufacturing facility can cost more than $1 billion.

Computer chips are valuable because of their technological capabilities; cost is often a secondary consideration. The production of circuit boards and other electronic components and accessories, on the other hand, focuses on cost reduction. To a large extent, circuit boards and other electronic components and accessories are commodity items, whose technical features can easily be duplicated by other manufacturers.

Sales & Marketing

Major customers are manufacturers of computers, telecommunication devices, and control devices that end up in other products such as machines, airplanes, cars, and various consumer products. Marketing and sales focus on a manufacturer's ability to produce the specific component required at a reasonable cost. Many products are made-to-order, although some commodity-type components, such as memory chips, may be manufactured in quantity without specific orders in hand. Sales are handled by senior managers who are often engineers, especially in small companies. Commodity-type products are often sold through distributors. Trade shows and personal contracts are important sources of sales.

Many small companies depend heavily on repeat sales to large customers. Even large companies depend on big orders: Intel can receive more than 15 percent of its sales from each of its largest two customers. Some supply contracts can cover several years because the producer must invest in expensive manufacturing equipment. These contracts call for the buyer to take minimum quantities per year or pay a penalty. Such contracts are often used by large buyers, sensitive to the volatility of supply and demand in the industry, who want to be assured of an adequate supply.

Human Resources

The manufacture of computer chips and other electronic components involves operating sophisticated machinery (to make chips), but can also involve a large amount of hand assembly (to make circuit boards). Some technical skills are needed, which accounts for slightly above-average earnings of about $20 hourly, or about 9 percent more than the national average. The industry has a very good safety record, with half the number of injuries as the national average.

The design of electronic components requires highly skilled engineers, who are often senior managers in small companies. Companies often try to retain such key employees by awarding them stock or stock options.

Industry Employment Growth

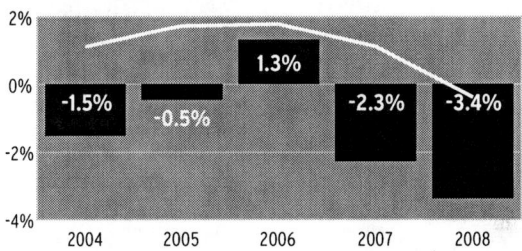

Average Hourly Earnings

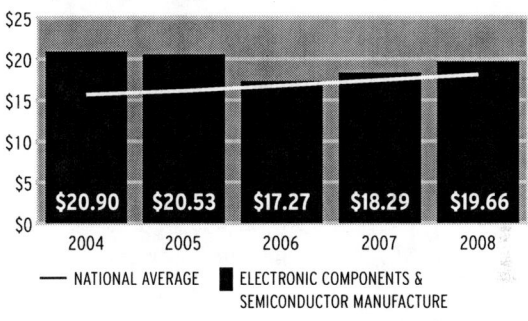

—— NATIONAL AVERAGE   ■ ELECTRONIC COMPONENTS & SEMICONDUCTOR MANUFACTURE

SOURCE: BUREAU OF LABOR STATISTICS

Call Preparation Questions

How does the company adjust when computer manufacturing demand slows?

Demand for electronic components depends directly on demand for computers and similar electronic devices.

How significantly does import competition affect the company's market share?

Much production of nonspecialized electronic components (including standard memory chips) has moved abroad to lower-cost manufacturers in Asia.

How does the company deal with product obsolescence? How are revenues affected?

Many electronics manufacturers specialize in a small number of product lines that depend on a particular technology application.

How is the company positioning itself to take advantage of demand in emerging markets?

Demand for semiconductors and other electronic components is expected to grow as the middle class expands in emerging economies around the globe.

What is the company's strategy for meeting growing consumer demand for new digital products and technology?

Sales of DVD players and digital TVs have increased steadily in the past few years.

Web Links

AeA (formerly American Electronics Association)

Public policy, research, and news.
www.aeanet.org

Consumer Electronics Association

News, market overview, technology and standards, magazines, and public policy.
www.ce.org

EDN

Industry news, research, and archives.
www.edn.com

EETimes Supply Network

Electronics business news.
eetimessupplynetwork.com

Electronic Industries Alliance

Industry links, business trends, government relations, and technology and standards.
www.eia.org

InformationWeek

Industry news, research, and archives.
www.informationweek.com

Semiconductor Industry Association

Industry statistics, forecasts.
www.sia-online.org

TechWeb

News about business technology, including computer processors and components.
www.techweb.com

Glossary of Acronyms

CCD — Charge-coupled devices
CMOS — Complimentary metal oxide semiconductor
DRAM — Dynamic random access memory
VOIP — Voice over Internet Protocol

HOOVER'S TOP COMPANIES

Largest Companies by Sales	($ mil.)
Intel Corporation	37,586.0
Texas Instruments Incorporated	12,501.0
QUALCOMM Incorporated	11,142.0
Micron Technology, Inc.	5,841.0
Advanced Micro Devices, Inc.	5,808.0
Freescale Semiconductor, Inc.	5,722.0
Broadcom Corporation	4,658.1
Kingston Technology Company, Inc.	4,500.0
NVIDIA Corporation	3,424.9
SanDisk Corporation	3,351.4

Largest Employers	Employees
Intel Corporation	83,900
Molex Incorporated	32,160
Amphenol Corporation	30,000
Texas Instruments Incorporated	29,537
Technitrol, Inc.	26,100
Vishay Intertechnology, Inc.	24,800
Freescale Semiconductor, Inc.	23,200
Micron Technology, Inc.	22,800
Amkor Technology, Inc.	20,500
QUALCOMM Incorporated	15,400

Fastest Growing* by Five-Year Sales Growth	(%)
Infinera Corporation	442.4
Entropic Communications, Inc.	337.1
Patriot Scientific Corporation	105.9
Cavium Networks, Inc.	85.0
Sigma Designs, Inc.	65.0
Acacia Technologies Group	63.8
NetLogic Microsystems, Inc.	59.6
Intellon Corporation	56.7
Laird Technologies, Inc.	55.2
MEMSIC, Inc.	54.2

Fastest Growing* by Five-Year Employee Growth	(%)
Entropic Communications, Inc.	71.4
OmniVision Technologies, Inc.	60.6
SiRF Technology Holdings, Inc.	49.2
Monolithic Power Systems, Inc.	48.1
MEMSIC, Inc.	48.0
Atheros Communications, Inc.	42.4
Techwell, Inc.	39.5
Powerwave Technologies, Inc.	39.3
Acacia Technologies Group	36.4
SanDisk Corporation	34.7

Top Public Companies by Market Value	($ mil.)
Intel Corporation	78,869.2
QUALCOMM Incorporated	75,911.0
Texas Instruments Incorporated	19,832.9
Marvell Technology Group Ltd.	7,655.6
Broadcom Corporation	7,230.8

* These rates are compounded annualized increases and may have resulted from acquisitions or one time gains. If less than 6 years of data are available, growth is for the years available.

SOURCE: HOOVER'S, INC., DATABASE

Electronic Components and Semiconductor Wholesalers

THIS INDUSTRY INCLUDES:

SIC CODES

5065   Electronic Parts and Equipment

NAICS CODES

42369   Other Electronic Parts and Equipment Merchant Wholesalers

More than 15,000 wholesale distribution outlets of electronic parts and equipment operate in the US, generating annual revenues of $140 billion. Large companies include Arrow Electronics and Avnet. The average distributor has 20 employees and annual sales less than $10 million. The industry is rapidly consolidating and has a large international component. The 50 largest firms hold about 65 percent of the market.

Competitive Landscape

Demand for electronic components is driven largely by business and consumer purchases of computers and telecommunications equipment. The profitability of individual companies depends on business volume and correct merchandising, or stocking the products buyers want. Large companies have advantages through buying in high volume at discounted prices, more-efficient inventory management, and the ability to fulfill large customer orders. Small wholesalers can compete by offering specialized products or better service.

Products, Operations & Technology

Major products include semiconductors (computer chips); connectors; and electromechanical devices. Other products include disk and tape drives, computer subsystems, microwave and fiber optic components, transistors, diodes, power supplies, and switches. Computer chips account for about 55 percent of industry revenue. In some cases components may be very small and inexpensive. Most distributors operate a single large distribution center, although a big distributor like Arrow operates 23 centers that serve customers in 40 countries. Distribution centers are often larger than 200,000 square feet.

In addition to products, wholesalers offer services like purchasing; marketing; warehousing; packing, shipping, and delivery; cus-

BUSINESS CHALLENGES

» Demand Depends on Cyclical Computer Manufacture

Demand for electronic components depends directly on demand for computers and other electronic devices, which can change rapidly. For example, US component production grew 60 percent per year for many years, but only 10 percent during the last recession. With more US electronics manufacture moving abroad, US demand for electronic components may never regain the former level of growth.

» International Trade Risks

The large international scope of the electronics industry creates potential problems for distributors through government regulation of imports and exports, the fluctuating value of currencies, and potential disruption of commerce due to political events. Annual US exports of electronic components, worth over $45 billion, are mainly to computer assembly plants in Mexico, Malaysia, Korea, Canada, the Philippines, and Taiwan.

» Risk of Inventory Obsolescence

When sales slow, electronic components distributors are often stuck with inventory that has diminishing value. Many electronic components (such as computer chips) have a short life cycle and steadily decreasing prices. Although many manufacturers take back a portion of obsolete inventory, the bulk of the inventory risk in the industry is borne by distributors.

tomized packaging, private labeling; minor repair and refurbishment; "kitting" (simple assembly); and other end-user support services.

The product mix for most wholesalers is always changing, due to changing market demand. Products are generally bought from manufacturers under non-exclusive authorized distributor agreements that establish marketing relationships with manufacturers, provide for joint marketing programs, and are renewable for one-year terms. Cancellation notice is usually from 30 to 180 days. These agreements are very important to protect wholesalers against price changes and obsolete inventory. They typically require a manufacturer to credit the wholesaler if the manufacturer cuts list prices (which happens frequently) and to accept inventory returns for a specified percentage of product purchased.

The design and operation of efficient supply chain systems is crucial for wholesalers because of the large numbers of parts and customers they deal with, the rapid pace of technological innovation, and the threat of declining prices. Arrow buys from 600 suppliers and sells to 175,000 customers. Sophisticated computerized inventory systems and distribution operations are essential. Typical systems provide online real-time information about inventory levels, pricing, customer order status, and supplier orders; analysis of inventory turns by product, supplier stock rotation, order backlog, and rejected materials; and other quantity and quality measures. Automated materials handling systems using bar code labels are often used in distribution centers. Because of high computer system efficiency, sales per employee are often around $500,000.

Sales & Marketing

Wholesalers sell parts to manufacturers of consumer electronics, industrial equipment, automotive electronics, and scientific and medical equipment. Over the past decade, because of the complexity of serving so many customers, electronic components manufacturers have increasingly used wholesalers to serve small and midsized OEMs; contract equipment manufacturers (CEMs); and value-added resellers (VARs). Consequently, many wholesalers are virtual marketing arms of large manufacturers and depend highly on them for products. Manufacturers, in turn, rely heavily on wholesalers for market intelligence.

Marketing and sales are conducted by a field sales force and sometimes by independent sales representatives. Internet sites are an increasingly important source of sales and service information, but websites with full capabilities are expensive to build and operate. Large distributors have a network of sales offices. Avnet operates more than 350 sales locations in the US and internationally. Many customers buy from distributors rather than directly from component manufacturers because they require faster delivery than the manufacturer can provide or because their order is of insufficient size for the manufacturer. Wholesalers in effect act as inventory managers for components that are often manufactured in large batches on an irregular schedule. To a large extent, wholesalers must anticipate the future needs of customers,

in turn increasing their risk of carrying unnecessary or obsolete inventory.

Human Resources

Jobs in wholesale distribution are mainly sales, customer support, and clerical, but require detailed technical knowledge of a wide range of products and therefore pay well. Wages are 45 percent higher than the average for all US workers. The industry's safety record is very good, with half the number of injury cases per year as the national average.

Industry Employment Growth

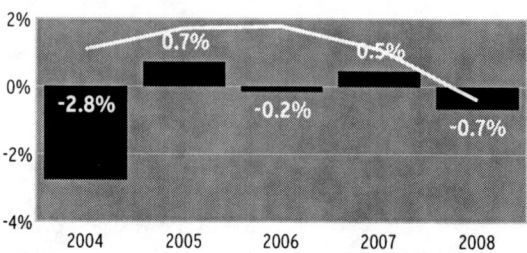

Average Hourly Earnings

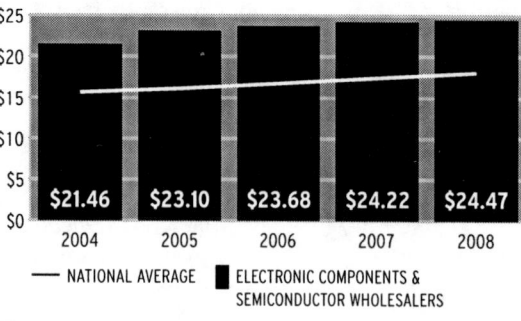

— NATIONAL AVERAGE ■ ELECTRONIC COMPONENTS & SEMICONDUCTOR WHOLESALERS

SOURCE: BUREAU OF LABOR STATISTICS

Call Preparation Questions

How do changes in computer demand impact company sales?

Demand for electronic components depends directly on demand for computers and other electronic devices, which can change rapidly.

How does the company mitigate risk of foreign currency fluctuations or government regulation of imports and exports?

The large international scope of the electronics industry creates potential problems for distributors through government regulation of imports and exports, the fluctuating value of currencies, and potential disruption of commerce due to political events.

How does the company deal with obsolete inventory? How are revenues affected?

When sales slow, electronic components distributors are often stuck with inventory that has diminishing value.

What strategies is the company implementing to improve supply chain efficiency?

Manufacturers are increasingly interested in supply chain efficiencies from distributors that will decrease inventory and speed product delivery.

How is the company positioning itself to take advantage of growing worldwide demand?

The demand for electronic components is expected to grow by 20 to 30 percent per year in the long-term.

Web Links

American Electronics Association

Public policy, research, and news.
www.aeanet.org

Consumer Electronics Association

News, market overview, technology and standards, magazines, and public policy.
www.ce.org

EDN

Offers news on the electronic industry.
www.edn.com

EETimes Supply Network

Industry news, industry directory and rankings.
eetimessupplynetwork.com

National Electronic Distributors Association

Industry position papers. Conference calendar.
www.nedassoc.org

Semiconductor Industry Association

Industry news, events, publications, and resources.
www.sia-online.org

Glossary of Acronyms

CEM — contract equipment manufacturer
EDI — electronic data interchange
ITC — International Trade Commission
NAWD — National Association of Wholesale Distributors
VAR — value-added reseller

HOOVER'S TOP COMPANIES

Largest Companies by Sales	($ mil.)
Avnet, Inc.	17,952.7
Arrow Electronics, Inc.	16,761.0
Nu Horizons Electronics Corp.	747.2
Richardson Electronics, Ltd.	568.4
Jaco Electronics, Inc.	193.7
Universal Power Group, Inc.	108.5
ADDvantage Technologies Group, Inc.	56.5
Western Switches and Controls, Inc.	10.1
Taitron Components Incorporated	7.5
Zunicom, Inc.	1.5

Largest Employers	Employees
Avnet, Inc.	12,800
Arrow Electronics, Inc.	12,700
Richardson Electronics, Ltd.	930
Nu Horizons Electronics Corp.	833
Jaco Electronics, Inc.	194
ADDvantage Technologies Group, Inc.	152
Zunicom, Inc.	77
Universal Power Group, Inc.	76
Western Switches and Controls, Inc.	32
Taitron Components Incorporated	31

Fastest Growing* by Five-Year Sales Growth	(%)
Nu Horizons Electronics Corp.	19.9
Universal Power Group, Inc.	16.6
Avnet, Inc.	14.7
Arrow Electronics, Inc.	14.1
ADDvantage Technologies Group, Inc.	11.2
Richardson Electronics, Ltd.	4.1

Fastest Growing* by Five-Year Employee Growth	(%)
Universal Power Group, Inc.	15.2
Nu Horizons Electronics Corp.	11.5
Avnet, Inc.	4.9
Zunicom, Inc.	2.8
Arrow Electronics, Inc.	2.5
ADDvantage Technologies Group, Inc.	2.1

Top Public Companies by Market Value	($ mil.)
Avnet, Inc.	4,143.5
Arrow Electronics, Inc.	2,247.8
Nu Horizons Electronics Corp.	109.3
Richardson Electronics, Ltd.	84.0
ADDvantage Technologies Group, Inc.	27.6

* These rates are compounded annualized increases and may have resulted from acquisitions or one time gains. If less than 6 years of data are available, growth is for the years available.

SOURCE: HOOVER'S, INC., DATABASE

Electronic Equipment Repair Services

The US electronic equipment repair service industry includes about 13,000 companies with combined annual revenue of $15 billion. Major companies include Cascade Asset Management, Am Signal, Reliable Richard's Service Corp, and American Electronic Services. Most are small, privately held businesses with one location, fewer than 20 employees, and revenue under $1 million. The industry is fragmented: the 50 largest firms account for 44 percent of industry revenue.

The industry includes companies that provide primarily repair services for electronic equipment like computers, consumer electronics, and communication products, and for precision equipment like medical and scientific instruments, but doesn't include household appliances or autos. The industry doesn't include companies that primarily manufacture or rebuild products, or sell new items with after-sale services and repairs.

Competitive Landscape

Demand is driven by the installed base of electronic equipment, equipment failure rates, and the cost advantage of regularly maintaining and fixing broken and idle equipment, rather than replacing it. The profitability of individual companies depends on service accuracy, speed, and volume. Large companies have advantages in breadth of services, worker allocation, and the number of manufacturers and types of products supported. Small companies can compete effectively by specializing by manufacturer or product type and providing superior service. The industry is labor-intensive: average annual revenue per worker is about $145,000.

Products, Operations & Technology

Major services are repair and maintenance of consumer electronics, computers, office machines, communication equipment, and precision devices. Computer repair and maintenance

BUSINESS CHALLENGES

» Dependence on Manufacturers

The electronic equipment repair services industry depends highly on manufacturer sales of new equipment to drive demand for warranty, repair, and maintenance work. Swings in production levels affect demand and vary greatly by product category. US production of computers and video and audio equipment is volatile, changing up to 50 percent a year; communication equipment output can vary up to 30 percent. Domestic output of business equipment can fluctuate 15 percent annually, and precision equipment, about 10 percent.

» Import Quality, Quantity

Much electronic equipment is produced abroad, but import quality and quantity vary, affecting work for repair services. Low-cost production in countries like China, the largest source of electronics imports, can lead to quality problems; Japan and Germany are known for high-quality, precision products. Some import categories depend on the economy: US imports of computers, communication equipment, and office machinery fell over 10 percent during the early 2001 recession. Import growth tends to be steady for navigational, measuring, electromedical, and control instruments.

» Competition with New Models

Manufacturers and OEMs of consumer electronics often price replacement parts so high that customers prefer to buy a new, rather than repair a broken, model. The cost to repair a DVD player, for example, may be only slightly less than the price of a new unit, many of which sell for under $100. Repair shops need to buy the replacement parts and then add labor charges, affecting customer repair-or-buy decisions.

provide 35 percent of industry revenue; precision devices, 35 percent; and communication equipment, almost 15 percent.

Industry companies repair and maintain equipment with complex electronic components, many of which include microchips and computer boards. Repair service restores equipment, making it operable again. Proactive maintenance service ensures that equipment works efficiently and prevents breakdowns. Service companies test products and diagnose problems, provide cost estimates to customers, obtain parts, and perform the stated repair or maintenance. Common industry metrics are estimate accuracy and service time-to-completion. Some companies guarantee estimates or not-to-exceed quotes. Estimates may be free or for a fee. Warranties typically cover work done, but not overall product operation.

Most companies limit the range of products they service. About 30 percent of companies service primarily computers; 25 percent, consumer electronics; and almost 25 percent, precision equipment. Consumer electronics include TVs, cameras, stereos, radios, and other audio/video equipment. Computer and related equipment includes storage, monitors, and other peripherals. Electronic office machines are mainly photocopiers. Communication equipment includes telephones, fax machines, communication transmission equipment, and two-way radios. Electronic precision equipment includes navigational devices (like sonar and radar); scientific and laboratory instruments; measuring and surveying instruments; and medical, surgical, and optical equipment.

Service companies get parts mainly from manufacturers or distributors, who also provide training and specifications for repair and maintenance of specific products. Some repair companies qualify as manufacturer designated authorized service centers by having staff meet product knowledge and service performance criteria. Authorization can apply to products under the original warranty, an extended warranty, or both. Because electronic equipment is complex, service firms hire skilled personnel with technical training or prior electronic equipment repair experience. Field technicians go to customer sites to repair or maintain equipment; bench technicians work at the service firm's facility. In small companies, technicians may do both. Most jobs are full-time, but some service centers require technicians to work shifts or be on-call for emergencies.

Technicians fix or replace mechanical, electric, and electronic parts or components. Repairs range from a simple solder or mechanical adjustment, to component or subsystem replacement, to complex calibrations. Maintaining or fixing computers and other software-dependent equipment often requires upgrading the software. Technicians use simple hand tools like screwdrivers and soldering irons; testing devices like multimeters to measure electrical properties, and oscilloscopes to monitor equipment signals; and safety tools like isolation transformers to protect against electric shock.

As the technology of electronic equipment has become increasingly complex, so have the tools to diagnose, repair, and maintain it. Software programs and specialized hardware are common for diagnosing and adjusting many types of electronic equipment. Many repair firms manage office functions with a small business computer system. Order management and service-related software enable communication with suppliers and customers, tracking of work-in-progress, and billing. Some repair shops' office functions remain paper-based.

Sales & Marketing

Typical customers are businesses, consumers, or both, depending on the product and the service company's focus. Major sales channels include a sales team and telemarketing. Business customers include offices and manufacturing, industrial, and commercial firms. In small repair shops, the owner may be the sole salesperson.

Major types of marketing are Yellow Pages, newspaper ads, and listings on product manufacturer or distributor promotional materials and ads. Some manufacturers and distributors have multiple levels of certification for repair firms; those that achieve the highest ranking receive priority listings on supplier marketing materials. In small repair shops, the same person may handle telemarketing, customer support, and office functions.

Internet leads are mainly through listings on manufacturer, distributor, and trade association websites. Larger service dealers, especially those with national presence, have their own websites.

Typical prices range from $75 to $500 per hour, depending on product complexity and availability of repairers. Some firms have flat rates for various types of repairs. Contract prices for regularly scheduled preventive maintenance depend on equipment quantity and type. Prices vary greatly by region and the presence of competition. Major competitors are retailers and wholesalers that provide after-sales service. Business customers are a form of competition when they bring repair services in-house.

Human Resources

Electronic and precision equipment repair staff require product knowledge and skills in servicing units with complex electronic components. Many employers prefer workers with an associate's degree in electronics, manufacturer or industry certification, and related job experience; some jobs require a bachelor's degree.

On-the-job training is common; some fields, like precision instrument repair, require internships or apprenticeships. Industry wages are higher than the US average.

Injury rates are about 30 percent lower than average. About half of injuries are due to sprains and strains from vehicle accidents. Unions like the International Brotherhood of Electrical Workers are active at larger service centers.

Industry Employment Growth

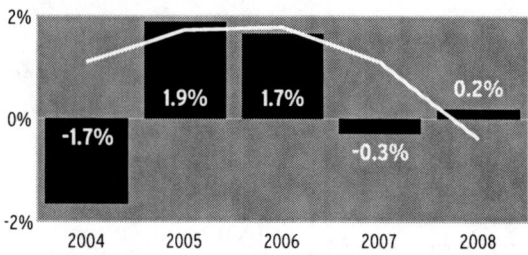

Average Hourly Earnings

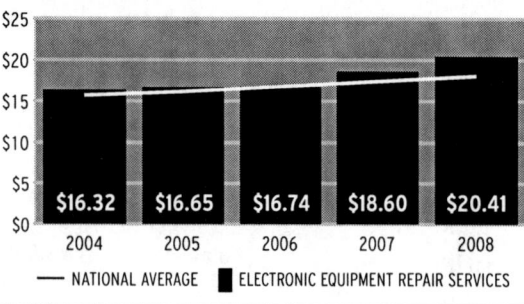

— NATIONAL AVERAGE ■ ELECTRONIC EQUIPMENT REPAIR SERVICES

SOURCE: BUREAU OF LABOR STATISTICS

Call Preparation Questions

How do fluctuations in new equipment sales affect demand for the repair center's services?

The electronic equipment repair services industry depends highly on manufacturer sales of new equipment to drive demand for warranty, repair, and maintenance work.

What differences in quality does the company see in imports from various parts of the world?

Much electronic equipment is produced abroad, but import quality and quantity vary, affecting work for repair services.

What concerns does the company have about the prices of replacement equipment versus repairs?

Manufacturers and OEMs of consumer electronics often price replacement parts so high that customers prefer to buy a new, rather than repair a broken, model.

What opportunities does the company see in providing high-level, specialized service?

Specialized, high-level service centers fix what others can't.

Web Links

Certified Service Center (a program/coalition)

List of certified service centers and how to become one.
www.c-csc.org/Consumer

Consumer Product Safety Commission

Product safety standards, recalls, legislation.
www.cpsc.gov

Electronics Technicians Association (ETA)

Industry news, certification training programs.
www.eta-i.org

International Society of Certified Electronics Technicians (ISCET)

Technical training and certification division of NESDA.
www.iscet.org/about

National Coalition for Electronics Education

Standards, content for certification programs by job title.
www.ncee-edu.org

National Electronics Service Dealers Association (NESDA)

News, magazine, membership list, consumer information.
www.nesda.com

Glossary of Acronyms

CET — Certified Electronics Technician
ETA — Electronics Technicians Association
ISCET — International Society of Certified Electronics Technicians
MST — Multimedia Systems Technician
NESDA — National Electronics Service Dealers Association
OEM — Original equipment manufacturer
SMC — Surface mounted components

HOOVER'S TOP COMPANIES

Largest Employers	Employees
QualxServ LLC	2,045
ExpressPoint Technology Services, Inc.	370
DataSpan	238
CSI Computer Specialists, Inc.	155
Barrister Global Services Network, Inc.	95
Flo-Tech LLC	64
Geek Squad	40

SOURCE: HOOVER'S, INC., DATABASE

Electronic Gaming Products

The electronic gaming products manufacturing industry includes about 100 companies with combined annual revenue in North America of about $7 billion and worldwide sales of about $20 billion. Major companies include Microsoft, Nintendo, Sony, and Logitech. The industry is highly concentrated: the top three companies have over 80 percent market share.

PCs also enable entertainment and game play, and about 15 percent of game software sold in the US is for PCs.

This profile doesn't include PCs used for gaming.

Competitive Landscape

Demand is driven primarily by personal income. The profitability of individual companies depends on effective marketing, competitive product design, and manufacturing efficiency. Market success drives additional revenue via royalties paid by third-party game developers. Because most manufacturing is by third parties, average revenue per employee is about $700,000.

Electronic gaming products compete with PCs, TV, and other forms of electronic and non-electronic entertainment for consumer leisure time.

Products, Operations & Technology

Major products are video game consoles (50 percent of revenues); portable players (25 percent); and peripheral hardware (25 percent). Video game consoles are computers specially designed to deliver entertainment and game software, using a TV as a monitor. Video game console sales consist of three competing products: Sony's PlayStation 3, Microsoft's Xbox 360, and Nintendo's Wii. Portable players are handheld gaming devices, like the Nintendo DS and Sony PSP (PlayStation Portable). Peripheral hardware includes devices that elevate the human-machine interaction (HMI) such as

BUSINESS CHALLENGES

» Dependence on Personal Income

Playing video games is a leisure activity and electronic gaming products a discretionary purchase. Core gamers are less likely to reduce purchases in a slow economy, but as video games become more mainstream, the impact of economic downturns increases.

» Cyclical Nature of Industry

Electronic gaming products have a historical life cycle of four to six years of strong sales followed by diminishing sales and heavily discounted prices. Sales of hardware and software slow near the end of a product's life cycle, as consumers anticipate the release of next-generation products. At the same time, software development costs increase as companies continue to develop for current platforms and ramp up investment in products for the new platform. Hardware companies face heavy investments in R&D and marketing prior to realizing any revenue from new platforms.

» Seasonal Sales

Industry sales in November and December may total 40 percent or more of annual sales. Missed deadlines for product launches just prior to the holiday selling season can be financially draining as sales opportunities are lost. Sunk costs in advertising and marketing may be wasted and the company's reputation may be damaged.

game pads, joysticks, and driving wheels. Peripherals also include upgrades to core products, such as larger hard drives, additional memory, and wireless connectivity.

Most parts are manufactured and assembled offshore. The essential components of a system include a central processing unit (CPU); memory; optical drive; hard drive storage device; chassis; power supply; and controller (sometimes referred to as a game pad). Products are manufactured in high volumes using highly automated assembly lines. Process controls and testing procedures minimize product defects.

In addition to upgrade products offered by manufacturers, peripheral devices are often manufactured and marketed by third-party vendors directly to consumers. Some peripheral manufacturers are granted licenses from console manufacturers that give access to proprietary design information. They may also be granted rights to use manufacturers' logos.

Hardware system costs may vary greatly depending on final design and components. Frequently, the initial selling price of next-generation hardware is below manufacturing cost. Companies anticipate falling component prices as product volume increases and therefore price products to grow market share. Royalty revenues from third-party game developers also help offset initial low gross margins.

CAD is used extensively in developing advanced technologies contained in video game hardware systems. Advances made available through CAD include high definition displays, multi-function audio and video capabilities, online gaming and other communication features, and wireless connectivity. Peripheral manufacturers may use reverse engineering to ensure functional equivalency with console manufacturer offerings.

Sales & Marketing

Typical customers include mass merchandisers, wholesale clubs, electronic superstores, specialty game stores, and Internet retailers. Retailers may operate online game stores, but brick-and-mortar outlets are the primary distribution channel of hardware products. Electronic gaming products may be on the shelves of 20,000 or more outlets. In-house sales forces and distributors are the primary sales channels.

Video games once were considered a product for those under 18, but the average video game buyer is about 37. Gamers usually prefer specific game genres (action, sports, simulation, strategy, children's entertainment) and choose hardware with rich content in that genre.

Major marketing vehicles include ads in platform-specific gaming magazines, special in-store promotions, and company websites. Pre-launch online and print previews and post-launch reviews are major vehicles for creating demand. Manufacturers may pay retailers for shelf position, special promotions, and merchandising programs.

Product prices range from $15 for a joystick to $600 or more for a robust console system. Prices decline as hardware moves through its life cycle (generally four to six years). Consumers anticipate the release of next-generation products and wait to buy.

Human Resources

Jobs in gaming hardware development are highly technical and include electrical engineers, computer hardware and software engineers, and electronic technicians. US wages average about $40 to $45 per hour. Virtually all manufacturing is done offshore. Design, integration, and testing are the primary focus of US engineering staffs.

Companies require employees to sign non-disclosure and confidentiality agreements to protect intellectual property rights. Virtually all employees are non-union in the US.

Call Preparation Questions

How does the economy affect the company's product sales?

Playing video games is a leisure activity and electronic gaming products a discretionary purchase.

How has the cyclical nature of electronic gaming products affected the company?

Electronic gaming products have a historical life cycle of four to six years of strong sales followed by diminishing sales and heavily discounted prices.

What percentage of company sales is in the holiday selling season?

Industry sales in November and December may total 40 percent or more of annual sales.

How does the company price its products for various consumer segments?

Console and peripheral devices are generally created for either heavy-use core gamers, or casual gamers.

What products does the company provide that support online gaming?

Online gaming is one of the fastest-growing segments of the electronic gaming industry.

Web Links

Entertainment Software Association

Industry trade association.
www.theesa.com

GameDaily

Industry News.
www.gamedaily.com

gamesindustry.biz

Industry News.
www.gamesindustry.biz

GameSpot

Industry News.
www.gamespot.com

Nintendo

News about Nintendo's hardware and software products.
www.nintendo.com

PlayStation

News about Sony's PlayStation 3 and other products.
www.ps3.com

Xbox

News about Microsoft's Xbox products and games.
www.xbox.com

Glossary of Acronyms

ESA — Entertainment Software Association
ESRB — Entertainment Software Rating Board
HMI — human-machine interaction
PSP — PlayStation Portable

HOOVER'S TOP COMPANIES

Largest Companies by Sales	($ mil.)
Microsoft Corporation	60,420.0
Mattel, Inc.	5,918.0
Hasbro, Inc.	4,021.5
LeapFrog Enterprises, Inc.	459.1
Mad Catz Interactive, Inc.	87.6
Nintendo of America Inc.	—
Sony Corporation of America	—

Largest Employers	Employees
Microsoft Corporation	91,000
Mattel, Inc.	31,000
Sony Corporation of America	27,000
Hasbro, Inc.	5,900
Nintendo of America Inc.	955
LeapFrog Enterprises, Inc.	844
Mad Catz Interactive, Inc.	138
Kids II, Inc.	135
Learning Resources, Inc.	122
Bandai America Incorporated	60

Fastest Growing* by Five-Year Sales Growth	(%)
Microsoft Corporation	13.4
Hasbro, Inc.	5.1
Mattel, Inc.	3.6

Fastest Growing* by Five-Year Employee Growth	(%)
Microsoft Corporation	10.6
Action Products International, Inc.	9.3
Mattel, Inc.	5.5
LeapFrog Enterprises, Inc.	0.4

Top Public Companies by Market Value	($ mil.)
Microsoft Corporation	251,744.0
Mattel, Inc.	5,736.0
Hasbro, Inc.	4,043.2
LeapFrog Enterprises, Inc.	128.2
Mad Catz Interactive, Inc.	34.2

* These rates are compounded annualized increases and may have resulted from acquisitions or one time gains. If less than 6 years of data are available, growth is for the years available.

SOURCE: HOOVER'S, INC., DATABASE

Engineering Services

The US engineering services industry includes over 45,000 companies with combined annual revenue of about $135 billion. Large companies include Jacobs Engineering Group and URS Corporation, and the engineering divisions of large construction companies like Fluor and Bechtel. Half the firms in the industry are small with fewer than five employees; less than 5 percent of engineering services firms have more than one office or location. The industry is highly fragmented: the 50 largest firms account for only 35 percent of industry revenue. About 100 firms have more than $100 million of annual revenue.

Competitive Landscape

Demand is driven largely by the construction needs of companies and governments and the desire of industrial customers to improve the efficiency of operations. Profitability depends on the ability to accurately predict costs for a project. Small firms, which can effectively compete with larger ones by having expertise in a particular field, are often hired as consultants on larger projects if they have special expertise. Large firms are advantaged in designing and managing large projects. Average revenue per employee is about $200,000 for large firms, $115,000 for small ones.

Products, Operations & Technology

Major engineering services include product and industrial process design, construction design and management, systems engineering, and maintenance and operations. Engineering companies may be involved in projects that require skills in analysis, design, project management, operations, or all four. Most firms specialize in a particular type of engineering. Most engineering work is per project, such as designing and constructing a highway or formulating an environmental plan for a wetlands area.

BUSINESS CHALLENGES

» Dependence on Construction, Industrial Production

Demand in major fields such as construction and industrial process design depends heavily on the health of the US economy. During economic slowdowns, engineering firms are disproportionately hurt. For example, from 2001 to 2003, nonresidential construction in the US dropped 25 percent due to effects of recession.

» Vulnerability to Project Cost Overruns

Project cost overruns are a primary cause of financial distress for engineering companies. Raytheon sold its engineering and construction unit after losses from a single power project, and Stone & Webster was bankrupted by cost overruns on a power plant decontamination project. In addition to paying for cost overruns, engineering firms can be penalized for not meeting deadlines.

» Vulnerability to Litigation

The nature of engineering work leaves firms open to liability lawsuits, both for poor work and inattention to regulations, as poor engineering work can result in injury and death. The increasing complexity of many engineering projects increases the likelihood of errors. Engineering service firms must comply with a large number of regulations, the improper handling of which can result in criminal fines and penalties.

Engineering firms basically sell the knowledge of their employees. The work is labor-intensive. Attracting and retaining qualified engineers is an ongoing concern. Due to the complexity of many jobs, engineering firms often hire subcontractors and consultants to perform specialized work. Material inputs are provided by subcontractors.

Computer systems are used extensively for analysis, design, budgeting, project planning and control, accounting, and communications. Nearly all engineering companies have a centralized IT staff. Wide-area networks with engineering software that enable firms to balance workload among locations and ultimately improve productivity, and CAD, which allows instantaneous information sharing between engineers, architects, and planners, have become staples.

Sales & Marketing

Typical customers include governments, industrial corporations, and real estate developers. Some companies rely on the federal government for the majority of business. Only about 5 percent of engineering services companies do business overseas.

Many firms depend on large customers (like the federal government) for repeat business. Because referrals are an important source of new customers, firms cultivate relationships with past customers, other engineering firms, architects, and construction companies. Firms may advertise their expertise in trade magazines. Many engineering contracts are obtained after a bidding process. In the private sector, a customer typically invites several firms to bid on a particular project. Public sector bids are usually open to all bidders who meet certain basic technical and financial qualifications. The bidding process usually involves preparing a detailed plan of action for a project and a cost estimate. Firms often collaborate to bid on large projects that require a range of expertise.

Contracts are awarded to an engineering firm under a variety of pricing schemes that assign the risk of cost overruns. Under a fixed-cost (or lump sum) contract, an engineering firm is responsible for any costs incurred in excess of those forecast, but can also make a bigger profit if costs are less. Under a time and materials (or cost-reimbursable) contract, the customer pays for all costs, plus a fee that may be a lump sum or a markup on labor costs. Under a guaranteed maximum price contract, the customer pays a fee plus all costs up to a maximum amount. Additional terms may be negotiated in any of these contracts to address how costs are handled if the customer changes the project's scope.

Human Resources

Most employees in engineering services have special technical or engineering skills and are accordingly well paid. Average earnings are well above the national average wage. Employment growth has been strong in recent years as the US economy required engineering for construction, industrial design, environmental services, and productivity enhancements. To attract and retain engineers and technicians, employers offer sizable fringe benefits.

The industry's safety record is exceptional, averaging only one case per year per 100 full-time employees, a rate that's less than one-fourth the national average for all industries.

Industry Employment Growth

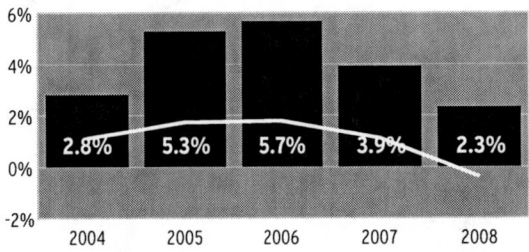

Average Hourly Earnings

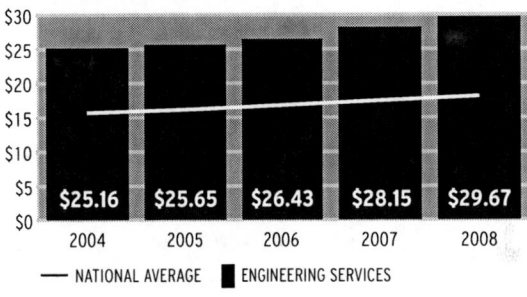

— NATIONAL AVERAGE ■ ENGINEERING SERVICES

SOURCE: BUREAU OF LABOR STATISTICS

Call Preparation Questions

How does the firm adapt to cyclical demand?

Demand in major fields such as construction and industrial process design depends heavily on the health of the US economy.

How accurately does the firm estimate costs?

Project cost overruns are a primary cause of financial distress for engineering companies.

How does the firm protect itself from litigation?

The nature of engineering work leaves firms open to liability lawsuits, both for poor work and inattention to regulations, as poor engineering work can result in injury and death.

What engineering design opportunities or challenges does the company expect from new security concerns?

Concerns over terrorism will change engineering focus.

How much work does the company receive from the federal government?

US government spending on infrastructure projects, such as highways and bridges, is expected to remain high during the next decade.

Web Links

American Association of Engineering Societies

Information on public policy, links, and communications.
www.aaes.org

American Council of Engineering Companies

Publications, news bulletins, and training information.
www.acec.org

American Institute of Chemical Engineers

Conference, publication, education, training, government and industry information.
www.aiche.org

American Society of Civil Engineers

Up-to-date information on civil engineering.
www.asce.org

American Society of Mechanical Engineers

News, links, and more.
www.asme.org

CENews.com

News about civil engineering.
www.cenews.com

Chemical Engineering

Engineering articles, news, product roundups, seminars and conferences, links, job advice, and more.
www.che.com

Engineering News-Record

News by specialized areas.
www.enr.com

National Academy of Engineering

Publications, news, events, directories, and research reports.
www.nae.edu

Society of Manufacturing Engineers

News, education, trade shows. Salary surveys.
www.sme.org

The Institute of Electrical and Electronics Engineers (IEEE)

Publications, product and services information, news and conferences.
www.ieee.org

Glossary of Acronyms

ASCE — American Society of Civil Engineers
ENR — Engineering News-Record
EPC — engineering, procurement, construction
CAD — computer-aided design
LD — liquidation damages

HOOVER'S TOP COMPANIES

Largest Companies by Sales	($ mil.)
Bechtel Group, Inc.	27,000.0
Fluor Corporation	22,325.9
KBR, Inc.	11,581.0
Jacobs Engineering Group Inc.	11,252.2
URS Corporation	5,383.0
CH2M HILL Companies, Ltd.	4,376.2
Parsons Corporation	3,600.0
Black & Veatch Holding Company	3,200.0
The Day & Zimmermann Group	2,200.0

Largest Employers	Employees
URS Corporation	56,000
KBR, Inc.	52,000
Bechtel Group, Inc.	42,500
Fluor Corporation	41,260
The Day & Zimmermann Group	24,000
CH2M HILL Companies, Ltd.	22,000
Parsons Corporation	11,500
Black & Veatch Holding Company	9,600
Stanley, Inc.	3,600

Fastest Growing* by Five-Year Sales Growth	(%)
Arrowhead Research Corporation	59.7
VSE Corporation	50.7
Stanley, Inc.	35.6
ENGlobal Corporation	31.7
Basin Water, Inc.	31.1
SRI International	25.4
Fuel Tech, Inc.	19.8
Jacobs Engineering Group Inc.	19.5
Parsons Corporation	18.6
Bechtel Group, Inc.	18.4

Fastest Growing* by Five-Year Employee Growth	(%)
Lauren Engineers & Constructors, Inc.	93.4
Basin Water, Inc.	51.7
Arrowhead Research Corporation	42.6
Stanley, Inc.	25.1
VSE Corporation	25.1
ENGlobal Corporation	21.8
URS Corporation	17.5
Fuel Tech, Inc.	16.2
CH2M HILL Companies, Ltd.	15.7
The Day & Zimmermann Group	9.5

Top Public Companies by Market Value	($ mil.)
Fluor Corporation	8,146.4
Jacobs Engineering Group Inc.	6,663.9
URS Corporation	4,573.6
KBR, Inc.	2,458.2
Tetra Tech, Inc.	1,526.2

* These rates are compounded annualized increases and may have resulted from acquisitions or one time gains. If less than 6 years of data are available, growth is for the years available.

SOURCE: HOOVER'S, INC., DATABASE

Entertainment and Games Software

THIS INDUSTRY INCLUDES:

SIC CODES
7372   Prepackaged
        Software

NAICS CODES
511210 Software
        Publishers

The US entertainment and games software industry includes about 1,000 companies with combined annual revenue of about $12 billion. Major companies include Electronic Arts, Activision Blizzard, THQ, and Take-Two Interactive, along with divisions of large integrated companies such as Microsoft, Sony, and Nintendo. The video game publishing segment is highly concentrated: the top 10 companies have over 80 percent market share. The game development segment is fragmented: most game development studios have a single location and fewer than 20 employees.

Competitive Landscape

Demand is driven primarily by personal income. The profitability of individual companies depends on an understanding of consumer needs, timely product development, and effective marketing. Large companies publish a portfolio of titles and have advantages of scale in manufacturing, marketing, distribution, and selling. Small development studios compete through creative designs and by partnering with large publishers.

Computer and video games compete as a leisure time activity with TV, movies, music, the Internet, and other forms of electronic and nonelectronic entertainment.

Products, Operations & Technology

Major entertainment and games software product segments are video game software (about 85 percent of revenues) for dedicated gaming machines that work with TVs, such as Sony's PlayStation, Microsoft's Xbox, and Nintendo's Wii; and PC game software (about 15 percent). Video game software also includes content for portable handheld devices such as PSP (PlayStation Portable); Nintendo's Game Cube and DS systems; and cell phones.

Development studios bring together the talents of game designers, producers, program-

BUSINESS CHALLENGES

» Dependence on Personal Income

Playing video games is a leisure activity and video game software a discretionary purchase. Core gamers are less likely to reduce purchases in a slow economy, but as video games become more mainstream, the impact of economic downturns increases.

» Control by Console Manufacturers

Software publishers and developers depend highly on hardware system sales. Game console manufacturers require royalties from platform licensees for each unit manufactured. Manufacturers may also require milestone review and approval during development for products developed for their platforms. Next-generation hardware releases are risky for developers who must create software content simultaneously with hardware development.

» Cyclical Nature of Industry

Video game hardware platforms have a historical life cycle of four to six years. Sales of hardware and software slow near the end of a product's life, as consumers anticipate the release of next generation products. In transitioning to new platforms, software development costs may increase as development continues for current generation platforms and as companies ramp up investment in products for the new platform. Game developers are challenged by higher costs at the same time revenues are slowing.

mers, graphic artists, sound engineers, and play testers who may work for months or years to deliver a completed software product. Development studios work with software development kits (SDK) issued by gaming machine makers. These kits provide tools and instructions to ensure products play efficiently on the selected hardware platforms. After extensive play testing and quality assurance checks, a "gold master" disk, along with documentation and packaging design, is prepared for each hardware platform release.

Prior to release for manufacture, publishers must obtain a game rating that advises the buyer of age appropriateness and thematic content, from the Entertainment Software Ratings Board (ESRB). This rating must be prominently displayed on the packaging at retail. Disk or cartridge duplication, packaging, printing, assembly, warehousing, and shipping are by third-party printers, replicators, and fulfillment houses. To protect hardware designs, game equipment makers specify a pre-approved third-party source or manufacture and assemble themselves. In addition to the cost of manufacturing, publishers pay royalties to platform licensors for each unit manufactured.

Development studios are of three types: 1) in-house development studios owned by publishers; 2) third-party studios that have close relationships with publishers and may be partially owned by the publishers; and 3) independent studios, which operate autonomously and may shop each development project to the highest bidding publisher. Typically, third-party and independent publishers are paid a royalty on sales generated from product sales. Advance royalties, used by development studios as the source of cash for development activities, are common.

Publishers are responsible for marketing, distributing, and selling software products from development studios. Publishers also influence product design and content, as they're attuned to market demands, and generally maintain a mix of internally and externally developed content to ensure creativity and originality. Many titles become franchise properties (such as Electronic Arts' "Madden NFL"), with each new edition adding features to improve game play and take advantage of new hardware capabilities.

Content distribution is divided between packaged and downloadable software. Software is packaged in CD; DVD; UMD (universal media disc); and cartridge forms. Downloadable software, bought at online retail outlets or directly from the publisher's online store, is a growing distribution option.

Consumers frequently reserve copies of new games at retail outlets prior to launch by paying a small purchase deposit and receiving added value, like special hints and tips for game play or extra maps. Pre-ordering helps publishers gauge demand for new products when setting initial manufacturing volumes.

Technology advancements propel the rapid rate of change in the video games industry.

Higher processing speeds, more advanced visualization technologies, and improvements in artificial intelligence enhance the gaming experience. Software game demand typically slows in anticipation of the introduction of hardware systems that incorporate the latest technical innovations.

Sales & Marketing

Typical customers include mass merchandisers, wholesale clubs, electronic superstores, specialty game stores, and Internet retailers. Publishers and retailers may operate their own online game stores, but brick-and-mortar outlets are the primary distribution channel of packaged products. A title with high US retail penetration may be on the shelves of 20,000 or more retail outlets. Companies use a variety of sales channels including in-house sales forces, manufacturer rep agencies, distributors, and online stores.

Once considered a product for those under 18, the average video game player is now about 30 and the average game buyer is about 37. Games are classified by genre with marketing and public relations campaigns targeted to gamers interested in a particular sector. Major genres include action, children and family entertainment, role-playing, shooters, simulations, sports, and strategy games.

Major marketing vehicles include ads in platform-specific gaming magazines, special in-store promotions, and company websites. Online and print previews and reviews in game magazines are a major component of creating demand. Similar to the movie industry, most advertising and public relations campaigns are prior to release of a title.

Video game software prices range from $3 to $70. Most products are initially released at price points of $19.95 to $59.95, but discounting occurs quickly if unit sales begin to slow. Retailers enjoy higher margins and unit sales on new releases and remove slow-moving inventory quickly; thus, shelf life of a title may be as little as three months. Publisher payments for shelf position, special promotions, and merchandising programs for newly released titles also incentivize retailers to focus on new products.

Human Resources

Jobs in development studios have a wide range of skill and experience requirements. Wages average about $25 per hour, about 50 percent above the average US production employee rate. Industry employees include programmers, game designers, producers, graphic artists, sound designers, play testers, and customer service personnel. Worker classification between exempt and non-exempt (eligible for overtime) employees was challenged in a class-action lawsuit that established a precedent for overtime payment for certain job classifications.

Colleges offer classes in video game development. Some larger publishers have funded programs at major universities to offer advanced degrees in the video game field. The International Game Developers Association (IGDA), an international industry trade association, promotes education and quality of worklife issues for industry employees. Over 8,500 of the 12,000 total members are employed in North America.

Industry Employment Growth

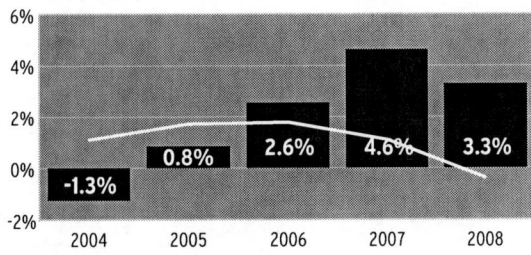

Average Hourly Earnings

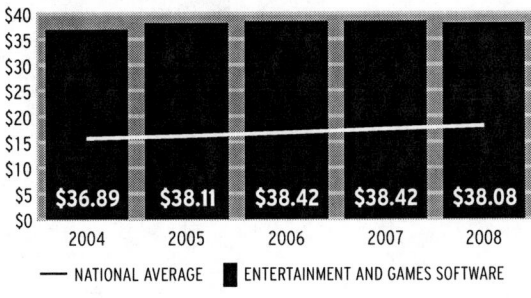

— NATIONAL AVERAGE   ■ ENTERTAINMENT AND GAMES SOFTWARE

SOURCE: BUREAU OF LABOR STATISTICS

Call Preparation Questions

How do economic conditions affect demand for the company's video games?

Playing video games is a leisure activity and video game software a discretionary purchase.

What hardware systems are most important for the company?

Software publishers and developers depend highly on hardware system sales.

What challenges the company in managing the transition to next-generation products?

Video game hardware platforms have a historical life cycle of four to six years.

What company products have an online game play component?

Online gaming continues to grow, as gamers who enjoy socializing or competing gravitate to it.

What role does licensing existing brands play in the company's strategy?

Finding affordable intellectual properties with brand recognition can be difficult, but leveraging an existing brand can reduce the risk of product failure.

Web Links

Entertainment Software Association

The industry's trade association; consumer statistics, policy issues.
www.theesa.com

Gamedailybiz

A comprehensive daily online publication dedicated to the gaming industry.
www.gamedaily.com/news/biz

Games for Windows

PC game industry magazine and web site.
www.gamesforwindows.com

GameSpot

Online industry publication.
www.gamespot.com

International Game Developers Association

Industry association with game development focus.
www.igda.org

Glossary of Acronyms

ESA — Entertainment Software Association
ESRB — Entertainment Software Ratings Board
IGDA — International Game Developers Association
MMOG — massively multi-player online game
PS3 — PlayStation3
PSP — PlayStation Portable
SDK — software development kit

HOOVER'S TOP COMPANIES

Largest Companies by Sales	($ mil.)
Electronic Arts Inc.	3,665.0
Activision Blizzard, Inc.	3,026.0
Take-Two Interactive Software, Inc.	1,537.5
THQ Inc.	1,030.5
Midway Games Inc.	157.2
Glu Mobile Inc.	89.8
Disney Interactive Studios	—
SEGA of America, Inc.	—
Sony Online Entertainment LLC	—

Largest Employers	Employees
Electronic Arts Inc.	9,000
Activision Blizzard, Inc.	7,000
Take-Two Interactive Software, Inc.	2,100
THQ Inc.	2,000
Midway Games Inc.	900
Hands-On Mobile, Inc.	817
Sony Online Entertainment LLC	700
Glu Mobile Inc.	417
LucasArts Entertainment Company Ltd.	300
Amaze Entertainment, Inc.	200

Fastest Growing* by Five-Year Sales Growth	(%)
PokerTek, Inc.	265.1
Glu Mobile Inc.	118.6
THQ Inc.	72.8
Silverstar Holdings, Ltd.	52.5
Conspiracy Entertainment Holdings, Inc.	38.4
Activision Blizzard, Inc.	26.1
Take-Two Interactive Software, Inc.	8.3
Electronic Arts Inc.	8.1

Fastest Growing* by Five-Year Employee Growth	(%)
Silverstar Holdings, Ltd.	131.7
Activision Blizzard, Inc.	39.5
THQ Inc.	24.0
Electronic Arts Inc.	13.8
Midway Games Inc.	10.4
Take-Two Interactive Software, Inc.	1.6

Top Public Companies by Market Value	($ mil.)
Electronic Arts Inc.	15,874.6
Activision Blizzard, Inc.	11,225.7
THQ Inc.	1,446.5
Take-Two Interactive Software, Inc.	921.5
PokerTek, Inc.	84.7

* These rates are compounded annualized increases and may have resulted from acquisitions or one time gains. If less than 6 years of data are available, growth is for the years available.

SOURCE: HOOVER'S, INC., DATABASE

Erosion Control

THIS INDUSTRY INCLUDES:

SIC CODES
8711   Engineering
        Services

NAICS CODES
541330 Engineering
        Services

The erosion control industry includes manufacturers and distributors of erosion control products and contractors for erosion control services; total annual revenues aren't well-defined, but are probably less than $2 billion. All companies are privately held or are divisions of larger companies.

Competitive Landscape

Demand is driven by construction activity, especially of highways. The profitability of individual companies depends on the volume of work, because large equipment costs are fixed. Large companies have an advantage in being able to handle large contracts. Small companies can compete effectively by specializing in a particular control method or by serving a small geographical area.

Products, Operations & Technology

The industry provides products and services to prevent soil erosion due to wind and water in places where natural ground cover has been removed or damaged. Without natural ground cover, rain can rapidly wash dirt from construction sites into storm drains and eventually into rivers and wetlands, where silt is a major environmental problem. Major causes of soil erosion are agricultural plowing and tilling; highway and road construction; real estate development; strip mining; artificial landscaping (such as for golf courses and landfills); other engineering projects; and natural causes such as the actions of rivers and the ocean.

Erosion control solutions are either "hard," such as retaining walls and interlocking bricks, or "soft," such as regrowth of natural vegetation. The four major categories of erosion control products are biodegradable ground cover, permanent ground cover, soil stabilization, and periodic erosion control applications. Many companies provide erosion control plant seeds that provide final vegetation cover. Most firms

BUSINESS CHALLENGES

» Heavy Dependence on Construction Activity

Construction activity can vary widely in local markets from year to year and follow longer economic cycles. The largest need for erosion control services results from highway construction and real estate development. In some local markets, the volume of construction activity can rise or fall more than 20 percent per year.

» Customer Concentration

Contractors who specialize in ground cover applications may get a major portion of work from local government bodies or large real estate developers. Dependence on a few large contracts is financially risky.

» Competition from Construction Companies

The basic technology of erosion control with ground cover is easy to get and use. Successful companies can rapidly face new competition, both from other contractors and their own customers. The growth of large regional and national home builders has provided more competition for erosion control companies, both because these larger companies do their own erosion control work, and because they may compete for work on third-party projects.

concentrate on products that provide biodegradable temporary ground cover over raw soil until natural vegetation grows to provide permanent protection. Typical products are woven biodegradable organic mats and sprayed-on organic materials. In situations where a natural cover will be inadequate to control erosion, either because the slope of the land is too steep or because the concentration of wind or water attack is too strong, other products, including interlocking paving stones and nondegradable grid systems made from concrete or plastic, combine to provide permanent ground stabilization and cover.

Most erosion control products are designed to protect surface soil from erosion. However, bulk products like dry cement bags, sand and rock bags, wind fences, mats, and concrete members are intended to stabilize soil contours like sand dunes, golf course formations, and water runoff channels, and are usually placed under the soil surface. To protect soil on dirt roads, landfills, and construction sites, products such as cement and acrylic polymer sprays may be applied periodically to act as glues that prevent dust formation, while plastic fences and other temporary barriers prevent soil runoff during construction activities.

Temporary ground cover products, usually organic products like straw, wood chips, or other natural fibers that are mulched and slurried with water, and "tackifiers" (degradable organic glues), are sprayed over the target area with a hydroseeder (a truck with a large tank, a pump, and a fire-hose-type spray nozzle). The target area is topsoiled and seeded with the eventual ground cover plants. In some cases, the erosion-control product, fertilizer, and plant seed are mixed and sprayed in one application. The same types of cover products are also woven into mats or blankets (collectively called "geotextiles") and unrolled over the target area. Permanent (non-biodegradable) erosion control systems, such as interlocking paving stones, gravel nets, and cement or recycled plastic elements, are often applied in an open matrix pattern that allows natural ground cover to grow around, and eventually, over them.

In addition to hydroseeders, other large equipment includes hydromulchers that produce and spread a water-mulch mixture, and straw blowers that shred bales of hay into small pieces, mix them with a tackifier, and blow them onto the target area. This erosion control equipment (large manufacturers are Bowie Industries, FINN Corp., and Reinco), which typically costs over $200,000, is sold by farm equipment and construction equipment dealers.

Sales & Marketing

Customers are real estate developers, home builders, and highway construction general contractors. Contracts for public highway work are typically won through a bidding process. Private work may involve bidding on contracts but may also be awarded on the basis of long-term relationships.

Human Resources

Erosion control companies require personnel with good engineering knowledge and pay them well. The actual installation work, however, requires few skills and brings low wages. Similar to landscaping workers, erosion control workers earn on average less than $13 hourly, which is below the national wage. The industry's annual injury rate is higher than the national norm and, similar to landscapers, is about six cases per 100 full-time workers. The actual incident rate is much higher, since the data doesn't include part-time workers. Due to seasonal demand, companies typically add part-time workers in summer.

Call Preparation Questions

How does the company mitigate the feast or famine cyclical volatility of the industry?

Construction activity can vary widely in local markets from year to year and follow longer economic cycles.

How reliant is the company on a few top customers?

Contractors who specialize in ground cover applications may get a major portion of work from local government bodies or large real estate developers.

How does the company compete with construction companies for erosion control business?

The basic technology of erosion control with ground cover is easy to get and use.

How could new high-tech tools help the company in its operations?

Erosion control companies are finding new uses for technology, like GPS; geographic information systems (GIS); and weather simulation models.

How does the company benefit from erosion control planning software?

A growing number of engineers and control experts are using computer software to map erosion patterns, forecast future damage, and test new prevention and rehabilitation techniques.

Web Links

BioCycle

Journal of compost and mulch recycling.
www.jgpress.com

Construction Financial Management Association

Publications, industry links, and news.
www.cfma.org

Erosion Control

Industry news.
www.erosioncontrol.com

International Erosion Control Association

Industry links.
www.ieca.org

National Soil Erosion Research Lab

Information on erosion control process research.
www.ars.usda.gov/main/site_main.htm?
modecode=36021500

US Department of Agriculture, Natural Resources Conservation Service

Soil conservation issues.
www.nrcs.usda.gov

Glossary of Acronyms

ESC — erosion and sedimentation control
GIS — geographic information system
GRP — Grasslands Reserve Program
NPDES — National Pollutant Discharge Elimination System
NWP — nationwide permits
TSP — technical service providers

HOOVER'S TOP COMPANIES

Largest Employers	Employees
Advanced Drainage Systems, Inc.	4,000
CONTECH Construction Products Inc.	2,000
S. W. Rodgers Company, Inc.	750
Tensar Corporation	715
TenCate Geosynthetics North America	648
American Soil Technologies, Inc.	19

SOURCE: HOOVER'S, INC., DATABASE

Fabricated Metal Parts Manufacturing

THIS INDUSTRY INCLUDES:

NAICS CODES
332   Fabricated Metal Product Manufacturing

The US fabricated metal products industry consists of about 60,000 companies that generate $300 billion of annual revenue. Large companies in specialty segments include Ball Corporation and Snap-On. Because of the special manufacturing processes involved, most companies make a limited range of products. The industry as a whole is fragmented: the largest 50 companies hold just 20 percent of the market, but concentration can be high in industry segments like cutlery, boilers, springs, and metal cans.

Competitive Landscape

Demand is driven largely by the needs of other industrial companies, and is therefore linked to economic growth. The profitability of individual companies depends on technical expertise and efficient manufacturing operations. The specialized nature and use of many products allows smaller companies to compete effectively. Despite gains in labor productivity, the industry is still fairly labor-intensive: average annual revenue per worker is close to $150,000.

Products, Operations & Technology

The industry consists of several distinct segments, including ornamental and structural metals ($60 billion); forging and stamping ($30 billion); metal valves ($30 billion); metal containers ($20 billion); hardware ($15 billion); springs and wire products ($15 billion); and fasteners ($10 billion). Many companies make products in smaller specialized segments.

Companies manufacture mainly simple metal parts used by industrial customers, such as those making autos, airplanes, machinery, appliances, and computers. Some companies make simple finished products like metal cans, tools, plumbing fixtures, and structural steel members. Most companies operate a single manufac-

BUSINESS CHALLENGES

» Demand Depends on US Manufacturing Activity
Demand for fabricated metal parts is heavily driven by US manufacturing levels, especially for equipment and machinery. US production of fabricated metal products dropped 9 percent during a recent recession. A greater reliance on low-cost overseas manufacture has cut the market for US metal products.

» Import Competition Keeps Prices Low
Imports of simple metal products, such as plumbing fixtures, tools, and hardware, have increased from nations like China that have access to low-cost raw materials and labor. Imports of fabricated metal products from China increased nearly 645 percent in the last decade.

» Fluctuating Raw Materials Costs
The cost of iron and steel can change 10 percent during a year. In addition, from time to time the US imposes various restrictions and tariffs on imports of steel from lower-cost countries to preserve jobs in the US steel industry.

turing facility. A typical company has about 25 employees, 20 of whom are production workers.

Basic raw materials are ferrous and nonferrous metals, like carbon, alloy and stainless steels, aluminum, titanium, brass, copper, and various alloys. Raw materials are bought in semifinished form (slabs, billets, and blooms) or finished form (plates, coils, sheets, wire, bars, rails, beams), either directly from primary metal processors like US Steel; Freeport McMoRan Copper & Gold (copper); and Alcoa (aluminum) or, most often, from large metals distributors (metals service centers).

Three major metal processing operations are fabrication, preparation, and finishing. Fabrication includes processes like punching, cutting, bending, welding, coil processing, roll forming, laser cutting, and stamping. Machining, a fabrication method, uses a wide variety of machine tools to cut or form material to precise specifications. Preparation includes cleaning and surfacing metal with chemicals. Finishing includes plating, polishing, coloring, and coating.

Many companies have highly automated production lines. Typical equipment includes presses, screw machines, rotary transfer machines, computer controlled (CNC) single- and multiple-spindle lathes, and turning and machining centers. Some companies use CAD and computer-aided manufacturing (CAM) equipment. Engineering skills are needed to design products and production processes.

Sales & Marketing

Many companies supply only a handful of products to a few large customers. To a large extent, such companies are de-facto manufacturing subsidiaries of their customers.

A combination of marketing channels are used, often including a company sales force and manufacturers' representatives. Trade shows are important, especially since companies often are selling their ability to produce according to customer requirements, rather than a standard line of products.

Most work is awarded via purchase orders or contracts that detail product specifications, volumes, and delivery schedules. Sales often depend on a company having the design, engineering, and manufacturing capabilities to make the product to specification and on time. Price is often a secondary consideration. Raw material price changes can often be passed to the customer.

Human Resources

Many production jobs in metal parts manufacture are semiskilled; accordingly, hourly pay is closer to the national average. Fringe benefits are about 25 percent of wages. Production work often involves operating large machines, which can be a safety hazard. The industry's safety record has improved in the past decade, but the injury rate is still more than 40 percent worse than the national average.

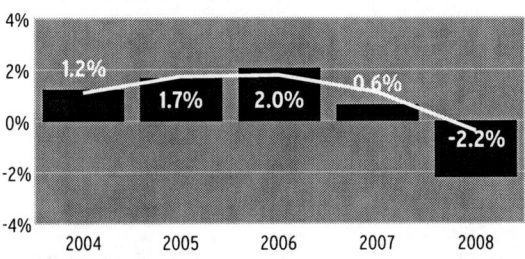

Industry Employment Growth

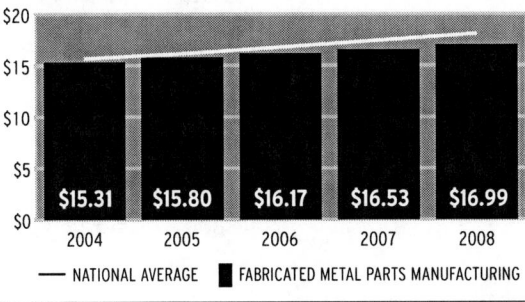

Average Hourly Earnings

— NATIONAL AVERAGE ■ FABRICATED METAL PARTS MANUFACTURING

SOURCE: BUREAU OF LABOR STATISTICS

Call Preparation Questions

How cyclical are the markets that the company sells to?

Demand for fabricated metal parts is heavily driven by US manufacturing levels, especially for equipment and machinery.

How are low-cost imports affecting the company's domestic market?

Imports of simple metal products, such as plumbing fixtures, tools, and hardware, have increased from nations like China that have access to low-cost raw materials and labor.

How does the company manage volatile raw material costs?

The cost of iron and steel can change 10 percent during a year.

How is the use of new metal alloys benefiting the company?

New metal alloys with desirable physical properties allow manufacturers to upgrade existing products and introduce new ones.

What opportunities does the company see to invest in machinery to produce increasingly complicated parts?

As machinery and other products become more sophisticated in function and design, the parts used to build them generally also become more complicated, requiring more engineering and tighter manufacturing specifications.

Web Links

American Iron and Steel Institute (Auto Steel)

Use of metal parts in automobile manufacturing. www.autosteel.org

METAL WEB NEWS – Current Metalworking News

Excellent source of recent news.
www.metalwebnews.com/news.html

National Association of Manufacturers

News.
www.nam.org

National Tooling and Machining Association

Reports, publications, events, government affairs and public relations.
www.ntma.org

Precision Machined Products Association

Reports and events, newsletter.
www.pmpa.org

Precision Metalforming Association

News, articles, links, and more.
www.pma.org

Thefabricator.com

Fabricating news.
www.thefabricator.com

Tooling and Manufacturing Association

Bulletin, trends survey, and industry links.
www.tmanet.com

Glossary of Acronyms

CAD — computer-aided design
CAM — computer-aided manufacturing
CNC — computer controlled
NAM — National Association of Manufacturers
PMPA — Precision Machined Products Association

HOOVER'S TOP COMPANIES

Largest Companies by Sales	($ mil.)
Commercial Metals Company	10,427.4
Crown Holdings, Inc.	8,305.0
Ball Corporation	7,561.5
Precision Castparts Corp.	6,852.1
The Timken Company	5,663.7
The Stanley Works	4,426.2
American Axle & Manufacturing Holdings, Inc.	3,248.2
Snap-on Incorporated	2,934.7
Mueller Industries, Inc.	2,558.4
Valmont Industries, Inc.	1,907.3

Largest Employers	Employees
The Timken Company	25,662
Crown Holdings, Inc.	21,800
Precision Castparts Corp.	21,600
The Stanley Works	18,225
Ball Corporation	15,500
Commercial Metals Company	15,276
Snap-on Incorporated	11,600
American Axle & Manufacturing Holdings, Inc.	9,800
Barnes Group Inc.	6,523
Valmont Industries, Inc.	6,029

Fastest Growing* by Five-Year Sales Growth	(%)
Metalico, Inc.	67.9
American Electric Technologies, Inc.	62.6
Lifetime Brands, Inc.	30.3
Commercial Metals Company	29.4
Dynamic Materials Corporation	29.3
Precision Castparts Corp.	26.5
RTI International Metals, Inc.	24.3
North American Galvanizing & Coatings, Inc.	21.0
Mueller Industries, Inc.	20.7
Thermodynetics, Inc.	20.3

Fastest Growing* by Five-Year Employee Growth	(%)
American Electric Technologies, Inc.	138.5
American Technologies Group, Inc.	130.5
Lifetime Brands, Inc.	17.5
Commercial Metals Company	14.2
Dynamic Materials Corporation	13.8
Precision Castparts Corp.	12.6
WSI Industries, Inc.	11.5
Metalico, Inc.	9.8
RTI International Metals, Inc.	9.4
Euramax International, Inc.	8.5

Top Public Companies by Market Value	($ mil.)
Precision Castparts Corp.	14,090.5
Ball Corporation	3,898.3
Crown Holdings, Inc.	3,056.5
Commercial Metals Company	2,961.6
The Stanley Works	2,797.7

* These rates are compounded annualized increases and may have resulted from acquisitions or one time gains. If less than 6 years of data are available, growth is for the years available.

SOURCE: HOOVER'S, INC., DATABASE

Farm Equipment Manufacture

THIS INDUSTRY INCLUDES:

SIC CODES
3523   Farm Machinery
        and Equipment

NAICS CODES
333111 Farm Machinery
        and Equipment
        Manufacturing

In the US, about 1,200 companies manufacture farm machinery and equipment, with total annual revenue of $15 billion. Large manufacturers, including Deere, AGCO, and CNH have worldwide operations. The industry is highly concentrated: the 20 largest companies hold over 80 percent of the market.

Competitive Landscape

Sales are directly tied to farm income and crop production projections for the next season, and can vary highly year to year. The profitability of individual companies depends on the volume of products sold, since many manufacturing costs are fixed. Big companies have large economies of scale, especially in manufacturing tractors and combination machines. Small companies can be successful by making specialized equipment, especially tractor attachments. Smaller companies, which are more labor-intensive, produce annual revenue per employee of about $150,000. Larger companies, more capital-intensive, produce about $350,000 per employee.

Products, Operations & Technology

Major products are tractors, self-propelled harvesting combines, tractor attachments, and other equipment used for crop production and farm animal management. Smaller utility vehicles and ATVs are coming into general use on farms. Tractors account for about 30 percent of the market, combines 25 percent.

Large companies, such as John Deere, AGCO, and CNH, produce a full array of products, while smaller companies generally make a single product line. Production of diesel engines is the major separator between large and small companies, because of the large amounts of capital and expertise required. Large companies have highly automated production lines and make products that can be mass-produced.

BUSINESS CHALLENGES

» Revenue Depends on Cyclical Farm Income

Industry revenue depends on the financial condition of crop farmers, which is highly cyclical. During the past 10 years, multiyear periods have occurred where crop prices rose or fell 10 to 15 percent, with a similar rise or fall in farm equipment production.

» Competition from Imports

Imported farm equipment holds almost a third of the US market. In the past five years, imports have almost doubled. The largest volume of imports comes from Japan, but the sharpest increases have been from China, Korea, and India.

» Competition from Used Equipment

Since farm equipment is designed to be durable, a large base of used equipment exists and sells for a fraction of the price of new. During periods of reduced farm income, farmers are much more sensitive to machinery prices. Ford 9N tractors, first produced in 1939, are still used.

Manufacturing at the low end consists of assembling parts, bolting, welding, and painting.

Steel is a major raw material in production, and steel prices can influence end product prices. Weight is not a major concern in tractor and implement design. In fact, weights are commonly placed on the front end of tractors to balance equipment on three point hitches on the rear. Because of the ruggedness requirements of farm implements, plastics aren't used extensively. Field maintainability requirements generally preclude use of aluminum, which also requires specialized equipment and expertise for welding.

Expertise in diesel engine technology is critical to manufacturers as products evolve to meet new environmental requirements for off-road diesels. Machinery innovations and integration of advanced technology based on GPS technology enable farmers to better control costs and improve yields. Newer tractors, sprayers, and combines are equipped with systems that allow automated steering under computer control using GPS. New technology allows multiple machines to be operated simultaneously from a single control and monitoring station. To achieve the extreme accuracy required for strip-till fertilizing and seeding, agribusinesses and equipment distributors are collaborating to construct tower networks using Real-Time Kinematic (RTK) technology. The systems are so accurate that repeated planting, spraying, and harvesting is possible in tracks that vary only by centimeters.

Sales & Marketing

Large manufacturers have regional sales operations that service networks of dealerships. Smaller manufacturers either sell to dealerships through distributors or direct sales forces. John Deere services about 1,600 equipment dealers throughout the US. Large companies advertise extensively in both national magazines and trade publications, and have extensive promotions at state and county agricultural fairs. To support sales, manufacturers have regional parts depots with repair technicians trained in their product lines.

Dealerships are privately owned, some established with financial support from the manufacturer. Most dealerships are also family-run organizations well-established within the geographic area where they operate. Dealerships sell directly to farms in their region and repair and provide warranty services on the equipment. Farmer-dealer relations are well-established and frequently go back generations. Larger manufacturers often provide inventory financing for their dealers.

As more crop production is coming from large farms and agribusinesses, equipment sales in the US are shifting toward the upper end of the market. Prices for large pieces of equipment are high: a 500-horsepower John Deere tractor can cost more than $250,000. Little price competition exists, and most equipment sells at or near the manufacturer's recommended sales price. Equipment buyers usually have a choice of two or three dealerships within a reasonable distance of their operation. The buyer depends on the dealer to resolve large or complex problems; because of the size of some of the equipment, it usually must be repaired onsite. Service and proximity are critical in buying decisions.

Human Resources

The workforces of the largest manufacturers are at least partially unionized. Wages in the industry average about $15 per hour, comparable to workers in fabricated metal products and durable goods manufacturing industries, but much lower than the average for auto workers of $29 per hour.

Most manufacturing facilities are located in smaller cities in the center of farming areas. These facilities draw on populations with farming experience to staff the plants. Typically farming experience includes working with and repairing farm machinery and using welding equipment.

Industry Employment Growth

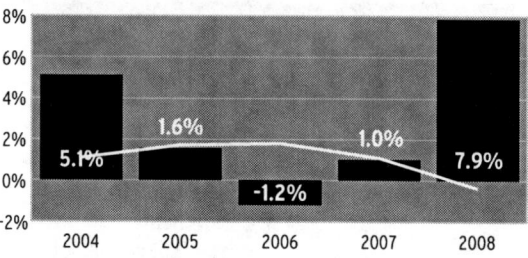

Average Hourly Earnings

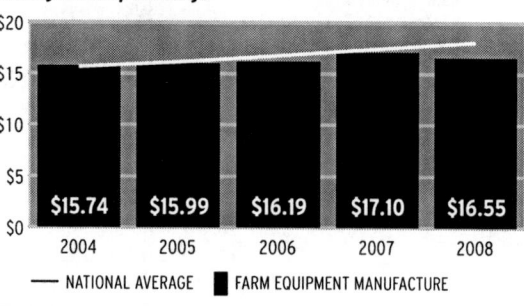

SOURCE: BUREAU OF LABOR STATISTICS

Call Preparation Questions

How does the company adjust to cyclical demand?

Industry revenue depends on the financial condition of crop farmers, which is highly cyclical.

How has growing import competition affected the company the last few years?

Imported farm equipment holds almost a third of the US market. In the past five years, imports have almost doubled.

What benefits or opportunities does the company see in buying and selling used equipment?

Since farm equipment is designed to be durable, a large base of used equipment exists and sells for a fraction of the price of new.

What plans, if any, does the company have to make add-on products for ATVs?

ATVs and utility vehicles (such as the Deere "Gator") are becoming increasingly popular as working vehicles on farms.

What opportunities or challenges does the company see in producing GPS-related products?

GPS is now accurate and inexpensive enough to have practical farm uses, although it's most effective on large farms.

Web Links

American Farm Bureau

General farming news.
www.fb.org

American Soybean Association

Soybeans are a major US export crop.
www.soygrowers.com

ASSEMBLY Magazine

News and some statistics.
www.assemblymag.com

Association of Equipment Manufacturers

Excellent statistics and analyses.
www.aem.org

Farm Equipment Manufacturers Association

Product and member searches, as well as news releases.
www.farmequip.org

Farm Industry News

News about new products and technology for the farm.
www.farmindustrynews.com

Farms.com

Commodity pricing and links to farm equipment resources.
www.farms.com

National Farmers Union

Family farm and ranch organization.
www.nfu.org

US Farm News

General farming news and statistics.
usfarmnews.com

USDA

Search for statistics on farm income and crop prices.
www.usda.gov

Glossary of Acronyms

ATV — all-terrain vehicle
CNH — Case New Holland
HP — horsepower
ROPS — roll over protection system
RTK — real-time kinematic

HOOVER'S TOP COMPANIES

Largest Companies by Sales	($ mil.)
Deere & Company	28,437.6
AGCO Corporation	8,424.6
Titan International, Inc.	837.0
Alamo Group Inc.	504.4
Lindsay Corporation	475.1

Largest Employers	Employees
Deere & Company	56,700
AGCO Corporation	13,700
Titan International, Inc.	2,700
Alamo Group Inc.	2,347
Chief Industries, Inc.	1,645
CTB, Inc.	1,260
Lindsay Corporation	1,239
Great Plains Manufacturing, Incorporated	700
Hog Slat, Incorporated	600
Sloan Implement	180

Fastest Growing* by Five-Year Sales Growth	(%)
Lindsay Corporation	23.8
AGCO Corporation	19.2
Alamo Group Inc.	14.2
Deere & Company	12.9
Titan International, Inc.	12.6

Fastest Growing* by Five-Year Employee Growth	(%)
Lindsay Corporation	14.9
Alamo Group Inc.	6.9
Deere & Company	5.6
AGCO Corporation	2.7

Top Public Companies by Market Value	($ mil.)
Deere & Company	16,283.7
AGCO Corporation	2,166.6
Lindsay Corporation	1,478.9
Titan International, Inc.	683.9
Alamo Group Inc.	178.3

* These rates are compounded annualized increases and may have resulted from acquisitions or one time gains. If less than 6 years of data are available, growth is for the years available.

SOURCE: HOOVER'S, INC., DATABASE

Farm Support Services

The US farm support service industry includes around 9,000 companies and 75,000 individuals with combined annual revenue of $15 billion. No major companies dominate. The industry is highly fragmented: the top 1 percent of companies employs 20 percent of the workforce. Around 80 percent of all companies employ fewer than 20.

This industry includes companies that support crop and animal farm operations but don't themselves harvest crops, raise farm animals, or own farmland.

Competitive Landscape

Demand is driven by domestic trends in crop and livestock production. The profitability of individual companies depends on establishing a value-added benefit to farms and keeping wages low. Large conglomerates like Cargill have advantages in vertical integration and economies of scope (offering a wide range of services). Small companies can compete effectively by specializing in a niche industry or service. The industry is labor-intensive: average revenue per worker for a typical company is $140,000.

Products, Operations & Technology

Major services include post-harvest crop activities like drying, cleaning, shelling, sorting, grading, and packing (45 percent of industry revenue); animal support activities like breeding livestock and pets, boarding and training horses, spraying cattle with insecticides, and stud services (25 percent); and soil preparation services like plowing, fertilizing, and planting, cultivating, and protecting crops (15 percent). Other services include machine-harvesting crops, crop farm management services, and farm labor contracting on citrus groves, vineyards, and orchards.

Of the 9,000 farm support service providers, half specialize in crops and half in livestock.

BUSINESS CHALLENGES

» Dependence on Agriculture Industry
By definition, farm support services depend heavily on the success of crop and livestock farms. Rising input and labor costs may actually help some service providers, as it may make sense for a farm to outsource certain labor- or capital-intensive tasks. However, the livelihood of many support services depends heavily on factors beyond the company's control, including grain prices, demand for meat and food crops, trends in imports and exports, fuel costs, and federal farm support programs.

» Cash Flow, Employment Highly Seasonal
Many farm services depend on a few critical weeks (planting and post-harvest) for the majority of profits. Employment levels can swing considerably depending on food demand, farm worker wages, and growing conditions. Because of the highly seasonal nature and the changes in year-to-year demand, few service providers can count on renewable contracts.

» Dependence on Low-Cost Labor
Other than specialty service providers, agricultural support service wages rarely exceed rates paid to hired farm workers. In general, farmers look at support services as a source of low-cost labor for tasks that the farm might otherwise do itself. Support service wages generally run 5 to 10 percent lower than wages for hired farm workers.

However, crop-related activities account for 75 percent of total farm support service revenue.

Crops are at their most delicate and fragile at initial planting and just after harvest. To minimize crop loss, farms often outsource planting, harvesting, and post-harvest tasks to companies (or neighboring farmers) that specialize in these critical stages. While many farms have expertise in pre- and post-harvest activities, outsourcing these can help maximize yield and lower farm labor costs.

Immediately following harvest, water retention and temperature control are the two most critical concerns. Fresh products can quickly become damaged due to excessive hot or cold temperatures, direct sunlight, or desiccation (water loss). Uneven temperatures can lead to excessive browning, uneven ripening, softening, and off-flavors. Many fruits, vegetables, and flowers shrivel after losing only a small percentage of their ideal moisture content. For example, lettuce won't spoil for 10 days when picked at temperatures less than 60 degrees and cooled within two hours, but if picked at 75 degrees and not cooled until after 10 hours, spoilage begins after two days.

To make the most of a harvest, farms, particularly large farms, often use third-party services that can quickly pick and/or transfer harvest crops into the processing stage. Depending on the crop, key tasks include force-air-cooling, drying, cleaning, threshing, grading, and sorting.

Inputs vary depending on the support services provided. Common inputs include diesel fuel, electricity, machine repairs, chemicals, water, and hired farm labor.

Recent technological advances include automated grading and sorting machinery, GPS tracking, improved cattle spray technology, and yield monitoring software that optimizes farm labor hours needed at harvest. Support service providers often become experts in the technological advancements of their chosen field and can access new products that may be out of reach for the typical farm. Some companies work in conjunction with agricultural research schools. Universities that specialize in post-harvest crop research and livestock support include the University of California at Davis and North Carolina State University.

Sales & Marketing

Typical customers are grain and oilseed farms, vegetable and melon farms, fruit and tree nut farms, livestock farms, concentrated animal feeding operations (CAFOs), and animal enthusiasts (for horse and companion animal breeding). Major sales channels include trade shows, brokers, the Yellow Pages, and networking among farm cooperatives.

Marketing efforts are limited. Word-of-mouth and customer referrals are the primary way to promote farm services. Most support service providers try to build a good reputation and strive for repeat business. Companies and individuals promote services on the Internet, but only a few companies sell directly online (beneficial insects, stud services).

Prices vary depending on the type of service provided. Per-acre fees are common for pre- and post-harvest activities. Farm labor contracting and management services are on a per worker, per hour basis, averaging around $6 to $10 an hour for workers and $15 to $20 an hour for experienced managers. Livestock activities like vaccination, branding, sheering, and boarding are usually charged by the animal serviced. Sheep sheering costs around $4 a head. Branding is often tied to registering cattle at the local or state level, and can cost anywhere from $10 to $20 per head.

Apart from regulatory compliance services that pass along a mandatory fee, companies generally must keep prices low to appeal to farmers. However, some companies specialize in top-of-the-line services that command a price premium, such as American Kennel Club (AKC) registered dogs, artificial insemination services, and farm management of high-end vineyards.

Human Resources

A major selling point of support services is the industry's low wages. Support activities for crop production pay an average $10 an hour, nearly 50 percent lower than the national average. Pay among livestock support services averages $13.50 an hour, 30 percent lower than the national average. Overtime, insurance, and other benefits are rare. During the planting season or at harvest, workers often put in 12- to 16-hour shifts, seven days a week. Annual personnel turnover is extremely high due to the seasonal nature of the work.

Compared to the national average, injury rates are 35 percent higher for livestock specialists and 15 percent higher for crop specialists. Most injuries are skin-related: burns, cuts, and scrapes that result in lost work days until the worker recovers.

Depending on the job, specialists may require advanced technical training or industry certification. Most workers have a high school education; managers may have an advanced science or viticulture degree. Apprenticeships are common, particularly in livestock support services.

Call Preparation Questions

How does the company forecast demand for its services?

By definition, farm support services depend heavily on the success of crop and livestock farms.

FAST FACTS

» The US farm support service industry includes around 9,000 companies and 75,000 individuals with combined annual revenue of $15 billion.

» No major companies dominate.

» Major services include post-harvest crop activities like drying, cleaning, shelling, sorting, grading, and packing (45 percent of industry revenue); animal support activities like breeding livestock and pets, boarding and training horses, spraying cattle with insecticides, and stud services (25 percent); and soil preparation services like plowing, fertilizing, and planting, cultivating, and protecting crops (15 percent).

» Typical customers are grain and oilseed farms, vegetable and melon farms, fruit and tree nut farms, livestock farms, concentrated animal feeding operations (CAFOs), and animal enthusiasts (for horse and companion animal breeding).

» Cash flow is highly seasonal for most farm support services, as all crop and livestock production has a natural season.

How seasonal are the company's hiring needs and cash flow?

Many farm services depend on a few critical weeks (planting and post-harvest) for the majority of profits.

How does the company ensure attractive wages for farms?

Other than specialty service providers, agricultural support service wages rarely exceed rates paid to hired farm workers.

What business opportunities or new services is the company considering?

Pre-harvest specialists that plow and fertilize farmland may be able to extend services to include soil decontamination.

Has the company considered creating products for retail sale?

Post-harvest crop specialists can consider extending their product reach to create fresh-from-the-farm products.

Web Links

National Cotton Ginners Association

Trade association for cotton ginning (post-harvest process).
cotton.org/ncga

UC Davis Post-harvest Research Center

Post-harvest research, news, and information.
postharvest.ucdavis.edu

USDA Agricultural Outlook

Monthly statistical reports on a variety of crops.
www.ers.usda.gov/publications/outlook

USDA Economic Research Service

Farm and market reports, news, links and data.
www.ers.usda.gov

USDA National Agricultural Statistics Service

Statistics and analysis on US agriculture.
www.nass.usda.gov

Glossary of Acronyms

APHIS — Animal and Plant Health Inspection Service
CAFO — concentrated animal feeding operation
HACCP — Hazard Analysis and Critical Control Point
MSPA — Migrant and Seasonal Agricultural Worker Protection Act
NGO — non-governmental organization
VOC — volatile organic compound

HOOVER'S TOP COMPANIES

Largest Employers	Employees
CHS Inc.	6,885
Dunavant Enterprises, Inc.	3,000
The Andersons, Inc.	2,953
Trout-Blue Chelan-Magi, Inc.	675
The Scoular Company	530
DeBruce Grain, Inc.	530
Farmers Cooperative Company	280
South Dakota Wheat Growers Association	270
Farmers Cooperative Society	200
Calcot, Ltd.	190

Top Public Companies by Market Value	($ mil.)
The Andersons, Inc.	298.8
CHS Inc.	232.1
Pro-Fac Cooperative, Inc.	40.1
Canal Capital Corporation	0.1

SOURCE: HOOVER'S, INC., DATABASE

Fast Lube/Auto Oil Change Service

The US automotive oil change and lubrication industry includes about 4,000 companies with combined annual revenues of $4 billion. Large chains include Jiffy Lube, Pennzoil 10-Minute Oil Change, Valvoline Instant Oil Change, and Texaco Xpress Lube. The industry is highly fragmented, despite the large chains: the 50 biggest companies hold less than 40 percent of the market. Fast lube operators, for the most part, are independent owners with one or two shops. Most companies operate a single location, with 10 employees and annual revenue of $600,000.

Competitive Landscape

Demand is driven by the amount of driving that consumers do and by new car sales. The profitability of individual companies depends on convenient location and good marketing. Large chains have an advantage in name recognition, but the operations of individual locations are similar. Small companies can compete successfully by owning favorable locations. Operations are labor-intensive: annual revenue per employee is just $60,000.

Products, Operations & Technology

Major services are oil changes, installation of new oil filters, chassis lubrication, and preventative maintenance. Routine maintenance services like adjusting tire pressure, changing windshield wipers, replacing light bulbs, and topping off auto fluid levels, are usually done in ten minutes or less. Typically, more than 70 percent of revenue is from oil changes.

A typical location performs about 1,200 jobs per month. Most locations operate two to five bays in a drive-through building, and many use basement construction so that oil can be changed below while other services are being completed above. However, to keep capital investments low and offer quick building relocation, vehicle lifts can be used rather than

basements. Locations can be built on a relatively small piece of property and require low capital investment, typically less than $250,000.

Managers closely monitor daily vehicle count (which ranges from 25 vehicles for new locations up to 100 for established locations); average ticket price (ranging from $25 to $45); and services provided. To track vehicle and customer spending habits and demographics, man-

BUSINESS CHALLENGES

» Dependent on Auto Travel Miles

The number of miles consumers drive and the average age of cars affect demand for oil changes and other services. The number of miles consumers drive has grown only slowly in recent years, but a greater number of older cars remain in operation. Total US highway miles driven increase about 2 percent per year.

» More Competition from Auto Dealers

Many car dealers use low prices on oil changes to draw customers to service departments. Car dealers also benefit from the increased complexity of new cars, which can often be serviced best by dealers, as they typically own the latest diagnostic computers. The push by dealers into the auto service business is likely to intensify, as many dealerships make higher profits on car service than sales. Dealerships have become more competitive by offering services like extended hours and short-wait oil changes.

» Reduced Demand via Better Oil Technology

New vehicles (including hybrids and cars that use fuel cells) are becoming more fuel- and maintenance-efficient, decreasing the need for fast lube services. Newer cars require oil changes less often. Traditionally, mechanics and car makers recommended 3,000 miles between oil changes, but major car makers now recommend 5,000 to 10,000 miles. New oil-filtering technology may even further reduce the need for oil changes for new passenger cars. Fast lubes may need to educate drivers on the value of having oil changes and other services sooner.

agement depends on computer technology, which details customers' required services for their particular vehicle make and model.

Sales & Marketing

Successful marketing depends largely on securing a favorable location, as customers are unwilling to go far out of their way for an oil change. Yellow Pages advertising, newspaper coupons, and direct mail are frequently used. Customer loyalty and repeat business are emphasized and encouraged through customer mailings and VIP cards.

Franchising is a major factor in the industry. Franchisers offer training, advertising, equipment, and other services. These agreements usually include upfront fees ranging from $12,500 at the low-end to $50,000 or $60,000 at Jiffy Lube; and ongoing royalty fees ranging from 3 to 8 percent of revenue, and national advertising fees of 1 to 5 percent of revenue. Some operators have exclusive territory agreements.

The industry is becoming mature since expanding rapidly over the past 15 years. For example, Jiffy Lube opened the first location in 1979. Fast lube locations compete for oil changes with do-it-yourselfers, independent mechanic shops, automobile dealerships, and full service gas stations.

Human Resources

Because most jobs in the fast lube business require minimal skills, pay is low, about 40 percent less than for the average US worker. With low pay, personnel turnover and training for new employees are constant concerns for managers. The industry, however, has a good safety record, with fewer injury cases than the national average. The annual injury rate for auto maintenance services, including fast lube, is just under the US average.

Industry Employment Growth

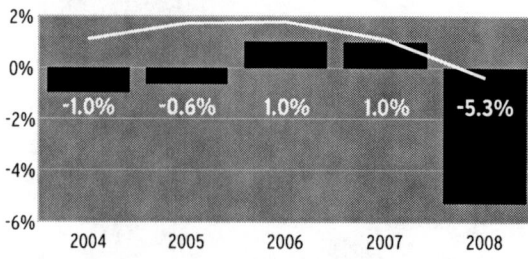

2004	2005	2006	2007	2008
-1.0%	-0.6%	1.0%	1.0%	-5.3%

Average Hourly Earnings

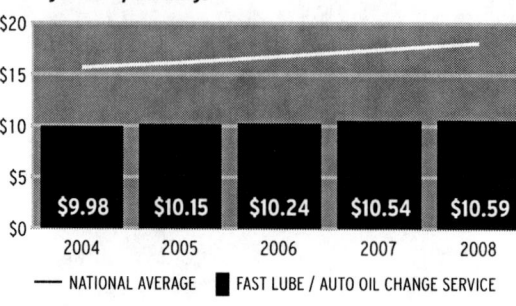

2004	2005	2006	2007	2008
$9.98	$10.15	$10.24	$10.54	$10.59

—— NATIONAL AVERAGE ■ FAST LUBE / AUTO OIL CHANGE SERVICE

SOURCE: BUREAU OF LABOR STATISTICS

Call Preparation Questions

How have recent demand changes affected company sales?

The number of miles consumers drive and the average age of cars affect demand for oil changes and other services.

How does the company address increasing auto dealer competition?

Many car dealers use low prices on oil changes to draw customers to service departments.

How are new oil technologies impacting oil change demand and company revenues?

New vehicles (including hybrids and cars that use fuel cells) are becoming more fuel- and maintenance-efficient, decreasing the need for fast lube services.

How is the company benefiting from the "do-it-for-me" trend in consumer attitudes?

Dual family incomes and the need for convenience have increased the desire for quick vehicle maintenance.

How successful are the company's brand management and promotion?

Some oil change chains are starting brand awareness advertising through direct mailing.

Web Links

Automotive News

Automotive industry news and links.
www.autonews.com

Automotive Oil Change Association

General industry information.
www.aoca.org

Jiffy Lube

Information about franchising and initial investments.
www.jiffylube.com

Kwik Industries Inc.

Information on oil lube industry and franchises.
www.kwikind.com

National Oil & Lube News

Industry news.
noln.net

National Petroleum News

News, information, and more on petroleum industry.
www.npnweb.com

Glossary of Acronyms

AOCA — Automotive Oil Change Association
ASA — Automotive Service Association
BPD — barrels per day
SSDE — Service Station Dealers Exemption

HOOVER'S TOP COMPANIES

Largest Employers	Employees
Jiffy Lube International, Inc.	3,000
Lucor, Inc.	2,011
Speedco, Inc.	1,100

SOURCE: HOOVER'S, INC., DATABASE

Financial Planners and Investment Advisors

About 10,000 firms in the US provide financial planning and investment advice to individuals and businesses, with combined annual revenue of $15 billion. Large companies include Value Line, Morningstar, and units of financial services companies. The industry is concentrated at the top, with the eight largest firms accounting for a quarter of industry revenue, but is otherwise highly fragmented. A large local firm may have 30 employees and generate $10 million of annual revenue.

Competitive Landscape

Demand is driven by consumer income and wealth and demographics. The profitability of individual firms depends largely on effective marketing. Large companies have some advantages in providing expertise in a wider range of investment options, and may charge lower fees. Small companies can compete successfully by providing better service and advice. In small and large firms, annual average revenue per employee is about $200,000.

Products, Operations & Technology

Financial planners help customers put together a plan to manage their financial resources; investment advisers suggest specific investments. About 60 percent of industry revenue comes from providing services to individuals. Financial planners help individuals form a plan that may include debt, asset, college, retirement, estate and tax planning, and may periodically check with the client to see how well the plan is being followed. Much of the planning revolves around an income and spending budget, with advice about the types of financial investments suitable for the client. For wealthy individuals, and for organizations like trusts, estates, and charitable foundations, financial planners offer more comprehensive and detailed planning, often of a tax-sensitive nature, and frequently recommend specific invest-

BUSINESS CHALLENGES

» Too Many Investment Alternatives

The explosion in the number of investment vehicles available in the past few years makes familiarity with them all impossible for a financial planner. An advantage of larger planning firms is their ability to cover many specialized investment areas. Smaller firms are less likely to be able to afford the computer technology and information services that allow them to keep up with so many investment choices.

» Potential Conflicts of Interest

Financial planners affiliated with brokerage and investment firms face potential conflicts of interest, especially if they're paid partly through commissions on sales of investments. While some clients are attracted by the wider range of resources large financial companies can offer, others prefer the independence of unaffiliated planners. Generally, legislators and regulators are demanding more separation between financial planners and the products they sell.

» Competition from Computerized Planning Packages

While many clients prefer the "handholding" a human adviser can bring, the proliferation of computerized planning tools threatens the lower and middle segments of the financial planning business because of lower cost. Instead of paying up to $2,000 for a plan from a human financial planner, Internet websites offer comprehensive financial planning for a $100 annual fee. These planning tools provide as much detail as a human adviser and can use live information on interest rates and equity values to update calculations.

ments, in which case they function as investment advisors.

Investment advisers recommend specific investments, sometimes to individuals but most often to managers of investment funds such as mutual funds. Investment advice is usually based on research, which can be of many kinds. Many advisers develop methods of research and analysis that are unique to their firm. Large firms operate like brokerage houses — with large numbers of general-knowledge advisers backed by a research and support staff. Advisers may be paid a flat fee (typically much higher than for basic financial planning); a fee based on the size of the assets under management (from 1 to 5 percent of assets); or a performance fee based on the success of the investment advice. In some cases, compensation is indirect, through commissions received from brokering investment transactions. Some advisers have authority to invest on their clients' behalf.

Sales & Marketing

Marketing is largely by referral, direct mail, and advertising in finance-oriented publications. Investment advisers depend heavily on referrals for new customers, but also may advertise their success in trade publications. Financial planning and investment advising are highly personal activities, where the adviser's personality is as important as the advice given. Wealthier clients, especially, may demand a high degree of personal attention. Financial planners typically are paid a flat fee of $300 to $2,000 for preparing an individual plan, or charge at the rate of $100 to $200 per hour.

The relationships between financial planners, investment advisers, and other parts of the financial services industry are complex. Since planners/advisers largely influence client investments, they're heavily courted by the brokerage and investment management parts of the industry. Many financial services companies have established their own financial planning/investment adviser departments to attract clients to the other services and investment products they offer.

Human Resources

Industry employment growth well exceeds the national rate. Wages are nearly 50 percent higher than the national average. Median employee income in financial planning is about $60,000 per year with about 40 percent of advisers self-employed.

To practice financial planning and investment advising, workers must pass the Registered Investment Adviser Exam before applying for state certification. Workers may also apply for certifications through the Certified Financial Planner Board of Standards to become a Certified Financial Planner (CFP), or the American Academy of Financial Management to be a Master Financial Planning Professional (MFPP).

Financial planners and investment advisers may face long hours, frequent travel to visit companies and talk to potential investors, and deadline pressures.

Industry Employment Growth

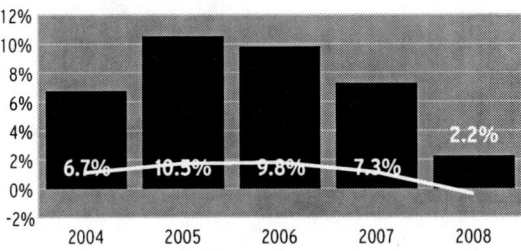

Average Hourly Earnings

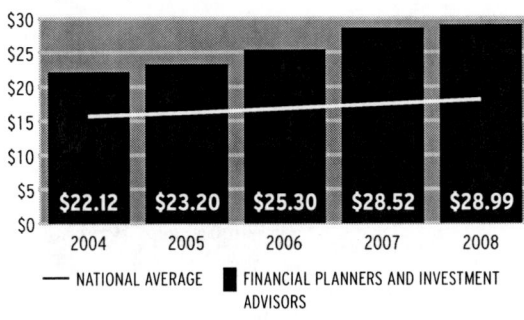

SOURCE: BUREAU OF LABOR STATISTICS

Call Preparation Questions

How does the firm stay abreast of the range of investment products available?

The explosion in the number of investment vehicles available in the past few years makes familiarity with them all impossible for a financial planner.

How is the firm reducing potential conflicts of interest between financial planners' income and customer needs?

Financial planners affiliated with brokerage and investment firms face potential conflicts of interest, especially if they're paid partly through commissions on sales of investments.

How does the firm mitigate competition from planning software and online planning sites?

While many clients prefer the "handholding" a human adviser can bring, the proliferation of computerized planning tools threatens the lower and middle segments of the financial planning business because of lower cost.

How do changes in tax regulations affect the firm's marketing?

Changes in tax regulations often have implications for investment strategies that consumers have difficulty understanding on their own.

What opportunities does estate planning present for the company?

Congress continues to pass new legal provisions that may affect estate planning strategies.

Web Links

CFA Institute

Professional organization.
www.cfainstitute.org

Financial Planning Association

Professional organization.
www.fpanet.org

Financial Planning Magazine

Articles.
www.financial-planning.com

Financial Services Online – Advisor's Weekly

Practical advice for financial planners.
fsc.fsonline.com/fsj

International Association of Registered Financial Consultants

Professional organization.
www.iarfc.org

Journal of Financial Planning

Practical aspects of being a financial planner.
www.fpajournal.org

National Association of Personal Financial Advisers

Organization of "fee-only" planners.
www.napfa.org

Securities and Exchange Commission (SEC)

Regulation of investment advisers.
www.sec.gov

Worth

Lists top financial advisors.
www.worth.com

Glossary of Acronyms

CFP — Certified Financial Planner
CFA — Chartered Financial Analyst
CHFC — Chartered Financial Consultant
FPA — Financial Planning Association
FPI — Financial Planners International
HNW — high-net-worth (with investable assets over $1 million)
IARD — Investment Adviser Registration Depository
LNW — low-net-worth ($100,000 to $1 million in investable assets)
NASDR — National Association of Securities Dealers Regulation
PFS — Personal Financial Specialist
SEC — Security and Exchange Commission
SMA — separately managed account

HOOVER'S TOP COMPANIES

Largest Companies by Sales	($ mil.)
TIAA-CREF	13,187.0
Principal Financial Group, Inc.	9,935.9
Ameriprise Financial, Inc.	7,149.0
BlackRock, Inc.	4,844.7
Mutual of America Life Insurance Company	1,810.2
SEI Investments Company	1,247.9
Affiliated Managers Group, Inc.	1,158.2
National Financial Partners Corp.	1,150.4
Robert W. Baird & Co. Incorporated	729.0
Fidelity Investments Institutional Services	—

Largest Employers	Employees
Fidelity Investments Institutional Services	38,000
Principal Financial Group, Inc.	16,585
Ameriprise Financial, Inc.	8,750
TIAA-CREF	7,500
BlackRock, Inc.	5,500
National Financial Partners Corp.	3,247
SEI Investments Company	2,300
Robert W. Baird & Co. Incorporated	2,161
Morningstar, Inc.	1,720
Affiliated Managers Group, Inc.	1,580

Fastest Growing* by Five-Year Sales Growth	(%)
Duff & Phelps Corporation	89.3
Epoch Holding Corporation	67.0
BlackRock, Inc.	53.0
U.S. Global Investors Funds	49.5
RiskMetrics Group, Inc.	42.6
Morningstar, Inc.	29.2
Investors Capital Holdings, Ltd.	21.5
Och-Ziff Capital Management Group LLC	20.6
National Financial Partners Corp.	19.9
Affiliated Managers Group, Inc.	18.5

Fastest Growing* by Five-Year Employee Growth	(%)
BlackRock, Inc.	43.3
Och-Ziff Capital Management Group LLC	33.3
Resource America, Inc.	24.6
Morningstar, Inc.	19.8
Pzena Investment Management, Inc.	16.4
National Financial Partners Corp.	15.5
Investors Capital Holdings, Ltd.	15.3
Epoch Holding Corporation	14.9
Affiliated Managers Group, Inc.	11.5
U.S. Global Investors Funds	10.6

Top Public Companies by Market Value	($ mil.)
Principal Financial Group, Inc.	5,852.4
Ameriprise Financial, Inc.	5,057.7
SEI Investments Company	3,003.7
Affiliated Managers Group, Inc.	1,919.7
Morningstar, Inc.	1,678.5

* These rates are compounded annualized increases and may have resulted from acquisitions or one time gains. If less than 6 years of data are available, growth is for the years available.

SOURCE: HOOVER'S, INC., DATABASE

Fitness Centers

About 15,000 companies and nonprofits in the US operate over 26,000 fitness and recreation centers, with combined annual revenue of $15 billion. Large companies include Bally Total Fitness, 24 Hour Fitness Worldwide, and Town Sports International, operator of the Sports Club brand. About 5,000 centers are operated by nonprofits like YMCAs. The industry is extremely fragmented: the 50 largest companies hold only about 30 percent of the market, and only a few dozen companies own more than 10 centers. A typical large fitness center has $3 million of annual revenue and 65 employees.

Competitive Landscape

Demand is partly linked to income levels and partly to market demographics. The profitability of individual companies depends on good marketing. Large companies have economies of scale in advertising and buying equipment. Small companies can compete effectively if they have favorable locations. The industry is highly labor-intensive: average annual revenue per worker is just $35,000.

Products, Operations & Technology

Major services include facilities for aerobic exercise and weightlifting. Running, swimming, racquet sports, yoga, karate, basketball, and swimming may also be offered. Small studios may cover just a few thousand square feet while multi-activity operations can cover 200,000 square feet. The operations of all fitness centers are similar: the operator makes space and equipment available for customers to engage in various types of fitness activities, provides staff to help customers properly use the equipment, maintains the facilities, and provides various other services such as professional trainers and class instructors, child care, food and drinks, showers and lockers, hot tubs and saunas, and sales of sports clothing and equipment.

BUSINESS CHALLENGES

» High Member Attrition Rate

About 35 to 40 percent of fitness club members don't renew memberships, making revenue uncertain and requiring high marketing costs to get new members. Attrition for members who make installment payments is even higher for some clubs. To fight attrition, clubs promote programs to monitor diets, fitness levels, and exercise regimes, and assess metabolic rates, oxygen use, and body fat.

» Large Required Capital, Training Costs

Because fitness centers must keep up with the latest fitness trends, including new equipment and classes, training employees and buying and maintaining equipment takes major capital investments. Commercial-grade fitness equipment costs from $5,000 to $10,000 per machine. Bally installs about $400,000 of equipment in a new fitness center.

» Changing Demographics

The number of people 20 to 45, historically the primary users of fitness clubs, will stagnate during the next 10 years. Now, aging baby boomers make up a large percentage of membership targets for health clubs. As people age, they're less likely to participate in high-impact sports, and more likely to use exercise equipment in a social setting.

Fitness equipment is usually leased and can be classified into aerobic exercisers (treadmills, stationary bicycles, stair climbers, rowing machines and elliptical cross trainers); weightlifting machines (sometimes called resistance equipment or plate-loaded equipment); and traditional weight-training equipment (barbells and various types of benches, bars, and racks). A typical Bally or Gold's Gym facility covers 25,000 square feet, divided fairly equally between aerobic machines, weight machines, and classrooms, with about $400,000 of equipment (mainly leased). Because of uneven customer traffic, many employees work part-time. The total cost to open a new Bally facility is $2 million. A large, mature facility may have 3,000 members.

Sales & Marketing

Marketing is through a variety of channels, including referrals from existing members, print advertising, radio and local TV ads, direct mail, and telemarketing. Companies target different audiences, according to the type of activities they offer. Competition is usually very strong because of the ease with which a club can be opened. Clubs can usually draw members from within a 15-minute driving distance, but not more, because convenience is a major factor in choosing a club. The attrition rate, the percentage of club members who don't renew each year, on average is a fairly high 35 to 40 percent, requiring constant new member recruitment. The structure of membership costs at many fitness centers with high initiation fees is designed mainly to reduce attrition.

Payments to acquire and maintain membership often mimic those of country clubs, with an initiation fee (sometimes called an "initial membership fee" or a "joining fee") and annual or monthly dues. Because membership costs are often high, many customers make monthly payments, either through direct withdrawals from their bank accounts or credit cards. Membership charges vary, depending on the type and quality of services provided. At high-end Sports Clubs, memberships may cost $2,500, with an initiation fee of $2,500. Clubs with a high initial fee of $500 to $1,000 typically have low monthly dues of $10 or so. Other clubs have low initial fees of $200 but monthly dues of $50. Some companies, like Bally, will finance the initiation fee over 36 months.

Human Resources

Employees at fitness centers require only a low level of skill and are paid a fairly low rate. Average wages are about 25 percent below the average wage for all US workers. Activities typically involve checking customers in, demonstrating equipment, selling products, and maintaining the club. Many employees work part-time and don't receive many fringe benefits. The annual injury rate for recreational industries, including fitness centers, is the same as the national average: just over four cases per 100 full-time workers.

Industry Employment Growth

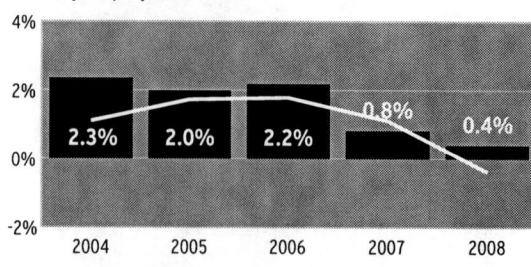

Average Hourly Earnings

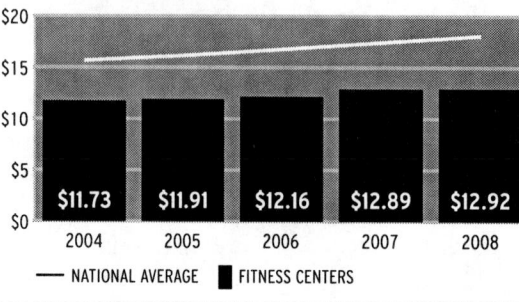

SOURCE: BUREAU OF LABOR STATISTICS

Call Preparation Questions

How does the club combat membership attrition?

About 35 to 40 percent of fitness club members don't renew memberships, making revenue uncertain and requiring high marketing costs to get new members.

How does the company manage the high costs of buying new equipment and training employees?

Because fitness centers must keep up with the latest fitness trends, including new equipment and classes, training employees and buying and maintaining equipment takes major capital investments.

What initiatives is the company taking to increase membership?

The number of people 20 to 45, historically the primary users of fitness clubs, will stagnate during the next 10 years.

How can the club benefit from the national concern over obesity?

Fitness centers may benefit from growing national concern over obesity in the US, as more organizations, companies, and individuals take action against the impact of weight-related illnesses.

Aside from membership, what revenue sources is the company benefiting from or planning to implement?

Retail can be a strong profitability factor. Clubs should train front desk staff to actively sell retail and service products.

Web Links

Club Industry's Fitness Business Pro

Industry news. Club Industry Top 100.
fitnessbusinesspro.com

FitCommerce.com

News and articles for fitness and wellness
professionals.
www.fitcommerce.com

Fitness Management

News and information for fitness facilities operators.
fitnessmanagement.com

IDEA Health and Fitness Association

Publications, events, and news.
www.ideafit.com

International Health, Racquet & Sportsclub Association

Industry news and statistics.
cms.ihrsa.org

Medical Fitness Association

Association of hospital fitness centers.
www.medicalfitness.org

SportsOneSource

Industry news.
www.sportsonesource.com

Glossary of Acronyms

ACE — American Council on Exercise
ASD — American Sports Data
CDCP — Centers for Disease Control and Prevention
IHRSA — International Health & Racquet Sportsclub
Association
MBS — mind-body-spirit
NIA — Neuromuscular Integrative Action

HOOVER'S TOP COMPANIES

Largest Companies by Sales	($ mil.)
24 Hour Fitness Worldwide, Inc.	1,280.0
Bally Total Fitness Holding Corporation	1,059.1
Life Time Fitness, Inc.	769.6
Town Sports International Holdings, Inc.	506.7
Health Fitness Corporation	70.0

Largest Employers	Employees
24 Hour Fitness Worldwide, Inc.	21,410
Bally Total Fitness Holding Corporation	19,200
Life Time Fitness, Inc.	15,000
Town Sports International Holdings, Inc.	9,000
The Wellbridge Company	3,000
The Sports Club Company, Inc.	2,619
TCA Holdings, LLC	2,200
AGT Crunch Acquisition LLC	2,200
Gold's Gym International, Inc.	2,000
Club One Inc.	1,500

Top Public Companies by Market Value	($ mil.)
Life Time Fitness, Inc.	513.0
Town Sports International Holdings, Inc.	78.6
Health Fitness Corporation	8.4

SOURCE: HOOVER'S, INC., DATABASE

Fitness Equipment

Fewer than 100 manufacturers of fitness equipment operate in the US, with combined annual sales of about $3 billion. Large companies include ICON Health & Fitness, Nautilus, Life Fitness, Precor, and Cybex International.

Competitive Landscape

Demand is driven partly by consumer income and partly by demographic trends. The profitability of individual companies depends on unique product designs and effective marketing. Large companies have some advantages in brand-name recognition, but small companies can compete effectively by making a unique product.

Products, Operations & Technology

Major products are motorized treadmills, stationary bikes, stair climbers, rowing machines, and elliptical "cross-trainers," collectively called aerobic exercisers; and weightlifting machines ("strength training"), and traditional weightlifting equipment ("free weights" and benches). In addition, there are a large number of ancillary products. This equipment allows individuals to exercise by themselves in a limited space. The two major market segments for fitness equipment are the home and the institutional exercise equipment market (including health clubs, corporations, apartments, and hotels). The home market is by far the largest and has grown significantly in the past decade. Products are made and marketed separately for the two segments; many manufacturers produce for only one.

Products for home use are mainly treadmills and exercise bikes. Cost is a primary consideration, so home equipment is generally built with lighter materials and comes in a wider range of prices, especially toward the lower end. Home exercise equipment is rarely used more than one hour per day. Products sold to fitness clubs include the entire range of fitness equipment,

BUSINESS CHALLENGES

» Demand Subject to Fashion

Fitness equipment manufacturers have had to contend with relatively rapid changes in consumer preferences. The popularity of various equipment types has changed over the years: exercise bikes were the most popular aerobic fitness equipment in the late 80s, followed by rowing machines. Bikes were still the most popular in the early 90s, closely followed by stair climbers, and treadmills became the most popular in the late 90s; elliptical trainers have become popular in the last few years.

» Technology Knowledge

Technology development is a driving force in the fitness equipment industry. Consumers demand enhancements through systems that reduce impact, monitor heart rate, and deliver better performance metrics. While mechanical expertise is necessary, new experiential and operations technologies will drive future growth. Fitness equipment manufacturing is dominated by megacompanies such as ICON that have more capital to allocate to R&D, which leads to quicker and more dramatic improvements in product design.

» Manufacturing Costs High for Small Product Runs

Because manufacturers generally produce a line of models that are constantly being replaced by newer versions, production runs are relatively small, which leaves few opportunities for companies to decrease manufacturing costs through automation or other manufacturing efficiencies.

with treadmills, exercise bikes, and stair climbers the most popular. Weightlifting machines and "free weights" appeal predominantly to men, a minority in most fitness clubs. Since a typical club owns dozens of pieces of fitness equipment, initial cost is a major consideration, but since equipment in a club is used very intensively, durability is even more important. A club treadmill or exercise bike may be used more than 12 hours per day, 7 days a week. Accordingly, equipment sold to clubs is more sturdily built and costs more than that sold to the home market.

Most fitness equipment consists of a mechanical portion that provides resistance to a muscular activity, and an electronic portion that interfaces with the user that allows resistance adjustment and provides a wide variety of information about the amount of exercise the user gets. Electronics, key in the growing popularity of exercise machines, counter the main complaint that stationary exercise is boring. Treadmills consist basically of a motor and a wide belt stretched between two rollers and supported by a deck. Because they absorb greater force from individuals running on them, treadmills must be built more sturdily than bikes and stair-steppers. Exercise bikes, ellipticals, and stair climbers use sprocket chains, pulleys, ratchets, and a variety of resistance mechanisms. Weightlifting machines consist mainly of levers, pulleys, and weights.

Most manufacturers have a single production plant that includes metal fabrication, plastics molding, and welding and painting operations. Handling metals, plastics, and paints means that environmental issues have to be addressed. Although manufacturers hold patents on various features of their equipment, patent protection isn't an important consideration because of the variety of ways that can be devised to produce the same basic exercise motions. Product innovation is important, however, because users, especially in clubs, become bored with equipment. Styling and various electronic features of exercise equipment, including sensors for measuring heart rate, and types of control and monitoring functions, are an important way for manufacturers to differentiate their products.

Sales & Marketing

Sales to the home market are primarily through mass merchants like Sears, Wal-Mart, Kmart, and Sports Authority. Manufacturers also sell directly to 25,000 retail stores that sell sporting equipment. Most of the large manufacturers also offer direct sales over the Internet. Some products are heavily advertised on TV and in health or fitness magazines. Prices for home treadmills generally range from $400 to $1500, although they can go higher. Prices for home bikes are generally between $200 and $700.

Sales to the club market are either by direct sales or through distributors. Because club equipment is expensive, some manufacturers

offer purchase and lease financing, either directly or through arrangements with a third party. Warranties and service contracts are an important feature of sales to clubs. Manufacturers train dealer personnel to provide maintenance and repair service to dealer customers. Club treadmills generally cost from $3,000 to $8,000, exercise bikes and stair-steppers around $2,000.

Human Resources

Precision assemblers, who work for manufacturers of more sophisticated fitness equipment, are skilled workers who put together a wide range of finished products from manufactured parts or subassemblies. US workers in machinery manufacture are paid wages slightly above the national average.

Industry Employment Growth

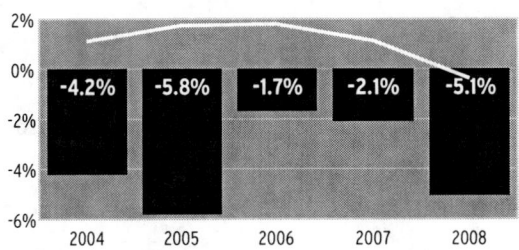

Average Hourly Earnings

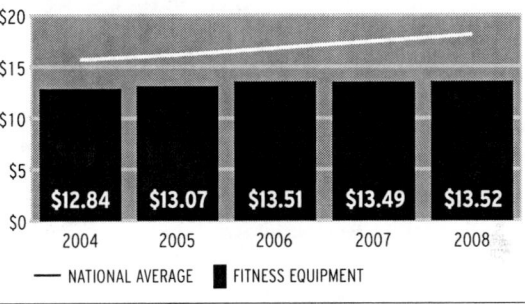

SOURCE: BUREAU OF LABOR STATISTICS

Call Preparation Questions

How does the company identify and design equipment for the latest exercise trends?

Fitness equipment manufacturers have had to contend with relatively rapid changes in consumer preferences.

How does the company stay on the cutting edge of technology?

Technology development is a driving force in the fitness equipment industry.

How does the company protect profits in this highly competitive industry?

Because manufacturers generally produce a line of models that are constantly being replaced by newer versions, production runs are relatively small, which leaves few opportunities for companies to decrease manufacturing costs through automation or other manufacturing efficiencies.

What are the company's plans for incorporating more video and audio electronics in its equipment?

To counteract consumer boredom, manufacturers have added electronic features that engage the user.

How can the company benefit from the national concern over obesity?

With a greater number of overweight Americans, demand for fitness equipment should stay high during the next decade.

Web Links

American Sports Data

Market research reports for a fee.
www.americansportsdata.com

Club Industry's Business Pro Magazine

News articles.
www.fitnessbusiness-pro.com

Cybex International

Manufacturer website. Equipment line.
www.cybexintl.com

Fitness Partner Connection

Reviews types of fitness equipment.
primusweb.com/fitnesspartner/library/equipment/equip.htm

ICON Health & Fitness

Manufacturer website. Equipment line.
www.iconfitness.com

IDEA Health & Fitness Association

Publications, events, and news.
www.ideafit.com

International Health, Racquet & Sportsclub Association (IHRSA)

Industry statistics, Club Business International Magazine.
cms.ihrsa.org

Sporting Goods Manufacturers Association (SGMA)

Market reports, some sporting goods news.
www.sgma.com

SportsOneSource

News articles.
www.sportsonesource.com

Glossary of Acronyms

IHRSA — International Health, Racquet and Sportsclub Association

NSGA — National Sporting Goods Association

SGMA — Sporting Goods Manufacturers Association

HOOVER'S TOP COMPANIES

Largest Companies by Sales	($ mil.)
Nautilus, Inc.	501.5
ICON Health & Fitness, Inc.	341.0
Escalade, Incorporated	185.6
Cybex International, Inc.	146.5
Life Fitness	198.1
Precor Incorporated	55.8

Largest Employers	Employees
ICON Health & Fitness, Inc.	2,500
Life Fitness	1,400
Nautilus, Inc.	1,262
Escalade, Incorporated	805
Cybex International, Inc.	608
Precor Incorporated	543
Fitness Quest Inc.	147
Keys Fitness Products, LP	84

Top Public Companies by Market Value	($ mil.)
Nautilus, Inc.	153.1
Escalade, Incorporated	117.2
Cybex International, Inc.	79.1

SOURCE: HOOVER'S, INC., DATABASE

Floor Coverings

The floor coverings industry in the US includes about 700 manufacturers; 4,000 wholesalers; and 15,000 retailers; with combined annual end-user sales of $25 billion. Major manufacturers include Shaw Industries, Mohawk Industries, Beaulieu Group, and Armstrong World Industries. Large retail franchise chains include Flooring America and Carpet One. The industry is highly concentrated at the manufacturing end, where the four largest companies hold close to 75 percent of the market, and highly fragmented at the retail end, where the top 50 companies hold just 10 percent.

Competitive Landscape

Demand for floor coverings depends on residential and commercial real estate construction and home sales, which can be cyclical. With many costs fixed, profitability of individual companies depends on their volume of business. There are large economies of scale in manufacturing and distribution. Annual revenue per employee at large carpet mills is close to $300,000. A typical wholesale location has annual revenue of $50 million, a typical retail location about $4 million.

Products, Operations & Technology

The industry produces and sells carpets and rugs, hardwood flooring, "resilient" plastic sheeting, and ceramic tiles. The majority (65 percent) of sales consists of carpeting and rugs. Tufted nylon carpeting accounts for about 50 percent of industry sales; rugs and other carpets, 15 percent; plastic sheeting and tiles, 23 percent; and wood flooring, 12 percent.

Most carpeting is made on large tufting machines that use rows of needles to sew loops of nylon thread into a latex "backing." The loops are cut to produce tufts and additional backing is glued on to the bottom to hold the tufts in place; polypropylene and polyester thread are

BUSINESS CHALLENGES

» Residential Sales Depend on Home Sales, New Construction

Consumers are most likely to replace flooring immediately after they buy a home. About 75 percent of carpeting goes into new homes and the residential replacement market. Home and carpet sales don't always decline during a recession, but can drop when mortgage rates rise.

» Commercial Floor Covering Sales Depend on Retail, Office Construction

Many wholesalers get a large amount of business from retail and office space refitting or new construction. The commercial market is largely independent of the residential and sensitive to office and retail vacancy rates, which can change rapidly. For example, the national vacancy rate for office space increased from 9 to 17 percent during the last recession.

» Competition from Home Center Chains

Floor covering wholesalers and traditional retailers lose market share to large home center chains like Home Depot and Lowe's. Lowe's operates 1,200 stores that sell floor covering, Home Depot 1,800. These and other large chains buy directly from manufacturers and sell to both retail and commercial customers.

also used. Rugs and woven carpeting are made on looms using wool, cotton, silk, or synthetic thread. Most carpeting is made as 100-foot rolls ("roll goods") of various widths — mainly 12 or 15 feet ("broadloom") — but modular carpet tiles are also made. Annual US production is about 2 billion square yards.

"Resilient" flooring is made as large sheets of plastic, either as a solid layer (vinyl) or as a sandwich with a design layer under the clear top layer (laminate); the finished product can be sheets or individual tiles. Ceramic tiles are baked clay, often with a glaze. Hardwood flooring may be solid wood or an engineered product with a layer of hardwood glued over a plywood core; the finished product can be in lengths or tiles. The manufacturing process for most of these products is simple and automated, leading to large economies of scale for high-volume producers and encouraging consolidation. A carpet manufacturer may produce hundreds of variations of the same product based on color, texture, pattern, and thread. Shaw produces more than 1,500 carpet styles.

Nylon thread, the major raw material for carpet manufacture, and the plastics used for vinyl and other synthetic flooring are made from crude oil and are therefore subject to cost changes that can be more than 10 percent in a six-month period. Major suppliers of nylon filament or resins are Koch Industries, Solutia, and Honeywell. Some large carpet manufacturers produce their own filament and thread.

Manufacturers, wholesalers, and retailers use computerized inventory systems due to the large number of products. The technology of tufting machinery continues to evolve, although the basic concept is old. Modern tufting machines can produce carpets and rugs with complex patterns, combinations of loops and tufts, varying pile depth, and up to six colors. Computer systems are used for carpet and rug design and machinery control.

Sales & Marketing

Floor coverings are sold to the residential "replacement" market, home builders, and managers and developers of commercial property, especially retail and office space. Smaller amounts are also sold to the auto, airline, and furniture industries and for sports and industrial use. Residential use accounts for about 75 percent of carpet sales. Within the commercial segment, carpet products may be made to specification (the "specified" market) or sold off the shelf (the "non-specified" market).

Distribution to end-users is via wholesale dealers, retailers, or directly from manufacturers. The residential replacement segment of the market is typically served through a traditional manufacturer-wholesaler-retailer chain, but the home builder and commercial segment cuts out the retailer and includes direct sales from manufacturers. Home centers like Home Depot and Lowe's buy directly from manufacturers and sell to both retail and commercial customers. Large manufacturers like Shaw operate a network of distribution warehouses that serve retailers and wholesalers. Retail outlets may be small showrooms or large flooring centers that stock the full range of floor coverings and accessories.

Wholesalers generally hold large inventories of standard product lines. Retailers may also hold some inventories of standard products but are mainly showrooms and rely heavily on wholesalers and manufacturers to fulfill their orders. About half of carpet sales require custom cutting, which may be done by the manufacturer or the wholesaler. Carpet dealers (wholesale or retail) typically sell brands in a variety of price ranges. Retail prices for carpet are expressed in dollars per square yard (or per square foot) and typically vary from $5 to $25 per square yard. Low-end retail prices per square foot can be 50 cents for vinyl tile, $2 for ceramic tile, and $2 for wood flooring. Most floor coverings require professional installation, which may be provided by the dealer or independent contractors.

Manufacturers and wholesalers typically use a sales force. Retailers often use newspaper, radio, and TV advertising. Trade shows are an important source of information about new product lines. Retail chains like Flooring America and Carpet One are cooperatives of independent stores, with the operator providing regional advertising and sales support.

Human Resources

Jobs in carpet manufacturing mills mainly involve tending the automated machinery and require relatively low skills. Pay is low, under $12 per hour, compared to the average national wage of $16. Jobs at floor covering retailers include salespeople with technical knowledge and sales skills, and materials handlers, who move, store, and deliver products. Average wages at floor covering stores are over $16 hourly. Jobs at wholesalers may involve operating warehousing equipment like forklifts and custom-cutting machinery, or computerized information systems, which require special skills. Home furnishing wholesalers pay workers an average $16 per hour.

Industry Employment Growth

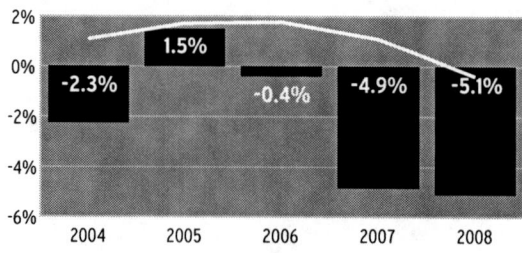

FAST FACTS

» The floor coverings industry in the US includes about 700 manufacturers; 4,000 wholesalers; and 15,000 retailers; with combined annual end-user sales of $25 billion.

» Major manufacturers include Shaw Industries, Mohawk Industries, Beaulieu Group, and Armstrong World Industries.

» The industry produces and sells carpets and rugs, hardwood flooring, "resilient" plastic sheeting, and ceramic tiles.

» Floor coverings are sold to the residential "replacement" market, home builders, and managers and developers of commercial property, especially retail and office space.

» Cash flow is seasonal because more homes are sold in summer and a large portion of floor covering replacements are made right after a home is bought.

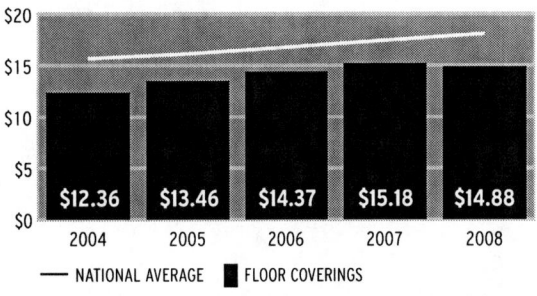

Average Hourly Earnings

	2004	2005	2006	2007	2008
FLOOR COVERINGS	$12.36	$13.46	$14.37	$15.18	$14.88

— NATIONAL AVERAGE ■ FLOOR COVERINGS

SOURCE: BUREAU OF LABOR STATISTICS

Call Preparation Questions

How has the company been affected by the recent drop in home sales?

Consumers are most likely to replace flooring immediately after they buy a home.

Does the company expect steady demand in the commercial market?

Many wholesalers get a large amount of business from retail and office space refitting or new construction.

How does competition from large retail chains impact the company?

Floor covering wholesalers and traditional retailers lose market share to large home center chains like Home Depot and Lowe's.

Will the company make or sell new types of floor coverings, like laminates?

As an alternative to hardwood and vinyl flooring, laminates provide an impact-resistant floor at reduced cost.

Web Links

Carpet and Rug Institute

Technical information about carpeting. Industry statistics.
www.carpet-rug.com

Floor Covering Weekly

Industry news.
www.floorcoveringweekly.com

Floor Daily

Industry news.
www.floordaily.net

National Association of Floor Covering Distributors

Good industry links.
www.nafcd.org

National Wood Flooring Association

Information about wood floors.
www.woodfloors.org/consumer

Resilient Floor Covering Institute

Information about vinyl and other resilient flooring.
www.rfci.com

World Floor Covering Association

Information about different types of flooring.
www.wfca.org

Glossary of Acronyms

NAR — National Association of Realtors
SF — square foot

HOOVER'S TOP COMPANIES

Largest Companies by Sales	($ mil.)
Mohawk Industries, Inc.	6,826.4
Armstrong World Industries, Inc.	3,393.0
Beaulieu Group, L.L.C.	1,100.0
Interface, Inc.	1,082.3
Lumber Liquidators, Inc.	482.2
The Dixie Group, Inc.	320.8
Shaw Industries, Inc.	—

Largest Employers	Employees
Mohawk Industries, Inc.	36,200
Shaw Industries, Inc.	30,000
Armstrong World Industries, Inc.	12,200
Beaulieu Group, L.L.C.	5,850
Interface, Inc.	3,838
Wilsonart International, Inc.	3,402
Mannington Mills, Inc.	2,200
Tandus Group, Inc.	1,623
The Dixie Group, Inc.	1,500
J&J Industries, Inc.	830

Fastest Growing* by Five-Year Sales Growth	(%)
Lumber Liquidators, Inc.	29.4
Mohawk Industries, Inc.	6.4
Interface, Inc.	3.2
Armstrong World Industries, Inc.	0.8

Top Public Companies by Market Value	($ mil.)
Mohawk Industries, Inc.	2,940.1
Armstrong World Industries, Inc.	1,233.4
Interface, Inc.	286.1
Lumber Liquidators, Inc.	283.0
The Dixie Group, Inc.	96.6

* These rates are compounded annualized increases and may have resulted from acquisitions or one time gains. If less than 6 years of data are available, growth is for the years available.

SOURCE: HOOVER'S, INC., DATABASE

Florists

THIS INDUSTRY INCLUDES:

SIC CODES
5992   Florists

NAICS CODES
4531   Florists

The retail florist industry includes about 22,000 retail flower shops with combined annual revenues of $7 billion. While there are no national florist chains, independent florists are usually linked into national wire services providers FTD and Teleflora, which connect customers with florists. 1-800-FLOWERS.COM has more than 100 franchised and company-owned shops. The industry is highly fragmented: the 50 largest companies hold just 6 percent of the market. Average annual sales per flower shop are about $300,000.

Competitive Landscape

Demand for flowers depends on discretionary consumer spending. The profitability of individual shops depends on effective marketing. Companies focus on a local or regional market and compete based on convenient location, price, and customer service. Florists also compete with supermarkets and mass merchandisers selling flowers, which can often sell at lower prices because of volume purchases from growers or wholesalers. The industry is highly labor-intensive: annual sales per employee are about $60,000.

Products, Operations & Technology

Major products are cut flower arrangements, potted plants, and loose cut flowers. Flower arrangements account for 55 percent of industry revenue, potted plants for 15 percent. Stores may also sell vases, artificial flowers, and other gift items. The top-selling flowers are roses, carnations, and lilies.

Florists buy product from one, or several, of 1,000 wholesalers and importers, who in turn buy from several thousand growers. Imports, mainly from South America, account for about 70 percent of cut flowers. Wholesalers typically deliver cut flowers several times per week. Store operations consist of caring for flowers, putting together flower arrangements, taking orders,

BUSINESS CHALLENGES

» Demand Depends on Consumer Income

Most consumers consider flowers a discretionary item, and demand depends on disposable income. During periods of higher energy or food prices and economic uncertainty, consumers are likely to cut flower purchases, or may opt for loose flowers, rather than more expensive cut flower arrangements.

» Competition from Supermarkets, Mass Merchandisers

The share of cut flowers sold through florists continues to decline as sales increase at supermarkets, discounters, and wholesale clubs. These alternative channels now account for over half of flower purchases and one-third of spending on cut flowers. Purchases at supermarkets or mass merchandisers are typically loose cut flowers bought impulsively.

» Slow Sales Growth

Overall sales by florists have been relatively flat, rising only 1 percent from 1997 to 2002. A 2005 survey by floral research firm Prince & Prince finds 69 percent of US florists reporting their businesses are stable or declining. Many florists consider a 2 to 3 percent sales increase successful.

serving walk-in customers, and delivering arrangements to consumer and commercial customers.

On-time local deliveries are an important aspect of customer service, particularly around major holidays. Florists often use multiple delivery vans to meet customer commitments; delivery costs fluctuate with gas prices.

Because high foot-traffic is desirable, florists may lease space in malls or other prime retail locations. Companies may operate local stores and non-permanent satellite operations on sidewalks, train stations, and other locations. The majority of companies operate a single store and even the largest companies operate less than ten stores on average. The average store has five employees.

Computer technology is used to send and receive orders via communication networks like FTD and Teleflora. Many stores operate an Internet site that allows customers to view selections and buy online. Other computer systems to boost productivity are route scheduling for local deliveries, customer information, and point-of-sale (POS).

Sales & Marketing

Customers are individual consumers and commercial institutions such as hotels, hospitals, and funeral homes. Consumer purchasers of flowers tend to be more affluent, highly educated, and older than the average US consumer. The fastest-growing segment is 55 or older, which is 36 percent of flower purchasers. Commercial customers typically are repeat accounts that get discounts. A store's physical location is the most important aspect of marketing. Websites have become important for local stores to accept orders.

In addition to fulfilling local orders, florists can receive "wire-ins" and can send "wire-outs" if they belong to networks like FTD and Teleflora. FTD, Teleflora, and other companies also act as "broker/order gatherers," using Internet sites to collect orders that are then "wired" to local florists for delivery. Typically, brokers keep 25 to 30 percent of the price of retail orders.

Typical prices are $30 to $40 for floral arrangements, less for bunches of loose cut flowers. Supermarkets are major competitors for consumer business, although they compete mainly in loose cut flowers.

Human Resources

The skill required of industry workers is fairly low and wages are accordingly below-average. Average hourly wages in 2005 were under $10, versus almost $16 for all US workers. Low wages promote high personnel turnover, in turn requiring a significant amount of training for new workers. To cope with varying demand, companies use a large number of part-time workers, especially around the big event days such as Valentine's Day.

Industry Employment Growth

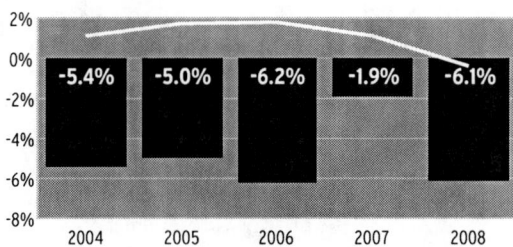

Average Hourly Earnings

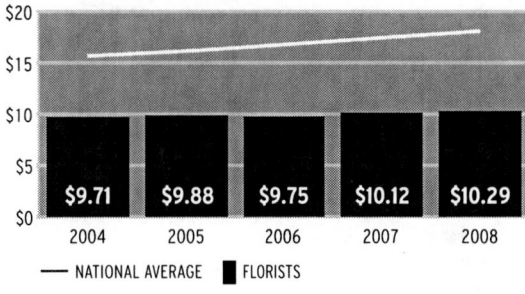

SOURCE: BUREAU OF LABOR STATISTICS

Call Preparation Questions

How is the current economic outlook affecting demand for the company?

Most consumers consider flowers a discretionary item, and demand depends on disposable income.

How has competition from supermarkets and mass merchandisers affected the company's business?

The share of cut flowers sold through florists continues to decline as sales increase at supermarkets, discounters, and wholesale clubs.

How is the company responding to slow growth in flower sales?

Overall sales by florists have been relatively flat, rising only 1 percent from 1997 to 2002.

What opportunities might the company expect by partnering with local businesses?

Florists can reach more consumers and generate incremental sales by developing relationships with complementary businesses in their local area.

Is the company marketing to older consumers? If so, to what benefit?

Consumers over 55 are the fastest-growing segment of flower buyers.

Web Links

1-800-FLOWERS.COM Investor Relations

Leading online retailer of flowers and gifts. phx.corporate-ir.net/phoenix.zhtml?c=67803&p=irol-IRHome

About Flowers.com

Sponsored by the Society of American Florists; contains industry statistics and advice on using flowers.

www.aboutflowers.com

American Floral Endowment

Market research on industry trends.

www.endowment.org

Florists' Review

A monthly magazine for florists.

www.floristsreview.com/main

FTD.com – Investor Relations

Wire service network of 20,000 florists in US and Canada.

phx.corporate-ir.net/phoenix.zhtml?c=96019 &p=irol-investors&type=528&homepage_link=FOOT

Society of American Florists

Trade association of florists, growers, and suppliers.

www.safnow.org

Teleflora

Wire service network of 25,000 florists in US and Canada.

www.teleflora.com/abouttf.asp

Wholesale Florist & Florist Supplier Association

News on floral industry wholesale trends.

www.wffsa.org

Glossary of Acronyms

AFE — American Floral Endowment
AIFD — American Institute of Floral Designers
POS — point-of-sale
SAF — Society of American Florists
WF&FSA — Wholesale Florist & Florist Supplier Association

HOOVER'S TOP COMPANIES

Largest Employers	Employees
1-800-FLOWERS.COM, Inc.	3,700
FTD Group, Inc.	745
Teleflora LLC	410
Provide Commerce, Inc.	175
Agriflora Corporation	120
Speaking Roses Inc.	30

SOURCE: HOOVER'S, INC., DATABASE

Food Distributors

The US wholesale food distribution industry includes about 38,000 companies with combined annual revenue of around $550 billion. Major companies include SYSCO, US Foodservice, SUPERVALU, and McLane Company. The industry is moderately concentrated: the 50 largest distributors hold about 50 percent of the total market.

This industry doesn't include revenue from retail or manufacturing operations.

Competitive Landscape

Demand is driven largely by demographic shifts, particularly trends in population and age, working women, race and ethnicity, household size, and levels of disposable income. The profitability of individual companies depends on a good product mix and efficient operations. Large distributors are advantaged by bulk purchasing and economies of scale in distribution. Smaller companies can compete effectively by specializing in organic, natural, or kosher products or focusing on a geographical area. Average annual revenue per worker for a typical company is $675,000.

Products, Operations & Technology

Major products are frozen, processed, and prepared foods; dairy items; poultry, fish, and meat; fresh produce; and baked goods.

Distributors are classified as "broadline," meaning that they sell to various customers; "product specialists," which sell a limited number of products; "market specialists" that sell to a particular type of customer, such as Chinese restaurants; or "system specialists" that sell to a particular kind of customer, such as hotels. Only about 150 large companies are broadline; the remaining wholesalers typically specialize in a specific market. Foodservice customers have surpassed grocery stores as the largest customer base for food wholesalers. Both SYSCO and US Foodservice sell mainly to food-

service institutions and chain restaurants; others sell mainly to supermarkets and grocery stores. Some large food retailers operate their own distribution operations.

Operations revolve around the logistics of getting food items from food producers to hundreds or thousands of retailers. Some distributors operate only locally (such as milk distributors). Many distributors receive products from all over the country but distribute only regionally.

Typically, distributors consolidate shipments from suppliers at regional warehouses and deliver daily to customers using a fleet of trucks, which can be owned, leased, or contracted. Suppliers include farmers (fruits and vegetables, dairy); food manufacturers; and importers. Supply contracts are common.

Some distributors also sell nonfood items like drink dispensers, cleaning supplies, and tobacco products, and services like inventory control systems, financing, equipment installation, menu planning, restaurant design, and management. A few large distributors are vertically integrated. Supplier side vertical integration occurs when wholesalers run their own crop or livestock farms, processing, and packaging facilities. Vertical integration can incorporate retail business, as some large wholesalers own and manage grocery outlets.

Major inputs include diesel fuel, electricity, pallets for receiving and storage, and vehicle repairs. Warehouses that handle large quantities range from 300,000 to 900,000 square feet. Large distributors may have several tiers of warehouses and may run separate warehouses for fast and slow turnover items. Large companies may buy and stock 50,000 items. Performance Food Group, a large foodservice provider, stocks 44,000 products and sells to 33,000 customers. Most small distributors concentrate in one product segment; have warehouses of 50,000 to 200,000 square feet; and may carry only a few thousand items.

To track prices, purchases, shipments, and product inventory, food distributors rely heavily on computer and communication technology and highly automated warehouses. Daily or weekly orders from large customers are typically electronic via private electronic data interchange (EDI) or Internet systems. Recent technological advances include wireless devices to track retail sales; radio frequency input device (RFID) tags that follow cases or kegs as they travel through the supply chain; and GPS that automatically determine truck routes and communicate with central dispatchers.

Sales & Marketing

Typical customers are food retailers (supermarkets, grocery and convenience stores) and the foodservice industry, which consists mainly of traditional outlets (restaurants, hospitals, schools, hotels, and industrial caterers), and chain restaurants (Burger King, Pizza Hut, etc.).

Major types of marketing include inviting retailers to attend "table-top" presentations at the distribution center, end-cap promotions, trade shows, and retailer discounts. Wholesalers must work closely with suppliers that invest heavily in advertising to ensure that stores are adequately stocked. Wholesalers may share the cost of regional or local advertising with suppliers. Much of distributors' volume is repeat business, and most have a sales force to look for new customers and sell new products to existing ones.

Prices to retail customers are typically quoted as market price plus fee and freight, with the fee varying according to quantity and other delivery characteristics. A typical wholesaler markup ranges from 20 to 40 percent, depending on the product.

Human Resources

Wholesale food distribution wages average $17 per hour, nearly 5 percent lower than the national average. Sales representatives are generally paid by a mix of base and commission. Incentive plans, once used mainly to tie key executives to total company results, are now used freely across employee groups, including hourly employees. Companies that distribute wholesale grocery foods pay about 20 percent more than those that distribute fruits and vegetables.

Food distributors require managerial, clerical, and technical skills. Truck drivers require driver training, certification, licensing, and physical strength to transport and deliver food.

The annual injury rate in wholesale food distribution is about 80 percent higher than the national average. Most injuries involve sprains, strains, cuts, lacerations, and soreness from moving, lifting, overexertion, or driving. Injuries from overexertion are more than double the national average.

Industry Employment Growth

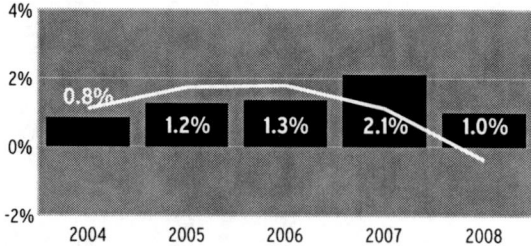

Average Hourly Earnings

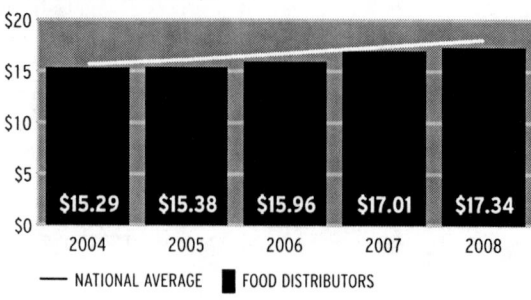

— NATIONAL AVERAGE   ■ FOOD DISTRIBUTORS

SOURCE: BUREAU OF LABOR STATISTICS

Call Preparation Questions

How is the company countering increased competition?

Large grocery chains, big-box retailers, and wholesale clubs can bypass distributors and deal directly with manufacturers.

How important are third-party logistics providers to the company's operations?

Food wholesalers are increasingly outsourcing some or all of their transportation and warehousing needs to third-party logistics providers.

How important are proprietary private-label brands to the company's overall success?

Big distributors, like SYSCO and SUPERVALU, receive higher margins on proprietary brands of products they sell to the foodservice industry.

Web Links

American Wholesale Marketers Association

Products, services, government and industry issues, education, and human resource information for convenience distributors.
www.awmanet.org

Food Logistics

Covers warehousing, material handling, transportation, distribution, information technology, and facility design news.
www.foodlogistics.com

Foodservice.com

Industry news, trade shows, classifieds, etc.
www.foodservice.com

Grocery Manufacturers Association

Association of food brokers. Good links to industry publications.
www.gmabrands.com/news

International Foodservice Distributors Association

Industry news and many useful links.
www.ifdaonline.org

Modern Distribution Management

Market data, like industry analysis reports, news, articles, and links.
www.mdm.com

Glossary of Acronyms

DC — distribution center
DSD — direct-store-delivery
EDI — electronic data interchange
ERP — enterprise resource planning
FDI — Food Distributors International
FMI — Food Marketing Institute
RFID — radio frequency identification
WMS — warehouse management systems

HOOVER'S TOP COMPANIES

Largest Companies by Sales	($ mil.)
SUPERVALU INC.	44,048.0
SYSCO Corporation	37,522.1
U.S. Foodservice, Inc.	20,200.0
Wakefern Food Corporation	9,900.0
Topco Associates LLC	8,800.0
C&S Wholesale Grocers, Inc.	7,302.0
Performance Food Group Company	6,304.9
Core-Mark Holding Company, Inc.	6,044.9
Associated Wholesale Grocers, Inc.	5,700.0
McLane Company, Inc.	4,471.4

Largest Employers	Employees
SUPERVALU INC.	192,000
Wakefern Food Corporation	50,000
SYSCO Corporation	50,000
U.S. Foodservice, Inc.	27,160
C&S Wholesale Grocers, Inc.	17,000
McLane Company, Inc.	15,115
Keystone Foods LLC	13,000
The Grocers Supply Co., Inc.	8,900
Spartan Stores, Inc.	8,100
Nash-Finch Company	7,475

Fastest Growing* by Five-Year Sales Growth	(%)
China Huaren Organic Products, Inc.	34.2
Synergy Brands, Inc.	23.2
The Grocers Supply Co., Inc.	19.6
United Natural Foods, Inc.	19.5
SUPERVALU INC.	18.1
Topco Associates LLC	17.1
Keystone Foods LLC	16.5
Dot Foods, Inc.	14.8
Associated Wholesale Grocers, Inc.	12.7
Centric Group, L.L.C.	11.8

Fastest Growing* by Five-Year Employee Growth	(%)
The Grocers Supply Co., Inc.	111.0
China Huaren Organic Products, Inc.	38.0
SUPERVALU INC.	27.3
Centric Group, L.L.C.	19.9
United Natural Foods, Inc.	16.1
Keystone Foods LLC	14.2
U.S. Foodservice, Inc.	13.4
Dot Foods, Inc.	9.6
Core-Mark Holding Company, Inc.	8.5
Associated Wholesale Grocers, Inc.	7.8

Top Public Companies by Market Value	($ mil.)
SYSCO Corporation	16,966.8
SUPERVALU INC.	5,923.3
Performance Food Group Company	964.3
United Natural Foods, Inc.	804.7
Nash-Finch Company	469.5

* These rates are compounded annualized increases and may have resulted from acquisitions or one time gains. If less than 6 years of data are available, growth is for the years available.

SOURCE: HOOVER'S, INC., DATABASE

Food Service Contractors

THIS INDUSTRY INCLUDES:

SIC CODES
5812   Eating Places

NAICS CODES
722310   Food Service Contractors

The food service contracting industry includes about 21,000 companies with combined annual revenue of $23 billion. Major companies include Compass Group USA, Aramark, Delaware North, and Sodexo, Inc. The industry is highly concentrated: the 50 largest companies account for about 90 percent of revenue.

Food service contractors provide restaurant, fast food, and cafeteria services to large businesses, institutions, and government agencies. This profile doesn't include food distributors, which supply food and equipment to restaurants.

Competitive Landscape

Demand is driven by employment trends and consumer tastes. The profitability of individual companies depends on efficient operations and food quality. Large companies have advantages in economies of scale in food and equipment purchasing, off-site food preparation, and distribution. Small companies can compete effectively by specializing in unique food products or local markets. The industry is labor-intensive: average annual revenue per worker is only $50,000.

Products, Operations & Technology

Major products are meals consumed on-premises (65 percent of revenue) and take-out food (30 percent). Other products include alcoholic drinks and grocery food items. Meals can vary depending on the setting and client, but typically focus on breakfast, lunch, and dinner standards. Food includes pizza, Mexican and Asian cuisine, sandwiches, salad bars, chicken, and hamburgers. Beverages include soft drinks, tea, coffee, bottled water, and juice.

Food service contractors prepare and serve meals cafeteria-style; in bulk quantity to students, hospital patients, and prisoners; and in fast-casual or quickservice restaurants (QSR). Fast-casual and QSRs can be either private-

BUSINESS CHALLENGES

» Demand Tied to Economic Cycles
The profitability of food service contractors fluctuates with the health of the national economy. A weak economy means fewer employees at the company cafeteria, less corporate spending on catering, fewer meals served at sports and entertainment venues, and more workers packing lunch versus eating out.

» Dependence on Low-Cost Labor
Wages in the food service contractor industry are 40 percent lower than the national average. About 20 percent of food service workers live in the US illegally. High demand for entry-level jobs attracts large numbers of illegal immigrants to the food contracting industry. Increased government enforcement of immigration laws has led to a crackdown on workers with forged or borrowed identification. Food service contractors may experience rising labor costs or a shortage of workers if the supply of illegal workers declines.

» Food Safety
Concerns over food-borne illnesses have prompted food service to improve health standards and carefully scrutinize vendor relationships. Bioterrorism is another contractor concern; food operators must carefully manage the supply chain to reduce the risk of contaminants poisoning thousands of patrons. More stringent safety regulations can add cost for food contractors and increase liability for non-compliance.

branded (Au Bon Pain, Bleeker Street Cafe) or a franchise (Burger King, Wolfgang Puck, Starbucks). Stand-alone QSRs tend to be less than 3,000 square feet. Cafeteria and public dining settings can be up to 40,000 square feet, with the dining area representing about 60 percent of total space, kitchen around 30 percent, and common areas 10 percent.

A large food service contractor operates thousands of facilities and serves millions of customers each day. A typical site serves around

500 to 1,500 people daily with an average transaction of $2.

Operations include food preparation, food service, and clean up. Food preparation involves cleaning, cutting, and cooking entrees, salads, soups, side items, and desserts. Major utility inputs include natural gas for cooking and electricity for refrigeration and cooling. Food ingredients are supplied by a food distributor. Increasingly, distributors are providing food service contractors with portion-controlled, pre-washed, and pre-assembled food items, reducing spoilage and limiting the time needed to prepare food onsite.

Large food service contractors employ a professionally trained chef on-site, whose primary responsibility is to oversee food preparation, limit spoilage, and reuse ingredients whenever possible. Cooks, food servers, and cleanup crew are typically paid hourly and require minimal skills.

Food service contractors rely heavily on point-of-sale (POS) technology to track sales and inventory. Software systems help food contractors reduce food costs and improve profitability by tracking individual products, sales trends, and revenue share figures. Contractors in the university sector are adopting fingerprint-based biometric identification, replacing traditional card-reading systems, allowing for a more rapid flow of customer traffic and eliminating the problem of lost or stolen cards.

Sales & Marketing

Typical customers are hospitals, corporate campuses, government agencies, sports and entertainment arenas, prisons, primary and secondary schools, airlines, and universities. Companies rely on a strong internal sales force to secure multi-year contracts and maintain client relationships.

Contractors often partner directly with the university, corporate partner, or hospital client to market the facility and increase patronage. Marketing typically involves radio, posters, billboards, and brochures. Food contractors may market a specific theme (such as healthy eating or "International Food Month") to increase customer interest.

Larger food service contractors create and manage interactive client websites. Key information includes current menu offerings, nutritional facts, special events, and the food contractor's corporate information.

Typical food service contracts range from $500,000 to $5 million annually and usually last five to 10 years with renewal options. Contracts

are awarded through a highly competitive bidding process. Contracts vary widely: some contractors may receive a monthly management fee or performance-related incentives; others may be required to pay the client an annual retainer, percentage of gross revenues, or share of profits.

Human Resources

Wages in the food service contracting industry are nearly 40 percent lower than the US average. Industry productivity has remained flat for the past five years. Employment is highly seasonal with peaks in spring and fall; employment drops 5 to 10 percent in winter months. The injury rate for special food services is 50 percent higher than the US average, primarily due to cuts and hand injuries during food preparation.

Industry Employment Growth

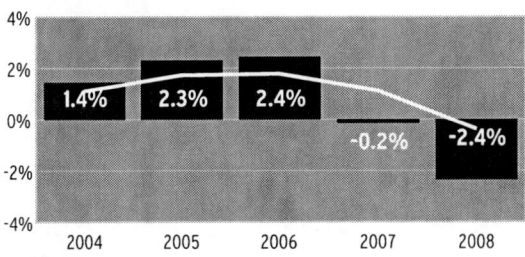

Average Hourly Earnings

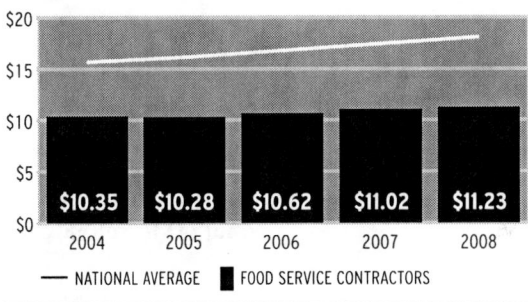

SOURCE: BUREAU OF LABOR STATISTICS

Call Preparation Questions

How does the state of the economy affect the company?

The profitability of food service contractors fluctuates with the health of the national economy.

Has the company been pressured to increase wages?

Wages in the food service contractor industry are 40 percent lower than the national average.

How is the company ensuring the safety of its food supplies?

Concerns over food-borne illnesses have prompted food service to improve health standards and carefully scrutinize vendor relationships.

FAST FACTS

» The food service contracting industry includes about 21,000 companies with combined annual revenue of $23 billion.

» Major companies include Compass Group USA, Aramark, Delaware North, and Sodexo, Inc.

» Major products are meals consumed on-premises (65 percent of revenue) and take-out food (30 percent).

» Typical customers are hospitals, corporate campuses, government agencies, sports and entertainment arenas, prisons, primary and secondary schools, airlines, and universities.

» Cash flow is highest in summer and fall, particularly for contractors specializing in sports and recreation facilities.

How is the company enhancing its food offerings?

Contractors trying to overcome the image of bland, mass-produced food are successfully offering customized food services and high-end ingredients.

Is the company serving patient meals in hospitals or considering that market?

Food service contractors are aggressively marketing the ability to provide onsite facilities management, which includes cleaning, HVAC maintenance, and laundering.

Web Links

Association of Correctional Food Service Affiliates (ACFSA)

International association of correctional food service professionals.
www.acfsa.org

Food Management

News and trends for non-commercial food service.
www.food-management.com

International Flight Services Association

Food service association for trains and airlines.
www.ifsanet.com

National Association of College and University Food Services (NACUFS)

Collegiate food services association.
www.nacufs.org

National Restaurant Association

Represents the food hospitality industry.
www.restaurant.org

Restaurant Hospitality Magazine

Ideas for full-service restaurants — includes corporate dining.
www.restaurant-hospitality.com

Glossary of Acronyms

ACFSA — Association of Correctional Food Service Affiliates
NACUFS — National Association of College and University Food Services
NRA — National Restaurant Association
POS — point-of-sale
PPFM — physical planning and facilities management
QSR — quickservice restaurant

HOOVER'S TOP COMPANIES

Largest Companies by Sales	($ mil.)
SYSCO Corporation	37,522.1
ARAMARK Corporation	12,384.3
Delaware North Companies, Inc.	2,000.0
Centerplate, Inc.	740.7
Sodexo, Inc.	—

Largest Employers	Employees
ARAMARK Corporation	250,000
Sodexo, Inc.	120,000
SYSCO Corporation	50,000
Delaware North Companies, Inc.	40,000
Centerplate, Inc.	29,050
Compass Group USA, Inc.	4,200
Guest Services, Inc.	3,500
Valley Services, Inc.	2,450
Ovations Food Services, L.P.	2,300
Five Star Food Service, Inc.	1,400

Fastest Growing* by Five-Year Sales Growth	(%)
SYSCO Corporation	7.5
Centerplate, Inc.	5.1
Delaware North Companies, Inc.	4.6
CURA Hospitality, Inc.	4.5

Fastest Growing* by Five-Year Employee Growth	(%)
Delaware North Companies, Inc.	7.4
SYSCO Corporation	0.4
Centerplate, Inc.	0.3

Top Public Companies by Market Value	($ mil.)
SYSCO Corporation	16,966.8

* These rates are compounded annualized increases and may have resulted from acquisitions or one time gains. If less than 6 years of data are available, growth is for the years available.

SOURCE: HOOVER'S, INC., DATABASE

Footwear Manufacture, Wholesale, and Retail

The US footwear industry consists of about 100 manufacturers; 1,500 wholesalers; and 30,000 retail outlets, with combined annual retail revenue of $25 billion. The major shoe companies in the US, including NIKE, Reebok, Brown Shoe, and Timberland, are mainly owners of brand names that "source" their shoes from independent manufacturers. The retail segment includes owners of large chains, like Foot Locker and thousands of small local retailers. The retail segment is highly concentrated: the largest 50 chains hold about 80 percent of the market. Many shoe companies operate in both the wholesale and retail segments.

Competitive Landscape

Demand is driven by fashion and demographics. The profitability of individual companies depends on their ability to design and market attractive shoe models. Big companies have economies of scale in distribution and marketing. Small companies can compete successfully through superior design or marketing.

Products, Operations & Technology

Major product segments are athletic, women's, and men's shoes. Athletic shoes account for about 30 percent of the retail market, women's casual and dress shoes for 25 percent, men's casual and dress shoes for 15 percent, and miscellaneous for the remainder.

Domestic manufacture of shoes has been rapidly declining and is now worth less than $3 billion annually. The typical US shoe manufacturer is small, with annual revenue of $10 million and fewer than 100 employees. US-made products are mostly private-label men's shoes. Average revenue per employee is $100,000. Materials, mainly leather, amount to 50 percent of costs. Shoe manufacture has moved to low-cost countries like China because of the large labor content in the manufacturing process, especially for athletic shoes. Despite

BUSINESS CHALLENGES

» Flat Prices: Greater Emphasis on Marketing

The profitability of US shoe companies depends on marketing skills because retail shoe prices have essentially been flat. In the last 10 years, retail prices declined 3 percent. With prices flat, manufacturers and retailers have had to rely on superior styling and marketing to increase sales.

» Reliance on Foreign Manufacture

US retailers depend on foreign manufacturers for most of their product, primarily from China, Italy, Brazil, and Spain. Almost all athletic shoes are imported into the US. Total shoe imports increased 40 percent between 1998 and 2006. Because of the high labor content, most manufacturing is in low-cost countries. The large dependence on foreign manufacturers increases the risk of supply disruptions and political interference.

» Vulnerability to Fashion Changes

Retail shoe sales are subject to uncertain consumer demand, which can leave manufacturers and retailers holding sizable inventories of unwanted goods. Consumer tastes are difficult to understand or predict. The development cycle in the industry, from initial shoe design to retail sale is about a year, long enough so that styles can become unpopular.

advances in automation, shoes are still largely assembled by hand, using cutting, glueing, and stitching machinery.

Retailers include regional and national shoe store chains, department and discount stores, and many independent local retailers. Chains typically locate stores in strip or enclosed malls, or as stand-alone operations. The retail shoe market is heavily segmented by type of consumer (sex, age, income level, urban/suburban, etc.) and price level. Better footwear prices range between $70 and $100; bridge footwear retails for between $100 and $200; designer footwear starts at about $200. Each brand includes numerous styles. With many choices of product, retailers develop "store model stocks" (the product mix) that will appeal to their target consumer audience.

The logistics of delivering product to retailers is extremely important for shoe companies, especially in view of the many brands, private labels, styles, colors, and sizes involved. Most shoe companies have several distribution centers, typically 500,000 to 1 million square feet, and sophisticated computer systems to track inventory, orders, and deliveries. Large retailers have similar distribution networks to service their retail outlets, usually with the aid of point-of-sale (POS) entry systems (scanners) at cash registers to track sales at individual outlets. Some shoe companies use electronic data interchange (EDI) or, more frequently, the Internet, to allow wholesale customers to place orders electronically. Problems with computer systems can have large financial consequences.

Sales & Marketing

Retail marketing makes heavy use of local print, TV and radio advertising, and instore displays. Brand name companies often provide promotional money to retailers. To move slower selling models, periodic price discounting is common. Retailers usually expend much effort to train sales personnel, the majority of whom work part-time at fairly low wages. Turnover of retail employees can be high.

Brand names are the most valuable asset of shoe companies, which design shoes, arrange for manufacture, and sell them to retailers. Shoes are sold to retailers using an in-house sales force and independent sales representatives. Many companies operate showrooms for wholesale buyers, and exhibit at regional and international trade shows, such as the New York Shoe Expo. Retailers usually place orders with shoe companies three to four months ahead of expected delivery time. Shoe companies, in turn, order raw materials and place orders with their (mainly foreign) manufacturers. Large shoe companies maintain a quality control staff near their foreign manufacturers. There are almost no long-term contracts in the industry, although long-term relationships are very important.

Human Resources

Most jobs in shoe retail stores require few special skills and accordingly pay fairly low wages, just over a third less than the average for all US workers. Because of uneven shopping demand during the day, week, and year, stores use a large number of part-time workers. Due to the low wages and uneven work schedules, personnel turnover can be 50 percent per year or more.

Industry Employment Growth

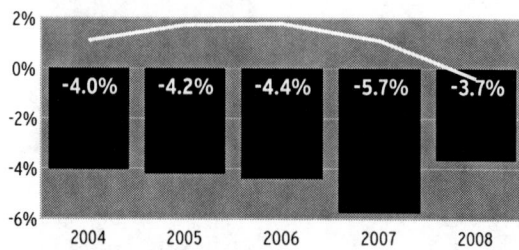

Average Hourly Earnings

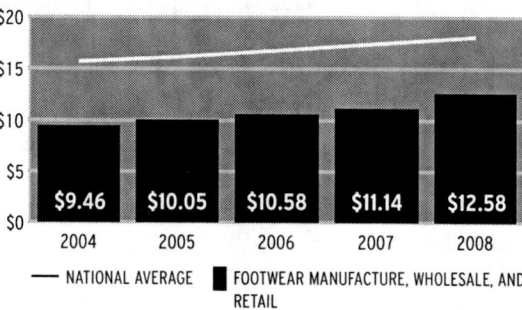

— NATIONAL AVERAGE ■ FOOTWEAR MANUFACTURE, WHOLESALE, AND RETAIL

SOURCE: BUREAU OF LABOR STATISTICS

Call Preparation Questions

What strategies does the company have to grow in the mature US market?

The profitability of US shoe companies depends on marketing skills because retail shoe prices have essentially been flat.

How would the company be affected by restrictions on US shoe imports?

US retailers depend on foreign manufacturers for most of their product, primarily from China, Italy, Brazil, and Spain.

How does the company manage shifts in consumer fashion trends?

Retail shoe sales are subject to uncertain consumer demand, which can leave manufacturers and retailers holding sizable inventories of unwanted goods.

How has the company benefited or been challenged by online sales?

Many shoe companies and retailers operate consumer Internet sites that allow online shopping.

What plans does the company have to enter or expand into international markets?

The popularity of American brands in international markets has provided a growth opportunity beyond the mature US market, especially for athletic shoes, high-end men's dress shoes, and specialty shoes like work boots.

Web Links

American Apparel & Footwear Association

Newsletter, regulatory and trade updates.
www.apparelandfootwear.org

Fashion Footwear Association of New York

New York Shoe Expo.
www.ffany.org/about_ffany.html

Footwear News

Articles and news.
www.footwearnews.com

Nike.com

Internet retailer.
www.nike.com

Shoes.com

Internet retailer.
www.shoes.com

Timberland.com

Internet retailer.
www.timberland.com

Glossary of Acronyms

AAFA — American Apparel and Footwear Association
DOC — Department of Commerce
EDI — electronic data interchange
SGMA — Sporting Goods Manufacturers Association
WTO — World Trade Organization

HOOVER'S TOP COMPANIES

Largest Companies by Sales	($ mil.)
NIKE, Inc.	18,627.0
Collective Brands, Inc.	3,035.4
Brown Shoe Company, Inc.	2,359.9
Retail Ventures, Inc.	1,871.9
New Balance Athletic Shoe, Inc.	1,630.0
Genesco Inc.	1,502.1
Skechers U.S.A., Inc.	1,440.7
DSW Inc.	1,405.6
The Timberland Company	1,364.6
The Finish Line, Inc.	1,277.2

Largest Employers	Employees
NIKE, Inc.	32,500
Collective Brands, Inc.	31,000
Retail Ventures, Inc.	17,342
Genesco Inc.	13,950
The Finish Line, Inc.	13,100
Brown Shoe Company, Inc.	13,100
Reebok International Ltd.	9,102
The Timberland Company	6,300
Nine West Group Inc.	6,000
DSW Inc.	5,800

Fastest Growing* by Five-Year Sales Growth	(%)
Crocs, Inc.	259.6
Zappos.com, Inc.	84.8
Heelys, Inc.	69.6
Deckers Outdoor Corporation	41.6
Rocky Brands, Inc.	19.6
Phoenix Footwear Group, Inc.	18.0
DSW Inc.	16.9
The Walking Company Holdings, Inc.	16.5
Genesco Inc.	12.6
NIKE, Inc.	11.7

Fastest Growing* by Five-Year Employee Growth	(%)
Crocs, Inc.	173.2
Zappos.com, Inc.	76.5
Phoenix Footwear Group, Inc.	66.9
Deckers Outdoor Corporation	28.2
Genesco Inc.	19.6
Skechers U.S.A., Inc.	18.5
DSW Inc.	17.2
The Walking Company Holdings, Inc.	13.2
The Timberland Company	9.0
Bakers Footwear Group, Inc.	8.9

Top Public Companies by Market Value	($ mil.)
NIKE, Inc.	26,958.3
Collective Brands, Inc.	1,122.0
Wolverine World Wide, Inc.	1,052.5
Deckers Outdoor Corporation	1,045.4
Brown Shoe Company, Inc.	722.9

* These rates are compounded annualized increases and may have resulted from acquisitions or one time gains. If less than 6 years of data are available, growth is for the years available.

SOURCE: HOOVER'S, INC., DATABASE

Freight Shipping Services

THIS INDUSTRY INCLUDES:

SIC CODES

4731   Arrangement of Transportation of Freight and Cargo

NAICS CODES

4885   Freight Transportation Arrangement

The freight shipping service industry includes about 17,000 companies with combined annual revenue of $34 billion. Major companies include CH Robinson Worldwide, UPS Supply Chain Solutions, and BAX Global, a US subsidiary of Deutsche Bahn. The industry is fragmented: the top 50 companies account for 45 percent of total industry revenue.

Freight shipping service providers, commonly known as freight forwarders and customs brokers, are companies that arrange the transportation of goods from shippers to receivers. The industry doesn't include carriers that directly handle cargo, logistics management consultants, or supply chain management software manufacturers.

Competitive Landscape

Demand is driven by domestic manufacturing output and levels of international trade. The profitability of individual companies depends on efficient operations, extensive relationships in shipper and carrier networks, and industry expertise. Large companies have advantages in account relationships and access to advanced logistics technologies. Small operations can compete effectively by serving a local market, specializing in cargo transfer with specific countries, and facilitating the transport of unusual goods. The industry is somewhat labor-intensive: average annual revenue per employee is $170,000.

Products, Operations & Technology

Major services are freight forwarding and customs brokering. Unlike fully integrated carriers that own truck, rail, air, or ocean assets and transport cargo, freight forwarders arrange the transportation of goods without owning any transportation equipment or handling ("fingerprinting") the cargo. Customs brokers add another layer of expertise by facilitating the clearing of goods through international customs

BUSINESS CHALLENGES

» Demand Tied to Economic Cycles

Freight shipping services depend highly on the volume of domestic and international trade. Economic slowdowns or a drop in consumer confidence typically results in less products being manufactured and shipped; thus, less business for companies that specialize in the efficient transfer of cargo. Shipping volume falls faster than manufacturing activity during an economic slowdown, as distributors and retailers have less inventory turnover.

» Dependence on Free Trade

Forwarders and customs brokers are highly dependent on the free flow of goods among nations. Embargoes, protectionist policies, and trade sanctions can limit or completely halt commerce among nations. Customs brokers that specialize in specific nations can see opportunities shut off entirely when free trade is blocked. Too much free trade can also harm the industry: the free flow of goods with limited customs barriers can reduce the need for experts to deftly navigate customs, tariffs, and filings.

» Increased Competition

The giants of the small package business, FedEx and UPS, have expanded operations to move heavy cargo. Both now maintain internal divisions focused on cargo forwarding. Excellent brand recognition and a network of existing customers have given these larger firms an immediate advantage. Some truck, rail, ship, and air carriers have used Internet technologies to develop internal forwarding and customs capabilities, and have eliminated relationships with third-party forwarders and brokers.

barriers. Most companies specialize in either freight forwarding or customs brokering, though companies and individuals can provide both.

Forwarders are well-versed in the schedules, rates, and availability of cargo carriers. They use this expertise to solve logistics challenges, lower expenses, and minimize delays for companies that ship or receive goods. Forwarders book cargo space with carriers; negotiate rates; arrange insurance; calculate the weight, volume, and cost of goods to be moved; prepare quotations, invoices, bills of lading, and letters of credit; and keep extensive records of all transported products. Forwarders may also act as freight consolidators, buying bulk cargo space on trucks, ships, and airlines only to resell it at a higher rate. Many forwarders specialize in a particular region, industry, or mode of transportation.

Customs brokers 'clear' goods through international customs on behalf of an importing or exporting business. Key responsibilities include preparing documents; submitting information electronically; paying taxes, duties, and excises on behalf of the client; and facilitating communication among the shipper, receiver, and government agencies. Government entities can be both international and domestic, as many goods require clearance and inspection from agencies like the FDA, USDA, or the US Fish and Wildlife Service. Just as forwarders tend to specialize, many customs brokers specialize in certain types of transactions, such as clothing, perishables, or obtaining clearance for the crew and manifest of large ocean vessels.

Shipping service providers can range from a sole, independent proprietor working out of a local office to large corporations with a network of hundreds of small offices and agents. Forwarding companies can also be a part of a freight services franchise. Local offices are largely autonomous: they serve local customers and are responsible for local marketing and for dealing with local contract carriers. In addition to their own offices, forwarders also may maintain a network of agents, especially in foreign locations.

Major technological advances center around proprietary computer systems that find the best routes for a shipment, present alternative fares and schedules, consolidate loads, confirm and bill orders, track and trace shipments, produce management reports, and allow logistics analysis. Some firms allow orders to be placed over the Internet, and by phone, fax, and electronic data interchange (EDI) with large customers. Customs brokers can be connected to the US Customs Automated Export System (AES), which allows shippers to electronically file a Shipper's Export Declaration and Ocean Manifest.

Sales & Marketing

Typical customers are shippers and receivers that need to move cargo within the US or internationally. Shippers include chemical companies, construction firms and building manufacturers, commodity importers and exporters, consumer products companies, food suppliers, and vehicle manufacturers.

Major types of marketing include online ads and rate quotes, telemarketing, and face-to-face visits with potential customers. Large shippers may negotiate national contracts with national or regional customers who are served through local offices.

Internet sales are common, especially for less-than-truckload (LTL) cargo. Potential customers can quickly get rate quotes and compare fees online. For specialized goods and heavier cargo, forwarders and brokers often use online forms to collect information and call back the prospect to discuss terms.

Prices vary depending on route, weight, volume, and demand. Freight shipping service providers make their money on the spread between the rates charged to customers and the rates they pay carriers. To get the most favorable rates, forwarders typically agree to provide a carrier with a minimum number of shipments. The forwarder and the carrier may also agree on general payment terms, but specific rates are negotiated at the time of service. Most sales are to repeat customers with whom the forwarder has long-term relationships. Customer contracts may call for discounts in return for a specific volume of business.

Human Resources

Wages average more than $18 an hour, slightly higher than the national average. Freight forwarding firms that are a part of a larger integrated carrier network may require many low-skilled material handlers and drivers. While background checks are required for customs brokers, a past criminal record doesn't preclude an individual from becoming licensed.

Since assetless forwarders don't handle cargo, the annual injury rate in the freight shipping industry is quite low: 60 percent below the national average. Most injuries involve sprains, strains, soreness, fractures, and bruises.

Industry Employment Growth

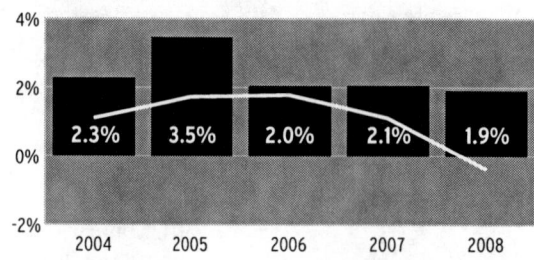

2004	2005	2006	2007	2008
2.3%	3.5%	2.0%	2.1%	1.9%

Average Hourly Earnings

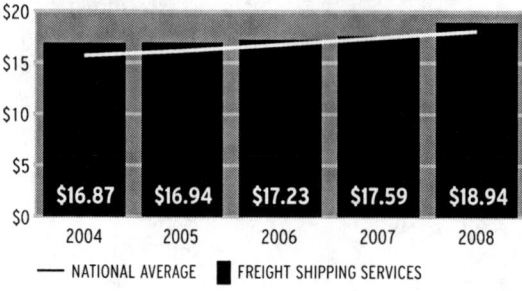

2004	2005	2006	2007	2008
$16.87	$16.94	$17.23	$17.59	$18.94

— NATIONAL AVERAGE ▪ FREIGHT SHIPPING SERVICES

SOURCE: BUREAU OF LABOR STATISTICS

Call Preparation Questions

How do economic slowdowns impact the company?

Freight shipping services depend highly on the volume of domestic and international trade.

How does the company handle slowdowns in global trade due to embargo and trade restrictions?

Forwarders and customs brokers are highly dependent on the free flow of goods among nations.

How has the entrance of FedEx and UPS impacted the company?

The giants of the small package business, FedEx and UPS, have expanded operations to move heavy cargo.

How has shipping deregulation benefited the company?

Deregulation of the trucking, rail, and airline industries has resulted in complex rates and a competitive free market.

What services beyond freight forwarding does the company offer?

Forwarders can take advantage of customers' greater logistics needs to provide services beyond basic freight scheduling.

Web Links

Airforwarders Association

Industry association representing the interest of air cargo forwarders.
www.airforwarders.org

American Association of Port Authorities

Port reports and news.
www.aapa-ports.org

American Trucking Associations

News for the trucking industry.
www.truckline.com

Intermodal Association of North America (IANA)

Trade association promoting the interests of intermodal transport.

www.intermodal.org

International Federation of Customs Brokers Associations

Worldwide industry group representing customs brokers associations.

ifcba.org

National Customs Brokers & Forwarders Association of America (NCBFAA)

Industry association for customs brokers and freight forwarders.

www.ncbfaa.org

NCBFAA Shippers Association (NCBFAASA)

Offshoot of the NCBFAA with a special focus on ocean shipping and forwarding.

www.ncbfaasa.org

Packaging Strategies

News and analysis on the world of packaging.

www.packagingstrategies.com

US Customs and Border Protection (CBP)

Division of Homeland Security that regulates and inspects US trade.

www.customs.gov

Glossary of Acronyms

AES — Automated Export System
EDI — electronic data interchange
FMC — Federal Maritime Commission
IANA — Intermodal Association of North America
IATA — International Air Transport Association
IFF — International freight forwarders
JIT — just-in-time
LTL — less than truckload
NCBFAA — National Customs Brokers & Forwarders Association of America
NVOCC — Non-Vessel Operating Common Carrier

HOOVER'S TOP COMPANIES

Largest Companies by Sales	($ mil.)
United Parcel Service, Inc.	51,486.0
C.H. Robinson Worldwide, Inc.	8,578.6
Expeditors International of Washington, Inc.	5,633.9
Pacer International, Inc.	2,087.7
Hub Group, Inc.	1,860.6
Greatwide Logistics Services, Inc.	1,140.0
ModusLink Global Solutions, Inc.	1,068.2

Largest Employers	Employees
United Parcel Service, Inc.	425,300
Expeditors International of Washington, Inc.	12,310
Caterpillar Logistics Services, Inc.	12,000
C.H. Robinson Worldwide, Inc.	7,332
APL Logistics, Ltd.	5,000
ModusLink Global Solutions, Inc.	3,200
Greatwide Logistics Services, Inc.	3,000
Cardinal Logistics Management Corporation	2,000
Phoenix International Freight Services, Ltd.	1,800
Pacer International, Inc.	1,443

Fastest Growing* by Five-Year Sales Growth	(%)
Echo Global Logistics, Inc.	261.7
NuState Energy Holdings, Inc.	93.6
AutoInfo, Inc.	42.3
ModusLink Global Solutions, Inc.	19.6
C.H. Robinson Worldwide, Inc.	18.9
Expeditors International of Washington, Inc.	16.5
United Parcel Service, Inc.	9.0
Janel World Trade Ltd.	7.8
Hub Group, Inc.	6.5
General Freight Services, Inc.	4.9

Fastest Growing* by Five-Year Employee Growth	(%)
General Freight Services, Inc.	37.3
Janel World Trade Ltd.	14.5
C.H. Robinson Worldwide, Inc.	12.7
Expeditors International of Washington, Inc.	9.4
Hub Group, Inc.	4.2
Greatwide Logistics Services, Inc.	3.5
United Parcel Service, Inc.	2.2

Top Public Companies by Market Value	($ mil.)
United Parcel Service, Inc.	37,619.1
C.H. Robinson Worldwide, Inc.	9,379.1
Expeditors International of Washington, Inc.	7,052.4
Hub Group, Inc.	980.8
Pacer International, Inc.	322.9

* These rates are compounded annualized increases and may have resulted from acquisitions or one time gains. If less than 6 years of data are available, growth is for the years available.

SOURCE: HOOVER'S, INC., DATABASE

Fruit and Tree Nut Farming

The fruit and tree nut farming industry includes about 100,000 farms with combined annual revenue of $17 billion. Major US companies include Dole Food Company, almond cooperative Blue Diamond Growers, the National Grape Cooperative and its Welch's subsidiary, and citrus cooperative Florida's Natural Growers. The industry is fragmented: the top 5 percent of farms generate around 40 percent of industry revenue.

Competitive Landscape

Demand is driven by US population growth and consumer trends in food consumption. The profitability of individual companies depends on maximizing crop yield and minimizing risk of disease. Large companies and farm cooperatives have advantages in highly mechanized operations, branded food products, and access to low-cost labor. Small operations can compete effectively by specializing in agritourism as well as organic, heirloom, or unusual fruits and nuts. The industry is highly labor-intensive: average annual revenue per employee (both farm operators and workers) is less than $20,000.

The fruit and nut industry competes with grain, vegetable, and melon farming for crop acreage, as farmers tend to plant and harvest crops with the highest yield and payout.

Products, Operations & Technology

Major products include grapes (30 percent of the market) and apples, almonds, oranges, and strawberries (10 percent each). Other fruits and nuts include blueberries, walnuts, peaches, cherries, and lemons.

A farmer commits to a crop based on available acreage, topography, soil, climate, and financial considerations. Fruit and nut farmers typically concentrate on a small handful of varietals that are the most commercially viable. For apples, a total of 15 varieties account for 90 percent of all apples produced. Three main types of

BUSINESS CHALLENGES

» Highly Volatile Yields, Prices

Fruit and nut crop yields and prices fluctuate sharply due to demand, acres planted, weather conditions, and inventory levels. Some years can produce bumper crops; other times, fruit and nuts are so blemished or damaged that the yield is negligible. Prices received for fruits and nuts commonly swing 100 percent or more from year to year. Tree nut farmers can offset this risk somewhat by maintaining stocks, which isn't an option for fruit farmers.

» Dependence on Low-Cost, Seasonal Labor

Most fruit and nut crops must be handpicked by laborers willing to tolerate inconsistent hours, hard work, and low pay. Farm workers can often find jobs offering comparable pay that is much less labor-intensive. Small or remote orchards can have difficulty finding low-cost laborers to pick fruits and nuts, and groves sometimes go unharvested due to a lack of field workers. Changes in immigration policies and enforcement can affect the availability of migrant workers.

» Weather and Disease

Fruit and nut crops are highly susceptible to damage from hurricanes, high winds, drought, and disease. Fungicides can help control disease outbreaks, but outbreaks still result in entire crops being cut down and replanted. Weather, as with almost all agricultural crops, is a constant challenge. The USDA manages crop insurance and crop disaster assistance programs for farmers facing natural disasters and disease outbreaks, but insurance payouts tend to favor field and grain crops.

strawberries dominate the market: June Bearing, Day Neutral, and Everbearing. California and Arizona orange farmers specialize in navel and Valencia sold whole at retail. Florida's warm and humid weather produces a thin-skinned orange that blemishes easily; thus, most Florida oranges are processed into juice.

Most fruit and nut farms must invest either in expensive picking equipment or seasonal farm labor. Almost all fruits and berries are handpicked. Berry crops require a large pool of seasonal labor and must be harvested every one to three days to maximize yield and encourage additional fruit production. If picked correctly, an acre of strawberries can yield 10,000 pounds of fruit.

The method of picking oranges hasn't changed much since the first grove was planted in Florida 300 years ago: workers handpick fruit from the lower branches and scale ladders up to 18 feet high, collecting the fruit into shoulder bags and filling large field tubs. Field workers can pick around 800 pounds of processed oranges an hour. Specially designed orange farm tractors, called "goats," transfer field tubs of oranges to truck trailers waiting at the edge of the field.

Mechanical tree "shakers" rustle the base of an almond tree, causing the shell to fall to the ground. The nuts dry on the ground, are swept into rows and picked up by machine.

With the exception of berries, fruit and nut trees typically require a long grow time before the first harvest. Almonds need at least seven years to grow from a sapling to a nut-producing tree. Navel oranges are seedless and sterile; the only way to produce new fruit is to graft cuttings onto other varieties of well-established citrus root stock. Grafted branches require at least five years before they start producing fruit. Common inputs include irrigation systems, seed and root stock, chemicals for weed control, fuel, electricity, farm supplies, machinery, and crop nutrients. Operator labor is a significant input, although nearly half of all fruit and nut farms are run by an operator whose primary profession isn't farming.

Recent technological advances include plant hybridization, genetic modification, crop irrigation, and mechanical harvesters. Some fruits hybridize easily, and farmers regularly experiment with new hybrids and genetically modified fruit that are cold- and heat-tolerant, uniform, and more flavorful. Automated irrigation helps ensure the optimal moisture of plants, trees, and fruit. Mechanical harvesters can improve a farm's yield and reduce dependence on seasonal labor.

Sales & Marketing

A farm's key customer depends on the crop and the farm's business model. Fruit and nut farmers often sell to a wide range of customers, including brokers, wholesalers, processors, retailers, restaurants, and directly to customers.

Most major fruit and nut categories have at least one exchange or cooperative. Cooperatives don't rely on third-party wholesalers or brokers; rather, they buy grower-owners' raw goods and turn them into branded products. Examples include Blue Diamond Almonds and Welch's, the product arm of the National Grape Cooperative.

Larger companies and cooperatives advertise through TV, radio, national newspapers, and magazines. Small farms have minimal sales and marketing needs, limiting efforts to word-of-mouth, magazine, or newspaper advertising. Some companies are advertising in new and unusual ways: Dole is experimenting with product placement in video games and Florida's Natural Growers are using YouTube to humorously mock imported oranges.

Farms may be required by state law to pay an assessment to a state commission based on production levels. State commissions such as the Washington Apple Commission promote, educate, and develop the state's apple market. National "checkoff" programs aren't as common: only blueberry, mango, and Hass avocado farmers are required to contribute to a national checkoff board for research and promotion.

Internet sales among fruit and tree nut farmers are much more common than in other agricultural sectors. Many large cooperatives and farmers sell products directly on the company website. Some farms have built a business entirely around Internet and mail-order sales. About 60 percent of all fruit and tree nut farmers have Internet access.

Typical prices received by farmers are 30 cents a pound for apples and peaches and $800 a ton for table grapes. Prices for strawberries can range from $40/cwt (per hundredweight) in summer to $150/cwt in winter. Prices for tree nuts range considerably from year to year, depending on the harvest. Almonds and walnuts average around $100 to $200/cwt; pecans, pistachios, and macadamias can reach $300 to $400/cwt.

The marketing spread (the grower's share of the retail price) averages 30 to 35 percent for most fruits and nuts. Citrus fruits have a much lower spread, around 15 to 20 percent.

Fruit and tree nut farmers compete mainly with produce from Asia and Central and South America. Some farmers compete with manufacturers that sell artificial fruit flavorings to food and beverage producers.

Human Resources

Fruit and tree nut farming wages average slightly less than $400 per week, nearly 50 percent lower than the national average. The industry is highly seasonal and labor-intensive. Of the 40 percent of fruit and tree nut farms that rely on hired labor, each farm employs an average of 15 workers, who average only 30 weeks of employment a year. To help recruit migrant workers, around 20 percent of farms provide free housing.

Operators must pay all workers, migrant or not, at least the federal or state minimum wage, whichever is higher. Enforcing this regulation is difficult: according to the Department of Labor, over 50 percent of all farm laborers aren't authorized to work in the US.

Fruit and tree nut farming requires mechanical, horticultural, and managerial skills. The average age of a fruit and tree nut operator is just under 60.

The annual injury rate in fruit and tree nut farming is 75 percent higher than the national average. Most injuries involve sprains, strains, cuts, bruises, and fractures resulting from equipment use and the physical demands of harvesting.

Call Preparation Questions

How much do the farm's yield and prices received change year to year?

Fruit and nut crop yields and prices fluctuate sharply due to demand, acres planted, weather conditions, and inventory levels.

How challenging is finding and keeping seasonal farmworkers?

Most fruit and nut crops must be handpicked by laborers willing to tolerate inconsistent hours, hard work, and low pay.

What percentage of the farm's revenues comes from unusual or heirloom varietals?

Fruit and tree nut farmers may find that rare and heirloom varietals can increase demand and revenues.

Web Links

Almond Board of California

USDA-initiated almond agency.
www.almondboard.com

California Walnut Commission

USDA-initiated walnut board.
www.walnuts.org

Florida Department of Citrus

Florida government agency that promotes, regulates, and researches the Florida citrus industry.
www.floridajuice.com

National Grape Cooperative

Grape-grower cooperative, including Welch's.
www.nationalgrape.com

North American Blueberry Council

National checkoff program for highbush blueberries.
www.blueberry.org

Glossary of Acronyms

AMS — Agricultural Marketing Service
CWT — hundredweight
FSA — Farm Service Agency
MSPA — Migrant and Seasonal Agricultural Worker Protection Act
TTB — Alcohol and Tobacco Tax and Trade Bureau

HOOVER'S TOP COMPANIES

Largest Companies by Sales	($ mil.)
Dole Food Company, Inc.	6,931.0
Roll International Corporation	1,980.0
Calavo Growers, Inc.	361.5
Alico, Inc.	116.4
Blue Diamond Growers	—
Cranberries Limited, Inc.	—
National Grape Cooperative Association, Inc.	—
Sunkist Growers, Inc.	—

Largest Employers	Employees
Dole Food Company, Inc.	45,000
Roll International Corporation	3,714
Blue Diamond Growers	1,500
National Grape Cooperative Association, Inc.	1,200
Calavo Growers, Inc.	830
Naumes, Inc.	700
Setton International Foods, Inc.	375
Lykes Bros. Inc.	250
Brooks Tropicals, Inc.	250
ML Macadamia Orchards, L.P.	249

Fastest Growing* by Five-Year Sales Growth	(%)
Alico, Inc.	19.2
Roll International Corporation	15.7
Dole Food Company, Inc.	9.8
Calavo Growers, Inc.	7.9

Fastest Growing* by Five-Year Employee Growth	(%)
Alico, Inc.	21.3
Roll International Corporation	17.6
Calavo Growers, Inc.	8.8

Top Public Companies by Market Value	($ mil.)
Alico, Inc.	349.7
Calavo Growers, Inc.	146.4

* These rates are compounded annualized increases and may have resulted from acquisitions or one time gains. If less than 6 years of data are available, growth is for the years available.

SOURCE: HOOVER'S, INC., DATABASE

Fruit and Vegetable Processing

The fruit and vegetable processing industry in the US includes about 2,000 companies with combined annual revenue of $40 billion. Large companies include Heinz, McCain, Del Monte, JR Simplot, grower cooperatives like Ocean Spray and Diamond Foods, and divisions of large food companies like ConAgra and General Mills. The industry is highly concentrated: the 50 largest companies hold more than 75 percent of the market. Smaller companies have local or regional operations that don't require the large distribution systems of the big companies.

Competitive Landscape

Demand is driven by food consumption, which depends on population growth. The profitability of individual companies depends on efficient operations because products are commodities subject to intense price competition. Companies compete largely based on cost and their ability to distribute the finished product. Large companies have advantages in distribution operations. Small companies can compete effectively in local or regional markets.

Products, Operations & Technology

The major processed crops in the US are tomatoes (solid tomato and tomato paste products); potatoes (French fries, potato chips); and oranges (orange juice). Other important processed products include corn; cucumbers (pickles); beans; grapefruit; apples (apple juice, applesauce); grapes (raisins); strawberries; pineapples; and nuts. The two major types of operation are canning and freezing. Canned goods account for about 60 percent of industry revenue. A typical canning operation has 100 workers and produces annual revenue of $250,000 per worker. Some processing plants have more than 1,000 workers. Freezing operations are similar in size, but produce slightly less revenue per worker, about $180,000.

BUSINESS CHALLENGES

» Crop Costs Variable

Crop yields and prices can change yearly due to weather, disease, and supply and demand. Processors sell large quantities of commodity products at fairly low prices; however, if a crop yield is poor, the processor usually can't raise prices enough to offset the lower volume because consumers will switch to alternative products.

» Dependence on Large Customers

Consolidation in the grocery and restaurant industries and the rise of mass food merchandisers, like Costco and Wal-Mart, has funneled demand through fewer but larger customers. Local and regional processors may depend on just a few customers for the bulk of business. Even national processors depend on large national accounts for much business: recently, just 15 customers accounted for 60 percent of sales for Del Monte; Wal-Mart accounted for 18 percent.

» Highly Seasonal Cash Flow

Many crops have a single harvesting season and are perishable, so that farmers must be paid, temporary workers hired, and canning materials bought over a period of just a few months. Some crops, like potatoes, have several harvests per year and can be inventoried, so production can be spread out. Because processing companies often have little collateral available, working capital loans are often perceived as risky.

Raw materials are usually acquired from contract growers, who grow specific varieties of plants according to processor requirements. In Maine, for example, farmers grow Russet Burbank and Shepody potatoes for French fry processors, and various specialty varieties for potato chip processors. Grower contracts are usually for one year and typically specify product quality, a base price, and various price adjustments. While growers contract for a certain acreage, quantities of product can't be specified because crop yields can be sharply affected by weather and other factors. Almost all tomatoes are grown under contract because of their high perishability, whereas a large open market exists for oranges and potatoes. Supply contracts for some fruits can extend up to ten years. Because fruit trees may not produce for several years, growers need long commitments. In long-term supply contracts, prices are negotiated annually.

Some canning operators produce their own cans, but most buy them from outside suppliers. Del Monte, the largest US canner, buys most of its cans under a 10-year contract with renewable five-year terms. Plant operations are usually highly seasonal, coinciding with the growth cycle of the crop; for many fruits and vegetables, this means harvesting and processing ("packing") from June to October. Temporary workers are hired and inventories grow substantially during the "pack" season. Some crops, such as potatoes, can have several harvests per year (although fall potatoes are by far the largest crop). To use plants most efficiently, many companies handle more than one crop, contracting for crops with differing harvest seasons.

While French fry, potato chip, and fruit processing plants produce a finished product, orange juice processors may produce bulk frozen concentrated orange juice (FCOJ) sold to remanufacturers that either package it as frozen orange juice or mix it with water and flavorings and package it as reconstituted, ready-to-serve (recon RTS) orange juice. About 70 percent of tomato processing is in the form of concentrated tomato paste (31 percent natural tomato soluble solids, or NTSS) that is shipped to remanufacturers. Economies in transportation generally favor the location of fruit and vegetable processing plants near production fields, but FCOJ is more cheaply shipped to processors near customer markets, and potato chip processors are usually located near customer markets because their finished product is fragile.

The technology to produce tomato products, French fries, potato chips, and orange juice is well-known and simple. Most processing operations are highly automated, but fruit sorting is still largely done by hand.

Sales & Marketing

Processed fruits and vegetables are marketed into three different channels: consumer, food service, and food processing. Food service (restaurants) has become the biggest market for French fries. Potato chips and orange juice are sold mainly as consumer products. Tomato products are sold into all three markets, but emphasis is on further processing into catsup, pasta sauces, and pizza toppings. Marketing for consumer products is often through food brokers, who place product with grocery chains. Local operators may sell directly to local chains. Food service and processing sales are handled by a sales force and wholesalers. Many processors produce private-label brands under contracts with local and regional retailers.

Human Resources

Most jobs in fruit and vegetable processing require only minimal skills and pay is therefore below average, around $13 hourly, three below the national wage. A large number of jobs are seasonal: Del Monte, one of the largest processors, doubles its workforce with temporary workers during pack seasons. Fringe benefits in the industry average a fairly high 33 percent addition to wages. The industry's safety record is poor: about eight injury cases a year per 100 full-time workers, three more than the national average.

Industry Employment Growth

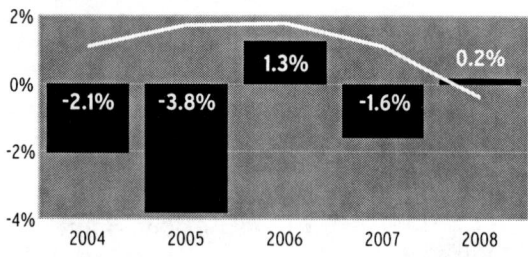

Average Hourly Earnings

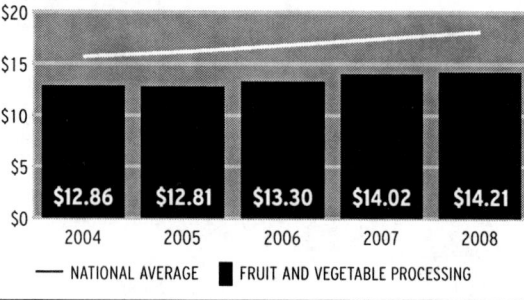

SOURCE: BUREAU OF LABOR STATISTICS

Call Preparation Questions

How does the company protect against changes in raw material and crop prices?

Crop yields and prices can change yearly due to weather, disease, and supply and demand.

How dependent is the company on a few large customers?

Consolidation in the grocery and restaurant industries and the rise of mass food merchandisers, like Costco and Wal-Mart, has funneled demand through fewer but larger customers.

How does the company manage seasonal cash flow?

Many crops have a single harvesting season and are perishable, so that farmers must be paid, temporary workers hired, and canning materials bought over a period of just a few months.

Web Links

California League of Food Processors

Industry statistics and news, mainly about tomatoes.
www.clfp.com

California Tomato Growers Association

Industry statistics and news.
www.ctga.org

Citrus Administrative Committee

Weekly citrus processing reports for Florida.
www.citrusadministrativecommittee.org

Florida Citrus Processors Association

Detailed weekly production reports.
www.fcplanet.org

Florida Department of Citrus

Industry production and retail sales statistics.
www.floridajuice.com

Global Potato News

National and international news.
www.potatonews.com

The Food Institute

Food industry news.
www.foodinstitute.com

The Grower magazine

Excellent grower industry links.
www.growermagazine.com/Links/tabid/70

The Produce News

News.
www.theproducenews.com

US Department of Agriculture

Economic Research Service. Briefing Rooms for potatoes, tomatoes, fruit, vegetables, etc.
www.ers.usda.gov/Briefing

USDA Market Reports

Government weekly price and volume reports.
www.marketnews.usda.gov/portal/fv

Glossary of Acronyms

ERS — Economic Research Service
FCOJ — frozen concentrated orange juice
NFC — not from concentrate (orange juice)
NTSS — natural tomato soluble solids
RECON RTS — reconstituted, ready-to-serve (orange juice)

HOOVER'S TOP COMPANIES

Largest Companies by Sales	($ mil.)
ConAgra Foods, Inc.	11,605.7
H. J. Heinz Company	10,070.8
Campbell Soup Company	7,998.0
Del Monte Foods Company	3,736.8
The Schwan Food Company	3,300.0
J.R. Simplot Company	3,000.0
Rich Products Corporation	2,650.0
The J. M. Smucker Company	2,524.8
TreeHouse Foods, Inc.	1,500.7
Goya Foods, Inc.	1,260.0

Largest Employers	Employees
H. J. Heinz Company	32,500
ConAgra Foods, Inc.	25,000
The Schwan Food Company	22,000
Campbell Soup Company	19,400
Del Monte Foods Company	18,100
J.R. Simplot Company	10,000
Rich Products Corporation	7,200
TreeHouse Foods, Inc.	3,400
The J. M. Smucker Company	3,250
Goya Foods, Inc.	3,000

Fastest Growing* by Five-Year Sales Growth	(%)
Cuisine Solutions, Inc.	25.8
TreeHouse Foods, Inc.	16.6
The J. M. Smucker Company	14.0
Overhill Farms, Inc.	11.8
Del Monte Foods Company	11.5
Goya Foods, Inc.	10.9
Seneca Foods Corporation	10.9
B&G Foods, Inc.	9.9
Rich Products Corporation	8.2
H. J. Heinz Company	4.1

Fastest Growing* by Five-Year Employee Growth	(%)
Seneca Foods Corporation	15.6
Cuisine Solutions, Inc.	14.5
Overhill Farms, Inc.	8.5
TreeHouse Foods, Inc.	6.1
B&G Foods, Inc.	3.9
Goya Foods, Inc.	3.7
The J. M. Smucker Company	3.2
Rich Products Corporation	2.1
Del Monte Foods Company	1.0

Top Public Companies by Market Value	($ mil.)
H. J. Heinz Company	14,648.3
Campbell Soup Company	12,762.6
ConAgra Foods, Inc.	11,324.6
The J. M. Smucker Company	2,724.6
Del Monte Foods Company	1,734.1

* These rates are compounded annualized increases and may have resulted from acquisitions or one time gains. If less than 6 years of data are available, growth is for the years available.

SOURCE: HOOVER'S, INC., DATABASE

Fuel Oil and LP Gas Dealers

The fuel oil and liquid petroleum gas dealer (fuel dealer) industry includes about 10,000 companies with combined annual revenue of $20 billion. Major companies include AmeriGas Partners, Ferrellgas Partners, and Star Gas Partners. The industry is fragmented and regional: the top 50 companies hold less than 40 percent of sales.

The majority of liquid petroleum gas dealers described in this profile are propane dealers, and LP gas refers to liquid propane gas. Major uses for LP gas include heating, powering large vehicles, and drying crops. Uses of fuel oil include space heating, water heating, cooking, and grilling.

Competitive Landscape

Residential, commercial, industrial, and agricultural heating needs drive demand. The profitability of individual companies depends on efficient operations, low-cost purchasing, and competitive pricing. Large companies have advantages in purchasing, finance, and distribution. Small companies can compete effectively by serving a local market, offering unique products, or providing special services. Average annual revenue per worker is about $250,000.

Fuel dealers compete with suppliers of other energy sources, including electricity and natural gas. The increased availability of natural gas has resulted in stagnant and declining markets for LP gas and fuel oil as home heating sources. In addition, companies may compete with farm cooperatives that sell energy to members.

Products, Operations & Technology

Major products sold include fuel oil (40 percent of industry sales); LP gas (40 percent); and auto fuel (10 percent). Fuel oil includes various grades (mostly No. 2 for heating) and kerosene. LP gas includes bulk and bottled forms. Auto fuels include diesel fuel and gas. LP gas dealers may rent storage tanks to customers or have

BUSINESS CHALLENGES

» Volatile Supply Costs

The cost of fuel oil and LP gas depends highly on the constantly fluctuating price of crude oil. Commodity prices for propane and fuel oil can change up to 80 percent in a single year; most suppliers increase wholesale prices accordingly. While dealers typically pass wholesale price increases to customers, most hesitate to raise prices enough to fully recover extreme rises in fuel costs. Customer price protection programs, which help retain customers, can hurt dealer profits when wholesale prices jump.

» Increasing Competition from Natural Gas

Growing availability of natural gas in the residential market has resulted in steady customer attrition for fuel dealers and flat market growth for LP gas dealers. Residential demand for fuel oil decreased 10 percent and propane demand was flat between 2000 and 2005, partially due to customers switching to natural gas. In general, LP gas and fuel oil are more expensive than natural gas. As a result of declining demand, most fuel dealers must rely on acquisitions to grow sales.

» Dependence on Weather

Abnormally warm winters can affect sales since most customers rely on fuel oil and propane for heating. Inclement weather during the grilling season (spring and summer) can reduce sales for smaller propane tanks. Because a large percentage of refineries are on the Gulf Coast, natural disasters can disrupt the supply chain.

portable tank exchanges. Companies may also sell, install, or service heating equipment.

Fuel oil and LP gas are derivatives of crude oil. Fuel oil is a distillate of crude oil, and is formed when oil is heated to a gas state and condensed. Of the six grades of fuel oil, No. 2 grade distillate is the type used for heating. LP gas is a by-product of natural gas production and petroleum refining. Extremely low temperatures or increased pressure converts gas to liquid, making it easier to transport. Fuel oil and

LP gas are not interchangeable and conversion to a different fuel requires new heating equipment.

Fuel dealers generally serve suburban and rural areas without access to natural gas. Many small companies are family-owned and handed down from one generation to the next. Demand for different types of fuel is regional and based on the type of heating equipment used in a particular market. Companies may consider geographical size, the number and density of potential customers, types of fuel usage, competition, typical weather conditions, and existing infrastructure for supply when considering new markets. Fuel oil dealers service an average of 2,600 residential accounts, sell about 3 million gallons of heating oil, and generate less than $5 million annually, according to Fuel Oil News.

While large LP gas dealers can have hundreds of distribution outlets, the average dealer has at least two with storage tanks to hold fuel, according to LP Gas. On average, tank capacity for small LP gas dealers is about 45,000 gallons, while capacity for large dealers is 500,000. Tank capacity for fuel oil dealers averages 230,000 gallons, but varies widely by region. Dealers may own or lease secondary storage facilities to hold fuel during periods of low demand, such as summer.

Companies use tanker trucks or bobtail trucks to transport fuel to customer tanks. Independent fuel oil dealers have about seven trucks. The average truck holds between 2,400 and 3,300 gallons, although larger transport trucks meant to service commercial customers can hold up to 9,000 gallons. Residential customer tanks typically hold between 250 and 550 gallons of fuel. Customers may receive multiple deliveries annually and can opt for automatic deliveries. Route planning is important to control costs and to minimize miles traveled between customers.

Dealers buy fuel from oil companies, natural gas processors, and wholesalers. To deliver fuel, dealers may rely on suppliers or use trucking or rail services. Supply agreements may range from six months to three years and include minimum or maximum purchases. Since fuel oil and LP gas are commodity products, pricing is typically based on the market price at the time of the contract or delivery date, plus a differential. Dealers may also buy fuel on the spot market to meet excess demand. Because fuel oil and LP gas are tied to crude oil, prices can be volatile and companies may use contract terms, options, or futures contracts to reduce risk.

Most fuel dealers use computerized information systems to manage receivables, payables, general ledger, and payroll. Companies may also use computer systems to monitor storage tanks remotely, forecast customer fuel use, and track customers. Routing software helps schedule deliveries more efficiently, GPS helps drivers navigate routes, and in-truck terminals give drivers billing capabilities.

Sales & Marketing

While the majority of customers are homeowners, fuel dealers also sell to agricultural, commercial, institutional, and industrial accounts. The average annual customer purchase for propane gas is about 800 gallons, according to LP Gas.

Because fuel oil and LP gas are mature markets, most companies focus on customer retention. In certain states, customers must fill rented LP gas tanks using the dealer owning the tank, which helps minimize customer turnover. Competition can be more intense for fuel oil customers, since most own their tanks. To develop loyalty, dealers may offer automated tank monitoring and refilling, or fixed-term contracts.

Word-of-mouth is extremely important. Other marketing and promotion vehicles include local newspaper, radio, TV, or print advertising; and direct mail. The Propane Education and Research Council (PERC) helps promote the use of propane gas and links interested customers with dealers via its website.

Large companies typically have Internet sites providing basic company, product, and local contact information. Some large dealers offer online billing. Few small dealers have websites because most operate within a limited geographic market.

Retail prices for fuels vary with market prices, except for customers with contracts at a set price. In the past five years, average prices for retail fuel oil ranged from $1.16 to $2.70 per gallon, and $1.12 to $2.01 for propane. Companies typically determine prices based on a margin over wholesale cost. When possible, companies pass wholesale price increases to customers.

Human Resources

Typical positions include repairmen, truck drivers, mechanics, and customer service and sales associates. Wages are about 10 percent lower than the average for all US workers. Some large companies have partially unionized workforces. Government regulations require training and certification for workers handling fuel.

The industry injury rate is 60 percent higher than the US average. Dealing with heavy equipment and handling hazardous substances accounts for the higher rate of strains, sprains, and burns.

Industry Employment Growth

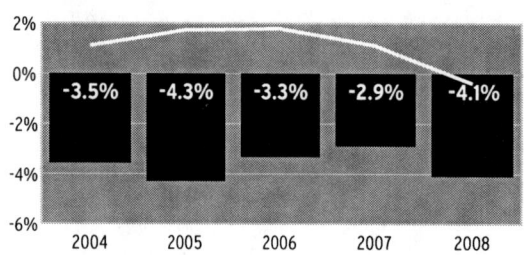

Average Hourly Earnings

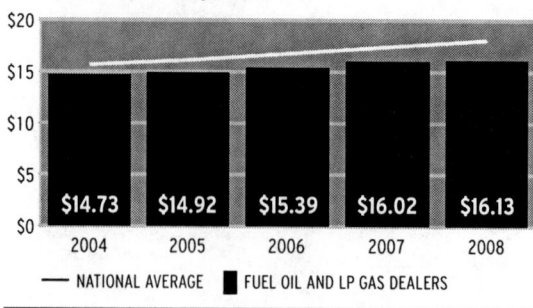

SOURCE: BUREAU OF LABOR STATISTICS

Call Preparation Questions

How does volatility in the crude oil market affect the company?

The cost of fuel oil and LP gas depends highly on the constantly fluctuating price of crude oil.

How has increased availability of natural gas affected the company's customer base?

Growing availability of natural gas in the residential market has resulted in steady customer attrition for fuel dealers and flat market growth for LP gas dealers.

How does weather affect demand in the company's market?

Abnormally warm winters can affect sales since most customers rely on fuel oil and propane for heating.

What storage issues does the company face?

Larger storage tanks allow companies to buy greater quantities of fuel and negotiate better prices with suppliers.

How does weak demand for fuel oil/LP gas affect the company's long-term strategy?

Companies can balance declining or stagnant demand for fuel oil and LP gas by offering complementary products and services.

Web Links

Energy Information Administration

Consumption, production, and pricing trends.
www.eia.doe.gov

Fuel Oil News

News, trends, statistics, industry study.
www.fueloilnews.com

LP Gas Magazine

News, trends, statistics, issues annual state of the industry report.
www.lpgasmagazine.com

National Biodiesel Board

Sales, trends, and news about biofuels.
www.biodiesel.org

National Oilheat Research Alliance

News, research, and education site.
www.nora-oilheat.org

National Propane Gas Association

News, trends, regulatory issues from trade association.
www.npga.org

Oilheating Manufacturers Association

News, statistics, consumer information.
www.oilheat.com

Propane Education and Research Council

Trends, surveys, and news.
www.propanecouncil.org

Glossary of Acronyms

API — American Petroleum Institute
EIA — Energy Information Administration
HVAC — heating, ventilation, and air conditioning
LP — liquid propane or liquid petroleum
LPG — liquid propane or liquid petroleum gas
MCF — thousand cubic feet
NBB — National Biodiesel Board
NFPA — National Fire Protection Association
NORA — National Oilheat Research Alliance
NPGA — National Propane Gas Association
OMA — Oilheat Manufacturers Association
PERC — Propane Education and Research Council

HOOVER'S TOP COMPANIES

Largest Companies by Sales	($ mil.)
Energy Transfer Partners, L.P.	9,293.9
UGI Corporation	6,648.2
Mansfield Oil Company	5,100.0
AmeriGas Partners, L.P.	2,815.2
Ferrellgas Partners, L.P.	2,290.7
Inergy Holdings, L.P.	1,878.9
Suburban Propane Partners, L.P.	1,574.2
Star Gas Partners, L.P.	1,543.1

Largest Employers	Employees
UGI Corporation	6,200
AmeriGas Partners, L.P.	6,200
Energy Transfer Partners, L.P.	5,316
Ferrellgas Partners, L.P.	3,508
Inergy Holdings, L.P.	3,104
Suburban Propane Partners, L.P.	2,985
Star Gas Partners, L.P.	2,817
MFA Oil Company	1,500
RBS Sempra Commodities	1,200
Petroleum Marketers, Inc.	1,100

Fastest Growing* by Five-Year Sales Growth	(%)
Energy Transfer Partners, L.P.	74.7
Mansfield Oil Company	55.8
Able Energy, Inc.	43.0
Inergy Holdings, L.P.	38.9
SMF Energy Corporation	29.3
UGI Corporation	17.0
Suburban Propane Partners, L.P.	15.3
Ferrellgas Partners, L.P.	13.4
Chesapeake Utilities Corporation	12.7
AmeriGas Partners, L.P.	11.6

Fastest Growing* by Five-Year Employee Growth	(%)
Able Energy, Inc.	74.1
Energy Transfer Partners, L.P.	29.0
Mansfield Oil Company	13.8
UGI Corporation	5.1
SMF Energy Corporation	3.8
AmeriGas Partners, L.P.	1.7
Inergy Holdings, L.P.	1.4
Star Gas Partners, L.P.	0.8

Top Public Companies by Market Value	($ mil.)
Energy Transfer Partners, L.P.	5,173.0
UGI Corporation	2,971.1
AmeriGas Partners, L.P.	1,734.8
Ferrellgas Partners, L.P.	1,244.1
Suburban Propane Partners, L.P.	1,120.2

* These rates are compounded annualized increases and may have resulted from acquisitions or one time gains. If less than 6 years of data are available, growth is for the years available.

SOURCE: HOOVER'S, INC., DATABASE

Funeral Operations

The US funeral industry includes 15,000 companies that generate about $15 billion of annual revenue from the operation of 16,000 funeral homes and 7,000 crematoriums and cemeteries. Large companies include Service Corporation International and Stewart Enterprises. The industry remains highly fragmented, despite strong consolidation in the 1990s. The top 50 companies hold only about 30 percent of the market. Most companies operate a single funeral home, with annual revenue close to $1 million.

Competitive Landscape

Demand for services is driven mainly by the number of older Americans. The profitability of individual companies depends on good marketing and efficient operations because local demand is relatively fixed. The main advantage of large companies is their ability to share resources (like cars, personnel, and marketing costs) among clusters of funeral homes. Small operators can compete successfully with national companies because the funeral business is intensely local. The industry is fairly labor-intensive: annual revenue per employee is $100,000.

Products, Operations & Technology

Companies in the industry sell products like caskets, burial vaults, burial garments, flowers, burial rights, memorial stones, and cremation urns. Services include body preparation, transportation, facility rental for wakes and memorial services, opening and closing burial plots, and cremation. Caskets are the largest cost item for most funerals. National suppliers include Batesville Casket, Aurora Casket, and Matthews International. Most funeral homes conduct fewer than 100 funerals a year and have a large investment in physical assets that are often idle.

In addition to providing products and services for current ("at-need") funerals, some

BUSINESS CHALLENGES

» Competition from Low-Cost Cremations

An increasing percentage of funerals involve cremation rather than the more expensive traditional casket and burial. About 25 percent of families choose cremation; the percentage of funerals with cremation doubled in the past two decades, and is expected to increase to 36 percent by 2010, according to the Cremation Association of North America.

» Market Growth Depends on Local Demographics

Demand for funeral services depends on local demographics. Advances in health care and the current age mix of the population indicate that the national mortality rate will be flat for a couple of decades, then rise rapidly due to aging baby boomers. In some retirement markets, the death rate exceeds the birth rate. Currently, there are about 2.5 million deaths in the US each year.

» Tighter Government Regulation

Past abuses led to regulation; present abuses and potential for geographic monopolies may lead to more. Federal and state regulations apply to industry marketing and practices, such as administration of pre-need funeral contracts. Additional regulation of pre-need contracts is possible. Also being discussed is legislation or regulation that would prohibit ownership of cemeteries by funeral home operators, or that would make common ownership of funeral homes in a particular geographical area ("clustering") more difficult.

companies sell "pre-need" services, including price-guaranteed prearranged funerals and sales of burial plots. These sales are generally paid for through monthly installments, although lump-sum payments may also be made. Because the installment payments may be insufficient to cover costs if the customer dies early, companies often use the installment payments to buy a life insurance policy on the customer. State laws may require companies to put a portion of the installment payments into a trust fund to ensure the delivery of future services, or may require companies to post surety bonds to ensure future performance.

Sales & Marketing

Major end-use customers are relatives of the deceased and, to a lesser degree, people making prior arrangements for their own funerals. Marketing funeral services is difficult, because death is an unpleasant topic for most consumers. Funeral homes typically draw business from the surrounding community, often according to religious faith. Location and reputation are important marketing factors. Funeral homes typically advertise through local newspapers and Yellow Pages. The marketing of pre-need services may be through telemarketing, direct mail, or home visits.

Prices vary depending on how elaborate a service package the consumer purchases. Caskets are expensive: the average consumer price is about $1,300. While funeral costs may be as high as $10,000, the average revenue per funeral is about $4,000, including casket.

Human Resources

Some industry jobs require low or average skills, but others require specialized training. Embalmers must pass collegiate science courses, such as human anatomy, pathology, and chemistry. Embalmers learn to work with a variety of toxic chemicals and to handle bodies with infectious diseases, including AIDS and tuberculosis. Industry wages are slightly below the national average for all US workers. Annual personnel turnover is slightly lower than the national average, and the safety record is better than the national average.

Industry Employment Growth

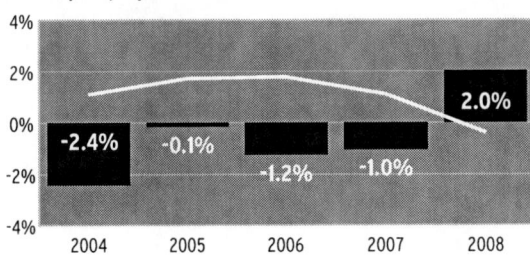

2004	2005	2006	2007	2008
-2.4%	-0.1%	-1.2%	-1.0%	2.0%

Average Hourly Earnings

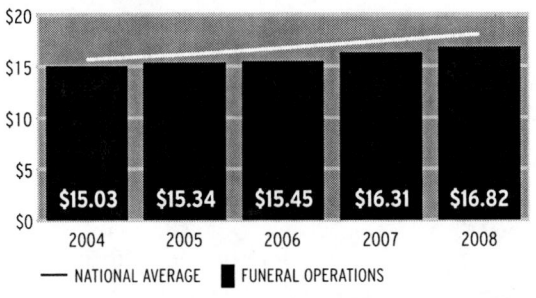

2004	2005	2006	2007	2008
$15.03	$15.34	$15.45	$16.31	$16.82

— NATIONAL AVERAGE ■ FUNERAL OPERATIONS

SOURCE: BUREAU OF LABOR STATISTICS

Call Preparation Questions

How is the increase in low-cost cremation services affecting the company?

An increasing percentage of funerals involve cremation rather than the more expensive traditional casket and burial.

What are mortality rates in the company's market area?

Demand for funeral services depends on local demographics.

How is the company challenged to meet stricter federal and state regulations?

Past abuses led to regulation; present abuses and potential for geographic monopolies may lead to more.

What plans does the company have to offer auxiliary services?

Funeral homes seek to extend their portfolios by providing services that families often use, including legal assistance, bereavement counseling, and family archiving of photographs and other memorabilia.

What opportunities or challenges does the company see in using Internet technology?

Some funeral homes provide the option, at a monthly cost, of memorial websites, where mourners can post pictures and comments about the deceased.

Web Links

Cremation Association of North America

Publications, statistics, FAQs, and links.
www.cremationassociation.org

Federal Trade Commission: Funerals – A Consumer Guide

Information on fair practices and disclosures.
www.ftc.gov/bcp/edu/pubs/consumer/products/pro19.shtm

funeralWire.com

Latest industry news.
www.funeralwire.com

International Cemetery and Funeral Association

Latest industry news.
www.icfa.org

International Conference of Funeral Service Examining Boards

Links, news, publications, careers, and statistics.
www.cfseb.org

National Funeral Directors Association

Publications, articles, and library information.
www.nfda.org

National Selected Independent Funeral Homes

Links and other information.
www.nsm.org

State Funeral Director Associations

Links to all state associations.
http://www.nfda.org/page.php?pID=296

Glossary of Acronyms

CAA — Cremation Association of America
CANA — Cremation Association of North America
CFSA — Casket and Funeral Supply Association
NCHS — National Center for Health Statistics
NFDA — National Funeral Directors Association
SCI — Service Corporation International

HOOVER'S TOP COMPANIES

Largest Companies by Sales	($ mil.)
Service Corporation International	2,155.6
Stewart Enterprises, Inc.	527.9
Carriage Services, Inc.	167.8
StoneMor Partners L.P.	145.3

Largest Employers	Employees
Service Corporation International	20,591
Stewart Enterprises, Inc.	5,400
StoneMor Partners L.P.	2,169
Carriage Services, Inc.	1,781
Forever Enterprises, Inc.	232

Fastest Growing* by Five-Year Sales Growth	(%)
StoneMor Partners L.P.	17.6
Carriage Services, Inc.	1.7
Stewart Enterprises, Inc.	0.2

Fastest Growing* by Five-Year Employee Growth	(%)
StoneMor Partners L.P.	19.7
Service Corporation International	11.0

Top Public Companies by Market Value	($ mil.)
Service Corporation International	1,239.9
Stewart Enterprises, Inc.	459.0
StoneMor Partners L.P.	172.3
Carriage Services, Inc.	169.1

* These rates are compounded annualized increases and may have resulted from acquisitions or one time gains. If less than 6 years of data are available, growth is for the years available.

SOURCE: HOOVER'S, INC., DATABASE

Furniture Manufacturing

Furniture manufacture in the US generates about $65 billion in sales from 20,000 companies. Large companies include Steelcase, Herman Miller, La-Z-Boy, Sealy, and Furniture Brands International. The average company operates a single plant and produces less than $50 million in annual revenue. Some sectors, such as metal office furniture, are highly concentrated, but the industry as a whole is fragmented: the largest 50 companies hold less than 40 percent of the market. The industry is fairly labor-intensive: average annual revenue per worker is about $130,000.

Competitive Landscape

The volume of home furniture sold depends heavily on the level of home sales, while office furniture sales depend on the health of the US economy. The profitability of individual companies is closely linked to volume, since many costs are fixed. Small companies can compete effectively if they produce specialty items or high-quality workmanship that can sell for a premium price. Imports have become a major competitive factor.

Products, Operations & Technology

Manufacturers generally specialize in either household furniture ($40 billion market) or office furniture ($25 billion). Within the household segment, wood furniture accounts for about 60 percent of sales; upholstered furniture 30 percent; and mattresses, metal furniture, and other products 10 percent. Products include "case goods" (bedroom, living room, and dining room furniture); upholstered items like sofas and recliners, kitchen cabinets, mattresses and box springs; and other items such as occasional furniture, home entertainment centers, and grandfather clocks. Products may be factory-finished or ready-to-assemble (RTA). Within the office segment, metal furniture accounts for a third of sales, wood furniture a

BUSINESS CHALLENGES

» Strong Dependence on Home Sales, Office Growth

Household and office furniture sales depend on the health of the US economy. Household furniture sales are strongly affected by home sales and new home construction. Office furniture sales are sensitive to job growth, corporate spending, and new business formations.

» Low-Cost Import Competition

Because of the high labor content of most furniture, manufacturers in low-cost countries like Mexico and China are able to compete in the US market despite the disadvantages of longer delivery times and higher transportation costs. For example, furniture imports grew 65 percent in the past five years, including a 150 percent increase from China.

» Dependence on Low Interest Rates

Because large furniture items are expensive, many consumers buy household furniture on credit. High interest rates discourage consumer buying and also affect home sales, which are closely tied to furniture sales.

third, and partitions, showcases, and shelving the other third.

Manufacturing operations are generally in company-owned factories of 50,000 to 200,000 square feet; Steelcase operates some factories with more than 1 million square feet. Larger companies also operate distribution centers and warehouses. Raw materials are the biggest cost item, usually representing about 50 percent of the wholesale price, and include steel, hardwoods, plywood and chipwood, textiles, polyurethane foam, springs, and various glues, paints and finishes.

Because of the vast number of items, styles, coverings, and finishes, much furniture is made-to-order, with delivery times varying between two weeks and several months (for some high-cost items). Despite automation, the made-to-order nature of much of the business means that labor content is high. Even the most efficient household furniture companies produce only $100,000 of sales per employee (compared to $200,000 in steel office furniture manufacture).

Sales & Marketing

In the household segment, larger manufacturers sell directly to retailers, who generally mark up furniture 100 to 150 percent. Some manufacturers, like Ethan Allen and Furniture Brands International, have independently owned captive retail outlets; Sealy sells to 7,000 retail outlets. Smaller manufacturers sell mainly through independent manufacturers' representatives. Trade shows are a primary sales tool for manufacturers: the most important US household trade show is the International Home Furnishings Market in High Point, NC, every fall and spring. In the office segment, distribution is through independent dealers and wholesalers.

Larger companies maintain showrooms in various locations around the country. Furniture lines are targeted to different retail segments based on price and quality. Furniture Brands produces furniture under a dozen brand names, each targeted to a different demographic retail segment.

Human Resources

Furniture manufacturing remains labor-intensive, despite growth in automation. Production workers are semiskilled, but wages are below the national average. Recent surges in furniture imports are consuming a large portion of the domestic furniture market, resulting in US furniture factory closings and job losses.

Due to the hazards of operating equipment and lifting heavy products, the industry's injury and illness rate is 60 percent higher than the national average.

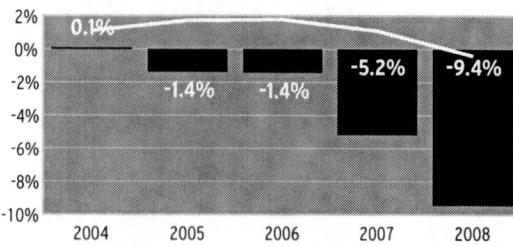

Industry Employment Growth

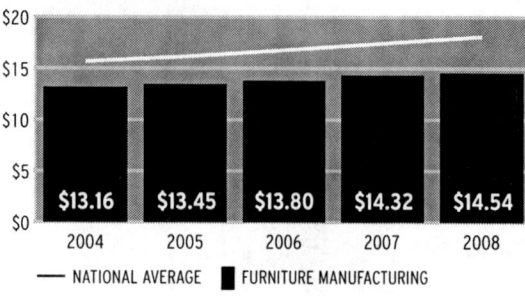

Average Hourly Earnings

— NATIONAL AVERAGE ■ FURNITURE MANUFACTURING

SOURCE: BUREAU OF LABOR STATISTICS

Call Preparation Questions

How does the company manage declines in consumer and business spending on furniture?

Household and office furniture sales depend on the health of the US economy.

How are low-cost imports affecting the company?

Because of the high labor content of most furniture, manufacturers in low-cost countries like Mexico and China are able to compete in the US market despite the disadvantages of longer delivery times and higher transportation costs.

What types of financing does the company offer customers?

Because large furniture items are expensive, many consumers buy household furniture on credit.

How automated is the manufacturing process, and to what benefit?

Newer computer-controlled machinery and automation processes can produce further efficiencies in an industry that, until recently, made almost everything by hand.

How useful is the company's website in helping customers and improving sales?

Small manufacturers can expand sales to retailers and directly to the public using the Internet.

Web Links

AKTRIN Furniture Information Center

Research reports and studies on the furniture industry for sale.
www.furniture-info.com/001-homepage.htm

American Home Furnishings Alliance

Government relations and publications.
www.ahfa.us

Business and Institutional Furniture Manufacturer's Association

News, events, statistics, standards, government issues, and links.
www.bifma.com

Furniture Today

Industry news.
www.furnituretoday.com

Furniture World

Industry news.
www.furninfo.com

International Sleep Products Association

Bedding and bed industry news and trade show calendar.
www.sleepproducts.org

Random Lengths

Wood and timber prices, market analyses, and more.
www.randomlengths.com

Western Home Furnishings Association

Industry information, meetings, events, services, products, and news.
www.whfa.org

Glossary of Acronyms

AHFA — American Home Furnishings Alliance
BIFMA — Business and Institutional Furniture Manufacturers Association
CAD — computer-aided design
HH&I — household and institutional
RTA — ready-to-assemble

HOOVER'S TOP COMPANIES

Largest Companies by Sales	($ mil.)
Leggett & Platt, Incorporated	4,076.1
Ashley Furniture Industries, Inc.	3,430.0
Steelcase Inc.	3,420.8
HNI Corporation	2,477.6
Herman Miller, Inc.	2,012.1
Furniture Brands International, Inc.	1,743.2
Haworth, Inc.	1,660.0
Sealy Corporation	1,498.0
La-Z-Boy Incorporated	1,450.9
Kimball International, Inc.	1,352.0

Largest Employers	Employees
Leggett & Platt, Incorporated	24,000
Ashley Furniture Industries, Inc.	17,000
Steelcase Inc.	13,500
HNI Corporation	13,300
Furniture Brands International, Inc.	11,900
La-Z-Boy Incorporated	10,057
Haworth, Inc.	8,000
Kimball International, Inc.	7,195
Herman Miller, Inc.	6,478
Ethan Allen Interiors Inc.	6,400

Fastest Growing* by Five-Year Sales Growth	(%)
Ashley Furniture Industries, Inc.	19.6
Select Comfort Corporation	18.9
Tempur-Pedic International Inc.	14.1
Simmons Company	10.9
Knoll, Inc.	9.9
Herman Miller, Inc.	8.5
HNI Corporation	7.1
Flexsteel Industries, Inc.	6.8
Steelcase Inc.	5.7
Hooker Furniture Corporation	5.0

Fastest Growing* by Five-Year Employee Growth	(%)
Decorize, Inc.	61.7
Ashley Furniture Industries, Inc.	16.3
Select Comfort Corporation	14.0
Knoll, Inc.	11.9
HNI Corporation	8.5
Simmons Company	5.6
Steelcase Inc.	1.9
Herman Miller, Inc.	0.5

Top Public Companies by Market Value	($ mil.)
Leggett & Platt, Incorporated	2,366.6
Herman Miller, Inc.	1,381.5
Steelcase Inc.	1,158.6
HNI Corporation	719.8
Ethan Allen Interiors Inc.	705.7

* These rates are compounded annualized increases and may have resulted from acquisitions or one time gains. If less than 6 years of data are available, growth is for the years available.

SOURCE: HOOVER'S, INC., DATABASE

Furniture Stores

The US furniture retailing industry includes about 20,000 companies with a combined annual revenue of $60 billion. Large companies include Ethan Allen, Ashley Furniture Industries, and Haverty Furniture Companies. The industry is fragmented: the 50 largest companies hold only about 30 percent of the market. The large majority of companies operate a single store. Most stores gross less than $1 million per year.

Competitive Landscape

Household furniture sales are closely linked to home sales. Office furniture sales are linked to employment growth and new business formations. The profitability of furniture stores depends on merchandising and marketing. Small stores can co-exist with large ones by carrying special goods that appeal to a particular type of customer. The average annual revenue per worker for a typical company is $200,000.

Products, Operations & Technology

A typical furniture store sells living room, dining room, kitchen and bedroom furniture, and mattresses. Products are sometimes classified as "case goods" (wood furniture) or upholstered products. Most retail furniture stores sell a broad range of products, but some concentrate on one furniture type, such as mattresses, sofas, or office or children's furniture. Store operations involve sales management, merchandising (deciding which products to sell), inventory management, and (sometimes) credit financing.

Many retailers have multiple stores fed by one or several regional warehouses, which in turn receive goods directly from multiple manufacturers. Typically, smaller stores are showroom galleries with little inventory of their own; customers receive the product from a central warehouse. Larger stores with an attached warehouse are more popular in suburban loca-

BUSINESS CHALLENGES

» Demand Strongly Depends on Economic Conditions

Furniture buying is strongly influenced by home sales, consumer income, new home construction, and employment. During weak economic cycles, the furniture industry is particularly sensitive because of the large price tag associated with purchases that are often seen as discretionary. Retailers need to carefully manage cash and keep debt low in order to survive economic downturns.

» Competition from Manufacturers

Some large manufacturers bypass retailers and sell directly to customers through dedicated retail outlets. Furniture Brands International distributes its products partly through independently owned, branded stores; Ethan Allen operates retail stores. Bassett Furniture Industries opened retail stores of its own in the past several years.

» Competition from Mass Merchants

While traditional home furniture retailers still own the largest piece of the market, those stores are losing market share to other retailers, such as specialty chains and mass merchants. For example, retailers such as Target have expanded their furniture offerings, and discount chain Big Lots has a larger furniture selection and some of its locations have dedicated furniture showrooms. The changing competitive landscape will be a longterm issue for traditional furniture retailers to monitor.

tions. While some furniture, like beds and mattresses, can be directly supplied from inventory, upholstered and wood furniture are often made-to-order by the manufacturer, with delivery times that can stretch to several months. Most purchases are delivered from a warehouse to the customer's home or office. Large-volume retailers may operate a fleet of delivery trucks.

Retailers buy much of their product at trade shows, of which there are a large number. The most important US trade show is the International Home Furnishings Market in High Point, North Carolina, in the spring and fall. Retailers typically buy product from dozens of manufacturers, and may have special sections in their store dedicated to a particular manufacturer brand. Some retailers like Ethan Allen have their own manufacturing operations and sell only their own products.

Large retailers generally buy directly from manufacturers, without wholesaler intervention. Associations like Associated Volume Buyers (AVB) allow smaller companies to buy from manufacturers at volume prices.

Retailers rely heavily on part-time staffers year round, as well as temporary workers during the peak holiday season. Employees often work on commission and receive employee discounts.

Some retailers are investing in technology such as retail inventory management systems that increase the inventory flow and monitor in-stock status at stores. Retailers also are investing in technology to improve their online sites, which serve as marketing and purchasing tools for customers.

Sales & Marketing

Stores generally target a particular type of consumer based on style and price. Selling furniture requires showrooms, which can be large, often between 40,000 and 100,000 square feet. Specialty retailers can be successful using much smaller stores, but must usually carry a more expensive line of products because turnover is lower.

Marketing is through local channels, including newspaper, radio, and TV. Retailers also use direct mail catalogs, electronic direct marketing, and strategic e-commerce relationships. Some large stores, like Jordan's Furniture (a unit of Berkshire Hathaway), provide entertainment to draw customers.

Many furniture retailers have established websites where consumers can view a range of products. These sites are usually just promotional, but some retailers also sell products over the Internet.

Product prices are dependent on several factors including the price of raw materials and lower-priced competition. Some retailers rely on advertised sales to attract customers, while others use a "everyday" pricing strategy with few or no sales.

Human Resources

Although store managers are responsible for operations during their shifts, most jobs in fur-

niture stores involve sales and the relatively low-paying roles of materials handling and delivery. Managers hire part-time workers to help staff stores that stay open long hours, on weekends, or during the local busy season, which usually correlates to spring and summer home buying. Average hourly pay is around $15, about $2 below the national wage. The industry's safety record is about average: four injury cases a year per 100 full-time workers.

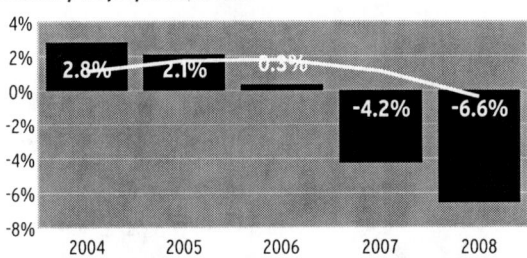

Industry Employment Growth

Average Hourly Earnings

— NATIONAL AVERAGE ■ FURNITURE STORES

SOURCE: BUREAU OF LABOR STATISTICS

Call Preparation Questions

What are the company's strategies for operating during industry or economic downturns?

Furniture buying is strongly influenced by home sales, consumer income, new home construction, and employment.

How is competition from manufacturers impacting the company?

Some large manufacturers bypass retailers and sell directly to customers through dedicated retail outlets.

How does the company differentiate itself from competitors?

While traditional home furniture retailers still own the largest piece of the market, those stores are losing market share to other retailers, such as specialty chains and mass merchants.

How successfully has the company's website increased sales?

Internet sales, still a small fraction of total sales, are increasing rapidly because prices are discounted by 30 to 40 percent.

How has celebrity or artist branding impacted company sales?

About 10 percent of furniture lines have license agreements to use famous names.

Web Links

AKTRIN Group of Information Centers

Sells research reports and studies on the furniture industry.
www.furniture-info.com/001-homepage.htm

Furniture Today

Weekly publication with news, useful links, and industry specific statistics.
www.furnituretoday.com

Furniture World

Industry news, articles on sales, marketing, and management.
furninfo.com

Independent Office Products and Furniture Dealers Association

News, links, and more.
www.iopfda.org

National Home Furnishings Association

Government and market information, news, and journal.
www.nhfa.com

National Retail Federation

Industry news.
www.nrf.com

North American Retail Dealers Association

News and publications on retailers.
www.narda.com

Western Home Furnishings Association

Industry information, meetings, events, services, products, and news.
www.whfa.org

World Furniture Online

International market outlooks and articles from nonprofit research organization based in Italy.
www.worldfurnitureonline.com

Glossary of Acronyms

AFMA — American Furniture Manufacturers Association

BIFMA — Business and Institutional Furniture Manufacturers Association

HOOVER'S TOP COMPANIES

Largest Companies by Sales	($ mil.)
Rooms To Go, Inc.	1,750.0
Pier 1 Imports, Inc.	1,511.8
Schottenstein Stores Corporation	1,300.0
Cost Plus, Inc.	1,023.9
Ethan Allen Interiors Inc.	980.0
Haverty Furniture Companies, Inc.	787.1
Restoration Hardware, Inc.	722.2
Levitz Furniture	294.8

Largest Employers	Employees
Pier 1 Imports, Inc.	16,400
Schottenstein Stores Corporation	8,050
Rooms To Go, Inc.	7,000
Cost Plus, Inc.	6,705
Ethan Allen Interiors Inc.	6,400
Haverty Furniture Companies, Inc.	4,500
Levitz Furniture	4,000
Restoration Hardware, Inc.	3,800
Raymour & Flanigan Furniture	3,100
Art Van Furniture, Inc.	3,000

Fastest Growing* by Five-Year Sales Growth	(%)
Design Within Reach, Inc.	27.6
Restoration Hardware, Inc.	12.5
Cost Plus, Inc.	8.1
Rooms To Go, Inc.	6.1
Schottenstein Stores Corporation	5.7
Haverty Furniture Companies, Inc.	2.0
Ethan Allen Interiors Inc.	1.6

Fastest Growing* by Five-Year Employee Growth	(%)
Design Within Reach, Inc.	14.3
Cost Plus, Inc.	7.8
Schottenstein Stores Corporation	5.9
Rooms To Go, Inc.	4.9
Restoration Hardware, Inc.	3.5
Haverty Furniture Companies, Inc.	3.0
Jennifer Convertibles, Inc.	2.1

Top Public Companies by Market Value	($ mil.)
Ethan Allen Interiors Inc.	705.7
Pier 1 Imports, Inc.	464.3
Restoration Hardware, Inc.	175.0
Haverty Furniture Companies, Inc.	155.6
Cost Plus, Inc.	93.2

* These rates are compounded annualized increases and may have resulted from acquisitions or one time gains. If less than 6 years of data are available, growth is for the years available.

SOURCE: HOOVER'S, INC., DATABASE

Gambling Operations

The US gambling (gaming) industry consists of about 500 commercial casinos and 160 Indian casinos, with combined annual revenue close to $85 billion. Companies with large casino operations include MGM MIRAGE and Harrah's Entertainment. About $35 billion of annual revenue is taken in by commercial casinos, $20 billion by state lotteries, about $25 billion by Indian casinos, and the rest by horse racing, bingo, charities, and bookmaking. (For gambling companies, "revenue" is the total amount bet minus winnings paid to gamblers.) Most casinos are small, limited by the size of the surrounding population. The industry has become highly concentrated: the top 20 companies hold more than 60 percent of the market.

Competitive Landscape

Growth in consumer income and state spending has driven expansion of the US gambling industry. The profitability of individual companies depends on efficient operations and effective marketing. Large operators have the financial resources to make large investments in facilities and efficient computer operations, and have cross-marketing opportunities. Small gambling facilities can thrive by catering to a local clientele. The industry is fairly labor-intensive: annual revenue per employee is $90,000.

Products, Operations & Technology

Gaming operators mainly provide a place or a means to play games of chance, where the odds of winning favor the "house." Popular casino games are slot machines (slots); video poker; and a variety of table games such as roulette, baccarat, Black Jack, and craps (dice). The house take on slot machines varies, but can be as high as 35 percent; that is, the house keeps 35 percent of all the money bet; the take on most table games is a bit lower. State lottery games are mainly numbers games. State lotteries often retain 40 percent of all money bet.

BUSINESS CHALLENGES

» Demand Linked to Economic Cycles

Gambling revenue is affected by the health of the economy, including the growth of personal income. During the last recession, industry jobs fell 6 percent. Because of high fixed-costs, the profitability of gambling operations depends on a high volume of customers.

» Dependence on Regulators

In states where gambling is legal, state commissions oversee gaming companies and have broad powers over their activities. State legislatures can easily raise tax rates on gambling machines. Continued industry growth depends on favorable legislation.

» Capital-Intensive

Companies have large capital investments in facilities and gaming equipment and usually a large amount of debt. Gambling companies routinely spend more than 10 percent of annual revenue on capital investments. To grow, companies typically need to raise substantial funds. Many companies have a high debt-to-equity ratio and are exposed to interest rate risk.

The actual operation of a casino involves acquiring and servicing gambling machines, training and supervising dealers and cashiers, entertaining customers, and managing cash. Large game equipment manufacturers are International Game Technology and the Bally Technologies. Gambling operators are free to set the odds of winning at a particular game as long as they prominently post a pay schedule on the machine. Operating licenses for some casinos require the operator to pay the state a percent of gross revenues, often in the range of 20 to 25 percent.

To attract and retain customers, some casino companies operate casino hotels that can accommodate large numbers of guests and that contain a variety of entertainment, restaurants, and retail stores in addition to their casino. A large hotel casino like the Trump Plaza in Atlantic City has about 900 hotel rooms; 2,800 slot machines; 100 table games; a theater; eight restaurants; four bars; and a number of retail stores. The trend in recent years has been toward larger casino hotels. Typically, 50 to 60 percent of revenue at a hotel casino comes from the casino.

Some casinos are located on land owned by legally-designated American Indian Tribes. Although these Indian casinos are regulated differently, they are operated like other casinos, usually under third-party operating contracts with regular commercial casino operators. Typical operating contracts give the operator 25 to 35 percent of net annual revenue and extend for a term of five years. Although not directly regulated by the state in which they operate, Indian casinos must have a revenue sharing agreement ("compact") with the state.

States operate a variety of state lottery games, most of which involve guessing a randomly drawn number. "Instant games" let the gambler buy a ticket with a hidden number that can be revealed by scratching off the covering. About 40 states operate lotteries, with combined annual sales of almost $50 billion and net profits of $20 billion. With a "take" close to 40 percent, lotteries typically return less money to players than casinos do. To counter moral objections, some states "earmark" the proceeds of lottery operations for specific laudable social spending projects, like education. Lottery tickets are sold through special computer terminals that retail outlets rent from the state.

Slot machines are now computerized, increasing their reliability, decreasing maintenance costs, and allowing operators to collect information using electronic game monitoring units (GMUs). Slot machines in casinos are typically replaced every three to five years by newer models, although their effective life is ten years. Computer technology has allowed the development of new games, such as video poker and "wide-area" games that hook several electronic machines together, and has increased player involvement with a game by offering improved graphic displays and sound. Video poker and other electronic gaming devices (EGDs) are now found in many places besides casinos.

Sales & Marketing

Most industry revenue comes from players of average means who bet only in small amounts, but who gamble regularly. Harrah's found that about 80 percent of its revenue and almost all of its profits came from around 30 percent of its gamblers who spent less than $500 per casino visit, but who visited frequently. Because regular gamblers lose money, gambling operators try to make the losing fun, presenting it as entertainment that is worth the price.

Promotional efforts for casinos target regional customers, who typically live within a three-hour car drive of a casino, and vacationers who select "destination" resorts that provide a variety of entertainment and activities, such as Las Vegas.

Casino marketing includes heavy advertising on radio and TV (in locales that allow it); direct mail; and Internet and telemarketing promotions that include offers of free casino chips, accommodations, or entertainment. Frequent gambler cards, which gamblers insert in slot machines before they play, allow gamblers to accumulate points toward rewards, and allow operators to monitor the playing habits of individual gamblers.

Human Resources

Most employees in the gambling industry work at casino hotels as regular hotel employees, who provide housekeeping and janitorial services, work as servers, or provide security. Casino employees who work the gaming activities need approval by regulatory authorities and require special training. Industry pay and benefits are generally low and personnel turnover high. The average wage for the industry is about 25 percent below the average for all US workers, although casino dealers get high pay. The rapid expansion of casino capacity in recent years has created a shortage of experienced casino employees. The industry's safety record is average.

Industry Employment Growth

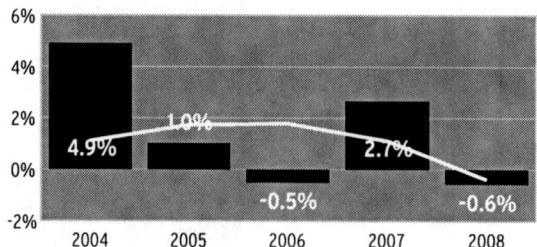

Average Hourly Earnings

— NATIONAL AVERAGE   ■ GAMBLING OPERATIONS

SOURCE: BUREAU OF LABOR STATISTICS

Call Preparation Questions

How does the company adjust to changes in leisure travel and spending?

Gambling revenue is affected by the health of the economy, including the growth of personal income.

How will the company be impacted if gambling is legalized in more states?

In states where gambling is legal, state commissions oversee gaming companies and have broad powers over their activities.

How important to the company is adding new games to attract customers and boost revenue?

Because slots, video poker, and other machine games are essentially computerized video games, developing new games and formats is easy.

Web Links

American Gaming Association

Industry Association. Excellent industry statistics.
www.americangaming.org

Gaming Magazine

Excellent news.
www.gamingmagazine.com

Michael Pollock's Gaming Industry Observer

A newsletter and research service that tracks trends that impact the gaming industry.
www.gamingobserver.com

National Center for Responsible Gaming

Pathological and youth gambling issues.
www.ncrg.org

National Indian Gaming Association

www.indiangaming.org

Nevada Gaming Commission

Regulations. Statistics about slot machine revenues.
www.gaming.state.nv.us

North American Association of State & Provincial Lotteries

State lottery statistics.
www.naspl.org

Glossary of Acronyms

AGA — American Gaming Association
EGD — electronic gaming device
GMU — game monitoring unit
IGRA — Indian Gaming Regulatory Act
NIGC — National Indian Gaming Commission
REVPAR — revenue per available room

HOOVER'S TOP COMPANIES

Largest Companies by Sales	($ mil.)
Harrah's Entertainment, Inc.	10,825.2
MGM MIRAGE	7,691.6
Las Vegas Sands Corp.	4,390.0
Wynn Resorts, Limited	2,987.3
Penn National Gaming, Inc.	2,557.4
Boyd Gaming Corporation	2,080.3
Station Casinos, Inc.	1,447.0
Ameristar Casinos, Inc.	1,267.9
Tropicana Entertainment, LLC	1,200.0
Isle of Capri Casinos, Inc.	1,125.3

Largest Employers	Employees
Harrah's Entertainment, Inc.	87,000
MGM MIRAGE	67,400
Las Vegas Sands Corp.	28,000
Wynn Resorts, Limited	20,600
Boyd Gaming Corporation	16,900
Penn National Gaming, Inc.	15,289
Station Casinos, Inc.	14,500
Tropicana Entertainment, LLC	11,000
Ameristar Casinos, Inc.	9,000
Isle of Capri Casinos, Inc.	8,559

Fastest Growing* by Five-Year Sales Growth	(%)
Wynn Resorts, Limited	395.5
Lakes Entertainment, Inc.	80.2
American Vantage Companies	57.6
Las Vegas Sands Corp.	44.7
Harrah's Entertainment, Inc.	21.2
Jacobs Entertainment, Inc.	20.0
Penn National Gaming, Inc.	17.1
Trans World Corporation	16.5
Youbet.com, Inc.	15.5
MGM MIRAGE	13.8

Fastest Growing* by Five-Year Employee Growth	(%)
Wynn Resorts, Limited	130.7
Las Vegas Sands Corp.	51.3
Youbet.com, Inc.	32.4
Canterbury Park Holding Corporation	19.7
Century Casinos, Inc.	17.5
Harrah's Entertainment, Inc.	15.7
MTR Gaming Group, Inc.	15.3
Lakes Entertainment, Inc.	10.3
Jacobs Entertainment, Inc.	10.3
Ameristar Casinos, Inc.	9.8

Top Public Companies by Market Value	($ mil.)
MGM MIRAGE	24,682.5
Wynn Resorts, Limited	4,733.7
Las Vegas Sands Corp.	3,806.1
Boyd Gaming Corporation	2,989.5
Penn National Gaming, Inc.	1,670.8

* These rates are compounded annualized increases and may have resulted from acquisitions or one time gains. If less than 6 years of data are available, growth is for the years available.

SOURCE: HOOVER'S, INC., DATABASE

Garden Centers and Farm Supply Stores

THIS INDUSTRY INCLUDES:

SIC CODES

5261   Retail Nurseries, Lawn and Garden Supply Stores

NAICS CODES

444220   Nursery, Garden Center, and Farm Supply Stores

The garden center and farm supply store industry includes about 17,000 stores with combined annual revenue of $25 billion. Major companies include Tractor Supply Company and Smith & Hawken (a division of Scotts Miracle-Gro). The industry is highly fragmented: the top 50 companies hold about 25 percent of industry sales.

The industry generally excludes nurseries, outdoor power equipment stores, farm equipment distributors, and farm cooperatives.

Competitive Landscape

Consumer income, home sales, and leisure activity trends drive demand in garden centers; the general health of the farming sector, which is tied to crop and livestock prices and consumer consumption patterns, drives demand in farm supply stores. The profitability of individual companies depends on effective merchandising and marketing, competitive pricing, and the ability to secure convenient locations. Large companies have advantages in purchasing, distribution, finance, and marketing and can better serve large customers. Small companies can compete effectively by offering specialty products, providing superior customer service, or serving a local market. Average annual revenue per worker is about $180,000.

Competition includes home centers, hardware stores, mass merchandisers, and Internet and catalog retailers. Farm supply stores also compete with farm cooperatives, which allow small farms to combine purchasing power and enjoy volume discounts.

Products, Operations & Technology

Major products sold include farm supplies (30 percent of industry sales); soil treatments (25 percent); and outdoor nursery stock (15 percent). Farm supplies include grain and animal feed. Soil treatments include fertilizers, lime, and other chemicals. Outdoor nursery

BUSINESS CHALLENGES

» Dependence on Real Estate, Construction

New home construction and existing home sales, important categories for garden centers and farm supply stores, drive growth for lawn and garden products. The real estate and construction industries are both cyclical and highly influenced by economic factors and consumer spending. During a recent recessionary period, employment in nurseries, garden centers, and farm supply stores decreased over 5 percent. Builders and consumers often cut landscaping and gardening projects or seek lower-cost retailers during tough economic times.

» Farm Industry Shrinking

The long-term decline of the farm industry has reduced demand for farm supplies, causing farm supply retailers to struggle for survival. The number of farms fell over 60 percent and the number of farm acres dropped over 20 percent between 1950 and 2006. As the suburbs expand, eager real estate developers continue to buy farms. More lucrative and less demanding non-farm employment opportunities have lured many farmers from the profession.

» Competition from Alternative Retailers

Garden centers and farm supply stores face strong competition for lawn and garden products from large, alternative retailers. Home centers, such as Home Depot and Lowe's, and mass merchandisers, including Wal-Mart, offer lawn and garden products and accessories at low prices. Large retailers often capitalize on seasonal demand and use aggressive pricing tactics to drive store traffic. As the farm industry continues to decline, farm supply stores rely increasingly on sales of gardening and landscaping supplies to offset decreasing revenues in traditional categories.

stock includes trees, shrubs, bedding plants, bulbs, sod, and seeds. Companies may also sell hardware, automotive fuel, pet food and supplies, and lawn and garden equipment and parts. Services include equipment repair, maintenance, or rental. Some garden centers offer landscaping design and installation services.

The industry consists primarily of independent retailers and regional chains, although Tractor Supply, a major farm supply company, has retail outlets in almost all states. Most stores have both indoor and outdoor retail space. Some garden centers have greenhouses or nurseries. Garden centers participating in a Lawn and Garden Retailer survey averaged 45,000 square feet with about 15,000 square feet of indoor and 30,000 square feet of outdoor retail space. Annual sales for garden centers averaged about $2 million with almost one-quarter of centers surveyed generating less than $100,000 annually. Locations include strip malls, stand-alone buildings, and indoor shopping malls (for stores specializing in garden accessories).

Average size for farm supply stores varies: large stores can exceed 50,000 square feet, while smaller stores can be just 1,500; Tractor Supply stores range from 15,500 to 18,500. Most farm supply stores are, or were, located in rural areas. Suburban developments have replaced vast amounts of farmland, forcing many farm supply stores to either move or alter merchandising strategy to include more non-farm goods. Common equipment includes trucks, skid loaders, and forklifts.

Companies buy merchandise from a variety of sources, including manufacturers, distributors, nurseries, feed suppliers, and equipment dealers. Buying cooperatives allow independent garden centers to enjoy volume discounts, centralized billing, and delayed invoicing. Many companies attend trade shows to review new products and make buying decisions.

Merchandise selection varies by season and geographic region. Popular garden center products include annuals, perennials, trees, shrubs, cut flowers, and ground coverings (soil, mulch, and rocks). Live plants, also known as "green goods," are perishable inventory and require adequate water, sunlight, and air circulation. Unsalable plants contribute to inventory "shrink." Important farm supply categories include animal care (feeds and supplements); seeds; fertilizers; tractors and parts; hardware; tools; and fuel. Changing customer demographics have caused many farm supply stores to stock a broader variety of merchandise, including lawn and garden care, pet care, and clothing items.

Some companies use computerized information systems to manage point-of-sale (POS); inventory; sales; accounting; purchasing; and distribution. While most of the top gardening centers have POS, about 40 percent don't, according to Today's Garden Center. Large compa-

nies may use electronic data interchange (EDI) to transmit purchase orders. Tractor Supply uses Web-based transportation management systems and radio frequency identification (RFID) to monitor merchandise movement through the supply chain.

Sales & Marketing

Typical customers for garden centers include homeowners and landscapers; farmers and ranchers for farm supply stores. The demographics for households that spend the most on lawns and gardens include adults over 55, married couples, college graduates, households with annual income over $75,000, and households with no children, according to the National Gardening Association (NGA). Farm supply store customers may be hobby or weekend farmers.

Marketing and promotional vehicles include local newspaper, radio, phone directory, and print advertising; direct mail; and in-store events and displays. Because most companies are small and regional, national advertising is cost-prohibitive. Companies may get marketing allowances from manufacturers to promote specific products. During key seasonal periods, garden center staff may host seminars, speak at community events, or give interviews with local press to generate interest and create "free" advertising.

Customer service is especially important for companies serving do-it-yourself (DIY) customers. Sales staff with horticultural expertise help customers select appropriate plants. Workers with farming experience can guide less experienced customers (such as hobby farmers) through DIY projects, such as fencing, and general maintenance tasks. Loyalty programs reward frequent customers and encourage repeat store visits.

Because garden centers and farm supply stores serve primarily local markets, Internet sales are limited. Shipping is expensive for animal feeds and can stress live plants. About 40 percent of garden centers sell some merchandise through websites, according to Lawn and Garden Retailer. Many company websites give basic information, including hours of operation, location, and product information.

Average annual spending by consumers on DIY lawn and garden products is $428, according to the NGA. The average sale in garden centers is about $50, according to the Garden Center Group.

Human Resources

Most jobs in garden centers and farm supply stores require few skills. As a result, wages are almost 30 percent lower than the average for all US workers. Companies may rely on part-time help during peak periods. To provide specialized expertise, some garden center staff may have formal education, experience, or certification in horticulture and landscaping. Most states require landscape architects to have licenses. Farm centers may employ workers with farming and ranching backgrounds. For example, each Tractor Supply store employs a farmer, a horse owner, and a welder.

The industry injury rate is about 15 percent higher than the average for all US workers, primarily due to vehicle-related accidents. Improper operation of lifting equipment contributes to the high injury rate.

Industry Employment Growth

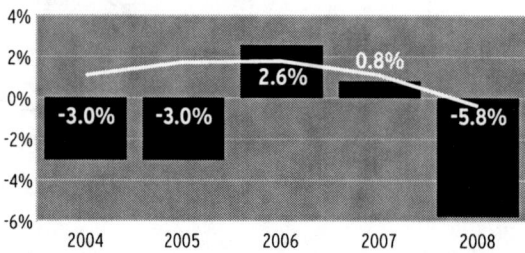

Average Hourly Earnings

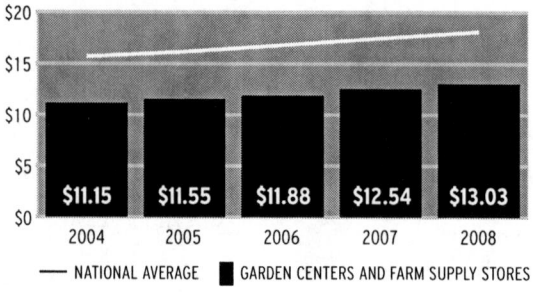

SOURCE: BUREAU OF LABOR STATISTICS

Call Preparation Questions

How do real estate and construction trends affect the company's sales?

New home construction and existing home sales, important categories for garden centers and farm supply stores, drive growth for lawn and garden products.

How have changes in the farm industry affected the company?

The long-term decline of the farm industry has reduced demand for farm supplies, causing farm supply retailers to struggle for survival.

How does the company compete against large home centers and mass marketers?

Garden centers and farm supply stores face strong competition for lawn and garden products from large, alternative retailers.

How important are specialty products to the company's merchandising mix?

Stocking specialty products or offering a wide selection of merchandise within a category helps garden centers and farm supply stores differentiate from competition.

Web Links

American Nursery and Landscape Association

Industry and legislative news and statistics from trade organization.
www.anla.org

Lawn & Garden Retailer

Industry news, trends, statistics, and annual survey.
www.lgrmag.com

National Gardening Association

Industry news, trends, statistics from trade organization.
www.garden.org

Nursery Retailer

Industry news and trends.
www.nurseryretailer.com

Today's Garden Center

Industry news, trends, Top 100 best practices garden centers.
www.todaysgardencenter.com

Glossary of Acronyms

CVM — Center for Veterinary Medicine
DIY — do-it-yourself
EDI — electronic data interchange
GWA — Garden Writers Association
GWAF — Garden Writers Association Foundation
LGR — Lawn and Garden Retailer
NGA — National Gardening Association
POS — point-of-sale
RFID — radio frequency identification

HOOVER'S TOP COMPANIES

Largest Employers	Employees
Tractor Supply Company	12,800
Hines Horticulture, Inc.	4,420
Color Spot Nurseries, Inc.	1,684
Petitti Garden Centers	700
Smith & Hawken, Ltd.	600
Calloway's Nursery, Inc.	600
Armstrong Garden Centers, Inc.	600
Adams Fairacre Farms	550
Earl May Seed & Nursery L.C.	500
SummerWinds Garden Centers, Inc.	350

Top Public Companies by Market Value	($ mil.)
Tractor Supply Company	1,244.8
Griffin Land & Nurseries, Inc.	162.2

SOURCE: HOOVER'S, INC., DATABASE

Gas Stations

THIS INDUSTRY INCLUDES:

SIC CODES

5541   Gasoline Service Stations

NAICS CODES

44719   Other Gasoline Stations

The gas station industry includes about 23,000 stores with combined annual revenue of an estimated $100 billion. While no major companies dominate, large oil companies own some stations. The industry is fragmented: the top 50 companies hold 30 percent of industry sales.

The industry generally excludes establishments that are combination gas station/convenience stores, and includes some truck stops.

Competitive Landscape

The volume of consumer and commercial driving drives demand. The profitability of individual companies depends on the ability to secure high-traffic locations, generate high-volume sales, and buy gas at the lowest possible cost. Large companies have advantages in purchasing and finance. Small companies can compete effectively by having superior locations. Average annual revenue per worker is $300,000.

As more retailers added gas to their merchandising mix, the competitive set for gas stations expanded to include convenience stores, mass merchandisers, warehouse clubs, and grocery stores.

Products, Operations & Technology

Major products sold include unleaded regular gas (35 percent of industry sales) and diesel fuel (30 percent). Gas stations also sell unleaded mid-grade and unleaded premium gas. Truck stops tend to sell more diesel fuel, since most commercial vehicles run on diesel. Companies may offer repair services or car washes. Some truck stops offer food, phones, showers, and lounges.

Gas stations include regional chains, independent retailers, and corporate-owned stations. Stations selling branded gas have fixed-term, contractual relationships with suppliers (typically large oil companies or distributors). While open dealers own their stations,

BUSINESS CHALLENGES

» Flat Demand

After several decades of growth, fuel consumption for all motor vehicles has stabilized, limiting market growth and causing many gas stations to struggle for survival. The average miles driven and gallons of gas consumed per vehicle were basically flat between 1997 and 2005. Improved fuel efficiency of some passenger cars (excluding vans, light trucks, and SUVs) and commercial trucks helped control consumption growth and offset the effects of low-mileage SUVs. Stagnant market growth especially harms gas stations, which typically carry low margins and depend on volume to generate profits.

» Volatile Costs Affect Thin Margins

With narrow margins, significant changes in manufacturer prices can affect profitability for gas stations. Manufacturer prices for gas can increase up to 45 percent in a single year, driven by highly volatile commodity prices for crude oil. While variable manufacturer prices can result in almost daily retail price changes, competition may limit how much stations can charge. In the wake of rising gas costs, stations may struggle to cover taxes and credit card commissions with the relatively small margin they make per gallon.

» Competition from Alternative Retailers

Gas stations face intense competition from alternative retailers that use gas sales to drive traffic. Convenience stores sell the majority of gas in the US. Mass merchandisers and warehouse clubs can offer gas at extremely low prices due to volume purchase discounts. Grocery stores with gas stations provide one-stop shopping for customers and often offer gas discounts to frequent shopper cardholders. Retailers specializing in auto services, such as oil changes, brake jobs, and tire services, compete with stations offering repairs.

lessee dealers lease stations from suppliers and receive a percentage of profits. Commissioned agent dealers are paid based on gallons sold. Major oil companies own and operate some stations.

Common locations include high-traffic intersections, major highways, interstates, and resort markets. Sites near highway entrance and exit ramps are popular due to ease of access. Because high-volume traffic is critical, competing gas stations may be located adjacent to one another at the same intersection. Almost all are self-service and allow customers to pump their own gas. Many stations operate 24 hours a day, 7 days a week.

Gas stations typically have one or more islands with multiple pumps that deliver gas from underground storage tanks (USTs). Most modern pumps have digital displays and accept credit or debit card payments (pay-at-the-pump). Vapor recovery systems linking pump nozzles and tanks prevent gas fumes from escaping into the air. Fiberglass or fortified steel USTs minimize gas leakage and ground contamination. Leakage of older steel USTs has caused major environmental problems, which can result in significant liability for some stations. The high cost of upgrading equipment to comply with environmental regulations has forced some small station owners out of business.

Truck stops serve much larger vehicles than traditional gas stations and require significantly more space. A typical stop has 80 or more large parking spaces, which help drivers better maneuver trucks. Stops may have weigh stations to help truckers minimize overweight violations. Many stops dedicate certain fuel lanes for trucks-only and most stops allow truckers to park overnight.

Suppliers include major oil companies, refineries, and distributors (also known as "jobbers"). Branded stations typically have multiyear purchasing contracts with suppliers. The price dealers pay for gas can vary: they may pay dealer tank wagon (DTW) prices, which are set by suppliers, or a fixed markup over the "rack," or market, price. Unbranded stations may buy from multiple suppliers and solicit bids to secure the best price. Generally, stations receive discounts for volume purchases. Purchased gas travels from distribution centers or terminals to individual stations via tanker trucks.

Branded gas may contain proprietary additives, such as detergents or combustion modifiers. Some stations offer private brands. Because high summer temperatures can react with volatile chemicals in gas to create ozone, gas sold in the summer is a different blend (and typically more expensive) compared to gas sold in the winter. A relatively small, but growing, number of stations offers alternative fuels, such as E85 (ethanol blend) and biodiesel fuels. Government environmental regulations have resulted in low sulfur formulations for diesel fuel, also known as ultra-low sulfur fuels (ULSF).

The majority of gas stations use cashless, pay-at-the-pump technology integrated with point-of-sale (POS) systems to monitor transactions. Some branded dealers offer contact-free payment through radio frequency identification (RFID) tags. A small number of stations are testing biometric identification, which allows customers to pay by fingerprint. Cardlock systems, which control unattended gas pumps, allow commercial customers to monitor and control fueling transactions. Computer information systems also help stations control pump operations, track inventory levels, and detect UST leaks. Integrated database programs administer customer loyalty programs.

Sales & Marketing

While most customers are car drivers, commercial truck drivers are also an important market; thus, most gas stations offer diesel fuel. Other customers include boat owners and RV owners.

Most customers choose gas stations according to location and price, so companies typically spend very little on marketing and promotion. Signage, including state DOT signs, is important for stations located off major highways. Large oil companies may advertise nationally to build awareness for branded gas. However, since many consumers view gas as a commodity, developing customer loyalty is a challenge. Branded dealers may offer special discounts or rebates on purchases made with company-issued credit cards to encourage purchase frequency. By accepting fleet cards, companies can generate more commercial business. Loyalty programs encourage repeat visits.

The retail price of gas is extremely volatile and ranged from less than $1 to over $4 for regular unleaded between 1998 and 2008. Due to competition, retail prices can change daily and vary significantly by location. Price zones set by oil companies can affect dealer prices. Some states require stations to post retail prices prominently.

Human Resources

Workers in gas stations require few skills; consequently, wages are about 40 percent lower than the average for all US workers. Because many stations operate 24/7, staffing can be difficult, forcing most companies to rely on part-time help. While the industry injury rate is significantly lower than average, gas station workers have a relatively high mortality rate. Low staffing (often just a single attendant) during late night hours makes stations prime targets for robberies, increasing worker risk.

Industry Employment Growth

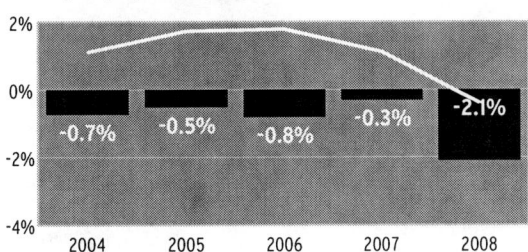

Average Hourly Earnings

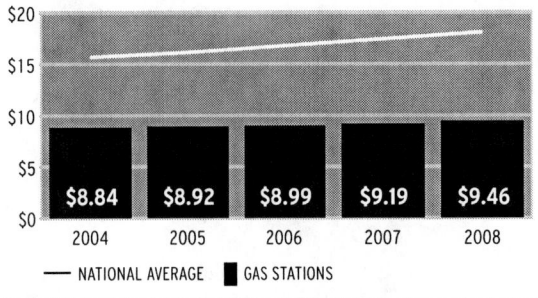

SOURCE: BUREAU OF LABOR STATISTICS

Call Preparation Questions

How has stagnant fuel consumption growth affected the company's performance?

After several decades of growth, fuel consumption for all motor vehicles has stabilized, limiting market growth and causing many gas stations to struggle for survival.

How does the company minimize the effect of volatile manufacturer prices for gas?

With narrow margins, significant changes in manufacturer prices can affect profitability for gas stations.

What is the company's competitive advantage?

Gas stations face intense competition from alternative retailers that use gas sales to drive traffic.

How much demand does the company foresee for alternative fuels?

With more concern about the environment and dependence on fossil fuels, the penetration of vehicles using fuels other than gas should grow, increasing demand for alternative fuels.

How important are non-fuel products to the company's sales?

To boost sales and traffic, gas stations can provide related products and services. An ATM attracts customers who need cash.

Web Links

American Petroleum Institute

Industry news, trends, statistics, and environmental and regulatory information.
www.api.org

Energy Information Administration

Gasoline and crude oil pricing and production trends. Alternative fuel trends.
www.eia.doe.gov

National Association of Convenience Stores

Industry news, trends, and statistics for all gas stations, including those with convenience stores.
www.nacsonline.com

National Association of Truck Stop Operators

Industry news and trends specific to truck stops and travel plazas.
www.natso.com

National Petroleum News

Industry news, trends, profitability studies.
npnweb.com

Society of Independent Gasoline Marketers of America

Industry news, trends, regulatory updates from trade association.
www.sigma.org

Glossary of Acronyms

API — American Petroleum Institute
DTW — dealer tank wagon
NACS — National Association of Convenience Stores
NPN — National Petroleum News
NATSO — National Association of Truck Stop Operators
POS — point-of-sale
RFID — radio frequency identification
SIGMA — Society of Independent Gasoline Marketers of America
ULSF — ultra-low sulfur fuels
UST — underground storage tank

HOOVER'S TOP COMPANIES

Largest Companies by Sales	($ mil.)
Exxon Mobil Corporation	477,359.0
Chevron Corporation	273,005.0
ConocoPhillips	246,182.0
Valero Energy Corporation	119,114.0
Sunoco, Inc.	54,146.0
Hess Corporation	41,209.0
Flying J Inc.	16,200.0
The Pantry, Inc.	8,995.6
TravelCenters of America LLC	7,658.4
Sinclair Oil Corporation	7,000.0

Largest Employers	Employees
Exxon Mobil Corporation	83,000
Chevron Corporation	65,000
ConocoPhillips	32,600
Shell Oil Company	24,008
Valero Energy Corporation	21,651
Casey's General Stores, Inc.	17,983
Flying J Inc.	16,000
The Pantry, Inc.	14,221
Sunoco, Inc.	14,200
Hess Corporation	13,300

Fastest Growing* by Five-Year Sales Growth	(%)
Love's Travel Stops & Country Stores, Inc.	40.0
Susser Holdings Corporation	29.8
Flying J Inc.	28.4
The Pantry, Inc.	26.7
Valero Energy Corporation	25.7
Sinclair Oil Corporation	25.0
Sunoco, Inc.	24.7
TravelCenters of America LLC	24.2
Hess Corporation	23.3
ConocoPhillips	18.6

Fastest Growing* by Five-Year Employee Growth	(%)
The Pantry, Inc.	9.6
Love's Travel Stops & Country Stores, Inc.	9.6
Casey's General Stores, Inc.	7.6
Hess Corporation	7.0
Susser Holdings Corporation	6.7
Flying J Inc.	6.4
Sunoco, Inc.	1.4
Chevron Corporation	1.4
Sinclair Oil Corporation	0.3

Top Public Companies by Market Value	($ mil.)
Exxon Mobil Corporation	397,234.1
Chevron Corporation	148,253.0
ConocoPhillips	78,783.6
Hess Corporation	17,493.8
Valero Energy Corporation	11,170.8

* These rates are compounded annualized increases and may have resulted from acquisitions or one time gains. If less than 6 years of data are available, growth is for the years available.

SOURCE: HOOVER'S, INC., DATABASE

Gift and Souvenir Stores

The gift, novelty, and souvenir store (gift store) industry includes about 30,000 stores with combined annual revenue of $13 billion. Major companies include Hallmark, Spencer Gifts, and Disney Stores (a division of The Walt Disney Company). The industry is fragmented: the top 50 companies represent 30 percent of industry sales.

The gift store industry does not include stationery stores.

Competitive Landscape

Consumer spending, special occasions, and tourist travel drive demand. The profitability of individual companies depends on effective merchandising and the ability to generate store traffic. Large companies have advantages in purchasing, distribution, and marketing. Small companies can compete effectively by selling specialty products, providing superior service, or delivering a unique customer experience. The industry is labor-intensive: average annual revenue per worker is about $80,000.

Gift stores compete with a wide range of businesses because they stock merchandise across many categories. Major competitors include mass merchandisers, department stores, Internet retailers, and toy stores.

Products, Operations & Technology

Major products sold by gift stores include souvenirs and novelty items (25 percent of sales); seasonal decorations (15 percent); greeting cards (15 percent); and giftware (10 percent). Novelty items include gift baskets and pre-filled balloons. Seasonal decorations include decorative cups, plates, and napkins. Giftware includes glassware and vases. Gift stores may also sell home accessories and provide services such as gift-wrapping and delivery.

Gift retailers include national and regional chains and independent retailers. Hallmark stores operate through licensing agreements

BUSINESS CHALLENGES

» Competition from Alternative Retailers

Gift stores face intense competition from mass merchandisers, department stores, and Internet retailers. Wal-Mart and Target are the top two destinations for gift shoppers, according to Unity Marketing. Reseller websites, such as eBay, have stolen sales from stores specializing in collectibles. The Internet offers alternatives to traditional greeting cards (such as e-cards and customized cards), which could limit growth in a key category for most gift retailers.

» Dependence on Consumer Spending

Most gifts are discretionary purchases and gift sales depend on consumer spending. During the last recession, employment in gift stores decreased more than 5 percent. While consumers may not eliminate gift purchases when the economy slows, many spend less and are less likely to buy additional items for themselves on impulse. Without established customer bases, new or struggling independent gift stores can be especially vulnerable during tough economic times.

» Reliance on Tourism

Souvenir stores and gift stores in vacation areas depend highly on the tourist market. Increases in fuel prices can affect car and air travel and reduce tourist traffic. Extended periods of bad weather or changes in traffic patterns can decrease accessibility for customers unfamiliar with a store's location.

with independent owners. The majority of companies operate a single location, according to Gifts and Decorative Accessories. Locations include strip malls, indoor shopping malls, resorts, hospitals, museums, and airports: souvenir stores may seek locations off interstates or near tourist destinations. Companies consider market demographics, neighboring tenants, visibility, traffic counts, major roadway access, and proximity to competitors when selecting new locations.

The average size for a gift store is 2,000 square feet, with 1,500 square feet dedicated to selling space. About half of stores have annual sales under $250,000. Gift superstores can exceed 10,000 square feet and generate over $1 million annually. Some chains, such as the Disney Store, have multiple store formats to serve different markets. Companies may also operate outlet stores to liquidate excess merchandise.

Inventory size and selection can vary. Merchandise changes constantly due to different market trends in each gift category. Many gift stores continuously add and drop product categories, as well as lines within categories. Popular categories include candles and candle accessories, greeting cards, holiday products, jewelry, photo frames, and collectibles. Some gift stores offer private-label merchandise.

While companies may buy inventory directly from manufacturers, manufacturers representatives and wholesalers play an important role because the gift manufacturing industry is highly fragmented. Over half of gift stores buy from between 20 and 60 vendors, with most companies buying from two to four for each category. Many seasonal products are imports from China, and companies may use foreign buying agencies to manage imports.

Order lead times can be long, especially for seasonal items. Most companies place orders in the summer for winter holiday merchandise. Gift stores may have a right of return for certain products, such as seasonal greeting cards. Many suppliers have minimum order quantities. Buyers typically attend trade shows, also known as "market," to review new products and make purchasing decisions. Major trade shows occur in the winter and summer.

Companies may use computerized information systems integrating point-of-sale (POS), inventory, and purchasing. Bar codes and scanners identify and track movement for individual items. Some companies use software to spot fast and slow moving merchandise, and help make better purchasing decisions. Gift stores may use database programs to manage customer information and loyalty programs. While electronic data interchange (EDI) is available, most small gift retailers are unable to leverage electronic order processing due to lack of standardization across the industry.

Sales & Marketing

While the typical customer can vary by store type, women in their 40s make most gift purchases. Specifically, women buy more than 80

percent of greeting cards, according to American Greetings.

Marketing and promotional vehicles include direct mail; newspaper, radio, TV, and outdoor advertising; and newsletters/flyers. Souvenir shops may rely on billboards and state DOT signs to draw tourists. Store image can be important to attract a specific demographic. Special events, such as holiday open houses, product demonstrations, and trunk shows drive traffic. Most gift stores hold sales at least two times annually, according to Gifts and Decorative Accessories.

Because gift stores typically stock a wide range of products, customers may need help when selecting merchandise. Seasoned, knowledgeable sales staff can help identify popular items, recommend gifts, and encourage impulse purchases. To reward loyal customers, companies may offer discount coupons or advance notice for sales.

Although more stores are using the Internet to sell products, only one-quarter of companies sell merchandise through websites and online purchases are generally a small percentage of sales. Because most gift stores are small, those with retail websites may link with larger websites to help drive site traffic.

The retail price for most items sold in gift stores is less than $25. The average cash/check sale is about $30 and the average credit card sale is $40. The average markdown is 40 percent off the retail price.

Human Resources

Workers in gift stores require few skills and wages are almost 40 percent lower than the US average. Companies rely highly on part-time help, and typically increase staff during peak periods, such as the winter holidays or summer vacation months. A typical Disney Store has 10 part-time sales associates. Most gift stores average two full-time and four part-time employees, according to Gifts and Decorative Accessories. The industry injury rate is significantly below the US average.

Industry Employment Growth

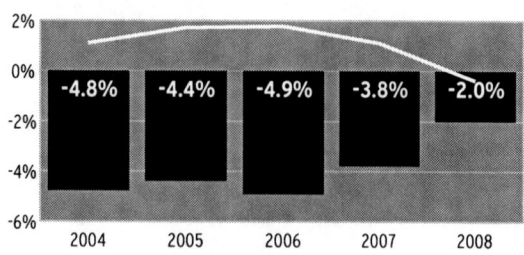

Average Hourly Earnings

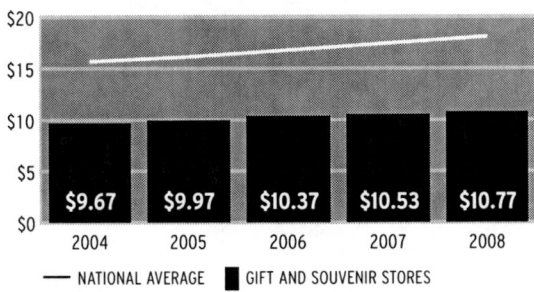

	2004	2005	2006	2007	2008
Gift and Souvenir Stores	$9.67	$9.97	$10.37	$10.53	$10.77

— NATIONAL AVERAGE ■ GIFT AND SOUVENIR STORES

SOURCE: BUREAU OF LABOR STATISTICS

Call Preparation Questions

What is the company's most serious competitive threat?

Gift stores face intense competition from mass merchandisers, department stores, and Internet retailers.

How do changes in consumer spending affect the company's sales?

Most gifts are discretionary purchases and gift sales depend on consumer spending.

How important is the tourist market to the company?

Souvenir stores and gift stores in vacation areas depend highly on the tourist market.

How does the Internet fit into the company's business plan?

Companies can leverage rapid growth in online retailing and reach customers beyond local markets by offering products for sale through the Internet.

What are some of the company's trademark specialty products?

Gift stores can better compete with large retailers by offering unique and hard-to-find items.

Web Links

Gift and Home Trade Association

Trade association for gift industry.
www.giftandhome.org

Gift Shop Magazine

Trends, operational information (requires free registration).
www.giftshopmag.com

Gifts and Decorative Accessories

Industry news, statistics, and annual retailer survey.
www.giftsanddec.com

Giftware News

Industry and product news and trends.
www.giftwarenews.com

Unity Marketing

Industry research — some available for purchase.
www.unitymarketingonline.com

Glossary of Acronyms

ADA — Americans with Disabilities Act
EDI — electronic data interchange
GHTA — Gift and Home Trade Association
POS — point-of-sale

HOOVER'S TOP COMPANIES

Largest Companies by Sales	($ mil.)
Hallmark Cards, Inc.	4,400.0
Amscan Holdings, Inc.	1,247.4
1-800-FLOWERS.COM, Inc.	919.4
FTD Group, Inc.	613.0
The Swiss Colony, Inc.	600.0
Brookstone, Inc.	562.8
Harry & David Holdings, Inc.	545.1
Spencer Gifts, LLC	168.0
Things Remembered	160.0

Largest Employers	Employees
Hallmark Cards, Inc.	15,900
Amscan Holdings, Inc.	12,569
Spencer Gifts, LLC	4,200
Party City Corporation	4,100
Things Remembered	4,000
1-800-FLOWERS.COM, Inc.	3,700
Brookstone, Inc.	3,504
Oriental Trading Company, Inc.	2,000
Harry & David Holdings, Inc.	1,507
iParty Corp.	887

Fastest Growing* by Five-Year Sales Growth	(%)
Amscan Holdings, Inc.	26.5
The Swiss Colony, Inc.	13.2
1-800-FLOWERS.COM, Inc.	10.2
iParty Corp.	9.4
Brookstone, Inc.	8.4
Hallmark Cards, Inc.	1.9

Fastest Growing* by Five-Year Employee Growth	(%)
Amscan Holdings, Inc.	44.4
1-800-FLOWERS.COM, Inc.	23.3
iParty Corp.	6.1
Brookstone, Inc.	3.2

Top Public Companies by Market Value	($ mil.)
1-800-FLOWERS.COM, Inc.	179.6
iParty Corp.	5.0

* These rates are compounded annualized increases and may have resulted from acquisitions or one time gains. If less than 6 years of data are available, growth is for the years available.

SOURCE: HOOVER'S, INC., DATABASE

Glass and Fiber Optic Manufacturing

The US glass industry includes 2,000 manufacturers with combined annual revenue of $25 billion. Large companies include PPG Industries, Owens-Illinois, and Corning. The industry is highly concentrated: the 50 largest companies hold close to 90 percent of the market. Most companies in the industry manufacture products from bulk glass bought from a handful of primary glass manufacturers.

Competitive Landscape

Demand comes from the construction, auto, bottling, and container industries. The profitability of individual companies depends on low-cost operations because most products are commodities that are bought based on price. Large manufacturers have large efficiencies of scale in operations, which is why the industry is so concentrated. Small manufacturers can compete effectively by producing specialty products or serving a local market. The industry is capital-intensive: annual revenue per worker is close to $200,000.

Products, Operations & Technology

Major products are glass containers, flat glass, fiberglass, and specialty products such as TV tubes, glass ware, lenses, mirrors, and optic fiber. Specialty products account for more than half of industry revenue, containers about 25 percent, and flat glass about 10 percent.

Bulk glass is made by melting quartz sand and adding various substances such as limestone, soda ash, metals, and other materials to produce a "melt." The melt is then formed, cooled, and further processed by grinding, cutting, and polishing into finished products. Glass furnaces, or "tanks," usually fired by natural gas or oil, melt the raw material mixtures at temperatures up to 1,600 degrees Celsius. Tanks for container glass may produce 500 tons per day, while flat glass tanks produce up to 1,000 tons per day.

BUSINESS CHALLENGES

» Dependence on Construction

Residential and commercial construction and renovation drive glass manufacturer sales of windows, mirrors, glass doors, and fiberglass insulation.

» Dependence on Manufacturing

Glass demand can be affected by changes in auto, textile, electronic equipment, and container production. Autos are an important glass market, both in initial production and glass replacement. Many glass manufacturers produce containers for food, beverage, and other industries. Glass fiber production includes glass wool insulation, fiberglass, and textile glass fiber.

» Increased Competition from Plastics, Aluminum

Plastics and aluminum have displaced glass in many applications during the past 20 years, especially in the container segment. Glass is still the preferred container for alcoholic beverages or acidic foods such as spaghetti sauce, but the continuing development of new plastics is a long-term threat. Plastics are likely to take a greater share of container markets, and plastic foams are cutting into the use of fiberglass insulation.

Molten glass is formed before it cools, using four major methods. Containers and TV tubes are produced by blowing molten glass into forms. Flat glass is usually produced by floating molten glass on top of a molten tin bath, then running it through rollers. Fiberglass is produced by pulling or spraying strands directly from the melt. Special shapes can be produced by pouring molten glass into ceramic molds. Because production of various glass products requires different kinds of equipment and manufacturing skills, most producers operate in only one segment of the industry. Because raw glass production technology is relatively unsophisticated and the raw materials inexpensive, manufacturers concentrate on production efficiencies.

Optic fiberglass is an ultra-high-purity silica glass that can be stretched into long, hair-thin fibers and used to transmit information over long distances, a replacement for copper wires. Fiber optic strands consist of an inner core of high purity glass with a high refractive index that transmits light, and an outer core of low refractive glass that keeps the light signal from seeping out the sides. The basic unit from which fibers are drawn is called a "preform," a glass cylinder that may be several inches thick and several meters long, with a core of high refractive glass and a clad of low refractive glass. The preform is placed inside a draw furnace, heated to 2,000 degrees Celsius, and stretched into hair-thin, flexible fibers that may be many miles long. Fibers are coated, colored, and bundled in a protective jacket to form optic fiber cables.

The basic technology of glass manufacture is well-known, but research into the properties of various glasses has resulted in a long list of possible new formulations and applications. To improve the efficiency of production, especially to make various specialty glasses, sensors and computer controls are used.

FAST FACTS

» The US glass industry includes 2,000 manufacturers with combined annual revenue of $25 billion.

» Large companies include PPG Industries, Owens-Illinois, and Corning.

» Major products are glass containers, flat glass, fiberglass, and specialty products such as TV tubes, glass ware, lenses, mirrors, and optic fiber.

» Major customers are the auto, construction, bottling, and container industries.

» Companies that supply the auto or construction industries may have seasonal cash flow related to the annual production cycles of those industries.

Sales & Marketing

Major customers are the auto, construction, bottling, and container industries. Manufacturers contract directly with large customers to supply products made to exact glass formula specifications. Manufacturers typically differentiate their products based on the raw glass used. Sales are usually handled by an in-house staff that must have technical expertise. Because of the low cost of the product, manufacturers seek out large contracts. Although primary glass manufacturers produce various standard grades of glass, their marketing is oriented toward their ability to provide special glass formulations.

Human Resources

Jobs in glass products manufacture largely involve controlling automated machinery. Wages are about 10 percent higher than the national average. The industry's injury rate is about 75 percent worse than the average.

Industry Employment Growth

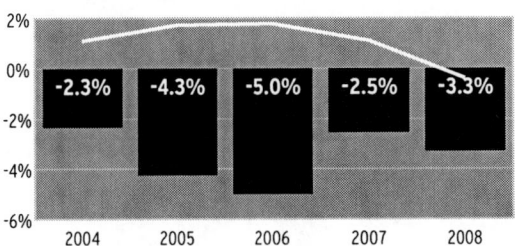

Average Hourly Earnings

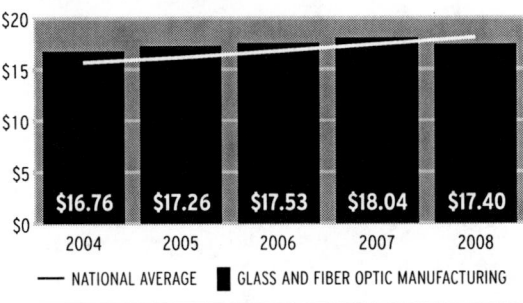

SOURCE: BUREAU OF LABOR STATISTICS

Call Preparation Questions

How have recent housing and construction trends impacted company sales?

Residential and commercial construction and renovation drive glass manufacturer sales of windows, mirrors, glass doors, and fiberglass insulation.

What industries has the company targeted for customer growth?

Glass demand can be affected by changes in auto, textile, electronic equipment, and container production.

How is competition with plastic and aluminum manufacturers impacting company market share and sales?

Plastics and aluminum have displaced glass in many applications during the past 20 years, especially in the container segment.

How is the company positioning itself to take advantage of growing global demand for architectural glass?

World demand for flat glass will rise more than 4 percent per year, according to Freedonia Group.

What future does the company see for glass products in computers?

Expansion of the computer industry provides glass manufacturers with a growing market.

Web Links

Fiber Optics Online

A premier sourcing site for the fiber optic communications industry.
www.fiberopticsonline.com

Glass on Web

News.
www.glassonweb.com

Glass Packaging Institute

Information on bottles and jars.
www.gpi.org

Glass Resource

Comprehensive information on specifications, processes, innovations, history, and types of glass.
www.glassresource.com

glassBYTEs

Latest auto and flat glass industry news.
www.glassbytes.com

Glasslinks

Wealth of links and information on flat and auto glass.
www.glasslinks.com

GlassOnline Magazine

News articles and more. Large news archive.
www.glassonline.com

How Fiber Optics Work

Description of how fiber optics work.
electronics.howstuffworks.com/fiber-optic.htm

National Glass Association

Flat glass news.
www.glass.org

USGlass Magazine

News on architectural and automotive glass.
www.usglassmag.com

www.fiber-optics.info

Links, trade journals, and glossary.
www.fiber-optics.info

Glossary of Acronyms

AVD — axial vapor deposition
IVD — inside vapor deposition
OEM — original equipment manufacturers
OVD — outside vapor deposition
TRI — toxic release inventory

HOOVER'S TOP COMPANIES

Largest Companies by Sales	($ mil.)
PPG Industries, Inc.	15,849.0
Owens-Illinois, Inc.	7,884.7
Corning Incorporated	5,948.0
Guardian Industries Corp.	5,470.0
Apogee Enterprises, Inc.	881.8
Saint-Gobain Containers, Inc.	869.3

Largest Employers	Employees
PPG Industries, Inc.	34,900
Corning Incorporated	27,000
Owens-Illinois, Inc.	23,000
Guardian Industries Corp.	19,000
Anchor Hocking Company	8,900
Saint-Gobain Containers, Inc.	8,500
Apogee Enterprises, Inc.	5,438
Pilkington North America Inc.	4,500
Schott Corporation	3,101
Vitro America Inc.	3,000

Fastest Growing* by Five-Year Sales Growth	(%)
Diversified Thermal Solutions, Inc.	124.5
Dynasil Corporation of America	49.4
Corning Incorporated	14.0
PPG Industries, Inc.	12.6
Owens-Illinois, Inc.	5.1
Guardian Industries Corp.	4.6
Apogee Enterprises, Inc.	2.7

Fastest Growing* by Five-Year Employee Growth	(%)
Dynasil Corporation of America	63.0
PPG Industries, Inc.	6.4
Corning Incorporated	5.6
Apogee Enterprises, Inc.	0.4

Top Public Companies by Market Value	($ mil.)
Corning Incorporated	14,752.4
PPG Industries, Inc.	6,966.9
Owens-Illinois, Inc.	4,568.2
Kaire Holdings Incorporated	2,700.0
Apogee Enterprises, Inc.	442.4

* These rates are compounded annualized increases and may have resulted from acquisitions or one time gains. If less than 6 years of data are available, growth is for the years available.

SOURCE: HOOVER'S, INC., DATABASE

Golf Courses

The 12,000 golf courses in the US generate combined annual revenue of about $18 billion. Large companies include ClubCorp and American Golf. About 3,000 courses, with $7 billion of revenue, are owned by non-profit entities such as municipalities and private clubs. The industry is highly fragmented: within the commercial segment, the 50 largest companies account for only about 25 percent of the market. Most companies operate just one or two courses. The average commercial course has annual revenue of about $1 million.

Competitive Landscape

Demand is driven by demographics and population growth. The profitability of individual companies depends on efficient operations and good marketing, because many costs are fixed. Large companies can have advantages in management experience. Small companies can compete successfully by operating in favorable locations or through superior marketing. The industry is very labor-intensive: annual revenue per employee is just $55,000.

Products, Operations & Technology

Golf courses receive revenue from membership dues, activity fees, sales of food and drinks, and sales of merchandise. Membership dues account for a third of industry revenue; activity fees ("greens fees"), 25 percent; food and drinks, 25 percent.

Golf courses can be classified as private or open to the public. Private courses may be associated with country clubs, golf clubs, or real estate developments. Courses open to the public may be associated with resorts or operated as local "daily fee" courses, including commercial and municipal courses. About 70 percent of US courses are open to the public. Private courses get revenue mainly from annual memberships, public courses mainly from daily fees.

BUSINESS CHALLENGES

» Participation Growth Slow

Participation in golf has been flat for the last decade. As many as 3 million people join the sport every year, but roughly the same number quit. Aging baby boomers were responsible for most growth in the number of golfers and in the development of real estate-related golf courses in the past decade.

» More Stringent Water Access Regulations

Access to adequate amounts of water for golf course irrigation is a major issue in some areas of the country, and owners always struggle with water quality and shortages. Strong population growth in the West and Southwest has increased demand for golf courses in areas that periodically suffer drought conditions. Municipal regulations can prevent golf course operators from using as much water as they need. Use of treated, recycled wastewater could reduce the need for golf courses to tap into drinking water systems for irrigation, ease bans on water consumption during droughts, and allow courses to better maintain greens during droughts.

» Land Use Restrictions

With the average golf course requiring 200 acres of land and located on prime land within metropolitan areas, fewer suitable locations exist in areas of highest demand. Preservationists are concerned with courses being built on historical sites, like Civil War battlegrounds or Indian mounds. Federal, local, and state agencies often require land to be set aside on new courses to protect endangered species of birds and plants.

The operations of all golf courses are similar and include activities aimed at customers such as scheduling, food service and merchandise sales, and groundskeeping activities such as mowing, fertilizing, tree care, watering, and maintenance. The costs to maintain a golf course are largely the same no matter how many golfers use the course. Access to enough water is a major consideration and can be a major cost. In warm and dry areas like Florida, Arizona, or Southern California, where golf can be played year-round, a popular course can host between 80,000 and 100,000 rounds per year. But the average course in the US hosts an average of 30,000 rounds per year, mainly because of adverse winter weather. Private courses are used even more lightly.

Sales & Marketing

A typical golfer is a 40-year-old male with a household income of $70,000, who plays 20 rounds a year. Local golf courses market themselves through local newspaper and magazine advertising, and by hosting local tournaments. Because many golfers have above-average income, courses may host promotional events together with car dealers, stock brokers, or other providers of up-scale products and services.

The median cost of a weekend round of golf at an 18-hole municipal golf course in the US is close to $35. Commercial fee courses may charge $30 during the week and over $50 on weekends. Many private clubs have initiation fees over $20,000 and monthly fees that vary from $200 to $500. Out of the 25 million golfers, about 6 million play regularly and account for 60 percent of all spending.

Human Resources

Golf course managers are often highly paid because efficient operations are so important, but many employees require few skills and accordingly receive relatively low pay. Average earnings for golf course workers are about 30 percent less than for the average US worker. Because demand varies sharply during the day, week, and year, many employees in food or merchandise sales are part-time workers. The industry's safety record is average.

Industry Employment Growth

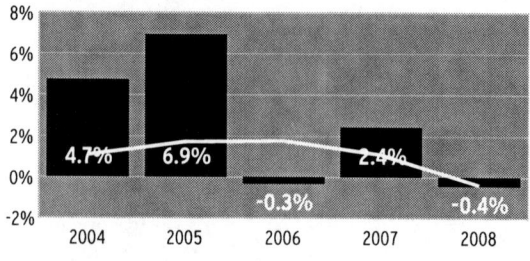

	2004	2005	2006	2007	2008
	4.7%	6.9%	-0.3%	2.4%	-0.4%

Average Hourly Earnings

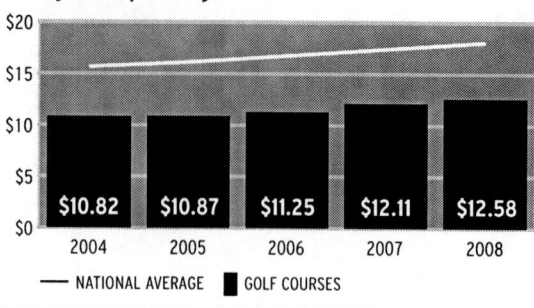

	2004	2005	2006	2007	2008
	$10.82	$10.87	$11.25	$12.11	$12.58

— NATIONAL AVERAGE   ■ GOLF COURSES

SOURCE: BUREAU OF LABOR STATISTICS

Call Preparation Questions

How is the company reducing annual turnover of members or customers?

Participation in golf has been flat for the last decade.

What arrangements does the company have for future water supplies?

Access to adequate amounts of water for golf course irrigation is a major issue in some areas of the country, and owners always struggle with water quality and shortages.

How does the company address concerns about land use and expansion?

With the average golf course requiring 200 acres of land and located on prime land within metropolitan areas, fewer suitable locations exist in areas of highest demand.

What new maintenance technologies is the company considering investing in? To what benefit?

Technology plays a significant role in managing and maintaining courses.

What plans does the company have to build or remodel practice range facilities on its courses?

Golfers are using practice or range facilities more, which also leads to increased rounds played and more commitment to the game.

Web Links

Golf Business Magazine

Official publication of the NGCOA.
www.golfbusinessmagazine.com

Golf Course Builders Association of America

Information from a nonprofit trade association of the world's foremost golf course builders and leading suppliers for the golf course construction industry.
www.gcbaa.org

Golf Course Industry

Online journal.
www.golfcoursenews.com

Golf Course Management

Articles.
www.gcsaa.org/GCM

Golf Digest Magazine

Online magazine.
www.golfdigest.com

Golf Range Association of America

Magazine, publications, links, and Top 100 Golf Ranges.
www.golfrange.org

National Golf Course Owners Association (NGCOA)

Publications, suppliers, news, and conferences.
www.ngcoa.org

National Golf Foundation

Industry trade group. Excellent statistics on golfers and golf courses.
www.ngf.org

Southern Golf

Guide to Gulf Coast golf.
www.southerngolf.com

The Golf Course Superintendents Association of America

Highlights, news, resource center, and government issues.
www.gcsaa.org

United States Golf Association

Equipment, greens, rules, championships, amateur status, associations, and news.
usga.org

Glossary of Acronyms

IPM — integrated pest management
NGF — National Golf Foundation
NGP — National Golf Properties
USGA — US Golf Association

HOOVER'S TOP COMPANIES

Largest Employers	Employees
ClubCorp USA, Inc.	16,000
American Golf Corporation	10,000
Troon Golf L.L.C.	1,500
Arnold Palmer Golf Management, LLC	1,000
Heritage Golf Group, LLC	800
KemperSports Inc.	250
Augusta National, Inc.	200
Club Management Enterprises, L.L.C.	70
Wildcat Golf Club	60
Redstone Golf Management, L.L.P.	30

SOURCE: HOOVER'S, INC., DATABASE

Government Contractors

The US federal government each year spends about $500 billion to buy goods and services, including $240 billion for Medicare, $150 billion for defense, and $100 billion for non-defense items. State and local governments spend an additional $150 billion on capital projects, such as highways, bridges, and public buildings. Government contractors include large corporations, like Lockheed Martin and Boeing; academic institutions, like the University of California and California Institute of Technology; health care companies, like AmeriSourceBergen; and tens of thousands of smaller companies.

The government contracting industry is highly fragmented, but at the federal level is concentrated at the top:the 100 largest federal contractors receive about 60 percent of procurement dollars.

Competitive Landscape

Demand is driven by the expanding needs of governments and the trend toward outsourcing. The profitability of individual contracts depends on efficiency, because most contracts have a fixed price. Large companies have advantages in getting large contracts and may have greater expertise in the contracting process, but small companies can compete successfully for most contracts by offering the lowest price. Although some government contracts can be handled only by large companies, small companies can be very competitive by supplying specialized products or services, or by working as subcontractors. Some programs set funds aside specifically for small businesses.

Products, Operations & Technology

In addition to supplying ordinary administrative goods and services, commercial vendors provide governments with specialized goods and services such as consulting, IT, research, construction, weapons, and medical care. Dif-

BUSINESS CHALLENGES

» Dependence on Government Revenues

The amount the federal government can spend each year depends on political factors and the economy's health. State and local governments are even more constrained because they're usually required to have a balanced budget, so spending falls if revenue falls. For example, after growing at an average annual rate of 7 percent between 1995 and 2000, state and local tax revenues were flat in 2002.

» Expense of Regulation Compliance

Government contractors must adhere to an additional layer of regulations and accounting procedures. The federal Cost Accounting Standards (CAS), overseen by the Cost Accounting Standards Board (CASB), require contractors to operate a more detailed set of accounting books. CAS focuses on allowable expenses, allocation of expenses to the correct time period, and correct classification of expenses. Defense contractors are audited by the Defense Contract Audit Agency (DCAA); nondefense contractors by other agencies.

» Customer Concentration

Many government contractors depend on the government for virtually all their revenue. While large contractors may operate several government programs that consist of many individual contracts and last for years, providing a dependable stream of revenue, smaller contractors may work on only a few contracts of short duration. The loss of contracts or the inability to get new ones is a major threat to profitability or even survival. Both large and small contractors are constantly seeking new contracts, but the overall success rate for companies bidding on a government contract is less than 50 percent.

ferent levels of government have different commercial needs. Local governments contract mainly for construction and waste management services. State governments spend heavily on construction; consulting; medical services (Medicaid); and information systems. The federal government uses commercial vendors most heavily for defense, medical services, consulting, R&D, and information systems.

Aside from Medicare, the federal government contracts with commercial vendors for about $200 billion of goods and services through Procurement Contracts issued by some 60 executive departments and agencies. The largest amounts are contracted by the Department of Defense (DoD); Department of Energy; General Services Administration (GSA); and NASA. Although contracts and purchases must usually be awarded to the lowest qualified bidder, various programs that favor small businesses are administered through the Small Business Administration (SBA). About 4 percent of total federal procurement dollars were awarded under such programs. Overall, 20 percent of procurement dollars go to small businesses, 70 percent to large ones, and the rest to nonprofits, foreign contractors, and other vendors.

Sales & Marketing

To supply goods and services, commercial vendors must follow special procedures meant to ensure fair competition and prevent waste and fraud. The cornerstone of all government contracting is the bidding process, which is open to any vendor that meets certain minimal standards. Regulations governing the solicitation and award of contracts vary by state and local jurisdiction, but generally follow the same guidelines as federal regulations.

For a company to become a vendor to the federal government, it must register and meet certain financial standards. Once approved, a vendor can respond to specific "solicitations" made by departments or agencies that are looking for goods or services and have issued a request for proposal (RFP). These requests are published on various websites, including www.fedbizopps.gov. For routine supplies and services, several vendors may be approved for each "Schedule."

Although federal departments and agencies can directly enter into contracts with commercial vendors, the federal procurement process is overseen by the General Services Administration (GSA) and governed by Federal Acquisition Regulations (FAR), which are very specific. Within each department and agency, only specified procurement officers can contract with vendors. Once contracts are signed, administrative officers monitor progress and performance, and contracts may be audited to ensure that

correct procedures and accounting rules are followed.

Some federal departments have additional procedures in addition to FAR; defense contractors must follow the Defense Federal Acquisition Regulation Supplement (DFARS). Defense contracts are facilitated by the Defense Contract Management Agency (DCMA) and audited by the Defense Contract Audit Agency (DCAA). The Department of Health and Human Services has HHS Acquisition Regulations (HHSAR). Special regulations for Medicare vendors are overseen by the Centers for Medicare & Medicaid Services.

Human Resources

Because they often supply expertise that governments don't have, contractors typically assign highly trained employees to work on contracts. Companies may hire consultants or outside experts specifically to work on a government contract.

Call Preparation Questions

How much of company revenue depends on government contracts?

The amount the federal government can spend each year depends on political factors and the economy's health.

How does the company manage the additional expense of complying with government contracting regulations?

Government contractors must adhere to an additional layer of regulations and accounting procedures.

How reliant is the company on any single government program?

Many government contractors depend on the government for virtually all their revenue.

Web Links

Consolidated Federal Funds Report

Details about federal spending.
www.census.gov/govs/www/cffr.html

Defense Contract Audit Agency

Provides accounting and financial advisory services regarding DoD contracts.
www.dcaa.mil

Defense Contract Management Agency

Independent combat support agency within the DoD.
www.dcma.mil

Department of Defense Business Opportunities

How to do business with the Department of Defense.
www.dod.gov/other_info/business.html

Federal Acquisition Regulation

Acquisition information.
www.arnet.gov

Federal Business Opportunities

Primary federal site for government procurement.
www.fedbizopps.gov

Federal Procurement Data System

Excellent federal procurement statistics. Top 100 contractors.
www.fpds.gov

General Services Administration

GSA secures the buildings, products, services, and technology for federal agencies.
www.gsa.gov

Government Executive Magazine

News about federal government procurement. Articles. Excellent industry links.
www.governmentexecutive.com/procurement

Legal Information Institute

Information about government contracts.
www.law.cornell.edu/topics/
government_contracts.html

National Association of State Budget Officers

State budget issues.
www.nasbo.org

Office of Management and Budget

Federal budget issues.
www.whitehouse.gov/omb

Glossary of Acronyms

CAS — Cost Accounting Standards
CASB — Cost Accounting Standards Board
DCAA — Defense Contract Audit Agency
DCMA — Defense Contract Management Agency
DFARS — Defense Federal Acquisition Regulation Supplement
DHS — Department of Homeland Security
DOD — Department of Defense
DOE — Department of Energy
FAR — Federal Acquisition Regulation
GSA — General Services Administration
HHS — Department of Health and Human Services
HHSAR — Health and Human Services Acquisition Regulation
IT — information technology
ITAA — Information Technology Association of America
NASA — National Aeronautics and Space Administration
OMB — Office of Management and Budget
RFP — request for proposal
SBA — Small Business Administration

HOOVER'S TOP COMPANIES

Largest Companies by Sales	($ mil.)
AT&T Inc.	124,028.0
Hewlett-Packard Company	118,364.0
International Business Machines Corporation	103,630.0
McKesson Corporation	101,703.0
Verizon Communications Inc.	97,354.0
AmerisourceBergen Corporation	70,189.7
The Boeing Company	60,909.0
Microsoft Corporation	60,420.0
Lockheed Martin Corporation	42,731.0
Kaiser Permanente	37,800.0

Largest Employers	Employees
Manpower Inc.	4,033,000
Kelly Services, Inc.	760,000
International Business Machines Corporation	426,969
Hewlett-Packard Company	321,000
AT&T Inc.	310,000
ARAMARK Corporation	250,000
Verizon Communications Inc.	235,000
The Boeing Company	162,200
Kaiser Permanente	159,766
Lockheed Martin Corporation	146,000

Fastest Growing* by Five-Year Sales Growth	(%)
AT&T Inc.	24.9
Fluor Corporation	20.5
Jacobs Engineering Group Inc.	19.5
Oracle Corporation	18.8
Bechtel Group, Inc.	18.4
The Shaw Group Inc.	16.2
Microsoft Corporation	13.4
McKesson Corporation	12.2
Manpower Inc.	12.1
General Dynamics Corporation	12.0

Fastest Growing* by Five-Year Employee Growth	(%)
The Shaw Group Inc.	139.2
AT&T Inc.	28.1
Hewlett-Packard Company	17.7
Oracle Corporation	15.7
Manpower Inc.	11.4
Microsoft Corporation	10.6
Fluor Corporation	8.8
General Dynamics Corporation	8.5
McKesson Corporation	6.1
International Business Machines Corporation	4.7

Top Public Companies by Market Value	($ mil.)
Microsoft Corporation	251,744.0
AT&T Inc.	167,950.8
Oracle Corporation	117,626.0
International Business Machines Corporation	112,698.3
Verizon Communications Inc.	100,602.0

* These rates are compounded annualized increases and may have resulted from acquisitions or one time gains. If less than 6 years of data are available, growth is for the years available.

SOURCE: HOOVER'S, INC., DATABASE

Grain Milling

The grain milling industry includes about 400 companies with combined annual revenue of $11 billion. Major companies include Archer Daniels Midland (ADM), ConAgra, Cargill, and General Mills. The industry is fragmented: the top 25 companies account for 25 percent of industry revenue.

Grain milling is the milling of flour and rice; the malting of grains (primarily barley); and the mixing of prepared flour mixes and dough. This industry doesn't include revenue from mills that prepare breakfast cereals, nor does it include meal ground from legumes or nuts.

Competitive Landscape

Demand is driven by consumer patterns in bread, whole grains, and rice consumption. The profitability of individual companies depends on managing grain prices and inventory effectively, and minimizing the risk of rodents, insects, and molds. Large companies have advantages in advanced milling technology and a diversified product line. Small operations can compete effectively by specializing in organic, non-genetically modified, or heirloom grains. The industry is capital-intensive: average annual revenue per employee is about $600,000.

Products, Operations & Technology

Major products include wheat flour (55 percent of the market); rice (20 percent); and cornmeal (10 percent). Other products include malted barley and prepared flour mixes.

Any grain can be ground into flour, but wheat is the most common milled grain. About three-quarters of all US grain products are made from wheat flour. Each year, mills grind around 900 million bushels of wheat, producing 20 million tons of flour.

Wheat is typically seeded in spring or fall and harvested in late summer. Trucks transfer harvested wheat from a farm or elevator to a mill. After weigh-in and inspection, trucks

BUSINESS CHALLENGES

» Volatile Grain Prices

Grain prices paid by milling companies fluctuate considerably from year to year, due in large part to inconsistencies in wheat supply and demand. Wheat supplies are subject to weather, and poor global harvests can drive up demand for US exports. Government subsidies for competing products, like corn for ethanol and soybeans, can also have a major impact on wheat supply and prices. Higher grain prices can affect operating costs and profit margins for milling companies. Established sales contracts between flour mills and key customers can limit a mill's ability to pass along increased raw material costs.

» Dependence on Consumer Trends

Wheat accounts for over half of total industry revenue, and consumers can be fickle about their overall wheat intake. Grain mills depend highly on consumer interest in eating wheat-based products like bread, pasta, and cereal. Low-carbohydrate diets, a shift from bleached white flour, or a switch from barley-based beer to wine can significantly impact profits. Most mills process only one type of flour per site; thus, consumer trends can impact capacity levels and profitability at individual facilities.

» Dependence on Fumigants

Grain storage bins attract rodents and insects, and most large millers rely on regular fumigation to prevent pest damage. The EPA is reviewing several chemicals used by mills as rodenticides, insecticides, and fumigants. Some consumer advocacy and environmental groups want the EPA to phase out all fumigants. Chloropicrin, once used as a chemical weapon, is used to treat empty bins, but is under EPA review and risk assessment.

dump the grain into a dump pit. A conveyor takes the seed from the pit to a cleaning house, where machines pull large and small particles from the grain. After cleaning, the wheat must be tempered for about 24 hours, a process that adds water to the wheat, raising its kernel moisture.

Mills grind, sift, purify, and sometimes bleach grain until the flour reaches the preferred grade. Finished flour is moved to a hopper, where it's bagged and held in inventory until delivered by truck or rail, or used in-house to make prepared dough. Bags can range from industrial-sized 50- or 100-pound sacks to three-pound bags for retail sale.

Wheat is separated into five main classes: hard red winter (HRW); hard red spring (HRS); soft red winter (SRW); soft white; and durum. Hard flours are best for baking bread; soft are used to make cakes, pastries, and tortillas; durum wheat is hard and high-protein and is used to make pasta. Hard wheat represents around 70 percent of all flour milled; soft wheat, 20 percent; and durum, 8 percent.

Grain mills tend to specialize in a single class of wheat. However, by altering the milling process, a mill can produce multiple products. White flour is made using only the endosperm portion of the wheat kernel. The unused bran and middlings, byproducts called millfeed, are sold as livestock feed. Whole wheat flour retains the bran and germ of the kernel and doesn't produce millfeed.

A 60-pound bushel of wheat typically yields 42 pounds of white flour and 18 pounds of millfeed. A commercial loaf of bread uses 1 pound of flour; thus, a bushel of wheat yields 42 loaves of white bread. Americans consume an average of 130 pounds of wheat and 20 pounds of rice each year.

Common inputs in the grain milling industry include electricity; packaging materials such as plastic, cardboard, and textile bags; wood for pallets; and equipment repairs. Grain is the largest material cost.

Recent technological advances include complex milling machinery that can quickly process large quantities of flour. Other important advances include highly precise temperature and humidity controls in the storage facility, and fumigants with reduced ozone emissions.

Sales & Marketing

Typical customers are commercial bakeries, fast food and quickservice restaurants, cereal manufacturers, and food companies. Companies that manufacture bread mixes, dough, or branded products sell directly to retailers. Milo, a sorghum derivative, is used to make wallboard and is sold to the construction industry.

Marketing includes trade publications, promotional events, trade shows, and customer vis-

its. Institutional and retail product sales are driven by a mix of a traditional internal sales force and third-party brokers. Some companies use solution-based selling to avoid selling commodities based solely on price. Large mills often develop consumer food products or partner with major food companies to develop co-branded products. Because most large mills sell consumer products, customer service typically includes a toll-free number and Web-based customer assistance.

Internet sales are limited. Companies rely more on traditional sales and marketing and use the Internet to promote products. Several large companies have developed restricted-access Intranets for customers to review and place orders, track rail cars, and manage inventory.

Typical product prices are $35 for a 100-pound sack of bread flour and $10 per hundredweight (cwt) for both cornmeal and rice. Prices are susceptible to commodity shortages and oversupply. Grain shortages can lead to price increases for bulk flour and consumer products like bread and beer.

Human Resources

Grain milling wages average $18 per hour, about 5 percent higher than the national average. Productivity has steadily increased in recent years, rising nearly 40 percent in the 10 years ending in 2005. Grain milling requires mechanical and technical skills. A few Midwestern universities offer advanced degrees in cereal grain science.

The annual injury rate in grain milling is about 15 percent higher than the national average. Most injuries involve sprains, strains, bruises, and contusions resulting from equipment use, falls, and overexertion. Amputations are eight times higher than the national average. Noise from machinery can be a problem at older mills, leading to employee hearing loss. Grain dust must be restricted and confined to reduce the risk of spontaneous explosions, which result in higher than average burns and deaths.

Industry Employment Growth

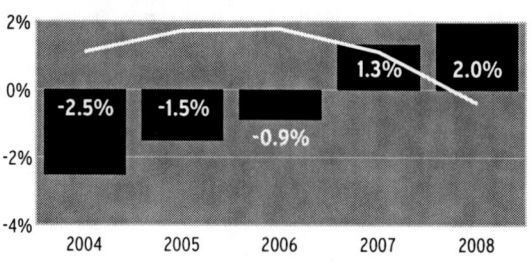

SOURCE: BUREAU OF LABOR STATISTICS

Call Preparation Questions

How does the mill manage highly volatile grain prices?

Grain prices paid by milling companies fluctuate considerably from year to year, due in large part to inconsistencies in wheat supply and demand.

How do consumer trends like low-carb diets affect company profitability?

Wheat accounts for over half of total industry revenue, and consumers can be fickle about their overall wheat intake.

How dependent is the company on traditional chemical fumigants?

Grain storage bins attract rodents and insects, and most large millers rely on regular fumigation to prevent pest damage.

How has the company responded to increased interest in local and healthy foods?

As more consumers seek locally grown and healthy foods, historic grain mills may draw more interest as tourist destinations.

Web Links

USDA Briefing Room on Rice

Historical levels, current status, and future projections for rice.

www.ers.usda.gov/Briefing/Rice

USDA Briefing Room on Wheat

Historical levels, current status, and future projections for wheat.

www.ers.usda.gov/Briefing/Wheat

USDA National Agricultural Statistics Service

Data on farmed wheat, rice, corn for meal, and barley.

www.nass.usda.gov

Glossary of Acronyms

ADM — Archer Daniels Midland

ESL — extended shelf life

FIFRA — Federal Insecticide, Fungicide, and Rodenticide Act

GIPSA — Grain Inspection, Packers and Stockyards Administration

HRS — hard red spring wheat

HRW — hard red winter wheat

SRW — soft red winter wheat

HOOVER'S TOP COMPANIES

Largest Companies by Sales	($ mil.)
Cargill, Incorporated	120,439.0
Archer Daniels Midland Company	69,816.0
Bunge Limited	52,574.0
General Mills, Inc.	13,652.1
ConAgra Foods, Inc.	11,605.7
Seaboard Corporation	4,267.8
Bartlett and Company	1,510.0
Riceland Foods, Inc.	947.0

Largest Employers	Employees
Cargill, Incorporated	160,000
General Mills, Inc.	29,500
Archer Daniels Midland Company	27,600
ConAgra Foods, Inc.	25,000
Bunge Limited	23,889
Seaboard Corporation	10,663
Riviana Foods Inc.	2,752
Riceland Foods, Inc.	1,900
Bartlett and Company	700
Producers Rice Mill, Inc.	600

Fastest Growing* by Five-Year Sales Growth	(%)
Bartlett and Company	37.3
Bunge Limited	18.9
Archer Daniels Midland Company	17.9
Cargill, Incorporated	17.2
Seaboard Corporation	16.6
MGP Ingredients, Inc.	13.3
General Mills, Inc.	5.4
Riceland Foods, Inc.	4.8

Fastest Growing* by Five-Year Employee Growth	(%)
Cargill, Incorporated	10.3
General Mills, Inc.	1.6
Archer Daniels Midland Company	1.5
Seaboard Corporation	1.5

Top Public Companies by Market Value	($ mil.)
Archer Daniels Midland Company	21,735.0
General Mills, Inc.	20,617.9
ConAgra Foods, Inc.	11,324.6
Bunge Limited	6,296.9
Seaboard Corporation	1,481.1

* These rates are compounded annualized increases and may have resulted from acquisitions or one time gains. If less than 6 years of data are available, growth is for the years available.

SOURCE: HOOVER'S, INC., DATABASE

Graphic Design Services

The US graphic design services industry includes about 16,000 companies with combined annual revenue of $8 billion. Major companies are units of large, integrated design firms that provide graphic design services in support of a primary specialty like architectural, environmental, or product design, such as Gensler, ERM, and IDEO, respectively. The industry consists of privately owned companies and is highly fragmented: the 50 largest firms account for less than 20 percent of total industry revenue. Most firms are small: a typical business has one location, fewer than four employees, and average annual revenue of around $500,000. About 30 percent of graphic designers are self-employed.

Competitive Landscape

Regional economic activity drives demand, because most graphic design firms are small and work locally. The profitability of individual companies depends on accurate bidding, timely delivery of projects, and a steady volume of work. Large companies have advantages in marketing and sales, breadth of services, delivery of complex projects, and supporting ongoing contracts. Small companies can compete effectively by responding quicker, adopting new trends, and specializing by services or markets. The industry is labor-intensive: average annual revenue per employee is around $130,000.

Customers and prospects become competitors when they bring design services in-house, rather than use graphic design firms. Freelance designers may be competitors or contract labor.

Products, Operations & Technology

Major industry services are general graphic design, commercial art and illustration, drafting, and photography. General graphic design services comprise 75 percent of industry revenue, and commercial art and illustration, over 15 percent. Some firms also offer other special-

BUSINESS CHALLENGES

» Demand Depends On Economic Activity

Most graphic design firms are small and rely on the local economy or a specific customer industry. Many clients, in turn, are consumer-oriented companies that depend on personal income to drive sales. In a healthy economy, businesses increase spending on advertising and promotion, which are key projects for graphic designers. Economic slowdowns mean cuts to marketing budgets and decreased demand for graphic designers.

» Competition from Customer In-house Staff

Easy-to-use design software and digital collaborative tools enable client companies to bring graphic design in-house for many projects; consequently, more corporations are adding designers to their marketing staffs. Design firms find themselves competing with potential clients, in addition to other businesses. Competition affects industry employment, which fell almost 14 percent in a recent five-year period.

» Competition from Online Companies

Web-based companies that provide graphic design and printing services are growing competitors, especially at the lower end of the market. Online companies, like VistaPrint, typically target small businesses with fewer than 10 employees, which is the focus of many graphic design firms. Online firms provide easy-to-use, do-it-yourself web applications and do-it-for-me design consulting services, mainly to produce business cards, brochures, and reports. VistaPrint's US revenue more than doubled in a recent two-year period.

ized, professional design services and some sell merchandise. The graphic design industry, once known as graphic arts, has evolved from producing only graphical images to providing more extensive design services — to such a degree that the printing industry now uses the moniker "graphic arts."

Graphic design services result in a wide variety of visual communication products, such as logos, signage, advertisements, book and CD covers, publication layouts, brochures, packaging, websites, new typefaces, and even election ballots. Some leading-edge firms also offer text content. The particular services a firm supplies depend highly on its staff's skills. Many firms specialize by content, such as corporate or product branding; signage and directional wayfinding systems ("environmental graphics"); or website graphic design. Other firms specialize by industry.

Businesses, institutions, and government agencies hire graphic designers to develop visual designs for printed, video, or multi-media communications. Graphic designers analyze customer needs, research the subject and audience, and plan, design, and create visual messages. Designers and their clients determine the appropriate types of media for communicating the messages, such as print, film, or electronic media. Graphic designers use a variety of visual elements and methods to convey the message, including color, typeface, illustration, photography, and animation. In addition to the creative and technical aspects of design, leading firms develop overall corporate visual communication strategies.

In developing a project, designers produce sketches by hand or computer. At various stages of the project, the design firm presents work to the clients for feedback and approval. As the project progresses, designers fine-tune the design details. The final version is ready-to-use ("camera-ready") for client production. Some full-service design firms also provide project management to coordinate the printing and production processes.

Major materials that the industry uses include art supplies, paper, typeface fonts, and stock images. Firms obtain art and paper supplies from distributors or through business accounts at art supply stores, and often favor certain suppliers regardless of location. Typeface fonts are available under license online, as are camera-ready stock images, which include photographs, illustrations, and video clips. Firms subscribe to color forecasting companies to receive information about color trends. Design firms use digital cameras for original photography and computer software for the bulk of design work.

Graphic design firms increasingly rely on technology — computers, cameras, and specialized equipment — to develop and deliver projects. Designers predominantly use Apple Computer's Mac operating system, due to the visual, easy-to-use interface and special graphics capabilities, such as handling large graphic and video files. Designers use special software to develop graphics and illustrations, layouts, web pages, animation, and interactive media designs. Software also helps size and change photographs.

Sales & Marketing

Typical customers are businesses, organizations, and government entities that need visual design of corporate and brand logos, product labels and packaging, advertising and promotion, computer graphics and websites, and publications and reports. Customers include a wide range of entities, such as advertising firms, publishers, manufacturers, health care facilities, retailers, and entertainment companies — virtually any organization that needs to convey visual components in communications with its audience.

Major types of marketing include advertisements in telephone directories and trade publications, and a firm's website, which showcases finished projects. Firms with a content specialty, such as health care or consumer electronics, market to organizations in the appropriate industry. In small graphic design firms, the owner often is the only salesperson, but larger companies also have a sales force. Graphic design firms build referral relationships with complementary companies and establish partnerships to attract and deliver a wider range of projects. Design firms also join local business associations to expand professional contacts and develop sales opportunities.

Prices range from hourly fees of $40 to over $300, or fixed-price projects from under $1,000 to thousands, depending on the scope and scale of the contract. Nationally known firms and principals can charge higher rates. Major competition comes from complementary industries that serve the business market and from client in-house graphic design staffs. Ad agencies, marketing groups, and architecture firms are among the industries that provide visual services and products and include graphic design in their repertoires. Companies as diverse as packaging manufacturers and commercial printers also offer graphic design services to clients for customization of their finished products.

Human Resources

Graphic design requires special training and most firms hire designers with college degrees in design or a related art field. Accordingly, wages are almost 30 percent higher than the national average. Employees doing solely CAD or drafting may have less education, but prior skills training is important. Designers need to be creative and have good problem-solving skills, and those who interact with clients need good verbal communication skills. Proficiency using computer graphics and design software is becoming a requirement.

Business skills can be challenging for the self-employed, who account for 30 percent of graphic designers. Large firms have the luxury of hiring people for specialized functions, like drafting, illustration, or CAD, but small firms benefit when employees have multiple skills. Most work is in an office or studio environment, so industry injury rates, not surprisingly, are negligible. Increasing use of computers by designers, however, causes concern about repetitive stress injury, a subject of employer and trade group awareness training.

Industry Employment Growth

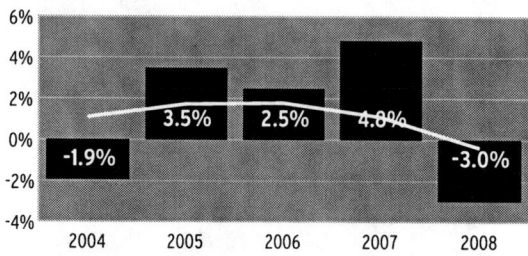

Average Hourly Earnings

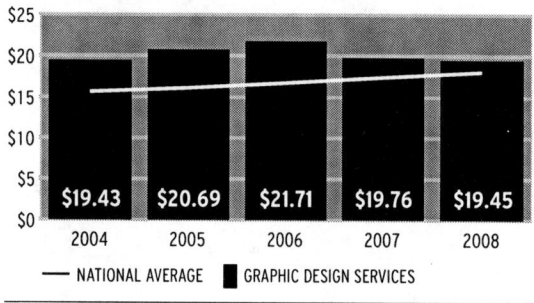

— NATIONAL AVERAGE ■ GRAPHIC DESIGN SERVICES

SOURCE: BUREAU OF LABOR STATISTICS

Call Preparation Questions

How dependent is the firm on business from local customers or one industry?

Most graphic design firms are small and rely on the local economy or a specific customer industry.

What changes has the firm seen in customer use of in-house design staff?

Easy-to-use design software and digital collaborative tools enable client companies to bring graphic design in-house for many projects; consequently, more corporations are adding designers to their marketing staffs.

How concerned is the company about competition from online companies?

Web-based companies that provide graphic design and printing services are growing competitors, especially at the lower end of the market.

What technical advantages or challenges does the firm have designing e-commerce websites?

Technically astute graphic design firms are adding transactional websites (e-commerce) to their services, helping client sales efforts.

Web Links

American Institute of Graphic Arts

Professional group's strategic initiatives, conferences, publications.
www.aiga.org

Creativepro.com

Graphics news, feature articles, technology reviews.
www.creativepro.com

Eye

Trendsetting magazine of graphic design and visual culture.
www.eyemagazine.com

Graphic Artists Guild

Extensive links to graphic design firms; legislative issues.
www.gag.org

Graphic Design USA

Industry news in the current Issue and e-newsletter links.
www.gdusa.com

Society for Environmental Graphic Design

News items about firms' project wins.
www.segd.org

Society for Publication Designers

Excellent industry resource links.
www.spd.org

Glossary of Acronyms

AIGA — American Institute of Graphic Arts
CAD — computer-aided design
E&O — errors and omissions insurance
GAG — Graphic Artists Guild
GDC — Society of Graphic Designers of Canada
GDUSA — Graphic Design USA

Grocery Stores and Supermarkets

THIS INDUSTRY
INCLUDES:

SIC CODES
5411   Grocery Stores

NAICS CODES
44511   Supermarkets and
        Other Grocery
        (except
        Convenience)
        Stores

The US retail grocery industry includes about 70,000 grocery stores (excluding convenience stores) with combined annual revenue of almost $500 billion. Large companies include Kroger, Safeway, SUPERVALU, and Ahold. The industry is concentrated: the 50 largest companies are about 70 percent of industry sales.

Competitive Landscape

Population growth and consumer tastes drive demand. Because margins are low, the profitability of individual companies depends on high volume sales and efficient operations. Large companies can offer a wide selection of products and have advantages in purchasing, distribution, marketing, and finance. Small companies can compete effectively by offering specialty products, serving a local market, or providing superior customer service. Annual revenue per worker averages $180,000.

Mass merchandisers and warehouse clubs have aggressively pursued the retail grocery market. As a result, Wal-Mart is the largest seller of groceries in the US. Other competition includes specialty food stores, convenience stores, drugstores, dollar stores, and, to some degree, restaurants.

Products, Operations & Technology

Major products sold include perishable foods (50 percent of industry sales); non-perishable foods (25 percent); and non-food items (20 percent). Perishables include meats/poultry/fish, produce, dairy, frozen foods, and deli items. Non-perishable foods (or dry grocery products) include most packaged goods, such as cereals, snacks, and soft drinks. Non-food items include health and beauty products, general merchandise, and medication (including prescription drugs).

The industry includes national and regional chains and independent retailers. Large companies may operate multiple chains under differ-

BUSINESS CHALLENGES

» Competition from Alternative Retailers

As alternative retailers realized the traffic-driving power of food sales, the competitive set for grocery stores expanded and the battle over food dollars became more intense. By buying in enormous volume, mass merchandisers and warehouse clubs have become low price leaders: Wal-mart is the largest food retailer in the US and holds an estimated 20 percent of the grocery market, according to Retail Forward. In addition, time-starved consumers are spending a greater percentage of food dollars away from home at restaurants. Take-out food has helped restaurants cut into grocery stores' share of the food market.

» Low Margins

Grocery stores operate with extremely low margins and depend on volume to generate profits. Gross margins are 25 percent of sales, lower than the 40 to 50 percent margin for most retailers. Profit margins can be razor-thin: in some cases, grocery stores net less than a penny per dollar of retail sales. Competition limits a company's ability to raise prices. On average, retail prices for food at home grow between just 2 and 3 percent annually.

» Large Companies Dominate

Small companies struggle to survive due to a combination of intense price competition and low margins in the grocery retailing industry. Efficiencies of buying and distribution allow large companies to set low prices without sacrificing margins. Manufacturers typically offer discounts and special terms for large purchases, requiring volume too high for many small retailers to sell. Large foreign companies have expanded by acquiring regional chains and opening new stores. Because industry dynamics favor large scale operations, small chains often become victims of consolidation.

ent banners. A typical grocery store averages 47,500 square feet; carries 45,000 different items; and generates almost $400,000 weekly, according to the Food Marketing Institute (FMI). Because grocery stores typically serve customers within a one- to two-mile radius, companies carefully consider demographics when selecting store locations.

Grocery stores typically group similar merchandise into aisles to aid shoppers. Stores may have bakeries, delis, pharmacies, and floral departments. Prepared foods sections serve consumers looking for ready-to-eat items. Companies may have sections dedicated to specialty categories, such as organic or ethnic products. Through third parties, companies may have in-store restaurants, banks, coffee shops, or gas stations. Most grocery stores have multiple check-out lanes to process orders and bag merchandise. Some retailers offer self-checkout lanes.

Because grocery retailing is generally a high volume/low margin business, effective supply chain management is key to keeping costs low. While large companies buy directly from manufacturers, small chains and independent retailers rely on wholesalers. Depending on product mix, companies may buy from many distributors and use food brokers. Volume discounts allow big chains to keep prices low. Manufacturers typically offer additional trade funds, which allow grocery stores to discount or promote certain products without sacrificing margins.

Most chains have distribution centers that receive and redistribute merchandise among individual stores. Companies may own or lease truck fleets to transport goods. To reduce transportation and distribution costs, large chains may arrange for direct shipment from manufacturers to stores for certain large orders. Because storage space is limited, individual stores may receive shipments frequently, particularly for perishable items.

Grocery stores must track a staggering number of individual products in various flavors, sizes, and packaging formats. Proper category management maximizes the use of valuable shelf space and helps minimize inventory shrink due to spoilage. Buyers and merchandising staff decide which items to stock, discontinue, or promote. Retailers typically feature and discount different products weekly. Many retailers charge manufacturers slotting fees to stock new products. Companies typically offer a mix of brand name and private-label products, and may customize merchandise selection based on the demographics of the surrounding market area.

Because of the large volume of grocery products companies must manage, retailers rely on computerized information systems to link operations and analyze data. Point-of-sale (POS) systems use scanners to read a product's Universal Product Code (UPC) and process sales transactions and credit card payments. Inventory management programs track products through the supply chain and may automatically reorder products when merchandise runs low. A small number of large retailers are experimenting with radio frequency identification (RFID) systems to monitor product movement. About 70 percent of large companies use electronic data interchange (EDI) to manage purchasing operations. Some companies are testing handheld scanners and cart-attached devices to track purchases as a customer shops.

Sales & Marketing

The typical grocery store customer is a female head of household, according to the Food Marketing Institute (FMI). Households with children spend about 30 percent more than childless.

Marketing and promotional vehicles include newspaper, print, and TV advertising; direct mail; and in-store events. Free standing insert (FSI) coupons delivered via newspaper, retail price discounts, and end-aisle displays are common promotions. Sampling events help retailers promote new products. Customer loyalty programs reward frequent shoppers with special discounts or gifts.

Most companies have Internet sites that communicate basic store operating information, such as hours of operation, location, and in-store events. Some websites post weekly promotions. Internet sales are a tiny part of the grocery market. A few retailers have partnered with third-party websites to offer online sales.

Consumers make about two trips to a grocery store and spend about $100 weekly. About half of a typical grocery purchase goes to perishables. Some companies use an everyday low pricing strategy (EDLP), while others set higher retail prices and use heavy discounts to drive sales volume.

Human Resources

Because most jobs in grocery stores require few skills, pay is low and turnover high. Wages are 35 percent lower than the average for all US workers. To fill shifts at odd hours, grocery stores rely on part-time help. Most positions involve cashiering, restocking, food preparation, and bagging. Union participation rate is 20 percent — higher than the US average of 12 percent.

The industry injury rate is 40 percent higher than the average for all US workers. Heavy lifting associated with restocking and cutting required for food preparation put workers at increased risk of injury.

Industry Employment Growth

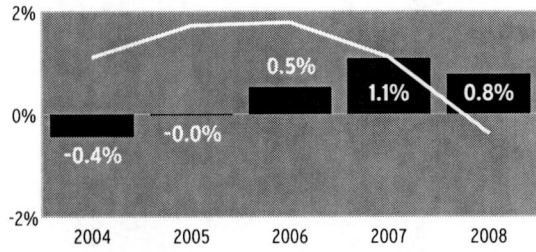

Average Hourly Earnings

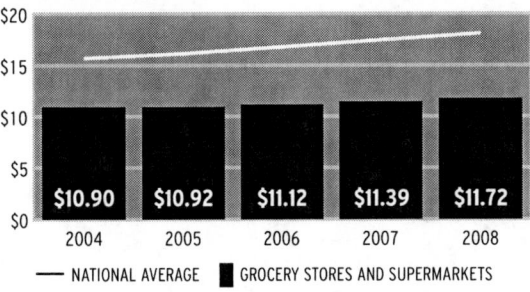

— NATIONAL AVERAGE ■ GROCERY STORES AND SUPERMARKETS

SOURCE: BUREAU OF LABOR STATISTICS

Call Preparation Questions

How has the company's competitive environment changed over time?

As alternative retailers realized the traffic-driving power of food sales, the competitive set for grocery stores expanded and the battle over food dollars became more intense.

What are the company's biggest challenges in maintaining margins?

Grocery stores operate with extremely low margins and depend on volume to generate profits.

How does the company effectively compete against large retailers?

Small companies struggle to survive due to a combination of intense price competition and low margins in the grocery retailing industry.

How have consumer health and wellness trends affected the company's business?

Companies can leverage increased consumer interest in health and wellness by improving and expanding perishable and organic merchandise departments and offering health-related services.

How important are prepared foods to the company's sales?

Grocery stores can offer consumers added convenience and better compete with restaurants by offering high-quality prepared foods.

Web Links

Food Marketing Institute

Industry information, statistics. Industry Associations.
www.fmi.org

Glossary of Supermarket Terminology

Definitions of terms, acronyms and jargon commonly used in the food industry.
www.fmi.org/glossary

Grocery Headquarters Magazine

Industry news and issues.
www.groceryheadquarters.com

Grocery Manufacturers Association

Largest industry organization of food producers.
www.gmabrands.com

National Grocers Association

Association of independent grocers. 2002 Marketing Survey.
www.nationalgrocers.org

Progressive Grocer Magazine

Industry news.
www.progressivegrocer.com/progressivegrocer

Supermarket News

Industry news.
www.supermarketnews.com

Glossary of Acronyms

EDI — electronic data interchange
ELP — everyday low price
FMI — Food Marketing Institute
FSI — free standing insert
GMA — Grocery Manufacturers of America
POS — point-of-sale
RFID — radio frequency identification
SKU — stock-keeping units
UPC — Universal Product Code

HOOVER'S TOP COMPANIES

Largest Companies by Sales	($ mil.)
The Kroger Co.	70,235.0
SUPERVALU INC.	44,048.0
Safeway Inc.	42,286.0
Publix Super Markets, Inc.	24,109.6
IGA, Inc.	21,000.0
Delhaize America, Inc.	17,289.2
Meijer, Inc.	13,900.0
H. E. Butt Grocery Company	13,500.0
Whole Foods Market, Inc.	7,953.9
Ahold USA, Inc.	—

Largest Employers	Employees
The Kroger Co.	323,000
Safeway Inc.	201,000
SUPERVALU INC.	192,000
Publix Super Markets, Inc.	144,000
Ahold USA, Inc.	142,916
Delhaize America, Inc.	109,000
IGA, Inc.	92,000
Meijer, Inc.	67,000
H. E. Butt Grocery Company	63,000
Whole Foods Market, Inc.	52,900

Fastest Growing* by Five-Year Sales Growth	(%)
Whole Foods Market, Inc.	20.4
SUPERVALU INC.	18.1
Super Center Concepts, Inc.	10.9
Ingles Markets, Incorporated	10.2
The Penn Traffic Company	9.6
K-VA-T Food Stores, Inc.	9.2
The Golub Corporation	8.4
Wegmans Food Markets, Inc.	8.3
Ruddick Corporation	7.9
Publix Super Markets, Inc.	7.3

Fastest Growing* by Five-Year Employee Growth	(%)
SUPERVALU INC.	27.3
Whole Foods Market, Inc.	15.7
Roundy's Supermarkets, Inc.	9.8
Super Center Concepts, Inc.	9.8
Ruddick Corporation	7.7
Ingles Markets, Incorporated	5.9
K-VA-T Food Stores, Inc.	5.2
The Golub Corporation	3.9
Wegmans Food Markets, Inc.	3.7
Publix Super Markets, Inc.	3.3

Top Public Companies by Market Value	($ mil.)
Publix Super Markets, Inc.	87,336.3
Safeway Inc.	20,596.0
The Kroger Co.	17,224.7
SUPERVALU INC.	5,923.3
Whole Foods Market, Inc.	2,895.5

* These rates are compounded annualized increases and may have resulted from acquisitions or one time gains. If less than 6 years of data are available, growth is for the years available.

SOURCE: HOOVER'S, INC., DATABASE

Gun Manufacturing

The US firearms industry includes about 200 companies with combined annual revenue of $2 billion. The largest gun manufacturers are Remington Arms and Sturm, Ruger & Company. Other companies that manufacture more than 50,000 weapons annually are Marlin Firearms, OF Mossberg & Sons, Smith & Wesson, US Repeating Arms, Savage Arms, Beretta USA, and Hi-Point Firearms. Winchester Ammunition and Remington are major manufacturers of ammunition. The industry is highly concentrated.

Competitive Landscape

Demand, which has been flat for years, is driven partly by hunters and partly by weapon upgrades by police departments. The profitability of individual companies is closely linked to marketing. Small companies can compete effectively by producing premium-priced high-quality or decorative guns. Although automation has increased, the industry is still fairly labor-intensive: average annual revenue per worker is about $150,000.

Products, Operations & Technology

The industry produces about 3 million guns per year: 620,000 pistols; 320,000 revolvers; 1,300,000 rifles; and 700,000 shotguns. About 60,000 machine guns are made, principally for the government. Sturm Ruger is the only company with large sales in each of the four categories. Remington makes mainly rifles and shotguns; Smith & Wesson mainly pistols and revolvers; other companies specialize in one category. Within a category, a company may make guns of different caliber and style. The most popular pistol calibers are 9 millimeter; .45; and .22. The most popular revolver calibers are .357; .45; and .38.

Gun manufacture is similar to the manufacture of other metal products with moving parts that require precision machining and assembly.

BUSINESS CHALLENGES

» Industry Highly Regulated

Because of the nature of the product, the industry is tightly regulated by federal and state governments. Manufacturers must be licensed, are prohibited from making certain products, can sell only to licensed dealers, and have to mark and track every individual gun. Gun ownership is a contentious political issue.

» Gun Manufacturers Targets of Lawsuits

Because guns are dangerous, manufacturers are regularly the target of lawsuits that look for large financial penalties. Such lawsuits typically allege defective manufacture or negligent distribution. Large legal awards could bankrupt manufacturers or increase the cost of insurance to prohibitive levels.

» Imports Taking Larger Market Share

Imports of small arms total around $850 million per year, accounting for about 30 percent of the US market, and increased over 55 percent from 2001 through 2005. Although Italy, Austria, and Germany remain the largest gun exporters to the US, imports have increased rapidly from low-cost countries like China and Brazil.

A typical gun contains between 50 and 100 parts. The precision parts are made from raw steel shapes using expensive computer-controlled machining stations. Because most manufacturers make several different models using the same machinery, production is in batches. Some manufacturers contract out all of their parts manufacturing to machine shops. Wood or plastic parts for stocks may be manufactured by outside contractors or produced in-house. Parts are assembled and finished by hand (sometimes with elaborate metal etching or other design work) and weapons are individually test-fired.

The technology used to produce guns is fairly standard, but requires sophisticated CAD and manufacturing (CAM) equipment. Because of the large number of parts required for each of dozens of gun models a company might produce, good inventory control systems are necessary. Computer systems are also used for the extensive documentation required to track each individual gun.

Sales & Marketing

Ultimate buyers of guns are sportsmen (target shooting); hunters; police departments; and government organizations; as well as foreign buyers. Manufacturers sell to wholesale distributors, who in turn sell to local retail gun outlets (dealers). Large manufacturers also use manufacturers representatives to maintain direct contact with retail dealers. Sturm, Ruger sold about 40 percent of its 2005 firearms production to three distributors: AcuSport Corp., Jerry's Sports Center, and Sports South Corp. Wal-Mart is one of the largest gun retailers in the US.

Consumer marketing is chiefly through advertising in a large number of specialty gun/sporting magazines like Guns & Ammo. Much of manufacturers' marketing effort is directed at retailers. Because of government restrictions, guns can't be mail-ordered or bought over the Internet, except through a local licensed dealer.

Human Resources

Jobs in gun manufacturing require special skills handling metal-working machinery or assembling or decorating guns. Average hourly pay is 20 percent higher than the national wage. The industry has improved quality and productivity in the past decade through greater automation and has shed almost 30 percent of previous jobs. The ammunition segment of the industry has a good safety record, but the rate of injuries at small arms factories is worse than average.

Industry Employment Growth

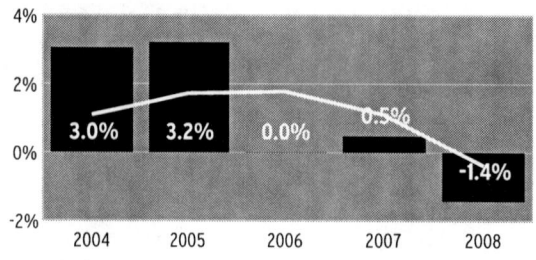

	2004	2005	2006	2007	2008
	3.0%	3.2%	0.0%	0.5%	-1.4%

Average Hourly Earnings

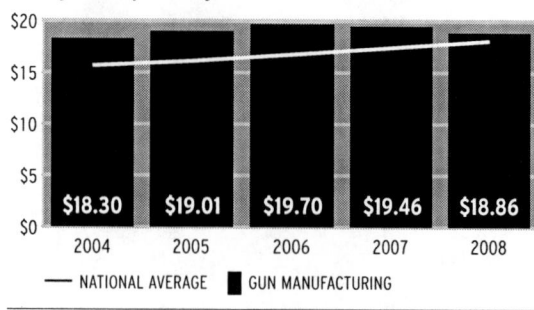

	2004	2005	2006	2007	2008
	$18.30	$19.01	$19.70	$19.46	$18.86

— NATIONAL AVERAGE ■ GUN MANUFACTURING

SOURCE: BUREAU OF LABOR STATISTICS

Call Preparation Questions

How would the company be affected by more government regulation or restrictions on weapons?

Because of the nature of the product, the industry is tightly regulated by federal and state governments.

What precautions has the company taken to defend itself against possible lawsuits?

Because guns are dangerous, manufacturers are regularly the target of lawsuits that look for large financial penalties.

How have imports affected sales of the company's products?

Imports of small arms total around $850 million per year, accounting for about 30 percent of the US market, and increased over 55 percent from 2001 through 2005.

Does the company support marketing to promote hunting or target shooting?

About 19 percent of the US population hunted in 2005, according to the annual sports participation survey of the National Sporting Goods Association (NSGA).

Does the company make and promote guns specifically for women?

Women's participation in hunting remained stable at around 11 percent in the past five years, while their participation in target shooting increased from 18 to 23 percent, according to the National Sporting Goods Association (NSGA).

Web Links

A.M. Best Insurance

Gun-related insurance news. Enter "gun" in search window.
www3.ambest.com/news/NewsSearch.aspx?both=1

Brady Center to Prevent Gun Violence

Information about anti-gun lawsuits.
www.gunlawsuits.org

Bureau of Alcohol, Tobacco, Firearms and Explosives

Regulatory news.
www.atf.gov

GunBroker.com

Firearm industry news.
www.gunbroker.com/user/IndustryNews.asp

National Association of Firearms Retailers

Legislative issues.
www.nafr.org

National Rifle Association

Lobbying/education organization. Good industry links.
www.nra.org

National Shooting Sports Foundation

Legislative issues.
www.nssf.org

National Sporting Goods Association

See Research & Statistics section for retail sales and participation data.
www.nsga.org

Professional Gun Retailers Association – American Firearms

Historical statistics. Manufacturer and distributor listings.
www.amfire.com

Ruger's Firearms News

Manufacturer news. Good industry links.
ruger.com/Firearms/N-Firearms_News.html

Sporting Arms and Ammunition Manufacturers' Institute (SAAMI)

Technical information about guns.
www.saami.org

StateGunLaws.org

Information about state gun-control laws.
www.stategunlaws.org

Glossary of Acronyms

ATF — Bureau of Alcohol, Tobacco, Firearms and Explosives
CAD — computer-aided design
NSGA — National Sporting Goods Association
NRA — National Rifle Association

HOOVER'S TOP COMPANIES

Largest Companies by Sales	($ mil.)
Remington Arms Company, Inc.	489.0
Smith & Wesson Holding Corporation	295.9
Sturm, Ruger & Company, Inc.	181.5

Largest Employers	Employees
Winchester Ammunition	6,200
Remington Arms Company, Inc.	2,550
Smith & Wesson Holding Corporation	1,453
Sturm, Ruger & Company, Inc.	1,100
Marlin Firearms Company	575
O.F. Mossberg & Sons, Inc.	500
Colt Defense Inc.	380
Savage Arms, Inc.	375
Beretta USA, Corp.	325
Browning Arms Company	250

Fastest Growing* by Five-Year Sales Growth	(%)
DAC Technologies Group International, Inc.	39.5
Smith & Wesson Holding Corporation	24.2
Remington Arms Company, Inc.	5.0
Sturm, Ruger & Company, Inc.	4.2

Fastest Growing* by Five-Year Employee Growth	(%)
Smith & Wesson Holding Corporation	20.8
Remington Arms Company, Inc.	1.8

Top Public Companies by Market Value	($ mil.)
Smith & Wesson Holding Corporation	304.7
Sturm, Ruger & Company, Inc.	113.7
DAC Technologies Group International, Inc.	5.1

* These rates are compounded annualized increases and may have resulted from acquisitions or one time gains. If less than 6 years of data are available, growth is for the years available.

SOURCE: HOOVER'S, INC., DATABASE

Hair Care Services

THIS INDUSTRY INCLUDES:

SIC CODES
7231   Beauty Shops
7241   Barber Shops

NAICS CODES
812111   Barber Shops
812112   Beauty Salons

In the US, about 80,000 hair care salons (75,000 beauty salons; 5,000 barber shops) generate combined annual sales of $16 billion. Large companies include Regis Corporation and Ratner Companies. The industry is highly fragmented: the 50 largest companies hold just 15 percent of the market. The large majority of salons are independently owned. A large salon has annual revenue of about $300,000 and 10 employees.

Competitive Landscape

Demand is partly driven by demographics and partly by population growth. The profitability of individual companies depends on technical expertise and marketing skills. Big companies have few advantages over small ones, which is why the industry remains fragmented. Small companies can compete successfully through technical superiority or favorable location. The industry is highly labor-intensive: average annual revenue per employee is just $35,000.

Products, Operations & Technology

Major products are hair cutting, hair coloring, nail care, skin care, and merchandise sales. A typical salon offers haircutting and styling, coloring, shampooing, and permanents. Some salons also offer nail care, facial treatments, makeup, bikini waxing, massage, tanning, and other types of spa treatments, but the lower volume of demand for such specialty services often makes them uneconomical. Sales of hair care products are an important revenue source for many salons, providing from 5 to 40 percent of revenue. Gross margins are higher for hair care products than for services.

The average salon occupies about 1,500 square feet and is located in a mall. A typical salon employs hairstylists who do the actual haircutting, colorists who specialize in hair coloring, and various assistants who wash and dry

BUSINESS CHALLENGES

» Pricing Depends on Local Economic Growth

The prices salons can charge depend heavily on the economic circumstances of the surrounding population. Local economic slowdowns rapidly impact demand because many customers have alternatives, such as visiting a salon less frequently or having their hair done at home. Overall, salon prices closely follow income gains.

» Dependence on Low-Paid Personnel

Because of relatively low pay, personnel turnover is a problem for salons, especially because customers may follow a popular stylist to another salon. At lower-end salon chains, adequately trained stylists are often in short supply because they can easily move to salons with better pay. In higher-end salons, new stylists often must work as apprentices before earning higher pay.

» Competition from Do-it-Yourself Products

Home hair care products are becoming easier to use and less expensive, with more variety of applications. More professional "salon only" hair care products are being offered at lower prices through mass channels directly to consumers, competing with salon retail sales. Some retail outlets get salon products from diverters that "collect" products from salons in small batches or from bulk diversion Internet sites.

hair. Average operating expenses, mainly rent and labor, are a high 80 percent of revenue. In most independently owned salons, the owner or owners are part of the work force. The average hourly pay for workers is low. Receptionists sometimes get a commission for hair care product sales. Tips are an important source of income for workers. Stylists, who often develop their own clientele of loyal customers, frequently work on commission, taking up to 50 percent of service revenue.

Haircutting, including washing, typically takes 45 minutes, while coloring may take as long as two hours. Many women have their hair cut every six to eight weeks and color done once a month. Customers often develop long-term relationships with their hair care professional and are extremely loyal.

Sales & Marketing

For many salons, marketing consists of word-of-mouth from existing customers, and occasional print advertising that includes discounts for new customers. Chains can use radio and TV advertising because the cost is spread among several salons. Women form the bulk of clientele at higher-priced salons, men and children at lower-priced salons.

Prices for hair care vary significantly. Regis operates several different chains that appeal to different customers. The average sale is about $25 at Regis Salons, $17 at Trade Secret, $13 at MasterCuts, and $11 at Supercuts. Many independent salons have higher average sales, with prices of $50 or more for cutting or coloring. Competition is strongest at the lower end of the business, where price and location make a big difference, as does the availability of walk-in service (higher-end salons usually require appointments).

Chains try to duplicate a successful concept: most are small enough to be directly managed by the owner. Multiple locations are the only way for most salons to expand, since most customers want small, intimate locations. Larger chains usually are highly regional and may have company-owned locations as well as franchises. Of the 8,000 salons that Regis operates in North America, about 2,300 are franchised. Franchisees typically pay an initial fee and ongoing royalties, and receive help with training, operations, advertising, and financial controls. Larger chains tend to work at the lower end of the market, where customers are most price-sensitive and have the least salon loyalty.

Human Resources

Because the work is physically demanding, many stylists work fewer than 40 hours per week. Stylists can receive relatively high pay, but other workers need no special skills and receive low pay, about 20 percent below the national average. Customers often follow if their stylist moves from one salon to another. The hair care industry's safety record is much better than average.

Industry Employment Growth

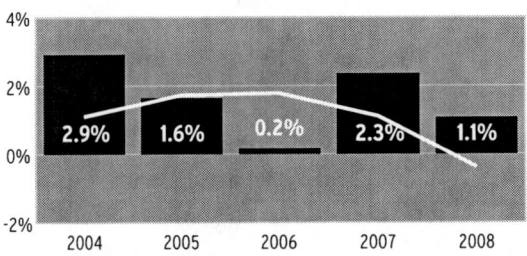

Average Hourly Earnings

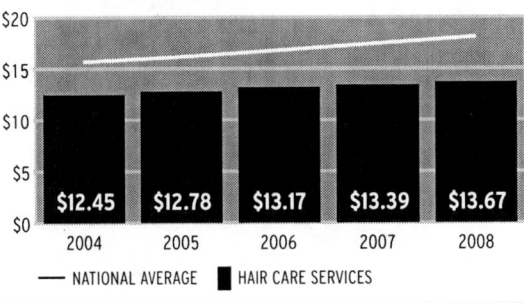

— NATIONAL AVERAGE ■ HAIR CARE SERVICES

SOURCE: BUREAU OF LABOR STATISTICS

Call Preparation Questions

How successfully has the company raised prices?

The prices salons can charge depend heavily on the economic circumstances of the surrounding population.

How successfully has the company decreased personnel turnover?

Because of relatively low pay, personnel turnover is a problem for salons, especially because customers may follow a popular stylist to another salon.

How have DIY products affected company sales?

Home hair care products are becoming easier to use and less expensive, with more variety of applications.

How does the company choose products to stock for retail sale?

Product sales (shampoos, rinses, conditioners, sprays, etc), while perhaps small in volume, are a major source of profits for many salons.

What types of special decor, services, or entertainment does the salon offer children?

Salons for children are typically brightly decorated and offer video games, puzzles, and TVs playing cartoons.

Web Links

Beautynet.com

Salon trends.
www.beautynet.com

Modern Salon magazine

Industry links, features.
www.modernsalon.com

Professional Beauty Association

News, industry updates.
www.probeauty.org/progress

Regis Corporation

Company news.
www.regiscorp.com

Salon Channel

Industry news.
salonchannel.com

Glossary of Acronyms

BLS — Bureau of Labor Statistics
SBA — Small Business Administration

HOOVER'S TOP COMPANIES

Largest Employers	Employees
Regis Corporation	65,000
Ratner Companies	12,542

SOURCE: HOOVER'S, INC., DATABASE

Handtool and Cutlery Manufacture

The US handtool and cutlery manufacturing industry includes about 1,400 companies with combined annual revenue of $10 billion. Large companies include Snap-on, Klein Tools, and the tools units of Stanley Works, Cooper Industries and Newell Rubbermaid. About a third of the companies are small, with fewer than five employees. The industry is fairly concentrated: the 50 largest companies hold more than 65 percent of the market.

Competitive Landscape

Demand depends heavily on the construction and building repair industries. The profitability of individual companies depends on marketing and efficient production. Large companies have economies of scale in purchasing and production. Small firms can compete by making specialty products. Production is highly automated: annual revenue per worker is about $250,000.

Products, Operations & Technology

Major products include handtools, cutlery, saw blades, and kitchen utensils. Handtools such as wrenches, hammers, scissors, vises, clamps, screwdrivers, pliers, chisels, and measuring devices, account for about 55 percent of industry revenue. Cutlery, including kitchen knives, sporting knives, razor blades, and "flatware" (table knives, forks and spoons), accounts for around 15 percent of industry revenue, while saw blades and kitchen utensils account for about 13 percent each, and various miscellaneous items for the rest.

Manufacturers use a variety of fabrication processes including forging, stamping, bending, forming, and machining to turn purchased metal into final products. Steel is the major raw material, often in the form of alloys with special properties such as hardness or resistance to corrosion. Plastic is frequently used for handles.

BUSINESS CHALLENGES

» Import Competition

Imports have taken a larger share of the US industry market, especially for lower-cost products like saw blades and cutlery. US imports of cutlery and handtools grew 45 percent in the past five years. Imports from China, the largest exporter to the US, doubled.

» Steel Prices Change Rapidly

Prices for steel, the major raw material for handtool and cutlery manufacture, can change more than 10 percent in 12 months. Prices depend on world demand and import restrictions. Prices for cold rolled steel sheet varied 7 percent during 2005, but 30 percent in 2004.

» Dependence on Cyclical Construction Industry

Demand from the construction industry accounts for a significant part of handtool industry revenue. The level of construction activity is cyclical and can vary sharply from year to year. During the last recession, industry production dropped 8 percent as office and commercial construction activity fell 20 percent.

Small manufacturers may buy semi-finished forgings or castings from outside suppliers; large manufacturers usually make their own. Because most handtools are fairly simple devices, the production process is uncomplicated and easily lends itself to automation. Companies typically make a range of products.

Some manufacturers make extensive use of robotics hardware and automation software that controls and tracks processes. Manufacturers use supply chain information systems that link to customers and suppliers to help ensure availability of materials to fulfill customer orders.

Sales & Marketing

Major end-use customers are in the construction, home improvement, auto repair, or industrial manufacture industries. Manufacturers sell primarily through distributors and dealers to reach the consumer and professional trade markets. Manufacturers may have a direct sales force to manage large accounts, such as national retailers. Prices for products range from a few dollars for a simple handtool to several hundred for high-end cutlery.

Promotion aims at the end-user, and jointly paid cooperative advertising is common with major retailers. Manufacturers participate in trade shows for industries that make significant use of their products, such as for the construction and tableware industries. Many tool manufacturers sponsor race cars and racing events.

Human Resources

Most production jobs in the handtool and cutlery manufacturing industry involve operating automated machinery and therefore require few special skills. Average wages in the industry are relatively low for a manufacturing operation, about 10 percent lower than for all US manufacturers. Fringe benefits are similarly low, about 20 percent of wages. The annual injury rate is high, 40 percent above the national rate.

Industry Employment Growth

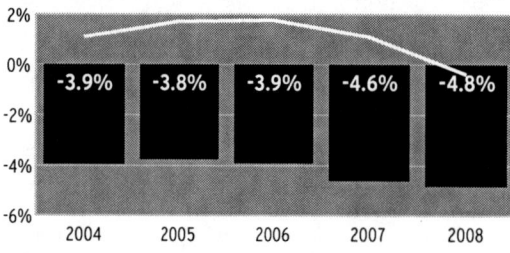

Average Hourly Earnings

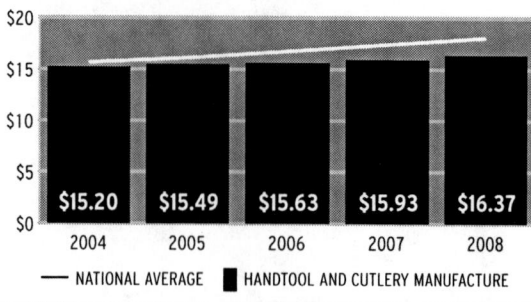

— NATIONAL AVERAGE ■ HANDTOOL AND CUTLERY MANUFACTURE

SOURCE: BUREAU OF LABOR STATISTICS

Call Preparation Questions

How will the company be affected if imports gain a larger market share?

Imports have taken a larger share of the US industry market, especially for lower-cost products like saw blades and cutlery.

How are changes in steel prices affecting the company?

Prices for steel, the major raw material for handtool and cutlery manufacture, can change more than 10 percent in 12 months.

How do fluctuations in construction industry demand impact company production and revenues?

Demand from the construction industry accounts for a significant part of handtool industry revenue.

What percentage of the company's products is outsourced or manufactured overseas?

Lower cost of labor and operations are driving more companies to manufacture in Asia, often in India or China.

How much company R&D is directed to ergonomic design?

Manufacturers have dual incentives to produce more ergonomic products: consumer demand is increasing, and ergonomic products lower the likelihood of lawsuits due to injury.

Web Links

American Edged Products Manufacturers Association

(Formerly the American Cutlery Manufacturers Association) Lists of manufacturers, trademarks and owners.

www.aepma.org

American Hardware Manufacturers Association

News.

www.ahma.org

American Knife and Tool Institute

News and events.

www.akti.org/news

Cookware Manufacturers Association

Shipment statistics, standards, trademark lists and industry self-monitoring.

www.cookware.org

Hand Tools Institute

Manufacturers, safety publications, and standards.

www.hti.org

Irwin Industrial Tools

Glossary of tool tips; articles on tool tips and safety.

www.irwin.com/irwin/consumer/jhtml/
newProductsSelected.jhtml?attrId=IrwinCat100368

Klein Tools

Tool catalog with photographs.

www.kleintools.com

Professional Tool & Equipment News

Auto repair tool and equipment market news.

www.pten.com

The Tool Directory

List of tools and manufacturers.

www.thetooldirectory.com/main.asp

Glossary of Acronyms

ANSI — American National Standards Institute
ISO — International Standards Organization

HOOVER'S TOP COMPANIES

Largest Companies by Sales	($ mil.)
Cooper Industries, Ltd.	6,521.3
Newell Rubbermaid Inc.	6,470.6
The Black & Decker Corporation	6,086.1
The Stanley Works	4,426.2
Snap-on Incorporated	2,934.7
The Toro Company	1,878.2
Lifetime Brands, Inc.	493.7
The L.S. Starrett Company	242.4
Makita U.S.A., Inc.	—
Robert Bosch Tool Corporation	—

Largest Employers	Employees
Cooper Industries, Ltd.	31,504
The Black & Decker Corporation	22,100
Newell Rubbermaid Inc.	22,000
The Stanley Works	18,225
Snap-on Incorporated	11,600
The Toro Company	5,133
Robert Bosch Tool Corporation	4,000
The L.S. Starrett Company	2,221
Makita U.S.A., Inc.	1,561
Lifetime Brands, Inc.	1,469

Fastest Growing* by Five-Year Sales Growth	(%)
AeroGrow International, Inc.	193.1
Lifetime Brands, Inc.	30.3
WSI Industries, Inc.	19.1
Q.E.P. Co., Inc.	11.0
The Stanley Works	10.6
Cooper Industries, Ltd.	9.9
P&F Industries, Inc.	7.5
The L.S. Starrett Company	6.6
The Black & Decker Corporation	6.3
Snap-on Incorporated	5.2

Fastest Growing* by Five-Year Employee Growth	(%)
Lifetime Brands, Inc.	17.5
WSI Industries, Inc.	11.5
The Stanley Works	6.2
Cooper Industries, Ltd.	3.8
Q.E.P. Co., Inc.	1.9

Top Public Companies by Market Value	($ mil.)
Cooper Industries, Ltd.	4,878.7
The Stanley Works	2,797.7
Newell Rubbermaid Inc.	2,710.0
The Black & Decker Corporation	2,512.5
Snap-on Incorporated	2,360.9

* These rates are compounded annualized increases and may have resulted from acquisitions or one time gains. If less than 6 years of data are available, growth is for the years available.

SOURCE: HOOVER'S, INC., DATABASE

Health Fundraising Organizations

THIS INDUSTRY INCLUDES:

SIC CODES
8399   Social Services

NAICS CODES
813212   Voluntary Health
          Organizations

About 2,000 health fundraising organizations ("voluntary health associations") operate in the US, with combined annual revenue of about $8 billion. Large associations include the American Cancer Society, March of Dimes, American Heart Association, and Cystic Fibrosis Foundation. The 50 largest organizations take in about 60 percent of industry revenue.

Competitive Landscape

The revenue of these organizations depends on consumer income and corporate profits. The long-term viability of individual organizations depends on strong marketing and public perceptions of usefulness. Large organizations have advantages in name recognition. Small organizations can compete successfully through superior marketing or by having a wealthy sponsor.

Products, Operations & Technology

Program services usually fall into three major categories: funding medical research, public education, and direct services such as testing programs, support groups, patient care, rehabilitation and training, etc. Research funding is usually accomplished through grants to individuals or institutions that apply for funds. Public education involves media advertising, publications, school programs, and awareness events often in conjunction with fundraising activities, and legislative lobbying activities. Lobbying usually takes the form of advocating increased government funding for research and support activities, and can be very effective for organizations with large numbers of members.

For large organizations, program services take close to 75 percent of revenue. Support services include management expenses, and fundraising expenses account for the rest of revenue. Management expenses for large organizations are typically around 5 percent of revenue; fundraising expenses, close to 15 percent.

BUSINESS CHALLENGES

» Contributions Depend on Economic Conditions

Charitable contributions typically shrink in more difficult economic times. In recent years, high charitable donations were tied to the wealth created by a rising stock market; however, many charities felt a significant drop in donations when the market moved lower. The stream of small donations at many charities is unaffected by investment losses, but big donors give less. In a declining economy, when charities receive fewer contributions, their services are more in demand. A soft economy can widen the distance between the amount of money pledged and the amount actually collected.

» Poor Reputation Accountability Hurts Donations

Accountability has historically been weak for all nonprofits. Private giving is discouraged by news of abuses that have squandered contributors' money. Nonprofits are just beginning to publish standardized financial statements (IRS Form 990) to provide more transparency. The next steps will include analyzing this information and rating all nonprofits according to agreed-upon standards of efficiency. The American Institute of Philanthropy (AIP) is one of several "watchdog" groups that rate the performance of charities.

» Lower Perceived Relevance of National Organizations

With the government now playing the leading role in funding health care and medical research, private companies and the general public see the mission of many national health fundraising organizations as less important. The original mission of the March of Dimes, for example, was achieved when polio was eradicated in the US. Rather than supporting national organizations, more individuals donate to local or regional entities.

Fundraising is a major activity of these organizations and is usually separated into soliciting support from individuals, corporations, and government, each of which require different approaches. Because of the increasing sophistication of fundraising methods, many organizations hire consultants to design (and sometimes run) their programs. Government accounts for less than 15 percent of industry revenue; private contributions account for about 70 percent; and individuals provide the bulk of support, although corporate support is important for many smaller organizations. Investment income is usually a minor source of funds.

Information systems are very important to fundraising organizations because they take small donations from a large number of people. Systems are important for accounting purposes and marketing campaigns, because previous donors are the most likely source of future contributions. Frequent communications, by mail, phone, and e-mail, are essential to maintaining support from a large number of members and other contributors. Specialized computer programs have been developed to handle fundraising and take donations over the Internet.

Sales & Marketing

Marketing programs are aimed at the charitable instincts of individual donors. Professional fundraising consultants are often used, as is telemarketing. A growing variety of methods has been developed to help individuals make contributions, including membership dues, direct solicitations via mail, affinity credit cards, car donations, door-to-door canvassing using "commissioned fundraisers," will bequests, life insurance policies, life income agreements, charitable remainder trusts, and special events such as walkathons, races, concerts, fairs, dinners, auctions, etc. Senior staff are often involved in fundraising from corporate and government sources.

Human Resources

Most health fundraising organizations operate with a relatively small staff. Even the largest may employ only a few hundred workers. Much of the work of fundraising and providing direct services is by unpaid volunteers. The average annual pay of full-time staff workers is about

$40,000. Senior managers generally earn between $50,000 and $60,000, less than they might earn in the private sector but benefits are usually very generous.

Because the work they do involves helping others, employees are often highly motivated and loyal, even if compensation is modest.

Industry Employment Growth

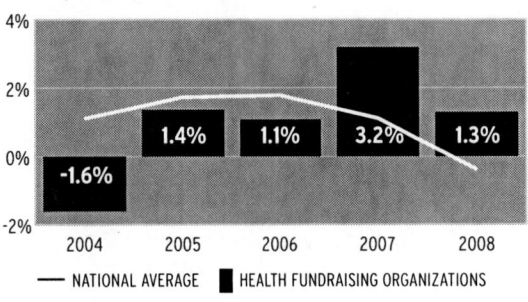

SOURCE: BUREAU OF LABOR STATISTICS

Call Preparation Questions

How does the organization adjust when revenues decrease?

Charitable contributions typically shrink in more difficult economic times.

What steps has the organization taken to improve accountability?

Accountability has historically been weak for all nonprofits.

How could the organization change its business model to improve fundraising efforts?

With the government now playing the leading role in funding health care and medical research, private companies and the general public see the mission of many national health fundraising organizations as less important.

Does the organization lobby Congress? If so, to what benefit?

With their large networks of dedicated supporters, the big national health fundraising organizations are a political force whose views are sought in public policymaking.

How are medical advances helping the organization's fundraising efforts?

The long-expressed desire to "find a cure" for a particular disease has become a practical matter of promoting increased research funding.

Web Links

American Cancer Society

News and events.
www.cancer.org

American Heart Association

News and events.
www.americanheart.org

American Lung Association

News and events.
www.lungusa.org

Arthritis Foundation

News and events.
www.arthritis.org

Association for Healthcare Philanthropy

Fundraising, education, and development.
www.ahp.org

Giving Institute: Leading Consultants to Non-profits

Statistics on national philanthropy.
www.aafrc.org

GuideStar.Org

Form 990 financial statements for 220,000 nonprofit organizations.
www.guidestar.org

Health Fundraising Organizations and Nonprofit Institutions: Association of Fundraising Professionals

www.nsfre.org

National Center for Charitable Statistics

Links, data, fact sheets, and other resources.
www.nccs.urban.org

NonProfit Times

Online newsletter, recent articles, links. The NP 100 largest charities.
www.nptimes.com

Glossary of Acronyms

ADA — American Diabetes Association
HFO — Health Fundraising Organizations
HIPAA — Health Insurance Portability and Accountability Act
PIF — pooled income fund
UW — United Way

HOOVER'S TOP COMPANIES

Largest Employers	Employees
The American National Red Cross	35,000
American Cancer Society, Inc.	7,000
Muscular Dystrophy Association	1,400
Health Research, Inc.	1,400
March of Dimes Birth Defects Foundation	1,300
The Leukemia & Lymphoma Society, Inc.	825
Cystic Fibrosis Foundation	550
American Lung Association	500
United States Fund for UNICEF	200
Easter Seals, Inc.	200
Alzheimer's Disease and Related Disorders Association, Inc.	200

SOURCE: HOOVER'S, INC., DATABASE

Health Supplement Stores

THIS INDUSTRY
INCLUDES:

SIC CODES
5499   Miscellaneous
        Food Stores

NAICS CODES
446191 Food (Health)
        Supplement Stores

The health supplement store industry includes about 10,000 stores with combined annual revenue of almost $5 billion. Major companies include GNC Corporation; VS Holdings (The Vitamin Shoppe); and Vitamin World. The industry is fragmented: the top 50 companies hold 40 percent of industry sales.

Competitive Landscape

Health and nutrition trends and consumer spending drive demand. The profitability of individual companies depends on product innovation, effective merchandising, and competitive pricing. Large companies have advantages in purchasing, distribution, finance, and marketing. Small companies can compete effectively by providing superior customer service, offering unique products, or serving a local market. The industry is labor-intensive: average annual revenue per employee is less than $100,000.

Health supplement stores compete with mass merchandisers, supermarkets, drugstores, mail order and Internet retailers, health food stores, and direct sellers.

Products, Operations & Technology

Major products sold in health supplement stores include vitamins, minerals, and dietary supplements (70 percent of industry sales) and grocery items (20 percent). The vitamin, mineral, and health supplement (VMHS) category includes "alphabet" vitamins, multi-vitamins, aromatherapy, herbal extracts, and macrobiotic, homeopathic, herbal and botanical remedies. Sports nutrition products include protein and weight gain supplements, sports drinks and bars, and high potency vitamins. Weight loss products include diet pills, shakes, bars, and teas; meal replacements; and low carb items. Other categories include beauty care, pet care, books, and magazines.

The health supplement store industry includes national and regional chains, franchises,

BUSINESS CHALLENGES

» Competition from Alternative Retailers

Health supplement stores compete with a wide range of alternative retailers, including Internet and catalog retailers, mass merchandisers, and direct marketers. Internet and catalog retailers often provide detailed product information and offer consumers the convenience of shopping from home. While large mass merchandisers typically offer a limited selection of health supplements, most sell many other product categories, experience higher store traffic, and offer extremely competitive prices. Direct marketers are important players in the herbal products segment and enjoy low overhead costs.

» Dependence on Consumer Spending

While demand can be volatile due to trends in nutrition, health supplement sales also depend on personal income. During the last recession, employment in health supplement stores declined 10 percent. Some products, especially highly specialized supplements with unique benefits, can be expensive. While consumers may not completely eliminate supplements during tough economic times, some may buy cheaper brands or look for less expensive remedies.

» Trends Drive Demand

Because scientific research and the media can influence public perception, demand for health supplements can be cyclical. Publicity about scientific studies, both favorable and unfavorable, can result in volatile sales. Conflicting reports and opinions can confuse consumers. St. Johns Wort, melatonin, and low carb products had strong sales initially, only to have performance wane in the wake of negative publicity. Demand for weight loss products tends to more volatile than other supplements and can be more sensitive to consumer trends.

and independent retailers. Typical locations include shopping malls, strip malls, outlet malls, stand-alone buildings, and high traffic areas. Companies may have different store layouts depending on location type. The typical health supplement store generates about $600,000 annually, according to Vitamin Retailer. Store size for large companies ranges from 1,000 to 3,600 square feet.

Companies buy inventory from manufacturers, distributors, wholesalers, and brokers. Merchandise mix can vary, depending on a company's strategy. Large companies may stock over 8,000 stock-keeping units (SKU) per store. The average health supplement store carries 10 lines (brands) of products, with multiple SKUs in each. Many large companies manufacture and sell private-label brands, which can be between 30 and 70 percent of sales. Because health supplements affect the human body and are sometimes perceived and used as medical remedies, product quality is extremely important. Large retailers often test merchandise to ensure ingredient purity and strength, product composition, and safety.

Computerized point-of-sale (POS) systems record customer transactions and process credit/debit purchases. Centralized order management systems allow companies to scan vendor inventory and automatically generate purchase orders. Inventory management systems track product movement and help buyers identify sales trends. Database programs store customer information and help companies develop loyalty programs.

Sales & Marketing

The typical customer for health supplement stores varies by product category: generally, women over 35 are more likely to buy vitamins, minerals, or other supplements. Sports nutrition products appeal to men 18 to 49, and diet products appeal to women 18 to 49.

Advertising and promotion includes newspaper, print, radio, and TV; catalogs; and direct mail. Companies may receive cooperative advertising or product demonstration funds from manufacturers. Because many supplements promise health or weight loss benefits, product advertising claims regarding efficacy (such as "lose 10 pounds in 2 days") can be controversial and have brought increased scrutiny to the industry. False advertising has led to many government-driven product recalls.

Superior customer service helps companies develop loyal followings. Well-educated sales associates can recommend the correct supplement depending on a customer's unique situation. And rapid introduction of products, trends, and constantly changing scientific data require a savvy sales staff to assist and educate customers. Frequent buyer programs encourage loyalty and help identify cross-selling opportunities and market-specific trends.

Large companies may partner with Internet sites, such as drugstore.com, to sell proprietary brands online. Web-based retailing allows companies to sell a wider variety of products than those offered in physical stores. Through the Internet, some companies allow customers to set up automatic delivery for supplements needed regularly.

The average retail price for brand name vitamins and supplements is just over $8, according to Private Label Buyer. Retail prices for private-label equivalents average $6.65. Private-label products often have higher gross margins than national brands.

Human Resources

A typical health supplement store employs three full-time and three part-time workers, according to Vitamin Retailer. When hiring sales staff, some companies look for individuals who are regular health supplement users or have backgrounds in nutrition. Companies may offer training to keep workers informed on the latest new products and market trends.

Industry Employment Growth

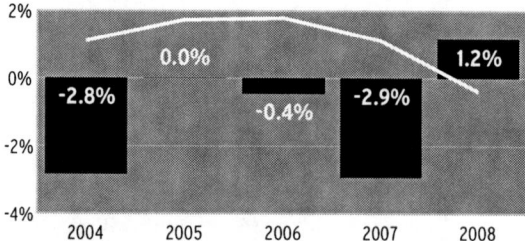

Average Hourly Earnings

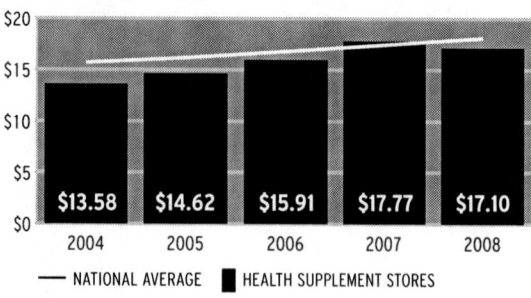

— NATIONAL AVERAGE   ■ HEALTH SUPPLEMENT STORES

SOURCE: BUREAU OF LABOR STATISTICS

Call Preparation Questions

What is the company's biggest competitive threat?

Health supplement stores compete with a wide range of alternative retailers, including Internet and catalog retailers, mass merchandisers, and direct marketers.

How do changes in consumer spending affect demand for the company's products?

While demand can be volatile due to trends in nutrition, health supplement sales also depend on personal income.

How do health and nutrition trends affect the company's supplements sales?

Because scientific research and the media can influence public perception, demand for health supplements can be cyclical.

What changes has the company seen in the diet and weight loss supplement category?

The growing obesity epidemic and associated health problems should increase demand for diet and weight loss products.

How important are new products to the company?

New products drive sales in the health supplement industry.

Web Links

Council for Responsible Nutrition

Trade organization, industry news, trends, regulatory information.

www.crnusa.org

Dietary Supplement Information Bureau

Trade organization, regulatory news, trends, studies.

www.supplementinfo.org

NPICenter

Industry and product news and trends for nutritional and dietary supplements and nutraceuticals.

www.npicenter.com

Nutrition Business Journal

Industry news and trends — subscription based. In-depth data available for purchase.

www.nutritionbusiness.com

Nutrition Industry Executive

Industry news and trends.

www.vitaminretailer.com/NIE

Vitamin Retailer

Industry news, trends, and statistics, including annual retailer survey.

www.vitaminretailer.com/VR

Glossary of Acronyms

CPSC — Consumer Products Safety Commission

CRN — Council for Responsible Nutrition

DSHEA — Dietary Supplement Health and Education Act

DSIB — Dietary Supplement Information Bureau

IHRSA — International Health, Racquet, and Sportsclub Association

NCHS — National Center for Health Statistics

POS — point-of-sale

SKU — stock-keeping unit

VMHS — Vitamin, Mineral, and Health Supplement

HOOVER'S TOP COMPANIES

Largest Companies by Sales	($ mil.)
NBTY, Inc.	2,179.5
GNC Corporation	1,552.8
VS Holdings, Inc.	537.9

Largest Employers	Employees
NBTY, Inc.	13,760
GNC Corporation	13,239
VS Holdings, Inc.	2,880

Fastest Growing* by Five-Year Sales Growth	(%)
NBTY, Inc.	12.8
VS Holdings, Inc.	11.6
GNC Corporation	1.7

Fastest Growing* by Five-Year Employee Growth	(%)
VS Holdings, Inc.	10.3
NBTY, Inc.	7.1

Top Public Companies by Market Value	($ mil.)
NBTY, Inc.	1,818.4

* These rates are compounded annualized increases and may have resulted from acquisitions or one time gains. If less than 6 years of data are available, growth is for the years available.

SOURCE: HOOVER'S, INC., DATABASE

Healthcare Sector

THIS INDUSTRY INCLUDES:

NAICS CODES
62   Health Care and Social Assistance

The US health care sector includes over 820,000 hospitals, doctor offices, emergency care units, nursing homes, and social services providers, with combined annual revenue of over $1.5 trillion. Major companies include Kaiser Permanente, Hospital Corporation of America (HCA), and Ascension Health. The sector is highly fragmented: the top 50 organizations hold just 15 percent of the market. Hospitals are the least fragmented industry: the top 50 hospitals account for 30 percent of total hospital revenue.

The industry includes about 6,000 general hospitals; 20,000 nursing homes; 15,000 diagnostic labs; 30,000 outpatient clinics; 120,000 dentist offices; 200,000 doctor offices; 75,000 day care facilities; and 50,000 family and social services providers.

The health care sector doesn't include health insurance providers, exercise facilities, or weight reduction services.

Competitive Landscape

Demand for health care services is driven by demographics and advances in medical care and technology. The profitability of individual companies depends on efficient operations and, in the case of many nonprofit health care providers, obtaining grants and federal funds. Large companies have advantages in accessing the latest medical research, buying supplies, offering a wide range of services, and negotiating contracts with health insurers. Small institutions can compete successfully by serving a limited geographical area, offering specialized services, or building a local reputation for quality care. Healthcare is labor-intensive: annual revenue per employee is $80,000. Revenue per employee is nearly $100,000 for ambulatory services and hospitals, and only around $45,000 for nursing homes, residential care facilities, and social assistance providers.

BUSINESS CHALLENGES

» Containing Rising Costs

Healthcare officials expect the cost of medical care to continue to grow between 7 and 10 percent annually through 2010. Physician care, hospital services, and prescription drugs are all expected to continue their unprecedented rise in costs. The average cost per stay at a community hospital was $1,800 in 1980; today, the average cost is nearly $10,000.

» Dependence on Federal Regulation

Government programs account for 45 percent of the nation's health care spending, up from 35 percent in the 1970s. This figure may rise if the US moves toward federally funded health care programs. With an annual budget of $400 billion, Medicare has an outsized influence on medical practices through its detailed reimbursement schedules. These schedules set an industry standard that insurers copy – standards that, according to many physicians and hospitals, fail to cover the rising cost of medical care. New treatments, even if already approved by the FDA and the medical community, have a limited market if not approved for Medicare reimbursement.

» High Cost of Uninsured

About 47 million people in the US are uninsured; however, many still receive health care, often by using high-cost resources such as ERs. Urban hospitals currently have to absorb these extra costs. Efforts to provide coverage to the uninsured have so far failed because the government would likely have to bear the cost. As a result, the costs of caring for the uninsured are "cost-shifted" to the insured.

Products, Operations & Technology

Major services include hospital medical care (40 percent of industry revenue) and outpatient care provided by physicians (20 percent). Other services include dental work, urgent care, elderly and hospice care, and social assistance.

Healthcare in the US is led by for-profit entities, an exception to the global norm of nationalized medicine. Of the 6,000 US hospitals, around 75 percent are for-profit. Most doctor offices, nursing homes, outpatient and urgent care centers, and day care facilities are run as for-profit enterprises.

US health care isn't, however, a completely private enterprise. Federal and state governments are heavily involved in the US health care sector, as a direct-care provider (the Department of Veterans Affairs); an operator of health insurance programs (Medicare for the elderly, Medicaid for the low-income and disabled), and as a provider of social services (Health and Human Services, state departments of Social Services).

In total, around 60 percent of Americans are covered by employee-sponsored health insurance and 5 percent on individual ("private non-group") insurance; 15 percent are enrolled in public insurance programs like Medicaid and Medicare. People over 65 are almost universally covered by Medicare. In spite of this combination of for-profit and government involvement, 45 million Americans are uninsured — more than 15 percent of the US population. This combination of employer-sponsored plans, individual insurance, subsidized insurance, and the uninsured spins a complex web of payers (private insurance companies and the government) and health care providers, known in the industry as a multi-payer system.

Individuals and businesses fund Medicare through payroll taxes. Businesses pay all or a portion of the premiums for employee-sponsored health care. A typical family of four pays $11,000 a year toward health insurance; on average, an employer covers around 75 percent of this cost. Beyond contributing to premiums, individuals also pay additional direct or out-of-pocket expenses to providers for health care services.

The government uses money generated from taxes to reimburse providers who care for patients enrolled in Medicare, Medicaid, VA hospitals, and State Children's Health Insurance Programs (S-CHIP). Tax dollars also support health insurance premiums for federal employees.

Private insurers accept premiums from individuals, business, and the government. In turn, insurers reimburse providers for taking care of insured patients. Healthcare providers care for individuals and are reimbursed by private insurers and the government.

In total, government expenditures account for around 45 percent of total health care costs and private expenditures the remaining 55 percent. The $1.5 trillion in annual US health care spending is around 15 percent of total GDP, highest among industrialized nations. On average, Americans spend nearly $6,000 a year on health care.

Despite these inefficiencies and the large numbers of uninsured, the US is clearly a leader in health care technology, scientific advances, and medical research. Many of these advances are led by research hospitals that maintain a staff of PhDs specializing in research and discovery. Molecular biology, largely federally funded, has advanced understanding of the cellular processes involved in disease, largely by identifying defective proteins and gene mutations. New drug treatments, often developed in partnership with pharmaceutical firms, counter the effects of these abnormalities. Advances in computer technology have produced new diagnostic imaging systems like ultrasound, MRI, CAT, and PET that can detect abnormalities in their earliest stages, often preventing the onset of diseases like cancer and organ failure. The R&D that drives these discoveries is costly, often resulting in expensive medicine.

Around 30 percent of US doctors use electronic medical records (EMRs). EMRs are networked systems that can help a physician track a patient's health, check for potential harmful drug interactions, and provide medical decision support. The use of EMRs among US physicians is much lower than many European and other nations: nearly all doctors in the Netherlands rely on EMRs, as do most doctors in the UK, Australia, New Zealand, and Germany.

Sales & Marketing

Typical customers are individuals requiring urgent medical care, routine check-ups, and long- or short-term help ranging from nursing home care, day care, and social services.

Marketing efforts vary depending on the type of service provided. Doctors typically stick with traditional approaches like Yellow Pages' ads, word-of-mouth, and referrals. A growing number of physicians have websites and even personal blogs — though doctors must avoid violating patient's rights and privacy laws when writing about specific cases or incidences. Hospitals market to doctors, insurers, and individuals using a variety of means, including medical presentations, brochures, magazine and newspaper ads, targeted press releases, informational websites, and TV ads.

Prices vary depending on the services offered, the length of the patient stay, the patient's insurance policy, and the level of government support. For hospitals, the average revenue per admission is close to $10,000. The average daily cost for a hospital stay is around

$1,500. Average revenue per outpatient visit is around $500. Medicare (and, in many cases, supplemental state insurance policies) sets limits on reimbursable charges. In a typical scenario, a 15-minute doctor visit costs around $75, but Medicare policies allow a physician to charge a patient only around $35. Medicare pays 80 percent of this; the patient pays the remainder. In essence, the doctor "loses" $40. To offset these losses, doctors often limit the number of Medicare patients they accept, shorten patient time, or raise prices on private payers through what's known as "cost shifting."

Human Resources

Overall wages in the health care sector are 4 percent higher than the national average. While the majority of skilled and nonskilled hospital employees earn low to modest pay, the high income of doctors and specialists more than offsets these low wages. Surgeons and anesthesiologists earn nearly $100 an hour (four times the national average), while home health aides earn less than $10 (nearly half the national average). Wages in nursing homes, residential care, and social services are 30 percent lower than the national average.

Injury rates are 15 percent higher compared to the national average. Common injuries include back strains and sprains from moving patients or from falls. Workers must be aware of assaults by frustrated or confused patients: injuries from violent assaults are surprisingly high in the health care sector, at around nine per 10,000 full-time workers (almost three times the national average).

Healthcare and social service employees require training and certification on a broad range of issues, including government regulations, insurance matters, limiting workplace injuries and medical mishaps, reducing the risk of liability, and overcoming language and cultural barriers. Over half of nursing and residential care employees have a high school diploma or less, as do a fifth of hospital workers.

Industry Employment Growth

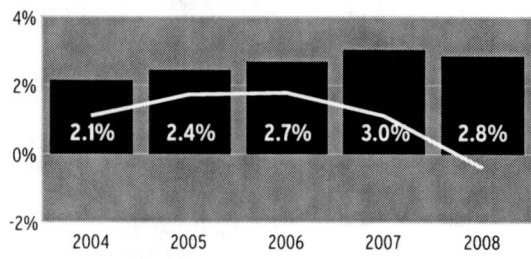

Average Hourly Earnings

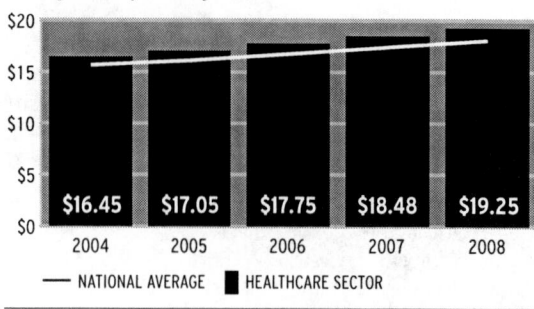

SOURCE: BUREAU OF LABOR STATISTICS

Call Preparation Questions

How are rising health care costs impacting the company?

Healthcare officials expect the cost of medical care to continue to grow between 7 and 10 percent annually through 2010.

How much of company revenue depends on government-funded programs?

Government programs account for 45 percent of the nation's health care spending, up from 35 percent in the 1970s.

What types of technology does the company plan to buy/use in the near future?

Only 25 percent of hospitals have a comprehensive Health Information Technology (HIT) system in place.

How does the aging US population impact business operations?

The aging US population both strains and presents opportunities for the American health care system over the next decade.

Web Links

Agency for Healthcare Research and Quality

News and announcements on the health care industry, research, funding opportunities, quality assessments, and clinical consumer health data.
www.ahrq.gov

American Association of Healthcare Administrative Management (AAHAM)

Patient accounts, billing admission, registration.
www.aaham.org

American Health Information Management Association

Professional organization specializing in health information management education for health care professionals. Hot topics, career information, certification, products, events, and specialty group links.
www.ahima.org

American Hospital Association

National organization formed in 1906 that represents and serves hospitals, health care networks and patients. Provides advocacy, campaigns for coverage, compliance assistance, press releases, health forums, and research and education.

www.aha.org

American Medical Association (AMA)

Industry news, links and information about many physician specialties.

www.ama-assn.org

Centers for Medicare & Medicaid Services

Federal government agency that oversees government health insurance for 74 million Americans through Medicare and Medicaid. Statistics, data, local information, laws, and links. Formerly called the Health Care Financing Administration.

www.cms.hhs.gov

Consumer Healthcare Products Association

Industry news, issues, and statistics.

www.chpa-info.org

Institute of Medicine

Studies about the quality of medical care in the US.

www.iom.edu

Managed Healthcare Executive

Magazine for managed health care industry.

www.managedhealthcareexecutive.com

National Center for Health Statistics (NCHS)

Surveys and data collection systems, health initiatives, research and development, publications and information products, news releases, and FEDSTATS.

www.cdc.gov/nchs

World Health Organization

International health comparisons.

www.who.int

Glossary of Acronyms

AHRQ — Agency for Healthcare Research and Quality

AMA — American Medical Association

BBA — Balanced Budget Act of 1997

CMS — Centers for Medicare and Medicaid Services

DHHS — Department of Health and Human Services

EMRS — electronic medical records

HIPAA — Health Insurance Portability and Accountability Act

HMO — health maintenance organization

MCO — managed care organizations

NIH — National Institutes of Health

PHRMA — Pharmaceutical Research and Manufacturers of America

PPN / PPO — Preferred provider network / organization

S-CHIP — State Children's Health Insurance Programs

WHO — World Health Organization

HOOVER'S TOP COMPANIES

Largest Companies by Sales	($ mil.)
Kaiser Permanente	37,800.0
HCA Inc.	26,858.0
Ascension Health	13,489.0
Community Health Systems, Inc.	10,840.1
Tenet Healthcare Corporation	8,663.0
Catholic Healthcare West	8,401.5
Sutter Health	7,651.0
Mayo Foundation	6,897.6
Providence Health & Services	6,348.0
Trinity Health	6,300.0

Largest Employers	Employees
Kaiser Permanente	159,766
Ascension Health	107,000
Tenet Healthcare Corporation	63,264
Mayo Foundation	54,914
Catholic Health East	54,000
Catholic Healthcare West	50,000
Providence Health & Services	45,000
Sutter Health	44,828
Trinity Health	44,500
Adventist Health System	43,000

Fastest Growing* by Five-Year Sales Growth	(%)
PTS, Inc.	146.6
American CareSource Holdings, Inc.	131.1
Virtual Radiologic Corporation	78.4
Hythiam, Inc.	74.8
NightHawk Radiology Holdings, Inc.	59.6
The Providence Service Corporation	46.8
Banyan Corporation	44.3
Psychiatric Solutions, Inc.	43.2
Health Grades, Inc.	35.2
PharmaNet Development Group, Inc.	34.2

Fastest Growing* by Five-Year Employee Growth	(%)
Prospect Medical Holdings, Inc.	74.6
NightHawk Radiology Holdings, Inc.	43.0
Duke University Health System	42.1
Continucare Corporation	32.2
Psychiatric Solutions, Inc.	28.0
LCA-Vision Inc.	27.5
Health Grades, Inc.	26.2
Transcend Services, Inc.	25.7
Commonwealth Biotechnologies, Inc.	25.4

Top Public Companies by Market Value	($ mil.)
DaVita Inc.	5,143.1
Pharmaceutical Product Development, Inc.	3,412.5
Covance Inc.	2,913.6
Charles River Laboratories International, Inc.	1,677.7
Community Health Systems, Inc.	1,334.2

* These rates are compounded annualized increases and may have resulted from acquisitions or one time gains. If less than 6 years of data are available, growth is for the years available.

SOURCE: HOOVER'S, INC., DATABASE

Hedge Fund Management

The US hedge fund industry includes about 9,000 companies with combined annual revenue of $60 billion. Almost all hedge funds are private companies. The industry is fragmented, as large size is often an impediment to high investment returns.

Competitive Landscape

Demand for hedge fund services is driven by the growth of investment capital managed by institutional investors. The profitability of individual funds depends on investment expertise. Large funds can more easily participate in big financial transactions. Small funds can compete effectively through specialized investment strategies. The industry is highly automated.

Hedge funds are unregulated investment pools that, unlike mutual funds, can engage in a wide variety of investment activities. Hedge funds are typically organized, marketed, and operated by an individual or institution that also serves as the fund's investment adviser.

Products, Operations & Technology

Hedge funds operate much like mutual funds, but are also able to trade financial derivatives and to take "short" positions. In contrast, mutual funds can own only registered securities such as stocks and bonds. Hedge funds typically specialize in a particular type of investing, such as stocks, bonds, commodities, futures contracts, distressed securities, mergers and acquisitions, arbitrage, or investing in other funds.

The daily operations of a hedge fund depend on the particular investment strategy it follows. Funds that specialize in arbitrage may use computer programs to automatically make hundreds or thousands of trades per day. Funds that specialize in mergers and acquisitions may extensively research possible acquisition candidates. Some hedge funds are characterized by intricate investment strategies devised through

BUSINESS CHALLENGES

» High Investment Risk

Because investors expect hedge funds to produce high returns, hedge fund managers may make risky investments. The availability of complex financial derivatives, in particular, easily allows fund managers to produce high investment returns if they're willing to assume high risk. Because the risks of many complex investments are uncertain, hedge funds may hold more risk than investors realize.

» Increased Industry Regulation

As the number of funds managed by the hedge fund industry climbs, industry regulation is more likely. Although the hedge fund industry is still small compared to the mutual fund industry, the SEC and other regulators are concerned that they have little knowledge of the risks the industry may pose to US financial markets. Regulation may at first consist only of simple reporting of the amounts being managed, but industry participants fear they'll eventually be asked to reveal investment strategies.

» Competition for Institutional Investors

Institutional investors have fueled the rapid growth of the hedge fund industry. Because of the limits on the number of investors many funds can have, large hedge funds depend on big investments from big institutions, particularly pension funds. The number of such large investors is limited.

sophisticated data analysis, but others merely buy and hold traditional stocks and bonds.

To access various securities exchanges, hedge funds need an arrangement with one or several securities broker-dealers who are members of the exchanges. Broker-dealers provide services such as execution of trades, custody of securities, securities lending for "short" sales, and margin lending. Broker-dealers may also introduce hedge funds to potential investors and provide a variety of administrative and advisory services.

The strategy of a hedge fund is devised and executed by the fund's investment adviser, who is usually the fund's organizer and operator. The adviser may be an individual or an institution. The investment adviser typically charges an annual investment management fee of 1 to 2 percent of the assets, and typically receives a share of profits (an "incentive allocation") of about 20 percent.

Disclosure of information to investors in hedge funds is often limited to the initial private placement memorandum (PPM) that typically describes in very general terms the types of investments a fund may make, and to account statements that may be prepared quarterly or annually. Investors are typically restricted in their ability to withdraw money from a hedge fund. Typically, funds are organized as limited partnerships, with the organizer and investment adviser as general partner.

Many hedge funds use computer technology extensively, both to analyze information to devise an investment strategy and to execute trades. Funds may have large and ongoing investments in computer and communication equipment. Funds that trade heavily may be connected directly to trading systems.

Sales & Marketing

Typical investors in hedge funds are wealthy individuals and institutions such as pension plans, universities, and foundations. To maintain an unregulated status, a hedge fund can't take on small, or "retail," investors.

To maintain their unregulated status, hedge funds can't publicly advertise for investors, and therefore typically gather investors through personal contacts or through introductions from broker-dealers. The Internet has become a medium for hedge funds to introduce themselves to potential investors.

Investors are attracted to hedge funds because of the possibility of higher investment returns than is available through more traditional investments such as mutual funds. Institutional investors are particularly attracted by the possibility of good returns even in periods when the value of stocks or bonds is falling.

Human Resources

Because managing a hedge fund typically requires only a small staff, and because of high management fees, managers of big hedge funds can afford to hire expensive workers with special skills, experience, or education.

Industry Employment Growth

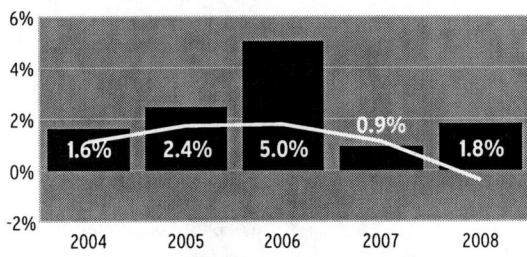

Average Hourly Earnings

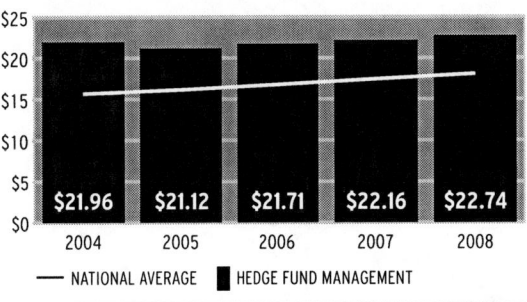

— NATIONAL AVERAGE ■ HEDGE FUND MANAGEMENT

SOURCE: BUREAU OF LABOR STATISTICS

Call Preparation Questions

How does the fund control the risk of its investments?

Because investors expect hedge funds to produce high returns, hedge fund managers may make risky investments.

What does the fund foresee as likely future regulation of the industry?

As the number of funds managed by the hedge fund industry climbs, industry regulation is more likely.

To what extent does the fund rely on institutional investors?

Institutional investors have fueled the rapid growth of the hedge fund industry.

Does the fund plan to participate in private equity deals?

While hedge funds invest mainly in tradable securities, some also have stakes in private equity, usually the province of private equity funds.

Does the fund have foreign investments and investors?

Because of the easy accessibility of foreign securities exchanges, many US hedge funds have foreign investments.

Web Links

Connecticut Hedge Fund Association

Lobbying organization.
www.cthedge.org

Hedge Fund Association

Facts about hedge funds, investment strategies.
www.thehfa.org

Hedge Fund Research

News, data, for registered users.
www.hedgefundresearch.com

Managed Funds Association

Lobbying organization. Issues.
www.mfainfo.org

Glossary of Acronyms

CDO — collateralized debt obligations
LTCM — long-term capital management
PPM — private placement memorandum

Highway and Street Construction

In the US, about 10,000 companies provide highway and street construction services, with combined annual revenues of about $70 billion. Large companies include APAC and divisions of large construction companies like Bechtel Group and Kiewit. The industry is fragmented: although a few companies have a large regional or national presence, 70 percent of the market is held by companies with fewer than 250 employees. A typical company has $5 million of annual revenue and fewer than 50 employees.

Competitive Landscape

Demand is largely driven by the availability of government roadbuilding funds. The profitability of individual companies depends on operating efficiencies and the ability to correctly estimate costs. Big companies have the resources and engineering skills necessary for large construction jobs. Small companies can compete effectively by bidding for smaller projects or by working as subcontractors on large projects. The work is capital-intensive: annual revenue per employee is about $200,000.

This is largely a local business with few economies of scale or technical complexities to encourage consolidation. Most contracts are fairly small and local marketing is important in acquiring them.

Products, Operations & Technology

Nationally, road construction work consists 55 percent of new construction, 30 percent of alterations or reconstruction, and 15 percent of maintenance and repair. The US has about 1.5 million miles of unpaved roads, and 2.5 million miles of paved roads. New street and highway construction can involve complicated engineering, and skilled operations like earthmoving, grading, and bridge, curb, sidewalk, and water drainage system construction. The typical small construction company does light new construction work and concentrates

BUSINESS CHALLENGES

» Dependence on State, Federal Budgets

Although funding for major highway construction projects isn't immediately affected by lower government revenues, repair projects are often postponed during periods of economic slowdown, as government budgets are squeezed. After increasing an average 10 percent during each of the prior five years, state and local highway spending was flat during the last recession. Most federal highway funding is awarded on the condition that state or local governments also provide money.

» Raw Material Costs Linked to Energy Prices

Higher oil prices can hurt highway contractors, raising costs for paving asphalt, bituminous concrete, plastic pipe products, material deliveries, and for running equipment fleets. Because asphalt cement is a byproduct of crude oil refining, asphalt prices can vary substantially with the price of oil.

» Seasonal Workflow

In much of the US, highway construction can't be done in the winter or rainy seasons, as low temperatures and excess precipitation make road construction difficult. Because the traditional peak season for public highway contracts is between April and August, contractors usually maintain a core labor force of skilled workers and hire extra workers during this season. Finding and training these seasonal workers is sometimes difficult, especially for smaller companies.

mainly on reconstruction and maintenance. Engineering design work is important for new construction.

Streets and highways consist of several different layers of materials, earth and various grades of gravel on the bottom. Paved roads have cement or asphalt (95 percent) on the top. The typical street or highway has a gravel base and several layers of asphalt. (An asphalt street is officially called a "bituminous roadway.") A heavily used highway, like the Baltimore Beltway, has three layers of asphalt: a 12-inch coarse layer; a 3-inch intermediate layer; and a 2-inch top layer. Concrete roadways are usually poured to a standard thickness of 9 inches.

Asphalt is a mixture of sand, gravel, or rock, asphalt cement, and various additives. Sand and gravel (called "aggregate") make up 90 percent of the asphalt. Asphalt cement (AC — sometimes called bituminous cement) is the black substance left over when crude oil is distilled into gasoline and other liquid products. Asphalt is made up as "hot mix asphalt" (HMA) in a special mixing facility where the paving aggregates are dried and heated, and then mixed with melted asphalt cement. The HMA is transferred to silos for short-term storage and delivered by truck to the worksite. Some construction companies operate their own HMA facilities, but most buy their asphalt from independent operators.

Most construction jobs specify the type and amount of aggregate and asphalt cement to be used. (The federal system for specifying asphalt quality is called Superpave.) At the worksite, HMA is loaded into a paving machine that actually lays down the surface. Rollers then smooth and compact the surface as the HMA cools. Construction materials account for about a third of project costs.

Reconstruction of asphalt roads involves grinding off the top layer and replacing it. The ground up old pavement, called reclaimed asphalt pavement (RAP), can be added to HMA to form new asphalt, usually for the coarse bottom layers, where it may constitute as much as 30 percent of the asphalt. Nationally, 80 percent of RAP is recycled; the rest is used as landfill.

Construction companies usually own some core pieces of heavy equipment (trucks, backhoes, paving machines, and rollers) and lease other pieces as needed, depending on the type of work. Many companies also do other kinds of construction work such as driveways, parking lots, sidewalks, foundations, concrete and masonry work, to efficiently use their assets and skills.

Sales & Marketing

Major customers are state, county, or municipal governments. States account for 70 percent of road construction dollars, municipalities for 15 percent, and county governments for 10 percent. Although the federal government dispenses about $25 billion each year for roadwork, most of the money is funneled through state and local projects. Municipalities mainly contract for street repaving; states for most new highway construction.

Construction companies acquire almost all of their business by bidding on fixed-cost contracts. The large companies often win a bid to be general contractor for a project and may hire smaller local companies to perform parts of the project. Large projects may be awarded under contracts that allow additional costs, because of the uncertainty of the obstacles that may be encountered, but projects like repaving are almost always of the fixed-cost variety.

Human Resources

The workload for most construction companies varies, affected both by the nature of the work and weather. Consequently, many companies maintain a core of skilled employees and hire additional ones as needed. Construction workers have relatively high hourly earnings, averaging over $20, about $4 more than the national wage. The construction industry's safety record is poorer than the norm, with six cases a year per 100 full-time workers, two more than the national average.

Industry Employment Growth

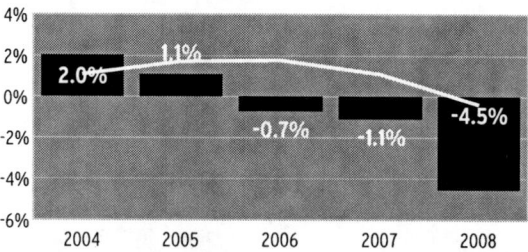

Average Hourly Earnings

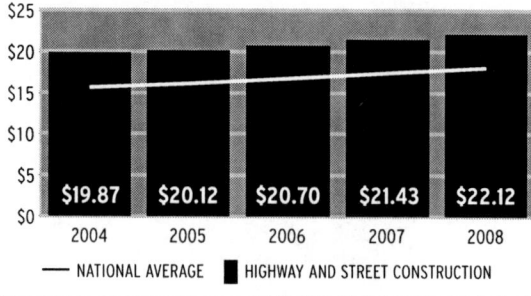

— NATIONAL AVERAGE ▪ HIGHWAY AND STREET CONSTRUCTION

SOURCE: BUREAU OF LABOR STATISTICS

Call Preparation Questions

How does the company manage changes or delays in government spending for highway and street construction?

Although funding for major highway construction projects isn't immediately affected by lower government revenues, repair projects are often postponed during periods of economic slowdown, as government budgets are squeezed.

How does the company mitigate fluctuating raw material costs?

Higher oil prices can hurt highway contractors, raising costs for paving asphalt, bituminous concrete, plastic pipe products, material deliveries, and for running equipment fleets.

How does the company handle the seasonal nature of contracts?

In much of the US, highway construction can't be done in the winter or rainy seasons, as low temperatures and excess precipitation make road construction difficult.

How is the company strategically positioning itself to win more federal, state, and local bids?

Political support for street and highway construction funding remains high among taxpayers.

What techniques, like asphalt test strips, does the company use to optimize material use and limit costs?

Running a test strip can assure the asphalt paving contractor of the quality, cost, and timing of a paving job.

Web Links

American Association of State Highway and Transportation Officials

Online journal, magazine, events, federal transportation regulations and transportation news.
www.transportation.org

American Road & Transportation Builders Association

Industry lobbying association with government affairs, industry links, and news.
www.artba.org

American Society of Highway Engineers

Newsletter, current events, and directories.
www.highwayengineers.org

Construction Financial Management Association (CFMA)

Construction finance information.
www.cfma.org

Engineering News-Record (ENR)

News items.
enr.construction.com/news/transportation

Federal Highway Administration

News, websites, legislation, and regulations. Articles on funding, legislation, etc.
www.fhwa.dot.gov

National Asphalt Pavement Association

News and information.
www.hotmix.org

Pavement magazine

Covering contractors who work in the paving, sealcoating, pavement marking and sweeping industry.
www.forconstructionpros.com/cover/Pavement/3FCP

The Asphalt Contractor Online

Facts, industry links, news, and industry acronyms.
www.forconstructionpros.com/cover/Asphalt-Contractor/2FCP

The Intermodal Transportation Database

Statistics relating to highway transportation.
www.transtats.bts.gov

Glossary of Acronyms

AC — asphalt cement (also called bituminous cement)
ARTBA — American Road and Transportation Builders Association
CSD — context-sensitive design
HMA — hot mix asphalt
ITS — intelligent transportation systems
RAP — reclaimed asphalt pavement

HOOVER'S TOP COMPANIES

Largest Companies by Sales	($ mil.)
Bechtel Group, Inc.	27,000.0
Peter Kiewit Sons', Inc.	6,200.0
Meadow Valley Corporation	205.9

Largest Employers	Employees
Bechtel Group, Inc.	42,500
Peter Kiewit Sons', Inc.	15,000
APAC, Inc.	9,500
Modern Continental Companies, Inc.	5,700
Colas Inc.	4,500
Skanska USA Civil	4,000
The Lane Construction Corporation	3,500
The Hubbard Group, Inc.	1,852
Balfour Beatty, Inc.	1,803

Fastest Growing* by Five-Year Sales Growth	(%)
Bechtel Group, Inc.	18.4
Peter Kiewit Sons', Inc.	10.9
Meadow Valley Corporation	6.4

Top Public Companies by Market Value	($ mil.)
Meadow Valley Corporation	65.8

* These rates are compounded annualized increases and may have resulted from acquisitions or one time gains. If less than 6 years of data are available, growth is for the years available.

SOURCE: HOOVER'S, INC., DATABASE

Hog and Pig Farming

THIS INDUSTRY INCLUDES:

SIC CODES
0213   Hogs

NAICS CODES
1122   Hog and Pig
        Farming

The US hog and pig farming industry includes about 65,000 farms with combined annual revenue of $14 billion. Major companies include Smithfield Foods, Tyson Foods, JBS Swift, and Cargill. The industry is highly concentrated: over 90 percent of industry revenue is generated by just 10 percent of farms. Smithfield Foods and Tyson Foods farm and process nearly half of the pork consumed in the US.

Hog farming involves six stages: breeding; gestation; birthing (known in the industry as farrowing); weaning; nursery; and grow finishing, where the hog reaches its ideal weight. While many large companies are often vertically integrated and ready the animal for consumption, this industry doesn't include slaughter.

Competitive Landscape

Demand is driven primarily by domestic and international trends in pork consumption. The profitability of individual companies depends on efficient operations and reducing the spread of disease. Large companies have advantages in vertically integrating operations from birthing to packaging and distribution. Small operations, typically family-owned farms, can compete effectively by specializing in a single stage of hog farming or raising humanely treated animals. Average annual revenue per worker on US farms is $175,000.

Hog and pig farms compete against other livestock, poultry, and fish operations.

Products, Operations & Technology

Major services include farrow-to-finish (45 percent of farms); growing pigs and hogs to finishing (25 percent); wean-to-finish (10 percent); and breeding (10 percent). Other services include farrow-to-wean and nursery operations.

The total US inventory of hogs and pigs (immature hogs weighing less than 125 pounds) is around 60 million head. Each year, the pork industry produces 20 billion pounds of pork, a

BUSINESS CHALLENGES

» Vulnerable to Raw Material Prices

Feed costs represent 50 to 60 percent of the total cost of production for pig and hog farmers. A typical grow-finish pig eats more than 500 pounds of corn, grains, and soybeans in just four months of finishing; 80 percent of a grow-finish hog's diet is corn feed. Corn production and prices are at a 10-year high, due in large part to current and projected demand for ethanol. Rising corn prices and lack of a food substitute can saddle hog farmers with high production costs and diminished profits.

» Competition from Alternative Products

Pork consumption has remained flat for many decades, in spite of the well-known "The Other White Meat" ad campaign. Per capita consumption has fallen 10 percent since 1960 to around 45 pounds per person annually. Chicken overtook pork in the late 1990s and is now tied with beef as the most popular meat in the US. The USDA projects that US demand for pork will continue to fall as the two fastest-growing demographics, Hispanics and the elderly, traditionally eat less pork than the national average. Competition has resulted in slower growth in consumer prices for pork products relative to other meats.

» Environmental Concerns

Industrial farms generate vast amounts of concentrated animal waste, which emit toxic gases while collecting in open-air lagoons or evaporating through sprays. Gases from these pools and sprays, primarily hydrogen sulfide and ammonia, are poisonous. Hurricanes can spread the waste from spray fields and lagoons into waterways and eco-systems, further fouling the environment. Concerns over the environmental impacts of waste lagoons is forcing companies to invest in alternative technologies, and has led several counties and states, including North and South Carolina, to impose moratoriums on new and expanded hog operations.

number which has remained flat for decades in spite of US population gains. The number of US hog farms has fallen about 90 percent since the 1970s and 1980s, as highly efficient industrial operations displaced small, typically family-run farms. Of US hog farms, 70 percent manage fewer than 100 hogs, yet account for just 1 percent of total industry revenue. The average farm manages 900 pigs and hogs.

A female hog (gilt) is ready to reproduce at eight months. Reproduction begins with mating a gilt and a boar or through artificial insemination. Gestation takes about four months. A sow nurses her pigs for two to three weeks before the litter is weaned. Sows can be bred again mere weeks after weaning a litter. The typical sow produces around 15 piglets annually, yielding 3,000 to 4,000 pounds of live offspring a year.

Pigs weigh 10 to 20 pounds when weaned from a mother. Young pigs are gathered into a nursery with pigs the same size, where they eat a high-energy feed of soybean meal and corn. Pigs typically gain three pounds for every pound of feed. Farmers move feeder pigs out of the nursery when they reach 50 to 60 pounds, at around two to three months old. The final stage, growing (also known as finishing), is a four-month process of intense feeding until the hog reaches 240 to 270 pounds, the ideal slaughter weight. Each day, around 400,000 hogs are transferred to slaughterhouses. Of US hogs, 10 percent are kept for breeding, and around 5 to 10 percent are removed from inventory due to death or disease.

Although farrow-to-finish is the most common hog farm operation, almost as many farms specialize in one or two of the key stages, selling off and transferring pigs at the end of each stage.

Major inputs include corn, soybeans, water, and medications such as antibiotics. Feed inputs can be in short supply due to weather and competition from other non-feed harvests. Hog farmers typically enter into contracts with corn and soybean providers to guarantee plenty of feed for the anticipated number of pigs and hogs.

Technology plays a critical role in the health of the hog farming industry, particularly as large farms have become highly efficient and automated. Genetic standardization of hog semen improves the likelihood of a lean, high-yield marketing hog and can raise the number of pigs per litter. Antibiotics speed growth and limit infectious disease outbreaks. Technical innovations in hog waste and lagoon management can limit pollution spills and lower the risk of chemical exposure to farm workers, fish, and livestock.

Sales & Marketing

Major customers depend on the steps in hog farming operations that a company focuses on. Small, specialized farrow-to-wean farms sell exclusively to nurseries, which sell directly to finishing farms. External customers of industrial farms can include livestock wholesalers, meat packaging companies, and distributors. However, often the customer is simply a vertically integrated business division of the same hog operation.

Contracts take two basic forms. In a marketing contract, a farmer and buyer agree on quantity and price before the farmer markets pigs and hogs. The farmer makes management decisions, retains product ownership as the pigs and hogs grow, and incurs costs of production. In production contracts, small farms pay a fee to an industrial farm to provide management, labor, facilities, and equipment. The contractor owns the product, assigns the source and quantity of raw material inputs, and determines the size of the harvest. A farm can hold both marketing and production contracts.

Hog producers market livestock at auctions, commodity markets, trade shows, and in magazine or trade publications. Smaller farms sometimes join forces as a cooperative and sell directly to a large operation's buying station, stockyard, or central processing plant. Smaller hog farms sometimes market directly to consumer and foodservice operators, emphasizing more sustainable, environmentally sensitive, and humane operations than industrial hog practices. Direct-to-consumer and Internet sales are rising, particularly on farms specializing in hormone-free, sustainable, and organic meat. Selling directly adds to a farm's overhead, but eliminates the distribution and retail margin, which can run as high as 60 percent.

Product prices are expressed in dollars per hundred pounds ($/cwt). Live hog market prices average $40 to $50/cwt, depending on the season; carcass hogs average $50 to $60/cwt. At the retail level, pork averages around $2.75 a pound (expressed by the industry in cents per retail pound). Prices are impacted by the supply of marketable hogs, feed costs, and weather conditions. Pork competes with other meat proteins such as beef, turkey, chicken, and fish.

Human Resources

Wages for livestock workers are 40 percent lower than the national average, but 5 percent higher than for agricultural field workers. Breeders make around $15 an hour and livestock managers around $20. CEOs of large-scale industrial farms earn millions each year; several hog farm executives have been named among the richest people in America.

The average hog farm employee works 43 hours a week. Working conditions can often be dangerous and stressful for farmhands, particularly around hog lagoons. The overall injury rate is more than twice the national average. Common workplace injuries include sprains, heat burns, bruises, and soreness. Environmental hazards include overexposure to ammonia, methane, carbon dioxide, and hydrogen sulfide, leading to increased risk of eye and respiratory irritation and asphyxiation. Turnover is extremely high, sometimes reaching 100 percent of the workforce.

Call Preparation Questions

How have rising feed costs impacted profitability?

Feed costs represent 50 to 60 percent of the total cost of production for pig and hog farmers.

How can the company increase public interest in pork?

Pork consumption has remained flat for many decades, in spite of the well-known "The Other White Meat" ad campaign.

How does the company manage hog waste?

Industrial farms generate vast amounts of concentrated animal waste, which emit toxic gases while collecting in open-air lagoons or evaporating through sprays.

Has the company explored innovative uses for hog waste?

Methane gas from decomposing hog waste can potentially generate a significant amount of electric power.

Is the company exploring new uses for hog byproducts?

Scientists are increasingly finding pharmaceutical uses for hog byproducts.

Web Links

Agricultural Electronic Bulletin Board

Up-to-date resource on agricultural and livestock markets.
agebb.missouri.edu

National Agricultural Statistics Service (NASS)

The USDA's equivalent of Census information.
www.nass.usda.gov

National Pork Producers Council

Alliance of 44 state pork councils and associations.
www.nppc.org

Pork.org – Blog

Editorials and insights from the hog industry.
blog.pork.org

Pork.org – News and Publications

News from the National Pork Board.
www.pork.org/NewsAndInformation

The Pig Site

Online news resource about pigs and hogs.
www.thepigsite.com

USDA Economic Research: Briefing Room

Overview and outlook of the US hog industry.
www.ers.usda.gov/Briefing/Hogs

Glossary of Acronyms

ARS — Agricultural Research Service
CAFO — concentrated animal feeding operation
CWT — hundredweight
DDGS — dried distillers grains with solubles
FIS — federally inspected slaughter
MRSA — methicillin-resistant staphylococcus aureus
NASS — National Agricultural Statistics Service

HOOVER'S TOP COMPANIES

Largest Companies by Sales	($ mil.)
Cargill, Incorporated	120,439.0
Tyson Foods, Inc.	26,862.0
Smithfield Foods, Inc.	11,351.2
Seaboard Corporation	4,267.8
JBS Swift & Company	—

Largest Employers	Employees
Cargill, Incorporated	160,000
Tyson Foods, Inc.	107,000
Smithfield Foods, Inc.	58,100
JBS Swift & Company	20,200
Seaboard Corporation	10,663

Fastest Growing* by Five-Year Sales Growth	(%)
Cargill, Incorporated	17.2
Seaboard Corporation	16.6
Smithfield Foods, Inc.	7.5
Tyson Foods, Inc.	1.8

Fastest Growing* by Five-Year Employee Growth	(%)
Cargill, Incorporated	10.3
Smithfield Foods, Inc.	5.7
Seaboard Corporation	1.5

Top Public Companies by Market Value	($ mil.)
Tyson Foods, Inc.	3,895.8
Smithfield Foods, Inc.	3,827.7
Seaboard Corporation	1,481.1

* These rates are compounded annualized increases and may have resulted from acquisitions or one time gains. If less than 6 years of data are available, growth is for the years available.

SOURCE: HOOVER'S, INC., DATABASE

Home Centers and Hardware Stores

The home center and hardware store industry (home improvement retailers) includes about 30,000 stores with combined annual revenue of about $200 billion. Major companies include The Home Depot, Lowe's Companies, True Value Company, and Ace Hardware. The industry is concentrated at the top but fragmented at the bottom: Home Depot and Lowe's are about 60 percent of industry sales.

Home centers offer more building supplies (such as lumber and flooring) than hardware stores. This profile excludes building supply wholesalers and distributors and lumberyards.

Competitive Landscape

Home remodeling and repair and new homebuilding drive demand. The profitability of individual companies depends on low-cost purchasing, effective merchandising, and competitive pricing. Large companies can offer wide selections, supply high-volume goods to builders, and have advantages in purchasing, finance, distribution, and marketing. Small companies can compete by offering specialty products, providing superior service, or serving a local market. Average annual revenue per worker is about $200,000.

Competition includes building supply distributors and wholesalers, mass merchandisers, warehouse clubs, and Internet retailers.

Products, Operations & Technology

Major products include lumber and building supplies (50 percent of sales); hardware, tools, and plumbing and electrical supplies (25 percent); and paint and lawn and garden products (5 percent each). Building supplies include doors, windows, masonry supplies, cabinets, and countertops. Lawn and garden supplies include lawn care machinery; outdoor nursery stock (trees and shrubs); and fertilizers. Companies may also offer installation, delivery, design, or tool rental services.

BUSINESS CHALLENGES

» Unfavorable Retail Pricing Trends

Declining and flat retail prices in key categories for home improvement retailers can affect profitability. Retail prices for tools and hardware were basically flat between 1998 and 2006, and down almost 10 percent for outdoor equipment and supplies. With limited retail pricing flexibility due to competition and increasing manufacturer prices, companies struggle to maintain margins.

» Dependence on the Residential Housing Market

Home sales, improvement and repair projects, and new residential construction drive sales for home improvement stores. The residential real estate market can be cyclical and influenced by economic conditions. Decreases in home turnover and slower price appreciation, which limits discretionary consumer spending, can lead to fewer home improvement projects. Home centers, particularly those that depend on builders and contractors, are vulnerable to changes in new housing starts.

» Dominance of Large Companies

Home Depot and Lowe's dominate the market. Volume discounts allow large companies to offer extremely competitive prices. Most large home centers provide a wider variety of products and carry building supplies that small hardware stores don't stock. Large companies also have the resources to cater to builders and contractors.

The industry includes national and regional chains and independent retailers. Membership in a cooperative, such as True Value or Ace, allows independent retailers to leverage a national name and benefit from volume discounts. Cooperative members may receive payouts or dividends based on how well the co-op performs.

Do-it-yourself (DIY) projects generally refer to customers buying products and performing work themselves. Do-it-for-me (DIFM) refers to projects where home improvement retailers supply and install products. Companies typically rely on third-party contractors for installations.

Large stores require significant amounts of real estate and are typically located in major retail centers to capitalize on heavy traffic. Locations for independent retailers include secondary strip malls and small town centers. A typical hardware store is about 8,500 square feet, generates just over $1 million annually, and averages $150 in sales per square foot, according to Hardware Retailing. Home centers are about 14,000 square feet, generate $4 million annually, and average $300 per square foot.

Inventory varies according to store type. Home centers stock more lumber and building supplies because many customers are building contractors. Large home centers can carry up to 45,000 stock-keeping units (SKUs) and typically have wide selections within product categories. While independent hardware retailers offer a more limited selection in stores, cooperatives offer members access to a broad range of inventory. Companies using a "good-better-best" merchandising strategy may carry products at different price/quality levels, including national brand names, exclusive brands, and private-label products. Periodically, companies may have line reviews for a category to decide which products or brands to add or drop.

Companies buy inventory from manufacturers, cooperatives, distributors, and importers. The supply side of the industry is fragmented; for example, Lowe's buys from about 7,000 vendors. Large chains and cooperatives typically have extensive distribution networks to facilitate shipping from suppliers to stores. Special distribution centers may stock large items, items requiring special handling, imports, special orders, or Internet sales. Effective supply chain management has allowed large companies to realize significant cost savings and keep prices low.

Integrated information systems have been extremely important to large companies by linking operations at point-of-sale (POS); warehouses; and distribution centers. Bar codes allow companies to track the flow of individual products and identify slow- and fast-turning items. Electronic ordering and automatic replenishment can be important for high-volume stores. Database management systems track important customer groups, such as frequent buyers or new home owners, and help companies create targeted marketing programs.

Sales & Marketing

Typical customers include home owners, building contractors, and repairmen. While home centers tend to attract commercial customers, hardware stores appeal to consumers looking for products needed for DIY projects or repairs.

Marketing and promotional vehicles include national or local TV, radio, print, and newspaper advertising; direct mail; sponsorships; and in-store displays. Vendors may provide cooperative advertising allowances. Partnering with home improvement TV shows, such as such as Home and Garden TV (HGTV), has helped large companies build brand awareness. Store events, such as instructional workshops, can drive traffic. Loyalty programs reward frequent customers and generate repeat business.

Good service is critical to appealing to both consumer and commercial customers. Companies in the consumer segment need workers who can help individuals seeking basic information and how-to instructions. Sales staff for commercial customers require in-depth knowledge of building supplies and typically deal with large quantities of products and specific timetables. Long-term relationships with contractors and builders are extremely important in the commercial sector.

Internet sales of hardware and home improvement products are growing rapidly. Most large companies have retail websites that may offer store and product information, project ideas, how-to instructions, buying guides, and installation quotes. Stores may use websites to sell products with volume too low to justify shelf space. Through the Internet, companies offering specialty merchandise, such as high-end bath fixtures, can reach beyond local markets.

The average transaction size for hardware stores and home centers is $15 and $41, respectively, according to Hardware Retailing.

Human Resources

Wages for home improvement retailers are 20 to 30 percent lower than the average for all US workers. Pay in home centers is slightly higher than that in hardware stores due to expertise required to deal with commercial accounts. Some companies rely on part-time workers, especially during key seasonal periods. The industry injury rate is about equal to the US average in hardware stores, but 75 percent higher than average in home centers. The hazards of dealing with pallet configurations and lifting heavy building supplies account for the higher than average rate of back injuries in home centers.

Industry Employment Growth

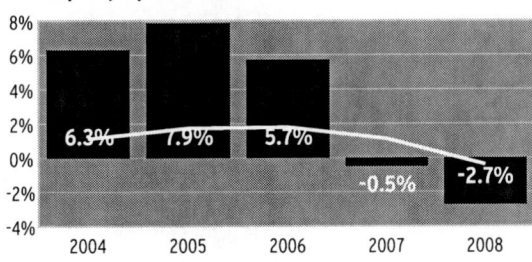

Average Hourly Earnings

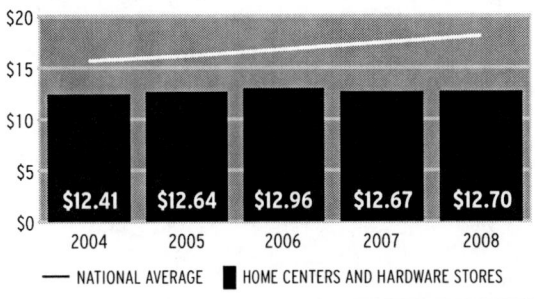

SOURCE: BUREAU OF LABOR STATISTICS

Call Preparation Questions

How have long-term pricing trends in the home improvement market affected the company?

Declining and flat retail prices in key categories for home improvement retailers can affect profitability.

How do residential housing trends affect the company's sales?

Home sales, improvement and repair projects, and new residential construction drive sales for home improvement stores.

How have large home centers, such as Home Depot and Lowe's, impacted the company?

Home Depot and Lowe's dominate the market. Volume discounts allow large companies to offer extremely competitive prices.

How important are installation services to the company's sales?

By offering products and installation, companies can provide a valued service and generate incremental sales.

How do specialty products help the company compete?

By specializing in a particular category, such as high-end fixtures or hardware, small companies can offer better selections and service.

Web Links

Home Channel News

News, surveys.
www.homechannelnews.com

Home Depot

Product trends from major home improvement retailer.
www.homedepot.com

National Association of Home Builders

Building news and trends from trade association.
www.nahb.org

North American Retail Hardware Association

News, industry statistics (annual survey), operating strategies, legislative issues from trade association. Publishes Hardware Retailer.
www.nrha.org

US Census – Construction Statistics

Construction trends.
www.census.gov/const/www

Glossary of Acronyms

DIY — do-it-yourselfer
DIFM — do-it-for-me
HGTV — Home and Garden TV
NRHA — North American Retail Hardware Association
POS — point-of-sale
SKU — stock-keeping unit

HOOVER'S TOP COMPANIES

Largest Companies by Sales	($ mil.)
The Home Depot, Inc.	77,349.0
Lowe's Companies, Inc.	48,283.0
Menard, Inc.	7,800.0
Ace Hardware Corporation	3,970.6
84 Lumber Company	3,100.0
Fastenal Company	2,340.4
True Value Company	2,040.6
Sutherland Lumber Company, L.P.	1,070.0
National Patent Development Corporation	132.9
Do it Best Corp.	—

Largest Employers	Employees
The Home Depot, Inc.	331,000
Lowe's Companies, Inc.	216,000
Menard, Inc.	40,000
Fastenal Company	12,013
84 Lumber Company	7,000
Ace Hardware Corporation	4,800
True Value Company	3,000
Sutherland Lumber Company, L.P.	2,140
Do it Best Corp.	1,549
National Patent Development Corporation	295

Fastest Growing* by Five-Year Sales Growth	(%)
National Patent Development Corporation	67.8
Fastenal Company	18.7
Lowe's Companies, Inc.	12.8
84 Lumber Company	7.7
The Home Depot, Inc.	5.8
Ace Hardware Corporation	5.6

Fastest Growing* by Five-Year Employee Growth	(%)
Fastenal Company	13.6
Lowe's Companies, Inc.	7.1
84 Lumber Company	3.8
The Home Depot, Inc.	3.4

Top Public Companies by Market Value	($ mil.)
The Home Depot, Inc.	51,460.5
Lowe's Companies, Inc.	37,251.9
Fastenal Company	5,176.3
National Patent Development Corporation	44.5

* These rates are compounded annualized increases and may have resulted from acquisitions or one time gains. If less than 6 years of data are available, growth is for the years available.

SOURCE: HOOVER'S, INC., DATABASE

Home Furnishings Stores

The US home furnishings store industry includes 22,000 stores with combined annual revenues of over $23 billion. Major companies include Bed Bath & Beyond, IKEA, and Williams-Sonoma. The industry is concentrated: the 50 largest companies have about 70 percent of industry sales.

Competitive Landscape

Demand is driven by consumer income. Large companies compete through volume purchasing, breadth of products, and effective merchandising and marketing. Small companies focus on a market segment and compete through depth of products and superior customer service. Average annual sales per employee is $125,000. Competition includes department stores, mass merchandisers, home improvement stores, and mail order retailers.

Products, Operations & Technology

Major product categories are domestics (20 percent of sales); decorative accessories (20 percent); dinnerware (10 percent); cookware (10 percent); other kitchen and bathroom accessories (15 percent); and window treatments (10 percent). Domestics are towels, sheets, blankets, and table linens. Decorative accessories include lamps, mirrors, pictures, clocks, and desk sets. Dinnerware includes china, glassware, and flatware. Window treatments are curtains, draperies, blinds, and shades.

Home furnishings retailers include national chains and independent stores. Major chains, such as Bed Bath & Beyond, offer "superstores" that vary from 20,000 to 70,000 square feet and are located in suburban strip malls. Other chains, such as Williams-Sonoma, operate stores of 5,000 to 15,000 square feet located primarily in enclosed shopping malls. Independent stores range from 2,000 to 20,000 square feet.

Large format stores typically carry 15,000 to 40,000 different items and can generate $5 to

BUSINESS CHALLENGES

» Consumer Income Drives Demand

Home furnishings are usually discretionary purchases that can be postponed when consumer income declines. Sales for home furnishings stores rose less than 1 percent during the 2001 recession, as consumers deferred purchases. Sales rose over 7 percent annually during the stronger economy of 2004 and 2005.

» Imports Driving Down Prices

Consumer prices for home furnishing products have been steadily falling the past five years, driven by low-cost imports and competition from national chains and mass merchandisers. Prices for window coverings fell 15 percent from 2000 to 2005; for linen, 18 percent; and for other home furnishings, 13 percent.

» Changing Consumer Preferences

Most home furnishings products have become fashion items subject to changing preferences for features, styles, and colors. Like apparel, a particular product category, design, or color can become "hot" and surge in demand before cooling. Retailers must anticipate consumer lifestyle trends when buying merchandise and respond quickly when demand shifts. Managers review daily reports from point-of-sale systems to detect changes in buying patterns.

$8 million in annual sales or $200 to $300 per square foot. Smaller stores have annual sales of $1 to $4 million and generate $250 to $400 per square foot.

Stores store inventory in attached warehouses. Chains usually have their own distribution facilities with centralized purchasing and inventory management. Goods may be purchased from distributors, importers, or directly from manufacturers. Independent retailers typically buy from several hundred suppliers, while large chains have several thousand suppliers. Most chains use third-party logistics companies for shipping goods to stores. To reduce inventory costs and respond quickly to demand shifts, some retailers are replenishing store inventories daily.

Home furnishings retailers use computer systems to manage point-of-sale (POS) transactions and inventory and warehouse operations. To improve customer service, many also use hand scanners and bar codes to look up prices on the store floor. Computers are also used to store customer data, handle credit approval, and manage bridal gift registries.

Sales & Marketing

The typical target customer is a woman, age 25 to 55, who is fashion- and brand-conscious and has better than average income. Based on local demographics, retailers vary the mix of styles and price points carried at each store.

Effective merchandising and customer service are key to attracting new customers and repeat visits. Retailers frequently change displays and product mix to reflect seasonal variations in demand and create a "fresh" appearance for the store. Sales staff receive product training to help customers in purchase selections. Customer service also includes generous return policies for merchandise.

Advertising typically includes full color newspaper inserts and direct mail. Retailers with catalog operations also use their catalogs as direct mail to drive store traffic. The Internet is also used for advertising and to provide shop-at-home convenience.

To encourage repeat store visits, retailers offer customer loyalty programs that include private-label credit cards, advance notice of sales, and frequent buyer discounts.

Industry trade shows are an important source of information on new products and market trends.

Human Resources

Skill levels for workers are relatively low and wages average about $12 per hour, below the national average of $16 for all workers, but comparable to the average for all US retail. Wage increases have been above average since 2004 as stores seek to improve customer service through more knowledgeable staff. Due to the seasonality of sales, stores employ a large number of part-time workers.

A typical home furnishings store has a manager, one to two assistant managers, and five to 15 employees.

Industry Employment Growth

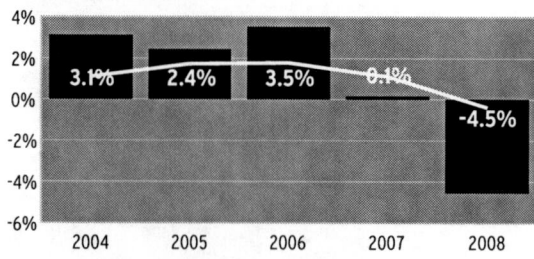

Average Hourly Earnings

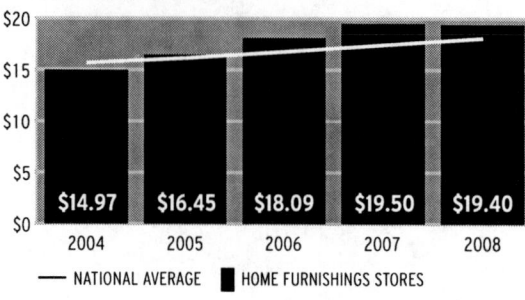

— NATIONAL AVERAGE ■ HOME FURNISHINGS STORES

SOURCE: BUREAU OF LABOR STATISTICS

Call Preparation Questions

How sensitive are the company's sales to economic conditions?

Home furnishings are usually discretionary purchases that can be postponed when consumer income declines.

How has the company responded to declining prices?

Consumer prices for home furnishing products have been steadily falling the past five years, driven by low-cost imports and competition from national chains and mass merchandisers.

How does the company keep pace with trends in consumer preferences?

Most home furnishings products have become fashion items subject to changing preferences for features, styles, and colors.

What role does customer service play in the company's competitive strategy?

Home furnishings stores can compete effectively with mass merchandisers by offering superior customer service through knowledgeable sales staff.

Does the company offer any exclusive brands?

To differentiate themselves from the competition and attract new customers, many home furnishings retailers are developing exclusive product offerings.

Web Links

Bed Bath & Beyond

Largest home furnishings chain.
www.bedbathandbeyond.com

Home Furnishings News

Weekly news and retail trends in home furnishings.
www.hfnmag.com

National Home Furnishings Association

Trade association for furniture and other home furnishings.
www.nhfa.org

National Retail Federation

Largest retail trade association.
www.nrf.com

Williams-Sonoma

High-end home furnishings retailer.
www.williams-sonomainc.com

Glossary of Acronyms

NHFA — National Home Furnishings Association
NRF — National Retail Federation
POS — point-of-sale

HOOVER'S TOP COMPANIES

Largest Companies by Sales	($ mil.)
Bed Bath & Beyond Inc.	7,048.9
Williams-Sonoma, Inc.	3,944.9
Pier 1 Imports, Inc.	1,511.8
Tuesday Morning Corporation	885.3
Overstock.com, Inc.	834.4
Lumber Liquidators, Inc.	482.2

Largest Employers	Employees
Williams-Sonoma, Inc.	39,000
Bed Bath & Beyond Inc.	39,000
Pier 1 Imports, Inc.	16,400
Tuesday Morning Corporation	9,300
Euromarket Designs, Inc.	6,000
The Container Store Inc.	3,529
Hanover Direct, Inc.	1,840
Tandus Group, Inc.	1,623
Anna's Linens	1,620
Arizona Tile Supply, Inc.	950

Fastest Growing* by Five-Year Sales Growth	(%)
Lumber Liquidators, Inc.	29.4
Overstock.com, Inc.	28.4
Bed Bath & Beyond Inc.	14.0
Williams-Sonoma, Inc.	10.8
Tuesday Morning Corporation	1.5

Fastest Growing* by Five-Year Employee Growth	(%)
Overstock.com, Inc.	16.7
Bed Bath & Beyond Inc.	8.0
Williams-Sonoma, Inc.	4.0
Tuesday Morning Corporation	2.8

Top Public Companies by Market Value	($ mil.)
Bed Bath & Beyond Inc.	7,337.8
Williams-Sonoma, Inc.	2,899.2
Pier 1 Imports, Inc.	464.3
Lumber Liquidators, Inc.	283.0
Overstock.com, Inc.	245.2

* These rates are compounded annualized increases and may have resulted from acquisitions or one time gains. If less than 6 years of data are available, growth is for the years available.

SOURCE: HOOVER'S, INC., DATABASE

Home Healthcare Services

The US home health care industry includes about 18,000 companies and agencies with combined annual revenue of $55 billion. Major companies include Apria Healthcare Group, Gentiva Health Services, and Lincare Holdings. The industry is highly fragmented: the 50 largest companies hold less than 25 percent of the market.

Competitive Landscape

Demand is driven by demographics, developments in portable medical technologies, and patients' preference for in-home care. The profitability of individual companies depends on effective marketing and efficient operations. Large companies have some economies of scale in sales and marketing. Small companies can compete successfully by serving a local market. The industry is labor-intensive: average annual revenue per worker is about $60,000.

Products, Operations & Technology

The home health care industry includes medical and skilled nursing services; medical equipment, supplies, and medication services; personal care (such as bathing and transportation); therapeutic services (like physical and respiratory therapy); and psychosocial services (including counseling and spiritual care). Most in-home patients receive medical/skilled nursing services (75 percent), followed by personal care (44 percent), and therapeutic services (37 percent). Companies treat patients who have a short-term need for care, such as after a hospital stay, as well as those with conditions like chronic obstructive pulmonary disease (COPD) who require long-term treatment. Heart disease, diabetes, and cerebral vascular disease are among the most prevalent admission diagnoses for home health care patients. Some 70 percent of patients are age 65 and older.

The back-office operations of companies are very basic, involving mainly personnel management and appointment scheduling, equipment maintenance, and insurance billing. Operations are highly local. Large companies generally operate a network of branch offices. Services are provided by nurses, aides, therapists, and medical technicians as part of a care plan prescribed by a doctor.

Similar to other health care providers, home health care companies rely heavily on computer systems for scheduling and billing. Because care is provided in patient homes, wireless communication systems are an important source of efficiencies.

BUSINESS CHALLENGES

» Dependence on Reimbursement Rates

The industry depends highly on the reimbursement rates that insurers allow for specific home health care services, especially Medicare. The rapid rise in national health care costs in recent years has made Medicare reimbursement a political issue. Because the industry already operates with low costs, any cuts in reimbursement rates directly impact profitability.

» High Personnel Turnover

Being a home health care aide can be physically and emotionally demanding. Patient loads are often excessive and opportunities for advancement are few. Finally, aides' wages and benefits are generally low compared to other available jobs. All of these factors combine to result in an annual personnel turnover rate of 50 percent or higher.

» Customer Concentration

Many companies in the industry have reimbursement arrangements with just a few third-party payers, and therefore depend heavily on those relationships. Payers like insurance companies, managed care organizations (MCOs), and Medicare can terminate contracts for various reasons. Disqualification from a large program like Medicare would devastate most home health care companies.

Sales & Marketing

Although patients are the users of home health care services, marketing is focused on those who authorize treatments or who pay for them, including doctors, hospitals, insurers, and managed care companies (MCOs). Sales are usually handled by a field sales force. The large companies in the industry benefit from being able to provide services to insurers with regional or national needs.

Local, state, and federal government programs provide about three-quarters of industry revenue, including about 37 percent from Medicare and 20 percent from Medicaid. Just more than 10 percent of revenue comes from private health insurers, the rest is from individuals in the form of co-payments. The Medicare program pays for more than 3 million patients per year, with an average of about 30 visits per client and an average payment per visit of about $130.

Human Resources

Staff at home health care companies are mainly home health aides (50 percent), nurses (20 percent), and various types of specialty therapists. Companies use a large number of part-time workers. Although registered nurses (RNs) are highly paid, their median per-hour rate is about $25, aides who feed and clean disabled adults are paid low wages. The median wage for home care aides is about $11 per hour. Overall, average pay for the industry is slightly lower than the national average wage. Annual personnel turnover of low-paid aides can be 50 percent or higher.

Home health care jobs can be physically demanding. Lifting and transferring patients without the aid of other workers or devices can lead to back injuries and muscle strains. The industry's injury rate, however, is similar to the US average.

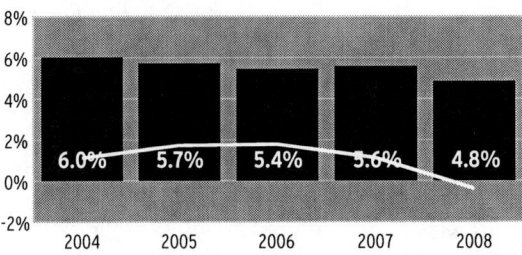

Industry Employment Growth

2004: 6.0% 2005: 5.7% 2006: 5.4% 2007: 5.6% 2008: 4.8%

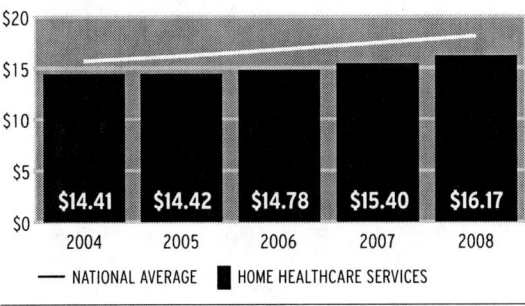

Average Hourly Earnings

2004: $14.41 2005: $14.42 2006: $14.78 2007: $15.40 2008: $16.17

— NATIONAL AVERAGE   ■ HOME HEALTHCARE SERVICES

SOURCE: BUREAU OF LABOR STATISTICS

Call Preparation Questions

How much of company revenue is from private insurance, managed care organizations (MCOs), Medicare, and Medicaid?

The industry depends highly on the reimbursement rates that insurers allow for specific home health care services, especially Medicare.

How does the company recruit and retain personnel?

Being a home health care aide can be physically and emotionally demanding.

How reliant is the company on any single funding source, such as Medicare?

Many companies in the industry have reimbursement arrangements with just a few third-party payers, and therefore depend heavily on those relationships.

Is the company able to provide multi-market services to large MCOs?

The prevalence of national and regional managed care organizations (MCOs), such as health maintenance organizations (HMOs) and preferred provider organizations (PPOs), affords an opportunity for large home health care companies to provide a complete range of services for MCO members.

What plans does the company have to enter specialized fields, like pediatrics?

Home health care for pediatric patients with long-term conditions is preferred by both doctors and parents over long hospitalizations.

Web Links

American Association for Homecare

News, government relations, and links.
www.aahomecare.org

American Health Care Association

News.
www.ahcancal.org/Pages

American Nurses Association

Articles and news.
www.nursingworld.org

National Association for Home Care & Hospice

News, facts, figures, statistics, and links.
www.nahc.org

US Department of Health & Human Services

News and health information.
www.hhs.gov

Visiting Nurse Associations of America

Directory and caregiver information.
www.vnaa.org

Glossary of Acronyms

ACLI — American Council of Life Insurance
CMS — Centers for Medicare and Medicaid Services
COPD — chronic obstructive pulmonary disease
HMO — health maintenance organization
LTC — long-term care
MCO — managed care organization
PPO — preferred provider organization
PPS — prospective payment system
RN — registered nurse

HOOVER'S TOP COMPANIES

Largest Companies by Sales	($ mil.)
Lincare Holdings Inc.	1,664.6
Apria Healthcare Group Inc.	1,631.8
Gentiva Health Services, Inc.	1,300.4
Chemed Corporation	1,148.9
Amedisys, Inc.	697.9
Odyssey HealthCare, Inc.	616.0
LHC Group, Inc.	383.3
Allied Healthcare International Inc.	298.6
American HomePatient, Inc.	293.0
Girling Health Care, Inc.	237.2

Largest Employers	Employees
Addus Healthcare, Inc.	20,000
Gentiva Health Services, Inc.	15,450
Girling Health Care, Inc.	15,000
Apria Healthcare Group Inc.	13,276
Chemed Corporation	11,783
Lincare Holdings Inc.	9,450
Amedisys, Inc.	8,900
Odyssey HealthCare, Inc.	4,834
Almost Family, Inc.	4,800
LHC Group, Inc.	4,498

Fastest Growing* by Five-Year Sales Growth	(%)
Amedisys, Inc.	40.1
LHC Group, Inc.	39.6
Chemed Corporation	30.0
Odyssey HealthCare, Inc.	17.6
Gentiva Health Services, Inc.	9.8
Almost Family, Inc.	9.0
Lincare Holdings Inc.	7.7
Apria Healthcare Group Inc.	5.4
New York Health Care, Inc.	2.7
Allied Healthcare International Inc.	0.3

Fastest Growing* by Five-Year Employee Growth	(%)
Amedisys, Inc.	31.8
LHC Group, Inc.	20.1
Almost Family, Inc.	9.9
Lincare Holdings Inc.	7.0
Gentiva Health Services, Inc.	5.3
Apria Healthcare Group Inc.	4.7
Chemed Corporation	4.1
American HomePatient, Inc.	0.4

Top Public Companies by Market Value	($ mil.)
Lincare Holdings Inc.	2,003.4
Amedisys, Inc.	1,279.4
Apria Healthcare Group Inc.	944.6
Chemed Corporation	891.4
Gentiva Health Services, Inc.	778.2

* These rates are compounded annualized increases and may have resulted from acquisitions or one time gains. If less than 6 years of data are available, growth is for the years available.

SOURCE: HOOVER'S, INC., DATABASE

Hospitals

The US hospital industry includes about 6,500 hospitals with combined annual revenue of around $575 billion. Major companies include Kaiser Permanente, HCA (Hospital Corporation of America), Ascension Health, Tenet Healthcare, and Catholic Health Initiatives. The industry is highly fragmented: the top 50 organizations hold less than 30 percent of the market.

Hospitals provide inpatient and outpatient services using specialized equipment. This industry doesn't include residential care facilities, outpatient care centers, or doctors' offices.

Competitive Landscape

Demand for hospital services is driven by demographics and advances in medical care and technology. The profitability of individual companies depends on efficient operations, since many hospitals offer similar services. Large companies have advantages in buying supplies, sharing best practices, and negotiating contracts with health insurers. Large hospitals may offer a wider variety of services. Small hospitals can compete successfully by serving a limited geographical area or offering specialized services. Hospitals are labor-intensive: annual revenue per employee is close to $100,000.

Products, Operations & Technology

Major services include in-patient hospital care (55 percent of industry revenue) and outpatient services that typically don't require an overnight stay (30 percent). Other sources of revenue include prescription drug sales, ambulatory surgeries, and contributions from private donors, nonprofit foundations, and the federal government.

Hospitals can be government- or privately-run, either by a charitable organization or a for-profit corporation. Around 60 percent of hospitals are non-governmental general medical and surgical hospitals, accounting for 75

BUSINESS CHALLENGES

» Rapidly Rising Hospital Costs

Due to advances in medical knowledge and shortages of trained personnel, costs to provide good medical care have increased rapidly. Total spending for hospital services in the US increased at annual rates above 8 percent in recent years. Costs rise both because new medical equipment is expensive and because hospitals remain labor-intensive.

» Vulnerable to Increased Government Regulation

The hospital industry is subject to numerous government regulations that specify operating and accounting procedures, essentially mandating certain costs. Through Medicare and Medicaid programs, which jointly provide nearly 60 percent of hospital revenues, the government largely determines industry profitability. Hospitals have little choice but to accept these payments because insurers control access to such large numbers of patients. Rising costs have made health care a political issue with uncertain future developments.

» Capital Spending Required

To compete locally, hospitals require large capital investments in facilities and equipment. Although payers like Medicare have resorted to fixed payments for specific treatments, doctors and patients demand the latest equipment and techniques, which can be expensive. Investments in computer systems have been especially important to comply with the records regulations of HIPAA and to improve clinical information flow.

percent of total industry revenue. Government-run hospitals like Veterans Administration (VA) hospitals account for nearly 20 percent of total revenue and 20 percent of all US hospitals. Around 900 private and 300 government hospitals provide psychiatric, substance abuse, and specialized services, generating around 7 percent of industry revenues.

Hospitals provide an efficient way for doctors to use facilities, equipment, and services too expensive to buy for private practices. Hospital operations revolve around routine patient care such as feeding and hygiene; treatment procedures (including medications); record-keeping; personnel management; purchasing; and billing. A typical large hospital may have 250 beds and annual revenue of $100 million; community hospitals generally have fewer than 100 beds.

Hospitals play close attention to costs, because they usually receive a fixed amount of revenue per patient and must bear actual costs themselves. There are some economies of scale: a 50-bed hospital often needs the same expensive equipment (such as an MRI machine) as a 200-bed hospital. Hospitals usually need to keep a nursing staff in proportion to the number of "licensed" beds. Occupancy rates are often no more than 50 percent of beds. The average hospital stay for an in-patient is five to six days.

Labor is the largest single operating cost item, often equal to more than 40 percent of revenue. Nurses, aides, and technicians comprise the majority of the workforce. While hospitals may employ their own doctors, most doctors who use their facilities have independent practices and use the hospital under contract. Doctors may be affiliated with several hospitals within the same area. Some hospitals are affiliated with medical schools to provide student training, and many others host research facilities.

Technology is important in hospital management, largely through computer systems that manage patient records and billings. Many hospitals also have computerized purchasing systems that keep inventories low. Recent technological advances include medical information systems that help doctors with diagnoses and treatment, and prescription systems that help prevent drug interactions and medication mistakes. Some hospitals use wireless technologies that doctors and nurses can use at bedside. Hospital equipment is often expensive and may have a short useful life because of rapid technological advances, especially complex imaging systems like MRI and CT or CAT Scan.

Sales & Marketing

Typical customers are individuals requiring immediate urgent care, scheduled surgeries with extended recovery time, and individuals needing routine outpatient services such as blood work, wellness checks, diagnosis, treatment, and rehabilitation.

Major types of marketing include TV ads, newspapers, and radio. Most marketing is for general branding and name recognition. Hospitals directly market and sell services to doctors (who refer patients) and to insurers (who pay for most services) rather than to the individuals who actually receive the services. Hospitals attract referrals from doctors by offering a wide array of facilities and equipment and hosting specialists on their staff. Contracts with health insurers, another important resource for patient referrals, typically specify the variety and costs of services provided to insured individuals.

The Internet plays an increasingly important role in marketing, particularly in urban areas where patients have choices in the type of care. Some hospitals use online screening forms to collect basic information about a patient's need, guiding the patient to an appropriate division or specialist. Hospitals regularly tout their expertise in online newsletters, publications, and public seminars.

Prices vary depending on the service, length of patient stay, and the patient's insurance policy. Average revenue per admission is close to $10,000; average revenue per outpatient visit is close to $500. Hospitals routinely negotiate rates with a patient's insurance provider or MCO. Payment terms to hospitals are much more standardized in federal programs like Medicaid (intended for low-income families) and Medicare (those 65 or over).

Human Resources

Although the majority of hospital employees earn low to modest pay, the high income of doctors and specialists contributes to higher overall earnings. Wages of workers in general medical and surgical hospitals are 35 percent higher than the national average. Pay at psychiatric and substance abuse hospitals are much lower, equal to the national average.

Injury rates are 40 percent higher in hospitals when compared to the national average. Common injuries include back strains and sprains from moving patients or from falls.

Hospital employees require training on a broad range of issues, including government regulations, insurance, limiting workplace injuries and medical mishaps, reducing liability, and overcoming language and cultural barriers. HR executives regularly schedule lunch seminars and presentations to maintain a highly educated staff. Initial training and orientation can last several weeks. Attrition can be costly, and turnover a problem in lower-wage positions.

Industry Employment Growth

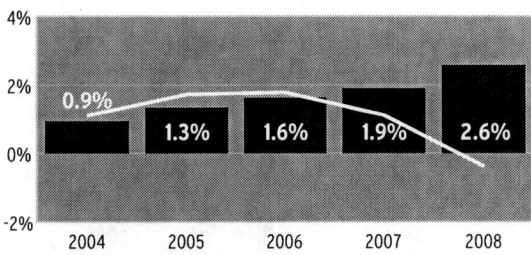

Average Hourly Earnings

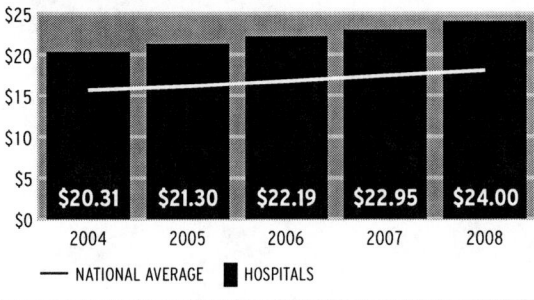

SOURCE: BUREAU OF LABOR STATISTICS

Call Preparation Questions

What trend is the hospital seeing in costs?

Due to advances in medical knowledge and shortages of trained personnel, costs to provide good medical care have increased rapidly.

How much of the hospital's revenue comes from Medicare reimbursements?

The hospital industry is subject to numerous government regulations that specify operating and accounting procedures, essentially mandating certain costs.

How much does the hospital invest in capital improvements?

To compete locally, hospitals require large capital investments in facilities and equipment.

What opportunities does the hospital see in serving the aging population?

National health care expenditures are expected to double over the next decade as the population ages.

How is the hospital benefiting from new IT systems?

Hospitals have been slow to adopt IT tools because of the expense in implementation and difficulty in managing complex medical information.

Web Links

Agency for Healthcare Research and Quality

News and announcements on the health care industry.

www.ahrq.gov

American College of Healthcare Executives

Virtual link to Congress, education, FAQs, Health Administration press, and career services.

www.ache.org

American Health Information Management Association

Professional organization specializing in health information management education for health care professionals. Hot topics, career information, certification, products, events, and specialty group links.

www.ahima.org

American Hospital Association

National organization formed in 1906 that represents and serves hospitals, health care networks and patients. Provides advocacy, campaigns for coverage, compliance assistance, press releases, health forums, and research and education.

www.aha.org

American Medical Association

Hundreds of links, news, and information about many physician specialties.

www.ama-assn.org

HospitalConnect

News links.

www.hospitalconnect.com

Modern Healthcare

Weekly business news related to the health care industry.

www.modernhealthcare.com

Glossary of Acronyms

AHA — American Hospital Association

BBA — Balanced Budget Act

CDCP — Centers for Disease Control and Prevention

CON — certificate of need

DRG — diagnosis-related group

EMR — electronic medical records

HCA — Hospital Corporation of America

HCFA — Health Care Financing Administration

HIPAA — Health Insurance Portability and Accountability Act

MCO — managed care organization

NCHS — National Center for Health Statistics

PPO — Preferred provider organizations

PPS — prospective payment systems

RFID — radio frequency identification

SCHIP — State Children's Health Insurance Program

HOOVER'S TOP COMPANIES

Largest Companies by Sales	($ mil.)
Kaiser Permanente	37,800.0
HCA Inc.	26,858.0
Ascension Health	13,489.0
Community Health Systems, Inc.	10,840.1
Tenet Healthcare Corporation	8,663.0
Catholic Healthcare West	8,401.5
Sutter Health	7,651.0
Mayo Foundation	6,897.6
Providence Health & Services	6,348.0
Trinity Health	6,300.0

Largest Employers	Employees
HCA Inc.	186,000
Kaiser Permanente	159,766
Ascension Health	107,000
Tenet Healthcare Corporation	63,264
Mayo Foundation	54,914
Catholic Health East	54,000
Catholic Healthcare West	50,000
Providence Health & Services	45,000
Sutter Health	44,828
Trinity Health	44,500

Fastest Growing* by Five-Year Sales Growth	(%)
Psychiatric Solutions, Inc.	43.2
Ardent Health Services LLC	32.2
Community Health Systems, Inc.	30.8
LifePoint Hospitals, Inc.	24.4
KishHealth System	16.7
PHC, Inc.	16.1
Vanguard Health Systems, Inc.	15.8
Health Management Associates, Inc.	14.2
Chindex International, Inc.	13.0
Children's Medical Center of Dallas	12.5

Fastest Growing* by Five-Year Employee Growth	(%)
Duke University Health System	42.1
Psychiatric Solutions, Inc.	28.0
Community Health Systems, Inc.	20.7
Chindex International, Inc.	12.9
Health Management Associates, Inc.	9.2
KishHealth System	8.5
Catholic Healthcare West	6.8
Henry Ford Health System	6.8
Children's Medical Center of Dallas	6.7
LifePoint Hospitals, Inc.	5.1

Top Public Companies by Market Value	($ mil.)
Universal Health Services, Inc.	1,719.1
Psychiatric Solutions, Inc.	1,557.8
Community Health Systems, Inc.	1,334.2
LifePoint Hospitals, Inc.	1,220.6
Tenet Healthcare Corporation	548.7

* These rates are compounded annualized increases and may have resulted from acquisitions or one time gains. If less than 6 years of data are available, growth is for the years available.

SOURCE: HOOVER'S, INC., DATABASE

Hotel and Motel — Lodging

The US hotel and motel industry consists of about 30,000 companies that operate 50,000 individual locations, with combined annual revenue over $90 billion. Large US companies include Marriott International, Hilton Hotels, Carlson Hotels, and Starwood Hotels & Resorts. The industry's 50 largest companies hold about 45 percent of the market. The majority of hotels are part of a chain. A typical hotel has about $7 million in annual revenue and 100 employees.

This industry doesn't include casino hotels, bed-and-breakfast inns, youth hostels, housekeeping cabins and cottages, and tourist homes. Casino hotels are included in the "Gambling Operations" industry profile.

Competitive Landscape

Business and tourist travel drive demand and are closely linked to the health of the economy. The profitability of individual companies depends on efficient operations, because many costs are fixed, and on effective marketing. Large companies have advantages in economies of scale in operations, can more easily raise capital, and have strong name recognition. Small companies can compete effectively in favorable locations and by providing specialty services. A hotel business requires large amounts of capital, but operations are labor-intensive: average annual revenue per employee is less than $65,000.

Products, Operations & Technology

Major industry product lines are room fees and sales of food, alcoholic drinks, and merchandise. Room fees account for 70 percent of industry revenue, food for 15 percent, and alcohol for 5 percent.

Basic operations of hotels and motels consist of providing sleeping accommodations, housekeeping, maintenance, and a variety of personal services. Hotels may provide restaurants, meeting rooms, event hosting, business services, and

BUSINESS CHALLENGES

» Demand Highly Sensitive to Personal Income, Corporate Profits

The hotel industry is sensitive to the health of the national economy, which affects the number and frequency of business and tourist travelers, the major customer segments. National personal income, employment levels, and corporate profits are key economic indicators influencing travel and hotel stays. US hotel employment declined three times faster than the national average during a recent recession, and the average US hotel's operating profit fell over 19 percent, according to PKF Hospitality Research. Hotels have high fixed-costs and need relatively high demand and occupancy rates to break even.

» Prices Restrained by Capacity Additions

The ease with which new hotels can be built in most markets limits price increases. The hotel industry is subject to long-term surges of capacity addition, typically coinciding with low interest rates. A surge of hotel construction in a recent decade cut the industry occupancy rate from 66 to 61 percent, according to the American Hotel and Lodging Association; average room rates grew 3 percent per year.

» Dependence on Reservation Systems

Access to one of several large computer reservation systems is critical to success for most hotels, as a vast majority of bookings is through the large systems. Hotel chains' and travel agencies' proprietary systems now compete with Web-based competitors, including Expedia, Travelocity, and Hotels.com. Hotels that don't reach agreements with these systems can have serious marketing challenges.

resort services like golf, tennis, swimming pools, and fitness centers. Labor is a significant operating expense, requiring efficient personnel management. Key industry metrics, in addition to retail sales, are occupancy rates, average room prices, and revenue per available room

(RevPAR), which is a hotel's occupancy rate multiplied by its average daily room rate (ADR).

Most companies own and operate their own hotels, but other arrangements are common. Some hotel companies are operators that receive the majority of their revenue from management fees. Companies may franchise their brands to other owners, manage hotels that belong to other owners, or lease hotels from other owners. Some companies also manage time-share properties.

Hotel websites with reservation capability have become major marketing and sales tools, as have listings on the major reservation and travel systems. Computer and communication systems are essential for most hotels to acquire guests via the large reservation systems; provide guest services; and track reservations, guests, and room charges. Due to the large proportion of business travelers and increasing use of the Internet by tourists, many hotels have installed Internet access networks, including wireless networks. With guests' greater cell phone use, some hotels install indoor cell antennas.

Sales & Marketing

Typical customers are business and leisure travelers: about 60 percent are business travelers and 40 percent are tourists. Major sales channels include websites and travel agencies. Instead of trying to appeal to all travelers, hotels usually specialize in a particular market segment defined by price, service level, and location. Price segments range from budget to luxury. Service levels are fullservice, limited service, and all-suites. Location categories include urban, suburban, airport, and resort. Large hotel chains often have several brands that operate in different or overlapping segments.

Major types of marketing include travel websites, agent networks, magazine and newspaper ads, and customer loyalty programs. Marketing choices depend on the type of hotel and customer. The industry relies heavily on travel websites like Travelocity and Expedia and on travel agents, who have exclusive access to major proprietary reservation systems. These systems have national and international reach, but hotels that host local businesses' events and meetings also advertise in local media. Loyalty programs reward customers who use the same hotel or chain on repeat stays.

Franchise marketing includes national TV and print advertising, and agreements or alliances with travel agents and reservation systems, airlines, credit card companies, other corporations, and business and travel associations. For hotel operators, primary attractions of joining a franchise are name recognition and participation in the chain's national reservation system.

Internet bookings are increasingly important to the industry as more consumers use self-service websites, and as more corporations use internal versions of major travel websites.

Generally, hotel price categories are luxury (often over $200 per night); upscale (usually over $100); moderate (about $60 to $100); and budget (under $60). Prices vary by region, season, and occupancy rates. Prices usually are higher in the Northeast and California, and in prime downtown areas of large cities. Urban bed and breakfast inns that cater to business travelers have become a niche competitor of hotels.

Human Resources

Hotel management and business degrees benefit the industry's professional positions, but most hotel jobs require few special skills. Accordingly, average industry pay is low: US hotel workers' wages are 30 percent below the national average. Largely due to low pay, annual personnel turnover in the hotel and restaurant industry is about 70 percent, which is over 60 percent higher than the national average. The hotel and motel industry's safety record, based on injury rates, is almost 30 percent worse than the national average. The majority of injuries are sprains and strains that result from falls. Unions are active in the industry.

Industry Employment Growth

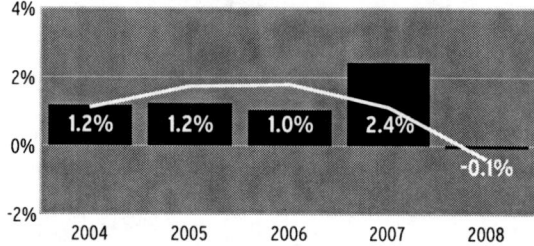

Average Hourly Earnings

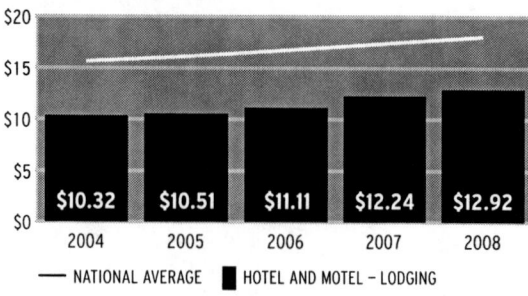

SOURCE: BUREAU OF LABOR STATISTICS

Call Preparation Questions

How does the company handle cyclical business and leisure travel?

The hotel industry is sensitive to the health of the national economy, which affects the number and frequency of business and tourist travelers, the major customer segments.

Which reservation systems are most important to the company's success?

Access to one of several large computer reservation systems is critical to success for most hotels, as a vast majority of bookings is through the large systems.

What plans does the company have to update or expand its loyalty program?

Hotels are updating loyalty programs and rewarding staff for enrolling new members.

Web Links

American Hotel & Lodging Association

News, statistics, publications, newsletters.
www.ahla.com

Cornell University School of Hotel Administration

Industry news, in-depth articles on hotel and restaurant management.
www.hotelschool.cornell.edu/industry

Hospitality Trends

Industry, management, technology news; market research.
www.htrends.com

Hotel & Motel Management

News, articles. List of top hotel companies.
www.hotelmotel.com

Hotel Interactive

News, articles.
www.hotelinteractive.com

Lodging Hospitality

Articles for hotel developers and operators.
www.lhonline.com

Lodging Magazine

News, trends, statistics, publications.
www.lodgingmagazine.com

Glossary of Acronyms

ADR — average daily rate
AHMA — American Hotel and Motel Association
REVPAR — revenue per available room

HOOVER'S TOP COMPANIES

Largest Companies by Sales	($ mil.)
Carlson Companies, Inc.	39,800.0
Marriott International, Inc.	12,879.0
Hilton Hotels Corporation	8,090.0
Starwood Hotels & Resorts Worldwide, Inc.	5,907.0
Host Hotels & Resorts, Inc.	5,288.0
Wyndham Worldwide Corporation	4,281.0
Global Hyatt Corporation	4,000.0
Columbia Sussex Corporation	1,730.0
HVM L.L.C.	1,090.0

Largest Employers	Employees
Carlson Companies, Inc.	160,000
Starwood Hotels & Resorts Worldwide, Inc.	155,000
Marriott International, Inc.	151,000
Hilton Hotels Corporation	135,000
Global Hyatt Corporation	90,000
Wyndham Worldwide Corporation	33,200
Interstate Hotels & Resorts, Inc.	25,500
Accor North America	22,800
Columbia Sussex Corporation	18,250
HVM L.L.C.	9,600

Fastest Growing* by Five-Year Sales Growth	(%)
Great Wolf Resorts, Inc.	38.7
LaSalle Hotel Properties	27.6
Bluegreen Corporation	20.5
Sunstone Hotel Investors, Inc.	16.0
Hilton Hotels Corporation	16.0
Gaylord Entertainment Company	15.7
Carlson Companies, Inc.	15.0
Strategic Hotels & Resorts, Inc.	11.5
Choice Hotels International, Inc.	11.0
Host Hotels & Resorts, Inc.	8.9

Fastest Growing* by Five-Year Employee Growth	(%)
InnSuites Hospitality Trust	143.5
Great Wolf Resorts, Inc.	33.8
Morgans Hotel Group Co.	30.1
Strategic Hotels & Resorts, Inc.	23.9
The Marcus Corporation	16.3
Hilton Hotels Corporation	12.8
Bluegreen Corporation	11.7
Wyndham Worldwide Corporation	10.3
Host Hotels & Resorts, Inc.	8.9
LaSalle Hotel Properties	7.2

Top Public Companies by Market Value	($ mil.)
Marriott International, Inc.	7,018.2
Host Hotels & Resorts, Inc.	3,976.5
Starwood Hotels & Resorts Worldwide, Inc.	3,272.6
Choice Hotels International, Inc.	2,061.4
Wyndham Worldwide Corporation	1,161.7

* These rates are compounded annualized increases and may have resulted from acquisitions or one time gains. If less than 6 years of data are available, growth is for the years available.

SOURCE: HOOVER'S, INC., DATABASE

Household Appliance Manufacture

The US household appliance manufacturing industry consists of about 300 companies with combined annual revenue of $25 billion. Major companies include Whirlpool, Electrolux, and GE. Most companies in the industry are small. The industry is highly concentrated: the top 20 companies hold 95 percent of the market.

Competitive Landscape

Demand is driven by growth in consumer income and by home sales. The profitability of individual companies depends on efficient operations and effective marketing. Large companies have economies of scale in production, marketing, and distribution. Small companies can compete effectively by producing specialty products, subcontracting to the larger manufacturers, or producing name brand goods under contract. The industry is fairly automated: annual revenue per employee is close to $250,000.

Products, Operations & Technology

Major products are refrigerators, household laundry equipment, ovens, ranges, and vacuum cleaners. Refrigerators and freezers account for 25 percent of industry revenue; washers and dryers 20 percent; ovens and ranges 15 percent; and vacuum cleaners 12 percent. Other appliances include dishwashers, fans, microwave ovens, and water heaters.

Most appliance makers produce the body of their product from steel and plastics, and buy components like electric motors, compressors, heat elements, and controls from suppliers. Manufacturing operations consist largely of shaping metal in stamping presses with custom-built dies and assembling components. Steel is the major raw material, either cold-rolled or galvanized. Plastics are used in making vacuum cleaner parts, as an insulating material in other products, and for the interiors of refrigerators. Painting operations are part of most manufacturing plants.

Manufacturers generally produce several models of a particular product in long production runs to achieve economies of scale. Annually, the industry produces about 10 million refrigerators, 10 million washing machines, 10 million ovens and ranges, and 7 million dryers.

Many appliance manufacturers also operate as their own distributor, and some operate retail outlets. Because of the strength of brand names, manufacturers may license a brand name or act as contract supplier for a brand name. For example, Whirlpool is a major producer of the Kenmore brand Sears owns.

BUSINESS CHALLENGES

» Competition from Low-Cost Imports

Due to low labor costs and large economies of scale in production, imports have become a major factor in the US market. Imports, which hold about 40 percent of the US appliance market, come both from foreign and US manufacturers with foreign plants. Half of imports come from China.

» Dependence on Cyclical Real Estate Market

Sales of major appliances are closely linked to sales of new and existing homes, as consumers are most likely to buy new appliances when they buy a home. US home sales increased 45 percent from 2000 to 2005, boosting appliance sales. A significant drop in home sales sharply affects appliance demand.

» Vulnerable to Changing Steel Prices

Because steel is the major raw material used to manufacture large appliances, even small changes in steel prices can largely affect company profitability. Steel prices have been highly cyclical in the past, sometimes increasing more than 30 percent within 12 months.

Because most household appliances are fairly simple devices, the applications of technology in this industry have focused mainly on improving the manufacturing process with greater automation. Computer technology has also been applied in the design process and in the greater sophistication of appliance controls.

Sales & Marketing

Manufacturers sell to appliance distributors — of whom there are about 1,000 — and also directly to large retailers. Distributors in turn sell to small retailers, home builders, property managers, and remodelers. Large retailers, like Sears and Home Depot, can account for a large percentage of a manufacturer's sales. A major retailer can represent over 10 percent of a large supplier's revenue and over 30 percent of a smaller supplier's. Retail stores tend to carry a limited number of appliance brands.

Due to acquisitions and long-term business agreements, major appliance manufacturers make and sell multiple brands that compete in the same category. For example, Whirlpool makes KitchenAid, and now owns Maytag's brands, which include Jenn-Air, Amana, Magic Chef, and Admiral appliances, as well as Hoover vacuums. GE also makes Hotpoint. Manufacturers develop and target brands to different consumer price-points or retail outlets, though consumers often perceive brands as competitors. Typical retail prices for large appliances range from $300 to $2,000.

Manufacturers conduct significant advertising on the national level to create brand awareness and demand, which translates into sales at the retail level. Often companies run cooperative advertisements with national retailers. Companies use TV, radio, and print ads, and may also provide in-store displays and product demonstration videos.

Human Resources

Appliance manufacturers pay moderate wages. Average wages are about 10 percent less than the national average. The annual injury rate for household appliance workers is slightly higher than the national average.

Industry Employment Growth

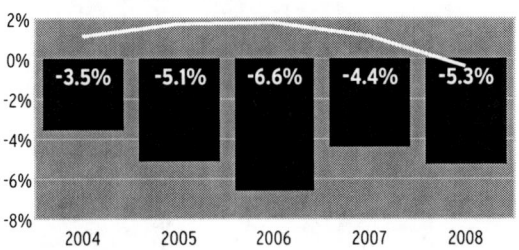

Average Hourly Earnings

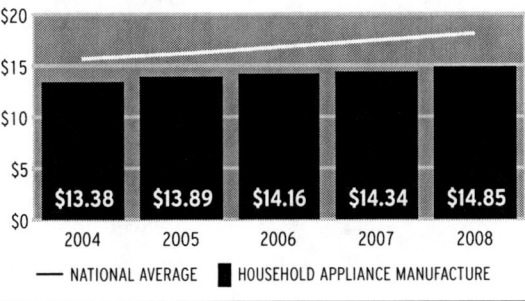

— NATIONAL AVERAGE ■ HOUSEHOLD APPLIANCE MANUFACTURE

SOURCE: BUREAU OF LABOR STATISTICS

Call Preparation Questions

How have imports affected the company's business?

Due to low labor costs and large economies of scale in production, imports have become a major factor in the US market.

How is the company affected by changes in the volume of housing sales?

Sales of major appliances are closely linked to sales of new and existing homes, as consumers are most likely to buy new appliances when they buy a home.

How have changes in steel prices affected company manufacturing costs?

Because steel is the major raw material used to manufacture large appliances, even small changes in steel prices can largely affect company profitability.

Does the company have significant revenue from foreign sales?

Selling in multiple countries and regions allows US appliance makers to compensate for varying economic conditions and consumer demand in any specific country.

Does the company make or buy products or components abroad?

Many appliance manufacturers outsource some or all of their production, especially to Asia.

Web Links

Appliance Design

Industry news. See production data in Shipments/Forecasts.
www.appliancedesign.com

Appliance Magazine

Monthly production statistics. Articles.
www.appliancemagazine.com

Association of Home Appliance Manufacturers

Legislative and regulatory news.
www.aham.org

Gas Appliance Manufacturers Association

Statistics about gas water heaters.
www.gamanet.org

US Consumer Product Safety Commission

Recalls and product safety news.
www.cpsc.gov/cpscpub/prerel/prerel.html

Whirlpool

Company site.
www.whirlpoolcorp.com

Glossary of Acronyms

CPSC — Consumer Product Safety Commission
GECI — GE Consumer and Industrial
WTO — World Trade Organization

HOOVER'S TOP COMPANIES

Largest Companies by Sales	($ mil.)
General Electric Company	182,515.0
Whirlpool Corporation	18,907.0
Jarden Corporation	5,383.3
NACCO Industries, Inc.	3,602.7
Conair Corporation	1,900.0
Salton, Inc.	676.4
Alliance Laundry Holdings LLC	443.3
Electrolux Home Products — North America	—

Largest Employers	Employees
General Electric Company	327,000
Whirlpool Corporation	70,000
Jarden Corporation	25,000
Electrolux Home Products — North America	22,000
NACCO Industries, Inc.	10,200
Conair Corporation	4,060
Royal Appliance Mfg. Co.	2,600
Alliance Laundry Holdings LLC	1,653
Shop-Vac Corporation	1,600

Fastest Growing* by Five-Year Sales Growth	(%)
Jarden Corporation	55.7
iRobot Corporation	41.5
Alliance Laundry Holdings LLC	11.7
Conair Corporation	10.1
Whirlpool Corporation	9.2
NACCO Industries, Inc.	7.2
General Electric Company	6.3

Fastest Growing* by Five-Year Employee Growth	(%)
iRobot Corporation	25.5
Jarden Corporation	19.5
Alliance Laundry Holdings LLC	4.9
Whirlpool Corporation	2.0
General Electric Company	1.7

Top Public Companies by Market Value	($ mil.)
General Electric Company	170,697.7
Whirlpool Corporation	3,018.5
Jarden Corporation	869.4
NACCO Industries, Inc.	664.0
iRobot Corporation	230.5

* These rates are compounded annualized increases and may have resulted from acquisitions or one time gains. If less than 6 years of data are available, growth is for the years available.

SOURCE: HOOVER'S, INC., DATABASE

Household Appliance Stores

THIS INDUSTRY INCLUDES:

SIC CODES
5722   Household
        Appliance Stores

NAICS CODES
443111 Household
        Appliance Stores

The US household appliance store industry includes 10,000 stores with combined annual revenue of $14 billion. No major companies dominate: the largest chains, like P.C. Richard and ABC Appliance, are regional and consist of 50 or fewer stores. The industry is highly fragmented: the 50 largest companies represent 35 percent of industry sales.

Competitive Landscape

Demand is driven by home sales, replacement due to product failure, and home remodeling. The profitability of individual companies depends on effective marketing and merchandising. Large companies can negotiate volume discounts from manufacturers. Small companies can compete effectively by offering superior customer service or specializing in product segments. The high value of major appliance purchases results in an average annual revenue per employee of $200,000.

Major competitors include department stores (Sears); home improvement stores (Home Depot, Lowe's); consumer electronics stores; warehouse clubs; and mass merchandisers. Sears also has a network of over 800 independent dealers that sell its Kenmore brand appliances in small markets.

Products, Operations & Technology

Major product segments include kitchen, laundry, and small household appliances, and TVs. Kitchen appliances account for 40 percent of sales, washers and dryers for 20 percent, other major household appliances for 15 percent, and TVs for 10 percent. Large appliances, with the exception of TVs, are often referred to as "white goods." Kitchen appliances include refrigerators, freezers, dishwashers, and microwaves. Other major household appliances include room air conditioners, dehumidifiers, and vacuum cleaners. Appliance retailers may also sell consumer electronics, including video and

BUSINESS CHALLENGES

» Growth Depends on Cyclical Home Sales

Sales of new and existing homes drive growth for appliance retailers, as consumers are highly likely to buy new appliances when buying a home. Appliance sales related to moving are about one-quarter of all appliance purchases. A soft housing market significantly depresses appliance sales.

» Imports Depress Retail Prices

Retail prices for major appliances declined 6 percent between 1998 and 2005, due primarily to an increase in imports of low-priced products. Of the US appliance market, 40 percent consists of imported products, mainly from China and Mexico; import volume almost tripled between 1996 and 2005 to over $13 billion. Increasing import volume and strong demand for low-end products contribute to flat and decreasing prices across most major appliance segments, challenging retailers to maintain profit margins.

» Competition from Large Retailers

Appliance retailers face intense competition from department, home improvement, and consumer electronics stores. Sears represents almost 40 percent of appliance sales, owns the top-selling Kenmore brand, and focuses on the value segment of the market. Lowe's and Home Depot are increasing market share by adding high-end brands like KitchenAid.

audio equipment. Stores typically offer extended warranties and delivery, installation, or repair services.

Appliance retailers include regional chains and independent retailers. Both chains and independents may have a "superstore" format, which can exceed 100,000 square feet. Superstores may be located in large strip malls or stand-alone locations in high traffic areas. Traditional appliance stores range from 8,000 to 30,000 square feet, and are usually located in smaller strip or shopping malls. Appliance retailers may have clearance centers to sell damaged, used, or discontinued merchandise.

An appliance superstore generates between $30 and $70 million annually, and averages $300 to $500 per square foot. A traditional appliance store generates between $2 and $12 million annually, and averages $200 to $500 per square foot.

Most appliance retailers carry product lines at a variety of price points. A smaller store can stock over 1,000 different products. Since most appliances require delivery, retailers display models in the store, with inventory in an attached or offsite warehouse. Large retailers may offer exclusive models to differentiate from competitors. Appliance retailers that derive a large percentage of sales from TVs and other consumer electronics must carefully assess demand, as rapidly changing technology can render inventory obsolete.

Smaller retailers may buy through established buying groups like Associated Volume Buyers (AVB) and United to maximize purchasing power and achieve volume discounts comparable to larger retailers. Large regional appliance retailers purchase products directly from manufacturers, like Whirlpool and GE, and through buying groups. Manufacturers in the appliance industry are highly concentrated; Conn's, a Southwestern appliance chain, buys over 60 percent of inventory from just six vendors.

Most appliance retailers use computer systems to manage point-of-sale (POS) transactions and inventory and warehouse operations. Retailers also use computers to store customer data and handle consumer credit approval.

Advances in technology have created demand for high-end appliances. Microprocessors and sensors allow appliances like washers, dryers, and dishwashers to perform at different levels depending on the characteristics of the load. Some high-end models of refrigerators now incorporate flat screen TVs in their doors.

Sales & Marketing

The typical customer is a 35 to 55 year old female homeowner looking to replace or upgrade an existing appliance. Buyers of small appliances are younger. Customers buying homes or remodeling are driving an increasing number of appliance purchases.

Marketing and promotion include local media (newspapers, radio, and TV); direct mail; and Internet advertising. Manufacturers often provide cooperative advertising allowances for joint promotions. Retailers may offer no interest financing or match competitive pricing on the spot to complete a sale.

Customer service is extremely important, as most products sold in appliance stores are high-ticket items, and the breadth of product offerings can be overwhelming for customers. A strong reputation based on service can help smaller appliance retailers develop a loyal customer base. Many appliance retailers are family-owned and have been in business for decades.

Most appliance retailers have websites that offer product, pricing, and store information. Due to high shipping costs and level of customer service required to complete a sale, appliance sales over the Internet are relatively low, although consumers do use the Internet to research products.

Human Resources

At an average of about $15 per hour, appliance store wages are high compared to the average $12 per hour for all retail workers, but lower than the US average for all industries. Many appliance stores use commissions to compensate sales associates. Stores may train employees to specialize in one or more particular product segments to provide the expertise needed to sell the relatively high priced products.

A typical appliance store has a manager, one to two assistant managers, and six to 20 employees. Superstores have larger staffs.

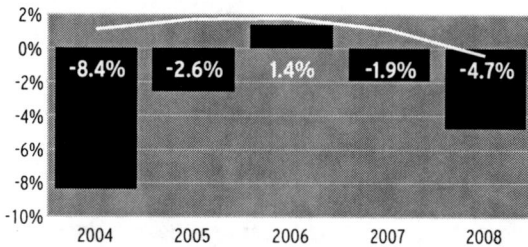

Industry Employment Growth

	2004	2005	2006	2007	2008
	-8.4%	-2.6%	1.4%	-1.9%	-4.7%

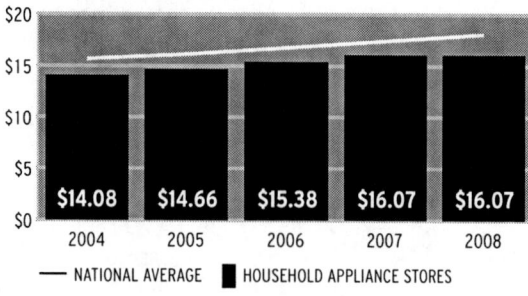

Average Hourly Earnings

	2004	2005	2006	2007	2008
	$14.08	$14.66	$15.38	$16.07	$16.07

— NATIONAL AVERAGE   ■ HOUSEHOLD APPLIANCE STORES

SOURCE: BUREAU OF LABOR STATISTICS

Call Preparation Questions

How are the company's sales affected by changes in home sales?

Sales of new and existing homes drive growth for appliance retailers, as consumers are highly likely to buy new appliances when buying a home.

How important is the high-end appliance segment to the company?

The premium segment of appliances represented almost 50 percent of the market in 2005, driven by growing consumer spending power and heightened interest in kitchen design.

What opportunity does the company see in targeting baby boomers?

Baby boomers are the demographic highly likely to remodel, downsize, or buy a second home, and are therefore likely to buy new appliances.

Web Links

Appliance Aid

Appliance recalls and court settlements.
www.applianceaid.com/news.html

Appliance Magazine

Industry news and trends.
www.appliancemagazine.com

Appliance Service News

Service news.
www.asnews.com

Association of Home Appliance Manufacturers

Industry statistics, household penetration, and trends.
www.aham.org

Consumer Reports

Appliance reliability and customer service surveys.
www.consumerreports.org

This Week in Consumer Electronics (TWICE)

Industry statistics and trends.
www.twice.com

Topix.net

Appliance news.
www.topix.net/business/appliances

Glossary of Acronyms

AHAM — Association for Home Appliance Manufacturers
AVB — Associated Volume Buyers
NARDA — North American Retail Dealers Association
NAR — National Association of Realtors
POS — point-of-sale
TWICE — This Week in Consumer Electronics

HOOVER'S TOP COMPANIES

Largest Companies by Sales	($ mil.)
The Home Depot, Inc.	77,349.0
Lowe's Companies, Inc.	48,283.0
Sears Holdings Corporation	46,770.0
Best Buy Co., Inc.	40,023.0
Conn's, Inc.	824.1

Largest Employers	Employees
Sears Holdings Corporation	337,000
The Home Depot, Inc.	331,000
Lowe's Companies, Inc.	216,000
Best Buy Co., Inc.	150,000
Conn's, Inc.	2,950
P.C. Richard & Son	2,700
ABC Appliance, Inc.	1,750
American TV & Appliance of Madison, Inc.	1,700
Metro Builders Supply, Inc.	250
HADCO	160

Fastest Growing* by Five-Year Sales Growth	(%)
Sears Holdings Corporation	15.0
Best Buy Co., Inc.	13.8
Conn's, Inc.	13.1
Lowe's Companies, Inc.	12.8
The Home Depot, Inc.	5.8

Fastest Growing* by Five-Year Employee Growth	(%)
Best Buy Co., Inc.	11.2
Lowe's Companies, Inc.	7.1
Conn's, Inc.	5.4
The Home Depot, Inc.	3.4

Top Public Companies by Market Value	($ mil.)
The Home Depot, Inc.	51,460.5
Lowe's Companies, Inc.	37,251.9
Best Buy Co., Inc.	17,659.0
Sears Holdings Corporation	4,992.2
Conn's, Inc.	431.8

* These rates are compounded annualized increases and may have resulted from acquisitions or one time gains. If less than 6 years of data are available, growth is for the years available.

SOURCE: HOOVER'S, INC., DATABASE

HVAC and Plumbing Contractors

THIS INDUSTRY INCLUDES:

SIC CODES

1711   Plumbing, Heating, and Air-Conditioning

NAICS CODES

23822   Plumbing, Heating, and Air-Conditioning Contractors

The annual revenues of the utility contractor industry in the US are more than $75 billion. This highly fragmented industry includes 40,000 mostly privately held companies that operate from a single location, and have annual sales under $5 million each. Companies that work mainly in the residential market are usually small, while large companies, including EMCOR Group and Comfort Systems USA, work mainly in the commercial field.

Competitive Landscape

Demand for services depends partly on new residential and commercial construction, but demand for maintenance and repair work is substantial. Larger companies may have a competitive advantage winning large projects that require design work and installation, and can provide services to corporations in several markets. Large companies operate through semi-autonomous local units. Profitability depends on the volume of work a company can acquire, since most costs are fixed.

Products, Operations & Technology

HVAC contractors install and service furnaces; air conditioning (AC) units; fans; and the associated ductwork and control units in residential and commercial buildings. While HVAC accounts for the bulk of industry revenues, many commercial HVAC contractors also have sheet metal operations to build custom HVAC ductwork. Plumbing contractors install bathroom and kitchen fixtures and the associated pipes in residential or commercial buildings, and may also install gas appliances and pipework.

Industry revenue is almost evenly split between commercial and residential segments; companies usually participate in only one, as the work differs fundamentally. Within both segments, revenues are further split between installation and maintenance; commercial com-

BUSINESS CHALLENGES

» Dependence on New Construction, Home Sales
Demand for HVAC services in the US depends partly on the volume of new construction, which can drop rapidly during an economic slowdown. During the last recession, the volume of commercial construction fell 25 percent. Although a large portion of industry revenue is from maintenance and repair of existing equipment, new construction can be the major source of new business for large commercial HVAC contractors. Plumbing work most often occurs when a home is sold.

» Dependence on Skilled Employees
Contractors often have difficulty finding workers with enough technical training. Because of rapid technological advances in HVAC equipment, mainly in the form of computerized sensors and controls, even experienced technicians may require frequent training. Five-year apprenticeships are required to be certified as a service/AC or testing and air balancing mechanic; two-year apprenticeships are required for certification as a residential AC specialist.

» Customer Consolidation
Increased consolidation among home builders is leaving some plumbing and HVAC contractors with fewer customers. In 2002, the 100 largest builders accounted for 33 percent of all residential construction. While builders typically use local contractors, larger builders prefer to deal with large contractors.

panies usually do both, in many cases providing continuing maintenance under long-term service contracts.

Most residential companies perform mainly maintenance work. There are about 43 million central air conditioners, 54 million furnaces, and 9 million heat pumps in US homes. Maintenance, repair, and replacement of these units generate about $30 billion in annual revenue.

For installation work, companies buy equipment such as furnaces, coolers, and air conditioners from distributors. The markup on such equipment is fairly low. Major equipment is custom-ordered for each project. Some sophisticated HVAC systems incorporate computerized monitoring and control components. Compressors, chillers, blowers, and other equipment are bought from manufacturers like Carrier, Trane, and YORK. Most materials are bought from specialty distributors like True Value, Graybar, and WESCO, or from home improvement centers like Home Depot and Lowe's.

Sales & Marketing

Major commercial customers include building owners and developers, manufacturers, general contractors, architects, and property managers, who are cultivated by a sales force. Large projects are often gotten through a bidding process. Both commercial and residential companies sell the expertise of their employees and their ability to complete a job on time and on budget. Small companies, often run by individual service technicians, depend heavily on Yellow Pages advertising, direct mail campaigns, and word-of-mouth.

Human Resources

Plumbing and HVAC contractor employees have special technical or engineering skills, and are therefore well-paid. Average hourly pay is over $20, $4 more than the national average wage. State certification programs maintain workforce quality, but also restrict entry into the business. Maintaining a high-quality workforce is a major concern for most contractors, as is safety. The industry's safety record is poor: eight injury cases a year per 100 full-time workers, compared with the national rate of just over four cases.

Industry Employment Growth

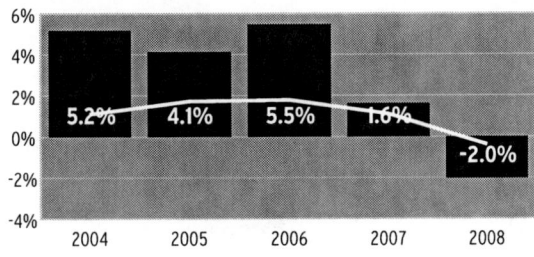

	2004	2005	2006	2007	2008
	5.2%	4.1%	5.5%	1.6%	-2.0%

Average Hourly Earnings

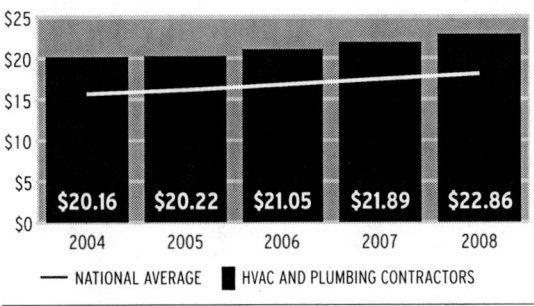

	2004	2005	2006	2007	2008
	$20.16	$20.22	$21.05	$21.89	$22.86

— NATIONAL AVERAGE ■ HVAC AND PLUMBING CONTRACTORS

SOURCE: BUREAU OF LABOR STATISTICS

Call Preparation Questions

What are the prospects for new construction in the company's market?

Demand for HVAC services in the US depends partly on the volume of new construction, which can drop rapidly during an economic slowdown.

How does the company find qualified employees?

Contractors often have difficulty finding workers with enough technical training.

How reliant is the company on its top few customers, and what are the chances of customer consolidation in the market?

Increased consolidation among home builders is leaving some plumbing and HVAC contractors with fewer customers.

What types of computer technology does the company use, and to what benefit?

Manual processes and paper-based systems can hinder customer service by making it difficult for HVAC companies to schedule and service maintenance contracts efficiently and on time.

What opportunities does the company see in providing temporary rental equipment to customers?

Some contractors provide rental units that customers can use while their main cooling system is being repaired.

Web Links

Air Conditioning Contractors of America

Links, industry-related news, and information about local chapters.
www.acca.org

Air Conditioning, Heating & Refrigeration News

Weekly news magazine serving the HVAC/R industry.
www.achrnews.com

American Subcontractors Association (ASA)

Good links to specialty contractor associations.
www.asaonline.com/Web

Associated Builders and Contractors

Up-to-date news by region.
www.abc.org

Contractor Magazine

News.
www.contractormag.com

Engineering News-Record

Lists top specialty contractors.
www.enr.com

EPA Indoor Air Quality Links

EPA documents about indoor air quality.
www.epa.gov/ebtpages/airindoorairpollution.html

Heating, Refrigeration and Air Conditioning Institute of Canada

Links, news releases, and issues.
www.hrai.ca/site/hrai/news_releases.html

Institute of Heating and Air Conditioning Industries

Seminars, education and more.
www.ihaci.org

Mechanical Contractors Association of America (MCAA)

News and links for mechanical, plumbing, and service contractors.
www.mcaa.org/news

Plumbing-Heating-Cooling Contractors Association

Legislative and education information.
www.phccweb.org

Sheet Metal and Air Conditioning Contractors' National Association (SMACNA)

Newsletters and legislative updates.
www.smacna.org/news/news.cfm

Glossary of Acronyms

HFC — hydrofluorocarbon
HVACR — heating, ventilating, air conditioning and refrigeration
IAQ — indoor air quality
NAR — National Association of Realtors

HOOVER'S TOP COMPANIES

Largest Companies by Sales	($ mil.)
EMCOR Group, Inc.	6,785.2
Comfort Systems USA, Inc.	1,328.5
American Residential Services L.L.C.	709.5
KSW, Inc.	77.3

Largest Employers	Employees
EMCOR Group, Inc.	29,000
American Residential Services L.L.C.	7,500
Comfort Systems USA, Inc.	6,647
Southland Industries Inc.	1,400
TDIndustries, Ltd.	1,300
KSW, Inc.	45

Fastest Growing* by Five-Year Sales Growth	(%)
Comfort Systems USA, Inc.	11.1
KSW, Inc.	10.7
EMCOR Group, Inc.	8.4

Fastest Growing* by Five-Year Employee Growth	(%)
Comfort Systems USA, Inc.	11.6
EMCOR Group, Inc.	5.6

Top Public Companies by Market Value	($ mil.)
EMCOR Group, Inc.	1,469.6
Comfort Systems USA, Inc.	412.2
KSW, Inc.	43.5

* These rates are compounded annualized increases and may have resulted from acquisitions or one time gains. If less than 6 years of data are available, growth is for the years available.

SOURCE: HOOVER'S, INC., DATABASE

Industrial Machinery Manufacturing

The manufacture of machinery in the US involves about 30,000 companies with combined annual revenue of $300 billion. Large companies include Caterpillar and Deere, and divisions of GE and other large corporations. The industry is highly fragmented because most companies specialize in producing a particular type of machinery. Most companies have annual sales between $10 and $500 million and operate in a relatively small field, but may produce dozens of variations and models of the same basic product.

Competitive Landscape

Demand for machinery depends strongly on the health of the US economy and various subsectors such as the construction industry. The profitability of individual companies is tied to engineering expertise and efficient production operations. Small companies can compete effectively if they produce machinery with unique characteristics. The industry is capital-intensive and fairly automated: average annual revenue per worker is about $225,000.

Products, Operations & Technology

The major subsections of the industry are farm and construction machinery, manufacturing machinery, metalworking machinery, commercial machinery, and general machinery such as engines and pumps. While some products, such as tractors or heaters, are finished products, others, like motors, are components used in further production, and some, like textile looms, are custom-designed for a particular manufacturing process.

Manufacture involves producing and assembling components. Companies either make or buy components and various types of mechanical, hydraulic, and electrical control systems. Manufacturing often involves forging, machining, and welding activities that require skilled labor. Products often have a high engineering

content. Product design usually involves CAD systems, which sometimes are hooked directly into a computer-aided manufacturing (CAM) process.

Production is typically on an assembly line, except for the largest pieces of machinery, which may be assembled at a customer's site. Machinery is typically complex, often consisting of thousands of moving parts. Computer controls have become an important feature of many products. Companies may produce many variations of a single product such as a motor, which limits the efficiency of assembly operations.

Sales & Marketing

Customers are industrial companies or commercial users. Sales are usually handled by an in-house sales force complemented with manufacturers' representatives and independent dealers. Salespeople often must have extensive engineering knowledge. Large process machinery, like a painting system for car manufacture, is usually sold directly to the end-user, while farm and construction machinery and smaller items like pumps and motors are sold almost exclusively through dealers. Trade shows are an important source of new customers. Advertising may be in trade publications.

Because machinery is highly technical, the availability of service and spare parts is important to generate sales and retain customers, and most manufacturers have regional or local service centers.

Technical innovation is critical in many industry segments. R&D costs are often high. Patents are used to protect unique design features.

Human Resources

Manufacturing components and assembling industrial machinery require skilled labor; pay is about 10 percent above the national average. To retain skilled workers, companies provide a relatively high level of benefits, an average addition of 30 to 35 percent to payroll costs. The safety record of the industry has improved in recent years, though it's still worse than the national average.

Average Hourly Earnings

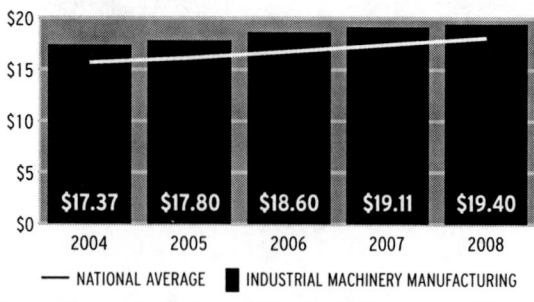

	2004	2005	2006	2007	2008
	$17.37	$17.80	$18.60	$19.11	$19.40

— NATIONAL AVERAGE ■ INDUSTRIAL MACHINERY MANUFACTURING

SOURCE: BUREAU OF LABOR STATISTICS

Call Preparation Questions

How responsive is the company to adjusting to demand changes?

Demand for machinery can drop rapidly during periods of slow or declining economic growth.

How successful is the company at differentiating its products from foreign competition?

Machinery imports account for about 30 percent of the US market. Japan, China, Germany, and Canada are major sources of imports.

How does the company manage raw material availability and price problems?

Costs for raw materials like aluminum, copper, and plastics can fluctuate sharply from year to year.

How automated is the company's production process, and what benefits are gained?

US manufacturers continue to improve productivity by adding more automated machinery.

How are new technologies affecting company machinery manufacturing and sales?

New technology is rapidly applied in new machinery. Digital image recognition is now used to sort and inspect fruits and vegetables.

Industry Employment Growth

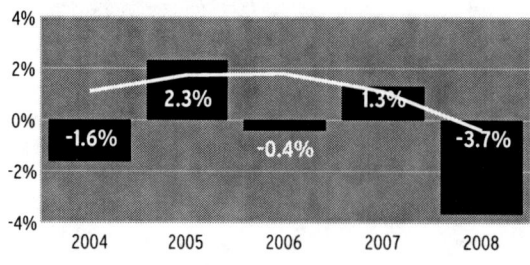

	2004	2005	2006	2007	2008
	-1.6%	2.3%	-0.4%	1.3%	-3.7%

Web Links

American Textile Machinery Association

Industry news, membership information, and trade events.

www.atmanet.org

Farm Equipment Manufacturers Association

Communication forum for the industry; facilitates the exchange of ideas and product information.

www.farmequip.org

Industrial Supply Association

News and links.

www.isapartners.org

Institute for Supply Management

Education, resources, news, supply-chain information, and manufacturing business reports. NAPM index of manufacturing activity.

www.ism.ws

National Association of Industrial Technology

Demographics, journals and publications like Industrial Technology Insider.

www.nait.org

National Association of Manufacturers

Policy issues, news, articles, surveys, links, and press releases.

www.nam.org

Society of Manufacturing Engineers

Industry news.

www.sme.org

Society of Manufacturing Engineers

Manufacturing news.

www.sme.org/cgi-bin/servicecenters.pl?/html/serv_center_media.htm

The Association for Manufacturing Technology

Product directory, newsletters, and policy guidelines.

www.amtonline.org

Glossary of Acronyms

AMT — Association of Manufacturing Technology
CAD — computer-aided design
CAM — computer-aided manufacturing
HVAC — heating, ventilation, air conditioning
ISM — Institute for Supply Management
RBI — Reed Business Information

HOOVER'S TOP COMPANIES

Largest Companies by Sales	($ mil.)
General Electric Company	182,515.0
United Technologies Corporation	58,681.0
Honeywell International Inc.	36,556.0
Deere & Company	28,437.6
Emerson Electric Co.	24,807.0
Danaher Corporation	12,697.5
Rockwell Automation, Inc.	5,697.8
NACCO Industries, Inc.	3,602.7
Joy Global Inc.	3,418.9
Bucyrus International, Inc.	2,505.8

Largest Employers	Employees
General Electric Company	327,000
United Technologies Corporation	223,100
Emerson Electric Co.	140,700
Honeywell International Inc.	128,000
Deere & Company	56,700
Danaher Corporation	50,000
Rockwell Automation, Inc.	21,000
Joy Global Inc.	11,800
NACCO Industries, Inc.	10,200
Bucyrus International, Inc.	6,050

Fastest Growing* by Five-Year Sales Growth	(%)
GT Solar International, Inc.	128.2
Bucyrus International, Inc.	49.3
Joy Global Inc.	23.0
Rudolph Technologies, Inc.	22.8
Aehr Test Systems	20.9
Danaher Corporation	19.1
Tegal Corporation	18.5
International Baler Corp.	18.4
Entegris, Inc.	17.4
Aetrium Incorporated	17.1

Fastest Growing* by Five-Year Employee Growth	(%)
Bucyrus International, Inc.	68.7
GT Solar International, Inc.	57.5
FormFactor, Inc.	34.7
Rudolph Technologies, Inc.	14.2
Danaher Corporation	13.6
Woodward Governor Company	12.7
Entegris, Inc.	12.0
Joy Global Inc.	10.4
Cascade Microtech, Inc.	9.9
Cascade Corporation	9.9

Top Public Companies by Market Value	($ mil.)
General Electric Company	170,697.7
United Technologies Corporation	50,595.2
Emerson Electric Co.	31,457.9
Honeywell International Inc.	24,116.5
Danaher Corporation	18,023.5

* These rates are compounded annualized increases and may have resulted from acquisitions or one time gains. If less than 6 years of data are available, growth is for the years available.

SOURCE: HOOVER'S, INC., DATABASE

Industrial Machinery Wholesalers

THIS INDUSTRY INCLUDES:

SIC CODES
5084 Industrial Machinery and Equipment

NAICS CODES
42383 Industrial Machinery and Equipment Merchant Wholesalers

The US industrial machinery wholesale industry consists of 25,000 companies with combined annual revenue of almost $115 billion. Large companies include MSC Industrial Supply, and the wholesale operations of manufacturers such as General Electric and NACCO Materials Handling Group. Independent distributors hold about 80 percent of the market. The industry is highly fragmented: the 50 largest companies account for over 25 percent of industry revenue.

Competitive Landscape

Demand depends heavily on US manufacturing activity. Profitability depends on product selection and efficient operations. Large companies have economies of scale in advertising and sales programs. Small companies can compete effectively by specializing in particular industries, end-use applications, or geographical areas, and by offering special services. The industry is highly automated: average annual sales per employee is $350,000.

Products, Operations & Technology

Major products are general purpose machinery such as pumps and engines, manufacturing machinery, machine tools, materials handling equipment like forklifts, and oil field equipment. General purpose machinery accounts for 30 percent of industry revenue, manufacturing machinery for 20 percent; other types of machinery make up the rest. About 10 percent of revenue comes from sales of used equipment.

Suppliers are machinery manufacturers or other wholesalers. Companies typically handle products from multiple manufacturers, often under non-exclusive distributor agreements that may require the distributor to provide various product services. If the focus is on standard equipment and parts, companies may operate one or more warehouses, but if the focus is on large machinery, little or no inventory may be

BUSINESS CHALLENGES

» Demand More Volatile than US Economy

Demand for industrial machinery is linked to overall manufacturing activity and the particular customer industries distributors serve. Demand can fluctuate rapidly during economic peaks or lulls, even more than the economy as a whole. For example, during the last recession, US production of industrial machinery dropped 40 percent, while total manufacturing output fell just 5 percent.

» Growing Importance of Foreign Suppliers

Foreign manufacturers are supplying a larger share of the US market for industrial machinery. Many US wholesalers lack the resources and knowledge to participate in the import market, which may involve foreign trade shows, buying offices, and financing and currency. In the last five years, forklift imports were up 35 percent; pump imports were up 50 percent.

» Competition from Rental Companies

In some segments, wholesalers compete with equipment leasing companies and rental operations. Customers sometimes rent equipment only when it is needed, rather than buying it. For example, United Rentals, National Equipment Services, and Hertz rent a full range of equipment. Retailer Home Depot now rents equipment, in addition to selling supplies.

carried. In addition to product sales, companies may provide related services, such as delivery, installation, training, parts, maintenance, and repair work.

Large wholesalers have data systems that link all their locations and operations and integrate tightly with customers and suppliers. Functions include ordering, inventory control, automatic replenishment, and special software systems such as vendor-managed inventory (VMI) and electronic data interchange (EDI). Some companies use elaborate Internet sites and electronic catalogs.

Sales & Marketing

Major customers are industrial manufacturers, warehouse operators, machine shops, and oilfield operators. Wholesalers may use a field sales force and internal phone operations. Advertising is primarily by manufacturers. Leasing and rental options can be important for sales of larger pieces of equipment. Manufacturer websites often lead customers to local distributors, and have become important sources of business.

Prices range from a few dollars for small items to tens of thousands for standard production machinery. Prices are usually marked up a fixed percentage from cost. The availability of the same products from other local distributors limits price mark-ups.

Human Resources

Many employees of industrial machinery wholesalers require special product knowledge, so are paid well. The average wage is 20 percent higher than the national average. Fringe benefits add upward of 25 percent to payroll costs. Large wholesalers have over 100 workers. Union membership is uncommon. The industry's safety record is slightly better than the national average.

Industry Employment Growth

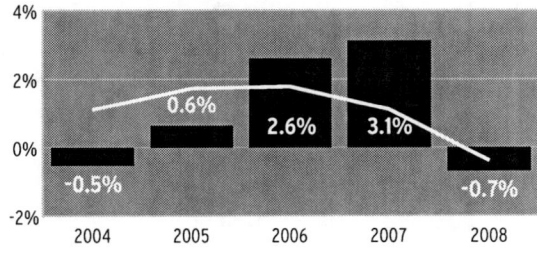

Average Hourly Earnings

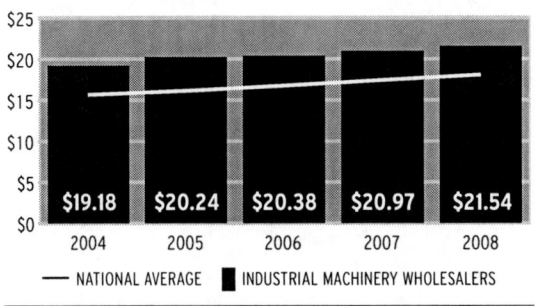

SOURCE: BUREAU OF LABOR STATISTICS

Call Preparation Questions

What is the outlook for demand in the company's customer markets?

Demand for industrial machinery is linked to overall manufacturing activity and the particular customer industries distributors serve.

What percentage of the company's products is imported?

Foreign manufacturers are supplying a larger share of the US market for industrial machinery.

Does the company offer leasing or rental options, in addition to sales?

In some segments, wholesalers compete with equipment leasing companies and rental operations.

Does the company operate a website for taking orders?

By allowing customers to search their catalogs and order online, more wholesalers are improving the efficiency of their operations.

How much revenue does the company get from selling used equipment?

Used and remanufactured industrial equipment accounts for about 10 percent of industry revenue.

Web Links

Associated Equipment Distributors

News articles from various publications.
www.aednet.org/aednews

Association for Manufacturing Technology

Product directory, news and policy guidelines.
www.mfgtech.org

Association of Equipment Manufacturers

News, trends and statistics about manufacturers of equipment for the construction, agricultural, mining, forestry and utility industries.
www.aem.org

Industrial Distribution

News, events, features concerning the industrial supply distribution and supply chain.
www.inddist.com

Industrial Supply Association

Newsletter and links for the industrial distribution supply chain.
www.ida-assoc.org

Institute for Supply Management

News, resources, supply-chain information and the "ISM Report on Business" for manufacturing activity.
www.ism.ws

Modern Distribution Management

Newsletter for the wholesale distribution channel.
www.mdm.com

National Association of Wholesaler-Distributors

News and industry issues supported by this lobbying group.
www.naw.org

North American Equipment Dealers Association

Issues, news and events focused on relationships with manufacturers.
www.naeda.com

Progressive Distributor magazine

Distribution industry news.
www.progressivedistributor.com/
progressive_distributor_body.htm

Glossary of Acronyms

CMI — customer-managed inventory
CRM — customer relationship management
EDI — electronic data interchange
MRO — maintenance, repair, and operations
RFID — radio frequency identification
SKU — stock-keeping unit
VMI — vendor-managed inventory

HOOVER'S TOP COMPANIES

Largest Companies by Sales	($ mil.)
General Electric Company	182,515.0
Illinois Tool Works Inc.	15,869.3
NACCO Industries	3,680.3
Lincoln Electric Holdings, Inc.	2,479.1
Rexnord Holdings, Inc.	1,853.5
RBS Global, Inc.	1,853.5
MSC Industrial Direct Co., Inc.	1,779.8
Kaman Corporation	1,253.6
Barry-Wehmiller Companies, Inc.	1,200.0

Largest Employers	Employees
General Electric Company	327,000
Illinois Tool Works Inc.	60,000
Tecumseh Products Company	10,300
NACCO Industries	10,200
Lincoln Electric Holdings, Inc.	9,329
Rexnord Holdings, Inc.	7,400
RBS Global, Inc.	7,400
EnPro Industries, Inc.	5,100
Barry-Wehmiller Companies, Inc.	5,000
MSC Industrial Direct Co., Inc.	4,261

Fastest Growing* by Five-Year Sales Growth	(%)
Energy Recovery, Inc.	81.9
Titan Machinery Inc.	38.7
Rexnord Holdings, Inc.	30.9
Presstek, Inc.	25.0
DXP Enterprises, Inc.	24.6
Hurco Companies, Inc.	24.3
Chart Industries, Inc.	22.9
RBS Global, Inc.	20.8
Lincoln Electric Holdings, Inc.	19.0
Altra Holdings, Inc.	18.9

Fastest Growing* by Five-Year Employee Growth	(%)
Titan Machinery Inc.	29.0
DXP Enterprises, Inc.	25.6
Presstek, Inc.	22.1
Chart Industries, Inc.	15.9
BTU International, Inc.	14.7
Kadant Inc.	13.5
Hurco Companies, Inc.	13.1
GSI Group Inc.	11.4
NN, Inc.	10.5
Lincoln Electric Holdings, Inc.	9.3

Top Public Companies by Market Value	($ mil.)
General Electric Company	170,697.7
Illinois Tool Works Inc.	18,639.2
MSC Industrial Direct Co., Inc.	2,222.6
Lincoln Electric Holdings, Inc.	2,165.6
Nordson Corporation	1,244.8

* These rates are compounded annualized increases and may have resulted from acquisitions or one time gains. If less than 6 years of data are available, growth is for the years available.

SOURCE: HOOVER'S, INC., DATABASE

Industrial Supply Wholesalers

THIS INDUSTRY INCLUDES:

SIC CODES
5085   Industrial Supplies

NAICS CODES
423840   Industrial Supplies
Merchant
Wholesalers

The US market for distributing industrial supplies includes about 10,000 companies with combined annual revenue of $70 billion. Large companies include WW Grainger, Applied Industrial Technologies, MSC Industrial Supply, and Industrial Distribution Group. The industry is both fragmented and concentrated at the top: the 50 largest companies hold about 50 percent of the total market, but 80 percent of companies have less than $5 million in annual sales.

Competitive Landscape

Demand is closely tied to the level of US manufacturing production. Because many operating costs are fixed, profitability depends on operational efficiency, particularly inventory management. Smaller companies can compete effectively by providing specialized supplies or superior service (delivery service and product expertise). Large distributors with a network of warehouses and outlets can maintain a lower inventory/sales ratio. The industry is highly automated: average annual revenue per worker is close to $500,000.

Products, Operations & Technology

Industrial supply companies sell a large number of products that industrial customers use for maintenance, repair, operations, and production (the industry refers to itself as the MRO supply or MROP supply industry). Examples include tools, pipe, and valve fittings; electrical products; fluid handling equipment; pumps, motors, fasteners, instruments; and safety and cleaning equipment and supplies. Large distributors may carry 500,000 different items (stock keeping units — SKUs). Products are grouped into product lines. Wholesalers are often referred to as either "general line," meaning they carry six or more different product lines, or as "specialty line," meaning they carry less than five product lines.

BUSINESS CHALLENGES

» Dependence on Manufacturing

Demand for industrial supplies depends on manufacturing activity. During the last recession, US industrial production fell 5 percent. More US manufacturing capacity is expected to move to lower-cost countries like Mexico and China.

» Industry Concentrations

Many distributors serve only customers in a particular industry, exposing distributors to greater demand volatility. Smaller wholesalers often get a large percentage of business from a few large customers, or from customers all in the same industry. Specialty line companies are especially vulnerable to a business slowdown in a particular industry or geographical area.

» Dependence on Skilled Labor

Despite advanced computer systems, distributors still depend heavily on personnel with wide knowledge of the industry they supply. Because of strong price competition, smaller companies depend heavily on providing superior customer service from experienced staff.

The operations of industrial supply wholesalers revolve around inventory management, including order taking and fulfillment, delivery, billing and collections, and inventory replenishment and control. A typical wholesaler must track thousands of orders because the average customer order consists of just two items and is valued at less than $150. Computer systems are vital to the wholesaler operations, both for processing customer orders and reordering products from suppliers. A typical local distributor may process 200 to 300 orders per day.

A typical industrial supply company has more than 1,000 customers and may buy materials from hundreds of suppliers, either manufacturers or other wholesalers. Companies may have authorized distributorship arrangements with manufacturers and provide training, maintenance, and repair for some equipment. Large distributors may have dozens of local retail outlets and a network of regional or local warehouses, but the typical distributor operates one combined retail/warehouse location. In 2003, Grainger operated almost 400 local branches with an average size of 20,000 square feet.

Customers include industrial companies and maintenance departments, janitorial service companies, and maintenance and repair companies. Small orders are often picked up by the customer ("will call" orders). Large orders may be delivered either by the wholesaler's own trucks or contract truckers. Wholesalers sometimes offer maintenance, security, or janitorial services as additional products. Price, product selection, customer service, and convenient location are major factors affecting sales. The staff usually needs to be highly knowledgeable about a large number of individual products.

Sales & Marketing

Sales and marketing are through a variety of channels, including customer visits, telemarketing, catalog mailings, advertising in phone directories, and trade shows. Catalogs are a particularly important marketing channel. MSC recently used a master catalog of 4,600 pages and 97 specialty catalogs, and mailed out 29 million publications. Although many local outlets have a fair amount of walk-in ("counter") business, wholesalers usually get the bulk of sales from accounts with large industrial customers.

The Internet is becoming an important source of sales and customer service for some distributors, due to the ease of presenting large amounts of information online. MSC receives over 15 percent of its revenue from its website, which generated $184 million in 2005. Despite the growth of Internet sales, most orders occur via phone or fax and require manual entry into the company's computer system.

Human Resources

Customer service jobs require special training to understand the large number of products. Warehouse jobs require no special skills. Average pay is 15 percent higher than the average national wage. Wholesalers in general have high personnel turnover, about 30 percent annually, and an average safety record.

Industry Employment Growth

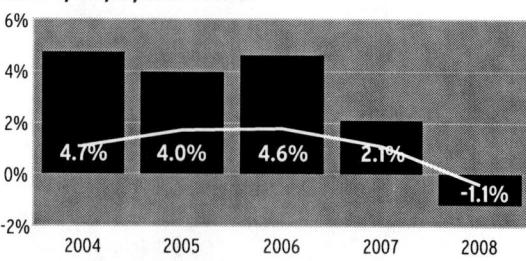

Average Hourly Earnings

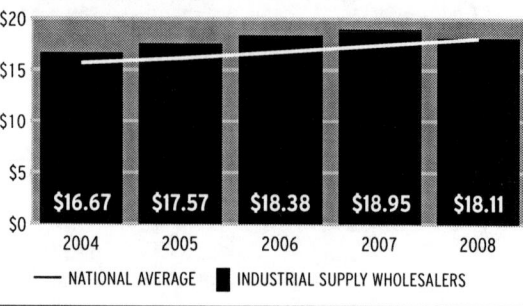

—— NATIONAL AVERAGE ■ INDUSTRIAL SUPPLY WHOLESALERS

SOURCE: BUREAU OF LABOR STATISTICS

Call Preparation Questions

What changes is the company seeing in the manufacturing industries it serves?

Demand for industrial supplies depends on manufacturing activity.

How reliant is the company on its largest customers?

Many distributors serve only customers in a particular industry, exposing distributors to greater demand volatility.

What opportunities does the company see in serving niche industries?

Low-cost items in niche markets often have the highest margins for a wholesaler.

How effective is the company's inventory management system?

To keep inventory as low as possible while minimizing stock-outs, some companies use computer software that predicts how many units of each item in inventory will be sold during a period, based on prior sales history.

Web Links

American Machine Tool Distributors' Association

Calendar, industry statistics, news, events, and industry links.
www.amtda.org

American Supply Association

Information and articles about plumbing, heating, cooling, and piping wholesalers.
www.asa.net

Fluid Power Distributor Association

Distributor lists, member lists, statistics, marketing, resources, and links.

www.fpda.org

Industrial Distribution

Industry news.

www.inddist.com

International Sanitary Supply Association

Online magazine that addresses distribution industry issues.

www.issa.com

Modern Distribution Management

News.

www.mdm.com

National Fastener Distributors Association

Publications, annual reports, new releases, and educational services.

www.nfda-fastener.org

Progressive Distributor

MRO distributor news.

www.progressivedistributor.com

Safety Equipment Distributors Association (SEDA)

Event information and member and resource links.

www.safetycentral.org

The National Association of Wholesaler-Distributors

Business books, research reports and audio and videotapes created for wholesalers and distributors.

www.naw.org/publications/pindex.php

Total US Manufacturing Technology Consumption

Historic consumption from the Association for Manufacturing Technology and the American Machine Tool Distributors' Association.

www.amtda.org/website/article.asp?id=137

Glossary of Acronyms

AMT — Association for Manufacturing Technology
ASA — American Supply Association
B2B — business to business
CRM — customer relationship management
EDI — electronic data interchange
HOS — hours of service
ISA — Industrial Supply Association
IDA — Industrial Distributors Association
ISM — Institute of Supply Management
MRO — maintenance, repair, and operations
MROP — maintenance, repair, operations and production
NAW — National Association of Wholesalers
RFID — radio frequency identification
SKU — stock-keeping units

HOOVER'S TOP COMPANIES

Largest Companies by Sales	($ mil.)
W.W. Grainger, Inc.	6,850.0
Applied Industrial Technologies, Inc.	2,089.5
MSC Industrial Direct Co., Inc.	1,779.8
Industrial Distribution Group, Inc.	537.5
Lawson Products, Inc.	485.2
The Hillman Companies, Inc.	445.6
DXP Enterprises, Inc.	444.5
Crown Bolt LLC	320.0

Largest Employers	Employees
W.W. Grainger, Inc.	18,036
Applied Industrial Technologies, Inc.	4,805
MSC Industrial Direct Co., Inc.	4,261
The Hillman Companies, Inc.	2,055
Forge Industries Inc.	1,837
DXP Enterprises, Inc.	1,603
Lawson Products, Inc.	1,400
Victory Packaging, Inc.	1,250
Industrial Distribution Group, Inc.	1,240
Crown Bolt LLC	900

Fastest Growing* by Five-Year Sales Growth	(%)
Crown Bolt LLC	25.5
DXP Enterprises, Inc.	24.6
MSC Industrial Direct Co., Inc.	16.1
The Hillman Companies, Inc.	9.2
W.W. Grainger, Inc.	8.0
Applied Industrial Technologies, Inc.	7.4
Lawson Products, Inc.	4.5
Abatix Corp.	2.9
Industrial Distribution Group, Inc.	1.8

Fastest Growing* by Five-Year Employee Growth	(%)
DXP Enterprises, Inc.	25.6
MSC Industrial Direct Co., Inc.	8.4
W.W. Grainger, Inc.	3.8
The Hillman Companies, Inc.	2.7
Applied Industrial Technologies, Inc.	2.0
Lawson Products, Inc.	0.5

Top Public Companies by Market Value	($ mil.)
W.W. Grainger, Inc.	5,895.7
Kaire Holdings Incorporated	2,700.0
MSC Industrial Direct Co., Inc.	2,222.6
Applied Industrial Technologies, Inc.	1,022.1
Lawson Products, Inc.	194.7

* These rates are compounded annualized increases and may have resulted from acquisitions or one time gains. If less than 6 years of data are available, growth is for the years available.

SOURCE: HOOVER'S, INC., DATABASE

Information Technology

The IT industry includes 95,000 companies that generate about $174 billion in annual revenue. Large companies include Accenture, Computer Sciences Corporation (CSC), and the technology consulting arms of IBM and Hewlett-Packard. The facilities outsourcing segment of the industry is highly concentrated: the 50 largest companies hold more than 80 percent of the market. The rest of the industry is fairly fragmented: the 50 largest companies hold less than half the market.

Some components of IT include manufacturers of hardware and software, providers of telecommunications devices and services, and Internet companies. These industries are reviewed in separate profiles.

Competitive Landscape

Demand for IT services is driven by rapid technological advances, but spending for these expensive products depends on the health of the US economy. The profitability of companies depends on offering technical expertise, innovative services, and effective marketing. Large companies have advantages in broad service offerings and global reach, which give them the ability to provide outsourcing services to big corporate customers. Small companies can compete effectively by specializing in market niches or by partnering with larger companies that want to broaden their mix of services. Average annual revenue per employee is close to $160,000.

Products, Operations & Technology

IT companies mainly provide consulting, systems integration, data processing, and technology outsourcing services to business customers. Roughly half of industry revenue comes from consulting and systems integration activities, while the rest comes from outsourcing. These companies help clients use computers, software, and communications sys-

BUSINESS CHALLENGES

» Revenue Depends on Corporate Technology Spending

Because spending for IT services comes mainly from corporation upgrades, much of it can be postponed during economic downturns. About half of all US capital investment in recent years has been computer-related, exposing IT spending to economic cycles. For example, corporate profits, an indicator of technology spending, fell nearly 10 percent during the late 2000s recession.

» Competition from Hardware, Software Suppliers

As computer and communication hardware and software become commodity-type products with lower margins, their manufacturers are providing more integration and maintenance services, in competition with traditional IT companies. Often manufacturers, particularly computer makers, have deeper financial resources and greater capacity to perform IT functions than their traditional IT counterparts. Other competitors that are not necessarily traditional IT firms nonetheless can offer services that overlap with an IT rival's own offerings.

» Customer Concentrations

Because IT companies, particularly smaller firms, may depend on only a few large customers for most of their revenue, customer consolidations or failures can have serious financial consequences. Many IT firms lost large contracts through the failure of telecom and energy customers in the early 2000s recession. In the late 2000s IT firms competed for customers as companies consolidated due to the economic downturn.

tems more efficiently. In addition to providing advice on using computer systems, they frequently recommend hardware and software systems to their customers. Firms provide a variety of associated services, including business function outsourcing, data warehousing, systems planning, enterprise resource planning, and training.

Companies may be pure consulting operations, or also operate outsourcing and data processing functions, such as IBM and

Hewlett-Packard. The types of contracts firms have with customers depend on the service being rendered. Data processing and outsourcing contracts typically last for many years because of the substantial initial cost. In a typical outsourcing contract, the IT company operates (and may own) the computer systems of a client, either operating them at the customer's location or at a centralized data center that serves multiple clients. Consulting contracts are shorter, usually lasting less than a year, and typically specify either a fixed project cost or services billed at hourly rates.

IT operations most often begin at a service provider's Web site. Large companies like IBM's Global Services division use the Internet to introduce prospective clients to their services. Once a contract is signed, an IT provider can assist customers with on-site staff, live teleconferencing or Webcast tutorials, and longer-term online support (via e-mail and instant messaging between IT staff and customers). Primary applications for IT include aligning IT initiatives with overall business goals, improving IT infrastructure efficiency, and creating a flexible service-oriented architecture that combines systems development with business processes.

Sales & Marketing

The customers of IT firms are often the IT departments of corporations and government agencies. Companies typically offer time-and-materials contracts or fixed-price contracts, or some combination of both. Major contracts are often secured after a bidding process. For contracts that also involve the purchase of hardware or software, consultants often partner with a specific hardware or software company to provide a comprehensive bid. Marketing is largely through personal selling by executives and senior managers, or through reputation within a particular industry.

Because the most effective use of computer technology is different for different industries, IT companies often specialize in a particular industry, such as health care or financial services, or in segments within an industry. Large com-

panies have service groups for different industries and market their services to those groups specifically. Due to the complexity of their services, companies often customize their prices for each service, accounting for the required skills and the estimated cost of providing the service.

Competition comes in multiple forms, including offshore providers, service arms of large global technology firms, niche providers, and companies that rely on their own internal IT resources.

Pricing can be competitive, particularly among large IT providers. Competitors put significant investments in creating closed and proprietary IT platforms in order to lock customers into a specific IT system. That can drive up prices as a result. Firms also work to develop differentiated and premium IT products that allow them to charge more.

Human Resources

IT companies need technologically skilled labor, and finding and keeping such labor is an ongoing concern. Firms find entry-level employees among recent college graduates who have degrees in computer science or mathematics. IT skills and experience bring premium pay, more than double the average for all US workers. A few key people often determine the success of a smaller firm. Annual turnover is an industry-wide issue, and firms have significant expenses for finding, training, and retaining qualified labor. The IT industry's safety record is excellent, with an extremely low incident of injuries.

The strong growth in demand for IT professionals in the past decade prompted many firms to recruit abroad. Firms sponsor foreign professionals and bring them to the US through visas under the H-1B program, which can allow visa holders to work in the US for up to six years.

Industry Employment Growth

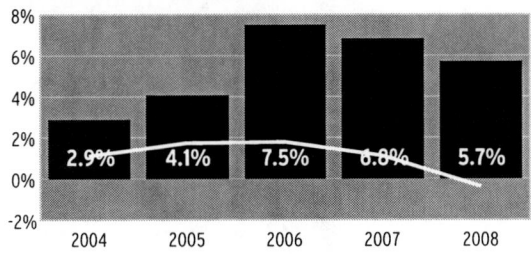

Year	Growth
2004	2.9%
2005	4.1%
2006	7.5%
2007	6.8%
2008	5.7%

Average Hourly Earnings

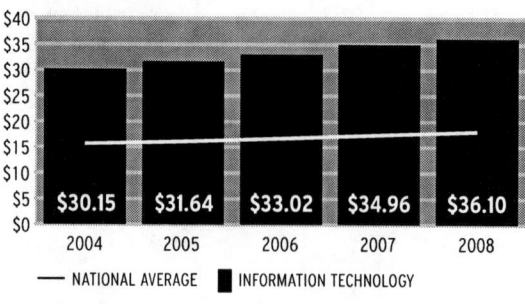

	2004	2005	2006	2007	2008
	$30.15	$31.64	$33.02	$34.96	$36.10

— NATIONAL AVERAGE   ■ INFORMATION TECHNOLOGY

SOURCE: BUREAU OF LABOR STATISTICS

Call Preparation Questions

How does the company manage shifts in corporate technology spending?

Because spending for IT services comes mainly from corporation upgrades, much of it can be postponed during economic downturns.

How vulnerable is the company to non-traditional competition?

As computer and communication hardware and software become commodity-type products with lower margins, their manufacturers are providing more integration and maintenance services, in competition with traditional IT companies.

How many customers does the company need to stay profitable?

Because IT companies, particularly smaller firms, may depend on only a few large customers for most of their revenue, customer consolidations or failures can have serious financial consequences.

How is heightened demand for security impacting the company?

The heightened focus on security will provide additional opportunities for IT companies, which will be called on to design and implement new computerized security systems for both businesses and governments.

What opportunities do networking and wireless technology present the company?

The rapid evolution of business networks to include wireless devices has created new opportunities for IT firms.

Web Links

CDW IT Monitor

Bimonthly IT industry outlook.
www.cdwitmonitor.com

Computerworld

Latest news, features, and opinions of IT, software, and computers.
www.computerworld.com

Forrester Research

Industry research and news.
www.forrester.com

Gartner

Industry research and news.
www.gartner.com

Government Computer News

Government IT news. See especially the Outsourcing and State & Local sections.

www.gcn.com

Information Technology Association of America

Articles, news, publications, government affairs, calendars, and events.

www.itaa.org

Information Technology Industry Council

News and IT government relations resources.

www.itic.org

InformationWeek

News. See especially Business Services section.

www.informationweek.com

ITworld

IT news, topics, and links.

www.itworld.com

TechWeb

News and technology on segments of electronic industry, like networks, wireless, and e-business.

www.techweb.com

The McKinsey Quarterly

Prescriptive IT articles.

www.mckinseyquarterly.com/Business_Technology

Glossary of Acronyms

PC — Personal Computer

SaaS — software-as-a-service

HOOVER'S TOP COMPANIES

Largest Companies by Sales	($ mil.)
Hewlett-Packard Company	118,364.0
International Business Machines Corporation	103,630.0
Accenture Ltd	25,313.8
Computer Sciences Corporation	16,499.5
SAIC, Inc.	8,935.0
SYNNEX Corporation	7,768.2
Unisys Corporation	5,233.2
Cognizant Technology Solutions Corporation	2,816.3
Perot Systems Corporation	2,779.0
World Wide Technology, Inc.	2,500.0

Largest Employers	Employees
International Business Machines Corporation	426,969
Hewlett-Packard Company	321,000
Accenture Ltd	186,000
Computer Sciences Corporation	89,000
Cognizant Technology Solutions Corporation	55,400
SAIC, Inc.	43,800
Unisys Corporation	30,000
Perot Systems Corporation	23,100
Keane Inc.	13,600
Syntel, Inc.	11,709

Fastest Growing* by Five-Year Sales Growth	(%)
Global Telecom & Technology, Inc.	448.6
Caneum, Inc.	187.6
Consonus Technologies, Inc.	156.3
Conversion Services International, Inc.	154.8
Catapult Systems Inc.	100.0
Prime Technology Group, Inc.	87.5
Lattice Incorporated	72.3
NetSol Technologies, Inc.	57.3
Sourcefire, Inc.	51.5
Perficient, Inc.	50.3

Fastest Growing* by Five-Year Employee Growth	(%)
Catapult Systems Inc.	68.1
Perficient, Inc.	56.9
Cognizant Technology Solutions Corporation	51.0
Zanett, Inc.	47.1
GSI Commerce, Inc.	44.5
Synchronoss Technologies, Inc.	40.8
SYNNEX Corporation	35.8
Bridgeline Software, Inc.	33.9
Sapient Corporation	33.8
MTC Technologies, Inc.	33.2

Top Public Companies by Market Value	($ mil.)
International Business Machines Corporation	112,698.3
Hewlett-Packard Company	92,446.2
NAVTEQ Corporation	7,481.1
Computer Sciences Corporation	6,165.6
Cognizant Technology Solutions Corporation	5,267.6

* These rates are compounded annualized increases and may have resulted from acquisitions or one time gains. If less than 6 years of data are available, growth is for the years available.

SOURCE: HOOVER'S, INC., DATABASE

Inland Barge Transport

THIS INDUSTRY INCLUDES:

SIC CODES
4449   Water
        Transportation of
        Freight

NAICS CODES
483211 Inland Water
        Freight
        Transportation

The US inland barge transport industry consists of about 350 companies with combined annual revenue of over $2 billion. Major companies include independents, such as Ingram Barge, American Commercial Lines, and Kirby Corporation, along with captive subsidiaries of large producers of energy or agriculture commodities, such as MEMCO Barge (owned by American Electric Power) and American River Transportation (owned by Archer Daniels Midland). The industry is highly concentrated: the largest 50 companies have over 85 percent of industry revenue.

Competitive Landscape

Demand is driven primarily by the level of agricultural exports, petroleum refining, coal usage, and chemical shipments. Large companies have advantages in handling a broad range of cargo types, along with economies of scale in purchasing and marketing. Small companies compete by specializing in particular cargo types or services, subcontracting to larger companies, and offering responsive customer service. Average annual revenue per employee is about $200,000 for small companies and over $300,000 for large companies.

Inland barge companies compete with other methods for transporting bulk materials and liquids, including trucks, railroads, and pipelines.

Products, Operations & Technology

Inland barge transport services include freight transportation (92 percent of industry revenue); towing and tugboat services (6 percent); and other related services. Freight transportation services consist of dry cargo (such as grain, coal, steel, fertilizers, and aggregates) and liquid cargo (refined petroleum products, petrochemicals, black oils, and agricultural chemicals). Dry cargo is the dominate type of

BUSINESS CHALLENGES

» Dependence on Petroleum Products, Coal Markets
Petroleum products and coal account for over half the tonnage shipped by inland barge companies. Bulk petrochemical shipments are driven by US production of paper, fibers, and plastics. Demand for black oil products, such as fuel oil, and refined petroleum products, such as gas, depends on weather conditions and auto and air travel. Coal demand is driven by electricity and steel production.

» Dependence on Agriculture Exports
Demand for dry cargo barge shipments in the US is affected significantly by the volume of agriculture exports, primarily grain, passing through the Port of New Orleans. Agriculture exports depend on the size of US and worldwide harvests, and on subsidies or tariffs imposed by US or foreign governments. These exports can be volatile: US annual grain exports have fallen as much as 11 percent and risen as much as 16 percent yearly since 2002.

» Environmental Concerns
Concerns over water and air pollution have led to regulations that affect operating procedures, costs, and vessel designs for inland barge companies. Mandated conversion to double-hull designs has helped reduce the oil spill rate from tank barges by over 90 percent since 1996. Companies are required to install vapor control equipment on barges to prevent emissions of gases during loading and unloading of petroleum products. Fishermen and environmentalists often oppose expansion of dams and locks on waterways due to the impact on fish and bird populations.

freight shipped by volume and dry cargo barges make up about 85 percent of the US barge fleet.

Dry cargo barges include both covered and open hopper barges, used for grain, coal, steel, and other bulk commodities, and deck barges, used to haul machinery and other oversized cargoes. A typical barge, which is 200 feet long and 35 feet wide, can carry 1,500 tons of cargo, or the equivalent of 15 railcars or 60 trailer trucks.

Liquid cargo is carried in tank barges. The capacity of a 30,000 barrel inland tank barge is the equivalent of 40 railroad tank cars or 150 tractor-trailer tank trucks. Depending on the requirements of the cargo being carried, tank barges may include heating or refrigeration systems, stainless steel tanks, aluminum tanks, or specially coated tanks. Older single-hull tank barges are being retrofitted or replaced with double-hull barges to minimize cargo leakage into waterways. Federal law requires all tank barges to have double hulls by 2015.

Barges are moved by towboats whose engines may vary from 500 to 9,000 horsepower. The more powerful towboats, known as line boats, are used along the lower Mississippi River to tow as many as 40 barges at a time. These line hauls operate like a freight train, picking up and dropping off barges as they move along the river. Midsize towboats, also called line boats, are used on the Upper Mississippi River and Illinois Waterway, where locks and dams limit the size of tows to about five barges. The smallest towboats, known as push boats, are used to move one or two barges at a time around ports and harbors.

Larger barge companies use technology to increase the efficiency of their operations and improve customer service. Computerized logistics systems help schedule and route shipments. GPS is used to track shipments and provide accurate navigation information to pilots. Wireless communications allow pilots to stay up-to-the-minute on river and weather conditions. Many companies also provide websites that allow customers to track shipments and expected delivery times.

Sales & Marketing

Customers for inland barge transportation include energy, agricultural, and industrial companies. Barge companies maintain ongoing relationships with customers and often depend highly on a small group of large customers.

Services are usually provided under long-term contracts, ranging from one to five years with renewal options. Contracts provide a fixed rate for cargo movement between a specified origin and destination, with adjustments for fuel prices and, in some cases, inflation. These contracts, also known as contracts of affreightment, don't usually have volume guarantees. A less frequently used form of long-term contract

is a time charter contract, where the customer pays a daily rate for use of a specified number of barges for a period of time.

Services are also provided under spot contracts where the rate is negotiated at the time of the cargo shipment. These rates depend on market conditions and are often volatile. Grain shipments are often handled under spot contracts. Barge companies will typically earn between 20 and 40 percent of their revenue from spot contract shipments.

Companies use a direct sales force, since the sale of services involves contract negotiations. A survey of inland tank barge operators by the US Maritime Administration finds that sales calls and contract negotiations are primary means of determining customer needs and satisfaction.

Inland barge companies compete with captive operations of large agriculture and energy companies, as well as with trucks, railroads, and pipelines. For large shipments, barges are the most economical from of transportation at less than $1 per ton mile. On a cost per ton mile basis, rail is three times and trucks are 30 times more expensive.

Human Resources

Captains and pilots of towboats earn an average annual salary of about $55,000 and must have US Coast Guard (USCG) certification. Deckhands on towboats earn less than the average for all US production workers due to the relatively unskilled nature of the work. All personnel handling liquid cargo require licenses from the USCG.

Crew member safety is an ongoing focus of the industry and USCG. Safety programs have resulted in a drop in annual towing vessel crew fatalities from 28 in 1997 to 9 in 2004.

Crew retention can be an issue, as crews typically work 20 days on, 10 days off, or 30 days on, 15 days off. To aid in retention, larger companies provide training programs for crew members to achieve required certifications and enable advancement opportunities for deckhands.

Call Preparation Questions

How dependent is the company on shipments of petroleum products and coal?

Petroleum products and coal account for over half the tonnage shipped by inland barge companies.

What is the company's outlook for US grain exports?

Demand for dry cargo barge shipments in the US is affected significantly by the volume of agriculture exports, primarily grain, passing through the Port of New Orleans.

How have environmental regulations changed the company's operations?

Concerns over water and air pollution have led to regulations that affect operating procedures, costs, and vessel designs for inland barge companies.

What opportunities does the company see in the growing US ethanol industry?

Rising demand for ethanol as a gas additive and blend could create higher demand for inland barge companies.

What role do new services play in the company's growth plans?

To supplement freight revenue and better service customers, barge companies are expanding services.

Web Links

American Commercial Lines

Large inland barge company.
www.aclines.com

Ingram Marine Group

Largest dry cargo barge operator.
www.ingrambarge.com

Inland Rivers Ports & Terminals, Inc.

Waterway trade association.
www.irpt.net

Kirby Inland Marine Transportation

Large US tank barge operator.
www.kirbycorp.com/2_inland

Marine Link.com

News of worldwide maritime industry.
www.marinelink.com

Maritime Administration

News on US maritime operations.
www.marad.dot.gov

The American Waterways Operators

Trade association for tugboat and barge operators.
www.americanwaterways.com

US Army Corps of Engineers

News on waterways projects and traffic data.
www.usace.army.mil

WorkBoat

Commercial marine industry publication.
www.workboat.com

Glossary of Acronyms

AWO — The American Waterways Operators

CERCLA — Comprehensive Environmental Response, Compensation, and Liability Act of 1981

OPA — Oil Pollution Act of 1990

USCG — United States Coast Guard

HOOVER'S TOP COMPANIES

Largest Companies by Sales	($ mil.)
Ingram Industries Inc.	2,100.0
Kirby Corporation	1,360.2
American Commercial Lines Inc.	1,196.8
Rand Logistics, Inc.	94.8

Largest Employers	Employees
Ingram Industries Inc.	5,700
Kirby Corporation	3,100
American Commercial Lines Inc.	3,000
United Maritime Group	1,035
Canal Barge Company, Inc.	385
Rand Logistics, Inc.	281
American Steamship Company	219
General Steamship Agencies, Inc.	115

Fastest Growing* by Five-Year Sales Growth	(%)
Rand Logistics, Inc.	454.9
Kirby Corporation	17.3
American Commercial Lines Inc.	14.1

Top Public Companies by Market Value	($ mil.)
Kirby Corporation	1,463.5
American Commercial Lines Inc.	309.9
Rand Logistics, Inc.	65.1

* These rates are compounded annualized increases and may have resulted from acquisitions or one time gains. If less than 6 years of data are available, growth is for the years available.

SOURCE: HOOVER'S, INC., DATABASE

Insurance Agencies

About 130,000 insurance agency and broker offices in the US generate annual revenues of $85 billion. Large companies include Marsh & McLennan, Arthur J. Gallagher, and Aon. Despite the prominence of large companies in the commercial segment, the industry remains highly fragmented: the largest 50 firms only hold 20 percent of the total market. The average office has five employees and generates less than a million dollars in annual revenue. An insurance agent works on the insurance company's behalf; an insurance broker on the customer's behalf. Many companies on the commercial side function mainly as brokers.

Competitive Landscape

Demand is related to consumer income and the volume of commercial activity. The profitability of individual agencies depends on effective marketing. Large agencies have advantages in name recognition, connections with more insurers, and the ability to craft more complex insurance packages. Small agencies can compete successfully by specializing in a product, industry, or market. Average annual revenue per employee is close to $200,000.

Products, Operations & Technology

The three broad categories of insurance are property and casualty (P/C), which generates about 60 percent of annual industry revenue; health, about 12 percent; and life, which generates 10 percent. Within the P/C segment, commercial insurance accounts for 60 percent of revenue. Because of the very different insurance issues involved in each, many agencies handle only one type of insurance. Agencies may also specialize in selling to individuals, businesses, or groups. Agencies that sell to individuals may provide highly personalized service.

P/C insurance includes auto (40 percent); homeowners'; commercial; workers' compensation; and other liability coverage. With these

BUSINESS CHALLENGES

» Revenue Depends on Economic Conditions

The revenue of many insurance agencies swings with economic conditions, especially in property and casualty insurance, because the volume of insurance-related transactions changes. A slower economy generally means fewer new homes built and sold, fewer cars bought, and fewer investment-type insurance products bought.

» Competition from Direct Sales

While the majority of insurance transactions involve an agent or broker, experts expect that fewer of these transactions will use an agent or broker as more consumers buy insurance through direct sources. Insurers can easily sell auto and term life insurance, the largest volume of insurance business, over the Internet without an insurance agent intermediary. Many insurance companies also sell a significant number of policies directly to consumers through direct mail and telemarketing.

» Competition from Banks, Brokerages

Deregulation of the financial services sector allows banks and stock brokers to sell insurance, providing consumers the same kind of personalized service as traditional agents. A growing number of banks and independent insurance agents are forming joint marketing ventures, and banks are buying agencies.

types, especially in the commercial segment, agencies frequently provide various fee services such as claims adjustment, risk assessment, and premium collection in addition to selling policies. Health insurance is sold primarily to companies or groups, but individual supplemental policies have become more popular in recent years as managed care providers have limited their coverage. Agencies that sell health insurance often offer administrative and consulting services in the employee benefit field.

Agencies selling life insurance essentially specialize in personal financial and retirement planning, and sell other investment products such as annuities. Annuities (fixed, variable, deferred, and payout) are an insurance product that essentially functions as a financial investment. Annuities generate more annual revenue for life insurance companies than do regular life insurance sales.

Agency agreements with insurance companies allow agents to bind insurance coverage on the company's behalf and specify the commission the agency receives from policies. Agencies usually have agreements with multiple insurance companies, although some work exclusively with one company and are essentially franchisees. Typically, agencies receive a large percentage of the initial premium from a new policy and a smaller percentage from renewal premiums, but the compensation formula varies according to the policy premium schedule. Brokers work on behalf of their customers, soliciting bids from several insurers, and are used extensively in the commercial segment of the industry. Broker compensation is through fees from the customer, although in some cases brokers may also receive commissions from insurers.

Sales & Marketing

Agencies that sell products to individuals depend heavily on referrals from existing customers and from accountants, real estate agents, stockbrokers, and financial planners. Because of the very personal and local aspect of the business, even large agencies work through small local offices. Agencies that sell or broker commercial or group health insurance typically use a direct sales force, advertise in local business publications, and may sponsor local business events. Large agencies also may have a national sales force that serves large corporations with national or international locations.

Human Resources

Jobs with insurance agencies are of two types, clerical and sales. Clerical jobs require computer skills, while sales jobs often require sophisticated financial knowledge. Most insurance agents receive a large portion of income from commissions on sales. Average hourly wages are around 19 percent above the national wage. The availability of insurance policies over the Internet and the new competition from banks and brokerages have limited the number of new agency jobs in the past few years.

Industry Employment Growth

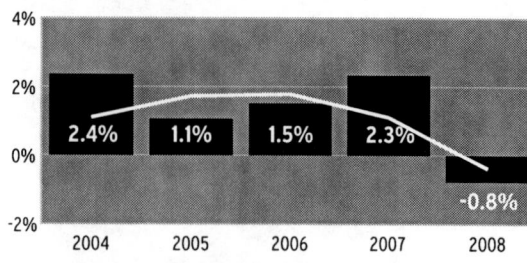

Average Hourly Earnings

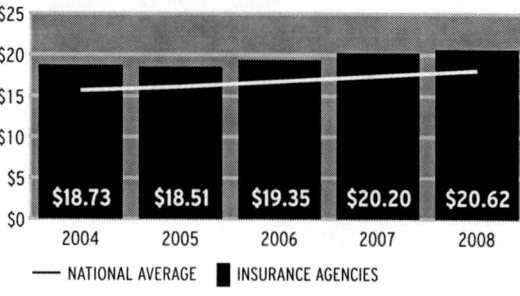

SOURCE: BUREAU OF LABOR STATISTICS

Call Preparation Questions

How does the company manage shifts in demand due to economic conditions?

The revenue of many insurance agencies swings with economic conditions, especially in property and casualty insurance, because the volume of insurance-related transactions changes.

How have agency sales been affected by the Internet?

While the majority of insurance transactions involve an agent or broker, experts expect that fewer of these transactions will use an agent or broker as more consumers buy insurance through direct sources.

How does the agency counter increased competition from banks and brokerage houses due to financial deregulation?

Deregulation of the financial services sector allows banks and stock brokers to sell insurance, providing consumers the same kind of personalized service as traditional agents.

How does the agency use the Internet to find new business or serve customers?

The Internet allows agencies to increase their level of service by giving customers greater access to products, services, and information.

How is the agency benefiting from deregulation of the financial services industry?

Deregulation allows agencies to sell investment products.

Web Links

A.M. Best Company

Insurance industry news.
www.ambest.com

Independent Insurance Agents and Brokers of America

Insurance industry studies.
www.independentagent.com

Insurance Information Institute

Links to state and national associations.
www.iii.org

Insurance News Net

Industry news by product line.
www.insurancenewsnet.com

Insurance Services Office

Information about the property & casualty insurance business; statistics.
www.iso.com

Insurance.com

Informational site for consumers.
insurance.com

National Association of Insurance Commissioners

Regulatory issues.
www.naic.org

Property and Casualty.com

Industry news.
www.propertyandcasualty.com/content/homepage

The Council of Insurance Agents & Brokers

Industry links and news.
www.ciab.com

The National Underwriter Company

Industry news and links to product line magazines.
cms.nationalunderwriter.com/cms/
nationalunderwriter/public%20website

Glossary of Acronyms

CIAB — Council of Insurance Agents and Brokers
IIABA — Independent Insurance Agents and Brokers of America
III — Insurance Information Institute
RMS — Risk and Insurance Management Society
SMART — State Modernization and Regulatory Transparency Act

HOOVER'S TOP COMPANIES

Largest Companies by Sales	($ mil.)
Marsh & McLennan Companies, Inc.	11,587.0
Aon Corporation	7,631.0
American Financial Group, Inc.	4,404.7
Factory Mutual Insurance Company	3,355.8
Selective Insurance Group, Inc.	1,696.0
Arthur J. Gallagher & Co.	1,645.0
Philadelphia Insurance Companies	1,529.6
National Financial Partners Corp.	1,150.4
Erie Indemnity Company	1,137.2
Crawford & Company	1,135.9

Largest Employers	Employees
Marsh & McLennan Companies, Inc.	56,000
Aon Corporation	42,500
Arthur J. Gallagher & Co.	9,300
Crawford & Company	9,280
Sedgwick Claims Management Services, Inc.	6,200
Brown & Brown, Inc.	5,047
Factory Mutual Insurance Company	4,500
Erie Indemnity Company	4,100
Hub International Limited	3,820
National Financial Partners Corp.	3,247

Fastest Growing* by Five-Year Sales Growth	(%)
Specialty Underwriters' Alliance, Inc.	375.6
Brooke Corporation	39.6
eHealth, Inc.	38.1
North Pointe Holdings Corporation	32.7
Mercer Insurance Group, Inc.	30.6
Claimsnet.com, Inc.	28.5
Philadelphia Insurance Companies	27.4
Sedgwick Claims Management Services, Inc.	24.9
ProCentury Corporation	24.3
First Mercury Financial Corporation	22.4

Fastest Growing* by Five-Year Employee Growth	(%)
Specialty Underwriters' Alliance, Inc.	84.6
North Pointe Holdings Corporation	35.3
Regions Insurance Group, Inc.	24.6
Crawford & Company	23.3
eHealth, Inc.	22.3
Mercer Insurance Group, Inc.	21.0
First Mercury Financial Corporation	19.7
National Financial Partners Corp.	15.5
Sedgwick Claims Management Services, Inc.	15.4
Philadelphia Insurance Companies	14.1

Top Public Companies by Market Value	($ mil.)
Marsh & McLennan Companies, Inc.	12,481.2
Aon Corporation	12,429.5
American Financial Group, Inc.	3,277.9
Brown & Brown, Inc.	2,958.3
Philadelphia Insurance Companies	2,836.6

* These rates are compounded annualized increases and may have resulted from acquisitions or one time gains. If less than 6 years of data are available, growth is for the years available.

SOURCE: HOOVER'S, INC., DATABASE

Insurance Carriers

In the US, about 5,000 companies provide insurance coverage of various sorts, with combined annual revenue of $1 trillion. Large companies include American International Group, MetLife, Aetna, and Allstate. The industry is highly concentrated: the 50 largest companies hold more than 60 percent of the market. Within product segments, concentration is even higher.

Competitive Landscape

Demand is driven by demographics and commercial transactions. The profitability of individual companies depends on effective marketing and on the ability to accurately estimate future payments. Large companies have big economies of scale in administration and in access to capital. Small companies can compete successfully by specializing in particular products or industries.

Products, Operations & Technology

Major products are accident and health insurance, property and casualty insurance, life insurance, and the sale of annuities. Premiums earned from these products account for about 30 percent, 28 percent, 10 percent, and 12 percent of industry revenue, respectively.

All insurance carriers operate in essentially the same way: they collect premiums today in exchange for paying claims or benefits in the future. Their revenue consists of insurance premiums and income from the large investment portfolios they hold. The number of insurance products is large, and each has different premium plans and claim options.

Accident and health insurance policies are of three major types. Fee-for-service plans make payments for medical services from any provider. Managed care plans (which generally have lower premiums) pay only for services from providers the insurer has contracts with. Supplemental health policies cover the policy-

BUSINESS CHALLENGES

» Investment Income Depends on Economic Conditions

The revenue of insurance companies depends highly on economic conditions. During economic slowdowns, fewer business transactions (like home sales) occur that require new insurance, and investment income can be sharply reduced if the stock market or interest rates are lower. Investment income typically accounts for more than a third of total revenue at large insurers.

» Individual Insurers May Have Catastrophic Losses

Large-scale claims have become more common and individual insurers may have concentrations of risk. Although insurers often spread risks through reinsurance, unknown risks can be large enough to drive insurers out of business. Fortress Re, a large aviation insurer, went out of business following 9/11.

» Rates Depend on Regulators

Because insurers have difficulty forecasting future claims for a variety of coverages, including auto and health insurance, they've frequently had to appear before state insurance commissions to ask for higher rates. Although insurance commissioners wish to maintain the financial health of insurers, they're also influenced by political considerations, and frequently grant lower rates that insurers ask for.

holder for medical services not covered by standard insurance plans or programs like Medicare.

Property and casualty (P/C) insurance covers mainly homes, cars, and commercial and industrial properties. Most such policies feature a choice between higher premiums and higher deductibles — the amount of a loss that the policyholder absorbs before insurance coverage begins. Many P/C policies provide different levels of coverage for losses of different sizes, and include "stop-loss" provisions that limit the exposure of the insurer. P/C insurers often limit their risk exposure on commercial policies by selling off "slices" to other insurers.

Life insurance products may be single or joint policies, whole life, term life, or variable life policies, among a long list of products. Term policies are the most straightforward life insurance product because a premium is paid solely in exchange for the possibility that the insurance holder will die during the term of the policy; any investment income is kept by the insurance company. Most other life insurance policies include some type of investment feature and therefore have higher premiums. Annuities are almost entirely an investment product, with a large upfront premium and investment-type returns every year.

Calculating future claims (set aside as loss reserves) is crucial in determining the size of the premiums that an insurance company must charge, and has a large effect on reported financial performance because additions to the loss reserve are income deductions. The annual loss ratio for an insurer (the ratio of losses to premiums) is often close to 80 percent. To calculate loss reserves, insurance companies calculate the incidence of a claim (the odds that a claim will occur) and the size of the claim that might be paid. When the incidence and claim size can be estimated with good accuracy (for example, for a life insurance policy), the insurance company can afford to charge a relatively low fixed premium for a policy that extends many years. When either incidence or claim size can't be forecast with reliability, premiums may be higher, or adjustable, or the policy term may be short. The addition of the loss ratio to the expense ratio (the ratio of expenses to premiums) and the policyholder dividend ratio (if the insurer pays such dividends) gives the combined ratio, a measure frequently used to describe company performance.

The operations of insurance companies are largely clerical and rely heavily on computer technology to store and access files on individual customers and policies. Most insurers have electronic communications links with major commercial customers. The Internet has become a major source of direct business for life and auto insurance.

Sales & Marketing

Insurance is marketed and sold through a company sales force and independent agents who may also sell policies from competitors. Allstate, for example, has a network of 12,000 exclusive and 15,000 independent agents. Life, home, and auto insurance are more likely to be sold by agents, while health and commercial and industrial coverage are usually sold by a sales force. Many companies also use direct response techniques, such as telemarketing, direct mail, and Internet sales. On the commercial side, companies maintain relations with large brokers, like Marsh & McLennan, who ask insurers to bid for business from customers. The Internet has become a major source of insurance sales for life and auto insurance. Marketing efforts focus both on new production and policy retention.

Human Resources

Jobs with insurance carriers are of three major types: clerical, investment management, or sales. Many jobs require special skills, as reflected in above-average earnings. Insurance carriers have very good safety records, with few on-the-job injuries.

Industry Employment Growth

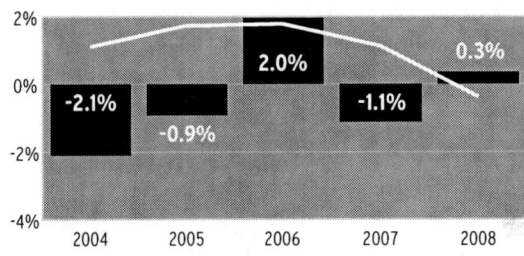

Average Hourly Earnings

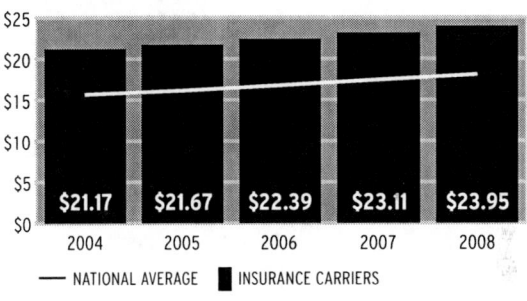

— NATIONAL AVERAGE ■ INSURANCE CARRIERS

SOURCE: BUREAU OF LABOR STATISTICS

Call Preparation Questions

How does the company manage shifts in revenue due to economic conditions?

The revenue of insurance companies depends highly on economic conditions.

How would an updated catastrophe modeling system help the company in underwriting?

Large-scale claims have become more common and individual insurers may have concentrations of risk.

What difficulties does the company face requesting rate increases from legislators?

Because insurers have difficulty forecasting future claims for a variety of coverages, including auto and health insurance, they've frequently had to appear before state insurance commissions to ask for higher rates.

Web Links

A.M. Best Company

Excellent industry news.
www.ambest.com

American Council of Life Insurers

Lobbying organization.
www.acli.org

Insurance Information Institute

Data about property and casualty insurers.
www.iii.org

Insurance Services Office

Information and data about the property & casualty insurance segment. Excellent links.
www.iso.com

Insure.com

Excellent glossary of insurance terms.
info.insure.com/glossary.cfm

International Risk Management Institute

Recent risk management issues.
www.irmi.com

National Association of Insurance Commissioners

Association of regulators.
www.naic.org

National Association of Mutual Insurance Companies (NAMIC)

News. Industry issues.
www.namic.org

Reinsurance Association of America

List of top reinsurers. Industry information.
www.reinsurance.org

The National Underwriter Company

Industry news and links to product line magazines.
www.nationalunderwriter.com

Glossary of Acronyms

ACLI — American Council of Life Insurers
ERM — enterprise risk management
FSMA — Financial Services Modernization Act
III — Insurance Information Institute
ISO — Insurance Services Office
NAIC — National Association of Insurance Commissioners
NAII — National Association of Independent Insurers
NAMIC — National Association of Mutual Insurance Companies
PCI — Property Casualty Insurers Association of America

HOOVER'S TOP COMPANIES

Largest Companies by Sales	($ mil.)
UnitedHealth Group Incorporated	81,186.0
State Farm Mutual Automobile Insurance	61,600.0
WellPoint, Inc.	61,251.1
MetLife, Inc.	50,989.0
Aetna Inc.	30,950.7
The Allstate Corporation	29,394.0
Prudential Financial, Inc.	29,275.0
Humana Inc.	28,946.4
Liberty Mutual Holding Company Inc.	25,961.0
The Travelers Companies, Inc.	24,477.0

Largest Employers	Employees
American International Group, Inc.	116,000
State Farm Mutual Automobile Insurance	68,000
UnitedHealth Group Incorporated	67,000
MetLife, Inc.	49,000
WellPoint, Inc.	42,900
Liberty Mutual Holding Company Inc.	41,000
Prudential Financial, Inc.	40,703
The Allstate Corporation	38,000
Nationwide Mutual Insurance Company	36,000
Aetna Inc.	35,200

Fastest Growing* by Five-Year Sales Growth	(%)
Specialty Underwriters' Alliance, Inc.	375.6
First Acceptance Corporation	203.1
Darwin Professional Underwriters, Inc.	165.4
Universal Insurance Holdings, Inc.	82.5
The Amacore Group, Inc.	70.3
Hallmark Financial Services, Inc.	60.5
Universal American Corp.	55.7
Tower Group, Inc.	45.3
Life Partners Holdings, Inc.	42.9
HealthSpring, Inc.	42.5

Fastest Growing* by Five-Year Employee Growth	(%)
The National Security Group, Inc.	92.9
Specialty Underwriters' Alliance, Inc.	84.6
FinCor Holdings, Inc.	51.2
Darwin Professional Underwriters, Inc.	50.9
Universal Insurance Holdings, Inc.	50.0
AmTrust Financial Services, Inc.	47.8
North Pointe Holdings Corporation	35.3
GAINSCO, INC.	32.5
Independence Holding Company	31.7
Centene Corporation	31.2

Top Public Companies by Market Value	($ mil.)
UnitedHealth Group Incorporated	32,335.4
MetLife, Inc.	27,665.9
The Travelers Companies, Inc.	26,446.5
Aflac Incorporated	21,389.6
WellPoint, Inc.	21,201.1

* These rates are compounded annualized increases and may have resulted from acquisitions or one time gains. If less than 6 years of data are available, growth is for the years available.

SOURCE: HOOVER'S, INC., DATABASE

Interior Design Services

THIS INDUSTRY INCLUDES:

SIC CODES
7389   Business Services

NAICS CODES
541410   Interior Design
          Services

The US interior design industry includes about 11,000 businesses with combined annual revenue of $7 billion. Major companies are units of larger architectural and design firms Gensler; Hellmuth, Obata + Kassabaum (HOK); Perkins + Will; Callison; and Leo A Daly. The industry is highly fragmented: the 50 largest firms account for only 10 percent of total revenue. Most firms are small: a typical business has one location, fewer than four employees, and average annual revenue of about $620,000. About 30 percent of interior designers are self-employed.

Competitive Landscape

Constructing and renovating residential, commercial, industrial, and institutional buildings drive demand for interior design services. The profitability of individual companies depends on accurate bidding, timely delivery, and a steady volume of projects. Large companies have advantages in marketing, developing partnerships, building a large client referral list, and getting priority service from suppliers. Small companies can compete effectively by providing better service, specializing, and using unique or custom product sources. Average annual revenue per worker for a typical business is $185,000.

Competitors include suppliers and consumers. Suppliers compete by expanding their services to include interior design; consumers compete by establishing their own independent businesses, typically a home-based operation focusing on interior decorating.

Products, Operations & Technology

Major services of interior designers are selling products as part of an integrated design service, providing fee-based consulting services, and managing subcontractors. Product sales contribute 60 percent of revenue; consulting

BUSINESS CHALLENGES

» Reliance on New Construction, Renovations

The interior design industry depends on new building construction and renovations as major sources of projects. US interior design industry revenue rose 41 percent from 1997 through 2002, due largely to a 35 percent increase in spending for construction and residential improvements. Spending more than doubled in the decade ending in 2005, despite a recession. New construction spending actually increased during the last recession, due to projects already in progress, but residential improvements declined 2 percent as homeowners delayed plans.

» Dependence on Consumer Income, Local Economy

Spending on interior design services is a discretionary expense that depends on personal income and the health of local economies. US personal income increased 66 percent from 1995 through 2005, a positive indicator for consumer discretionary spending. Since most interior design firms work locally or regionally, local economic activity also influences demand. In recent years, economic growth has been strongest in Nevada, Florida, and Arizona, and weakest in Michigan, Ohio, and Pennsylvania.

» Low Barriers to Entry

Independents or small startups can enter the interior design market easily, especially for interior decorating. In many states, an interior design business can be started without certification or industry-specific experience, and startups don't need employees or an official office. The number of businesses in the industry increased almost 20 percent in a recent five-year period, despite a trend toward large companies acquiring small and midsized firms.

fees, 35 percent; and subcontracting services, 5 percent.

Homeowners, businesses, and government entities engage interior designers to plan, design, and supervise physical and aesthetic projects for interiors of buildings. Clients may hire interior decorators, who are part of this industry, to consult solely on the aesthetics of interior spaces, not the physical structure.

Designers evaluate clients' functional needs, style preferences, and budgets, and customize interiors to meet those requirements. Designers determine how the intended use of an interior will affect a variety of issues, such as foot-traffic patterns, floor layout, heating and air conditioning, lighting and electrical outlets, public and private spaces, furniture, and decor. Designers ensure that their plans comply with local building, health, and safety codes.

Interior design firms may specialize by client (residential, commercial, or government) or project type (new construction or renovations). Some firms may specialize in industries or projects that have unique requirements, such as health care and hospitals, retail stores, or the hotel and hospitality industry. Large firms may offer full-service, integrated design services across many industries and types of projects, while small firms typically have a narrower focus.

Depending on the project, designers may specify and buy wall and ceiling materials, flooring, fabric, furniture, lighting, appliances, cabinets, doors, accessories, and other interior design materials. Design firms with commercial and industrial building clients often conform to the standards of the Construction Specifications Institute. Firms generally buy wholesale from suppliers on a per-project basis. Designers maintain samples and marketing materials to show clients, but don't stock inventory, other than what the firm orders for specific projects. Designers keep photographs of completed projects to help clients visualize how materials will look in use.

Regional style preferences exist among clients and designers, although every market has a mixture. Traditional styling is popular in the South; Colonial in New England; eclectic in New York City; contemporary and Mediterranean on the West Coast; and Spanish in the Southwest. Regional magazines like Sunset (for the western US) and Southern Living play a big role as style-setters.

Interior designers have long used drawing as a planning tool and a way to communicate designs to clients, and increasingly use CAD and specification software. Larger firms may have CAD talent on staff, but smaller firms typically outsource the creation of technical drawings. Cutting-edge architect firms that also have interior design services are beginning to use 3D visualization software that simulates the experience of walking through a finished interior. The Internet is enabling design firms to expand their teams and partnerships in other areas of the country and world, to reach a dispersed client base and to buy materials electronically.

Sales & Marketing

Typical customers of interior design services are commercial and industrial companies, homeowners, and institutions, including government. Some design firms specialize by customer segment or industry, such as health care facilities, which have unique needs. Customers typically engage interior designers early in the planning stages for new buildings or major renovations, although many homeowners use design services simply for redecorating, often as a result of minor remodeling.

Major types of marketing are through ads in Yellow Pages and local real estate and home fashion magazines. Referrals are a major source of customers, so building relationships and partnerships is very important. Interior design firms seek good relationships with architects, builders, realtors, and product providers for interiors, such as furniture stores. Design firms use newsletters, open houses at completed projects, and social events to build and maintain client and professional relationships. Members of the American Society of Interior Designers receive marketing tools from the organization and participate in their regional chapter's projects, such as the designer house of the year. Individual firms seek publicity by entering design contests and submitting photos for publication in leading architectural and design magazines.

Sales efforts of larger firms typically focus on the commercial and institutional segments, and rely on senior executives' contacts and a direct sales force. In smaller firms, the owner or partners are the only salespeople and use a highly personal, one-on-one, consultative approach with prospects and clients. Institutional projects go through a controlled proposal and bidding process, as do many corporate jobs, although executives' preferences often are the deciding factors with commercial customers.

Pricing may be based on hourly fees, a fixed-price bid, or a percentage markup on materials and services. Hourly consultation fees range from $40 to hundreds of dollars. Fixed-price projects range from $1,000 to hundreds of thousands. Designers price products by adding a markup of 5 to 100 percent to the cost they incur for items, such as flooring, wall tiles, furniture, lamps, and carpeting. Some firms prefer to take a flat percentage fee based on the total cost of purchases and services of any subcontractors they hire, such as electricians, painters, or installers.

Design firms typically buy wholesale, but the smallest companies may not receive much discount and may buy decorative items at retail. Retailers and manufacturers compete for product sales, because clients can buy directly from stores or producers' showrooms.

Human Resources

Interior design requires special training and most firms hire designers with college degrees. Accordingly, average annual wages are at least 10 percent higher than the US average. In addition to formal training, as prerequisites for achieving registration or licensure, many states and most Canadian provinces require on-the-job experience of one to three years ("apprenticeship") and passing the standard exam of the National Council for Interior Design Qualification. Designers need to take continuing education courses for license renewal.

Business skills can be challenging for the self-employed, who account for 30 percent of interior designers. Large firms have the luxury of hiring people for specialized functions, like drafting or computer-aided design (CAD), proposal development, or product selection, but small firms must rely on employees who perform multiple functions. Most work occurs in an office or client environment, so industry injury rates are negligible.

Industry Employment Growth

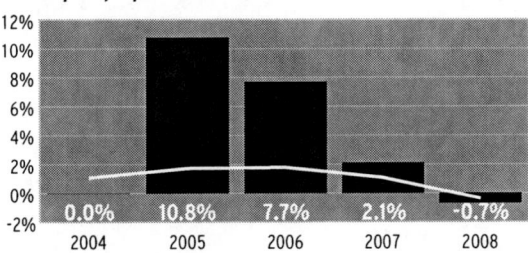

Average Hourly Earnings

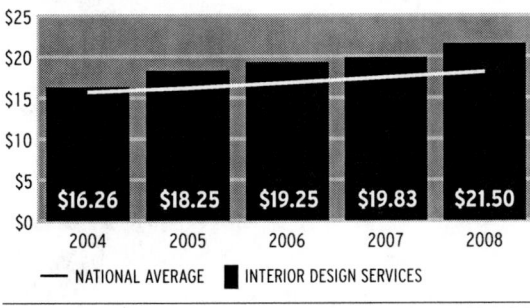

— NATIONAL AVERAGE ■ INTERIOR DESIGN SERVICES

SOURCE: BUREAU OF LABOR STATISTICS

Call Preparation Questions

How important to the firm are projects for new construction, compared to renovations?

The interior design industry depends on new building construction and renovations as major sources of projects.

How have the local economy and consumer spending affected the firm?

Spending on interior design services is a discretionary expense that depends on personal income and the health of local economies.

How does the firm differentiate itself?

Providing the best responsiveness to clients is a differentiating factor in interior design, because service defines the business.

What plans does the firm have to incorporate universal design into its services?

Interior designers whose projects conform to universal design principles can quickly become experts in the field.

Web Links

American Society of Interior Designers

News for designers and business resources.
www.asid.org

Interior Design Magazine

News, features, and trends.
www.interiordesign.net

International Interior Design Association

Awards, news, and continuing education information.
www.iida.org

National Council for Interior Design Qualification

Certification program.
www.ncidq.org

The Interior Design Society

Resources for residential designers.
www.interiordesignsociety.org

Glossary of Acronyms

ASID — American Society of Interior Designers
CAPS — certified aging-in-place specialist
CSI — Construction Specifications Institute
IIDA — International Interior Design Association
NAHB — National Association of Home Builders
NCIDQ — National Council for Interior Design Qualification

HOOVER'S TOP COMPANIES

Largest Employers	Employees
M. Arthur Gensler Jr. & Associates, Inc.	2,210
HOK Group, Inc.	1,839
Leo A Daly Company	950
Callison Architecture, Inc.	800
The Perkins & Will Group, Ltd.	450
Hirsch Bedner Associates Design Consultants	350
Mancini Duffy	170
Wolcott Architecture Interiors	47

SOURCE: HOOVER'S, INC., DATABASE

Internet and Catalog Retailers

THIS INDUSTRY INCLUDES:

SIC CODES
5961   Catalog and Mail-Order Houses

NAICS CODES
4541   Electronic Shopping and Mail-Order Houses

The Internet and catalog retailing industry in the US includes 16,000 companies with combined annual revenue of over $160 billion. Major companies include Lands' End, LL Bean, Amazon, Overstock, and Hanover Direct. The industry is concentrated: the top 50 companies account for about 60 percent of industry revenue. Over the past five years, the industry has shifted from catalog to Internet sales.

Competitive Landscape

Demand is driven by consumers' personal income. Profitability of individual companies depends on effective marketing to build a customer base. Larger firms enjoy central purchasing efficiencies and economies of scale in inventory management, customer service, and telecommunications. Smaller firms compete on outstanding customer service and providing niche products. Average annual revenue per worker for a typical company is about $400,000.

While most brick-and-mortar retailers have an online presence and many also offer catalog sales, this profile focuses on retailers who use the Internet or catalogs as their sole or primary sales channel.

Products, Operations & Technology

Although catalog and Internet retailers sell a variety of products and services, some of the largest product categories are drugs, health, and beauty aids; computer hardware and software; and clothing. While many Internet and catalog companies specialize in a single product category, larger companies are expanding offerings to maintain growth and leverage brand awareness. Amazon has expanded from being an online bookstore to offering items in more than 30 categories, including loose diamonds.

Catalog retailers specialize in target marketing, which identifies specific customers and customer groups most likely to buy their products. Catalogers mail about 300 million cata-

BUSINESS CHALLENGES

» Demand Depends on Consumer Income

Catalog and Internet retailers sell primarily discretionary goods and services, so demand varies with changes in personal income. Consumers delay or cut back on computers, new clothing, home furnishings, and other discretionary items when the economy weakens. Total US retail sales grew only 2.4 percent per year during the 2001 recession, but averaged 6 percent per year before and after.

» Competition from Traditional Retailers

Traditional retailers are becoming the dominant online retailers by leveraging high consumer awareness. Consumers are moving to large brands that have online capability and that they're familiar with. Internet retailing is growing rapidly, accounting for 5 percent of all retail sales in 2005. Traditional retailers that offer multi-channel marketing will profit from serving online customers.

» Security, Privacy Concerns

A fundamental requirement for e-commerce is the secure transmission of private information over public networks. Credit card fraud is much higher for Web retailers than traditional stores. The industry has historically suffered from a general public mistrust of entering personal and credit card information online. Security measures have been installed by most online retailers, but information security and privacy remain consumer concerns.

logs a year to existing customer base and targeted prospects. Catalog firms maintain a proprietary customer list of those who have bought in the past. This list is supplemented by purchased and rented lists of consumers with desired buying behavior, and names from print advertising and promotional inserts.

Consumers buy merchandise by calling a toll-free number and placing their order at the firm's call center. The order is entered into an online order entry and inventory control system. Customers provide shipping and payment information, generally a credit card number.

In-stock items are usually shipped the next day from the company's warehouse(s) or distribution center(s) or from a third party through a sponsoring agreement. Company warehouses can be as large as 600,000 square feet and contain thousands of different products. Shipments are made via the US Postal Service (USPS) or a commercial shipping firm, and fulfillment may be enhanced by providing the customer a delivery date and delivery shipment notification.

Most catalogers have unconditional return policies. Disputes regarding purchases and deliveries are resolved by the credit card issuing bank. Credit card association procedures require the retailer to prove the sale and delivery of the disputed merchandise.

The Internet retailer's process is similar to catalog retailers' except that the merchandise is ordered online. The customer puts items for purchase in an online shopping cart and then provides shipping and payment information before checking out. Internet retailers typically have call centers for customer service calls. Customers order online by going directly to a firm's website, through third party websites by "click thrus" where the retailer pays a commission, and from online advertising. Catalogs are one of the largest factors in generating online orders. Consumers who receive catalogs are twice as likely to buy online as those who don't get catalogs, according to the USPS.

Catalog and Internet retailers have invested heavily in management information systems that allow easy access to data, including customer purchase history, product availability, product specifications, and shipment dates. Information systems are used to automate warehouse operations, inventory management, and call center operations. The customer database is the source for marketing and promotional campaigns. Due to customer privacy and security issues, Internet retailers have invested in encryption technology to protect sensitive customer information transmitted over the Web.

Sales & Marketing

Consumers are the major customers of catalog and Internet retailers, although business-to-business Internet retailing is increasing. According to the Direct Marketing Association, the typical catalog customer is a married, employed woman in her 50s who makes more than

$50,000 and lives in the suburbs with her working husband.

Many companies have an advertising campaign that uses national, regional, and local media, including network and cable TV and consumer magazines. Internet retailers also use sponsored links, e-mail, and cooperative advertising with vendors. Internet retailers sponsor ads on other websites, and create "pop-up" ads and special portals for online shopping.

Catalogs are mailed to customers multiple times each year. The types of catalogs are regular product, seasonal, and sale catalogs, and abridged versions typically mailed to prospective customers. Catalog and Internet companies maintain extensive databases of their customers, including shopping and buying habits, and demographic data. The database is routinely updated and refined based on most recent and frequency and size of purchases, and specific products purchased.

Human Resources

Average hourly earnings for the industry are below the US average, reflecting the emphasis on primarily unskilled workers. Turnover is high, primarily due to low wages and the seasonality of the industry; most companies use contract and temporary personnel during fourth quarter.

Industry Employment Growth

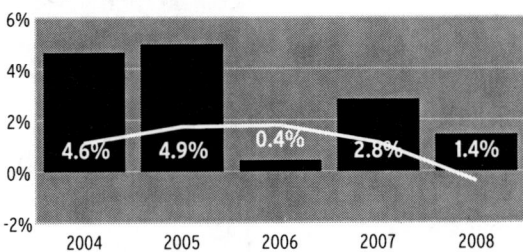

Average Hourly Earnings

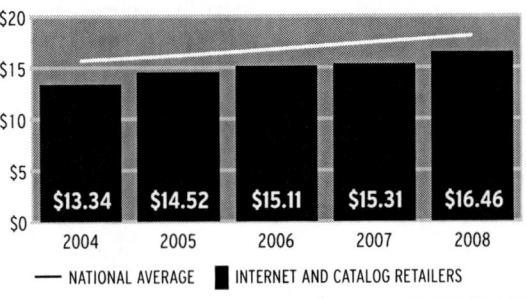

SOURCE: BUREAU OF LABOR STATISTICS

Call Preparation Questions

How does the current economic environment affect the company's sales outlook?

Catalog and Internet retailers sell primarily discretionary goods and services, so demand varies with changes in personal income.

How does the company compete with online sales by traditional retailers?

Traditional retailers are becoming the dominant online retailers by leveraging high consumer awareness.

How is the company improving its site and information security?

A fundamental requirement for e-commerce is the secure transmission of private information over public networks.

How is the company increasing the amount consumers buy?

Over half of Internet shoppers place items in their carts but then abandon them without buying anything.

What is the company's mix of sales channels and how do they support each other?

Catalog retailers have adapted to online marketing successfully; they enjoy the advantages of having an established infrastructure and have extensive experience selling to customers remotely.

Web Links

DIRECT

News and reports about direct marketing, online retailing.
www.directmag.com

Direct Marketing Association

News and links.
www.the-dma.org

eWeek

Electronic commerce news.
www.eweek.com

Internet Retailer

Industry news, events, articles, listing of top 300 Internet retailers.
www.internetretailer.com

National Retail Federation

Retail industry news, legislative issues.
www.nrf.com

RetailNet

Catalog industry news.
www.retailnet.com

Shop.org

Association for retailers online.
www.shop.org

Glossary of Acronyms

DMA — Direct Marketing Association
NRF — National Retail Federation
SKU — stock-keeping unit

HOOVER'S TOP COMPANIES

Largest Companies by Sales	($ mil.)
Amazon.com, Inc.	19,166.0
Liberty Interactive Group	10,084.0
eBay Inc.	8,541.3
Cabela's Incorporated	2,552.7
L.L. Bean, Inc.	1,620.0
HSN, Inc.	1,157.4
Overstock.com, Inc.	834.4
ValueVision Media, Inc.	781.5
Lands' End, Inc.	—

Largest Employers	Employees
Amazon.com, Inc.	17,000
eBay Inc.	16,200
Cabela's Incorporated	15,000
HSN, Inc.	6,600
L.L. Bean, Inc.	5,700
Columbia House Company	2,300
Hanover Direct, Inc.	1,840
LTD Commodities, LLC	1,500
ValueVision Media, Inc.	1,200

Fastest Growing* by Five-Year Sales Growth	(%)
Bodybuilding.com, LLC	44.6
eBay Inc.	31.6
Amazon.com, Inc.	29.5
Overstock.com, Inc.	28.4
PetMed Express, Inc.	27.9
drugstore.com, inc.	18.1
SourceForge, Inc.	18.0
Liberty Interactive Group	15.4
Cabela's Incorporated	12.9
ValueVision Media, Inc.	7.1

Fastest Growing* by Five-Year Employee Growth	(%)
Cabela's Incorporated	21.9
Amazon.com, Inc.	19.0
Overstock.com, Inc.	16.7
drugstore.com, inc.	16.6
ValueVision Media, Inc.	9.7
PetMed Express, Inc.	9.5
eBay Inc.	8.7

Top Public Companies by Market Value	($ mil.)
Amazon.com, Inc.	21,947.8
eBay Inc.	17,897.1
Cabela's Incorporated	434.4
Liberty Interactive Group	424.1
drugstore.com, inc.	310.2

* These rates are compounded annualized increases and may have resulted from acquisitions or one time gains. If less than 6 years of data are available, growth is for the years available.

SOURCE: HOOVER'S, INC., DATABASE

Internet Service Providers

The US Internet services provider industry includes about 4,000 companies that generate combined annual revenue of $30 billion. Large companies include AOL, AT&T, Comcast, Microsoft, and Verizon. The industry is highly concentrated: the 50 largest companies hold about 80 percent of the market; the four largest companies hold more than 50 percent.

The industry includes companies that provide access to the Internet, but not electronic commerce companies such as Amazon and eBay that sell products or services over the Internet.

Competitive Landscape

Demand is driven by consumer and business demands for information. The profitability of individual companies depends heavily on efficient operations and good marketing, as most costs are fixed. Big ISPs have large economies of scale in operations, purchasing, and marketing. Small companies can compete successfully by serving small markets or providing technical expertise to customers.

Products, Operations & Technology

Major products are Internet access, website design and hosting, and technical support services. Internet access accounts for about 60 percent of industry revenue. Internet access allows individuals or companies to connect to the Internet over ordinary and special telephone lines, cable, or wireless connections (including satellite). Website hosting allows users to have an address on the Internet (a website) by maintaining files on a specialized computer called a server, while Web design and technical services involve designing and constructing websites, and consulting on various communications and operations issues. Some Internet access companies provide content services, like chat rooms, bulletin boards, and music downloads.

The Internet is a collection of computers (big mainframes or small personal computers)

BUSINESS CHALLENGES

» Competition from Telecom Companies

In view of the growing importance of the Internet to their businesses, many companies bypass ISPs and connect directly to the Internet through the large telecom companies that provide the backbone of the network. In coming years, even small and midsized companies are likely to follow suit. Many customers now have sufficient technology expertise in-house to manage direct connections.

» Large Required Capital Investments

As consumers and businesses use the Internet more and demand more services, ISPs continually have to invest in new equipment. Although prices for computer servers continue to fall, periodic investments require access to large amounts of capital. The need for large capital investments has driven consolidation in the industry.

» Higher E-mail Volume

Business e-mail increases at more than double-digit rates annually, according to Gartner. Such rapid growth puts greater burdens on companies to manage the large volume of mail crossing their servers.

connected by communication lines. By making files on a computer available to others, individuals and companies can communicate with each other. Three major systems operate on the Internet: the e-mail system that allows users to send messages to each other; the file transfer system, called FTP, that allows users to exchange many types of files; and the World Wide Web (by far, the largest part of the Internet), that allows users to see special graphical files called Web pages.

Several special types of computers operate the Internet. Servers (computers with many hard-disk drives), hold most of the information, while routers (computers with rapid processing capabilities) direct information to the correct communications channel. The speed with which customers can gain access to the Internet depends on the bandwidth of their connection. Most consumers using ordinary phone lines can take information off the Internet at a speed of 56 kilobytes per second, which is called narrowband access. DSL phone lines, cable, fiber optic, and satellite links can accommodate speeds from 300 kilobytes per second to more than 10 megabytes per second, which is known as broadband access. Although broadband is rapidly gaining in popularity, a large portion of industry revenue still comes from narrowband dial-up access.

Sales & Marketing

Services are sold differently to consumers, small businesses, and large businesses. Marketing for consumer Internet services is through magazine advertising and direct mail. Because Internet use requires a computer, service companies often target new computer buyers. Most access providers operate in a limited local or regional area. Cable and telephone companies market Internet access to their existing TV or telephone subscribers through direct mail. Business Internet services are marketed through advertising and a sales force, and on the Internet. Because businesses typically want broadband access, they usually contract with the local telephone or cable company. Web hosting is typically marketed on the Internet, since customers need not be local.

Internet access is sold by subscription, with fees charged monthly. Generally speaking, businesses buy fast, expensive access to the Internet, while consumers buy slow, but inexpensive, access. Businesses may pay from $300 to more than $1,000 per month for a high-speed Internet connection, while the monthly charge for an ordinary consumer telephone connection is currently about $20 per month. Internet access over high-speed cable TV lines typically costs $40 per month. Monthly charges for website hosting typically range from $15 to $300 per month, depending on the size and complexity of the website, and the volume of communications it generates. Subscription renewal rates are typically high because Internet access and website hosting are commodity products that are invisible as long as they work properly. Web design and technical services are usually billed at hourly rates.

Human Resources

Employees at ISPs have special technical expertise and are accordingly well-paid, earning 40 percent more than the average US worker. With rapid changes in computer and communi-

cations technology, workers need continuing training. ISPs have an excellent safety record.

Industry Employment Growth

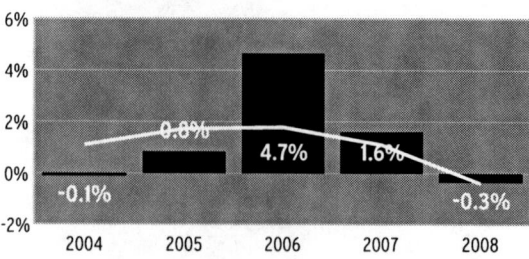

Average Hourly Earnings

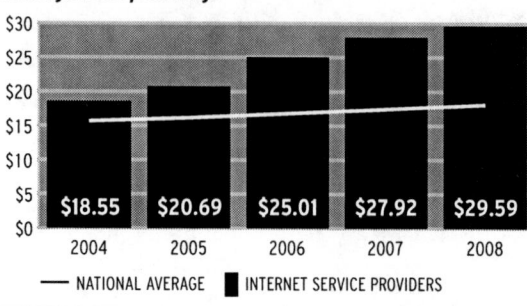

SOURCE: BUREAU OF LABOR STATISTICS

Call Preparation Questions

How does growing competition from large telecom companies affect the company's customer retention rate?

In view of the growing importance of the Internet to their businesses, many companies bypass ISPs and connect directly to the Internet through the large telecom companies that provide the backbone of the network.

What plans does the company have for major equipment purchases near-term?

As consumers and businesses use the Internet more and demand more services, ISPs continually have to invest in new equipment.

How is the company dealing with the increasing volume of emails?

Business e-mail increases at more than double-digit rates annually, according to Gartner.

How would the company be benefited or challenged by entering or starting an Internet data center?

Some service providers have expanded the concept of Web hosting by establishing high-security data centers to house their own and customers' computer servers.

What opportunities does the company see in designing virtual private networks (VPN) for clients?

ISPs can create networks on the Internet that are as secure as private intranets within companies.

Web Links

eMarketer

Find out who's making money on the Web, how much goes toward advertising, and who users are.
www.emarketer.com

Federal Communications Commission

Broadband access issues.
www.fcc.gov

In-Stat

News and information about the Internet industry.
www.instat.com

Internet Society

Good links to sites with statistical information about the Internet and its history.
www.isoc.org

InternetNews – ISP News

Daily news on ISPs.
www.internetnews.com/isp-news

ISP-Planet

News, links, and resources for ISPs.
www.isp-planet.com

Light Reading

Newsmagazine about ISP, telecommunication, and next-generation services. News and policy issues. Good listing of Internet backbone companies.
www.lightreading.com

National Cable & Telecommunications Association

Policy issues related to broadband access. Data on cable Internet access.
www.ncta.com

US Internet Service Provider Association

Reports and media on ISPs.
www.usispa.org

Glossary of Acronyms

DSL — digital subscriber line
FTP — file transfer protocol
VPN — virtual private network
WPA — WiFi protected access

HOOVER'S TOP COMPANIES

Largest Companies by Sales	($ mil.)
AT&T Inc.	124,028.0
Verizon Communications Inc.	97,354.0
Microsoft Corporation	60,420.0
Time Warner Inc.	46,984.0
Comcast Corporation	34,256.0
Qwest Communications International Inc.	13,475.0
Cablevision Systems Corporation	7,230.1
Charter Communications, Inc.	6,479.0
Embarq Corporation	6,124.0
Windstream Corporation	3,171.5

Largest Employers	Employees
AT&T Inc.	310,000
Verizon Communications Inc.	235,000
Comcast Corporation	100,000
Microsoft Corporation	91,000
Time Warner Inc.	86,400
Qwest Communications International Inc.	37,000
Cablevision Systems Corporation	22,935
Embarq Corporation	18,000
Charter Communications, Inc.	16,500
Windstream Corporation	7,570

Fastest Growing* by Five-Year Sales Growth	(%)
Telkonet, Inc.	244.6
WPCS International Incorporated	79.8
Windstream Corporation	58.1
NeuStar, Inc.	34.3
Cogent Communications Group, Inc.	29.4
j2 Global Communications, Inc.	27.5
AT&T Inc.	24.9
180 Connect Inc.	16.3
LodgeNet Interactive Corporation	15.6
Comcast Corporation	13.3

Fastest Growing* by Five-Year Employee Growth	(%)
WPCS International Incorporated	46.1
NeuStar, Inc.	32.5
AT&T Inc.	28.1
j2 Global Communications, Inc.	23.7
Cogent Communications Group, Inc.	12.6
LodgeNet Interactive Corporation	12.6
Microsoft Corporation	10.6
Internap Network Services Corporation	5.7
Mediacom Communications Corporation	3.8
United Online, Inc.	1.5

Top Public Companies by Market Value	($ mil.)
Microsoft Corporation	251,744.0
AT&T Inc.	167,950.8
Verizon Communications Inc.	100,602.0
Time Warner Inc.	36,095.3
Comcast Corporation	34,789.4

* These rates are compounded annualized increases and may have resulted from acquisitions or one time gains. If less than 6 years of data are available, growth is for the years available.

SOURCE: HOOVER'S, INC., DATABASE

Investment Banking

THIS INDUSTRY
INCLUDES:

SIC CODES
6211   Security Brokers,
        Dealers, and
        Flotation
        Companies

NAICS CODES
52311   Investment
        Banking and
        Securities Dealing

The investment banking industry in the US is comprised of fewer than 2,000 companies, with combined annual revenue of about $110 billion. Major companies include Morgan Stanley and Goldman Sachs. Investment banking is heavily concentrated: the largest 50 firms hold 90 percent of the market.

Competitive Landscape

Demand is driven by economic activity that results in company mergers, acquisitions, or public financing. The profitability of an investment bank depends on its ability to accurately assess both the value of a business transaction and the readiness of the market to buy the attendant debt or equity. Big firms have an advantage because large customer transactions require firms with substantial financial resources. Small investment banks can compete by participating in syndications and operating in regional markets or specialized industries. Although labor-intensive, the industry produces very high value: average annual revenue per employee at large firms is close to $1 million.

Products, Operations & Technology

The primary revenue sources of the investment banking industry are from placing new debt and equity issues with public and private investors, and the fees associated with M&As. Investment banks also buy new debt and equity issues for their own accounts, acting as the market "maker," and actively trade other financial instruments. Most investment banks are active securities and currency traders and provide asset management services for wealthy clients and retirement and investment funds. Of industry revenue, 30 percent comes from M&A fees and associated stock transactions; 15 percent from helping corporations and governments issue bonds; 20 percent from active trading in financial instruments; and 10 percent from interest income.

BUSINESS CHALLENGES

» Revenue Depends on Volume of Economic Activity

Investment banking activity, along with the US economy, is cyclical and volatile. For example, during the last recession, revenues of the four largest investment banks fell 25 percent and profits almost 40 percent. As the economy shows strong growth, investment bank revenues and profits generally outpace the economy.

» Regulatory Oversight and Litigation Intensify

Regulatory oversight of investment banking has intensified. Investment bankers are likely targets of litigation due to stricter federal sentencing guidelines, larger financial penalties, and greater public awareness. Three areas in particular have attracted attention: manipulation of "hot" IPO prices, biased research, and insufficient risk assessment or disclosure.

» Dependence on Market Volatility

Market fluctuations and volatility may adversely affect the value of banks' interest rate and credit products, currency, commodity, and equity positions, and the institutions' merchant banking investments. Conversely, certain trading businesses depend on market volatility to provide trading and arbitrage opportunities, and decreases in volatility may reduce these and adversely affect the results of these businesses.

The industry assembles and supplies the capital required by businesses to expand, merge, and acquire other businesses. Investment banks are intermediaries between corporations issuing new debt and equity securities and investors that buy the securities. An investment bank underwrites new securities by buying them from the issuing company at a negotiated price, then reselling them to its investor base, other investment banks, and the investing public. It may act as the maker of the market for the new securities, facilitating trades between buyers and sellers. Investment banks perform a variety of other financial services, such as M&A advice and market analysis.

The major investment banks have a research staff that performs the risk, economic, and financial analysis used to support internal operations, from acquisitions and mergers to formulating trading positions in world, US, and regional markets. The profitability of an investment bank is directly related to the quality of its research analysis. Big investment banks employ a large number of salespeople, analysts, and traders in a network of offices, and may operate a trading "floor." Smaller banks operate out of regular offices. Labor is the chief operating expense.

Investment banks use cutting-edge communication and computing technology to support their operations. Dedicated, fully redundant, high-speed networks interconnect all major offices (domestic and foreign). Computing facilities and critical data are distributed among operations and backup sites. Backup facilities can be placed in service automatically in real-time without loss of data. Within a few days of 9/11, trading and support operations resumed when the markets reopened using backup facilities without loss of customer data.

Sales & Marketing

Investment banking is largely a matter of developing relationships with potential buyers of new securities and with corporations or governments that want to issue new securities or acquire other companies. Investment bank sales staffs develop relationships with corporate finance departments in target industries to promote their services for facilitating mergers and acquisitions and acquiring capital. Other salespeople develop relationships with individual investors. Institutional salespeople develop business relationships with large institutional investors, such as money managers, pension fund managers, or mutual fund companies. Private client service representatives provide brokerage and money management services for high-wealth individuals. Salespeople make money through commissions on trades made through their firm.

Because investment banking fees are fairly standard throughout the industry, banks rely heavily on their reputation of effectiveness to attract customers, and accordingly advertise their role in securities issuances and acquisition or merger "deals." Fees are often negotiated according to the size of a deal and the share price that the investment banker can get from investors. Fees of 0.5 to 1 percent of the transaction size are common.

Human Resources

Investment banks compete vigorously for the top graduates of business, finance, economics, and legal schools. Average starting compensation for MBAs from top 10 business schools average about $145,000 per year. Average employee income in investment banks is about $220,000 per year. While compensation in the industry is high, the pressure to perform is intense, resulting in high turnover.

Call Preparation Questions

How cyclical is the firm's business?

Investment banking activity, along with the US economy, is cyclical and volatile.

How does the firm ensure regulatory compliance?

Regulatory oversight of investment banking has intensified.

How does market volatility affect the firm?

Market fluctuations and volatility may adversely affect the value of banks' interest rate and credit products, currency, commodity, and equity positions, and the institutions' merchant banking investments.

How much of an overseas presence does the firm have?

While competition for business in the US and Europe is intense, major investment banks are looking to expand into underserved foreign markets.

What types of bankruptcy advice does the firm provide?

A new bankruptcy law, expected to remove many restrictions prohibiting investment banks from acting as advisors during bankruptcies, will allow banks to leverage their industry research staff to help companies reorganize under bankruptcy rules.

Web Links

American Bankers Association

News, economic indicators, and events.
www.aba.com

BizJournals

Investment banking news.
www.bizjournals.com/industries/industries/
banking_financial_services/investment_banking

BVMarketData

Contains a variety of databases offering financial and transactional data relating to the sales of public and privately held companies, control premiums, minority discounts, and marketability discounts.
www.bvmarketdata.com

Corporate Financing Week

M&A news. Requires subscription.
www.corporatefinancingweek.com

Financial Industry Regulatory Authority

A private-sector provider of financial regulatory services.
www.finra.org

Forbes Magazine

Industry news.
www.forbes.com

Investor's Business Daily

Industry news.
www.investors.com

Investorwords.com

A complete glossary of investor terms.
www.investorwords.com

New York Stock Exchange

World's leading and most technologically advanced equities market.
www.nyse.com

Red Herring

Investment banking in technology industries.
www.redherring.com

Securities and Exchange Commission

Regulatory issues.
www.sec.gov

The Deal.Com

Investment news. Requires subscription.
www.thedeal.com

Thomson ONE Banker

Delivers critical information and analysis tools for investment banking professionals.
banker.thomsonib.com

Glossary of Acronyms

FINRA — Financial Industry Regulatory Authority
IPO — initial public offering
M&A — mergers and acquisitions
NASD (NOW FINRA) — National Association of Securities Dealers
SEC — Securities and Exchange Commission
SRO — self-regulating organization

HOOVER'S TOP COMPANIES

Largest Companies by Sales	($ mil.)
Morgan Stanley	62,262.0
The Goldman Sachs Group, Inc.	53,579.0
The Charles Schwab Corporation	5,393.0
The Jones Financial Companies, L.L.L.P.	4,146.9
E*TRADE Financial Corporation	3,323.0
Raymond James Financial, Inc.	3,204.9
TD AMERITRADE Holding Corporation	2,787.0
LPL Investment Holdings Inc.	2,717.6
Credit Suisse (USA), Inc.	—
UBS Investment Bank	—

Largest Employers	Employees
Morgan Stanley	46,964
The Jones Financial Companies, L.L.L.P.	38,100
The Goldman Sachs Group, Inc.	30,067
UBS Investment Bank	17,000
The Charles Schwab Corporation	13,300
Credit Suisse (USA), Inc.	10,899
Raymond James Financial, Inc.	6,900
TD AMERITRADE Holding Corporation	3,882
E*TRADE Financial Corporation	3,800
Stifel Financial Corp.	2,834

Fastest Growing* by Five-Year Sales Growth	(%)
Duff & Phelps Corporation	89.3
Merriman Curhan Ford Group, Inc.	68.3
International Assets Holding Corporation	63.5
Evercore Partners Inc.	54.2
Liquidnet Holdings, Inc.	46.3
LPL Investment Holdings Inc.	32.9
Stifel Financial Corp.	32.0
GFI Group Inc.	31.0
Paulson Capital Corp.	30.9
TD AMERITRADE Holding Corporation	30.7

Fastest Growing* by Five-Year Employee Growth	(%)
National Holdings Corporation	62.0
Evercore Partners Inc.	55.5
LPL Investment Holdings Inc.	47.8
International Assets Holding Corporation	42.8
FBR Capital Markets Corporation	40.4
TD AMERITRADE Holding Corporation	37.5
Merriman Curhan Ford Group, Inc.	37.0
Stifel Financial Corp.	25.0
GFI Group Inc.	22.6
Greenhill & Co, Inc.	19.0

Top Public Companies by Market Value	($ mil.)
The Goldman Sachs Group, Inc.	34,956.0
The Charles Schwab Corporation	18,710.3
Morgan Stanley	15,452.1
TD AMERITRADE Holding Corporation	9,887.5
Raymond James Financial, Inc.	3,965.9

* These rates are compounded annualized increases and may have resulted from acquisitions or one time gains. If less than 6 years of data are available, growth is for the years available.

SOURCE: HOOVER'S, INC., DATABASE

Janitorial Services and Carpet Cleaning

The US commercial janitorial industry consists of about 40,000 companies with combined annual revenue of $30 billion. The industry includes divisions of larger service companies like ServiceMaster, ABM Industries, and UNICCO. Only 150 companies have annual revenue over $10 million. The industry is highly fragmented: the 50 largest companies control less than 30 percent of the market. A large local operation may have 100 employees and annual revenue of $3 million, but most companies are smaller.

Competitive Landscape

The level of commercial business activity and income growth drive demand for cleaning services. The profitability of individual companies depends on good marketing. Large companies have an advantage in serving large customers. Small companies can compete effectively in local markets, especially for small business and residential customers. The industry is highly labor-intensive: average annual revenue per employee is only $20,000.

Products, Operations & Technology

Janitorial services include general services of cleaning, trash pickup, floor polishing, and the specialty services of cleaning carpet and ducts and washing windows. Operations consist of crews cleaning buildings and houses by hand or with the help of basic equipment like floor polishers. Operations are highly labor-intensive.

Carpet cleaning firms account for about 10 percent of industry revenue. This work uses specialty equipment and is less labor-intensive than regular janitorial work. Water, steam, and/or various chemicals are injected into a carpet and removed by vacuum along with dirt and stains. Some companies use proprietary application/extraction systems. The rate of customer dissatisfaction with the cleaning results is high. Only a few hundred of the 7,000 firms in this industry segment have annual revenue

BUSINESS CHALLENGES

» Revenue Depends on Business Activity

Demand for commercial cleaning services depends on the amount of office space that businesses occupy, which varies according to the health of the economy. During the last recession, office vacancy rates in some markets exceeded 20 percent. Demand for residential cleaning services is linked to income growth; during economic downturns, consumers cut cleaning services.

» Dependence on Low-Cost Labor

Due to the relatively low prices that cleaning companies can charge, they depend on a supply of low-cost workers. With average annual revenue of just $20,000 per worker, companies must pay low wages. Because of poor working conditions and low wages, personnel turnover is high.

» Competition from Diversified Companies

Large customers are increasingly negotiating multifunction, multisite contracts with large service companies that can provide a full range of services. Janitorial companies usually don't have the range of expertise to compete with diversified companies for such contracts. Bundled services may include electrical and mechanical maintenance, energy management, pest control, security, parking, snow removal, recycling, and grounds maintenance.

over $1 million. In the residential segment, companies like Chem-Dry and Duraclean provide equipment and supplies to small franchise operations.

Sales & Marketing

Industry firms provide services to commercial, industrial and/or residential customers. Companies usually market to commercial companies or building operators through sales visits. Janitorial service companies bid on contracts usually based on an annual fixed-price, with a 30- to 90-day cancellation notice and automatic renewal. Some contracts are cost-plus-fee, which indicate that customers reimburse wages, payroll taxes, insurance charges, and other expenses, plus a stated profit margin. Contracts usually specify a particular cleaning program, with a detailed list and schedule of tasks to perform.

Human Resources

Most janitorial and carpet cleaning workers receive low wages and work a short workweek, because cleaning at businesses must occur after business hours. Pay is low, about 40 percent less than the national average. The industry has an acknowledged problem with illegal immigrants. Companies have the typical problems associated with a workforce that earns minimum wage: high turnover and uneven service quality. Small firms often employ family members and therefore have lower turnover. Due to the low revenue received per worker, only a small amount of supervision is possible: just one supervisor per 25 workers. The industry's safety record is better than average.

Industry Employment Growth

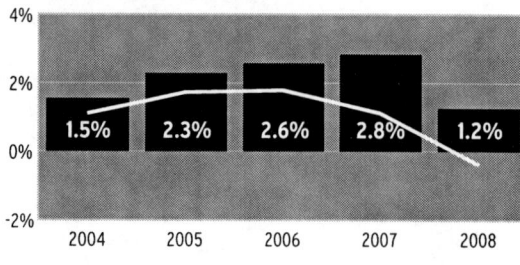

2004	2005	2006	2007	2008
1.5%	2.3%	2.6%	2.8%	1.2%

Average Hourly Earnings

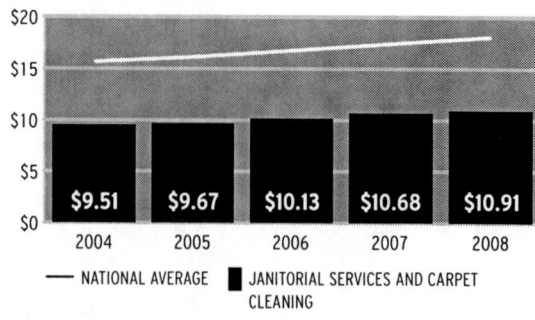

2004	2005	2006	2007	2008
$9.51	$9.67	$10.13	$10.68	$10.91

— NATIONAL AVERAGE   ■ JANITORIAL SERVICES AND CARPET CLEANING

SOURCE: BUREAU OF LABOR STATISTICS

Call Preparation Questions

How have changing economic conditions impacted the company's business?

Demand for commercial cleaning services depends on the amount of office space that businesses occupy, which varies according to the health of the economy.

How does the company find and train enough workers?

Due to the relatively low prices that cleaning companies can charge, they depend on a supply of low-cost workers.

How does the company compete with companies that offer a variety of services, like maintenance or security, in addition to cleaning?

Large customers are increasingly negotiating multifunction, multisite contracts with large service companies that can provide a full range of services.

How successfully has the company won new outsourcing contracts?

Companies that can't afford the time or money to maintain their own maintenance staff are increasingly outsourcing janitorial and other facilities services.

What strategy does the company have to service different types of customer industries?

Companies that provide diversified services can serve a larger variety of customers.

Web Links

ABM Industries

Largest janitorial services company in the US.
www.abm.com/Home

Building Owners & Managers Association

Research and statistics.
www.boma.org

Cleaning & Maintenance Management Online

Industry news.
www.facility-maintenance.com

Cleaning Specialist

Industry news.
www.icsmag.com

International Facilities Management Association

Industry journal.
www.ifma.org

Professional Carpet & Upholstery Cleaning Association

Member information.
www.pcuca.org

Glossary of Acronyms

BRI — building-related illness
IAQ — indoor air quality
SBS — sick building syndrome
SEIU — Service Employees International Union

HOOVER'S TOP COMPANIES

Largest Companies by Sales	($ mil.)
ABM Industries Incorporated	3,623.6
The ServiceMaster Company	3,356.7
JohnsonDiversey, Inc.	3,130.0

Largest Employers	Employees
ABM Industries Incorporated	107,000
The ServiceMaster Company	29,000
UGL Unicco	20,500
JohnsonDiversey, Inc.	11,500
Crothall Services Group, Inc.	11,000
Control Group	6,500
Diversco, Inc.	4,500
Harvard Maintenance, Inc.	3,000
The BMS Enterprises, Inc.	1,700
Stanley Steemer International, Inc.	1,500

Fastest Growing* by Five-Year Sales Growth	(%)
ABM Industries Incorporated	9.9
JohnsonDiversey, Inc.	7.3

Fastest Growing* by Five-Year Employee Growth	(%)
ABM Industries Incorporated	21.1

Top Public Companies by Market Value	($ mil.)
ABM Industries Incorporated	832.2

* These rates are compounded annualized increases and may have resulted from acquisitions or one time gains. If less than 6 years of data are available, growth is for the years available.

SOURCE: HOOVER'S, INC., DATABASE

Jewelry Manufacturing

The US jewelry manufacturing industry includes about 1,900 companies with combined annual revenue of over $6 billion. Major companies include Tiffany, Zale, and Richline Group (Aurafin and Bel-Oro International). The industry is concentrated: the 50 largest firms account for 60 percent of industry revenue. However, nearly two-thirds of companies have fewer than five employees.

The industry includes companies primarily engaged in manufacturing, engraving, chasing, or etching jewelry and personal goods, such as compacts or cigarette cases, and stamping coins. Products are made with precious metal solid or precious metal clad jewelry, and can be with or without stones.

Competitive Landscape

Demand for jewelry is driven by personal income and world gold and silver prices. The profitability of individual companies depends on efficient operations and cost controls. Large companies have advantages in offering a broader product line to meet consumers' changing desires, and in efficient production and distribution operations. Small companies can compete effectively by offering individualized and unique product lines. Average annual revenue per worker for a typical large company is over $200,000.

Products, Operations & Technology

Major products are gold and platinum jewelry (70 percent of industry revenue); silver jewelry (10 percent); and other jewelry, including other metal types, precious stones, and pearls (11 percent). In addition to jewelry, personal goods products, such as cigarette cases and lighters, vanity cases and compacts; trimmings for umbrellas and canes; and jewel settings and mountings are included.

Jewelry products have traditionally been unbranded. The basic manufacturing steps are de-

BUSINESS CHALLENGES

» Dependence on Personal Income

Jewelry sales are strongly tied to the health of the US economy, particularly changes in disposable personal income. Jewelry is a luxury item and consumers often postpone purchases or trade down to less expensive items during difficult economic times. During the 2002 recession, US jewelry manufacturing employment fell 16 percent.

» Volatile Raw Materials Pricing

Raw materials comprise about 57 percent of jewelry revenues. The most important raw material, representing nearly one-third of total materials, is precious metal. Prices for precious metals, including gold, platinum, silver, and other metals, have been volatile in recent years. Gold ore prices have nearly doubled in the last five years. Soaring metal prices pressure manufacturing margins.

» Import Competition

Imports, which continue to represent a larger percentage of the total jewelry market in the US, are 50 percent higher than domestic production. Over the past five years, imports have grown over 50 percent, while domestic production has been flat or slightly declining. Competition from imports has been particularly difficult for manufacturers of lower cost jewelry sold through mass merchandisers.

signing, molding, casting, polishing, finishing, and plating. Most jewelry is produced by casting machines. After the design is finalized, a high technology mold is used to make a wax reproduction of the jewelry. The master mold, with all of the fine details, sets the base for the total manufacturing process. Molding and casting are complex processes that require high levels of skill and experience. Significant hazardous waste is produced in the polishing, cleaning, and stripping steps.

The largest raw material is precious metal, such as gold or platinum, representing 32 percent of inputs. Precious, semi-precious, and synthetic stones and pearls represent 22 percent. These raw materials are bought primarily from the mining industry. Gold, silver, platinum, and palladium are all readily available and come in many forms such as bars, ingots, sheets, strips, solders, platings, and electrodes. Precious stones, such as diamonds, can be in short supply due to political conditions in producing countries and trade regulations. Diamond supply is controlled by the Diamond Trading Company, which is a part of De Beers of South Africa. Manufacturers buy directly from De Beers.

Gold is an ideal raw material for jewelry as it doesn't corrode, rust, or tarnish and, although it's strong, it's also the most malleable of all metals. Platinum is relatively rare and more valuable than gold. Platinum's popularity is driven by its durability and attractive silver-white color. Platinum is heavy and is offered in purer form than gold. Silver is also popular, with its bright and durable characteristics, but isn't as popular as gold and platinum because it does tarnish and lose its shininess. Ten-karat gold has become an increasingly popular alternative to 14-karat due to its greater durability and lower price.

Technology is a critical component of product design and manufacturing. CAD software is used to create virtual models of new jewelry pieces. Process control systems automate steps in mold- and model-making.

Sales & Marketing

Typical customers are jewelry retailers, including specialty, department, discount stores and mass merchants, as well as jewelry wholesalers. The largest jewelry retailers include Tiffany, Zale, and Sterling Jewelers.

Since jewelry often isn't branded and therefore difficult for consumers to evaluate, most manufacturers don't focus on consumer marketing. Nearly all manufacturers attend key trade shows, such as the yearly JCK (Jewelers Circular Keystone) Las Vegas Show, to sell to retailers and wholesalers. The trade show is a comprehensive jewelry gathering, bringing domestic and international jewelry buyers and retailers together.

With the onset of Web-based jewelers, shoppers now have the power to research, select, personalize, and pay for an expensive piece of jewelry online. Internet companies like Blue Nile and Bidz.com make buying jewelry online easier.

Product prices are impacted by changes in raw material costs. High material costs have led

manufacturers to move toward mixed metals to offer products at lower price points. Product quality is identified on the piece with appropriate markings to assure authenticity.

Human Resources

Both low skilled workers, such as assemblers and polishers, and highly trained creative workers, such as mold- and model-makers, are required. Jewelers usually learn their trade in vocational or technical schools and then develop their skills through informal apprenticeships and on-the-job training. Average industry wages are 11 percent below the average for all US production workers.

Since jewelry manufacturing has strict safety guidelines and has become highly automated, total injury rates are about half those for all US manufacturing.

Industry Employment Growth

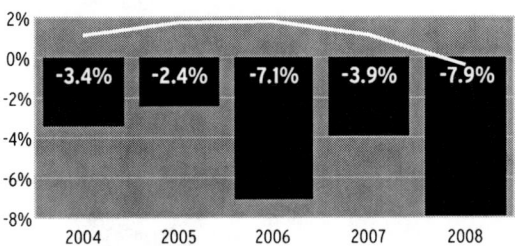

Average Hourly Earnings

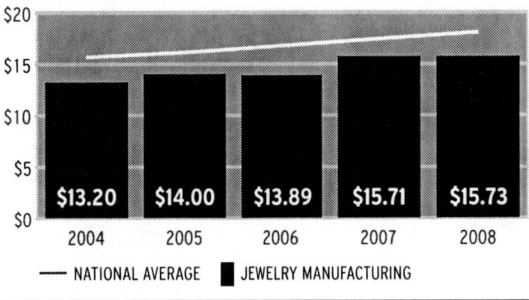

SOURCE: BUREAU OF LABOR STATISTICS

Call Preparation Questions

What trend is the company seeing in consumer demand for its products?

Jewelry sales are strongly tied to the health of the US economy, particularly changes in disposable personal income.

What trend is the company seeing in raw material costs?

Raw materials comprise about 57 percent of jewelry revenues.

How have jewelry imports affected the company's business?

Imports, which continue to represent a larger percentage of the total jewelry market in the US, are 50 percent higher than domestic production.

What new channels of distribution has the company developed?

Jewelry-selling parties offer a comfortable environment for women to try on jewelry.

How has the company differentiated its products?

Jewelry companies begin to focus on building brand names to differentiate themselves, maintain higher price points, and drive sales.

Web Links

American Gem Trade Association

Primary association for gemstone category. www.agta.org

Fair Trade Jewelry

Articles, news and regulations. www.fairjewelry.org

Jewelry Facts

News, articles, and industry facts. www.jewelryfacts.net

Jewelry Retailers Association

National association for the retail jeweler. www.jewelers.org

Manufacturing Jewelers and Suppliers of America Journal

Major industry trade association journal. www.mjsajournal.org/ntm.php

Perl Auction

News and articles about jewelry and diamonds. www.perlauction.com

Tiffany and Company

Company website. www.tiffany.com/International.aspx

Zale Corporation

Company website. http://www.zalecorp.com/brands/brands2.aspx?pid=9

Glossary of Acronyms

CAD — computer-aided design
CAM — computer-aided manufacturing
DTC — Diamond Trading Company
JCK — Jewelers Circular Keystone
WJA — Womens Jewelers Association

HOOVER'S TOP COMPANIES

Largest Companies by Sales	($ mil.)
Tiffany & Co.	2,938.8
Zale Corporation	2,138.0
Visant Holding Corp.	1,270.2
Herff Jones Company of Indiana, Inc.	532.9
James Avery Craftsman, Inc.	80.0

Largest Employers	Employees
Zale Corporation	15,500
Tiffany & Co.	8,800
Visant Holding Corp.	5,691
Herff Jones Company of Indiana, Inc.	3,000
Andin International, Inc.	1,500
James Avery Craftsman, Inc.	1,000
Michael Anthony Jewelers, Inc.	450
The Aaron Group, LLC	300
Yurman Design, Inc.	200

Fastest Growing* by Five-Year Sales Growth	(%)
Tiffany & Co.	11.5
Visant Holding Corp.	7.0

Fastest Growing* by Five-Year Employee Growth	(%)
Visant Holding Corp.	11.7
Tiffany & Co.	6.5

Top Public Companies by Market Value	($ mil.)
Tiffany & Co.	5,043.5
Zale Corporation	699.3

* These rates are compounded annualized increases and may have resulted from acquisitions or one time gains. If less than 6 years of data are available, growth is for the years available.

SOURCE: HOOVER'S, INC., DATABASE

Jewelry Retail

THIS INDUSTRY INCLUDES:

SIC CODES
5944   Jewelry Stores

NAICS CODES
44831   Jewelry Stores

The US jewelry retail industry generates annual revenues of about $25 billion from 30,000 specialty stores. Large companies include Zale, Tiffany, and Sterling Jewelers. The industry is fragmented: the top 50 jewelry chains hold less than half of the market.

Competitive Landscape

Jewelry sales depend partly on consumer income. Small jewelers can effectively compete with large chains because price isn't the main factor determining sales. Profitability depends on merchandising and effective marketing. Average industry revenue per worker is about $160,000.

Jewelry is also sold in department and discount stores, and by mass merchants. Because regular gross margins are very high, often 50 percent, mass merchants have been able to cut prices and take market share. Wal-Mart is the largest jewelry retailer in the US.

Products, Operations & Technology

Jewelry is often classified as bridal merchandise (engagement, bridal and anniversary rings — about 35 percent of the market); fashion jewelry (rings, bracelets, earrings, pins, gold chains); and watches, silver flatware, and other giftware. Diamond jewelry and loose diamonds account for the largest share of total jewelry store sales (46 percent); gold jewelry for 11 percent; colored gemstone jewelry (rubies, sapphires, emeralds, etc.) 9 percent; and watches 4 percent.

Jewelry is expensive, intimidating, difficult for consumers to evaluate, and usually not branded. Purchases therefore require a good deal of service and expertise. Consumers are most likely to buy jewelry from a merchant they feel is trustworthy: either a well-known local jeweler or a retailer such as Tiffany.

Jewelers' operations consist of buying jewelry from manufacturers and wholesalers, train-

BUSINESS CHALLENGES

» Sales Tied to Economic Growth

Jewelry sales are tied to the health of the US economy, particularly changes in disposable personal income and consumer confidence. Sales of expensive jewelry, especially, depend on good economic growth. For example, during the last recession, jewelry store sales dropped 5 percent.

» Competition from Mass Merchants

Specialty jewelry stores continue to lose market share to mass merchants like Wal-Mart. Specialty stores account for only about half of all jewelry sales in the US. The share sold by traditional department stores has also been declining.

» Influence of DeBeers

The world diamond supply and pricing are strongly affected by DeBeers, the South African group, which controls 65 percent of the world's rough diamond supply. However, DeBeers faces increased competition from Canada, Australia, Angola, and Russia, and has encountered legal obstacles in the US and the EU because of its business practices.

ing sales staff, and marketing products through various channels. Many jewelers also operate repair services, which can account for 10 percent of annual revenue. Company buyers must be both technically skilled and aware of fashion trends. Most retailers buy merchandise fully finished from many different manufacturers. Some retailers also create pieces themselves. Tiffany manufactures about 30 percent of its jewelry, and has licensing arrangements with several jewelry designers who sell their designs only through the company. Retailers also sell merchandise on consignment from manufacturers.

Sales & Marketing

Selling costs are high for jewelry retailers, who generally wish to project an upscale image, because high quality sales space, furnishings, and expert sales personnel are expensive.

Marketing is typically through newspaper and magazine advertising, although some retailers also use direct mailing, and is typically directed at a particular demographic group. Whitehall, for example, targets middle- and upper-middle-income women over 25.

Larger companies like Zale Corporation operate several chains that target different shoppers. The average sales price of an item is less than $200 at its Peoples Jewelers chain and close to $1,000 at its Bailey Banks & Biddle chain.

Human Resources

Employees of higher-priced jewelry stores usually require special training and may be bonded for security reasons. Because of the special expertise required, most workers at high-end stores are full-time. Salespeople often work on commission. Typical hourly wages are below the national average. Retail jewelry stores have an exceptionally good safety record.

Industry Employment Growth

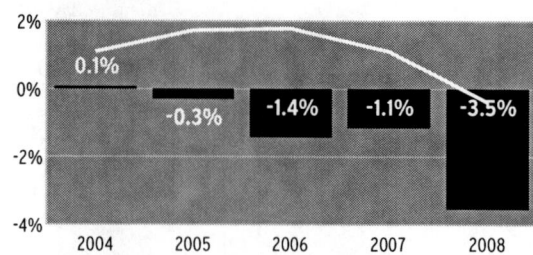

Average Hourly Earnings

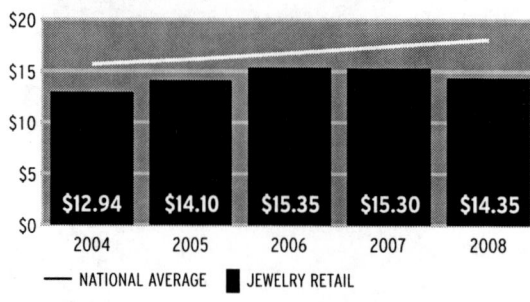

SOURCE: BUREAU OF LABOR STATISTICS

Call Preparation Questions

How does the company manage changes in the economy and consumer spending?

Jewelry sales are tied to the health of the US economy, particularly changes in disposable personal income and consumer confidence.

How will the jeweler compete against big-box retailers like Wal-Mart?

Specialty jewelry stores continue to lose market share to mass merchants like Wal-Mart.

How reliant is the company on its suppliers?

The world diamond supply and pricing are strongly affected by DeBeers, the South African group, which controls 65 percent of the world's rough diamond supply.

Does a third party handle extending credit or does the company manage credit risk itself?

Jewelers offering private credit cards have targeted promotional materials to customers to enhance connection with the store; some have also been able to sell other types of merchandise to them.

How successful is the company's Internet strategy?

Luxury jewelry giant Tiffany and many other jewelers have set up websites to sell a limited amount of jewelry.

Web Links

American Gem Society

Education in diamond grading.
www.americangemsociety.org

Gemological Institute of America

Education about precious stones.
www.gia.edu

Jewelers Circular Keystone

Primary industry magazine; industry news; list of associations; trade fair calendar.
www.jckonline.com/jckgroup

Kitco

Precious metal and jewelry news, charts, and pricing.
www.kitco.com

Modern Jeweler

News.
www.modernjeweler.com

Professional Jeweler Magazine

News, articles, search engines, statistics, and more.
www.professionaljeweler.com

Glossary of Acronyms

DTC — Diamond Trading Company
POS — point-of-sale
WGC — World Gold Council

HOOVER'S TOP COMPANIES

Largest Companies by Sales	($ mil.)
Tiffany & Co.	2,938.8
Zale Corporation	2,138.0
Finlay Enterprises, Inc.	835.9
ValueVision Media, Inc.	781.5
Helzberg Diamonds	479.7
Blue Nile, Inc.	295.3
Fred Meyer Jewelers Inc.	259.0
Bidz.com, Inc.	207.4

Largest Employers	Employees
Tiffany & Co.	8,800
Fred Meyer Jewelers Inc.	3,000
Helzberg Diamonds	2,500
Bidz.com, Inc.	240
Blue Nile, Inc.	198

Fastest Growing* by Five-Year Sales Growth	(%)
Bidz.com, Inc.	34.2
DGSE Companies, Inc.	23.4
Blue Nile, Inc.	18.0
Tiffany & Co.	11.5
ValueVision Media, Inc.	7.1

Fastest Growing* by Five-Year Employee Growth	(%)
Bidz.com, Inc.	18.8
Blue Nile, Inc.	16.5
ValueVision Media, Inc.	9.7
Tiffany & Co.	6.5
DGSE Companies, Inc.	4.5

Top Public Companies by Market Value	($ mil.)
Tiffany & Co.	5,043.5
Zale Corporation	699.3
Blue Nile, Inc.	360.2
ValueVision Media, Inc.	208.9
Bidz.com, Inc.	105.4

* These rates are compounded annualized increases and may have resulted from acquisitions or one time gains. If less than 6 years of data are available, growth is for the years available.

SOURCE: HOOVER'S, INC., DATABASE

Kidney Dialysis Centers

THIS INDUSTRY INCLUDES:

SIC CODES
8092   Kidney Dialysis
        Centers

NAICS CODES
621492 Kidney Dialysis
        Centers

The commercial kidney dialysis industry includes about 3,200 dialysis centers with combined annual revenue of $10 billion. Large companies include Fresenius Medical Care, DaVita, and Diversified Specialty Institutes. The industry has become highly concentrated: the four largest companies operate more than 70 percent of all centers. A typical kidney dialysis center has 20 employees and $3 million of annual revenue.

Competitive Landscape

Demand depends on the number of people who suffer from kidney disease. The profitability of individual companies is linked to efficient operations and good marketing. Large companies have economies of scale in administrative costs, which has driven consolidation in the industry. Small operators can compete successfully if they have centers in desirable locations or good relations with doctors who refer patients. The industry is moderately labor-intensive: average annual revenue per worker is about $140,000.

Over 300,000 patients use dialysis centers in the US, a number expected to grow 4 to 5 percent per year. In addition to the 3,200 commercial dialysis centers, about 1,000 are operated by hospitals and nonprofit organizations.

Products, Operations & Technology

The industry provides a special treatment called hemodialysis for patients who suffer from end stage renal disease (ESRD). Hemodialysis, the most common form of treatment for ESRD, is not a cure but a blood-filtering process that prolongs life. ESRD patients must undergo dialysis for the rest of their lives. Without dialysis treatment or a kidney transplant, ESRD is a terminal disease. Less than 5 percent of patients receive a kidney transplant, because of the scarcity of donors. Diabetes and high blood pressure are the top two causes of kidney dis-

BUSINESS CHALLENGES

» Dependence on Insurer Reimbursement Rates

Medicare, which has a fixed reimbursement rate for dialysis treatment, provides the majority of revenue for most kidney dialysis centers. Because private insurers often peg their own reimbursements to the Medicare rate, revenue per patient for dialysis centers is effectively set by the government. Inflation-adjusted reimbursement rates for dialysis have fallen in the past decade.

» Operating Costs Continue Rise

Operating costs for dialysis centers rise faster than revenues. Government mandates on staffing levels and quality control measures have limited opportunities for cost-cutting through staff reductions. A shortage of nurses has pushed up labor costs. Average wages in outpatient care centers rose 25 percent from 2000 to 2005.

» Competition from Hospitals

Many hospitals have upgraded their dialysis facilities to recapture lost revenue. Independent kidney dialysis centers grew rapidly as an alternative to hospital facilities that were inefficient and inconvenient. However, now some hospitals operate free-standing dialysis centers in addition to in-house centers, in competition with commercial centers.

ease; diabetes alone accounts for over a third of all new cases.

The hemodialysis process involves passing a patient's blood through a machine that includes pumps; monitors; a dialysis filter (dialyzer); and various chemical solutions to remove toxins, fluids, and chemicals. The treatment process lasts three to five hours and patients require treatment three times per week. Machines are made by several companies, including Baxter, DaVita, and Fresenius. Dialysis filters cost about $20 each.

A typical dialysis center provides 30 to 50 treatments per day, using 15 to 20 "stations." Center operations involve acquiring and maintaining dialysis machines and other equipment, managing staff, scheduling appointments, providing treatments, and billing. Although larger centers would be more efficient, the size of centers is limited by the distance patients can reasonably travel to get there. A new center can cost more than $1 million to build and equip. In addition to dialysis treatments, centers may provide lab testing services, support for home dialysis, in-hospital dialysis services for acutely sick patients, and infusion services for drugs such as erythropoietin (EPO). Some companies also manage in-hospital centers for a fee.

The technology of hemodialysis is well-known, although the effectiveness of the process has been improved with better filters and dialysis chemicals. An alternative to hemodialysis is "peritoneal dialysis," which spreads chemicals through the abdomen. Kidney transplantation, the only current cure for ESRD, is becoming more effective but is limited by the availability of suitable donor kidneys.

Sales & Marketing

The primary source of patients for a particular center is referrals from doctors, especially those who specialize in treating kidney disease (nephrologists). Most doctors prefer to have their patients treated at centers where they or other members of their practice can supervise the care. The industry advertises little, if at all.

Dialysis centers market their services to physician groups, hospitals, and managed-care companies. A large percentage of patients may come from just a few doctors. Large chains often hire a nephrologist to be medical director of a local dialysis center, with the expectation that many of the doctor's patients will be treated at the center. Many independent centers are owned by doctors who use them to treat their patients.

Human Resources

A qualified physician or group of physicians must act as medical director for each center. Each center must have an administrator to manage each center, typically a registered nurse

(RN). The staff includes other RNs, licensed practical or vocational nurses, technicians, social workers, dietitians, biomedical equipment technicians, and clerical staff. The ratio of nurse to patients is about 1:4. Due to the specialized and highly trained staff, wages are about 25 percent higher than the average for all US workers. The safety record of the industry is better than average.

Industry Employment Growth

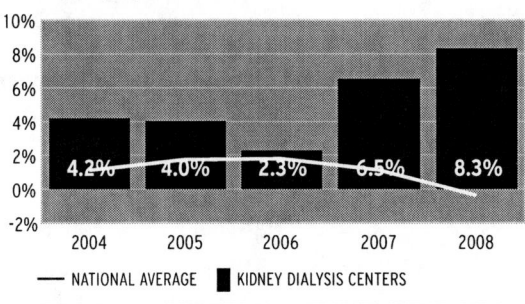

— NATIONAL AVERAGE ■ KIDNEY DIALYSIS CENTERS

SOURCE: BUREAU OF LABOR STATISTICS

Call Preparation Questions

How dependent is the company on Medicare reimbursement rates?

Medicare, which has a fixed reimbursement rate for dialysis treatment, provides the majority of revenue for most kidney dialysis centers.

How does the company manage rising operational costs?

Operating costs for dialysis centers rise faster than revenues.

What steps has the company taken to counteract increased competition from hospitals?

Many hospitals have upgraded their dialysis facilities to recapture lost revenue.

How is the company positioning itself for the expected growth in demand?

The market for dialysis treatment is expected to grow 5 percent per year, as higher rates of diabetes and high blood pressure produce more end-stage renal disease (ESRD).

How important is managing in-hospital centers to the company?

Because of their expertise in managing efficient dialysis centers, commercial companies sometimes have contracts to manage in-hospital dialysis centers.

Web Links

American Society of Nephrology

Industry news, information, links.
www.asn-online.org

Centers for Medicare & Medicaid Services – ESRD

Medicare regulations and programs about ESRD.
www.cms.hhs.gov/ESRDGeneralInformation

National Kidney and Urologic Diseases Information Clearinghouse

Excellent explanation of dialysis treatment and how it works.
kidney.niddk.nih.gov

National Kidney Foundation

News about dialysis and industry.
www.kidney.org/news/newsroom

National Renal Administrators Association

Legislation and links.
www.nraa.org

Renal Physicians Association

Issues for nephrologists.
renalmd.org

The Kidney Foundation of Canada

Canadian information.
www.kidney.ca

US Renal Data System

Excellent patient and industry statistics in annual reports.
www.usrds.org

Glossary of Acronyms

CKD — chronic kidney disease
CMS — Centers for Medicare & Medicaid Services
EPO — erythropoietin
ESRD — end-stage renal disease
HIPAA — Health Insurance Portability and Accountability Act

HOOVER'S TOP COMPANIES

Largest Companies by Sales	($ mil.)
Fresenius Medical Care	6,663.0
DaVita Inc.	5,660.2
Dialysis Clinic, Inc.	583.3
Dialysis Corporation of America	86.8
Renal Advantage Inc.	12.5

Largest Employers	Employees
DaVita Inc.	31,000
Dialysis Clinic, Inc.	5,000
Dialysis Corporation of America	653
Renal Advantage Inc.	165

Fastest Growing* by Five-Year Sales Growth	(%)
Dialysis Corporation of America	23.4
DaVita Inc.	22.9

Fastest Growing* by Five-Year Employee Growth	(%)
Dialysis Corporation of America	22.2
DaVita Inc.	5.2

Top Public Companies by Market Value	($ mil.)
DaVita Inc.	5,143.1
Dialysis Corporation of America	67.1

* These rates are compounded annualized increases and may have resulted from acquisitions or one time gains. If less than 6 years of data are available, growth is for the years available.

SOURCE: HOOVER'S, INC., DATABASE

Labor Unions

THIS INDUSTRY INCLUDES:

SIC CODES

8631   Labor Unions and
        Similar Labor
        Organizations

NAICS CODES

81393   Labor Unions and
        Similar Labor
        Organizations

The labor union industry includes 15,000 organizations; the largest unions have annual revenue between $100 and $300 million. Major organizations include the American Federation of Labor and Congress of Industrial Organizations (AFL-CIO); the National Education Association; the Service Employees International Union; and the National Association of Letter Carriers.

Competitive Landscape

Business and job growth drive demand. The profitability of individual organizations depends on ability to grow membership. Large unions have stronger bargaining power and advantages in marketing and finance. Small unions can serve a local market or individuals in specialized industries or professions.

Products, Operations & Technology

The majority of revenue comes from member dues, including fees from individual workers and other unions. Unions may also generate revenue from investment income. Industry sectors with strong union participation include government and education, training, library, and protective services.

National unions may have local, state, regional, or international chapters, also known as affiliates or delegates. Unions may belong to larger unions, such as the American Federation of Labor and Congress of Industrial Organizations (AFL-CIO). An individual union's membership can vary: local chapters may have less than 100 members while national organizations claim millions.

Unions represent groups of workers within common industries or professions. Closed shop employers require union membership of workers, but union membership is optional in open shop employers. Some states have Right-To-Work (RTW) laws, and prohibit union membership as a condition of employment. In RTW

BUSINESS CHALLENGES

» Increasing Employment Costs

Many employers are struggling to cover rising employment costs and demanding more concessions from unions during contract negotiations. Overall employment costs, which include wages and benefits, have grown slightly higher than the rate of inflation, with benefit costs increasing over 30 percent between 2001 and 2007. Because union workers typically earn more than non-union, bargaining for significant increases in compensation can be a challenge. Even concessions considered necessary for a company's survival can anger union membership.

» Membership Depends on Industry Dynamics

As US industries evolve and adapt to increasingly competitive markets, many companies are making fundamental changes that can affect union membership. Automation and technology have replaced many jobs with machines in many union-dominated industries, including auto manufacturing and railroad and postal operations. To cut costs, many corporations in manufacturing and service sectors have moved traditional union jobs to lower wage countries. Mergers by large corporations reduce union negotiating power. Weak industry performance can reduce labor needs and erode a union's membership base. Struggling industries are also likely to resist unions' attempts to organize new chapters.

» Increased Use of Temporary Workers

To reduce costs and increase flexibility, employers are hiring more contractors, freelancers, and temporary workers, thereby reducing the need for unionized labor. As one of the fastest-growing segments of the labor market, temporary workers allow corporations to avoid complicated union relationships and benefit expenses. Without union contracts, employers can freely adapt workforce needs to changes in demand.

states, unions may represent workers without union affiliation.

Unions negotiate with management to establish general employment terms, including fair wages, health benefits, pension plans, safety requirements, job security, and overtime compensation. Contracts may include worker involvement in major corporate policy decisions. Due to collective bargaining, union workers generally earn more than non-union. Unions also enforce contract terms and typically have established grievance procedures for violations. Contracts are generally renegotiated every few years. If unions and management can't agree, the union may order a work stoppage or a strike. Forms of protest include picket lines and boycotts.

Unions also lobby for legislation favorable to the members and industries represented. Unions may endorse politicians and political causes that support membership goals. Many political candidates eagerly pursue union endorsements, as memberships can represent a large number of constituents and provide grassroots campaign support. Unions may have separate political action committees (PACs) to raise and donate funds to favorable political parties.

Unions often dedicate local resources to organizing new chapters. To start a new chapter, interested workers must file a petition to hold a union election with the National Labor Relations Board (NLRB). The petition must have support from at least 30 percent of the workforce. The NLRB conducts elections and, with a majority vote, certifies unions as designated bargaining representatives. Depending on contract terms, unions may administer certain benefits (such as pensions and health insurance plans) typically managed by employers. Some unions offer worker training, education, and certification.

Unions employ labor lawyers and mediators to negotiate contracts and resolve disputes. Other jobs may require expertise in accounting; administrative, health care plan, or pension management; and health and safety procedures.

Unions may use computerized information systems to manage basic accounting and financial data. Database systems track membership information and dues. Unions may collect dues through automatic deduction programs administered through employer payroll systems.

Sales & Marketing

Workers more likely to be union members include men 45 to 64, public sector employees, and African Americans. Membership may include both active or retired members.

Unions may use the Internet to communicate general organization information, including mission statements, constitutions, member benefits, political affiliations, and local chapter contacts. Websites allow unions to post critical information, such as contract negotiation status, faster than traditional methods allow. To solicit membership opinions, unions may conduct Internet surveys. Blogs, chatrooms, and bulletin boards foster communication among members.

Marketing includes newsletters, direct mail, e-mail, and phone calls. Local chapters of large unions may develop grassroots efforts to organize new chapters. Unions may issue reports or press releases to communicate opinions and positions on important membership issues.

Members typically contribute monthly dues based on a percentage or number of hours of pay. Consequently, the gross amount of dues increases as overall pay increases. Members may pay an initiation fee to join.

Human Resources

Unions generally require workers with professional skills. Wages for workers employed by union offices are almost 10 percent higher than the average for all US workers. Jobs may require specialized education or experience in fields such as employment and labor law, government and international affairs, worker health and safety issues, or PR. Unions may dedicate resources to managing Social Security, Medicare, pension, retirement, and health insurance programs. Union representatives typically receive extensive training in negotiation and dispute resolution.

An elected board of officials governs each union chapter and ensures that the organization adheres to a set of rules or a constitution.

Industry Employment Growth

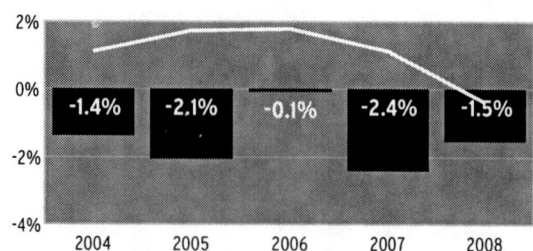

2004	2005	2006	2007	2008
-1.4%	-2.1%	-0.1%	-2.4%	-1.5%

Average Hourly Earnings

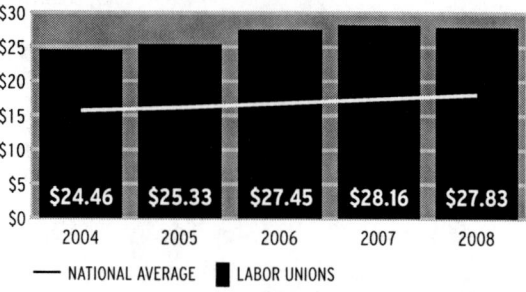

2004	2005	2006	2007	2008
$24.46	$25.33	$27.45	$28.16	$27.83

— NATIONAL AVERAGE ■ LABOR UNIONS

SOURCE: BUREAU OF LABOR STATISTICS

Call Preparation Questions

How have changes in employment costs affected the organization's bargaining position?

Many employers are struggling to cover rising employment costs and demanding more concessions from unions during contract negotiations.

How do industry dynamics affect the organization's membership?

As US industries evolve and adapt to increasingly competitive markets, many companies are making fundamental changes that can affect union membership.

How has the shift to employing more temporary workers affected the organization's membership?

To reduce costs and increase flexibility, employers are hiring more contractors, freelancers, and temporary workers, thereby reducing the need for unionized labor.

How successfully has the organization formed new chapters?

With employment declining in key industries, unions can target workforces in new areas to grow membership.

What partnerships could help the organization grow membership?

By merging with similar organizations or targeting workers in alternative industries, unions can develop bigger, stronger membership bases.

Web Links

Bureau of Labor Statistics

Labor force statistics and Monthly Labor Review publication.
www.bls.gov

Bureau of National Affairs (BNA)

News and statistics (some require purchase).
www.bna.com

Department of Labor

Labor news, trends, statistics, union financial and collective bargaining agreement reports.
www.dol.gov

Labor Notes

News from pro-union non-profit organization.
labornotes.org

National Institute for Labor Relations Research

News and research from anti-union non-profit organization.
www.nilrr.org

National Labor Relations Board

National union statistics and trends, legislative activity, and news from federal governmental agency.
www.nlrb.gov

Glossary of Acronyms

DOL — Department of Labor
NALC — National Association of Letter Carriers
NEA — National Education Association
NLRB — National Labor Relations Board
PAC — political action committee
RTW — right-to-work
SEIU — Service Employees International Union Committee
UAW — The International Union, United Automobile, Aerospace and Agricultural Implement Workers of America

HOOVER'S TOP COMPANIES

Largest Employers	Employees
International Union, UAW	3,000
National Education Association	735
Communications Workers of America	650
International Brotherhood of Teamsters	649
AFL-CIO	480
American Federation of State, County and Municipal Employees, AFL-CIO	450
American Federation of Teachers	320
Screen Actors Guild	294
United Mine Workers of America	250
Writers Guild of America, west, Inc.	160

SOURCE: HOOVER'S, INC., DATABASE

Landscaping Services

The US landscaping services industry includes about 50,000 companies with combined annual revenue of $40 billion. Large companies include the TruGreen Landcare division of ServiceMaster, The Davey Tree Expert Company, The Brickman Group, and Asplundh Tree Expert. The vast majority of companies are small with annual revenue less than $2 million. The industry is highly fragmented: the top 50 companies hold only 15 percent of the market.

Competitive Landscape

Demand is driven partly by construction of new commercial properties and partly by the economy's overall health. Because management and equipment costs are mainly fixed, the profitability of individual companies depends on demand volume and operations' efficiency. Small companies can easily compete with big ones, except in providing services to large customers. Big companies operate mainly through local branches or offices that have operations almost identical to those of local companies. Annual revenue per employee is about $70,000.

Products, Operations & Technology

Landscaping services include commercial and residential landscape maintenance, landscape installation, irrigation systems, tree services, chemical lawn care, and "line-clearing": branch removal around utility lines. Larger companies may offer several of these services, but most provide just one. Landscape installation and maintenance account for the bulk of industry revenue; tree services account for about 30 percent. In winter, many companies provide snow removal services.

For a typical commercial client, a landscape maintenance company might provide mulching, fertilizing, and flower planting in spring; mowing, pruning, irrigation, and fertilizing in summer; and leaf clearing in fall. Services are typically provided weekly by a work

BUSINESS CHALLENGES

» Demand for Landscape Services Tied to Economy

Although basic landscape maintenance like mowing is relatively unaffected by economic cycles, customers pull back on optional services during economic difficulties. Demand for new landscape installations is closely tied to residential and commercial real estate construction, which are cyclical.

» Industry Depends on Cheap Labor

Landscaping depends on a cheap source of seasonal labor. Companies typically retain a core of experienced supervisors throughout the year and hire temporary laborers as demand increases in spring and summer. Immigrants (sometimes illegal) form a large part of the seasonal labor force and are often trained on the job.

» Demand Highly Seasonal

Most landscaping work is done in the second and third quarters. Commercial contracts may provide level monthly revenue but costs are highest in summer. Companies must be able to manage seasonal cash flow and a seasonal labor force. The industry workforce increases about 50 percent between January and June; for companies in cold-weather states, the job swing is even greater.

crew of four to 10, depending on the size of the property. Typical equipment consists of mowers, blowers, spreaders, and trimmers, brought to the site in a trailer (Wells Cargo is a major trailer manufacturer). A large local company may own 10 trucks and trailers, operate six work crews, and service 50 to 100 customers.

Common residential services are mowing, leaf clearing, and chemical lawn care, provided regularly, usually by a one or two person crew with a tanker truck. Tree services such as planting, fertilizing, pruning, and removal require special skills and equipment. Line-clearing is done mainly with bucket (aerial lift) trucks, chain saws, and chippers to shred the removed branches.

Labor is the major expense for most landscape companies. Most workers usually aren't unionized and are paid low wages because of the simple nature of the work. Crew leaders and supervisors are more highly paid because their knowledge is crucial to performing work efficiently. In many parts of the country, a large number of workers are foreigners who work seasonally under H-2B temporary visas. Companies sometimes knowingly or unknowingly hire illegal immigrants. Because of low pay, turnover among workers can be high. Because of the seasonal nature of the work, many companies use a large amount of part-time help. Tree and lawn maintenance work can be dangerous because of the equipment used.

Technology used in the industry is very basic. Trucks, mowers, and blowers are the major pieces of equipment used. Toro is a major equipment manufacturer and supplier. Tree care companies and companies that specialize in line-clearing use trucks with hydraulic lifts. Large cranes may sometimes be needed for pruning or removing large trees, but are typically rented.

Sales & Marketing

Major customers are homeowners and commercial property managers such as building and office park managers, housing associations, businesses, municipalities, colleges, and utilities. About 25 percent of US households use professional landscaping services each year. Maintenance contracts may last for one or several years but are usually cancelable with short notice. Commercial contracts are often won after a bidding process. Because contracts typically specify a fixed annual price, proper cost estimation for a particular job is crucial; large companies use sophisticated computerized cost-estimating programs. Contracts usually cover basic services, while additional work is covered by one-time work orders. In one year, Brickman received one-third of its revenue from work orders; two-thirds from contracts.

The average annual household maintenance contract is close to $600, according to the American Nursery and Landscape Association (ANLA). A typical household landscape installation costs close to $4,000.

Sales are usually handled by senior managers in the off-season. Companies with a large residential clientele may advertise in local newspapers, and use Yellow Pages listings and telemarketers. Some large companies, notably TruGreen, operate in some markets through franchises.

Much sales effort goes into keeping existing customers. In one year, Brickman retained 90 percent of its commercial customers, while TruGreen retained 60 percent of its residential customers.

Human Resources

Because of the relatively low skill required, workers in the industry receive fairly low wages, about 25 percent less than the average US worker. Workers for line-clearing companies at times work in hazardous conditions, but the overall industry illness and injury rate is close to the average for all US workers.

Many seasonal landscaping workers from other countries (mainly Mexico) are able to enter the US on H-2B visas.

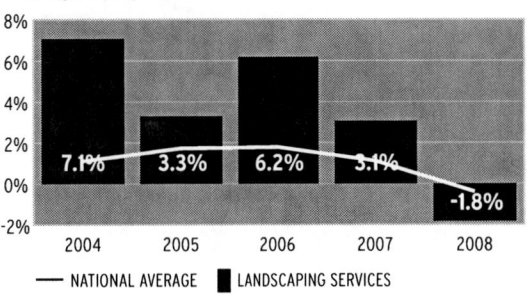

Industry Employment Growth

2004: 7.1% | 2005: 3.3% | 2006: 6.2% | 2007: 3.1% | 2008: -1.8%

— NATIONAL AVERAGE ■ LANDSCAPING SERVICES

SOURCE: BUREAU OF LABOR STATISTICS

Call Preparation Questions

How does the company adjust to lower demand during economic downturns?

Although basic landscape maintenance like mowing is relatively unaffected by economic cycles, customers pull back on optional services during economic difficulties.

How much difficulty does the company have finding workers?

Landscaping depends on a cheap source of seasonal labor.

How does the company manage seasonal swings in revenue?

Most landscaping work is done in the second and third quarters.

Does the company market its services to corporate or government customers?

The landscaping industry has grown rapidly in recent years partly because it offers a specialized service that customers want to outsource.

Has the company explored the possibility of offering other services, like janitorial?

Some landscaping companies have expanded the range of services they offer.

Web Links

American Nursery & Landscape Association

News. Industry statistics for households.
www.anla.org

Association of Professional Landscape Designers

Resources and events.
www.apld.com/resources.asp

Grounds Maintenance

Industry news. Excellent association list. Survey information for sale.
www.grounds-mag.com

Landscape Management

Industry news. Excellent annual state-of-the-industry survey reports.
www.landscapemanagement.net/landscape

Lawn & Landscape

Industry news.
lawnandlandscape.com

PRO Magazine

Landscaping and grounds maintenance market news.
www.promagazine.com

The American Society of Landscape Architects

News.
www.asla.org/nonmembers/publicrelations/
pressreleases/press.htm

The Professional Landcare Network (PLANET)

Legislative issues and updates.
www.landcarenetwork.org/cms/home.html

Toro Landscaping Equipment

Manufacturer of professional landscaping equipment.
www.toro.com/professional/lce

Tree Care Industry Association

Tree care industry issues.
www.treecareindustry.org

Yard and Garden

News.
www.yardngarden.com

Glossary of Acronyms

ANLA — American Nursery & Landscape Association

HOOVER'S TOP COMPANIES

Largest Companies by Sales	($ mil.)
The ServiceMaster Company	3,356.7
Asplundh Tree Expert Co.	2,370.0
ValleyCrest Companies	1,010.0
The Davey Tree Expert Company	506.1
The Brickman Group, Ltd.	332.2

Largest Employers	Employees
The ServiceMaster Company	29,000
Asplundh Tree Expert Co.	28,606
ValleyCrest Companies	10,500
The Davey Tree Expert Company	5,600
The Brickman Group, Ltd.	5,047

Fastest Growing* by Five-Year Sales Growth	(%)
The Davey Tree Expert Company	9.6
Asplundh Tree Expert Co.	7.1

Fastest Growing* by Five-Year Employee Growth	(%)
Asplundh Tree Expert Co.	0.4

* These rates are compounded annualized increases and may have resulted from acquisitions or one time gains. If less than 6 years of data are available, growth is for the years available.

SOURCE: HOOVER'S, INC., DATABASE

Legal Services

THIS INDUSTRY INCLUDES:

SIC CODES

7389   Business Services

8111   Legal Services

NAICS CODES

54111   Offices of Lawyers

541199   All Other Legal
         Services

The US legal services (law firm) industry includes about 170,000 law offices that generate annual revenue of over $180 billion. Large firms include Skadden, Arps, Slate, Meagher & Flom; Latham & Watkins; Baker & McKenzie; Jones Day; and Sidley Austin. The industry is highly fragmented: the 50 largest firms hold less than 15 percent of the market. About 2,000 law firms have annual revenue over $10 million.

Competitive Landscape

Demand depends on the volume of commercial and civil legal transactions and court and criminal cases. The profitability of individual firms depends on the partners' reputation and ability, and effective case management. Large firms have advantages in serving corporate customers with a wide range of needs. Small firms can compete successfully providing specialized expertise or superior outcomes and operating in a local market. The industry is labor-intensive, but employee contribution is high: average annual revenue per worker is about $165,000.

Products, Operations & Technology

The industry's major service is the practice of law, which is providing legal services to individuals, businesses, government, and nonprofits. Services to businesses account for almost 50 percent of industry revenue; individuals, including estates, 40 percent; government, 4 percent; and nonprofits, 3 percent. Miscellaneous legal services provide an additional 3 percent.

Law firms operate as partnerships. Operations support the provision of legal advice and other services, such as document preparation and production, legal filings, and litigation. Most work falls under the general categories of transactional or litigation law. Transactional matters occur between at least two parties and usually require contract preparation or filings with government agencies. Litigation includes

BUSINESS CHALLENGES

» Dependence on Local Economy, Specific Industries

Law firms with a large transactional business, such as for real estate or financial matters, are strongly affected by swings of the local and national economy. US GDP, an indicator of potential demand for legal services, can fluctuate up to 5 percent yearly; law office employment, a reflection of demand, can vary up to 3 percent. Changes in local demand for transactional services affect the amount of business law firms do, which impacts billing rates and employment levels.

» Specialization Brings Higher Fees, Risks

Rising costs and competition lead general law practices to enter more specialized areas of law. Specialists' fees are typically higher than generalists' and less competition exists in a given market. Specialization carries greater risks, however, as specialists suffer when consumer or commercial activity declines in their area of law. Specialists' fees contributed to US consumer costs for legal services rising more than 50 percent in a recent decade, double the inflation rate.

» Legislative Reaction to Large Monetary Awards

Corporations and influential individuals pressure state legislators to amend tort laws, which apply to civil wrongdoing and can result in defendants' paying large settlements in liability lawsuits. Tort law critics argue for reform, most notably in the areas of asbestos litigation, medical malpractice, and other class actions. Trial attorneys argue that large awards are necessary to deter civil wrongdoing by companies and individuals, especially large firms and the rich and powerful. Many states have begun tort reform by setting limits on the dollar amount a jury can award as punitive damages.

civil lawsuits and criminal cases. Civil matters include commercial disputes and personal and property damage. Criminal matters are law violations brought to court by government authorities. Document preparation is the major activity for most legal services firms. Many law offices also provide legal opinions and advice and may become involved in business clients' operations and strategy. Metrics include annual caseload and outcomes, such as total dollar amount of settlements favoring clients.

Due to the complexity and number of federal, state, and local laws and regulations, attorneys generally specialize in a particular area of law. Specialization can be in commercial, M&As, antitrust, bankruptcy, intellectual property, international, real estate, labor, securities, estate, tort (related to civil wrongdoing), tax, or criminal matters. Firms may also develop industry-specific expertise, particularly in heavily regulated industries, such as telecommunications, banking, or transportation. Large law firms may have expertise in many areas, while small firms may specialize in one or two. Specialization includes knowledge of relevant laws, the court interpretations of those laws, and the operations of particular law courts.

Most law firms use nonlegal staff to handle administrative functions, client service issues, and related tasks, such as title searches and document preparation. Legal assistants perform multiple administrative functions. Paralegals work for litigation attorneys and typically facilitate depositions and research court records. Office managers handle banking, billing, payables, and day-to-day operations. Some firms, especially those working on contingency, outsource legal assistant and paralegal functions to companies in lower-cost, English-speaking countries like India.

Computer and communication technology are essential for many law firms to handle administrative functions, conduct legal research, and, in some cases, to file documents with courts. Computerized phone systems and software track lawyers' time talking and working on behalf of specific client assignments and send time-accounting data to billing systems. Videoconferencing technology is used for meetings, training sessions, depositions, and settlement conferences. Portable wireless messaging devices are increasingly common for attorney use. Some firms enable clients to access certain systems to exchange e-mail, review and edit documents, and receive copies of filings.

Sales & Marketing

Typical customers are corporations, individuals, and government; some firms specialize by segment. The major sales channel is senior partners, who maintain a wide range of contacts and memberships in professional and civic organizations. Customer referrals are an important source of sales for smaller firms.

Major types of marketing include customer visits, community sponsorships, PR, and ads in Yellow Pages, newspapers, and magazines. Some law firms also advertise on radio and TV, most notably those that specialize in personal injury law. Law firms market to other attorneys through law industry associations, conferences, and journals, because a large amount of new business comes from professional referrals. Most law firms provide pro bono (free) legal services, such as to nonprofits and needy individuals.

Human Resources

Attorneys need law school degrees and state licensing; paralegals typically have associate or undergraduate degrees and undergo special training, often at a local college. Average industry wages, including for attorneys, paralegals, and other support staff, are about 55 percent higher than the national average. Personnel turnover varies, depending on the area and economy, but can be high for newly hired lawyers and more experienced attorneys who don't become a partner. Injury rates are negligible, due to the sedentary work.

Competition for new law school graduates is high, especially among larger firms that recruit from top-rated universities. Starting salaries for new lawyers at top firms often exceed $120,000 annually. Personnel management is a major concern at most law firms, because productivity directly relates to hourly billings, and competition can be high among staff attorneys who want to earn partnership. The ratio of nonpartner attorneys (associates) to partners is often 4:1 at the biggest firms and 2:1 at small firms.

Industry Employment Growth

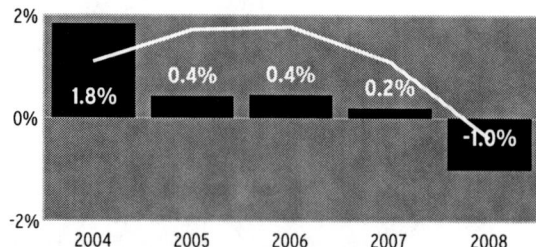

Average Hourly Earnings

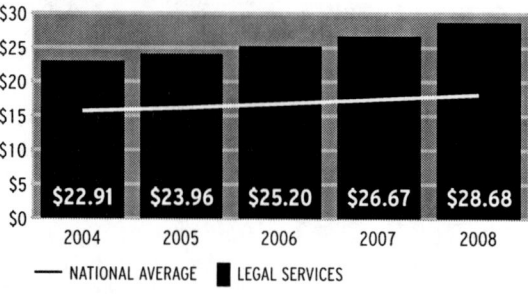

— NATIONAL AVERAGE   ■ LEGAL SERVICES

SOURCE: BUREAU OF LABOR STATISTICS

Call Preparation Questions

How vulnerable is the firm to changes in the local economy?

Law firms with a large transactional business, such as for real estate or financial matters, are strongly affected by swings of the local and national economy.

How has the firm's mix of business changed in the last few years?

Rising costs and competition lead general law practices to enter more specialized areas of law.

Does the firm expect to increase its expertise in specific fields like technology law?

Demand for legal services is expected to increase, due to the greater complexity of conducting business, particularly for global companies and in specialty industries related to science and technology.

Web Links

ABA Journal

News.
www.abajournal.com

American Bar Association – Lawlink

Excellent links in the legal services industry by category.
www.abanet.org/tech/ltrc/lawlink/home.html

Federal Bar Association

Publications, links, hot topics, and more.
www.fedbar.org

FindLaw

Thousands of links to legal sites, cases, codes, forms, law reviews, law schools, bar associations, law firms, experts, and much more.
www.findlaw.com

Law.Com

Industry news, news archive.
www.law.com

The American Lawyer

Industry news.
www.law.com/jsp/tal

The National Law Journal

Latest news, articles, features, and surveys.
www.law.com/jsp/nlj

US Law Firms and Lawyer Associations

List of links for legal associations, including specialties.
www.hg.org/lawfirms-assoc.html

Glossary of Acronyms

ACC — Association of Corporate Counsel
ADR — alternative dispute resolution

ATRA — American Tort Reform Association
IP — intellectual property
LPO — legal process outsourcing
MDP — multidisciplinary practice

HOOVER'S TOP COMPANIES

Largest Companies by Sales	($ mil.)
Skadden, Arps, Slate, Meagher & Flom LLP	2,170.0
Latham & Watkins LLP	2,005.0
Baker & McKenzie	1,829.0
Jones Day	1,441.0
Sidley Austin LLP	1,386.0
White & Case LLP	1,373.0
Greenberg Traurig, LLP	1,200.0
Mayer Brown	1,183.0
Weil, Gotshal & Manges LLP	1,175.0

Largest Employers	Employees
Baker & McKenzie	8,000
Jones Day	4,977
Skadden, Arps, Slate, Meagher & Flom LLP	4,721
Latham & Watkins LLP	4,500
White & Case LLP	4,372
Sidley Austin LLP	3,806
Mayer Brown	3,400
Weil, Gotshal & Manges LLP	2,800
Foley & Lardner LLP	2,621
Paul, Hastings, Janofsky & Walker LLP	2,500

Fastest Growing* by Five-Year Sales Growth	(%)
Latham & Watkins LLP	19.1
Milbank, Tweed, Hadley & McCloy LLP	18.8
Skadden, Arps, Slate, Meagher & Flom LLP	16.1
Paul, Hastings, Janofsky & Walker LLP	14.9
White & Case LLP	14.6
Sidley Austin LLP	11.0
Baker Botts L.L.P.	9.6
Mayer Brown	9.5
Foley & Lardner LLP	8.0
Weil, Gotshal & Manges LLP	7.5

Fastest Growing* by Five-Year Employee Growth	(%)
Latham & Watkins LLP	6.3
Sidley Austin LLP	6.2
Mayer Brown	5.4
Foley & Lardner LLP	4.4
Skadden, Arps, Slate, Meagher & Flom LLP	3.6
Jones Day	2.6
Patterson Belknap Webb & Tyler LLP	1.6
Baker Botts L.L.P.	1.2

Top Public Companies by Market Value	($ mil.)
Pre-Paid Legal Services, Inc.	425.2

* These rates are compounded annualized increases and may have resulted from acquisitions or one time gains. If less than 6 years of data are available, growth is for the years available.

SOURCE: HOOVER'S, INC., DATABASE

Lighting Equipment Manufacture

The US lighting equipment manufacturing industry includes about 1,100 companies with combined annual revenue of about $12 billion. Major companies include Acuity Brands, Hubbell, and Philips Lighting. Divisions of large integrated companies such as General Electric also manufacture lighting equipment. The industry is concentrated: the largest 50 companies have about 70 percent market share.

Competitive Landscape

Demand depends primarily on residential, industrial, and commercial construction activity. Large companies have advantages in purchasing power, manufacturing volume, and distribution efficiencies. Small companies compete by offering specialized products and superior customer service in regional markets. Annual revenue per employee is about $200,000.

Products, Operations & Technology

Major product categories are lamp bulbs and parts (about 20 percent of revenues) and lighting fixtures (about 80 percent). Lamp bulbs consist primarily of incandescent, fluorescent, and three types of high intensity discharge (HID) lamps: metal halide, sodium, and mercury vapor. Lighting fixtures consist of metal, glass, and plastic products in various decorative styles.

Residential fixtures may be highly decorative while industrial, commercial, and institutional applications tend to be more basic. Portable fixtures, such as table and floor lamps, are used primarily in residential applications. Incandescent bulbs are the primary choice for residential applications, while longer-lasting, more expensive, fluorescent and HID bulbs dominate industrial, commercial, and institutional applications.

Raw materials for lamp bulbs include glass, tungsten, copper, and inert gases such as argon

BUSINESS CHALLENGES

» Competition from Imports

Imports are an increasing percentage of US lighting equipment consumption. To capitalize on low-cost labor sources, US companies have moved high-volume product lines offshore. Foreign competitors have also expanded their share of North American markets. Imports now comprise about 40 percent of total US consumption of lighting equipment products, up from 35 percent in 2002.

» Heavy Dependence on New Construction

About 80 percent of lighting fixtures is sold for new construction or add-on projects; only 20 percent for renovation. This dependence on construction activity can result in manufacturing overcapacity during downturns in the residential and commercial building markets.

» Volatile Raw Material Prices

Prices for metals, glass, and petroleum-based materials, used to make lighting equipment, can vary widely. Raw material expenditures represent roughly 45 percent of total sales revenue. The highly competitive nature of the market makes recovering higher material costs by passing them customers difficult.

and nitrogen. Lighting fixture manufacturers use steel, aluminum, copper, brass, and plastics as components of finished products.

Incandescent lamp bulbs are the highest unit volume form of lighting due to their low cost to manufacture and install. The incandescent bulb has three basic components: the filament, bulb, and base. The filament is drawn by pulling tungsten mixed with a binder material through a die into a fine wire form, which is then annealed to soften the wire and welded to lead-in wires. Glass bulbs are produced by moving a continuous ribbon of glass past air nozzles that blow the glass through holes in the conveyor belt into molds, creating the glass casings. After the glass casings are cooled and cut, they're coated with silica to reduce glare from the uncovered filament. Manufacturing the base also uses molds to provide the screw shape that fits the socket of a light fixture. Automated machines fit the three pieces together, and then they're sealed, tested, and packaged for shipment.

Fluorescent and HID bulbs, while manufactured similarly, require a ballast to start and regulate the flow of current so that the bulb operates at maximum efficiency. Advantages of these bulbs include greater energy efficiency, better lighting disbursement, less heat generation, and longer life.

Lighting fixtures are manufactured using a series of steps that may include cutting, bending, machining, spinning, anodizing, polishing, and painting, depending on the materials used and final design configurations.

Larger companies have their own distribution centers. Smaller companies use third party distribution centers or ship direct from the factory. Transportation is by common carrier or company-owned vehicles.

Manufacturing processes are highly automated. Lamp bulb production may be accomplished at speeds as high as 50,000 per hour. Computer-controlled metal-working machinery combines precision and manufacturing speed for fixture components. Most orders are made to stock and enterprise resource planning (ERP) systems aid in production planning, inventory management, and order fulfillment.

Sales & Marketing

Major customers include retail home improvement centers, electrical distributors and wholesalers, lighting showrooms, contractors, and lighting design firms. Residential (about 20 percent of total revenues) and nonresidential markets represent two distinct segments within the lighting industry. Nonresidential markets include industrial, institutional and commercial, outdoor, and vehicular applications. Companies use a combination of direct sales personnel and manufacturer reps to reach these markets.

Marketing includes advertising in industry trade publications, participating in trade shows, distributing product catalogs, using corporate websites, and advertising on TV or in newspapers. Marketing programs for residential applications are targeted directly to the end consumers, while lighting products for commercial applications are targeted to engineers, designers, and general contractors.

Product prices for lamp bulbs range from less than a dollar for an incandescent bulb to a few hundred for high intensity discharge (HID) bulbs. Fixture prices typically cost from a few to several hundred dollars, depending on style and end-use.

Human Resources

Production employees in lighting equipment manufacturing earn about $32,000, slightly below the national average for all manufacturing employees. Fringe benefits average about 25 percent of payroll. Large companies have some unionized locations; most small manufacturers are non-union.

Industry employment shrunk from approximately 79,000 employees to 61,000, a 23 percent reduction, from 2001 through 2005; productivity increased approximately 3.3 percent annually.

Injury rates in the industry average about 10 percent lower than the average for all US manufacturing companies.

Industry Employment Growth

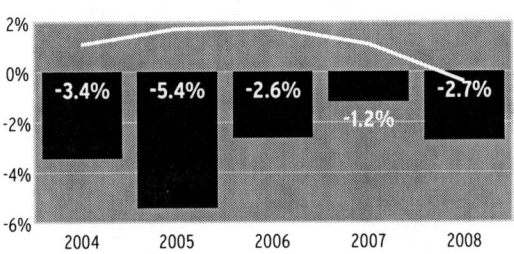

Average Hourly Earnings

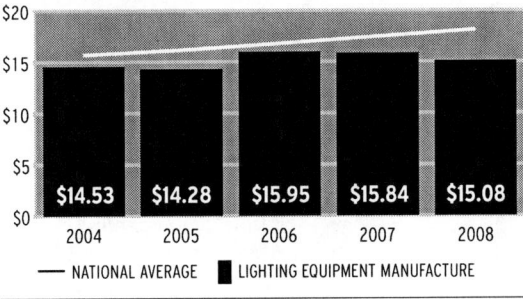

— NATIONAL AVERAGE   ■ LIGHTING EQUIPMENT MANUFACTURE

SOURCE: BUREAU OF LABOR STATISTICS

Call Preparation Questions

How have imports affected the company's US operations?

Imports are an increasing percentage of US lighting equipment consumption.

How dependent is the company on new construction spending?

About 80 percent of lighting fixtures is sold for new construction or add-on projects; only 20 percent for renovation.

FAST FACTS

» The US lighting equipment manufacturing industry includes about 1,100 companies with combined annual revenue of about $12 billion.

» Major companies include Acuity Brands, Hubbell, and Philips Lighting.

» Major product categories are lamp bulbs and parts (about 20 percent of revenues) and lighting fixtures (about 80 percent).

» Major customers include retail home improvement centers, electrical distributors and wholesalers, lighting showrooms, contractors, and lighting design firms.

» Revenues are somewhat seasonal with peak demand in spring and summer when construction is highest.

How has the company been challenged by managing raw material costs?

Prices for metals, glass, and petroleum-based materials, used to make lighting equipment, can vary widely.

Does the company export US-manufactured products?

The economies of China, Indonesia, and other Asia Pacific countries are growing faster than the US economy.

Does the company offer products that qualify for government incentives?

About 22 percent of US electric consumption is for lighting, causing federal, state, and local governments to offer incentives to replace existing lighting systems with more energy-efficient models.

Web Links

Acuity Brands

Large manufacturer of lighting fixtures.
www.acuitybrands.com

American Lighting Association

News of lighting manufacturers, distributors, and retailers.
www.americanlightingassoc.com

Energy Star

Information regarding energy efficiency and greenhouse emissions for lighting and other electrical industries.
www.energystar.gov

Hubbell

Large manufacturer of lighting and other electrical products.
www.hubbell.com

Illuminating Engineering Society of North America

News about technical and product developments in the lighting industry.
www.iesna.org

Glossary of Acronyms

CERCLA — Comprehensive Environmental Responsibility, Compensation and Liability Act

CFL — compact fluorescent light

CLC — Certified Lighting Consultant

ERP — enterprise resource planning

HID — high intensity discharge

NPEP — National Partnership for Environmental Priorities

PTL — Pick to Light

SSL — solid state lighting

VDP — Voice Directed Picking

WMS — warehouse management system

HOOVER'S TOP COMPANIES

Largest Companies by Sales	($ mil.)
Hubbell Incorporated	2,704.4
Acuity Brands, Inc.	2,026.6
Cooper Lighting, LLC	582.1
OSRAM SYLVANIA Inc.	633.3
AZZ incorporated	320.2
LSI Industries Inc.	305.3
Philips Lighting Business Unit	—

Largest Employers	Employees
Hubbell Incorporated	13,000
OSRAM SYLVANIA Inc.	9,500
SLI Holdings International, LLC	7,000
Cooper Lighting, LLC	6,739
Acuity Brands, Inc.	6,500
Philips Lighting Business Unit	3,891
Catalina Lighting, Inc.	2,623
LSI Industries Inc.	1,500
AZZ incorporated	1,422
Advanced Lighting Technologies, Inc.	1,168

Fastest Growing* by Five-Year Sales Growth	(%)
Lime Energy Co.	65.5
Orion Energy Systems, Inc.	54.7
Xenonics Holdings, Inc.	44.8
Craftmade International, Inc.	13.9
AZZ incorporated	11.8
Hubbell Incorporated	8.8
LSI Industries Inc.	7.5

Fastest Growing* by Five-Year Employee Growth	(%)
Craftmade International, Inc.	35.0
Orion Energy Systems, Inc.	22.2
Xenonics Holdings, Inc.	17.8
AZZ incorporated	7.5
Hubbell Incorporated	4.8
Nexxus Lighting, Inc.	2.4

Top Public Companies by Market Value	($ mil.)
Acuity Brands, Inc.	1,749.2
AZZ incorporated	429.6
Orion Energy Systems, Inc.	257.2
Hubbell Incorporated	218.9
Lighting Science Group Corporation	188.8

* These rates are compounded annualized increases and may have resulted from acquisitions or one time gains. If less than 6 years of data are available, growth is for the years available.

SOURCE: HOOVER'S, INC., DATABASE

Linen and Uniform Supply Services

The linen and uniform supply industry includes about 2,500 companies with combined annual revenue of $9 billion. Major companies include Cintas, ARAMARK, G&K Services, and Alsco. The industry is highly concentrated: the 50 largest companies account for 75 percent of revenue.

The industry's two main services are industrial laundry and linen supply. Industrial laundry services clean and supply heavy work garments, such as overalls, bib trousers, and protective gear; and laundered and unlaundered mats. Linen supply companies handle easier-to-clean, ironed items, such as aprons; hospital scrubs and gowns; and bedding, tableware, and cloth napkins ("flatware"). Because the two cleaning processes use different washing techniques and machinery, less than 15 percent of companies offer both services.

Competitive Landscape

Demand is driven by employment trends, as swings in labor and service hiring impact uniform and garment needs. The profitability of individual companies depends on efficient operations and maintaining low labor costs. Large companies have advantages in centralized laundry plant operations. Small companies can compete effectively through excellent service and custom solutions. The industry is highly labor-intensive: average annual revenue per worker is $70,000.

Linen and uniform supply companies compete with makers of disposable supplies. Competition also comes from large institutions with on-premises laundries (OPL).

Products, Operations & Technology

Major services include cleaning and renting industrial garments (33 percent of the market); flatware (20 percent); linens (15 percent); and industrial mats (10 percent). Other services include supplying wiping cloths, mops, cleaning

BUSINESS CHALLENGES

» Dependence on Manufacturing Industry

Sales in the industrial sector, primarily garments and dust control, consistently account for two-thirds of revenue for the overall linen and uniform supply industry. Employment patterns in manufacturing and industrial production can greatly impact the profitability of individual companies. A shift from permanent to temporary workers can also have an effect, as contract workers typically furnish their own uniforms.

» Dependence on Low-Cost Labor

Average pay for production workers in the linen supply industry is 30 percent lower than the national average. Many large companies are fighting unionization attempts. New and proposed state immigration bills levy fines against companies that employ undocumented workers, which make up a sizable portion of workers in the linen supply industry. Companies claim that employees are treated and paid fairly, and that labor costs must remain low to maintain profitability. Wages average about 15 percent of sales.

» Ongoing EPA Scrutiny

The EPA continues to place industrial launderers on its list of targets for additional regulation. Every two years, the agency reviews around six to 10 industries vulnerable to further government oversight. The most recent round of reviews kept industrial launderers on the watch list for possible future rule development, but off the list of industries immediately subject to heavier EPA regulation.

products, and lint-free "clean room" garments. Linens and uniforms may be sold; rented (includes cleaning); or leased (without cleaning) to customers. Large companies typically process about 10 million pounds of laundry annually.

A typical contract begins with an onsite visit from a service manager, who assesses client needs and measures each employee for appropriate fit. Employees typically receive one change of uniform per day. A route representative picks up garments weekly and delivers them to a central laundry facility. Route representatives typically manage around 100 customers.

At the laundering facility, items are sorted by type and soil level, placed in carts or slings (bags), and weighed for billing purposes. Sorted items are placed on conveyor belts and enter either a washer-extractor or a tunnel washer, a computerized laundry machine where workers continually add batches of soiled laundry. Garments requiring pressing enter large flatwork ironers. Items that don't need ironing are moved by sling to large tumblers that can dry up to 400 pounds in a batch. Garments are sorted according to size and inspected for tears and excessive wear. Workers repair items as needed before route representatives return clean items to customers.

Major linen and uniform supply industry costs include cleaning and drying equipment, water, electricity, and detergents. Other major inputs include delivery vehicles, gas, and textiles such as cotton and synthetic fibers. Most companies own the equipment they use. A complete industrial laundering system can cost upward of $2 million; used and refurbished systems can lower the cost considerably. Workers need only basic technical skills as most computerized equipment is user-friendly.

Companies invest in technical innovations that can recycle water and lower the time it takes to clean garments. Radio frequency identification (RFID) tracking technology can help lower sorting and packaging mistakes to improve inventory management and delivery service. Some companies now outfit fleet vehicles with GPS to monitor route efficiency.

Sales & Marketing

Typical linen supply customers are hospitals, universities, hotels, and restaurants. Industrial laundry customers include manufacturing plants, automobile service shops, and construction crews.

Companies generate sales leads through referrals, internal sales force visits to new businesses, and telemarketing. Large contracts may require a competitive bidding process. Marketing is a mix of direct mail catalogs, print advertising, and sponsorships.

In addition to a service manager and route representative (driver), companies typically provide 24-hour telephone customer service. Service managers typically meet weekly with

clients to ensure that delivery and quality are meeting customer needs.

The Internet plays a significant role in industry sales. Most major companies sell products online and use the Internet to showcase products and generate rental and lease leads. Companies with advanced technical resources may offer a secure web platform for customers to select and manage uniform assignments for each employee.

Uniform rental is highly competitive and price-sensitive. Prices vary based on the size of an order and whether the linens and uniforms are sold, rented, or leased. Customers are charged by either unit or weight, depending on the item. Contracts typically last three to five years; large contracts range anywhere from $10,000 to $3 million.

Human Resources

Most jobs in the linen supply industry require minimal skills and pay low wages. Pay is nearly 30 percent lower than the national average. A constant workload and difficult working conditions often result in adversarial relationships between workers and management. Nearly half of all workers are represented by UNITE HERE, the largest US laundry union, or by the Teamsters union, which represents drivers. Common job injuries include back and neck strain, skin and eye irritation from chemical exposure, and mishaps involving heavy machinery.

Industry Employment Growth

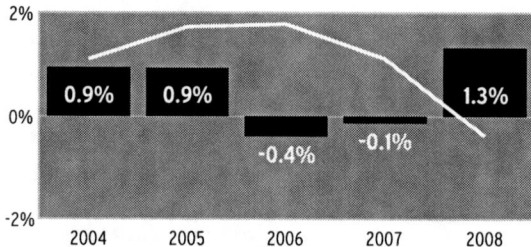

Average Hourly Earnings

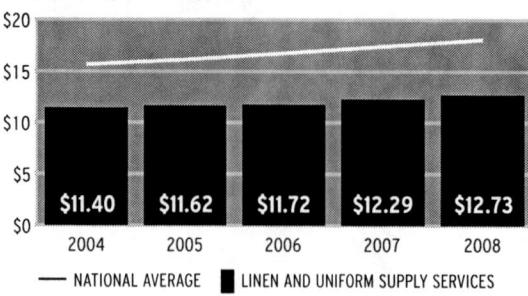

SOURCE: BUREAU OF LABOR STATISTICS

Call Preparation Questions

How dependent is the company on sales to the manufacturing industry?

Sales in the industrial sector, primarily garments and dust control, consistently account for two-thirds of revenue for the overall linen and uniform supply industry.

How important is the availability of low-cost labor to the company?

Average pay for production workers in the linen supply industry is 30 percent lower than the national average.

How concerned is the company that the EPA will tighten environmental regulations?

The EPA continues to place industrial launderers on its list of targets for additional regulation.

What opportunities does the company see in the health care market?

Healthcare is a high-growth market for linen and uniform supply companies.

What is the company doing to expand its product offerings?

Linen suppliers and industrial garment suppliers are expanding the products and services they offer.

Web Links

Cintas

One of largest uniform suppliers in US.
www.cintas.com

Industrial Launderer

Industry magazine.
ilmagonline.com

Laundry ESP

Laundry Environmental Stewardship Program.
laundryesp.com

Textile Rental Services Association of America (TRSA)

Association representing the textile rental industry.
www.trsa.org

Uniform and Textile Service Association (UTSA)

International trade association.
www.utsa.com

UNITE HERE

Industrial laundry workers union.
www.unitehere.org

Glossary of Acronyms

ALSCO — American Linen Supply Company
NOG — not our goods (laundering-only contract)
OPL — on-premises laundry
POTW — publicly owned treatment works
SFA — sales force automation
TRSA — Textile Rental Services Association
UTSA — Uniform and Textile Service Association

HOOVER'S TOP COMPANIES

Largest Companies by Sales	($ mil.)
ARAMARK Corporation	13,200.0
Cintas Corporation	3,937.9
Alsco, Inc.	1,160.0
UniFirst Corporation	1,023.2
G&K Services, Inc.	1,002.4
Angelica Corporation	430.0

Largest Employers	Employees
ARAMARK Corporation	260,000
Cintas Corporation	34,000
Alsco, Inc.	12,000
UniFirst Corporation	10,000
G&K Services, Inc.	7,800
Angelica Corporation	6,400
AmeriPride Services Inc.	6,025
Mission Linen Supply	3,000
Prudential Overall Supply	1,600
Morgan Services, Inc.	900

Fastest Growing* by Five-Year Sales Growth	(%)
UniFirst Corporation	11.4
Cintas Corporation	7.9
G&K Services, Inc.	7.3
Angelica Corporation	3.4

Fastest Growing* by Five-Year Employee Growth	(%)
Angelica Corporation	4.3
UniFirst Corporation	4.3
Cintas Corporation	3.1

Top Public Companies by Market Value	($ mil.)
Cintas Corporation	4,537.0
UniFirst Corporation	619.1
G&K Services, Inc.	592.5

* These rates are compounded annualized increases and may have resulted from acquisitions or one time gains. If less than 6 years of data are available, growth is for the years available.

SOURCE: HOOVER'S, INC., DATABASE

Local Bus Transportation

About 4,000 companies in the US provide local bus service, with combined annual revenue of $9 billion. Large companies include FirstGroup America and Atlantic Express. Most companies are small, with annual revenue less than $5 million. The average bus operator has fewer than 100 buses and operates a single maintenance location.

Competitive Landscape

Demand depends mainly on the demographic makeup and growth of the local population. The profitability of individual companies depends on efficient operations, as the business is capital-intensive. Small companies can compete by providing specialized services. Large companies can have advantages in buying fuel and in maintaining fleets. Because of the heavy use of part-time workers, annual revenue per worker is a low $35,000 for school bus operators.

Products, Operations & Technology

Most industry revenue comes from operating school buses. Companies may also provide municipal bus service; charter bus service; vehicle maintenance; paratransit services (for handicapped students and senior citizens); and bus sales. National and regional companies often provide all these services; small companies usually provide only school bus and charter services.

Companies acquire buses, hire and train drivers, operate maintenance facilities, and pick up and discharge passengers along routes and according to schedules determined by contract customers like school districts or municipalities. Drivers are the largest single cost for bus operators. To drive vehicles that carry more than 14 passengers, drivers must have a commercial driver's license (CDL). A national company that operates 4,800 vehicles of various types may have 5,200 drivers and 450 mechan-

BUSINESS CHALLENGES

» School Bus Services Tied to Local Demographics

Growth of the local school-aged population determines demand for school bus transport. On average, the school-aged population in the US will be flat from 2000 to 2010. If local school demand is stagnant, companies have limited growth options.

» Vulnerability to Safety Issues

School bus companies and operators are liable for injuries suffered on their buses. The issue of whether to mandate the use of safety belts on school buses hasn't been settled in many states. Although safety belts might reduce injuries, the belts could easily be vandalized and misused. Bus operators could be responsible for enforcing their use, which would require a monitor on each bus, at higher cost.

» Dependence on Specialized Labor

Due to the specialized training required to earn a license to drive commercial or school buses, companies can't easily replace drivers. Turnover among bus drivers can be high, especially among school bus drivers, who often have low pay and short hours. Labor negotiations sometimes cause disruptions: about 40 percent of school bus drivers belong to unions, versus 15 percent of commercial bus drivers.

ics. To a large extent, bus operators are in the personnel management business.

Companies acquire buses from manufacturers like Blue Bird and Thomas Built that put a customized body on a truck chassis from suppliers like GM or International Truck and Engine. About 40,000 new school buses are sold every year. Most of these are large type "C" or "D" buses that can seat 60 to 78 passengers and cost $50,000 to $70,000 and have an effective life of 15 years, but about a quarter are smaller type "A" buses that carry about 20 passengers. The market in used school buses is large; a 10-year-old school bus that seats 70 can be bought for $10,000.

Municipal commercial "transit" buses cost upward of $100,000 and luxury charter "coaches" can cost upward of $300,000. Most buses run on diesel fuel. An average school bus only travels 15,000 miles per year and the average annual operating cost, including driver, fuel, and maintenance, is close to $25,000. The full cost of operating a bus is about $1.50 per mile. The average age of school bus fleets is close to seven years.

Bus companies use logistics software to help reconcile rider needs with bus and driver availability, and bus scheduling and routing. Some public-serving companies make schedules available on websites. Other than logistics, most bus companies are relatively low-tech, although newer buses can be ordered with on-board computer technology, such as GPS and scanners for student ID cards.

Sales & Marketing

Major customers are school districts, municipalities, private employers, and government agencies. Most US school districts contract for school bus services rather than owning and operating buses themselves because they need the buses only a few hours per day. Contractors can supply the service more cheaply because they can use the buses and drivers for charters and commercial services during non-school hours. In contrast, most large cities operate their own municipal bus service. Private operators like First America provide mainly municipal bus service to smaller communities.

Contracts with school districts and municipalities are won through either a bidding process, where the lowest responsible bidder is awarded the contract (more usual for municipal services), or through a Request for Proposal (RFP) process (more usual for school districts) where various competitors are asked to submit proposals and price is only one determining factor. Contracts are usually awarded for one to five years. Safety and reliability are key in securing contracts for school bus services. School districts are notoriously conservative and likely to have long-term relationships with school bus operators, routinely renewing contracts.

Human Resources

Most school bus drivers work no more than 20 hours per week, usually receive minimal benefits, and are paid by the hour. Wages for school bus drivers vary considerably across the country, and are about 20 percent lower than for the average US worker. Training for school bus drivers is usually one to four weeks. Annual personnel turnover is a high 30 percent, because of low pay. High turnover and absenteeism are key management concerns. The safety record of the industry is 45 percent worse than average.

Wages for municipal bus drivers are higher than for school bus drivers. City bus drivers work full-time and receive benefits equivalent to those received by municipal employees, equal on average to about 50 percent of their wages. Maintenance workers receive about $25,000 yearly. The local bus transportation industry has about 18 percent more injuries a year than the national average.

Industry Employment Growth

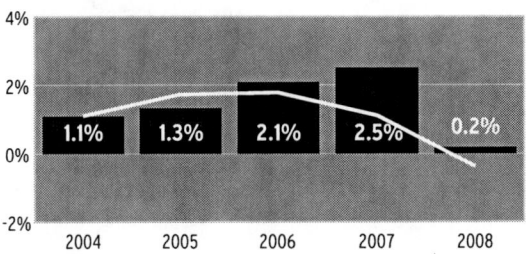

Average Hourly Earnings

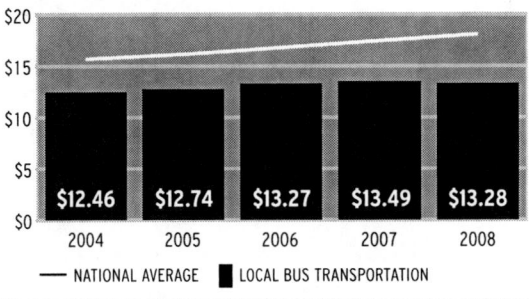

— NATIONAL AVERAGE ■ LOCAL BUS TRANSPORTATION

SOURCE: BUREAU OF LABOR STATISTICS

Call Preparation Questions

If in the school market, how have changes in the demographics of school-aged children affected the company?

Growth of the local school-aged population determines demand for school bus transport.

What steps has the company taken to increase safety and reduce risk?

School bus companies and operators are liable for injuries suffered on their buses.

How does the company recruit and retain drivers?

Due to the specialized training required to earn a license to drive commercial or school buses, companies can't easily replace drivers.

What growth opportunities does the company have providing paratransit services?

Special transport of the handicapped, disabled, and elderly will continue to grow significantly as more Americans age in the next decade.

What are the company's strategies for winning contracts in large school districts?

The majority of large school district bus fleets are publicly run, providing an opportunity for private operators who can offer lower costs.

Web Links

American Public Transportation Association

Statistics.
www.apta.com

Federal Transit Administration

Information on public municipal bus systems.
www.fta.dot.gov

Mass Transit

News.
www.masstransitmag.com

National Association for Pupil Transportation

Legislative news.
www.napt.org

National Highway Traffic Safety Administration

Safety issues.
www.nhtsa.dot.gov

National School Transportation Association

News, legislative issues.
www.yellowbuses.org

National Transportation Safety Board

Safety issues.
www.ntsb.gov

School Bus Fleet

Articles and news.
www.schoolbusfleet.com

School Bus Information Council

National statistics. Safety issues.
www.schoolbusinfo.org

Glossary of Acronyms

ADA — Americans with Disabilities Act
CDL — commercial driver's license
FMCSA — Federal Motor Carrier Safety Administration
FTA — Federal Transit Administration
NHTSA — National Highway Traffic Safety Administration

HOOVER'S TOP COMPANIES

Largest Companies by Sales	($ mil.)
FirstGroup America, Inc	3,319.0
Coach USA, LLC	783.5
MV Transportation, Inc.	514.6
Atlantic Express Transportation Corp.	433.5
Veolia Transportation, Inc.	—

Largest Employers	Employees
Atlantic Express Transportation Corp.	7,600
MV Transportation, Inc.	6,100
Coach USA, LLC	5,000

Fastest Growing* by Five-Year Sales Growth	(%)
FirstGroup America, Inc	30.8
Atlantic Express Transportation Corp.	4.4

* These rates are compounded annualized increases and may have resulted from acquisitions or one time gains. If less than 6 years of data are available, growth is for the years available.

SOURCE: HOOVER'S, INC., DATABASE

Lumber Wholesalers

About 6,000 lumber wholesalers operate in the US, with combined annual revenue of $75 billion. Most are privately held with annual revenue of less than $10 million. Despite some large regional companies, the industry is local and fragmented: the 50 largest companies hold about 40 percent of the market.

Competitive Landscape

Demand for lumber and plywood is strongly affected by the level of residential real estate construction. Only the largest companies have more than 100 employees, while the typical wholesaler has only 10. National and regional wholesalers usually have several offices that serve local customers. Most companies operate locally, serving local customers and buying from local mills. Large wholesalers are more likely to serve large customers, with operations in multiple markets.

Products, Operations & Technology

Lumber wholesalers buy truck or railcar loads of lumber and other wood products from sawmills and plywood plants, and resell them to retail lumberyards, home improvement centers, large homebuilders, industrial users, and building products distributors. Although some wholesalers have lumberyard operations, wholesaling is mainly a trading operation. Some wholesalers specialize in lumber, others in plywood panels, milled wood, and various engineered products like veneers; I-joists; laminated lumber (glulam); and oriented strandboard (OSB). Larger companies usually handle both. Plywood, milled wood, and engineered products now account for more than half of industry revenue.

Sales & Marketing

Sales operations are usually by phone and fax. Wholesalers establish and maintain contacts with producers and customers, and moni-

BUSINESS CHALLENGES

» High Dependence on Cyclical Construction Industry
Demand for lumber is highly cyclical, depending on the level of new home construction and volume of home sales; repair and remodeling are somewhat less cyclical. The level of new home construction can vary more than 20 percent over a two-year period.

» Volatile Lumber Prices
Lumber supply and prices can be volatile, affected by construction levels, variability of domestic supply, Canadian imports, weather, and environmental regulations. The industry's fragmentation means that the market has difficulty predicting supply, which fluctuates monthly; lumber prices can change by 40 or 50 percent in a couple of months.

» Customer Concentration
Smaller wholesalers may get a large share of revenue from just a few customers. Only a relatively small number of wholesalers have a national presence: most operate locally and have a large amount of repeat business with big customers.

tor their anticipated production and consumption. A large number of sales are back-to-back trades, where the wholesaler is able to execute buy (from the producer) and sell (to the customer) orders immediately, and product goes directly from a producer's mill to a customer. A smaller percentage is transit business, where the wholesaler buys product at a favorable price without yet having a buyer, but expects to sell the product while still in transit. Wholesalers with a lumberyard also sell out of inventory. A large company, like Forest City Trading Group, has about 3,500 repeat customers and 1,500 one-time customers each year. Only 15 percent of its sales typically are made out of the company's lumberyards. Marketing consists largely of advertising in industry trade publications and participating in numerous trade shows and conventions.

Annual lumber production in the US is about 50 billion board feet, of which 70 percent is softwood and 30 percent hardwood, with a total value of $30 billion. Plywood panel production is about 20 billion square feet, with a value of $10 billion. Annual sales of engineered products like OSB are about $10 billion.

Human Resources

Lumber wholesaling consists mainly of white-collar desk jobs that involve trading, using computers and telephones, but require no advanced education. Warehouse and inventory jobs primarily involve moving lumber, contributing to an industry injury rate that is 50 percent higher than average. The industry's average hourly pay is less than a dollar above the national wage.

Industry Employment Growth

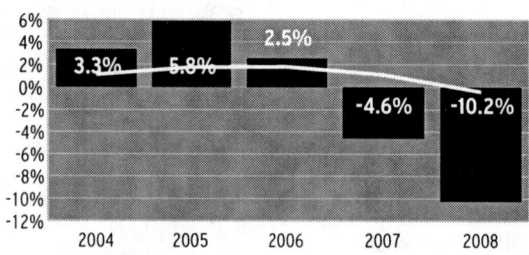

Average Hourly Earnings

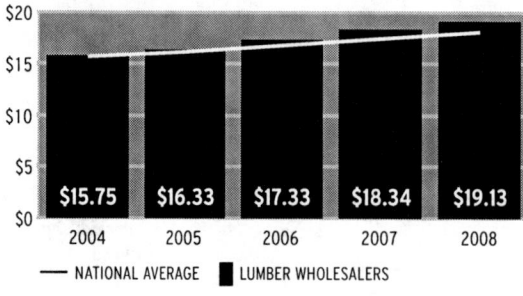

SOURCE: BUREAU OF LABOR STATISTICS

Call Preparation Questions

How does the company manage seasonal cash flow?

Demand for lumber is highly cyclical, depending on the level of new home construction and volume of home sales; repair and remodeling are somewhat less cyclical.

How does the company protect itself from price fluctuations?

Lumber supply and prices can be volatile, affected by construction levels, variability of domestic supply, Canadian imports, weather, and environmental regulations.

How reliant is the company on a top few customers?

Smaller wholesalers may get a large share of revenue from just a few customers.

What opportunities do engineered wood products (EWP) present for the company?

Demand for standardized engineered prefabricated wood products, like trusses, has grown rapidly in recent years because they can be made from smaller trees than comparable lumber, and are usually lighter and cheaper.

How could alliances with other wholesalers benefit the company?

Although many small wholesalers specialize in just one type of wood product, the fact that many customers require a full range of building materials presents an opportunity for expansion, potentially through alliances with other wholesalers or producers of other products.

Web Links

APA – The Engineered Wood Association

Good description of various engineered wood products.
www.apawood.org

Foreign Affairs and International Trade Canada

Information about Canadian softwood lumber.
www.dfait-maeci.gc.ca/eicb/softwood/menu-en.asp

Lumber + Building Materials Daily (LBM Daily)

News.
www.lbmdaily.com

North American Wholesale Lumber Association

Monthly bulletin. Industry links.
www.lumber.org

Random Lengths

Wood and timber prices, market analyses, and more.
www.randomlengths.com

TIMBERWeb

International lumber news.
www.timberweb.com/News/IndustryNewsList.html

US Forest Service

Production, trade, consumption and pricing.
www.fs.fed.us

US International Trade Commission

Export and import data.
dataweb.usitc.gov

Western Wood Products Association

Forecast of demand.
www.wwpa.org

Glossary of Acronyms

BLS — Bureau of Labor Statistics
DOC — Department of Commerce
EWP — engineered wood products
ITC — International Trade Commission
LVL — laminated veneer lumber
MBF — thousand board feet
MSF — thousand square feet
OSB — oriented strandboard

HOOVER'S TOP COMPANIES

Largest Companies by Sales	($ mil.)
Pro-Build Holdings Inc.	5,000.0
BlueLinx Holdings Inc.	2,779.7
North Pacific Group, Inc.	1,200.0
Builders FirstSource, Inc.	1,034.5
Huttig Building Products, Inc.	671.0

Largest Employers	Employees
Pro-Build Holdings Inc.	17,000
Stock Building Supply Inc.	10,936
Pacific Coast Building Products, Inc.	3,500
Builders FirstSource, Inc.	3,300
BlueLinx Holdings Inc.	2,800
Foxworth-Galbraith Lumber Company	2,300
Huttig Building Products, Inc.	1,900
Lumber Products	850
North Pacific Group, Inc.	780
Brockway-Smith Company	775

Fastest Growing* by Five-Year Sales Growth	(%)
Jewett-Cameron Trading Company Ltd.	3.0
Moore-Handley, Inc.	2.2
North Pacific Group, Inc.	1.0

Fastest Growing* by Five-Year Employee Growth	(%)
Pro-Build Holdings Inc.	15.3

Top Public Companies by Market Value	($ mil.)
BlueLinx Holdings Inc.	81.2
Builders FirstSource, Inc.	55.3
Jewett-Cameron Trading Company Ltd.	17.5

* These rates are compounded annualized increases and may have resulted from acquisitions or one time gains. If less than 6 years of data are available, growth is for the years available.

SOURCE: HOOVER'S, INC., DATABASE

Machine Tool Manufacture

The US machine tool manufacturing industry consists of about 7,000 companies with combined annual revenue of $25 billion. Large companies include Kennametal, Thermadyne, and Hardinge, as well as divisions of integrated companies such as Ingersoll. The industry is fragmented: the largest 50 companies hold less than 30 percent of the market. Large companies may have annual revenue over $100 million, but a typical company has revenue under $10 million.

Competitive Landscape

Demand is closely linked to US industrial activity. The profitability of individual companies depends on the complexity of their product designs and their manufacturing efficiency. Large companies have the resources to make complex, automated machinery. Small companies can compete successfully by making specialty products, replacement parts, or accessories. The industry is fairly capital-intensive: average annual revenue per employee is close to $150,000.

Products, Operations & Technology

Major products include dies, molds, cutting tools, and machining centers. Dies and molds account for about 50 percent of industry revenue, cutting tools for 20 percent, machining centers for 15 percent, and 15 percent for miscellaneous machine tools. The industry itself relies on machine tools to make products. Manufacturing facilities basically are specialized foundry and machine shops.

Dies and molds are used to make products by taking on the outside shape of the product. Dies are used to stamp shapes into metals, plastics, and other materials, often with the aid of a hydraulic press. Molds hold a shape while a molten substance like metal, glass, or plastic is poured or blown inside. Dies and molds are typically cast from metal into rough form and finished with machine tooling. Because dies and

BUSINESS CHALLENGES

» Demand Highly Cyclical

Demand for machine tools, which depends heavily on US manufacturing, is significantly impacted by cyclical changes in the manufacturing sector. During periods of lower manufacturing activity, customers make do with the machine tools they already own, rather than buy new. For example, during the last recession, when US manufacturing activity fell 5 percent, production of machine tools fell 25 percent.

» Competition from Imports

Imported machine tools account for almost 30 percent of the US market, of which Japan, Canada, and Germany are the major sources. Sophisticated machining centers are a major import. In recent years, machine tool imports increased 10 percent per year.

» Vulnerability to Raw Material Prices

Fluctuations in raw material costs, particularly steel and aluminum, can sharply affect profitability. Raw materials account for over half of production costs for manufacturers of machining centers. Steel prices can vary more than 30 percent within 12 months.

molds must be specially made for each product, there are few economies of scale in their production. They are often made by small companies that specialize in a particular type of application and who work in close cooperation with the customer.

Machining centers are used to cut away material from a semi-finished product by drilling, cutting, milling, grinding, and other operations. Two major types are vertical machining centers (VMC) and horizontal machining centers (HMC). "Multi-tasking" machining centers can perform several operations in sequence on a "workpiece." Many machining centers are operated with computer numerical controls (CNC). To improve precision, machining centers are heavy and consist of a stage that holds the workpiece, and one or several high speed power devices that apply various cutting tools. In addition to large amounts of steel, major components used in production are electric motors and computer controls.

Cutting tools are made from hard materials like high-speed steel (HSS) or tungsten carbide, but are worn down in the manufacturing process and must frequently be replaced. Manufacturers of machining centers supply cutting tools for their machines, but independent manufacturers also produce a large variety of cutting tools that can be used in machining centers. Cutting tools like drill bits and saw blades are also used in other types of machines besides machining centers. Because of the very high melting point of carbides, the manufacture of carbide tools requires special manufacturing techniques such as liquid phase sintering and chemical vapor deposition (CVD).

Finished products typically are heavily used and therefore wear out rapidly. Cutting tools, especially, must regularly be replaced, but dies and molds also wear out or are replaced by new designs. Machining centers have a typical useful life of three to five years.

Computer and material technologies are very important for manufacturers of machine tools and other metalworking machinery. Manufacturers of cutting tools must know which materials are most suitable for a wide variety of applications. Computer controls are essential for operating machining centers and producing dies and molds. Dies and molds, which may be small enough to produce pieces of jewelry or large enough to make car panels, are often made using computer-aided design and manufacturing processes (CAD/CAM) that can produce prototypes and finished products directly from computer designs.

Sales & Marketing

Major customers are manufacturing companies and independent machine shops. Standard products like cutting tools are typically sold through distributors. Machining centers are often made-to-order and sold through an internal sales force, distributors, and/or manufacturer representatives. Because dies and molds are made-to-order, manufacturers sell directly to customers. Advertising is primarily in trade publications. Participation in industry trade shows is important.

The price range for individual cutting tools, such as a carbide drill bit, is around $100 to $200. Dies and molds cost thousands, depending on size and precision. Prices for machining centers typically range from $20,000 to

$100,000, but can be much higher for complex integrated machines.

Human Resources

Production workers are skilled and fairly well paid. Wages are about 15 percent higher than the national average. The industry injury rate is 40 percent higher than the national average. Industry employment has fallen in the past five years, due both to greater foreign competition and increased automation.

Industry Employment Growth

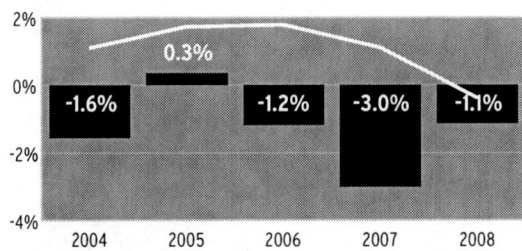

Average Hourly Earnings

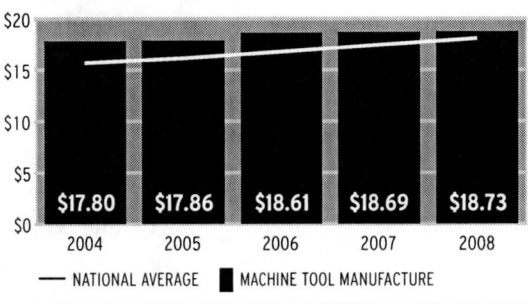

SOURCE: BUREAU OF LABOR STATISTICS

Call Preparation Questions

How much has company revenue changed in the past 12 months?

Demand for machine tools, which depends heavily on US manufacturing, is significantly impacted by cyclical changes in the manufacturing sector.

How much competition does the company get from imports?

Imported machine tools account for almost 30 percent of the US market, of which Japan, Canada, and Germany are the major sources.

How does the company mitigate shifts in prices of raw material, like steel?

Fluctuations in raw material costs, particularly steel and aluminum, can sharply affect profitability.

Does the company expect Internet sales to be a significant source of revenue?

Internet commerce sites are expanding the sales territory of many machine tool makers.

How large is the company's export business?

Because of short delivery times, US manufacturers are advantaged in exporting machine tools to Canada and Mexico.

Web Links

American Machine Tool Distributors' Association

Statistics about national machining center "consumption."
www.amtda.org

Association for Manufacturing Technology

Industry news.
www.amtonline.org

Cutting Tool Engineering

News and articles.
www.ctemag.com

International Tungsten Industry Association

Information about tungsten carbide manufacture.
www.itia.org.uk

MetalForming Magazine

Technical articles.
www.metalformingmagazine.com

Modern Machine Shop Online

Industry news and articles.
www.mmsonline.com

Tooling & Manufacturing Association

Association of Chicago-area tool manufacturers.
www.tmanet.com

Glossary of Acronyms

CAD — computer-aided design
CAM — computer-aided manufacture
CNC — computer numerical controls
CVD — chemical vapor deposition
EDM — electrical discharge machining
HMC — horizontal machining center
HSS — high-speed steel
VMC — vertical machining center

HOOVER'S TOP COMPANIES

Largest Companies by Sales	($ mil.)
Kennametal Inc.	2,705.1
Sandvik Coromant Company	895.2
ROFIN-SINAR Technologies Inc.	575.3
Thermadyne Holdings Corporation	494.0
Hardinge Inc.	356.3

Largest Employers	Employees
Kennametal Inc.	13,673
Sandvik Coromant Company	4,000
Thermadyne Holdings Corporation	2,950
Gleason Corporation	2,508
ROFIN-SINAR Technologies Inc.	1,775
Hardinge Inc.	1,519
Giddings & Lewis Machine Tools, LLC	1,000
Simonds International Corporation	960
DoALL Company	927
Greenlee Textron Inc.	900

Fastest Growing* by Five-Year Sales Growth	(%)
ROFIN-SINAR Technologies Inc.	17.4
Hardinge Inc.	16.1
Kennametal Inc.	9.0
Thermadyne Holdings Corporation	3.6

Fastest Growing* by Five-Year Employee Growth	(%)
ROFIN-SINAR Technologies Inc.	8.3
Hardinge Inc.	5.7
Thermadyne Holdings Corporation	1.0

Top Public Companies by Market Value	($ mil.)
Kennametal Inc.	2,501.7
ROFIN-SINAR Technologies Inc.	884.5
Hardinge Inc.	192.6
Thermadyne Holdings Corporation	153.7

* These rates are compounded annualized increases and may have resulted from acquisitions or one time gains. If less than 6 years of data are available, growth is for the years available.

SOURCE: HOOVER'S, INC., DATABASE

Magazine Publishers

About 1,000 companies in the US publish magazines, journals, and tabloids, with combined annual revenue of about $40 billion. Large companies include PRIMEDIA, Meredith, and the magazine divisions of integrated media companies like Time Warner and The Washington Post Company. While the total number of magazines published in the US is greater than 10,000, only about 2,000 have significant circulation. The industry is concentrated: the 50 largest companies hold almost 70 percent of the market.

Competitive Landscape

Demand for magazines is driven largely by growth in consumer income. The profitability of individual companies depends highly on marketing expertise. Small companies can compete by specializing in niche topics and markets, while larger companies benefit from a wide selection of magazine titles to offer advertisers. Large companies also have economies of scale in production and distribution. The industry is labor-intensive: average annual revenue per worker is $120,000.

Products, Operations & Technology

Products include weekly and monthly general interest magazines, industry trade publications, and various non-print information products like CDs and Internet websites. General interest magazines account for about 60 percent of industry revenue, trade publications for 15 percent.

Most companies have an editorial staff that prepares features and a business staff that handles promotion, production, circulation, and advertisement sales. Freelance writers are often used in addition to in-house staff. Printing may occur at one or several locations, depending on how widely the magazine is distributed. Some publishers operate their own printing operations, but most have contracts with outside

BUSINESS CHALLENGES

» Dependence on Advertising

Advertising accounts for the bulk of magazine publisher revenue. More than 85 percent of total ad spending is by 12 industries, making magazine publishers susceptible to downturns in those particular industries. Ad spending is measured by the number of pages sold ("ad pages").

» Paid Circulation Slows

Total industry circulation revenue has slowly declined in the past decade and circulation has been flat. The annual paid circulation for magazines covered by Audit Bureau of Circulations has been virtually flat for 10 years, at 365 million copies. Magazines aren't a growth industry, although the value of magazines as an advertising medium has increased. Circulation is defined by subscription and single-copy (newsstand) sales.

» Customer Consolidation

Consolidation affecting distributors, retailers, and ad agencies has left many magazine publishers with little power for price negotiation and with smaller profit margins.

printers who can make more efficient use of expensive printing equipment. Even companies that use outside printers must often buy their own paper, usually coated stock that fluctuates significantly in price.

Magazines have two major sources of revenue: circulation and advertising. Overall, about 35 percent of industry revenue comes from circulation sales, either single-copy sales or subscriptions. For many large-circulation titles, like Sports Illustrated, single-copy revenues are less than 10 percent of subscription revenue. But for a large number of titles, like Cosmopolitan, single-copy sales provide the bulk of circulation revenues. Subscriptions are very valuable to publishers, even though they're often achieved by giving subscribers a large discount from the single-copy price. The value derives from having a steady readership — with typical renewal rates of 70 percent — and access to information about the magazine's readers. Many publishers rent their subscriber list to marketers. Some magazines have no circulation revenue; they're specialized controlled circulation publications sent free to individuals who have signed up to receive them.

Advertising is usually a greater source of revenue for publishers than circulation, overall accounting for 50 percent of industry revenue. To a large extent, magazines are a vehicle to present advertising to a selected group of consumers. The largest advertisers in consumer magazines are car, computer, financial services, and drug companies. The average ratio of advertising to editorial pages (those with content) in consumer magazines is about 1:1; in other words, 50 percent of a typical magazine is devoted to ads. The two types of advertising are formatted display ads and direct-response promotions, which include tear-outs and inserted postcards for the reader to respond to by phone, mail, or e-mail. Advertising rates depend on the size, color, and positioning of ads, as well as a magazine's circulation.

Publishers and independent firms closely measure circulation because of its importance to advertisers. Publishers usually guarantee a certain circulation ("rate base") that may be lower than actual circulation. Publishers can estimate circulation fairly accurately by counting subscriptions, single-copy sales to retailers, and returns from retailers. Third-party firms, the most prominent of which are the Audit Bureau of Circulations (ABC) and BPA Worldwide, also conduct independent surveys. Advertisers measure the cost of reaching a target audience by dividing the cost of a magazine ad by the number of thousands of readers who will see it, expressed as a cost per thousand (CPM). For example, a $30,000 ad that reaches 1 million readers has a CPM of $30. Extensive research defines the precise demographics of a magazine's readers — by criteria such as age, sex, income, education, location, and interests — so that publishers can offer advertisers a highly qualified audience. The Publishers Information Bureau (PIB) tracks the quantity and types of advertising pages in many consumer magazines. The Standard Rate and Data Service (SRDS) compiles information about ad rates.

Magazine publishers use computer technology heavily to create and edit content and page design, prepare copy for printing, and manage distribution. Some magazines publish a digital version on their websites. Ad content is digitized, and printing presses are typically computer-controlled.

Sales & Marketing

Magazine publishers try to sell their products to consumers who fall within specific demographic categories. Marketing is through advertising (TV, billboards, and in other magazines); direct mail; and point-of-sale promotion (for single-copy sales). Sweepstakes, an important source of new subscribers for many magazines, have been scaled back because of lawsuits over deceptive advertising. Single-copy sales are a valuable source of new subscribers, which is why magazines feature their own ads and inserts. Distribution of subscription copies is usually through the US Postal Service (USPS) at a special rate. Distribution of single-copies is usually handled by national distributors and regional wholesalers that have access to about 150,000 retail sites, including newsstands and checkout displays at supermarkets and other retail stores.

Magazine distribution is highly concentrated, with five national companies controlling about 90 percent of the market. The largest national distributors are Anderson News, with 40 percent market share, and The News Group, with 25 percent. Distributors typically buy magazines at a 40 percent discount from the cover price. Only 35 percent of newsstand magazines are actually sold, down from 50 percent ten years ago. Retailers return unsold magazines to distributors, who shred and sell them as scrap paper. The sales efficiency of some titles is as low as 20 percent; that is, 80 percent of printed copies remain unsold.

Human Resources

Magazine employees are well-paid, earning average hourly wages about 40 percent above the national average. The annual personnel turnover rate for the information industry, including magazine publishing, is less than 25 percent, significantly lower than the national average of 40 percent. Information workers have a very good safety record, with a third the number of injuries as the national average.

Industry Employment Growth

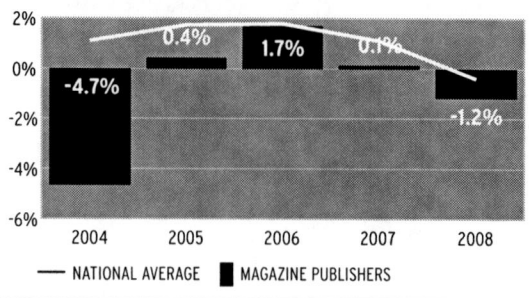

SOURCE: BUREAU OF LABOR STATISTICS

Call Preparation Questions

How does the company mitigate downturns in advertising by major customers?

Advertising accounts for the bulk of magazine publisher revenue.

What strategies does the company use to increase circulation?

Total industry circulation revenue has slowly declined in the past decade and circulation has been flat.

How do bar coding and other marking technologies benefit the company?

Bar coding allows retailers and publishers to track magazine sales just like any other stock item, allowing more sophisticated product selection.

What plans does the company have to expand its product line?

Established publishing companies have low entry barriers for creating new magazines.

Web Links

Audit Bureau of Circulations

Industry circulation auditing company.
www.accessabc.com

Folio

News and articles.
www.foliomag.com

I Want Media

Media news.
www.iwantmedia.com

Magazine Publishers of America

News and articles.
www.magazine.org

MagMall

Extensive listing of magazines by category.
www.magmall.com

MediaFinder

Publisher of various magazine directories.
www.mediafinder.com

Publishers Information Bureau

Source of advertising information — pages and revenue.
www.magazine.org/pib

PubList.com

Database of periodicals.
www.publist.com

Glossary of Acronyms

ABC — Audit Bureau of Circulations

B2B — business-to-business
CPM — cost per thousand
CRMA — City and Regional Magazine Association
MPA — Magazine Publishers of America
PIB — Publishers Information Bureau
SRDS — standard rate and data service
USPS — United States Postal Service

HOOVER'S TOP COMPANIES

Largest Companies by Sales	($ mil.)
Time Inc.	4,608.0
The Washington Post Company	4,461.6
The Hearst Corporation	4,380.0
The Reader's Digest Association, Inc.	2,786.4
Meredith Corporation	1,586.5
Marvel Entertainment, Inc.	676.2
Morningstar, Inc.	502.5
The Condé Nast Publications	—
Johnson Publishing Company, Inc.	453.3

Largest Employers	Employees
The Washington Post Company	19,000
The Hearst Corporation	17,070
International Data Group, Inc.	13,640
Dominion Enterprises	5,700
The Reader's Digest Association, Inc.	4,700
The Condé Nast Publications	4,000
Meredith Corporation	3,570
Morningstar, Inc.	1,720
Time Inc.	1,258
PRIMEDIA Inc.	1,150

Fastest Growing* by Five-Year Sales Growth	(%)
Morningstar, Inc.	29.2
FriendFinder Networks Inc.	24.6
Marvel Entertainment, Inc.	14.2
Meredith Corporation	8.0
The Hearst Corporation	4.2
Martha Stewart Living Omnimedia, Inc.	2.9
The Reader's Digest Association, Inc.	2.4
Johnson Publishing Company, Inc.	1.3
Value Line, Inc.	0.1

Fastest Growing* by Five-Year Employee Growth	(%)
Morningstar, Inc.	19.8
Meredith Corporation	9.7
Martha Stewart Living Omnimedia, Inc.	8.7

Top Public Companies by Market Value	($ mil.)
Marvel Entertainment, Inc.	2,411.0
Morningstar, Inc.	1,678.5
Meredith Corporation	1,026.8
Salon City, Inc.	984.1
Value Line, Inc.	446.8

* These rates are compounded annualized increases and may have resulted from acquisitions or one time gains. If less than 6 years of data are available, growth is for the years available.

SOURCE: HOOVER'S, INC., DATABASE

Managed Healthcare

THIS INDUSTRY INCLUDES:

SIC CODES

6321   Accident and Health Insurance

6324   Hospital and Medical Service Plans

NAICS CODES

524114   Direct Health and Medical Insurance Carriers

The US managed health care industry includes about 3,000 companies with combined annual revenue of about $350 billion. Large participants include Aetna, UnitedHealth, and Humana, and nonprofits such as Kaiser Permanente and state Blue Cross Blue Shield organizations. The industry has become concentrated: the 50 largest companies hold more than 60 percent of the market.

Competitive Landscape

Demand is driven by the rising costs of providing medical care. The profitability of individual companies depends on efficient operations and the ability to negotiate favorable contracts with health care providers. Large companies and organizations have advantages in negotiating contracts with health care providers. Small companies can compete successfully only by providing special coverage plans, or in small markets. The industry is highly automated: annual revenue per employee is close to $1 million.

Products, Operations & Technology

The industry provides various types of health insurance plans that have built-in cost containment measures, unlike traditional indemnity plans that pay whatever costs are incurred. Among the major products are HMOs; preferred provider organizations (PPO); point-of-service (POS) plans; and indemnity benefit plans. Companies usually offer a number of such plans and each may operate dozens of them.

HMO plans, sometimes called "closed system" plans, have the most active cost-containment features. Consumers choose a primary care doctor from the HMO's network of providers, who acts as a gatekeeper for any other medical services the consumer may need. PPO plans, also called "open access" plans, allow consumers to use any services within a network of providers, without a gatekeeper. Ser-

BUSINESS CHALLENGES

» Rapidly Rising Healthcare Costs

Healthcare spending by private health insurers increased 70 percent between 1998 and 2004. National health care costs rose almost 60 percent, and are expected to grow 7 percent annually through 2010. In 2004, private health insurance accounted for 36 percent of national health care costs.

» Tighter Government Regulation

Government mandates concerning medical practice and management are increasingly complex and extensive, burdening health care and related companies, including MCOs, with compliance. Healthcare providers and insurers need expert advice to stay current with regulations and considerable staff to process required forms and data. The absence of a government-run national health care system contributes to the growth of MCOs, regardless of often restrictive regulations.

» Premiums Lag when Costs Rise

Because health insurance premium rates are usually based on actual historical rather than prospective future costs, premiums can be insufficient when costs rise rapidly.

vices outside the provider network are available, but cost more. POS plans are hybrids of HMOs and PPOs. They typically feature a primary care doctor who makes referrals for services within the provider network, but also allow consumers to avoid the gatekeeper and directly use services within the network, though at higher cost. POS plans also allow consumers to go outside the network at a still higher cost. The higher costs in PPO and POS plans take the form of higher deductibles, higher co-payments, or lower reimbursement rates.

The industry grew rapidly in the 1990s on the premise that the traditional way of delivering health care was financially wasteful, since health care providers (doctors, hospitals, etc.) had no incentive to keep treatment costs to a minimum. Managed care companies attempt to control costs in four ways: by providing financial incentives to providers and users to minimize the amount of care used, contracting for services at discounted rates, reviewing expenses to determine the legitimacy of costs, and establishing low-cost treatment protocols providers are expected to follow.

Managed health care companies are administrative intermediaries between health care providers and users. They sign annual contracts for services with doctors, hospitals, testing labs, and other providers, usually at a fixed cost, and resell them to plan members for a fixed monthly premium. The risk that actual expenses will be higher than the contracted reimbursement rate is borne mainly by providers, although most plans provide a stop-loss provision that shares excess expenses with providers after a certain expense limit is reached. The risk that premiums are insufficient to cover administrative costs is typically borne by the company.

In addition to using financial incentives to limit unnecessary medical care, managed health care companies use "utilization management" to review and standardize care. Committees of doctors and administrators review the actual services used in the network to determine if they're being used appropriately, and to recommend standards of care that doctors and hospitals are expected to follow. Committees also determine drug formularies that specify which drugs should be used to treat specific conditions. The statistical information collected for utilization management is also used for risk management and underwriting, the process of determining what payments to offer providers and what premiums to charge consumers.

Computerized information and communication systems are vital to managed health care companies to process claims and manage records, and for statistical collection and analysis.

Sales & Marketing

Managed health care plans are sold mainly to employers or other groups that want to provide health care insurance to employees or members. Plans intended for large employers are sold directly by sales representatives or through insurance brokers. Such sales involve two steps: the employer must sign on, and then employees must be convinced to join. Plans designed for small groups and individuals are often sold through independent agents, telemarketing, or direct mail, and may involve TV and print advertising. Average annual premiums for US employer-sponsored plans in 2005 were $4,023 for an individual plan and $10,880 for a family plan, according to the annual survey of Employer Health Benefits by the California HealthCare foundation.

To attract customers, managed health care companies build networks of providers (doctors, hospitals, diagnostic labs). Contracts with providers are usually non-exclusive and typically renew annually at renegotiated rates; contract terms differ for the various plans a company offers. A typical independent doctor has contracts with several managed care plans.

Contracts with doctors, hospitals, and other providers usually take the form either of "capitation," a fixed payment per month based on the number of members in the plan (whether they use the service or not), or a "fixed-fee schedule" that specifies the amount the plan pays for actual services rendered. Capitation is the major incentive used by HMOs to limit referrals by primary care doctors, who keep a greater amount of the capitation for primary care patients if they minimize treatments and referrals. Capitation limits risk for the managed health care company. Fixed-fee schedules are the major form of contract for PPOs.

Human Resources

Most jobs in managed health care companies are clerical, but involve computer skills or technical knowledge of insurance products and government regulations, and are therefore fairly well-paid. Average hourly pay is about 28 percent higher than the average national wage. The industry's safety record is good, with only one-fourth the number of injuries as the national average.

Industry Employment Growth

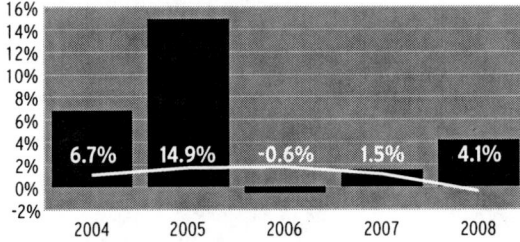

2004	2005	2006	2007	2008
6.7%	14.9%	-0.6%	1.5%	4.1%

Average Hourly Earnings

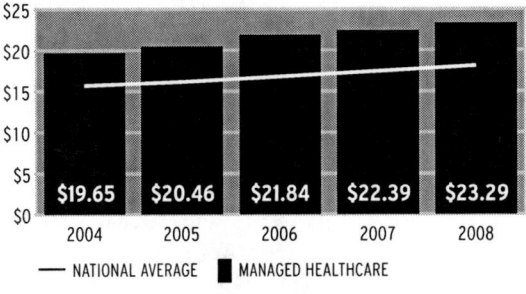

2004	2005	2006	2007	2008
$19.65	$20.46	$21.84	$22.39	$23.29

— NATIONAL AVERAGE   ■ MANAGED HEALTHCARE

SOURCE: BUREAU OF LABOR STATISTICS

Call Preparation Questions

How do rising health care costs impact the company?

Healthcare spending by private health insurers increased 70 percent between 1998 and 2004.

How are tighter government regulations impacting the company?

Government mandates concerning medical practice and management are increasingly complex and extensive, burdening health care and related companies, including MCOs, with compliance.

How does the company mitigate lags in health care costs and premium increases?

Because health insurance premium rates are usually based on actual historical rather than prospective future costs, premiums can be insufficient when costs rise rapidly.

Web Links

America's Health Insurance Plans (AHIP)

Industry association representing 1,000 companies. Legislative positions, some statistics.
www.ahip.org

American Association of Preferred Provider Organizations

News and policy issues.
www.aappo.org

BCBS Health Issues

News about national health care issues.
bcbshealthissues.com

Health Affairs

News and policy issues.
www.healthaffairs.org

Managed Care Key Terms and Concepts

Explanation of managed care financial terms and ratios.
www.mcareol.com/factshts/factkeyt.htm

Managed Care Magazine

Capitation, articles, and etc.
www.managedcaremag.com

Glossary of Acronyms

CDHP — consumer-directed health plans
CSHSC — Center for Studying Health System Change
CMS — Centers for Medicare and Medicaid Services
HCFA — Health Care Financing Administration
HIPAA — Health Insurance Portability and Accountability Act
MCP — managed care plans
NCQA — National Committee for Quality Assurance
PBM — Pharmacy Benefit Manager
PPO — preferred provider organization
URAC — Utilization Review Accreditation Committee

HOOVER'S TOP COMPANIES

Largest Companies by Sales	($ mil.)
UnitedHealth Group Incorporated	81,186.0
WellPoint, Inc.	61,251.1
Kaiser Foundation Health Plan, Inc.	37,800.0
Aetna Inc.	30,950.7
Humana Inc.	28,946.4
CIGNA Corporation	17,623.0
Aflac Incorporated	16,554.0
Health Net, Inc.	15,366.6
Health Care Service Corporation	14,348.4
Blue Cross and Blue Shield Association	—

Largest Employers	Employees
Kaiser Foundation Health Plan, Inc.	159,766
Blue Cross and Blue Shield Association	150,000
UnitedHealth Group Incorporated	67,000
WellPoint, Inc.	42,900
Aetna Inc.	35,200
CIGNA Corporation	26,600
Humana Inc.	25,000
Highmark Inc.	18,500
Health Care Service Corporation	16,500
Coventry Health Care, Inc.	15,000

Fastest Growing* by Five-Year Sales Growth	(%)
The Amacore Group, Inc.	70.3
Universal American Corp.	55.7
WellCare Health Plans, Inc.	44.2
HealthSpring, Inc.	42.5
Alliance HealthCard, Inc.	37.2
Centene Corporation	34.3
Molina Healthcare, Inc.	31.4
WellPoint, Inc.	29.6
UnitedHealth Group Incorporated	23.0
AMERIGROUP Corporation	22.7

Fastest Growing* by Five-Year Employee Growth	(%)
Independence Holding Company	31.7
Centene Corporation	31.2
Kaiser Foundation Health Plan, Inc.	27.6
The Regence Group	25.0
AMERIGROUP Corporation	24.7
Molina Healthcare, Inc.	23.8
Coventry Health Care, Inc.	23.5
WellCare Health Plans, Inc.	22.8
Magellan Health Services, Inc.	19.8
HealthSpring, Inc.	19.2

Top Public Companies by Market Value	($ mil.)
UnitedHealth Group Incorporated	32,335.4
Aflac Incorporated	21,389.6
WellPoint, Inc.	21,201.1
CIGNA Corporation	15,022.3
Aetna Inc.	13,004.6

* These rates are compounded annualized increases and may have resulted from acquisitions or one time gains. If less than 6 years of data are available, growth is for the years available.

SOURCE: HOOVER'S, INC., DATABASE

Manufactured Housing

In the US about 200 companies make manufactured housing (MH) — previously called "mobile homes" — with combined annual sales of about $7 billion. Large manufacturers include Champion Enterprises, Palm Harbor Homes, Fleetwood Enterprises, and Clayton Homes. The industry is highly concentrated: the top 20 manufacturers account for more than 80 percent of production.

Competitive Landscape

The high cost of conventional housing and the availability of credit drive demand for manufactured housing. The profitability of individual companies depends on efficient operations and access to dealers. Large companies benefit in distribution, the creation of large dealer networks, and ability to locate factories close to dealers. Small companies can compete successfully in local markets.

Products, Operations & Technology

The industry manufactures single- or double-wide rectangular housing units, which are later installed on a site to form a dwelling. The resulting house may consist of a single or several units, called "floors," even though they sit side-by-side, fastened together at the installation site. Units cost from $15,000 to $170,000 and range from 400 to 4,000 square feet. A large majority are double-wide instead of single width. Most have three or more bedrooms, two full bathrooms, central air conditioning, and average 1,500 square feet.

MH is built on assembly lines in factories, generally using the same materials as for a site-built house. The efficiency of working in standardized fashion in a controlled environment substantially reduces construction costs. Manufacturing costs are about $30 per square foot, versus $60 per square foot or more for a site-built house. A unit can be assembled in one or two days from various pre-assembled compo-

BUSINESS CHALLENGES

» Highly Cyclical Demand

US production of MH has been highly cyclical in the past 15 years. Production was up 150 percent in the 1990s, and down 20 percent in subsequent years. Shipments are somewhat seasonal, with larger volume usually in summer and lower volume in winter.

» Sales Depend Highly on Credit Financing

Because MH is often bought by customers with low income, credit financing availability is important. Many lenders had deep losses and have left the industry. When fewer financing sources are available, unit sales may be lower and manufacturers may raise prices to compensate.

» Dependence on Dealer Network

To ensure an outlet for their product, a number of large manufacturers have expanded ownership of dealers or negotiated exclusive access. Manufacturers without a dealer network are limited to sales through a smaller number of independent dealers.

nents. All units are built on a permanent steel chassis (Ford is the largest supplier) that allows the finished unit to be transported to the installation site, where it is placed on a foundation (most often concrete blocks), and secured with tiedown straps. Some units are placed on permanent masonry foundations.

The manufacturing operation is a highly streamlined process that uses computer technology. Designers use CAD software to create house designs. The shop floor operations use computer-aided-manufacturing (CAM) software.

Sales & Marketing

Manufacturers market and sell to retail dealers, and may also operate their own retail outlets; Clayton operates about 400 sales centers. Dealers often stock a few showroom models and order only after a customer has made a purchase. Manufacturers generally keep no inventory and produce homes based on orders. The need for continual orders at the factory has pushed consolidation in the industry. Delivery time for a new order is around 90 days. As in the car business, ownership passes from the manufacturer to the dealer and then to the customer.

Dealers arrange transportation and installation, including utility hookup, and often provide air conditioning and furniture options. Because transportation from factory to installation site can be expensive and is paid by the retailer, most dealers buy from factories located no more than 250 miles away. As a result, manufacturers have factories in many locations across the country. Dealers frequently have multiple outlets, and most sell products made by several manufacturers. The average manufactured home retail price is close to $60,000, but prices can go much higher. Retail markup by dealers is close to 50 percent.

Human Resources

Industry workers earn an average of $14 hourly, $3 less than for all manufacturing, and $2 less than the US national average. The industry injury rate is 15 cases per 100 full-time workers, more than double the rate for manufacturing workers as a whole, and triple the national average. The annual personnel turnover rate is about the same as for other manufacturing segments.

Industry Employment Growth

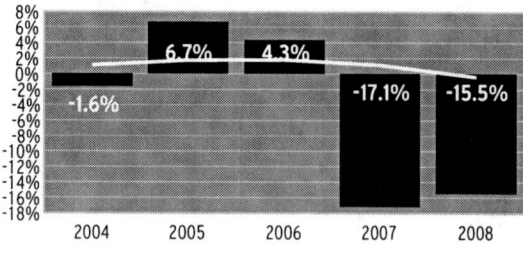

-1.6%	6.7%	4.3%	-17.1%	-15.5%
2004	2005	2006	2007	2008

Average Hourly Earnings

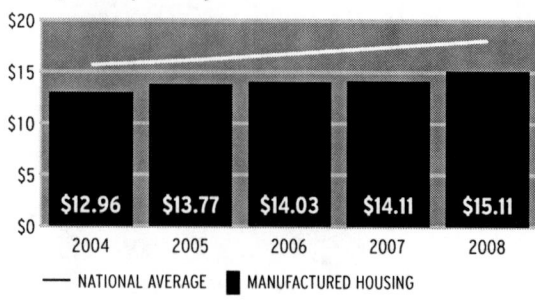

2004	2005	2006	2007	2008
$12.96	$13.77	$14.03	$14.11	$15.11

— NATIONAL AVERAGE   ■ MANUFACTURED HOUSING

SOURCE: BUREAU OF LABOR STATISTICS

Call Preparation Questions

How does the company manage cyclical demand?

US production of MH has been highly cyclical in the past 15 years.

How have recent trends in financing affected the company?

Because MH is often bought by customers with low income, credit financing availability is important.

What challenges has the company had building networks and relationships with dealers?

To ensure an outlet for their product, a number of large manufacturers have expanded ownership of dealers or negotiated exclusive access.

How does the company benefit from shifts in demographics?

MH is popular for retirement, improving the outlook as baby boomers get closer to retirement age.

How is the company advantaged or challenged by diversifying its product lines?

Manufacturers diversify by offering financing and insurance, and producing different types of manufactured units and components.

Web Links

Manufactured Housing Institute

News, industry links, and statistics.
www.manufacturedhousing.org/site_map.asp

Manufactured Housing Network

Links to manufacturers and retailers.
www.mhn.net/mhnbackup.htm

Manufactured Housing Statistics

From US Census Bureau.
www.census.gov/const/www/mhsindex.html

MobileHome.Net

Industry links and state associations.
www.mobilehome.net

Modern Homes Magazine

Feature articles on manufactured housing.
www.manufacturedhousing.org/modern_homes

National Modular Housing Council

News and policy information for modular home
manufacturers.
www.modularcouncil.org

U.S. Department of Housing and Urban Development

Federal information concerning manufactured
homes.
www.hud.gov/homes/manufactured.cfm

Glossary of Acronyms

CB — Census Bureau
FEMA — Federal Emergency Management Agency
HUD — Department of Housing and Urban
Development
LBP — lender best practices
MHA — Manufactured Housing Association
MHI — Mobile Home Institute
OFHEO — Office of Federal Housing Enterprise
Oversight

HOOVER'S TOP COMPANIES

Largest Companies by Sales	($ mil.)
Fleetwood Enterprises, Inc.	1,660.0
Champion Enterprises, Inc.	1,033.2
Palm Harbor Homes, Inc.	555.1
Skyline Corporation	301.8
Cavalier Homes, Inc.	164.4
Cavco Industries, Inc.	141.9
Clayton Homes, Inc.	—

Largest Employers	Employees
Clayton Homes, Inc.	12,000
Champion Enterprises, Inc.	6,500
Fleetwood Enterprises, Inc.	6,400
Palm Harbor Homes, Inc.	3,800
Skyline Corporation	2,000
Horton Industries, Inc.	1,900
Wick Building Systems, Inc.	1,400
Cavco Industries, Inc.	1,075
Fairmont Homes, Inc.	850
Liberty Homes, Inc.	800

Top Public Companies by Market Value	($ mil.)
Cavco Industries, Inc.	226.1
Skyline Corporation	224.2
Palm Harbor Homes, Inc.	116.8
Champion Enterprises, Inc.	49.0
Nobility Homes, Inc.	43.1

SOURCE: HOOVER'S, INC., DATABASE

Manufacturing Sector

The US manufacturing sector consists of about 300,000 companies with combined annual sales of over $4.5 trillion. Major manufacturers include GM, Ford, Boeing, GE, IBM, Hewlett-Packard, Tyson Foods, Procter & Gamble, Pfizer, DuPont, and Caterpillar. Although fragmented into many industries served by numerous competitors, the manufacturing sector is concentrated at the top: the largest 50 companies produce more than 25 percent of total sales.

Competitive Landscape

Demand ultimately depends on consumer spending, but changes in demand often aren't felt immediately because most manufacturers make intermediate products. The profitability of individual companies depends on efficient production and distribution. Large companies often have large economies of scale in purchasing, production, and marketing. Small companies can compete effectively by producing specialized products. The industry is capital-intensive and highly automated: annual revenue per employee varies greatly due to the large variety of production operations but averages more than $350,000.

Computer systems and controls have steadily increased the labor productivity of US manufacturers, a 50 percent improvement in the last 10 years. Even so, US labor costs remain high and many labor-intensive manufacturers have moved production operations to lower-cost countries like China.

Products, Operations & Technology

Major manufactured products include transportation equipment, computers and electronics, food, chemicals, machinery, and products made of metal, plastic, and paper. Cars and planes account for about 16 percent of US manufacturing output, food and beverages for 15 percent, chemicals for 15 percent, and comput-

ers and electronics for 9 percent. The net output of the manufacturing sector, after subtracting sales among manufacturers, is about $1.5 trillion, or 16 percent of US GDP.

Production operations transform input materials, including unfinished products and components, into finished products, using energy, machinery, and labor. Inputs may be raw materials (iron ore, petroleum feedstock); crops (cotton, rubber, foods); or semi-processed components (steel bars, plastic pellets, electronics, car subassemblies). To ensure availability of input materials, supply contracts are common. Energy, used mainly to power equipment or produce heat, is a major cost for many manufacturers. The steady rise in the cost of energy has encouraged companies to design energy-efficient production processes.

Several basic manufacturing methods are used, including continuous process and batch operations. Continuous process operations, like assembly lines, have proven to be the most efficient way to make many products, with economies increasing as greater volume is produced. These economies of scale encourage companies to grow. Batch operations are more common when customized products are made. The efficiency of production varies from company to company, and in many cases both the process and the final products are protected by patents. The manufacturing process produces goods with varying degrees of quality. A top priority for most manufacturing companies is to increase the yield of high-quality products.

The greatest production efficiencies are often achieved by companies that specialize in a particular product. Few US manufacturers today produce everything from raw materials to finished goods. A result of specialization is that most manufacturers make products for other manufacturers. Specialization often allows a manufacturer to have expertise in manufacturing similar products or products with similar uses.

The US manufacturing industry has become highly automated in all aspects. US manufacturers spend over $7 billion annually in capital expenditures for computer equipment. Manufacturing was a lead industry in the application of enterprise resource planning (ERP) technology and in its evolution to an enterprise services architecture (ESA). Applying these technologies has streamlined business processes and reduced the number of labor hours required per unit of production.

Most manufacturers have automated their backoffice processes including accounting, order entry, inventory management, and HR. These processes are integrated, operating on common databases. Many companies have implemented ERP systems having suites of applications adapted to the manufacturing industry and based on industry best practices. Adopting industry standard packages lowers the cost of automation and gives the company flexibility in leveraging third-party applications.

To minimize investment in materials inventory, most manufacturing companies practice some form of just-in-time (or lean) manufacturing. This requires the company to carefully coordinate deliveries from suppliers to minimize raw materials inventory and to coordinate deliveries to customers to minimize finished goods inventory. Supply chain management systems allow manufacturers, suppliers, and customers to share information on orders, schedules, and inventories to reduce inventory costs and maintain timely order fulfillment.

To remain competitive in a global economy, US manufacturers have automated production operations using machinery, robotics, and computer control systems. Much of the equipment used in manufacturing includes programmable logic controllers (PLCs) containing microprocessors that can be programmed. These controllers can be networked to pass status and control information from machine to machine. In some larger operations, controllers are linked to servers that control processes among multiple machines. Factory systems are usually tied together using TCP/IP networking. Some factories are evolving to use wireless technology, driven in part by increasing use of radio frequency identification (RFID) tags.

Factory floor hardware, including portable computers, is generally ruggedized so that it can perform in adverse environments. The ruggedization can include shock mounting, heat sinks, fans, and hermetically sealed units.

Sales & Marketing

Most manufacturers sell to other manufacturers or to wholesalers. Developing and maintaining long-term relationships with repeat customers is a major goal of marketing and sales. Sales may be handled by an in-house sales force or independent manufacturers representatives.

Industry trade shows and advertising in trade publications are important sources of new customers. Single or multi-year sales contracts are often used for large orders, and may commit the buyer to take a certain amount of product. Many products are made-to-order according to buyer specifications. For highly technical products, the sales process is often handled by engineers.

Although pricing is important, product quality and on-time delivery are often more important. Price pressures are high for US-based manufacturers that compete with low-cost foreign producers. US manufacturers are increasingly focusing on specialty products that have a high technology and a low labor content, to avoid low-cost foreign competitors.

Human Resources

As manufacturing has become more automated, the role of many workers has changed from direct operations to machinery control. Wages are accordingly a bit higher than for all US workers. The design of new products and the supervision of production facilities require that manufacturers maintain a high level of engineering expertise.

Many manufacturing operations create safety issues for workers. The overall injury rate for workers in manufacturing is only slightly above that for all US workers, but the rate for individual industries can be much higher.

Industry Employment Growth

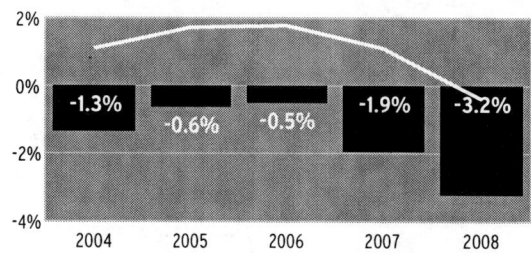

Average Hourly Earnings

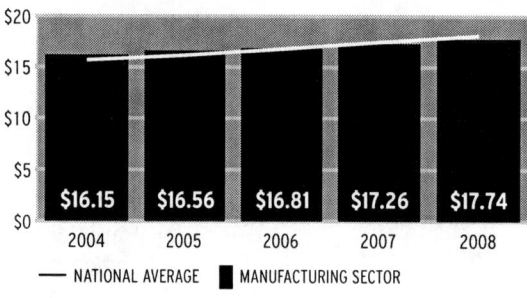

SOURCE: BUREAU OF LABOR STATISTICS

Call Preparation Questions

How does the company manage fluctuations in consumer spending or economic downturns?

Production in the manufacturing sector depends on consumer spending and retail sales, and can change rapidly during an economic slowdown.

How is the company affected by imports from low-cost countries?

US imports of manufactured goods have increased rapidly, because products with large labor content are much cheaper to produce in low-cost countries like China and Mexico.

How does the company typically finance large R&D or capital investments?

Manufacturing companies must make large investments in production equipment and computer systems to improve efficiency, and in R&D to develop new products.

What technologies could the company use to streamline processes and reduce costs?

US manufacturers use technology to lower costs, improve products, and optimize supply chain performance.

How are improvements in logistics, like GPS, benefiting the company?

To minimize inventories and speed distribution, many manufacturers invest in distribution technology and better logistics communication.

Web Links

AFL-CIO

Labor issues.
www.aflcio.org

Economic Statistics Briefing Room

Latest economic indicators.
www.whitehouse.gov/fsbr/production.html

Institute for Supply Management

Former National Association of Purchasing Management. Indexes of manufacturers purchasing activity, price activity. Benchmark data for select industries.
www.ism.ws

Manufacturing & Technology News

News archive.
www.manufacturingnews.com

Manufacturing.Net

News, news archive. Stock prices. Good discussion of issues in Automation & Control, Design, Mfg. Processes, Plant Operations, and Supply Chain.
www.manufacturing.net

National Association of Manufacturers

Policy issues.
www.nam.org

The Conference Board

Economic information, news, and events.
www.conferenceboard.org

Glossary of Acronyms

ISM — Institute for Supply Management
NAM — National Association of Manufacturers
WTO — World Trade Organization

HOOVER'S TOP COMPANIES

Largest Companies by Sales	($ mil.)
General Electric Company	182,515.0
General Motors Corporation	148,979.0
Ford Motor Company	146,277.0
Hewlett-Packard Company	118,364.0
International Business Machines Corporation	103,630.0
The Procter & Gamble Company	83,503.0
Johnson & Johnson	63,747.0
Dell Inc.	61,133.0
The Boeing Company	60,909.0
Caterpillar Inc.	51,324.0

Largest Employers	Employees
International Business Machines Corporation	426,969
General Electric Company	327,000
Hewlett-Packard Company	321,000
General Motors Corporation	243,000
Ford Motor Company	213,000
The Boeing Company	162,200
The Procter & Gamble Company	138,000
Johnson & Johnson	118,700
Caterpillar Inc.	112,887
Tyson Foods, Inc.	107,000

Fastest Growing* by Five-Year Sales Growth	(%)
International Baler Corp.	18.4
Caterpillar Inc.	17.7
Cascade Corporation	16.6
The Procter & Gamble Company	14.0
Dell Inc.	11.5
Key Technology, Inc.	10.2
Hewlett-Packard Company	10.1
Johnson & Johnson	8.8
Quipp, Inc.	8.6
NACCO Industries, Inc.	7.2

Fastest Growing* by Five-Year Employee Growth	(%)
Hewlett-Packard Company	17.7
Dell Inc.	17.7
Caterpillar Inc.	10.3
Cascade Corporation	9.9
The Procter & Gamble Company	7.1
Columbus McKinnon Corporation	5.5
The InterTech Group, Inc.	5.0
Key Technology, Inc.	4.8
International Business Machines Corporation	4.7
International Baler Corp.	4.4

Top Public Companies by Market Value	($ mil.)
The Procter & Gamble Company	184,419.5
General Electric Company	170,697.7
Johnson & Johnson	162,163.1
Pfizer Inc.	119,471.7
International Business Machines Corporation	112,698.3

* These rates are compounded annualized increases and may have resulted from acquisitions or one time gains. If less than 6 years of data are available, growth is for the years available.

SOURCE: HOOVER'S, INC., DATABASE

Market Research Services

The marketing research services industry in the US includes more than 5,500 companies with combined annual revenue of over $12 billion. Large companies include ACNielsen, Burke, Maritz Research, and Millward Brown, all of which are privately held. The industry is slightly concentrated: the top 50 companies have about 55 percent of industry revenue. The average marketing research firm has annual revenue of about $2.3 million.

Competitive Landscape

Demand is driven primarily by the health of the US economy and corporate profits. The profitability of individual companies depends on the quality of the research services delivered and the ability to manage costs. Large companies have advantages in providing a variety of research and ancillary services to large customers, and in achieving economies of scale in marketing and computerized operations. Small companies can compete successfully by specializing in a research methodology or in emerging niche knowledge areas. The industry is labor intensive: annual revenue per employee is less than $100,000.

Products, Operations & Technology

Major services are marketing research, which accounts for over 90 percent of industry revenue, and public opinion polling. Other services include media monitoring and analytic services. Many research firms specialize in 1) a discipline, such as customer satisfaction, human resources, or advertising tracking; 2) an industry segment, such as technology or pharmaceuticals; or 3) marketing services, such as focus groups, polling, or psychographics.

Most market research firms perform primary research — they gather and analyze original data. Primary research can either be custom for a particular client, or syndicated and sold to a number of clients. Secondary research uses pre-

BUSINESS CHALLENGES

» Dependence on Corporate Profits

Marketing research is sometimes seen as an expendable expense that may be cut in economic downturns or when corporations are struggling financially. Some research firms were hurt in the last recession when corporate profits fell. Firms specializing in ad tracking and branding were particularly hurt, as ad budgets are one of the first areas for spending cutbacks.

» Retaining Qualified Staff

Success depends on employee skill and knowledge. Senior research analysts and consultants are valued for their knowledge and client relationships. Companies compete for a limited number of qualified professionals, and thus try to retain high performers. Experienced staff is kept at many firms even in slow economic times. Noncompete agreements are frequently required of associates.

» Maintaining Large Clients

For many research companies, the projects of large corporations fund their infrastructure. Large client projects fund technology investments that can be leveraged for other client projects. Projects for large clients can easily surpass a million dollars and require the services of many employees. The loss of a large client affects numerous professionals and decreases the profitability of the firm, unless a new client of comparable size is found.

viously published data and provides primarily background information. Research firms conduct both consumer research projects and business to business analyses.

Marketing research begins with outlining a problem to explore, assessing a new product idea or concept, or testing a hypothesis. The firm works with the client to determine the project objectives, designs an appropriate research methodology and sample plan, chooses a data collection technique, performs the research, analyzes the results, and then communicates those results and recommendations to the client. Research firms generally outline these steps in a contract proposal that includes a project plan and price.

The two primary forms of market research are qualitative and quantitative. Large full-service firms typically offer both; smaller firms specialize in one. Qualitative research is used for exploratory purposes with a small number of respondents, such as focus groups of eight to 12, or one-on-one in-depth interviews. Qualitative research is effective to test concepts such as new ads or marketing messages. Results aren't representative of the general population. Quantitative research, used to draw conclusions and test particular hypotheses, is statistically based and uses random sampling techniques with a large number of respondents so results can be inferred to the entire population.

Market research firms consist of a staff of professionals with various levels of experience and expertise, support personnel with technical and clerical skills, and IT for collecting, tabulating, and analyzing data. Large firms with many professionals may have some economies of scale and produce higher annual revenue per employee ($150,000 for the top 20 firms) than small firms ($70,000 for firms not in top 50). Quantitative projects can involve several interviewers, data tabulation personnel, as well as a senior researcher and support staff. Qualitative projects generally involve one or a few research professionals.

Information technology has made quantitative research more efficient. Computer-assisted phone interviewing (CATI) places phone calls by calling the correct area codes and exchanges and randomly assigning the last four digits. In this way, even unlisted numbers are included in consumer samples. Statistical software has made data tabulation and analysis much quicker. The Internet is also being increasingly used as a data collection tool, primarily with the establishment of web panels. Companies acquire the emails of consumers who agree to serve on the panel and participate in selected studies. Large firms also use project accounting software to track project component costs and billings.

Sales & Marketing

Customers are primarily commercial businesses that want to understand the behavior of their customers and prospective customers, either consumers or other businesses. Government agencies, nonprofit organizations, and associations also use marketing research ser-

vices. Firms rely on sales professionals, generally referred to as business development managers, or senior managers to generate new business and maintain and grow relationships with existing clients.

Market research firms publish articles in trade publications, participate in client industry conferences and trade shows, and mail marketing materials to prospective customers.

Service prices are determined by the research methodology and the staff time involved in the project. While market research firms don't generally have billable hours, contract prices are based on the time various professionals are expected to spend on the project and the perceived value-added to the client for the service. Some projects are subject to competitive bids or are in response to requests for proposal (RFP). Contracts are usually fixed-price and government projects may have penalty clauses for not meeting contracted timelines.

Human Resources

The major resource of market research firms is their staff's talent and expertise. Most senior researchers have advanced degrees. Attracting and retaining accomplished professionals can be a major concern for individual companies. Wages are above the national norm and account for up to 40 percent of revenue. The industry injury rate is minimal.

Industry Employment Growth

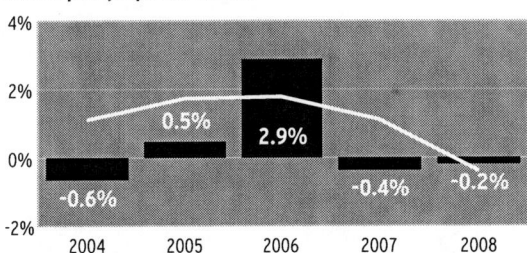

Average Hourly Earnings

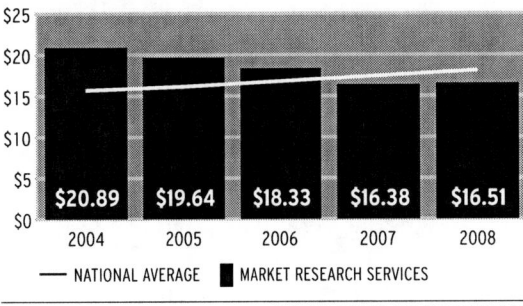

— NATIONAL AVERAGE ■ MARKET RESEARCH SERVICES

SOURCE: BUREAU OF LABOR STATISTICS

Call Preparation Questions

How volatile is demand for the company's services?

Marketing research is sometimes seen as an expendable expense that may be cut in economic downturns or when corporations are struggling financially.

FAST FACTS

» The marketing research services industry in the US includes more than 5,500 companies with combined annual revenue of over $12 billion.

» Large companies include ACNielsen, Burke, Maritz Research, and Millward Brown, all of which are privately held.

» Major services are marketing research, which accounts for over 90 percent of industry revenue, and public opinion polling.

» Customers are primarily commercial businesses that want to understand the behavior of their customers and prospective customers, either consumers or other businesses.

» Cash flow can be uneven due to the project-based nature of the work.

What is the competitive strength of the company?

Success depends on employee skill and knowledge.

How important are large customers to the company?

For many research companies, the projects of large corporations fund their infrastructure.

How has the company improved its survey response rates?

As the response rates of traditional surveying methods such as phone and mail decrease, research companies are increasingly looking to Internet panels as a way to collect data.

To what extent does the firm act as a consultant with clients?

In collecting and analyzing data, market research firms gain valuable insight into a variety of business issues and markets.

Web Links

American Association for Public Opinion Research

News about polling; polling updates.
www.aapor.org

American Marketing Association

News and events.
www.marketingpower.com

Council of American Survey Research Organizations

Industry standards, events, code of ethics.
www.casro.org

Market Research World

News, resources, links, glossary of terms, library of articles.
www.marketresearchworld.net

Marketing Research Association

Industry news, events, links.
www.mra-net.org

Glossary of Acronyms

AAPOR — American Association for Public Opinion Research

AMA — American Marketing Association

CASRO — Council of American Survey Research Organizations

CATI — computer-assisted telephone interviewing

PRC — Professional Research Certification

HOOVER'S TOP COMPANIES

Largest Companies by Sales	($ mil.)
IMS Health Incorporated	2,329.5
Maritz Inc.	1,560.0
Gartner, Inc.	1,279.1
ACNielsen Corporation	$679.5
Information Resources, Inc.	368.8
Arbitron Inc.	368.8
Forrester Research, Inc.	240.9
Harris Interactive Inc.	238.7
Merkle Inc.	181.0

Largest Employers	Employees
ACNielsen Corporation	21,068
IMS Health Incorporated	7,950
The Kantar Group	5,800
Information Resources, Inc.	4,300
Gartner, Inc.	4,198
Maritz Inc.	3,920
Arbitron Inc.	1,616
Datascension, Inc.	1,500
Harris Interactive Inc.	1,350
Merkle Inc.	900

Fastest Growing* by Five-Year Sales Growth	(%)
Greenfield Online, Inc.	54.0
Datascension, Inc.	25.2
Merkle Inc.	24.8
comScore, Inc.	18.5
National Research Corporation	16.9
Keynote Systems, Inc.	15.0
Forrester Research, Inc.	13.8
Harris Interactive Inc.	12.8
IMS Health Incorporated	11.0
Gartner, Inc.	8.3

Fastest Growing* by Five-Year Employee Growth	(%)
comScore, Inc.	50.0
Greenfield Online, Inc.	42.3
Merkle Inc.	25.9
Keynote Systems, Inc.	16.2
Forrester Research, Inc.	12.4
National Research Corporation	9.4
IMS Health Incorporated	7.3
Gartner, Inc.	5.0
Arbitron Inc.	0.7

Top Public Companies by Market Value	($ mil.)
IMS Health Incorporated	2,751.3
Gartner, Inc.	1,673.9
Forrester Research, Inc.	650.1
Greenfield Online, Inc.	384.4
comScore, Inc.	371.4

* These rates are compounded annualized increases and may have resulted from acquisitions or one time gains. If less than 6 years of data are available, growth is for the years available.

SOURCE: HOOVER'S, INC., DATABASE

Material Handling Equipment Distribution

About 4,000 distribution outlets for material handling equipment in the US generate combined annual sales of $15 billion, about half due to lift truck sales. Most distributors are privately owned, single-location companies, although manufacturers like NACCO also own some dealers. Among the largest lift truck manufacturers are NACCO Industries in the US, Jungheinrich AG in Europe, and Toyota Industries in Asia. The industry is highly fragmented: the 50 largest companies hold about 35 percent of the market.

Competitive Landscape

Demand depends on the quantity of goods moving through the US economy. The profitability of individual distributors depends on good marketing. Small distributors can compete by specializing in a specific industry or type of equipment, or by offering excellent service programs. Large distributors can negotiate favorable agreements with manufacturers. Average annual revenue per employee is over $250,000.

Products, Operations & Technology

Products include lift trucks and inventory handling systems like conveyors, sorters, storage racks, carousels, and shelving systems. Distributors usually operate in either the lift truck segment or in the inventory systems segment, but not both. Products are used in both manufacturing and inventory facilities. Well-known lift truck brands are Hyster, Yale, Crown, Clark, Caterpillar, Komatsu, Toyota, Nissan, and Raymond.

Most distributors have only one or two distribution outlets. A typical manufacturer sells products through a network of many distributors. For example, Clark Material Handling has over 200 dealers. Distributors are usually independent, but are often affiliated with a particu-

BUSINESS CHALLENGES

» Highly Dependent on Flow of Goods

Demand for material handling equipment depends on the level of goods moving through the US economy from domestic production, imports, and sales. US manufacturer shipments of goods fell 6 percent during the last recession; imports of durable goods fell 5. In a stagnant economy, customers defer purchases of new equipment.

» Competition from Rental Companies

Equipment rental companies provide an alternative to buying forklifts or other equipment from a distributor. Big companies, like United Rentals and NationsRent, rent a limited line of popular forklifts along with other types of industrial and construction equipment. Smaller rental companies may specialize in specific types of material handling equipment.

» Competition from Manufacturers

Some material handling equipment manufacturers have opened retail outlets and use Internet sites for direct sales, bypassing distributors. With sophisticated websites, manufacturers can fill orders directly from customers of any size. Distributors with large service operations are essential for manufacturers, but smaller companies that handle only sales may be cut out.

lar manufacturer. Some manufacturers own their own dealerships.

In addition to the sale of new and used equipment, dealerships lease and rent equipment either long- or short-term. Lift truck dealers operate much like traditional car dealers, providing sales, service, spare parts, financing (often in cooperation with the manufacturer); taking trade-ins; and selling used trucks. A large base of existing trucks provides dealers with a big market for replacement parts, maintenance, and retrofitting. The margins on service are better than those on original sales. A dealer's territory is limited by its ability to provide service.

Sales & Marketing

Major customers are manufacturing plants and inventory-handling facilities. Distributors compete with other independent distributors and with manufacturer-owned dealers.

A typical customer is a distribution center that services 100 stores a day with 300,000 cases, 21,000 pallets, and 20,000 stock-keeping units (SKUs). Most facilities have a flow-through design, with receiving at one end and shipping at the other. Facilities use single and double-deep pallets and pushback racks, and forklifts to move material.

Because the industry is diverse and fragmented, prices vary greatly, depending on the size and complexity of the equipment. High-volume, lower-priced products can be susceptible to competitive pricing, but more expensive equipment is less vulnerable to price pressures.

A key element in sales of complicated inventory or process systems is physical configuration of the customer's production floor or warehouse space. With construction and real estate costs increasing, customers have distributors help them design and build the best layout and material handling system to maximize use of a compact space.

Human Resources

Wholesalers' average hourly pay is about 25 percent higher than the national average wage. Distributor sales and service personnel of complex products and systems need more advanced training and skills than their peers who work with low-level products. Turnover in the wholesale business is around 28 percent, lower than the 40 percent rate for the entire private sector. The industry's safety record is par with the national average.

Call Preparation Questions

How do fluctuations in the flow of goods from manufacturing and foreign trade affect the company?

Demand for material handling equipment depends on the level of goods moving through the US economy from domestic production, imports, and sales.

How much competition does the company get from equipment rental companies?

Equipment rental companies provide an alternative to buying forklifts or other equipment from a distributor.

How much competition does the company see from direct sales by manufacturers?

Some material handling equipment manufacturers have opened retail outlets and use Internet sites for direct sales, bypassing distributors.

How might the company benefit by offering maintenance/repair services and selling spare parts?

Big distributors sell more parts and provide more repairs, industrial maintenance, and equipment rental.

How is the trend toward "lean manufacturing" impacting the company?

Changes in US industrial practice over the past decade have increased demand for effective material handling and inventory management.

Web Links

LiftTruck.com

Safety information and training.
www.lifttruck.com

Material Handling Equipment Distributors Association

Current industry news.
www.mheda.org

Material Handling Industry of America

Good industry statistics. List of members based on product categories.
www.mhia.org

Material Handling Product News

Journal news.
www.mmh.com/prodspot

Modern Materials Handling

News.
www.mmh.com

Glossary of Acronyms

DC — distribution center
ISM — Institute for Supply Management
MHEDA — Material Handling Equipment Distributors Association
MHEM — material handling equipment manufacturing
MHIA — Material Handling Industry of America
NAWD — National Association of Wholesaler-Distributors
SKU — stock-keeping unit
WMS — warehouse management system

HOOVER'S TOP COMPANIES

Largest Companies by Sales	($ mil.)
Kaman Corporation	1,253.6
Columbus McKinnon Corporation	623.3
Quipp, Inc.	24.6
Paragon Technologies, Inc.	21.5
International Baler Corp.	12.8
Dematic Corp.	—
FKI Logistex North America	—

Largest Employers	Employees
Kaman Corporation	3,618
Columbus McKinnon Corporation	3,250
Dematic Corp.	1,500
FKI Logistex North America	1,100
Quipp, Inc.	106
International Baler Corp.	62
Paragon Technologies, Inc.	49

Fastest Growing* by Five-Year Sales Growth	(%)
International Baler Corp.	18.4
Quipp, Inc.	8.6
Kaman Corporation	7.0
Columbus McKinnon Corporation	6.6

Fastest Growing* by Five-Year Employee Growth	(%)
Columbus McKinnon Corporation	5.5
International Baler Corp.	4.4
Quipp, Inc.	2.0

Top Public Companies by Market Value	($ mil.)
Columbus McKinnon Corporation	588.3
Kaman Corporation	461.8
Paragon Technologies, Inc.	19.1

* These rates are compounded annualized increases and may have resulted from acquisitions or one time gains. If less than 6 years of data are available, growth is for the years available.

SOURCE: HOOVER'S, INC., DATABASE

Meat Products Manufacture

In the US, 3,000 companies produce meat products, with combined annual revenues of about $85 billion. Large companies include Tyson Foods and Smithfield Foods. Tyson is the largest beef company, Smithfield the largest pork company. The slaughtering segment of the industry is highly concentrated: the 50 largest companies hold 90 percent of the market. The secondary processing segment is less concentrated, with the top 50 companies holding 60 percent of the market.

Competitive Landscape

Demand is driven by consumer income and by exports. Because meat is largely a commodity, the profitability of individual companies depends on efficient operations and an effective distribution network. Large companies have big economies of scale in production and distribution. Small companies can compete effectively in a local area or by producing unique products.

Products, Operations & Technology

Major products are wholesale meat parts ("boxed" beef or pork) that will be cut or processed further, ground beef for commercial use, and "case-ready" (ready for supermarket display cases) items for retail use. The industry produces about 40 billion pounds of beef products per year, and 30 billion pounds of pork products.

Several distinct steps are involved in processing live animals into finished meat products. Live animals are typically bred and raised on individual farms until they reach a minimum size (45 pounds for hogs and about 500 pounds for steers). They're then transported to feedlots (or feedyards) for "finishing," where they're fed high-quality grain feed mixtures until they reach their finished weight (250 pounds for hogs and 1,200 pounds for steers). The animals are then slaughtered and the

BUSINESS CHALLENGES

» Dependence on Federal Regulators

Each year, more than 4 million Americans get sick from eating bacteria-tainted foods, and over 1,200 die. The USDA, which regulates various aspects of meat processing operations and has the power to shut plants down, has promoted a Hazard Analysis and Critical Control Point system (HACCP) in slaughter and meat processing plants to reduce food contamination.

» Competition from Other Foods

Consumer tastes have shifted to lower consumption of red meats like beef and pork. For example, per capita consumption of chicken in the US grew 70 percent in the last 20 years to 85 pounds, while beef consumption fell 15 percent to 65 pounds. Soy-based meat alternatives, once niche products, are becoming more common and generate almost $1 billion in annual sales.

» Risk of Catastrophic Animal Diseases

Exposure to animal diseases like foot-and-mouth (FMD) or mad cow disease, also known as bovine spongiform encephalopathy (BSE), could devastate meat product sales. FMD and BSE ravaged cattle herds in Europe in recent years. Swine flu has periodically led to wholesale destruction of animals in Asia.

"dressed" carcasses are either processed further in the same plant or sold to outside processors.

The economics of raising steers and hogs are dictated largely by the price of feed and by "feed efficiency," the rate at which feed is turned into weight gain. High-quality feeds for both steers and hogs are combinations of corn (mainly), soybean meal, and various additives. "Finishing" steers need 6 pounds of feed for 1 pound of weight gain, hogs only about 2.5 pounds of feed. Fed cattle are ready for slaughter at 20 months after birth, hogs at seven. Most beef packers don't produce their own cattle, but buy them from large feedlot operators. Some pork packers produce a large percentage of their own hogs, either on their own feedlots or through production contracts with independent farmers, who they supply piglets and feed to. Packers employ experienced animal buyers who make daily competitive purchases from feedlots, sales barns, and other supply points. Live cattle and hog costs are based on the expected yield (of usable meat) and quality (meat grade) of the animals, and on basic supply-demand considerations.

Sales & Marketing

Meat packers sell to large customers such as grocery chains, meat distributors, food service distributors, restaurant and hotel chains, and processors. Price and quality are the main competitive factors. Because fresh meats are perishable, large processors have extensive distribution systems, including refrigerated warehouses and refrigerated distribution trucks. Large companies maintain regional sales/service centers. Sales are made by in-house sales staff, and through food brokers and distributors. There are few long-term supply contracts, even with major customers. Most orders are placed shortly before shipment.

Human Resources

Production workers in meat packing and processing plants are semiskilled. Many work with dangerous equipment like knives and other power tools, in unpleasant conditions. Wages are below the national average and have increased at a below-average rate in recent years.

The industry rate of illness and injury in meat packing plants is nearly double the average for all US workers.

The periodic shortage of labor, due to the unpleasant nature of much of the work in slaughtering and processing, has sometimes led to the hiring of illegal immigrants.

Industry Employment Growth

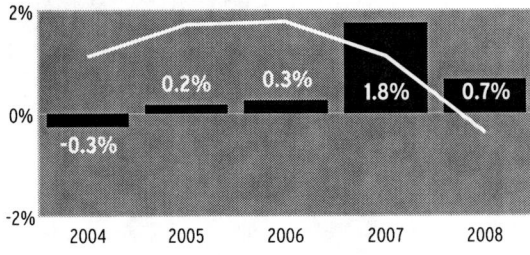

Average Hourly Earnings

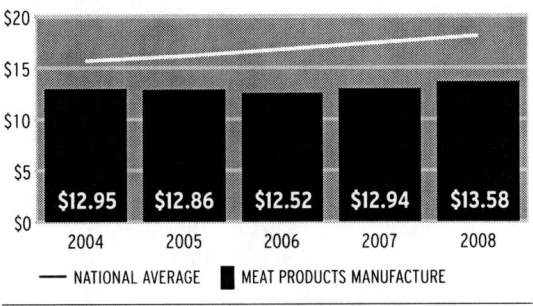

SOURCE: BUREAU OF LABOR STATISTICS

Call Preparation Questions

How does the company reduce risk of food contamination and subsequent recalls or litigation?

Each year, more than 4 million Americans get sick from eating bacteria-tainted foods, and over 1,200 die.

How does the company mitigate shifts in meat consumption?

Consumer tastes have shifted to lower consumption of red meats like beef and pork.

How do ongoing threats of animal diseases, like mad cow, impact the company?

Exposure to animal diseases like foot-and-mouth (FMD) or mad cow disease, also known as bovine spongiform encephalopathy (BSE), could devastate meat product sales.

How are genetic engineering and advanced breeding techniques benefiting the company?

Advanced breeding processes have developed meat animals with lower fat content, faster weight gain, and greater quality consistency.

How is the company advantaged by branding meats, such as Angus?

Differences in meat quality have allowed packers to create brand name products, such as Angus beef, which consumers are willing to pay a premium for.

Web Links

Agriculture and Agri-Food Canada

www.agr.ca

American Meat Institute

News, industry issues.
www.meatami.com

Canada Beef Export Federation

Industry statistics.
www.cbef.com

Canadian Meat Council

Industry statistics. Issues.
www.cmc-cvc.com/english/industry_statistic_e.asp

Cattle Buyers Weekly

Top 30 beef packers in 1999.
www.cattlebuyersweekly.com/information/
marketshare/beefpackers.html

CattleFax

Current volume and price reports.
www.cattlefax.com/quicklinks-data/usda-reports

ERS Livestock, Dairy, and Poultry Outlook

This monthly government report provides forecasts
of production, consumption, trade, prices received,
and more.
www.ers.usda.gov/Publications/ldp

Food Safety

Government interagency information and links.
www.foodsafety.gov

Grain Inspection, Packers & Stockyards Administration

USDA agency. Trade practices and competition
issues.
www.gipsa.usda.gov

Meat & Poultry

News. Industry situation.
www.meatpoultry.com

National Agricultural Statistics Service

USDA agency. Animal and meat statistics.
www.nass.usda.gov/QuickStats/indexbysubject.jsp?
Pass_group=Livestock+%26+Animals

National Cattlemen's Beef Association

Good industry links. Industry statistics. Issues.
www.beef.org

National Meat Association

Lobbying organization. Industry links.
www.nmaonline.org

National Pork Producers Council

Lobbying organization. Industry issues.
www.nppc.org

Texas Cattle Feeders Association

Good information about feedlot operations. Industry
statistics.
www.tcfa.org

US Meat Export Federation

Meat export issues. Export statistics.
www.usmef.org

Glossary of Acronyms

BSE — bovine spongiform encephalopathy
COOL — country of origin labeling
FSIS — Food Safety and Inspection Service
HACCP — Hazard Analysis and Critical Control Point
ITC — International Trade Commission

HOOVER'S TOP COMPANIES

Largest Companies by Sales	($ mil.)
Tyson Foods, Inc.	26,862.0
Smithfield Foods, Inc.	11,351.2
Pilgrim's Pride Corporation	8,525.1
Hormel Foods Corporation	6,754.9
OSI Industries, LLC	4,620.0
Seaboard Corporation	4,267.8
Foster Poultry Farms	1,890.0
Koch Foods Incorporated	1,800.0
JBS Swift & Company	—
Perdue Incorporated	—

Largest Employers	Employees
Tyson Foods, Inc.	107,000
Smithfield Foods, Inc.	58,100
Pilgrim's Pride Corporation	44,750
OSI Industries, LLC	22,000
Perdue Incorporated	21,000
JBS Swift & Company	20,200
Hormel Foods Corporation	19,100
Koch Foods Incorporated	14,000
ContiGroup Companies, Inc.	13,500
Sanderson Farms, Inc.	10,739

Fastest Growing* by Five-Year Sales Growth	(%)
Darling International Inc.	19.7
Seaboard Corporation	16.6
Sanderson Farms, Inc.	14.6
Koch Foods Incorporated	13.4
Hormel Foods Corporation	10.0
Pilgrim's Pride Corporation	9.7
Smithfield Foods, Inc.	7.5
Foster Poultry Farms	5.7
Cagle's, Inc.	4.8
Tyson Foods, Inc.	1.8

Fastest Growing* by Five-Year Employee Growth	(%)
Koch Foods Incorporated	36.6
OSI Industries, LLC	12.9
Darling International Inc.	8.8
Sanderson Farms, Inc.	7.5
Smithfield Foods, Inc.	5.7
Hormel Foods Corporation	2.8
Pilgrim's Pride Corporation	2.5
Seaboard Corporation	1.5

Top Public Companies by Market Value	($ mil.)
Tyson Foods, Inc.	3,895.8
Hormel Foods Corporation	3,831.1
Smithfield Foods, Inc.	3,827.7
Seaboard Corporation	1,481.1
Darling International Inc.	951.1

* These rates are compounded annualized increases and may
have resulted from acquisitions or one time gains. If less
than 6 years of data are available, growth is for the years
available.

SOURCE: HOOVER'S, INC., DATABASE

Medical and Imaging Laboratories

THIS INDUSTRY INCLUDES:

SIC CODES
8071   Medical Laboratories
8093   Specialty Outpatient Facilities
8099   Health and Allied Services

NAICS CODES
6215   Medical and Diagnostic Laboratories

The commercial medical and diagnostic laboratory industry in the US consists of about 5,000 companies with combined annual revenue of $3 billion. Major companies include Quest Diagnostics and Laboratory Corporation (LabCorp) in the medical lab segment, and Alliance Imaging and RadNet in the imaging segment. The industry is fairly fragmented: the 50 largest companies hold just over 40 percent of the market. Medical labs account for about two-thirds of industry revenue; imaging centers account for one-third.

Competitive Landscape

Demand is linked to the number of people receiving medical treatment. The profitability of individual companies depends on efficient operations and good marketing. There are large economies of scale in the operation of medical labs, which can receive samples from a wide geographical area. Small medical labs can compete effectively by providing specialized analyses, or by serving geographical regions with few medical facilities. Imaging centers don't have similar economies of scale because they must be located close to patients, so small firms can compete effectively with large ones in a particular area. The industry is fairly labor-intensive: annual revenue per worker is $140,000.

Products, Operations & Technology

Medical labs (often called "clinical labs") receive specimens of body fluids (most often blood) or tissues collected from patients, and perform a wide variety of tests to determine the presence and amount of various biochemicals to help doctors diagnose and treat medical conditions. Laboratory Corporation offers about 4,000 different tests. The tests performed are often classified as either "routine" or "esoteric/specialty," according to the difficulty of analysis and the frequency of use in medicine. As technology improves and medical

BUSINESS CHALLENGES

» Dependence on Government Regulations, Approvals

Federal and state laws regulate many aspects of the operations of clinical labs and imaging centers, both to assure quality and control costs. Medicare and Medicaid determine what tests they'll pay for and impose their own fee schedules, which are often copied in the private sector. "Certificate of need" laws control the equipment an imaging center may have. The FDA must approve all new tests and test equipment.

» Competition from Hospitals, Office Labs

Commercial clinical labs face stiff competition from labs operated by hospitals and doctor offices. Estimates vary, but suggest that hospital labs hold 60 percent of the total market, commercial labs about a third, and office labs the rest. Because the Clinical Laboratory Improvement Amendments require all labs to be certified, an expensive process, many smaller office labs have closed.

» Rapid Technological Innovation

Rapid changes in medical practice can render current equipment and methods obsolete and can require expensive retooling. New clinical tests can be expensive to license or may be unavailable at all if the manufacturer has an exclusive arrangement with one customer. Esoteric tests, which command a premium payment, may be replaced by simpler, low-cost tests.

knowledge advances, esoteric tests (such as HIV tests) can become routine. The large companies get about 80 percent of their revenue from routine tests. Some companies, like Specialty Laboratories, operate only in the esoteric segment.

Routine tests include cholesterol tests, blood cell counts, pap smears, urinalyses, microbiology cultures, pregnancy tests, HIV tests, and tests to measure the levels of sugar, enzymes, and other chemicals in blood. Such tests are done mainly with highly automated equipment and results are generally reported in 24 hours. Esoteric tests like gene tests and immunological tests require technicians with advanced training who often use highly sophisticated equipment. Anatomic pathology testing requires the preparation of microscope slides and may include interpretation by pathologists.

The main operational challenges of clinical labs involve collecting and correctly handling a large number of small specimens, mainly in small blood tubes. In a recent year, Quest processed 130 million specimens in 30 major clinical labs, or about 12,000 per lab per day. Specimens may be collected from hospitals, clinics, and doctor offices, and from satellite service centers where patients are sent by doctors to have blood drawn. Quality control and accurate reporting are major concerns. Most test results are reported electronically.

Imaging centers use special equipment to visualize structures and processes inside the human body, including MRI, CT, and PET scanning; and x-rays, mammography, ultrasound, fluoroscopy, and nuclear medicine. MRI has become the method of choice for imaging soft tissues. Equipment is often very expensive, made by divisions of GE, Hitachi, Siemens, or Phillips. The quality of MRI images depends on the strength of the magnets in the equipment, usually from 0.5 to 1.5 tesla. Imaging centers operate much like a clinic because they schedule appointments with patients, often treat patients with sedatives or contrast agents before a procedure, and may hold patients afterward in a recovery area. Imaging centers may simply forward images directly to the ordering doctor, or may contract with radiologists to interpret the images.

Sales & Marketing

While most clinical and imaging tests are ordered by doctors, marketing efforts are directed toward the third-parties that pay for the services, such as Medicare; Medicaid; managed care organizations (MCOs); and other insurers. Labs and imaging centers also contract with commercial customers such as hospitals, clinics, doctor offices, and employers for services they may eventually bill to a third party insurer. In the private sector, fee schedules are negotiated, often as a discount from a standard schedule. With Medicare and Medicaid, the fee schedule is imposed by the government but may differ in different parts of the country. In addition to such "fee-for-service" contracts, labs may contract with MCOs on a "capitated" basis,

meaning that the lab receives a set fee each month according to how many patients are enrolled in a managed care plan, regardless of how many tests are performed. In a recent year, Quest received about 40 percent of revenues from third party payers, 30 percent from commercial customers, 15 percent from Medicare/Medicaid, 5 to 10 percent from private individuals; and 5 to 10 percent from capitation fees. Imaging centers may have contracts with hospitals or clinics that extend three to five years and can't be canceled.

Human Resources

Most jobs in labs and imaging centers have a moderate technical component and require special training. Pay is accordingly above-average, about 10 percent above the average US wage. With a limited number of employers in each local market, personnel turnover is probably relatively low.

Employment in the industry has steadily increased in recent years, despite consolidation and greater reliance on automated equipment, as the health care industry has made greater use of diagnostic tools.

Industry Employment Growth

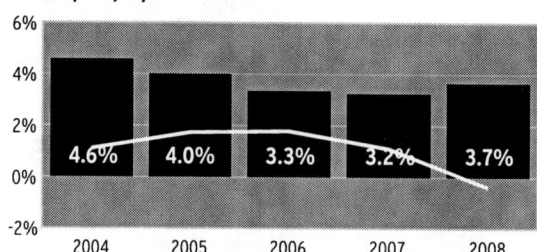

Average Hourly Earnings

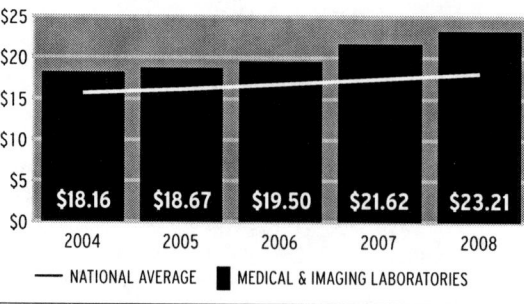

— NATIONAL AVERAGE ■ MEDICAL & IMAGING LABORATORIES

SOURCE: BUREAU OF LABOR STATISTICS

Call Preparation Questions

What difficulties has the company had adhering to state and federal regulations?

Federal and state laws regulate many aspects of the operations of clinical labs and imaging centers, both to assure quality and control costs.

How does the company differentiate itself?

Commercial clinical labs face stiff competition from labs operated by hospitals and doctor offices.

How does the company mitigate rapid obsolescence of equipment?

Rapid changes in medical practice can render current equipment and methods obsolete and can require expensive retooling.

How does the company gain access to newly developed tests and equipment?

Rapid advances in understanding human physiology and pathology are creating a need for new kinds of tests and stronger demand for existing tests.

What advantages could the company gain from expanding operations to include non-medical testing?

Using clinical tests by employers (for drug and alcohol abuse); insurance companies (for life insurance policies); police departments (DNA fingerprinting, forensics investigation); and security agencies (identification) is expected to increase.

Web Links

American Clinical Laboratory Association

Monthly news and articles.
www.clinical-labs.org/news/index.shtml

American College of Radiology

Professional organization.
www.acr.org

FDA Center for Devices and Radiological Health

www.fda.gov/cdrh

Lab Tests Online

Explanation of a wide variety of lab tests. News about new tests.
www.labtestsonline.org

National Imaging Associates

Latest developments from a managed care perspective.
www.radmd.com

NEMA – Medical Market Data

Imaging equipment manufacturers.
www.nema.org/econ/data/prod/medical

Radiological Society of North America

Professional organization.
www.rsna.org

Glossary of Acronyms

CDC — Centers for Disease Control
CLIA — Clinical Laboratory Improvement Amendments
CMS — Centers for Medicare and Medicaid Services
HIPAA — Health Insurance Portability and Accountability Act
HHS — Health and Human Services

HOOVER'S TOP COMPANIES

Largest Companies by Sales	($ mil.)
Quest Diagnostics Incorporated	7,249.5
Laboratory Corporation of America Holdings	4,505.2
RadNet, Inc.	502.1
Alliance HealthCare Services	444.9
Bio-Reference Laboratories, Inc.	301.1
InSight Health Services Holdings Corp.	242.6
Genoptix, Inc.	116.2
Bostwick Laboratories, Inc.	102.8
MEDTOX Scientific, Inc.	80.3
Clarient, Inc.	43.0

Largest Employers	Employees
Quest Diagnostics Incorporated	42,800
Laboratory Corporation of America Holdings	26,000
InSight Health Services Holdings Corp.	2,148
Alliance HealthCare Services	2,070
Bio-Reference Laboratories, Inc.	1,648
Bostwick Laboratories, Inc.	753
MEDTOX Scientific, Inc.	523
Genoptix, Inc.	155
Clarient, Inc.	139
Psychemedics Corporation	97

Fastest Growing* by Five-Year Sales Growth	(%)
Genoptix, Inc.	258.9
Bostwick Laboratories, Inc.	84.2
Clarient, Inc.	35.8
RadNet, Inc.	29.6
Bio-Reference Laboratories, Inc.	22.5
MEDTOX Scientific, Inc.	9.1
Laboratory Corporation of America Holdings	8.9
Quest Diagnostics Incorporated	8.9
Psychemedics Corporation	8.8
Alliance HealthCare Services	1.5

Fastest Growing* by Five-Year Employee Growth	(%)
Genoptix, Inc.	37.2
Bio-Reference Laboratories, Inc.	13.6
Clarient, Inc.	11.6
InSight Health Services Holdings Corp.	4.8
Laboratory Corporation of America Holdings	4.1
Quest Diagnostics Incorporated	2.8
MEDTOX Scientific, Inc.	2.0

Top Public Companies by Market Value	($ mil.)
Quest Diagnostics Incorporated	9,882.3
Laboratory Corporation of America Holdings	6,969.2
Genoptix, Inc.	568.5
Alliance HealthCare Services	489.9
Bio-Reference Laboratories, Inc.	338.8

* These rates are compounded annualized increases and may have resulted from acquisitions or one time gains. If less than 6 years of data are available, growth is for the years available.

SOURCE: HOOVER'S, INC., DATABASE

Medical Equipment Distributors

The medical equipment and supplies distribution industry in the US includes about 6,000 companies with combined annual revenue of about $53 billion. The largest national distributors include Owens & Minor, Henry Schein, Patterson Dental, and PSS/World Medical. The industry is highly concentrated: the top 50 companies hold almost 65 percent market share. Most companies participate at a regional or local level and have revenues of about $5 million.

Competitive Landscape

Demand depends on the number of people in the US receiving medical treatment. The profitability of individual companies depends on merchandising and efficient delivery systems. Large companies have economies of scale in purchasing, and highly developed infrastructure that allow for efficient distribution. Small companies can compete effectively by specializing in a product line or servicing a local customer base. Annual revenue per employee is about $500,000.

Products, Operations & Technology

Major products include medical and surgical supplies (about 45 percent of the market) and instruments and equipment (about 40 percent). Other products include orthopedic and prosthetic appliances, dental products, and veterinary supplies. Some companies carry over 100,000 items while others specialize in niche markets and may carry only a few different stock items to serve a local market's specific needs.

Distributors buy high volumes of product from manufacturers, store these products at company-operated distribution centers, and deliver to customers as required. Products are generally delivered by company-owned or leased trucks. Common carriers are used as needed.

BUSINESS CHALLENGES

» Cost-Containment Efforts Cap Equipment Prices

Total health care costs continue to grow rapidly, and distributors are pressured by both manufacturers and insurers to contain costs. Although costs for medical equipment haven't grown very fast, they're subject to overall efforts to contain health care costs. In recent years, national spending for medical equipment increased just 4 percent per year, but average prices for medical equipment were almost flat.

» Competition from GPOs

Many of the nation's hospitals and physician offices belong to group purchasing organizations (GPO), which can negotiate bulk sales at reduced prices directly from manufacturers. Distributors are still involved in actual delivery to customers for a fee, but don't have the opportunity to resell at a higher price.

» Maintaining Supplier Base

Major national distributors may carry two or three manufacturers' products, each of whom account for 10 to 15 percent of total sales revenue. Small specialty wholesalers may, in some instances, depend completely on one or two companies for their entire revenue stream. The loss of a major supplier can significantly impact a company's financial performance.

Computer and Internet technologies play a major role. Distributors operate proprietary systems that allow customers to place orders directly and receive products the next business day. Inventory monitoring, automated vendor purchase order creation, order analysis, pricing, delivery scheduling, and automated billing are components of the most refined systems.

Sales & Marketing

Major end-users are physician offices, hospitals, dental offices, alternate care facilities such as same-day surgical centers, clinics, and extended care facilities. In the US, about 230,000 physician offices; 130,000 dental practices; and 5,800 hospitals operate. Many belong to buying groups known as Group Purchasing Organizations (GPO) that negotiate pricing directly with manufacturers and then contract with distributors for distribution at a fixed price. Alternatively, GPOs may set up long-term contracts directly with distributors based on cost-plus percentage.

Marketing is through trade publications, product literature delivered directly to provider locations, product presentations by company and supplier sales personnel, seminars, and trade shows. Selling is by a combination of field sales consultants who make frequent calls on the customer, and telesales and electronic ordering when negotiated long-term contractual agreements are in place. Sales transactions vary from a few dollars for routine consumable supplies to several thousand for sophisticated analytical or diagnostic equipment.

Distributors also compete directly with manufacturers with a dedicated sales force. Highly complex and expensive equipment, such as MRI machines, are sold by manufacturers salespeople.

Human Resources

Workers in the industry are relatively well-paid because the products sold require employees with detailed product knowledge. Entry level sales positions often require degrees in biology, chemistry, or engineering. Telemarketers and warehouse personnel comprise the remainder of the workforce. Average employee pay in the industry is about $55,000 per year.

Training expenses can be significant. Manufacturers hold training sessions for distributors when products are introduced. In-house training of new hires can be lengthy because of the total number of products a salesperson must represent to potential customers.

Industry Employment Growth

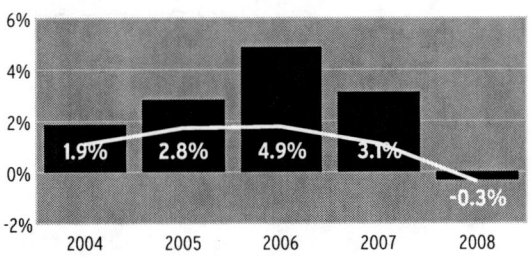

Average Hourly Earnings

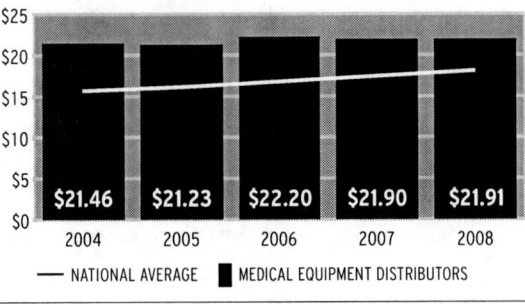

SOURCE: BUREAU OF LABOR STATISTICS

Call Preparation Questions

How have health care cost-containment efforts impacted company growth?

Total health care costs continue to grow rapidly, and distributors are pressured by both manufacturers and insurers to contain costs.

What percentage of company sales is through group purchasing organizations (GPOs)?

Many of the nation's hospitals and physician offices belong to group purchasing organizations (GPO), which can negotiate bulk sales at reduced prices directly from manufacturers.

How dependent is the company on a handful of key suppliers?

Major national distributors may carry two or three manufacturers' products, each of whom account for 10 to 15 percent of total sales revenue.

What opportunity does the company see in sales to outpatient surgery centers and other alternate care facilities?

Many non-invasive, and even some invasive, procedures have been transferred out of the hospital and into walk-in facilities that perform same-day services.

Does the company carry products for cosmetic and other elective applications?

Cosmetic and elective surgery centers are growing as demand increases.

Web Links

Dail-E News

News site associated with Repertoire.
www.mdsi.org/dailenews.asp

Health Industry Distributors Association

Contains industry news, education, and resource listings.
www.hida.org

Medical Device Manufacturers Association

Medical product news, industry issues.
www.medicaldevices.org/public

Medical Distribution Solutions, Inc. (MDSI)

Resource center; list of distributors, manufacturers.
www.mdsi.org

Repertoire

Magazine serving the health care distribution industry.
www.repertoiremag.com

Glossary of Acronyms

GPO — group purchasing organization
HIDA — Health Industry Distributors Association
MDMA — Medical Device Manufacturers Association

HOOVER'S TOP COMPANIES

Largest Companies by Sales	($ mil.)
McKesson Corporation	101,703.0
Cardinal Health, Inc.	91,091.4
Owens & Minor, Inc.	7,243.2
Henry Schein, Inc.	6,394.9
VWR International, LLC	3,540.0
Patterson Companies, Inc.	2,998.7
PSS World Medical, Inc.	1,855.8
Rotech Healthcare Inc.	559.3
Darby Dental Supply	350.0

Largest Employers	Employees
Cardinal Health, Inc.	43,500
McKesson Corporation	32,900
Henry Schein, Inc.	12,000
VWR International, LLC	6,960
Patterson Companies, Inc.	6,850
Rotech Healthcare Inc.	4,800
Owens & Minor, Inc.	4,800
PSS World Medical, Inc.	3,593
CCS Medical Holdings, Inc.	1,434
Universal Hospital Services, Inc.	1,318

Fastest Growing* by Five-Year Sales Growth	(%)
Henry Schein, Inc.	13.8
Patterson Companies, Inc.	12.6
McKesson Corporation	12.2
Universal Hospital Services, Inc.	11.4
Owens & Minor, Inc.	11.3
Cardinal Health, Inc.	9.9
PSS World Medical, Inc.	9.5
VWR International, LLC	6.2
SRI/Surgical Express, Inc.	2.3
NationsHealth, Inc.	1.5

Fastest Growing* by Five-Year Employee Growth	(%)
Owens & Minor, Inc.	13.9
Universal Hospital Services, Inc.	9.8
Patterson Companies, Inc.	7.5
McKesson Corporation	6.1
VWR International, LLC	5.1
Henry Schein, Inc.	4.4
PSS World Medical, Inc.	3.9

Top Public Companies by Market Value	($ mil.)
Cardinal Health, Inc.	18,419.2
McKesson Corporation	14,506.5
Patterson Companies, Inc.	4,100.2
Henry Schein, Inc.	3,161.3
Owens & Minor, Inc.	1,560.3

* These rates are compounded annualized increases and may have resulted from acquisitions or one time gains. If less than 6 years of data are available, growth is for the years available.

SOURCE: HOOVER'S, INC., DATABASE

Medical Supplies and Devices

The medical supplies and devices manufacturing industry includes about 12,000 companies with combined annual revenue of $78 billion. Large manufacturers include Johnson & Johnson, Baxter, Medtronic, and Boston Scientific. The industry is slightly concentrated: the 50 largest companies hold close to 60 percent of the market.

Medical supply and device manufacturers produce instruments, apparatus, and supplies used in the medical field. The industry doesn't include the manufacture of X-ray or electromedical equipment and devices, such as ultrasound equipment, pacemakers, and electrocardiographs.

Competitive Landscape

Demand is driven by population demographics and advances in medical knowledge and technology. The profitability of individual companies depends on the ability to develop superior products. Large companies have economies of scale in manufacturing and R&D. Small companies can compete successfully by specializing in a particular market segment, or through technical innovation. Annual revenue per employee is about $250,000.

Products, Operations & Technology

Major products include surgical and medical instruments such as syringes, hypodermic needles, and catheters (nearly 40 percent of industry revenue), and surgical appliances and supplies such as sutures, surgical dressings, and orthopedic devices (also about 40 percent). Other sources of revenue include lab equipment and furniture (centrifuges, scales, operating tables, hospital beds); ophthalmic goods (prescription glasses, contact lenses); and dental equipment and supplies.

Syringes are typically produced in assembly lines. The basic stages include needle formulation, plastic component molding, piece assembly, packaging, labeling, and shipping. Needles are produced from molten steel drawn through a die. The steel is rolled into a continuous, hollow wire and cut to form the needle. Plastic barrels and plungers can be made through extrusion or injection modeling. The barrel moves down a conveyor and is held in place to receive the plunger, needle, and safety cap. The completed syringes are packed into boxes, stacked on pallets, and sent to distributors.

Sterility and safety are key in manufacturing. Steel is often coated with nickel to prevent corrosion, and the production plant must be

BUSINESS CHALLENGES

» Dependence on Regulators

All new medical devices require approval from the FDA to be marketed, and from Medicare and other insurers that ultimately pay for use. Although FDA and Medicare have streamlined procedures, review for new devices can be lengthy and approval uncertain. Devices that get FDA approval may be unsuccessful if insurers judge them to be too expensive. The costs associated with such regulation can be high, particularly with higher-risk, Class III devices.

» Healthcare Cost-Containment

Because of rapidly increasing health care costs, private insurers and government programs like Medicare have moved to limit payments for many medical treatments that require medical supplies or devices. Doctors and hospitals, in turn, have a greater incentive to resist price increases. Wholesale prices for surgical instruments, for example, increased only 5 percent in the last 10 years.

» Product Obsolescence Risks

Medical device manufacturing is highly specialized, and rapid industry innovation greatly increases the risk of technological obsolescence. Most medical device companies are small and specialize in just one type of device, targeted toward one particular market, so they can't spread the risk of obsolescence across multiple products and markets.

free of disease-causing agents. Workers wear masks and sterile garments to prevent the spread of germs. Quality control agents use precise instrumentation like calipers, micrometers, or microscopes to ensure that products are the appropriate thickness, length, and width.

For many technically advanced products, manufacturing is labor-intensive. Many small manufacturers outsource manufacturing to facilities operated by contract manufacturers. Manufacturers of low-tech product like latex gloves, tape, syringes, and gauze are most concerned with maintaining a highly efficient, low-cost manufacturing environment. Companies that specialize in diagnostic and therapeutic devices generally emphasize technological innovation and precision.

Major inputs include stainless steel, silicone or latex rubber, plastic, aluminum, polymers, and natural fabrics. Electricity and natural gas typically provide the power for manufacturing.

The industry is technologically advanced, and new product development is a major activity for most manufacturers. Patents are valuable and patent disputes frequent. Large companies often buy small companies that have developed promising new technologies.

Sales & Marketing

Typical customers are national medical supply distributors like Cardinal Health, Owens & Minor, and Henry Schein. Large companies may distribute products directly to hospital chains or other major customers.

Major types of marketing include advertising on TV, and in magazines and newspapers. Manufacturers market products through a combination of direct sales and sales representatives that target hospitals, insurers, and individual doctors. Companies with products tied directly to a particular medical condition often sponsor medical conferences. The general adoption of a specialized technique — for example, the use of metal stents to open clogged arteries — can dramatically increase sales. The actual cost of manufacturing a medical device is often small relative to the marketing costs. Because of the large expense involved in such testing and documentation, small manufacturers often form marketing alliances with larger companies.

Manufacturer sales tend to be through traditional channels, though some medical supply resellers specialize exclusively in online sales. The Internet plays an important role in marketing product uses, features, and benefits to dis-

tributors, hospitals, and physicians. The FDA regulates online sales and marketing of medical devices by third parties. Companies may try to sell devices like contact lenses without a prescription, or may sell items like magnets and patches that purport to cure diseases, aches, and pains.

Prices vary depending on the type of product. A box of 1,000 syringes may cost around $8 to a wholesaler, while an artificial hip may cost $10,000 or more.

Human Resources

Wages for workers in medical products manufacturing are 10 percent lower than the national average. Pay for surgical and medical instruments manufacture is even lower at more than 15 percent below the national average. Because of relatively small production runs, much of the work is labor-intensive, prompting manufacturers to move production to lower-cost countries like Ireland, Mexico, and China. Most workers in medical products manufacture require only average skills.

The industry has a good safety record: injury rates are more than 40 lower than the national average. Common injuries include strains, sprains, cuts, and wrist pain from working with machinery, moving containers, and overexertion.

Industry Employment Growth

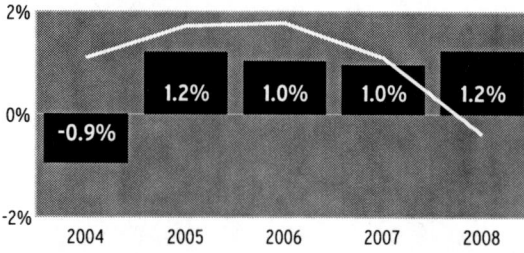

Average Hourly Earnings

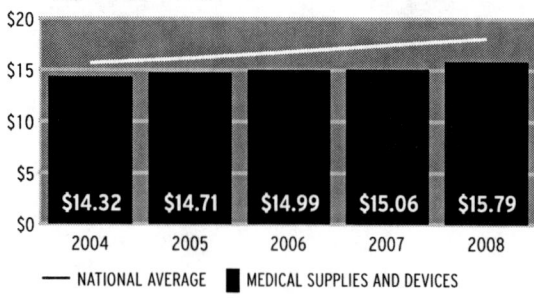

SOURCE: BUREAU OF LABOR STATISTICS

Call Preparation Questions

What difficulties has the company had meeting FDA and insurer approval?

All new medical devices require approval from the FDA to be marketed, and from Medicare and other insurers that ultimately pay for use.

Has the company been able to raise prices enough to cover cost increases?

Because of rapidly increasing health care costs, private insurers and government programs like Medicare have moved to limit payments for many medical treatments that require medical supplies or devices.

How does the company mitigate rapid obsolescence of products?

Medical device manufacturing is highly specialized, and rapid industry innovation greatly increases the risk of technological obsolescence.

What are the company's more recent technological innovations?

Manufacturers of implantable medical devices and diagnostic equipment are rapidly adopting wireless capabilities into their designs.

Web Links

FDA Center for Devices and Radiological Health (CDRH)

Medical devices news releases, regulations, MedWatch warnings and recalls.
www.fda.gov/CDRH

Independent Medical Devices Association

Online publications, links.
www.imda.org

Medical Device Link

News and articles.
devicelink.com

Medical Device Manufacturers Association

Industry News.
www.medicaldevices.org

Medical Devices Today

News and analysis on the medical device industry.
www.medicaldevicestoday.com

Repertoire

News and analysis for medical products distributors and manufacturers.
www.repertoiremag.com

Repertoire Dail-E News

Industry news.
dailenews.mdsi.org

Glossary of Acronyms

AHA — American Hospital Association

CDRH — Center for Devices and Radiological Health

CMS — Centers for Medicare and Medicaid Services

GMP — Good Manufacturing Practices

HHS — Department of Health and Human Services

OEM — original equipment manufacturer

PMA — Pre-Market Approval

HOOVER'S TOP COMPANIES

Largest Companies by Sales	($ mil.)
Johnson & Johnson	63,747.0
Medtronic, Inc.	13,515.0
Baxter International Inc.	12,348.0
Boston Scientific Corporation	8,050.0
Becton, Dickinson and Company	7,155.9
Stryker Corporation	6,718.2
St. Jude Medical, Inc.	4,363.3
Zimmer Holdings, Inc.	4,121.1
Medline Industries, Inc.	2,830.0
Bausch & Lomb Incorporated	2,500.0

Largest Employers	Employees
Johnson & Johnson	118,700
Baxter International Inc.	46,000
Medtronic, Inc.	40,000
Becton, Dickinson and Company	28,018
Boston Scientific Corporation	27,500
Stryker Corporation	17,594
Teleflex Incorporated	14,000
Bausch & Lomb Incorporated	13,000
St. Jude Medical, Inc.	12,000
C. R. Bard, Inc.	10,200

Fastest Growing* by Five-Year Sales Growth	(%)
Acclarent, Inc.	953.6
MAKO Surgical Corp.	438.5
Biophan Technologies, Inc.	242.1
NxStage Medical, Inc.	236.2
Hansen Medical, Inc.	199.0
Nephros, Inc.	128.9
DexCom, Inc.	111.1
Conceptus, Inc.	109.4
Inovio Biomedical Corporation	88.8
Sirona Dental Systems, Inc.	80.6

Fastest Growing* by Five-Year Employee Growth	(%)
Micrus Endovascular Corporation	81.6
Sirona Dental Systems, Inc.	78.2
NuVasive, Inc.	70.1
AcuNetx, Inc.	50.0
HealthTronics, Inc.	43.9
Cook Group Incorporated	42.9
Hologic, Inc.	40.4
AngioDynamics, Inc.	36.0
Natus Medical Incorporated	35.2
ev3 Inc.	34.8

Top Public Companies by Market Value	($ mil.)
Johnson & Johnson	162,163.1
Medtronic, Inc.	55,593.9
Baxter International Inc.	33,011.1
Becton, Dickinson and Company	19,509.4
Stryker Corporation	15,836.2

* These rates are compounded annualized increases and may have resulted from acquisitions or one time gains. If less than 6 years of data are available, growth is for the years available.

SOURCE: HOOVER'S, INC., DATABASE

Mental Health and Substance Abuse Services

About 15,000 mental health and substance abuse facilities operate in the US with combined annual revenue of over $17 billion. Major facilities include The Betty Ford Center, the Richard J Caron Foundation, and Res-Care. The industry is highly fragmented: the top 50 companies account for only about 20 percent of industry revenue. Most facilities are single location offices operated by a government agency, charitable foundation, or private health care firm. About 70 percent are operated by tax-exempt organizations.

The industry includes establishments that provide residential and rehabilitation care with minimal medical care, and outpatient facilities with medical staff to provide treatment.

Competitive Landscape

Demand for mental health and substance abuse facilities is driven by population demographics, availability of new drugs and treatments, and funding policies of health care insurance programs. The profitability of individual facilities depends on controlling costs and attracting physician referrals. Large companies have advantages in group purchasing and in marketing to physician and managed health care companies. Small facilities compete effectively by providing superior patient service, integrating treatment with follow-up procedures, and specializing by treatment or demographic group. Mental health and substance abuse facilities are labor-intensive: average revenue per worker is about $50,000.

Products, Operations & Technology

Revenue is derived from patient care services (37 percent); government grants and contributions (27 percent); and residential care services (25 percent). Other revenue sources include private contributions and sales of prescription drugs. Tax-exempt facilities receive about 55 percent of revenue from patient care services

BUSINESS CHALLENGES

» Rising Treatment Costs

Rising health care costs make affordable treatment difficult; efforts to control costs can affect the profitability of mental health and substance abuse facilities. The government estimates that fewer than a third of adults with a diagnosable mental disorder use mental health services. While most insured Americans have addictive and mental health coverage, insurance plans generally limit the disorders covered, implement higher cost-sharing for mental health issues, and limit the duration of covered services.

» Dependence on Government Funding

Medicare and Medicaid make up about 40 percent of all mental health and substance abuse payments. As the nation's largest health care program, Medicare decisions on payment rates and covered procedures also influence coverage by private health insurance providers. New treatments have a limited market if Medicare doesn't accept them for reimbursement; reduced reimbursement rates for existing procedures affect the profitability of mental health and substance abuse treatment providers. Some state legislatures have also cut funds for alcohol and substance abuse programs.

» Complexity of Managed Care Contracts

Managed health care is the norm in the US; facilities can have hundreds of managed care contracts with various HMOs and other medical providers. Managed care net revenue can account for about 50 percent of facility revenue. Meeting the billing and documentation requirements of multiple managed care providers increases the administrative costs of mental health and substance abuse facilities.

and 40 percent from contributions and grants; patient care services account for over 95 percent of revenue for taxable facilities.

The most common addiction treatments are for alcohol, marijuana, heroin, and crack cocaine abuse. The most common mental health issues are depression and anxiety. Dementia is a common problem for those over 60. Other mental health problems include eating disorders; phobias; schizophrenia; bi-polar disorders; obsessive-compulsive disorder (OCD); and post-traumatic stress disorder (PTSD).

Outpatient facilities offer alcohol or drug treatment, and mental health, counseling, and rehabilitation services. Substance abuse treatment is generally provided through outpatient, rather than residential, facilities. Substance abuse patients are typically treated for a short period at a hospital and then moved to an outpatient center.

Residential care facilities include mental health facilities, residential drug and alcohol treatment centers, and halfway houses. Metrics for residential and rehabilitation care facilities include occupancy rate, generally about 75 to 80 percent, and average length of stay. Inpatient stays for alcohol detoxification treatments generally run 28 days; 10 for mental health disorders.

Treatment plans include 12-step principles of self-help organizations such as Alcoholics Anonymous (AA); detoxification; counseling; therapy; and physiological assessment and support. Inpatient facilities generate about $400 to $575 per patient per day; outpatient revenue is much less.

With the increased importance of managed health care plans, information systems and support technology are critical to most health care providers. Advanced medical information technology improves care and tracks patient treatments, prescriptions, and safety concerns. Information systems also help satisfy comprehensive documentation requirements.

Sales & Marketing

Clinical studies estimate that about one in four Americans has either a mental or addictive disorder and 15 percent use mental health services. Patients come to mental health and substance abuse facilities on their own or by a physician referral. About 25 percent of substance abuse admissions are for alcohol abuse, almost 50 percent for illicit drug abuse, and the remainder for both alcohol and drug abuse. In the US, about 43 percent of substance abuse admissions are by those 31 to 45; almost 30 percent are from those 25 and younger.

Marketing focuses on attracting and maintaining a physician referral network. Clinical development managers manage referral sources at local hospitals. Some companies have dedicated sales associates to market company facilities. Many firms have websites to provide

behavioral health professionals with educational tools and details of the facility's services.

Inpatient treatments are substantially more expensive than outpatient care. Prices at well-known inpatient facilities, such as the Betty Ford Clinic, which caters to the affluent, can exceed $25,000 per month. Prices at most facilities vary by type of treatment and can range from $2,000 to $4,000 per week.

Human Resources

Almost half of all mental health and substance abuse employees are social service workers whose wages compare to the national norm. Healthcare providers with special medical and counseling skills, such as psychiatrists, earn much higher than the national average. Mental health and substance abuse facilities struggle with the national nursing shortage. Turnover among less skilled workers can be high.

Due to the violent nature of some patients, mental health professionals' injury rates are high. They're four times more likely to be injured at work than other physicians, and five times more likely than the US workforce on average.

Industry Employment Growth

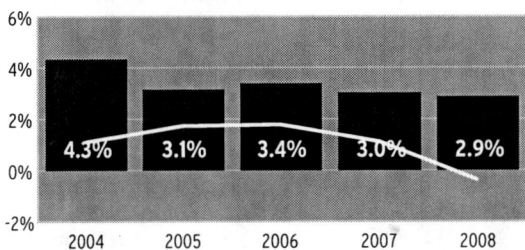

Average Hourly Earnings

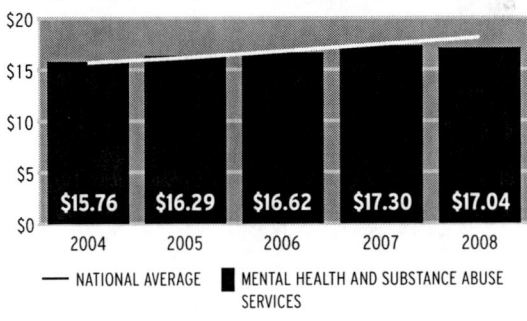

SOURCE: BUREAU OF LABOR STATISTICS

Call Preparation Questions

How have efforts to control health care costs affected the company?

Rising health care costs make affordable treatment difficult; efforts to control costs can affect the profitability of mental health and substance abuse facilities.

How much of company revenue depends on government programs?

Medicare and Medicaid make up about 40 percent of all mental health and substance abuse payments.

How many MCOs does the company work with?

Managed health care is the norm in the US; facilities can have hundreds of managed care contracts with various HMOs and other medical providers.

How has demand for the company's substance abuse services changed over the past 10 years?

Demand for substance abuse services has increased over the last 10 years, as prevalence rates increased despite efforts by health and government agencies to reduce substance abuse.

How important are elderly patients to the company?

As America ages, the number of adults who need help for anxiety, depression, and dementia will increase, benefiting facilities that educate the elderly about common mental issues and that offer accessible and affordable treatment.

Web Links

American Psychiatric Association

News, articles, research papers.
www.psych.org

American Psychiatric Foundation

News, reports, statistics.
www.psychfoundation.org

American Psychological Association

News, articles, topic index.
www.apa.org

National Council for Community Behavioral Healthcare

Articles, links.
www.thenationalcouncil.org

National Institute of Mental Health

News, health information.
www.nimh.nih.gov

Psychiatric Times

News, articles.
www.psychiatrictimes.com

Substance Abuse & Mental Health Services Administration

News, statistics, programs, topic index, facility locater, links.
www.samhsa.gov

Glossary of Acronyms

CDC — Centers for Disease Control

HIPAA — Health Insurance Portability and Accountability Act

HMO — health maintenance organization

PPO — preferred provider organization

SAMHSA — Substance Abuse and Mental Health Services Administration

HOOVER'S TOP COMPANIES

Largest Companies by Sales	($ mil.)
Northwestern Human Services, Inc	311.5
Macomb-Oakland Regional Center, Inc.	178.4
Res-Care, Inc.	146.4
Telecare Corporation	75.9
Richard J. Caron Foundation	59.7
The Betty Ford Center	40.0

Largest Employers	Employees
Res-Care, Inc.	42,000
Northwestern Human Services, Inc	6,500
Telecare Corporation	2,050
Richard J. Caron Foundation	450
Macomb-Oakland Regional Center, Inc.	300
The Betty Ford Center	220

Top Public Companies by Market Value	($ mil.)
Res-Care, Inc.	733.7

SOURCE: HOOVER'S, INC., DATABASE

Metal Coating, Engraving, and Heat Treating

The metal coating, engraving, and heat treating industry includes about 6,000 companies with combined annual revenue of about $19 billion. Large companies include Precoat Metals and North American Galvanizing & Coatings. The industry is fragmented: the largest 50 companies hold about 40 percent market share. A typical company has 20 employees and less than $3 million in annual sales.

Competition comes from metal manufacturers and fabricators that have in-house capability. Other competitors are large steel mills and aluminum producers, like Nucor and Alcoa, that have operations that incorporate these value-added services.

Competitive Landscape

Demand depends on the level of manufacturing production and construction activity. The profitability of individual companies is linked to manufacturing process efficiencies. Most companies are small and compete by focusing on a specialty customer niche within a local or regional area. The industry is somewhat labor-intensive: annual revenue per employee is about $130,000.

Products, Operations & Technology

Major services are engraving and coating (50 percent of revenues); electroplating, galvanizing, and anodizing (30 percent); and heat treating (20 percent). Major customer industries for metal fabricators are the auto, aerospace, building construction, highway construction, petrochemical processing, and utility markets.

The basic steps in the process include material cleaning; preparing, or priming, the surface; applying coating or other treatments (galvanizing, etching, electroplating, or anodizing); curing or drying; and inspection. In the case of heat treating, the material is heated to a high temperature under carefully controlled conditions then cooled rapidly to set the desired

BUSINESS CHALLENGES

» Volatile Energy, Raw Material Prices

Natural gas and raw material costs (mostly zinc or other metal platings and petroleum-based coatings) can vary greatly month to month and year to year. Over the past five years, zinc prices increased 200 percent; gas prices increased 400 percent.

» Dependence on Manufacturing Sector

The industry is hypersensitive to the health of the US manufacturing sector. During the last recession, when US manufacturing output decreased 4 percent, industry output dropped 14 percent. Machinery and aerospace manufacture are especially important drivers of demand.

» High Regulatory Compliance Costs

Companies may spend as much as 3 percent of revenues on compliance issues. Handling, treating, and disposing of toxic chemicals and wastes are expensive. Significant capital expenditures for treatment equipment can also affect cash flow or create debt on company balance sheets.

properties. Facilities vary in size but a typical facility ranges from 40,000 to 60,000 square feet and is company-owned.

Various alloys of steel and aluminum with unfinished surfaces are transported to facilities specifically designed to perform these services. The company provides the raw materials, such as primers, paints, coatings, caustics, and zinc, to complete the service, while the fabricator typically owns the metal inventory. This arrangement is known as "tolling" or "toll conversion," and companies that perform this third-party outsourcing are "converters" or "jobbers."

In most cases, the finished product is shipped directly to the fabricator's customer. In some cases, the product may be returned to the fabricator for subsequent processing, especially for heat treated products (steel, aluminum, and bronze) where heat treating is used to impart properties of strength and formability prior to further processing.

Automated application systems, computerized process controls, and advanced environmental treatment systems are being adopted, but the industry remains labor-intensive. Most productivity improvements require large capital investments, making operations dependent on high processing volumes to recoup invested capital.

Sales & Marketing

Target customers are typically metal fabricators within a local or regional area. Sales are generated by a direct sales force. In many operations, the owner is the general sales manager and is deeply involved with customers because of detailed knowledge of the business and the company's capabilities.

Most business is performed under contracts negotiated at the senior management level. Contracts are usually for one year, renewable automatically or upon review, with clauses to protect against raw material and energy cost increases. While contracts may be long-term, they don't usually contain volume guarantees because of customer dependence on market forces beyond their control.

Marketing generally consists of company brochures detailing facility capabilities offered both in print and online. Association trade shows, technical forums, and customer visits are the primary forms of face-to-face contact with customers and potential customers.

Human Resources

Workers are relatively low-skilled and earn average hourly wages 20 percent lower than the average for all manufacturing industries.

Worker safety is a major focus within the industry. The industry's annual injury rate is 30 percent higher than that for all of US manufacturing. Employees routinely contact hazardous chemicals, coatings, and byproducts such as hexavalent chromium. Company safety programs require workers to wear protective clothing and respirators at certain times. Material Safety Data Sheets (MSDS) are available to workers so they understand the risks and safe handling procedures of compounds.

Industry Employment Growth

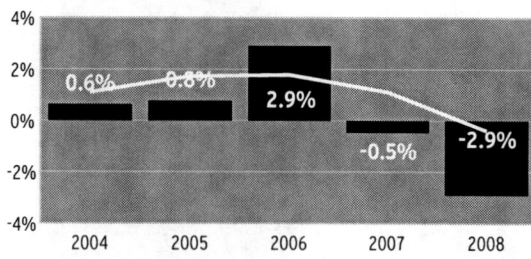

Average Hourly Earnings

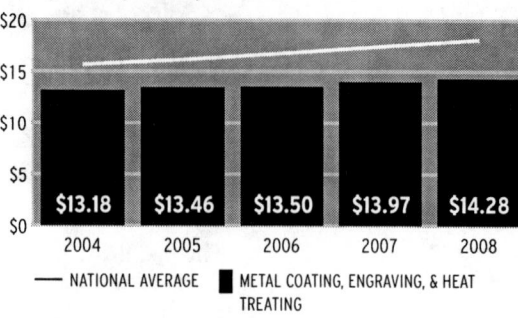

— NATIONAL AVERAGE ■ METAL COATING, ENGRAVING, & HEAT TREATING

SOURCE: BUREAU OF LABOR STATISTICS

Call Preparation Questions

How does the company cope with volatile energy and raw material prices?

Natural gas and raw material costs (mostly zinc or other metal platings and petroleum-based coatings) can vary greatly month to month and year to year.

What drives demand for the company's products?

The industry is hypersensitive to the health of the US manufacturing sector.

How do environmental and safety issues affect the company's performance?

Companies may spend as much as 3 percent of revenues on compliance issues.

How is the company challenged by selling the advantages of outsourcing?

Third-party coaters and finishers have successfully added customers who formerly carried out these processes internally.

What materials does the company process?

Companies in this industry traditionally work with metal substrates, but treatments for vinyl, wood, and other synthetic materials offer expansion opportunities.

Web Links

American Galvanizers Association

National trade association for galvanizers.
www.galvanizeit.org

Metal Center News

News of the metal fabrication industry.
www.metalcenternews.com

Metal Finishing

News of metal finishers.
www.metalfinishing.com

National Association for Surface Finishing

Surface finishing industry news.
www.nasf.org

National Association of Manufacturers

Lobbyist organization of manufacturers.
www.nam.org

National Metal Finishing Resource Center

Industry news and issues.
www.nmfrc.org

Glossary of Acronyms

EIA — Energy Information Administration
LME — London Metal Exchange
MEK — methyl ethyl ketone
MSDS — Material Safety Data Sheets
NCCA — National Coil Coaters Association
PEL — permissible emission level
VOC — volatile organic compounds

HOOVER'S TOP COMPANIES

Largest Companies by Sales	($ mil.)
Sequa Corporation (Precoat Metals)	969.4
Brush Engineered Materials Inc.	955.7
Steelscape, Inc.	500.0
Material Sciences Corporation	235.0
MetoKote Corporation	128.3
North American Galvanizing & Coatings, Inc.	86.1

Largest Employers	Employees
Sequa Corporation (Precoat Metals)	10,000
Brush Engineered Materials Inc.	2,201
MetoKote Corporation	2,000
Pioneer Metal Finishing Corporation	650
Material Sciences Corporation	543
Steelscape, Inc.	500
Oerlikon Balzers Coating USA Inc.	400
North American Galvanizing & Coatings, Inc.	400
Lincoln Industries	340
The Techs	230

Fastest Growing* by Five-Year Sales Growth	(%)
North American Galvanizing & Coatings, Inc.	21.0
Brush Engineered Materials Inc.	20.7
Sequa Corporation (Precoat Metals)	3.0

Fastest Growing* by Five-Year Employee Growth	(%)
North American Galvanizing & Coatings, Inc.	3.5
Brush Engineered Materials Inc.	3.4

Top Public Companies by Market Value	($ mil.)
Brush Engineered Materials Inc.	757.8
Material Sciences Corporation	104.3
North American Galvanizing & Coatings, Inc.	61.4

* These rates are compounded annualized increases and may
have resulted from acquisitions or one time gains. If less
than 6 years of data are available, growth is for the years
available.

SOURCE: HOOVER'S, INC., DATABASE

Metal Ore Mining

The US metal ore mining industry includes about 250 companies with combined annual revenue of over $7 billion. Major companies include Freeport McMoRan Copper & Gold and Newmont Mining. Metal ore mining is highly concentrated: the largest 10 gold companies account for 80 percent of revenue, and the largest 10 copper and nickel companies account for 95 percent of revenue.

Competitive Landscape

Demand is driven by industrial demand and economic growth, both domestic and foreign. Individual company profitability depends on volume and operating efficiency. Large companies can afford to discover and develop new deposits and increase reserves. Small companies typically own just one mine, limit exploration to that one property, and operate it as efficiently as possible. Metal ore mining is capital-intensive: annual revenue per employee is about $300,000.

The industry includes companies that mine and process gold, silver, copper, nickel, lead, zinc, iron ore, and other metals.

Products, Operations & Technology

Major products include gold bullion (35 percent of revenue); iron ore (25 percent); and metal concentrates (20 percent). Iron ore is used to make steel for many industries. Precious metals such as gold and silver are used in jewelry and electronics; copper is commonly used in construction.

Almost all US metal ore mining companies use open-pit mines, where the surface is removed to reach ore deposits. Benches are cut into the mine walls to provide access to progressively deeper ore. The ore is extracted by drilling holes in the rock for explosives. After blasting, the ore is removed using huge earth-moving equipment such as power shovels and draglines. This equipment is bought from

BUSINESS CHALLENGES

» Cyclical Industrial Demand

Demand for metal ore is sensitive to cyclical demand from the construction, electronics, electrical, transportation, and jewelry industries. Demand for gold and silver is also affected by speculative pressures. During the last recession and its aftermath, gold mining dropped 25 percent and copper mining dropped 22 percent. Annual production for various metals has fluctuated as much as 12 percent over the past 10 years.

» Volatile Metal Prices

Given the high fixed-costs of mining, industry profitability can be sharply affected by changes in metal prices. Over the past 10 years, iron ore has fluctuated as much as 19 percent in a year, copper 30 percent, and gold 18 percent. From 2001 to 2005, prices for gold bullion increased 50 percent, while prices for copper ore increased 100 percent.

» Industry Sensitive to Energy Prices

Energy, including electricity, diesel fuel, and natural gas, is approximately 20 to 25 percent of the industry's production costs; any sudden changes in prices greatly affect company profitability. Extraction, reclamation, and transportation all use substantial amounts of energy. Companies often have price protection programs to help mitigate price increases, but margins may still be squeezed during large energy price hikes. To help offset volatile energy costs, Phelps Dodge purchased a power plant in New Mexico for its copper plants in Arizona.

major mining and drilling equipment manufacturers. Once the metal is exposed, smaller shovels are used to load it into trucks, rail cars, and conveyors for transport to a mill for processing. Mines are large, typically hundreds of acres, and produce up to half a million tons of ore.

Some companies have their own processing facilities and others sell the unrefined ore to third-party processors. Most gold and copper are processed by the mining company. Processing is called beneficiation and involves removing unwanted parts to improve the quality and purity of the metal. Steps include crushing, washing, filtering, sorting, sizing, separating, and acid leaching.

Processing depends upon the grade of ore. Higher grade oxide ores are processed in mills by grinding the ore into a fine powder and mixing it with water before passing it through a leaching circuit. Lower grade oxide ores are processed using heap leaching, which consists of stacking crushed ore on pads and using a weak leaching solution to dissolve the metal. Chemicals used in the leaching process differ by the metal mined, primarily cyanide solutions for gold and sulphuric acid for copper.

Waste material, created by mining and processing, can be up to 99 percent of the rock volume in the case of precious metals, such as gold and silver. Mine tailings contain impurities and chemical residues that were used in beneficiation. Acid drainage into groundwater, caused by leakage or seepage during leaching, can be an environmental problem.

Mining exploration focuses on finding large-scale deposits of metals and costs about 5 percent of company revenue. About a third of exploration is at existing mines. For new exploration, a feasibility study is completed and exploration conducted using airborne geophysical data, satellite and location devices, field-portable systems, and onsite geological prospecting. Companies often joint venture on exploration projects and then pay royalties to each other for mineral rights. Mining companies either own the property outright or pay royalties or lease payments to the owners for mining rights. Mining is sometimes allowed on government land after rights are secured and royalties paid.

Ore reserves are estimated quantities of proven, probable, or possible material that may be economically mined in the future. Estimates of reserves are based on engineering evaluations and data derived from drilling holes. Mining companies must continually replace areas depleted by production, which makes reserves a major financial asset.

Technology investments focus on production improvements and exploration efficiency. Technologies providing constant improvement of existing processes are the norm, rather than breakthroughs. Reducing the temperature of high pressure leaching, which reduces the amount of water and acid needed in beneficiation, is an example of a recent process improvement.

Sales & Marketing

Metal ore customers are metal traders, wholesalers, and refiners/processors that purchase unrefined metals to produce gold bullion, silver ingots, and refined copper, nickel, and other metals.

Metals are internationally traded commodities. Prices are effectively determined by three major metal exchanges — the New York Commodity Exchange (COMEX); the London Metal Exchange (LME); and the Shanghai Futures Exchange (SHFE). Prices generally reflect the worldwide balance of supply and demand, but are also significantly influenced by currency and bullion speculation. Contracts are generally for one year.

Companies use multiple trade shows, both domestic and international, to market to customers.

Human Resources

Production worker hourly wages are well above the national average, as sophisticated equipment and machinery require technical skills and training. Almost 30 percent of metal mining workers belong to a labor union, compared to 15 percent of total US workers. Annual injury rates are about the national average for all industries. Mining injuries are typically due to overexertion, involve industrial equipment, and require missing a large number of days from work.

Industry Employment Growth

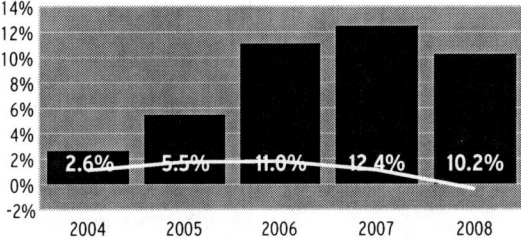

	2004	2005	2006	2007	2008
	2.6%	5.5%	11.0%	12.4%	10.2%

Average Hourly Earnings

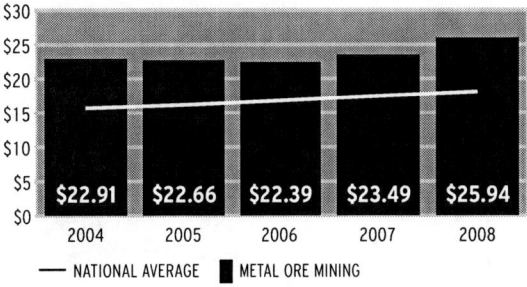

	2004	2005	2006	2007	2008
	$22.91	$22.66	$22.39	$23.49	$25.94

— NATIONAL AVERAGE ■ METAL ORE MINING

SOURCE: BUREAU OF LABOR STATISTICS

Call Preparation Questions

How does the company manage cyclical demand?

Demand for metal ore is sensitive to cyclical demand from the construction, electronics, electrical, transportation, and jewelry industries.

How is the company affected by swings in metal prices?

Given the high fixed-costs of mining, industry profitability can be sharply affected by changes in metal prices.

Does the company use GPS? If so, how and to what benefit?

Metal and mineral mining companies are increasingly using global positioning, communications, and imaging satellites to improve exploration, production, and reclamation efforts.

Web Links

American Geological Institute

Legislative news.
www.agiweb.org

Metal Producing & Processing

Industry news.
www.metalproducing.com

Mine Safety and Health Administration (MSHA)

Safety rules and regulations related to the mining industry.
www.msha.gov

Mining Technology

Updates on industry technology worldwide.
www.mining-technology.com

National Mining Association

Industry news, articles, archives.
www.nma.org

Office of Surface Mining Reclamation and Enforcement

Reclamation information from Department of Interior.
www.osmre.gov

The Mining News

Industry news, articles, archives.
www.theminingnews.org

Glossary of Acronyms

COMEX — New York Commodity Exchange
LME — London Metal Exchange
NMA — National Mining Association
SHFE — Shanghai Futures Exchange
SMCRA — Surface Mining Control and Reclamation Act

HOOVER'S TOP COMPANIES

Largest Companies by Sales	($ mil.)
Freeport-McMoRan Copper & Gold Inc.	17,796.0
Newmont Mining Corporation	6,199.0
Cliffs Natural Resources Inc.	3,609.1
USEC Inc.	1,614.6
Haynes International, Inc.	637.0
Stillwater Mining Company	619.2
Globe Specialty Metals, Inc.	452.6
Kennecott Utah Copper Corporation	—

Largest Employers	Employees
Freeport-McMoRan Copper & Gold Inc.	25,400
Newmont Mining Corporation	15,000
Cliffs Natural Resources Inc.	5,298
The Doe Run Company	4,271
USEC Inc.	2,866
Golden Star Resources Ltd.	2,800
Stillwater Mining Company	1,625
Kennecott Utah Copper Corporation	1,400
Globe Specialty Metals, Inc.	1,373
Haynes International, Inc.	1,138

Fastest Growing* by Five-Year Sales Growth	(%)
Globe Specialty Metals, Inc.	104.0
Solitario Exploration & Royalty Corp.	100.0
Gold Reserve Inc.	56.2
Freeport-McMoRan Copper & Gold Inc.	51.7
Cliffs Natural Resources Inc.	33.3
Royal Gold, Inc.	33.2
Golden Star Resources Ltd.	31.9
MESABI TRUST	30.0
Nanophase Technologies Corporation	17.7
Stillwater Mining Company	17.6

Fastest Growing* by Five-Year Employee Growth	(%)
Uranium Resources, Inc.	115.2
Brazauro Resources Corporation	67.0
Globe Specialty Metals, Inc.	29.0
Golden Star Resources Ltd.	22.9
Cliffs Natural Resources Inc.	13.9
Newmont Mining Corporation	2.9
Haynes International, Inc.	2.0
USEC Inc.	1.9
Royal Gold, Inc.	1.6
Stillwater Mining Company	0.6

Top Public Companies by Market Value	($ mil.)
Newmont Mining Corporation	15,740.2
Freeport-McMoRan Copper & Gold Inc.	9,385.0
Cliffs Natural Resources Inc.	2,907.0
Royal Gold, Inc.	1,063.9
Stillwater Mining Company	892.6

* These rates are compounded annualized increases and may have resulted from acquisitions or one time gains. If less than 6 years of data are available, growth is for the years available.

SOURCE: HOOVER'S, INC., DATABASE

Metal Valve Manufacture

The US metal valve manufacturing industry consists of about 1,100 companies with combined annual revenue of $22 billion. Major companies include units of integrated process control companies such as Parker Hannifin, Curtiss-Wright, and Flowserve, as well as valve manufacturers such as American Valve and William Powell Company. The industry is concentrated: the largest 50 companies have about 65 percent market share.

Competitive Landscape

Demand depends primarily on the level of manufacturing and construction activity. Construction activity in the chemical, petroleum, utilities, water treatment, and housing industries is especially important. Large companies have advantages in efficiency of operations and economies of scale. Offshore subsidiaries are frequently used for low-cost manufacturing. Smaller producers compete by focusing on specialized product offerings and superior customer service. Annual revenue per employee is about $200,000.

Metal valves compete with other materials, primarily plastics, in the residential market and with high-strength composites, fluorocarbons, and elastomers for high-end uses.

Products, Operations & Technology

Major product categories are industrial valve applications used primarily in water works and municipal water systems (about 40 percent of US shipments); fluid power valves used in compressed or pressurized applications (30 percent); and plumbing-related valves and fixtures (20 percent). Valves control the flow of liquids, gases, slurries, or dry materials through a pipe or similar passageway, and may also control the rate of flow, volume, pressure, and direction. Some of the most common types of valves are gate, ball, butterfly, pressure relief, and custom engineered for special applications. Valve acti-

BUSINESS CHALLENGES

» Low-Cost Manufacturing Sources

Imports from low-wage countries make up an increasing percentage of US metal valve consumption. US-owned companies acquire foreign manufacturers, create joint ventures, and set up green-site manufacturing operations in low-wage countries to ensure competitiveness. Between 2002 and 2005, imports increased 50 percent to reach about 30 percent of all US metal valve consumption.

» Volatile Raw Material Prices

Raw material costs are about 40 percent of metal valve sales revenue. Raw materials consist primarily of iron, steel, aluminum, and copper. Prices for these primary metals fluctuate widely, making quoting prices difficult for manufacturers to ensure adequate gross margins, especially on extended deliveries.

» Disrupted Distribution Channels

Large customers, such as oil, gas, and utility companies with integrated supply chains, may dictate that suppliers work with a specific distributor. These demands may disrupt long-standing relationships between valve manufacturers and their existing distribution partners. New distributors must be trained and supported, even though they carry a few products for a single customer. Supporting specialized channels can raise overall distribution costs for valve manufacturers.

vation is controlled by an actuator that may be manual, pneumatic, hydraulic, or electric. Valve sizes range from fractions of an inch to 25 to 30 feet in diameter.

Raw materials are primarily aluminum, copper, iron, and steel. Bronze and brass, frequently used in valve manufacturing, are copper-based alloys. Raw materials are bought from primary metal producers or secondary processors that alloy ingredients.

Manufacturing facilities frequently include foundry operations. Most valve housings are castings made from molten metals poured into molds, often made of baked green sand. Manufacturing processes include designing and building the molds into which the molten metal will be poured. After the valve housing is removed from the mold, the interior surface is cleaned, trimmed, and machined to ensure exact dimensions. To enable flow to occur as designed, flow control inserts are placed inside the housing and actuator mechanisms are attached. Quality assurance and testing ensure structural integrity, dimensions, and optimal performance.

Most valves are standard products and built to stock. However, some specialty applications may be one-of-a-kind designs and can be very expensive. Facilities range from 40,000 to several hundred thousand square feet.

Companies use sophisticated computer programs to aid in the design process and quality control, and in-the-field monitoring of performance criteria. In critical applications, such as gas pipelines or nuclear power plants, computer monitoring, assessment, and continuous self-adjustment are major components of the total valve solution.

Sales & Marketing

Major customers are general contractors serving the petroleum, chemical, utility, and residential housing industries and government municipalities. Specifying engineers frequently work directly with valve manufacturers to determine performance specifications and provide these specifications to contractors for bid. Aftermarket sales are supported by distributors or sold directly to end-users.

Products are sold through direct sales forces, manufacturer reps, and distributors as authorized resellers. Relationships with specifying engineers, architects, and purchasing organizations are critical. Prices may range from a few dollars for a valve used in residential applications to several hundred thousand for a critical application in oil or gas transmission. Customer services include technical assistance in evaluating performance criteria, recommending designs to meet requirements, suggesting cost-saving possibilities, and evaluating post-sales performance.

Marketing generally includes company brochures and product catalogs detailing product offerings both in print and online. Press releases are common for products introduced at industry trade shows.

Human Resources

Metal valve manufacturing requires average skills, and production workers earn comparable wages to the national average for all workers. Most companies aren't unionized, although some larger companies are.

Industry injury rates are comparable to the average rate for all US manufacturing. Worker safety exposures include burns from molten metal, strains and sprains from heavy lifting, and cuts and abrasions from operating grinders, lathes, and other machinery.

Industry Employment Growth

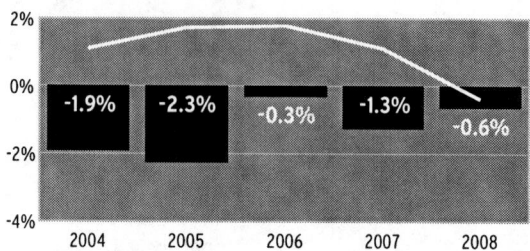

Average Hourly Earnings

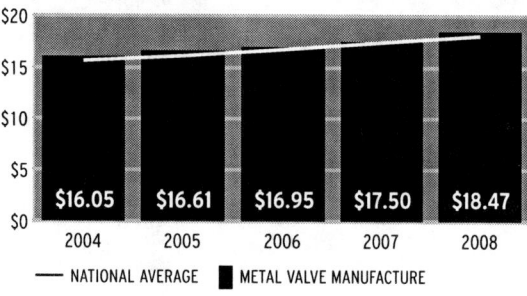

— NATIONAL AVERAGE ■ METAL VALVE MANUFACTURE

SOURCE: BUREAU OF LABOR STATISTICS

Call Preparation Questions

How has the company been affected by imports?

Imports from low-wage countries make up an increasing percentage of US metal valve consumption.

How does the company mitigate volatile raw material prices?

Raw material costs are about 40 percent of metal valve sales revenue. Raw materials consist primarily of iron, steel, aluminum, and copper.

What criteria does the company use to select its distribution network?

Large customers, such as oil, gas, and utility companies with integrated supply chains, may dictate that suppliers work with a specific distributor.

How important are exports to the company?

International demand for valve products is increasing due to infrastructure investment in China, Indonesia, India, and other countries.

What customer support services does the company offer?

Post-sales support through technical training and consulting enhances a company's position with customers.

Web Links

Institute for Supply Management

Former National Association of Purchasing Management. Indexes of manufacturers purchasing activity, price activity. Benchmark data for select industries.

www.ism.ws

National Association of Manufacturers

Lobbying organization for manufacturers.

www.nam.org

National Fluid Power Association

Manufacturers of hydraulic and pneumatic valves.

www.nfpa.com/OurIndustry/OurInd-_IndustryDataResources_FactsFigures.asp

Valve Magazine

Quarterly publication for buyers, specifiers, users, and distributors of industrial valves and actuators.

www.valvemagazine.com

Valve Manufacturers Association of America

Information on North American valve and actuator manufacturers.

www.vma.org

Valve World

Community for valve professionals.

www.valve-world.net

Glossary of Acronyms

ISO — International Standards Organization
LME — London Metal Exchange
NAM — National Association of Manufacturers
NYMEX — New York Mercantile Exchange
VMA — Valve Manufacturers Association

HOOVER'S TOP COMPANIES

Largest Companies by Sales	($ mil.)
Flowserve Corporation	4,473.5
Crane Co.	2,604.3
Mueller Industries, Inc.	2,558.4
Dresser, Inc.	2,000.0
Mueller Water Products, Inc.	1,859.3
Curtiss-Wright Corporation	1,830.1
McWane, Inc.	1,700.0
Watts Water Technologies, Inc.	1,382.3
Swagelok Company	1,300.0
Gibraltar Industries, Inc.	1,232.3

Largest Employers	Employees
Flowserve Corporation	15,000
Crane Co.	12,000
Watts Water Technologies, Inc.	7,800
McWane, Inc.	7,500
Curtiss-Wright Corporation	7,500
Mueller Water Products, Inc.	6,500
Dresser, Inc.	6,400
Mueller Industries, Inc.	4,700
Swagelok Company	4,000
Gibraltar Industries, Inc.	3,950

Fastest Growing* by Five-Year Sales Growth	(%)
Mueller Water Products, Inc.	44.0
Dynamic Materials Corporation	29.3
RTI International Metals, Inc.	24.3
Sun Hydraulics Corporation	21.0
Mueller Industries, Inc.	20.7
Curtiss-Wright Corporation	19.7
Watts Water Technologies, Inc.	17.6
CIRCOR International, Inc.	17.2
Swagelok Company	14.0
Flowserve Corporation	13.2

Fastest Growing* by Five-Year Employee Growth	(%)
Sono-Tek Corporation	16.3
Swagelok Company	15.5
Dynamic Materials Corporation	13.8
Curtiss-Wright Corporation	12.8
RTI International Metals, Inc.	9.4
Watts Water Technologies, Inc.	9.1
Omega Flex, Inc.	8.6
CIRCOR International, Inc.	8.2
Crane Co.	7.4
McWane, Inc.	6.1

Top Public Companies by Market Value	($ mil.)
Flowserve Corporation	2,843.6
Curtiss-Wright Corporation	1,504.7
Crane Co.	1,008.4
Watts Water Technologies, Inc.	911.9
Mueller Industries, Inc.	847.2

* These rates are compounded annualized increases and may have resulted from acquisitions or one time gains. If less than 6 years of data are available, growth is for the years available.

SOURCE: HOOVER'S, INC., DATABASE

Mortgage Banking

The US mortgage banking industry includes 6,000 firms with total annual revenue that varies between $50 and $100 billion. Large companies include units of Wells Fargo, JPMorgan Chase, Citigroup, and Bank of America.

Competitive Landscape

Demand for mortgage services is driven by home sales and the refinancing that occurs when mortgage rates are low. The profitability of individual companies depends on volume, interest rate spreads, and efficient operations. Large companies have big economies of scale in operations. Small companies compete successfully by funneling mortgages to the large companies. The industry is fragmented at the bottom but highly concentrated at the top: the largest 50 companies hold more than 70 percent of the market.

Products, Operations & Technology

Mortgage bankers lend money to homeowners through a mortgage, with the home as collateral. The traditional mortgage has a fixed interest rate and level monthly payments that pay off the loan over 30 years, but loans with adjustable interest rates (ARMs) and variable payment schedules have become common in recent years.

While mortgage loans are usually made to buy a home (a "purchase" mortgage), they're also made to refinance an existing mortgage (typically at a lower interest rate), or to provide cash to the homeowner (a home equity loan).

The main functions of mortgage bankers are loan production, underwriting, and servicing. Large mortgage bankers may also create and trade mortgage-backed securities.

Loan production is sales. Mortgage bankers advertise heavily and may have a network of retail offices and Internet sites where consumers can apply for a mortgage. Mortgage bankers

BUSINESS CHALLENGES

» Demand for Mortgages Depends on Economic Factors

Although demand for mortgages is fairly steady from year to year, refinance mortgage activity can swing wildly. Demand for mortgage loans, which is affected by interest rates and home prices, can change more rapidly than companies can adjust their expenses.

» Heavy Industry Dependence on Fannie Mae, Freddie Mac

Many mortgage bankers depend on these two "agencies" for new funds, by selling them their mortgages. The two companies effectively set mortgage and business standards, and the interest rate at which they can sell securities sets mortgage rates for the industry. Despite backing by the US government, these agencies have been seriously weakened by the subprime mortgage crisis, further destabilizing the mortgage industry.

» Mortgage Quality Affects Value

Low credit standards can increase loan production, but the value of those loans can fall rapidly. Low-quality mortgages have higher delinquency and foreclosure rates, producing higher loss reserves and servicing expenses for mortgage bankers who own or service them. Loans that require little or no down payment are very exposed to a drop in home prices.

charge fees for processing mortgage applications and for loan origination — when an approved loan actually "closes."

Loan underwriting consists of determining the risk of a particular loan. Underwriters typically consider the market value of the home, the loan-to-value ratio of the loan, and the borrower's creditworthiness. Mortgage bankers may use their own credit scoring system to determine the borrower's creditworthiness, or one provided by a number of analytical companies such as Fair Isaac (the FICO score). The risk of default on a mortgage determines whether the mortgage bank approves the loan and at what interest rate. Borrowers with low creditworthiness ("subprime") may still be approved for a mortgage if the interest rate is high enough to compensate for the extra risk.

Loan servicing includes sending bills, receiving payments, accounting, efforts to collect if the borrower misses payments ("delinquency"), and the operations involved in foreclosure proceedings if the lender must take title to the property. Many mortgage bankers service mortgages owned by other investors, charging an annual fee of 0.25 to 0.50 percent (25 to 50 "basis points") of the unpaid loan amount.

Both mortgages and the "mortgage servicing rights" (MSR) attached to them are bought and sold in the secondary mortgage market. A mortgage banker may keep a new mortgage in its own loan portfolio, sell it, or include it with other mortgages in a "pool" that serves as collateral for a mortgage-backed security (MBS). By "securitizing" mortgages, mortgage bankers create an investment instrument that's easily bought and sold by other investors.

Fannie Mae (Federal National Mortgage Association) and Freddie Mac (Federal Home Loan Mortgage Corporation) are large buyers of home mortgages in the secondary market. Unlike other securitizers of mortgages, they issue securities that aren't backed by specific mortgage pools, but the securities they issue are considered safe investments because both companies have the implicit support of the US government.

The operations of mortgage bankers, whether they mainly originate mortgages, service mortgages, or manage a portfolio of mortgage loans and securities, depend heavily on sophisticated computer systems, which are the source of the large economies of scale in the industry.

Sales & Marketing

TV and radio ads are commonly used, as are direct mail and telemarketing. The Internet has become a major source of mortgage applications because consumers can readily compare rates offered by different originators. In addition to acquiring mortgages through their own retail network, some mortgage bankers have networks of "correspondent" originators and independent brokers who feed them loans, and have wholesale relationships with homebuilders and realtors.

Human Resources

Because most jobs in the industry require special skills in financial sales, credit analysis, loan processing, loan servicing, or portfolio

management, wages are accordingly high. Demand for workers can be cyclical because home purchases and mortgage refinancing can vary sharply from year to year. During periods of strong demand, companies may use a large number of part-time workers, and turnover can be high for experienced personnel.

Industry Employment Growth

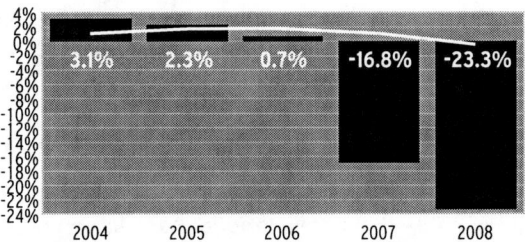

Average Hourly Earnings

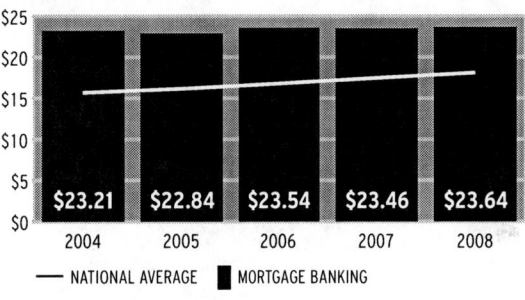

— NATIONAL AVERAGE ■ MORTGAGE BANKING

SOURCE: BUREAU OF LABOR STATISTICS

Call Preparation Questions

How will the company adjust to lower revenue if interest rates rise?

Although demand for mortgages is fairly steady from year to year, refinance mortgage activity can swing wildly.

How reliant is the company on industry leaders like Fannie Mae and Freddie Mac?

Many mortgage bankers depend on these two "agencies" for new funds, by selling them their mortgages.

How much has the company been involved with subprime mortgages?

Low credit standards can increase loan production, but the value of those loans can fall rapidly.

What involvement does the company have with securitizing mortgages?

Mimicking the traditional activity of Fannie Mae and Freddie Mac, many large mortgage bankers package mortgages into pools as collateral for mortgage-backed securities.

To what extent does the company still rely on paper documentation?

The increasing use of computer systems at all stages of the mortgage process reduces paper documentation.

Web Links

Department of Housing and Urban Development

Recent regulatory initiatives.
www.hud.gov

Inside Mortgage Finance

News about mortgage finance.
www.imfpubs.com

Mortgage Bankers Association

News, industry data, issues.
www.mbaa.org

National Association of Realtors

News and data on home prices and home sales.
www.realtor.org

National Mortgage News

Subscription service. Free headlines and brief description.
www.nationalmortgagenews.com

Office of Federal Housing Enterprise Oversight (OFHEO)

Home price index.
www.ofheo.gov

Glossary of Acronyms

ARM — adjustable-rate mortgage
FICO — Fair Isaac (credit score)
GFE — good faith estimate
GMP — guaranteed mortgage package
GSE — government sponsored enterprise
HOEPA — Home Ownership and Equity Protection Act
HUD — Department of Housing and Urban Development
LTV — loan-to-value ratio
MBA — Mortgage Bankers Association
MBS — mortgage-backed securities
MSR — mortgage servicing right
OFHEO — Office of Federal Housing Enterprise Oversight
RESPA — Real Estate Settlement Procedures Act

HOOVER'S TOP COMPANIES

Largest Companies by Sales	($ mil.)
Federal National Mortgage Association	51,777.0
HSBC North America Holdings Inc.	43,197.9
Federal Home Loan Mortgage Corporation	43,104.0
Residential Capital, LLC	8,169.0
National City Mortgage Co.	4,603.6
Synovus Mortgage Corp.	4,150.1
SunTrust Mortgage, Inc.	1,257.7
Centerline Holding Company	572.9

Largest Employers	Employees
HSBC North America Holdings Inc.	53,000
Residential Capital, LLC	13,700
GMAC Mortgage, LLC	7,500
PHH Mortgage	5,900
National City Mortgage Co.	5,800
Federal National Mortgage Association	5,700
Federal Home Loan Mortgage Corporation	5,000
Allied Home Mortgage Capital Corporation	4,300
Wells Fargo Home Mortgage	4,000
Capmark Financial Group Inc.	3,000

Fastest Growing* by Five-Year Sales Growth	(%)
ASI Technology Corporation	63.3
American Mortgage Acceptance Company	41.8
Centerline Holding Company	37.5
Security National Financial Corporation	16.8
NovaStar Financial, Inc.	13.1
Federal Agricultural Mortgage Corporation	11.2
Federal Home Loan Mortgage Corporation	3.8

Fastest Growing* by Five-Year Employee Growth	(%)
Centerline Holding Company	17.8
Security National Financial Corporation	13.0
Federal Agricultural Mortgage Corporation	11.7
Federal National Mortgage Association	1.8

Top Public Companies by Market Value	($ mil.)
Federal National Mortgage Association	824.9
Centerline Holding Company	385.3
Security National Financial Corporation	25.0
Federal Agricultural Mortgage Corporation	17.5
ASI Technology Corporation	12.8

* These rates are compounded annualized increases and may have resulted from acquisitions or one time gains. If less than 6 years of data are available, growth is for the years available.

SOURCE: HOOVER'S, INC., DATABASE

Motion Picture Production and Distribution

The US motion picture production and distribution industry includes about 11,000 companies with combined annual revenue of $33 billion. Major companies include Disney, Sony Pictures, MGM, Paramount, FOX, Universal, and Warner Bros. The top motion picture studios are generally part of larger media companies. The industry is highly concentrated: the 50 largest companies account for about 80 percent of industry revenue. Most companies are small and privately held. Most of the industry, including many independent firms, engages in both production and distribution; about 500 firms are solely distributors.

Competitive Landscape

Consumer spending drives demand. The profitability of individual companies depends on creativity, marketing, and distribution. Large companies often have the advantages of long-term contracts with key actors and directors, a permanent staff of technical employees, and wide distribution networks. Small companies can compete successfully by creating marketable movies, often for niche audiences, on low budgets. Although production work is labor-intensive, the value of the product results in high average annual industry revenue of $300,000 per employee.

Products, Operations & Technology

The motion picture industry produces mainly first-run movies and secondary releases, distributed first through theatres and later on various media through a variety of commercial outlets. Secondary releases, mainly on DVD through wholesale and retail channels, contribute 50 percent of industry revenue, while first-runs account for about 20 percent. Other products include commercials, music videos, special features, and post-production and technical services. Some companies sell merchandise or earn fees from licensing brand names to third-party manufacturers. Distribution of pre-

BUSINESS CHALLENGES

» High Production Costs

The high expense of financing movies well in advance of revenue has prompted producers to find ways to spread the financial burden and lower costs. Producers may seek financing from a variety of backers, simplify production and processes, or find lower-cost locations. Foreign tax incentives lure US companies to film in other countries, in what the industry calls "runaway" productions.

» High Failure Rate

Despite a large number of outlets for movies, many productions are financial failures. Illegal copies or a disappointing first-run in theatres can limit a project's prospects for revenue from secondary releases, such as on TV and DVD. Producers and big studios spend large amounts on market research and forecasting models, but the industry has poor ability to predict public acceptance of any single production. Producers and studios constantly look for new and interesting script ideas and monitor consumer preferences and demographic and cultural trends.

» Dependence on Distributors

Distributing movies has become more complicated, due to the larger number of possible outlets. This market fragmentation increases dependence on distributors. The big distribution organizations like Disney, FOX, Viacom, and Time Warner have an advantage due to their reach. Only large distributors have established relationships and efficient access to hundreds of movie theatres, cable channels, and foreign markets.

viously released products is through theatres; wholesalers and retailers; network, local, cable, and satellite TV; the Internet; and other distributors. Companies that both produce and distribute product account for 97 percent of industry revenue.

Production may be on a proprietary or fee-for-service (contract production) basis. Because long-term profit from successful motion pictures can be very high compared to upfront production costs, companies often prefer to produce movies on a proprietary basis and own the product. When customers own the product, they pay fees for production and distribution services, a common arrangement for non-movie products, such as commercials, educational features, music videos, and direct-to-video DVDs. Independent production companies increasingly contract with major studios for distribution services, which include marketing.

Creating a movie goes through four phases: development, pre-production, production, and post-production. In development, the producer creates or acquires a screenplay, gets tentative commitments from a director and principal actors, and develops a budget. Once these elements are in place, the producer secures financing from a movie studio or independent source. Much of the work of producers involves assembling a pre-production package that financial backers will approve.

After project approval and financing, the movie goes into pre-production. The producer finalizes director, cinematographer, and lead actor contracts, and most details of the screenplay; hires a production crew; ensures development of a detailed schedule that identifies timing and need for cast, costumes, equipment, and other production elements; and monitors rehearsals. Filming ("principal photography") for a movie may run from a few weeks to several months.

Once shooting is complete, the movie goes into post-production, which includes processes and tasks such as editing, music scoring, audiovisual synchronization, special effects, and titles. The result of the cumulative post-production work is a master negative that will serve as the source for exhibition copies of the movie. The industry refers to expenses through production of the master negative as "negative costs." An independent company may produce one movie per year; larger studios may produce over a dozen.

Distribution of finished product typically goes through the large studios, which have relationships with extensive numbers of theatres, TV networks, major retailers, and other secondary outlets. Distribution of first-release motion pictures includes marketing to theatres ("exhibitors") that rent ("license") movies; obtaining exhibitor contracts; advertising; and providing promotional materials and copies of the film. Contracts specify what percentage of gross ticket sales go to the exhibitor, the distributor, and the production company.

License fees from multi-phased distribution are important to the financial success of most projects. Usually, movies first go into theatrical release, then to video or DVD after about six months, then to cable and pay-per-view TV channels, and eventually to free TV. A production company typically sells licenses separately for distribution through these different outlets. To ensure revenue, independent producers may enter a "negative pickup" contract through which they sell their ownership rights in the master negative, as of a specific date, to a studio or an independent distributor before completing the film. Typically, the new owner pays costs, the producer finishes the film, and the two parties split net profit.

The industry uses advanced technology for business forecasts and production. Computer forecasting models help predict success of projects and decision-support tools help determine a marketing and distribution strategy. The technology in movie production changes rapidly, due to the increasing power, visual, and sound capabilities of computers. Many crews use digital cameras to shoot movies and specialized computer software for editing. Special effects are mainly computer-generated imagery (CGI). Digital files have enabled electronic distribution to customers.

Sales & Marketing

Typical customers for first-run movies are theatres and independent distributors. Large studios market to a wide network of theatres, while small production companies typically use independent distributors. Major studios usually have distribution contracts in place prior to filming, but smaller independent producers often find distributors during the production process or subsequently "acquire" them after screenings at film festivals like Sundance and Cannes.

Major types of marketing are exhibition showings to theatre owners and independent distributors; TV, magazine, and newspaper ads; in-theatre previews ("trailers"); and a movie's website. Production companies rely primarily on executive relationships and a sales force to secure exhibitors and distributors, but may also use brokers and agents, particularly for other countries.

Marketers add citations to marketing materials for movies that win awards at events like the Oscars and Golden Globes and at festivals like Cannes and Sundance. Consumer tastes, culture, and trends have more to do with what movies a studio decides to produce than awards do. A project may take years from concept to opening day. Awards, however, may affect the release of a movie that the company has completed, but not yet released, or may extend a movie's first-run release.

Product prices are actually license fees from theatres and secondary outlets. Production companies license theatre corporations to show movies, usually on a film-by-film and theatre-by-theatre basis for a specific timeframe and within geographical film licensing zones. In zones with competing theatres, competitors may bid for the exclusive right to show a new movie or the distributor may allocate films to theatres. In zones with no competitors, theatre owners choose the films they want and negotiate the license fee with the distributor. License fees for theatres depend on admission revenue and usually are on a sliding scale — often over 70 percent of initial admissions, declining to 30 percent by the seventh week. License fees may also be based on admission revenue minus a certain allowance for expenses.

Production companies also negotiate license fees for secondary-release distribution in other media formats, such as DVD or computer games, and outlets other than theatres, such as broadcast media and retail stores. Secondary releases, especially consumer products like DVDs, comprise about 50 percent of industry revenue and are important sources of sales commissions.

Human Resources

Industry employees are highly skilled specialists, many performing jobs unique to movie production, and accordingly receive pay 50 percent higher than the average national wage. Employment levels of full-time workers vary as much as 8 percent yearly and don't follow national trends. Annual personnel turnover is high, due to competitive hiring. Actors and production crews occasionally are injured while filming.

Production companies manage relationships with many talent agencies and unions. Talent agencies represent creative personnel, including actors and cinematographers, in finding roles and production opportunities. A variety of unions represents actors, writers, directors, and production personnel for most movie work. Many production personnel, including actors, work on a project basis and may be unemployed for parts of the year. Companies manage large numbers of temporary workers, in addition to permanent staff.

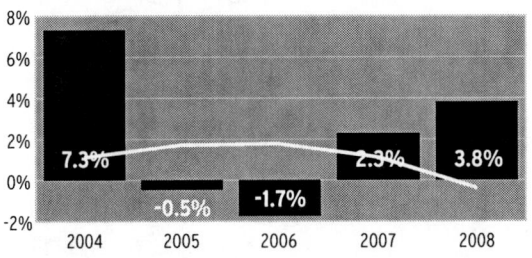

Industry Employment Growth

SOURCE: BUREAU OF LABOR STATISTICS

Call Preparation Questions

How is the company addressing the high cost of financing movies?

The high expense of financing movies well in advance of revenue has prompted producers to find ways to spread the financial burden and lower costs.

How does the company determine the potential success of a movie?

Despite a large number of outlets for movies, many productions are financial failures.

What strategies does the company use to reach the large number of potential outlets for its products?

Distributing movies has become more complicated, due to the larger number of possible outlets.

What opportunities does the company have to expand into new media and distribution channels?

The growth of distribution outlets has created strong demand for more entertainment products in a variety of media.

How does the company take advantage of its film library?

Demand from cable channels has greatly increased the value of the libraries of old movies that many major studios have produced or acquired.

Web Links

Alliance of Motion Picture and Television Producers (AMPTP)

Collective bargaining issues.
www.amptp.org

Directors Guild of America (DGA)

Monthly news related to directing.
www.dga.org/index2.php3

Motion Picture Association of America (MPAA)

Industry issues, statistics.
www.mpaa.org

Motion Picture Editors Guild

News about editing and post-production.
www.editorsguild.com/v2

Screen Actors Guild (SAG)

News and issues related to acting.
www.sag.org

Variety

Film news, box-office and production charts.
www.variety.com

Writers Guild of America, West

Industry news.
www.wga.org

Glossary of Acronyms

AFM — American Film Market
AMPTP — Alliance of Motion Picture and Television Producers
CGI — computer-generated imagery
DGA — Directors Guild of America
MPAA — Motion Picture Association of America
SAG — Screen Actors Guild

HOOVER'S TOP COMPANIES

Largest Employers	Employees
Universal Studios, Inc.	15,000
Sony Pictures Entertainment Inc.	5,700
Lucasfilm Ltd.	1,500
DreamWorks Animation SKG Inc.	1,450
Pixar Animation Studios Inc.	850
Ingram Entertainment Holdings Inc.	670
CKX, Inc.	619
DreamWorks SKG	600
New Line Cinema Corporation	550
Lions Gate Entertainment Corp.	444

Top Public Companies by Market Value	($ mil.)
DreamWorks Animation SKG Inc.	1,969.0
Lions Gate Entertainment Corp.	1,157.0
Liberty Capital Group	424.1
CKX, Inc.	338.7
Rentrak Corporation	128.3

* These rates are compounded annualized increases and may have resulted from acquisitions or one time gains. If less than 6 years of data are available, growth is for the years available.

SOURCE: HOOVER'S, INC., DATABASE

Motor, Generator, Pump, and Compressor Manufacturing

US manufacture of electric motors, generators, pumps, and compressors involves about 1,000 companies, with combined annual revenue of $20 billion. Big manufacturers include AO Smith, IDEX Corp, Franklin Electric, and operating divisions of large companies like GE, Ingersoll Rand, and Emerson Electric. The industry is highly concentrated: the 50 largest companies control about 80 percent of each market segment. A typical operation has $6 million of annual revenue, a single manufacturing location, and fewer than 50 employees.

Competitive Landscape

Industrial and manufacturing companies drive demand. The profitability of individual companies depends on efficient production. Small companies can compete by specializing. While larger companies, like GE, produce mainly a standard line of products, smaller companies are more likely to adapt products for customers' special needs. The industry is fairly automated: average annual revenue per worker is close to $200,000.

Products, Operations & Technology

Products include about $9 billion of electrical motors and generators, $7 billion of pumps, and $4 billion of air and gas compressors. Fractional horsepower motors (fractions of one horsepower) account for the majority of motor and generator production; followed by integral horsepower motors (multiples of one horsepower); "prime mover" generators (powered by prime movers like diesel or steam engines); and motor-generator sets. Almost all motors and generators are sold to industrial users (both as components in product manufacture and for industrial process use), as sources of power for industrial use, and as emergency electrical sources for commercial users.

The three major types of pumps and compressors are rotary gear, centrifuge, and piston

BUSINESS CHALLENGES

» Dependence on Manufacturing Sector

Because most motors, generators, pumps, and compressors are sold to industrial customers, the industry depends highly on US manufacturing levels. Typically, US manufacturing activity grows between 4 and 6 percent per year. During the last recession, manufacturing dropped 5 percent.

» Competition from Low-Cost Imports

US manufacturers face more competition from imports of low-end products with a high labor content. A large number of US imports now come from Mexico, where many US firms have located production facilities. Malaysia and China have increased production of low-end products like small electric motors and compressors.

» Customer Concentration

Large manufacturers with a complete product line have a diversified customer base, but smaller companies that specialize in a particular type of product, or that produce customized versions, may receive a large amount of business from just a few customers or from customers in a narrow line of business.

(reciprocating) types. Customers buy 40 percent of pumps for industrial process applications, such as moving water and chemicals; 10 percent for oilfield applications; 15 percent for household water and drainage systems; and 10 percent for product dispensing systems (such as gas and soda pumps), car circulation systems, and industrial spraying equipment. About 60 percent of compressors are used in refrigeration systems and industrial and commercial process systems, and 20 percent in industrial spraying systems, mainly paint spraying.

The very large number of specialized uses for basic industrial machines has prevented the emergence of dominant competitors. Good economies of scale in manufacturing exist for some commodity-type products like medium electric motors, but the large variety of types and sizes of products limit production runs, and therefore limit cost advantages for large producers. Even a $100 million company may produce dozens of variations of its major product.

The production process is similar in that it requires precision machining of metal components, so that various moving parts work with the most efficient use of energy. Most generators, pumps, and compressors are powered by motors. Usually there are only a few moving parts, but these must fit precisely. The products also have various electrical controls and are typically sold to other manufacturers that incorporate them into other products.

A production plant typically has various machine tool stations and metal presses, where raw materials, like steel, brass, aluminum, and copper, and semi-finished parts like castings are shaped. In assembly areas, the manufactured parts and other purchased parts are combined into the finished product. Although most precision work is done automatically by sophisticated machinery, a large amount of manual labor is required to feed the machinery and assemble the product.

Manufacturers use computer technology to improve the inventory, manufacture, and service components of the business. Electronic data interchange (EDI) helps manufacturers exchange order and product information with suppliers and customers, while shop-floor automation and resource systems help in production and planning. Material handling and logistics systems aid in moving, storing, shipping, and tracking delivery of products.

Sales & Marketing

Although some manufacturers make finished products for the consumer market, most sales are to OEMs, industrial, and commercial customers. Over half of motor sales are to the replacement market. Sales and marketing is typically through an in-house sales force, wholesale distributors (who may stock product or be "non-stocking" order takers) and manufacturers representatives. Most companies have only a small sales force because they're small and rely heavily on distributors. Regional and national trade shows are an important source of new business.

Human Resources

Production requires semi-skilled workers who receive wages close to the national average for all US workers. The injury rate of the pump

and compressor industry is close to the national average, but the injury rate of the motor and generator industry is almost 30% higher. Annual employee turnover in the manufacturing sector is 30 percent.

Most companies have an engineering staff to improve products and adapt existing products to customer needs. Some production jobs in the industry involve servicing sophisticated production machinery and therefore require technical knowledge and expertise. Many jobs, however, simply involve assembling components and are relatively low-paid. Employment has been decreasing as customers have moved their own manufacturing operations overseas.

Industry Employment Growth

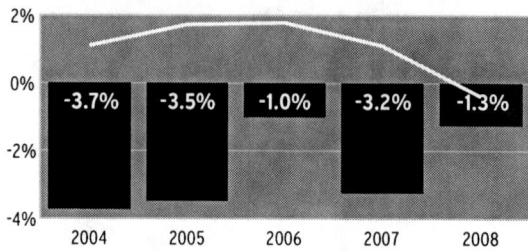

Average Hourly Earnings

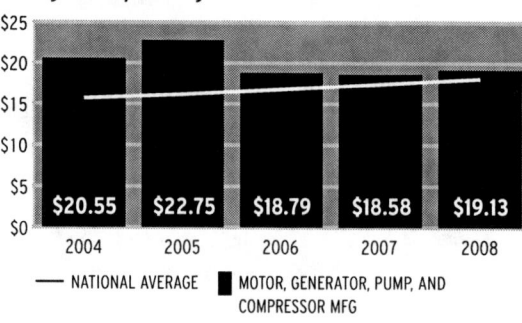

— NATIONAL AVERAGE ■ MOTOR, GENERATOR, PUMP, AND COMPRESSOR MFG

SOURCE: BUREAU OF LABOR STATISTICS

Call Preparation Questions

How does the company manage shifts in product demand from the manufacturing sector?

Because most motors, generators, pumps, and compressors are sold to industrial customers, the industry depends highly on US manufacturing levels.

What impact has foreign competition had on company market share and sales?

US manufacturers face more competition from imports of low-end products with a high labor content.

How much of company revenue is from a few large customers?

Large manufacturers with a complete product line have a diversified customer base, but smaller companies that specialize in a particular type of product, or that produce customized versions, may receive a large amount of business from just a few customers or from customers in a narrow line of business.

What opportunities does the company see in the municipal water treatment market?

Stricter wastewater regulations necessitate a more elaborate infrastructure for compliance, including special pumps and motors, creating an increase in the number and size of treatment facilities.

What opportunities or challenges might the company expect in supplying products to the medical industry?

Automated machinery used in medical testing kits for blood and other fluids relies heavily on precision pumps and motors.

Web Links

Appliance Magazine

News and statistics about consumer end-use markets.

www.appliancemagazine.com

Compressed Air and Gas Institute

Technical information about compressors.

www.cagi.org

Hydraulic Institute

Technical information about pumps and compressors.

www.pumps.org

Motor and Motion Association

Technical information about small motors.

www.smma.org

National Electrical Manufacturers Association

Motor & Generator section has list of major manufacturers by category.

www.nema.org

Sustainable Facility

News for the energy industry.

www.sustainablefacility.com

Glossary of Acronyms

EDI — electronic data interchange

FDI — foreign direct investment

OEM — original equipment manufacturer

HOOVER'S TOP COMPANIES

Largest Companies by Sales	($ mil.)
Pentair, Inc.	3,352.0
AMETEK, Inc.	2,531.1
A. O. Smith Corporation	2,304.9
Regal Beloit Corporation	2,246.3
Gardner Denver, Inc.	2,018.3
Baldor Electric Company	1,954.7
IDEX Corporation	1,489.5
Tecumseh Products Company	1,133.4
Robbins & Myers, Inc.	787.2
Franklin Electric Co., Inc.	602.0

Largest Employers	Employees
Regal Beloit Corporation	17,900
A. O. Smith Corporation	16,800
Pentair, Inc.	16,000
AMETEK, Inc.	11,300
Tecumseh Products Company	10,300
Baldor Electric Company	8,083
Gardner Denver, Inc.	6,200
IDEX Corporation	5,009
Robbins & Myers, Inc.	3,357
Franklin Electric Co., Inc.	3,200

Fastest Growing* by Five-Year Sales Growth	(%)
Distributed Energy Systems Corp.	62.7
American Superconductor Corporation	39.9
Allied Motion Technologies Inc.	37.5
Gardner Denver, Inc.	35.6
Regal Beloit Corporation	29.4
Baldor Electric Company	28.3
AMETEK, Inc.	18.3
IDEX Corporation	13.3
Tech/Ops Sevcon, Inc.	11.2
Franklin Electric Co., Inc.	11.1

Fastest Growing* by Five-Year Employee Growth	(%)
Gardner Denver, Inc.	34.4
Regal Beloit Corporation	27.6
Baldor Electric Company	21.6
Allied Motion Technologies Inc.	8.2
IDEX Corporation	7.9
AMETEK, Inc.	7.4
Pentair, Inc.	6.8
American Superconductor Corporation	5.2
Franklin Electric Co., Inc.	3.8
The Dewey Electronics Corporation	3.4

Top Public Companies by Market Value	($ mil.)
AMETEK, Inc.	3,224.2
Pentair, Inc.	2,326.2
IDEX Corporation	1,939.3
Robbins & Myers, Inc.	1,556.5
Gardner Denver, Inc.	1,208.7

* These rates are compounded annualized increases and may have resulted from acquisitions or one time gains. If less than 6 years of data are available, growth is for the years available.

SOURCE: HOOVER'S, INC., DATABASE

Motorcycle Manufacturing

THIS INDUSTRY INCLUDES:

SIC CODES
3751   Motorcycles, Bicycles, and Parts

NAICS CODES
336991   Motorcycle, Bicycle, and Parts Manufacturing

US motorcycle manufacturers include about 60 companies with combined annual revenue of about $6 billion. The industry is highly concentrated. Harley-Davidson dominates the US manufacturing sector. The remainder are foreign-based companies with final assembly operations in the US, parts and accessories manufacturers, or custom builders who make built-to-order products for motorcycle enthusiasts.

Competitive Landscape

Personal income and interest rates drive demand. Motorcycles are considered discretionary items in the US since few are used as a primary means of transportation. About one-fourth of motorcycle purchases are financed. The profitability of individual companies depends on volume and sales of high-margin accessories and add-ons. Small manufacturers compete by offering highly customized products. Annual sales per employee averages about $400,000.

Products, Operations & Technology

Major products include touring and cruiser motorcycles designed for comfort and long distance rides (67 percent of industry revenue); off-road cycles designed for dirt and mountain terrain (25 percent); dual sport designed for both road and off-road usage (3 percent); and scooters (5 percent). Motorcycle engines are measured in cubic centimeters (cc) and range from 50cc to 2300cc. Heavyweight bikes have engines with 650cc or greater.

Motorcycles are typically produced on assembly lines, similar to how the auto industry makes cars. Parts are received from outside sources (either third-party companies or other corporate-owned plants), usually on a just-in-time basis. Beginning with the basic steel or aluminum frame, the product proceeds from station to station where components are added to produce a finished product. These compo-

BUSINESS CHALLENGES

» Dependence on Personal Income

Because motorcycles are considered a discretionary purchase, sales depend highly on disposable personal income. Consumers are likely to delay purchases of motorcycles during economic downturns. Motorcycle sales and personal income grew every year in the US from 2001 to 2006.

» Competition from Imports

Imports make up about 60 percent of all US sales in the motorcycle industry. Japan and China are the leading exporters to the US market. Imports increased about 45 percent from 2002 through 2006, from about $4 to $5.8 billion. US manufacturers market features, such as performance and customization, to avoid competing on price with imports.

» Consumer Safety

A major reason consumers give for not buying motorcycles is concern for safety. Concerted efforts, including a Congress-funded study matched by industry participants, are underway as the industry attempts to improve rider safety. Motorcycle fatalities rose for the ninth straight year in 2006.

nents include telescopic forks for holding the front wheel, handlebars, brakes, engines, transmissions, drive shafts, wheels, seats, and fairings (plastic or fiberglass coverings). Paints and coatings are applied in separate operations.

Raw materials include steel and aluminum forgings and castings, chromed metal parts, plastics, fiberglass, vinyl, leather, paints, epoxies, and other coatings. Material costs represent about 55 percent of revenues.

Low-volume manufacturing by custom bike builders does not justify investment in assembly line processes. The cost of less efficient production processes is covered by the higher selling price of custom bikes.

Engineering and technology advancements have driven assembly costs down over the years. Just-in-time inventory management reduces inventory costs, but requires tighter tolerances on machined parts for assembly. CAD parts and products has reduced the rate of non-conforming parts and increased manufacturing efficiencies.

Sales & Marketing

Motorcycle owners have higher than average educational backgrounds and earnings. According to Harley-Davidson, its typical buyer is a mid-40's male with annual income of about $82,000.

Products are sold primarily through the 4,500 motorcycle dealers located throughout the US. Most dealers carry multiple brands, though 80 percent of Harley-Davidson dealers carry Harley products exclusively. In addition to selling motorcycles, dealers may also sell other power sports equipment such as ATVs, snowmobiles, jet skis, and golf carts. The typical dealer also provides after-market service, parts, and accessories for the product line.

Primary marketing vehicles include TV, print, and outdoor advertising. Rallies and events promote brand loyalty among enthusiasts, such as the over 500,000 people who attend the annual Harley-Davidson rally in Sturgis, South Dakota. Manufacturers support co-op advertising to dealers, generally based on the prior year's sales performance. Manufacturer websites direct potential buyers to nearby dealer locations and offer descriptions, performance specifications, and other information to help potential buyers make informed decisions.

Motorcycle selling prices vary widely depending on type, performance criteria, extras, and brand. Typical prices for touring or cruising motorcycles range between $6,500 and $28,000. Custom-built motorcycles range from $35,000 to $80,000. Scooters and off-road products range from $3,000 to $15,000.

Human Resources

Motorcycle manufacturing requires special production skills in machining, welding, and assembly. Production workers gain such skills at trade schools, community colleges, and through in-house training programs. Production workers earn about $21 per hour, about 25 percent higher than the average US hourly manufacturing wage.

Worker injury rates are about 20 percent higher than the average of the overall US manufacturing sector. The majority of production workers in the US are represented by unions. However, most companies are owner-operated manufacturers and non-union.

Call Preparation Questions

How does the general economy affect the company's business?

Because motorcycles are considered a discretionary purchase, sales depend highly on disposable personal income.

How do imports affect the company's business?

Imports make up about 60 percent of all US sales in the motorcycle industry.

How does concern about motorcycle safety affect the company's sales?

A major reason consumers give for not buying motorcycles is concern for safety.

How does the company increase profit margins?

Like auto manufacturers, motorcycle manufacturers enjoy higher margins on extras and upgrades.

What attracts buyers to the company's products?

Motorcycle enthusiasts who like to express their individuality buy customized products.

Web Links

American Motorcyclist Association

Product updates and industry information.
www.ama-cycle.org

Motorcycle Industry Council

Industry trade organization.
www.mic.org

Motorcycle Safety Foundation

Information about rider safety training programs.
msf-usa.org

Motorcycle.com

News and reviews.
www.motorcycle.com

MotorcycleUSA.com

News and reviews.
www.motorcycle-usa.com

webBikeWorld

Sales statistics and other industry information.
www.webbikeworld.com/Motorcycle-news/blog

Glossary of Acronyms

AMA — American Motorcyclist Association
CAD — computer-aided design
CERCLA — Comprehensive Environmental Response, Compensation, and Liability Act
CC — cubic centimeter
MIC — Motorcycle Industry Council
MSF — Motorcycle Safety Foundation
NHTSB — National Highway Transportation Safety Board

HOOVER'S TOP COMPANIES

Largest Employers	Employees
Harley-Davidson, Inc.	10,100
Yamaha Motor Corporation, U.S.A.	3,700
Paladin Holdings, Inc	858
Global Motorsport Group, Inc.	680
American Ironhorse Motorcycle Company	500
Ultra Motorcycle Inc.	25

Top Public Companies by Market Value	($ mil.)
Harley-Davidson, Inc.	3,950.0

SOURCE: HOOVER'S, INC., DATABASE

Movie Theatres

The US movie theatre industry includes about 2,000 companies with combined annual revenue of $11 billion and around 5,000 indoor theatres and 300 drive-ins. Major companies include Regal Entertainment, AMC Entertainment, and Cinemark. The industry is highly concentrated: the 50 largest firms own half of the nation's theatres and earn around 85 percent of industry revenue. A typical company is small, with average annual revenue under $700,000, one theatre, and fewer than 20 employees.

Competitive Landscape

Personal income and leisure time drive demand. The profitability of individual companies depends on securing access to popular movies and sales of high-margin food and beverages. Large companies have advantages in negotiating with movie distributors; marketing; and economies of scale in purchasing. Small companies can compete effectively by specializing in movie type or audience, or providing better service and amenities. Average annual revenue per worker is $80,000.

Products, Operations & Technology

Major services are sales of tickets, food, and beverages. Ticket admissions account for almost 70 percent of industry revenue; food and beverage for more than 25 percent; and on-screen advertisements, over 1 percent. Other services include facility and concession rental during non-peak hours, amusement machine use, and merchandise sales. Drive-ins have fewer services than indoor theatres and on average earn 80 percent of revenue from admission sales, 15 percent from food and beverages, and less than 5 percent from facility rental.

Movie theatre operations center on licensing and showing ("exhibiting") films to consumers, and obtaining and selling concession items. Theatres acquire from distributors the right to

BUSINESS CHALLENGES

» Dependence on Movie Production, Distribution Companies

Theatres rely on movie production companies and distributors for films, license rights, and marketing. Theatres need movies that appeal to local markets. Distributors decide which venues can license specific films, so theatres' relationships and negotiations with movie suppliers are important. Theatres increasingly depend on production studios and distributors to market first-run films. A studio's or distributor's problems, such as strikes or finances, can directly affect theatre revenue.

» Dependence on Consumer Spending

As a discretionary spending item, movie-going depends on personal income and competes for the consumer dollar with other forms of paid entertainment. Changes in average national income typically indicate fluctuation in movie theatre business. During the last recession, US personal income declined 3.5 percent and movie theatre employment dropped 2.7 percent, reflecting lower attendance and revenue. When consumer spending is healthy, theatres typically increase per-customer revenue through concession sales.

» Competition from Alternate Distribution Channels

Movie production companies can generate revenue from multiple distribution channels, rather than relying primarily on theatres, as they did historically. Production companies' distribution strategies typically include additional revenue streams from releases for cable TV, in-home video and DVD, satellite and pay-per-view services, and Internet downloads. Total home video spending increased almost 50 percent in a recent five-year period, according to Veronis Suhler Stevenson. Although theatres remain important first-run outlets, they risk becoming less important to production companies' revenue strategies.

use (license) a movie in specific geographic zones for a determined duration. Distributors define the zones, which typically vary from two to 15 miles in radius. Theatre companies that are the only exhibitor in a zone have an advantage in negotiating and selecting which new ("first-run") films to exhibit. Distributors typically rank zones by their population density, audience demographics, and potential box office revenue.

Most theatres license films from independent distributors, although large theatre chains rent directly from distributors owned by the major movie production companies. License contracts typically are on a theatre-by-theatre and film-by-film basis. Theatres negotiate license fees with distributors using one of three types of formulas: a percentage-of-revenue rate set prior to exhibition ("firm term"); a rate set at completion of the engagement ("review or settlement"); or an agreed "sliding scale" formula that will apply decreasing rates to successive weeks of an engagement. Sliding scale rates are typically 50 to 70 percent of box office revenue at the start of a film's run, dropping to around 30 percent after a month or two. Theatres pay more to license potential blockbuster movies, which typically have longer engagements.

Major operational metrics are ticket sales ("box office revenue" or "admissions"); food and beverage ("concession") sales; and revenue-per-customer. Metrics for size of business are total number of screens (auditoriums) and ratio of screens to theatres. The largest companies have a screen-to-theatre ratio of over 12 to 1, but the national average historically has been below seven. A multiplex theatre has more than one screen; a megaplex, 10 to 20. The largest company has over 6,000 screens in its US circuit. Most companies locate theatres near areas of high consumer traffic, such as shops and restaurants. Theatre facility formats include the older sloped-floor auditorium or modern stadium seating.

Concession items consist mainly of popcorn, candy, and soft drinks; some theatres, particularly "art" theatres, sell wine and beer, and some offer children's meals. Because concession items have higher margins than ticket sales, theatres focus on food and beverages to increase the average purchase per customer. Theatres incent concession staff to increase sales and service speed. Theatres buy food and beverages from concession distributors, which make weekly or as-needed deliveries. Chains negotiate bulk rates and order directly from manufacturers, but receive the shipments from distributors, paying them a percentage for warehouse and delivery services.

Technology has become important for selling tickets and measuring business performance. Companies' e-commerce websites enable customers to buy and print tickets in advance or pick them up at the theatre, sometimes at self-service kiosks. Point-of-sale systems track ticket and concession sales, triggering automatic replenishment orders to suppliers. Systems integrate sales data real-time from a theatre, its website, and third-party ticketing services to provide staff with current ticket and seating availability. The data also enable management to change schedules and screenings and to support negotiations for film bookings with distributors. Many companies send sales data electronically to firms that measure and rank movie theatres.

Most theatres continue to exhibit content that production companies recorded on 35mm film, although digital formats are increasing. Other than referring to the technical recording format, the industry uses the term "film" synonymously with "motion picture" or "movie."

Sales & Marketing

Typical customers are consumer movie-goers, with younger patrons the most frequent. Theatres increasingly market to businesspeople for gift card purchases and to businesses for facility rentals. Corporate event sales are relatively low and primarily serve to earn revenue when the theatre is otherwise idle.

Major types of marketing are newspaper ads and movie schedule listings, and Internet advertising. Film distributors pay for most newspaper ads and for radio and TV spots to promote special movies and events. Theatres pay for newspaper directory listings. Newspaper ads often include placing movie descriptions and schedules on the news publication's website. Theatre websites allow customers to see previews ("trailers"), read about actors, access schedules, and buy advance tickets or gift cards. Large chains often have promotional programs with distributors that include movie-goer contests; third-party cross-promotions, such as merchandise sales; and radio, TV, or cell phone ads.

Theatres also show coming attractions, and chains run trailers of movies playing at their nearby venues. Advance sales of tickets, gift, and discount cards also occur via phone, fax, e-mail, and postal mail. Many companies offer loyalty programs for frequent movie-goers and cross-promotional specials among same-ownership theatres. Some companies sell gift cards at major retailers.

Large companies have formed partnerships for sales and delivery of on-screen display advertisements in theatres and other venues. Several of the largest firms are partnering to develop digital technology for delivery and exhibition of digitally formatted movies.

Typical prices nationwide range from $5 to $10 for admission and $2 to $6 for a drink, popcorn, or candy. Prices in major cities can be almost twice as much as in low-cost geographies. Theatres compete with other forms of leisure activity, including non-fee activities like sports and hobbies, and for-fee entertainment like concerts, sports events, and amusement parks. Further competition comes from other forms of movie exhibition, including DVD, TV, video on-demand, and Internet downloads.

Human Resources

Most industry employees need only on-the-job training, because the jobs require minimal sales or service skills. Theatres give ongoing training to concession-counter personnel on suggestive and up-selling methods that help increase sales. The backoffice business staff and the projectionists who run the film or digital equipment require special training. Some projectionists are union members. In-theatre management is responsible for controlling operations and quality assurance. Average industry wages are low, less than half the national wage, mainly due to the part-time status of most customer-facing jobs. Over 90 percent of many theatre staff is part-time. Injury rates are low, but tend to be sprains and strains from personnel falling on floors.

Industry Employment Growth

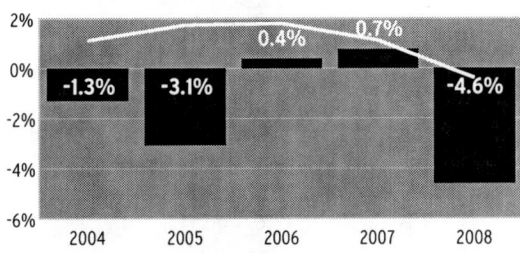

Average Hourly Earnings

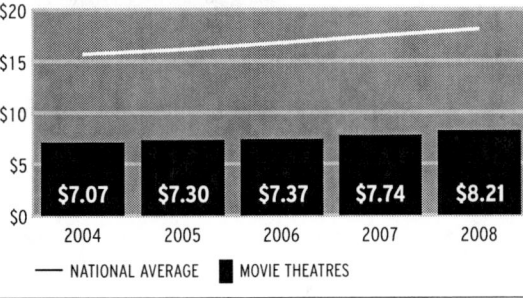

SOURCE: BUREAU OF LABOR STATISTICS

Call Preparation Questions

How dependent is the theatre on movie production and distribution companies?

Theatres rely on movie production companies and distributors for films, license rights, and marketing.

How do changes in personal income affect movie attendance?

As a discretionary spending item, movie-going depends on personal income and competes for the consumer dollar with other forms of paid entertainment.

How concerned is the company about theatres being one of many distribution channels for movies?

Movie production companies can generate revenue from multiple distribution channels, rather than relying primarily on theatres, as they did historically.

How does the company compete with large theatre chains?

Smaller and midsized companies can specialize to differentiate themselves from large movie chains and appeal to underserved markets.

What kinds of facility upgrades could help the company compete more effectively?

Most large chains have already remodeled or replaced old theatres and continue to build modern ones, so smaller and midsized companies can often compete if they upgrade facilities.

Web Links

Cinema Advertising Council

In-theatre advertising statistics, research, technology.
www.cinemaadcouncil.org

Fandango

Third-party ticketing agency.
www.fandango.com

Motion Picture Association of America (MPAA)

Movie industry news, issues, statistics, ratings descriptions.
www.mpaa.org

National Association of Theatre Owners

Issues, news, and statistics from trade association.
www.natoonline.org

National CineMedia (NCM)

Digital delivery of cinema advertising and non-movie content for events.
www.ncm.com

The Motion Picture Theatre Associations of Canada

Statistics, lists of provincial associations.
www.mptac.ca

United Drive-In Theatre Owners Association

Drive-in theatre business FAQs, statistics.
uditoa.org

Variety

Film news, box-office and production charts.
www.variety.com

Glossary of Acronyms

AFM — American Film Market

AMC — AMC Entertainment

AMPTP — Alliance of Motion Picture and Television Producers

CGI — computer-generated imagery

DMA — designated market area

MPAA — Motion Picture Association of America

MPTAC — The Motion Picture Theatre Associations of Canada

NAC — National Association of Concessionaires

NATO — National Association of Theatre Owners

NCM — National CineMedia

HOOVER'S TOP COMPANIES

Largest Companies by Sales	($ mil.)
National Amusements Inc.	5,224.6
Regal Entertainment Group	2,771.9
AMC Entertainment Holdings, Inc.	2,504.3
Cinemark Holdings, Inc.	1,742.3
Carmike Cinemas, Inc.	474.4
Reading International, Inc.	119.2

Largest Employers	Employees
National Amusements Inc.	133,269
Regal Entertainment Group	23,292
AMC Entertainment Holdings, Inc.	20,200
Cinemark Holdings, Inc.	13,600
Carmike Cinemas, Inc.	6,838
Kerasotes ShowPlace Theatres, LLC	2,200
Reading International, Inc.	1,523
Landmark Theatres	1,000
Brenden Theatre Corporation	510
CinemaStar Luxury Theaters, Inc.	350

Fastest Growing* by Five-Year Sales Growth	(%)
Cinemark Holdings, Inc.	12.7
Reading International, Inc.	6.6
Regal Entertainment Group	2.2

Fastest Growing* by Five-Year Employee Growth	(%)
Reading International, Inc.	5.3
Cinemark Holdings, Inc.	2.3

Top Public Companies by Market Value	($ mil.)
Regal Entertainment Group	1,325.3
Cinemark Holdings, Inc.	808.6
Reading International, Inc.	209.7
Carmike Cinemas, Inc.	46.8

* These rates are compounded annualized increases and may have resulted from acquisitions or one time gains. If less than 6 years of data are available, growth is for the years available.

SOURCE: HOOVER'S, INC., DATABASE

Moving and Storage

The US moving and household storage industry consists of 8,000 companies with about $13 billion in combined annual revenue. Large companies include UniGroup (owner of United and Mayflower); SIRVA (Allied, Global, and North American); Atlas; and Bekins. Despite recent consolidation, the industry is largely fragmented: the 50 largest companies hold only about 45 percent of the market.

Competitive Landscape

Home sales, residential rental turnover, and corporate relocations drive demand for moving and storage services. The profitability of individual companies depends on good marketing, as services are largely the same. Small companies can compete with large ones by offering competitive prices and better service for local moves. Large companies have economies of scale in being able to consolidate loads on long hauls. The industry is fairly labor-intensive: average annual revenue per employee is about $120,000.

Products, Operations & Technology

Companies in this industry move household and office goods, and specialty items like pianos and trade show exhibits, either locally or interstate. Moving companies also provide long- and short-term storage for the items that they move. About 45 percent of industry revenue comes from long-distance moving. Most of the companies in this industry are privately owned.

The industry is divided into three tiers. The top tier includes long-distance moves handled by a dozen large van lines like North American, Allied, Atlas, United, Mayflower, Bekins, and Wheaton, which each have annual revenue of $500 million to $1 billion. Shorter interstate moves, the second tier, are handled by about 2,000 smaller movers, who may also make long-distance moves. The third tier is local movers, thousands of small, local companies. The typi-

BUSINESS CHALLENGES

» Dependent on Relocations, Home Sales

The moving industry depends highly on home sales, which can vary as much as 10 percent per year nationally, and on corporate relocations. Corporate moving is often related to office vacancy rates. In local markets, home sales can vary by more than 20 percent per year. In Las Vegas, home sales jumped 30 percent in one year.

» Vulnerable to Fuel, Insurance Costs

Changing fuel and insurance costs heavily affect profitability in the moving industry. During periods of increasing fuel prices, competition keeps operators from complete cost recovery. The industry is only marginally profitable because of strong competition from small companies.

» Poor Public Image

Surveys show that damage claims are frequent, and about 30 percent of customers are unhappy with their moving experience. Thousands complain to consumer and regulatory agencies each year, saying movers demand extra fees once goods are on their truck or that they refuse to pay for damaged or missing property. Problems continue because government regulations are weak, consumer advocates say, and many police agencies treat complaints as a civil dispute between a customer and a business.

cal local mover has 15 employees, two to three trucks, and annual revenue of less than $1 million. A large van line may have 11,000 tractors and trailers and more than 6,000 drivers.

The large van lines operate mainly through independently owned agents who, in most cases, actually own the trucks, hire the drivers, and operate locally — much in the manner of a franchise. The van lines themselves provide mainly logistical support and sell services (like moving insurance) to their agents. North American and Atlas each have 600 local agents in the US, United has 500, and Allied has 50.

Despite sophisticated computerized techniques for scheduling and planning, this industry remains a low-technology business. Many companies leverage their internal logistics expertise and shipping and tracking systems (STS) to build new lines of business, such as outsourcing logistics and delivery fleets. Long-distance companies may use GPS to track cross-country shipments.

Sales & Marketing

Household moves provide the bulk of industry revenue, but business customers provide a steadier flow of business. Without steady business, expensive trucks and drivers are underused. Getting new customers is the major concern for household movers, since current customers are unlikely to produce repeat business. Large business customers, on the other hand, may have a constant need for moving services, especially if they routinely relocate employees. National companies have the resources to advertise widely to both household and corporate prospects, using national media and direct mail. Telephone directory advertising is important to local operators.

More household moves occur locally or regionally than nationally. Every year, 42 million Americans, representing about 17 million households, move; 60 percent are within the same county; 20 percent outside the county, but within the same state; and 20 percent to another state or country.

Human Resources

Personnel turnover and training are key difficulties for movers, who offer fairly low pay and can't guarantee steady employment. Average hourly wages for industry employees are about 10 percent lower than the national average. Annual personnel turnover for the transportation and warehousing industries is high at almost 36 percent. Moving companies have an annual injury rate 40 percent higher than average.

Industry Employment Growth

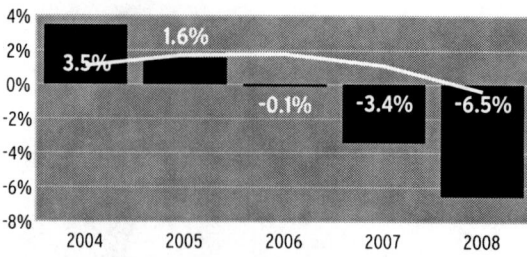

Average Hourly Earnings

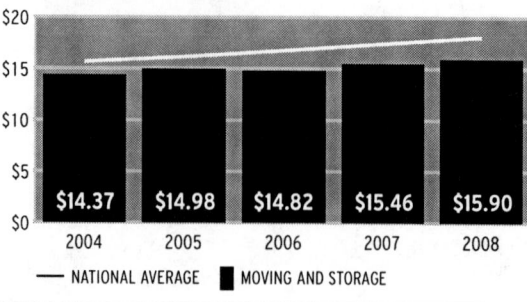

— NATIONAL AVERAGE ■ MOVING AND STORAGE

SOURCE: BUREAU OF LABOR STATISTICS

Call Preparation Questions

How does the company manage changes in demand due to fluctuations in home sales and economic cycles?

The moving industry depends highly on home sales, which can vary as much as 10 percent per year nationally, and on corporate relocations.

How has the company been affected by changes in fuel costs?

Changing fuel and insurance costs heavily affect profitability in the moving industry.

How does the company ensure customer satisfaction?

Surveys show that damage claims are frequent, and about 30 percent of customers are unhappy with their moving experience.

Has the company leveraged internal logistics expertise to expand services?

Large van lines are sophisticated logistics companies, with onboard tracking monitors that enable customers to access van location and projected arrival information.

How has the company taken advantage of Web or other online technologies?

A Web-based commercial moving and storage business can give a tremendous ROI, if it offers the right content and ease-of-use.

Web Links

American Moving and Storage Association

Consumer and cost information. List of movers.
www.moving.org

Federal Motor Carrier Safety Administration

Regulates aspects of trucking and household moving.
www.protectyourmove.gov

Moving Terminology

From American Moving and Storage Association.
www.moving.org/Article/default.asp?CEQ_ArticleID
=30&VAR_prHeadline=Moving%20Terminology

Relocation.com

A moving resource for consumers.
www.relocation.com

Self Storage Association

A nonprofit trade association for the self-storage industry.
www.selfstorage.org

Glossary of Acronyms

FMCSA — Federal Motor Carrier Safety Administration
FSMP — Full Service Moving Project
HOS — hours of service
NAR — National Association of Realtors
SSA — Self Storage Association
STS — shipping and tracking systems

HOOVER'S TOP COMPANIES

Largest Companies by Sales	($ mil.)
SIRVA, Inc.	3,969.9
UniGroup, Inc.	2,200.0
Public Storage	1,745.6
Atlas World Group, Inc.	942.6
Graebel Companies, Inc.	334.2
Extra Space Storage Inc.	273.3
U-Store-It Trust	236.4
Sovran Self Storage, Inc.	203.0

Largest Employers	Employees
Public Storage	5,700
SIRVA, Inc.	3,800
Extra Space Storage Inc.	1,853
Graebel Companies, Inc.	1,771
UniGroup, Inc.	1,350
The Suddath Companies	1,200
Sovran Self Storage, Inc.	1,057
U-Store-It Trust	989
Starving Students Inc.	600
Beltmann Group Incorporated	600

Fastest Growing* by Five-Year Sales Growth	(%)
Extra Space Storage Inc.	49.7
U-Store-It Trust	24.0
Public Storage	14.8
SIRVA, Inc.	12.7
Sovran Self Storage, Inc.	12.4
UniGroup, Inc.	5.2

Fastest Growing* by Five-Year Employee Growth	(%)
Extra Space Storage Inc.	48.9
Smart Move, Inc.	46.8
U-Store-It Trust	21.1
Public Storage	18.9
Sovran Self Storage, Inc.	10.4
UniGroup, Inc.	0.2

Top Public Companies by Market Value	($ mil.)
Public Storage	13,378.2
Extra Space Storage Inc.	885.4
Sovran Self Storage, Inc.	792.6
U-Store-It Trust	256.4

* These rates are compounded annualized increases and may have resulted from acquisitions or one time gains. If less than 6 years of data are available, growth is for the years available.

SOURCE: HOOVER'S, INC., DATABASE

Museums, Zoos, and Parks

The industry includes about 4,000 museums, 500 zoos, and 500 nature parks, with combined annual revenue close to $9 billion. National parks and museums are not included. Large institutions with more than $100 million of annual revenue include the Zoological Society of San Diego (San Diego Zoo), The Metropolitan Museum of Art, and The Art Institute of Chicago. Museums account for about 70 percent of industry revenue, zoos for 20 percent. Most museums, zoos, and parks are nonprofit. The industry is fragmented: most institutions operate a single facility.

Competitive Landscape

Demand is partly linked to growth in local income and to tourist travel. The profitability of individual institutions depends largely on good marketing. Large institutions have the advantage of name recognition. Small institutions can compete successfully by concentrating on specialty topics, or by operating in a favorable location. The industry is capital- and labor-intensive: average annual revenue per worker is $75,000.

Products, Operations & Technology

Museums, zoos, and parks provide exhibits, and may also sell food and merchandise. Some parks provide overnight accommodations or campsites. Operations revolve around the care and exhibition of objects or animals, which require workers with special knowledge or skills. Academic research may also be an important function.

The number of visitors varies substantially by institution type. Zoos typically have 500,000 annual visitors; science museums 180,000; botanical gardens 120,000; children's museums 85,000; and art museums 60,000, according to the American Association of Museums. History museums have the lowest annual attendance, about 15,000.

BUSINESS CHALLENGES

» Heavy Dependence on Economic Climate

Visitor attendance and other fundraising activities by institutions are heavily influenced by economic health, specifically government budgets, corporate profits, a volatile stock market, and personal disposable income. Many institutions receive only a small part of their revenue from admission fees, leaving them vulnerable to reduced charitable contributions and memberships.

» Cost of New Art, Exhibits

The cost of acquiring and exhibiting new works of art or animals has increased much faster than institution revenues. After languishing for many years, the Art Price Index for the US art market doubled in the last 10 years, according to Artprice.com. In 2005, global art prices increased about 10 percent.

» Reliance on Major Donors

Smaller establishments may rely on a few large donors for their operating budget, such as state or local governments that have increasingly reduced appropriations to institutions. Private donors may verbally commit to contributions but there are rarely contractual assurances. Business consolidations may remove a major corporate donor from a local market.

Marketing and fundraising are major activities for many institutions. Professional fundraising organizations are often used. Food and merchandise sales are also often run by outside vendors.

Computer systems are used to track members, store information about inventory (museums), and coordinate operations such as animal feeding and care (zoos). Security systems are essential for both museums and zoos. Large museums may have sophisticated equipment to help analyze and restore objects.

Sales & Marketing

Marketing is targeted at visitors and other sources of funds, including individuals, corporations, grant-making charities, and governments. Visitor marketing includes billboard and radio advertising, extensive newspaper advertising, direct mail, and relationships with tourism and travel companies. Many institutions have special programs aimed at schools. Joint marketing efforts with corporations that sponsor events and exhibits are becoming popular.

Fundraising efforts include the sale of memberships through direct mail and telemarketing campaigns; grant applications to corporations, charities, and governments; and appeals to wealthy donors. The board members of many museums are expected to make substantial annual contributions. Other revenue comes from fundraising events. Some institutions also rent their facilities for corporate events or private parties.

Many institutions serve as tourist destinations in their own right, such as the San Diego Zoo and The Metropolitan Museum of Art. Admission fees vary widely. At major institutions, admission varies from $15 to $40 per day, but is generally lower at smaller institutions. The median cost for museum admission is $5.

Human Resources

While museum curators, park naturalists, and zoo specialists are usually well-paid, the vast majority of work at these establishments is unskilled and receives low pay. Industry pay is about 15 percent lower than for the average US worker. Turnover is high, worsened by the summer seasonality. The safety record of the industry is average.

Industry Employment Growth

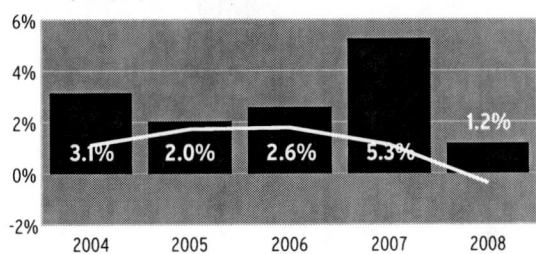

Average Hourly Earnings

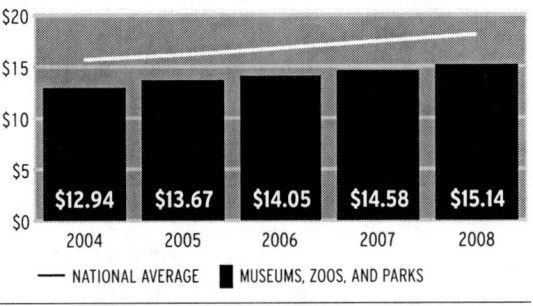

SOURCE: BUREAU OF LABOR STATISTICS

Call Preparation Questions

What portion of the institution's revenues comes from fundraising?

Visitor attendance and other fundraising activities by institutions are heavily influenced by economic health, specifically government budgets, corporate profits, a volatile stock market, and personal disposable income.

How has the institution found the capital to keep its collections or exhibits up-to-date?

The cost of acquiring and exhibiting new works of art or animals has increased much faster than institution revenues.

To what extent does the institution rely on a single large financial supporter?

Smaller establishments may rely on a few large donors for their operating budget, such as state or local governments that have increasingly reduced appropriations to institutions.

How effective are corporate sponsorships as a source of funding for the institution?

Corporate sponsorship of specific exhibits has become a new source of revenue for some museums, zoos, and parks.

Does the institution believe that online viewing of its collection can encourage attendance?

In an effort that aids scholarly research and makes more material accessible to the public, some museums have created digital records of their collections, some of which can be viewed online.

Web Links

American Association of Museums

Museum resources and listings, news, general research information, statistics.
www.aam-us.org/pressroom.cfm

American Public Gardens Association

Industry information.
www.aabga.org

Art Museum Network

Art museum news.
www.artmuseumnetwork.com

Association of Zoos and Aquariums

News of zoos and aquariums, conservation, various foundations.

www.aza.org

Botanic Gardens Conservation International

A resource for botanic garden operators.

www.bgci.org/worldwide/home

Canadian Association of Zoos and Aquariums

Promotes the welfare of and encourages the advancement and improvement of zoology, recreation, education, conservation and science.

www.caza.ca

Canadian Botanical Conservation Network (CBCN)

Aiding botanical gardens, arboreta and related organizations, individuals and others to increase their participation in plant conservation and biodiversity programs.

www.rbg.ca/cbcn/en

GuideStar

Recent financial details (Form 990 data) for many non-profits.

www.guidestar.org

World Association of Zoos and Aquariums

News and links.

www.waza.org/news

Glossary of Acronyms

AAM — American Association of Museums
AWA — Animal Welfare Act
AZA — American Zoo and Aquarium Association

HOOVER'S TOP COMPANIES

Largest Employers	Employees
Smithsonian Institution	6,300
The Colonial Williamsburg Foundation	3,100
The Metropolitan Museum of Art	2,372
Zoological Society of San Diego	2,300
American Museum of Natural History	1,262
Museum of Fine Arts, Boston	1,000
The Field Museum of Natural History	600
The Museum of Modern Art	530
United States Holocaust Memorial Museum	500
The Frick Collection	300

SOURCE: HOOVER'S, INC., DATABASE

Music Production and Distribution

THIS INDUSTRY INCLUDES:

SIC CODES

3652   Phonograph Records and Prerecorded Audio Tapes and Disks

8999   Services

NAICS CODES

5122   Sound Recording Industries

The music production and distribution industry includes about 2,600 companies with combined annual revenue of about $15 billion. Major companies include Universal Music Group, Sony Music Entertainment, EMI, and Warner Music Group. The industry is highly concentrated: eight companies account for 80 percent of industry revenue.

Competitive Landscape

Demand is driven by consumer spending. The profitability of individual companies depends on discovering and promoting new musical talent and generating revenue from the company's asset base of recordings and publications. Large companies have advantages in marketing and distribution. Smaller companies, referred to as Indies, compete by focusing on artists within local markets or music genres. The industry is capital-intensive: average annual revenue per employee is about $475,000.

Products, Operations & Technology

The major products of the industry are musical recordings (70 percent of revenue) and the publication of lyrics and musical scores (20 percent). Other products and services include the production of master recordings, the manufacture and packaging of physical CDs, and the production of databases to distribute downloads of recordings.

Major studios have musical artists — singers, rappers, and musicians — under contract to produce recordings that are either marketed as stand-alones or combined with other recordings as albums. The studios then promote the new recordings by sponsoring concert tours; providing music to radio stations to play on air; and advertising via radio, TV, print, and the Internet. Studios also promote the sale of music from their catalogs of recordings that are more than 18 months old.

BUSINESS CHALLENGES

» Declining Revenue

The revenue from music sold on CDs or downloaded legitimately peaked in 1999, the year that the first major file-sharing service was initiated. Although that service was forced to close in 2002, sales of legitimate CDs and downloads have been declining because of the pervasiveness of illegal copying. The music industry estimates that for every legal download from iTunes, as many as 100 tracks are illegally swapped on peer-to-peer networks, and that 35 percent of CDs sold are illegal copies.

» Distribution of Small Labels

The shift from specialty music stores to high-volume discount chains makes gaining shelf space harder for small labels. The demise of Tower Records and Musicland has decreased the number of outlets offering large selections of music that can be browsed by customers, forcing many smaller labels to depend on Internet distribution. Digital distribution sites, such as iTunes, tend to offer more favorable distribution terms to major studios with large catalogs of songs.

» Copy Protection Controversy

Most music that's legally downloaded is "copy protected," which prevents it from being played on multiple devices. Many users see this as infringing on their ownership rights, and maintain they should be able to play the music on their PC, home stereo, car stereo, or portable device. This consumer perception of the "unfairness" of copy protection may encourage further use of illegal downloads and file sharing.

Small studios may only produce sound recordings or may also promote and distribute them. Small, integrated studios focus on finding new (undiscovered) talents and promoting them in selected markets. The studios may specialize in a particular music genre, such as hip-hop or jazz, and develop relationships with local entertainment businesses, such as nightclubs, casinos, and concert halls. Smaller studios also develop relationships with radio and TV stations that specialize in particular genres. The studios also acquire rights to the lyrics and scores produced by and for their musicians.

Some musical groups, such as the Rolling Stones, are popular enough that all of their work is in demand. These groups usually retain rights to their own works, may have their own recording studios and labels, and contract with integrated studios to distribute their recordings.

About 85 percent of music is distributed on CDs to retailers for sale to the public. Traditionally, stores specializing in music were the major venue for music sales, but the entry of discount retailers and Internet-based retailers with huge selections at discounted prices has driven many music specialty stores out of business.

The process of creating music CDs can involve several different companies. A performance by an artist is recorded in a sound studio on multiple tracks (two to 24 tracks are common). Sound engineers can then enhance each track and optimize the mix to create a sound track on a premaster CD. The sound engineers in the mixing process can edit individual tracks, even correcting notes, and can add or delete tracks as desired. The premaster CD, along with packaging materials, is sent to a CD production plant (or CD replication plant) that creates a glass master for the production process. Once replicated, individual CDs are then wrapped in the production packaging and shipped to distributors.

The digital distribution of music through the Internet is growing and replacing physical distribution of CDs. After the premaster CD is created, it's forwarded to electronic distribution centers operated by content providers that maintain a library of recorded music for sale to consumers.

Sales & Marketing

Consumers of recorded music span all age groups and are about evenly divided between males and females. According to the Recording Industry Association of America (RIAA), about 20 percent of music purchases in 2005 were made by teenagers, 25 percent by people in their 20s, and 25 percent by those 45 or older. The younger demographics drive purchases of particular music genres; the top selling genres are rock and rap/hip-hop, which represented 45 percent of purchases in 2005.

New music is promoted heavily by the integrated studios. Promotion typically involves print, TV, radio, and Internet advertising. Since music genres are often bought by specific age

or ethnic groups, advertising is aimed at the target groups. In addition, new releases can be promoted through concert tours and broadcast of music videos on TV. While paying radio DJs and TV hosts to play specific music is illegal (known as "payola"), studios can promote their labels, releases, and tours through paid advertising and generally distribute courtesy copies of releases to broadcasters.

Prior to 2000, new albums were typically $15 to $20. Major studios set a Minimum Advertised Price (MAP) for each new album and threatened to halt distribution to any retailer selling below that price. The government ordered the industry to cease the practice in 2000 as a restraint of trade. This order, combined with the growth of sales through discount retailers, has lowered the typical price of CDs to $9 to $15.

Human Resources

Performers, songwriters, and producers under contract to a studio are generally paid directly by the studios for their work. The Alliance of Artists and Recording Companies (AARC) collects royalties from the recording companies and distributes them to artists not currently under contract.

Most professional musicians are members of the American Federation of Musicians (AFM) of the US and Canada. The AFM helps musicians negotiate fair agreements, protects ownership of recorded music, secures health care and pension benefits, and lobbies legislators on behalf of the members. Recording studio personnel aren't generally unionized; however, they require a unique blend of technical and artistic skills and can be difficult to recruit.

Industry Employment Growth

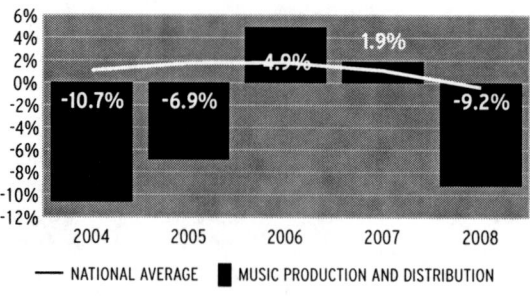

SOURCE: BUREAU OF LABOR STATISTICS

Call Preparation Questions

How have the studio's sales been affected by piracy?

The revenue from music sold on CDs or downloaded legitimately peaked in 1999, the year that the first major file-sharing service was initiated.

How does the studio get its products in front of the public?

The shift from specialty music stores to high-volume discount chains makes gaining shelf space harder for small labels.

Does the studio have a program for copy protection that will get wider consumer acceptance?

Most music that's legally downloaded is "copy protected," which prevents it from being played on multiple devices.

How is the studio using its music catalog to generate revenues?

Studios accumulate recordings of music and libraries of musical scores and lyrics to which they have ownership rights.

How is the company taking advantage of the Internet to grow sales?

The Internet has become a critical venue to sell and distribute music, both on CDs and downloads.

Web Links

American Federation of Musicians

Trade union for musicians.
www.afm.org

Billboard Magazine

Industry magazine with articles, Top 200 list, and statistics.
www.billboard.com

Mix Magazine

Magazine serving the recording and production side of the industry.
mixonline.com

Recording Industry Association of America

Trade association with news, issues, and statistics.
www.riaa.com

The Alliance of Artists and Recording Companies

News on royalty agreements for music industry.
www.aarcroyalties.com

Glossary of Acronyms

AARC — The Alliance of Artists and Recording Companies

AFM — American Federation of Musicians

BMG — Bertlesmann Music Group

DRM — digital rights management

IPTV — Internet protocol television

RIAA — Recording Industry Association of America

HOOVER'S TOP COMPANIES

Largest Companies by Sales	($ mil.)
Warner Music Group Corp.	3,491.0
EDCI Holdings, Inc.	384.6

Largest Employers	Employees
Sony Music Entertainment Inc.	10,000
Universal Music Group	9,661
Warner Music Group Corp.	3,800
EDCI Holdings, Inc.	2,200
The Welk Group, Inc.	1,350
Muzak Holdings LLC	1,261
EMI Music Publishing	629
Bad Boy Worldwide Entertainment Group	600
Alfred Music Publishing Co., Inc.	275
Integrity Media, Inc.	218

Top Public Companies by Market Value	($ mil.)
Warner Music Group Corp.	1,170.5
EDCI Holdings, Inc.	470.1

SOURCE: HOOVER'S, INC., DATABASE

Music Stores

The music store industry includes about 4,000 stores with combined annual revenue of about $4 billion. Major companies include Trans World Entertainment Corporation (which operates FYE, For Your Entertainment; and Wherehouse) and CD Warehouse. The industry is highly concentrated: the top 50 companies have 80 percent of industry revenue.

Competitive Landscape

Consumer spending and entertainment trends drive demand. The profitability of individual companies depends on effective merchandising and competitive pricing. Large companies have advantages in purchasing, distribution, finance, and marketing. Small companies can compete effectively by stocking specialty products, providing superior customer service, or serving a local market. The industry is labor intensive: average annual revenue per employee is $115,000.

Traditional competition for music stores includes consumer electronics stores, mass merchandisers, warehouse clubs, Internet retailers, and mail order clubs. Internet sites facilitating or selling direct downloads of music are changing the dynamics of the entire industry, and have detrimentally affected music stores by replacing CD sales.

Products, Operations & Technology

Products sold by music stores include CDs, records, and tapes (60 percent of revenue) and DVDs, videotapes, and laserdiscs (20 percent). The vast majority of music products are CDs. Other products and services include books, toys, video games, and DVD rentals. Some stores sell used CDs or DVDs. Companies may offer digital music downloads through websites or in-store kiosks.

Music stores include national and regional chains, franchises, and independent retailers. Superstores are designed more as entertain-

BUSINESS CHALLENGES

» Competition from Alternative Retail Outlets

Music stores face intense competition from consumer electronics stores, mass merchandisers, warehouse clubs, and Internet retailers. Music stores capture less than half of all US music purchases, according to the Recording Industry Association of America (RIAA). Large retailers, like Best Buy and Target, typically stock the top-selling CDs in each major category and sell them at deep discounts to drive traffic. Major music studios view large alternative retailers as attractive partners due to their high sales volume, and may provide them with exclusive products. Retail Internet sites allow customers to sample and buy a wide variety of music without leaving home.

» Competition from Digital Downloading

Digital music downloading, both legal and illegal, has negatively affected US CD sales across the industry. Sales of physical CDs declined 20 percent between 2000 and 2005, according to RIAA. Digital downloads, which are less than 10 percent of the recorded music market, have been increasing at double- and triple-digit rates. The ability to download single songs has been a driving force in the declining CD market, as most consumers are interested in only a few songs from an album. Sales growth for devices with MP3-playing capability, like iPods and some cell phones, will continue to drive demand for digital music. Illegal downloading continues to be an ongoing problem for the music industry.

» Hits Drive Cyclical Sales

Forecasting music store sales is difficult because new music releases can be cyclical and big hits are hard to predict. Music stores rely on hits to drive sales, and depend on studios to produce and market albums and artists. Hits can be hard to come by, as the music market is trend-driven and "hot" acts can quickly fizzle. In addition, studios may not introduce new releases in a timely manner, affecting sales in music stores.

ment centers and can range from 15,000 to 25,000 square feet. A typical chain store may be located in a mall or be freestanding and about 6,000 square feet. CD Warehouse franchise stores are between 1,200 and 2,500 square feet. Companies target high traffic areas, and may enjoy category exclusivity in some leased locations, preventing other entertainment-oriented retailers from opening in the same shopping complex.

Interactive kiosks or listening stations allow customers to sample or download music or video. Stores often arrange music by genre, then alphabetically by artist. Companies can design store layouts to maximize cross-marketing opportunities. Special displays highlight new releases and special promotions. In-store cafes encourage customers to linger.

Large companies typically buy directly from major music studios or publishers, while small companies may rely on distributors. Large music studios (or labels) dominate the music production industry. Music stores may depend on distributors for music from independent artists (artists not affiliated with a major label) or specialty genres, such as religious or ethnic music. Most major music suppliers allow music stores to exchange or return unsold merchandise, but typically assess a penalty or fee for such transactions.

Because the music market is fragmented and differs by region, inventory size and selection can vary. Major categories include rock; rap/hip-hop; R&B (rhythm and blues)/urban; country; and pop. Music superstores may carry between 50,000 to 100,000 titles, and typically offer selections across a wide range of categories. Independent music stores may specialize in a genre, like punk or alternative music, and offer a deep selection within a limited number of categories.

Sales & Marketing

While music appeals to a broad demographic, individual genres attract different followings. For example, growing popularity for female country artists increased the number of female country music fans. Younger customers, particularly teenagers, drive sales of rock, rap, and hip-hop music.

Marketing and promotional vehicles include newspaper, print, and TV advertising; direct mail; and in-store displays. Companies, especially large chains, may receive cooperative marketing support from both major studios and independent labels. Stores can host in-store appearances and live performances by recording artists to draw store traffic. Small music stores may feature local talent, often overlooked by larger retailers, to compete effectively at the

market level. Local festival and event sponsorships help build community relations. Companies may also develop partnerships with media providers and execute joint promotions.

Knowledgeable sales staff and superior customer service can help music stores differentiate from other retailers. Educated sales associates with a passion for music can satisfy the needs of dedicated fans. Stores may provide advance notification for big releases to frequent customers to help develop loyalty. In-house newsletters can focus on specialty music genres and help a company become a designated expert in a particular category.

Most music retailers have Internet sites communicating basic store and product information. Websites may sell select music downloads. Music stores with a used product trade may use the Internet to expose pre-owned inventory to a wider geographic market.

The average retail price for a music CD ranges from $12 to $15. CDs featuring music with targeted appeal, such as classical music, can retail for close to $20. Companies may promote new releases or clearance CDs for less than $10. Most music Internet sites allow customers to download individual songs for under $1.

Human Resources

Generally, workers in music stores require few skills, and wages are about half of the US average. Music retailers depend highly on part-time workers, and may add temporary staff during the winter holiday. Stores with a specialized or unique music selection may employ sales staff with extensive knowledge in a particular genre.

Industry Employment Growth

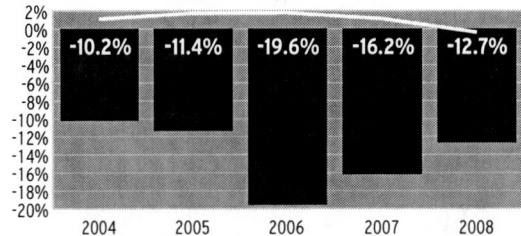

Average Hourly Earnings

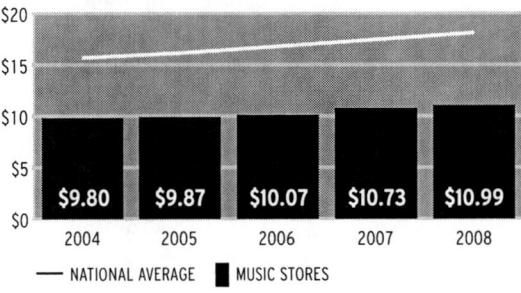

SOURCE: BUREAU OF LABOR STATISTICS

Call Preparation Questions

Who are the company's most significant retail competitors?

Music stores face intense competition from consumer electronics stores, mass merchandisers, warehouse clubs, and Internet retailers.

How has digital downloading affected the company?

Digital music downloading, both legal and illegal, has negatively affected US CD sales across the industry.

How does the cyclical nature of the music industry affect the company?

Forecasting music store sales is difficult because new music releases can be cyclical and big hits are hard to predict.

How do local marketing opportunities help the company compete with large retailers?

By supporting local groups and artists, small music stores can differentiate from large chains and mass merchandisers, which typically focus on national best sellers.

How important are sales in categories other than music?

Music stores can compensate for declining CD sales by stocking complementary entertainment-related items, like DVDs, video games, or books.

Web Links

Almighty Institute of Music Retail

Retail database site — news.
www.almightyretail.com

Arbitron

Information provider for media usage — listening trends.
www.arbitron.com

Billboard

Music publication for industry, company, and artist-specific news.
www.billboard.com

Coalition of Independent Music Stores

Consortium of top independent music stores — tracks top sellers for independent artists.
www.cimsmusic.com

Music Industry Today

News, trends.
music.einnews.com

Nielsen SoundScan

Information provider for music sales — weekly national sales data, trends.
www.soundscan.com

Recording Industry Association of America

Trade group for recording industry — news, trends, statistics.
www.riaa.com

Glossary of Acronyms

DRM — digital rights management
POS — point-of-sale
RIAA — Recording Industry Association of America
UMVD — Universal Music and Video Distribution

HOOVER'S TOP COMPANIES

Largest Companies by Sales	($ mil.)
Apple Inc.	32,479.0
Amazon.com, Inc.	19,166.0
Trans World Entertainment Corporation	1,265.7
Hastings Entertainment, Inc.	547.7
Napster, Inc.	127.4

Largest Employers	Employees
Apple Inc.	35,100
Amazon.com, Inc.	17,000
Trans World Entertainment Corporation	7,500
Hastings Entertainment, Inc.	6,080
Alliance Entertainment, LLC	900
Virgin Entertainment Group, Inc.	700
Berean Christian Stores	410
Napster, Inc.	133
Books on Tape	101
CD Warehouse	99

Fastest Growing* by Five-Year Sales Growth	(%)
Apple Inc.	39.2
Amazon.com, Inc.	29.5
Hastings Entertainment, Inc.	2.0
Napster, Inc.	1.1

Fastest Growing* by Five-Year Employee Growth	(%)
Apple Inc.	27.2
Amazon.com, Inc.	19.0

Top Public Companies by Market Value	($ mil.)
Apple Inc.	113,918.9
Amazon.com, Inc.	21,947.8
Trans World Entertainment Corporation	131.0
Hastings Entertainment, Inc.	90.8
Napster, Inc.	68.3

* These rates are compounded annualized increases and may have resulted from acquisitions or one time gains. If less than 6 years of data are available, growth is for the years available.

SOURCE: HOOVER'S, INC., DATABASE

Musical Instrument Manufacture

THIS INDUSTRY INCLUDES:

SIC CODES
3931   Musical
        Instruments

NAICS CODES
339992 Musical
        Instrument
        Manufacturing

The US musical instrument manufacturing industry includes about 550 companies with combined annual revenue of $2 billion. Large companies include Harman, Fender, and Steinway (formerly Selmer Industries). The industry is highly concentrated: the 50 largest companies hold more than 80 percent of the market.

Competitive Landscape

Demand is largely driven by consumer income and education demographics. The profitability of individual companies depends on cost efficiencies. Many large companies benefit by offering a wide range of products. Small companies can compete effectively by specializing in high-end or niche instruments. The industry is labor-intensive: average annual revenue per employee is about $125,000.

Products, Operations & Technology

Major products are string instruments (including violins and guitars); electronic keyboards; pianos; and woodwinds. String instruments account for about 20 percent of the market; keyboards, pianos, and woodwinds for 10 percent each. Other products include brass wind instruments, percussion instruments, and organs. Replacement parts and accessories, such as strings, mouthpieces, and music stands, account for a significant portion of industry sales, about 25 percent.

Lower-cost instruments are often made on assembly lines, while higher-quality instruments are produced at clusters of workstations. Typical tools include cutting tools, molds, sanders, lathes, presses, and drills. Production involves manufacture of components and final assembly. Components, especially electronics, are often bought from other manufacturers.

Raw materials vary, depending on the instrument type and quality. Professional wind instruments are usually made using silver, gold or brass (70 percent copper and 30 percent zinc).

BUSINESS CHALLENGES

» Competition from Imports

Imports account for about 50 percent of the US market for musical instruments, partly because of lower foreign manufacturing costs. China is the largest source of imports, followed by Japan. China and other Asian manufacturers make mainly low-end and midrange instruments that account for the bulk of the US market.

» Stagnant Retail Demand

Retail sales of musical instruments in the US have been stagnant the past decade. Because of the difficulty of learning, interest in playing music has declined. The number of children in the music-learning age category has been flat. In the past five years, jobs at musical instrument stores dropped 10 percent.

» Flat Retail Prices Squeeze Instrument Manufacturers

With retail prices for musical instruments flat, US manufacturers have largely had to absorb cost increases. In the past five years, manufacturers have been able to raise wholesale prices about 2 percent per year, less than the inflation rate. Labor and materials each account for about 40 percent of the cost of musical instrument manufacture.

Student versions are often made of nickel brass or silver-plated brass. High-end pianos and string instruments contain hardwoods such as maple, beech, spruce, and basswood, while lower-quality versions contain cheaper woods and plastics.

The fundamental physical construct of an instrument doesn't vary from one maker to another. The key differences among high-end and low-end versions of an instrument are the quality of the materials and level of craftsmanship. Because most instruments contain many intricate parts, labor content is high.

Technology is used in automation of assembly lines and through the use of computer-controlled machine tools. Computer systems are used in distribution to dealers and to manage inventory. Large retail chains require manufacturers to use business-to-business electronic ordering and purchasing systems.

Sales & Marketing

Major customers are music distributors, music retailers, schools, churches, and professional artists. Depending on the customer, sales are handled by independent dealers, retail showrooms, an internal sales force, or telemarketing.

Many companies offer a low-, medium-, and high-end version of an instrument type. This wide range of quality and craftsmanship results in high variation in pricing for consumers. Domestically produced pianos can cost as little as $2,000 for a basic upright to $150,000 for a limited edition grand piano. Band instruments can range from $200 for student versions to $25,000 for specialized instruments for professional artists.

Human Resources

Instrument production workers range from semi-skilled assembly workers to skilled artisans. Earnings are close to the US average for all workers. Fringe benefits run about 20 percent of total compensation. The industry injury rate is 35 percent higher than the national average, in part due to the chemicals and solvents used in the finishing process.

Call Preparation Questions

How is the company competing against low-priced imports?

Imports account for about 50 percent of the US market for musical instruments, partly because of lower foreign manufacturing costs.

Does the company expect the US market to expand or shrink?

Retail sales of musical instruments in the US have been stagnant the past decade.

How successfully has the company cut production costs?

With retail prices for musical instruments flat, US manufacturers have largely had to absorb cost increases.

Has the company had success with self-playing instruments?

While sales of traditional pianos have declined steadily, sales of electronic player pianos have increased rapidly.

Web Links

American Music Conference

Consumer interest group promoting music education.
www.amc-music.org

Fender Musical Instruments

Leading guitar manufacturer.
www.fender.com

Musikmesse

Host of music instrument trade shows in Munich and Shanghai.
musik.messefrankfurt.com/global/en/home.html

NAMM – National Association of Music Merchants

Industry association promoting the international music products and music retail industry.
www.namm.org

Steinway Musical Instruments

Manufacturer of high-end pianos.
www.steinway.com

Yamaha Corporation of America

World's largest manufacturer of musical instruments.
www.yamaha.com

Glossary of Acronyms

MAP — minimum advertised price
MIDI — musical instrument digital interface
MITA — Musical Instrument Technicians Association

HOOVER'S TOP COMPANIES

Largest Companies by Sales	($ mil.)
Steinway Musical Instruments, Inc.	406.3
LOUD Technologies Inc.	208.3

Largest Employers	Employees
Peavey Electronics Corporation	2,400
Steinway Musical Instruments, Inc.	2,363
Fender Musical Instruments Corporation	1,742
Gibson Guitar Corp.	1,000
C. F. Martin & Co., Inc.	831
D'Addario & Company, Inc.	815
LOUD Technologies Inc.	658
Allen Organ Company	505
Taylor-Listug, Inc.	376
S.K.B. Corporation	370

Top Public Companies by Market Value	($ mil.)
Steinway Musical Instruments, Inc.	223.3
LOUD Technologies Inc.	31.4

SOURCE: HOOVER'S, INC., DATABASE

Musical Instrument Stores

THIS INDUSTRY INCLUDES:

SIC CODES

5736   Musical Instrument Stores

NAICS CODES

451140   Musical Instrument and Supplies Stores

The musical instrument store industry includes about 4,500 stores (known in the industry as "dealers") with combined annual revenue of $5 billion. Major companies include Guitar Center, Sam Ash Music, and online dealers American Musical Supply and Sweetwater Sound. The industry is fragmented: the 50 largest companies hold 45 percent of the market.

Competitive Landscape

Consumer income and changes in musical tastes drive demand for musical instruments. The profitability of individual companies depends on effective merchandising. Small companies can compete effectively by specializing in personalized service or high-end instruments. Average annual revenue per employee is $150,000.

Products, Operations & Technology

Major products include guitars, pianos, sound equipment, parts and accessories, and school music products. Guitar sales account for about 25 percent of sales, traditional pianos for 20 percent, audio equipment for 15 percent, and electronic keyboards 10 percent. Other products include repairs, equipment leasing, and sheet music.

Musical instrument stores include full-line stores and specialty stores such as keyboard, school band music, and pro audio stores. Full-line stores offer a complete range of musical instruments and accessories. Keyboard stores specialize in traditional upright, grand, self-playing, and electronic pianos. School music stores sell band instruments to universities, high schools, and amateur players. Pro audio stores specialize in selling sound system equipment.

Full-line musical stores include national chains and independent dealers, as well as big-box retailers with a musical instrument department. National full-line chains operate in

BUSINESS CHALLENGES

» Stagnant Consumer Demand

US sales of musical instruments have been stagnant for the past decade. With a wide range of choices for leisure activities, fewer children play musical instruments regularly. Only 30 percent of children play a musical instrument, yet 90 percent play video games an average of seven hours a week.

» Competition from Big-Box Retailers

Mass merchants such as Wal-Mart, Target, and Costco have entered the musical instrument market, selling entry-level guitars, electronic keyboards, and band instruments. Best Buy recently launched a musical instrument "store-within-a-store" concept. Over the past decade, the number of full-line and specialty music instrument stores declined 7 percent.

» Competition from Used Instrument Sales

Musical instrument buyers are increasingly purchasing used products in pawn shops, thrift stores, and on Internet sites like eBay and Craigslist. As prices drop and the Internet demystifies the instrument buying experience, consumers are increasingly willing to purchase used instruments. Putting the buying and selling of instruments into the hands of consumers often bypasses the traditional instrument dealer.

stand-alone buildings and strip malls, with stand-alone stores ranging from 12,000 to 30,000 square feet. Chains may also operate midsized stores within indoor shopping malls, and often own specialty stores under a different brand name. Specialty stores typically operate within 2,000 to 4,000 square feet of retail space, either as small stand-alone buildings or within strip malls. Many specialty stores supplement retail sales with an online store or through auction sites like eBay.

Full-line stores, school music stores, and sound stores all generate an average of approximately $1 million annually and average $210 in revenue per square foot. Keyboard stores generate more revenue: an average of $1.5 million annually and $225 per square foot.

Small specialty retailers are often family-owned businesses with a staff as few as two people. Chain stores typically employ 20 to 40, including an hourly commissioned sales staff, a salaried management team, and a warehouse manager.

Inventory assortment varies widely depending on the sales channel, store size, and product mix. Large full-line stores carry between 5,000 and 8,000 stock-keeping units (SKUs) in a physical store, but can offer up to 40,000 SKUs in an online catalog. Smaller specialty stores, particularly keyboard stores, may carry only 250 to 500 SKUs.

Full-line stores operate centralized distribution centers to support retail store operations. Products flow through the distribution facility and are drop-shipped to individual dealers. Large chains rely on automated merchandise replenishment systems to analyze and forecast sales for each product. Corporate buyers are assigned to manage sales for entire product categories such as guitars, accessories, and electronic instruments.

Small dealers juggle multiple ordering systems operated by distributors and manufacturers. Product orders can be placed online through a wholesaler or manufacturer's website, or via a print catalog.

Sales & Marketing

The typical musical instrument customer is a parent buying an instrument or accessories for a young child or teenager.

Full-line stores manage in-store promotional events such as concerts, sweepstakes, inventory reduction programs, and celebrity appearances. Large chain stores often feature elaborate "Battle of the Bands" talent contests or establish social networking sites designed for musicians. Other large store marketing vehicles include newspaper, print, radio advertising, concert tour promotions, VIP purchasing programs, direct mail, and one-to-one e-mail marketing.

Small stores typically rely on referrals, repeat business from loyal customers, and service programs such as lessons, repairs, and rentals. Large contracts with neighboring universities or area churches can provide a significant boost to small specialty stores. Many specialty retailers establish exclusive contracts with instrument manufacturers.

The typical price of a traditional piano is around $8,000. Guitar prices average around $250, and violins typically about $300. Most

musical instrument product categories have a low-, medium-, and high-end offering, with top-of-the-line products priced at five to ten times higher than the average price.

Human Resources

Average wage is 30 percent lower than the US average. Music stores try hard to recruit musicians and enthusiasts to provide better customer service, but turnover is very high. The industry injury rate is much lower than the average within the retail trade.

Industry Employment Growth

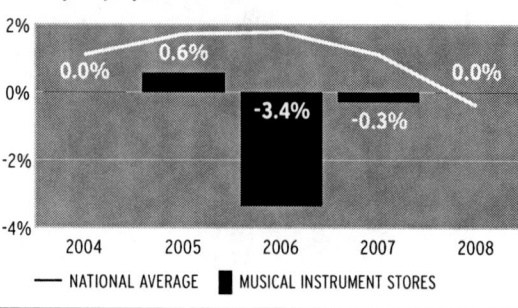

SOURCE: BUREAU OF LABOR STATISTICS

Call Preparation Questions

How has the national decline in learning musical instruments affected the company?

US sales of musical instruments have been stagnant for the past decade.

How does the company compete with mass merchandisers?

Mass merchants such as Wal-Mart, Target, and Costco have entered the musical instrument market, selling entry-level guitars, electronic keyboards, and band instruments.

How has the company responded to consumers buying used, rather than new, instruments?

Musical instrument buyers are increasingly purchasing used products in pawn shops, thrift stores, and on Internet sites like eBay and Craigslist.

Is the company considering international expansion?

Large music store chains — particularly Guitar Center — are exploring expansion opportunities in Japan, Europe, and Canada.

Besides product retailing, what revenue streams does the company pursue?

Specialty stores seeking new revenue streams have turned to value-added services such as music lessons, repairs, tuning, and rentals.

Web Links

American Music Conference

Consumer interest group promoting music education.

www.amc-music.org

International Music Products Association (NAMM)

Industry association promoting international music products and music retail.

www.namm.org

Music Trades Journal

Journal of the Music Products and Retail Industries.

www.musictrades.com

The Alliance of Independent Music Merchants (AIMM)

Alliance of manufacturers and independent musical instrument dealers.

www.musicmerchants.com

Glossary of Acronyms

MAP — minimum advertised price
MIDI — musical instrument digital interface
MITA — Musical Instrument Technicians Association
NAMM — International Music Products Association
SKU — stock-keeping unit

HOOVER'S TOP COMPANIES

Largest Employers	Employees
Guitar Center, Inc.	9,540
Schmitt Music Company	400
Sweetwater Sound Inc.	225
Fletcher Music Centers, Inc.	205
Cascio Music Company, Inc.	125

SOURCE: HOOVER'S, INC., DATABASE

Mutual Fund Management

The US mutual fund management industry includes fewer than 1,000 companies with combined annual revenue of $100 billion. Large companies include Fidelity, Vanguard, American Funds, and T Rowe Price. The industry is highly concentrated.

Mutual fund management companies serve the 8,000 mutual funds registered in the US.

Competitive Landscape

Demand is affected by the growth of retirement capital and returns on alternative investments. The profitability of individual companies depends on investment expertise and effective marketing. Large companies have economies of scale in operations and marketing; small companies can compete effectively by producing higher investment returns. The industry is highly automated.

Products, Operations & Technology

Major management services include the initial formation of a mutual fund, sales and redemption of shares, investment advisory services, and day-to-day management.

Each mutual fund is a separate open-end investment company, with shareholders (the investors) and a board of directors, but no operating staff. All services are provided by outside contractors. The sponsor of a fund usually serves as investment adviser and manager of the fund, and receives an annual fee typically calculated as a percentage of fund's assets. Large mutual fund operators may sponsor and manage dozens of funds, collecting a management fee from each. In addition to paying a management fee, mutual funds pay the underwriters who sell their shares, the custodian of their portfolio, the transfer agent, and an independent auditor. The expense ratio for a fund is the sum of all annual expenses divided by the average net assets of the fund. The average industry expense ratio is under 1 percent.

BUSINESS CHALLENGES

» Revenues Depend on Portfolio Size

The fees mutual fund managers receive are linked to the size of the funds they manage. Declines in the value of the securities in a fund, or withdrawals by investors, directly affect management revenue. Funds with poor investment performance can quickly lose investors.

» Competition from Alternative Investments

Other types of investments can pull money out of mutual funds. Because many mutual funds are structured as low-risk investments suitable for retirement-oriented investors, they typically produce only moderate gains. Hedge funds, real estate, commodities, and securities like certificates of deposit (CDs) often offer the possibility of higher returns. During periods of low interest rates, investors are more likely to want higher returns than mutual funds offer.

» Managers Depend on Regulatory Approval

Mutual fund advisers are bound by restrictions imposed by the SEC and other regulatory bodies. Managers can be fined for infractions, and in extreme cases be barred from the industry. Because of the large amount of retirement money invested in mutual funds, continued scrutiny by regulators and legislators is certain.

A mutual fund typically specializes in one particular type of investment or investment strategy, such as investing only in government bonds or only in the stocks of small companies. By sponsoring a range of such specialized funds (a family of funds), managers allow investors to create their own diversified fund portfolio. Typically, close to half of all mutual fund assets are invested in US stocks, with the other half split among foreign stocks, corporate bonds, municipal bonds, government securities, and money market instruments.

While many mutual funds are actively managed in an attempt to get superior investment returns, some are operated as index funds, which try merely to match the return of a well-known basket of securities such as the S&P 500. Index funds generally have low expenses because they minimize trading and don't need sophisticated investment advice.

Mutual fund managers rely heavily on computer systems to manage portfolios and make trades, analyze and implement investment strategies, ensure regulatory compliance, and provide accounting and reporting to investors. Internet sites are an important tool for sales to investors.

Sales & Marketing

Mutual fund managers sell shares in their funds directly and through brokers. Buyers may be individuals or institutions such as insurance companies or pension plans. Large fund companies like Fidelity have advantages in name recognition and can sell funds directly. Large companies typically advertise using TV, newspaper, and direct mail. Smaller funds rely more heavily on brokers to sell their shares. Managers often have relationships with independent financial and retirement fund advisers to make their funds available to participants in corporate pension plans such as 401(k) plans.

The Internet has become an important source of sales for mutual funds, and investors can manage their mutual fund investments through the website of their mutual fund management company, without broker intervention.

Mutual fund managers may receive two types of fees. Sales "loads" are charged to investors when they buy shares (so-called front-loads) or when they sell shares (back-end loads). Loads may amount to several percent of the shares' value and are intended to pay for the sales effort, which historically was often through an outside party like a stockbroker. Many mutual funds now are "no-load" that pay no sales fees to the fund manager, because loads deter sales. Annual management fees, including an investment advisory fee, may also be as high as several percent of the assets managed, but for large index funds that require minimal management, annual management fees may be less than one-half percent.

Human Resources

Most employees in the mutual fund industry handle clerical and administrative tasks but require special skills and education and are accordingly well-paid. Average industry wages are 50 percent higher than for the average US worker. The managers who make investment decisions for individual funds may be very highly paid, with part of their pay linked to the performance of their fund.

Industry Employment Growth

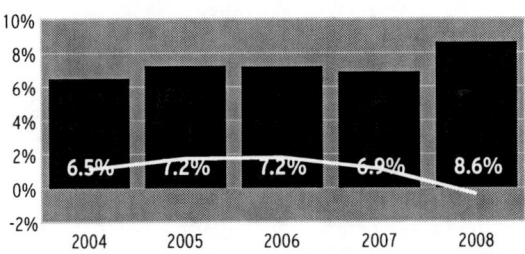

6.5%   7.2%   7.2%   6.9%   8.6%

Average Hourly Earnings

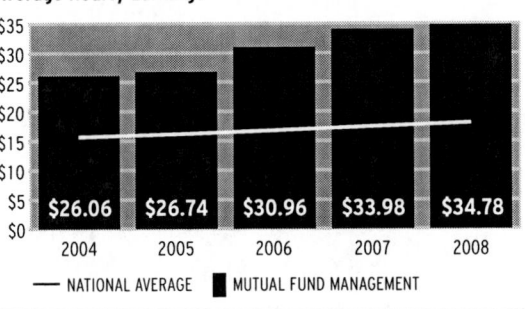

$26.06 $26.74 $30.96 $33.98 $34.78

— NATIONAL AVERAGE   ■ MUTUAL FUND MANAGEMENT

SOURCE: BUREAU OF LABOR STATISTICS

Call Preparation Questions

How rapidly does the company expect to increase the size of its funds?

The fees mutual fund managers receive are linked to the size of the funds they manage.

How does the company counter the allure of higher-return investments?

Other types of investments can pull money out of mutual funds.

Which regulations does the company find most restrictive?

Mutual fund advisers are bound by restrictions imposed by the SEC and other regulatory bodies.

To what extent does the company portray itself as a manager of retirement assets?

The growth in assets of mutual funds has been driven mainly by the growth of retirement funds such as pension plans, IRAs, and corporate 401(k) plans.

How actively does the company sell itself to corporate 401(k) plans?

Sales of mutual funds to corporate 401(k) plans continue to be a strong source of fund assets.

Web Links

Fidelity

News from large mutual fund company.
personal.fidelity.com/myfidelity/InsideFidelity/
index_NewsCenter.shtml?refhp=p

Investment Company Institute

Largest industry association. Key issues. Excellent statistics.
www.ici.org

Morningstar

Mutual fund news, ratings, statistics.
www.morningstar.com

SEC

SEC comments about mutual funds.
www.sec.gov/answers/mutfund.htm

Vanguard

News from large mutual fund company.
onlinepressroom.net/vanguard

Glossary of Acronyms

ICA — Investment Company Act
ERISA — Employee Retirement Income Security Act
ETFS — exchange-traded funds
NAV — net asset value
CD — certificate of deposit

HOOVER'S TOP COMPANIES

Largest Companies by Sales	($ mil.)
FMR LLC	14,900.0
The Capital Group Companies, Inc.	9,900.0
Franklin Resources, Inc.	6,032.4
AllianceBernstein L.P.	4,719.7
Legg Mason, Inc.	4,634.1
Invesco Ltd.	3,307.6
T. Rowe Price Group, Inc.	2,116.3
Eaton Vance Corp.	1,095.8
Janus Capital Group Inc.	1,037.9
The Vanguard Group, Inc.	—

Largest Employers	Employees
FMR LLC	46,400
The Vanguard Group, Inc.	11,500
The Capital Group Companies, Inc.	9,000
Franklin Resources, Inc.	8,800
AllianceBernstein L.P.	5,580
Invesco Ltd.	5,475
T. Rowe Price Group, Inc.	5,385
Legg Mason, Inc.	4,220
American Century Companies, Inc.	1,837
Waddell & Reed Financial, Inc.	1,702

Fastest Growing* by Five-Year Sales Growth	(%)
Diamond Hill Investment Group, Inc.	110.5
U.S. Global Investors Funds	49.5
Legg Mason, Inc.	23.5
Calamos Asset Management, Inc.	19.2
Franklin Resources, Inc.	18.1
T. Rowe Price Group, Inc.	16.2
Eaton Vance Corp.	15.9
FMR LLC	15.8
Waddell & Reed Financial, Inc.	15.3
AllianceBernstein L.P.	11.5

Fastest Growing* by Five-Year Employee Growth	(%)
Diamond Hill Investment Group, Inc.	26.4
Calamos Asset Management, Inc.	14.8
Eaton Vance Corp.	11.9
FMR LLC	10.7
U.S. Global Investors Funds	10.6
T. Rowe Price Group, Inc.	7.2
Franklin Resources, Inc.	6.2
AllianceBernstein L.P.	6.0
Waddell & Reed Financial, Inc.	4.0
GAMCO Investors, Inc.	2.8

Top Public Companies by Market Value	($ mil.)
Franklin Resources, Inc.	20,514.7
T. Rowe Price Group, Inc.	9,103.0
Legg Mason, Inc.	7,756.4
Invesco Ltd.	6,160.1
Eaton Vance Corp.	2,539.3

* These rates are compounded annualized increases and may have resulted from acquisitions or one time gains. If less than 6 years of data are available, growth is for the years available.

SOURCE: HOOVER'S, INC., DATABASE

Natural Gas Production and Distribution

About 10,000 companies in the US explore, produce, transmit, and locally distribute natural gas, with combined annual revenue of $100 billion. Exploration and production are conducted by large, vertically integrated petroleum companies like ConocoPhillips and Chevron, by large independents such as Anadarko and Devon Energy, and by thousands of smaller exploration companies. Transmitting gas from production to consumption areas is handled by about 1,000 pipeline operators. Local distribution is handled by thousands of utilities. Regional energy companies like Dominion Resources and ONEOK combine transmission, storage, and distribution operations. The US consumes about 20 trillion cubic feet (tcf) of natural gas annually.

Competitive Landscape

Demand for natural gas depends partly on the health of the US economy and partly on the price of crude oil, a competitive product. The profitability of natural gas companies depends largely on the efficiency of their operations. There are large economies of scale in the production, processing, and distribution of gas, but small companies can effectively compete with large ones in exploration, where technical ability is more important than size.

Products, Operations & Technology

Raw natural gas is a mixture of methane, ethane, propane, butane, and other hydrocarbons, along with various contaminants such as nitrogen compounds, sulfur compounds, and water. Processed natural gas is mainly methane, with a small amount of ethane and other components. Because it is mainly methane, processed natural gas burns very cleanly and efficiently. Natural gas is found in various geological formations, often along with crude oil. Natural gas is used by consumers and businesses to provide heat and hot water, by utilities to power turbines that produce electricity, and

BUSINESS CHALLENGES

» **Volatility of Natural Gas Prices**

Because of changing crude oil prices and distribution bottlenecks, prices for natural gas can vary substantially from month to month. In the last few years, the average US wellhead price varied from $2 to $10 per thousand cubic feet (mcf) with changes of more than 50 percent within a 12-month period.

» **Dependence on Regulators**

State and federal regulators control the interstate distribution and retail pricing of natural gas. In recent years, the goal of government efforts was to deregulate the industry, but deregulation difficulties in California slowed the process. State and federal legislation could reintroduce tighter regulations. Political pressures for re-regulation increase when prices are high.

» **High Required Capital Investment**

The US natural gas industry estimates that it will need to raise at least $150 billion over the next 20 years to expand its gas delivery infrastructure to meet predicted demand growth.

by industrial users to power furnaces and as a feedstock to produce other chemicals.

Gas exploration is conducted by large and small companies, usually on leased land. Leases specify an expiration period and a royalty rate to be paid on any gas produced. Small companies often sell production from their wells to larger companies that have invested substantial capital in processing and pipeline facilities. Exploration involves various seismic (sound wave) techniques to visualize the geological formations underground, and the drilling of "wildcat" wells in promising locations.

The success rate of exploratory wells may be no better than 20 percent, although new seismic techniques can improve the odds. Development wells drilled into an existing field have a much higher success rate. The US has about

300,000 production wells. Gas extracted with crude oil from oil wells (called "associated" gas) must be separated at the wellhead. A bit more than 25 percent of natural gas production in the US comes from oil wells. State excise taxes on extracted gas are sizable.

The amount of gas exploration activity varies with the price of gas. The number of rotary drilling rigs increases or decreases as gas prices are up or down. Producers are very concerned about acquiring new gas sources to add to reserves, often describing additions to reserves as a percentage of annual sales. Producers also report the amount of developed and undeveloped lease acreage they hold. Large, vertically integrated producers refer to their operations as "upstream" (exploration and production) and "downstream" (marketing, transportation, and storage).

Production from gas wells is routed via a system of small pipelines to one of about 600 processing plants in the US, where most of the components other than methane are removed. Many of these components have economic value, especially ethane, propane, and butane, called "natural gas liquids" (NGL). Ethane is an important feedstock for the production of ethylene, a basic industrial chemical.

Once processed to a suitable level of purity, natural gas can be moved by pipeline from production to consumption areas. Transmission companies move natural gas via large underground pipelines. There are about 300,000 miles of large-diameter gas transmission pipeline in the US. Compressing stations are located every 70 to 100 miles along a pipeline to keep the gas flowing. Gas transmission companies don't own the gas they deliver. Acquiring rights-of-way and local permits for new construction is often difficult.

In addition to transmission pipelines, many transmission companies also own and operate natural gas storage facilities — usually underground depleted gas fields or salt caverns. Storage facilities are especially important in the Midwest and Northeast, where demand for natural gas in winter exceeds the daily delivery capacity of existing pipelines. Most transmission companies have long-term contracts with buyers, like local distribution companies, gas marketers, electricity generators, and industrial users, that specify transportation volumes and whether delivery is "firm" or "interruptible" during periods of high volume use.

Local distribution companies (LDCs) buy gas directly from producers or gas marketers and distribute it to local customers generally classified as residential, commercial, or industrial. The "penetration" of a local distributor is the percentage of homes in its territory that use natural gas. Large industrial users and electricity generators often bypass the local distributor and deal directly with pipeline companies and marketers. Gas is supplied to residential and small commercial users on a "firm" basis, and to large commercial and industrial users on a "firm" or "interruptible" basis, with different price structures. Distributors measure delivery capacity in terms of "peak-day capability" (usually expressed as thousand cubic feet per day — mcfd), which is a combination of contracted pipeline capacity, underground storage release capacity, and peaking supplies (generally LNG in storage containers).

Sales & Marketing

Gas marketers are middlemen, essentially trading companies that can control short- or long-term supplies of gas, pipeline capacity, and storage. They are often affiliates of pipeline companies, but can also be units of producers or distributors, or may be completely independent.

Natural gas is a commodity, so sales depend largely on its price and convenience versus alternative products like coal and fuel oil. The marketing efforts of local distributors usually focus on converting consumers who use fuel oil or electricity for heating and hot water. Environmental concerns have become a strong element encouraging greater use of natural gas by electric utilities.

The price of natural gas is heavily influenced by the price of crude oil. There are several different gas prices: the wellhead price is the price paid before processing and distribution; citygate is the price paid by local distributors after pipeline transportation to their local area; the delivered price is the price paid by users. An important wholesale reference price is the "Henry Hub" price, the price of processed natural gas at the Henry Hub in Louisiana, at the intersection of several major pipelines. Large users with long-term contracts, like electric generating utilities, usually pay the lowest delivered cost, while residential consumers pay the highest.

Human Resources

Jobs in gas extraction, production, and distribution are largely technical and therefore well-paid. The steady loss of jobs in production and distribution is due largely to increased automation, which allows fewer workers to control process flows.

Industry Employment Growth

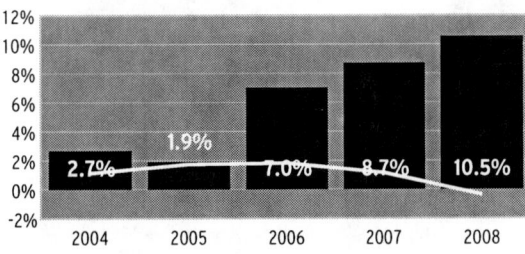

Average Hourly Earnings

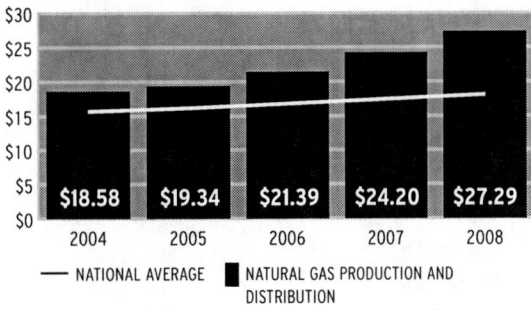

— NATIONAL AVERAGE ■ NATURAL GAS PRODUCTION AND DISTRIBUTION

SOURCE: BUREAU OF LABOR STATISTICS

Call Preparation Questions

How does the company hedge against price changes?

Because of changing crude oil prices and distribution bottlenecks, prices for natural gas can vary substantially from month to month.

What new or prospective regulations concern the company the most?

State and federal regulators control the interstate distribution and retail pricing of natural gas.

What capital investments is the company planning? Using what financial sources?

The US natural gas industry estimates that it will need to raise at least $150 billion over the next 20 years to expand its gas delivery infrastructure to meet predicted demand growth.

How much infrastructure investment does the company plan to accommodate greater demand for natural gas in electricity generation?

The Department of Energy forecasts that 60 percent of new electricity generation capacity added in the next 20 years will be gas-fired.

Is gas demand steady in the company's market throughout the year?

With demand for gas becoming more even throughout the year, supply bottlenecks that affect prices are disappearing.

Web Links

American Gas Association (AGA)

Lobbying organization. Industry issues.
www.aga.org

American Public Gas Association

News, links, and FAQs.
www.apga.org

Baker Hughes Drilling Rig Counts

Number of gas drilling rigs in use.
www.bakerhughes.com/investor/rig

EIA- Annual Gas Outlook

Government forecast.
www.eia.doe.gov/oiaf/aeo/gas.html

Interstate Natural Gas Association of America (INGAA)

Pipeline operators.
www.ingaa.org

National Energy Marketers Association

www.energymarketers.com

Natural Gas Supply Association (NGSA)

Exploration and production companies. News, statistics, industry background information.
www.ngsa.org

Natural Gas Weekly Update

From US Department of Energy. Prices, capacity.
tonto.eia.doe.gov/oog/info/ngw/ngupdate.asp

NaturalGas.org

Good description of operations. By NGSA.
www.naturalgas.org

Platts Global Energy

Natural gas news.
www.platts.com/Natural%20Gas/Resources

Glossary of Acronyms

AGA — American Gas Association
BCF — billion cubic feet
BOE — barrel of oil equivalent (6000 cubic feet is equivalent to 1 barrel of oil)
BTU — British thermal unit
EIA — Energy Information Administration
FERC — Federal Energy Regulatory Commission
LDC — local distribution company
MCF/D — thousand cubic feet per day
MCF — thousand cubic feet
MMBTU — billion British thermal units
MMCF — million cubic feet
NGL — natural gas liquids
OPS — Office of Pipeline Safety
TCF — trillion cubic feet

HOOVER'S TOP COMPANIES

Largest Companies by Sales	($ mil.)
Marathon Oil Corporation	78,569.0
Enterprise GP Holdings L.P.	35,469.6
Murphy Oil Corporation	27,512.5
Occidental Petroleum Corporation	24,480.0
Constellation Energy Group, Inc.	21,193.2
Enterprise Products Partners L.P.	16,950.1
The Williams Companies, Inc.	16,833.0
ONEOK, Inc.	16,157.4
Anadarko Petroleum Corporation	15,723.0
Devon Energy Corporation	15,365.0

Largest Employers	Employees
Marathon Oil Corporation	29,524
Sempra Energy	14,314
Constellation Energy Group, Inc.	10,200
Occidental Petroleum Corporation	9,700
CenterPoint Energy, Inc.	8,568
NiSource Inc.	7,607
Murphy Oil Corporation	7,539
UGI Corporation	6,200
Chesapeake Energy Corporation	6,200
Spectra Energy Corp	5,100

Fastest Growing* by Five-Year Sales Growth	(%)
EnerJex Resources, Inc.	3,500.0
Crusader Energy Group Inc.	300.0
Concho Resources Inc.	249.0
Dune Energy, Inc.	248.0
Teton Energy Corporation	245.2
Avalon Oil & Gas, Inc.	200.0
Evolution Petroleum Corporation	156.1
Transmeridian Exploration Corporation	155.3
Atlas Pipeline Partners, L.P.	147.6
Petrohawk Energy Corporation	143.1

Fastest Growing* by Five-Year Employee Growth	(%)
Double Eagle Petroleum Co.	141.0
Petrohawk Energy Corporation	116.2
Arena Resources, Inc.	97.7
GMX Resources Inc.	94.7
Cheniere Energy, Inc.	85.4
RAM Energy Resources, Inc.	81.0
W&T Offshore, Inc.	68.5
Atlas America, Inc.	53.5
EXCO Resources, Inc.	51.2
Chesapeake Energy Corporation	46.6

Top Public Companies by Market Value	($ mil.)
Occidental Petroleum Corporation	52,876.6
Devon Energy Corporation	29,155.5
Apache Corporation	24,945.9
XTO Energy Inc.	20,440.1
Marathon Oil Corporation	19,316.2

* These rates are compounded annualized increases and may have resulted from acquisitions or one time gains. If less than 6 years of data are available, growth is for the years available.

SOURCE: HOOVER'S, INC., DATABASE

Newspapers and News Organizations

THIS INDUSTRY INCLUDES:

SIC CODES

2711   Newspapers:
        Publishing, or
        Publishing and
        Printing

NAICS CODES

51111   Newspaper
        Publishers

The US newspaper publishing industry includes about 2,000 companies with combined annual revenue of $50 billion. Large companies include Gannett, McClatchy, Advance Publications, Tribune Company, The Washington Post, and The New York Times. The industry is highly concentrated: the top 50 companies control almost 80 percent of the market. Many of the larger companies also own and operate TV stations.

A few newspapers, including the The Wall Street Journal, USA Today, The Los Angeles Times, The Washington Post, and The New York Times, have daily circulation greater than 1 million, but most have circulation under 50,000. The combined daily circulation of US newspapers is just under 55 million.

Competitive Landscape

The health of the economy drives both advertising and readership. The profitability of individual companies depends on marketing expertise, as most costs are fixed. Large companies benefit from economies of scale in sharing resources and by providing a range of outlets for advertisers. Small publishers can compete successfully by serving smaller markets. The industry is fairly labor-intensive: average annual revenue per employee is about $120,000.

Products, Operations & Technology

Products include daily, weekly, monthly, and Sunday newspapers; Internet news services; and distribution services. Large circulation newspapers are usually produced daily; community newspapers are usually produced weekly. Almost 70 percent of industry revenue comes from sales of advertising space ("advertising revenue"), and only about 20 percent from subscription and single-copy sales ("circulation revenue"). Some papers are controlled-circulation papers — they're free to a targeted

BUSINESS CHALLENGES

» Dependence on Ad Revenue

Almost three-quarters of newspaper revenue come from advertising, which typically falls during business slowdown. About 60 percent of newspaper ad revenue is from local and national retailers, including clothing, shoe, and grocery stores; car dealers; and travel agencies. Newspapers base much of their ad rates on circulation rates.

» Volatile Raw Material Prices

Newsprint and ink costs dramatically impact newspaper publishers – newsprint is the second-largest cost after personnel and fluctuates greatly. Prices for newsprint routinely vary 50 percent or more within a year, and have sometimes increased 100 percent. Newspaper publishers have fewer sources from which to buy paper, due to supplier consolidation in the paper industry. A large share of the US market is served by Canadian producers.

» Declining Readership

Readership has steadily declined for many newspapers over the past decade, and the average age of readers has increased. Only about half of the adult population regularly reads a newspaper. Due to competition from TV and the Internet, many people no longer buy newspapers to get news. To bolster readership, many newspapers now operate sophisticated marketing programs.

audience and receive revenue only from advertising.

Local news is usually gathered through a network of reporters and correspondents, and through regular public sources such as police, fire, court, and legislative proceedings. Regional, national, and international news are acquired through correspondents (if the newspaper is large) and through subscriptions to news services such as Associated Press (AP); Reuters; United Press International (UPI); and Dow Jones. Editors review stories from reporters, contributors, and news services and decide which to put in the newspaper.

Advertising is usually sold through a dedicated sales staff. Total US newspaper advertising is about 45 percent local retail, 35 percent classified ads, and 15 percent national. Classified ads are often separated into cars, apartments, real estate, recruitment, and personal. "Run-of-paper" advertising is printed in the body of the newspaper and produces most ad revenue. "Preprint" advertising is supplied by advertisers and inserted into the newspaper. Run-of-paper advertising is measured as "advertising inches" or "advertising linage" — six-column inches.

Production has two phases: composition and printing. Papers are generally composed on sophisticated computer systems, which allows the final composition to be electronically transmitted (sometimes via satellite) to a number of printing plants. Printing is done in large plants (close to a million square feet) on expensive offset presses. The size and type of press determines the number of pages printed at one time and if color can be used. While large newspapers have their own printing plants, many smaller papers have their printing done by independent contractors. The chief raw material is newsprint (for magazines it's called "body paper"), which is bought from newsprint companies under long-term contracts but at market prices.

The physical distribution of newspapers has two components: transportation to agents and distribution by agents. Most papers use independent transportation and distribution companies under contracts of varying duration.

The industry uses computer technology throughout its business, in content creation, page design, pre-print preparation, advertising content, printing, and distribution. Many newspapers publish to the Web, but their business models vary. Some require paid access; some allow access only to hardcopy subscribers; others offer the current issue free, but charge for access to archives.

Sales & Marketing

Circulation determines both advertising and circulation revenue, since advertising rates are based on circulation. Newspapers boost circulation by direct mail solicitation, telemarketing, and TV, radio, and billboard advertising. More than 80 percent of newspapers are sold through home delivery plans, versus single-copy sales at newsstands. Papers usually run separate plans for the Sunday edition, which often has a

higher circulation than the daily paper. Because circulation is so crucial, many newspapers have their "daily-paid circulation" measured by a private company, Audit Bureau of Circulations (ABC).

Human Resources

Newspaper employees span a wide range of skill sets, from highly skilled editors, writers, and printers, to large numbers of low-paid delivery personnel. The average wage is close to the average for all US workers. The annual personnel turnover rate for the information industry, including newspapers, is about 30 percent, significantly lower than the national average of 50 percent. Information workers have an illness and injury rate well below that of most other workers.

Industry Employment Growth

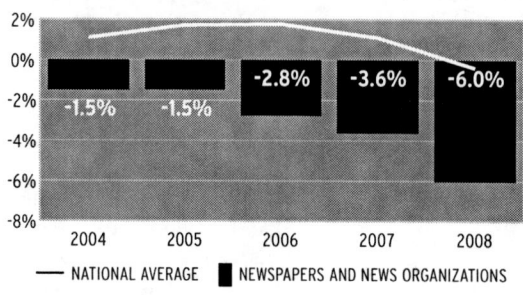

SOURCE: BUREAU OF LABOR STATISTICS

Call Preparation Questions

How does the company deal with shifting advertising demand?

Almost three-quarters of newspaper revenue come from advertising, which typically falls during business slowdown.

How does the company mitigate high newsprint and ink costs?

Newsprint and ink costs dramatically impact newspaper publishers — newsprint is the second-largest cost after personnel and fluctuates greatly.

What strategies does the company have to retain readership and growth?

Readership has steadily declined for many newspapers over the past decade, and the average age of readers has increased.

What new sources of revenue is the company developing?

To offset financial concerns, publishers now provide contract publishing services for other companies, rework classified ad space, and create new publications.

Does the company plan new distribution channels for its news service?

Alternative distribution, such as the Internet, can best be developed by companies already in the news business.

Web Links

American Society of Newspaper Editors

Issues confronting editors.
www.asne.org

Association for Education in Journalism and Mass Communication

Association of journalists; excellent links.
www.aejmc.org

Editor & Publisher

Trade magazine; news archives.
www.editorandpublisher.com

I Want Media

Media news.
www.iwantmedia.com

National Newspaper Association

Lobbying group for community papers.
www.nna.org

Newspaper Association of America

Excellent industry statistics.
www.naa.org

Glossary of Acronyms

ABC — Audit Bureau of Circulations
AP — Associated Press
ASNE — American Society of Newspaper Editors
JOA — joint operating agreements
NAA — Newspaper Association of America
PRN — PR Newswire
UPI — United Press International

HOOVER'S TOP COMPANIES

Largest Companies by Sales	($ mil.)
News Corporation	32,996.0
Advance Publications, Inc.	7,970.0
Gannett Co., Inc.	6,767.6
Tribune Company	5,063.0
The Washington Post Company	4,461.6
The New York Times Company	2,948.9
The McClatchy Company	1,900.5
Lee Enterprises, Incorporated	1,028.9
The E. W. Scripps Company	1,001.8
Cox Newspapers, Inc.	—

Largest Employers	Employees
News Corporation	64,000
Gannett Co., Inc.	46,100
Advance Publications, Inc.	29,100
Tribune Company	19,600
The Washington Post Company	19,000
The McClatchy Company	15,748
Cox Newspapers, Inc.	15,000
The New York Times Company	10,231
The E. W. Scripps Company	8,500
Lee Enterprises, Incorporated	8,200

Fastest Growing* by Five-Year Sales Growth	(%)
Dolan Media Company	38.4
GateHouse Media, Inc.	25.0
The McClatchy Company	11.6
News Corporation	11.4
The Washington Post Company	9.5
Lee Enterprises, Incorporated	9.4
Advance Publications, Inc.	4.4
Daily Journal Corporation	3.5
Journal Register Company	2.6
American Community Newspapers Inc.	1.9

Fastest Growing* by Five-Year Employee Growth	(%)
The McClatchy Company	32.7
News Corporation	16.3
Journal Register Company	7.7
The Washington Post Company	7.6
GateHouse Media, Inc.	4.1

Top Public Companies by Market Value	($ mil.)
The Washington Post Company	3,085.9
Gannett Co., Inc.	1,729.2
The New York Times Company	1,000.9
Journal Communications, Inc.	414.5
Dolan Media Company	197.4

* These rates are compounded annualized increases and may have resulted from acquisitions or one time gains. If less than 6 years of data are available, growth is for the years available.

SOURCE: HOOVER'S, INC., DATABASE

Nonmetallic Mineral Mining and Quarrying

The nonmetallic mineral mining and quarrying industry in the US includes about 4,000 companies with annual revenues of about $20 billion. Major companies include Vulcan Materials, Martin Marietta Materials, and subsidiaries of foreign firms such as Hanson Building Materials (UK); Oldcastle Materials (Ireland); and Rinker Materials (Australia). The industry is highly fragmented, with many small firms serving local geographic markets; about 75 percent of operations have fewer than 20 employees.

Competitive Landscape

Demand is driven by construction spending and agricultural spending on fertilizers. Large companies have some economies of scale in purchasing and administrative systems, and have the production volume to supply large construction projects, such as new highways. Small companies typically own just one mine and compete in a local market based on superior customer service. Annual revenue per employee averages about $200,000.

Products, Operations & Technology

Major products include crushed and broken limestone (30 percent of revenue); construction sand and gravel (25 percent); crushed and broken granite (10 percent); and phosphate rock and potassium salts (10 percent). Other products include soda ash, bentonite, clay, and other broken stone. Phosphates and potassium salts are used to make fertilizers. Crushed stone, sand, and gravel are also referred to as aggregates.

Most quarries are open-pit mines where the surface is blasted to reach stone mineral and stone deposits. Benches are cut in to the walls to enable access to deeper deposits. The rock is blasted from the mine face, loaded into trucks, and carried to the primary crusher, which breaks it into smaller pieces. These smaller

BUSINESS CHALLENGES

» **Cyclical Construction Spending**

The nonmetallic mineral mining industry is cyclical and highly dependent on US construction spending. About 20 percent of US demand is for residential construction and another 20 percent for commercial. Local construction activity determines the success of individual companies.

» **Dependence on Public Spending**

More than half of nonmetallic mining demand is driven by public works' spending on highways and public buildings. While total public construction spending in the US has risen almost 90 percent over the past 10 years, local projects depend on government budgets and priorities, which can change with each election.

» **Environmental Issues**

Mines and quarries have to coexist with local communities and the agricultural industry, requiring compliance with environmental regulations and zoning restrictions. Agriculture needs fertile areas and flood plains for farming, which are also the best locations for aggregates and concrete producers. Dust control is an issue in the Southwest, where both Arizona and California regulators are putting stricter standards on the industry. Southern California instituted new regulations in 2005, reducing particulate emissions by about 60 percent.

pieces are carried to the surface by conveyor and sorted by size. The aggregate is then transported to customers, usually by truck. Some mines further process onsite, whereas smaller mines may ship the aggregate to third-party processing facilities. Processing includes further crushing, sorting, washing, and leaching.

Transportation costs can exceed the price of products, so aggregates typically supply a local market within 50 miles of the mine. About 80 percent of aggregates is transported by truck. About 15 percent of aggregates is used for roads and ramps at the production site.

Mines and quarries can be quite large, but their use depends on local demand. Each year hundreds of mines are idled, closed, or abandoned and hundreds more opened or reactivated. The changing locations of construction and highway projects drive these decisions. Environmental regulations require companies to return abandoned quarries back to their original look and use.

Technology improvements focus on extracting and removing aggregates, making the industry more efficient and reducing the need for labor. Such improvements have caused an 18 percent rise in production in the past ten years while total employment has risen just 2 percent. Research and development expenditures are small, generally less than 1 percent of revenue.

Sales & Marketing

The major customer is the local construction industry; about 40 percent of crushed stone produced is used for roads and highways, 20 percent for residential construction, 20 percent for commercial construction, and 20 percent for public works such as airports and schools. About 400 tons of aggregates are used to construct the average home; about 38,000 tons are used in the construction of every mile of interstate highway.

Marketing and advertising expenses are low, relative to other administrative costs. Companies respond to public works requests for competitive bids and develop close relationships with local builders to learn of upcoming construction projects.

Products are commodities and companies compete primarily on price. The average price per ton of aggregate is about $6 and rose about 3 percent a year between 2000 and 2004. Prices have risen more rapidly since 2004 due to high construction demand and increased fuel prices.

Human Resources

Production worker hourly wages are higher than the national norm as some technical skills are required to operate mining equipment. Fringe benefits average 28 percent of payroll. About 20 percent of workers are unionized.

While annual injuries and illnesses are about the national norm, one-third of injuries result in over 31 days of missed work. Two-thirds of reported injuries are caused by contact with machinery or overexertion.

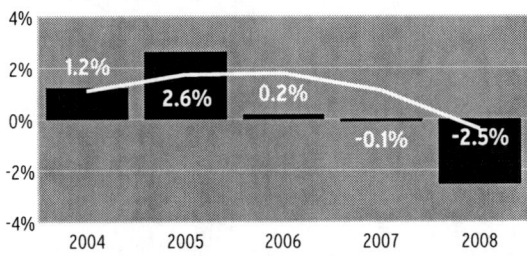

Industry Employment Growth

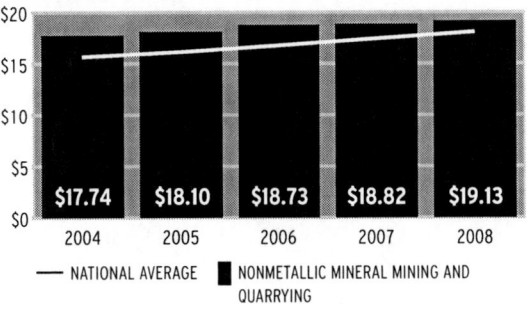

Average Hourly Earnings

— NATIONAL AVERAGE   ■ NONMETALLIC MINERAL MINING AND QUARRYING

SOURCE: BUREAU OF LABOR STATISTICS

Call Preparation Questions

How does the company respond to cyclical industry demand?

The nonmetallic mineral mining industry is cyclical and highly dependent on US construction spending.

How important are public works projects to the company?

More than half of nonmetallic mining demand is driven by public works' spending on highways and public buildings.

How has the company been affected by more aggressive local environmental regulations?

Mines and quarries have to coexist with local communities and the agricultural industry, requiring compliance with environmental regulations and zoning restrictions.

How much of the company's business depends on building and repairing roads?

America's highway and transportation infrastructure needs repair.

What recycling initiatives has the company undertaken?

Higher cost for new aggregates makes recycling of aggregates, primarily concrete and asphalt, more economically feasible.

Web Links

American Society of Civil Engineers

Engineering news, legislative updates.
www.asce.org

Martin Marietta Materials

Large producer of aggregates and other minerals.
www.martinmarietta.com

National Stone, Sand, and Gravel Association

Industry news, legislative news, industry operations and updates.
www.nssga.org

Pit & Quarry

Industry news, highway funding news, merger & acquisition updates.
www.pitandquarry.com

Vulcan Materials

Leading US producer of construction aggregates.
www.vulcanmaterials.com

Glossary of Acronyms

NSSGA — National Stone, Sand, and Gravel Association

TEA 21 — Transportation Equity Act for the 21st Century

HOOVER'S TOP COMPANIES

Largest Companies by Sales	($ mil.)
Vulcan Materials Company	3,651.4
Martin Marietta Materials, Inc.	2,120.1
AMCOL International Corporation	744.3

Largest Employers	Employees
Oldcastle Materials, Inc.	14,500
Vulcan Materials Company	10,522
Rinker Materials Corporation	10,085
Martin Marietta Materials, Inc.	5,255
New Enterprise Stone & Lime Co., Inc.	3,500
Unimin Corporation	3,400
Knife River Corporation	2,370
AMCOL International Corporation	2,017
Rogers Group, Inc.	1,500
Luck Stone Corporation	1,200

Fastest Growing* by Five-Year Sales Growth	(%)
AmerAlia, Inc.	31.4
United States Lime & Minerals, Inc.	26.1
AMCOL International Corporation	20.0
Vulcan Materials Company	4.8
Martin Marietta Materials, Inc.	4.4

Fastest Growing* by Five-Year Employee Growth	(%)
Vulcan Materials Company	14.3
AMCOL International Corporation	12.2
United States Lime & Minerals, Inc.	10.6

Top Public Companies by Market Value	($ mil.)
Vulcan Materials Company	7,672.6
Martin Marietta Materials, Inc.	4,025.1
AMCOL International Corporation	1,084.3
United States Lime & Minerals, Inc.	191.7

* These rates are compounded annualized increases and may have resulted from acquisitions or one time gains. If less than 6 years of data are available, growth is for the years available.

SOURCE: HOOVER'S, INC., DATABASE

Nonprofit Institutions

THIS INDUSTRY INCLUDES:

SIC CODES

8641   Civic, Social, and
        Fraternal
        Associations

NAICS CODES

81341   Civic and Social
        Organizations

The nonprofit industry includes about 1.5 million organizations across the US with combined annual revenue of more than $1 trillion. Major organizations include Goodwill Industries, Ascension Health, National Cancer Institute, New York University, and the Bill & Melinda Gates Foundation. The industry is highly fragmented: large organizations with assets of $10 million or more represent just 6 percent of the industry, but account for more than 80 percent of the sector's total annual revenue.

Although technically distinct, the terms "nonprofit," "tax-exempt," and "charitable" are often used interchangeably. Nonprofits are sometimes referred to as "501(c)" entities, after the section of the Internal Revenue Code that defines their tax status.

Competitive Landscape

Demand is driven by the need to represent special interests or provide social services that can't be met by the market or government. Organizations receive nonprofit status because their primary purpose is religious, charitable, scientific, literary, or educational in nature. Their purpose must be to serve the public good versus a private interest.

The success of nonprofits often depends on efficient operations and their ability to match expenses with fluctuating revenues. Large nonprofits have advantages in fundraising due to strong name recognition. Small nonprofits can be successful if they serve a dedicated membership or have a dependable source of revenue. The industry is labor-intensive: the average annual wage for a nonprofit sector employee is about $35,000.

Products, Operations & Technology

Nonprofits are classified into nine service categories, including arts, culture, and humanities; education; environment; health; human services; international, foreign affairs; mutual,

BUSINESS CHALLENGES

» Uncertain Revenue

The amount of revenue available every year is uncertain for most nonprofits. Unlike most for-profits, nonprofits don't depend on product sales, relying instead on the generosity of contributors. Even nonprofits with large endowment funds have uncertain revenue because their investment income depends on the state of the financial markets.

» Contributions Depend on Economic Conditions

Charitable contributions typically shrink in more difficult economic times. In recent years, the level of charitable donations was impacted by the stock market and other investments. During difficult economic periods, the stream of small donations at many charities is unaffected, but big donors give less.

» Dependence on Big Donors

Many nonprofits depend on a few large donors for a large share of revenue. Large donors may verbally commit to continue contributions, but few nonprofits have contractual assurances. In recent years, some donors who made multi-year promises were unable to fulfill them when the value of their financial assets dropped.

membership benefit; and religion related, according to the National Taxonomy of Exempt Entities (NTEE), developed by the National Center for Charitable Statistics. The largest segment in terms of revenue is health, which generates more than half of all revenue reported by charitable organizations. The largest category in terms of number of firms is human services, which accounts for 38 percent of all nonprofits.

Specific operations of nonprofits are defined by the types of services they offer. For example, the health segment includes hospitals, nursing facilities, blood banks, substance abuse treatment services, medical research groups, and organizations focused on the prevention and treatment of diseases. The human services category comprises organizations offering programs and services focused on specific community needs such as housing and shelter; job training and placement; public safety, disaster preparedness, and relief; recreation and sports; and crime prevention.

Grantmaking organizations (also called charitable foundations) are special types of nonprofits that give money to other nonprofits. About 110,000 of these organizations, with annual revenue of $83 billion (largely from investments), actively seek to give money away through grants by soliciting Requests for Proposals (RFPs) from potential recipients. Examples are the Bill & Melinda Gates Foundation, the Ford Foundation, the J. Paul Getty Trust, and the Howard Hughes Medical Institute. US foundations manage more than $500 billion in combined assets.

Nonprofit institutions' operations are typically labor-intensive. Though staffs likely include paid workers, the industry relies heavily on volunteers. More than 60 million Americans volunteer for nonprofits, donating nearly 13 billion hours annually, which is equivalent to 7.6 million full-time employees.

Nonprofits use technology to network with volunteers, members, employees, and donors; solicit online support and contributions; and manage financial, donor, client, and volunteer data.

Sales & Marketing

Customers of nonprofits include the clients they serve, as well as donors who support them financially and volunteers who contribute their time and talents to them. Fundraising is a major activity for most nonprofits, often contracted out to specialized for-profit fundraising firms. Aside from fees for services rendered, funds are raised through advertising, grant applications, public relations, promotional events, direct-mail requests, and other media solicitations. Direct mail solicitation is a major source of funds, and "tray counts" measure mail response to direct mailings. Some nonprofits team with for-profits to provide for-profit services to fund their charitable efforts.

The Internet has become a major source for individual contributions. Nonprofits solicit donations and interact with visitors on websites and send fundraising appeals and personalized gift receipts to contributors via e-mail.

Nonprofits compete with each other for the clients they serve. Additionally, they compete with other fundraising organizations for donors

and with other personal and professional obligations for volunteers.

Human Resources

Top leaders at US charities earn an average salary of about $150,000. CEO compensation accounts for just more than 3 percent of an average organization's total spending. Lower-level positions at nonprofits often pay less than in the for-profit sector. Salaries at nonprofits differ widely, however, based on geographic location and charitable mission. Educational organizations (private colleges) have the highest salaries, religious ones, the lowest. The average CEO pay at an educational institution is $140,000 more than that paid to the average leader of a religious nonprofit.

Call Preparation Questions

What percentage of revenue is from contributions, gifts, and grants; program services; membership dues; and investment income?

The amount of revenue available every year is uncertain for most nonprofits.

How does the nonprofit deal with lower revenue during an economic slowdown?

Charitable contributions typically shrink in more difficult economic times.

How seasonal is the nonprofit's cash flow?

Many nonprofits depend on a few large donors for a large share of revenue.

What benefits does the aging population present the company in terms of donations?

Older people and their estates represent a significant portion of the donor base for many nonprofits.

What charitable gaming programs does the nonprofit offer?

Many charities depend on bingo or other forms of charitable gambling.

Web Links

American Institute of Philanthropy

Watchdog group that rates charities. www.charitywatch.org

Association of Fundraising Professionals

Advocacy, research, and education information. www.afpnet.org

BBB Wise Giving Alliance

Rating system for major charities. From a merger of National Charities Information Bureau and Better Business Bureaus' Foundation. us.bbb.org/WWWRoot/SitePage.aspx?site=113 &id=4ef08b14-37cb-4974-a385-7f41f63b16b0

Foundations.Org

Large listing of foundations.
www.foundations.org

Guide Star

Form 990 financial statements for 220,000 nonprofit organizations.
www.guidestar.org

National Center for Charitable Statistics

Links, data, fact sheets, and other resources.
www.nccs.urban.org

National Council of Nonprofits

Projects, public policy, and association links.
www.councilofnonprofits.org

Network for Good

Grant guides, ideas, resources, facts, figures, Internet resources, events, deadlines, products and services.
www.networkforgood.org

Nonprofit Resource Center

Links for many nonprofit topics.
www.not-for-profit.org

Society for Nonprofit Organizations

Resources and publications.
www.snpo.org

The Council on Foundations

Policies, resources, news, reports, and legal updates.
www.cof.org

The Foundation Center

Philanthropy News Digest. Excellent news articles.
foundationcenter.org/pnd

The NonProfit Times

Online newsletter and recent articles.
www.nptimes.com

www.freeERISA.com

Lists organizations' IRS Form 5500 mostly for pension plans/funds; also has tax-exempt organizations.
www.freeerisa.com

Glossary of Acronyms

AFP — Association of Fundraising Professionals
NGO — non-government organization
NTEE — National Taxonomy of Exempt Entities
RFP — request for proposal

HOOVER'S TOP COMPANIES

Largest Employers	Employees
Goodwill Industries International, Inc.	87,444
The Salvation Army	59,651
Boys & Girls Clubs of America	47,000
The American National Red Cross	35,000
Volunteers of America	15,000
Knights of Columbus	12,000
CARE USA	10,000
UNICEF	7,100
American Cancer Society, Inc.	7,000
Smithsonian Institution	6,300

SOURCE: HOOVER'S, INC., DATABASE

Nurseries

In the US, about 25,000 farming operations produce nursery and greenhouse crops with a total annual wholesale value of $14 billion. Large companies include Hines Horticulture, Monrovia Nursery, and Color Spot Nurseries. In this highly fragmented industry, only 2,000 operations have annual revenue over $1 million. The largest 2,000 farms produce 65 percent of industry revenue. Most producers are small, with nurseries attached to a retail store.

Competitive Landscape

Demand is driven by consumer income and commercial real estate construction. The profitability of individual companies depends on anticipating demand for various types of plants, and an efficient distribution system. Large operators have economies of scale in distribution. Small operators can compete successfully by raising specialty plants or serving a local market.

Products, Operations & Technology

Products include flowers and flowering plants, shrubs, food plants like tomatoes, Christmas trees, sod and seeds. Large commercial growers concentrate on producing container-grown ornamental plants for indoor and outdoor use, including bedding plants (usually grown in flats and transplanted into beds by the end-user); shrubs; and flowering potted plants. Products include annuals like marigolds and petunias; perennials like daylilies and clematis; evergreens like azalea, box wood, pines, spruce, and juniper; tropical flowering plants like Bougainvillea and hibiscus; "holiday" or "seasonal" plants like Easter lily and poinsettia; and specialty plants like bonsais, ferns, and trellises. Cut flowers are a smaller segment. Because of weather limitations, most single-location growers can produce only several hundred varieties of plants, but national growers can produce several thousand.

BUSINESS CHALLENGES

» Demand Subject to Economic Conditions

Residential and commercial construction drive demand for plants for landscaping and indoor decoration, as new housing developments and suburban office parks need trees, shrubs, and flowering plants. Because indoor plants often have an effective life of only a few weeks, requiring frequent replacement throughout the year, the expense of maintaining them can be too high during periods of economic difficulty.

» Dependence on Large Customers

Many growers get a large percentage of revenue from a few large customers, such as national garden center chains, mass merchandisers like Wal-Mart, and supermarket chains. In local markets, hotels and real estate developers may be major customers. To service bigger customers, larger nursery companies like Hines and Color Spot have grown through acquisitions.

» Highly Seasonal Demand

Most nurseries do the bulk of their business in spring, although some remain open year-round. Most flower sales occur around Christmas/Chanukah, Mother's Day, Easter, Valentine's Day, and Thanksgiving. Because of seasonal demand, labor needs and cash flow are very uneven throughout the year.

Commercial operations revolve around the growing cycle. Growers buy plant "plugs" from suppliers who germinate them from seed in large, controlled-environment facilities for four to 10 weeks before shipping them around the country. Growers transplant these "prefinished" plants into containers and grow them until they're ready to be shipped to customers. Large growers may have their own plug operations for some plants, but also buy from suppliers. A large nursery can cover from 10 to 1,000 acres, but 50 to 100 is typical for a big commercial operation, with 500,000 square feet of greenhouse space. Relatively more greenhouse space is used in colder climates.

Growing time is six to nine weeks for bedding plants, eight to 14 weeks for flowering potted plants, 10 to 14 months for shrubs, and seven to nine years for Christmas trees. The prime commercial planting season generally extends from February to May when seasonal labor is hired, though planting continues year-round, with producers getting more "turns" (inventory turnover) depending on their crop. Many growers increase their workforce by as much as 80 percent at the peak in April. Transplanting and caring for containerized plants is highly labor-intensive. Although growers take pains to produce a uniformly high-quality product, many plants don't grow properly and must be discarded.

Automation has proven to be difficult, aside from the widespread use of irrigation and fertilization systems. Greenhouse operations can be technically sophisticated, with automatic irrigation, fertilization, air and lighting systems driven by a variety of sensors. Innovations demanded by big-box retailers, like custom labeling, bar codes, scanners, and electronic data interchange between suppliers and buyers, are now used by many producers. Computerized information systems are becoming more important, especially for big growers who have to track a large volume of containers and a large variety of plants.

Sales & Marketing

Commercial nurseries market and sell to independent or chain garden centers; home centers like Home Depot, Homebase, and Lowe's; mass merchants like Wal-Mart; drug and grocery chains; wholesalers; landscapers; and large end-users like hotels, office parks, and golf courses. Although plant "plugs" can easily be shipped long distances, grown plants are usually shipped no more than 150 miles because of perishability problems and shipping costs. Once at a retail location, many bedding plants have a shelf life of just a few weeks.

Sales are usually by a direct sales force who has established relations with large buyers. Marketing is through numerous trade shows, advertising in trade publications, catalogs, and direct mail. Close planning with large buyers is required to ensure that the right product mix is produced, but demand for different products can vary substantially from year to year. Large growers like Hines and Color Spot use sales merchandisers who provide instore service to large customers, including instore display maintenance, restocking, promotions, and consumer information.

Human Resources

Although supervisors must have strong technical knowledge, most workers in the industry are unskilled laborers who receive low wages. Because of strongly seasonal demand, many workers are hired for just a few months of the year.

Industry Employment Growth

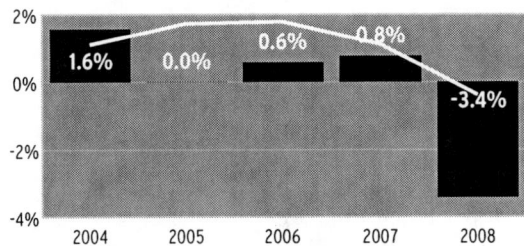

Average Hourly Earnings

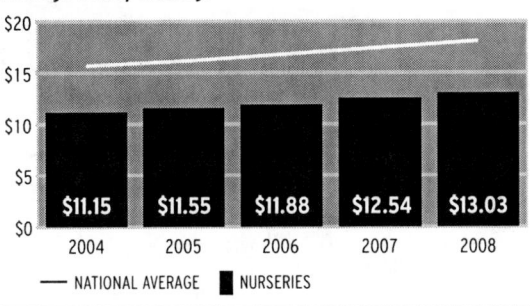

SOURCE: BUREAU OF LABOR STATISTICS

Call Preparation Questions

How do shifts in local or regional construction impact the company?

Residential and commercial construction drive demand for plants for landscaping and indoor decoration, as new housing developments and suburban office parks need trees, shrubs, and flowering plants.

How reliant is the company on a few top customers?

Many growers get a large percentage of revenue from a few large customers, such as national garden center chains, mass merchandisers like Wal-Mart, and supermarket chains.

How does the company ensure cash flow during slower seasons?

Most nurseries do the bulk of their business in spring, although some remain open year-round.

How does the company plan to capitalize on the aging population's demand for nursery products?

The most avid gardeners are consumers over 50, a group that will grow from 74 million today to 97 million by 2010, an increase of about 30 percent.

Is the company investing in automated irrigation and fertilizer systems?

Greenhouses have had to automate to allow for mass production and compete with large garden centers.

Web Links

American Nursery & Landscape Association (ANLA)

News and resources.
www.anla.org

American Nurseryman

Online magazine.
www.amerinursery.com

EPA Office of Pesticide Programs

www.epa.gov/pesticides

Nursery and Green Industry Links

Portal to nursery related sites.
www.pottedliners.com/links.htm

Society of American Florists

Data and news about the cut-flower segment of the industry.
www.safnow.org

The Green Beam

Publishers of NMPro and other publications.
www.greenbeampro.com

USDA National Agricultural Statistics Service

Statistics on greenhouses and nurseries.
www.nass.usda.gov

Glossary of Acronyms

APHIS — Animal and Plant Health Inspection Service
BLS — Bureau of Labor Statistics
EDI — electronic data interchange
NGA — National Gardening Association
OPP — Office of Pesticide Programs of the EPA

HOOVER'S TOP COMPANIES

Largest Employers	Employees
Hines Horticulture, Inc.	4,420
Ball Horticultural Company	3,000
Monrovia Nursery Company	2,000
Color Spot Nurseries, Inc.	1,684
Skinner Nurseries	238
Albin Hagstrom & Son, Inc.	235
Griffin Land & Nurseries, Inc.	174
White Flower Farm, Inc.	151
Fred Gutwein & Sons, Inc.	60

Top Public Companies by Market Value	($ mil.)
US Farms, Inc.	346.3
Griffin Land & Nurseries, Inc.	162.2

SOURCE: HOOVER'S, INC., DATABASE

Nursing Homes and Assisted Living

The nursing care industry includes about 35,000 companies that operate 70,000 facilities with combined annual revenue of $130 billion. Major companies include Sunrise Senior Living, Kindred Healthcare, Golden Horizons (owned by GGNSC Holdings), and SunBridge Healthcare. The industry is highly fragmented: only 13 of the 50 largest senior housing owners and operators manage portfolios of more than 100 properties.

Competitive Landscape

Demand for nursing care is linked to the demographics of the US population. The profitability of individual nursing facilities depends on efficient operations, as revenue per patient is largely controlled by the big government insurance programs, Medicare, and Medicaid. Large companies have some economies of scale in administration and purchasing, but small operators can compete effectively by offering better service. The industry is highly labor-intensive: annual revenue per worker is less than $45,000.

Products, Operations & Technology

The industry includes skilled nursing facilities for recovery from acute or chronic medical conditions, mental health and substance abuse facilities, and various types of community care and assisted living arrangements. A wide array of health care and dependent-care services are provided including 24-hour nursing care; help with daily living tasks such as bathing, eating, and dressing; housekeeping; food service; and leisure activities.

Nursing homes represent 25 percent of the total number of nursing and residential care facilities; residential mental health and substance abuse centers, 40 percent; community care centers, 25 percent; and other care facilities, 10 percent. Large firms may operate hundreds of domestic and foreign nursing facilities, either company-owned or leased.

BUSINESS CHALLENGES

» Heavy Dependence on Government Regulations

Many nursing facilities receive a majority of revenue from Medicare and Medicaid. Because of this dependence, nursing facilities are vulnerable to changing government rules and reimbursement rates. National concern over rising health care costs creates pressure to limit reimbursement rates, while highly publicized cases of patient abuse at nursing facilities causes calls for additional regulation.

» Labor-Intensive Industry

Labor is the largest single cost of nursing facilities. Companies try to reduce this cost by using lower-paid aides instead of expensive skilled nurses and through greater efficiency of operations, although regulators require minimum staffing levels. The industry is operating with a shortage of nurses and aides that's anticipated to expand as the US population ages and demand for nursing care increases.

» High Risk Workplace

The nursing and residential care industry's annual injury and illness rate is nine per 100 workers, more than double the national average. Nursing aides, orderlies, and attendants are most at risk from injury due to manually lifting patients and working closely with mentally ill or violent patients.

Nursing homes typically care for patients recovering from major medical procedures and older patients with chronic disabilities and deteriorating mental and physical capacities. Facilities provide nursing care, physical therapy, meals, recreational activities, personal services, and assistance with activities of daily living (ADL). Bed occupancy rates are typically between 80 and 85 percent.

Community care facilities include community-based residential facilities and adult family homes where small groups of individuals live and receive care, assisted living complexes where aides help residents with some daily activities, and residential care apartment complexes (RCAC) that provide independent apartments and some nursing care. Occupancy rates for assisted living facilities are typically between 90 and 95 percent.

Nursing care facilities often contract services from other health care providers to broaden their range of services without incurring added labor and equipment costs. Providers include pharmacies, medical directors, hospice care services, and a variety of physician specialists including dentists, podiatrists, therapists, psychiatrists, and opthamologists. Large facilities and chains are more likely to contract with outside health care providers than are small independent facilities.

Technology includes computers, electronic medical records, medical equipment, and security and fire systems. Due to the industry's low profitability and reliance on government or community funding, many facilities struggle to afford technology upgrades such as new computer systems and specialized medical equipment. Adoption of electronic medical records has also been slow, due to the high labor and funding investment required to convert patient records from paper to electronic files. Due to recent fires at nursing homes, regulators are requiring facilities to install fire alarms and sprinkler systems, which can be expensive depending on the construction of the facility.

Sales & Marketing

Through sales staff, nursing facilities market their services to health insurers, hospitals, individual doctors in fields like surgery and gerontology that are likely to need long-term care for their patients, local agencies for the aging, social workers, and financial planners serving aged clients. Like other health care providers, nursing care companies often enter into contracts with insurers to provide care at specified rates for members.

Marketing for most assisted living and residential care facilities is aimed at individuals and includes direct mailings; print advertisement in newspapers, magazines, and Yellow Pages; billboards; and public events such as open houses, health fairs, and community outreach events. A growing number of companies are developing websites to inform the public about their care, housing, and service options and attract new residents.

High-end residential care facilities market to the affluent. These properties depend less on Medicare, Medicaid, and private insurance and

tend to have lower but more profitable growth. Many provide various levels of care ranging from subacute nursing facilities to retirement communities with nursing-support services.

Average revenues are about $170 per day for nursing homes and $85 for assisted living facilities.

Human Resources

The average nursing care facility has 100 to 250 workers; the largest establishments may employ over 1,000. Adequate staffing is often a major problem, because of the labor-intensive nature of nursing care and the industry's low wages. Although supervisory jobs may be held by skilled nurses, most workers are aides with little special education or training. Nurses and aides typically receive lower pay than they would in an acute-care hospital. Wages are generally 20 percent less than for the average US worker.

Annual personnel turnover can be high, as much as 100 percent for aides at some facilities. High turnover results in near constant training of new workers, which is costly. Nonprofit nursing homes tend to have higher staffing levels and lower turnover than for-profit.

Facilities may employ unionized nurses and support workers, resulting in periodic labor and wage negotiations.

Industry Employment Growth

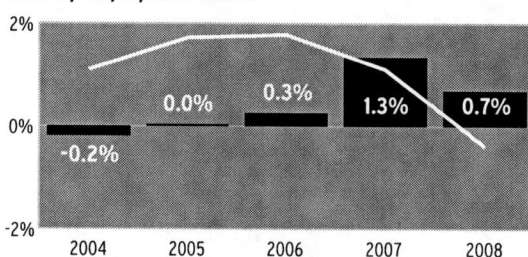

Average Hourly Earnings

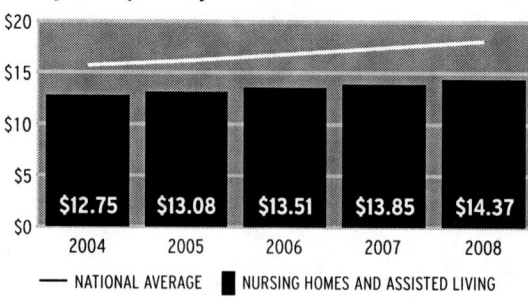

SOURCE: BUREAU OF LABOR STATISTICS

Call Preparation Questions

How have changes in Medicare or Medicaid programs affected the company?

Many nursing facilities receive a majority of revenue from Medicare and Medicaid.

What is the company doing to improve worker safety?

The nursing and residential care industry's annual injury and illness rate is nine per 100 workers, more than double the national average.

How large a demand increase does the company expect in its markets, and what plans does it have for expansion?

Between 2005 and 2015, the number of Americans 65 and over will increase more than 25 percent, raising demand for nursing services.

Web Links

Administration on Aging

Aging stats and news.

www.aoa.gov

American Association of Homes and Services for the Aging (AAHSA)

Regulatory, legislative issues, more.

www.aahsa.org

American Health Care Association – National Center for Assisted Living

State affiliates, educational resources, consumer information, news, regulatory reviews, and links.

www.ncal.org

Assisted Living State Regulatory Review

State-by-state regulatory review summarizes assisted living regulations and provides contact information for the state agencies.

www.ncal.org/about/state_review.cfm

Consumer Consortium on Assisted Living

News, links, and resources for comparing the quality of assisted living facilities.

www.ccal.org

HHS Division on Aging

Latest key statistics on nursing homes and care facilities.

www.os.dhhs.gov/aging

National Investment Center for the Seniors Housing & Care Industry

Quarterly updated information on loan volume and performance, occupancy and move-in rates, construction starts and capitalization rates for the seniors housing and care industry.

www.nic.org

Glossary of Acronyms

ADL — activities of daily living

AHCA — American Health Care Association

CCRC — continuing care retirement communities

CMS — Centers for Medicare & Medicaid Services

LTC — long-term care

RCAC — residential care apartment complexes

SNF — skilled nursing facility

HOOVER'S TOP COMPANIES

Largest Companies by Sales	($ mil.)
Kindred Healthcare, Inc.	4,151.4
Manor Care, Inc.	3,890.0
GGNSC Holdings LLC	2,490.0
Life Care Centers of America	2,120.0
Select Medical Holdings Corporation	1,991.7
Brookdale Senior Living, Inc.	1,928.1
Sunrise Senior Living, Inc.	1,652.6
Sun Healthcare Group, Inc.	1,587.3
SavaSeniorCare, LLC	1,270.0
Genesis HealthCare Corporation	—

Largest Employers	Employees
Manor Care, Inc.	61,700
Res-Care, Inc.	42,000
Sunrise Senior Living, Inc.	41,000
GGNSC Holdings LLC	41,000
Kindred Healthcare, Inc.	38,200
Genesis HealthCare Corporation	37,700
Sun Healthcare Group, Inc.	36,850
Brookdale Senior Living, Inc.	32,700
Life Care Centers of America	31,153
SavaSeniorCare, LLC	22,000

Fastest Growing* by Five-Year Sales Growth	(%)
Brookdale Senior Living, Inc.	54.0
Emeritus Corporation	28.9
Sunrise Senior Living, Inc.	26.7
Capital Senior Living Corporation	25.2
Skilled Healthcare Group, Inc.	18.3
The Ensign Group, Inc.	17.7
Five Star Quality Care, Inc.	13.9
AdCare Health Systems, Inc.	9.5
Advocat Inc.	8.1
Life Care Centers of America	7.7

Fastest Growing* by Five-Year Employee Growth	(%)
Five Star Quality Care, Inc.	52.7
Brookdale Senior Living, Inc.	46.0
Sunrise Senior Living, Inc.	28.3
Emeritus Corporation	15.3
Capital Senior Living Corporation	10.6
Res-Care, Inc.	7.7
The Ensign Group, Inc.	6.4
GGNSC Holdings LLC	2.5
Sun Healthcare Group, Inc.	2.0
Life Care Centers of America	0.8

Top Public Companies by Market Value	($ mil.)
Sunrise Senior Living, Inc.	1,551.1
Emeritus Corporation	981.6
Sun Healthcare Group, Inc.	736.6
Res-Care, Inc.	733.7
National HealthCare Corporation	659.6

* These rates are compounded annualized increases and may have resulted from acquisitions or one time gains. If less than 6 years of data are available, growth is for the years available.

SOURCE: HOOVER'S, INC., DATABASE

Office Supply and Paper Distribution

The wholesale and retail distribution of office paper and other office products generates annual sales of about $55 billion in the US. Large companies include Office Depot, Staples, OfficeMax, Unisource, and the distribution arms of large paper manufacturers. The industry includes "contract stationers," wholesale-retail chains, small dealers, and mail order companies that sell through catalogs or the Internet. The industry has become concentrated: the 50 largest wholesalers hold about 70 percent of the market. A large regional distributor has annual revenue close to $30 million.

Competitive Landscape

Demand is closely tied to the level of business activity. The profitability of individual companies depends on merchandising and an efficient delivery system. Big companies have economies of scale in distribution because they can supply a wide range of products to the same customer. Small companies can compete successfully by distributing specialty products or providing superior customer service. Operations are highly automated. Within the wholesale segment of the industry, annual revenue per employee is about $300,000.

Products, Operations & Technology

The industry distributes general office supplies, technology products, and office furniture. Paper and paper forms and envelopes account for about 35 percent of wholesale revenue. Technology products include personal computers and software, printers, calculators, telephones, etc. Toners and ink cartridges account for 10 percent of revenue.

Big chains, like Office Depot, buy products directly from manufacturers, but also buy specialty items from big wholesalers. Office Depot stocks 13,000 items at its customer service centers. A large wholesaler like United Stationers may buy from 500 manufacturers, stock 40,000

BUSINESS CHALLENGES

» Demand Linked to Cyclical Business Activity

Demand for office and paper supplies depends strongly on the level of business activity. Demand may grow sharply as businesses stock new offices, but drops when economic activity slows. During the last recession, wholesale trade in paper and paper products fell 7 percent.

» Low Profit Margins

With industry gross margins typically around 20 percent of sales, paper distributors must operate highly efficient distribution systems. Price competition is very strong. Despite attempts to differentiate themselves by providing faster service, most distributors have no special advantage over competitors, leaving price the main source of competition.

» Market Saturation by Superstores

Office supply superstores that expanded too aggressively have been cutting back and closing locations. Although the industry is still expected to grow an average of 7 percent annually in the coming years, overbuilding and expansion have exceeded demand in some markets.

items, and distribute to 20,000 resellers. Local retail outlets usually buy products from several wholesalers. Small retailers are increasingly being squeezed out by the superstore chains, which can undercut prices on most items. To remain competitive, many small retailers maintain and repair computers and other office equipment, and sell other consumer merchandise.

Large customers are usually serviced by contract stationers, while small, medium, and consumer customers are served by retail stores, catalogs, and the Internet. Many wholesalers service several different market segments, selling to big contract customers, big non-contract customers, and smaller companies. Contract stationer sales are usually discounted substantially from manufacturers' list prices. Contracts typically last several years. Operations for all suppliers are dominated by the logistics of moving large numbers of items to many customers.

End-use customers expect rapid delivery, usually the next day, requiring distributors to maintain large inventories and operate a large delivery fleet.

Distributors must fill and track orders for many items, from many customers, and manage their own inventory levels. Orders are received via telephone, fax, mail, and electronically. United Stationers receives 90 percent of its orders electronically. To achieve next-day delivery, national distributors have large warehouse networks that can usually distribute efficiently within a 400-mile radius.

Companies rely heavily on sophisticated computer systems that provide a direct link to suppliers, and on automated warehouse systems. Electronic data interchange (EDI) systems between customers and suppliers are common and Internet ordering systems are becoming more important.

Sales & Marketing

Customers are big businesses, small businesses, and individuals. Office products distributors rely heavily on catalogs, containing thousands of items, to get sales from both contract and non-contract customers. A wholesaler may distribute a variety of catalogs to customers; Office Depot may mail 300 million catalogs per year. Contract stationers use an internal sales force. Internet operations are an important new outlet for both wholesale and retail sales, but the need for an efficient distribution system means that Internet sales are handled mainly by the big chains and large distributors.

Human Resources

Jobs in office supply involve clerical activities, physical product movement, and retail customer service. These are generally unskilled

jobs that have relatively low pay and accordingly have relatively high turnover. In the retail segment, uneven customer demand during the day and week is accommodated by the use of part-time workers, who receive minimal benefits and have high turnover.

Demand for office supplies is highly sensitive to the level of economic activity.

Industry Employment Growth

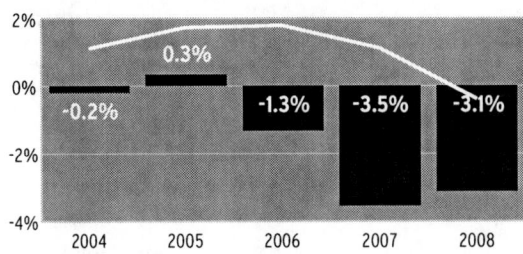

Average Hourly Earnings

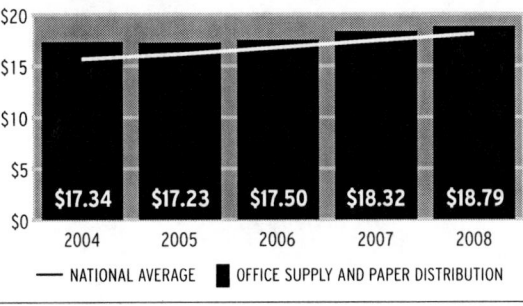

SOURCE: BUREAU OF LABOR STATISTICS

Call Preparation Questions

How does the company mitigate cyclical business demand for office supplies?

Demand for office and paper supplies depends strongly on the level of business activity.

How is the company strengthening profit margins?

With industry gross margins typically around 20 percent of sales, paper distributors must operate highly efficient distribution systems.

How is rapid industry expansion affecting the store's market share and profits?

Office supply superstores that expanded too aggressively have been cutting back and closing locations.

Does the company have a website that can take orders, and if so, to what advantage?

Office supply chains like Staples are advantaged over pure-Internet retailers, as most have a brand name, an infrastructure, buying power, database expertise, and direct marketing experience.

What opportunities or challenges does the company see in private-label branding?

Large wholesale-retailers, like Office Depot, have their own private-label products that typically have lower prices than other brands, but that produce higher profits.

Web Links

Independent Office Products and Furniture Dealers Association

Lobbying organization. Monthly "Office Products Industry Report." Statistics available to buy.
www.iopfda.org

National Purchasing Association

Purchasing association for small and medium office supply companies.
www.npaoffice.com

National School Supply and Equipment Association

Trade shows and industry publications.
www.nssea.org

Office Products Wholesalers Association

Industry calendar.
www.opwa.org

TriMega Purchasing

Purchasing association for larger contract stationers.
www.trimega.org

Glossary of Acronyms

EDI — electronic data interchange
FPI — Federal Prison Industries
GP — Georgia-Pacific
IP — International Paper
RFID — radio frequency identification

HOOVER'S TOP COMPANIES

Largest Companies by Sales	($ mil.)
Staples, Inc.	23,083.8
Office Depot, Inc.	14,495.5
OfficeMax Incorporated	8,267.0
Unisource Worldwide, Inc.	5,300.0
United Stationers Inc.	4,986.9
Corporate Express US, Inc.	4,367.1
IKON Office Solutions, Inc.	4,168.3
ACCO Brands Corporation	1,578.2
Gould Paper Corporation	1,160.0

Largest Employers	Employees
Staples, Inc.	75,588
Office Depot, Inc.	49,000
OfficeMax Incorporated	36,000
IKON Office Solutions, Inc.	15,000
Corporate Express US, Inc.	10,000
Unisource Worldwide, Inc.	6,500
United Stationers Inc.	6,100
ACCO Brands Corporation	6,000
School Specialty, Inc.	2,800
Gould Paper Corporation	431

Fastest Growing* by Five-Year Sales Growth	(%)
Stamps.com Inc.	39.4
Acme United Corporation	15.4
Staples, Inc.	11.9
Midland Paper Company Inc.	11.6
ACCO Brands Corporation	7.4
United Stationers Inc.	5.3
School Specialty, Inc.	4.6
Office Depot, Inc.	3.2
Gould Paper Corporation	0.6
OfficeMax Incorporated	0.1

Fastest Growing* by Five-Year Employee Growth	(%)
Midland Paper Company Inc.	18.6
Stamps.com Inc.	18.4
School Specialty, Inc.	7.7
Staples, Inc.	5.7
Acme United Corporation	5.1
ACCO Brands Corporation	4.7
Office Depot, Inc.	1.6
OfficeMax Incorporated	1.4
United Stationers Inc.	0.8

Top Public Companies by Market Value	($ mil.)
Staples, Inc.	11,406.8
Office Depot, Inc.	822.7
United Stationers Inc.	788.0
OfficeMax Incorporated	565.3
School Specialty, Inc.	559.0

* These rates are compounded annualized increases and may have resulted from acquisitions or one time gains. If less than 6 years of data are available, growth is for the years available.

SOURCE: HOOVER'S, INC., DATABASE

Oil and Gas Exploration and Production

The oil and gas exploration and production industry consists of about 7,000 companies with combined annual revenue of around $890 billion. Major companies include Murphy Oil, Chesapeake Energy, Devon Energy, Anadarko Petroleum, and Occidental Petroleum. Other companies include the exploration and production divisions of integrated companies such as Exxon Mobil, Chevron, and ConocoPhillips. The industry is moderately fragmented: 10 percent of companies generate 60 percent of revenue.

This industry segment doesn't include transmission, refining, or retailing of petroleum and natural gas products.

Competitive Landscape

Demand is driven by economic activity, population growth, and energy efficiency for residential, industrial, and transportational uses of oil and gas. Profitability of individual companies is driven by the success rate of new wells drilled and the ability to increase production from existing wells. Large companies are advantaged by access to capital, including the ability to buy or merge smaller companies. Small companies compete by focusing on, and developing expertise in, a few geographic areas. The industry is capital intensive: average annual revenue per employee is about $5 million.

Oil and gas compete with other energy sources, such as coal, nuclear power, and hydroelectric power, for industrial and home heating applications. Renewable fuels, such as ethanol and biodiesel, and hybrid-electric cars, which use stored electricity from batteries instead of or in addition to gas or diesel, are emerging alternatives for transportation applications.

Products, Operations & Technology

Major products of the oil and gas exploration and production industry are crude oil (about 45

BUSINESS CHALLENGES

» Volatility of Oil, Gas Prices

About 35 percent of the world oil supply of 85 million barrels of oil per day comes from areas with political instabilities (the Persian Gulf, Venezuela, and Nigeria). Given the fragile balance of supply and demand, perceived threats to the supply can cause large price disturbances. Capital availability and investment decisions are driven by estimates of future prices and probable production levels.

» Environmental Concerns

Petroleum and natural gas well blowouts in the past have caused oil and natural gas well drilling to be associated with toxic spills and site contamination. High-visibility accidents have occurred despite requirements for well safeguards and restrictions on drilling in populated and environmentally sensitive areas. Environmental restrictions and regulations limit exploration opportunities for companies and add cost to drilling operations.

» Forecasting Petroleum, Natural Gas Prices

Exploration and production investment is a long-term gamble on petroleum and natural gas prices. As prices increase, the amount of capital available for drilling increases and the size of reserves required for a well to be profitable decreases. Since a well can take two years to bring into full production and most are expected to have a productive life of 15 to 30 years, company management requires a good sense of the long-term market.

percent of industry revenue) and natural gas (55 percent). About 33 percent of US petroleum production comes from offshore wells and 67 percent from land-based wells. About 15 percent of US natural gas production comes from offshore wells.

Crude oil and natural gas are found in underground basins that meet certain geologic conditions. All exploration companies have staff geologists, and many hire companies specializing in geological research to identify areas with high potential for petroleum-bearing formations. Since the first US oil well was drilled in 1858, there have been hundreds of thousands of drillings (in 2006, the number of wells drilled approached 50,000, increasing to over 53,500 in 2007). Geologists use the geologic data from these drillings to identify areas with promise. To further improve the probability of finding petroleum, geologists can create 3D maps of underground rock formations using seismic waves from controlled explosions or sound generators (vibroseis).

Once a company selects an area to explore, it must obtain a lease on the mineral rights. Most companies hire a land services company to research the ownership of mineral rights. In most states, the mineral rights can be separated from the surface rights and owned by different parties. Land services companies employ landmen to present lease proposals to the mineral rights owners. The leases are for a fixed period, typically two to five years, and pay the owner a fixed fee for the right to drill during that period. The lease also defines access rights and rights to install and operate a well, along with royalty payments to the mineral rights owner for any hydrocarbon products extracted.

The exploration site is cleared and leveled and a drilling rig and crew brought in. Rotary rigs consist of a derrick and power source (usually two or more diesel engines), along with ancillary equipment, such as desanders and desilters, mud pumps, stacks of pipe, and living quarters for the crew. The crew commonly has 20 to 30 members and operates in 8-hour shifts, 24/7 until completion. A typical land-based well costs about $300 per foot to drill, and many wells cost $1 to $2 million to bring to production. The majority of commercial oil fields have been found at depths of 2,000 to 15,000 feet. Natural gas fields are generally between 2,000 and 25,000 feet. As a well is being drilled, geologists examine the cuttings evacuated from the borehole to evaluate the type and content of rock at each depth. Most exploration companies use a combination of their own rigs and crews and third-party drilling companies.

Gas flowing from a well has to be treated on-site to remove liquids and corrosive gases before it can be moved through a pipeline to a treatment plant.

Offshore drilling can be done in the shallow waters of the continental shelf or in deep seas. In shallow waters up to 500 feet, a drilling rig, such as a jackup rig, is towed to the drilling site and part of the platform sunk to the bottom. Legs are lowered from the upper platform to

the sunken platform and the upper platform is then jacked up to the desired height above the water. Drilling is then conducted in a manner similar to onshore drilling. In deeper waters, submersible rigs or deepwater drillships may be used. Usually three shifts of crews are on for the offshore rigs — two living aboard, the third ashore. The shifts are rotated in two-week intervals. Large rigs can have as many as 200 workers living aboard.

Wells require periodic workovers to maintain production levels. During service, a workover rig or a smaller service unit is used to raise and lower equipment into the well. Sand, rock, and other debris can be removed from the well using oil- or water-based mud or a nitrogen foam pumped into the well under high pressure. In some instances, wells can be drilled nearby and water or a gas (carbon dioxide or nitrogen) can be pumped in to drive the petroleum or natural gas toward the production well.

IT is used extensively to create the seismic 2D and 3D subsurface maps of potential drilling areas. To monitor production, companies operate Supervisory Control and Data Acquisition (SCADA) networks, which connect sensors and other equipment at each production site back to a staffed central control facility. The communication network may be older legacy wireline, microwave connections, or a modern wireless system.

Sales & Marketing

Crude oil is sold to either major oil or crude oil gathering companies that then sell it in bulk to refiners. Crude may be sold at the wellhead or at the refinery with the seller responsible for transportation. Most oil in the US is moved through the 85,000 miles of crude oil gathering pipelines. Once a well is brought into production, it's either connected to a nearby pipeline or crude is aggregated at the site and trucked to a pipeline or refinery. Pricing depends on the specific grade of crude, the location in regard to pipelines and refineries, and the local market price.

Most domestically produced natural gas is moved to market by pipeline. Gas may be sold at the wellhead to an end-user (who pays the pipeline company for transport), or to an aggregator (which may be the pipeline company), which then resells to gas processing plants that make the gas acceptable for transmission on interstate pipelines. In the US, about 90,000 miles of natural gas gathering pipelines plus 280,000 miles of interstate gas transmission pipelines and 850,000 miles of distribution pipelines exist. Price is determined by spot prices, which fluctuate seasonally, and regional index prices.

Human Resources

Production workers in oil and gas extraction require special skills and experience, resulting in average hourly wages that are about 40 percent higher than the national average for all industries. Most labor is in drilling, which is usually conducted 24/7, until the well is either brought into production or declared dry and capped. The industry injury and illness rate of about two per 100 employees is lower than in most manufacturing and mining industries.

Industry Employment Growth

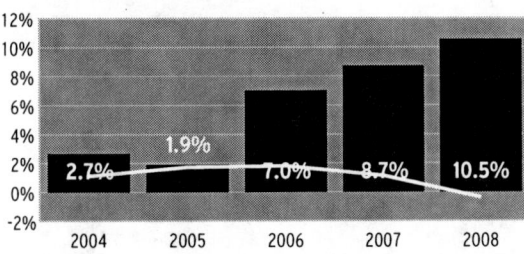

Average Hourly Earnings

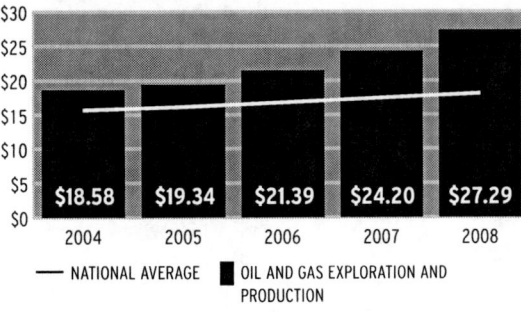

— NATIONAL AVERAGE ■ OIL AND GAS EXPLORATION AND PRODUCTION

SOURCE: BUREAU OF LABOR STATISTICS

Call Preparation Questions

How does political instability affect the company's ability to forecast oil prices?

About 35 percent of the world oil supply of 85 million barrels of oil per day comes from areas with political instabilities (the Persian Gulf, Venezuela, and Nigeria).

How have environmental concerns affected the company's exploration activities?

Petroleum and natural gas well blowouts in the past have caused oil and natural gas well drilling to be associated with toxic spills and site contamination.

What factors influence the company's investment decisions for exploration and production?

Exploration and production investment is a long-term gamble on petroleum and natural gas prices.

How many of the company's customers prefer long-term supply contracts?

Many users, such as power companies, are willing to execute long-term contracts for natural gas to assure a long-term supply at a stable price.

Does the company prefer to lease or own drilling equipment?

Drilling rigs can cost $10 to 20 million and require full-time crews and support staff.

Web Links

American Petroleum Institute

Oil and natural gas trade association.
www.api.org

Department of Energy

Annual Energy Review — Petroleum.
www.eia.doe.gov/emeu/aer/petro.html

E&P – Global Exploration and Production News

Exploration and production company news.
www.eandpnet.com

Oil and Gas Investor Magazine

News about exploration and production company
activities.
www.oilandgasinvestor.com

Oil and Gas Journal

Current news and market data.
www.ogj.com

World Oil Magazine

Source of oil news and statistics for buyers and
sellers.
www.worldoil.com

Glossary of Acronyms

ANWR — Arctic National Wildlife Refuge
BLM — Bureau of Land Management
CERCLA — Comprehensive Environmental Response,
Compensation and Liability Act
WTI — West Texas Intermediate

HOOVER'S TOP COMPANIES

Largest Companies by Sales	($ mil.)
Exxon Mobil Corporation	477,359.0
Chevron Corporation	273,005.0
ConocoPhillips	246,182.0
Marathon Oil Corporation	78,569.0
Murphy Oil Corporation	27,512.5
Occidental Petroleum Corporation	24,480.0
Anadarko Petroleum Corporation	15,723.0
Devon Energy Corporation	15,365.0
Apache Corporation	12,389.8
Chesapeake Energy Corporation	11,629.0

Largest Employers	Employees
Exxon Mobil Corporation	83,000
Chevron Corporation	65,000
ConocoPhillips	32,600
Marathon Oil Corporation	29,524
Occidental Petroleum Corporation	9,700
Murphy Oil Corporation	7,539
Chesapeake Energy Corporation	6,200
Devon Energy Corporation	5,000
Anadarko Petroleum Corporation	4,300
Apache Corporation	3,639

Fastest Growing* by Five-Year Sales Growth	(%)
EnerJex Resources, Inc.	3,500.0
Crusader Energy Group Inc.	300.0
Concho Resources Inc.	249.0
Teton Energy Corporation	245.2
Avalon Oil & Gas, Inc.	200.0
Evolution Petroleum Corporation	156.1
Transmeridian Exploration Corporation	155.3
Petrohawk Energy Corporation	143.1
Lucas Energy, Inc.	138.5
Encore Energy Partners LP	135.1

Fastest Growing* by Five-Year Employee Growth	(%)
Hyperdynamics Corporation	149.0
Double Eagle Petroleum Co.	141.0
Petrohawk Energy Corporation	116.2
Arena Resources, Inc.	97.7
GMX Resources Inc.	94.7
RAM Energy Resources, Inc.	81.0
Constellation Energy Partners LLC	75.6
W&T Offshore, Inc.	68.5
SandRidge Energy, Inc.	57.7
EXCO Resources, Inc.	51.2

Top Public Companies by Market Value	($ mil.)
Exxon Mobil Corporation	397,234.1
Chevron Corporation	148,253.0
ConocoPhillips	78,783.6
Occidental Petroleum Corporation	52,876.6
Devon Energy Corporation	29,155.5

* These rates are compounded annualized increases and may
have resulted from acquisitions or one time gains. If less
than 6 years of data are available, growth is for the years
available.

SOURCE: HOOVER'S, INC., DATABASE

Oil and Gas Field Services

The US oil and gas field services and equipment industry includes 8,000 companies with combined annual revenue of $89 billion. Large global suppliers include Halliburton, Schlumberger, and Baker Hughes. Despite recent consolidation, the industry is still fragmented and characterized by small specialty firms: over half of companies have fewer than five employees.

Competitive Landscape

Demand is driven by oil and gas prices. The profitability of individual companies depends on technical expertise and efficiency of operations. Large companies can offer a broad range of services. Small firms can compete effectively by specializing in a particular type of service or geographic area. The industry is relatively labor-intensive: average annual revenue per employee is about $410,000.

Products, Operations & Technology

Oil and gas field service companies provide drilling and support services for oil and gas wells and make drilling equipment. Drilling provides about 35 percent of industry revenue, support services 45 percent, and equipment manufacture 20 percent. Major support services include preparing wells for production, maintaining and enhancing the output of producing wells, and exploration.

Drilling a well with a drilling rig involves creating a hole using a drill bit attached to a rotating drill "string" made up of 30-foot sections of pipe. Heavy fluids ("drilling mud") are pumped down the hole during drilling to carry cuttings to the surface. Periodically, the drill pipe is pulled out and a larger diameter pipe, known as "casing," is cemented in place to protect the hole against collapse.

After drilling is finished, a well is prepared for production in a process known as "well completion." The casing is perforated at the production depth and a smaller diameter pipe

BUSINESS CHALLENGES

» Drilling Rig Activity Tied to World Energy Prices

Investment in drilling is closely linked to world energy prices, which are volatile and can change dramatically within a year: spot prices for West Texas Intermediate in the US rose 98 percent from mid-2007 to mid-2008, for example. As a result, the active rig count in the US has risen and fallen over 25 percent a year multiple times the past 10 years. As fuel prices rise, searching for more marginal supply sources becomes more profitable.

» Declining US Oil Production

Although new methods have improved production from existing fields, US crude oil production declined 27 percent from 1995 to 2005 as oil fields were depleted. More recently, the production decline has slowed to about 1 percent annually. Despite new exploration activity and high gas prices, which are driving a political movement to open offshore reserves to exploration, proven crude oil reserves have declined for the past 50 years and have leveled over the past decade at between 21 and 22 billion barrels.

» Political Instability of International Markets

Large US firms typically do over 60 percent of their business internationally, often in regions with political uncertainty. Drilling in Latin America, the Middle East, Russia, China, and Nigeria are all subject to political risks that can impact oil prices and service demand. In some countries, employees may be personally at risk, from kidnapping or politically motivated violence.

("tubing") is inserted to allow oil and gas to flow up the well. Finally, a "Christmas tree" structure of multiple valves is attached to the top of the tubing to control the flow of oil and gas from the well.

Offshore drilling requires specialized equipment such as drillships, semi-submersible rigs, "jack-up" rigs, equipment barges, and helicopter services. Directional drilling uses special "downhole" motors or directional sleeves to drill wells at an angle.

"Workover" of the 900,000 producing wells in the US typically involves pumping steam and chemicals into a well to remove obstacles and enhance flow. "Well servicing" involves repairing or replacing down-hole equipment and plugging wells at the end of their productive life. Exploration services use sophisticated seismic equipment to identify underground geological formations that might hold oil or gas.

Specialized manufactured products include drill bits, drilling pipe, derricks, portable rigs, well monitoring instruments, valves, tubing, and drilling fluids. Rotary drilling rigs consist of a derrick, motors, pumps, winches, and other equipment. About 2,300 land drilling rigs operate in the US and Canada, and about 68 offshore drilling rigs. Workover rigs are typically smaller, truck-mounted units.

Computer technology and sophisticated sensors (including downhole "wireline" instruments) are used to explore, monitor drilling progress, assess the condition of existing wells, and monitor and control product flow from producing wells.

Sales & Marketing

Customers are major oil and gas companies and smaller independent oil and gas producers. Sales are through direct contacts or competitive bidding.

Contracts for drilling typically specify prices in terms of a "dayrate." Multi-well drilling contracts generally have fixed dayrates, while the dayrates in "well-to-well" contracts change according to market demand. During periods of high demand, dayrates for offshore drilling can exceed $300,000 for floating rigs and $100,000 for jackup rigs. Dayrates for land drilling and workover services are less, but high demand can push rates above $15,000. Some drilling contracts are priced according to "footage" instead of dayrate, or a combination.

Customer service is key in winning business, and companies must maintain equipment service and storage centers near production areas. Mobile units typically service wells within 100 miles of their base location.

Human Resources

Drilling oil and gas wells requires special technical skills and experience. Workers earn wages 20 percent above the US average. Fringe benefits average an extra 22 percent of payroll.

Drilling oil and gas wells is hazardous, and safety is an ongoing concern of companies. Workers engaged in non-drilling services have an average injury rate, but the injury rate for workers involved in drilling activities, while falling in recent years, remains about 25 percent higher than the national average.

Industry Employment Growth

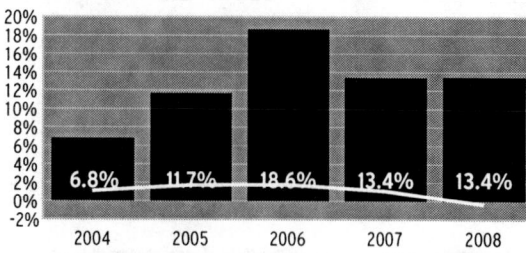

2004	2005	2006	2007	2008
6.8%	11.7%	18.6%	13.4%	13.4%

Average Hourly Earnings

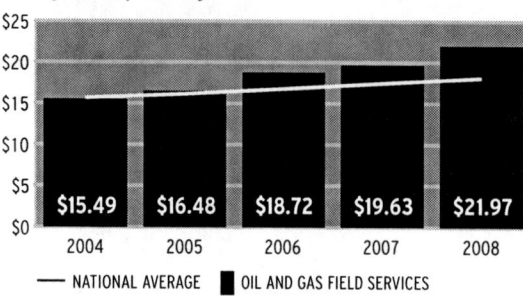

2004	2005	2006	2007	2008
$15.49	$16.48	$18.72	$19.63	$21.97

— NATIONAL AVERAGE ■ OIL AND GAS FIELD SERVICES

SOURCE: BUREAU OF LABOR STATISTICS

Call Preparation Questions

What changes in energy prices does the company anticipate over the next year? How will higher or lower prices impact demand for the company's services?

Investment in drilling is closely linked to world energy prices, which are volatile and can change dramatically within a year: spot prices for West Texas Intermediate in the US rose 98 percent from mid-2007 to mid-2008, for example.

How does a decline in US oil production impact demand for company products and services?

Although new methods have improved production from existing fields, US crude oil production declined 27 percent from 1995 to 2005 as oil fields were depleted.

What risks does the company face from political instability in oil-rich regions?

Large US firms typically do over 60 percent of their business internationally, often in regions with political uncertainty.

How will the government's goal to reduce oil imports from the Middle East impact demand for company products and services?

The US government has set a goal to reduce dependence on Middle East oil by 75 percent by 2025.

How will the company benefit if new federal lands are opened to oil and gas exploration?

Much of the remaining oil and gas resources in the US to be discovered — 78 percent of the oil and 62 percent of the gas — are expected to be found beneath federal lands and coastal waters.

Web Links

American Petroleum Institute

Policy issues and educational material.
api-ec.api.org

Baker Hughes.com

Current and historical statistics on worldwide rig counts.
www.bakerhughes.com/bakerhughes

Energy Information Administration

Description of drilling and production processes. Industry statistics.
www.eia.doe.gov/pub/oil_gas/petroleum/
analysis_publications/oil_market_basics

Oil & Gas Journal

Industry news. Annual subscription to industry statistics.
ogj.pennnet.com

Rigzone.com

News and statistics, company directories, and product information.
www.rigzone.com

Society of Petroleum Engineers

Glossary of terms and descriptions of processes.
www.spe.org

World Oil.com

News and statistics about oil exploration and production.
worldoil.com

Glossary of Acronyms

API — American Petroleum Institute
BPD — barrels per day
CERCLA — Comprehensive Environmental Response, Compensation, and Liability Act
EIA — Energy Information Administration
SPE — Society of Petroleum Engineers

HOOVER'S TOP COMPANIES

Largest Companies by Sales	($ mil.)
Schlumberger Limited	27,564.8
Halliburton Company	18,279.0
National Oilwell Varco, Inc.	13,431.4
Baker Hughes Incorporated	11,864.0
Smith International, Inc.	10,770.8
Weatherford International Ltd.	9,600.6
Transocean Inc.	6,377.0
Cameron International Corporation	5,848.9
BJ Services Company	5,426.3
FMC Technologies, Inc.	4,550.9

Largest Employers	Employees
Schlumberger Limited	80,000
Halliburton Company	51,000
Baker Hughes Incorporated	39,800
Weatherford International Ltd.	38,000
National Oilwell Varco, Inc.	31,198
Nabors Drilling USA, LP	22,599
Transocean Inc.	21,100
Smith International, Inc.	19,865
BJ Services Company	16,700
Cameron International Corporation	15,400

Fastest Growing* by Five-Year Sales Growth	(%)
Houston American Energy Corp.	121.2
Hiland Partners, LP	105.4
Hercules Offshore, Inc.	90.3
Bronco Drilling Company, Inc.	86.8
Allis-Chalmers Energy Inc.	83.3
Complete Production Services, Inc.	77.9
TGC Industries, Inc.	70.4
Targa Resources Partners LP	60.2
Superior Well Services, Inc.	58.9
Atlas Energy Resources, LLC	50.2

Fastest Growing* by Five-Year Employee Growth	(%)
Allis-Chalmers Energy Inc.	108.7
Boots & Coots International Well Control, Inc.	71.6
Bronco Drilling Company, Inc.	62.7
TGC Industries, Inc.	61.7
Superior Well Services, Inc.	43.8
National Oilwell Varco, Inc.	42.8
OMNI Energy Services Corp.	34.2
Cal Dive International, Inc.	29.1
Hiland Partners, LP	26.6
Dawson Geophysical Company	26.2

Top Public Companies by Market Value	($ mil.)
Schlumberger Limited	50,546.3
Transocean Inc.	45,410.5
Halliburton Company	16,271.1
Noble Corporation	15,157.3
National Oilwell Varco, Inc.	10,200.1

* These rates are compounded annualized increases and may have resulted from acquisitions or one time gains. If less than 6 years of data are available, growth is for the years available.

SOURCE: HOOVER'S, INC., DATABASE

Optometrists and Opticians

The retail optical industry in the US includes about 14,000 optician stores with combined annual revenue of $7 billion, and 16,000 offices of optometrists with combined annual revenue of $6 billion. Large opticians include Luxottica (LensCrafters and Pearle Vision), Eye Care Centers of America, and US Vision. The optician segment of the market is fairly concentrated: the 50 largest chains hold about 60 percent of the market. The optometrist segment is highly fragmented.

Optometrists work mainly as solo practitioners or in small group practices. A typical group practice has less than $500,000 in annual revenue and four employees. About 1,000 practices have annual revenue over $1 million. Many optometrist practices include retail sales.

Competitive Landscape

Demand is driven by demographics, fashion, and changing health care practices. Most important is the aging US population, which is increasing demand for eye exams and glasses. The profitability of optometrist practices depends on efficient operations and whether they also sell glasses and contact lenses. There are few economies of scale in retail operations, except that large stores can offer a larger choice of product styles. Small retailers can often compete successfully with large chains by offering a different product mix. Eyeglass purchases are mildly cyclical with the economy, as many consumers view extra glasses as an expense that can be deferred.

Products, Operations & Technology

Optometrists perform routine eye examinations, mainly to write prescriptions for corrective lenses, and can treat some simple eye conditions. Complicated conditions like glaucoma, cataracts, or retinal detachments are referred to ophthalmologists. Optometric eye examinations are fairly standard, usually take

BUSINESS CHALLENGES

» Growth of Eye Care Insurance Coverage may Lower Prices

As more consumers receive eye care coverage from their health insurer, the average price retailers get is likely to decline. Payments for eye exams and glasses from health insurers are often 25 percent lower than the regular prices optometrists and opticians charge. To get business from members of managed care plans, optometrists and opticians have little choice but to accept the discounted prices.

» Improved Corrective Eye Surgery may Shrink Optical Market

Although corrective eye surgery like LASIK has so far had no major impact on sales of glasses and contact lenses, the volume of such surgery is expected to increase as quality improves and costs decrease. LASIK eye surgery has rapidly grown into a multi-billion dollar industry.

» Competition from Mass Merchants

Mass merchants like Wal-Mart have opened optical departments within their stores in recent years and generally offer lower prices than many independent stores or chains. Although these companies compete mainly at the lower end of the market, they affect higher-end prices as well.

less than 20 minutes, and are charged at a flat fee. Revenue from eye exams depends almost entirely on how many customers an optometrist can see. Both optometrists and ophthalmologists may also sell glasses and contact lenses directly from an office dispensary. Because of space constraints, retail sales in office practices are usually limited to contact lenses.

Opticians sell eyeglasses and contact lenses in retail stores based on prescriptions written by optometrists or ophthalmologists. Optometrists may also own and operate retail stores. Lenses ("ophthalmic lenses") and frames account for the bulk of store sales. Frames, which come in enormous variety and a wide range of prices, are often branded and can produce high markups, while contact lenses and lenses for glasses are mostly commodity items with fairly low margins. A typical store may hold an inventory of 500 frames in 100 different styles. Eye Care Centers of America carries 450 styles and 2,000 frames in some of its superstores. The price range of frames a store carries depends on the demographics of local shoppers. Opticians also sell non-prescription products like sunglasses and generic reading glasses (magnifiers). Average annual revenue per worker is close to $100,000.

Contact lenses come in hard or soft varieties, may be colored, and may allow extended wear or be disposable. The lenses for glasses also come in various colors and with various coatings and may contain areas of different correction (bi- or tri-focals). "Progressive" lenses are bifocals with the corrective areas smoothly blended into each other. Simple conditions, like near- or far-sightedness, can be corrected with either contact lenses or glasses, while some can best be corrected with glasses.

Because the lenses for glasses must be ground, coated, and shaped to fit a particular frame, some retail stores have an attached optical laboratory, while others send such work out to a company-owned or independent laboratory. Some stores with an attached lab can produce a finished pair of glasses in an hour, but the usual turnaround time is several days.

Lenses for glasses are made of plastic and are bought from a few large manufacturers like Sola. Frames are usually bought from a dozen manufacturers but may carry a large number of brand names. Contact lenses are made by companies like Bausch & Lomb, Johnson & Johnson, and CIBA.

Only ophthalmologists are allowed to perform LASIK surgery (laser-assisted in-situ keratomileusis) to correct vision defects. In LASIK surgery, the outer layer of the cornea is cut and folded back and a laser is used to precisely vaporize tissue in the middle layer, changing the shape of the cornea. The cost of LASIK surgery, generally between $1,000 and $2,000, isn't covered by most health insurance plans. Because of the high cost of the laser devices, ophthalmologists often lease the equipment or share it with other ophthalmologists in outpatient centers.

Sales & Marketing

Optometrists operate a practice very much like doctors and dentists, keeping medical records, scheduling appointments, getting new patients by referral, and getting much of their revenue through repeat visits from patients. Many optometrists combine their examination practice with the operation of a retail optical store.

Optician stores operate much like other retail stores, locating in areas of high shopper traffic like shopping malls or near office buildings. Much of their business is walk-ins. Because state regulations require a prescription for corrective lenses, many stores have an optometrist on-site or in an adjacent office. Some large chains bundle a retail store with an optometrist and a lab, for the fastest service. Some chains operate stores within larger department or warehouse stores.

Marketing for independent stores is largely limited to Yellow Pages advertising and window displays. Chains use local TV, radio, and newspaper advertising and often group several stores within a market to make advertising more cost-effective.

Because many health insurance plans (but not Medicare) cover routine eye exams and corrective lenses, optometrists and opticians enter into agreements with insurers to provide services and products at rates often lower than their regular rates. Consumers covered under vision care plans visit eye care providers three to four times in a five-year period, versus just twice for non-covered consumers. In 2003, Eye Care Centers of America received 30 percent of its retail sales from insurance plans.

Internet sales of contact lenses have become common in recent years, because they can be ordered exactly according to prescription and don't require fitting from an optician. Opticians aren't likely to lose much revenue to Internet merchants, as contact lenses provide only a small percentage of sales at optical stores, but many optometrists get substantial revenue from contact lens' sales.

Human Resources

Most jobs in optometrist offices and optical goods stores require only a moderate amount of skill and training and are relatively low paid. Average earnings in both segments of the industry are about 20 percent lower than for the average US worker.

Industry Employment Growth

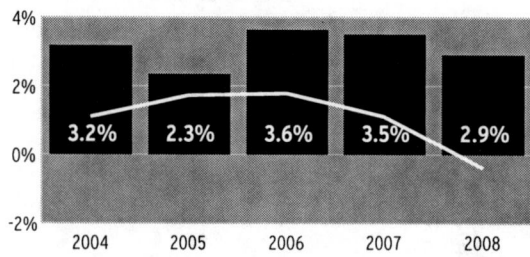

Average Hourly Earnings

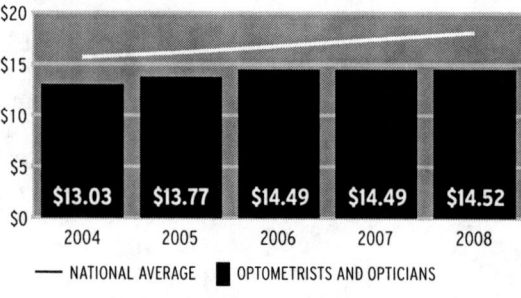

—— NATIONAL AVERAGE ■ OPTOMETRISTS AND OPTICIANS

SOURCE: BUREAU OF LABOR STATISTICS

Call Preparation Questions

How is the growth of eye care insurance impacting prices the practice charges?

As more consumers receive eye care coverage from their health insurer, the average price retailers get is likely to decline.

How is the company's market affected by the growth of corrective surgery?

Although corrective eye surgery like LASIK has so far had no major impact on sales of glasses and contact lenses, the volume of such surgery is expected to increase as quality improves and costs decrease.

How strong is competition from the large national chains in the company's market?

Mass merchants like Wal-Mart have opened optical departments within their stores in recent years and generally offer lower prices than many independent stores or chains.

What plans does the company have to expand treatment options?

Some states are considering allowing optometrists, who already generally treat infections like conjunctivitis, to treat complex eye conditions like glaucoma.

Web Links

20/20 Magazine

Fashions and trends in the industry.
www.2020mag.com

All About Vision

Information about LASIK surgery, eyeglasses, eye exams, and more.
www.allaboutvision.com/visionsurgery

American Academy of Ophthalmology

News releases.
www.aao.org/aao/newsroom

American Optometric Association

Good descriptions of eye conditions.
www.aoa.org

FDA LASIK Eye Surgery Site

Government information on LASIK.
www.fda.gov/cdrh/lasik

Jobson Medical Information

Data for the optical community.
www.jmihealth.com/hcp/optical

Opticians Association of America

Issues and legislation.
www.oaa.org

Opticians Association of Canada

Vision testing by opticians. Press releases.
www.opticians.ca

Review of Optometry

Periodic articles about optometry practice.
www.revoptom.com

Glossary of Acronyms

AAO — American Academy of Ophthalmology

HOOVER'S TOP COMPANIES

Largest Employers	Employees
LensCrafters, Inc.	14,000
Eye Care Centers of America, Inc.	4,800
Pearle Vision, Inc.	3,700
National Vision, Inc.	2,547
U.S. Vision, Inc.	1,966
Emerging Vision, Inc.	134

SOURCE: HOOVER'S, INC., DATABASE

Outpatient Surgical Centers

The outpatient and ambulatory surgical center (ASC) industry in the US includes about 1,500 companies that operate 3,500 freestanding centers, with combined annual revenue close to $9 billion. Major companies include Tenet Healthcare, Community Health Systems, Trinity Health, and Universal Health Services. The industry is highly fragmented: the 50 largest companies hold only about 30 percent of the market. A typical center has 30 employees and $5 million of annual revenue.

Competitive Landscape

Demand is linked to the number of people receiving medical care. The profitability of individual centers depends on efficient operations and good marketing. Chains that operate several centers have few advantages over single centers because there are few economies of scale in operations. Average annual revenue per employee is about $150,000.

Products, Operations & Technology

Surgical centers, otherwise known as ambulatory surgical centers (ASCs), are used by doctors to perform a variety of surgical procedures that don't require patients to stay overnight in a hospital. Typical procedures include eye, orthopedic and hand, and plastic surgery; pain management (spinal injections); podiatry; ear-nose-and-throat surgery; and abortions, endoscopy, and laparoscopy. Outpatient surgical centers are a lower-cost and more convenient alternative to hospitals. Hospitals generally have a higher cost structure, are often located downtown rather than in the suburbs, have limited availability of operating rooms, and can't always guarantee schedules because of possible preemption by emergency surgery.

Most centers have from two to six operating rooms, and areas for reception, preparation, recovery, and administration. The staff includes nurses, technicians, and administrative person-

BUSINESS CHALLENGES

» Investment Required in Expensive Equipment

To attract referrals, ASCs must provide the latest equipment and support. Medicare and other health insurance plans make standard overhead reimbursements for various types of surgical procedures, no matter the actual cost. By keeping costs low, profits can be high, but facilities without up-to-date equipment don't attract referrals.

» Dependence on Reimbursement Rates

Efforts to contain the rising cost of US health care services could result in lower future profitability for ASCs through reduced payments from medical insurers. Medicare, the largest payer, is being pressured politically to restrain rising costs and could do so unilaterally by reducing the reimbursement schedule for or limiting future increases.

» Vulnerability to Self-Referral Regulations

In general, Medicare regulations forbid doctors from referring patients to treatment facilities in which they own a financial interest. Current regulations allow surgeons to refer patients to outpatient, or ASC, in which they hold an interest if certain very specific conditions are met, the so-called "ASC Safe Harbor," but a blanket exemption from the self-referral regulations doesn't exist. The arrangements of any specific center might be challenged under the Fraud and Abuse law.

nel. Aside from anesthesiologists, doctors usually aren't part of the working staff (but are often involved in ownership and management). Surgeons and anesthesiologists typically arrange to meet patients at the center, perform the procedures, and leave. The average procedure takes 60 minutes. The daily operations of a center involve mainly personnel management, scheduling, and billing. Typically, 35 percent of facility costs are for labor, 35 percent for equipment and supplies. Centers typically lease space, because a facility usually needs only 10,000 to 20,000 square feet.

Revenues depend on the volume of referrals to the surgical center, with a typical center performing 2,000 procedures per year, although volume can be much higher. St. Luke's Ambulatory Surgical Center performs close to 7,000 procedures per year. A large percentage of revenue may stem from a small number of surgeons who each perform hundreds of procedures per year.

Sales & Marketing

ASCs market their services to doctors who refer patients and to third-party payers, such as insurers and employers, usually through individual sales calls. Marketers solicit business from individual surgeons or physician groups that perform a large volume of procedures, and centers gear their equipment and personnel to support the procedures these groups perform.

Surgical centers bill a "facility fee" for their services according to the type of procedure performed. (Doctors bill separately for their own fees.) Typically, deductibles and co-payments are billed to patients, but the bulk of charges are billed directly to Medicare, Medicaid, and other insurers. A large operator may receive 30 percent of revenue from Medicare, and 70 percent from traditional insurers, managed care plans, workers' compensation insurance, Medicaid, and other sources. Insurers have a set schedule of fees they pay for various procedures, which can sometimes be negotiated when a contract is signed between a payer and surgical center. Medicare fee schedules are set by the federal government. Medicare currently maps all procedures into eight groups and pays a flat fee according to group. Typical Medicare fees range from $300 to $1,000. Overall, facility fees can range up to $2,500 for a procedure, but the average fee is about $1,000.

Human Resources

Employees of outpatient surgical centers are mainly nurses, clerks, and technical support personnel, similar to the employees of a doctor's office. Because of the technical skills required, workers are paid above-average wages, generally 25 percent higher than for all US workers. Locally, skilled nurses may be in short supply.

Industry Employment Growth

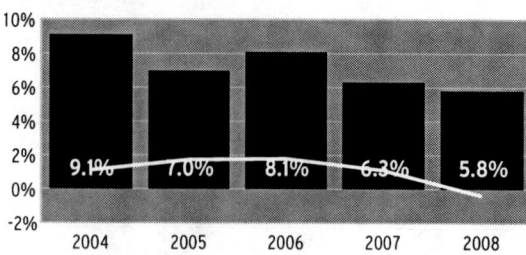

Average Hourly Earnings

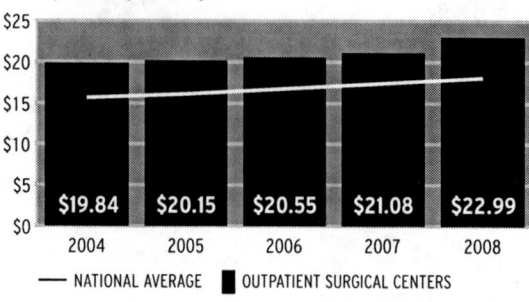

SOURCE: BUREAU OF LABOR STATISTICS

Call Preparation Questions

How often does the company buy major pieces of equipment?

To attract referrals, ASCs must provide the latest equipment and support.

How heavily does the center depend on payments from medical insurers or Medicare?

Efforts to contain the rising cost of US health care services could result in lower future profitability for ASCs through reduced payments from medical insurers.

How would the center be affected by stronger enforcement of anti-referral regulations?

In general, Medicare regulations forbid doctors from referring patients to treatment facilities in which they own a financial interest.

What percentage of available services do insurers cover?

Medicare, often the benchmark for other health insurance plans, now approves more than 2,000 procedures performed at ASCs.

Does the company plan to perform a larger variety of procedures?

Advances in surgical technique, anesthesia, and patient care have allowed more surgical procedures to be done as outpatient.

Web Links

Accreditation Association for Ambulatory Health Care

Industry issues.
www.aaahc.org

Ambulatory Surgery Center Association

Regulatory developments.
www.ascassociation.org

American Association for Accreditation of Ambulatory Surgery Facilities

Operational standards.
www.aaaasf.org

Centers for Medicare & Medicaid Services

Ambulatory Surgical Centers page.
www.cms.hhs.gov/center/asc.asp

National Survey of Ambulatory Surgery

Data on procedures and outcomes. From the National Center for Health Statistics.
www.cdc.gov/nchs/about/major/hdasd/nhds.htm

Outpatient Surgery Magazine

Operating and regulatory issues discussed.
www.outpatientsurgery.net

Glossary of Acronyms

ASC — ambulatory surgical centers
ASPS — American Society of Plastic Surgeons
CMS — Centers for Medicare & Medicaid Services
HHS — Health and Human Services
HIPAA — Health Insurance Portability and Accountability Act

HOOVER'S TOP COMPANIES

Largest Companies by Sales	($ mil.)
AmSurg Corp.	600.7
LCA-Vision Inc.	292.6
U.S. Healthworks, Inc.	250.0
NovaMed, Inc.	128.6

Largest Employers	Employees
AmSurg Corp.	2,460
U.S. Healthworks, Inc.	2,200
LCA-Vision Inc.	784

Top Public Companies by Market Value	($ mil.)
AmSurg Corp.	731.5
Healthways, Inc.	640.1
LCA-Vision Inc.	369.1
NovaMed, Inc.	104.4

SOURCE: HOOVER'S, INC., DATABASE

Paint and Coating Manufacturing

**THIS INDUSTRY
INCLUDES:**

SIC CODES

2851   Paints, Varnishes,
Lacquers, Enamels,
and Allied
Products

NAICS CODES

32551 Paint and Coating
Manufacturing

The US paint and coatings industry includes about 1,400 companies with combined annual sales of $20 billion. Large companies include Sherwin-Williams, Benjamin Moore, RPM International, Valspar, and divisions of DuPont, BASF, and PPG. The industry is highly concentrated: the largest 50 companies hold 80 percent of the market. Most manufacturing plants are midsized, with 20 to 250 employees and average annual sales of $30 million.

Competitive Landscape

Demand is driven by industrial production and the housing market. The profitability of individual companies depends on technological expertise and efficient production. Small companies can compete successfully with large ones because of the large number of paints and coatings used for a wide variety of applications, including decoration, water resistance, and corrosion resistance. The industry is highly automated: average annual revenue per employee is about $430,000.

Products, Operations & Technology

Major products are "architectural coatings" (house paints), product finishes, industrial coatings, and miscellaneous products like varnish removers and paint thinners. House paints account for about 40 percent of industry revenue; product finishes (for cars, furniture, etc.) for 25 percent; industrial coatings for 20 percent.

Paints and coatings consist of three major components: a resin or polymer that will ultimately form the coating layer, a pigment that provides color, and a solvent or vehicle that holds the resin and pigment in liquid form and evaporates once the liquid mixture is applied. Additives can be used to alter the flow characteristics of the paint or the glossiness of the applied product. Paints are often classified according to whether the solvent is water or a

BUSINESS CHALLENGES

» **Slow, Cyclical Demand**

Demand for paints is cyclical and strongly tied to the general US economy because demand for housing, cars, and other industrial goods fluctuates. Paints and coatings are a mature business. US paint production was flat for a number of years before falling sharply in the last recession. The principal end-use markets, such as appliances and industrial products, grow no faster than the US population, about 1 percent per year.

» **Raw Material Prices Fluctuate**

Because many paint resins and solvents are made from industrial chemicals derived from crude oil or natural gas, the cost of production can vary significantly. Manufacturers have only a limited ability to pass higher costs to customers. Crude oil prices routinely change 10 to 20 percent during a year.

» **Uncertain Outcome of Lead Paint Litigation**

Adverse legal judgments against former manufacturers of paints containing lead could devastate the industry. Although paints have been lead-free for years, lead paint persists in many older houses and institutions and is a major cause of lead poisoning. Many major and regional paint manufacturers, retailers, and trade associations have been targeted by lawsuits.

volatile hydrocarbon. In practice, paints with a hydrocarbon solvent are called "solvent" paints — what consumers think of as oil-based — while paints with water as the solvent are called water-based. Certain kinds of resins such as latex and acrylic remain dissolved in water until they dry; other resins, like epoxy and alkyds, are best dissolved in hydrocarbon solvents.

Paint manufacturers are mainly in the business of mixing components (pigments, resins, solvents, additives) into solutions that have the special characteristics required by customers. Titanium oxide is the most widely used pigment (white). Raw materials, which account for 50 percent of the selling price for many products and many which are made from petroleum, are usually procured from a number of industrial chemical suppliers. Large paint manufacturers make some of their own component materials, while small manufacturers often buy and mix components.

While the basic methods of mixing components to make paints are well known, the technology of producing new types of paints for special applications--such as paints that can be "cured" with ultra-violet light--requires special chemical and engineering knowledge. Computer technology is used to control the manufacturing process, which requires precise measurement of the component ingredients. Research and development of new products and applications is essential to success in a field where the overall use of paints is growing only slowly.

Sales & Marketing

Major customers are retailers of consumer paints, and OEMs like the big car companies. In the consumer segment, large manufacturers sell branded products directly to home centers, mass merchants, and hardware stores. A few sell through retail outlets that bear the brand name. Sherwin-Williams owns about 3,000 retail paint stores; Benjamin Moore sells to 4,000 independent stores. Smaller manufacturers with lower volume distribute through wholesalers. In the OEM segment, sales are directly to manufacturers by sales teams with technical knowledge; companies may sell existing products or formulate a product especially for the customer. Technical expertise and the amount of technical support provided are key selling tools.

Pricing is affected both by the strength of demand and raw material costs, which are linked to the price of crude oil. Prices for home paints increase readily during periods of high new home construction and home sales. But prices for product finishes are influenced more by the buying power of large customers like car companies.

Human Resources

Many jobs in the industry involve operating automated machinery and require special technical skills. Earnings are therefore somewhat above-average. Improved workplace control of toxic substances has reduced the annual rate of injury to the national average.

Industry Employment Growth

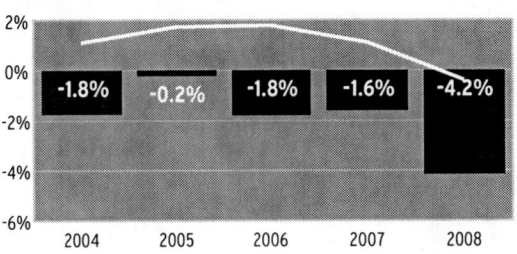

Average Hourly Earnings

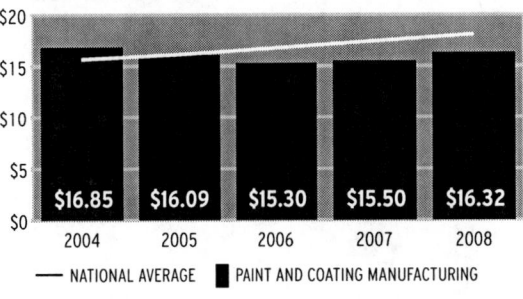

— NATIONAL AVERAGE ■ PAINT AND COATING MANUFACTURING

SOURCE: BUREAU OF LABOR STATISTICS

Call Preparation Questions

How does the company manage seasonal or cyclical demand?

Demand for paints is cyclical and strongly tied to the general US economy because demand for housing, cars, and other industrial goods fluctuates.

How do fluctuations in raw material prices impact the company?

Because many paint resins and solvents are made from industrial chemicals derived from crude oil or natural gas, the cost of production can vary significantly.

How is the company reducing the risk of environmental contamination and liability?

Adverse legal judgments against former manufacturers of paints containing lead could devastate the industry.

What growth opportunities does the company see in plastic coatings?

To serve the plastics industry, coating manufacturers are increasingly interested in finding ways to better adhere coatings to plastics.

To what extent is the company involved in developing new paint and coating technologies?

Environmental and efficiency concerns have prompted the development of new types of paints and paint applications.

Web Links

Federation of Societies for Coatings Technology

Sponsor of the International Coatings Expo, the largest industry trade show.

www.coatingstech.org

Glossary of Paint and Coating Terms

Commonly used terms in the paints and coatings industry to describe the characteristics, use, and components of paints and coatings.

www.paint.org/ind_info/terms.cfm

Insider News

Free weekly e-mail newsletter that includes up-to-the-minute paint and coatings industry news.

www.pcimag.com/HTML/BNP_GUID_9-5-2006_A_10000000000000047814

National Paint & Coatings Association

Industry association. Issues, industry information, industry calendar, links.

www.paint.org

Paint & Coating Industry

Articles and news.

www.pcimag.com

Paint & Decorating Retailers Association (PDRA)

Links, news, reports, industry data, and trends on paint retail.

www.pdra.org

Paint Quality Institute

Magazine, facts, news, trends, and technology updates.

www.paintquality.com

Painting & Decorating Contractors of America (PDCA)

News, government affairs, and links.

www.pdca.org

SpecialChem

Industry news.

www.paintandcoatings.com

The Society for Protective Coatings

News on OSHA and environmental issues.

www.sspc.org

Glossary of Acronyms

APM — auto parts manufacturers
NPCA — National Paint and Coatings Association
OEM — original equipment manufacturer
PRP — potentially responsible party
VOC — Volatile Organic Compounds

HOOVER'S TOP COMPANIES

Largest Companies by Sales	($ mil.)
E. I. du Pont de Nemours and Company	31,836.0
PPG Industries, Inc.	15,849.0
Rohm and Haas Company	9,575.0
The Sherwin-Williams Company	7,979.7
RPM International Inc.	3,643.8
The Valspar Corporation	3,482.4

Largest Employers	Employees
E. I. du Pont de Nemours and Company	60,000
PPG Industries, Inc.	34,900
The Sherwin-Williams Company	31,572
Rohm and Haas Company	15,710
RPM International Inc.	10,360
The Valspar Corporation	10,000
Akzo Nobel Inc.	8,210
ICI Paints in North America	7,000
Benjamin Moore & Co.	2,951
OMNOVA Solutions Inc.	2,630

Fastest Growing* by Five-Year Sales Growth	(%)
LaPolla Industries, Inc.	44.8
PPG Industries, Inc.	12.6
NoFire Technologies, Inc.	11.8
RPM International Inc.	11.8
ADM Tronics Unlimited, Inc.	11.6
The Valspar Corporation	9.1
Rohm and Haas Company	8.3
The Sherwin-Williams Company	8.1
OMNOVA Solutions Inc.	5.0
E. I. du Pont de Nemours and Company	2.8

Fastest Growing* by Five-Year Employee Growth	(%)
OMNOVA Solutions Inc.	13.5
The Valspar Corporation	9.3
PPG Industries, Inc.	6.4
RPM International Inc.	6.2
The Sherwin-Williams Company	5.2

Top Public Companies by Market Value	($ mil.)
E. I. du Pont de Nemours and Company	22,830.1
Rohm and Haas Company	12,063.5
The Sherwin-Williams Company	6,992.8
PPG Industries, Inc.	6,966.9
RPM International Inc.	2,997.3

* These rates are compounded annualized increases and may have resulted from acquisitions or one time gains. If less than 6 years of data are available, growth is for the years available.

SOURCE: HOOVER'S, INC., DATABASE

Paper Products Manufacture

About 4,000 companies manufacture paper products in the US, with combined annual product revenue of $160 billion. Large companies include International Paper, Kimberly-Clark, Georgia-Pacific, and Avery Dennison. The industry is only moderately concentrated as a whole, but is highly concentrated in specific product segments, where the largest 50 companies often hold close to 70 percent of the market. A typical manufacturer of paper products has 150 employees, a single plant, and $40 million of annual sales.

Competitive Landscape

Demand is driven by general commercial activity and population growth. The profitability of individual companies depends on efficient operations, as products are sold mainly based on price. Big companies have advantages in distribution and can supply large customers. There are few economies of scale in manufacturing; large and small producers operate the same kinds of plants — large producers just have more of them. Small companies can compete successfully by making specialty products or serving a small geographical market. The industry is capital-intensive: average annual revenue per worker is close to $300,000, although the figure varies by product segment.

Products, Operations & Technology

Major product categories are paperboard containers, coated papers, tissue products, stationery, and paper bags. Paperboard containers include single-layer boxes and multi-layer corrugated boxes and account for about 30 percent of industry revenue. Coated papers account for 15 percent of revenue, tissue products for 5 percent, stationery for 5 percent. Tens of thousands of different paper products are produced, but most manufacturers concentrate on a very limited product line.

BUSINESS CHALLENGES

» Slow Demand Growth

Demand for paper products has been flat for a decade. Production of paper products was flat in the last 10 years, while total US industrial production increased 40 percent. Although demand for tissue products increased, demand for packaging products decreased as customers used less packaging per unit. Demand for business and printing paper has lagged as digital communications have become more popular.

» Volatile Raw Material Prices

Prices for wood pulp can fluctuate sharply from year to year, depending partly on energy costs; changes of 25 percent within a year aren't unusual. Paper manufacturers pass these costs to converters, which may be unable to pass all increases to customers.

» Competition from Canadian Imports

Imports of paper from Canada total about $13 billion per year. With a large supply of low-cost lumber to use, Canadian pulp and paper mills can often undercut prices of US manufacturers.

The manufacture of paper products is mainly a commodity business. Manufacturing processes are standardized, as are the products. Paper products are made in three stages. First, wood is turned into pulp at pulp mills. Then, pulp is turned into large rolls of commodity product at paper or paperboard mills. Finally, the large rolls are used to make finished products at converter plants. While the large national companies typically have vertically integrated operations (they own their own forests, cut their own trees, make their own pulp, etc.), most smaller companies operate only converter plants, buying the paper or paperboard raw material from the large producers.

Paper is made from cellulose tree fiber, by dicing and pounding wood, and treating it with water, chemicals, heat, and mechanical beaters to dissociate the fibers. The resulting wood pulp is spread onto large moving screens to drain, then flattened by rollers, dried, and collected in large rolls. Many different types and thicknesses of paper are produced according to the type of raw wood used, the pulping process, the chemicals used and added, and the rolling process. The kraft (which means "strength" in German) chemical pulping process is the most common manufacturing process, using soft woods (mainly pine) to produce paperboard and heavy paper (used in grocery bags, etc.). Paperboard can be used directly to make cardboard containers (often with one white side made from recycled office paper), or can be glued together (two flat outside layers of "linerboard" and an inner layer of "corrugated medium") to make containerboard, used to make corrugated boxes.

Because the finished product is inexpensive and bulky, transportation costs can be a significant part of the total delivered cost. Due to high transportation costs, small manufacturers can compete effectively with big producers in their local market. The effective sales area for corrugated boxes, for example, is only about 150 miles from the production plant.

Pulp and paper mills are capital-intensive operations that may operate just one giant machine. Converting plants are more labor-intensive because of the large number of different customer orders they typically handle. Production machinery, both at mills and converting plants, is large and expensive. A corrugated-box producer will typically operate a production line with several large specialized machines (corrugating, gluing, slotting, shearing, stitching, etc.) that can be adjusted to make boxes of many different grades and sizes.

The technology of making various paper products is well-known. Most R&D is oriented toward greater production efficiency rather than new products. Computer technology is used mainly to track the receipt and completion of customer orders.

Sales & Marketing

The major customers are commercial companies that use paper and boxes as containers to hold, deliver, and display products. Other customers are commercial printers, resellers of stationery, and wholesalers and retailers of tissue products for both the "at-home" consumer market and "away-from-home" commercial and industrial market. Sales are usually handled by an in-house sales force, within the geographical area serviced by the local paper mill or convert-

ing plant. National companies often have national accounts they supply from their various local locations.

Standard items may be sold through distributors. Most manufacturing at converting plants is done to order, since most customers have unique quality, size, volume, and printing requirements. While price is an important factor in sales, the timeliness and reliability of production and delivery are often more important, for what is usually a low-cost product.

Human Resources

Production workers in paper mills and converting plants are mainly machine operators. Wages are slightly above the national average. Working conditions have improved rapidly in the past decade. The industry injury rate is average.

A large number of workers in the industry are unionized. Wages have increased in line with the rest of the economy in recent years, even though overall employment in the industry has been flat.

Industry Employment Growth

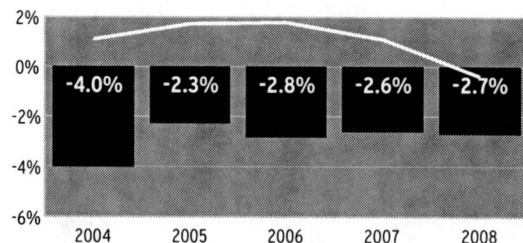

Average Hourly Earnings

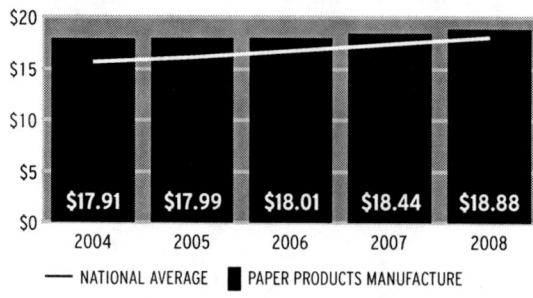

SOURCE: BUREAU OF LABOR STATISTICS

Call Preparation Questions

How is the company managing weak demand for basic paper products?

Demand for paper products has been flat for a decade.

How does the company protect against raw material price fluctuations?

Prices for wood pulp can fluctuate sharply from year to year, depending partly on energy costs; changes of 25 percent within a year aren't unusual.

How are imports impacting the company's markets?

Imports of paper from Canada total about $13 billion per year.

Does the company plan to invest in advanced printing capabilities?

Retailers of consumer products are demanding more sophisticated printing capabilities from packaging suppliers.

How is the company positioned to take advantage of growing demand for complex products, like laminated papers?

While demand for basic products like corrugated boxes has grown only slowly, markets for coated papers, labels, and papers laminated with other materials like metal foils, glues, and plastics have expanded more rapidly.

Web Links

American Forest & Paper Association

Good descriptions of paper products and production processes.
www.afandpa.org

Converting Industry.Com

Industry news. Extensive links to machinery suppliers.
www.convertingindustry.com/02industrynews.htm

Packaging Online

News.
www.packaging-online.com

Paper Age

Magazine with news, price indexes.
www.paperage.com

PaperBoard Packaging Council

Lobbying group.
www.ppcnet.org

Resource Information Systems Inc.

News, articles, industry links. Pulp and Paper Week Online.
www.risiinfo.com/pages/ind/pulp

Glossary of Acronyms

AF&PA — American Forest & Paper Association
CRM — customer relationship management
G-P — Georgia-Pacific
IP — International Paper
PPPC — Pulp and Paper Products Council
RFID — radio frequency identification

HOOVER'S TOP COMPANIES

Largest Companies by Sales	($ mil.)
International Paper Company	24,829.0
Kimberly-Clark Corporation	19,415.0
Smurfit-Stone Container Corporation	7,420.0
Avery Dennison Corporation	6,710.4
MeadWestvaco Corporation	6,637.0
Central National-Gottesman Inc.	3,000.0
Rock-Tenn Company	2,838.9
Packaging Corporation of America	2,316.0
NewPage Group Inc.	2,168.0
Georgia-Pacific LLC	—

Largest Employers	Employees
Kimberly-Clark Corporation	53,000
International Paper Company	51,500
Georgia-Pacific LLC	50,000
Avery Dennison Corporation	37,300
MeadWestvaco Corporation	24,000
Smurfit-Stone Container Corporation	22,700
Rock-Tenn Company	10,700
NewPage Group Inc.	8,500
Packaging Corporation of America	8,350
National Envelope Corporation	5,000

Fastest Growing* by Five-Year Sales Growth	(%)
NewPage Group Inc.	17.7
Orchids Paper Products Company	16.1
P. H. Glatfelter Company	15.9
Rock-Tenn Company	14.6
Central National-Gottesman Inc.	13.4
Schweitzer-Mauduit International, Inc.	7.3
Avery Dennison Corporation	7.1
Kimberly-Clark Corporation	6.2
Clearwater Paper Corporation	6.0

Fastest Growing* by Five-Year Employee Growth	(%)
NewPage Group Inc.	71.2
Avery Dennison Corporation	64.3
P. H. Glatfelter Company	11.8
Rock-Tenn Company	4.7
Appleton Papers Inc.	3.7
Central National-Gottesman Inc.	3.3
Packaging Corporation of America	1.1
Schweitzer-Mauduit International, Inc.	0.8

Top Public Companies by Market Value	($ mil.)
Kimberly-Clark Corporation	21,813.3
International Paper Company	5,044.5
Avery Dennison Corporation	3,101.5
Packaging Corporation of America	2,961.5
Smurfit-Stone Container Corporation	2,705.5

* These rates are compounded annualized increases and may have resulted from acquisitions or one time gains. If less than 6 years of data are available, growth is for the years available.

SOURCE: HOOVER'S, INC., DATABASE

Parking Facility Management

The parking facility management industry includes about 3,000 companies with combined annual revenue of over $8 billion. Major companies include Standard Parking, Apco System Parking, and Central Parking. The industry is concentrated: the top 50 companies have 75 percent of the market, although the vast majority of companies are small and operate a single parking facility generating about $600,000 in annual revenue.

The parking facility management industry provides temporary parking spaces for vehicles on an hourly, daily, weekly, or monthly basis, and doesn't include long-term vehicle storage.

Competitive Landscape

Demand is driven by the occupancy rates of commercial real estate: large buildings require parking spaces for commuters, customers, and related area industry. The profitability of individual companies depends on operational efficiency and customer service. Large companies have advantages in relationships with large property managers and owners, and economies of scale in operating efficiency. Small companies can compete effectively by catering to customer needs and operating a desirable location. The industry is labor-intensive: average annual revenue per employee for a typical company is less than $60,000.

Products, Operations & Technology

Major services are auto parking services in parking lots and garages. Ancillary services, such as oil changes, auto detailing, and dry cleaning pickup, are offered at many urban parking facilities, but their revenue is less than 5 percent of total industry revenue. Companies with facilities at airports frequently offer shuttle buses between the parking facility and airport terminal.

Parking facility companies generally operate through two arrangements: management con-

BUSINESS CHALLENGES

» Dependence on Commercial Real Estate Market

Occupancy in urban buildings is a major driver of the parking facility management industry, as higher occupancy yields more cars and higher collected fees. As building construction increases and occupancy rates rise, parking space demand and rates increase. Large clients are increasingly focused on financial performance and how parking revenues contribute to a building's value, so meeting occupancy goals is key to client retention.

» Reliance on Business, Tourist Travel

Many parking management companies have facilities at airports, hotels, and in downtown areas close to tourist destinations. Economic issues that hinder travel affect occupancy in these parking facilities. Companies with airport locations suffered post-9/11, as increased security reduced parking spaces and passenger volume. High energy prices increase the cost of both air and car travel, causing some businesses and vacationers to cut the number of trips.

» High Insurance Costs

Parking facility management companies buy comprehensive liability insurance to cover claims at their lots and garages. Property insurance covers damage or loss to owned or leased properties. Workers compensation and umbrella liability insurance are a normal cost of doing business. Due to the high cost of coverage, companies are typically responsible for a large deductible amount, such as the first $250,000 of any loss.

tracts or leases. Under management contracts, obtained through competitive bidding, companies receive a base monthly fee for managing the parking facility and additional fees for ancillary services. Companies may also receive incentives based on performance objectives. Revenue and expenses flow to the property owner. Contracts are generally for one to three years, may contain renewal clauses, and can usually be terminated without cause with 30 days notice. Under lease agreements, parking operators pay either a fixed annual rent, a percentage of parking collections, or a combination to the property owner. Parking companies collect all revenue and are responsible for operating expenses. Parking facility management companies sometimes own parking facilities, but ownership requires substantial capital investment.

Over 100 million parking spaces exist in the US, with about two-thirds in parking lots and garages. Costs for new parking facilities range from about $1,500 per space for surface facilities to about $7,500 per space for multi-level garages. Operating costs for parking facilities are primarily staffing, utilities, and equipment maintenance and repair. Staffing requirements include fee collection, maintenance and upkeep, customer services, and facility management.

About 90 percent of parking facility management companies operate a single facility; less than 5 percent operate more than 10, but these have an average of over 100 facilities. These large multi-facility firms generate about 40 percent more revenue per employee than single facility firms.

Technology increases customer convenience, reduces labor costs, and improves cash management at parking facilities. Automated gates and machines that print tickets, calculate fees, and collect receipts are common. Electronic funds transfer (EFT) options and bar code technology are increasing. Advanced information systems connect local offices and garages with parking management company central offices, making backoffice functions such as accounting, financial reporting, and marketing more efficient. Completely automated parking facilities have been introduced in the US.

Sales & Marketing

Typical customers are commercial real estate companies and managers of office buildings, airports, stadiums, shopping centers, and municipalities. Large companies have dedicated personnel for business development and customer service. Executives are often assigned to large national accounts. Office parking facilities often sign contracts with corporations to reserve a number of parking spaces for their employees.

Most companies use websites and direct mail for marketing, and may offer discounts or membership rates to corporate customers. Companies with airport or hotel locations may have promotional agreements with third-parties, particularly airlines or travel agencies.

Ancillary services can enhance parking facility customer service. Some facilities offer auto services such as oil changes, detailing, and car washes. Urban parking structures sometimes offer taxi dispatch and dry cleaning pickup, and airport locations often have shuttle services.

Consumer parking fees have risen steadily, about 4 percent annually over the past six years. Hourly fees are the norm at most parking facilities, although long-term facilities such as airport parking facilities have daily rates. Monthly rates are common in major urban locations that service commuters and residents.

Human Resources

Parking companies operating a single facility average about 12 employees. Typical personnel include cashiers, porters, valet attendants, maintenance staff, and managers. Most workers are relatively unskilled and average wages are below the national average. At some companies, up to a third of employees are unionized. Industry injury rates are about half the national average.

Industry Employment Growth

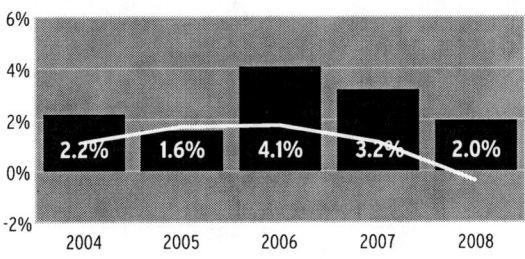

| 2004 | 2005 | 2006 | 2007 | 2008 |
| 2.2% | 1.6% | 4.1% | 3.2% | 2.0% |

Average Hourly Earnings

| 2004 | 2005 | 2006 | 2007 | 2008 |
| $10.29 | $9.89 | $9.86 | $10.08 | $10.86 |

— NATIONAL AVERAGE ■ PARKING FACILITY MANAGEMENT

SOURCE: BUREAU OF LABOR STATISTICS

Call Preparation Questions

How dependent is company revenue on office occupancy rates?

Occupancy in urban buildings is a major driver of the parking facility management industry, as higher occupancy yields more cars and higher collected fees.

How dependent is company revenue on travel volume?

Many parking management companies have facilities at airports, hotels, and in downtown areas close to tourist destinations.

What type of insurance does the company have?

Parking facility management companies buy comprehensive liability insurance to cover claims at their lots and garages.

What ancillary services does the company provide?

Adding services that complement parking, such as shuttle services, meter collection, valet parking, and auto servicing, can help parking facility managers deepen client relationships.

What trend has the company seen in outsourcing parking by property owners?

Historically, many property owners managed their parking facility internally.

Web Links

Canadian Parking Association

Information about Canadian parking industry.
www.canadianparking.ca

International Parking Institute

State association links, publications, regulations.
www.parking.org

National Parking Association

News, events.
www.parking-net.com

Parking Today

News snapshots, company updates, conferences.
www.parkingtoday.com

Security Management

Articles about parking lot security.
www.securitymanagement.com

Glossary of Acronyms

EFT — electronic funds transfer
MPS — mobile parking service
PCI DSS — Payment Card Industry Data Security Standard

HOOVER'S TOP COMPANIES

Largest Companies by Sales	($ mil.)
Central Parking Corporation	1,109.4
Standard Parking Corporation	700.8
Ace Parking Management, Inc.	370.0
Parking Company of America Management, LLC	29.8
Diamond Parking, Inc.	10.0

Largest Employers	Employees
Central Parking Corporation	18,940
Standard Parking Corporation	12,600
Ace Parking Management, Inc.	3,500
Diamond Parking, Inc.	800
Parking Company of America Management, LLC	700

Top Public Companies by Market Value	($ mil.)
Standard Parking Corporation	311.6

SOURCE: HOOVER'S, INC., DATABASE

Performing Arts Companies

The US performing arts industry includes about 9,000 companies with combined annual revenue of $11 billion. Major companies include the Metropolitan Opera Association; New York Shakespeare Festival Management (doing business as The Public Theater); Boston Symphony Orchestra; and San Francisco Ballet Association. Most companies are privately held or nonprofit, and include local, regional, and state orchestras, dance, and theater companies. The industry is fragmented: the 50 largest companies account for under 30 percent of revenue. Two-thirds of year-round performing arts companies have annual revenue under $500,000.

The industry provides live entertainment and includes about 3,000 theater companies; 200 dinner theaters; 200 opera and 600 dance companies; 4,600 musical groups and artists, including 850 symphonies and chamber music organizations; and 60 circuses. The industry doesn't include firms that primarily promote shows, sell tickets, or produce recorded entertainment.

Competitive Landscape

Personal income and leisure time drive demand for performing arts. The profitability of individual companies depends on producing performances that audiences want to see and on efficient operations. Large companies have advantages in marketing, fundraising, and attracting star performers. Small companies can compete effectively by specializing in new, unique, or popular works. The industry is highly labor-intensive: average annual revenue per worker is $90,000.

Products, Operations & Technology

Major products of the performing arts industry are admissions; entertainment contract fees; private contributions; royalty, licensing, and residual fees; and government grants. Admissions account for 40 percent of industry rev-

BUSINESS CHALLENGES

» Competition for Consumer Spending

As a discretionary spending item, attending performances depends on personal income and competes for the consumer dollar with other entertainment and pastimes. Primary competition for consumer spending comes from movies, TV, spectator and active sports, hobbies, and other personal interests. The performing arts industry is highly susceptible to economic downturns: in the last recession, industry employment, an indicator of demand, fell six times faster than the national average and took three years longer to recover.

» Dependence on Third-Party Funding

Performing arts companies depend on third-party sources for investment and supplemental funding, as revenue can't cover expenses. Corporate and individual sponsorships, foundation and government grants, and gifts help underwrite operations; private contributions account for 15 percent of industry revenue. Changes in corporate profits, the stock market, and government budgets are indicators of near-term financial support from private and public sources.

» Powerful Unions

Trade unions are powerful in the performing arts industry, due to their large membership and ability to call a strike, effectively bringing shows and theaters to a standstill. The Actors' Equity Association has over 46,000 members, including actors, singers, dancers, and stage managers, on whose behalf it negotiates contracts and working conditions with producers, theaters, and performing arts companies. A notable impasse between producers and the stagehand union led to a 19-day strike that stopped production of about 70 percent of New York's Broadway shows around Thanksgiving 2007.

enue; contract fees, 25 percent; and private contributions, 15 percent. Other revenue sources include food, beverage, and merchandise sales; facility rental; membership dues; and fees for entertainer management, advertising, and endorsements.

Performing arts companies prepare productions primarily for presentation to live audiences. Theater companies and dinner theaters account for 50 percent of industry revenue; musical groups and artists, about 40 percent; and dance companies, just under 5 percent. Companies create or license rights to plays, dances, songs, or other content. They recruit producers, third-party sponsors, and other sources of funding, including grants. Companies hire directors and conductors, performers, costume and set designers, and production crews either per project or on a seasonal or full-time basis. Companies may hire independent grant writers and outsource production and technical work to firms that provide stage, set-building, sound, lighting, or other specialized crews.

About 80 percent of performing arts companies operate to some degree year-round and about 45 percent have fewer than five employees. Ticket sales ("box-office receipts"); audience size; number of performances; and budget are major industry metrics. Most companies schedule a group of shows well in advance for each performance "season."

Auditions are the main way companies find performers, and rehearsals are the primary means to ensure quality performances. Companies interact with professional performers' agents or managers, who represent entertainers, find appropriate theatrical roles or music engagements, and negotiate on their clients' behalf. Through auditions, companies identify the primary performer for a theatrical role or musical position and a substitute (called an understudy, standby, swing, or cover), who can fill in as needed. Solo performers and some performing arts companies, particularly those that do road-shows, use booking agents to find and secure engagements ("gigs" in the music industry). Companies comply with unions' rules, which include minimum salaries and working conditions for members.

Most symphonies, operas, and theater companies are hierarchical organizations with executive boards and administrative and artistic or music directors, who run the operations, and affiliates, who provide financial support and volunteer. Many smaller organizations combine administrative and artistic responsibilities in a single job and operate somewhat differently than larger groups. An ensemble group's members stay together from season to season, usually share decision-making, and often are community-oriented. A repertory company has a single group of entertainers who perform a variety of shows; performers may be resident with the company or hired for the performance season. Summer stock groups generally present the same or similar repertoire each year, but with different — often new or young — performers each summer. Broadway producers run show-specific organizations, with upfront funding from investors.

Technology is increasingly important to performing arts companies for creative development, production, and business operations. Artistic directors rely on digital technology for sound, lighting, and special effects. Marketing, sales, and grant submission have online components. Company websites feature information about performers, works performed, schedules, favorable reviews, and tickets. Computers are essential to most companies' scheduling, capacity planning, ticket sales, and reporting. A current and correct view of profitability after each performance helps measure progress against budget, and contributes to decisions about canceling or continuing a show or the season.

Sales & Marketing

Customers vary greatly by age, income, and education, depending on type of performance and venue. Major sales channels are ticket agencies, travel agencies, and venue box offices. Many performing arts companies hire third-party booking agents to represent them in obtaining engagements. Performance companies sell advertising in program booklets ("playbills" in the theater segment) to help cover publication costs.

Major types of marketing include newspaper, magazine, radio, and TV advertising. Other marketing is through visibility from corporate sponsorships, fundraising events, benefit performances, and membership drives. Companies use affiliate memberships as fee-based loyalty programs: members receive special attention, such as discounted tickets, priority seating, and invitations to social events. The industry commonly uses third-party marketing companies and consultants.

Internet sales are increasingly important. Online sources include Ticketmaster and regional and local entertainment and ticketing websites. Many websites give consumers the option to print their tickets or receive them via standard mail or delivery services, for a fee.

Ticket prices range from $15 to over $100 per performance, depending on the company, key performers, and locale. Yearly theater or concert subscriptions can cost hundreds. Many companies discount tickets for students, seniors, groups, or corporate sponsors' employees. Processing fees and delivery can each add over 10 percent to the cost of a ticket. Ticket scalping is common in some cities and for popular performers and can drive a single ticket's street price into hundreds or thousands of dollars.

Human Resources

Professional performers typically have formal training or a college degree in their specialties and need to excel, because competition for roles and positions is intense. Management, conductors, producers, and directors generally have college degrees and those in artistic roles have experience as performers. Wages in the performing arts industry are more than 25 percent higher than the national average.

Personnel turnover is high, because most companies hire performers per project or per season. Industry injury rates are over 10 percent lower than the national average and consist mainly of sprains and strains, due to performers' positioning or movement. Trade unions are highly influential in the industry.

Industry Employment Growth

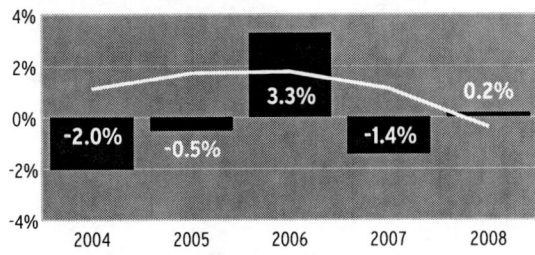

Average Hourly Earnings

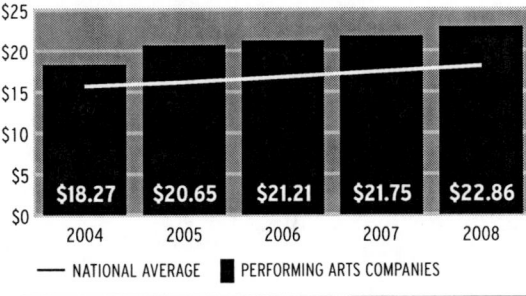

— NATIONAL AVERAGE ■ PERFORMING ARTS COMPANIES

SOURCE: BUREAU OF LABOR STATISTICS

Call Preparation Questions

How do changes in the economy affect attendance at the company's performances?

As a discretionary spending item, attending performances depends on personal income and competes for the consumer dollar with other entertainment and pastimes.

How important to the company are third-party investors and financial supporters?

Performing arts companies depend on third-party sources for investment and supplemental funding, as revenue can't cover expenses.

How do trade unions affect the company?

Trade unions are powerful in the performing arts industry, due to their large membership and ability to call a strike, effectively bringing shows and theaters to a standstill.

What opportunities does the company see to develop new audiences?

Opportunities exist to develop new audiences, especially as the population ages and retirees become the fastest-growing segment.

How important are new works for the company?

Leading-edge groups, often small in size and budget, have long included new works in their repertoire, but more companies are now doing so.

Web Links

Actors' Equity Association (AEA)

Trade union news, resources, casting calls.
www.actorsequity.org

American Association of Community Theater (AACT)

Resources, festivals for community theater groups.
www.aact.org

Association of Performing Arts Presenters

Advocacy initiatives for performing arts industry; news; "Inside Arts" magazine.
www.artspresenters.org/newsroom/pressreleases.cfm

Dance/USA

Statistics, resources, issues.
www.danceusa.org

League of American Orchestras

Statistics, resources, issues.
www.americanorchestras.org

National Endowment for the Arts (NEA)

News, funding for performing and other arts.
www.nea.gov

OPERA America

Information for companies, artists, audiences; links.
www.operaamerica.org

Professional Association of Canadian Theatres

Resources, advocacy, links.
www.pact.ca

Society of Stage Directors and Choreographers (SSDC)

News, strike lists for independent union.
www.ssdc.org

Theater Communications Group

News about not-for-profit theater.
www.tcg.org

Variety

News on music performers, groups, awards.
www.variety.com

Glossary of Acronyms

AACT — American Association of Community Theater
AEA — Actors' Equity Association
NEA — National Endowment for the Arts
SSDC — Society of Stage Directors and Choreographers

HOOVER'S TOP COMPANIES

Largest Employers	Employees
Los Angeles Philharmonic Association	2,000
The Shubert Foundation, Inc.	1,700
Metropolitan Opera Association, Inc.	1,500
The John F. Kennedy Center for the Performing Arts	1,144
Lyric Opera of Chicago	790
Lincoln Center for the Performing Arts, Inc.	525
Jujamcyn Theaters	473
On Stage Entertainment, Inc.	400
The Second City, Inc.	300
New York Philharmonic	200

SOURCE: HOOVER'S, INC., DATABASE

Personal Care Products Manufacturing

THIS INDUSTRY INCLUDES:

SIC CODES
2844   Perfumes, Cosmetics, and Other Toilet Preparations

NAICS CODES
325620   Toilet Preparation Manufacturing

The personal care products industry includes about 750 companies with combined annual revenue of $40 billion. Major companies include Procter & Gamble, Johnson & Johnson, and Estée Lauder. The industry is concentrated: the 50 largest firms account for nearly 70 percent of industry revenue.

This industry includes companies engaged primarily in preparing, blending, compounding, and packaging toilet preparations. Products produced include makeup, shampoo, creams and lotions, perfume, skin care products, sunscreen, mouthwash, and shaving products.

Competitive Landscape

Demand is driven by population growth and consumer preferences. The profitability of individual companies depends on product innovation, effective sales and marketing, and efficient operations. Large companies have scale advantages in purchasing, manufacturing, distribution, and marketing. Small companies can compete effectively by offering specialized products. The industry is capital-intensive: average annual revenue per worker is over $600,000.

Products, Operations & Technology

Major products include cosmetics, hair products, and creams and lotions. Cosmetics (makeup, deodorant, and nail products) are 33 percent of industry revenue; hair products, 25 percent; and creams and lotions, 21 percent. Other products include perfume (10 percent); mouthwashes (2 percent); and shaving preparations (2 percent).

Cosmetics, such as lipstick, follow current fashion trends and come in a wide variety of colors. Lipstick is made of dyes and pigments in a fragranced oil-wax base. Ingredients are melted separately, and then oils and solvents are ground together with desired color pigments. The manufacturing process includes three distinct steps: melting and mixing the lipstick, molding by

BUSINESS CHALLENGES

» Volatility of Raw Material Prices
Raw material price increases and competitive consumer price pressures squeeze margins for personal care products manufacturers. Suppliers pass price increases for surfactants, palm oil, chemical additives, plastic packaging, and other raw materials to finished goods manufacturers. At the same time, strong competition within the cosmetics industry forces manufacturers to absorb higher costs rather than increase retail prices.

» Demand Tied to Economic Cycle
Sales of high-end personal care products are susceptible to decreased consumer spending. Luxury items within the industry, such as high-end perfume, makeup, or skin care products, are particularly vulnerable to economic downturns. Consumers tend to reduce discretionary purchases and may switch to less expensive beauty products during tough economic times. Overall personal care products industry production declined during the last recession.

» Dependence on New Product Development
New products and innovation drive growth for personal care products companies. New products flood the market every year; in the prestige fragrance market, more than 200 products are introduced annually, a high percentage of which aren't financially successful. Products that are first to market and have a visible consumer benefit are most successful. All manufacturers invest heavily in new product development, but the effectiveness of these investments can vary widely.

pouring the mixture into the tube, and packaging the product for sale. Lipstick manufacturing can be highly automated, producing up to 2,400 tubes per hour, if it's a color or product in high demand; less popular colors are produced manually at 150 tubes per hour. Lipstick has strict quality control procedures, as it's the only ingested cosmetic product.

Hair products are initially created by cosmetic chemists in the laboratory, where they develop the product characteristics and performance attributes. Product characteristics are thickness, color, and fragrance. Performance attributes are cleaning capability and rinsibility.

Shampoo is composed of water (80 percent); detergent called surfactants; foam boosters; thickeners; conditioning agents; preservatives; and other additives. The shampoo manufacturing process involves compounding (following all formula instructions to make large batches of 3,000 gallons or more); mixing; testing quality; filling bottles; and packaging.

Cream and lotions, such as sunscreens, are made with both synthetic and natural ingredients; formulas must be approved by the FDA. Formulations for sunscreens are generally geared toward a specific SPF rating or the needs of a specific consumer group, such as children. Water is purified and then mixed with other ingredients, generally purchased externally, to match the specific formula. Sunscreen is then pumped from mixing tanks through stainless steel pipes into molded plastic containers. The process is highly automated.

Raw materials, readily available from numerous sources, are generally bought externally. Raw materials include both natural ingredients found in various plant and animal sources, and synthetic materials produced and formulated by raw material suppliers. Purchased raw materials include fragrance oils, detergents, active ingredients, additives, and basic chemicals. New ingredients are continually developed by raw material suppliers and, with advances in polymers, silicones, and surfactants, are becoming less irritating and expensive and more environmentally friendly.

Extensive consumer testing assesses demand for new products and ensures compliance with consumer safety regulations. Testing includes evaluating irritation potential for skin and eyes; toxicity (both ingested and inhaled); and reactions with chemicals and to light. Products with efficacy claims, such as antiperspirants, sunscreens, and anti-aging skin creams, are classified as drugs and must go through more extensive testing to get FDA approval.

Information systems support all business processes including product development, marketing, sales, order processing, production, distribution, and finance. Supply chain management systems help optimize inventory levels and reduce delivery times among manufacturers, suppliers, and retailers.

Sales & Marketing

Typical customers are department stores, mass market retailers, direct sales, specialty retailers, and professional hair and beauty salons. Large companies use an in-house sales force, and their own product distribution. Large and small companies use independent distributors.

Major marketing vehicles include TV, magazine, and newspaper advertising; direct mail; and instore promotions. Because brand awareness is critical to the success of many personal care products, the industry spends heavily on advertising and promotions.

Prestige brands are premium-priced products found in high-end department stores, such as Nordstrom, Macy's, and Bloomingdales. Prestige brands include Estée Lauder, Clinique, Lancôme, and Chanel. Mass market brands tend to be lower priced and are found in wide distribution in chain drugstores, grocery stores, and mass merchandisers. Mass market brands include Clairol, Revlon, L'Oréal, and Maybelline. Beauty stores may carry private-label products, along with professional or salon-only brands, such as Matrix and Redken. Direct sales brands are available only through a direct sales force and include Avon, Mary Kay, and Arbonne.

Internet sales are beginning to affect the traditional markets; however, the inability to simulate actual color or smell over the Internet inhibits sales of many products.

Personal care product prices vary widely between mass market and prestige brands. Lipstick prices range from about $5 to $22; shampoo, $3 to about $15; and cream and lotion prices can vary from around $4 to $60.

Human Resources

Personal care product manufacturing is highly automated. Labor productivity has increased nearly 50 percent in the last five years, significantly higher than the 18 percent increase for the US economy as a whole.

Most production jobs require few skills due to the high level of automation. The average hourly wage for production workers is below average for all US workers. The high level of automation has resulted in injury rates less than half the US average for all production workers.

R&D engineers and scientists have advanced degrees and are highly sought after in the industry.

Industry Employment Growth

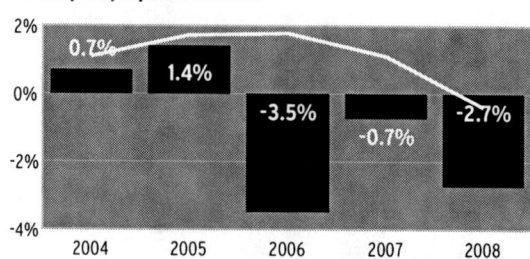

Average Hourly Earnings

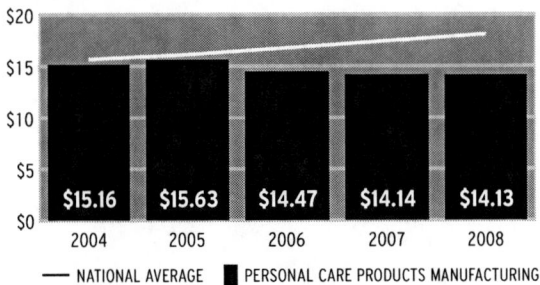

	2004	2005	2006	2007	2008
PERSONAL CARE PRODUCTS MANUFACTURING	$15.16	$15.63	$14.47	$14.14	$14.13

— NATIONAL AVERAGE ■ PERSONAL CARE PRODUCTS MANUFACTURING

SOURCE: BUREAU OF LABOR STATISTICS

Call Preparation Questions

How vulnerable is the company to changes in consumer spending?

Sales of high-end personal care products are susceptible to decreased consumer spending.

How successful is the company's new product development?

New products and innovation drive growth for personal care products companies.

How is the company taking advantage of the aging US population?

The aging US population creates a larger consumer segment for anti-aging face, hair, and body care products.

Web Links

Consumer Healthcare Products Association

Association for manufacturers and distributors of nonprescription, OTC medicines and nutritional supplements.
www.chpa-info.org/ChpaPortal

Cosmetic Ingredient Review

Reviews and assesses the safety of ingredients used in cosmetics.
www.cir-safety.org

Cosmetic News

Industry news website, targeted at all beauty professionals.
www.cosmeticnews.com

Personal Care Products Council

Trade association for cosmetic and personal care products industry.
www.personalcarecouncil.org

Glossary of Acronyms

CIR — Cosmetic Ingredient Review
CTFA — Cosmetic, Toiletry and Fragrance Association
INCI — International Nomenclature Cosmetic Ingredient
PCPC — Personal Care Products Council
REACH — Registration, Evaluation, and Authorization of Chemicals

HOOVER'S TOP COMPANIES

Largest Companies by Sales	($ mil.)
The Procter & Gamble Company	83,503.0
Johnson & Johnson	63,747.0
Avon Products, Inc.	10,690.1
The Estée Lauder Companies Inc.	7,910.8
Alberto-Culver Company	1,443.5
Revlon, Inc.	1,346.8
Nu Skin Enterprises, Inc.	1,247.7
Elizabeth Arden, Inc.	1,141.1
Melaleuca, Inc.	859.0
Inter Parfums, Inc.	389.6

Largest Employers	Employees
The Procter & Gamble Company	138,000
Johnson & Johnson	118,700
Avon Products, Inc.	42,000
The Estée Lauder Companies Inc.	32,000
Nu Skin Enterprises, Inc.	8,700
Revlon, Inc.	5,600
Alberto-Culver Company	3,800
Elizabeth Arden, Inc.	2,650
Melaleuca, Inc.	2,400
Inter Parfums, Inc.	248

Fastest Growing* by Five-Year Sales Growth	(%)
Inter Parfums, Inc.	24.5
The Female Health Company	23.0
Physicians Formula Holdings, Inc.	20.7
Parlux Fragrances, Inc.	16.3
Natural Health Trends Corp.	15.6
The Procter & Gamble Company	14.0
Melaleuca, Inc.	9.3
Avon Products, Inc.	9.2
Johnson & Johnson	8.8
Elizabeth Arden, Inc.	8.7

Fastest Growing* by Five-Year Employee Growth	(%)
Inter Parfums, Inc.	19.2
Elizabeth Arden, Inc.	13.8
Physicians Formula Holdings, Inc.	2.0
Johnson & Johnson	1.4

Top Public Companies by Market Value	($ mil.)
The Procter & Gamble Company	184,419.5
Johnson & Johnson	162,163.1
Avon Products, Inc.	10,244.0
The Estée Lauder Companies Inc.	5,427.2
Alberto-Culver Company	2,665.8

* These rates are compounded annualized increases and may have resulted from acquisitions or one time gains. If less than 6 years of data are available, growth is for the years available.

SOURCE: HOOVER'S, INC., DATABASE

Personnel Staffing Agencies

THIS INDUSTRY INCLUDES:

SIC CODES

7363   Help Supply Services

NAICS CODES

5613   Employment Services

In the US, over 40,000 personnel staffing offices generate total annual revenue of more than $130 billion. Large firms include Adecco, Manpower, Randstad, and Kelly Services. The average agency has one office, $2 million in annual sales, and 15 employees. Despite strong consolidation in recent years, the industry remains fairly fragmented: the 50 largest firms hold about 40 percent of the market. Agencies with multiple offices may have agency-owned branches, independently owned franchise offices, or licensed area-representative offices.

Competitive Landscape

Job growth drives demand for the personnel staffing industry. The profitability of individual companies depends on good marketing. Large companies enjoy economies of scale in marketing and back-office operations. Small companies can compete successfully by specializing in an industry or by job function.

Products, Operations & Technology

The industry is divided into three major segments: permanent placement of workers, temporary placement of workers, or leasing of full-time workers. In terms of revenue, the temporary and leasing segments dominate, with about $70 billion and $55 billion of annual revenue, respectively, while permanent placement produces only $5 billion of annual revenue. However, these figures are misleading because temporary and leasing agencies count as revenue the wages and benefits they collect from employers and pass along to workers, while revenue for placement agencies only includes placement fees.

Placement agencies find workers to fill permanent positions at customer companies. These agencies may specialize in placing senior managers (executive recruiters, headhunters); midlevel managers; technical workers; or clerical and other support workers. Temporary help

BUSINESS CHALLENGES

» Revenue Depends on Employment Growth

The revenue of personnel agencies depends on the number of jobs they fill, which in turn depends on economic growth. During economic slowdowns, many client companies stop hiring altogether. In years of good economic growth, the number of jobs in the US economy grows 1 to 2 percent per year. During the last recession, job growth was zero.

» Competition from Internet Job Sites

Internet employment sites expand companies' ability to find workers without the help of traditional agencies. Personnel agencies often work as intermediaries, helping employers accurately describe job openings and screen candidates. Increasing the use of sophisticated, automated job description and candidate-screening tools could make many traditional functions of personnel agencies obsolete.

» Competition from Customers

To avoid large personnel agency fees, big companies may use in-house personnel staff, current employee referrals, or human resources consulting companies to find and hire new personnel. Because personnel agencies typically charge a fee of 20 to 30 percent of the annual salary of a new worker, companies with many jobs to fill have a large financial incentive to avoid agencies.

agencies provide workers for customers for limited periods, often to substitute for absent permanent workers or to help during periods of peak demand. These workers, who are employees of the temporary help agency, may be clerical, technical, or industrial. Employee leasing agencies, sometimes known as professional employer organizations (PEOs), provide workers on long-term or permanent assignment. While working under customer management, leased workers are employees of the leasing agency.

The two major activities of personnel agencies are recruiting potential employees and potential employers. Agencies advertise for and solicit workers through networks of contacts, newspaper advertising, and increasingly on the Internet, and interview, test, and counsel workers before sending them to the customer for approval. Ninety percent of staffing agencies provide some sort of training, especially data entry and basic computer skills. They also provide pre-employment screening, which can include skills tests, drug screenings, and criminal checks, to ensure that applicants are qualified.

Temporary help agencies recruit workers who want a succession of part-time assignments, and often provide extensive training in specific skills such as word processing and spreadsheet use, and other specific computer applications. PEOs have greatly expanded their scope in the past decade by contracting with customers to run entire functions for them, typically complicated ones like HR, but they also work in accounting, manufacturing, and production. In many cases, the PEO hires the customer's existing workers and leases them back to the customer. As employers, both temporary agencies and PEOs are liable for withholding taxes, unemployment and social security payments, worker compensation, and other liabilities.

The personnel placement industry has been radically changed by the Internet. Many companies list available positions with one or several Internet personnel sites like monster.com or jobs.com, and on their own site. Personnel agencies operate their own sites and often still work as intermediaries by helping employers accurately describe job openings and screening candidates who submit applications. However, as sophisticated automated job description and candidate screening tools become available, many traditional functions of personnel agencies will become obsolete.

Sales & Marketing

Major end-use customers are commercial, financial, and industrial corporations. Marketing involves direct sales' presentations, referrals from existing clients, radio commercials, and print ads. Agencies compete both for customers and workers. Depending on market supply and demand at any given time, agencies may allocate more resources either to finding potential employers or potential workers.

Permanent placement agencies work either on a retainer or a contingency basis (often 30 percent of annual salary). Clients may retain an agency for a specific job search or on contract for a specific period. Temporary agencies charge customers a fixed price per hour or a standard markup on prevailing hourly rates. Leasing agencies typically charge a fee related to the total compensation of workers.

Human Resources

Industry wages are low, the personnel turnover rate of permanent staff is low, and the absenteeism and safety record is about average. Wages are 20 percent below the national average for all workers. The annual personnel turnover rate is half the national average for private industry. The absenteeism and safety record are slightly better than average.

Industry Employment Growth

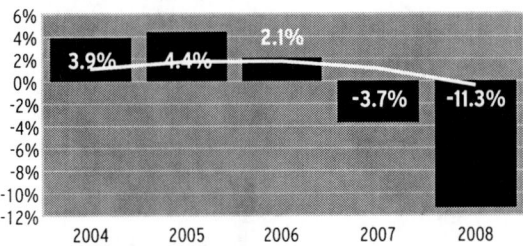

Average Hourly Earnings

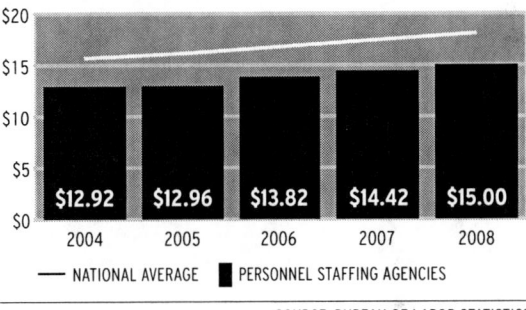

SOURCE: BUREAU OF LABOR STATISTICS

Call Preparation Questions

How much is the agency's business affected by economic cycles?

The revenue of personnel agencies depends on the number of jobs they fill, which in turn depends on economic growth.

How does the company combat competition from Internet agencies?

Internet employment sites expand companies' ability to find workers without the help of traditional agencies.

How does the agency win business from companies that use mainly in-house staff to find new hires?

To avoid large personnel agency fees, big companies may use in-house personnel staff, current employee referrals, or human resources consulting companies to find and hire new personnel.

Is the agency able to outsource HR functions for customers?

The trends of outsourcing entire departments and dependence on temporary and leased workers will expand opportunities for personnel agencies.

What steps has the agency taken to take advantage of better online technology?

New online technology is improving staffing efficiency.

Web Links

American Staffing Association

Reports.
www.americanstaffing.net

CareerBuilder.com

Internet staffing site.
www.careerbuilder.com

ExecuNet

Trends in executive marketplace.
www.execunet.com/r_trends.cfm

Jobs.com

Internet staffing site.
www.jobs.com

Monster.com

Internet staffing site.
www.monster.com

National Association of Professional Employer Organizations

Industry news.
www.napeo.org

Staffing Industry Analysts, Inc.

News.
www.staffingindustry.com

Glossary of Acronyms

CRM — customer relation management
DOL — Department of Labor
EEOC — Equal Employment Opportunity Commission
IDC — International Data Corporation
IT — information technology
NABE — National Association of Business Economics
PEO — Professional Employer Organization

HOOVER'S TOP COMPANIES

Largest Companies by Sales	($ mil.)
Adecco S.A.	30,955.9
Manpower Inc.	21,552.8
Allegis Group, Inc.	5,570.0
Kelly Services, Inc.	5,517.3
Robert Half International Inc.	4,600.5
MPS Group, Inc.	2,171.8
Spherion Corporation	2,017.1
Express Employment Professionals	2,000.0
TrueBlue, Inc.	1,384.3

Largest Employers	Employees
Manpower Inc.	4,033,000
Kelly Services, Inc.	760,000
Express Employment Professionals	375,000
Robert Half International Inc.	272,300
Spherion Corporation	258,000
Adecco S.A.	37,000
Medical Staffing Network Holdings, Inc.	29,150
Barrett Business Services, Inc.	27,400
MPS Group, Inc.	22,200
On Assignment, Inc.	20,350

Fastest Growing* by Five-Year Sales Growth	(%)
Command Center, Inc.	218.7
Dice Holdings, Inc.	105.7
Fortune Industries, Inc.	59.2
Insight Global, Inc.	58.9
Global Technology Resources, Inc.	57.4
CareerBuilder LLC	48.0
EDI Specialists, Inc.	46.9
Kenexa Corporation	43.1
Resources Connection, Inc.	33.0
ICONMA, LLC	31.6

Fastest Growing* by Five-Year Employee Growth	(%)
ICONMA, LLC	93.1
Global Technology Resources, Inc.	49.0
Barrett Business Services, Inc.	48.4
Kenexa Corporation	40.8
CareerBuilder LLC	38.1
Resources Connection, Inc.	24.3
Dice Holdings, Inc.	23.5
EDI Specialists, Inc.	22.5
Allegis Group, Inc.	16.8
Manpower Inc.	11.4

Top Public Companies by Market Value	($ mil.)
Robert Half International Inc.	3,142.6
Manpower Inc.	2,650.0
Resources Connection, Inc.	938.2
MPS Group, Inc.	922.5
TrueBlue, Inc.	396.6

* These rates are compounded annualized increases and may have resulted from acquisitions or one time gains. If less than 6 years of data are available, growth is for the years available.

SOURCE: HOOVER'S, INC., DATABASE

Pest Control Services

About 10,000 companies provide residential, commercial and industrial pest control services in the US, with combined annual revenue of about $7 billion. The largest pest control companies are Terminix and Orkin. The rest are mainly privately owned regional and local firms. The industry is fragmented: the 50 largest firms control less than 50 percent of the market. A typical pest control firm has 20 employees, one office location, and annual revenue close to $2 million.

Competitive Landscape

Demand is driven by home sales and the occupancy of commercial and industrial properties. The profitability of individual companies depends on providing good service. Large companies benefit from brand recognition and economies of scale in advertising, franchising or backoffice operations. Small companies can compete successfully because large companies have no advantage in providing good service. Average annual revenue per employee is about $85,000.

Products, Operations & Technology

Pest control firms — also called pest control operators (PCOs) — are in the business of identifying the presence of pests and applying poisonous chemicals to kill them. Firms hire and train employees to detect and identify pests, and to choose and apply chemicals, which typically involves certification.

Companies buy chemicals and other control systems from distributors or directly from the large number of chemical manufacturers. Chemicals are identified as general- or restricted-use, which are the more dangerous chemicals that can be applied only by a certified worker ("applicator"). Labor costs are the largest operating expense for pest control firms.

The two distinct markets are residential, and commercial and industrial. In the residential

BUSINESS CHALLENGES

» Revenue Depends on Home Sales, Commercial Occupancy

Local house sales and commercial construction and occupancy rates drive demand for pest control services. Homeowners order services due mainly to pre-sale property inspections; they and commercial building managers order services for ongoing prevention and control. Annual home sales are often near 6 million, but can drop 10 percent during a recession or when mortgage rates rise. Commercial work, which is steadier than residential, is partly affected by building vacancy rates, which rose above 20 percent in some markets in the 2001 recession.

» Tougher Pesticide Restrictions

Due to public concern and government review of agricultural pesticides, the range of available insecticides and pesticides is decreasing. The reevaluation of all pesticides as part of the 1996 Food Quality Protection Act will probably lead to tighter restrictions or outright bans on some chemicals used in pest control, particularly organophosphates. While the EPA's focus is on agricultural chemicals, many are also used in residential and commercial pest control. Technological developments in alternative pest control include ultrasonic, thermographic, and acoustic detection devices to find pests, such as termites, cockroaches, and mice.

» Customer Dissatisfaction

Customers often switch extermination services if they find pests are still present, or if they don't feel they're getting the best customer service. Customers expect pest control companies to eliminate pests, but exterminators can rarely produce total elimination. Homeowners who suffer termite damage often make financial claims against pest control companies. Almost 70 percent of customers stop using a pest control company due to an attitude of indifference from a company employee, according to Techletter.

market, firms provide services to individual homeowners and concentrate on controlling termites. In the commercial and industrial market, firms provide services to apartment buildings, office buildings, institutions, hotels, and to the food industry — with a concentration on controlling rodents, cockroaches and flies. Larger companies serve both markets, but small companies typically operate in the residential market. Services to commercial customers often involve regular preventative measures like spraying and inspection. Services to homeowners usually involve just a single job unless a bait system is used.

The two major methods for dealing with termites are chemical barrier and bait. The traditional chemical barrier system involves injecting liquid chemicals (termiticides) into the ground around a house's foundation, thereby isolating the house from any underground termite nests, and directly applying chemicals to any infested areas inside the house. Newer bait systems consist of a number of plastic stations, initially containing wood bait, which workers insert into the ground around a building and inspect at regular intervals, usually monthly. If inspection reveals termite activity, a worker replaces the wood with termite bait, which consists of any of a number of slow-acting chemicals that will eventually poison the termites. Termites take the poison back to their nest, where they pass the poison to other termites through exchange of secretions and food, eventually killing the entire nest.

Homeowners usually prefer bait systems, because they use a much smaller volume of toxic chemicals. The disadvantage of bait systems is that they are only effective after termites find the stations, which may take a while even if termites are present in the soil. Bait systems may cost over $1,000 to install and $20 to $30 per month to monitor.

Methods for dealing with other types of pests are generally straightforward. For insects, workers often spray contact poisons on surfaces that pests might cross. For rodents, workers leave poisoned food in containers that only rodents can access. Typically the rodents digest the food and leave the area in search of water, perishing outdoors.

Sales & Marketing

Major end-user customers are commercial/industrial building managers and residential homeowners. Services to commercial customers are provided under annual con-

tracts. Residential contracts may cover monthly bait system checks, quarterly insect spraying, and yearly termite inspection, for example, but many residential services are one-time jobs.

Marketing to the residential and commercial segments is different: an internal sales force calls on commercial customers, while advertising and professional contacts influence residential customers. Large companies may advertise on TV and radio, but most companies use the Yellow Pages. Real estate brokers and inspectors are key sources of referrals. Commercial sales are often made based on price for a specified schedule of services. Residential sales also involve price, but reputation is important, which is why the large national companies have been able to grow. Various types of guarantees are an important part of residential and commercial add-on sales.

Human Resources

The three grades of state certification for employees in pest control are technician, applicator, and supervisor, all which require training, work experience, and an exam. No special education is required, but the unpleasant and physically demanding nature of the work reduces the pool of potential employees.

The average wage is slightly lower than the national average, as is typical in many service industries, but is quite a bit higher than minimum wage, due to the skilled nature of the occupation. Wages increased rapidly in recent years, reflecting strong demand as a result of record home sales.

Industry Employment Growth

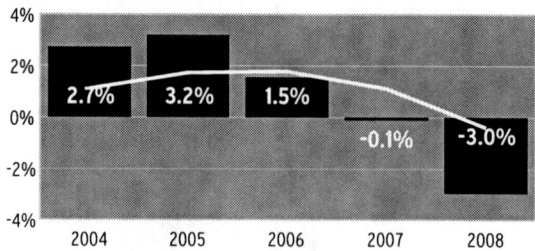

Average Hourly Earnings

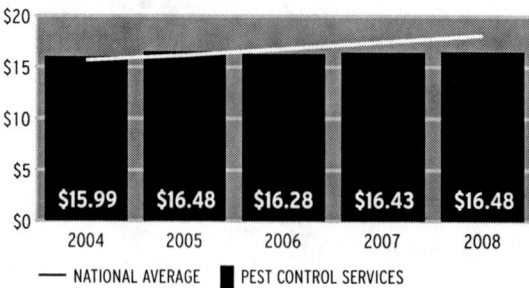

— NATIONAL AVERAGE ■ PEST CONTROL SERVICES

SOURCE: BUREAU OF LABOR STATISTICS

Call Preparation Questions

How dependent is the company on home sales or commercial construction for new customers?

Local house sales and commercial construction and occupancy rates drive demand for pest control services.

How are tighter pesticide regulations affecting company use of chemicals?

Due to public concern and government review of agricultural pesticides, the range of available insecticides and pesticides is decreasing.

What strategies does the company use to retain customers?

Customers often switch extermination services if they find pests are still present, or if they don't feel they're getting the best customer service.

What opportunities does the HACCP program create for the company?

The Hazard Analysis and Critical Control Point (HACCP) systems, which the FDA is implementing with the food industry to reduce contamination, will probably produce more work for pest control firms.

What impact does the use of less toxic pesticides have on the company?

To decrease toxicity, the industry is moving toward less toxic chemicals, applied more often.

Web Links

Association of American Pest Control Officials

aapco.ceris.purdue.edu

Bio-Integral Resource Center

Resource for information about sustainable, environmentally friendly IPM.
www.birc.org

EPA Office of Pesticide Programs

Good information about current regulatory actions and trends.
www.epa.gov/pesticides

National Pest Management Association

Industry association.
www.pestworld.org

National Pesticide Information Center

Links to manufacturers and state regulators.
npic.orst.edu

Orkin

Pest control company.
www.orkin.com

Pest Control Portal

Excellent industry links.
www.pestcontrolportal.com

Pest Control Technology Magazine

News. Industry issues.
www.pctonline.com

Terminix

Pest control company.
www.terminix.com

Glossary of Acronyms

BLS — Bureau of Labor Statistics
CB — Census Bureau
ESA — Endangered Species Act
FIFRA — Federal Insecticide, Fungicide, and Rodenticide Act
FQPA — Food Quality Protection Act
HACCP — Hazard Analysis and Critical Control Point
IPM — integrated pest management
NPMA — National Pest Management Association
PCO — pest control operator

HOOVER'S TOP COMPANIES

Largest Companies by Sales	($ mil.)
Rollins, Inc. (Orkin)	1,020.6
Sunair Services (Middleton Pest Control)	56.6
Copesan Services, Inc.	56.0
The Terminix International Company L.P.	43.1
Swisher International, Inc.	41.8

Largest Employers	Employees
Rollins, Inc. (Orkin)	8,400
The Terminix International Company L.P.	1,043
Sunair Services (Middleton Pest Control)	538
Copesan Services, Inc.	250
Swisher International, Inc.	65

Fastest Growing* by Five-Year Sales Growth	(%)
Sunair Services (Middleton Pest Control)	57.2
Rollins, Inc. (Orkin)	8.6

Fastest Growing* by Five-Year Employee Growth	(%)
Sunair Services (Middleton Pest Control)	6.1
Rollins, Inc. (Orkin)	5.0

Top Public Companies by Market Value	($ mil.)
Rollins, Inc. (Orkin)	1,808.7
Sunair Services (Middleton Pest Control)	26.6

* These rates are compounded annualized increases and may have resulted from acquisitions or one time gains. If less than 6 years of data are available, growth is for the years available.

SOURCE: HOOVER'S, INC., DATABASE

Pet Food Manufacture

The US pet food manufacturing industry includes about 175 companies with combined annual revenue of $11 billion. Large companies include divisions of Nestlé (Nestlé Purina PetCare Company); Procter & Gamble (Iams); Colgate-Palmolive (Science Diet and Prescription Diet); and Del Monte (9Lives, Gravy Train, Milk-Bone, and Meow Mix). The industry is highly concentrated: the 50 largest companies hold almost 100 percent of the market.

Competitive Landscape

Pet ownership drives demand. The profitability of individual companies depends heavily on effective marketing. Large companies have advantages of scale in manufacturing, marketing, and distribution. Small companies can compete effectively by offering specialized products or by serving a local market. Pet food manufacturing is capital-intensive; average annual revenue per employee is over $700,000. The pet food industry is highly competitive, with large companies spending millions on marketing to maintain share.

Products, Operations & Technology

Major products are dry dog food, canned cat food, dry cat food, and canned dog food. Dry dog food accounts for about 50 percent of industry revenue, canned cat food for 20 percent. Dry foods include semi-moist products. Canned cat foods may be fish-based or meat-based. Other types of pet food include pet treats and food for birds; fish (fresh and saltwater); small animals; and reptiles.

Pet food manufacturing is a highly automated process that makes low-cost products. Ingredients are mixed, cooked, and canned, or may be extruded under heat and pressure, shaped, dried, and packaged. Dies allow manufacturers to change the shape of products. Flavorings and additional nutrients for dried foods are often sprayed on after extrusion.

BUSINESS CHALLENGES

» Fewer Dog Owners

Demand for dog food may level, as fewer new owners choose dogs as pets. A projected decrease in the number of households with children, the demographic most likely to own dogs, may further decrease the population of potential dog owners. And increasing urbanization doesn't favor ownership of large dogs, the biggest consumers of pet food.

» Slow Growth in Wholesale Prices

Heavy competition within the pet food industry has limited wholesale price growth. Wholesale prices increased just 10 percent in the last 10 years. Growth in private-label pet food, which can be highly profitable to retailers, has contributed to low prices.

» Escalating Marketing Costs

The cost of introducing and maintaining brand names in the intensely competitive packaged goods environment continues to grow. Retailers charge heavy distribution allowances for new products and demand funds for price promotion. Small companies have difficulty competing due to heavy spending by national brand names.

Major raw materials are grains (corn, wheat, soybeans); chicken meal; meat meal; fish meal; fats and oils; metal cans; and plastic or paper bags. Because many of the ingredients are waste products (like chicken feathers) from human food manufacturing operations, costs are low. Companies buy most ingredients from commodity companies, grain cooperatives, and processors of meat byproducts (rendering plants).

Packaging represents almost 30 percent of costs. Technology in plastic material has allowed some companies to use pouches and plastic film, according to Food and Drug Packaging. Plastic pouches are faster to sterilize and easier to open than cans. Plastic film bags can be resealed, and are more durable than paper bags.

Although more expensive than paper, plastic packaging can be cut into different shapes and offers improved graphics.

Pet food companies invest significant amounts of capital in manufacturing equipment. Large plants can produce multiple products, and require skilled engineers and maintenance staff. Small companies, without the financial resources, may use contract manufacturers, and have higher costs. Plants need to be close to both suppliers of raw materials and distributors to reduce freight costs.

Finished products are usually shipped from warehouses to customer distribution centers, retail stores, or regional pet supply distributors. Small companies often ship via a common carrier like UPS. Distributor relationships are important for small companies that may lack the resources to service a large customer base. Protecting a company's position with a distributor can be a challenge, as the average pet supply distributor stocks over 12,000 products.

R&D focuses on nutrition for pets. Scientists and nutritionists adjust product formulation, and experiment with various ingredients, vitamins, and minerals, to find different ways of providing nutritional and health benefits. Companies often use third-party laboratories to test reformulated product or new products on live pets.

Computer systems control the production machinery and manage warehouse operations. Companies may use electronic data interchange (EDI) to buy ingredients or process orders from customers. Bar codes identify and track products.

Sales & Marketing

Major customers are supermarket chains, pet supply distributors, mass merchandisers, warehouse clubs, large pet supply retailers like PetSmart and PETCO, and veterinary chains. Large companies use an in-house sales force; smaller companies may use independent food brokers. Trade shows are important for smaller companies.

Marketing and promotion are through TV and magazine ads, coupons, direct mail, and in-store promotion. Websites may offer product information and promotions. Branding is

important. Companies may produce brands targeted at different types of outlets, including supermarket brands like Alpo and Purina, premium brands like Eukanuba and Nutro, and low-priced private-label brands.

Retail pricing is market-driven, due to the relatively low cost of production. While a 20-lb bag of premium dry dog food can retail for $20, a comparable supermarket brand costs $10, and a private-label brand costs $7. Periodically, companies give retailers allowances, known as trade promotions, to promote specific products and reduce prices.

Human Resources

Most pet food production personnel need minimal skills and are paid accordingly. Hourly pay is slightly below the national average, and fringe benefits run about 25 percent of total compensation. The industry injury rate is slightly higher than the national average.

Industry Employment Growth

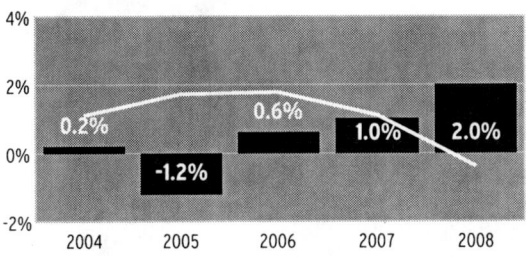

Average Hourly Earnings

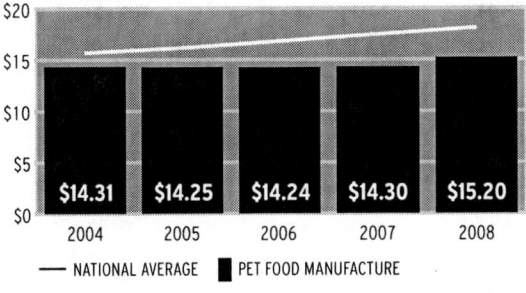

— NATIONAL AVERAGE ■ PET FOOD MANUFACTURE

SOURCE: BUREAU OF LABOR STATISTICS

Call Preparation Questions

How has limited growth in the population of dog owners affected the company?

Demand for dog food may level, as fewer new owners choose dogs as pets.

How has slow growth in wholesale prices affected the company's profitability?

Heavy competition within the pet food industry has limited wholesale price growth.

How have rising marketing costs affected the company?

The cost of introducing and maintaining brand names in the intensely competitive packaged goods environment continues to grow.

How is the company taking advantage of the growth in premium products that provide health and nutrition benefits?

Premium pet foods are 35 percent of the market and expected to reach 40 percent by 2008.

What plans does the company have to enter or expand into international markets?

Pet ownership continues to increase in Europe and developing countries.

Web Links

American Pet Products Association

Pet ownership and spending statistics.
www.americanpetproducts.org

Pet Age

Pet food retail and distributor information.
www.petage.com

Pet Food Institute

Pet food sales statistics and trends, pet ownership trends.
www.petfoodinstitute.org

Pet Industry Distributors Association

Distributor trade association.
www.pida.org

Pet Product News

Industry trends and statistics.
www.petproductnews.com

Glossary of Acronyms

APPMA — American Pet Products Manufacturers Association

API — Animal Protection Institute

BSE — bovine spongiform encephalopathy (mad cow disease)

EDI — electronic data interchange

OTA — Organic Trade Association

PFI — Pet Food Institute

PIDA — Pet Industry Distributors Association

HOOVER'S TOP COMPANIES

Largest Employers	Employees
Nestlé Purina PetCare Company	7,000
Doane Pet Care Company	2,202
The Hartz Mountain Corporation	1,600
United Pet Group, Inc.	1,215
The Iams Company	1,000
Blue Seal Feeds, Inc.	500
Texas Farm Products Company	300
American Nutrition, Inc.	150
Old Mother Hubbard, Inc.	136
Redbarn Pet Products, Inc.	100

SOURCE: HOOVER'S, INC., DATABASE

Pet Stores

The US pet and pet supply store industry includes about 7,500 stores with combined annual revenue of almost $8 billion. Major companies include PetSmart, PETCO Animal Supplies Stores, Pet Supplies "Plus," and Petland. The industry is concentrated: the 50 largest companies hold 60 percent of sales.

Competitive Landscape

Pet ownership drives demand, and spending generally resists economic cycles. Profitability for individual companies depends on the ability to generate store traffic and effective merchandising. Large companies offer low prices and wide selections of both products and services. Small companies compete effectively by serving a local market, selling unique products, offering specialized services, or providing pet expertise. The industry is labor-intensive, with annual revenue per employee of about $100,000. Revenue per employee for small, independent pet stores is significantly lower than for major chains. Competitors include grocery stores, warehouse clubs, mass merchandisers, Internet retailers, and some veterinary clinics.

Products, Operations & Technology

Major product segments include pet food, pet supplies, aquarium products and fish, and pets. Pet food accounts for 40 percent of sales, pet supplies for 40 percent, aquarium products and fish for 10 percent, and pets for 5 percent. The pet food segment primarily consists of dog and cat food. Pet supplies include pet toys, collars and leashes, cages and habitats, and vitamins and supplements. Types of pets sold include dogs, cats, fresh and saltwater fish, birds, reptiles, and small animals (mostly hamsters and gerbils).

Pet stores include national chains, franchises, and independent retailers. National chains operate a "superstore" format, which can exceed 20,000 square feet. Pet superstores are located in high traffic areas, usually in large strip malls, co-anchored by other strong superstores. Pet store franchises vary in size, but generally have smaller stores of about 8,000 square feet. Smaller stores allow franchises to locate in smaller shopping centers, closer to neighborhoods. Independent pet stores serve small markets, and average 3,000 square feet.

Pet superstores generate about $3 million of revenue annually, with sales per square foot about $200. A typical pet store franchise has

BUSINESS CHALLENGES

» Low Growth in Key Segments of Pet Ownership

Lack of growth in dog ownership will affect overall demand for pet supplies. Dogs drive pet food consumption, and dog owners spend more on supplies than any other pet owners. Increasing urbanization, while conducive to owning cats and fish, makes dog ownership difficult, and the number of households with children, the demographic most likely to own dogs, is expected to decline through 2010.

» Slow Growth in Retail Prices

Retail prices for pets and pet supplies increased just over 4 percent from 2002 to 2005, well below the inflation rate. Industrywide discounting and growth of private-label products for dog and cat food have suppressed retail prices. Low-priced imports have driven overall retail prices down for pet accessories. Declining pet ownership and slow growth in retail pricing will eventually affect profitability.

» Competition from Alternative Channels

Pet stores face intense competition from mass merchandisers, warehouse clubs, grocery stores, and Internet retailers. Mass merchandisers and warehouse clubs offer lower prices on pet food, and represent almost 40 percent of pet product sales. Grocery stores offer convenience, and Internet retailers offer a wide range of supplies at extremely competitive prices. Recognizing the profitability of pet products, even hardware stores are establishing pet sections.

$2 million of annual revenue, or $250 per square foot. Smaller independent pet stores generally have revenue under $1 million, with sales per square foot under $200.

Pet superstores carry large inventories, and can offer almost 13,000 different products. Superstores may offer veterinary services, grooming, and obedience classes. Pet store franchises let independent owners customize inventory for a local market, with large franchises capable of offering 10,000 different products. Both chains and franchises offer private label products. Independent pet stores may carry unique inventory, like exotic animals (pythons, chinchillas, bearded dragons) or organic pet food. Most pet stores are known for selling premium pet foods, which are generally not available through grocery stores and mass merchandisers due to manufacturer restrictions.

Chains and franchises buy large quantities of key products like dog and cat food directly from manufacturers at deep discounts. Independent pet stores purchase directly from smaller manufacturers or distributors. Pet stores typically mark up dog and cat food between 20 and 30 percent; other pet foods and supplies are marked up between 80 and 90 percent. Trade shows are an extremely important source of information, since the pet supply industry is highly fragmented.

Many pet stores must provide care and maintenance for live animals. Some pets are highly perishable or require special care and feeding. In general, independent pet stores generate a higher percentage of sales from live pets than do pet superstores.

Chains and franchises employ computerized inventory management systems to track tens of thousands of items from thousands of different suppliers. Independent pet stores also use computers to track how fast items move. Chains may also use electronic data interchange (EDI) to automate the purchasing process. Radio frequency identification (RFID) improves the efficiency of PetSmart's distribution system.

Sales & Marketing

The typical pet store customer is a family with children with higher-than-average income. Over half of US households own a pet; the most popular are dogs, cats, or fish.

The primary marketing and promotional vehicles include TV, print, and radio advertising, direct mail, and newspaper circulars. To generate store traffic, pet stores may hold special events like pet adoption drives. Major chains offer customer loyalty programs that offer discounts and rebates. Loyalty programs also allow companies to collect consumer information and perform market research. Independent pet stores rely heavily on referrals from other customers and repeat business.

Some companies have Internet retail websites or link to complementary websites. Other companies provide information only about store locations, products, services, or pet care. Internet operations are especially important to highly specialized independent pet stores, which may serve customers outside their local market area. Sales of pet food are limited over the Internet due to the high shipping charges customers must pay.

Pet stores discount dog and cat food to drive store traffic and generate incremental sales from complementary pet supplies with higher margins. Pet store dog and cat food pricing is typically competitive with that of grocery stores, but higher than mass merchandisers. Some chains price lower than grocery stores. In addition, pet stores may offer competitive pricing on veterinary services, boarding, and grooming.

Human Resources

Most pet store employees require minimum skills and are paid accordingly. Wages are about a third less than for the average US worker. Pet stores rely greatly on part-time help. About half of all employees at both PetSmart and PETCO are part-time. A high employee turnover rate of 50 percent for all retail workers makes hiring and training an ongoing part of operations. Employees of highly specialized independent pet stores, especially stores selling exotic animals or expensive aquarium systems, require more extensive knowledge and training.

Industry Employment Growth

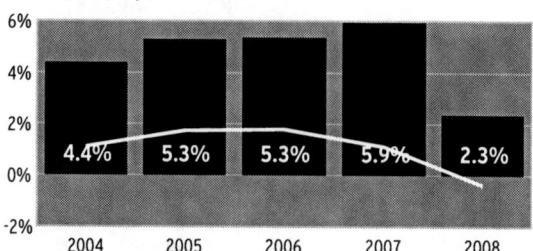

Average Hourly Earnings

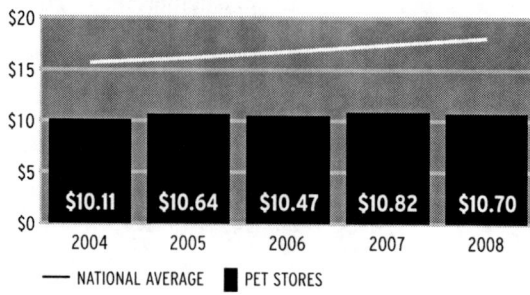

SOURCE: BUREAU OF LABOR STATISTICS

Call Preparation Questions

How have changes in the ownership of different pets affected demand in the company's market?

Lack of growth in dog ownership will affect overall demand for pet supplies.

How has slow growth in retail pricing of pets and pet supplies affected company performance?

Retail prices for pets and pet supplies increased just over 4 percent from 2002 to 2005, well below the inflation rate.

How does the company compete with other types of retailers selling the same products?

Pet stores face intense competition from mass merchandisers, warehouse clubs, grocery stores, and Internet retailers.

What role do pet services have in the company's business?

Busy owners look for services providing convenience, like pet day care or walking.

How important are specialty pets or products for the company?

With the declining number of pet stores offering live animals, opportunities exist to sell specific pets and provide expertise on pet care.

Web Links

American Pet Products Association

Trade association providing basic industry statistics.
www.americanpetproducts.org

Humane Society

Animal protection organization, information on care and treatment of pets.
www.hsus.org

Pet Age

Industry trends, issues annual retailer report focusing on independent pet stores.
www.petage.com

Pet Business

Retail industry trends.
www.petbusiness.com

Pet Industry Distributors Association

Trade association for pet product wholesalers and distributors. Good supply chain information.
www.pida.org

Glossary of Acronyms

APPMA — American Pet Products Manufacturers Association
EDI — electronic data interchange
PIDA — Pet Industry Distributors Association
PIJAC — Pet Industry Joint Advisory Council
RFID — radio frequency identification

HOOVER'S TOP COMPANIES

Largest Companies by Sales	($ mil.)
PetSmart, Inc.	4,672.7
PETCO Animal Supplies, Inc.	2,400.0
PetMed Express, Inc.	188.3
Pet Supermarket, Inc.	161.0
PetCareRx.com	60.0
KV Vet Supply Company	14.6
Petland, Inc.	7.9

Largest Employers	Employees
PetSmart, Inc.	43,000
PETCO Animal Supplies, Inc.	20,100
Pet Supermarket, Inc.	800
PetMed Express, Inc.	216
PetCareRx.com	100
KV Vet Supply Company	100

Fastest Growing* by Five-Year Sales Growth	(%)
PetMed Express, Inc.	27.9
PetSmart, Inc.	11.6

Fastest Growing* by Five-Year Employee Growth	(%)
PetSmart, Inc.	12.8
PetMed Express, Inc.	9.5

Top Public Companies by Market Value	($ mil.)
PetSmart, Inc.	3,070.4
PetMed Express, Inc.	263.2

* These rates are compounded annualized increases and may have resulted from acquisitions or one time gains. If less than 6 years of data are available, growth is for the years available.

SOURCE: HOOVER'S, INC., DATABASE

Petroleum Refining

About 145 petroleum refineries operate in the US, owned by 60 companies, with combined annual revenue of $160 billion. Large refiners include Valero, ConocoPhillips, ExxonMobil, BP, and Chevron. Annual revenue fluctuates substantially because of the shifting price of crude oil. The industry is highly concentrated: the five largest refiners hold about 50 percent of all US refining capacity.

Competitive Landscape

Demand, largely driven by US consumption of gas and diesel fuel, has been relatively flat in recent years. The profitability of refineries depends on efficient operations and the best mixture of products. Although there are significant economies of scale in refinery operations, a small refinery can compete effectively with large ones if it's located in a favorable market area, or if it produces specialty products that are in high demand. The industry is highly automated: average annual revenue per worker is over $3 million.

Products, Operations & Technology

Major products are gas, 60 percent by volume; diesel fuel, 20 percent; propane, 7 percent; heating oil, 5 percent; and jet fuel, 3 percent. Diesel fuel and heating oil are jointly called "distillates." A refinery uses crude oil as raw material. The output of a particular refinery depends on the grade of crude oil it uses and the downstream processing operations it has installed.

Refineries come in many different sizes, from 5,000 barrels per calendar day (BBL/CD) of distillation capacity up to 500,000. A typical refinery has a capacity between 50,000 and 150,000 BBL/CD.

Crude oil is composed mainly of hydrocarbons of various weights. When the crude oil is heated, the different hydrocarbons boil at different temperatures and can therefore be drawn

BUSINESS CHALLENGES

» Long-Term US Demand Flat

US gas consumption has been essentially flat in recent years, rising less than 1 percent per year. Demand for heating oil has decreased as homeowners switch to natural gas. Concerns about foreign fuel dependency and environmental issues have prompted actions to increase fuel efficiency in vehicles.

» Crude Oil Prices, Availability Uncertain

The average refinery cost of crude oil in the US is volatile: prices can change 50 percent within a year. Imports provide over 60 percent of US crude oil consumption and are vulnerable to political disruptions and transportation delays. To ensure uninterrupted operations, refiners may have to hold larger raw material inventories, increasing their susceptibility to market price changes.

» Long-Term Low Industry Profitability

Low gross margins in refining operations (often less than 5 percent), combined with the high debt levels typical in this capital-intensive industry, often produce losses for refiners. In general, refiners are more profitable when gas prices are rising.

off and re-liquefied. Refineries are rated according to this crude distillation capacity. Since lighter hydrocarbons are usually more valuable than heavy ones, most refineries further process the middle and heavy distillates in various "downstream" operations that extract further light hydrocarbons ("cracking" long hydrocarbons into smaller pieces) and turn heavier ones into usable products. Common downstream operations include vacuum distillation, catalytic cracking, hydrocracking, and coking. In addition, to remove the sulfur that is a common contaminant in crude oil, many refineries use a hydrodesulfurizing process. All of these processes occur in separate production units that are interconnected and that generally operate on a continuous-flow basis. Most refineries also operate gasoline-blending processes and have significant storage facilities. Small refineries may run only a distillation operation, with no downstream processing.

Crude oil may arrive at a refinery by pipeline, oceangoing tanker, barge, truck, or tank car. The composition of the crude oil (gravity and sulfur content) partly determines its cost. Light (high-gravity) and intermediate crude oils, like West Texas Intermediate (WTI) and Nigerian Bonny Light, have a high natural yield of light and middle distillates. Crude oils from the Middle East, including Saudi Arabian Light, have a lower yield of light and middle distillates. Crude oils from Mexico and Venezuela are generally heavy and have a high sulfur content. (Low-sulfur crude oil is called "sweet"; high-sulfur oil is "sour.") The difference in price between light and heavy crude oils is the "light/heavy spread," and is important to refineries that can efficiently process heavy crude oil.

Crude oil costs vary according to origin because of transportation costs and the grade of the oil. US refinery prices for WTI crude are usually lower than prices for oil from Nigeria, and higher than oil from Saudi Arabia, Mexico, and Venezuela. Crude oil costs can change as much as 50 percent within 12 months.

While large integrated oil companies, like ExxonMobil and BP, supply their refineries with oil from their own exploration and production operations, many refiners must buy oil from other producers or wholesalers. To ensure adequate supplies, anticipated need is filled under short or long-term supply contracts (that typically contain a price adjustment mechanism) and through purchases on the spot market. In view of the volatility of crude oil prices, refiners may engage in futures contracts on commodity markets like the New York Mercantile Exchange. Refiners are very sensitive to market prices of crude oil and can adjust their refineries to accept oil of varying grades, depending on availability and comparative prices.

Sales & Marketing

Refiners sell to retailers, wholesalers, and industrial end-users, but may also operate their own gas stations. Many gas stations also operate convenience stores that sell non-gasoline merchandise. (See the Industry Profile, "Convenience Stores.") Because most refinery products are commodities, sales are made based mainly on price. Refiners discount price for customers who take a large volume of product. Supply contracts with customers typically specify minimum product volumes and last three to ten

years. Actual prices charged depend mainly on the acquisition costs of crude oil.

Refineries are usually located close to customer markets, because it's cheaper to move crude oil than to move highly flammable products like gas and jet fuel. Products may be distributed to customers via pipeline, rail tank cars, trucks, barges, and oceangoing tankers. Refiners usually own storage tanks and operate terminal facilities.

Human Resources

Many employees in refineries have special technical or engineering skills and are accordingly well paid. Fringe benefits average an extra 30 percent of payroll. The average large refinery has about 600 workers, a number that has been steadily falling in recent years, as centralized computer control of refinery operations has become more common and as refineries have become larger. Refinery workers are among the safest in US industry, with an annual rate of illness and injury per 100 workers of only 2.5 cases (total US industry average 6.3).

Industry Employment Growth

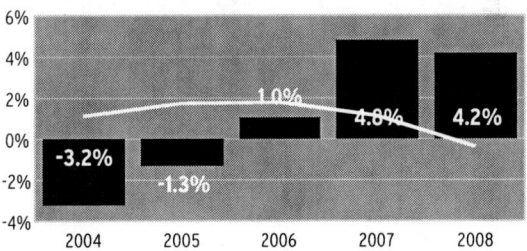

Average Hourly Earnings

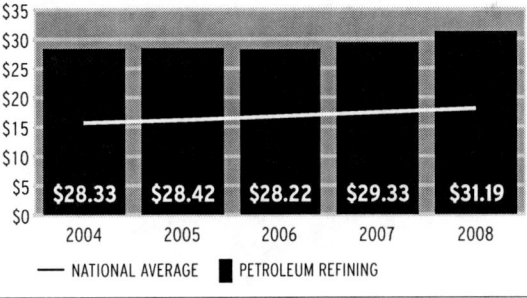

SOURCE: BUREAU OF LABOR STATISTICS

Call Preparation Questions

How has the company managed flat demand for petroleum products?

US gas consumption has been essentially flat in recent years, rising less than 1 percent per year.

How does the company protect profit margins?

Low gross margins in refining operations (often less than 5 percent), combined with the high debt levels typical in this capital-intensive industry, often produce losses for refiners.

What plans does the company have to produce more specialty products?

Some refiners are producing a higher mix of specialty products like waxes, lubricants, and chemical feedstocks, products that generally have higher margins than gas and heating oil.

Does the company plan to upgrade or add new processing technology to its refineries?

Better knowledge of the chemistry of refining continues to produce new refining processes that use energy and raw materials more efficiently.

Web Links

American Petroleum Institute

Policy issues.

api-ec.api.org

Energy Information Administration

Excellent description of refining processes. Detailed industry statistics and prices.

www.eia.doe.gov/pub/oil_gas/petroleum/
analysis_publications/oil_market_basics

National Petrochemical & Refiners Association

Lobbying organization. Industry issues.

www.npradc.org

National Petroleum Council

Advisory council to the Secretary of Energy. Policy issues.

www.npc.org

Oil & Gas Journal

Industry news. Annual subscription to industry statistics for $50.

ogj.pennnet.com/home.cfm

Short-Term Energy Outlook

Department of Energy's (DOE) energy forecast.

www.eia.doe.gov/emeu/steo/pub/contents.html

WorldOil.com

News and statistics about oil exploration and production.

www.worldoil.com

Glossary of Acronyms

API — American Petroleum Institute

BBL/CD — barrels per calendar day

BPD — barrels per day

CERCLA — Comprehensive Environmental Response, Compensation, and Liability Act

EIA — Energy Information Administration

MTBE — methyl tertiary butyl ether

PADD — Petroleum Administration Defense District

RFG — reformulated gasoline

UST — underground storage tank

HOOVER'S TOP COMPANIES

Largest Companies by Sales	($ mil.)
Exxon Mobil Corporation	477,359.0
BP, p.l.c.	361,143.0
Chevron Corporation	273,005.0
ConocoPhillips	246,182.0
Valero Energy Corporation	119,114.0
Koch Industries, Inc.	98,000.0
Hess Corporation	41,209.0
Tesoro Corporation	28,309.0
Western Refining, Inc.	10,725.6

Largest Employers	Employees
BP, p.l.c.	97,000
Exxon Mobil Corporation	83,000
Koch Industries, Inc.	80,000
Chevron Corporation	65,000
ConocoPhillips	32,600
Valero Energy Corporation	21,651
Hess Corporation	13,300
Sinclair Oil Corporation	7,000
Tesoro Corporation	5,500

Fastest Growing* by Five-Year Sales Growth	(%)
Rentech, Inc.	90.1
Western Refining, Inc.	59.8
Alon USA Energy, Inc.	34.0
Holly Corporation	33.1
CVR Energy, Inc.	31.8
Ergon, Inc.	26.6
Tesoro Corporation	26.2
Valero Energy Corporation	25.7
Sinclair Oil Corporation	25.0
Arabian American Development Company	24.2

Fastest Growing* by Five-Year Employee Growth	(%)
Western Refining, Inc.	657.0
Alon USA Energy, Inc.	38.1
Koch Industries, Inc.	36.3
Calumet Specialty Products Partners, L.P.	35.2
Tesoro Corporation	18.3
Hess Corporation	7.0
Holly Corporation	5.5
Arabian American Development Company	5.1
Ergon, Inc.	4.6
Chevron Corporation	1.4

Top Public Companies by Market Value	($ mil.)
Exxon Mobil Corporation	397,234.1
Chevron Corporation	148,253.0
ConocoPhillips	78,783.6
Hess Corporation	17,493.8
Valero Energy Corporation	11,170.8

* These rates are compounded annualized increases and may have resulted from acquisitions or one time gains. If less than 6 years of data are available, growth is for the years available.

SOURCE: HOOVER'S, INC., DATABASE

Petroleum Wholesale Distribution

The wholesale distribution of petroleum products in the US includes about 5,300 companies with annual revenue of around $300 billion. Revenue can vary significantly from year to year because the price of crude oil can vary by 50 percent within a year. Major companies include SemGroup, Global Partners, Colonial Group, and Apex Oil. The industry is highly concentrated: the 50 largest companies hold more than 70 percent of the market. A typical wholesaler has annual revenue between $1 and $25 million.

Competitive Landscape

Demand for petroleum comes mainly from auto and truck use and home heating. Profitability is determined by the spread between purchase price and selling price and on the volume of product. Most companies are local and operate a single "bulk station" (tank farm), although the large companies may operate a dozen facilities and serve several states. There are economies of scale because large wholesale purchasers generally can negotiate bigger price discounts from suppliers, and because the fixed cost of bulk holding facilities can be spread over a larger number of gallons.

Products, Operations & Technology

Products include gas, diesel fuel, propane, heating oil, jet fuel, kerosene, and lubricants. Gas accounts for 60 percent of volume, diesel fuel for 20 percent, propane for 7 percent, and heating oil for 5 percent. Diesel fuel and heating oil are collectively called "no. 2 distillates." Petroleum distributors, also called jobbers or marketers, buy petroleum products from oil refiners and resell them to residential, industrial, or commercial consumers like gas stations, convenience stores, trucking companies, and farming operations. Large retail customers often bypass wholesalers and buy directly from oil companies.

BUSINESS CHALLENGES

» Long-Term US Demand Flat

US gas consumption has been essentially flat in recent years, rising an average 1 percent a year. Demand for heating oil has decreased as homeowners switch to natural gas. Concerns about foreign fuel dependency and environmental issues are prompting actions to increase fuel efficiency in vehicles, potentially reducing future US demand for gas.

» Petroleum Prices Can Be Volatile

Because of changing crude oil prices, constraints in refining capacity, and changing retail demand, wholesale prices for heating oil and gas often vary 50 percent during the year. Rapid changes in product costs require wholesalers to frequently adjust consumer prices and the value of their inventory with hedging activities.

» Competition from Suppliers

Wholesalers compete with the distribution/retail operations of the large oil companies. Although some large companies have shed their retail gasoline chains in recent years to concentrate on production and refining, others have aggressively expanded their retail operations.

Wholesale distributors operate "bulk plants" (tank farms) from which they distribute product to customers. They may also distribute products directly from their suppliers' "rack" or regional pipeline terminal; about 50 percent of all gasoline is distributed straight from the rack. Improvements in distribution technology allow some distributors to deliver a greater volume of gasoline directly from the rack, avoiding the risk and expense of holding their own inventory. Distributors usually own and operate a fleet of delivery trucks, although outsourcing the transportation from rack to customer is common. The average wholesaler sells approximately 12 million gallons of petroleum products per year. About 60 percent of distributors sell both motor fuels and heating oil.

Some distributors are "quasi-wholesale" because they also sell gasoline at retail. Wholesalers may own and operate c-stores or other gasoline operations. Major oil companies own less than 20 percent of all service stations in the US; the rest are owned by independent owners and petroleum distributors. Some distributors retail petroleum by supplying and owning the pumps, underground storage tanks (USTs), and other equipment used by independent c-stores, then sharing in the gasoline profits under what are called special purpose leases.

Sales & Marketing

Sales are through supply contracts with customers that specify approximate or minimum volumes but usually not price. New customers are acquired through sales calls, telemarketing, direct mail, newspaper advertising and Yellow Pages' advertising. Referrals from realtors can be an important source of new residential customers.

Petroleum products are commodities in the sense that there are a limited number of formulations, many of which can be used interchangeably. Prices can fluctuate greatly based on changing supply and demand, which are affected by world economic and political conditions. Prices from suppliers are usually quoted as "rack" prices, which vary across the country according to local refining and pipeline transportation costs. Local wholesale prices charged to customers mainly consist of rack prices and delivery costs.

Wholesalers frequently have multiyear supply contracts with suppliers that specify minimum quantities and provide financial incentives for higher levels of purchases.

Human Resources

A large number of workers in petroleum distribution are truck drivers who have special skills and are accordingly well-paid. Because of changing demand for products, drivers are sometimes in short supply. Turnover among truckers in general is high, but is probably lower among employees of smaller distributors. Much of the work associated with scheduling deliveries involves skills with computer operations.

Industry Employment Growth

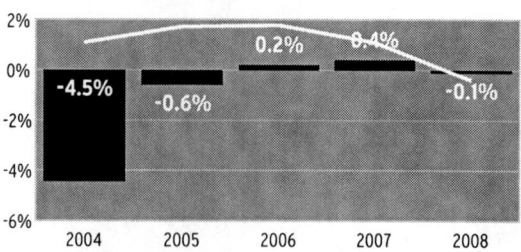

Average Hourly Earnings

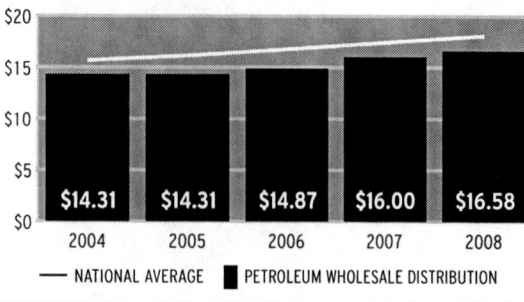

— NATIONAL AVERAGE ■ PETROLEUM WHOLESALE DISTRIBUTION

SOURCE: BUREAU OF LABOR STATISTICS

Call Preparation Questions

How is the company mitigating relatively flat demand for petroleum?

US gas consumption has been essentially flat in recent years, rising an average 1 percent a year.

How does the company protect itself from fluctuating petroleum prices and supplies?

Because of changing crude oil prices, constraints in refining capacity, and changing retail demand, wholesale prices for heating oil and gas often vary 50 percent during the year.

How does the company compete with petroleum producers that supply the same markets?

Wholesalers compete with the distribution/retail operations of the large oil companies.

What opportunities does the company see in providing pump maintenance or repair?

Petroleum distributors frequently sell services to customers, including maintenance and repair of pumps and furnaces.

What advantages does diversification provide the distributor?

Large distributors that distribute multiple brands can gain a competitive edge.

Web Links

Alexander's Gas & Oil Connections

News, trends, calendar, information on exploration and production.
www.gasandoil.com/goc

American Petroleum Institute

News, research, consumer information, and more.
api-ec.api.org

Energy Information Administration

Industry supply, consumption and pricing information.
www.eia.doe.gov

Energy Information Administration – Short-Term Energy Outlook

From the US Department of Energy.
www.eia.doe.gov/emeu/steo/pub/contents.html

Environmental Protection Agency – Office of Underground Storage Tanks

In-depth information about the EPA's standards for USTs.
www.epa.gov/OUST

National Petroleum News

Industry news.
www.npnweb.com

Oil & Gas Journal

Petroleum news, oil and gas technology, energy data for exploration, drilling, pipeline, and production.
ogj.pennnet.com/home.cfm

Oil and Gas Online

Daily news and product updates, information on manufacturing, technology, equipment, supplies, and discussion forums, online chat, newsletter and software.
www.oilandgasonline.com

Petroleum Marketers Association of America

Industry resources, links, and excellent legislative news.
www.pmaa.org

Petroleum Marketing Monthly

Updated information, from US Petroleum page.
www.eia.doe.gov/oil_gas/petroleum/
data_publications/petroleum_marketing_monthly/
pmm.html

WorldOil.com

US and world statistics on oil production, oil supply, monthly gas prices and trends, geophysical activity, rotary drilling and workover rigs.
worldoil.com/InfoCenter/statistics_main.asp

Glossary of Acronyms

API — American Petroleum Institute
BPD — barrels per day
EIA — Energy Information Administration
MTBE — methyl tertiary butyl ether
UST — underground storage tank

HOOVER'S TOP COMPANIES

Largest Companies by Sales	($ mil.)
World Fuel Services Corporation	18,509.4
SemGroup, L.P.	14,200.0
Transammonia, Inc.	8,339.4
Global Partners LP	6,757.8
Colonial Group Inc.	6,200.0
Mansfield Oil Company	5,100.0
Apex Oil Company, Inc.	5,000.0
Center Oil Company	4,900.0
Delek US Holdings, Inc.	4,615.2
Gulf Oil Limited Partnership	—

Largest Employers	Employees
Delek US Holdings, Inc.	3,708
SemGroup, L.P.	2,272
Alon Brands, Inc.	2,014
Oxbow Corporation	1,200
Magellan Midstream Partners, L.P.	1,127
NuStar GP Holdings, LLC	1,104
NuStar Energy L.P.	1,104
Colonial Group Inc.	1,100
World Fuel Services Corporation	916
TransMontaigne Partners L.P.	776

Fastest Growing* by Five-Year Sales Growth	(%)
NuStar GP Holdings, LLC	130.4
Titan Global Holdings, Inc.	110.2
NuStar Energy L.P.	92.8
Oxbow Corporation	61.7
Mansfield Oil Company	55.8
Delek US Holdings, Inc.	52.3
World Fuel Services Corporation	47.4
Martin Midstream Partners L.P.	44.5
TransMontaigne Partners L.P.	32.1
Clean Energy Fuels Corp.	26.3

Fastest Growing* by Five-Year Employee Growth	(%)
Oxbow Corporation	22.5
SemGroup, L.P.	21.4
World Fuel Services Corporation	19.0
Delek US Holdings, Inc.	18.6
Global Partners LP	15.6
Martin Midstream Partners L.P.	15.4
Mansfield Oil Company	13.8
Holly Energy Partners, L.P.	10.2
TransMontaigne Partners L.P.	5.1

Top Public Companies by Market Value	($ mil.)
Buckeye Partners, L.P.	2,258.9
NuStar Energy L.P.	2,236.2
Magellan Midstream Partners, L.P.	2,016.3
NuStar GP Holdings, LLC	1,410.6
Delek US Holdings, Inc.	284.0

* These rates are compounded annualized increases and may have resulted from acquisitions or one time gains. If less than 6 years of data are available, growth is for the years available.

SOURCE: HOOVER'S, INC., DATABASE

Pharmaceutical Manufacture and Sale

About 1,500 companies in the US manufacture and market medicinal drugs, with combined annual US revenue over $200 billion. Large US manufacturers include Merck, Pfizer, Bristol-Myers Squibb, Abbott, and Eli Lilly. The industry is highly concentrated: the 50 largest companies control more than 80 percent of the market.

The traditional drug manufacturing industry increasingly overlaps with the biotechnology industry, which is a source of many new medical treatments. To a large extent, traditional drug manufacturers are becoming development and marketing companies that acquire new drugs from smaller research companies.

Competitive Landscape

The industry is marked by rapid advances in scientific knowledge that produce ever-more effective medicines. Profitability is determined mainly by the ability to discover new drugs. The industry is dominated by the large manufacturers/marketers that manufacture drugs, have large research operations, and also have large clinical testing, marketing, and distribution capabilities. Small companies are mainly research operations or manufacturers of nonprescription products. Because of the high value of the product, average revenue per employee is a very high $600,000.

Products, Operations & Technology

Drugs are chemicals with beneficial biological activity. Modern drug development is an outgrowth of recent research into the specific causes of illness and disease, coupled with advances in chemistry and industrial technology that allow scientists to manufacture chemicals to improve these conditions. The explosion of scientific knowledge about human biology in the past 40 years, and in particular, the discovery that the chemistry of proteins is involved in

BUSINESS CHALLENGES

» Heavy Government Regulation, Political Pressure on Prices

The pharmaceutical industry is heavily regulated by the FDA and subject to state and federal laws. The high profitability of many drug companies at a time of rising health care costs makes the industry a prime target for political interference. In recent years, US spending on prescription drugs increased 8 percent per year. In many other countries, drug prices are government-controlled.

» Revenue Depends on Patent Protection

Profits from sales of prescription drugs usually plummet once lower-cost generic alternatives are available. Generic drugs now account for more than half of all prescriptions filled in the US. Traditional drug companies must constantly discover or acquire new drugs. Manufacturers of generic drugs, on the other hand, have a constant source of new products as patents expire.

» High Cost of R&D

Large drug companies typically spend about 5 percent of their revenues on R&D, a very high ratio, but without any certainty that profitable new products will result. Most new candidate drugs eventually prove unsuitable and are abandoned. Including the cost of failed drugs, the industry estimates that the cost to develop a successful drug is $500 million or more.

many illnesses and diseases, has provided a wide array of protein "targets" for drugs to act on.

R&D is the major activity of most drug companies. While some drugs can now be designed from the ground up to fulfill a specific biological function, drug development in most cases still involves testing a large number of chemicals "in vitro" (in a test tube) to see if they have biological activity. Many of these chemicals are derived from natural sources, especially plants. A company may test thousands of chemicals before finding a few that have the desired effect.

The entire drug development process may take many years (while patent protection is running down), with only a small percentage of candidate drugs surviving the testing and approval process. On average, the industry claims, discovering and developing a new drug takes ten to 15 years and costs $500 million.

Major areas of current research include the cardiovascular system (high blood pressure, high cholesterol); cancer; the endocrine system (diabetes, osteoporosis); the gastrointestinal system (ulcers); infections; and antidepressants.

The actual manufacture of drugs involves one of three major methods: synthesis (using well-known chemical reactions to build a drug from simpler components); extraction (using solvents to remove and purify a drug from a natural source); or biotechnology (such as gene-splicing to produce large quantities of drugs from bacterial fermentation, or the production of monoclonal antibodies using mouse or human cells). Small companies may use a contract manufacturer to produce their products.

Because large research budgets don't guarantee new products, many large companies supplement their own efforts by buying or licensing products from other companies. Companies often buy smaller ones that have a promising research program, to ensure a future stream of products.

Sales & Marketing

The success of a prescription drug depends largely on whether doctors will prescribe it, which in turn depends on their familiarity with it. The big drug companies have large sales forces to regularly call on doctors, hospitals, wholesalers, pharmacists, and managed care organizations. Drug companies also advertise heavily in medical journals, send direct mail advertising and samples to doctors, and participate at medical meetings. Some prescription drugs are marketed directly to consumers via TV and magazine.

Small companies can't match the large sales force that big companies have and therefore often license their drugs to big companies, or enter into marketing agreements with them.

Companies distribute drugs directly to large users like managed care organizations, hospital chains, and retail drug chains, but also through a network of about 200 US drug wholesalers; among the largest are AmerisourceBergen, Cardinal Health, and McKesson.

Human Resources

Drug companies generally have a large staff of scientists and technicians with special skills; average pay in the industry is accordingly high. Fringe benefits in the industry, on average, are a 24 percent addition to payroll. The rapid expansion of drug research in the past decade has sometimes created shortages of qualified personnel.

Industry Employment Growth

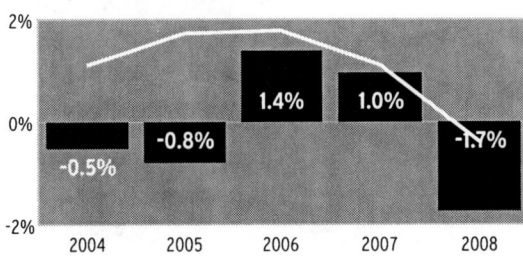

Average Hourly Earnings

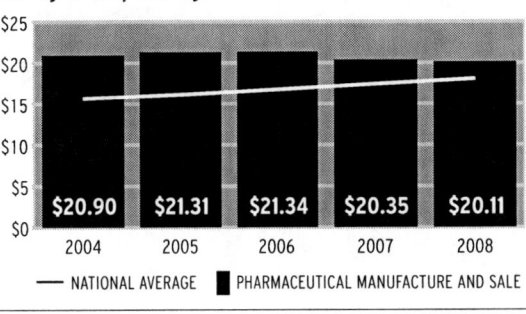

— NATIONAL AVERAGE   ■ PHARMACEUTICAL MANUFACTURE AND SALE

SOURCE: BUREAU OF LABOR STATISTICS

Call Preparation Questions

How is the company challenged by government regulations?

The pharmaceutical industry is heavily regulated by the FDA and subject to state and federal laws.

How is the company preparing to handle expiration of its key patents?

Profits from sales of prescription drugs usually plummet once lower-cost generic alternatives are available.

What percentage of revenues does the company invest in R&D?

Large drug companies typically spend about 5 percent of their revenues on R&D, a very high ratio, but without any certainty that profitable new products will result.

How are rapid advances in biochemistry, immunology, and other fields impacting the company's ability to create new products?

Rapid scientific advances in biochemistry, molecular and cell biology, immunology, genetics, and information technology are making possible more-effective, precise drugs with fewer side effects.

Web Links

American Pharmacists Association

Government affairs, recalls, alerts, and product news.
www.aphanet.org

BioSpace.com

Industry and company news.
www.biospace.com

Canada's Research-Based Pharmaceutical Companies

Canadian news and issues.
www.canadapharma.org

Canadian Generic Pharmaceutical Association

Canadian news and issues.
www.canadiangenerics.ca/en

Centers for Medicare & Medicaid Services

Data, statistics and policy.
www.cms.hhs.gov

Consumer Healthcare Products Association

Industry news.
www.chpa-info.org

FDA News

News headlines (subscription service).
www.fdanews.com

Healthcare Distribution Management Association

Press releases, public policy, industry statistics, and analysis.
www.healthcaredistribution.org

Pharmaceutical Research and Manufacturers of America

Publications, policy views, and press releases.
www.phrma.org

PhRMA Pharmaceutical Industry Profile 2006

www.phrma.org/files/
2006%20Industry%20Profile.pdf

US Food and Drug Administration

News, recalls, and safety information.
www.fda.gov

US Patent and Trademark Office

Information on patents.
www.uspto.gov

Glossary of Acronyms

DTCA — direct to customer advertising
HPD — high potent drugs
NDA — New Drug Application (filed with the FDA)
NIH — National Institutes of Health

HOOVER'S TOP COMPANIES

Largest Companies by Sales	($ mil.)
Johnson & Johnson	63,747.0
Pfizer Inc.	48,296.0
Abbott Laboratories	29,527.6
Merck & Co., Inc.	23,850.3
Wyeth	22,833.9
Bristol-Myers Squibb Company	20,597.0
Eli Lilly and Company	20,378.0
Schering-Plough Corporation	18,502.0
Amgen Inc.	15,003.0
Genentech, Inc.	13,418.0

Largest Employers	Employees
Johnson & Johnson	118,700
Pfizer Inc.	86,600
Abbott Laboratories	69,000
Merck & Co., Inc.	59,800
Schering-Plough Corporation	55,000
Wyeth	50,527
Baxter International Inc.	46,000
Bristol-Myers Squibb Company	42,000
Eli Lilly and Company	40,600
Amgen Inc.	17,500

Fastest Growing* by Five-Year Sales Growth	(%)
Tercica, Inc.	1,966.7
Halozyme Therapeutics, Inc.	344.8
Samaritan Pharmaceuticals, Inc.	295.8
NovaBay Pharmaceuticals, Inc.	293.3
Auriga Laboratories, Inc.	290.6
Alnylam Pharmaceuticals, Inc.	243.9
Affymax, Inc.	233.7
Santarus, Inc.	210.5
CombinatoRx, Incorporated	189.8
Osiris Therapeutics, Inc.	115.4

Fastest Growing* by Five-Year Employee Growth	(%)
NutraCea	255.8
Mylan Inc.	120.7
Bio-Engineered Supplements & Nutrition, Inc.	75.7
Sucampo Pharmaceuticals, Inc.	72.4
CytRx Corporation	69.9
Barr Pharmaceuticals, Inc.	67.3
Anesiva, Inc.	61.3
Peplin, Inc.	57.4
Zila, Inc.	32.7
ISTA Pharmaceuticals, Inc.	11.8

Top Public Companies by Market Value	($ mil.)
Johnson & Johnson	162,163.1
Pfizer Inc.	119,471.7
Genentech, Inc.	87,304.2
Abbott Laboratories	82,853.3
Merck & Co., Inc.	64,073.8

* These rates are compounded annualized increases and may have resulted from acquisitions or one time gains. If less than 6 years of data are available, growth is for the years available.

SOURCE: HOOVER'S, INC., DATABASE

Photo Studios and Commercial Photography

The photographic services industry in the US includes about 14,000 companies with combined annual revenue of $7 billion. Large companies include CPI Corp, Lifetouch, and Olan Mills portrait studios, and Getty Images and Corbis commercial services. The portrait studio segment is concentrated with the four largest companies holding a third of the market. The commercial segment is highly fragmented: the top 50 companies hold less than a quarter of the market. While a few companies have annual revenue well over $100 million, most are small, with revenue under $500,000.

The transition from film-based imagery to digital photography and the associated technologies now available to the industry and its consumer base have revolutionized the industry in recent years.

Competitive Landscape

Demand is closely tied to consumer income and corporate marketing activity. The profitability of individual companies depends heavily on effective marketing. Large companies have economies of scale in marketing and production. Small companies can compete effectively by offering specialized services or holding favorable locations. The industry is labor-intensive: average annual revenue per worker is $75,000 for portrait studios, $120,000 for commercial firms.

Products, Operations & Technology

Major products are family portraits and images for corporate advertising and marketing materials. Portrait studios account for 70 percent of industry revenue. Peripheral sales (frames, albums, and related products) make up less than 5 percent of total revenues.

Family portrait companies specialize in just one segment of the industry, while many commercial firms also produce family portraits in addition to commercial work. In the commer-

cial segment, most companies work on assignment to produce original photographs, and a few large firms like Getty and Corbis license photographs they buy from outside sources.

Studio operations generally require 300 to 1,000 square feet, but studios with multiple camera setups may be larger. Larger studios may have their own processing lab, but most send their images to an independent central laboratory that has high speed, cost-effective image processing equipment. Digital photographers can circumvent laboratory processing by submitting images (proofs) to customers on CDs, although many still create hard-copy proofs. The shift to digital images creates a level playing field for the small studio because high

BUSINESS CHALLENGES

» Competition from Consumer Technology Pressures Prices

Photography fees have been flat the past few years. Today, consumers can photograph, process, edit, and distribute high-quality pictures using low-cost digital and computer technologies and bypass professional photo services. In recent years, photographer fees have been almost flat. Competition is greatest for retail photo studios but also affects commercial providers.

» Commercial Demand Tied to Economic Growth

Demand for commercial photography services, mainly for advertising, depends on the economic environment. Advertising spending falls sharply during recessions. During the last recession, production of newspapers, large carriers of commercial photography, fell 15 percent.

» Demographic Trends Unfavorable

Families with young children are the single most important demographic for the photo industry. The under-5 age segment of the US population will grow just 1 percent per year through 2010. Those 21 to 45 (decision-making parents of the five and under group) will remain relatively constant over the next five years.

volume studios receive discounts from processing labs.

Commercial photographers may operate an indoor studio but also often work onsite. In addition to providing original digital images, services may include pre-production work such as image processing, brochure design and layout, and image archiving. Commercial work is usually in close cooperation with the corporate customer, an advertising agency, or a commercial printer.

Photo studios (and their service labs) now compete with their customers for certain services. Photos can be printed by customers with a photo printer and distributed via the Internet, completely eliminating the traditional photo print.

Advances in the ability to manipulate the "as taken" photograph allow both image and productivity enhancements. Photo shoots can take place in studios where previously they had to be done remotely to produce a true image complete with backgrounds. Images can now be substantially touched up and improved, with undesirable characteristics and blemishes removed.

Sales & Marketing

Major customers are families with children and corporations that produce marketing materials. In the portrait market, seniors are the fastest-growing demographic segment and studios are developing special incentives, reduced pricing, and tailored product offerings to win their business. In the commercial market, studios may act as a subcontractor to ad agencies or commercial printers, rather than work directly with the end client.

Marketing is through a variety of channels. The large companies operate approximately 4,500 portrait studios within major retail outlets such as Wal-Mart, Sears, JCPenney, and Target. In addition to their visible retail presence, these companies use newspaper ads with coupons, inserts, and special offerings. Other large companies such as Olan Mills focus on schools and churches as their primary market.

The commercial or independent studio uses referrals; advertising in customer specific journals and magazines (wedding publications, for example); and direct mail campaigns to target market segments. Virtually all studios have websites that they consider an important marketing tool.

Most selling is by the owner/operator. A sales force is uncommon except in large companies focusing on church and school markets.

Retail photo transactions vary from as little as $15 to several thousand dollars. The average transaction value at the major retail studios is about $65. Commercial studios have a substantially higher transaction value because much of their revenue is generated from corporate clients and is highly customized work.

Due to affordable digital technologies, more photographers are entering the retail photo studio arena, contributing to downward price pressures.

Human Resources

Photography is a relatively low-wage industry and the skills required beyond the photographers themselves are clerical or customer service-related. Since the business for portrait studios is highly seasonal, many part-time employees are involved. As many as 30 percent of the industry's employees are seasonal, hired for strong fourth quarter consumer holiday demand.

Most jobs in the industry require little training and accordingly provide low wages. While commercial studios are generally owner-operated by photographers, the mass retail studios are staffed by "for hire" employees at much lower pay. The average wage is 15 percent lower than the national average.

Industry Employment Growth

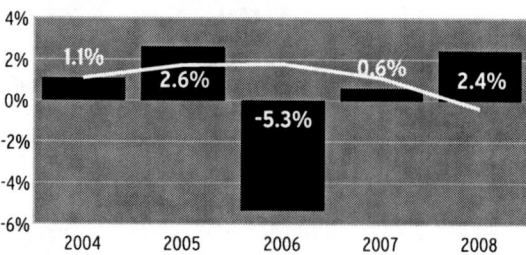

Average Hourly Earnings

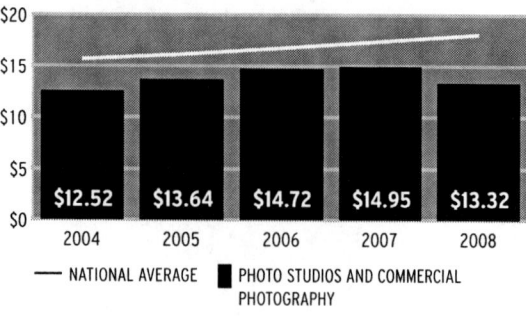

— NATIONAL AVERAGE ▪ PHOTO STUDIOS AND COMMERCIAL PHOTOGRAPHY

SOURCE: BUREAU OF LABOR STATISTICS

Call Preparation Questions

How has the company dealt with the digital photography revolution and its impact on pricing?

Photography fees have been flat the past few years.

What is the outlook for the company's commercial business?

Demand for commercial photography services, mainly for advertising, depends on the economic environment.

How is the company responding to changing US demographics?

Families with young children are the single most important demographic for the photo industry.

How is the company taking advantage of the transition to digital technology?

The transition from film-based to digital photography over the past five years has revolutionized the industry.

How is the company generating additional revenue from its image archives?

To achieve greater visibility for their images, some studios partner with online content aggregators, companies that resell photographic images to the general public through the Internet.

Web Links

DigiCamNews

The latest in news and product information.
www.digicamnews.net

Digital Photography Review

Reviews and news of the digital photography industry.
www.dpreview.com

Newsline International

Features daily news of the photo industry.
www.photomarketing.com/newsletter/
ni_Newsline.asp

Photo Marketing Association International

Features PMA Data Watch, a weekly capsule of relevant news to the industry.
www.pmai.org

Professional Photographers of America

14,000 member association representing interests of professional photographers.
www.ppa.com

Glossary of Acronyms

DPI — dots per inch
PMA — Photo Marketing Association
PPA — Professional Photographers of America

HOOVER'S TOP COMPANIES

Largest Employers	Employees
Lifetouch Inc.	20,000
CPI Corp.	12,854
Olan Mills, Inc.	4,000
Getty Images, Inc.	1,935
Corbis Corporation	1,100

SOURCE: HOOVER'S, INC., DATABASE

Photofinishing and Camera Stores

The photofinishing and retail camera industry includes about 8,000 locations with combined annual revenue of $7 billion. Ritz Camera Centers operates over 1,300 stores. The industry is concentrated: the 50 largest companies hold more than 60 percent of the market. A typical store has five employees and about $500,000 in annual revenue.

Competitive Landscape

Demand depends on consumer income. Profitability of individual companies is linked to marketing, and, for photofinishers, efficiency of operations. Large companies can have economies of scale in purchasing and operations. Small companies can compete successfully by offering superior service. The industry is fairly labor-intensive: annual revenue per employee is about $100,000.

Major competitors are big-box retailers, like Wal-Mart and Target, and electronic superstores, such as Best Buy and Circuit City. Photo kiosks and mini-labs are also found in many major drugstore chains. Digital photography has had a major impact on the industry.

Products, Operations & Technology

Film processing and printing account for about 50 percent of industry revenue, sales of cameras and film for 40 percent. Stores also offer repair services and sell related items like picture frames and albums. Photofinishing labs may provide direct retail services or may process films and images for other retailers.

A typical store occupies about 3,000 to 5,000 square feet and stocks 2,000 to 3,000 items, which are distributed from central warehouses of big companies. Smaller companies buy from distributors or directly from manufacturers.

Many camera stores have photofinishing mini-labs or kiosks. Photofinishing labs use automated printing systems and paper made by manufacturers like Kodak and Fuji. Camera

BUSINESS CHALLENGES

» Competition from Online Services
Online retailers and photofinishing services are capturing increasing market share every year. Consumers buy cameras, printers, and supplies online, upload images, and have printed copies sent directly to their doorstep without ever setting foot in a retail outlet.

» Growth of In-Home Photofinishing
The shift from film to digital technology has driven significant downsizing of the photofinishing industry: total US employment in photofinishing fell 55 percent from 2000 to 2005. With digital cameras and printers, consumers can choose to not print digital images, print digital images at home, or send them to a photofinisher via the Internet or CD.

» Mass Retailers Expanding Photo Services
Mass retailers have a major presence in the photofinishing and retail camera and supplies industry. Electronic superstores and mass retail outlets push large volumes of goods and services through their photo sections. Their purchasing, merchandising, and marketing power make it difficult for the small camera shop or photofinisher to remain competitive.

stores are often located in malls or heavily trafficked business districts. As with other retailers, operations center on merchandising, marketing, inventory control, and customer service.

The technology of photography and photofinishing has shifted almost entirely from film to digital processing. Stores provide services such as computerized image processing and instant printing that formerly had to be sent to outside labs. Stores can receive images for printing on CDs or via the Internet.

Sales & Marketing

The typical consumer is 21 to 54 with a family. Capturing memories is the most frequently cited reason for photo activity in this age group.

Many consumers rely on independent product reviews to help in their buying decisions and also seek advice from store personnel. Professional photographers are more likely than amateurs to buy equipment and supplies online.

Marketing for camera stores often centers on merchandising programs offered by suppliers. Manufacturers often sponsor in-store demonstrations, point-of-purchase displays, special promotions, and rebates. Newspaper inserts with discount coupons are popular methods of reaching the consumer.

Sales personnel of larger photofinishing labs call on private studios, commercial photographers, and retail outlets to sell processing and printing services or to sell self-processing kiosks into the retail channel. Many of these contacts are made at industry trade shows. Most photofinishing marketing is geared toward digital users, although traditional film processing remains available from most labs because of existing infrastructure.

Human Resources

Employees of camera stores are highly paid because of the specialized product knowledge required. The average camera store employee earns about 30 percent more than the average US worker.

Production employees in the US photofinishing industry are paid 15 percent less than average.

Industry Employment Growth

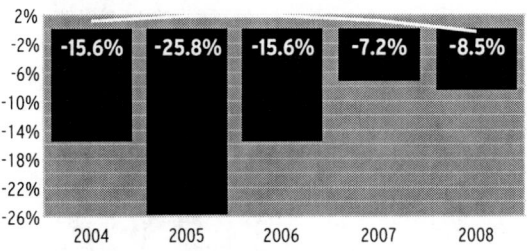

Average Hourly Earnings

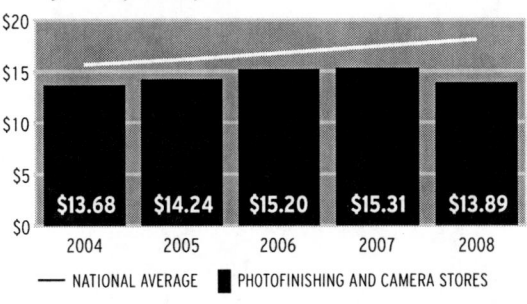

— NATIONAL AVERAGE ■ PHOTOFINISHING AND CAMERA STORES

SOURCE: BUREAU OF LABOR STATISTICS

Call Preparation Questions

How have online photofinishing and supply services affected the company's business?

Online retailers and photofinishing services are capturing increasing market share every year.

How is in-home photofinishing impacting the company's business?

The shift from film to digital technology has driven significant downsizing of the photofinishing industry: total US employment in photofinishing fell 55 percent from 2000 to 2005.

How has competition from mass retailers affected the company's business?

Mass retailers have a major presence in the photofinishing and retail camera and supplies industry.

Does the company operate in-store kiosks or mini-labs to print images?

Many camera shops provide in-store printing; offering this convenience is a way to generate store traffic.

How does the company maximize the impact of product introductions to drive sales?

Retailers must effectively market product introductions to encourage upgrades and drive store traffic.

Web Links

DigicamNews

The latest in news and product information.
digicamnews.net

Digital Imaging Marketing Association

Industry association promoting digital imaging opportunities.
www.imagesite.com/orgs/dima

Digital Photography Review

Reviews and news of the digital photography industry.
www.dpreview.com

Newsline International

Photo industry source for recent news.
www.photomarketing.com/dailynews/nl_default.htm

PMA – The Worldwide Community of Imaging Associations

Industry association for photo industry retailers and processors.
www.pmai.org

This Week in Consumer Electronics (TWICE)

Online consumer electronics weekly magazine with digital imaging section.
www.twice.com/community/820/Digital+Imaging/23114.html

Glossary of Acronyms

DIMA — Digital Imaging Marketing Association
IPI — Independent Photo Imagers
POS — point-of-sale
RCRA — Resource Conservation and Recovery Act

HOOVER'S TOP COMPANIES

Largest Companies by Sales	($ mil.)
Ritz Camera Centers, Inc.	1,180.0
MOTO Franchise Corporation	—

Largest Employers	Employees
Ritz Camera Centers, Inc.	10,150

SOURCE: HOOVER'S, INC., DATABASE

Physician Offices

Over 200,000 physician offices operate in the US with combined annual revenue of over $280 billion. About 75 percent of all physician offices are small, with fewer than 10 employees (including the doctors); only about 1,300 offices have more than 100 employees. The industry is highly fragmented: the top 50 firms account for less than 10 percent of industry revenue. The average annual revenue for small offices is about $650,000.

Competitive Landscape

Demand for physician services is driven by population growth and demographics. The profitability of individual practices depends on the reputation and expertise of the physician and staff. Large practices have advantages in leveraging administrative processes and expensive diagnostic equipment. Small practices compete effectively by providing specialized skills and good customer service. Physicians generally have several direct competitors in the immediate geographic area. Average annual revenue per worker for a small physician's office is about $135,000.

Products, Operations & Technology

Operations of physician offices revolve around patient care, appointment scheduling, records management, and insurance processing. Typically, a patient makes an appointment several days or weeks before being seen, a medical record file is retrieved, the patient sees the doctor for less than 20 minutes, the doctor orders tests or prescribes treatment, the doctor's consultation and any test results or treatments are entered into the medical records, and the cost of the visit is billed to an insurance plan.

The type of patient care that doctors provide depends on their area of expertise, advances in diagnostic and treatment knowledge, and on the type of insurance plan that covers the patient, as some plans limit the types of tests paid

BUSINESS CHALLENGES

» Dependence on Reimbursement Rates

Although doctors serve individuals, bills are usually paid by various third-party health care insurers. In addition to Medicare and Medicaid, doctors typically have contracts with insurers and MCOs that specify reimbursement rates. Consolidation of third-party payers in the past decade has produced a number of large payers that frequently follow Medicare's lead in setting rates. Efforts to curb health care costs have put downward pressure on Medicare reimbursements to physicians in recent years.

» Operational Costs Increasing

Insurers dictate reimbursement rates, which have risen only modestly in recent years, but doctors' own costs for labor, supplies, and liability insurance have increased faster. Malpractice insurance premiums rose sharply in recent years, sometimes such that doctors have given up especially vulnerable specialties like neurosurgery or obstetrics.

» Supplier Concentration

Many doctors, especially surgeons, depend heavily on outside resources such as surgical units (either in hospitals or ambulatory surgical centers); imaging laboratories (for CAT scans or MRIs); diagnostic laboratories; or admitting facilities (hospitals or nursing homes). Within a local market, only one or a few such resources may be available.

for and the types of treatments covered. Typically, the physicians in a group practice all specialize in the same general area of medicine. Offices with a mixture of specialties are more common in smaller communities.

To provide a broad range of care, most doctors in private practice have affiliations with local hospitals. While general practitioners usually deliver most treatments in their office, surgeons often deliver treatment in a hospital or an ambulatory surgical center. Some doctor's offices have basic laboratory and X-ray equipment, but more sophisticated testing is usually handled by independent laboratories.

The explosion of medical knowledge during the past 20 years has forced doctors to specialize in smaller areas of medicine, while making it more difficult for doctors to stay abreast of the latest diagnostic and treatment developments in their field. Diagnostic devices and treatments are often introduced to doctors by sales representatives of device makers and drug companies.

The administrative functions of most physician offices are highly computerized, relying on software created specifically to manage medical offices. Many visits to a doctor's office last only 15 minutes, but require scheduling, reminding, retrieving medical records, ordering tests, rescheduling, billing, billing reconciliation, reconciling payment, and accounting. Without computer systems, this volume of administrative activity would be prohibitively expensive. Using computers to aid medical treatment has become more common, especially as medical records become available in computerized form, providing doctors easier access to records and allowing "expert systems" to flag possible drug interactions and suggest diagnoses and treatments.

Sales & Marketing

Doctors get new patients largely through referrals from existing patients and other doctors, and from being included on approved lists of corporate insurance plans. Doctors who contract with managed care plans may get new patients from the membership. TV and print advertising, formerly banned, have become common, as has direct mailing. Location is important for many patients, as are the hospitals and insurance plans with which the doctor has contracts.

While health care prices are set by physicians, most insurance plans' fee schedules determine what physicians will receive for their services. Medicare also sets price schedules for procedures.

Human Resources

Most jobs in physician offices are clerical and involve scheduling, keeping medical records, and billing. In most offices these activities are highly computerized and require computer skills. In small practices, workers usually need to be able to operate all of these systems. In larger groups, specialization of function is more common.

Because of the repetitive nature of much of the work and the limited prospects for career advancement, employee turnover can be high. Since workers in this field are very knowledgeable about medical insurance plans, fringe benefits are usually high, averaging close to 30 percent of compensation. Average industry wages are higher than the national average.

As insurance payments to physicians decline, many offices are having physician assistants take on routine medical tasks. More medical care is performed by nurses or physician assistants to allow doctors to see more patients and have time for more complex medical issues.

Industry Employment Growth

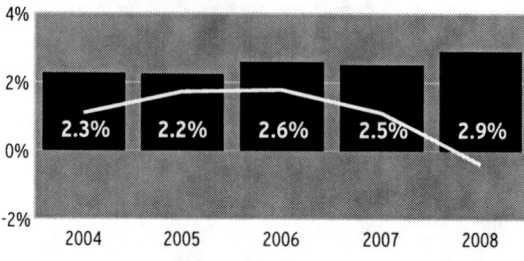

Average Hourly Earnings

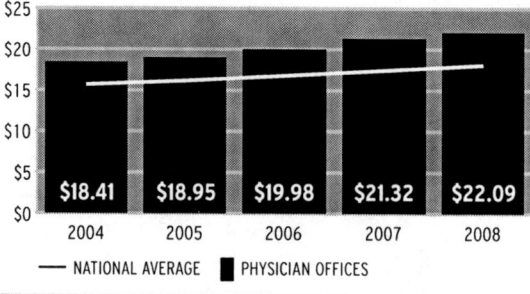

SOURCE: BUREAU OF LABOR STATISTICS

Call Preparation Questions

How are reimbursement rates affecting the office's profitability?

Although doctors serve individuals, bills are usually paid by various third-party health care insurers.

How does the office manage rising operating costs of insurance, labor, etc?

Insurers dictate reimbursement rates, which have risen only modestly in recent years, but doctors' own costs for labor, supplies, and liability insurance have increased faster.

What arrangements does the office have for access to specific hospitals, ambulatory surgical centers, imaging labs, etc.?

Many doctors, especially surgeons, depend heavily on outside resources such as surgical units (either in hospitals or ambulatory surgical centers); imaging laboratories (for CAT scans or MRIs); diagnostic laboratories; or admitting facilities (hospitals or nursing homes).

What plans does the office have to capitalize on growing demand for health care?

National health care expenditures are expected to double over the next decade, due mainly to an aging population.

How is the office benefiting from growing demand for preventative medicine?

Advances in scientific knowledge show that many medical disorders can be prevented or delayed through early intervention, such as lowering cholesterol.

Web Links

Agency for Healthcare Research and Quality

News and announcements on the health care industry, research, funding opportunities, quality assessments, and clinical consumer health data.
www.ahrq.gov

American Academy of Family Physicians

Statistics, articles, news.
www.aafp.org

American Medical Association

Hundreds of links, news, and information about many physician specialties.
www.ama-assn.org

American Medical News

Government and medical news.
www.ama-assn.org/amednews

Centers for Medicare & Medicaid Services

Formerly the Health Care Financing Administration. Statistics, data, local information, laws, and links.
www.cms.hhs.gov

Facts About Family Medicine

American Academy of Family Physicians (AAFP) data tables on physician and patient distribution, income, expenses, office visits, hours worked, graduate programs, and specialties.
www.aafp.org/facts

Massachusetts Medical Society

Industry issues.
www.massmed.org

Modern Healthcare

Weekly business news.
www.modernhealthcare.com

Modern Physician

Industry news.
www.modernphysician.com

The New England Journal of Medicine

Periodic articles about health care issues.
content.nejm.org

Glossary of Acronyms

AMA — American Medical Association

HHS — Health and Human Services

EMR — electronic medical record

HIPAA — Health Insurance Portability and Accountability Act

IPA — Independent Practice Association

PPM — physician practice management

PPO — preferred provider organization

HOOVER'S TOP COMPANIES

Largest Companies by Sales	($ mil.)
Kaiser Foundation Health Plan, Inc.	37,800.0
US Oncology, Inc.	3,000.8
Dean Health Systems, Inc.	1,300.0
MEDNAX, Inc.	1,068.3
Prospect Medical Holdings, Inc.	329.5
Continucare Corporation	254.4
IntegraMed America, Inc.	152.0
OnCure Medical Corp.	100.0

Largest Employers	Employees
Kaiser Foundation Health Plan, Inc.	159,766
US Oncology, Inc.	9,000
Dean Health Systems, Inc.	4,100
MEDNAX, Inc.	3,914
Prospect Medical Holdings, Inc.	1,853
IntegraMed America, Inc.	881
Continucare Corporation	589
OnCure Medical Corp.	400

Fastest Growing* by Five-Year Sales Growth	(%)
Prospect Medical Holdings, Inc.	37.7
Continucare Corporation	20.2
MEDNAX, Inc.	14.2
US Oncology, Inc.	12.7
IntegraMed America, Inc.	11.5
Kaiser Foundation Health Plan, Inc.	10.9

Fastest Growing* by Five-Year Employee Growth	(%)
Prospect Medical Holdings, Inc.	74.6
Continucare Corporation	32.2
Kaiser Foundation Health Plan, Inc.	27.6
US Oncology, Inc.	17.6
MEDNAX, Inc.	14.0
IntegraMed America, Inc.	10.1

Top Public Companies by Market Value	($ mil.)
Continucare Corporation	145.7
IntegraMed America, Inc.	98.6
Prospect Medical Holdings, Inc.	51.3

* These rates are compounded annualized increases and may have resulted from acquisitions or one time gains. If less than 6 years of data are available, growth is for the years available.

SOURCE: HOOVER'S, INC., DATABASE

Plastic and Rubber Products Manufacturing

In the US, about 16,000 companies produce plastic and rubber products, with combined annual revenue of $215 billion. Large producers include divisions of DuPont, Pactiv, Textron, and Mark IV Industries. The industry is highly fragmented with hundreds of niches, determined by material type, manufacturing process, and end-use.

Competitive Landscape

Because plastic products are widely used in industry and as consumer products, demand depends on the health of the US economy. The profitability of individual companies depends on product mix and production efficiency. Large companies have economies of scale in buying raw materials and in manufacturing commodity products like bottles and plastic film. Small companies can compete effectively by producing specialized products. Annual revenue per worker is about $220,000.

Products, Operations & Technology

Major products include plastic bottles, plastic film and sheets, plastic pipe and foams, and rubber hoses. Plastic products account for 80 percent of the industry. Plastics and rubber have a wide range of physical properties, making them suitable for different uses. Most producers specialize in a few product lines, as the equipment and tooling needed to manufacture to customer specifications can be expensive. Production usually occurs in single-use plants that can range from 50,000 to 500,000 square feet, depending on the product. The typical manufacturer has a single plant and fewer than 50 employees.

Injection and compression molding are the principal methods of plastic processing. In injection molding, plastic material is put into a hopper that feeds into a heated injection unit. The heat softens the plastic into a fluid, which is injected into a cold mold. The plastic cools

and hardens, then is ejected. Timing is essential to ensure that the plastic is in the correct state for softening and hardening. Compression molding uses plastic molding powder squeezed into a mold shape through force; pressure, heat, and timing are key. One new process method is reaction injection molding, which uses liquids that chemically react to turn into plastic inside the mold. Because this method requires little heating, it uses considerably less energy. Process methods and equipment are chosen to suit the type of product made, such as the blow molding process, which adds compressed air to form hollow articles like bottles.

Raw plastic materials include vinyl; acrylics; polyvinyl chloride (PVC); polystyrene; polypropylene (PP); high-density polyethylene (HDPE); polyethylene terephthalate (PET);

polycarbonate; epoxies; urethanes; and dozens of other plastics. Raw materials are the major manufacturing expense, often equal to 50 percent of revenue. These plastics may be bought from suppliers or made from polymer resins bought from large chemical producers such as DuPont, ExxonMobil, Dow, and Bayer, which typically synthesize them from oil or natural gas. The type of resin used depends on the end-use, such as acetal in auto parts and polyethylene in toys. Prices for resins are tied to crude oil prices. Some plastics, such as PET, often used for bottles and sheets, can be recycled.

Most rubber is synthetic, produced in manufacturing plants that synthesize it from petroleum and other minerals. Natural rubber is made from the sap of cultivated trees in Asia and Africa. Whether natural or synthetic, rubber in its native form is useless until chemicals are added to make it soft, resilient, or hard. The different types of synthetic rubbers are styrene butadiene (SBR); polybutadiene (BR); ethylene propylene rubber (EPR, both EPM and EPDM); acrylonitrile butadiene rubber (NBR); polychloropene (CR); butyl (IIR); and specialty elastomers.

Some plastics makers, such as of food packaging, use information management tools that link manufacturing operations to customers. These systems improve customer service by ensuring timely product distribution while reducing supply chain costs and improving productivity. Some companies may also use CAD systems to design products, or use 3D simulation software for computer modeling of various products or manufacturing processes.

Sales & Marketing

Primary markets for plastic and rubber products are packaging (bottles and wrapping); construction (pipes and insulation); electrical and electronics; and consumer products. Customers include OEMs such as auto, aircraft and medical device companies, and consumer product companies, such as Procter & Gamble, or soft drink bottlers that use bottles and containers.

Except for commodity products that are sold based on lowest price, manufacturers typically sell their ability to make a product according to the customer's specifications, with price a secondary consideration. Sales are handled by an in-house sales force with technical knowledge and by independent manufacturers representatives. Companies may advertise in trade magazines and at trade shows. Some producers have multi-year supply contracts with customers, but one-year contracts are more common. Man-

ufacturing plants for bulky products, such as bottles, are often located close to customers because of high shipping costs.

Human Resources

Jobs in plastics manufacture involve feeding and tending machinery that usually works in batches. Much of the work requires only modest skills, and wages are accordingly below average relative to manufacturing jobs in general. The industry injury rate is worse than average.

Industry Employment Growth

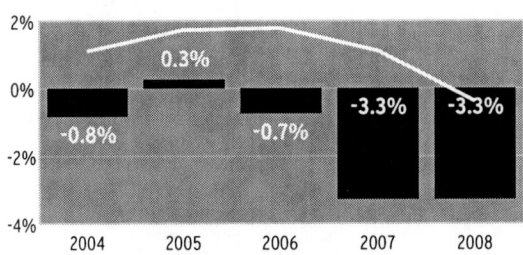

Average Hourly Earnings

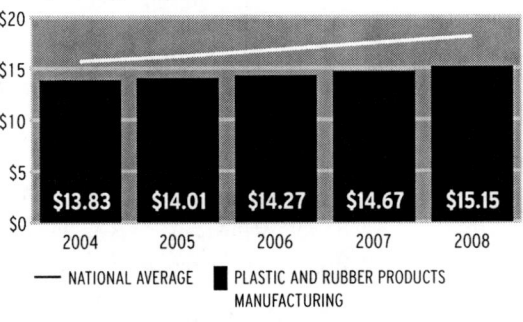

SOURCE: BUREAU OF LABOR STATISTICS

Call Preparation Questions

How does the company protect itself from the changing costs of raw materials like oil?

Because many plastic and rubber products are derived mainly from oil and natural gas, price and availability depend on the price of these feedstocks (raw materials).

How seasonal is demand and subsequent cash flow?

Some plastics have seasonal demand because they're used in construction.

Has the company taken market share from traditional materials, like glass and metal?

Demand for rubber and plastics to replace metal parts in autos and aircraft continues, as manufacturers prefer low-weight components.

Web Links

Plastics Division, American Chemistry Council

Industry statistics.
www.americanchemistry.com/s_plastics

FAST FACTS

» In the US, about 16,000 companies produce plastic and rubber products, with combined annual revenue of $215 billion.

» Large producers include divisions of DuPont, Pactiv, Textron, and Mark IV Industries.

» Major products include plastic bottles, plastic film and sheets, plastic pipe and foams, and rubber hoses.

» Primary markets for plastic and rubber products are packaging (bottles and wrapping); construction (pipes and insulation); electrical and electronics; and consumer products.

» Producers may have high levels of inventory (raw materials) and receivables.

Plastics Machining & Fabricating Magazine

News, feature articles, events, and links.
plasticsmachining.com/magazine/index.shtml

Plastics Technology magazine

Today's top news and feature articles on mergers and acquisitions, technology, US and global business.
www.plasticstechnology.com

Plastics.com

Industry news, links, and manufacturer rankings.
www.plastics.com

PlasticsNews.com

Industry news.
www.plasticsnews.com/subscriber/headlines.phtml

Rubber Manufacturers Association

Publications, links, market information services, and government news.
www.rma.org

Rubber Statistics – International Rubber Study Group

Spreadsheets and reports on the production, consumption, and prices of natural and synthetic rubber.
www.rubberstudy.com/statistics-geninfo.aspx

RubberNews.com

Rubber and plastics industry news.
www.rubbernews.com

RubberWorld.com

Industry news and manufacturer information.
www.rubberworld.com

The Society of the Plastics Industry

Basic industry information, definitions, statistics. Excellent industry issues.
www.plasticsindustry.org

The Vinyl Institute

News, definitions and uses of vinyl, environmental issues, and publications.
www.vinylinfo.org

Glossary of Acronyms

BR — polybutadiene
CR — polychloropene
EPR — ethylene propylene rubber
HDPE — high-density polyethylene
IIR — butyl
MSDS — Material Safety Data Sheets
NBR — acrylonitrile butadiene rubber
NESHAP — National Emission Standards for Hazardous Pollutants
PET — polyethylene terephthalate
PNC — plastic nanocomposites
PP — polypropylene
PVC — polyvinyl chloride
SBR — styrene butadiene

HOOVER'S TOP COMPANIES

Largest Companies by Sales	($ mil.)
E. I. du Pont de Nemours and Company	31,836.0
Textron Inc.	14,246.0
Newell Rubbermaid Inc.	6,470.6
Tenneco Inc.	5,916.0
Sealed Air Corporation	4,651.2
Pactiv Corporation	3,567.0
Graham Packaging Holdings Company	2,493.5
Solo Cup Company	2,106.3

Largest Employers	Employees
E. I. du Pont de Nemours and Company	60,000
Textron Inc.	43,000
Newell Rubbermaid Inc.	22,000
Tenneco Inc.	21,000
Nypro Inc.	18,000
Sealed Air Corporation	17,700
Pactiv Corporation	13,000
Tupperware Brands Corporation	12,800
Berry Plastics Corporation	12,700
Solo Cup Company	8,700
Solo Cup Company	8,700

Fastest Growing* by Five-Year Sales Growth	(%)
Greystone Logistics, Inc.	74.6
Graham Packaging Holdings Company	22.4
Solo Cup Company	20.3
Mark IV Industries, Inc.	16.1
Raven Industries, Inc.	14.1
Nypro Inc.	14.0
AptarGroup, Inc.	13.2
Tupperware Brands Corporation	13.0
Chase Corporation	12.2
Tenneco Inc.	9.5

Fastest Growing* by Five-Year Employee Growth	(%)
Greystone Logistics, Inc.	45.6
Prime Plastic Products, Inc.	20.0
Graham Packaging Holdings Company	14.9
Nypro Inc.	10.4
AptarGroup, Inc.	8.0
Tupperware Brands Corporation	4.6
Raven Industries, Inc.	4.4
EnPro Industries, Inc.	3.5
Advanced Drainage Systems, Inc.	2.6

Top Public Companies by Market Value	($ mil.)
E. I. du Pont de Nemours and Company	22,830.1
Sealed Air Corporation	3,740.0
Textron Inc.	3,720.2
Pactiv Corporation	3,272.0
Newell Rubbermaid Inc.	2,710.0

* These rates are compounded annualized increases and may have resulted from acquisitions or one time gains. If less than 6 years of data are available, growth is for the years available.

SOURCE: HOOVER'S, INC., DATABASE

Plastic Resins and Synthetic Fibers

About 1,000 companies in the US manufacture plastic resins and synthetic fibers, with combined domestic annual revenue of $60 billion. Large companies include Eastman Chemical, Solutia, and PolyOne, and operating divisions of large chemical companies like DuPont, Dow Chemical, and BASF. The industry is highly concentrated: the top 50 companies hold 85 percent of the market.

Competitive Landscape

Demand depends on the level of manufacture of plastic products, which is closely linked to US industrial production. Because resin manufacture is a high-volume process, the profitability of individual companies depends on operating efficiencies. Large companies have significant economies of scale in production and in the purchase of raw materials. Smaller companies can compete effectively by producing specialty resins and fibers. Many smaller companies buy commodity resins from large producers and rework them into specialty compounds. The industry is highly automated: annual revenue per worker is over $700,000 in large production plants, close to $500,000 in smaller ones.

Products, Operations & Technology

The two basic types of plastic resins are thermosets, which harden permanently after they are cured by heat, and thermoplastics, which may be hard or soft after being cured, but can be remelted or dissolved in a solvent. Thermosets include acrylics, amino resins, epoxy, unsaturated polyesters, polyurethanes and vinyl esters. Polyethylene (PE); polypropylene (PP); polyvinyl chloride (PVC); and polystyrene (PS) are themoplastics. A third type of resin, elastomers, are thermoplastics that remain elastic after being cured, such as polyurethane foam. By mixing various resins ("compounding") and adding colorants and other chemicals, compa-

BUSINESS CHALLENGES

» Volatile Demand

US production of products made from plastic resins can vary sharply from year to year, making demand difficult to predict. Output can change more than 10 percent from year to year for the industry as a whole, much more for individual companies. During the last recession, US resin production dropped more than 20 percent.

» Volatile Raw Material Prices

Resin manufacturers can be exposed to rapid changes in raw material inventory values, and may be unable to pass cost increases to customers. The major raw materials for resin manufacture are derived from oil and natural gas, and these costs can swing sharply with the price of crude oil.

» Customer Industry Concentration

Although most resin producers sell to a large number of customers, specialization in particular types of applications often results in sales to customers in the same industry. Major end-use industries are auto parts, computers, packaging, building materials, aircraft parts, textiles, and telecommunication equipment. Lower demand from a single end-use market can strongly affect individual producers.

nies can produce plastics with a wide range of physical and chemical properties.

Resins are made from industrial chemicals like methanol, propane, ethane, phenol, urea, and ethylene glycol, through chemical reactions that produce long molecules (polymers) with a carbon-hydrogen backbone. Although production methods vary, most resins are made by mixing chemicals in a reaction vessel ("kettle"), or a series of reaction chambers, and adding heat. Depending on how the finished product will eventually be used, the resin may be processed into chips, films, foam, powder, paste, or liquid. Resins are semifinished products that don't take on their final chemical form until they are "cured" by further treatment with air, chemicals, or heat. The curing process links the polymer molecules to create a solid plastic product.

Synthetic fibers are manufactured from plastic resins that are either melted or dissolved and then forced through small holes in a "spinneret" to create continuous filaments. In a melt-spinning operation, typically used to produce nylon and polyester, melted resin extruded through the spinneret solidifies by cooling. In dry-spinning, used to make acetate, acrylic, and spandex, resin that has been dissolved in a solvent and extruded through the spinneret is hardened by rapid evaporation of the solvent. In wet-spinning, used to make acrylic, rayon, and spandex, a dissolved resin is precipitated in a chemical wash after extrusion through the spinneret.

Manufacturing plants typically run batch operations, although foams and fibers may be produced in continuous-run operations. Most plants are highly automated. Production capacity is measured in hundreds of millions of pounds. Although the actual production of resins is relatively simple, formulating ingredients to achieve a product with particular characteristics is technically demanding. Producers typically have an engineering staff, and small companies may spend up to 10 percent of revenue on R&D.

Sales & Marketing

Sales of resins and fibers are typically handled by an internal sales staff, supplemented with independent agents and distributors. Trade shows are an important source of new customers. Sales are to industrial customers, which use the resins and fibers to produce plastic products and textiles. Although some resins and fibers are sold in standard, commodity formulations, many are specialized for particular applications. Producers often work closely with customers to determine the best specifications for a product.

Companies typically serve a large number of customers, but may have concentrations within a particular end-use market, such as carpeting, electronics, building materials, or car parts. Due to the high raw materials content of the finished products (reflected in low gross margins), product prices are very sensitive to raw material costs.

Human Resources

Operating highly automated resin and fiber production facilities requires strong technical

and engineering skills. Wages are 25 percent above the average for all US workers. Companies can afford to pay for skilled labor because productivity is very high.

The safety record of the industry is better than average.

Industry Employment Growth

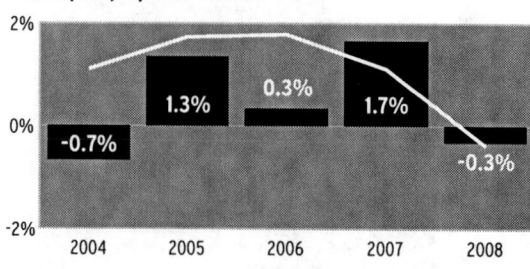

Average Hourly Earnings

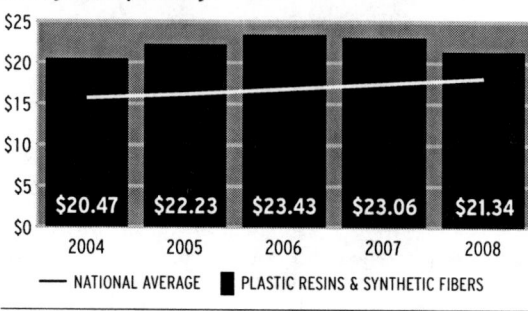

— NATIONAL AVERAGE   ■ PLASTIC RESINS & SYNTHETIC FIBERS

SOURCE: BUREAU OF LABOR STATISTICS

Call Preparation Questions

How does the company manage sharp swings in demand?

US production of products made from plastic resins can vary sharply from year to year, making demand difficult to predict.

How does the company protect itself from higher raw material prices?

Resin manufacturers can be exposed to rapid changes in raw material inventory values, and may be unable to pass cost increases to customers.

How dependent is the company on a few large buyers or a particular industry?

Although most resin producers sell to a large number of customers, specialization in particular types of applications often results in sales to customers in the same industry.

What advantages or challenges does the company see in producing high-strength plastics?

The technology of adding various fibers to resins or infusing resins into a fiber matrix continues to produce plastics with strength characteristics that make them suitable as substitutes for metals and other structural materials.

What future does the company see for plastic micro-fibers?

Technological advances now allow synthetic fiber manufacturers to produce fibers that are thinner than silk but have high strength.

Web Links

American Composites Manufacturers Association

Lobbying organization. Market statistics.
www.cfa-hq.org

American Fiber Manufacturers Association

Excellent industry background information. Industry news. Industry statistics for sale.
www.fibersource.com/afma/afma.htm

Energy Information Administration

Crude oil and natural gas prices.
www.eia.doe.gov

Environmental Protection Agency

www.epa.gov

ICIS Chemical Business Americas

Authoritative chemical industry news, by free trial or subscription.
www.icis.com

Modern Plastics Worldwide

Industry news.
www.plasticstoday.com

Plastics Division of the American Chemistry Council (ACC)

Industry statistics.
www.americanchemistry.com/plastics

Plastics.com

Industry news.
www.plastics.com

The Society of the Plastics Industry

Indoors issues. Excellent links. Some statistics. Financial & operating ratios for sale.
www.socplas.org

Glossary of Acronyms

APC — American Plastics Council
EIA — Energy Information Administration
ISM — Institute for Supply Management
OSB — oriented strand board
PE — polyethylene
PP — polypropylene
PS — polystyrene
PVC — polyvinyl chloride

HOOVER'S TOP COMPANIES

Largest Companies by Sales	($ mil.)
The Dow Chemical Company	57,514.0
E. I. du Pont de Nemours and Company	31,836.0
3M Company	25,269.0
Chevron Phillips Chemical Company LLC	12,986.0
Huntsman Corporation	10,215.0
Eastman Chemical Company	6,726.0
Dow Corning Corporation	4,940.0
Cytec Industries Inc.	3,639.9
Georgia Gulf Corporation	3,157.3
PolyOne Corporation	2,738.7

Largest Employers	Employees
3M Company	79,183
E. I. du Pont de Nemours and Company	60,000
The Dow Chemical Company	45,856
Huntsman Corporation	12,900
Eastman Chemical Company	10,800
Dow Corning Corporation	10,000
Cytec Industries Inc.	6,800
Ferro Corporation	6,275
Solutia Inc.	6,000
Carpenter Co.	5,900

Fastest Growing* by Five-Year Sales Growth	(%)
Zoltek Companies, Inc.	23.9
Georgia Gulf Corporation	20.7
Cytec Industries Inc.	19.9
Chevron Phillips Chemical Company LLC	18.9
ICO, Inc.	16.7
Landec Corporation	16.3
ICC Industries Inc.	15.8
Dow Corning Corporation	13.6
The Dow Chemical Company	12.0
Rogers Corporation	8.5

Fastest Growing* by Five-Year Employee Growth	(%)
Georgia Gulf Corporation	34.0
Zoltek Companies, Inc.	11.0
Cytec Industries Inc.	10.9
Huntsman Corporation	9.3
Dow Corning Corporation	4.0
3M Company	3.4
ICO, Inc.	3.3
Rogers Corporation	3.1
Momentive Performance Materials Inc.	2.7

Top Public Companies by Market Value	($ mil.)
3M Company	39,906.5
E. I. du Pont de Nemours and Company	22,830.1
The Dow Chemical Company	13,948.4
Eastman Chemical Company	2,297.8
Cytec Industries Inc.	998.7

*These rates are compounded annualized increases and may have resulted from acquisitions or one time gains. If less than 6 years of data are available, growth is for the years available.

SOURCE: HOOVER'S, INC., DATABASE

Poultry Processing

The poultry processing industry comprises about 500 companies with combined annual revenue of $40 billion. Large companies include Tyson Foods, Pilgrim's Pride, and Perdue Farms. The industry is highly concentrated: the 50 largest companies hold more than 90 percent of the market.

Competitive Landscape

Demand is driven by population growth and export markets. The profitability of individual companies depends on efficient production and distribution, because the finished product is a commodity. Big companies have large economies of scale in production and distribution. Small companies can compete successfully by serving a limited geographical area or by producing a specialized product. Average annual revenue per employee at big processors is $150,000.

Products, Operations & Technology

Major products are fresh or frozen young chickens, fresh or frozen turkeys, cooked or smoked poultry, and other birds such as ducks, geese, and Cornish hens. Young chickens account for about 65 percent of industry revenue, processed meats 25 percent, and turkeys less than 10 percent.

Chickens grown for eating (rather than laying eggs) are called broilers. About 9 billion broilers are produced in the US each year; the average broiler weighs 5 pounds. The large producers use industrial techniques that have been developed to produce chicken products at the lowest possible cost. These involve large feeding operations — using chicken breeds that efficiently turn feed into meat — and large distribution systems that can rapidly put fresh chicken parts (a highly perishable product) on supermarket shelves.

A typical chicken (or turkey) operation involves distinct steps. Chicks are produced from

BUSINESS CHALLENGES

» High Capacity Limits Prices

Poultry product prices are largely subject to the factory capacity available to produce products and to consumer demand. Broiler production in the US grew rapidly from 6 billion in 1990 to almost 9 billion. Although both domestic consumption and exports have grown, production capacity has increased faster. Wholesale chicken prices are driven more by production costs than consumer demand, limiting profitability.

» Variability of Feed Prices

Prices for corn and soybean meal, the major chicken feeds, can vary as much as 40 percent throughout the year. Processors often can't pass along cost increases because consumers will switch to other products.

» Food Safety

Although various methods are used to clean chickens after slaughter, contaminated meat still sometimes reaches consumers. Increased incidents of contamination have led to heightened consumer concern and tighter health and safety regulations for meat labeling and testing. Among the most important harmful bacteria are salmonella, listeria, and the 0157:H7 strain of E. coli.

eggs laid by breeder flocks, which are usually owned by the processor but may be maintained on contracted breeder farms. Eggs are collected and moved to hatcheries, where they're incubated and hatched in a process that takes about 21 days. A large producer like Pilgrim's Pride may own a dozen hatcheries. The yield of eggs that hatch from those that are "set" is close to 85 percent. Day-old chicks are inspected, vaccinated, and transported to "grow-out" farms, where they're placed in chicken houses and fed to maturity. Males and females are segregated because they grow at different rates.

Grow-out operations are typically run by contract growers, with feed, veterinary services, and technical advice supplied by the processor.

A large processor like WLR uses hundreds of contract growers in various states to supply just a few processing plants. Contract growers are paid based on the live weight of chickens they deliver, usually with a minimum guaranteed rate and various incentives. Because feed composition is critical to the rate at which chickens convert feed to body weight, processors have their own formulations and operate their own feed mills. Corn and soybean meal are the major ingredients of feeds and the largest cost of producing chickens. Feed conversion rates are close to 2.00; that is, it takes 10 pounds of feed to produce a 5 pound chicken. Chickens are fed at grow-out farms for eight to ten weeks until they reach processing weight, depending on the breed. Cornish Cross Broiler pullets can attain a weight of 6 pounds in 56 days, HY-Y Broilers take a week longer to attain the same weight but have larger breasts and less fat. Some processors have developed proprietary chicken breeds.

Mature birds are trucked to processing plants that are highly automated, where they are killed, de-feathered, and chilled. The amount of further processing, such as deboning, quartering, breading, and spicing, depends on the product ordered by the customer. Final products may be ice-packed, deep chilled or frozen, whole, cutup, or boneless. Further processing may be done in cooking or smoking facilities. Products are packaged, labeled, and shipped in refrigerated trucks. Some processors have their own cold storage facilities. Waste parts like feet, heads, organs, etc. are processed into animal or pet food.

Computer technology is necessary to track customer orders, which may include dozens of different product configurations, and to operate the elaborate distribution systems that must deliver product rapidly.

Sales & Marketing

Chicken (and turkey) products are sold to supermarkets, fast food outlets, restaurants, and institutional customers such as schools, governments, and food distributors. Chickens are a commodity product, even though some processors have been able to establish a retail brand name. Buyers usually do business with a number of different processors. Processors use an internal sales force to contact buyers and also use independent brokers. There are virtually no long-term supply contracts. Price competition is intense. Prices vary somewhat by region of the country. Buyers frequently use the USDA National Weekly Pricing Report as a benchmark for negotiating prices. Frozen broilers are traded on commodity futures markets.

Human Resources

A typical chicken processing plant employs 500 workers, who are paid low wages, only 65 percent of the average US wage. The work is generally unpleasant and personnel turnover is high. The work can be dangerous because knives and other cutting tools are used. The annual rate of illness and injury is 40 percent higher than for all US workers. Safety has increased substantially in the past decade, due to automation.

Employment in the industry has grown only slowly, partly because of the greater use of highly efficient automated processing machinery. Many processing plants are unionized, with workers often represented by the Teamsters Union or the United Food and Commercial Workers Union. The use of illegal immigrant workers is sometimes a problem.

Industry Employment Growth

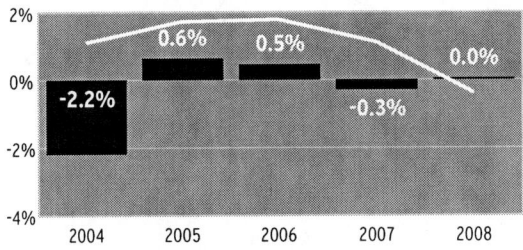

Average Hourly Earnings

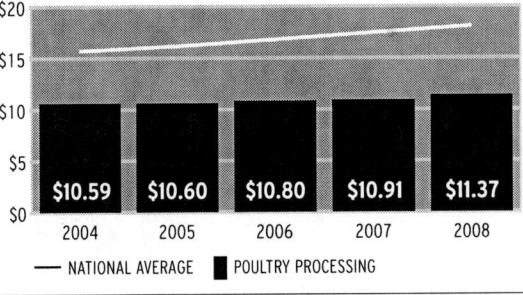

SOURCE: BUREAU OF LABOR STATISTICS

Call Preparation Questions

How does the company estimate demand, prevent overcapacity, and protect prices?

Poultry product prices are largely subject to the factory capacity available to produce products and to consumer demand.

How does the company protect itself from fluctuating feed prices?

Prices for corn and soybean meal, the major chicken feeds, can vary as much as 40 percent throughout the year.

How does the company reduce the risk of food safety problems?

Although various methods are used to clean chickens after slaughter, contaminated meat still sometimes reaches consumers.

What advantages do different chicken breeds offer the company?

Different breeds of chicken have different growth and taste characteristics.

Web Links

Agriculture and Agri-Food Canada

Industry statistics.
www.agr.gc.ca/index_e.phtml

American Meat Institute

News.
www.meatami.com

Food Safety and Inspection Service

News releases and recalls.
www.fsis.usda.gov

Further Poultry Processors Association of Canada

Poultry production charts.
www3.sympatico.ca/fppac/homepg.htm

Meat & Poultry

Industry news.
www.meatpoultry.com

National Agricultural Statistics Service

Production statistics.
www.nass.usda.gov

National Chicken Council

Industry statistics.
www.eatchicken.com

National Turkey Federation

Press news releases.
www.turkeyfed.org

Poultry Industry Council

Canadian poultry information.
www.poultryindustrycouncil.ca

USDA Agricultural Marketing Service

Extensive pricing information.
www.ams.usda.gov

USDA Glossary of Poultry Terms

www.ams.usda.gov/poultry/mncs/
glossaryofterms.htm

WATT Poultry

Industry news.
www.wattpoultry.com

Glossary of Acronyms

AMS — Agricultural Marketing Service
ARS — Agricultural Research Service
B/S — boneless, skinless
CAFO — concentrated animal feeding operations
COOL — country of origin labeling
ERS — Economic Research Service
HACCP — Hazard Analysis and Critical Control Point system
NTF — National Turkey Federation
RTC — ready-to-cook
WOG — without giblets

HOOVER'S TOP COMPANIES

Largest Companies by Sales	($ mil.)
Tyson Foods, Inc.	26,862.0
Smithfield Foods, Inc.	11,351.2
Pilgrim's Pride Corporation	8,525.1
Perdue Incorporated	4,300.0
Koch Foods Incorporated	1,800.0
Sanderson Farms, Inc.	1,723.6
Butterball, LLC	1,406.5
Mountaire Corporation	1,210.9
Jennie-O Turkey Store, Inc.	1,162.2
ContiGroup Companies (Wayne Farms)	—

Largest Employers	Employees
Tyson Foods, Inc.	107,000
Smithfield Foods, Inc.	58,100
Pilgrim's Pride Corporation	44,750
Perdue Incorporated	21,000
Koch Foods Incorporated	14,000
ContiGroup Companies (Wayne Farms)	13,500
Sanderson Farms, Inc.	10,739
Jennie-O Turkey Store, Inc.	7,000
Mountaire Corporation	6,000
House of Raeford Farms, Inc.	5,000

Fastest Growing* by Five-Year Sales Growth	(%)
Koch Foods Incorporated	13.4
Pilgrim's Pride Corporation	9.7
Smithfield Foods, Inc.	7.5
Cagle's, Inc.	4.8
Tyson Foods, Inc.	1.8

Fastest Growing* by Five-Year Employee Growth	(%)
Koch Foods Incorporated	36.6
Smithfield Foods, Inc.	5.7
Pilgrim's Pride Corporation	2.5

Top Public Companies by Market Value	($ mil.)
Tyson Foods, Inc.	3,895.8
Smithfield Foods, Inc.	3,827.7
Sanderson Farms, Inc.	633.4
Cagle's, Inc.	28.7

* These rates are compounded annualized increases and may have resulted from acquisitions or one time gains. If less than 6 years of data are available, growth is for the years available.

SOURCE: HOOVER'S, INC., DATABASE

Primary Metals Manufacturing

The US primary metals industry includes 5,000 companies with combined annual sales of about $140 billion. Large companies include Nucor and US Steel (steel); Alcoa (aluminum); and Freeport-McMoRan Copper & Gold. The industry is highly concentrated: the 50 largest producers hold more than 90 percent of the raw steel market. Secondary production of products from raw steel and other metals is also concentrated.

Competitive Landscape

Demand comes largely from the manufacturers of durable goods like motor vehicles, machinery, containers, and construction steel. The profitability of individual companies depends largely on efficient operations, because most products are commodities sold based on price. Big companies have large economies of scale in production. Accordingly, most producers of secondary products buy raw metal from the large producers. Small companies can compete by operating efficient local mini-mills or producing specialty products. The industry is highly automated: average annual revenue per worker is close to $300,000.

Products, Operations & Technology

The industry includes manufacturers and processors of steel, iron, aluminum, copper, and specialty metals like titanium, molybdenum, and beryllium. Steel products account for about 50 percent of the market. Companies are involved in three major types of activities. Primary processing is the separation of metal from ores in a furnace to produce slabs or ingots of metal. Secondary processing involves mainly the rolling or drawing of metal slabs into sheets, plates, foil, bars, and wire. Foundry operations produce metal shapes by pouring molten metal into casts or molds. Some producers have fully integrated operations, from mining raw materials to manufacturing fin-

BUSINESS CHALLENGES

» Demand Depends on Manufacturing, Construction

Demand for primary metals depends on the health of the US manufacturing sector, particularly the manufacture of motor vehicles, metal products, and machinery, and on commercial construction. Demand can be highly cyclical: during the last recession, US production of primary metals dropped 15 percent.

» Competition from Imports

Imports of primary metals, mainly raw steel and steel products, often depress US metals prices. Volume varies from year to year, but imports typically account for 20 to 30 percent of the US market. Import quotas and tariffs can be imposed when foreign manufacturers "dump" steel on the US market.

» Dependence on Regulators

Dependence on regulators, especially import regulations in the form of quotas and tariffs, protect US steel manufacturers from the full effects of international competition. Regulations vary, as they're subject to political forces and new legislation. International economic difficulties, the need for hard currency, and the desire to maintain employment for workers, often tempt foreign producers to sell product to the US at low prices. The US often responds with tighter restrictions and fees on imports.

ished products, but most operate in just one type of activity.

Steel production first involves converting iron ore or scrap iron into molten steel. The ore-based process uses a blast or oxygen furnace in a blast mill, and the scrap-based process uses an electric arc furnace in a mini-mill. Next, molten steel is poured and solidified in a continuous caster to produce semi-finished products, like steel slabs, billets, and blooms. These materials are put through a mechanical and heat treatment known as hot rolling, and some hot-rolled sheets are rolled again at lower temperatures (cold rolling) to form finished flat products such as plates, coils, or sheets, or long products such as wire, bars, rails, or beams. These products may then be coated with protective anticorrosion material.

The production of aluminum, copper, and other metals are similar. Metal is separated from an ore by melting it. Metal alloys are produced by adding various elements to the main metal. For example, 17 percent chrome and 8 percent nickel are added to iron to create stainless steel. The different properties and characteristics of metal are produced by altering the chemical composition and the different stages of the process, such as rolling, finishing, and heat treatment.

Primary production of metals requires large amounts of ore and large amounts of energy, so producers often locate near ore deposits (copper companies); coal fields; or sources of cheap electricity (aluminum companies). To ensure a supply of raw materials, many primary producers control their own ore deposits. Transporting the finished product is typically by rail. Producers can make thousands of different products because metals can be made in many different grades of hardness or other properties. A producer of castings and forgings, such as Citation, sells 20,000 products to 2,000 customers.

The technology of making metals with desired physical and chemical properties is highly complex. Modern production technology allows better control of the process and is more energy-efficient, but is also expensive to install. Many modern plants are highly automated, partly to reduce the need for expensive labor. Computerized inventory systems are used to track thousands of products at multiple locations.

Sales & Marketing

Primary customers are manufacturers of autos, appliances, machinery, aircraft, wire, metal containers, and the commercial construction industry. Metals and secondary products may be sold directly to large users like the auto industry, or wholesalers called metals service centers, which buy and stock metals in standard forms and grades for resale to local manufacturers. The auto industry is the largest single end-use customer for steel, using sheets for car bodies and castings for engines, axles, power trains, and brake housings. The construction industry uses steel girders and plates. Aluminum is produced primarily as sheets and plates for aircraft and truck bodies, and as rigid container sheet (RCS) for pressing into bever-

age cans. Copper is used primarily for making electrical wire, cable, and piping.

Because of the relatively small number of producers, advertising is unnecessary. Companies market their production capabilities and competition is usually based on delivered price. Producers may have long-term supply contracts with large users. Market prices for steel products such as cold-rolled sheets can vary by 20 to 30 percent within a year; prices for aluminum and copper can fluctuate even more sharply.

Human Resources

Despite many jobs in primary metal production requiring special technical skills, average industry wages are only 10 percent higher than the US average. The safety of the industry has improved, but working with hot metals is inherently dangerous. The industry injury rate is double the national average.

Fringe benefits are generally high, but differ in the various industry segments. As a percent of payroll, fringe benefits average 27 percent for steel products manufactured from purchased metal, 36 percent for aluminum production, and a very high 42 percent for iron and steel mills. The high levels of fringe benefits are a major issue, because they deter outside buyers, including foreign operators, from acquiring US mills.

Industry Employment Growth

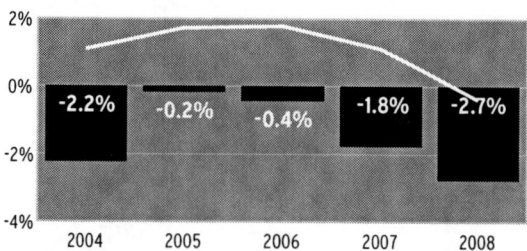

Average Hourly Earnings

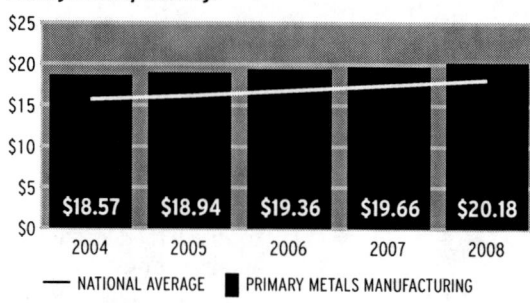

SOURCE: BUREAU OF LABOR STATISTICS

Call Preparation Questions

What is the company's strategy for dealing with cyclical changes in metal demand?

Demand for primary metals depends on the health of the US manufacturing sector, particularly the manufacture of motor vehicles, metal products, and machinery, and on commercial construction.

How is the company taking advantage of increased demand for specialty steel?

More US companies have moved into manufacturing and processing higher-grade products, such as stainless and high-strength steel.

How does the company manage exposure to higher energy costs?

Making steel requires a large amount of energy, around 3 percent of total US energy consumption.

Web Links

American Iron and Steel Institute

Industry news, statistics, links.
www.steel.org

American Metal Market LLC

Extensive industry news (by paid subscription) and issues.
www.amm.com

Association for Iron & Steel Technology

Steel industry news, technology.
www.aist.org

Forging Industry Association

Technical explanations and statistics.
www.forging.org

International Iron and Steel Institute (IISI)

World news.
www.worldsteel.org

Stainless Steel World

Industry news.
www.stainless-steel-world.net

Steel Recycling Institute

Facts and figures on steel recycling and the recycling process.
www.recycle-steel.org

SteelLinks.com

Search engine dedicated to the steel industry.
www.steellinks.com

The Aluminum Association

Industry news.
www.aluminum.org

United Steelworkers

Labor issues and trade news for the steel industry.
www.usw.org

Glossary of Acronyms

AISI — American Iron and Steel Institute
OEM — original equipment manufacturer
RCS — rigid container sheet
SSINA — Specialty Steel Industry of North America
USW — United Steelworkers

HOOVER'S TOP COMPANIES

Largest Companies by Sales	($ mil.)
Alcoa Inc.	26,901.0
United States Steel Corporation	23,754.0
Nucor Corporation	23,663.3
Freeport-McMoRan Copper & Gold	17,796.0
Commercial Metals Company	10,427.4
Steel Dynamics, Inc.	8,080.5
AK Steel Holding Corporation	7,644.3
Aleris International, Inc.	5,989.9
Gerdau Ameristeel Corporation	5,806.6
Allegheny Technologies Incorporated	5,309.7

Largest Employers	Employees
Alcoa Inc.	87,000
United States Steel Corporation	28,000
Freeport-McMoRan Copper & Gold	25,400
Nucor Corporation	18,000
Commercial Metals Company	15,276
Gerdau Ameristeel Corporation	10,140
Allegheny Technologies Incorporated	9,600
Aleris International, Inc.	8,800
Worthington Industries, Inc.	6,900
AK Steel Holding Corporation	6,800

Fastest Growing* by Five-Year Sales Growth	(%)
Aleris International, Inc.	54.2
Steel Dynamics, Inc.	52.3
Academy Corporation	35.9
RathGibson, Inc.	31.1
Nucor Corporation	30.4
Commercial Metals Company	29.4
Universal Stainless & Alloy Products, Inc.	26.5
Gerdau Ameristeel Corporation	24.5
Allegheny Technologies Incorporated	22.3
Century Aluminum Company	20.3

Fastest Growing* by Five-Year Employee Growth	(%)
Steel Dynamics, Inc.	94.4
Aleris International, Inc.	40.2
Nucor Corporation	26.2
Commercial Metals Company	14.2
Academy Corporation	13.8
Gerdau Ameristeel Corporation	12.1
Universal Stainless & Alloy Products, Inc.	7.6
RathGibson, Inc.	4.9
Century Aluminum Company	4.2
Worthington Industries, Inc.	0.6

Top Public Companies by Market Value	($ mil.)
Nucor Corporation	14,505.7
Freeport-McMoRan Copper & Gold	9,385.0
Alcoa Inc.	9,011.6
Gerdau Ameristeel Corporation	6,149.6
United States Steel Corporation	4,322.6

* These rates are compounded annualized increases and may have resulted from acquisitions or one time gains. If less than 6 years of data are available, growth is for the years available.

SOURCE: HOOVER'S, INC., DATABASE

Printer Manufacturing

The US printing machinery and equipment industry includes about 460 companies with combined annual revenue of about $3 billion. Major companies include offset equipment manufacturer Goss International and digital printer manufacturers Hewlett-Packard and Presstek. The industry is concentrated: the 50 largest companies have over 70 percent market share.

The printing machinery and equipment industry doesn't include home and office printers connected to PCs or small office/home office (SOHO) desktop publishing systems.

Competitive Landscape

Demand is driven by commercial print volume, which depends primarily on advertising and other business needs for printed material. About 35,000 commercial printers serve US business needs; about 1,400 daily newspapers with daily circulation over 50 million also drive industry demand. Profitability of individual companies depends primarily on manufacturing efficiencies. Large companies have advantages of economies of scale in purchasing and manufacturing. Small companies can compete effectively by marketing and manufacturing products for niche markets, such as ticket printing for sports events. Average annual revenue per worker for printer manufacturers is about $200,000.

Products, Operations & Technology

Major products are printing presses (about 25 percent of industry revenue); prepress equipment (25 percent); binding machinery (10 percent); and parts and accessories (15 percent). The predominant printing press technology used is offset lithography, but the industry is transitioning to digital presses for many applications. Other types of printing technologies include rotogravure and flexography. Rotogravure is used for high-quality printing and is expen-

BUSINESS CHALLENGES

» Shift to Digital Technology

Digital technologies are changing the printing industry. Digital printers continue to increase in speed and print quality and are replacing traditional mechanical printing equipment in many applications. Digital printers provide print shops greater flexibility by making shorter print runs cost-effective and enabling customization of individual documents. Digital print files allow print shops to provide services remotely. Printer manufacturers must develop new digital products or integrate digital technology into existing products to remain competitive.

» Online Advertising

Advertising represents the single largest source of print business; as such, printing equipment manufacturers are directly impacted by changes in advertising. The print sector of the ad industry has been steadily losing market share to online advertising. Loss of ad revenue makes remaining profitable difficult for newspapers and magazines; many have online versions of their publications to satisfy changing customer demands and derive ad revenue online.

» Lower Print Demand

As a percentage of ad and marketing communications, print volume is losing ground to the Internet. The growth of the printing industry has slowed, despite a robust business climate over the past several years. Between 1999 and 2003, the industry lost an estimated $16 billion in printing services due to alternate forms of information transfer, according to InfoTrends/Cap Ventures and Frank Romano, a professor at the Rochester Institute of Technology. The shift from print to electronic communication has continued since 2003 and results in lower demand for printer manufacturers.

sive. Flexography is used primarily for printing on packaging materials.

The offset printing process begins by transferring the image to be printed to a set of plates, usually made of aluminum, plastic, or paper. This preparation of plates is known as the prepress operation. In most instances, digital imaging is used to transfer the image to the plates using negatives. The latest prepress technology uses a direct "computer-to-plate" (CTP) process.

Printing presses are designed to feed paper stock in one of two ways: sheet fed (pre-cut sheets) or web (continuous rolls). As paper is fed into the press, a series of rollers apply water and ink to the plates; ink is applied to the imaged area while water keeps ink off the non-image areas of the plates. The plate transfers the image to a rubber blanket, which in turn, transfers the image to the paper. The term "offset" is applied to this process because the plates containing the images don't directly contact the paper. After the ink is applied, the paper passes through a gas-fired oven and a series of metal "chill rollers" to quickly dry and cool the paper and ink, preventing smudging. For color printing, color control and registration is achieved through computer-controlled alignment and release of inks.

Printing presses are high-tech equipment: web presses can print up to 32 letter-sized pages on a continuous feed sheet at speeds of up to 40,000 per hour. Some presses may weigh several tons, but contain parts to tolerances of thousandths of millimeters. Quality control checks are performed on parts frequently during the manufacturing process to ensure performance specifications are met. Some manufacturers build their own subassemblies to ensure quality control; others rely on outside vendors that specialize in manufacturing precision parts.

Peripheral equipment used in feeding, sorting, folding, collating, stamping, addressing, and bundling printed materials are about half of the US manufactured product mix, as most printing presses are produced offshore. These peripheral components must perform precise material handling at high speeds to keep up with presses and are computer-controlled, sophisticated machinery.

Inputs for printing machinery include steel structural components, rollers, cylinders, pneumatic parts, electronics, and computers. Material costs represent about 50 percent of revenue. Some offset presses may have 100,000 parts being controlled and synchronized by electronic processors and computers. Machining, structural fabrication, assembly, electronics and computer integration, and system testing are the most common manufacturing processes. Lead times for delivery of custom equipment may exceed one year, while some presses, espe-

cially standard digital models, are essentially off-the-shelf items.

Companies use computer information systems to manage large parts inventories and schedule and track customer orders through the manufacturing process. CAD systems are used to develop new equipment and components. Customer service systems track spare part inventories and help schedule service technicians.

Sales & Marketing

Typical customers are print shops, newspaper publishers, and book binderies. About 35,000 print shops and more than 1,400 daily newspapers with a daily circulation of more than 50 million copies operate in the US. Printing equipment is used largely by printers of magazines, newspapers and inserts, direct mailers, flyers, product brochures, phone books, reference materials, event tickets, paperbacks, and hard-bound books.

Printing machinery and equipment manufacturers use a combination of in-house sales forces, manufacturer reps, and distributors to sell products. Primary marketing tools are printed product brochures, websites, and trade shows. Annual trade shows of the printing industry are particularly effective vehicles for new product introductions. The Graphic Arts Show Company hosts the annual GRAPHEXPO in Chicago and every four years stages PRINT, a much larger convention.

Most companies market on both their own and distributor websites. Websites serve as a venue for sales of new and used equipment, and for replacement parts.

Prices for printing equipment vary. Equipment may be bought for as little as a few thousand dollars for auxiliary products or as much as several million for a state-of-the-art high speed press. Prices for printing services have been relatively flat for the past several years, making raising prices difficult for printing equipment manufacturers.

Human Resources

The industry requires mechanical, electrical, and computer engineering skills to design and integrate systems and to conduct R&D. Production employees need skills including welding, cutting, bending, punching, drilling, and machining metals using computer-controlled equipment. Production workers average about $18 per hour, close to the national average for all production workers. Fringe benefits for all employees average about 20 percent of wages.

Training is often on the job because of the unique requirements for assembling printing machinery. Some trade schools and community colleges offer courses for the printing industry. Rochester Institute of Technology houses one of the most prominent printing education centers.

Call Preparation Questions

What digital products does the company offer?

Digital technologies are changing the printing industry.

How has online advertising affected demand for the company's products?

Advertising represents the single largest source of print business; as such, printing equipment manufacturers are directly impacted by changes in advertising.

What trend has the company seen in overall US print volume?

As a percentage of ad and marketing communications, print volume is losing ground to the Internet.

What post-sales support does the company offer customers?

Manufacturers may support customers with post-sales programs for user training, preventive maintenance, technical support, and audits.

What opportunities does the company see in partnering with offshore manufacturers?

Most printing presses are manufactured offshore, so US manufacturers of peripheral equipment are partnering with foreign press manufacturers to offer integrated solutions to customers.

Web Links

American Printer Magazine

Technology, product, and management of print industry.
www.americanprinter.com

Printing Impressions

Monthly online publication on industry trends, technologies, and news.
www.piworld.com

Printing Industry of America/Graphic Arts Technical Foundation

Printing industry trade association with over 16,000 members.
www.gain.net

Printing News

Weekly news for the print industry of CT, NJ, NY, and PA.
printingnews.com

The Association for Suppliers of Printing, Publishing and Converting Technologies

Association for machinery, equipment, and suppliers to the printing industry.
www.npes.org

Glossary of Acronyms

CTP — computer-to-plate
DI — direct imaging
POD — print-on-demand
SOHO — small office/home office
USPS — United States Postal Service
VOC — volatile organic compounds

HOOVER'S TOP COMPANIES

Largest Companies by Sales	($ mil.)
Hewlett-Packard Company	118,364.0
Xerox Corporation	17,608.0
Goss International Corporation	1,110.0
Presstek, Inc.	254.8
Baldwin Technology Company, Inc.	236.3
Pamarco Technologies, Inc.	75.0
Graphic Controls LLC	68.0
Delphax Technologies Inc.	44.6
Heidelberg USA, Inc.	—
Ricoh Americas Corporation	—

Largest Employers	Employees
Hewlett-Packard Company	321,000
Xerox Corporation	57,400
Ricoh Americas Corporation	11,000
Goss International Corporation	4,000
Océ North America, Inc.	3,000
Pamarco Technologies, Inc.	1,050
Heidelberg USA, Inc.	1,000
Presstek, Inc.	712
Baldwin Technology Company, Inc.	699
Delphax Technologies Inc.	286

Fastest Growing* by Five-Year Sales Growth	(%)
Presstek, Inc.	25.0
Baldwin Technology Company, Inc.	12.0
Hewlett-Packard Company	10.1
Xerox Corporation	2.3
Goss International Corporation	0.5

Fastest Growing* by Five-Year Employee Growth	(%)
Presstek, Inc.	22.1
Hewlett-Packard Company	17.7
Baldwin Technology Company, Inc.	5.0

Top Public Companies by Market Value	($ mil.)
Hewlett-Packard Company	92,446.2
Xerox Corporation	6,892.3
Presstek, Inc.	177.3
Baldwin Technology Company, Inc.	33.4

* These rates are compounded annualized increases and may have resulted from acquisitions or one time gains. If less than 6 years of data are available, growth is for the years available.

SOURCE: HOOVER'S, INC., DATABASE

Private Schools K-12

About 27,000 private primary and secondary schools operate in the US with combined annual revenue of $25 billion. About 80 percent of these schools are affiliated with religious organizations, 30 percent with the Roman Catholic Church. While most private schools are tax-exempt, nonprofit entities, some operate on a for-profit basis.

Competitive Landscape

Demand is driven by perceived inadequacies in the public school system. The success of an individual school depends largely on its reputation for quality. Large schools can offer a wider range of instruction and have some economies of scale. Small schools can be successful by providing instruction in a special field. Schools are highly labor-intensive.

Products, Operations & Technology

Private schools provide primary and secondary education through a curriculum that is similar to that in public schools. About 60 percent of private schools provide education only through the primary grades (from kindergarten through the fifth or sixth grades); 10 percent provide only secondary education. Operations are similar to those at public schools: schools hire teachers, administrators, and support staff; buy educational and other materials; and buy or rent buildings and other space for classrooms and other student activities. Larger schools may operate food and sleeping facilities.

About half of private school students attend Catholic schools, which have an average of about 300 students. Other private schools are typically smaller, with an average of 130 students. The average public school has 530 students. The student-teacher ratio is 17:1 at Catholic schools; 12:1 at other religious schools; and 9:1 at independent schools. The national average for public schools is 16:1.

BUSINESS CHALLENGES

» High Costs Restrict Enrollment

Although the cost to attend many private religious schools is modest, only $2,000 for local Catholic elementary schools on average, the cost to attend a large number of the 6,000 independent private schools is beyond the means of most Americans. The average annual cost to attend a private boarding school is about $20,000; for a non-boarding school, about $9,000.

» Changing Demographics

The number of school-aged children in the US will change little near-term. Between 2000 and 2010, the total number of children 5 to 19 will increase just 1 percent. While the number of white and black children will each decrease 1 percent, the number of Hispanic children will increase 27 percent, pressuring enrollment at Catholic schools.

» Competition from Public Magnet, Charter Schools

Magnet and charter schools are efforts by the public school system to compete with traditional local public schools, but within the public system. Magnet schools offer advanced or specialized classes that draw students from a wide area. Publicly funded charter schools, operated by community-based groups, private business, or groups of educators and parents, are free from many of the regulations that burden ordinary public schools. Over half the states have passed legislation authorizing charter schools, and about 2,000 charter schools operate nationwide. To the extent that magnet and charter schools succeed in correcting some of the deficiencies of the public school system, they directly compete with private schools.

Parents send their children to private schools because of the perception that they provide a better academic or moral education. Some private schools provide intensive instruction unavailable in regular public schools, such as in music or art. Various objective measures, like test scores and eventual college attendance, seem to bear out the academic superiority of private schools. Catholic high schools have a graduation rate of 95 percent, versus 66 percent for public high schools, and the average SAT score is typically 10 percent higher at private schools, but parents' attitude and involvement may account for these differences.

Schools have two types of costs: instruction (teachers, equipment, libraries), which accounts for 62 percent of the total; and support services (counseling, health services, activities, athletics, maintenance, administration, etc.). Private schools spend less per student per year (about $3,500) than public schools (about $6,200). Per student spending at private schools varies from $2,000 in Catholic elementary schools to more than $9,000 in independent secondary schools.

To match or surpass public schools, many private schools spend heavily on computer and communication technology, mainly to allow students access to e-mail and the Internet. Some private schools use computers extensively for instruction and administration.

Sales & Marketing

Since most private schools have a religious affiliation, they market their services mainly through their church (or similar institution). Independent schools market through ads in newspapers and education magazines, inclusion in catalogs, and contacts with public schools. Word-of-mouth is one of the strongest marketing forces.

Admission policies vary widely. Some private schools will accept any applicant who satisfies minimal requirements. Some schools have more applicants than they can accept.

Human Resources

The lower spending per student in private schools results in part from lower salaries and benefits paid to teachers. In Catholic schools the average teacher salary is about $25,000; in independent schools about $30,000. The average teacher salary in public schools is over $35,000. Despite lower pay, surveys show that private school teachers are more satisfied with their jobs, both because of the more favorable climate for teaching and because they have more control over the curriculum they teach.

Call Preparation Questions

How have high tuition costs modified the composition of the school's student body?

Although the cost to attend many private religious schools is modest, only $2,000 for local Catholic elementary schools on average, the cost to attend a large number of the 6,000 independent private schools is beyond the means of most Americans.

Does the school expect changes in the local school-age population?

The number of school-aged children in the US will change little near-term.

What effect has competition from public magnet and charter schools had on enrollment?

Magnet and charter schools are efforts by the public school system to compete with traditional local public schools, but within the public system.

Has the school increased recruiting of foreign students?

US private boarding schools attract a large number of students from other countries.

How does the school keep the student-teacher ratio low?

Parents say a safer environment and a better focus on academic achievement, as well as low class size at independent private schools, are primary reasons why private schooling is superior to public; the student-to-teacher ratio is about 9:1.

Web Links

Independent Schools Association of the Central States

Excellent statistics about 200 independent schools in the Midwest.
www.isacs.org

National Catholic Educational Association

Statistics about Catholic schools.
www.ncea.org

National Center for Education Statistics – Elementary/Secondary Surveys

Includes statistics from the Private School Surveys.
http://nces.ed.gov/surveys-/SurveyGroups.asp?group=1

National Christian School Association

Information.
www.nationalchristian.org

Private Schools: A Brief Portrait

Data from The Condition of Education 2002.
nces.ed.gov/pubs2002/2002025_Analyses.pdf

The National Association of Independent Schools (NAIS)

Information on private schools.
www.nais.org

US Department of Education – Office of Non-Public Education

Studies and statistics.
www.ed.gov/about/offices/list/oii/nonpublic

Glossary of Acronyms

FTE — full-time equivalent teacher
NAIS — National Association of Independent Schools
NCEA — National Catholic Educational Association
NELS — National Educational Longitudinal Study
NCES — National Center for Education Statistics

Professional Services

THIS INDUSTRY
INCLUDES:

NAICS CODES
54   Professional,
      Scientific, and
      Technical Services

Professional services account for a large part of the US economy, generating about $600 billion in annual revenue for 600,000 individual firms. The largest segments are legal services ($130 billion); engineering services ($120 billion); computer-related services ($110 billion); accounting ($60 billion); management consulting ($60 billion); advertising ($50 billion); and scientific research ($25 billion).

Brokerage services, if added to this industry, would add another $200 billion of revenue, including securities brokerage ($80 billion); insurance brokerage ($60 billion); and real estate brokerage ($40 billion).

Most professional firms are small. Only about 5,000 firms have annual revenue over $10 million. The vast majority have a single office.

Competitive Landscape

Demand is driven heavily by the health of the US economy and particularly by corporate profits. While some professional services are necessary for the normal functioning of most companies, some of the most profitable services aren't considered essential and are often postponed when corporate profits are low. The profitability of professional service firms is closely tied to good marketing, because many costs are fixed. Small firms can compete successfully with large firms in their segment if they offer special expertise.

Products, Operations & Technology

Professional firms provide services that require special expertise but are needed only occasionally. Because of this intermittent, or single, use, firms can make their expertise available to many customers and serve several customers at the same time.

The services sold are often expert advice, but routine operations, transactions' processing, design work, and project supervision are also common. Most work is project-oriented, al-

BUSINESS CHALLENGES

» Corporate Spending Sharply Affects Revenue
Many corporate customers cut outside expenses or delay major projects when profits are low. The revenue of many professional firms dropped during the early 2000s recession; particularly hard-hit were engineering, computer-related services, and ad firms. Spending decreased 20 percent for corporate construction and 8 percent for business equipment.

» Greater Liability for Professional Advice
Because of the greater involvement of professional firms in the operations of corporate customers, firms face greater risk of blame or liability when their advice proves faulty. Customers are quicker to blame advisors, and regulators are more likely to impose penalties. Arthur Andersen essentially went out of business after its involvement with accounting irregularities at Enron.

» Industry Concentration
Many professional firms specialize in providing services to companies in a particular industry, such as real estate, manufacturing, or technology, and are disproportionately hurt if that industry is in a downturn. Large firms often serve a range of industries, but midsized firms have often grown by expanding within an industry and are particularly vulnerable.

though many legal and accounting services are delivered on a continuing basis.

Professional firms consist mainly of a staff of professionals with various levels of expertise, and support personnel with technical or clerical skills. A typical customer project is supervised by senior staff and executed by a team of junior professionals and support staff. In some cases a project team can include hundreds of individuals and require complex coordination.

Large offices with many professionals have significant economies of scale and usually produce higher annual revenue per person ($150,000) than small offices ($70,000), partly because they're more likely to work on large projects for corporate customers. Despite the advantages of size, the various segments of the industry are highly fragmented. In accounting and scientific research, the largest 20 firms hold 45 percent of the market, and in advertising 40 percent; but engineering, management consulting, and computer services hold only 25 percent, and legal services a mere 6 percent. The fragmentation is due to the high degree of specialization of most firms. There are dozens of areas of legal work firms can specialize in, such as antitrust, arbitration, intellectual property, and litigation.

Sales & Marketing

Most professional work is for corporate customers, although a big portion of legal work is for individuals. Consequently, most marketing is aimed at establishing long-term relationships with corporate customers or enhancing the firm's reputation. New customers may come through referrals from other firms, sales calls on potential customers, or bids on new projects. Bidding is common in the engineering, computer services, management consulting and advertising sectors. A bid generally consists of a plan for how a project will be done and a cost estimate. Firms are often invited to bid on a project in competition with other firms through a request for proposal (RFP).

Larger firms often advertise their areas of expertise in industry publications. Small firms typically rely more on referrals and Yellow Pages' advertising. Industry conferences and meetings are also important sources of new customer contacts.

Many firms, legal, accounting, and engineering firms in particular (and especially small ones), get a large amount of work on a recurring basis from existing customers. Large firms frequently have long-term relationships with corporate or government customers that they maintain by supplying a range of services. The loss of a large customer "account," as happens most often in the advertising and accounting segments, can have a major effect on revenue.

The size of professional firms depends partly on the breadth of expertise a firm can offer, partly on how many customers a firm wants to serve, and partly on how easily it can reproduce its basic service unit. Most law firms consist of a single lawyer with one or two support staff, while a large firm like Jones Day employs more than 2,000 lawyers in 30 offices. Size is important for large corporate customers, which want to hire a firm that can provide a full range of services.

Some of the largest professional firms, such as PricewaterhouseCoopers, with billions of annual revenue, are collections of semi-autonomous offices that all offer similar services.

Because many projects require a breadth of expertise that individual firms may not have, partnerships or alliances with other firms are common. Small firms may get a major part of revenue providing services to other professional firms, particularly in the legal and engineering service segments.

Human Resources

Attracting, training, and retaining expert staff is one of the largest problems for professional firms, especially for those with just a handful of professionals. Many firms are organized as partnerships and attract new professional staff with the offer or possibility of being a partner.

Salaries are usually high because of the high expertise of the employees. Compared to the US average hourly wage of $15, accountants in 2002 were paid an average $24, engineers $33, and lawyers $44.

Industry Employment Growth

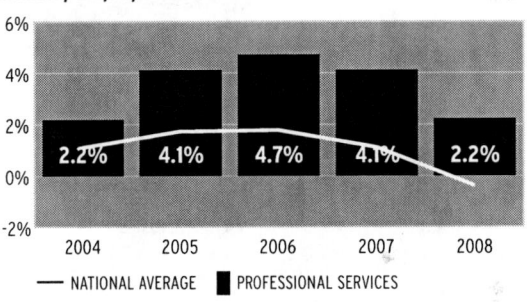

SOURCE: BUREAU OF LABOR STATISTICS

Call Preparation Questions

How does the firm mitigate the risk that customers will sue?

Because of the greater involvement of professional firms in the operations of corporate customers, firms face greater risk of blame or liability when their advice proves faulty.

How reliant is the firm on a particular industry or a few top customers?

Many professional firms specialize in providing services to companies in a particular industry, such as real estate, manufacturing, or technology, and are disproportionately hurt if that industry is in a downturn.

How is the increased complexity of corporate regulations impacting the firm?

The operations of corporations (the major customers of most professional service firms) and the regulatory climate have become more complicated in the past decade, leading more corporations to seek expert outside advice.

How is the firm benefiting from the trend in corporate outsourcing?

The drive for greater efficiency through outsourcing corporate functions will continue to put more work in the hands of professional firms.

Web Links

AccountingWEB

Industry news, links, services.
www.accountingweb.com

Advertising Age

News. Industry data on advertising, media, and marketing industries.
adage.com/dataplace

American Bar Association

Ethics, news, education.
www.abanet.org

American Institute of Architects

Primary site for information, articles, and statistics.
www.e-architect.com/news/research/home2.asp

American Institute of Certified Public Accountants

Industry news and current issues.
www.aicpa.org

Association of Management Consulting Firms

Publishes annual operating ratios for consulting firms.
www.amcf.org

Engineering News-Record

News by specialized areas, articles. Listings of Top Firms.
www.enr.com

Information Technology Association of America

Articles, news, publications, government affairs, calendars, and events.
www.itaa.org

InformationWeek

News. See especially Business Services section.
www.informationweek.com

Kennedy Consulting Research & Advisory

Industry news and articles. Consulting magazine.
www.kennedyinfo.com/consulting

The American Lawyer

Industry news.
www.americanlawyer.com

Glossary of Acronyms

IT — information technology
RFP — request for proposal

HOOVER'S TOP COMPANIES

Largest Companies by Sales	($ mil.)
International Business Machines Corporation	103,630.0
Deloitte Touche Tohmatsu	27,400.0
Bechtel Group, Inc.	27,000.0
Fluor Corporation	22,325.9
Computer Sciences Corporation	16,499.5
Omnicom Group Inc.	13,359.9
SAIC, Inc.	8,935.0
Affiliated Computer Services, Inc.	6,160.5
McKinsey & Company	5,330.0
KPMG L.L.P.	4,100.0

Largest Employers	Employees
International Business Machines Corporation	426,969
Deloitte Touche Tohmatsu	165,000
Computer Sciences Corporation	89,000
Collectors Universe, Inc.	72,000
Omnicom Group Inc.	70,000
Affiliated Computer Services, Inc.	65,000
PricewaterhouseCoopers LLP	45,940
SAIC, Inc.	43,800
Bechtel Group, Inc.	42,500
Fluor Corporation	41,260

Fastest Growing* by Five-Year Sales Growth	(%)
Acacia Research Corporation	113.0
TransPerfect Translations, Inc.	46.1
ExlService Holdings, Inc.	45.6
Lionbridge Technologies, Inc.	26.6
TechTeam Global, Inc.	24.2
Bechtel Group, Inc.	18.4
Getty Images, Inc.	13.1
Deloitte Touche Tohmatsu	12.7
McKinsey & Company	12.2
Omnicom Group Inc.	9.2

Fastest Growing* by Five-Year Employee Growth	(%)
Collectors Universe, Inc.	628.8
TransPerfect Translations, Inc.	47.4
ExlService Holdings, Inc.	39.7
TechTeam Global, Inc.	16.6
Lionbridge Technologies, Inc.	8.3
Affiliated Computer Services, Inc.	7.7
Deloitte Touche Tohmatsu	6.7
Omnicom Group Inc.	6.3
McKinsey & Company	5.4
International Business Machines Corporation	4.7

Top Public Companies by Market Value	($ mil.)
International Business Machines Corporation	112,698.3
Omnicom Group Inc.	8,272.5
Fluor Corporation	8,146.4
Computer Sciences Corporation	6,165.6
Affiliated Computer Services, Inc.	4,865.0

* These rates are compounded annualized increases and may have resulted from acquisitions or one time gains. If less than 6 years of data are available, growth is for the years available.

SOURCE: HOOVER'S, INC., DATABASE

Professional Sports Teams and Organizations

THIS INDUSTRY
INCLUDES:

SIC CODES
7941   Professional
        Sports Clubs and
        Promoters

NAICS CODES
711211 Sports Teams and
        Clubs

The professional sports teams industry includes about 800 organizations with combined annual revenue of over $16 billion. The dominant professional sports leagues in the US are the National Football League (NFL); the National Basketball Association (NBA); Major League Baseball (MLB); and the National Hockey League (NHL). Other less popular professional sports leagues include the Women's National Basketball Association (WNBA); Major League Soccer (MLS); and the National Lacrosse League. The industry is concentrated: the top 50 organizations have 60 percent of industry revenue.

The industry includes both major league and minor league sports teams, but not "non-team" professional sports, such as golf, tennis, and boxing.

Competitive Landscape

Demand is driven by consumer income and corporate entertainment spending. The profitability of individual teams depends on achieving high fan attendance and a large TV audience, both of which are enhanced by effective marketing and competitive play. Teams in large metropolitan areas have advantages in the population base and TV audience they can draw on, though they may face competition from other teams. Teams in smaller markets, along with less popular sports and minor league teams, can compete by building fan loyalty through local marketing promotions and an appeal to civic pride. Average annual revenue per worker across all sports teams is over $325,000.

Products, Operations & Technology

Major revenue sources for professional sports teams are admissions (about 40 percent of revenue); TV and radio fees (40 percent); advertising and endorsement fees (10 percent); and food and concession sales (5 percent).

BUSINESS CHALLENGES

» Dependence on TV Revenues

Major league sports rely on TV contracts for nearly half of their revenue, so TV considerations affect league operations. TV timeouts for commercials have become a standard part of football, basketball, and hockey games. Baseball's World Series shifted from day to night games to reach the primetime TV audience. Since the TV networks have lost money on sports broadcasting in recent years and TV viewership isn't growing, future TV contracts may not be as lucrative for the leagues.

» High Player Salaries

The importance of star players in attracting fans and TV revenues has led to bidding wars among teams and rapid escalation of salaries for top talent. The average annual player salary across all four major leagues is over $3 million, led by the NBA with an average player salary of about $5 million. Salaries can range from $300,000 for a backup player to over $20 million for a superstar. Most players employ professional sports agents to negotiate favorable contract terms. Owner attempts to control rising payroll costs have led to some form of team salary cap for all the leagues, except MLB.

» Player Drug Use

Negative publicity about players "cheating" by using performance enhancing drugs has tarnished the reputations of the major leagues. In response, all have implemented stricter policies prohibiting steroid use. These policies mandate random drug testing for all players and suspensions for the first offense. Multiple offenses can result in annual or lifetime suspensions, depending on the league. Current policies require drug testing via urine samples only, which can't detect players using human growth hormone (HGH). Blood samples are required to test for HGH.

Other revenue comes from program sales, merchandise sales, and facility rental fees.

Major League Baseball (MLB); the National Basketball Association (NBA); and the National Hockey League (NHL) consist of 30 teams each, while the National Football League (NFL) has 32. Within each league, teams are assigned to conferences and divisions for regular season play. The number of games played by each team in the regular season varies from 16 for the NFL to 162 for MLB; NBA and NHL teams play 82 games each.

Teams prepare for the regular season through training camps and preseason exhibition games. Coaches assess player talent during the preseason to determine the depth chart for each position — which players will be starters and which will be backups. Some players are cut from the team to get to the active roster the league allows. The number of players allowed on the active roster ranges from 12 for the NBA to 53 for the NFL.

The winners of each division and other teams with the best won-loss records during the regular season qualify for the playoffs. The number of playoff teams depends on the league: eight for MLB, 12 for the NFL, and 16 each for the NBA and NHL. The playoffs culminate with the crowning of a league champion.

Due to its large number of games, MLB has a total attendance greater than the other three leagues combined. In 2006, MLB had an attendance of over 76 million, or about 31,000 fans per game. The NFL averaged about 68,000 fans per game, but only 17 million in total attendance due to fewer games. Both the NBA and NHL averaged about 17,000 fans per game and 21 million in total attendance.

Venues for professional sports include stadiums and arenas, of which 70 percent are publicly owned. NFL stadiums range from 60,000 to 91,000 seats, while MLB stadiums seat 34,000 to 57,000; NBA and NHL arenas vary from about 16,000 to 22,000. Public facilities may be operated by the team owner (about 45 percent); the municipality (35 percent); or a facility management company (20 percent). Constructing new stadiums and arenas typically costs $400 to $600 million.

Professional sports teams use information technology to analyze team and player statistics, develop marketing programs, and automate accounting and administrative functions. Many teams use data mining software to gain insight into customer demographics and develop targeted marketing promotions and campaigns. Video technology helps coaches analyze games and provides instant replay capabilities to officials. Some teams are experimenting with "smart tickets" incorporating radio frequency identification (RFID) tags to speed admissions and prevent counterfeiting. Most teams have an official website where fans can learn about players, review game schedules, order tickets, and buy team merchandise.

Sales & Marketing

Customers for professional sports teams are individual fans and corporations that buy tickets for business entertainment or employee rewards. Typical fans are male, who range from 53 percent of fans for MLB to 60 percent for the NBA. Baseball fans tend to be older than fans for the other major sports; more than half of MLB TV viewers are over 50, compared to just 40 percent of NFL viewers.

Marketing programs consist primarily of local newspaper, billboard, radio, TV, and direct mail advertising. Teams invest in community relations through support of local charities and player appearances at community events. Teams also encourage positive press coverage by sports reporters for local newspapers and TV stations by arranging interviews with players and management.

Average ticket prices range from about $20 for MLB to about $60 for the NFL. Minor league baseball tickets are typically $7, to compete with movie theaters as a family entertainment activity. Due to the limited number of games played, most NFL franchises sell all or nearly all of their seats through season ticket packages. The other leagues depend more on individual game ticket sales, though the most desirable seats may be available only through season ticket packages. Teams charge higher prices for premium seating, such as club seats and luxury suites, which are typically sold to corporations for entertaining clients. Luxury suite prices range from $25,000 to $350,000 per season.

Human Resources

The success of professional sports teams depends on the skills of their players and how well they develop new talent and recruit established talent. Each league has a player development system and teams employ scouting staffs to assess new talent. The NFL and NBA rely primarily on college sports to develop players, though the NBA has also established the NBA D-League and recruits talent from international professional leagues. Both MLB and the NHL have traditionally relied on a minor league system to develop players signed out of high school; however, both are increasingly drafting college players and recruiting players internationally.

All four major leagues have player unions and collective bargaining agreements (CBAs) that govern salaries and contract terms. CBAs set minimum salaries for players, define pension benefits, and define when and how a player may negotiate with other teams. Players typically sign multiyear contacts that may include a signing bonus and incentive bonuses for performance on the field. The rules for a player be-

FAST FACTS

» The professional sports teams industry includes about 800 organizations with combined annual revenue of over $16 billion.

» The dominant professional sports leagues in the US are the National Football League (NFL); the National Basketball Association (NBA); Major League Baseball (MLB); and the National Hockey League (NHL).

» Major revenue sources for professional sports teams are admissions (about 40 percent of revenue); TV and radio fees (40 percent); advertising and endorsement fees (10 percent); and food and concession sales (5 percent).

» Customers for professional sports teams are individual fans and corporations that buy tickets for business entertainment or employee rewards.

» At roughly two-thirds of revenue, payroll is the most significant cost of professional sports teams.

coming a free agent, able to negotiate with other teams at the end of their contract term, vary from league to league.

Teams are generally led by a general manager, hired by the owner, who manages both the athletic and business staff. Athletic staff consists of a head coach or manager and various assistant coaches. Business staff handles marketing and finance functions.

Industry Employment Growth

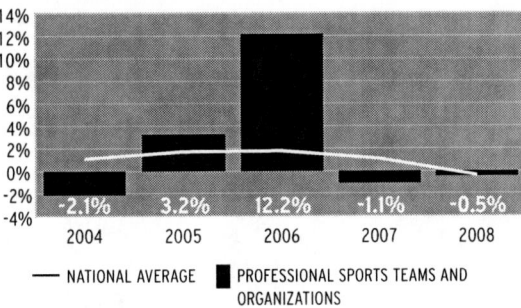

— NATIONAL AVERAGE ■ PROFESSIONAL SPORTS TEAMS AND ORGANIZATIONS

SOURCE: BUREAU OF LABOR STATISTICS

Call Preparation Questions

How much of the team's revenue is due to TV contracts?

Major league sports rely on TV contracts for nearly half of their revenue, so TV considerations affect league operations.

How does the team determine how much to spend on player salaries?

The importance of star players in attracting fans and TV revenues has led to bidding wars among teams and rapid escalation of salaries for top talent.

How has the team been challenged by enforcing anti-drug policies?

Negative publicity about players "cheating" by using performance enhancing drugs has tarnished the reputations of the major leagues.

What new venues is the team considering to broadcast its games?

The proliferation of cable TV channels and the ability to view live video on the Internet create new vehicles for teams to reach their audience.

How important are families to the team's marketing efforts?

Major league teams in smaller markets, minor league teams, and teams not in the "big four" major leagues, can build fan loyalty by appealing to families.

Web Links

ESPN

News on teams and players.
espn.go.com

MLB.com

Official site of Major League Baseball.
mlb.mlb.com

NBA

Official site of the National Basketball League.
www.nba.com

NFL Players Association

The Official Site of the NFL Players Association.
www.nflplayers.com

NFL.com

Official site of the National Football League.
www.nfl.com

NHL.com

The National Hockey League official site.
www.nhl.com

Sportbusiness.com

News on the business of sports worldwide.
www.sportbusiness.com

Sports Illustrated

Team and player news.
sportsillustrated.cnn.com

Street and Smith's SportsBusiness Journal

News on business aspects of professional sports.
www.sportsbusinessjournal.com

Glossary of Acronyms

CBA — collective bargaining agreement
HGH — human growth hormone
MLB — Major League Baseball
MLS — Major League Soccer
NBA — National Basketball Association
NFL — National Football League
NHL — National Hockey League
RFID — radio frequency identification

HOOVER'S TOP COMPANIES

Largest Organizations by Sales	($ mil.)
National Football League	6,900.0
Major League Baseball	6,500.0
National Basketball Association, Inc.	4,400.0
National Hockey League	2,747.0
San Francisco Forty Niners, Ltd.	595.2
New York Yankees Partnership	327.0
Dallas Cowboys Football Club, Ltd.	269.0
Boston Red Sox Baseball Club Limited Partnership	263.0
Hicks Sports Group Holdings LLC	—

SOURCE: HOOVER'S, INC., DATABASE

Public Relations

The US PR industry includes almost 7,000 companies with combined annual revenue of over $6 billion. The industry includes large companies such as Omnicom, WPP Group, and Interpublic as well as many privately held firms. The industry is fragmented: the top 50 companies have about 35 percent of industry revenue. A typical PR agency has annual revenue of less than $1 million and fewer than 10 employees.

Competitive Landscape

Demand is driven primarily by the health of the US economy and corporate profits. The profitability of individual companies depends on the value of the creative services delivered and efficient use of personnel. Large companies have advantages in having multiple subsidiaries that offer different marketing services to large customers and some economies of scale in marketing. Small companies can compete successfully by specializing in a particular industry or geographic market. The PR industry is labor-intensive: average annual revenue per employee is less than $150,000.

Products, Operations & Technology

About three-quarters of PR agencies provide a full range of services including media relations, crisis management services, lobbying services, event management, and fundraising services. The remaining agencies specialize in one or more of these services. PR agencies manage the communication between clients and their audiences. PR specialists work with various media to educate, correct mistakes, and build or improve the image of an organization, person, or product.

PR agencies consist mainly of a staff of professionals with various levels of expertise, and support personnel with technical and clerical skills. PR specialists interface with clients and media outlets to communicate their clients' messages. PR agencies work with media outlets

BUSINESS CHALLENGES

» Dependence on Corporate Profits

Marketing communication and PR are sometimes viewed as discretionary and may be cut in economic downturns or when corporations are struggling financially. Cutting spending with PR agencies allows companies to reduce expenses without layoffs. Many PR agencies had contracts cut in the last recession when corporate profits fell.

» Retaining Qualified Staff

Success depends on the intellectual capital and expertise of a company's employees. PR specialists build valued relationships with media members that can be easily transferred to other agencies. Companies compete for a limited number of qualified professionals, and experienced staff are kept even in slow economic times. Noncompete agreements are frequently required of associates. Failure to retain experienced staff or train additional staff can hurt future business.

» Retaining Large Clients

While client relationships are often longstanding, many companies periodically put their marketing communications services business up for competitive review. Despite a good relationship, companies may decide a fresh and different approach is appropriate and dismiss the incumbent PR agency. The business is highly competitive and small agencies often successfully steal business from larger PR agencies.

and develop relationships with those outlets to provide vehicles for their communications. PR specialists write press releases and stories for printed media, conduct interviews promoting their clients, and develop opportunities for their clients to speak directly to media channels. Some PR firms specialize in political lobbying and fundraising for particular causes or issues. Some firms specialize in representing celebrities.

The widespread dissemination of information and news via the Internet and digital communications is changing the traditional role of PR. Rather than just cultivating relationships with media outlets, PR agencies are focusing more attention on Internet messaging, "blogging," and webinars to communicate client messages directly to target audiences.

Sales & Marketing

Customers are primarily commercial businesses, government agencies, and individuals that want to establish, extend, or repair a brand or image. Small agencies may have only a handful of clients and even large agencies often rely on a few large clients. Agencies generally don't work for companies that compete with existing clients; some companies hire multiple agencies for different aspects of their marketing communications.

Customers are acquired through competitive bids when contracts come up for periodic review, agency reputation, and personal contacts. Agency management works on developing relationships with media outlets and selected industry stakeholders to attract business. PR firms use websites as marketing.

Prices for PR services typically range from $100 to $250 per hour. Most agencies negotiate for a monthly retainer from clients. Depending on the size of the retainer, agencies may bill separately for hours above the monthly amount included in the retainer.

Human Resources

The major resource of PR agencies is their staff's talent and creative expertise. Attracting and retaining accomplished professionals can be a major concern for individual companies. Wages are well above the national norm and account for up to 60 percent of revenue. The industry injury rate is minimal.

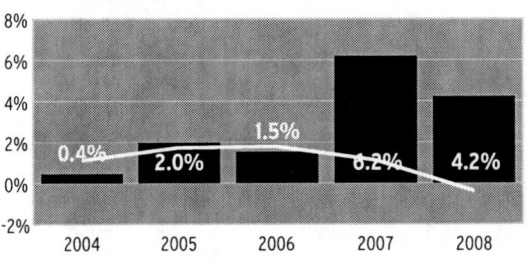

Industry Employment Growth

Year	Growth
2004	0.4%
2005	2.0%
2006	1.5%
2007	6.2%
2008	4.2%

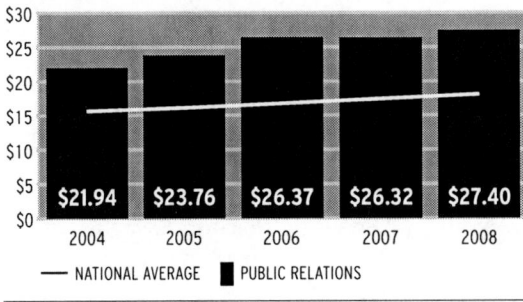

Average Hourly Earnings

Year	Public Relations
2004	$21.94
2005	$23.76
2006	$26.37
2007	$26.32
2008	$27.40

— NATIONAL AVERAGE   ▪ PUBLIC RELATIONS

SOURCE: BUREAU OF LABOR STATISTICS

Call Preparation Questions

How does the agency cope with economic swings?

Marketing communication and PR are sometimes viewed as discretionary and may be cut in economic downturns or when corporations are struggling financially.

How does the agency retain senior staff?

Success depends on the intellectual capital and expertise of a company's employees.

How does the agency retain its best clients?

While client relationships are often longstanding, many companies periodically put their marketing communications services business up for competitive review.

How is the agency ensuring that its clients' messages are received?

With the introduction of media platforms through the Internet, media usage has changed dramatically, giving consumers control.

How does the agency use podcasting for clients?

Podcasting, a multimedia file that's distributed by subscription over the Internet and played back on a PC or mobile device, has moved from the domain of technical enthusiasts to the business mainstream.

Web Links

AdWeek

Public Relations news, mergers, campaign examples.
www.adweek.com

American Marketing Association

News and events.
www.marketingpower.com

Council of Public Relations Firms

Industry events, news, publications.
www.prfirms.org

PR Week

Latest news of US PR industry.
www.prweek.com/us

Public Relations Society of America

Events, public relations tactics.
www.prsa.com

Ragan Report

Links to newsletters, training, conference listing.
www.ragan.com

Glossary of Acronyms

AMA — American Marketing Association
PRSA — Public Relations Society of America

HOOVER'S TOP COMPANIES

Largest Employers	Employees
WPP Group p.c	79,352
Omnicom Group Inc.	70,000
The Interpublic Group of Companies, Inc.	43,000
Young & Rubicam Brands	12,700
Maritz Inc.	3,920
Edelman	3,100
Hill & Knowlton, Inc.	1,585
The WORLDCOM Public Relations Group, Inc.	1,500
Waggener Edstrom Worldwide, Inc.	574
APCO Worldwide Inc.	450

Top Public Companies by Market Value	($ mil.)
Omnicom Group Inc.	8,272.5
The Interpublic Group of Companies, Inc.	1,886.6

* These rates are compounded annualized increases and may have resulted from acquisitions or one time gains. If less than 6 years of data are available, growth is for the years available.

SOURCE: HOOVER'S, INC., DATABASE

Pulp and Paper Mills

THIS INDUSTRY INCLUDES:

SIC CODES

2611   Pulp Mills
2621   Paper Mills
2631   Paperboard Mills

NAICS CODES

3221   Pulp, Paper, and
        Paperboard Mills

The US pulp, paper, and paperboard mill industry consists of about 270 companies with total combined annual revenue of more than $70 billion. Major companies include Wausau Paper and units of integrated manufacturers International Paper, Georgia-Pacific, and Weyerhaeuser. An average mill has about 300 employees and annual revenue of $125 million. The industry is highly concentrated: the top 20 companies produce 75 percent of industry revenue.

Competitive Landscape

Demand depends on both consumer and business use of paper products. The profitability of individual companies depends largely on production efficiency. Mills owned by large paper companies have advantages by being vertically integrated; the parent corporation may own timber farms, sawmills, pulp and paper mills, conversion plants, and other end-product manufacturing facilities. Small mills can compete successfully in regional markets, in close proximity to timber sources or customers. Mills are highly automated and capital-intensive: average annual revenue per employee is about $450,000.

Products, Operations & Technology

Major product segments are wood pulp, paper, paperboard, and newsprint. Paper accounts for 60 percent of industry revenue, paperboard 30 percent, and newsprint 5 percent. Other products include non-wood pulp, from cotton, straw, rag, flax, de-inked scrap paper and bagasse (the outer stalk of sugar cane), and byproducts such as turpentine and tall oil. Within the paper segment, major products are tissue papers, uncoated sheet papers, and coated printing papers. Paperboard is used mainly to make boxes and other containers.

Wood pulp is the major intermediate product used to make paper, paperboard, and

BUSINESS CHALLENGES

» Revenue Depends on Economic Activity

Demand for paper varies with the health of the national economy. Demand for printing papers depends on magazine advertising, while demand for packaging depends on consumer spending. During the early 2000s recession, US paper production dropped 8 percent.

» Import Competition Restrains Prices

Imports, mainly from Canada, account for about 20 percent of the US market. Imports can often undercut US prices because of lower costs for Canadian timber. US pulp prices were flat during the past decade.

» Fluctuating Product Prices

Prices for mill products can change rapidly in a 12 month period. Prices for wood pulp, for example, can rise or fall more than 25 percent in one year. Prices for end-products are less volatile, but often change 10 percent in a year. The uncertainty over prices discourages investment in the industry.

newsprint. Most mills produce a combination of products, but pulp mills tend to specialize by type of pulp. Other raw materials include chemicals and recycled paper. Softwoods, such as Southern pine, Hemlock, Douglas fir, and Jack pine, are primary wood sources. Mills buy wood in bolts and logs, and in chips, slabs, cores, sawdust, bark, and other forms of mill residue. Chemicals include chlorine, sodium hydroxide, sodium chlorate, aluminum sulfate, and lime. Electricity is a source of both heat and power for mills.

The cost of raw materials varies. For pulp mills, the cost of materials represents almost half the value of revenue; electricity and fuel account for around 10 percent. Companies protect against fluctuations in availability by entering into purchase agreements. Some larger companies assure supply by owning timberland.

The production process involves preparation of raw materials, the pulping operation, and the wet end and dry end operations of the paper-making machine. Wood is cleansed, cut, and sorted by size. The pulping operation breaks down the wood, separating the cellulose fibers from other impurities. Pulping involves a variety of chemical or mechanical techniques, depending on the type of paper or cellulose product being produced; the kraft process produces general purpose paper.

Wood pulp feeds through a paper-making machine that handles wet and dry processes, matting the cellulose fibers into sheets. The wet end operation removes water by spraying the pulp onto a long, wide screen called a wire. The pulp fibers bond into a mat, which felt-covered press rollers then squeeze to remove more water. At the end of the wet process, the pulp mat still contains about 60 percent water. In the dry end operation, the pulp mat passes through steam-heated metal cylinders up to 30 feet wide, which seal the pulp fibers close together, transforming the fiber mats into large sheets of paper. The calender part of the paper-making machine consists of heavy cast iron rollers that compress the paper to a consistent thickness. Paper may retain a matte finish, or papermakers may add coatings, such as fine clay, for a glossy finish. Finished paper is rolled into large spools.

The technology to produce paper is well-known, but many variations are used to produce specialty papers and increase production efficiency. Papermaking machines are highly automated, using computer controls.

Sales & Marketing

Major customers include manufacturers of "converted" paper products, such as paper bags, stationery, boxed tissue paper, coated and treated papers, and cardboard containers. Some converters use paper in construction products like insulation, sound-proofing, and wallboard.

Pulp mills tend to use an in-house sales force in the US and may have sales offices in Europe and Asia, in addition to agents and brokers. Paper and paperboard mills tend to sell through distributors. Mills may sell under "evergreen" contracts that are renewable annually, or on a spot basis. Product prices can fluctuate monthly and yearly. Prices for wood pulp, for example, can rise or fall more than 25 percent in one year. Prices are quoted by the ton. Typical newsprint prices are $600 per ton.

Human Resources

Pulp, paper, and paperboard mills pay high wages and have lower than average personnel turnover. Wages are 35 percent higher than the national average. Compensation is relatively high because employees include highly educated R&D chemical and process engineers, in addition to papermaking machinery operators and material handlers.

The industry injury rate is below the national average. Mills have steady employment throughout the year. Many hourly mill workers are members of the Paper, Allied-Industrial, Chemical & Energy Workers International Union.

Industry Employment Growth

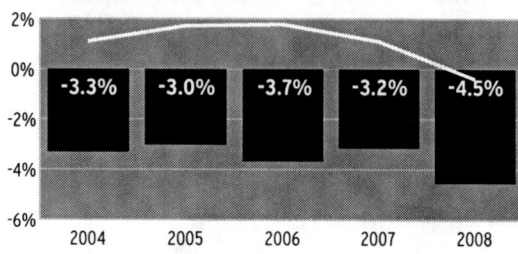

Average Hourly Earnings

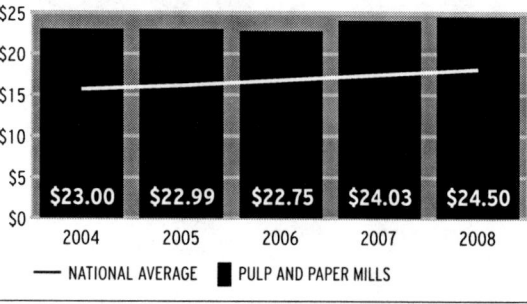

SOURCE: BUREAU OF LABOR STATISTICS

Call Preparation Questions

What does the company expect in demand trends in the next couple of years?

Demand for paper varies with the health of the national economy.

How are growing imports impacting the pulp and paper market?

Imports, mainly from Canada, account for about 20 percent of the US market.

How much have company prices changed in the past year?

Prices for mill products can change rapidly in a 12-month period.

What segments of the paper market does the company target?

Specialty or premium papers have higher profit margins than commodity items.

Has the company investigated using alternative materials for paper production?

Sugar cane fiber (bagasse) is an alternative source of raw material for pulp mills.

Web Links

American Forest and Paper Association

Paper products descriptions; industry policy; links; fun facts.
www.afandpa.org

Forest Products Association of Canada

Canadian industry facts.
www.fpac.ca

Neenah Paper

Glossary of paper terms.
www.neenahpaper.com/Glossary

PaperAge

Magazine with news releases, price indices, industry definitions.
www.paperage.com

PaperMoney Newsletter

Industry financial news.
www.globalpapermoney.org

PaperOnWeb.com

Comprehensive site; manufacturer and service provider lists; extensive industry and technical information.
www.paperonweb.com

Pulp & Paper Canada

Industry news.
www.pulpandpapercanada.com

Pulp and Paper Products Council

Pulp and paper product definitions.
www.pppc.org

Pulp and Paper Safety Association

Home page summarizes safety issues.
www.ppsa.org

Pulpwatch.com

International news, links and glossary.
www.pulpwatch.com

Resource Information Systems Inc.

News headlines, statistics, Pulp and Paper Week for subscribers.
www.risiinfo.com/pages/ind/pulp

Glossary of Acronyms

AF&PA — American Forest & Paper Association
ECF — elemental chlorine free
GP — Georgia-Pacific
IP — International Paper

NBSK — northern bleached softwood kraft
PPPC — Pulp and Paper Products Council
RFID — radio frequency identification

HOOVER'S TOP COMPANIES

Largest Companies by Sales	($ mil.)
International Paper Company	24,829.0
Weyerhaeuser Company	8,018.0
Temple-Inland Inc.	3,884.0
Verso Paper Corp.	1,766.8
Wausau Paper Corp.	1,240.4
Clearwater Paper Corporation	1,173.3
P. H. Glatfelter Company	1,157.8
The Newark Group, Inc.	1,028.9
Neenah Paper, Inc.	732.3
Georgia-Pacific LLC	—

Largest Employers	Employees
International Paper Company	51,500
Georgia-Pacific LLC	50,000
Weyerhaeuser Company	37,900
Temple-Inland Inc.	12,000
P. H. Glatfelter Company	3,704
Schweitzer-Mauduit International, Inc.	3,465
The Newark Group, Inc.	3,166
Wausau Paper Corp.	3,000
Verso Paper Corp.	2,900
Clearwater Paper Corporation	2,490

Fastest Growing* by Five-Year Sales Growth	(%)
P. H. Glatfelter Company	15.9
Schweitzer-Mauduit International, Inc.	7.3
Clearwater Paper Corporation	6.0
Wausau Paper Corp.	5.5
The Newark Group, Inc.	5.2
Verso Paper Corp.	4.7
Neenah Paper, Inc.	0.6

Fastest Growing* by Five-Year Employee Growth	(%)
P. H. Glatfelter Company	11.8
Schweitzer-Mauduit International, Inc.	0.8

Top Public Companies by Market Value	($ mil.)
Weyerhaeuser Company	6,467.6
International Paper Company	5,044.5
P. H. Glatfelter Company	691.1
Temple-Inland Inc.	505.9
Boise Inc.	34.3

* These rates are compounded annualized increases and may have resulted from acquisitions or one time gains. If less than 6 years of data are available, growth is for the years available.

SOURCE: HOOVER'S, INC., DATABASE

Radio Broadcasting and Programming

The US radio broadcasting and programming industry includes about 6,800 companies with combined annual revenue of $16 billion. Major companies include Clear Channel Communications, Cumulus Media, Citadel Broadcasting, and CBS Radio. The industry is concentrated: the 50 largest companies account for about 75 percent of revenue, with the top four earning almost 45 percent of the total. A typical midsized radio station has annual revenue of around $5 million.

The industry includes radio networks and stations, but not companies that broadcast only on the Internet or that primarily produce taped radio programs for sale.

Competitive Landscape

Business advertising and consumer demographics drive demand. The profitability of individual companies depends on advertisement volume, programming mix, and efficient operations. Large companies have advantages of market dominance, often owning the only radio stations in a geography. Small companies can compete effectively with special programming or broadcasters who attract large audiences. Average annual revenue per worker is $140,000.

Pay-for-service radio is a recent strategic development in the industry.

Products, Operations & Technology

Major industry product lines are broadcasts ("air time") and programming, production, and post-production services. Other products include program rights, merchandise sales, equipment rental, and sales of website advertising space. Air time, which includes advertising and network compensation, provides over 90 percent of industry revenue. Local advertising accounts for 65 percent of total revenue; national and regional ads, for 25 percent. Programming and broadcasting services provide over 5 percent of revenue. Radio broadcasting companies include

BUSINESS CHALLENGES

» Dependence on Ad Revenue

Broadcast radio stations depend heavily on advertisers for revenue, because delivery is usually free to users. Ads account for 90 percent of the US radio broadcasting and programming industry revenue. Ad spending, however, is closely related to the health of the national economy, as reflected in corporate profits and GDP. The broadcast radio industry competes for advertiser dollars with a variety of other media, including TV, outdoor display, newspapers, magazines, direct mail, and Internet sites.

» Increased Competition for Audience

Broadcast radio competes for audience with many forms of media transmission, in addition to broadcast TV and movies, the traditional competitors. Relatively new competitors include satellite radio or digital audio radio service (DARS), which offers CD-quality sound; cable radio; Internet radio; and satellite and cable TV. The growth in broadband, wireless, and satellite transmission threatens conventional broadcasting as the primary media delivery system to consumers. Radio station ad revenue depends on market share, which competing outlets can erode.

» Dependence on Federal Regulations

Radio stations are subject to government regulation mainly through the FCC, which grants and renews licenses and imposes some limitations on ownership concentration in local markets. The license renewal process is mandatory on a prescribed schedule, but a station can lose its license in the interim for failing to adhere to requirements. FCC regulatory changes can significantly affect the industry, as in 1996 when limitations on ownership concentration eased, fueling consolidation.

radio stations, which comprise over 85 percent of industry firms, and radio networks, which account for the remainder.

Industry companies produce or acquire radio programs and/or operate radio broadcasting studios and transmission facilities. Radio networks and stations provide a variety of programs for consumers and sell advertising time ("inventory") to businesses and organizations.

Ad sales and audience size are major industry metrics. Stations attract advertisers' targeted audiences by airing programs that appeal to them. A station earns a reputation for the type of programs ("format") it typically broadcasts. Radio stations sell air time directly or to brokers under Time Brokerage Agreements. The broker finds programming and sells advertising slots. Ad rates generally depend on the size of a station's audience, as measured by ratings firm Arbitron. Funding for public radio stations comes mainly from listener contributions and the Corporation for Public Broadcasting, but many stations also run subtle advertising.

Multiple radio stations often are owned by a large broadcast group that achieves advantages of scale in negotiating advertising and programming contracts and in centralizing backoffice operations, like accounting and finance. Broadcast companies are small compared with firms in other industries. Most large independent groups (non-network-owned) have annual revenue of less than $1 billion. Radio stations may affiliate exclusively with one network to receive its programming, or buy programs from multiple networks; some networks also own stations.

Program sources include local productions and syndicated and network shows. Stations often produce local news, sports, "talk," and local-interest programs, but may buy shows from local sources, such as sports teams. Stations buy syndicated programs from owners or independent producers or through brokers. Radio groups often produce their own shows for distribution to stations they own and for syndication to affiliates or other stations. Syndicated shows are available for cash or for "cash-plus-barter," which includes commercials that the syndicator sells. Radio music programming includes various categories, such as classical, oldies, country, or top 40. The majority of music programming is local, with fees paid to music distributors. Radio personalities are a major draw for stations, especially during morning and evening rush hours ("drive time"), when the largest number of listeners tune in.

The potential audience a radio station can reach depends largely on its location and the strength and quality of its transmission signal. The FCC allocates broadcast spectrum, regulates transmission signals, and issues licenses. A Class B radio station is a major station that covers a regional urban market. Because smaller radio stations are cheaper to buy, some radio

groups buy several in one market and simulcast the same signal through multiple stations to achieve wider coverage at lower cost. A low-power radio station broadcasts at 10 to 100 watts and reaches audiences up to a five-mile radius. A high-power radio station broadcasts at up to 50,000 watts and reaches audiences up to 70 miles away. Radio stations transmit either an AM signal, for wider coverage, or an FM signal, for better quality.

Technology and equipment are changing rapidly, enabling stations to convert to digital production and broadcasting. Digital signals, compared with analog signals, are higher quality, easier to edit and to enhance with special effects, and use less broadcast spectrum. Satellite or subscription radio uses digital signal transmission from a communications satellite, unlike conventional radio, which is "terrestrial" and uses radio frequencies.

Sales & Marketing

Typical customers are businesses and organizations that advertise and subscribers who pay a service fee. The ultimate end-users are consumers who listen to get information or for entertainment. Major sales channels are advertising brokers, a direct sales force for large accounts, and internal sales staff for telemarketing and incoming orders. Companies in the retail, auto, communications, media, and financial industries are the top advertisers on radio. Ads are available "upfront" — well before a program airs — or on a "spot" basis; 75 percent of radio advertising is local spot. Fees for upfront ads are often lower than for spot ads. Media representatives like Interep and Katz Media are major agencies that sell ad time, primarily to national advertisers.

Major types of marketing include advertising on the station's own broadcasts and on other media, including TV, newspapers, magazines, and trade publications. Sponsoring events is a common promotional strategy. Cross-promoting is common among stations owned by the same group.

Internet sales are increasingly important, because many media buyers prefer to buy air time ads electronically. Prices for radio ad time vary greatly, from hundreds to thousands per minute, depending on the station, locale, audience demographics and size, time-of-day, and many other factors. Complex formulas produce a cost per rating point (CPP) or cost per thousand impressions (CPM). Ratings by firms like Arbitron influence rate formulas, but ad prices are highly volatile. Ads generally are 15, 30, or 60 seconds long. Radio broadcast companies compete with other media, including Internet ads, for advertiser dollars.

Human Resources

Much of the work at radio stations requires highly technical skills or on-air broadcasting experience; accordingly, hourly earnings are 30 percent above the national average. Most jobs are in ad sales, program production, and broadcasting, which require very different skills. Turnover can be high, especially at small stations, which often serve as low-paying entry jobs for broadcasters who plan to move to larger markets to advance their careers. Strong competition for top employees exists in large metropolitan areas. Unions are influential, especially in negotiating contracts with networks and stations on behalf of members. Unions can keep members from working at companies without valid contracts. Due to the nature of the work, industry injury rates are low, about one-fifth the national average.

Industry Employment Growth

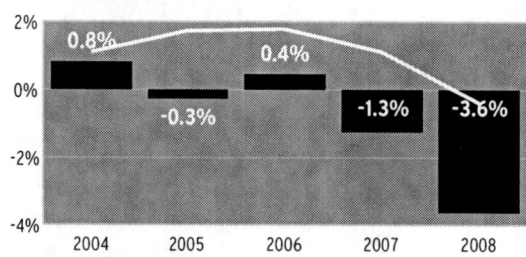

Average Hourly Earnings

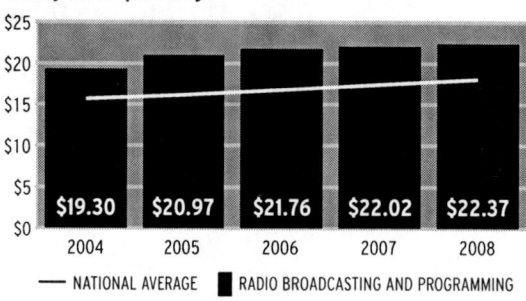

SOURCE: BUREAU OF LABOR STATISTICS

Call Preparation Questions

How important is advertising to the company's total revenue?

Broadcast radio stations depend heavily on advertisers for revenue, because delivery is usually free to users.

What media are the company's biggest competitors for audiences?

Broadcast radio competes for audience with many forms of media transmission, in addition to broadcast TV and movies, the traditional competitors.

How do government regulations affect the company's operations?

Radio stations are subject to government regulation mainly through the FCC, which grants and renews licenses and imposes some limitations on ownership concentration in local markets.

How would the company be advantaged by converting to digital broadcast technology?

Conversion to digital technology improves production, broadcast operations, and listener reception.

How satisfied is the company with its current formats?

Opportunities exist in formats that are growing in popularity.

Web Links

American Federation of Television & Radio Artists

Labor union news, contract negotiation, stop-work orders.
www.aftra.com/aftra/aftra.htm

Arbitron

Radio ratings, news, market research.
www.arbitron.com

Corporation for Public Broadcasting

Public radio grants, press releases.
www.cpb.org/pressroom

FCC

Federal regulations for broadcasting.
www.fcc.gov

I Want Media

Media news, resources.
www.iwantmedia.com

National Association of Broadcasters

Industry lobbying news, positions.
www.nab.org

Radio & Television Business Report

Industry news and analysis by subscription.
www.rbr.com

Radio Advertising Bureau

Ad news, facts, sales and marketing resources.
www.rab.com

Society of Broadcast Engineers

Trade association certification programs.
www.sbe.org

Glossary of Acronyms

CPP — cost per rating point
CPM — cost per thousand impressions
DARS — digital audio radio service
NAB — National Association of Broadcasters
RAB — Radio Advertising Bureau

HOOVER'S TOP COMPANIES

Largest Companies by Sales	($ mil.)
CBS Corporation	13,950.4
Clear Channel Communications, Inc.	6,688.7
SIRIUS XM Radio Inc.	1,664.0
Citadel Broadcasting Corporation	719.8
Westwood One, Inc.	451.4
Cox Radio, Inc.	444.9
Entercom Communications Corp.	438.8
Emmis Communications Corporation	361.2
Radio One, Inc.	316.4
Cumulus Media Inc.	311.5

Largest Employers	Employees
CBS Corporation	23,970
Clear Channel Communications, Inc.	23,400
Cumulus Media Inc.	3,400
Citadel Broadcasting Corporation	3,392
Westwood One, Inc.	2,400
Entercom Communications Corp.	2,343
Cox Radio, Inc.	2,136
Emmis Communications Corporation	1,900
Radio One, Inc.	1,690

Fastest Growing* by Five-Year Sales Growth	(%)
SIRIUS XM Radio Inc.	164.3
Global Traffic Network, Inc.	68.1
Citadel Broadcasting Corporation	13.2
Regent Communications, Inc.	6.8
Salem Communications Corporation	5.4
Saga Communications, Inc.	4.6
Beasley Broadcast Group, Inc.	3.1
Spanish Broadcasting System, Inc.	2.4
Entercom Communications Corp.	1.8
Cumulus Media Inc.	0.1

Fastest Growing* by Five-Year Employee Growth	(%)
Global Traffic Network, Inc.	44.5
SIRIUS XM Radio Inc.	25.9
Saga Communications, Inc.	6.0
Spanish Broadcasting System, Inc.	5.7
Beasley Broadcast Group, Inc.	0.8
Cumulus Media Inc.	0.2

Top Public Companies by Market Value	($ mil.)
CBS Corporation	5,021.3
Citadel Broadcasting Corporation	543.6
SIRIUS XM Radio Inc.	438.2
Entercom Communications Corp.	36.3
Clear Channel Communications, Inc.	—

* These rates are compounded annualized increases and may have resulted from acquisitions or one time gains. If less than 6 years of data are available, growth is for the years available.

SOURCE: HOOVER'S, INC., DATABASE

Railroad Equipment Manufacturing

The railroad equipment manufacturing industry includes about 200 companies with combined annual revenue of $9 billion. Major railcar companies include Trinity Industries and Greenbrier; GE Infrastructure and Electro-Motive Diesel (EMD) are the only two major US locomotive companies. The railroad equipment ("rolling stock") industry is highly concentrated: the 50 largest companies account for nearly 90 percent of revenue.

The US freight railroad industry includes around 1.3 million cars and 30,000 locomotives. On average, around 1,000 locomotives and 60,000 railcars are built or rebuilt each year, according to the Association of American Railroads (AAR).

Competitive Landscape

Demand for freight rolling stock is driven by fuel prices, as high gas prices shift freight transport from trucks to rail. Demand for passenger rail rolling stock is driven by public investment in regional rail transportation. The profitability of individual companies depends on securing long-term sales contracts with railroad companies and leasing agencies. Large companies have advantages in manufacturing economies of scale. Small companies can compete effectively through consulting services and custom-building locomotive and passenger railcars. The industry is highly capital-intensive: average annual revenue per worker is $350,000.

Products, Operations & Technology

Major products are new and rebuilt locomotives (about 30 percent of revenue); new and rebuilt freight, passenger, street, and rapid-transit cars (about 35 percent); and railroad parts and accessories (about 25 percent). Other products include railroad vehicles, airbrakes, and rail maintenance equipment, such as ballast spreaders and rail layers.

BUSINESS CHALLENGES

» Demand Tied to Economic Cycles

Railroads and railroad equipment manufacturing are cyclical. Orders, deliveries, and backlogs tend to peak in five- to 10- year cycles, according to the Railway Supply Institute. Railroads depend on a healthy economy to deliver homebuilding materials, cars, raw materials, and coal for energy plants. An economic downturn inevitably slows demand for rail traffic and purchases of rolling stock.

» Volatile Raw Material Prices

Steel, fabricated steel plates, and scrap metal represent from 65 to 85 percent of a rolling stock company's manufacturing costs. Due to record demand and short supply, steel prices increased 70 percent over the past five years. Steel shortages create significant backlogs for rolling stock manufacturers and threaten manufacturer ability to meet customer expectations.

» Dependence on Component Suppliers

Around 50 percent of all rolling stock consists of materials produced by third-party component suppliers. Manufacturers and government regulators often require that components meet specific grade, size, and quality standards. Only a few key suppliers can fulfill these requirements, and in recent years, a number of key rolling stock suppliers have been acquired or ceased operations. The combination of increased demand and industry consolidation has caused industrywide shortages of new and refurbished components.

Major freight car producers deliver around 5,000 to 15,000 new railcars annually. Freight rail companies tend to specialize in one or two types of cars, such as hoppers, tanks, auto carriers, or intermodal shippers. The two major locomotive manufacturers produce about 500 new freight locomotives each year. Demand for light rail fluctuates year to year, but on average, a major light rail manufacturer produces several thousand units annually. Almost all rolling stock companies rebuild the products they manufacture.

Building a new locomotive takes about 30 days, and less than a week to build a railcar. Manufacturers typically operate a main production site and several smaller facilities dedicated to key processes such as wheel, brake, and axle subassembly; repairs; and components and parts. Completed subassemblies are shipped by rail or truck to the main manufacturing plant for final assembly.

At the manufacturing plant, workers weld, fabricate, and assemble parts in component-specific production bays. The train takes shape as the chassis and wheels are placed on rails and subassemblies, airbrakes, wheel trucks, circuitry, and computer network systems are added. The assembled rolling stock is moved by rail to an onsite test track. Once the train passes extensive electrical, load, and track tests, it's moved to a painting booth and delivered by rail to the customer.

Major raw materials include steel, normalized steel plate, and castings. The cost of raw materials and specialty components represents 70 percent of rolling stock manufacturing costs. Many manufacturers manage internal component divisions rather than relying solely on third-party providers. Steel is in short supply with fewer suppliers and increased global demand. Most manufacturing contracts contain price variability provisions where raw material costs increases or decreases are passed directly on to customers.

Information technology plays an increasingly important role for efficient railroad equipment manufacturing. Companies are investing in supply chain management software to maintain adequate inventory and are streamlining operational processes to reduce the time it takes to make a locomotive or railcar. GE Transportation has set a goal to reduce the time to manufacture a locomotive from 26 to 10 days. Technological advances in component integration and testing are the main drivers in this ambitious goal.

Sales & Marketing

Typical customers are large, nationwide train operators (Class I railroads); railroad leasing companies; and the rolling stock company's own leasing division. Light rail is often funded through a mix of federal and state funds, local bonds, and city sales tax.

Companies typically manage an internal sales force and, on occasion, use independent sales representatives. Large manufacturers sometimes advertise on TV to promote a new product line, but most marketing is through trade shows and industry-oriented publications. Sales efforts are driven by word-of-mouth and long-standing contractual relationships.

Rolling stock manufacturers generally don't rely on the Internet to drive sales. Some companies are exploring buying and selling components through Internet auctions. More innovative manufacturers are experimenting with new media channels such as video websites and corporate blogs.

Typical product prices are $2 million for a new locomotive and $75,000 for a new railcar. The cost of a rebuilt locomotive can range from $50,000 to $500,000, with an average cost of $150,000. A locomotive or railcar is often rebuilt four or five times in its lifetime. Railroads and leasing companies generally choose to rebuild over buying new if the cost of the rebuild is less than two-thirds that of buying new.

Human Resources

Wages in the rolling stock industry are approximately equal to the national average and around 20 percent higher than the overall manufacturing sector. Wages are higher in part due to the technical and specialized nature of rolling stock assembly.

The overall injury and illness rate is more than 10 percent higher than the national average. High rates of illnesses and hearing loss incidents — more than triple the national average — account for the majority of injuries and illnesses.

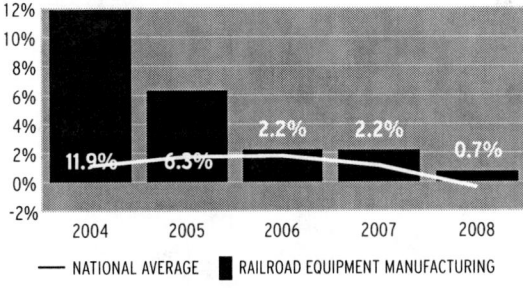

Industry Employment Growth

SOURCE: BUREAU OF LABOR STATISTICS

Call Preparation Questions

How does the company respond to slowdowns in the railroad industry?

Railroads and railroad equipment manufacturing are cyclical.

How does the company maintain profitability in light of higher steel costs?

Steel, fabricated steel plates, and scrap metal represent from 65 to 85 percent of a rolling stock company's manufacturing costs.

How dependent is the company on key component suppliers?

Around 50 percent of all rolling stock consists of materials produced by third-party component suppliers.

Does the company own components and parts divisions?

Locomotive and railcar companies are acquiring or buying stakes in components and parts makers, which can increase access to key parts such as airbrakes, wheelbases, and couplers.

Does the company lease the rolling stock it produces?

Railcar manufacturers are finding value in leasing the cars they make. Gross margins for leasing services can approach 50 percent.

Web Links

American Public Transportation Association

Transit and inner-city rail information.
www.apta.com/railstation.cfm

Association of American Railroads

Industry news and updates.
www.aar.org/Homepage.aspx

Federal Railroad Administration

Issue Briefs.
www.fra.dot.gov/us/content/37

National Transit Database

Statistics from the Federal Transit Administration.
www.ntdprogram.gov/ntdprogram

Rail Theory Forecasts

Supplier news.
www.railtheoryforecasts.com/supplier.html

Railway Supply Institute

Industry association for railway and rapid transit equipment suppliers.
www.rsiweb.org

Surface Transportation Board

Industry statistics and annual reports for Class I railroads.
www.stb.dot.gov/stb/industry/econ_reports.html

Glossary of Acronyms

AAR — Association of American Railroads
BTS — Bureau of Transportation Statistics
FRA — Federal Railroad Administration
NTSB — National Transportation Safety Board
RSI — Railway Supply Institute
STB — Surface Transportation Board

HOOVER'S TOP COMPANIES

Largest Companies by Sales	($ mil.)
Trinity Industries, Inc.	3,882.8
Westinghouse Air Brake Technologies	1,574.8
The Greenbrier Companies, Inc.	1,290.1
American Railcar Industries, Inc.	808.8
FreightCar America, Inc.	746.4
GE Infrastructure	294.5
New York Air Brake Corporation	292.4
A & K Railroad Materials, Inc.	150.0
Portec Rail Products, Inc.	109.5

Largest Employers	Employees
Trinity Industries, Inc.	13,070
Westinghouse Air Brake Technologies	7,295
The Greenbrier Companies, Inc.	4,174
New York Air Brake Corporation	3,194
ACF Industries LLC	2,800
GE Infrastructure	2,360
American Railcar Industries, Inc.	2,238
FreightCar America, Inc.	1,429
A & K Railroad Materials, Inc.	500

Fastest Growing* by Five-Year Sales Growth	(%)
American Railcar Industries, Inc.	30.0
FreightCar America, Inc.	25.0
Trinity Industries, Inc.	22.1
Westinghouse Air Brake Technologies	17.0
Portec Rail Products, Inc.	16.9
The Greenbrier Companies, Inc.	16.3

Fastest Growing* by Five-Year Employee Growth	(%)
FreightCar America, Inc.	10.9
Westinghouse Air Brake Technologies	10.2
The Greenbrier Companies, Inc.	6.8

Top Public Companies by Market Value	($ mil.)
Westinghouse Air Brake Technologies	1,904.3
Trinity Industries, Inc.	1,287.6
The Greenbrier Companies, Inc.	333.0
American Railcar Industries, Inc.	224.3
FreightCar America, Inc.	217.6

* These rates are compounded annualized increases and may have resulted from acquisitions or one time gains. If less than 6 years of data are available, growth is for the years available.

SOURCE: HOOVER'S, INC., DATABASE

Railroads

THIS INDUSTRY INCLUDES:

SIC CODES
4011   Railroads, Line-
        Haul Operating

NAICS CODES
482   Rail
        Transportation

The rail transportation industry includes about 350 companies with combined annual revenue of $50 billion. Major cargo companies include Union Pacific, BNSF Railway, and Norfolk Southern. Amtrak is the sole nationwide passenger rail service. The industry is highly concentrated: the 50 largest companies hold nearly 100 percent of the market.

The government classifies freight railroads based on annual revenues. Seven line-haul Class I railroads operate nationwide on high-density, intercity traffic lanes. Class I carriers comprise just 1 percent of freight railroads but account for over 90 percent of the industry revenue. The 30 regional Class II railroads typically operate routes of about 500 miles within two to four states. Over 300 short-line Class III railroads haul cargo 250 or fewer miles on local rail lines. Amtrak is included in this industry, but commuter, switching and terminal, and tourist railroads aren't.

Competitive Landscape

Demand is driven by consumer spending and fuel prices, as high gas prices shift freight transport from trucks to rail. The profitability of individual companies depends on efficient operations and controlling maintenance expenses. Large companies have advantages in owning substantial miles of railroad track connecting major cities. Small companies can compete effectively by servicing local routes and transporting a wide variety of commodities. The industry is highly capital-intensive: average annual revenue per worker for a typical Class I railroad is $250,000.

Railroads compete with trucks, vessels and barges, and pipelines to transport commodities and finished goods. According to the Association of American Railroads (AAR), railroads account for 40 percent of total US freight ton-miles, the most of any mode of transport, but generate less than 10 percent of all intercity freight revenues.

BUSINESS CHALLENGES

» High Capital Spending

Railroads invest an average of 18 percent of revenues into infrastructure improvements, far greater than the national average of 4 percent. Half of Class I capital commitments go toward maintaining tracks, 20 percent toward adding new lines, and 20 percent to buying new locomotives and cars. The cost to acquire railroad rolling stock was flat from 1997 to 2003, but has risen dramatically in recent years. Since 2004, new train car prices have risen over 25 percent.

» Vulnerability to Government Regulation and Litigation

Differential pricing practices, critical commodity routes with no alternate transportation choices, and a highly consolidated industry create a climate ripe for lawsuits and instigate calls for renewed railroad regulation. Shareholders are pressuring railroads to increase fees to seek relief from capacity constraints and higher infrastructure costs. Railroads must carefully seek ways to increase shipping fees without encouraging supplier lawsuits or calls for regulation.

» Rail Capacity Constraints

Rail lines are operating at near capacity, as high fuel prices shift freight travel from long-haul trucks to rail. The Energy Information Administration projects that US coal production will increase nearly 50 percent by 2030, which will further strain rail capacity. Technological advances in container shipping have created a new industry for intermodal transport, but have pressured demand for existing capacity. Railroads are investing in additional track, but are unable to keep up with current demand.

Products, Operations & Technology

Major services are the transport of commodities, including coal, crushed rock, and chemicals; containers of consumer goods; automobiles; and passengers. Rail transport of commodities accounts for nearly 80 percent of all railroad revenue. Coal accounts for 40 percent of these commodities by tonnage. Container transport, also known as intermodal rail traffic, moves consumer goods to ships and trucks without unloading the freight between modes of travel. Intermodal rail traffic of goods and commodities accounts for over 20 percent of rail transportation revenue. Amtrak, the sole nationwide passenger travel service, is a $2 billion business.

Moving commodities by rail begins at the source of raw materials. Trains typically carry only a single commodity from its origin to the line's terminus. Intermodal rail travel typically begins at port with cranes moving mixed consumer goods in containers from ship to railcar. Most train cargo is transported by diesel-electric locomotives moving about 100 railcars. Heavy freight operations may require up to four locomotives. The trip terminates at a classification yard, where cargo is diverted or unloaded, and train cars are uncoupled and either moved to storage tracks or reassembled for a new route. The time required for this final process, known as terminal dwell, is an important measure of railroad efficiency. Class I trains spend an average of 24 hours in terminal dwell.

Freight cars come in many forms. Autoracks are multi-level cars that transport automobiles. Well cars are designed to carry shipping containers and can be double-stacked. Tank cars carry petroleum, chemicals, and gases. Boxcars are versatile cars used to transport general freight. Flatcars hold loads that are too large to be enclosed in boxcars. Hoppers have opening doors on the underside of the car to transport and discharge loose commodities such as coal, grain, ore, and ballast. The average freight car capacity is just over 90 tons and cars typically have a useful life of 20 to 40 years.

Important operating metrics include average line-haul speed or velocity, a measure of train efficiency, and ton-miles, the movement of one ton a distance of one mile. The average Class I velocity is around 25 miles per hour. Revenue per ton-mile, a proxy for rail rates, is a measure of revenue a railroad brings in for its services and averages around 3 to 4 cents. Revenue ton-miles, on the other hand, are the total number of ton-miles moved within the industry or by a single company. The railroad industry moves nearly 2 trillion ton-miles annually.

Railroads invest heavily in infrastructure needs: steel, concrete, wood, and rock ballast for rail lines; signal cables; new locomotives and rail cars; and switch and cross ties. State governments often subsidize the investment in track infrastructure.

Technological improvements have led to huge productivity gains within the railroad industry. Automated real-time inspection systems detect rail failures; GPS and radio frequency identification (RFID) tags allow for real-time freight tracking. Class I railroads use complex computer workstations and telecommunication networks to efficiently schedule and manage freight traffic.

Sales & Marketing

Typical freight rail customers are international transporters; truckload and parcel companies; auto manufacturers; lumber and wood conglomerates; and agricultural, fuel, and chemical companies.

National railroads and Amtrak advertise through business magazines, TV, and national newspapers. Regional and local freight lines typically do not advertise. Class I freight operations rely heavily on the Internet to attract new customers by publicizing train schedules and shipment prices. Existing customers use online tools to request shipments, monitor specific rail cars, and pay freight bills. Some major rail companies now require customers to use the Internet to conduct business.

Product prices can vary widely, but average three to four cents per ton-mile. Most trips cost about $1,000 to $5,000 per railcar, depending on the product and distance traveled. Large customers are served through contracts lasting three to 10 years. Railroads charge customers different prices depending on the cargo and local competitive conditions. Shippers that have no choice but to use a single railroad line to move commodities, referred to as "captive shippers," typically pay 20 percent more than competitive rates.

Human Resources

Wages in the rail industry are nearly 40 percent higher than the national average. Cargo trains often operate 24 hours a day, 7 days a week, requiring many rail transportation employees to work extended hours, including nights, weekends, and holidays. On-board staff typically work 40 to 50 hours a week, and 80 percent of all rail workers are unionized. Many freight railroads face an aging workforce: over one-third of all workers are eligible for retirement within 10 years.

The injury and illness rate for railroad workers is 20 percent higher than the national average, with a significant number of injuries lasting longer than 30 days. In spite of this higher incidence, the railroad injury rate is lowest among all forms of freight transport.

Industry Employment Growth

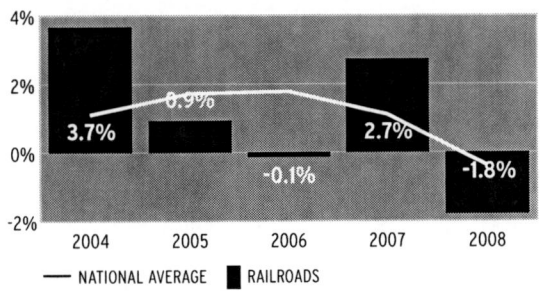

SOURCE: BUREAU OF LABOR STATISTICS

Call Preparation Questions

How much does the company expect to spend in the coming year on infrastructure improvements?

Railroads invest an average of 18 percent of revenues into infrastructure improvements, far greater than the national average of 4 percent.

Is the company experiencing capacity constraints?

Rail lines are operating at near capacity, as high fuel prices shift freight travel from long-haul trucks to rail.

What plans does the company have to use alternative fuels, such as biodiesel?

Biodiesel can reduce railroad carbon emissions by about 15 percent per route.

Web Links

Association of American Railroads

Industry news and updates.
www.aar.org

Brotherhood of Locomotive Engineers and Trainmen

News aggregator covering railroad companies.
www.ble.org/pr/headlines.asp

Federal Railroad Administration

Issue briefs.
www.fra.dot.gov/us/content/37

Railroad Performance Measures

Performance metrics for all Class I railroads.
www.railroadpm.org

Railway Age

Rail industry news and statistics.
railwayage.com

Surface Transportation Board

Industry statistics and annual reports for Class I railroads.
www.stb.dot.gov/stb/industry/econ_reports.html

Glossary of Acronyms

AAR — Association of American Railroads
FRA — Federal Railroad Administration
NTSB — National Transportation Safety Board
PTC — Positive Train Control
RFID — radio frequency identification
RRB — Railroad Retirement Board
STB — Surface Transportation Board

HOOVER'S TOP COMPANIES

Largest Companies by Sales	($ mil.)
Burlington Northern Santa Fe Corporation	18,018.0
Union Pacific Corporation	17,970.0
CSX Corporation	11,255.0
Norfolk Southern Corporation	10,661.0
Kansas City Southern	1,852.1
Genesee & Wyoming Inc.	602.0
OmniTRAX, Inc.	300.0
RailAmerica, Inc.	—

Largest Employers	Employees
Union Pacific Corporation	50,089
Burlington Northern Santa Fe Corporation	40,000
CSX Corporation	35,000
Norfolk Southern Corporation	30,806
Kansas City Southern	6,485
Genesee & Wyoming Inc.	2,307
RailAmerica, Inc.	2,000
Watco Companies, Inc.	1,051
Pan Am Systems, Inc.	1,000
OmniTRAX, Inc.	172

Fastest Growing* by Five-Year Sales Growth	(%)
Kansas City Southern	26.1
Genesee & Wyoming Inc.	19.7
Burlington Northern Santa Fe Corporation	13.9
Norfolk Southern Corporation	10.5
Union Pacific Corporation	9.2
CSX Corporation	7.6
Providence and Worcester Railroad Company	2.6

Fastest Growing* by Five-Year Employee Growth	(%)
Kansas City Southern	34.3
Union Pacific Corporation	2.2
Norfolk Southern Corporation	0.8

Top Public Companies by Market Value	($ mil.)
Burlington Northern Santa Fe Corporation	25,679.4
Union Pacific Corporation	24,054.2
Norfolk Southern Corporation	17,231.3
CSX Corporation	12,301.6
Kansas City Southern	1,742.4

* These rates are compounded annualized increases and may have resulted from acquisitions or one time gains. If less than 6 years of data are available, growth is for the years available.

SOURCE: HOOVER'S, INC., DATABASE

Real Estate Brokerage and Management

The US real estate management industry includes 220,000 companies generating about $160 billion in annual revenue. Of these, 60,000 are local real estate brokers, another 50,000 are involved in non-owner property management and appraisals, and the other 110,000 are owner/managers of residential and nonresidential properties, such as apartments, office and retail buildings, shopping malls, theaters, industrial space, assisted living facilities, and retirement communities. Only the largest real estate companies, such as Equity Office Properties, Coldwell Banker, and Simon Property Group, have revenues exceeding $1 billion; most have annual revenues less than $10 million.

The range size of companies in this very fragmented industry is enormous. A large apartment owner such as AIMCO manages over 300,000 apartments, while most companies are small and own or manage a single building. Even the largest property owners hold only a small fraction of the total US market, which includes 34 million apartments; 700,000 office buildings; 1.3 million retail buildings; and 2.5 million other commercial buildings. The average size of retail and office properties has not changed significantly in 20 years: 10,000 square feet for retail buildings and 15,000 square feet for office buildings.

Competitive Landscape

The profitability of real estate management companies (which have mainly fixed costs) depends on demand for the properties they're associated with or the volume of transactions they handle, both of which are usually higher during periods of strong economic growth and can be negatively affected by a recession or by too much new construction. Large companies have only modest economies of scale and benefit mainly from better name recognition than smaller competitors.

BUSINESS CHALLENGES

» Profitability Linked to Economic Cycles

Returns on real estate investment fluctuate with the health of the national economy. During recessions, the value of commercial real estate can fall 20 percent or more and the number of transactions decline sharply. Vacancy rates can change rapidly, with large regional differences.

» Lack of Access to Capital

Because investing in real estate can be risky, capital to fund acquisitions or construction can be difficult to get. Real estate is often highly leveraged and illiquid. In down markets, equity in real estate projects can rapidly disappear, leaving lenders with sharply devalued properties. During the late 2000s recession, many banks had to be bailed out by the federal government because of bad real estate loans.

» Property Obsolescence

Although the economic lifespan of many types of real estate properties is upward of 30 years, the period during which they can command the highest rents or prices is often less than ten. Improvements in construction and amenities can relegate older properties (especially malls and office buildings) to second-class status if a competing property is built in the vicinity.

Products, Operations & Technology

Real estate management companies provide services and are labor-intensive operations. Their daily activities typically involve gathering information, coordinating activities with other service providers, maintaining contact with customers, preparing documents, and conducting financial transactions.

Most real estate companies specialize in a segment of the industry, reflecting the different management requirements of each segment. Managing shopping malls, for example, is very different from managing office buildings. Many real estate companies engage in related activities that grow out of their particular area of expertise. A large residential real estate broker may also provide mortgage loans, homeowners insurance, and relocation services. A commercial broker may provide commercial financing, investment services, real estate research, and appraisals. Apartment and office building owners may also buy, sell, develop, and renovate properties, build new ones, and manage property for others. Assisted-living community operators may also operate nursing homes and provide other health-related services.

Residential real estate brokers bring buyers and sellers of individual properties together, assist them in setting a price and arrange for appraisals, inspections, and other services. Most transactions include two brokers: one assisting the buyer and one the seller. The seller's broker charges the seller a brokerage fee, usually 6 percent of the sales price (for expensive properties the fee may be lower), that is split with the buyer's broker. Since the buyer's broker is paid by the seller, the buyer's broker has a conflict of interest, and some buyers prefer to hire a broker not paid on commission.

Commercial real estate brokers facilitate both the lease and sale of commercial properties, and frequently also provide ancillary advisory and appraisal services. Brokerage fees are often negotiated (rather than being based on a standard formula) but can be as high as one-third of the first year's rent.

Property management companies are involved with marketing (ensuring that the property is as fully occupied as possible); financing (determining and negotiating lease length and amount); and building operations (hiring and supervising local staff, and providing utilities, maintenance, and other building services). Most owners of real estate actively manage their own properties, but a large number of passive owners hire a property manager to operate their buildings. Individual investors own most small apartment properties in the US (90 percent). Vacancy and lease rates are major concerns for property owners and managers. Because most property expense items are fixed, revenue losses from vacant space go straight to the bottom line. For an apartment owner, a 5 percent change in the vacancy rate can produce a 20 percent change in return on equity.

REITs are a type of real estate company organized to comply with certain IRS guidelines that provide favorable taxation if 90 percent of profits are passed to shareholders as dividends.

Publicly traded REITs (the real estate equivalent of mutual funds), which typically specialize in office buildings, apartments, or retail properties, have become a popular vehicle for real estate investing.

Sales & Marketing

Real estate brokers advertise heavily in local media, especially newspapers, use direct mail, and belong to local Multiple Listing Services. Owners of commercial real estate typically find tenants through brokers, who in turn make referrals to each other within a local market. Commercial brokers and property management companies cultivate long-term relationships with property owners and real estate developers.

The Internet has become a major marketing tool for residential and commercial brokers and real estate investors.

Human Resources

Industry employment has grown much faster than the national average, as consumers and businesses increasingly buy and rent properties. Wages are below the national average, despite sporadically growing faster than the national rate during the past decade. Median employee income of real estate brokers is about $60,000 per year with many working part-time; income of real estate managers is about $40,000 per year with over half being self-employed.

Real estate brokers and managers are required to be state-licensed. Most state licenses must be renewed after a limited time and require 10 to 20 hours of continued education annually, including real estate law updates. Brokers and managers also receive certification through industry organizations, such as the National Association of Realtors (NAR) and the Real Estate Buyers Agent Council (REBAC).

The industry is highly competitive, due to the low barriers to entry and education requirements. As a result, almost 90 percent of brokers and agents fail in their first year. Of the ones that succeed, about 70 percent have annual income below $30,000.

Industry Employment Growth

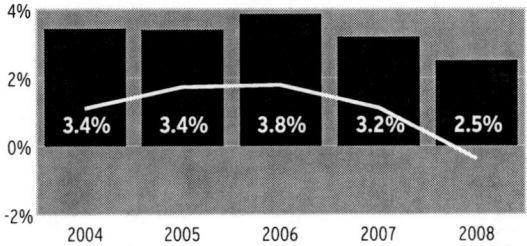

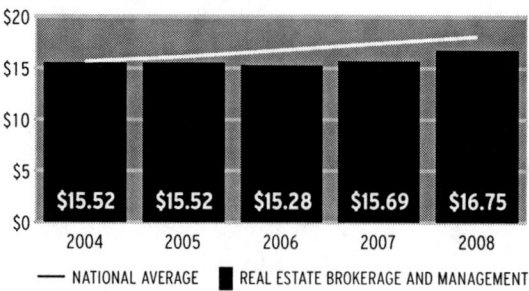

Average Hourly Earnings

	2004	2005	2006	2007	2008
REAL ESTATE BROKERAGE AND MANAGEMENT	$15.52	$15.52	$15.28	$15.69	$16.75

— NATIONAL AVERAGE ■ REAL ESTATE BROKERAGE AND MANAGEMENT

SOURCE: BUREAU OF LABOR STATISTICS

Call Preparation Questions

How does the company protect itself from revenue fluctuations caused by economic cycles?

Returns on real estate investment fluctuate with the health of the national economy.

What types of financing does the company use to buy property?

Because investing in real estate can be risky, capital to fund acquisitions or construction can be difficult to get.

What alternative revenue sources does the company have or plan to implement?

More property owners and managers can increase revenues by offering additional services, such as telecommunications and laundry services.

Web Links

Building Owners and Managers Association

FAQ's, reports, research, statistics, and news on the office building industry.
www.boma.org

Commercial Property News

Commercial real estate news.
www.cpnonline.com/cpn/print

Journal of Property Management

Journal for sale online.
www.irem.org/sechome.cfm?sec=jpm

National Association of Realtors

Legislative issues. Industry statistics.
www.realtor.org

National Association of Residential Property Managers

Association membership for property managers.
www.narpm.org

Glossary of Acronyms

CBD — central business district
CMBS — commercial mortgage-backed securities
IAQ — indoor air quality

IREM — Institute of Real Estate Management
NAHB — National Association of Home Builders

HOOVER'S TOP COMPANIES

Largest Companies by Sales	($ mil.)
Realogy Corporation	5,967.0
CB Richard Ellis Group, Inc.	5,128.8
Tishman Realty & Construction Co., Inc.	3,560.0
Jones Lang LaSalle Incorporated	2,697.6
HomeServices of America, Inc.	1,868.5
AIMCO Properties, L.P.	1,721.2
Colliers International Property Consultants, Inc.	1,600.0
Forest City Enterprises, Inc.	1,295.6
The Inland Real Estate Group of Companies, Inc.	—
Lefrak Organization Inc.	—

Largest Employers	Employees
Jones Lang LaSalle Incorporated	32,700
CB Richard Ellis Group, Inc.	29,000
Lefrak Organization Inc.	16,200
Cushman & Wakefield, Inc.	11,000
Colliers International Property Consultants, Inc.	10,092
Realogy Corporation	7,500
AIMCO Properties, L.P.	6,000
Binswanger Corporation	5,200
Newmark Knight Frank	4,500
Forest City Enterprises, Inc.	4,484

Fastest Growing* by Five-Year Sales Growth	(%)
The InterGroup Corporation	29.0
ZipRealty, Inc.	26.0
CB Richard Ellis Group, Inc.	25.8
Meruelo Maddux Properties, Inc.	23.6
Jones Lang LaSalle Incorporated	23.2
Studley, Inc.	16.0
First Hartford Corporation	15.1
Tishman Realty & Construction Co., Inc.	11.1
Consolidated-Tomoka Land Co.	9.5
Tejon Ranch Co.	8.3

Fastest Growing* by Five-Year Employee Growth	(%)
CB Richard Ellis Group, Inc.	41.4
Jones Lang LaSalle Incorporated	21.9
First Hartford Corporation	11.8
Tejon Ranch Co.	6.8
Tishman Realty & Construction Co., Inc.	2.7
Consolidated-Tomoka Land Co.	1.2
American Realty Investors, Inc.	1.0
Forest City Enterprises, Inc.	0.3

Top Public Companies by Market Value	($ mil.)
Forest City Enterprises, Inc.	3,116.3
CB Richard Ellis Group, Inc.	1,133.3
Jones Lang LaSalle Incorporated	957.4
Tejon Ranch Co.	690.4
Grubb & Ellis Company	415.5

* These rates are compounded annualized increases and may have resulted from acquisitions or one time gains. If less than 6 years of data are available, growth is for the years available.

SOURCE: HOOVER'S, INC., DATABASE

Real Estate Investment Trusts (REITs)

THIS INDUSTRY INCLUDES:

SIC CODES

6798   Real Estate Investment Trusts

NAICS CODES

52599   Other Financial Vehicles

The roughly 600 REIT companies in the US have combined annual revenue of $25 billion. Large companies include Equity Office Properties, Equity Residential Properties, Simon Property Group, and Vornado Realty Trust. Following strong consolidation, the industry has become highly concentrated at the top. The largest 50 REITs hold over 80 percent of the market. The larger REITs are publicly traded, but many smaller ones are privately held.

Competitive Landscape

The health of the economy drives demand for REITs as investment vehicles. Profitability depends on the value of the properties in the portfolio, which in turn highly depends on real estate vacancy rates. Large companies have advantages in deal-making, and economies of scale in marketing, computer and infrastructure investment, and operations. Smaller companies can compete by specializing not only in real estate type, but by geography, though geographic focus can increase risks.

Products, Operations & Technology

REITs are corporations that derive most of their revenue from owning or managing real estate, or from mortgages secured by real estate. The value of all real estate owned by REITs is close to $500 billion. A company organized as a REIT under IRS regulations can avoid paying income taxes if it pays out at least 90 percent of its net income (excluding capital gains) as dividends to shareholders. The benefit of being a REIT is that corporate income isn't taxed; the disadvantage is that the company can't fund growth with retained earnings.

To qualify as a REIT, the IRS requires a company to have at least 100 shareholders. REITs typically invest in a single type of real estate, such as office buildings, industrial buildings (warehouses), shopping centers, malls, or apartments. Simon Property Group, for example, in-

BUSINESS CHALLENGES

» Concentration in Specific Property Types

Most REITs specialize in a particular property type, such as office buildings, warehouses, shopping malls, or apartment buildings. While this specialization appeals to many investors who wish to participate in a specific sector of the real estate industry, it also increases the risk that economic events affect the value of a REIT's portfolio. For example, the 9/11 attacks subsequently affected the profitability of hotels, in turn decreasing the value of hotel REITs.

» Vulnerability to Cyclical Economic Conditions

The value of real estate is notoriously cyclical, varying with the strength of the regional or national economy. Vacancy rates for properties can climb rapidly, especially for office buildings and warehouses, if the economy falters. For example, the vacancy rate for office space in large markets like San Francisco and Dallas rose to 25 percent in the recent recession. Rents can also fall rapidly in economically impacted markets; office rents can fall 10 percent or more in a single year.

» Leverage Could Increase

Because the value of their assets is so high, REITs have a constant temptation to leverage equity by using debt to finance new real estate purchases. Although debt-to-equity ratio of REITs is usually between 1 and 2, a growing REIT may borrow more, especially when interest rates are low.

vests only in regional malls. Equity Office Properties invests in office buildings, and AvalonBay invests in apartment buildings. Some REITs, like Vornado Realty, hold a diverse portfolio of properties.

Office and industrial properties account for 30 percent of REIT holdings, retail properties for 25 percent, apartments for 20 percent, and a collection of hotels, hospitals, self-storage centers, and other types of real estate for the rest. The vast majority of companies are so-called "equity REITs" that own and manage property.

A small number are "mortgage REITs" that own mortgages rather than property. Another small percentage are "hybrid REITs" that hold both property and mortgages.

Sales & Marketing

REITs allow the public to easily invest in commercial real estate and are a new source of funds for the real estate industry. The stock price of a publicly traded REIT is often compared to the net asset value (NAV) of the stock (the per share market value of the company's net assets). A stock price higher than the NAV is considered bullish. Operating performance is often measured by "funds from operations" (FFO); that is, net income before depreciation and excluding gains from property sales.

Human Resources

REIT employees earn high wages, have low job turnover, and an excellent absenteeism and safety record. Industry workers earn an average of over $19 an hour, about $4 more than the national average for all private businesses. Annual personnel turnover for the finance and insurance industries, including REITs, is about 8 percent below the national average. Most employees need special knowledge of real estate markets, finance, and investment.

Call Preparation Questions

What strategies does the company use to mitigate risk associated with concentration in specific types of real estate?

Most REITs specialize in a particular property type, such as office buildings, warehouses, shopping malls, or apartment buildings.

How does the company protect itself from the revenue fluctuations caused by economic cycles?

The value of real estate is notoriously cyclical, varying with the strength of the regional or national economy.

How does the company plan to finance projected growth?

Because the value of their assets is so high, REITs have a constant temptation to leverage equity by using debt to finance new real estate purchases.

What opportunities does the company have for growth?

Although REITs are large owners of real estate, they own only a minority of US real estate assets.

What benefits or challenges does the company see in promoting itself as an investment alternative to the stock market?

The retreat of the stock market from the highs of recent years has prompted more investors to consider investing in REIT stocks.

Web Links

Building Owners and Managers Association

FAQs, reports, research, statistics, and news on the office building industry.
www.boma.org

Commercial Property News

Commercial real estate news.
www.cpnonline.com/cpn/print

InRealty.com

Links to many retailer organizations.
www.inrealty.com

Institute of Real Estate Management

Directories, government relations, features, news, and reports.
www.irem.org

MPF YieldStar

Produces the US Apartment Market Report.
www.realpage.com/yieldstar/publications.asp

National Association of Real Estate Investment Trusts

Research and statistics. Glossary. Issues.
www.nareit.com

National Association of Realtors

Legislative issues. Industry statistics.
www.realtor.org

National Association of Residential Property Managers

News and other information relevant to property management.
www.narpm.org

National Multi Housing Council

Industry statistics. Policy issues.
www.nmhc.org

National Real Estate Investor

Commercial real estate information by segment: industrial, office, multifamily, etc.
www.nreionline.com

ONCOR International

Excellent office market reports.
www.oncorintl.com

shoppingcenters.com

Directory of Major Malls — Shopping Center Digest.
www.shoppingcenters.com

Society of Industrial and Office Realtors

Industrial and office market reports.
www.sior.com

Glossary of Acronyms

CBD — central business district
FFO — funds from operations
FRTIB — Federal Retirement Thrift Investment Board
NAREIT — National Association of Real Estate Investment Trusts
NAV — net asset value
RER — Real Estate Roundtable
SOX — Sarbanes-Oxley
TSP — thrift savings plan
UPREIT — umbrella partnership REIT

HOOVER'S TOP COMPANIES

Largest Companies by Sales	($ mil.)
ProLogis	5,654.8
Host Hotels & Resorts, Inc.	5,288.0
Simon Property Group, Inc.	3,783.2
General Growth Properties, Inc.	3,361.5
Annaly Capital Management, Inc.	3,166.4
Vornado Realty Trust	2,697.1
Thornburg Mortgage, Inc.	2,640.3
Equity Residential	2,103.2
Public Storage	1,745.6
Apartment Investment and Management	1,457.9

Largest Employers	Employees
Public Storage	5,700
Simon Property Group, Inc.	5,300
Equity Residential	4,800
Apartment Investment and Management	4,400
General Growth Properties, Inc.	4,200
Vornado Realty Trust	4,020
The Macerich Company	3,014
American Campus Communities, Inc.	2,301
Rayonier Inc.	2,000
Plum Creek Timber Company, Inc.	2,000

Fastest Growing* by Five-Year Sales Growth	(%)
Bimini Capital Management, Inc.	465.8
CapitalSource Healthcare REIT	246.4
Realty Finance Corporation	237.2
Gramercy Capital Corp.	202.4
JER Investors Trust Inc.	155.8
DCT Industrial Trust Inc.	147.7
Ashford Hospitality Trust, Inc.	94.3
BioMed Realty Trust, Inc.	85.6
Douglas Emmett, Inc.	78.0
Deerfield Capital Corp.	33.6

Fastest Growing* by Five-Year Employee Growth	(%)
Bimini Capital Management, Inc.	464.8
Alesco Financial Inc.	251.6
Supertel Hospitality, Inc.	184.4
Digital Realty Trust, Inc.	66.3
Health Care REIT, Inc.	55.3
Extra Space Storage Inc.	48.9
Feldman Mall Properties, Inc.	40.3
New York Mortgage Trust, Inc.	37.1
First Potomac Realty Trust	15.0

Top Public Companies by Market Value	($ mil.)
Public Storage	13,378.2
Simon Property Group, Inc.	12,522.3
Vornado Realty Trust	9,371.5
Boston Properties, Inc.	6,664.9
ProLogis	3,708.7

* These rates are compounded annualized increases and may have resulted from acquisitions or one time gains. If less than 6 years of data are available, growth is for the years available.

SOURCE: HOOVER'S, INC., DATABASE

Recreational Vehicle Dealers

Over 3,000 RV dealers operate in the US with combined annual revenue of over $15 billion. Most RV dealers are privately held; larger dealers include Freedom Roads, Lazy Days' RV Center, and General RV Center. Major RV manufacturers, such as Fleetwood and Winnebago, also own some dealerships. The industry is fragmented: the top 50 dealers account for about a third of industry revenue. Most dealerships have about 10 employees, but large dealerships can have over 150.

Competitive Landscape

Demand is driven by consumer income and US population demographics. The profitability of individual companies depends on effective marketing and inventory management. Large dealerships have advantages in breadth of product line, repair center capability, and marketing efficiencies. Small dealers compete by providing superior customer service. Average annual revenue per employee is under $300,000 for small dealerships and over $600,000 for large ones.

Products, Operations & Technology

Major products include new motor homes (about 35 percent of sales); used RVs (25 percent); and new travel trailers (20 percent). Other dealership services include repair and maintenance, sales of RV parts, and extended warranty service contracts. Some dealers, especially in northern climates, also sell snowmobiles or other products during the winter.

Most dealers have non-exclusive sales contracts with multiple RV manufacturers, although some carry just one brand. Individual dealerships can carry more than 20 different RV brands. Dealers sell a wide variety of products, from small camper trailers that are towed, to self-contained motor homes. Dealerships can be large, approaching 125 acres to house vehicle inventory and multiple service bays.

BUSINESS CHALLENGES

» Revenue Depends on Economy

RVs are considered a luxury and a discretionary purchase; as such, sales depend highly on general economic conditions. Consumers postpone purchases when the economy contracts; demand increases when the economy booms. During each of the last two economic recessions, RV sales decreased significantly.

» Sensitivity to Interest Rates

Both dealers and consumers are sensitive to interest rates for RV financing. Dealers carry substantial inventories financed by third parties, and consumers generally finance motor home and large trailer purchases. High interest rates raise consumer costs, which can lead to delayed purchases or selection of less expensive RVs, resulting in lower sales.

» Poor Gas Mileage

RVs get relatively poor gas mileage; fuel costs are a major burden for RV and camper owners. Mileage varies from six miles per gallon for gas units to 10 for diesel. While existing RV owners are often resilient to fuel price increases, high fuel prices can discourage new RV purchases or rentals.

RVs are delivered by private parties who are paid to drive the RV from the manufacturer to the dealer and note any problems encountered on the drive. Time from dealer order to delivery can be several weeks. Most trailers, vans, and small RVs are sold off the lot. Larger motor homes can be custom-ordered through RV brokers or dealers. Most equipment is installed by the manufacturer; only small items, such as jacks, are added by the dealership.

Dealers offer maintenance services and sell replacement parts. Most dealers provide service and warranty work on the vehicle chassis and engine. Some large dealers also service the "home" or inside of the vehicle.

RV dealers buy used RVs as trade-ins for bigger vehicles. Dealers clean and repair used RVs for resale. RVs' trade-in value is largely a function of mileage, especially for gasoline-powered vehicles. Diesel vehicles have much higher trade-in values and aren't as adversely affected by road conditions.

High-tech amenities add to the comfort and price of vehicles. Recent innovations include plasma TVs, moving walls that expand the RVs interior, GPS, and better appliances. Dealerships are increasingly using the Internet to communicate with customers and suppliers. Dealers also develop databases of customers and prospects to use in marketing maintenance services and vehicle upgrades.

Sales & Marketing

Almost one in 12 US vehicle-owning households owns an RV. The typical RV customer is 50, married, owns a home, and has an annual household income around $70,000.

Major types of marketing include broadcast TV, radio, and direct mail. The Recreation Vehicle Industry Association sponsors a national campaign, called "Go RVing," which helps promote the industry to first time buyers. Individual dealers supplement national ads with local TV, radio, and business journal ads. Trade shows are very important, especially in winter months; the Florida RV Supershow attracts almost 50,000 attendees.

Internet marketing is increasing in importance: many dealers use the Internet as a virtual showroom for prospects and to develop an ongoing relationship with customers to sell services and upgrades.

Product prices range from $2,000 for a new camper trailer to more than $100,000 for a large motor home.

Human Resources

RV dealership employees earn slightly more than the national average. Mechanics generally are certified and attend periodic training for technical updates. Worker injuries are higher than the national norm, led by falls and sprains. Dealership payrolls can be seasonal, especially in northern climates. Part-time employees may be used to clean returned rental or trade-in vehicles.

Industry Employment Growth

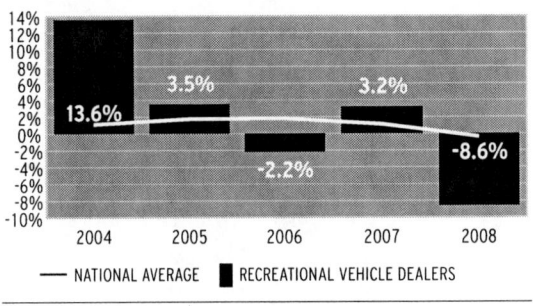

SOURCE: BUREAU OF LABOR STATISTICS

Call Preparation Questions

How are current economic conditions affecting the dealership's business?

RVs are considered a luxury and a discretionary purchase; as such, sales depend highly on general economic conditions.

How sensitive are dealer costs and sales to interest rates?

Both dealers and consumers are sensitive to interest rates for RV financing.

How do changes in gas prices affect the dealership?

RVs get relatively poor gas mileage; fuel costs are a major burden for RV and camper owners.

What maintenance services does the dealership offer?

Warranty work helps develop a loyal customer base and increase future sales, and is an excellent source of income and a good way to drive aftermarket sales.

How much of dealer sales is from customers who upgrade to bigger and more expensive RVs?

As consumers experience the RV lifestyle, they frequently want bigger models with greater amenities.

Web Links

MotorHome Magazine

Industry news, articles, accessories.
www.motorhomemagazine.com

National RV Dealers Association

News, case studies, dealer advice.
www.rvda.org

Recreation Vehicle Industry Association

News, events, market data, articles.
www.rvia.org

RV Forums

Message boards, rally schedule.
www.rvforums.net

RV Travel

News and travel advice for RVers.
www.rvtravel.com

RV-n-Motorhomes

Industry trends and statistics.
www.rv-n-motorhomes.com/RV-Facts-Statistics.html

Glossary of Acronyms

NCC — net carrying capacity
OEM — original equipment manufacturer
NHSA — National Highway Safety Administration
UVW — unloaded vehicle weight

HOOVER'S TOP COMPANIES

Largest Companies by Sales	($ mil.)
Fleetwood Enterprises, Inc.	1,660.0
FreedomRoads, L.L.C.	1,650.0
Winnebago Industries, Inc.	604.3

Largest Employers	Employees
Fleetwood Enterprises, Inc.	6,400
FreedomRoads, L.L.C.	4,000
Winnebago Industries, Inc.	2,250
La Mesa RV Center, Inc.	700
Lazy Days' R.V. Center, Inc.	669
Giant Inland Empire RV	550
General RV Center	300
Buddy Gregg Motor Homes	110

SOURCE: HOOVER'S, INC., DATABASE

Recreational Vehicle Manufacture

The RV manufacturing industry in the US consists of about 800 companies with combined annual revenue of $12 billion. Large companies include Thor, Fleetwood, Monaco Coach, and Winnebago. The industry is highly concentrated: the 20 largest manufacturers hold about 80 percent of the market.

Competitive Landscape

Demand is driven by consumer income and demographics, as RV buyers are mainly older. The profitability of individual companies depends on the ability to design desirable products. Large companies have economies of scale in production and distribution. Small companies can compete successfully by concentrating on a product line or by specializing in components.

Products, Operations & Technology

Major products are motor homes, travel trailers, and folding (or "camping") trailers. Motor homes account for about 45 percent of industry revenue, travel trailers for 45 percent, and folding trailers for 10 percent. Some manufacturers also make "park" models, which are essentially small mobile homes.

Motor homes are complete, self-propelled units. Travel trailers are complete units that must be towed by a car or truck. "Fifth-wheel" trailers are towed from a mount in a pick-up truck and extend over the bed of the truck. Folding trailers have walls that unfold to form the camping unit. Within the motor home segment, Class A models are full-size units built on a medium-duty truck chassis, while Class C models are smaller units built on a van chassis. Motor homes range from 16 to 40 feet long.

RVs are built on truck or van chassis bought from suppliers like GM and Ford. A chassis basically includes the frame, suspension, exhaust system, brakes, engine, transmission, rear axle, drive train, fuel system, wheels, and tires. A

BUSINESS CHALLENGES

» Revenue Sensitive to Economic Conditions

RV demand is difficult to forecast from year to year. Because they're considered a luxury, RVs are in lower demand during periods of economic difficulty. Consumers are less likely to buy RVs when the stock market is down, gas prices are high, employment low, or personal disposable income tight. During each of the last two recessions, RV shipments fell more than 20 percent.

» Dealers, Consumers Depend on Financing

Because they need to carry substantial inventories, RV dealers are sensitive to lending conditions. Few manufacturers supply financing for dealers, although many cooperate with lenders via repurchase agreements. Consumers also require financing, especially for more expensive motor homes. Sales suffer when interest rates are high or credit is tight.

» Dependence on Chassis Manufacturers

RV manufacturers depend on GM, Ford, or other car manufacturers for adequate supplies of chassis and engines. Shortages sometimes arise when RV manufacturers have demand surges. During shortages, RV manufacturers may get only a fraction of the number of chassis they need, because the allocation system is based on previous purchases.

chassis with engine is the largest single manufacturing cost for motor homes. Aluminum panels and extrusions, insulation, plumbing, wiring, cabinets, and appliances are also major cost items. Large manufacturers produce many of the components themselves and may also supply other manufacturers.

The industry annually produces about 50,000 new motor homes; 200,000 travel trailers; and 30,000 folding trailers. The major manufacturers produce a number of models and sizes of RVs under various brand names. Production facilities operate assembly lines that can be fairly easily reconfigured to produce different models. Production runs are fairly small. In 2004, Winnebago, the largest motor home manufacturer, built about 12,000 units under 16 model names. Production is usually started only after dealer orders are received. Many manufacturers have a backlog of orders.

Computers are used to manage the large number of parts and to design new models.

Sales & Marketing

Sales are made to about 3,000 independent RV dealers, but marketing is aimed at end-use customers. Advertising through RV magazines is important. The large manufacturers also advertise on cable TV and in local media outlets in conjunction with local dealers. Multi-year dealer agreements establish dealer sales territories and minimum inventory levels that dealers must hold, and often require dealers to provide product servicing. The big manufacturers have large networks of dealers, typically more than 500 and up to 1,500. New dealers are often acquired at periodic trade shows, such as the National RV Trade Show. Dealers are a primary source of market information.

Sales to dealers are for cash, but the large manufacturers help dealers get "floor plan" financing (financing for their inventory) from banks by entering repurchase agreements that commit them to buy back financed units if the dealer is unable to repay the bank.

The range in product prices is large. The average retail price for a Class A motor home is more than $150,000. Class C motor homes sell for about $70,000; travel trailers for less than $30,000; and folding trailers for under $10,000.

Human Resources

Production workers are mainly full-time who are paid wages just under the national average for all workers. The work is mainly repetitive assembly-line work that requires few special skills.The industry injury rate is more than three times higher than the national average, largely due to handling of materials and use of machinery.

Industry Employment Growth

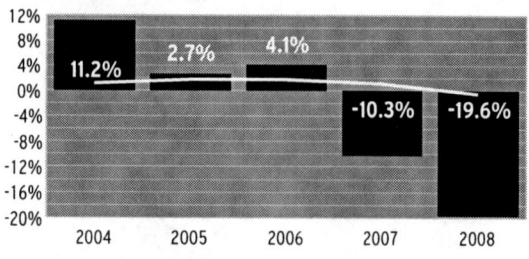

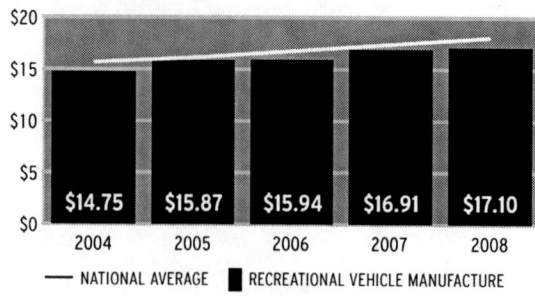

Average Hourly Earnings

	2004	2005	2006	2007	2008
	$14.75	$15.87	$15.94	$16.91	$17.10

— NATIONAL AVERAGE ■ RECREATIONAL VEHICLE MANUFACTURE

SOURCE: BUREAU OF LABOR STATISTICS

Call Preparation Questions

How accurately can the company forecast annual demand?

RV demand is difficult to forecast from year to year.

How do the company's dealers handle inventory financing when interest rates rise?

Because they need to carry substantial inventories, RV dealers are sensitive to lending conditions.

How does the company ensure adequate supplies of chassis?

RV manufacturers depend on GM, Ford, or other car manufacturers for adequate supplies of chassis and engines.

How does the company target aging baby boomers?

The segment of the population most likely to buy RVs, Americans over 50 with above-average wealth, according to the Recreation Vehicle Industry Association, is expected to grow rapidly.

What types of new electronics does the company plan to include in its products?

Various types of electronic add-on devices have made RVs more comfortable and versatile. GPS is common.

Web Links

MotorHome Magazine

Industry news, articles, RV accessories.
www.motorhomemagazine.com

National Association of RV Parks & Campgrounds (ARVC)

Industry calendar. Links to state associations.
www.arvc.org

Recreation Vehicle Industry Association (RVIA)

Industry production statistics.
www.rvia.org

Recreational Park Trailer Industry Association (RPTIA)

Demographics, resources, publications, and press releases.

media.rptia.com

Recreational Vehicle Rental Association (RVRA)

Consumer information about rentals.

www.rvra.org

RV America Online – The Home of the RV Industry

On Line features extensive resources for people exploring the RV lifestyle.

www.rvamerica.com

RV Trade Digest

Articles.

www.rvtradedigest.com

RVmanufacturers.com

List of different types of RVs.

www.rvmanufacturers.com/rv_types.cfm

The National RV Dealers Association (RVDA)

RV dealer financials and statistics. Dealer inventory report.

www.rvda.org

Trailer Life Magazine

Industry news.

www.trailerlife.com

Glossary of Acronyms

ARVC — National Association of RV Parks & Campgrounds
RVDA — Recreation Vehicle Dealers Association
RVIA — Recreation Vehicle Industry Association
RVRA — Recreational Vehicle Rental Association

HOOVER'S TOP COMPANIES

Largest Companies by Sales	($ mil.)
Thor Industries, Inc.	2,640.7
Fleetwood Enterprises, Inc.	1,660.0
Monaco Coach Corporation	1,272.1
Winnebago Industries, Inc.	604.3
Jayco, Inc.	585.0
Newmar Corporation	125.0
Tiffin Motorhomes, Inc.	497.8
Forest River Inc.	—

Largest Employers	Employees
Thor Industries, Inc.	7,064
Fleetwood Enterprises, Inc.	6,400
Forest River Inc.	5,800
Monaco Coach Corporation	5,348
Winnebago Industries, Inc.	2,250
Jayco, Inc.	1,770
Country Coach, Inc.	1,500
Newmar Corporation	1,000
Fairmont Homes, Inc.	850
Tiffin Motorhomes, Inc.	545

Top Public Companies by Market Value	($ mil.)
Thor Industries, Inc.	1,087.7
Winnebago Industries, Inc.	329.9

SOURCE: HOOVER'S, INC., DATABASE

Recreational Vehicle Parks

THIS INDUSTRY INCLUDES:

SIC CODES

7033   Recreational Vehicle Parks and Campsites

NAICS CODES

721211   RV (Recreational Vehicle) Parks and Campgrounds

Over 4,000 RV parks and campgrounds in the US have combined annual revenue of about $2 billion. Major companies include Kampgrounds of America (KOA) and Thousand Trails. Most RV parks and campgrounds are single locations and privately held. The RV parks and campgrounds industry is highly fragmented: the 50 largest companies account for about 25 percent of industry revenue. A typical campground has less than $500,000 in annual revenue and about five employees.

Competitive Landscape

Demand is driven by personal income and tourist travel. The profitability of individual campgrounds depends on site occupancy rate and effective marketing. Large campgrounds have advantages in diversity of site offerings and amenities. Small campgrounds can compete effectively by marketing to their target demographic and through favorable site location. Campground operations are labor-intensive: average annual revenue per employee is less than $100,000.

Products, Operations & Technology

Major services are campground rentals (77 percent of industry revenue) and groceries and meals (9 percent). Other revenue sources include dues and fees for membership campgrounds. Campground rental generally includes utility hookups for power, water, sewage, and propane gas.

Typical RV park amenities include a grocery store or snack bar, coin-operated laundry facilities, and a swimming pool or natural swimming area. More expensive campgrounds offer golf course, tennis, and spa facilities.

Most RV parks and campgrounds are independently owned; even many chain campgrounds are independently owned franchises. Campgrounds generally offer inexpensive recreation-oriented accommodations near na-

BUSINESS CHALLENGES

» RV Ownership Tied to Consumer Income

Growth in demand for RV parks depends on continued growth in RV ownership. RVs are costly to own and operate and are considered a discretionary purchase. As personal income declines, consumers postpone buying RVs. Owners may also cut the length and number of RV trips during difficult economic periods.

» Poor RV Gas Mileage

RVs get relatively poor gas mileage, making operating costs sensitive to fuel prices. Mileage varies from about six miles per gallon for large gas units to over 10 for diesel motor homes. RV owners are generally resilient to fuel price increases, but may decide to take fewer or shorter trips, impacting those campgrounds more distant from metropolitan areas.

» Restrictions on National Parks Access

National parks are the leading destination of RV owners, and many RV parks and campgrounds are located close to them. Overcrowding in some national parks during the busy summer months has led to proposals to restrict vehicle traffic. Industry associations are working with government agencies to resist any movement to restrict RV access to national parks.

tional and state parks or major travel routes. Individual campgrounds may have from a couple dozen to several hundred campsites and hookups. Most parks have at least 150 hook-up spaces and are between 10 to 30 acres. Employees are usually family members of the owner who maintain facilities and operate any store or concession areas.

Information technology is increasingly important in both marketing and operations. Many campgrounds have websites, some with virtual tours of the facilities. Some have online reservation systems to accommodate their guests. High-tech amenities such as wireless Internet access are becoming more common at RV campgrounds.

Sales & Marketing

Almost one in 12 US vehicle-owning households owns an RV. The typical RV campground customer is 50, married, owns a house, and has an annual household income of around $70,000.

Major types of marketing include the campground website, industry aggregate sites and listings, billboards, and direct mail to prior visitors. Industry associations advertise nationally in support of RV dealers and the RV lifestyle. Word-of-mouth endorsements and reviews on industry websites are important. Large franchises have affiliate programs offering savings by member vendors and commissions for referrals. Affiliates include car rental companies, pharmacies, insurance agencies, and RV supply dealers.

Campground prices range from about $10 for a simple hookup to close to $100 for more luxurious campgrounds with spas and golf courses. Rates can vary by season, and campgrounds may offer discounts for senior citizens, RV clubs (such as Good Sam Club), and long stays.

Human Resources

RV campground workers are low-skilled; workers generally perform maintenance tasks or help with concession operations. Wages are much lower than the national average. Most establishments are owner- or family-operated with only a limited number of permanent or seasonal workers. Employment is highly seasonal: industry employment in winter is less than half the level in summer.

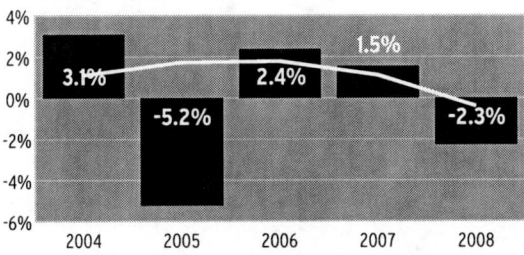

Industry Employment Growth

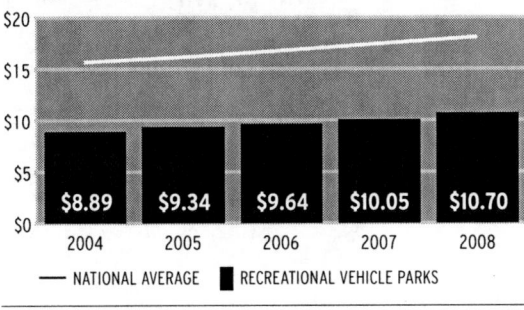

Average Hourly Earnings

—— NATIONAL AVERAGE   ■ RECREATIONAL VEHICLE PARKS

SOURCE: BUREAU OF LABOR STATISTICS

Call Preparation Questions

How has the park's business been affected by RV sales?

Growth in demand for RV parks depends on continued growth in RV ownership.

How has the park's business been affected by fluctuating fuel prices?

RVs get relatively poor gas mileage, making operating costs sensitive to fuel prices.

How dependent is the campground on national park visitors?

National parks are the leading destination of RV owners, and many RV parks and campgrounds are located close to them.

What amenities has the park added in the past year?

RV campgrounds are adding more amenities to attract new customers and encourage repeat visits.

What role do "park models" play at the campground?

Some RV parks are equipping their campgrounds with recreational park trailers, called "park models," which are similar to a fully-equipped cottage.

Web Links

Affinity Group

Holding company for several RV membership groups.
www.affinitygroup.com

Go Camping America

Directory of RV parks and campgrounds, trip planning, links.
www.gocampingamerica.com

GO RVing

Information on renting and buying RVs, trip planning, links.
www.gorving.com

National Association of RV Parks and Campgrounds

News, links.
www.arvc.org

Recreational Park Trailer Industry Association

News, listing of parks and dealers.
www.rptia.com

RV Park Hunter

Listing of RV parks by state with photos.
www.rvparkhunter.com

RV Park Reviews

Pictures and reviews of parks around US and Canada.
www.rvparkreviews.com

Glossary of Acronyms

BLM — Bureau of Land Management
GCWR — gross combined weight rating
KOA — Kampgrounds of America
LTVA — long-term visitor access
TIA — Travel Industry of America

HOOVER'S TOP COMPANIES

Largest Employers	Employees
Thousand Trails, Inc.	2,400
Kampgrounds of America, Inc.	400
Outdoor Resorts of America, Inc.	125
Pismo Coast Village, Inc.	58

SOURCE: HOOVER'S, INC., DATABASE

Rehabilitation Therapy Practices

THIS INDUSTRY INCLUDES:

SIC CODES

8049   Offices and Clinics of Health Practitioners, Not Elsewhere Classified

NAICS CODES

621340   Offices of Physical, Occupational and Speech Therapists, and Audiologists

The rehabilitation therapy industry in the US consists of about 20,000 practices with combined annual revenue of about $11 billion. Major companies include Select Medical, HealthSouth, Physiotherapy Associates, RehabCare Group, and US Physical Therapy. The industry is highly fragmented: no company has more than 5 percent market share and the top 50 companies have less than 25 percent.

Competitive Landscape

Demand is driven by the aging US population and medical advances that increase patient survival rates and prolong life. The profitability of individual practices depends on efficient use of personnel. Large companies have some economies of scale in financial and administrative systems, but the typical practice has fewer than 10 employees. Small companies compete by developing positive relationships with local health care providers and delivering superior customer service. The industry is highly labor-intensive: average revenue per employee is about $70,000.

Therapy practices compete with similar services provided by hospitals, physician offices, nursing homes, home health care services, chiropractors, and educational institutions that employ their own therapists.

Products, Operations & Technology

Rehabilitation therapy practices treat patients suffering from physical, mental, emotional, or communication disabilities. Services are primarily provided by physical therapists (60 percent of therapists); occupational therapists (20 percent); and speech therapists (15 percent). Other services are provided by audiologists, and art, dance, or music therapists. Fees for patient services make up over 90 percent of industry revenues; other revenues include lab test fees and sales of medical equipment and supplies, such as orthopedic appliances.

BUSINESS CHALLENGES

» Pricing Pressure

Insurance company and Medicare efforts to contain health care costs have limited price growth for rehabilitation therapy services. Increased competition from hospitals and physician offices has also pressured prices. From 2000 to 2005, consumer prices for therapy services rose only 15 percent, compared to a 26 percent rise for all medical services.

» Dependence on Government Reimbursements

Since elderly adults can be a large portion of demand for rehabilitation therapy services, practices depend highly on Medicare's reimbursement policies. The complexity of reimbursement rules adds overhead to billing operations and often results in payment delays. Policy changes, such as a financial cap on reimbursements or reduced fee schedules, can greatly affect revenues for therapy practices.

» Competition from Hospitals, Physicians

Hospitals and physician offices seeking to grow revenues are adding rehabilitation therapy. Rehabilitation therapy is a relatively easy service to add, since it doesn't require a large investment in specialized equipment or facilities. Competition from physicians is especially difficult for therapy practices, since physicians are their primary source of patient referrals.

Physical therapists provide services that restore function, alleviate pain, and reduce permanent physical disabilities of patients suffering from injuries or illness. Treatment begins with a review of the patient's medical history and a test of the patient's physical condition. A treatment plan is documented that describes specific tasks and anticipated outcomes. Treatment often includes exercises to improve flexibility, strength, and endurance. Physical therapists also use massage, electrical stimulation, hot or cold treatment, and ultrasound to relieve pain. These treatments may also be performed by a physical therapist assistant supervised by a physical therapist.

Occupational therapists treat many of the same physical conditions as physical therapists, but also work with individuals suffering from mental or emotional disabilities. Their goal is to improve patients' ability to perform tasks in daily living and work environments, which can range from dressing and eating to using a computer or making to-do lists. Occupational therapists teach patients with permanent physical disabilities to use adaptive equipment, such as wheelchairs and aids for eating and dressing. Some therapists work with employers to arrange jobs for disabled individuals and identify modifications to the work environment to accommodate their needs.

Speech therapists, also called speech-language pathologists, work with people who have problems speaking correctly, such as lisping or stuttering; have problems understanding or producing language; want to modify an accent; have attention, memory, or problem-solving disorders; or have swallowing difficulties. These problems may result from stroke or brain injury, learning disabilities, mental retardation, cerebral palsy, cleft palate, hearing loss, or emotional problems. Speech therapists assess each patient's condition and develop and deliver a treatment plan of exercises and drills tailored to their needs.

A typical physical therapy clinic occupies 1,500 to 3,000 square feet of leased space in an office building or shopping center. Most clinics operate five days per week and average about 20 patient visits per day. To increase patient convenience, a practice may also operate satellite clinics within a given geographic market.

Accurate and timely billing and reimbursement processes are critical for therapy practices, since nearly all services are paid for by managed care programs, commercial health insurance, Medicare/Medicaid, or workers' compensation insurance.

Computers are used to automate some treatments by occupational therapists and speech therapists, particularly treatments to help clients improve decision-making and problem-solving. Computer systems are also used to schedule appointments, track treatments and outcomes, and automate billing and reimbursement processes. Therapists working with hospitals and physician offices may also enter clinical data into an electronic health record for the patient.

Sales & Marketing

Customers for therapy services range from small children with physical or learning disabilities to elderly adults suffering from illness or mental deterioration. Victims of accidents span all age ranges. Medical developments that increase survival rates for trauma victims and babies born with severe birth defects create additional demand for rehabilitative services.

Referrals from physicians are the primary source of new patients for rehabilitation therapy practices. Other referral sources are patients, social workers, therapists at nursing homes, and physician practice administrators. To be eligible for reimbursement, Medicare and managed care plans require referral from a primary care physician. Many states have laws allowing some level of direct access by patients to physical therapists who meet certain eligibility requirements.

Marketing often includes Yellow Pages and local newspaper advertising, but the main focus is on contact with physicians through local professional meetings and direct mailings.

Treatments are usually charged per procedure. A typical treatment plan consists of one hour per day, two to three times per week, for two to six weeks, and costs $80 to $100 per visit. Medicare patients are charged based on fee schedules set by the government. Managed care plans negotiate discounted rates for members.

Human Resources

The education and training required for physical therapy providers to obtain licensing results in wages 20 percent higher than the average for all US workers. Within therapy practices, physical therapists typically earn about 5 percent more than occupational therapists or speech therapists and 60 percent more than physical therapist assistants.

The injury and illness rate for rehabilitation therapy services is much lower than the rate for all US workers, despite the physical demands of lifting patients and manipulating muscles and limbs.

Industry Employment Growth

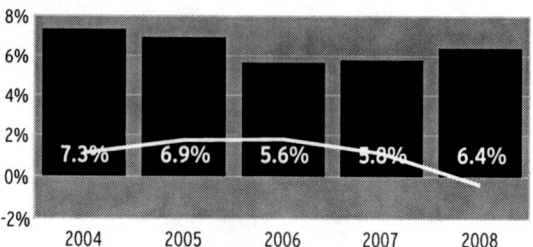

	2004	2005	2006	2007	2008
	7.3%	6.9%	5.6%	5.8%	6.4%

Average Hourly Earnings

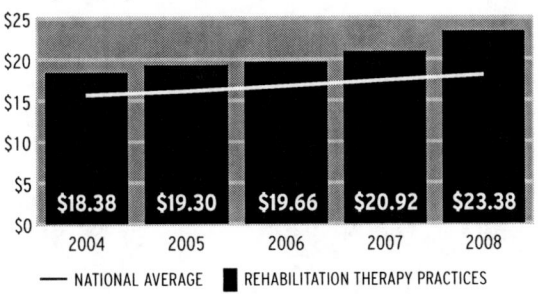

$18.38	$19.30	$19.66	$20.92	$23.38
2004	2005	2006	2007	2008

— NATIONAL AVERAGE ■ REHABILITATION THERAPY PRACTICES

SOURCE: BUREAU OF LABOR STATISTICS

Call Preparation Questions

How have prices for the company's services changed over the past year?

Insurance company and Medicare efforts to contain health care costs have limited price growth for rehabilitation therapy services.

How do changes in Medicare reimbursement policies affect the practice?

Since elderly adults can be a large portion of demand for rehabilitation therapy services, practices depend highly on Medicare's reimbursement policies.

What opportunities does the company see in providing preventative consulting services?

Rather than just treating patients injured on the job, some therapy practices are providing businesses with consulting and education services on how to avoid workplace injuries.

How is the company growing services for elderly patients?

The aging US population increases demand for therapy services.

Web Links

American Physical Therapy Association

Trade association for physical therapists. www.apta.org

Healthcare Industry Today

News on physical therapy industry. health.einnews.com/news/physical-therapy

The American Occupational Therapy Association

Trade association for occupational therapists. www.aota.org

Therapy Times

News on all therapy disciplines. www.therapytimes.com

Glossary of Acronyms

ABPTS — American Board of Physical Therapy Specialties

APTA — American Physical Therapy Association

CMS — Centers for Medicare and Medicaid

DPT — Doctor of Physical Therapy

HIPAA — Health Insurance Portability and Accountability Act

NPI — national provider identifier

HOOVER'S TOP COMPANIES

Largest Companies by Sales	($ mil.)
Select Medical Holdings Corporation	1,991.7
HealthSouth Corporation	1,842.4
Concentra Inc.	832.0
RehabCare Group, Inc.	743.1
Hanger Orthopedic Group, Inc.	703.1
Kennedy Krieger Institute	190.5
U.S. Physical Therapy, Inc.	151.7
HearUSA, Inc.	102.8

Largest Employers	Employees
HealthSouth Corporation	22,000
Select Medical Holdings Corporation	21,100
RehabCare Group, Inc.	14,000
Concentra Inc.	11,585
Hanger Orthopedic Group, Inc.	3,303
Physiotherapy Associates, Inc.	3,000
Kennedy Krieger Institute	1,780
U.S. Physical Therapy, Inc.	1,579
HearUSA, Inc.	654

Fastest Growing* by Five-Year Sales Growth	(%)
HearUSA, Inc.	11.5
U.S. Physical Therapy, Inc.	9.9
Hanger Orthopedic Group, Inc.	5.1
Select Medical Holdings Corporation	3.5

Fastest Growing* by Five-Year Employee Growth	(%)
U.S. Physical Therapy, Inc.	8.4
HearUSA, Inc.	6.3
Concentra Inc.	3.1
Select Medical Holdings Corporation	0.5
Hanger Orthopedic Group, Inc.	0.4

Top Public Companies by Market Value	($ mil.)
HealthSouth Corporation	964.7
Hanger Orthopedic Group, Inc.	471.8
RehabCare Group, Inc.	267.6
U.S. Physical Therapy, Inc.	170.1
HearUSA, Inc.	49.9

* These rates are compounded annualized increases and may have resulted from acquisitions or one time gains. If less than 6 years of data are available, growth is for the years available.

SOURCE: HOOVER'S, INC., DATABASE

Residential Real Estate Construction

About 170,000 companies build or renovate homes in the US, with combined annual revenue close to $500 billion. Large builders include Centex, Pulte, Lennar, and DR Horton. Most builders are small, with about 10 employees, build from five to 20 homes per year, and have annual revenue under $3 million. Only about 2,000 companies have annual revenue greater than $10 million. The industry remains fragmented: although large companies may build more than 20,000 homes per year, the top 10 builders together hold only 20 percent of the market.

Competitive Landscape

Demand for new housing depends on population growth and is linked to low interest rates. Large builders have some advantages in purchasing and marketing, but building methods are essentially the same for large or small builders. While larger builders have efficiencies because they can repeatedly build the same home models, they generally develop projects on large pieces of land. Small builders, therefore, build most homes in dense urban markets where little land is available.

Products, Operations & Technology

Major products are single family homes and multifamily buildings. Of an average 1.7 million homes built each year, 80 percent are single family and 20 percent are units in large apartment-style buildings. Multifamily units can be either apartments or condos. Home remodeling accounts for about 20 percent of industry revenue. Companies generally specialize in either single family or multifamily work.

The building process consists of distinct steps: land acquisition; land development (roads, sewers, utilities); permit acquisition ("entitlement"); construction; and marketing and sales. The time from initial land acquisition to final sale of a home is usually 12 to 24

BUSINESS CHALLENGES

» Highly Cyclical Demand for New Housing

Demand for new residential buildings can change rapidly, depending on the economy and interest rates: from 1984 to 1991, annual US home construction dropped 35 percent; from 1996 to 2006, it increased 40 percent; and from 2006 to 2007, it fell 25 percent. In local markets, changes in demand can be even more severe.

» Profitability Strongly Affected by Home Prices

Because a large number of homes are built speculatively, builders bear the risk that changing market conditions will produce lower selling prices than they'd anticipated. In some markets, home prices can be highly cyclical. Even in markets where prices don't fall, builders may anticipate getting a higher price than they eventually receive.

» Dependence on Local Economy

Despite national trends, demand for housing can be very volatile in local markets. Even in a large market, demand for new single-family homes can change by 50 percent in just two years; in smaller markets the change can be 100 percent. This demand volatility is due mainly to population shifts.

months, but can be longer for large projects or in congested areas with a lengthy entitlement process. Some companies work as general contractors for developers (as is typical in commercial construction), but most companies are "operative builders," who build and sell homes for their own account.

Actual construction consists of foundation work; framing (exterior walls and roof); and build-out (interior finishing, including electrical work, plumbing, floors, walls, ceilings, and carpentry). Construction time is about four to six months for a single-family home, nine to 15 for a high-rise. Construction costs for single-family homes (including land acquisition) typically equal 80 percent of the eventual sales price. Building materials generally account for

70 percent of construction costs, labor for 30 percent. Subcontractors are often hired to perform specialized work.

Larger homebuilders generally develop projects on raw tracts of land and enjoy economies of scale in construction that allow low pricing. Big builders may also engage in other types of construction to capitalize on project management expertise and counter residential real estate cycles. Some large companies also provide property management services, like security systems, pest control, and pool maintenance.

IT budgets are typically small, averaging less than 1 percent of revenue; IT functions are often outsourced. The industry's technology spending and use focuses on communications and security equipment in the office and on the jobsite, and computers and software to manage customers, inventory, subcontractors, marketing, and administrative functions. Adoption of mobile technologies including cell phones with two-way radios and Internet access is streamlining communication in the industry. Construction companies that have in-house architectural or engineering staff use specialized design software such as CAD and 3D modeling to create floor plans and technical drawings.

Sales & Marketing

Typical customers are home buyers and property investors. The typical new home buyer has a median annual household income of $55,000 and is about 40.

In some cases, homes are pre-sold, but most home construction is speculative ("on spec"), based on the expectation that a buyer will be found after a home is built. Large builders have a sales force, use model homes to market, advertise heavily, and frequently provide financing, either through an affiliated mortgage company or a third-party lender. Smaller companies typically sell through real estate brokers and don't provide financing, although they may recommend a third-party lender. Builders often specialize in certain market segments (low- or high-end, retirement communities, etc.) to capitalize on their marketing expertise.

Traditional marketing includes newspaper, magazine, radio, and TV advertising; direct mail; billboards; brochures and local home guides; and consumer trade shows and real estate exhibits such as Parade of Homes. Builders use design showrooms and model homes to attract, educate, and sell customers on floor plans, options, and upgrades. Builder websites have become a major marketing tool, as a growing number of home buyers use the Internet to research builders and new home communities before visiting showrooms and models.

The median price of a new single family home in the US was $248,000 in 2007 and grows an average 5 percent annually. Pricing varies by location: homes in metropolitan areas are typically priced about 2 to 3 percent higher than homes in suburban areas. By region, new homes in the Northeast and West are priced higher than the national average, with homes in the Midwest and South priced below. Land acquisition and development costs affect values; builders tend to price new homes higher in areas with minimal land for development such as in metropolitan and other high population density regions, to recoup the inflated cost of limited or high-demand land.

Human Resources

Many jobs in residential real estate construction require less extensive training or experience than specialized trade crafts, like electrical or plumbing work, where licensing is required. Unlike commercial construction, where operating heavy machinery is important, most residential work involves manual labor or hand tools.

Companies often keep a core of full-time employees and hire additional workers for individual projects. The industry employs about 900,000, with slight declines in winter months when construction slow and increases in spring and summer when construction demand rises.

Fringe benefits paid to workers are low, about a 20 percent addition to payroll costs. The safety record of the industry has improved substantially during the last decade: in 2006, the annual rate of illness and injury per 100 workers was five, down from 8.2 in 2000, and slightly better than the manufacturing industry at six.

Industry Employment Growth

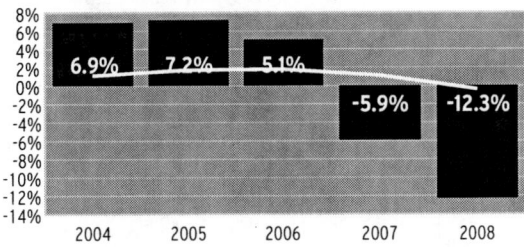

Average Hourly Earnings

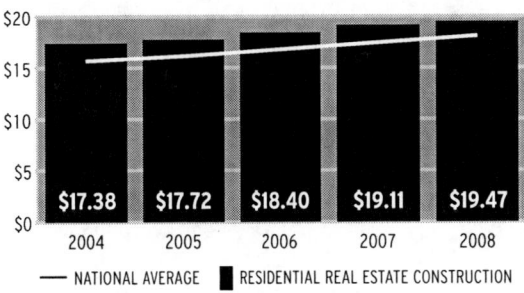

SOURCE: BUREAU OF LABOR STATISTICS

Call Preparation Questions

How does the company prepare for real estate cycles?

Demand for new residential buildings can change rapidly, depending on the economy and interest rates: from 1984 to 1991, annual US home construction dropped 35 percent; from 1996 to 2006, it increased 40 percent; and from 2006 to 2007, it fell 25 percent.

What opportunities does remodeling present for the company?

The remodeling market grew nearly 50 percent from 1991 to 2001 and an additional 30 percent from 2002 to 2007.

If used, how effective has Internet marketing been for the company?

The Internet can dramatically improve traffic to builder sales centers, increase conversion rates, and improve customer satisfaction by enabling builders to stay connected with customers through the entire home ownership cycle.

Web Links

Associated Builders and Contractors (ABC)

Information about legislative issues affecting contractors, PACs, up-to-date news by region.
www.abc.org

Builder Online

News. Statistics, website links, the 100 largest homebuilders and the top 5 builders in the 50 largest markets.
www.builderonline.com

McGraw-Hill Construction Dodge

Construction statistics, forecasts, news, regional publications, and job project pipeline information for members.
www.fwdodge.com

National Association of Homebuilders

NAHB boasts over 235,000 members, and its website provides an array of information on issues affecting the nation's homebuilders. News, useful tables, key data, and links to local homebuilder associations are included.
www.nahb.org

National Association of Realtors

News, economic summaries, government affairs, and reports on real estate.
www.realtor.org

Glossary of Acronyms

AGCA — Associated General Contractors of America
BCI — Building Cost Index
CCI — Construction Cost Index
EIA — Environmental Impact Assessment
EIS — Environmental Impact Statement

ENR — Engineering News-Record
NAHB — National Association of Home Builders
PPI — Producer Price Index

HOOVER'S TOP COMPANIES

Largest Companies by Sales	($ mil.)
Centex Corporation	8,275.6
D.R. Horton, Inc.	6,646.1
Pulte Homes, Inc.	6,289.5
Lennar Corporation	4,575.4
NVR, Inc.	3,714.1
Hovnanian Enterprises, Inc.	3,308.1
Toll Brothers, Inc.	3,158.2
KB Home	3,033.9
The Ryland Group, Inc.	1,976.1
M.D.C. Holdings, Inc.	1,458.1

Largest Employers	Employees
Pulte Homes, Inc.	8,500
Centex Corporation	6,530
Lennar Corporation	4,704
NVR, Inc.	4,119
Palm Harbor Homes, Inc.	3,800
D.R. Horton, Inc.	3,800
WCI Communities, Inc.	3,200
Toll Brothers, Inc.	3,160
KB Home	3,100
Hovnanian Enterprises, Inc.	2,816

Fastest Growing* by Five-Year Sales Growth	(%)
Comstock Homebuilding Companies, Inc.	50.2
Stratus Properties Inc.	18.6
Woodbridge Holdings Corporation	14.7
TOUSA, Inc.	9.1
Avatar Holdings Inc.	8.9
Orleans Homebuilders, Inc.	8.5
Meritage Homes Corporation	0.7
NVR, Inc.	0.2

Fastest Growing* by Five-Year Employee Growth	(%)
California Coastal Communities, Inc.	22.3
TOUSA, Inc.	14.3
Tejon Ranch Co.	6.8
Stratus Properties Inc.	6.7
Comstock Homebuilding Companies, Inc.	3.7
WCI Communities, Inc.	2.5

Top Public Companies by Market Value	($ mil.)
D.R. Horton, Inc.	4,122.9
Toll Brothers, Inc.	3,707.7
Centex Corporation	2,984.6
Pulte Homes, Inc.	2,821.8
NVR, Inc.	2,524.4

* These rates are compounded annualized increases and may have resulted from acquisitions or one time gains. If less than 6 years of data are available, growth is for the years available.

SOURCE: HOOVER'S, INC., DATABASE

Restaurants

The restaurant industry includes about 500,000 restaurants with combined annual revenue of almost $400 billion. Major companies include McDonald's; YUM! Brands (KFC, Pizza Hut, Taco Bell); and Darden Restaurants (Olive Garden, Red Lobster). The industry is highly fragmented: the 50 largest companies hold just 20 percent of the market.

The industry consists of fullservice restaurants (FSR) and limited service eating places, which include quickservice restaurants (QSR); cafeterias; buffets; snack bars; and non-alcoholic beverage bars.

Competitive Landscape

Demographics, consumer tastes, and personal income drive demand. The profitability of individual companies can vary: while QSRs rely on efficient operations and high volume sales, FSRs rely on high-margin items and effective marketing. Large companies have advantages in purchasing, finance, and marketing. Small companies can offer superior food or service. The industry is highly labor-intensive: annual revenue per worker is between $40,000 and $45,000.

Restaurants compete with companies that serve meals or prepared foods, including grocery stores, warehouse clubs, delis, and convenience stores. In addition, restaurants compete with home cooking.

Products, Operations & Technology

Products include appetizers, entrée/main dishes, desserts, and beverages. Companies may specialize in a certain type of cuisine (such as Italian, Chinese, or barbecue); entrée (sandwiches, steak, seafood); or other food item (pretzels, smoothies). Industry revenue is roughly evenly split between FSRs and limited service. In QSRs, customers generally order and pay before eating. While most QSRs are fast food restaurants, QSRs also include fast casual

BUSINESS CHALLENGES

» Volatile Supply Costs

Unstable manufacturer prices for raw ingredients used in restaurants can significantly impact restaurant profitability. Commodity markets affect wholesale prices for beef and poultry, where prices can change more than 20 percent in a single year. Supply issues can affect the cost of seafood. The wholesale price of flour, eggs, dairy products, fats, and oils can also increase rapidly and affect restaurant margins. Consumer price sensitivity can limit a restaurant's ability to completely pass through cost increases.

» Increasing Competition

Restaurants face increasing competition from a broad range of businesses vying for consumers' food dollars. Grocery stores and warehouse clubs are providing more ready-to-eat meals and sides, often at a better value than restaurants. Convenience stores, gas stations, coffee shops, and delis sell sandwiches and beverages, cutting into restaurants' share of the lunch market. Home cooking is also a source of competition, as consumers make over three-quarters of meals at home, according to NPD Group.

» Demand Dependent on Consumer Spending

Restaurant meals are generally more expensive than home cooking, and sales depend on consumer spending. During a recent recessionary period, sales growth in restaurants slowed and QSR employment declined as consumers cut unnecessary expenses. Slow restaurant traffic during tough economic times can depress sales.

restaurants, which offer higher quality, more expensive food without table service. In FSRs, waiters take orders, serve beverages and meals, present the check, and process payment. FSRs include casual dining (full bar); family dining (limited bar); and fine dining establishments.

The industry includes national and regional chains, franchises, and independent operators. The majority of companies are independently owned and operated, although many QSRs are franchises of large national chains. Franchises allow individual owners to leverage a well-known brand name and benefit from the purchasing efficiencies and operational expertise of the franchiser. Franchise agreements generally cover a specific geographical market and outline restaurant operating requirements, such as hours of operation, menu offerings, and pricing. Annual sales average $833,000 for FSRs and $694,000 for QSRs, according to the National Restaurant Association (NRA). A well-established, midsized chain FSR can generate between $3 and $5 million annually.

The food preparation area of a restaurant is known as the "back of house," while the dining area is known as the "front of house." Food prep areas include the kitchen, cold storage, and dishwashing areas. Dining space may include bars, outdoor seating, or banquet rooms. Upscale restaurants often feature unique decor to create a distinctive ambiance. An FSR's square footage and the number of seats and tables dictate how many patrons it can serve and directly affect sales. Because the restaurant industry is highly competitive, site selection is critical: companies may consider population density, household income, competition, visibility, accessibility, and traffic.

Food preparation varies depending on restaurant type. QSRs typically offer a limited number of simple items, which allows companies to train unskilled workers to prepare food. Most chains have strict operating procedures for food preparation to ensure consistent quality and food safety. FSRs offering expensive fare or a wide variety of menu options have more complex operations and require larger staff. An executive chef, assisted by a sous chef, oversees kitchen operations and may be involved in the business end of restaurant management. Line cooks are responsible for various kitchen stations, such as the grill, sauté, or fryer. Prep cooks prepare ingredients for cooking. Pastry chefs create desserts.

Companies typically buy supplies from food distributors. Some restaurants buy directly from local farms or farmers markets. Large chains may contract with suppliers to minimize volatile commodity costs. Companies carefully manage inventory of perishable food products, such as fresh seafood and dairy goods, to reduce losses due to spoilage.

When developing menus, restaurants consider ingredient availability, cooking equipment, labor requirements, physical space, and cost. The mix of menu options must balance popularity and profitability. Some companies change menu selections seasonally, with some high-end restaurants creating new menus daily. While menu options can vary widely, frequently consumed restaurant foods include hamburgers, french fries, pizza, salads, sandwiches, chicken, and seafood. Alcoholic beverages are important contributors to total sales, particularly for FSRs and especially for high-end restaurants. Companies may offer an alternative menu for children or those with special dietary needs.

Computerized information systems can improve and link food preparation and serving operations. Touchscreen ordering programs ensure accurate communication of customer orders. Timing systems monitor meal progress and can alert staff if an order is running behind schedule. Reservations programs maximize traffic flow and seating. Inventory management systems track supply levels and can help reduce waste due to spoilage. Cost accounting programs help companies determine the profitability of individual menu items. Handheld point-of-sale (POS) devices allow servers to place orders and print checks tableside, improving accuracy and reducing ordering time. Some handhelds can also print customer checks and process credit card payments.

Sales & Marketing

While restaurants appeal to a broad demographic, young adults without children are most likely to dine out, according to NPD Group. Young men are an important segment for QSRs, tourists are more likely to visit FSRs, and households with children tend to order take out.

Marketing and promotional vehicles include TV, print, radio, and outdoor advertising; direct mail; and newspaper insert coupons. Franchises typically contribute to corporate advertising funds and may run separate local marketing programs. Relationships with hotels can help drive tourist traffic. Word-of-mouth is especially important for small, independent restaurants with limited marketing budgets. Companies may also implement loyalty programs by offering discounts and free food for frequent visits.

Customer service is a critical element of the dining experience for FSRs, particularly in the high-end segment. Expensive restaurants may assign multiple waiters to a single table to ensure attentive service. Customers may expect waitstaff to have in-depth knowledge of menu offerings and recommend wine pairings. Developing personal relationships with regular patrons helps create a loyal customer base. Most QSR customers expect fast service and accurate order fulfillment.

Restaurants use Internet sites to post basic information, including menus, directions, and hours of operation. Some companies allow customers to make reservations or place take out, dine-in, or delivery orders through websites.

Customers can sign up for e-mail and cell phone notifications that communicate daily specials.

For chain FSRs, checks average about $8 for family and $18 for casual restaurants, according to Restaurants and Institutions. In the most expensive restaurants, checks regularly exceed $100 and entrées alone can cost $40 or more. Checks average $5 to $6 in fast food restaurants, according to Banc of America Securities. Fast casual restaurant checks range from $7 to $10, according to Technomic.

Human Resources

Many entry-level jobs, such as servers, dishwashers and bus staff, require few skills, with some positions paying at or slightly above minimum wage. Most servers rely on tips to supplement income. Wages are about half the average for all US workers; as a result, the industry depends on part-time help. In some areas, companies rely on undocumented workers to maintain staffing. Unpredictable restaurant traffic and rapid worker turnover make staffing and scheduling a constant challenge.

Jobs generally requiring experience or expertise include chefs, restaurant managers, and sommeliers. Some chefs have degrees from culinary schools or international training. The annual salary for an executive chef averages about $78,000 and a sous chef earns about $42,000, according to StarChefs.com. Executive chefs have about 20 years experience, with those in the most exclusive restaurants earning well over $100,000 annually. Restaurant managers earn between $40,000 and $55,000 annually, and may participate in profit-sharing plans.

Industry Employment Growth

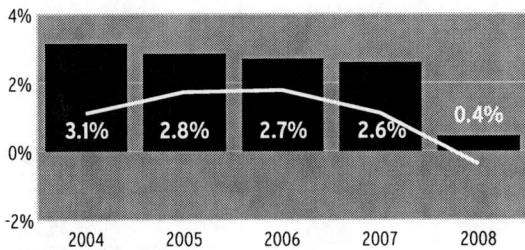

Average Hourly Earnings

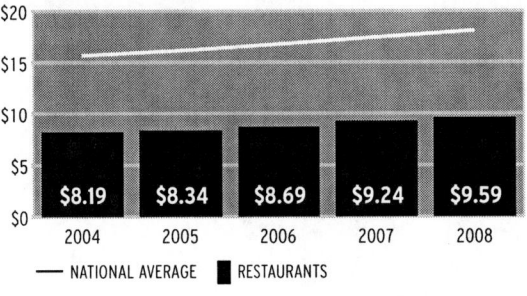

SOURCE: BUREAU OF LABOR STATISTICS

Call Preparation Questions

How have changes in food and beverage costs affected the company's profitability?

Unstable manufacturer prices for raw ingredients used in restaurants can significantly impact restaurant profitability.

How has the company's competition changed over time?

Restaurants face increasing competition from a broad range of businesses vying for consumers' food dollars.

How does the economy influence the company's sales?

Restaurant meals are generally more expensive than home cooking, and sales depend on consumer spending.

How is the company addressing the growing popularity of eco-friendly food?

Companies can leverage growing consumer interest in the environment and healthy eating by adding "green" menu choices.

How has the trend of smaller portion sizes affected the company's menu?

Restaurants can capitalize on consumers' desire to sample different flavors and types of food by offering small portions.

Web Links

Nation's Restaurant News

Industry news and trends.
www.nrn.com

National Restaurant Association

Industry news, trends, research, and consumer information from trade association.
www.restaurant.org

NPD Group

Eating and cooking trends.
www.npd.com

Restaurant Finance Monitor

Industry and company-specific news.
www.restfinance.com

RestaurantOwner.com

Restaurant operations, business tools, and surveys.
restaurantowner.com

Restaurants and Institutions

Industry news and trends.
www.rimag.com

Technomic

Industry and category sales, forecasts, and other market research.
www.technomic.com

Glossary of Acronyms

FSR — fullservice restaurant
NRA — National Restaurant Association
POS — point-of-sale
QSR — quickservice restaurant

HOOVER'S TOP COMPANIES

Largest Companies by Sales	($ mil.)
McDonald's Corporation	23,522.4
YUM! Brands, Inc.	11,279.0
Darden Restaurants, Inc.	6,626.5
Brinker International, Inc.	4,235.2
OSI Restaurant Partners, LLC	4,150.0
Chick-fil-A, Inc.	2,640.9
Jack in the Box Inc.	2,539.6
Burger King Holdings, Inc.	2,455.0
Wendy's International, Inc.	2,450.2
Cracker Barrel Old Country Store, Inc.	2,384.5

Largest Employers	Employees
McDonald's Corporation	400,000
YUM! Brands, Inc.	301,000
Darden Restaurants, Inc.	179,000
Brinker International, Inc.	113,900
Cracker Barrel Old Country Store, Inc.	65,000
Chick-fil-A, Inc.	50,000
Bob Evans Farms, Inc.	49,149
Ruby Tuesday, Inc.	47,800
Wendy's International, Inc.	44,000
Jack in the Box Inc.	42,700

Fastest Growing* by Five-Year Sales Growth	(%)
Healthy Fast Food, Inc.	900.0
uWink, Inc.	88.0
Organic To Go Food Corporation	63.9
Granite City Food & Brewery Ltd.	43.9
Kona Grill, Inc.	35.5
Chipotle Mexican Grill, Inc.	33.4
The Johnny Rockets Group, Inc.	33.2
Panera Bread Company	29.6
BJ's Restaurants, Inc.	29.4
Buffalo Wild Wings, Inc.	27.3

Fastest Growing* by Five-Year Employee Growth	(%)
DineEquity, Inc.	500.1
Granite City Food & Brewery Ltd.	84.4
Fog Cutter Capital Group Inc.	79.4
Ruth's Hospitality Group, Inc.	59.8
Wendy's/Arby's Group, Inc.	39.5
Buffalo Wild Wings, Inc.	28.9
BJ's Restaurants, Inc.	26.1
Noodles & Company	24.6
Texas Roadhouse, Inc.	24.1
Red Robin Gourmet Burgers, Inc.	23.6

Top Public Companies by Market Value	($ mil.)
McDonald's Corporation	69,360.5
YUM! Brands, Inc.	13,898.5
Darden Restaurants, Inc.	4,459.5
Burger King Holdings, Inc.	3,617.3
Wendy's/Arby's Group, Inc.	2,273.6

* These rates are compounded annualized increases and may have resulted from acquisitions or one time gains. If less than 6 years of data are available, growth is for the years available.

SOURCE: HOOVER'S, INC., DATABASE

Retail Sector

The US retail industry includes about 1 million outlets with combined annual revenue of over $4 trillion. Major companies include Wal-Mart, Home Depot, Kroger, Costco, and Target. While large companies dominate some retail sectors (such as mass merchandisers and grocery stores), other sectors (such as auto dealers and convenience stores) are fragmented. Many specialty retailers are single-store operations.

The US retail industry includes auto dealers and Internet and catalog retailers and generally excludes food and drinking establishments, such as restaurants and bars.

Competitive Landscape

Personal income, consumer confidence, and interest rates drive demand. The profitability of individual companies depends on efficient supply chain management and effective merchandising and marketing. Large companies have advantages in purchasing, distribution, and marketing. Small companies can compete effectively by selling unique merchandise, providing superior customer service, offering a distinctive shopping experience, or serving a local market. Annual revenue per worker averages $250,000, but ranges from $600,000 for new car dealers to less than $200,000 for grocery stores.

Products, Operations & Technology

Major retail sectors include motor vehicles and parts dealers (25 percent of sales); general merchandise and food and beverage stores (15 percent each); convenience stores (10 percent); building material and garden supply stores and non-store retailers (8 percent each). Motor vehicles and parts dealers include new and used car dealers. General merchandise stores include department stores, discount department stores, warehouse clubs, and superstores. Food and beverage stores include grocery; specialty food; and beer, wine, and liquor stores. Convenience stores may sell gas. Non-store retailers include

BUSINESS CHALLENGES

» Retail Demand Depends on the Economy

Economic factors, including personal income, consumer confidence, job growth, and interest rates, can greatly affect consumer spending and the retail sector. During recessionary periods, retail sales growth can slow drastically and even decline. Retail spending grows rapidly during periods of strong economic growth, as consumers spend a greater share of income and increase their personal debt. Rising interest rates affect consumer credit and consumer ability to finance large retail purchases, such as cars.

» Industry Concentration

In many retail segments, large companies dominate and hold the majority of the market. Even specialty retailers in fragmented markets must compete with mass merchandisers and warehouse clubs that offer a smaller selection of comparable merchandise at low prices. Suppliers favor large retailers by offering volume discounts. With limited marketing funds, small retailers struggle to compete with the large advertising budgets enjoyed by major retailers.

» Seasonal Cash Flow

For many retailers, cash flow is uneven because of seasonal demand. Due to increased demand during the winter holidays, many retailers, including toy, jewelry, and consumer electronics stores, generate a disproportionate share of revenue during fourth quarter. Back-to-school and spring and fall fashion introductions drive sales peaks for apparel retailers. Even general merchandise stores must build and finance inventory in seasonal merchandise categories to prepare for key selling periods.

Internet retailers, mail order catalogs, vending machine operators, and fuel dealers. Other retail sectors include health and personal care stores (drugstores); clothing and accessory stores; furniture and home furnishings stores; electronics and appliances stores; and sporting goods, books, hobby, and music stores.

Retailers buy goods from suppliers or wholesalers and resell them for a profit. The industry includes national and regional chains, franchises, and independent retailers. Franchises allow independent operators to leverage a well-known brand name and benefit from the parent company's purchasing and operational efficiencies. Because franchise owners pay royalties and bear much of the financial burden of opening a retail outlet, franchising is a cost-effective way for companies to expand.

The degree of specialization differentiates types of retailers. Department and general merchandise stores offer a wide range of items, while specialty retailers offer a broad selection within a product category. Numerous market segments can exist within a category. For example, clothing stores may focus on a particular gender (men, women, children); price tier (high, medium, low); style (traditional, contemporary, designer); or size (petite, tall, plus-size). At some discount retailers, such as dollar stores, merchandise can vary from week to week.

For brick-and-mortar retailers (those with physical stores), location is key to driving customer traffic. Typical sites include enclosed, outdoor, and strip malls, and stand-alone sites. Large retailers typically occupy desirable anchor spots in shopping malls. When selecting locations, retailers consider local demographics (population growth, income); traffic patterns; proximity to complementary and competitive retailers; and lifestyle. Retail format can vary: gigantic superstores offer massive selections, while kiosks allow companies to set up scaled-down versions of retail operations in small spaces. Specialty retailers may also lease locations within larger retailers.

Selecting the appropriate merchandise is critical. Buyers may attend trade shows or search through product catalogs or supplier websites to review upcoming new products. Vendors may set up individual meetings with large retailers to review product offerings. Because most companies place orders many months in advance of product receipt, buyers must have thorough knowledge of market and consumer trends to make good buying decisions. Volume discounts are common and favor large retailers. In industries where suppliers are numerous, retailers often buy from distributors or wholesalers, which consolidate merchandise and simplify purchasing. Retailers with multiple stores often operate their own warehouses or distribution centers to receive and store merchandise from suppliers.

Effective supply chain management controls the flow of merchandise from suppliers to individual retail outlets and helps keep operating costs low. Many companies, particularly large retailers, have implemented sophisticated information systems that integrate data from manufacturers, distributors, warehouses, transporters, and retail outlets to track merchandise movement, monitor inventory levels, and ensure timely delivery of stock to stores. Inventory management helps companies identify slow- and fast-moving items and spot shrinkage due to damage, spoilage, or theft. Rapid inventory turnover is especially critical for retailers selling perishable items, such as fresh foods or dairy products. Retailers periodically discount or "mark down" items that aren't selling to clear floor space for new merchandise.

When developing store layouts, retailers allocate space to basic merchandise, special promotions, checkout, and storage. Companies evaluate how efficiently they're using space by monitoring sales per square foot. Most retailers group similar merchandise and may place complementary items adjacent to one another to generate incremental sales. Well-designed layouts and window displays attract and maximize store traffic. Store atmosphere can vary significantly, based on the type of shopping experience retailers want to deliver. For example, a high end clothing store may feature lavish decor and expensive fixtures, while warehouse clubs offer little more than the basics. Checkout procedures can also vary: high volume retailers, such as grocery stores, typically have a centralized checkout area with multiple lanes to process as many transactions as possible. Department stores usually have checkout stations throughout the store. Some retailers offer self-checkout.

Computer information systems generally support the most basic retail operations. Point-of-sale (POS) technology records sales transactions and processes payments. Fully integrated information systems link POS, inventory, forecasting, purchasing, and many backoffice functions, such as payroll, finance, and accounting. Electronic data interchange (EDI) allows retailers to place purchase orders electronically. Automatic replenishment systems help companies maintain desired inventory levels of key products. To access real-time sales data, large companies link individual store systems to corporate systems.

To better manage merchandise movement, many large retailers have implemented enterprise resource planning (ERP), which improves companies' visibility into the supply chain by connecting retailer systems with manufacturers, raw material suppliers, distributors, and transporters. Some companies participate in cooperative supply chain networks that share sales data and forecasts from retailers and supply and production data from raw material suppliers and manufacturers. Known as just-in-time (JIT) merchandising, coordinating demand and supply information allows supply chain participants (including retailers) to reduce inventory carry costs and minimize write-offs and discounting.

Universal product codes (UPC), implemented with bar codes on product packaging, provide standard identification for retail products and allow retailers to scan items electronically. In addition to bar codes, a growing number of retailers are using radio frequency identification (RFID) devices, which can transmit and store product information. While more expensive to implement than bar code processing, RFID gives companies greater tracking abilities since RFID codes can be unique to an individual item. In addition, RFID allows retailers to monitor product movement more efficiently because supply chain participants can scan merchandise by the pallet.

Advances in payment system technology have allowed many retailers to improve the checkout process. RFID allows retailers to offer contactless payment through special tags or cards. Some companies, such as grocery stores, have added self-checkout lanes. Biometric identification allows customers to pay with a fingerprint. Handheld checkout devices eliminate the need for dedicated stations.

Sales & Marketing

Customer demographics vary by retailer and can be different within a retail segment. For example, while women buy more clothing and beauty products, men are more likely to buy motorcycles and consumer electronics. Among alcoholic beverage consumers, liquor consumers tend to be older, wine consumers older and female, and beer consumers younger and male. Demographic trends, including the aging US population, growth of minority populations, and Generation Y, affect retailer strategy and marketing.

Common marketing and promotional vehicles include TV, print, radio, and newspaper advertising; direct mail; and in-store events. Small retailers benefit from grassroots marketing, word-of-mouth, and local event sponsorship. Retailer brand names and brand name merchandise help attract a distinct clientele. Loyalty programs, which reward frequent or large purchases, help retailers develop a customer base. Gift cards are a popular way to generate repeat visits. Retailers may hold special sales or events to drive store traffic, introduce items, or clear out excess merchandise. Discounts or markdowns are common in some categories, such as women's apparel.

Large retailers rely on extensive consumer research to guide merchandising and pricing decisions. Syndicated data helps companies track competitors' performance and evaluate the effectiveness of marketing programs.

Customer service tends to be more important for expensive products (such as cars) or sophisticated products (electronics). Pricey or complicated products may have a longer selling cycle and require more personal attention from sales staff. For volume-driven retailers, such as grocery stores, customers are more likely to appreciate fast, efficient service. Many retailers measure customer service through surveys or follow-up phone calls.

The Internet has greatly affected the retail operating model by expanding consumer access to goods and allowing consumers to compare prices more effectively. Internet-only retailers, such as Amazon, can offer a vast selection of merchandise and enjoy low overhead due to the absence of physical stores. Many traditional retailers have established websites to develop an online presence, offer an expanded merchandise selection not available in stores, and compete with Internet-only retailers. Links from complementary websites help expose retailer websites to a broader audience. Companies can also offer links to other websites and may receive commissions for referral sales.

In some categories, online retailing has allowed suppliers to bypass traditional retail channels and reach consumers directly, although suppliers are often hesitant to sell directly for fear of losing product distribution. Some companies have drop ship agreements with suppliers, which allow the retailer to process online orders and the supplier to ship merchandise directly to customers.

Retailers may offer merchandise in multiple price tiers to appeal to a broad customer base. Brand name merchandise (including designer brands) is typically the most expensive. Large retailers may offer private-labels or store brands, which offer comparable quality but lower prices than brand names. Discount brands appeal to price-conscious customers. Companies may use promotional funding from manufacturers to discount retail prices.

Human Resources

The retail sector is the US' largest employer and provides over 15 million jobs. Typical jobs include sales, cashiering, and stocking. Most jobs require few skills and pay low wages. Wages are more than 25 percent lower than the average for all US workers. As a result, employee turnover exceeds 50 percent annually, higher than the average for all industries. Retailers rely heavily on part-time help because sales volume varies during the day and week, and seasonally.

In certain high-end retail segments, such as original art, some consumer electronics, and luxury autos, sales staff require specialized education or training. Expensive or complicated merchandise may involve a longer sales cycle and extensive customer relationship development. Companies specializing in high-end merchandise may use commissions as compensation to motivate sales staff.

The industry injury rate is slightly higher than the average for all US workers, primarily due to lifting-related injuries from restocking jobs.

Industry Employment Growth

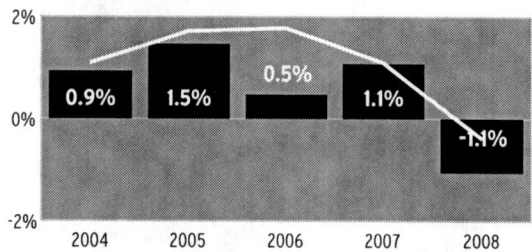

Average Hourly Earnings

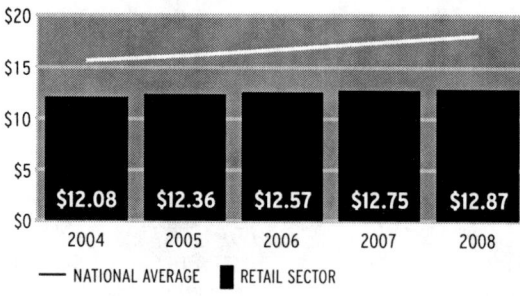

SOURCE: BUREAU OF LABOR STATISTICS

Call Preparation Questions

How sensitive is the company's business to the economy?

Economic factors, including personal income, consumer confidence, job growth, and interest rates, can greatly affect consumer spending and the retail sector.

How does the company compete with large retailers?

In many retail segments, large companies dominate and hold the majority of the market.

How do seasonal sales affect the company?

For many retailers, cash flow is uneven because of seasonal demand.

How effective are the company's loyalty programs?

Loyalty programs can help retailers retain customers, encourage repeat store visits, and increase purchase amounts.

How has the Internet affected the company's operations?

Widespread acceptance of the Internet as a retail channel has made websites an essential marketing vehicle for many retailers.

Web Links

Chain Store Age

News, trends, and statistics for chain retailers. www.chainstoreage.com

Chain Store Guide

Summaries of many retail categories. Available with free subscription. www.csgis.com

Internet Retailer

News and trends for online sales. www.internetretailer.com

LP Magazine

News on loss prevention for retailers. www.lpinformation.com

National Association of Retail Merchandising Services

Weekly and quarterly news and trends.
www.narms.com

National Retail Federation

Industry news, trends, statistics from trade association. Retailer surveys available for purchase.
www.nrf.com

Retail Traffic

Retail real estate trends.
retailtrafficmag.com

Retailing Today

News, trends, and statistics with free subscription.
www.retailingtoday.com

Shopping Centers Today

News and trends from International Council of Shopping Centers.
www.icsc.org/sct

Stores Magazine

News, trends, and statistics — National Retail Federation magazine.
www.stores.org

Glossary of Acronyms

EDI — electronic data interchange
ERP — enterprise resource planning
ICSC — International Council of Shopping Centers
JIT — just-in-time
NRF — National Retail Federation
POS — point-of-sale
RFID — radio frequency identification
UPC — universal product codes

HOOVER'S TOP COMPANIES

Largest Companies by Sales	($ mil.)
Wal-Mart Stores, Inc.	378,799.0
The Home Depot, Inc.	77,349.0
Costco Wholesale Corporation	72,483.0
The Kroger Co.	70,235.0
Target Corporation	63,367.0
Lowe's Companies, Inc.	48,283.0
Sears Holdings Corporation	46,770.0
SUPERVALU INC.	44,048.0
Safeway Inc.	44,104.0
Publix Super Markets, Inc.	24,109.6

Largest Employers	Employees
Wal-Mart Stores, Inc.	2,100,000
Target Corporation	366,000
The Home Depot, Inc.	331,000
The Kroger Co.	323,000
Lowe's Companies, Inc.	216,000
Safeway Inc.	201,000
Costco Wholesale Corporation	137,000
Kohl's Corporation	125,000
IGA, Inc.	92,000
Meijer, Inc.	67,000

Fastest Growing* by Five-Year Sales Growth	(%)
Super Center Concepts, Inc.	10.9
Ingles Markets, Incorporated	10.2
The Penn Traffic Company	9.6
K-VA-T Food Stores, Inc.	9.2
Wal-Mart Stores, Inc.	9.0
The Golub Corporation	8.4
Wegmans Food Markets, Inc.	8.3
Ruddick Corporation	7.9
Publix Super Markets, Inc.	7.3
The Kroger Co.	6.3

Fastest Growing* by Five-Year Employee Growth	(%)
Roundy's Supermarkets, Inc.	9.8
Super Center Concepts, Inc.	9.8
Wal-Mart Stores, Inc.	8.4
Ruddick Corporation	7.7
Ingles Markets, Incorporated	5.9
K-VA-T Food Stores, Inc.	5.2
The Golub Corporation	3.9
Wegmans Food Markets, Inc.	3.7
Publix Super Markets, Inc.	3.3
Safeway Inc.	3.2

Top Public Companies by Market Value	($ mil.)
Wal-Mart Stores, Inc.	201,590.0
Publix Super Markets, Inc.	87,336.3
The Home Depot, Inc.	51,460.5
Target Corporation	46,709.0
Lowe's Companies, Inc.	37,251.9

* These rates are compounded annualized increases and may have resulted from acquisitions or one time gains. If less than 6 years of data are available, growth is for the years available.

SOURCE: HOOVER'S, INC., DATABASE

Roofing, Siding, and Sheet Metal Contractors

THIS INDUSTRY INCLUDES:

SIC CODES

1761   Roofing, Siding, and Sheet Metal Work

NAICS CODES

23816   Roofing Contractors

23817   Siding Contractors

The roofing and siding industry includes 30,000 companies with combined annual revenue of about $25 billion. Most companies are small, local contractors, with annual revenue less than $1 million. Large commercial roofers include Centimark and Tecta America. Commercial and residential roofing are quite different, and most companies specialize in one or the other.

Competitive Landscape

Demand for roofing services is closely tied to local real estate construction. This highly fragmented industry has few large companies and little repeat business. Roofing technology is relatively simple and there are no economies of scale aside from the ability to handle several projects at once. Companies compete based mainly on price.

Because roofs need regular maintenance and often must be replaced every 20 years or so, roofing provides relatively steady work compared to other work that depends chiefly on new construction.

Products, Operations & Technology

Roofing and siding contractors install and repair commercial and residential roofs and siding, although the majority of industry revenue is from roofing. Contractors often provide siding and sheet metal work in addition because the work techniques are similar. Almost 70 percent of industry revenue comes from commercial jobs, of which 75 percent involve reroofing, repair, and maintenance and 25 percent new construction. The average useful life of a commercial roof is about 14 years. Reroofing, maintenance, and repairs are often more profitable than new construction, as companies often negotiate these contracts rather than soliciting bids from several competitors. Roof repair involves simple tasks like caulking, fixing leaks, and re-coating. Roof restorations are bigger

BUSINESS CHALLENGES

» Dependence on Local Real Estate Activity

Demand for roofing services is closely tied to the state of the local economy, including new residential and commercial real estate construction. New construction can swing wildly from year to year in local markets, sometimes more than 50 percent. Commercial roofing construction and demand for replacement roofing for commercial buildings are less volatile sources of business than residential roofing construction.

» Material Costs Tied to Oil Prices

Crude oil is a major ingredient of asphalt, plastics, and rubber roofing materials. Two of the most widely used roofing materials, asphalt shingles, primarily used on residential homes, and EPDM rubber, used primarily on commercial buildings, are made from petroleum products. Sometimes roofers can pass higher labor and material prices to contractors or consumers. However, when prices rise quickly, some roofers, especially smaller operators with less leverage, can get caught with the costs between the time they agree on a price for a project and the time they finish.

» Mold Liability

Exposure to moisture and mold lawsuits is growing as the size of jury awards escalates and juries take mold-related health problems more seriously. Mold claims have been brought against roofing contractors, who are liable for defective construction that allows moisture entry.

jobs, involving resurfacing and major repairs. Reroofing costs twice as much as restoring, and involves replacing all major materials.

Roofing work is labor-intensive. The availability of skilled roofing labor is an ongoing concern.

The two main types of commercial roofing systems are built-up and single-ply. Common commercial roofing materials used are synthetic rubber (EPDM); asphalt; coal tar; metal (steel, alloys, aluminum); acrylic (urethane); sprayed polyurethane foam; shingles (fiberglass asphalt, cement-based, wood, slate); and modified bitumen (asphalt mixed with chemicals).

Built-up roofs are constructed on the roof by the contractor using rolls of component materials such as felts and asphalt. Single-ply roofs are prefabricated membranes of flexible sheets of compounded synthetic materials like thermosets, thermoplastics, or modified bitumens. Asphalt shingles, for residential construction, are one of the most widely used roofing materials. Nearly 12 billion square feet of various asphalt shingle products are manufactured annually, enough to cover more than 5 million homes every year. Asphalt roofing products are classified into four broad groups: shingles, residential roll roofing, built-up roofing, and modified bitumen membranes.

The different types of siding materials include cedar, vinyl, steel, brick, stone, aluminum, and fiber cement. Vinyl is the most popular exterior siding on homes today because it's maintenance-free. Brick, stone, and cedar are also popular, but more expensive. Steel siding is used in dry areas frequented by damaging hailstorms. Aluminum is now rarely used. Insulation and vapor barriers must be installed with most siding and roof systems. In addition to sheet metal roofs and siding, roofing contractors often use metal for gutters and drains.

Sales & Marketing

Major customers include real estate developers and building managers. Roofing companies negotiate or bid on fixed-price contracts with customers. Contracts typically require partial payment upfront on small jobs or progress payments on large ones. Companies with annual sales under $5 million typically don't employ a sales force, but rely on referrals and personal contacts. Marketing to residential customers is difficult because repeat customers are few (a good roof can last 15 years without repair). Telemarketing is often used to find new residential and commercial customers. Roofers may have inspection and maintenance contracts with commercial customers, providing a steady stream of business.

In markets with lots of residential construction, roofers may be hired as subcontractors. But many large homebuilders do their own roofing work. Senior managers play a major role in marketing, negotiating, and bidding contracts. Experience is key when estimating material, labor, and equipment costs.

Human Resources

Jobs in roofing require special training or experience, and are therefore relatively well-paid. Roofing work is seasonal. Many companies keep a core of full-time workers and hire extra for each project. Workers employed on a project basis have no long-term fringe benefits.

Greater safety concerns, in an industry that still has a relatively high number of fatal accidents, brought annual accident rates down from 14 cases per 100 workers in 1990, to eight in 2004.

Industry Employment Growth

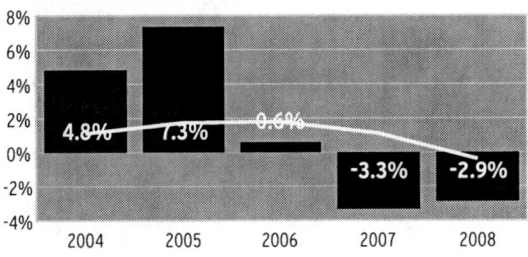

Average Hourly Earnings

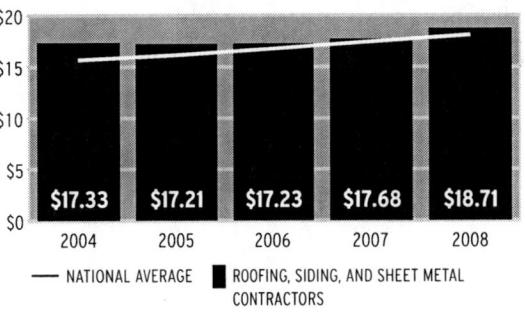

SOURCE: BUREAU OF LABOR STATISTICS

Call Preparation Questions

What is the company's strategy for countering the industry's cyclic nature?

Demand for roofing services is closely tied to the state of the local economy, including new residential and commercial real estate construction.

How does the company protect itself from the fluctuating prices of asphalt and other construction materials?

Crude oil is a major ingredient of asphalt, plastics, and rubber roofing materials.

What protection does the company have against mold lawsuits?

Exposure to moisture and mold lawsuits is growing as the size of jury awards escalates and juries take mold-related health problems more seriously.

What new labor-saving or safety technology has the company adopted in recent years, and to what benefit?

Hot asphalt roofing, though widely used, requires heavy manual labor involving many worker safety hazards.

Has the shift to alternative roofing materials benefited or challenged the company?

Higher-priced metal roofing, laminated shingles, and cedar tile are becoming more popular in residential housing due to their appearance and durability.

Web Links

Cedar Shake and Shingle Bureau

Benefits, installation, specifications, care, maintenance, FAQs, technical support on cedar shakes and shingles.
www.cedarbureau.org

Industry News – Roofing Contractor Online

Latest industry news.
www.roofingcontractor.com

National Roofing Contractors Association

Directories, conference, technical, and consumer information, government relations, and publications.
www.nrca.net

Professional Roofing Magazine

Useful articles and other information.
www.professionalroofing.net/

Roofing Siding Insulation Magazine

News.
www.rsimag.com/rsi

Single Ply Roofing Industry

Latest news on single-ply roofing markets.
www.spri.org/media

SNIPS

Sheet metal, roofing, and HVAC association.
www.snipsmag.com

Vinyl in Design

Highlights the history, manufacturing process and environmental performance of vinyl as a building material. Extensive technical and performance information on vinyl siding and roof membranes.
www.vinylbydesign.com

Glossary of Acronyms

EPDM — synthetic rubber
PSF — pounds per square foot

HOOVER'S TOP COMPANIES

Largest Employers	Employees
Tecta America Corp.	3,500
Duro-Last Roofing, Inc.	525
D. C. Taylor Co.	350
The Holland Roofing Group LLC	100
Campbell Roofing & Construction, Inc.	100
THL Enterprises, Inc.	50
Pickens Roofing Inc.	50
Garcia Roofing, Inc.	50
Cabral Roofing & Waterproofing Corp.	48

SOURCE: HOOVER'S, INC., DATABASE

Sales Promotion Services

The sales promotion services industry includes about 4,500 companies and departments of many advertising companies with combined annual revenue of about $10 billion. Major companies include subsidiaries of large marketing firms such as Maritz, and subsidiaries of major advertising agencies such as Omnicom and WPP. The industry is highly fragmented: the top 50 companies account for less than 30 percent of industry revenue. Most companies are small and independent with limited geographic coverage and product offerings.

The industry provides promotional products imprinted with the name, logo, and/or marketing message of clients.

Competitive Landscape

Demand is driven by economic growth and by corporate profits. The profitability of individual companies depends on efficient order fulfillment and marketing. Large companies have economies of scale in procurement and the ability to offer other marketing services. Small companies specialize by type of sales promotion product and differentiate themselves on customer service, particularly speed of delivery. The industry is labor-intensive: average annual revenue per employee is about $125,000.

Products, Operations & Technology

Major products are shirts, writing instruments, desk/office accessories, glassware, and caps/headgear, all customized with the customer's name, logo, and/or message. The most popular products are shirts (offered by almost 75 percent of companies); writing instruments (about 50 percent); and desk/office accessories (25 percent). Other products include other apparel, calendars, and magnets.

Sales promotion services companies have offices with showrooms to display the products and services offered. Companies process a large number of small custom-imprinted orders. Customers place an order with the sales promotion firm, which then orders the items from various suppliers that engrave, imprint, or embroider the logo or marketing message. Turnaround time from final order to delivery is generally two to three weeks; rush orders can be filled within two to three days, depending on the product.

BUSINESS CHALLENGES

» Dependence on Corporate Profits

The sales promotion services industry depends on the health of the national economy and business profitability. Specific companies can be very sensitive to particular industries as most sales promotion companies are small and many cater to just a few industries. Sales promotion products are often viewed as discretionary expenses that can be cut during economic downturns. Most sales promotion companies suffered sales declines in the last recession.

» Customer Consolidations

The sales promotion services industry's best customers are undergoing substantial consolidation. Major customers of sales promotion items, such as banks and pharmaceutical, telecommunication, and high-tech companies, are frequent merger or acquisition targets. Customer consolidation usually leads to lost business for sales promotion suppliers.

» Emergence of Outside Competitors

While most sales promotion services companies would consider other similar companies as major competitors, non-industry competitive threats are emerging. Mail-order companies have added corporate sales divisions that sell corporate apparel, national office suppliers are also beginning to offer some promotional items, and many ad agencies offer promotional products as part of integrated advertising programs. These new competitors are able to leverage their brand recognition and existing relationships with customers to expand into sales promotion products.

Sales promotion products may be made in the US or imported from overseas. Most promotion services companies have numerous suppliers and buy from them using purchase orders. The industry experiences little seasonality.

Large sales promotion services companies have begun to install a common information platform to integrate business and make reporting more efficient. Large companies have installed integrated systems for order entry, warehouse management, sales, and purchasing management. Other systems are designed to reduce order processing time and improve customer billing. Some companies have pull order-flow processing systems designed to process a large number of small orders efficiently.

Sales & Marketing

Customers range from small service and manufacturing companies to major corporations, primarily in health care, banking, insurance, pharmaceutical, education, and high technology. Large sales promotion services companies can have more than 80,000 customers. Major sales channels include catalogs, websites, and internal call centers. Many companies have inside salespeople; senior management is often involved in sales to major potential customers.

Catalogs are the predominant marketing tool of the sales promotion industry. Trade shows are common and used to exhibit product offerings and enhance strategic customer relationships.

The Internet has become the primary way to take orders in the sales promotion services industry. While catalogs remain the preferred product listing, more orders are now online than by phone. Many large companies have invested in e-commerce systems to allow for easy online order entry.

Sales promotion products are generally low priced, ranging from less than a dollar for items such as pens and key chains, to $20 for some kinds of apparel. Product design, quality, speed of delivery, and price are competitive elements.

Human Resources

Employees in the sales promotion services industry require no special skills or training. Positions include salespeople who are trained in sales techniques and about the company's products, order processing specialists, and warehouse workers. Average industry wages are slightly below the US average wage. The industry injury rate is minimal.

Industry Employment Growth

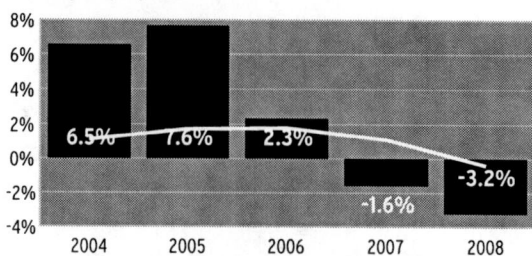

	2004	2005	2006	2007	2008
	6.5%	7.6%	2.3%	-1.6%	-3.2%

Average Hourly Earnings

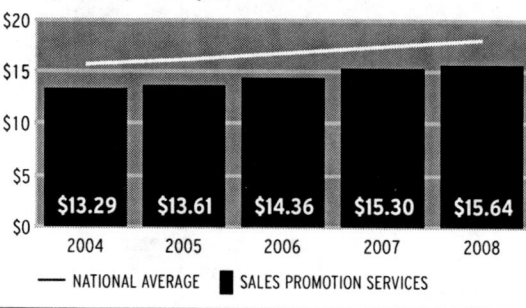

	2004	2005	2006	2007	2008
	$13.29	$13.61	$14.36	$15.30	$15.64

— NATIONAL AVERAGE ■ SALES PROMOTION SERVICES

SOURCE: BUREAU OF LABOR STATISTICS

Call Preparation Questions

What trend is the company seeing in sales?

The sales promotion services industry depends on the health of the national economy and business profitability.

How have customer M&As affected the company's business?

The sales promotion services industry's best customers are undergoing substantial consolidation.

What is the greatest competitive threat to the company?

While most sales promotion services companies would consider other similar companies as major competitors, non-industry competitive threats are emerging.

What products has the company developed?

Sales promotion companies are developing new products in response to market trends.

How is the company attracting business from startup companies?

Promotional items are particularly attractive to new businesses looking to establish their company identity and brand.

Web Links

Advertising Age

General advertising news, statistics.
www.adage.com

Advertising Specialty Institute

Industry news, links, events, annual industry reviews.
www.asicentral.com

American Advertising Federation

Government relations information and news.
www.aaf.org

American Marketing Association

Industry revenues, publications, links.
www.marketingpower.com

Institute of Sales Promotion

British site — has a best practices section.
www.isp.org.uk

Promotional Products Association International

Industry information, case studies, history.
www.ppai.org

Glossary of Acronyms

AMA — American Marketing Association
ASI — Advertising Specialty Institute
PPAI — Promotional Products Association International

HOOVER'S TOP COMPANIES

Largest Companies by Sales	($ mil.)
Valassis Communications, Inc.	2,381.9
Acosta, Inc.	4,014.2
Guthy-Renker Corporation	1,800.0
Maritz Inc.	1,560.0
Vertis, Inc.	1,365.2
Affinion Group, Inc.	1,320.0
Vertrue Incorporated	800.0
Greenbax Enterprises, Inc.	760.2
ValueClick, Inc.	625.8

Largest Employers	Employees
Acosta, Inc.	11,000
SPAR Group, Inc.	8,800
Valassis Communications, Inc.	7,500
Vertis, Inc.	5,800
Greenbax Enterprises, Inc.	5,000
CoActive Marketing Group, Inc.	4,545
Maritz Inc.	3,920
Affinion Group, Inc.	3,300
Vertrue Incorporated	2,500
O.C. Tanner Co.	1,650

Fastest Growing* by Five-Year Sales Growth	(%)
Affinity Solutions	86.2
Vertical Branding, Inc.	46.9
ValueClick, Inc.	46.6
Webloyalty.com, Inc.	36.6
Paid, Inc.	21.2
Valassis Communications, Inc.	21.0
Adstar, Inc.	16.9
Guthy-Renker Corporation	9.5
O.C. Tanner Co.	9.2
CoActive Marketing Group, Inc.	7.3

Fastest Growing* by Five-Year Employee Growth	(%)
Webloyalty.com, Inc.	23.5
Valassis Communications, Inc.	17.0
ValueClick, Inc.	16.8
Affinion Group, Inc.	4.9
Rewards Network Inc.	3.7
EMAK Worldwide, Inc.	2.7

Top Public Companies by Market Value	($ mil.)
ValueClick, Inc.	593.3
Alloy, Inc.	119.9
Rewards Network Inc.	69.9
Valassis Communications, Inc.	63.4
PDI, Inc.	57.0

* These rates are compounded annualized increases and may have resulted from acquisitions or one time gains. If less than 6 years of data are available, growth is for the years available.

SOURCE: HOOVER'S, INC., DATABASE

Sawmills and Plywood Mills

The lumber and plywood manufacturing industry in the US comprises about 5,000 companies with combined annual revenue of $45 billion. Large companies include divisions of Weyerhaeuser, Louisiana-Pacific, and Georgia-Pacific. The industry is moderately concentrated: the 50 largest companies hold about 50 percent of the market.

Competitive Landscape

Demand is closely tied to the level of home construction. The profitability of individual mills depends on efficient operations, because the products are commodities sold based on price. Large companies have big economies of scale in sawmill operations. Large mills can have annual revenue per employee of close to $300,000, while small mills may achieve only half as much. Local mills can often compete successfully with those of large companies because they can efficiently serve a local market. Sawmills can operate with only a modest investment of capital, but plywood mills require expensive equipment and therefore are usually plants with high annual volume.

Products, Operations & Technology

Sawmills process raw logs in a few simple operating steps. Logs are debarked and cut into "cants" that are further cut into finished pieces of lumber, using either circle saws or bandmills. Once lumber is cut to size, it may be sold as "green" lumber or may be stacked and dried to a specific moisture content through air- or kiln-drying. Kiln-drying involves stacking wood in shed-like structures and ventilating with hot air for ten to 30 days. Many sawmills produce a range of "dimension" lumber, lumber of various standard lengths, widths, and thicknesses. Some sawmills specialize in producing only "stud" lumber, lengths of 5 to 10 feet with a cross section of 2 by 4 inches or 2 by 6 inches. Because their product is smaller, studmills can use smaller, cheaper logs.

BUSINESS CHALLENGES

» Volatile Timber Costs, Lumber Prices

Lumber supply and prices can be volatile, affected by demand, domestic supply, Canadian imports, weather, and environmental regulations. The fragmented nature of the industry makes predicting supply, which fluctuates monthly, difficult. Lumber prices can change 40 or 50 percent in a matter of months. The costs of timber and the prices received for lumber and other wood products can be volatile but don't necessarily change in tandem. Lumber prices generally swing more widely than do timber costs, squeezing sawmill operators when demand falls.

» High Dependence on Home Construction

Demand is closely tied to the level of home construction. About 75 percent of lumber and wood panel is used in residential construction, either in homebuilding or indirectly as wood furniture and cabinets. The level of home construction typically varies in multi-year cycles, and can fall 20 percent per year. Home repair and remodeling form a smaller but less cyclical market.

» Uncertain Timber Supply

Because timber is too expensive to ship long distances, sawmills are vulnerable to regional shortages. Local timber supplies have frequently been interrupted over the last decade due to fires, environmental litigation, or increased government regulation.

Plywood mills are more complex than sawmills. Raw logs are debarked, cut to size, and heated with steam or hot water. The resulting "flitch" is rotated on a large lathe and pressed against a long, sharp blade, to peel off a continuous layer of wood called a veneer. Softwood veneers are usually 1/10 of an inch thick and may be more than 100 feet long. The veneer is cut to size and dried. Sheets of veneer are then sprayed with glue (usually a phenol-formaldehyde (PF) resin or a urea-formaldehyde (UF) resin), stacked on top of each other with the grain of the wood in alternating directions, and sandwiched in a hot-press that forces the pieces together and cures the glue. The ends are then trimmed and the product may be sanded. The standard size for plywood is 4 feet by 8 feet, with a 3/8 inch thickness most common.

Oriented strandboard (OSB) is manufactured similarly. Debarked logs are cut into 100-inch lengths and fed into a waferizer where they're sliced into thin strands (also called flakes or wafers) that are several inches long. The strands are dried, mixed with resin and other additives in large blenders, and formed into mats on trays or moving belts. Several layers are laid down, with the wood strands in alternating orientation, and the mats are rolled and cured in a hot-press. OSB is generally made in the same sizes as plywood and has similar strength characteristics, but is cheaper because it can be made from smaller, lower-quality logs.

Other types of panels, including particleboard, hardboard, and medium density fiberboard (MDF), are made from wood residues like sawdust, shavings, and chips that are ground to a desired size, dried, mixed with resin, and hot-pressed. (The ingredients to manufacture these panels, and OSB, are called the "furnish.") Such boards aren't as strong as plywood and OSB. Engineered wood products (EWP), such as glue laminated timber (glulam); laminated veneer lumber (LVL); and engineered I-joists, are produced from lumber that is dried, glued, and hot-pressed to create beams with greater structural strength than dimension lumber.

A large sawmill may have an annual capacity of 350 million board feet (mmbf). The output of panel mills is measured in millions of square feet. A large plywood mill may have a capacity of 300 million square feet; some OSB plants have a capacity of 600 million square feet.

Sawmills are located close to their source of timber because of the high costs of transportation. Large operators often use timber from their own lands. Both large and small operators also buy timber from private lands and federal and state forests. Logs are bought at market prices. Average "stumpage" prices paid for sawtimber from private lands in Louisiana in one year were $395 per thousand board feet (mbf) for Southern pine and $285 for oak. Prices for sawtimber from federal forests were $315 for Douglas fir, $268 for Southern pine, and $317 for oak. Prices can vary sharply from year to year. Softwoods like Douglas fir and Southern pine are used for most lumber and structural panel manufacture. Hardwoods like oak and maple are used to make veneered panels for cabinet and furniture manufacture.

Sales & Marketing

Residential real estate construction is the largest user of lumber and panels. About 65 percent of lumber, 85 percent of structural panels (plywood and OSB), and 40 percent of non-structural panels are used in residential construction. The manufacture of furniture and wood pallets accounts for the rest of lumber and panel consumption. Most smaller companies sell their production to lumber wholesalers, which may specialize in either dimension lumber or panels. In small markets, sawmills may sell directly to lumberyards or homebuilders. Large producers also sell to wholesalers, but may sell directly to retail chains, like Home Depot, or to large homebuilders. The geographic area of distribution (of what are commodity products) is limited by transportation costs. Distribution beyond the immediate market is usually by rail. Sales are handled by an in-house sales staff. Large plants try to operate with an order backlog of several weeks, adjusting their production mix accordingly but operating at high volume for greatest efficiency.

Human Resources

Sawmill operations are physically demanding, but require a relatively low level of skill and therefore pay relatively modest wages, about 20 percent below the national average. Fringe benefit costs are an average 26 percent addition to wages. The injury rate is 60 percent higher than the national average at plywood mills, 100 percent higher at sawmills.

Industry Employment Growth

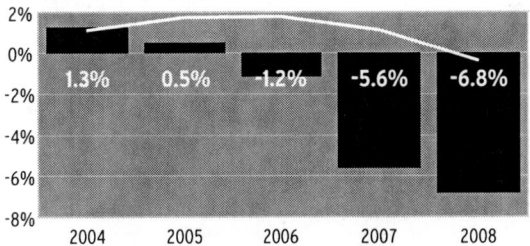

	2004	2005	2006	2007	2008
	1.3%	0.5%	-1.2%	-5.6%	-6.8%

Average Hourly Earnings

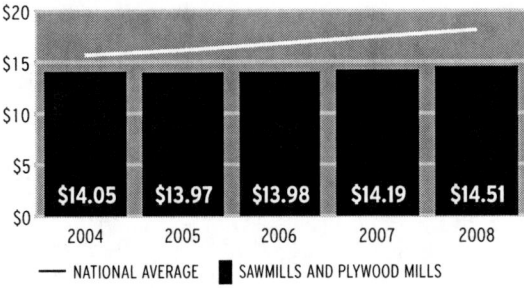

	2004	2005	2006	2007	2008
	$14.05	$13.97	$13.98	$14.19	$14.51

— NATIONAL AVERAGE ■ SAWMILLS AND PLYWOOD MILLS

SOURCE: BUREAU OF LABOR STATISTICS

Call Preparation Questions

How does the company protect against cost and price movements?

Lumber supply and prices can be volatile, affected by demand, domestic supply, Canadian imports, weather, and environmental regulations.

How does the company adjust to periods of lower demand?

Demand is closely tied to the level of home construction.

Where does the company get its timber? How prepared is the company to manage a timber shortage?

Because timber is too expensive to ship long distances, sawmills are vulnerable to regional shortages.

How flexible is the company at changing its product mix to accommodate market demand?

Some sawmills and panel manufacturers have increased margins by producing customized products for particular uses, such as engineered woods, I-joists, trusses, sanded and stained plywood, and stained or painted lumber.

Web Links

American Forest & Paper Association

Industry news.
http://www.afandpa.org

Engineered Wood Association

Good description of plywood, OSB, glulam, LVL.
www.apawood.org

Southeastern Lumber Manufacturers Association

Industry info and news.
www.slma.org

US Forest Service – Forest Products Laboratory

Historical statistics. Timber forecast.
www.fpl.fs.fed.us

Western Wood Products Association

Annual statistics. Forecast. Data by subscription.
www.wwpa.org

Glossary of Acronyms

AF&PA — American Forest & Paper Association
EWP — engineered wood products
IP — International Paper
ITC — International Trade Commission
LVL — laminated veneer lumber
MBF — thousand board feet
MMBF — million board feet
MDF — medium density fiberboard
MSF — thousand square feet

OSB — Oriented strandboard
PF — phenol-formaldehyde resin
SLA — Softwood Lumber Agreement
UF — urea-formaldehyde resin
VOC — volatile organic chemicals
WTO — World Trade Organization
WWPA — Western Wood Products Association

HOOVER'S TOP COMPANIES

Largest Companies by Sales	($ mil.)
Weyerhaeuser Company	8,018.0
Pro-Build Holdings Inc.	5,000.0
Universal Forest Products, Inc.	2,232.4
Louisiana-Pacific Corporation	1,376.2
Roseburg Forest Products Co.	1,300.0
Sierra Pacific Industries	1,010.0
Columbia Forest Products Inc.	1,000.0
Potlatch Corporation	440.0
Georgia-Pacific LLC	—

Largest Employers	Employees
Georgia-Pacific LLC	50,000
Weyerhaeuser Company	37,900
Pro-Build Holdings Inc.	17,000
Universal Forest Products, Inc.	8,400
Louisiana-Pacific Corporation	5,100
Columbia Forest Products Inc.	4,500
Sierra Pacific Industries	4,400
Roseburg Forest Products Co.	3,800
Potlatch Corporation	3,800
Simpson Investment Company	2,024

Fastest Growing* by Five-Year Sales Growth	(%)
Pope Resources	10.0
Roseburg Forest Products Co.	5.8
Deltic Timber Corporation	4.2
Universal Forest Products, Inc.	3.3

Fastest Growing* by Five-Year Employee Growth	(%)
Pope Resources	21.6
Pro-Build Holdings Inc.	15.3
Columbia Forest Products Inc.	6.1
Sierra Pacific Industries	2.4
Roseburg Forest Products Co.	2.0

Top Public Companies by Market Value	($ mil.)
Weyerhaeuser Company	6,467.6
Potlatch Corporation	1,033.7
Deltic Timber Corporation	638.3
Universal Forest Products, Inc.	484.4
Louisiana-Pacific Corporation	161.1

* These rates are compounded annualized increases and may have resulted from acquisitions or one time gains. If less than 6 years of data are available, growth is for the years available.

SOURCE: HOOVER'S, INC., DATABASE

Scrap Metals-Recycling

THIS INDUSTRY INCLUDES:

SIC CODES

5093 Scrap and Waste Materials

NAICS CODES

42393 Recyclable Material Merchant Wholesalers

56292 Materials Recovery Facilities

The US scrap industry includes about 8,000 companies with combined annual revenue of $30 billion. Large national scrap processors include Sims Metal Management, Schnitzer Steel, Alcan, and The David J. Joseph Company. A typical local scrap processor has annual revenue under $5 million. The industry is fragmented and local, because the low value-to-weight ratio of most scrap discourages long-distance transportation. The top 50 companies hold only about 40 percent of the market.

Competitive Landscape

Demand from the steel, auto, and construction industries drive the recycling industry. The profitability of individual companies depends on cultivating relations with suppliers and buyers. Most companies are small and compete by specializing in one type of material in their local market. Large companies have economies of scale and have the financial ability to invest in new, faster machinery.

Products, Operations & Technology

Scrap metal recycling companies collect, process, and resell materials like metals, glass, plastics, and paper. Recycling iron and steel scrap comprises about half of the industry's revenue. One company, Alcan, recycles about 40 percent of all aluminum cans in the US.

The scrap recycling industry processes about 145 million tons of material annually, including 75 million tons of iron and steel (ferrous metals); 50 million tons of paper and paperboard (cardboard); 10 million tons of nonferrous metals like aluminum, copper, stainless steel, lead and zinc; 4 million tons of glass; and 300,000 tons of plastics (PET and HDPE bottles). Almost all old cars are recycled, 90 percent of appliances, 65 percent of aluminum cans, 45 percent of paper, and 30 percent of bottle glass.

Scrap metal is classified as "industrial" or "obsolete." Industrial scrap is left over from in-

BUSINESS CHALLENGES

» High Dependence on End-Use Industries

Demand for scrap steel comes mainly from the US steel industry, which in turn depends heavily on the auto, machinery, and construction industries. The shift of more auto production to foreign plants will negatively affect scrap metal demand long-term. The shift toward more steel production using electric arc furnaces, on the other hand, will boost demand.

» Scrap Metal Prices Fluctuate

Scrap prices can change quickly, making revenues unpredictable both monthly and yearly. During the 1998 Asian financial crisis, scrap metal prices dropped 40 percent in one year. Strong export demand can also boost prices. China is the world's largest scrap metal importer.

» Competition from Scrap Imports

The amount of scrap imported from Asia, Europe, and Russia can significantly affect prices in the domestic market. Many dealers fault the steel industry for continuing to use imported scrap to keep costs down.

dustrial manufacturing operations like cutting, casting, stamping, and boring; the auto industry is the largest single source. Obsolete scrap is metal recovered from old or used consumer and industrial products, mainly cars, cans, and appliances, but also machinery, railroad cars and rails, construction girders, wire, pipes, and ships. To be suitable for reuse, scrap metal must be cut to convenient sizes, sorted according to metal or grade, and often formed into bales, pellets, or briquettes that end-users can put directly into their operations. The smaller and denser the scrap, the more valuable it is, because end-users can use it more efficiently.

Collecting scrap metal occurs at junkyards, recycling centers, or directly at industrial sites. Scrap metal processors often have long-standing relationships with industrial producers of scrap, and have drop-boxes on their sites for efficient collection. Because the quality of new steel made from scrap depends on the quality of the scrap, there is an extensive metal scrap grading system, with more than 80 grades of unprocessed ferrous scrap, including sheet iron; "white goods" (appliances); "unclean motor block"; and "whole prepared car bodies."

Metals processors use crane-mounted "alligator" or scissor shears and stationary guillotine shears to cut large pieces of scrap, such as girders, into smaller pieces. Cars, appliances, and other light scrap are processed by shredders that break the scrap into fist-sized pieces in less than a minute. Shredding operations use magnets to separate ferrous metals and nonferrous metals from residual "shredder fluff," which is put into landfills. Many nonferrous metals have a higher value than ferrous iron or steel, and are therefore sorted and separated using more labor-intensive methods. Light-gauge metals may be processed in balers, large hydraulic presses that compress the metal into uniform blocks. Nonferrous metals are often melted or pressed into ingots or "pigs" for the end-user.

Non-metal materials like paper, glass, plastics, and rubber undergo less processing than metals before being shipped. Paper and cardboard are collected at recycling centers or from commercial locations, then sorted and baled. Glass is collected similarly, sorted by color and then crushed into small pieces called "cullet." Plastics, mainly from bottles, are sorted by type and then baled, although some processors cut them into flakes or pellets. Rubber tires are processed by removing steel belts mechanically, then shredding the tire into chips varying from three inches to the size of a grain of sand.

Sales & Marketing

End-users of scrap metals are metal manufacturers. Traditional steel makers add scrap to other raw materials when making new steel. For operators of steel mini-mills that use electric arc furnace (EAF) technology, scrap is the main raw material. Mini-mill production has rapidly increased in the US during the past 20 years, and now accounts for about half of domestic steel production. Paper companies process scrap paper back into pulp, largely for use in making cardboard containers; glass makers mix as much as 20 percent of cullet with raw materials to make new glass bottles; and plastics manufacturers can add scrap directly to their operations. Recycled rubber is used by paving manufacturers to make asphalt, and by rubber flooring manufacturers to make rubberized mats.

The industry's fragmented nature means that sales are typically handled by dealers and brokers, and increasingly on the Internet. Large scrap processors cultivate established relationships with big customers, but long-term contracts are rare. Big customers, such as steel mini-mills, typically place orders that must be filled in 30 to 90 days at a fixed price.

Prices for scrap metal can change rapidly because they depend on demand for newly made products and on import and export prices. Prices for some materials like paper can be negative, meaning that sellers essentially must pay buyers to take the product, often the case for mixed office paper. Prices for processed scrap metal and other scrap products are usually negotiated directly with large customers because of grade variations and because transportation costs are a significant part of the delivered price. The spread between prices for unprocessed and processed scrap is often large, as processors try to protect themselves against sudden price changes.

Human Resources

Although metal recycling involves the operation of power equipment, most jobs require few skills and are accordingly not well-paid. Wages are about 15 percent lower than the national average.

Industry Employment Growth

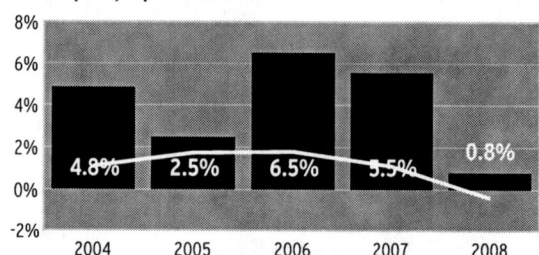

Average Hourly Earnings

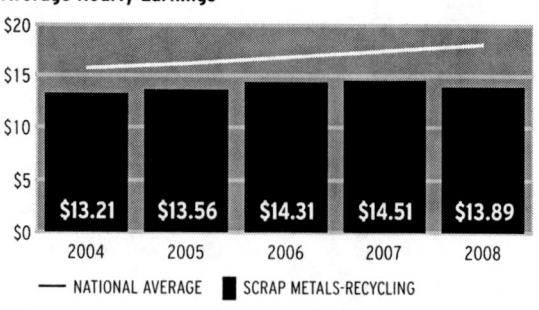

— NATIONAL AVERAGE   ■ SCRAP METALS-RECYCLING

SOURCE: BUREAU OF LABOR STATISTICS

Call Preparation Questions

If a steel recycler, how does the company mitigate fluctuations in domestic demand for scrap steel?

Demand for scrap steel comes mainly from the US steel industry, which in turn depends heavily on the auto, machinery, and construction industries.

How effectively does the company hedge against price changes?

Scrap prices can change quickly, making revenues unpredictable both monthly and yearly.

How are scrap imports impacting the company's market share?

The amount of scrap imported from Asia, Europe, and Russia can significantly affect prices in the domestic market.

How is the company challenged or advantaged by exporting scrap?

As the world's largest user of steel, the US also produces the largest amount of scrap metal.

If a steel recycler, how is the expansion of mini-mills impacting the company?

US steel production from mini-mills has steadily increased, due to technological advances that minimize waste in processing scrap.

Web Links

American Metal Market

International metals news and prices (by subscription).
www.amm.com

Institute of Scrap Recycling Industries

Background information, news, and scrap recycling statistics.
www.isri.org

MetalPrices

Prices from the London Metal Exchange.
www.metalprices.com

MetalWorld

Exchange site. Links to associations, dealers.
www.metalworld.com

Recycler's World

Comprehensive information and trading site by commodity and association; specific information on individual types of recycling.
www.recycle.net

Recycling Today

Industry news, trends, and statistics.
www.recyclingtoday.com

Scrap

Industry news and commodity inventories/prices.
www.scrap.org/topstories

Steel Recycling Institute

Facts and figures on steel recycling and the recycling process.
www.recycle-steel.org

Glossary of Acronyms

EAF — electric arc furnace
IISI — International Iron and Steel Institute
ISRI — Institute of Scrap Recycling Industries
UBC — used beverage cans

HOOVER'S TOP COMPANIES

Largest Companies by Sales	($ mil.)
Nucor Corporation (David J. Joseph Company)	23,663.3
Steel Dynamics, Inc.	8,080.5
Sims Metal Management	7,375.2
Harsco Corporation	3,967.8
Schnitzer Steel Industries, Inc.	3,641.6
Soave Enterprises L.L.C.	1,770.0
Philip Services Corporation	602.8
Wise Metals Group LLC	986.7
Joseph Behr and Sons, Inc.	356.2

Largest Employers	Employees
Harsco Corporation	21,500
Nucor Corporation (David J. Joseph Company)	18,000
Philip Services Corporation	12,000
Sims Metal Management	6,000
Schnitzer Steel Industries, Inc.	3,669
Steel Dynamics, Inc.	3,490
Soave Enterprises L.L.C.	2,200
Wise Metals Group LLC	1,151
Joseph Behr and Sons, Inc.	367
Keywell L.L.C.	229

Fastest Growing* by Five-Year Sales Growth	(%)
Steel Dynamics, Inc.	52.3
Schnitzer Steel Industries, Inc.	48.9
Nucor Corporation	30.4
Harsco Corporation	13.4
Soave Enterprises L.L.C.	12.1

Fastest Growing* by Five-Year Employee Growth	(%)
Steel Dynamics, Inc.	94.4
Schnitzer Steel Industries, Inc.	26.8
Nucor Corporation	26.2
Harsco Corporation	1.2
Soave Enterprises L.L.C.	0.9

Top Public Companies by Market Value	($ mil.)
Nucor Corporation	14,505.7
Harsco Corporation	2,219.2
Steel Dynamics, Inc.	2,032.7
Schnitzer Steel Industries, Inc.	1,477.1
Industrial Services of America, Inc.	27.3

* These rates are compounded annualized increases and may have resulted from acquisitions or one time gains. If less than 6 years of data are available, growth is for the years available.

SOURCE: HOOVER'S, INC., DATABASE

Seafood Processing and Distribution

The US seafood processing and distribution industry consists of 600 fresh and frozen seafood processors; 100 canneries; and 2,500 distributors; with a final commercial value of $12 billion. Annual revenue is around $9 billion for fish processors and $12 billion for distributors, although many companies are involved in both businesses. Major companies include Red Chamber, Trident Seafoods, Tri Marine International, and the US business division of Maruha Nichiro Holdings. The industry is relatively fragmented: the 50 largest processors control about 45 percent of its total market and the 50 largest wholesalers account for one-third of the distribution market.

This industry includes the processing and wholesaling of both wild-caught and farm-raised seafood. It doesn't include commercial fisheries or aquaculture operations.

Competitive Landscape

Demand is driven by domestic trends in fish consumption and, for processors, competition from imports. The profitability of individual companies depends on throughput and route efficiencies. Large companies have advantages in vertical operations and economies of scale. Small companies can compete effectively by specializing in sustainable practices or servicing a local market. Average revenue per employee is $225,000 for a typical processing facility and $500,000 for a typical seafood wholesaler.

Products, Operations & Technology

Major products include frozen fish (30 percent of processing revenue); frozen shellfish (20 percent); fresh fish and shellfish (15 percent); and canned seafood (15 percent). Other products include industrial goods like fish meal and fish oil.

Important frozen fish products are ground-fish (cod, haddock, pollock, and whiting) that is

BUSINESS CHALLENGES

» Variable Supply and Demand

Processors and wholesalers depend heavily on the success of commercial fisheries. The challenges that shape commercial fishing – regulations, legislation, changes in fish availability due to overfishing and migratory patterns, and vessel fuel prices – have a trickle-down effect on processors and wholesalers. Retailers and consumers can also impact profitability: consolidation among major grocery chains has increased retail buying power, and changing consumer tastes can influence processor operations and profitability. Large processors lower these risks by becoming vertically integrated, while wholesalers mitigate this challenge by offering a wide range of seasonal seafood products.

» Vulnerable to Energy Costs

Processors and wholesalers depend highly on the cost of diesel fuel, as diesel is the primary fuel for powering both fishing vessels and distribution trucks. In times of high fuel prices, commercial fisheries and processors must negotiate an appropriate fuel surcharge. Vertically integrated processors, catcher-processors, and seafood wholesalers directly incur the cost of fuel.

» Competition from Imports

The US imports 80 percent of its seafood, half of which is farmed. Low-cost fish and shrimp from Asian fisheries and fish farms compete directly with the US seafood industry. Processors and wholesalers are limited in how much they can raise prices to consumers, who in general favor lower prices over domestic products.

either battered and breaded, processed plain, cut into fillets or steaks, or formed into sticks. Alaskan pollock, the largest processed product in both revenue and weight, generates around $500 million annually in fresh and frozen form. Annual revenue from fresh and frozen salmon is around $200 million. Breaded fish and shrimp generates around $700 million in annual revenue. Key canned products include tuna ($700 million annually) and salmon ($250 million).

Seafood processors work onshore, at bay on floating offshore processors, and on at-sea catcher-processing vessels. Most processors are located onshore in permanent structures. Workers unload fish from the dock, load them in a hopper, degut fish on "slime lines," and prepare fillets. Other tasks include shoveling chipped ice, recording weights, moving stock, and grading seafood. Secondary processing can include breading, canning, cooking, and extracting protein. Work is done in a highly automated, assembly line fashion modified to fit the type of seafood processed. A large onshore processor can prepare 50,000 pounds of fish a day.

Floating (offshore) processors are ships or barges that have been converted into fish processing factories. Floating processors usually dock in remote, sheltered bays in key fishing regions for up to three months at a time. Processors receive fish from commercial fishing vessels, which allows the fishery to bypass the time and expense of docking onshore. The floating processor may also provide the fishery with additional food and fuel. Workers haul in the seafood, sort and process it, and freeze it below deck. Once the ship's holds are full, it docks briefly at port to unload its frozen catch for further onshore processing or shipping. The floating processor immediately returns to sea to resume operations.

An at-sea processor combines fishing and processing operations. Alaskan at-sea processors catch, process, freeze, and store groundfish like cod and pollock, producing fillet products and surimi (minced fish used to make imitation crab meat). The average at-sea catching-processing vessel is around 300 feet long and employs a crew of 125 each fishing season. Excursions range from 10 days to two months.

Large processors often manage vertically integrated operations that can include commercial fishing, primary and secondary processing, import/export services, wholesaling, co-packing, and branded consumer products.

While large processors often wholesale the fish they process, most wholesalers are small, family-run operations. Wholesalers buy processed fish, store the seafood under constant frozen or refrigerated conditions, and rely on a fleet of trucks to deliver fresh fish to its customer base. Because of the perishable nature and heavy weight of fresh seafood, wholesalers usually operate in a relatively small local market.

Common inputs in both processing and wholesaling include packaging materials, bunker or diesel fuel, ice, and machinery or truck repairs.

Recent technological advances include computer-aided automation in sorting, processing, and canning. For at-sea processors, new fish-sensing technologies and advanced hauling gear have improved catches, increased productivity, and reduced the number of unwanted fish and bycatch (non-targeted, unwanted species). Wholesalers now rely on on-truck GPS navigation, which can reduce driver error and increase the number of stops per route. Improvements in refrigeration and freezing have helped reduce the risk of spoiling.

Sales & Marketing

Typical processing customers include fast food chains, food processors, fish oil manufacturers, and wholesalers. Wholesalers sell to grocery stores, high-end and independent restaurants, fish exporters, and fishmongers. Some wholesalers sell directly to consumers, but these companies tend to specialize in a local market or unusual fish (high-grade sashimi or hard-to-catch species). In some urban areas, auction sales in seafood fish exchanges play an important role in connecting processors to wholesalers and brokers. Processors and wholesalers market their services at trade shows and via direct mail catalogs and in-person visits to key customers.

Processing plants usually enter supply contracts with customers for all or a portion of their production. Contracts typically address volume requirements; however, prices are usually determined by current market conditions. Processors may employ buying agents or brokers to secure large, multi-year contracts.

Processors and wholesalers increasingly use the Internet to conduct business, selling fish directly to consumers, grocery stores, and restaurants. Sales can sometimes be prearranged as processors and wholesalers anticipate seasonal catch.

Prices can range considerably due to changes in demand, supply, and competitive forces. Wholesalers can buy scallops from Massachusetts for $6 to $7 a pound, Maine lobster for $4 a pound, and Alaskan king crab for around $3 a pound. Wholesale prices for gulf shrimp, salmon, swordfish, and yellowfin tuna are around $4 a pound. Processors sometimes sell large quantities of fish like cod and pollock by hundredweight (cwt). Processor and wholesaler prices are typically quoted in ex-warehouse value, where the buyer is responsible for all transportation and logistics fees. NOAA projects that primary processing and wholesaling has a value-add of 12 percent to the industry's total economic value. Secondary wholesaling and processing adds an additional 10 percent.

Human Resources

The processing industry relies heavily on seasonal and temporary labor. Workers include local residents and college students seeking adventure. Most processors provide workers with free or low-cost shared housing and food; some offer laundry service, clothing, and rain gear. Drugs and alcohol are forbidden on floating and at-sea processing vessels; companies conduct drug tests and search packages to ensure that employees stay drug-free.

Annual personnel turnover is extremely high due to the seasonal nature of the work, the demanding conditions, and the repetitive tasks. Processors work hard to ensure that employees last to the end of the fishing season, offering perks and bonuses to workers who stay on board. Workers who quit or are fired typically must pay their way back home.

Most jobs in the industry require minimal skill and accordingly pay low wages. Wages average $13, around 40 percent less than the national average. However, overtime pays at time-and-a-half. When fishing is at its peak, workers often work 12 to 16 hour shifts, seven days a week. At-sea processors typically offer workers a percentage of the catch once it exceeds a certain threshold.

For processors, injury rates are more than twice the national average. Common injuries involve cuts on fingers, sprains and strains from lifting, and bruises and back injuries from falling on wet floors. Injuries due to repetitive motions are four times higher than the national average.

Industry Employment Growth

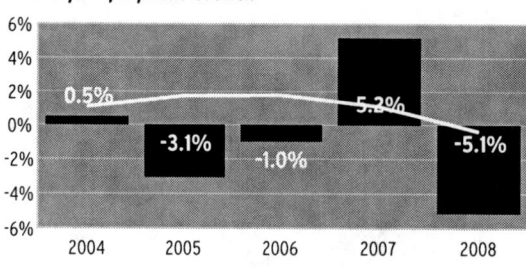

Average Hourly Earnings

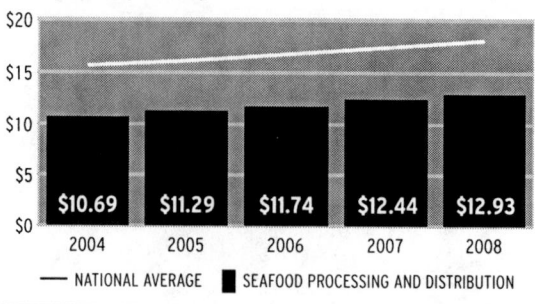

SOURCE: BUREAU OF LABOR STATISTICS

Call Preparation Questions

How dependent is the company on the success of commercial fishing operations?

Processors and wholesalers depend heavily on the success of commercial fisheries.

How do rising fuel costs challenge company profitability?

Processors and wholesalers depend highly on the cost of diesel fuel, as diesel is the primary fuel for powering both fishing vessels and distribution trucks.

How has the rise in fish and shellfish imports shaped the company's strategy?

The US imports 80 percent of its seafood, half of which is farmed.

What new technologies is the company exploring to limit fuel waste?

Wholesalers can reduce on-truck refrigeration costs up to 80 percent by switching from mechanical blower systems to cold plate technology.

What opportunities does the company see in the trend toward sustainable fish coalitions?

Processors are forming sustainable fish coalitions with like-minded wholesalers and commercial fisheries.

Web Links

AboutSeafood.com

Consumer and industry news from the National Fisheries Institute.
www.aboutseafood.com

American Fisheries Society

Scientific society. Conservation policy positions.
www.fisheries.org/afs

At-Sea Processors Association (APA)

Trade association for Alaskan pollock and whiting catcher-processors.
www.atsea.org

National Fishery Market News

NMFS dockside and wholesale seafood prices.
www.st.nmfs.gov/st1/market_news

National Marine Fisheries Service (NMFS)

Industry statistics and issues, including aquaculture and processing.
www.nmfs.noaa.gov

NMFS Fish Watch

Industry news with a focus on sustainability.
www.nmfs.noaa.gov/fishwatch

Pacific Seafood Processors Association (PSPA)

Alaskan and Pacific Northwest processor trade association.
www.pspafish.net

Seafood.com

Industry news.
www.seafood.com

West Coast Seafood Processors Association (WCSPA)

Trade association for California, Oregon, and Washington processors.
www.wcspa.com

Glossary of Acronyms

APA — At-sea Processors Association
CWT — hundredweight
HACCP — Hazardous Analysis and Critical Control Point
IFQ — individual fishing quota
NMFS — National Marine Fisheries Service
PSPA — Pacific Seafood Processors Association
PUFI — processed under federal inspection
WCSPA — West Coast Seafood Processors Association

HOOVER'S TOP COMPANIES

Largest Employers	Employees
Bumble Bee Foods, LLC	3,000
American Seafoods Group LLC	2,600
Trident Seafoods Corporation	2,510
Red Chamber Co.	1,600
Pacific Seafood Group	1,000
Gorton's	975
Icelandic USA, Inc.	900
Westward Seafoods, Inc.	600
Icicle Seafoods, Inc.	500
Morey's Seafood International LLC	400

SOURCE: HOOVER'S, INC., DATABASE

Search, Detection, and Navigation Equipment Manufacture

THIS INDUSTRY INCLUDES:

SIC CODES

3663   Radio and Television Broadcasting and Communications Equipment

3812   Search, Detection, Navigation, Guidance, Aeronautical, and Nautical Systems, Instruments, and Equipment

NAICS CODES

334220   Radio and Television Broadcasting and Wireless Communications Equipment Manufacturing

334511   Search, Detection, Navigation, Guidance, Aeronautical, and Nautical System and Instrument Manufacturing

The US search, detection, and navigation equipment manufacturing industry includes about 500 companies with combined annual revenue of about $37 billion. Major companies include Garmin, Furuno, and Raymarine. Divisions of large integrated companies such as Boeing, Northrop Grumman, and Raytheon also manufacture search, detection, and navigation equipment, primarily for national security and defense applications. The industry is highly concentrated: the largest eight companies have about 75 percent market share, and the largest 50 have about 95 percent market share.

Competitive Landscape

Demand depends on discretionary consumer income, general economic conditions, and federal budgets for defense and homeland security. Large companies have advantages in purchasing power, manufacturing volume, and distribution efficiencies. Small companies compete by offering specialized products and subcontract manufacturing to larger system integrators. Annual revenue per employee is about $270,000.

Products, Operations & Technology

Major products include radar (RAdio Detection And Ranging); sonar (SOund NAvigation Ranging); and GPS instruments and systems. Manufacturers develop a wide array of products for commercial and military markets. Products for commercial markets include depth finders; fish finders; air traffic control systems; navigational aids for ships, planes, and land vehicles; and speed detection devices. Military applications include most of these products, along with radar defense systems.

Radar was discovered in the late 1800s. Many advancements have been made in the technology, but the underlying scientific principle remains: a radio (electromagnetic) signal traveling at the speed of light is emitted from a transmitter and, when a solid object is in its

BUSINESS CHALLENGES

» Dependence on Federal Budgets

The Departments of Defense and of Homeland Security use navigation, search, and detection systems extensively and comprise a large percentage of industry revenues. Major changes in their budgets can significantly impact the industry. Overall US government spending on national defense is projected to be flat 2005 through 2009.

» Rapid Product Innovation

Search, detection, and navigation equipment companies compete in both commercial and government markets based on product innovation. Some companies spend as much as 10 percent of revenue on new technology developments. The rapidity of innovation results in shorter commercial product life cycles, lower prices for older products, and higher risk for complex custom systems.

» Acquiring Technical Talent

The industry's products are among the most technologically advanced in the scientific field, and companies compete for top engineering and computer talent. Companies sponsor intern and work-study programs with universities aimed at attracting the best of the estimated 15,000 annual US computer and electrical engineering graduates. While outsourced engineering resources from India and China have proven viable for some industries, concerns over intellectual property protection and national security issues have limited the use of foreign resources by search, detection, and navigation equipment manufacturers.

path, the signal rebounds (echoes) off the solid object and returns to a receiver. The direction and time required to receive the echo is used to calculate the exact location, distance, and speed of the object.

Sonar operates under a similar principle, employing sound waves that travel much slower than radio waves. Sonar, therefore, typically is good for underwater search and detection applications where slow moving ships, fish, or permanent objects are targets.

GPS technology was developed for the US government in the late 1970s and became available for public use in 1994. A series of 24 satellites orbit at about 12,000 miles above the earth's surface to support land, sea, and air navigation. Unlike radar and sonar, GPS is purely a directional and distance aid and does not provide any search or detection capability.

GPS satellites transmit electromagnetic signals, which are picked up by receivers (the commercial product) and tuned to compatible frequencies. Users must receive a signal from at least three of the orbiting satellites and, through the mathematical concept of triangulation, can determine, within 10 meters (and much more precisely if required), their exact location on earth, and the direction and time to any other location. The federal government removed some substantial restrictions for commercial users in 2000 by eliminating Selective Application (SA), a feature that limited non-military users to an accuracy of 100 meters and restricted use in certain areas of the world.

Raw materials and parts used in the manufacturing process include printed circuit boards; receivers; transmitters; semiconductors; liquid crystal displays; miscellaneous components and accessories for electronic circuitry; sheet metal; and other metal assemblies, primarily of aluminum and steel. Raw material costs are about one-third of revenues.

Commercial products are typically built to stock with emphasis on low cost. Manufacturing processes are highly automated for smaller stationary and portable units. Some manufacturers produce 300,000 or more units monthly to keep up with demand. The manufacturing process involves assembling and integrating parts (receivers, transmitters, controllers, switches, screens and monitors), followed by enclosing contents in metal or plastic covers. Quality is checked using statistical testing.

Large systems for defense applications are custom-made and may take several years to manufacture to complex design specifications. Prime contractors often use subcontractors to fill an order. Due to extended development and manufacturing times, contracts may be awarded in phases. The government monitors, inspects, and signs off on periodic progress reviews and awards progress payments. Subsequent phases proceed based on satisfactory

performance to date. Some projects involve leading-edge technology developments, so the initial contract award is for R&D only. Upon successful proof of concept, the company is then awarded a manufacturing contract as the next step of a multi-phase contract.

Company R&D drives revenues. Commercial manufacturers bring many new products to market annually via new additions, upgrades, and modifications to existing technologies. Companies may benefit from R&D paid for by government agencies.

High-volume manufacturers use enterprise resource planning (ERP) systems extensively, which improve purchasing and inventory management from raw material receipt through finished goods delivery. Transportation and shipping software aid in efficient product distribution to warehouses and retailers. Companies are also automating the product development process through electronic design software, 3D visualization software, and automated testing systems.

Sales & Marketing

Major customers include government agencies, such as the Department of Defense (DoD); FAA; and NASA; prime contractors; and commercial auto, aircraft, and marine manufacturers and distributors. Companies use a combination of direct sales personnel, manufacturer reps, and distributors to sell their products. Competitive bids are frequently used to award government contracts. Sales personnel work with the buying agency's purchasing and engineering personnel to be named as a supplier in the request for proposals (RFP).

Companies that can't meet the entire scope of government agency bids often focus on providing components as a subcontractor. These companies may be chosen by the prime contractor based on historical quality, reliability, and price. Subcontractors market and sell to both prime contractors and the government agency issuing the request for work.

Marketing is via advertising in industry trade publications, participating in trade shows, distributing product catalogs, and using corporate websites. Commercial suppliers may also use TV and newspaper advertising and promote products in the showrooms of marine and aviation dealers.

Product prices for commercial products range from less than $100 to several hundred per unit. Large, complex radar systems used for defense applications may run into the billions.

Human Resources

Production employees earn about $48,000 annually, about 50 percent higher than the national average for all manufacturing employees.

Fringe benefits average about 30 percent of pay-roll. Large companies have some unionized locations; most small manufacturers are non-union. Injury rates in the industry average about 80 percent lower than the average for all US manufacturing companies.

Industry Employment Growth

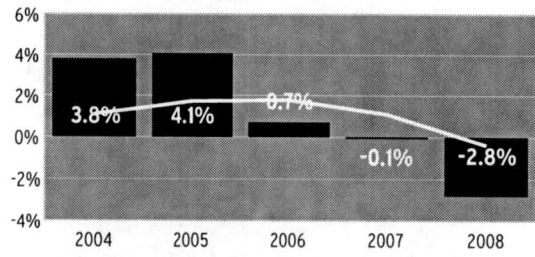

Average Hourly Earnings

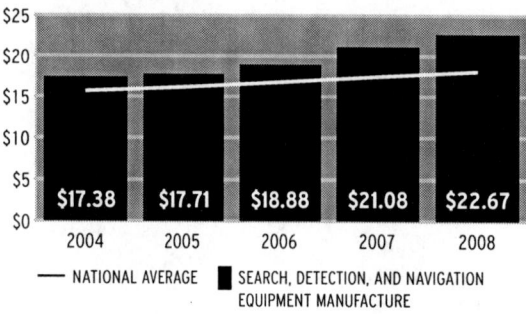

— NATIONAL AVERAGE ▮ SEARCH, DETECTION, AND NAVIGATION EQUIPMENT MANUFACTURE

SOURCE: BUREAU OF LABOR STATISTICS

Call Preparation Questions

How dependent is the company on government contracts?

The Departments of Defense and of Homeland Security use navigation, search, and detection systems extensively and comprise a large percentage of industry revenues.

How is the company driving product innovation?

Search, detection, and navigation equipment companies compete in both commercial and government markets based on product innovation.

How difficult is recruiting computer and engineering talent?

The industry's products are among the most technologically advanced in the scientific field, and companies compete for top engineering and computer talent.

How does the export market impact company sales?

Exports represent a growing opportunity for US manufacturers.

How does the company benefit from increased spending on homeland security?

Since 9/11, the US government has increased investment in border security. Airport and sea port access has become more tightly controlled.

Web Links

Aerospace Industries Association

Trade association representing the aerospace industry.

www.aia-aerospace.org

Aviation Week

Information on both civil and military aviation.

www.aviationweek.com

Cobra

Leading consumer navigation products manufacturer.

www.cobra.com

Defense Daily Network

Updates on defense procurements, including search, detection, and navigation systems.

www.defensedaily.com

Garmin

Leading GPS manufacturer.

www.garmin.com

Glossary of Acronyms

AIA — Aerospace Industries Association
COTS — commercial-off-the-shelf
ERP — enterprise resource planning
GAO — Government Accountability Office
PND — portable navigation device

HOOVER'S TOP COMPANIES

Largest Companies by Sales	($ mil.)
Northrop Grumman Corporation	33,887.0
Raytheon Company	23,174.0
ITT Corporation	11,694.8
Harris Corporation	5,311.0
Garmin Ltd.	3,494.1
DRS Technologies, Inc.	3,295.4
FLIR Systems, Inc.	1,077.0
Argon ST, Inc.	340.9
Herley Industries, Inc.	152.5
Magellan Navigation, Inc.	—

Largest Employers	Employees
Northrop Grumman Corporation	123,600
Raytheon Company	73,000
ITT Corporation	40,800
Harris Corporation	16,500
DRS Technologies, Inc.	10,200
Garmin Ltd.	8,434
FLIR Systems, Inc.	1,943
The O'Gara Group, Inc.	1,450
Argon ST, Inc.	990
Herley Industries, Inc.	903

Fastest Growing* by Five-Year Sales Growth	(%)
ICx Technologies, Inc.	252.9
The O'Gara Group, Inc.	62.0
Argon ST, Inc.	45.0
DRS Technologies, Inc.	37.3
FLIR Systems, Inc.	28.1
Harris Corporation	20.5
ITT Corporation	15.8
Sierra Monitor Corporation	9.1
Herley Industries, Inc.	6.7
Northrop Grumman Corporation	5.3

Fastest Growing* by Five-Year Employee Growth	(%)
Argon ST, Inc.	35.1
FLIR Systems, Inc.	28.0
DRS Technologies, Inc.	22.2
Harris Corporation	9.4
Innovative Solutions and Support, Inc.	7.9
Herley Industries, Inc.	5.0
ITT Corporation	0.9
Northrop Grumman Corporation	0.2

Top Public Companies by Market Value	($ mil.)
Raytheon Company	20,416.0
Northrop Grumman Corporation	14,728.7
ITT Corporation	8,356.4
Harris Corporation	6,837.4
FLIR Systems, Inc.	4,337.8

* These rates are compounded annualized increases and may have resulted from acquisitions or one time gains. If less than 6 years of data are available, growth is for the years available.

SOURCE: HOOVER'S, INC., DATABASE

Seasoning and Dressing Manufacturing

THIS INDUSTRY INCLUDES:

SIC CODES

2035 Pickled Fruits and Vegetables, Vegetable Sauces and Seasonings, and Salad Dressings

2082 Malt Beverages

2087 Flavoring Extracts and Flavoring Syrups

2099 Food Preparations

2899 Chemicals and Chemical Preparations

NAICS CODES

31194 Seasoning and Dressing Manufacturing

The seasoning and dressing manufacturing industry includes about 600 companies with combined annual revenue of $13 billion. Major companies include Kraft, Heinz, and McCormick. The industry is concentrated: the top 50 companies account for over 60 percent of industry revenue.

The seasoning and dressing manufacturing industry includes companies that make spices, dry gravy mixes, seasoning mixes, salad dressings, sauces, and natural extracts. The industry doesn't include companies that make tomato-based sauces (including pasta sauce, ketchup, and salsa) or pourable gravies.

Competitive Landscape

Demand is driven by consumer tastes and health considerations. The profitability of individual companies depends on efficient operations, effective marketing, and a strong sales force. Large companies have advantages in purchasing, distribution, and marketing. Small operations can compete effectively by manufacturing exotic sauces, sourcing and selling rare herbs, or formulating custom spice blends, extracts, and mixes. Average annual revenue per employee is $425,000.

Products, Operations & Technology

Major products include spices (15 percent of industry revenue); non-tomato-based prepared sauces (10 percent); pourable and spoon-type salad dressing (10 percent); powdered seasoning mixes (10 percent); and natural flavoring extracts (10 percent). Other products include mayonnaise, mustard, vinegar, cider, imitation flavoring extracts, powdered gravy and sauce mixes, and pepper.

To manufacture spices, blowers or gravity separators clean impurities from herbs, seeds, or peppercorns. Spices may need a special soak or treatment to eliminate bacteria. Imported spices may require additional fumigation, in-

BUSINESS CHALLENGES

» Highly Competitive Industry

The seasonings and dressing industry is mature and highly competitive. Industry leaders compete for shelf space and customer mindshare. Smaller companies must have a truly compelling product and a willingness to pay for shelf space to be considered by wholesalers and retailers. Manufacturers also compete with retail private-label offerings, even if the manufacturer doesn't produce private-label seasonings and dressings. Companies must differentiate brands to avoid competing on price: many consumers think of sauces, dressings, and spices as commodities bought solely based on price.

» Volatile Ingredient Prices

Prices for commodity inputs such as soybean oil, high fructose corn syrup, herbs, and spices can increase significantly due to poor farm yields, unpredictable weather patterns, and government farm subsidies. Ingredient prices typically represent 50 to 70 percent of a seasoning and dressing manufacturer's total cost of goods sold. Consumers may decide to forgo purchases of sauces or spices if they cost too much. Food manufacturers and restaurants may import ingredients if domestic costs are too high, or alter recipes to incorporate cheaper spices, dressings, and sauces.

» Dependence on Consumer Tastes

Consumer tastes and buying habits for seasonings and dressings are often unpredictable. Public attitude about particular products can change quickly, as seen in the decline in mayonnaise consumption over the past 10 years. Manufacturers often spend millions to reformulate products or develop new brands to capitalize on dietary fads (low-carb, organic, fat-free, sugar-free). Dietary trends can become quickly passé; or replaced by new and emerging health concerns.

spection, or gamma irradiation before being cleaned. Pepper, cumin, and cinnamon are sometimes ground into a fine powder using cold-mill rollers. A sifter sorts the spices by size and, for spice blends, conveys them to a mixing station. Sorted and blended spices move by conveyor to the packing station. Packaged spices can range from small one-ounce jars to 50-pound cases and canisters.

Mayonnaise is made with continuous blending machines that create an emulsion. The emulsified blend moves through a series of pumps and heat exchangers to maintain a constant temperature as flavorings are piped in through openings in the blending machine. A viscometer tests consistency, altering water or oil levels to produce an even, smooth spread. Most continuous blending machines can produce both mayonnaise and thick salad dressings made with cooked food starches.

Once blended, the finished product moves by tubes or extruders to a bottling station. Pre-sterilized jars or bottles move along a conveyor as overhead spouts drop pre-measured amounts of dressing into each container. Containers are mechanically sealed and labeled before being boxed, placed on pallets, and warehoused. Large companies typically maintain multiple factories and warehouses strategically located throughout the US.

Inputs for dressings include soybean oil, modified food starch, eggs, high fructose corn syrup, herbs, salt, and vinegar. Inputs for seasonings are the spices or herbs themselves. Both seasonings and dressings require material input costs for items like cardboard, metal, glass, and plastic bags.

Recent technological advances include more consistent dressing viscosity; new zero-bacteria emulsions; new methods to dispense product (squeeze bottles, sprays); improved packaging that requires less plastic; and reformulated recipes that reflect healthier eating habits. Companies are successfully substituting artificial and modified food starches with natural gums and thickeners, which often improves the taste but reduces a product's shelf life. Large seasoning and dressing companies use restricted-access Intranets, supply chain management systems, and electronic data interchange (EDI) systems to facilitate e-commerce transactions and track inventory.

Sales & Marketing

Typical customers are food distributors, grocery stores, warehouse clubs, restaurant chains, dollar stores, and convenience stores (c-stores). Many companies sell products directly to food manufacturers for use in processed foods. Industrial and foodservice customers represent 60 percent of all spice sales; retail sales account for the rest. Within the retail category, grocery stores account for around 70 percent of total sales and Wal-Mart another 10 to 20 percent. Products are sold by a mix of internal sales forces, food distributors, and third-party brokers. Companies typically assign a sales force and national sales manager to Wal-Mart (and other major retailers) to handle high volume needs.

In addition to their own product line, many companies produce private-label seasonings and dressings for grocery and c-stores. Private-label condiments, gravies, dressings, and sauces are a $500 million industry. Private-label brands typically cost 20 to 40 percent less than name-brand products.

Major marketing includes TV and radio advertising; coupons in newspapers, magazines, and on the Internet; celebrity tie-ins; cookbooks and seasonal recipes featuring branded spices and sauces; in-store discounts and end-cap promotions; volume discounts; and product-specific websites. Many companies rely on food trade shows to generate interest and sales around new product launches and innovations. Since seasonings and dressings complement main dishes, salads, side dishes, and desserts, companies regularly co-promote products with food manufacturers and fruit and vegetable companies. A diversified manufacturer may tie its spice or sauce line to other food divisions owned by the parent company.

Customer service operations can be extensive. Companies must have staff in place to handle customer inquiries and manage product recalls. Recalls are frequent in the seasonings and dressings industry and often result from mislabeling ingredients, a failure to fully disclose allergens, and the risk of E.Coli contamination.

Many companies invest in Internet promotions, developing informative and interactive websites to promote brand awareness. Several specialty purveyors sell spices on the Internet, serving both food enthusiasts and industrial customers.

Mayonnaise and thick and pourable salad dressings typically cost $2 to $3 per eight-ounce bottle. Dry seasoning mixes cost around $1 each. Dried herbs typically cost $3 to $4 for a one-half ounce jar; organic herbs cost around $2 more. Natural liquid extracts like almond and vanilla cost around $4 to $5 an ounce. Rare spices like saffron can be as high as $100 per ounce. Retailer consolidation has shifted buying power from manufacturers to retailers. Competition is intense among manufacturers, but seasoning and dressing companies face little competition outside the industry.

Human Resources

Seasoning and dressing manufacturing wages average $25 per hour, about 25 percent higher than the national average. Spice and extract companies pay about 20 percent more than companies producing mayonnaise and dressing. Production workers must have mechanical, scientific, and technical skills and be physically able to operate machinery and lift heavy objects.

The annual injury rate in seasoning and dressing manufacturing is about 15 percent higher than the national average. Most injuries involve sprains, strains, bruises, and heat burns from handling equipment; overexertion; and exposure to harmful substances. Amputations are five times higher than the national average.

Call Preparation Questions

What competitive issues is the company facing?

The seasonings and dressing industry is mature and highly competitive.

How does the company manage changes in commodity costs?

Prices for commodity inputs such as soybean oil, high fructose corn syrup, herbs, and spices can increase significantly due to poor farm yields, unpredictable weather patterns, and government farm subsidies.

How do shifts in consumer eating habits change the company's product mix?

Consumer tastes and buying habits for seasonings and dressings are often unpredictable.

What new healthy products does the company manufacture?

Building on the sales success of organic and low- and reduced-fat dressings, manufacturers are testing and launching new low-sodium dressings, sauces, seasonings, and marinades.

How important is co-marketing with other foods to the company's marketing strategy?

Seasoning and dressing manufacturers are promoting the health benefits of pairing sauces, dressings, and spices with fruits and vegetables.

Web Links

American Spice Trade Association (ASTA)

Industry association for the US spice industry.
www.astaspice.org

Association for Dressing and Sauces (ADS)

International trade association of salad dressing, mustard, condiment sauce, and mayonnaise manufacturers.
www.dressings-sauces.org

Spices Board of India

Import and export information from a major US spice partner.
www.indianspices.com

USDA: The Spice Market in the United States

Comprehensive overview of how spices are manufactured and sold.
www.ers.usda.gov/Publications/AIB709

Glossary of Acronyms

ADS — Association for Dressing and Sauces
ASTA — American Spice Trade Association
FOB — freight on board
HFCS — high fructose corn syrup
IRI — Information Resources Incorporated
RTE — ready-to-eat

HOOVER'S TOP COMPANIES

Largest Companies by Sales	($ mil.)
Kraft Foods Inc.	42,201.0
ConAgra Foods, Inc.	11,605.7
H. J. Heinz Company	10,070.8
McCormick & Company, Incorporated	3,176.6
TreeHouse Foods, Inc.	1,500.7
Goya Foods, Inc.	1,260.0
Sensient Technologies Corporation	1,252.6
Lancaster Colony Corporation	980.9
Griffith Laboratories Inc.	635.0
B&G Foods, Inc.	486.9

Largest Employers	Employees
Kraft Foods Inc.	98,000
H. J. Heinz Company	32,500
ConAgra Foods, Inc.	25,000
Lancaster Colony Corporation	3,500
Goya Foods, Inc.	3,000
Griffith Laboratories Inc.	2,500
Portion Pac, Inc.	1,700
T. Marzetti Company	1,420
The C.F. Sauer Company	900
Ken's Foods, Inc.	760

Top Public Companies by Market Value	($ mil.)
Kraft Foods Inc.	39,450.7
H. J. Heinz Company	14,648.3
ConAgra Foods, Inc.	11,324.6
McCormick & Company, Incorporated	3,506.9
Sensient Technologies Corporation	1,150.0

SOURCE: HOOVER'S, INC., DATABASE

Securities Brokers

The securities brokerage industry in the US includes fewer than 4,000 companies, with combined annual revenue of more than $100 billion. Large companies include Charles Schwab and brokerage units of large financial services companies like Citigroup, Morgan Stanley, and Fidelity Investments. The industry is highly concentrated: the top 50 companies hold over 80 percent of the market.

Competitive Landscape

Demand is driven by the returns of securities markets relative to alternative investments. The profitability of individual companies depends on efficient operations and good marketing. Large companies have economies of scale in operations and high name recognition. Small companies can compete effectively by offering better customer service. The industry is highly automated: average annual revenue per worker is close to $300,000.

The traditional brokerage industry that sold stocks to individual investors has largely evolved into companies that either broker large stock trades for institutional investors or sell a variety of investment products to individuals. Instead of buying individual securities, many individuals now invest in mutual funds.

Products, Operations & Technology

Major services are stock brokerage, investment advice, brokerage of bonds and derivatives, and the brokerage of mutual funds. Stock brokerage accounts for about 50 percent of industry revenue, investment advice for 15 percent, and brokerage of debt securities for 15 percent.

Brokerage includes helping individuals and institutions buy and sell securities, without taking an ownership position in the securities. Brokers accomplish this by belonging to securities exchanges, such as the New York Stock Exchange (NYSE), the NASDAQ, regional

BUSINESS CHALLENGES

» Exposure to Economic Conditions

Industry profitability depends on transaction volume and the size of customer accounts, both of which can rapidly change. In recent years, a high proportion of transaction volume came from hedge funds, which can quickly shift into other investments if conditions change. During the 2001 recession, consumer stock holdings dropped 50 percent.

» Competition from Bank Products

Investing in bank products, such as money market accounts and CDs, appeals to customers as an alternate to securities because of guaranteed returns and federal insurance. During the last recession, consumer deposit accounts grew 30 percent despite falling interest rates. In recent years, consumers held almost as much money in deposit accounts as in stocks. Higher interest rates encourage investment in bank products.

» Direct Customer Access to Exchanges

The rapid evolution of computer technology allows customers to trade their own securities without broker intervention. Brokers were essential when securities were traded on exchange floors, but aren't needed for electronic trading. Aside from regulatory concerns and the need for a clearing mechanism for payments, there are no impediments to direct electronic trading either by individuals or institutions.

exchanges, commodity exchanges, and various dealer groups. In cases where a broker doesn't have direct access to an exchange, transactions are through a secondary broker.

Typically, a broker who receives an order from a customer will communicate with a company employee located at a particular exchange, who will execute the order at the exchange and report details of the transaction to the broker. Customers typically keep their securities in an account with the broker. Brokers charge customers commissions for conducting transactions and fees for maintaining their accounts.

In addition to the basics, full-service brokers may loan customers part of the purchase price of a security, a process known as margin lending, and may loan securities so that customers can speculate on a fall in prices, so-called short selling. Full-service brokers may also provide securities research, investment advice, and money management services. Some brokers also function as securities dealers (buying and selling securities for their own account), as managers of funds, or as investment bankers. Brokers also act as stock underwriters, selling new shares of stock issued by corporations.

Computer technology has been a major factor in the rapid evolution of the brokerage industry. Computer systems handle back-office functions, including customer account reporting and regulatory oversight requirements. High-speed communication networks are used to communicate with securities exchanges and dealers. A large number of securities transactions are conducted on electronic exchanges. Many customers can now conduct transactions and manage their accounts directly through brokerage Internet sites.

Sales & Marketing

Major brokerage customers are institutions and individuals. Institutions own the majority of securities in the US and account for the largest volume of brokerage transactions. Institutions include mutual funds, pension funds, insurance companies, corporations, banks, foreign institutions, and other investment funds such as hedge funds. Because institutions and individuals require different types of services (institutions mainly want fast execution and low prices), brokers generally specialize in serving one or the other. Brokers who serve mainly individuals are called retail brokers.

Retail brokers advertise extensively in newspapers, magazines, and on TV, and use targeted mail. Because referrals are an important source of customers, they also host promotional events such as golf tournaments and financial seminars, and cultivate ties with accountants and financial advisors. Institutional brokers advertise in trade publications and use an internal sales force.

Trading commissions have steadily decreased in the past decade, as the efficiency of executing trades has improved. Commissions on retail stock trades of fewer than 1,000 shares are typically a flat $10 to $30 per trade, depending on the other services a customer uses. Institutional commissions are priced per share, sometimes as low as one penny per share.

Human Resources

Retail brokerages often employ brokers who develop their own clientele and who are compensated through a share of the fees and commissions their clients generate. Average annual pay for the industry as a whole is close to $100,000. Clients often trust their broker and will follow if their broker changes companies. Top brokers may be heavily recruited by other brokerages.

Industry Employment Growth

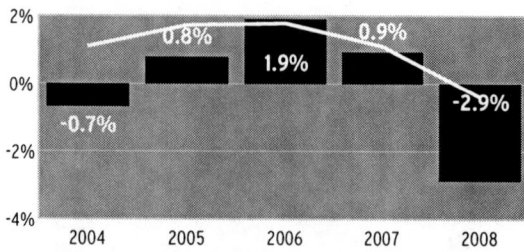

Average Hourly Earnings

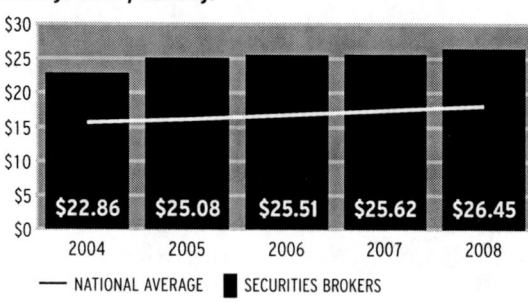

— NATIONAL AVERAGE ■ SECURITIES BROKERS

SOURCE: BUREAU OF LABOR STATISTICS

Call Preparation Questions

How much change in brokerage volume has the company seen in the past year?

Industry profitability depends on transaction volume and the size of customer accounts, both of which can rapidly change.

How is competition from bank products affecting the company's business?

Investing in bank products, such as money market accounts and CDs, appeals to customers as an alternate to securities because of guaranteed returns and federal insurance.

How does the company expect that electronic exchanges will impact it?

The rapid evolution of computer technology allows customers to trade their own securities without broker intervention.

How much of the company's trading volume is handled through its website?

Many brokers have developed elaborate Internet sites that allow their retail customers to trade stocks, mutual funds, and other securities directly.

What percentage of the company's trading volume is from securities other than stocks?

In addition to common stocks, customers of many brokerage houses can trade a wide variety of other securities.

Web Links

Financial Industry Regulatory Authority (FINRA)

Industry association and private regulator.
www.finra.org

Forbes Magazine

Industry news.
www.forbes.com

Investor's Business Daily

Industry news.
www.investors.com

InvestorWords

A complete glossary of investor terms.
www.investorwords.com

NASDAQ

Leading US electronic stock exchange.
www.nasdaq.com

New York Stock Exchange

World's leading equities market and private regulator.
www.nyse.com

Securities and Exchange Commission

Regulatory issues.
www.sec.gov

Security Industry Association

Industry lobbying group. Historical data. Legislative issues.
www.siaonline.org

Glossary of Acronyms

CFTC — Commodity Future Trading Commission
ECN — electronic communication network
FSA — Financial Services Authority
NASD — National Association of Securities Dealers
SIA — Securities Industry Association

HOOVER'S TOP COMPANIES

Largest Companies by Sales	($ mil.)
Merrill Lynch & Co., Inc.	54,046.0
The Goldman Sachs Group, Inc.	53,579.0
FMR LLC	14,900.0
UBS Investment Bank	12,760.3
Northern Trust Corporation	5,734.2
The Charles Schwab Corporation	5,393.0
The Jones Financial Companies, L.L.L.P.	4,146.9
E*TRADE Financial Corporation	3,323.0
Raymond James Financial, Inc.	3,204.9
TD AMERITRADE Holding Corporation	2,787.0

Largest Employers	Employees
FMR LLC	46,400
The Jones Financial Companies, L.L.L.P.	38,100
The Goldman Sachs Group, Inc.	30,067
Wachovia Securities, LLC	19,900
UBS Investment Bank	17,000
Raymond James Financial, Inc.	6,900
Morgan Keegan & Co., Inc.	3,400
LPL Investment Holdings Inc.	2,621
Thomas Weisel Partners Group, Inc.	650
Sanders Morris Harris Group Inc.	617

Fastest Growing* by Five-Year Sales Growth	(%)
Merriman Curhan Ford Group, Inc.	68.3
optionsXpress Holdings, Inc.	38.6
Stifel Financial Corp.	32.0
TD AMERITRADE Holding Corporation	30.7
Jesup & Lamont, Inc.	22.3
Investors Capital Holdings, Ltd.	21.5
Northern Trust Corporation	17.2
Merrill Lynch & Co., Inc.	14.3
E*TRADE Financial Corporation	10.6
MarketAxess Holdings Inc.	9.7

Fastest Growing* by Five-Year Employee Growth	(%)
TD AMERITRADE Holding Corporation	37.5
Merriman Curhan Ford Group, Inc.	37.0
optionsXpress Holdings, Inc.	29.1
Stifel Financial Corp.	25.0
Investors Capital Holdings, Ltd.	15.3
Northern Trust Corporation	10.1
Merrill Lynch & Co., Inc.	7.4
BGC Partners, Inc.	6.0
The Jones Financial Companies, L.L.L.P.	6.0
E*TRADE Financial Corporation	5.7

Top Public Companies by Market Value	($ mil.)
The Goldman Sachs Group, Inc.	34,956.0
The Charles Schwab Corporation	18,710.3
Merrill Lynch & Co., Inc.	18,290.9
Northern Trust Corporation	11,640.9
TD AMERITRADE Holding Corporation	9,887.5

* These rates are compounded annualized increases and may have resulted from acquisitions or one time gains. If less than 6 years of data are available, growth is for the years available.

SOURCE: HOOVER'S, INC., DATABASE

Security System Services

The security systems services industry in the US includes about 5,000 companies with total annual revenue of about $10 billion. Large companies include ADT Security Services, Protection One, and Brink's Home Security. The industry is concentrated: the 20 largest companies hold more than half the market.

Competitive Landscape

Demand is driven partly by home sales, new home construction, and new commercial and office construction. The profitability of monitoring companies depends on the volume of customers, as most costs are fixed. Large companies have advantages of scale in operating monitoring centers and in national advertising and brand recognition. Small companies often compete by selling customer contracts to the large monitoring companies, or reselling the monitoring companies' services, which they buy wholesale.

Products, Operations & Technology

Major products are the manufacture, sales, installation and monitoring of electrical security systems. The industry consists of commercial and residential segments, each of which uses different types of equipment and monitoring. Most companies operate in only one segment. The commercial segment accounts for about 60 percent of industry revenue. The main components of a security system are door, window and motion sensors, control keypads, alarms, and communications modules.

Commercial systems are installed by a large number of electrical contractors and security specialists. Commercial security systems are often integrated with fire alarm, access control, and closed-circuit television (CCTV) systems, and may be monitored by the customer on the premises or by a monitoring company at a remote station. Many commercial systems are linked directly to local police departments.

BUSINESS CHALLENGES

» Demand Linked to Home Sales, New Home Construction

Homeowners are most likely to install a security system when they buy or build a home. About 20 percent of US households are protected by professionally-installed and -monitored electronic burglar alarm systems. The volume of home construction and home sales largely determines industry growth.

» Keeping Up with New Technology

Security companies have to invest significantly to keep up with the latest technology as security systems become more complex. Biometrics identification, GPS tracking, and buildings with automated systems are examples of fast-growing, new security technologies.

» False Alarms

False alarms are a major problem: The International Association of Chiefs of Police says about 95 percent of alarm calls to police are false. False alarms consume resources of the monitoring company and local fire and police departments. The high rate of false alarms is so costly that many local jurisdictions impose fines or refuse service to residences with repeat false alarms. To help minimize the risk of false alarms, companies can give detailed operating instructions to consumers, and allow a testing period for them to use, check, and acclimate to the system. Some laws require security companies to verify alarms before dispatching the police.

Because the components of security systems are fairly simple, a large number of manufacturers produce them, including ADEMCO and Philips Electronics.

Residential systems use the same types of components as commercial systems, but are usually simpler. Residential systems often integrate fire detection and intrusion detection. While some systems merely set off alarms within the home when triggered, others connect through telephone lines directly to police or fire stations or to a service center. Due to the high number of false alarms, service centers are the preferred connection. The major source of revenue for large companies in the residential segment is from renewable contracts (subscriptions) for monitoring fire and security systems.

Depending on the service options the subscriber requests, operators at service centers take various actions when an alarm triggers. For example, they may notify the subscriber, dispatch company personnel to investigate the site, or notify fire or police departments. National companies have a network of regional service centers; each may monitor several hundred thousand residential and commercial subscribers. If service centers meet certain physical and staffing criteria, they can receive approval of the Underwriters Laboratories (UL). Since deterrence is the primary goal for buyers of security systems, warning decals and yard signs are a prominent feature of security packages.

Staying on top of technological innovations is important for manufacturers, dealers, and monitoring services. The miniaturization of sensors and detectors and advances in communications that permit wireless systems have made security systems affordable to a wider section of the population, but have also reduced the need for professional installation services. Monitoring companies use sophisticated computer systems to manage the large number of accounts they service.

Sales & Marketing

Commercial marketing usually consists of a direct sales force that calls on owners and operators of commercial buildings. Contracts to wire and monitor large buildings are usually awarded after a bidding process. Additionally, most manufacturers and monitoring companies sell products and services through a large network of independent dealers who perform the installations. Residential marketing usually includes advertising, telemarketing, dealer programs, and a commissioned sales force.

Residential security systems often come in a package deal that includes installation and monitoring. Residential monitoring contracts typically have an initial term of two to four years, followed by annual renewals. Monthly monitoring fees are typically between $25 and $50. The security system itself costs only a few hundred dollars if bought by the homeowner; the main expense is the ongoing monitoring. Some companies retain ownership of the standard systems they install and provide free in-

stallation as inducement for customers to sign up for the monitoring service. Newer security sytems with wireless technology eliminate the need for professional installation.

Companies closely monitor their subscriber attrition rate, which is the annualized percentage of accounts lost due to home turnover or cost concerns. Since the average home in the US is sold every seven years, natural attrition is fairly high: around 15 percent per year. Attrition rates are usually higher for single-family residences, lower for multifamily buildings, at around 6 percent, because the landlord passes the cost to the tenants as part of the rent.

Large companies sell wholesale monitoring services to smaller companies for resale to customers, because the smaller companies have too few customers to afford to operate their own service centers. Some local companies also resell their monitoring contracts to the large monitoring companies.

Human Resources

Jobs in this industry require technical skills, and therefore are relatively well-paid. Because most security systems are low-voltage systems, installers in most states do not need to be licensed electricians. Workers in the monitoring segment of the industry need computer skills.

Demand for security systems depends partly on local population growth. In recent years, states with the highest population growth were Nevada, Arizona, and Florida; Massachusetts, New York, and Ohio had the lowest growth.

Industry Employment Growth

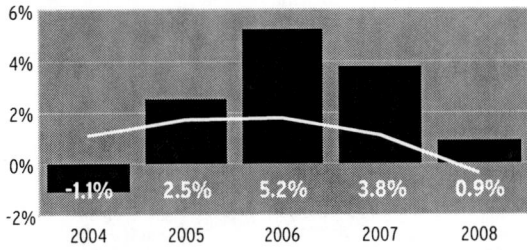

| | -1.1% | 2.5% | 5.2% | 3.8% | 0.9% |
| 2004 | 2005 | 2006 | 2007 | 2008 |

Average Hourly Earnings

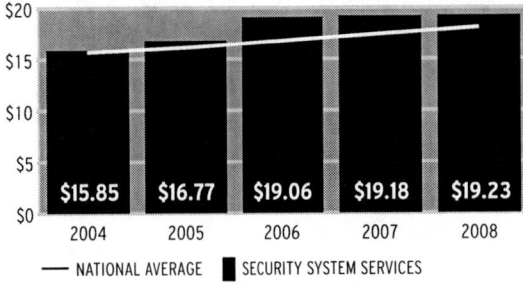

| $15.85 | $16.77 | $19.06 | $19.18 | $19.23 |
| 2004 | 2005 | 2006 | 2007 | 2008 |

— NATIONAL AVERAGE ■ SECURITY SYSTEM SERVICES

SOURCE: BUREAU OF LABOR STATISTICS

Call Preparation Questions

How is the company affected by the level of home sales?

Homeowners are most likely to install a security system when they buy or build a home.

What is the company's strategy for integrating new security technologies into its products or services?

Security companies have to invest significantly to keep up with the latest technology as security systems become more complex.

How does the company address the issue of the high rate of false alarms?

False alarms are a major problem: The International Association of Chiefs of Police says about 95 percent of alarm calls to police are false.

What plans does the company have to offer new types of monitoring products?

Affordable integrated monitoring systems now include devices that measure environmental factors, such as humidity and quality of air and water.

Web Links

Central Station Alarm Association

Excellent presentation of industry issues.
www.csaaul.org

Locksmith Ledger International

Locksmith news.
www.locksmithledger.com

National Burglar & Fire Alarm Association

Industry association. Statistics. Company links.
www.alarm.org

Security Industry Association

Directories and news.
www.siaonline.org

Security Sales & Integration

Industry news.
www.securitysales.com

SecurityInfoWatch.com

News.
www.securityinfowatch.com

Glossary of Acronyms

AFIS — automatic fingerprint identification systems
CSAA — Central Station Alarm Association
DIY — do-it-yourself
ECV — enhanced call verification
NBFAA — National Burglar and Fire Alarm Association
PV — photovoltaic
RMR — recurring monthly revenue
SIA — Security Industry Association

HOOVER'S TOP COMPANIES

Largest Companies by Sales	($ mil.)
United Technologies Corporation	58,681.0
Honeywell International Inc.	36,556.0
Tyco International Ltd.	20,199.0
Protection One, Inc.	347.9
LoJack Corporation	222.8
Defender Direct	77.0
Henry Bros. Electronics, Inc.	57.8
Devcon International Corp.	55.8
The O'Gara Group, Inc.	38.3
Brink's Home Security Inc.	—

Largest Employers	Employees
United Technologies Corporation	223,100
Honeywell International Inc.	128,000
Tyco International Ltd.	113,000
Brink's Home Security Inc.	3,300
Protection One, Inc.	2,500
The O'Gara Group, Inc.	1,450
Defender Direct	1,000
LoJack Corporation	913
Devcon International Corp.	703
American Medical Alert Corp.	580

Fastest Growing* by Five-Year Sales Growth	(%)
The O'Gara Group, Inc.	62.0
Defender Direct	53.1
Henry Bros. Electronics, Inc.	25.2
American Medical Alert Corp.	19.3
LoJack Corporation	13.9
United Technologies Corporation	13.6
Honeywell International Inc.	9.6
Protection One, Inc.	3.7
Devcon International Corp.	0.9
Synergx Systems Inc.	0.3

Fastest Growing* by Five-Year Employee Growth	(%)
Defender Direct	103.7
American Medical Alert Corp.	24.5
Devcon International Corp.	19.0
Henry Bros. Electronics, Inc.	14.3
LoJack Corporation	7.3
Honeywell International Inc.	3.5
United Technologies Corporation	1.9

Top Public Companies by Market Value	($ mil.)
United Technologies Corporation	50,595.2
Honeywell International Inc.	24,116.5
Tyco International Ltd.	17,372.8
LoJack Corporation	307.9
Protection One, Inc.	300.9

* These rates are compounded annualized increases and may have resulted from acquisitions or one time gains. If less than 6 years of data are available, growth is for the years available.

SOURCE: HOOVER'S, INC., DATABASE

Shipbuilding and Repair

THIS INDUSTRY INCLUDES:

SIC CODES

3731   Ship Building and Repairing

NAICS CODES

336611   Ship Building and Repairing

The US ship building and repair industry includes about 500 companies with combined revenue of about $15 billion. Major companies include Northrop Grumman, General Dynamics, Todd Shipyards, and Conrad Industries. The industry is highly concentrated: the largest 50 companies account for about 90 percent of revenue.

Competitive Landscape

Demand for military ship building is largely determined by the US military budget, and to a much lesser extent, the military spending of foreign governments allied with the US. Commercial ship building demand is determined by international and domestic trade, the health of the global economy, and rate of fleet replacement due to age or obsolescence. Small companies usually specialize in building and repair of small commercial vessels. Large companies tend to offer a wide range of building and repair services for both commercial and military vessels, and enjoy economies of scale in purchasing, design, and manufacturing. Due to a highly labor-intensive manufacturing process, the average annual revenue per employee is about $175,000.

Products, Operations & Technology

Revenue is generated by the design and construction of new commercial and military vessels, and the renovation and repair of existing ships. Commercial products include tankers, passenger vessels and cruise ships, barges and bulk carrier barges, and cargo and container vessels. Military products include aircraft carriers, attack submarines, transport and ammunition ships, cruisers, destroyers, amphibious assault ships, and mine hunters. For most large ship builders, commercial ship building accounts for 40 percent or less of sales.

Ship building takes place at large, coastal shipyards. Large companies typically have at

BUSINESS CHALLENGES

» Dependence on Government Contracts

The US Department of Defense (DoD) is the largest buyer of military vessels. Purchases are determined by the defense needs and strategies of the US government, the congressional budgeting and appropriations process, and the timing of awarded contracts. Changes in US policy or military strategy could affect numerous defense contracts and programs.

» Fluctuations in Raw Materials Prices

Builders of military and commercial vessels can be affected when prices of raw materials increase. Fixed-price contracts expose ship builders to potential cost overruns if prices for basic materials rise. Prices for materials like steel, aluminum, and plastics can vary as much as 60 percent in a single year.

» Increasing Foreign Competition

US commercial ship builders face increased competition from foreign companies for international business. Overseas ship builders often receive subsidies from their governments, and benefit from much lower labor costs; China and Vietnam have emerged as strong participants in the sector. US builders of large military vessels face little to no competition from foreign competitors, largely due to concerns of national security. Foreign competition isn't an issue for domestic commercial vessel sales, as the Jones Act limits how much repair work can be performed on US commercial vessels in foreign ports, and restricts trade between US ports to US-flagged vessels.

least one major shipyard on the East and West coasts, and on the Gulf coast. Smaller ship builders usually have one or more facilities that service a single US coast. Ship building facilities include dry docks, shipways, wharves, outfitting piers, cranes, and covered or indoor facilities for assembly and construction. Other operations include steel fabrication, pipe, and sheet metal shops, and repair and maintenance facilities. In some cases, labor requirements have been reduced by using modular construction techniques.

Lead times for new military vessels can be quite long. Extremely complicated vessels such as Virginia-class attack submarines can be built at a rate of about one per year. Large commercial container ships capable of carrying thousands of shipping containers can be built at a rate of about two per year.

Maintenance, overhaul, and repair schedules and specifications for commercial vessels usually are negotiated during the competitive bidding process. Maintenance is then determined by the agreed upon contract. Commercial vessels typically have a service life of about 25 to 30 years.

Builders of large naval vessels provide life cycle support services for the vessels they deliver to the US Navy. These services include configuration and data management, fleet services, integrated logistics support, and life cycle engineering and design. Large naval surface vessels such as a battleship may be commissioned for 40 years or longer.

While large military vessels are usually maintained by life cycle support services provided by the original builder, contracts for smaller or older vessels can be open to competitive contract bidding. These contracts are usually awarded based on repair capability and the shipyard's geographic proximity to a given vessel's location of service.

Raw materials include steel, aluminum, electronics, and plastics. Due to the large scale of the manufacturing process, shipbuilding depends on subcontractors, and in some cases, corporate partnerships. Builders of military ships work closely with the US military on vessel engineering and design. Both military and commercial ships are delivered directly from shipyards to military or commercial customers.

Computer technology is used to design and engineer finished products. Due to the complicated nature of the industry, shipbuilders use IT systems that track project progress in real-time to ensure that projects are completed on time and on-budget. Technology also is used to ensure the security of government and defense contractor networks that transmit sensitive information. The US government works closely with defense contractors to ensure that networks are protected.

R&D is critical to the industry due to the high level of product complexity. Costs associated with R&D are often built into fixed-price or cost-plus contracts for military products. R&D for both government and commercial products can also be self-funded.

Sales & Marketing

The US government is the largest buyer of US-built military ships. Customers for commercial ships include fishing fleets, cruise lines, cargo shipping companies, barge operators, and ferry operating entities of state governments.

The field of companies capable of delivering large military marine vessels to the US government is small. Military vessel makers' sales and marketing is done primarily by company executives. Companies that provide vessels for the US military often have high-level, retired military officers on their boards of directors who are familiar with US military requirements, strategies, and equipment. Establishing and maintaining relationships with the various agencies inside the US government relevant to military contracts, as well as directly lobbying legislators inside Congress, is important to the sales of military vessels.

Sales of commercial vessels are also largely carried out by company executives. The types of vessels offered are often highlighted in company brochures and on company websites.

Military vessels are primarily sold to the US government through fixed-price or incentive contracts that limit increases in contract value to specification changes by the government. Prices for military and commercial ships vary greatly depending on size, complexity, and intended use. A Virginia-class attack submarine costs about $2.3 billion; a 420-foot Coast Guard cutter, upward of $600 million. A large commercial cargo vessel can cost more than $150 million; a double hulled tanker vessel, more than $60 million.

Human Resources

The average hourly wage of production workers is about $20, over 20 percent above the average for US manufacturing overall. Ship building workers tend to be highly skilled trade specialists, including pipefitters, electricians, welders, machinists, shipwrights, and crane operators. Many of the trades used by the industry are represented by labor unions. Competition for skilled workers can be significant. Companies usually target recruiting efforts in coastal regions where qualified workers are concentrated.

Due to the sensitive nature of defense contracts, some ship building workers may be required to have US government security clearances.

Worker safety is a significant issue in the ship building and repairing industry; non-fatal injury and illness rates are nearly three times higher than that of private industry overall. Strains and sprains make up a majority of workplace injuries. To mitigate the number of workplace injuries, ship building companies routinely inspect workplace procedures and have safety training meetings.

Industry Employment Growth

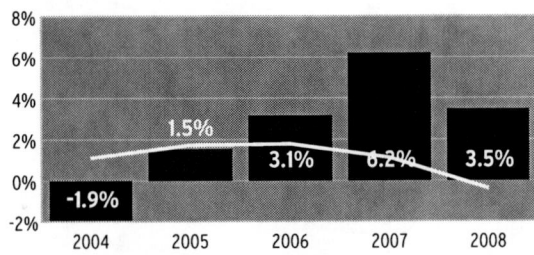

Average Hourly Earnings

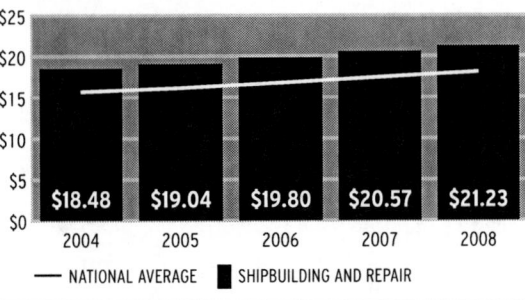

— NATIONAL AVERAGE ■ SHIPBUILDING AND REPAIR

SOURCE: BUREAU OF LABOR STATISTICS

Call Preparation Questions

How does the company mitigate the unpredictable nature of defense contracts?

The US Department of Defense (DoD) is the largest buyer of military vessels.

How does the company manage rising material costs?

Builders of military and commercial vessels can be affected when prices of raw materials increase.

What challenges does the company face from foreign competition?

US commercial ship builders face increased competition from foreign companies for international business.

What opportunities is the company exploring in using composite materials?

The use of structural composite materials in ship building is being explored.

How is the company planning to benefit from increased global trade?

As the consumer economies of nations such as China, India, Brazil, and Russia continue to grow and become more influential, global trade is expected to increase.

Web Links

American Shipbuilding Association

Trade association for American shipbuilders. usships.org

General Dynamics

www.generaldynamics.com

Global Security

News, information, and links for defense, space, intelligence, WMD, and Homeland Security issues. www.globalsecurity.org

Manufacturing.gov

Information on issues facing US manufacturers. www.manufacturing.gov

Marine Log

Shipbuilding and shipping news, information, links, and events. www.marinelog.com

National Defense Industrial Association

Industry events, meetings, news, and links. www.ndia.org

Northrop Grumman

www.northropgrumman.com

Glossary of Acronyms

DOD — Department of Defense
LCS — Littoral Combat Ship
RFP — request for proposal

HOOVER'S TOP COMPANIES

Largest Companies by Sales	($ mil.)
General Dynamics Corporation	29,300.0
Northrop Grumman Shipbuilding	1,378.5
Bollinger Shipyards, Inc.	222.0
Earl Industries, LLC	200.9
Conrad Industries, Inc.	168.5
Todd Shipyards Corporation	139.1

Largest Employers	Employees
General Dynamics Corporation	92,300
Northrop Grumman Shipbuilding	18,000
Bollinger Shipyards, Inc.	2,900
Todd Shipyards Corporation	800
Earl Industries, LLC	650
Conrad Industries, Inc.	498
Maritime Services Corporation	250
Cascade General, Inc.	250

Top Public Companies by Market Value	($ mil.)
General Dynamics Corporation	22,270.7
Todd Shipyards Corporation	92.5

SOURCE: HOOVER'S, INC., DATABASE

Shoe Stores

The shoe store industry includes about 30,000 stores with combined annual revenue of almost $25 billion. Major companies include Payless ShoeSource, Brown Shoe Company (which owns Famous Footwear and Naturalizer), Foot Locker, and DSW. Shoe manufacturers, such as Nike, also have retail operations. The industry is concentrated: the top 50 companies have about 80 percent of industry revenue.

Competitive Landscape

Fashion trends and personal income drive demand. The profitability of individual companies depends on effective merchandising and competitive pricing. Large companies have advantages in purchasing, distribution, and marketing. Small companies can compete effectively by stocking specialty products, providing superior customer service, or serving a local market. The industry is labor intensive: average annual revenue per worker is just over $100,000.

Shoe stores compete with department stores, mass merchandisers, apparel retailers, Internet retailers, and some shoe manufacturers.

Products, Operations & Technology

Major products sold by shoe stores include women's casual and dress shoes (25 percent of industry revenue); men's athletic shoes (20 percent); men's casual and dress shoes (15 percent), and women's athletic shoes (10 percent). Other products include handbags, hosiery, and jewelry. Companies may specialize in men's, women's, children's, or athletic shoes. Over half of all shoe retailers are family shoe stores, which offer merchandise for multiple targets.

Shoe stores include national and regional chains, franchises, and independent retailers. Superstores can range between 10,000 and 25,000 square feet; many chains between 1,500 and 3,000. Typical locations include strip malls, stand-alone locations, and indoor shopping

BUSINESS CHALLENGES

» Competition from Alternative Retailers

Shoe stores compete with a wide range of retailers, including department stores, mass merchandisers, shoe manufacturers, and Internet retailers. Department stores and mass merchandisers can use the apparel business to drive shoe sales and offer customers one-stop shopping for complete outfits. Shoe manufacturers have opened both traditional retail and outlet locations, and offer a wide selection within a specific brand. Online shoe sales are growing, driven by Internet-only retailers and sites established by traditional apparel and department stores.

» Flat Pricing Squeezes Margins

Shoe stores face a major challenge in growing profitability due to limited flexibility in retail pricing. In the last 10 years, retail prices for footwear declined 3 percent. In general, flat retail pricing requires shoe stores to rely on volume and multiple purchases to grow earnings. Increased competition from numerous alternative retailers has contributed to keeping retail prices low.

» Anticipating Fashion Trends

Companies must gauge demand based on constantly evolving fashion trends. Clothing trends drive sales for different shoe styles and colors, and fashion fads can die quickly. Most shoe stores must order merchandise well in advance, without the benefit of known consumer acceptance. In addition, fast response to a trend can be difficult because most shoes are imports, requiring long order lead times.

malls, particularly fashion malls; companies may also lease locations inside apparel retailers. Shoe retailers consider traffic, demographics, and neighboring tenants when considering new locations, and may cluster stores in a market to reduce advertising and distribution costs.

Shoe retailers often display single pairs (or samples) of shoes and store additional sizes in stockrooms. Self-service shoe stores allow customers to select and try on shoes without assistance by storing available sizes on the selling floor. Attractive displays and a distinctive store environment can be important to the shopping experience. Many shoe stores have glass exteriors that showcase key merchandise, helping drive traffic.

Companies typically buy shoes directly from manufacturers, such as Nike or Brown Shoe. Large shoe retailers may receive favorable purchasing terms, including volume rebates and short lead times for orders. Buyers identify fashion and color trends by researching styles in TV, movies, magazines, and music. Most buyers attend trade shows, such as the New York Shoe Expo, to review the latest merchandise. Companies order shoes between three and six months in advance, and closely monitor sell-through rates to determine reorders.

Major categories for shoes include athletic, casual, weekend, career, and special occasion. Companies may refer to athletic shoes as "white shoes" and non-athletic shoes as "brown shoes." Even small companies manage relatively large inventories because the shoe business involves different styles, sizes, and colors. Shoe superstores may carry between 20,000 and 30,000 pairs. Payless stocks just over 7,000 pairs. Most shoe stores offer national brand name shoes. Some large companies use agents to help develop and produce private-label products.

Many large chains tailor merchandise to match local market demographics. Because seasonality and trends drive demand for new styles, companies constantly rotate inventory and promote new products. Some chain stores receive new merchandise as often as twice a week. Large chains may test market new styles in a subset of stores before offering merchandise nationally.

Integrated computer systems manage point-of-sale (POS), inventory, distribution, and financial operations. Daily analysis of POS data allows companies to react quickly to market conditions and make fast decisions on pricing, reorders, and markdowns. Inventory management systems help shoe stores develop store specific merchandising plans and identify losses. Companies may track merchandise by universal product codes (UPC), and use electronic data interchange (EDI) and advance shipment notification (ASN) to aid in purchasing and in monitoring deliveries.

Sales & Marketing

While the typical customer for a shoe store varies by store type, women between 18 and 49 make the majority of footwear purchasing decisions. Appearance-conscious young women are important targets for the shoe industry. On average, women spend $40 on a pair of shoes, according to Greenfield.

Major marketing and promotional vehicles include TV, radio, newspaper, and print advertising, direct mail, and in-store displays. Brand name shoes are important. Giveaways and promotional events draw store traffic. Shoe retailers may encourage multiple purchases through loyalty clubs or by offering discounts. Seasonal decor highlights new merchandise. High-end shoe stores may hold trunk shows to feature special designers.

Customer service can be important, especially for stores relying on sales associates to size customers, make recommendations, and retrieve merchandise from stockrooms. Some companies use customer satisfaction surveys to monitor service levels.

Most shoe stores have Internet sites providing basic store information, including hours of operation and locations. Most large companies sell merchandise through websites or link with existing retail sites, such as Amazon. The Internet is especially important for shoe stores with specialized inventory, such as large size shoes.

Discount shoe stores typically sell brand name shoes at 20 to 60 percent off department store prices. Better footwear prices range between $70 and $10; bridge footwear retails for between $100 and $200; designer footwear starts at about $200. Shoe stores typically hold clearance sales at the end of seasons.

Human Resources

Workers in shoe stores require few skills, and wages are just over a third less than the US average. A typical mall-based shoe retailer may employ one manager, one assistant manager, and five sales associates. The industry relies highly on part-time workers. Compensation for sales associates can include commissions or incentives. Employee discounts encourage staff to wear merchandise to help promote sales. The industry injury rate is significantly below the US average.

Industry Employment Growth

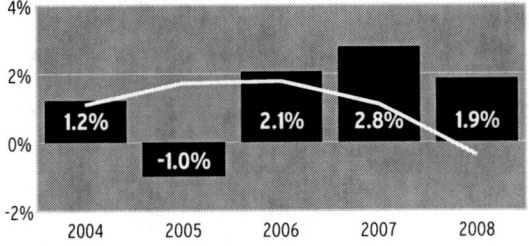

Average Hourly Earnings

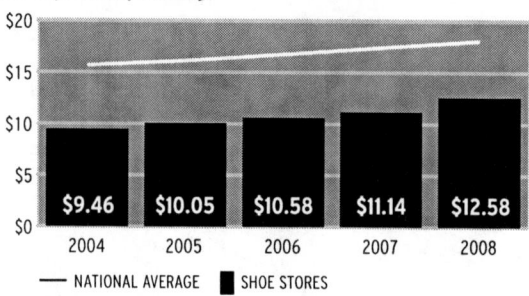

	2004	2005	2006	2007	2008
SHOE STORES	$9.46	$10.05	$10.58	$11.14	$12.58

— NATIONAL AVERAGE ■ SHOE STORES

SOURCE: BUREAU OF LABOR STATISTICS

Call Preparation Questions

How have retail pricing trends affected the company's profitability?

Shoe stores face a major challenge in growing profitability due to limited flexibility in retail pricing.

How does the company anticipate trends in shoe demand?

Companies must gauge demand based on constantly evolving fashion trends.

How does the company maximize accessory sales?

Companies can generate incremental sales by offering a wide range of accessories to complement shoes.

What types of specialty shoes does the company sell?

Shoe stores can better compete against alternative retailers by offering unique specialty products, such as comfort or orthopedic shoes, or shoes by up-and-coming designers.

Web Links

American Apparel and Footwear Association

Statistics, news, and trends.
www.apparelandfootwear.org

Footwear Plus

Trade publication for news and trends.
www.footwearplusmagazine.com

National Shoe Retailers Association

News and trends through Shoe Retailing Today publication.
www.nsra.org

Glossary of Acronyms

AAFA — American Apparel and Footwear Association
ASN — advance shipment notification
EDI — electronic data interchange
NSRA — National Shoe Retailers Association
POS — point-of-sale
WSA — World Shoe Association

HOOVER'S TOP COMPANIES

Largest Companies by Sales	($ mil.)
Foot Locker, Inc.	5,437.0
Collective Brands, Inc. (Payless ShoeSource)	3,035.4
Brown Shoe Company, Inc.	2,359.9
Retail Ventures, Inc.	1,871.9
Genesco Inc.	1,502.1
DSW Inc.	1,405.6
Schottenstein Stores Corporation	1,300.0
The Finish Line, Inc.	1,277.2
Zappos.com, Inc.	840.0
Shoe Carnival, Inc.	658.7

Largest Employers	Employees
Foot Locker, Inc.	44,415
Collective Brands, Inc. (Payless ShoeSource)	31,000
Retail Ventures, Inc.	17,342
Genesco Inc.	13,950
The Finish Line, Inc.	13,100
Brown Shoe Company, Inc.	13,100
Schottenstein Stores Corporation	8,050
DSW Inc.	5,800
Shoe Carnival, Inc.	4,300
Bakers Footwear Group, Inc.	2,450

Fastest Growing* by Five-Year Sales Growth	(%)
Zappos.com, Inc.	84.8
DSW Inc.	16.9
The Walking Company Holdings, Inc.	16.5
Genesco Inc.	12.6
The Finish Line, Inc.	11.0
Schottenstein Stores Corporation	5.7
Brown Shoe Company, Inc.	5.1
Shoe Carnival, Inc.	4.9
Bakers Footwear Group, Inc.	4.7
Foot Locker, Inc.	3.8

Fastest Growing* by Five-Year Employee Growth	(%)
Zappos.com, Inc.	76.5
Genesco Inc.	19.6
DSW Inc.	17.2
The Walking Company Holdings, Inc.	13.2
Bakers Footwear Group, Inc.	8.9
Shoe Carnival, Inc.	6.1
Schottenstein Stores Corporation	5.9
The Finish Line, Inc.	5.7
Foot Locker, Inc.	2.0
Brown Shoe Company, Inc.	1.8

Top Public Companies by Market Value	($ mil.)
Foot Locker, Inc.	2,153.4
Collective Brands, Inc. (Payless ShoeSource)	1,122.0
Brown Shoe Company, Inc.	722.9
Genesco Inc.	692.1
Retail Ventures, Inc.	345.2

* These rates are compounded annualized increases and may have resulted from acquisitions or one time gains. If less than 6 years of data are available, growth is for the years available.

SOURCE: HOOVER'S, INC., DATABASE

Site Preparation Contractors

The site preparation contractor industry includes over 30,000 businesses with combined annual revenue of $37 billion. Major companies include units of Bechtel, Fluor, Granite Construction, Jacobs Engineering Group, and URS Corporation. Most firms are privately owned. The industry is fragmented: over 75 percent of businesses are small, with fewer than 10 employees. Many independent site prep contractors operate as unincorporated sole proprietors, without permanent employees.

Competitive Landscape

Construction and demolition projects drive demand for site prep contractors. The profitability of individual companies depends on accurate bidding and optimal deployment of personnel and equipment. Large companies have advantages in servicing multiple types of projects simultaneously. Small companies can compete effectively by subcontracting their services to larger firms, specializing by type of work, or becoming a preferred contractor for local builders and developers. Average annual revenue per employee for a typical company is a low $130,000, because the work is labor-intensive.

Small firms often compete with solo owner-operators who hire temporary workers and rent equipment as needed.

Products, Operations & Technology

Major services are land clearing and excavation, preparation for construction, and demolition. Excavation services account for 60 percent of industry business, heavy construction for 30 percent, and wrecking and demolition, 8 percent. Other services include preparing for water, sewer, and pipeline construction, and support for oil, gas, and mining operations.

Most firms specialize in preparation work for buildings or infrastructure projects. Constructing buildings represents about 50 percent of

BUSINESS CHALLENGES

» Highly Dependent on New Construction

The site prep contracting business depends greatly on new construction of commercial and industrial buildings, housing, and public infrastructure. New construction represents about 75 percent of the industry's revenue in the US. Total construction spending doubled in the decade ending in 2005.

» Subject to Seasonal Demand

Industrywide, demand is strongest spring through early fall, requiring careful management of seasonal cash flow and labor. For companies in cold weather regions, demand can cease during harsh winters. Due to seasonality, the industry workforce fluctuates at least 20 percent between low and peak seasons, but for companies in cold regions, the change is even greater.

» Full Deployment of Personnel, Equipment

The seasonality of the industry challenges firms to avoid idle equipment and under-using full-time personnel when demand is low. Each piece of earthmoving and demolition equipment costs thousands, and full-time project managers and engineers earn high wages. Underused resources strain the financial health of firms, especially smaller ones that can service only one or two projects at a time.

site prep work. Infrastructure projects include highways, sewer and water mains and facilities, and driveways.

Contractors use wrecking equipment to demolish buildings and structures, and a variety of earthmoving equipment for excavation and land grading. Specialty contractors install septic systems, move houses, or rent equipment with operators. Companies win jobs through a bidding process, either on a per-hour or fixed-price basis. Firms often work as subcontractors, which accounts for about half of industry revenue.

For large projects, surveyors measure site elevations and engineers determine how best to do the work. Contractors acquire local construction permits as needed on a per-job basis. Firms transport equipment to the job site using trailers, flatbed carriers, or tractor-trailers.

Machine operators, manual laborers, and supervisors work on the job site. Typical functions include bulldozing to clear and grade land, digging or drilling to prepare for foundations, and wrecking or blasting for demolition. Workers prepare waste, such as dirt, rock, felled trees, and demolition debris, which may contain hazardous materials, for removal and hauling according to local ordinances.

Larger firms may work anywhere in the country or internationally, and typically manage multiple types of projects in multiple locations simultaneously. Midsize firms may work regionally, as well as locally, whereas smaller firms usually operate within a radius of less than 30 miles.

Equipment includes bobcats, backhoes, bulldozers, excavators, scrapers, graders, and loaders for putting debris into trucks for hauling. Major earthmoving equipment manufacturers are Caterpillar, Komatsu, and CNH Global. A small bulldozer costs around $15,000 and runs six hours on a tank of gas. Depending on the machine, purchase prices can vary by 4 to 10 percent during a year, while operational costs can vary greatly due to changes in gas prices. Smaller companies may rent machinery from sources like United Rentals and NationsRent.

Site prep machinery is incorporating more technology, including computerized sensors and controls, that enable the operator to work more efficiently. Sophisticated machines with GPS help in grading and leveling. Office technology includes software for project planning and management, site elevation schematics, billing, and receivables. Some smaller firms may prefer traditional manual processes for project plans and management, but use standard accounting and billing software.

Sales & Marketing

Typical customers are developers and builders of privately owned housing and commercial buildings, civil engineering and heavy construction firms, and government agencies. Smaller firms may cater exclusively to individual home and business property owners, or to larger contractors for whom the firms work as subcontractors. About 75 percent of the site prep industry's business comes from the private sector, and 25 percent from primarily state and local governments.

Major types of marketing include ads in the Yellow Pages, newspapers, and construction trade journals. The most important sales channel is developing and maintaining personal contacts with construction contractors, builders, and architects. Many firms receive most of their business through trade and customer referrals.

Smaller companies often compete with individual operators who work on a per-hour basis on equipment that the end-user customer, such as homeowners or independent developers, rents. These operators rarely have insurance or business licenses, issues that smaller companies can exploit in marketing and bidding. The largest contractors may compete with site prep units of very large construction firms.

Prices vary greatly by type and scope of project and location: from less than $100 per hour for a simple job by a solo operator, to thousands to prepare for a housing development, or millions for a major interstate highway project. Large firms price on a per-project basis, but smaller firms prefer to charge by the hour. Smaller firms may drop prices during off-season months to help ensure a steady revenue stream.

Human Resources

Most site prep employees are machine operators or manual laborers, though many firms employ engineers and estimators. Manual laborers use mainly physical skills and machinery operators require equipment-specific training, while highly paid engineers who plan and manage projects have college degrees. The industry pays on average about 20 percent higher wages than the US average. Fringe benefits add an average of 24 percent to compensation. Firms maintain a core workforce they supplement with seasonal labor, which can represent an increase of over 20 percent in headcount. Companies screen employees for drug use and legal work status.

Industry injury rates are 20 percent higher than the US average, due to the nature of the work. Many injuries are a result of coming into contact with site prep machinery, or sprains and strains from overexertion. The severity of injuries keeps industry workers off the job five days longer than the national average.

Industry Employment Growth

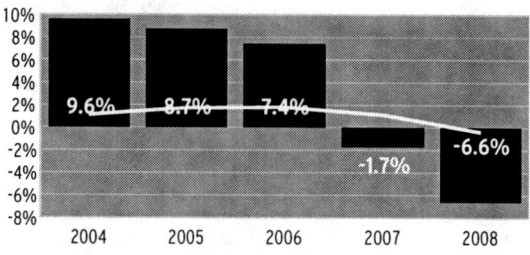

Average Hourly Earnings

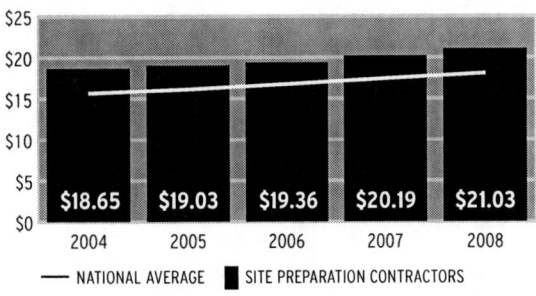

	2004	2005	2006	2007	2008
	$18.65	$19.03	$19.36	$20.19	$21.03

— NATIONAL AVERAGE ■ SITE PREPARATION CONTRACTORS

SOURCE: BUREAU OF LABOR STATISTICS

Call Preparation Questions

How dependent is the firm on new construction?

The site prep contracting business depends greatly on new construction of commercial and industrial buildings, housing, and public infrastructure.

How does the firm deal with seasonal fluctuations in demand?

Industrywide, demand is strongest spring through early fall, requiring careful management of seasonal cash flow and labor.

How is the company challenged by fully using personnel and equipment?

The seasonality of the industry challenges firms to avoid idle equipment and under-using full-time personnel when demand is low.

How is the firm taking advantage of new technologies?

Leading firms are using sophisticated technologies, like 3D visualization software and GPS, to win business and gain efficiencies.

Web Links

American Subcontractors Association

News, issues, and operational advice.
www.asaonline.com

Associated General Contractors of America

Issues of importance to construction contractors.
www.agc.org

Builder Online

News. Statistics, website links, the 100 largest homebuilders and the top 5 builders in the 50 largest markets.
www.builderonline.com

Engineering News-Record

Construction news.
www.enr.com

Glossary of Acronyms

GC — general contractor

NAHB — National Association of Home Builders

HOOVER'S TOP COMPANIES

Largest Companies by Sales	($ mil.)
Bechtel Group, Inc.	27,000.0
Fluor Corporation	22,325.9
KBR, Inc.	11,581.0
Jacobs Engineering Group Inc.	11,252.2
Peter Kiewit Sons', Inc.	6,200.0
Parsons Corporation	3,600.0
Granite Construction Incorporated	2,674.2
J.F. Shea Co., Inc.	2,260.0
Zachry Group	2,188.0
TIC Holdings, Inc.	2,000.0

Largest Employers	Employees
Jacobs Engineering Group Inc.	43,700
Bechtel Group, Inc.	42,500
Peter Kiewit Sons', Inc.	15,000
Parsons Corporation	11,500
Zachry Group	11,500
TIC Holdings, Inc.	9,000
J. Ray McDermott, S.A.	7,100
SNC-Lavalin Constructors Inc.	5,000
High Industries, Inc.	2,479
S & B Engineers and Constructors, Ltd.	2,400

Top Public Companies by Market Value	($ mil.)
Fluor Corporation	8,146.4
Jacobs Engineering Group Inc.	6,663.9
KBR, Inc.	2,458.2
Granite Construction Incorporated	1,681.1
Sterling Construction Company, Inc.	244.3

SOURCE: HOOVER'S, INC., DATABASE

Ski Facilities

The US ski resort industry includes about 350 companies, over 400 ski areas, and combined annual revenue of $2 billion, not including hotels or real estate. Major companies include Intrawest, Vail Resorts, and Booth Creek Ski Holdings. The industry is highly concentrated: the 50 largest firms earn over 80 percent of industry revenue and own 20 percent of ski facilities. Most ski areas are independently owned and operated.

Competitive Landscape

Good snow conditions and personal income drive demand. The profitability of individual companies depends on effective marketing and efficient skiing and business operations. Large companies have advantages in marketing and in sharing resources and staff among multiple skiing sites. Small companies can compete effectively by catering to the local population or providing customized services. The industry is labor-intensive: average annual revenue per worker is around $45,000.

Products, Operations & Technology

Major services at ski resorts are facility use, sales of food and beverages, instruction fees, merchandise sales, and equipment rentals. About 60 percent of industry revenue comes from usage or admission fees (including lift tickets); less than 15 percent from sales of food and beverages; 10 percent from instruction fees; and 10 percent from merchandise sales and equipment rentals. Additional revenue can come from membership dues, arcade machines, concession fees, and advertisement and endorsement fees. In addition to skiing-related services, some companies also rent or sell condominiums or houses at ski areas, but usually through a subsidiary or related company.

Of ski facilities, 60 percent operate year-round, while 40 percent open only for ski season. A typical ski season runs from

BUSINESS CHALLENGES

» Vulnerability to Weather Conditions

The amount and timing of snowfall is critical to a ski area's success. Avid skiers perceive early-season snow conditions as an indicator of an area's desirability for the entire ski season. Warm weather and drought can inhibit a ski facility's ability to make snow, and many small companies don't own or use snowmaking equipment, which is expensive. Excessive snow can prevent visitors from reaching ski areas and increases the cost of grooming trails. Experts worry that climatic warming trends threaten the ski industry.

» Dependence on Affluent Consumers

Skiing is expensive, making the industry dependent on consumers with high income. The average household income of US skiers is over $85,000, according to the National Sporting Goods Association, nearly double the median US household income. Average per-day ski tickets cost $50 to $100, but skiers can spend considerably more a day, including food, services, and incidentals.

» Unfavorable Demographics

Growth in the ski industry's key customer demographic is static: typical customers are singles to age 34 and active families with children, but the number of adults in those groups isn't increasing. The US government predicts flat growth in the population ages 20 to 44 from 2000 to 2010, and only 4 percent growth by 2020. In contrast, forecasters expect the total population to increase 10 percent near-term, with increasing numbers above age 45 as baby boomers age.

mid-November to mid-April in the highest elevations. Staff prepares and maintains trails; gives skiing lessons; runs restaurants and food concessions; rents, sells, "tunes," and repairs ski equipment; and operates onsite retail shops. Companies may outsource some services or lease concessions to third parties. During off-season, many facilities feature hiking, mountain biking, and swimming, and host conferences and vacationers.

Ski areas may focus on a major type of skiing: downhill ("Alpine"); cross-country ("Nordic"); freestyle; or snowboarding; or offer a combination. Most types of skiing require special surface preparation and equipment, such as ski lifts, tows, and trail-grooming machines. Equipment can be costly: an extensive snowmaking system can cost over $1 million for a large mountain. Many small companies can't afford to buy or use snowmaking equipment, even if its absence means fewer skiers.

Ski facilities' major metrics are skier visits (or "skier days") and revenue per visit. A skier visit includes the use of a ticket or free pass for any part of a single day. US skier visits number over 50 million in most years.

Ski areas can be on private or public land and can vary from a single run on a few acres to numerous runs on thousands of acres. When snowfall is inadequate, facilities that use snowmaking equipment require large quantities of water to convert into snow. A 200-foot-by-200-foot area requires 75,000 gallons of water to create a six-inch-deep snow layer, according to the Colorado Department of Public Health and Environment. Because water resources can be limited, ski facilities enter water usage agreements with nearby towns, affected states, and, in the case of public land, with federal agencies. Some ski facilities have their own lakes or reservoirs. Snowmaking, grooming, and chairlift equipment are energy-intensive to operate, but can be competitively advantageous. For example, high-speed chairlifts can carry four skiers up a mountain three times faster than older models.

Ski resorts depend on technology for marketing, sales, and operations. Websites often feature 360-degree video tours of the ski area and live shots of current weather and slope conditions, in addition to providing information and enabling reservations and ticket purchases. Some companies have point-of-sale ticket kiosks in regional stores, visitor centers, and hotels. Many ski areas scan tickets to track visitor activity and spending data, which feed into customer relationship management systems for better understanding of consumer preferences. Some companies issue branded temporary credit cards for onsite use. Computer controls manage and monitor sophisticated chairlifts and skiing-related heavy equipment.

Sales & Marketing

Typical customers are singles ages 18 to 34 and active families with children, although patrons vary greatly in age and skiing ability. Families account for almost half of skier visits. Over 65 percent of skiers are college-educated and almost half of those are in professional or managerial jobs, according to the National Sporting Goods Association (NSGA).

Customers include local day skiers, multi-day skiers who generally drive less than a day to the area, and vacationers ("destination" visitors), who typically arrive via a nearby airport and stay a week or more. The most skier visits come from customers who drive to skiing areas and are day skiers, with the exception of the destination resorts in the Rocky Mountains, according to Sitour USA. Customers at drive-up resorts include a higher percentage of snowboarders than at destination resorts. Over 6 million downhill skiers and over 5 million snowboarders participated in their snowsports more than once in the US in a recent year, according to the National Sporting Goods Association (NSGA).

Major sales channels include travel agencies, websites and e-mail, and internal sales forces. As part of growth strategies, sales efforts aim to attract new skiers and customers from other ski areas and to increase revenue per skier visit. Customers select a ski facility for its terrain and challenges, slope grooming and upkeep, types of lifts and services, geographic accessibility, typical snowfall and weather, and amenities on-site and nearby.

Major types of marketing include public relations article placement; advertisements in ski, lifestyle, and leisure magazines; direct marketing to targeted audiences; promotional and loyalty programs, and direct sales to corporations and organizations for conventions and meetings. Large ski resorts market internationally and nationally, but most companies market regionally. Hosting Winter Olympics is a major marketing coup that enhances a company's brand well beyond the event. Resorts form partnerships with consumer-oriented companies to gain revenue from brand name placement at the ski area and for cross-marketing opportunities. Ski facilities generally outsource customer service operations and rely on extensive use of visitor surveys to gauge customer satisfaction.

Internet marketing is increasing in importance in the industry. Ski areas' websites enable consumers to view virtual tours and current weather videos, read about services and amenities, buy tickets, and make reservations. Many ski areas provide content or links to websites of travel agencies, hotels, visitor centers, and retailers, but prefer to make the sale on their own sites. Ski facilities generally offer special pricing and activity packages for online sales as an incentive for customers to use this low-cost sales medium.

Typical lift-ticket prices for an adult range from $50 to $100 per day and from $500 to $2,000 for a season pass. Prices vary widely, depending on the ski facility, but tend to increase yearly. Rocky Mountain resorts generally have the highest prices. Most ski facilities offer a variety of ticket packages at various prices. Pre- and early-season purchases have lower prices, as do lift tickets for children and seniors. Most ski areas discount tickets during non-holiday weekdays or when weather is unfavorable.

Human Resources

Skiing is a specialized business that requires employees to have industry-specific knowledge and skills. Most workers need to be knowledgeable of the sport and skilled skiers, especially instructors and ski patrol members who respond to emergencies. Operators of chairlift, snow grooming, and snowmaking equipment need special training and can earn certification by industry groups or manufacturers. Safety and emergency response training are high priorities. To ensure a skilled workforce, regional universities near high-density snow resort areas offer courses that focus on snowsport businesses and range from management to ski instruction.

Average industry pay is about 40 percent lower than the national wage. Annual personnel turnover is high, because the majority of workers are seasonal. Early-season employee attrition is problematic. The largest resorts may retain about a third of their staff year-round to provide summer services and prepare for upcoming winter seasons. About 40 percent of companies close off-season and lay off workers. Included among seasonal help are managers, supervisors, and line employees from restaurants, retail, and skiing operations. Ski areas increasingly use online job services to recruit workers in advance of skiing season and to backfill jobs due to attrition.

Industry Employment Growth

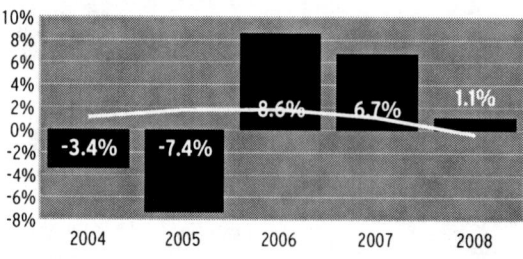

Average Hourly Earnings

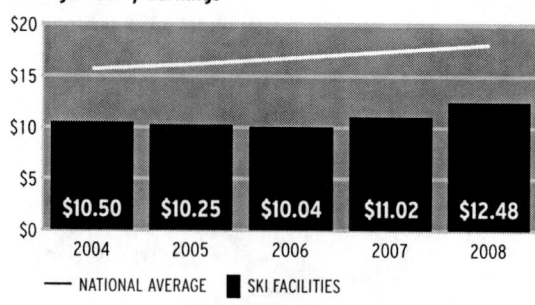

SOURCE: BUREAU OF LABOR STATISTICS

Call Preparation Questions

How satisfied is the company with the amount and timing of snowfall during the current (or most recent) ski season?

The amount and timing of snowfall is critical to a ski area's success.

How does the company attract higher-income consumers?

Skiing is expensive, making the industry dependent on consumers with high income.

How might the company diversify its services to appeal to the growing population over 45?

Growth in the ski industry's key customer demographic is static: typical customers are singles to age 34 and active families with children, but the number of adults in those groups isn't increasing.

What opportunities does the company see for off-season revenue?

About 40 percent of ski areas close off-season, but those that stay open find revenue opportunities in promoting multi-season recreation, events, and vacations.

How does the company decide which new amenities or services to offer?

Ski facilities continuously add features and services that help attract and keep skiers at the mountain longer.

Web Links

California Ski Industry Association (CSIA)

Industry news, regional ski area list.
www.californiasnow.com/press.asp

Colorado Ski Country USA

Regional resort list, snow levels, ticket passes, events.
www.coloradoski.com

National Ski Areas Association (NSAA)

Industry news, statistics, safety and environmental issues.
www.nsaa.org/nsaa/home

Ski & Snowboard Canada

Canadian Ski Council's site; news, events, ski area list.
www.skicanada.org/site

Ski Area Management (SAM magazine)

Industry news.
www.saminfo.com

Ski Central

Ski-related search engine with numerous categories, links.
www.skicentral.com/skiing.html

Ski Resort Glossary

Industry terms, definitions.
www.jobmonkey.com/ski/html/glossary.html

United States Ski and Snowboard Association (USSA)

Olympic event calendar, club directory, links.
www.ussa.org

Glossary of Acronyms

CSIA — California Ski Industry Association
NSAA — National Ski Areas Association
NSC — National Safety Council
NSGA — National Sporting Goods Association
NSP — National Ski Patrol
USSA — United States Ski & Snowboard Association

HOOVER'S TOP COMPANIES

Largest Employers	Employees
Vail Resorts, Inc.	15,300
Booth Creek Ski Holdings, Inc.	4,109
Mammoth Mountain Ski Area	450
Aspen Skiing Company	400
Western Standard Corporation	260
Winter Sports, Inc.	200
Snowdance, Inc.	100

SOURCE: HOOVER'S, INC., DATABASE

Snack Foods Manufacturing

The snack food manufacturing industry includes about 400 companies with combined annual revenue of $23 billion. Major companies include PepsiCo's Frito-Lay, Kraft's Nabisco subsidiary, and Kellogg's Retail Snacks business. The industry is concentrated: the top 50 companies account for 75 percent of industry revenue.

The snack food manufacturing industry includes companies that make roasted nuts and nut mixes; potato, tortilla, and corn chips; popped popcorn; and peanut butter. This industry doesn't include companies that make cookies, candy, crackers, pies, or chocolate-covered snacks.

Competitive Landscape

Demand is driven by consumer tastes and health considerations. The profitability of individual companies depends on efficient operations, effective marketing, and a strong sales force. Large companies have advantages in raw material purchasing, manufacturing efficiencies, distribution, and marketing budgets. Small operations can compete effectively by self-distributing products, selling online, or marketing snacks as gift items. Average annual revenue per employee is $500,000.

Snack food manufacturing competes against other "impulse" food items, including cookies and crackers, baked goods, fruits and vegetables, and fast food items.

Products, Operations & Technology

Major products are potato chips (30 percent of industry revenue); tortilla chips (20 percent); and bulk nuts (10 percent). Other products include canned nuts, corn chips, peanut butter, popcorn, and hard pretzels.

Salty snack foods are found in 99 percent of all American households. Research from the USDA and the Snack Food Association (SFA) finds that the average American household

BUSINESS CHALLENGES

» Volatile Ingredient Prices

The price of critical commodity inputs such as corn, tree nuts, soybean and cottonseed oil, and potatoes can increase significantly due to poor farm yields, unpredictable weather patterns, and market reactions to government farm subsidies. Tree nuts can represent up to 50 percent of the total cost of goods sold. While potatoes are a less expensive input, the price of white potatoes has fluctuated 20 percent or more in seven of the past eight years.

» Highly Competitive Industry

The snack food industry competes with a number of other impulse purchases and snacking options, including cookies, crackers, candy, energy bars, in-store bakery items, fast food, and baking at home. Salty snacks are among the first foods eliminated or restricted for those on a weight-management plan. Snack food brands face growing competition from private label offerings, which offer comparable value at a lower price.

» Vulnerability to Litigation, Regulation

Increased awareness of obesity has made snack food manufacturers much more vulnerable to litigation and federal regulation. Manufacturers routinely face lawsuits from individuals who blame them for manufacturing addictive, unhealthy products. Olestra, a fat substitute used to make "light" chips, was once regarded as a revolutionary breakthrough, but manufacturers now face lawsuits over its potential digestive effects. Companies emphasize the importance of industry self-regulation and try to stay one step ahead of potential lawsuits and federal clampdowns on advertising, ingredients, and labeling claims.

spends around $80 on 32 pounds of salty snacks each year. Potato chips are the most popular US snack, representing 40 percent of all snack food consumption. Each year, Americans consume 4.6 pounds of potato chips per capita from nearly 20 pounds of farmed potatoes.

To make potato chips, manufacturers receive daily truckloads of fresh potatoes. Sources depend on the season: potatoes come from Florida in April and May, from Virginia and North Carolina in the summer, and the Dakotas in winter. Potatoes are stored in warehouses at 40 to 45 degrees and warmed to room temperature prior to processing.

A conveyor belt moves the potatoes through the various stages of manufacturing. Vibrating conveyors remove debris and push the potato to an automatic peeling machine. After peeling, potatoes are washed with cold water and enter a revolving impaler. Straight blades produce regular chips; rippled blades make ridged potato chips. A secondary wash rinses off excess starch from the newly sliced potatoes. "Natural" potato chips aren't washed and retain this starch.

The sliced potatoes move through air jets that remove excess water and enter a long trough filled with hot cottonseed, corn, or blended oil. Paddles push the chips along as they fry. Salt and flavorings are added as the chips cool. Cooled chips are conveyed to a packing machine, where computer-aided machines pack the chips and add air and nitrogen to the package prior to sealing. Workers handpack the bags into cartons and place them on pallets for warehousing. Rejected potatoes and peels are sent to farms for animal feed. The starch removed during rinsing is sold to starch processors.

A snack food manufacturer must have advanced quality control measures in place at all stages of processing. Optical sensors spot and discard defective chips. Quality control managers inspect incoming ingredients, test the viscosity of oils, and taste-sample every product, typically on the hour.

To reduce product shipping costs, companies typically operate multiple manufacturing plants across the US. Most plants are capable of manufacturing a range of products, though each plant usually specializes in one or two popular brands. Large companies manage a network of distribution centers for warehousing products prior to store delivery.

Common inputs for snacks include white potatoes; corn and wheat flour; cottonseed, corn, and soybean oil; shelled peanuts; flavorings like herbs, salt, and spices; and packaging materials. Key energy inputs include water, electricity, diesel, and natural gas.

Recent technological advances include automated quality control instrumentation, advancements in creating crunchier chips, baked snacks, and genetically modified (GM) potatoes and corn that result in more uniform chips and snacks. Most large companies manage real-time sales tracking using a network of handheld wireless devices and centralized enterprise resource planning (ERP) systems.

Sales & Marketing

Typical customers are grocery wholesalers, warehouse club stores, food service distributors, vending machine distributors, and convenience stores ("c-stores"). Depending on the customer's needs, sales can be consumer-sized or in bulk quantities. Supermarket sales account for around 50 percent of all snack sales. Warehouse clubs and mass merchandisers represent around 10 to 15 percent of sales; vending and food service, 5 to 10 percent.

Several companies specialize in producing private-label brands for supermarkets and c-stores. Market share can vary depending on the product: for potato chips, tortilla chips, and pretzels, private-labels account for around 5 percent of sales. Private-label market share for ready-to-eat (RTE) popcorn is 10 percent and 25 percent for mixed nuts.

Major sales channels include independent distributors, third-party brokers, internal sales forces, and direct store delivery (DSD) programs, where products are stocked and pulled by the company's own distribution arm. Many companies rely on a combination of these channels.

Major types of marketing include TV and radio ads; coupons in newspapers, magazines, and on the Internet; movie, TV, and celebrity tie-ins; "merchandising" through in-store discounts and end-cap promotions; sweepstakes; and product-specific websites. Since most large snack manufacturers are a division of a food conglomerate, end-caps and in-store promotions often feature complementary products (Pepsi and Doritos). Brand extension is common (Planters Peanut Oil, Skippy Snack Bars). Companies seek to maximize merchandising lift, the marginal gain in product sales volume from a price discount, feature in a store advertisement, or in-store promotion.

Customer service operations are extensive, as bad publicity can severely damage a brand. Media reports of foreign objects or animals in a snack bag can quickly overwhelm customer service operations. Most companies manage toll-free help lines and Web-based e-mail submission forms to address product questions and concerns.

Companies invest heavily in Internet promotions, developing interactive web sites around well-known brands. Most large processors manage restricted-access Intranets or electronic data interchange (EDI) systems to facilitate e-commerce transactions and manage inventory. Some small snack companies may specialize in online sales; typically, these sales are marketed as gift tins or baskets.

Typical product prices are $0.30 an ounce for potato, tortilla, and flavored corn chips and $0.25 to $0.50 an ounce for roasted nuts, depending on the variety. Private-labels cost 20 to 40 percent less than name brand. New reduced calorie or low-salt offerings are often more expensive per ounce. Distributors typically mark up prices 20 to 30 percent from the manufacturer's price; retailers add another 10 to 20 percent. Retailer consolidation has shifted the buying power from manufacturers to retailers.

Human Resources

Snack food manufacturing wages average $15 per hour, 15 percent lower than the national average. Production workers must have basic mechanical and technical skills to operate machinery and the physical strength to lift heavy objects. The Snack Food Association (SFA) has partnered with several universities, providing online education for managers. Courses include new product development, business plan writing, and international trade.

The annual injury rate in snack food manufacturing is nearly 20 percent higher than the national average. Common injuries are sprains and strains, cuts, and fractures. Injuries can be severe: twice as many cases last more than a month compared to the national average, and amputations are five times higher than the national average.

Industry Employment Growth

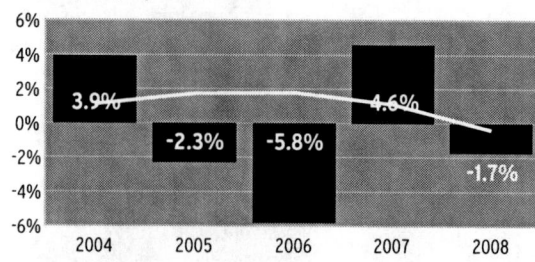

Average Hourly Earnings

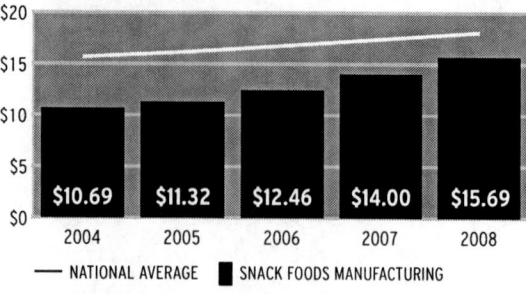

SOURCE: BUREAU OF LABOR STATISTICS

Call Preparation Questions

How does the company limit the risk of volatile commodity prices?

The price of critical commodity inputs such as corn, tree nuts, soybean and cottonseed oil, and potatoes can increase significantly due to poor farm yields, unpredictable weather patterns, and market reactions to government farm subsidies.

How difficult is raising prices to consumers?

The snack food industry competes with a number of other impulse purchases and snacking options, including cookies, crackers, candy, energy bars, in-store bakery items, fast food, and baking at home.

How challenging are the risks of increased litigation and regulation?

Increased awareness of obesity has made snack food manufacturers much more vulnerable to litigation and federal regulation.

What is the company's convenience store sales strategy?

Manufacturers have paid too little attention to maximizing the sales potential of snack foods at convenience stores (c-stores) and drugstores.

How can the company capitalize on the health benefits of tree nuts?

High in Omega-3s, tree nuts are one of the few true healthy snacks; however, the product category has lacked innovation for many years.

Web Links

American Bakers Association (ABA)

Trade association for bakeries and snack manufacturers.
www.americanbakers.org

American Institute of Baking (AIB)

Broad industry association that includes packaging companies and food suppliers.
www.aibonline.org

Private Label Magazine

News and insights into private label manufacturing.
www.privatelabelmag.com

Snack Food and Wholesale Bakery

News, interviews, and features on salty and sweet snacks.
www.snackandbakery.com

Snack Food Association

International trade association for the snack food industry.
www.sfa.org

Tortilla Industry Association

Industry association for tortilla and tortilla products.
www.tortilla-info.com

TrueNorth Snacks

All-natural snack line from Frito-Lay.
www.truenorthsnacks.com

Glossary of Acronyms

DSD — direct store delivery
EDI — electronic data interchange
ERP — enterprise resource planning
FALCPA — Food Allergen Labeling and Consumer Protection Act
GM — genetically modified
SFA — Snack Food Association
TIA — Tortilla Industry Association
USPB — United States Potato Board

HOOVER'S TOP COMPANIES

Largest Companies by Sales	($ mil.)
PepsiCo, Inc.	43,251.0
Kraft Foods Inc.	42,201.0
Kellogg Company	12,822.0
J & J Snack Foods Corp.	629.4
John B. Sanfilippo & Son, Inc.	541.8
Diamond Foods, Inc.	531.5
Kettle Foods, Inc.	184.7
Wise Foods, Inc.	82.7
Snyder's of Hanover, Inc.	—

Largest Employers	Employees
PepsiCo, Inc.	185,000
Kraft Foods Inc.	98,000
Kellogg Company	26,000
J & J Snack Foods Corp.	2,800
Wise Foods, Inc.	2,000
Utz Quality Foods, Inc.	1,800
John B. Sanfilippo & Son, Inc.	1,500
Herr Foods Inc.	1,200
Golden Enterprises, Inc.	991
Diamond Foods, Inc.	628

Fastest Growing* by Five-Year Sales Growth	(%)
Diamond Foods, Inc.	11.6
J & J Snack Foods Corp.	11.5
PepsiCo, Inc.	9.9
The Inventure Group, Inc.	8.9
Kellogg Company	7.8
Kraft Foods Inc.	6.4
John B. Sanfilippo & Son, Inc.	5.2
Golden Enterprises, Inc.	3.3

Fastest Growing* by Five-Year Employee Growth	(%)
PepsiCo, Inc.	8.6
J & J Snack Foods Corp.	6.0
The Inventure Group, Inc.	1.3
Kellogg Company	0.8

Top Public Companies by Market Value	($ mil.)
PepsiCo, Inc.	84,731.7
Kraft Foods Inc.	39,450.7
Kellogg Company	17,202.8
J & J Snack Foods Corp.	640.6
Diamond Foods, Inc.	393.5

* These rates are compounded annualized increases and may have resulted from acquisitions or one time gains. If less than 6 years of data are available, growth is for the years available.

SOURCE: HOOVER'S, INC., DATABASE

Soap and Detergent Manufacture

The soap and detergent manufacturing industry includes about 700 companies with combined annual revenue of $17 billion. Major companies in the consumer sector include divisions of Procter & Gamble (P&G); Unilever; and Dial. Major companies in the commercial sector include divisions of Ecolab and US Chemical. The industry is highly concentrated: the top 50 companies hold almost 90 percent of the market.

Competitive Landscape

Population growth, particularly among households with children, drives demand in the consumer sector, and economic growth drives demand in the commercial sector. The profitability of individual companies depends on efficient operations and effective sales and marketing. Large companies have scale advantages in purchasing, manufacturing, distribution, and marketing. Small companies can compete effectively by offering specialized products, providing superior customer service, or serving a local market. The industry is capital-intensive: average annual revenue per worker is more than $700,000.

The industry is about evenly split between the consumer and commercial segments. Both segments are highly competitive, and large companies spend millions to maintain market share.

Products, Operations & Technology

Major products include laundry detergent, soap, dishwashing detergent, and toothpaste. Laundry detergent accounts for 40 percent of industry revenue, soap for 20 percent, and dishwashing detergent for 15 percent. Laundry detergent comes in powder or liquid form, and may contain bleach additives or color brighteners. Dishwashing detergent comes in powder, liquid, or gel form. Soap comes in bars or liquids, and may have moisturizing, antibacterial,

or deodorant benefits. Companies in the commercial sector may also sell dispensing equipment and provide related training.

Detergent production starts by combining liquid and dry ingredients. Spray drying produces powder detergents by spraying the liquid mixture through nozzles under high pressure to create small droplets. The droplets fall through hot air and dry into hollow granules. Heat-sensitive ingredients, such as bleach or fragrance, are added after spray drying. Agglomeration produces higher density detergent powders by using a liquid binder and a different mixing process known as "rolling" or "shear mixing." Dry blending mixes dry raw materials with small quantities of liquids. Detergents are packaged in cartons, bottles, pouches, or bags.

Soap production starts by heating fatty acids or fats and oils, and combining them with alkali, such as sodium or potassium. The process, known as saponification or neutralization, produces a combination of soap and water (known as neat soap) plus glycerin, which can be resold. Neat soap is converted into dry soap pellets through vacuum drying. An amalgamator mixes pellets with fragrances and colors. Rolling mills and refining plodders refine the mixture to achieve uniform texture. The final mixture is extruded, cut into bars, and stamped into shapes in a soap press. Soap bars are wrapped and packaged into single or multiple packs.

Soaps and detergents are made of surfactants or surface-active agents, chemicals that help water soak and clean surfaces. Many surfactants are petroleum-based. Oleochemicals are surfactants derived from natural fats and oils. Soap reacts with minerals in hard water, diminishing cleaning properties. Builders boost the efficiency of surfactants by counteracting hard water, emulsifying oil and grease, and preventing soil from redepositing. Phosphates, an environmentally controversial chemical, are a commonly used builder.

Raw materials include surfactants, solvents, phosphates, silicates, alkalis, salts, and perfumes. Suppliers include major chemical manufacturers like Shell Chemical and Dow. P&G has a separate business unit that manufactures key chemicals as part of a global supply network. Companies may rely on or provide third-party contract manufacturing services. Large companies may own multiple plants, including many facilities outside the US.

Soap and detergent manufacturing is highly automated, and involves significant capital investment in plants and equipment. Computers control production equipment and inventory management. Due to the high level of automation, the average plant has fewer than 20 employees.

R&D involves creating, testing, and improving product formulation, and evaluating environmental compatibility. Technological advances have reduced the amount of product needed, thereby reducing the amount of packaging. Micro encapsulation technology allows manufacturers to deliver unstable ingredients, like vitamin C, through soap to the skin. Manufacturers also test new enzymes and bleaches that improve the efficacy of products.

Sales & Marketing

Major customers for the consumer segment include supermarket chains, mass merchandisers, drugstores, and warehouse clubs; major customers for the commercial segment include industrial and commercial laundries, hotels, restaurants, and health care providers. Most companies also sell to third-party distributors.

Marketing and promotional vehicles for the consumer segment include TV and magazine advertising, coupons, direct mail, and websites. Brand names, such as Tide and Dial, are extremely important in the consumer segment.

Large companies use an in-house sales force. Large and small companies use independent distributors to service smaller accounts. In the commercial segment, trade shows are an important sales vehicle. Superior service is also critical in maintaining long-term relationships with large customers.

Retail pricing for laundry detergent averages $5, dishwashing detergent $2, and soap $2.50. Private-label products sell for 20 to 50 percent less than branded versions.

Human Resources

Due to the high level of automation at many manufacturing facilities, most production jobs require few skills and wages for production personnel are slightly below the national average. Fringe benefits average 20 percent of payroll. Automation has also resulted in an average injury rate well below the US average for all workers. Research and development employees often have advanced degrees in chemistry or microbiology.

Some US manufacturing facilities are covered by labor agreements. Companies with operations outside the US may be subject to local work councils or labor unions.

Industry Employment Growth

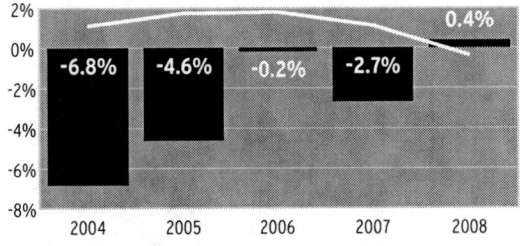

Average Hourly Earnings

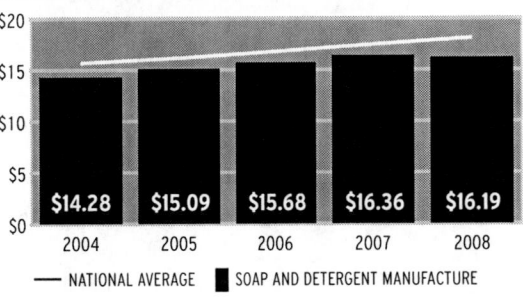

— NATIONAL AVERAGE ■ SOAP AND DETERGENT MANUFACTURE

SOURCE: BUREAU OF LABOR STATISTICS

Call Preparation Questions

How has slow growth in wholesale pricing affected the company's profitability?

Market maturity and heavy competition have depressed growth in wholesale prices for soaps and detergents.

What challenges does the company face complying with environmental regulations?

Manufacturers must comply with differing state and country environmental regulations.

What trends has the company seen with multi-purpose products?

As consumers demand higher performance from cleaning products, manufacturers of large brands deliver line extensions that serve multiple needs.

How important are specialty products to the company?

Market maturity has driven manufacturers to offer specialized products to generate growth.

Web Links

American Oil Chemists' Society

Information on surfactants and other raw materials. Technological trends.

www.aocs.org

Chemical Week Magazine

Publications, articles, indexes, news, and numerous links to related sites.

www.chemweek.com

Ecolab

Industrial and commercial soap and detergent manufacturer.

www.ecolab.com

Household and Personal Products Industry (HAPPI)

Industry trends.

www.happi.com

Soap and Detergent Association

Trade association representing manufacturers, government regulations, consumer affairs, trends.

www.sdahq.org

soapdetergents.com

International open marketplace and resource center for soap, detergents, and household cleaning products.

www.soapdetergents.com

Glossary of Acronyms

HAPPI — Household and Personal Products Industry
HE — high efficiency (washers)
IRI — Information Resources, Inc.

LAS — linear alkylbenzene sulfonates (commonly used petroleum-based surfactant)
P&G — Procter & Gamble
SDSI — Safer Detergents Stewardship Initiative

HOOVER'S TOP COMPANIES

Largest Companies by Sales	($ mil.)
The Procter & Gamble Company	83,503.0
Colgate-Palmolive Company	15,329.9
Avon Products, Inc.	10,690.1
S.C. Johnson & Son, Inc.	8,750.0
Alticor Inc.	7,168.0
Ecolab Inc.	6,137.5
The Clorox Company	5,273.0
Bath & Body Works, Inc.	2,422.4
Church & Dwight Co., Inc.	2,422.4

Largest Employers	Employees
The Procter & Gamble Company	138,000
Avon Products, Inc.	42,000
Colgate-Palmolive Company	36,000
Ecolab Inc.	26,050
Alticor Inc.	14,000
S.C. Johnson & Son, Inc.	12,000
The Clorox Company	8,300
Church & Dwight Co., Inc.	3,700
The Sun Products Corporation	3,000
The Dial Corporation	2,900

Fastest Growing* by Five-Year Sales Growth	(%)
Pacific Sands, Inc.	58.5
Kyzen Corporation	20.7
Church & Dwight Co., Inc.	18.0
Natural Health Trends Corp.	15.6
The Procter & Gamble Company	14.0
Ecolab Inc.	10.3
Avon Products, Inc.	9.2
Colgate-Palmolive Company	9.1
The Clorox Company	4.9
Zep Inc.	2.4

Fastest Growing* by Five-Year Employee Growth	(%)
Ecolab Inc.	7.8
The Clorox Company	3.0

Top Public Companies by Market Value	($ mil.)
The Procter & Gamble Company	184,419.5
Colgate-Palmolive Company	34,366.8
Avon Products, Inc.	10,244.0
Ecolab Inc.	8,302.4
The Clorox Company	7,205.6

* These rates are compounded annualized increases and may have resulted from acquisitions or one time gains. If less than 6 years of data are available, growth is for the years available.

SOURCE: HOOVER'S, INC., DATABASE

Specialty Food Stores

The specialty food store industry includes about 20,000 stores with combined annual revenue of $20 billion. Major companies include Whole Foods Market and Trader Joe's. The industry is fragmented: the 50 largest companies have less than 50 percent of sales.

The industry includes gourmet food stores, natural/organic food stores, health food stores, meat or seafood markets, fruit and vegetable markets, bakeries, and candy and nut stores.

Competitive Landscape

Consumer spending and tastes drive demand. The profitability of individual companies depends on effective merchandising and the ability to generate store traffic. Large companies can offer a wide selection of products and have advantages in purchasing, distribution, and marketing. Small companies can compete effectively by offering specialty products, providing superior service, or serving a local market. The industry is labor-intensive: average annual revenue per worker is about $100,000.

Competition includes traditional grocery stores, mass merchandisers, and warehouse clubs. Specialty food stores also compete with any venue serving food, including restaurants.

Products, Operations & Technology

Major products sold by specialty food stores include meat, fish, and poultry (40 percent of sales); produce (15 percent); and baked goods and candy (10 percent each). Other products include dry grocery products, dairy products, prepared foods, and kitchenware. Companies may place special orders for customers looking for unique items.

Specialty food stores include chains, independent retailers, franchises, and cooperatives. Franchises include companies such as Great Harvest Bakery, Cinnabon, and Rocky Mountain Chocolate Factory. Specialty food cooperatives are typically member-owned and -operated.

BUSINESS CHALLENGES

» Competition from Alternative Retailers

Specialty food stores face intense competition from grocery stores and mass merchandisers. Grocery stores hold almost 70 percent of specialty food sales, according to Mintel. To capitalize on growing demand, some large retailers are expanding specialty food selections and carrying more organic and gourmet products. In 2006, Target launched a certified organic line of private-label foods and Wal-Mart announced plans to expand organic food sections.

» Dependence on Consumer Spending

While food purchases are generally stable regardless of economic conditions, consumer spending can affect sales of specialty foods. Most specialty foods are considered luxury items and typically have higher retail prices than traditional grocery items. Consumers may switch to less expensive food products or stop buying high-end items when money is tight.

» Regulatory Changes Affect Operations

Changes in government regulations can affect the availability, formulation, and marketing of specialty food products. Certain segments of the specialty food industry, especially natural and organic foods, are highly regulated. The organic food market is relatively young, and future modifications to standards are likely. Regulatory changes could require reformulating or discontinuing products, altering handling procedures, and keeping additional records.

Store size and format can differ significantly. A large specialty grocery store can exceed 20,000 square feet, while a candy store can be less than 1,000. Companies may use a kiosk format to offer a small selection of products and to fit into non-traditional spaces.

Store layout is typically organized by product type, and companies often place complementary departments near each other to promote incremental sales. Specialty food stores may have instore bakeries, kitchens, or delis (also known as charcuteries). Retailers offering organic food must follow strict procedures to prevent contact with non-organic foods and substances. Organic merchandise also requires companies to keep records regarding product handling and vendor relationships.

Merchandise mix helps determine locations. For example, specialty grocery stores with a broad range of products may seek out strip malls or areas with other large retailers to help drive traffic. Because customers are willing to travel to buy unique merchandise, stores specializing in a few categories (meat or produce markets) may be farther from major shopping areas. When evaluating store locations, companies typically consider population density, traffic patterns, tenant mix, visibility, and accessibility. Because specialty food products tend to appeal to affluent consumers, companies may also consider education and income levels for the surrounding area.

Specialty grocery stores offer categories similar to traditional supermarkets, but stock unique or hard to find products within each category. Popular specialty food categories include specialty coffee/tea, olive oil/specialty oil, cheese, and chocolate. Companies may also focus on a particular category, such as baked goods. Stores specializing in ethnic foods offer imported merchandise. Perishables, such as produce and meat, require careful inventory management due to potential spoilage. Some specialty food stores offer private-label products.

While companies may buy directly from manufacturers, distributors and farm cooperatives are important because the supply and retail segments for many categories in the specialty food industry are highly fragmented. Large companies may have multi-year contracts with key suppliers and enjoy volume discounts. Small companies may join cooperatives to leverage increased purchasing power. Chains often have separate distribution centers for products requiring special handling, such as seafood.

Most specialty food retailers use computerized information systems to manage point-of-sale (POS) transactions and inventory movement. POS systems use scanners to track individual items by Universal Product Codes (UPC). Integrated systems linking sales and inventory allow companies to identify fast- and slow-moving products and minimize out-of-stocks and excess inventory. Large companies may use price-optimization software to maximize profitability. Voice-activated stock picking improves the efficiency of warehouse operations.

Sales & Marketing

The typical specialty food customer is a young, affluent adult. Surprisingly, gender doesn't play a significant role in demographics, as specialty food appeals to both men and women, according to Mintel. Specialty food consumers cook meals from scratch almost three times weekly. Ethnic food stores typically rely on a customer base of immigrants.

Marketing and promotional vehicles include instore signage, newspaper and print advertising, direct mail, and coupons. Grassroots marketing and word-of-mouth are important to generate awareness, as most companies have relatively small marketing budgets. Product tastings, cooking classes, and sampling help create excitement and draw traffic. Stores may sponsor local events or charities to develop community support.

Superior service can be especially important because the specialty food customer is typically a food enthusiast. Knowledgeable workers help customers find uncommon ingredients, make meal suggestions, and help with recipes. Upon request, a retailer may place special orders for products not normally stocked.

Specialty food stores may have websites offering store and product information, price promotions, recipes, or nutritional advice. Companies with highly specialized merchandise can reach customers beyond local markets by offering products for sale through the Internet. Through websites, specialty food retailers may also sell exotic foods not found in stores.

The average transaction in a specialty food store is about $30, according to Mintel. Specialty food products are typically premium priced compared to traditional grocery products.

Human Resources

In general, workers in specialty food stores require minimal skills and wages are 30 percent lower than the average for all US workers. Companies may rely on part-time or temporary workers. Positions involving direct food handling, such as meat-cutting or food preparation, require training in safety and sanitation procedures. Unions have tried to organize workers of some large specialty food retailers.

The industry injury rate is slightly higher than the US average, with more employees suffering from cuts and carpal tunnel syndrome. Jobs involving handling and processing meat, poultry, and seafood account for the higher injury rate.

Industry Employment Growth

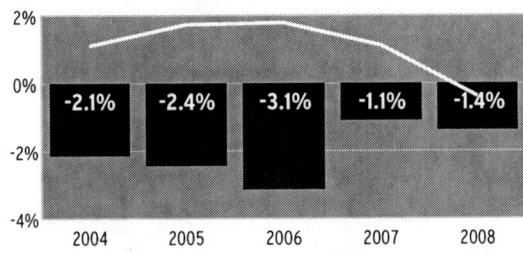

	2004	2005	2006	2007	2008
	-2.1%	-2.4%	-3.1%	-1.1%	-1.4%

Average Hourly Earnings

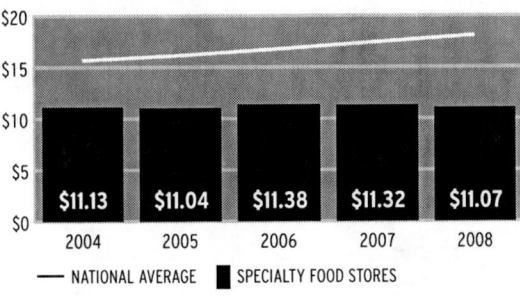

	2004	2005	2006	2007	2008
	$11.13	$11.04	$11.38	$11.32	$11.07

— NATIONAL AVERAGE ■ SPECIALTY FOOD STORES

SOURCE: BUREAU OF LABOR STATISTICS

Call Preparation Questions

How does the company compete with large retailers, such as grocery stores and mass merchandisers?

Specialty food stores face intense competition from grocery stores and mass merchandisers.

How do changes in consumer spending affect the company's business?

While food purchases are generally stable regardless of economic conditions, consumer spending can affect sales of specialty foods.

How have regulatory changes affected how the company operates?

Changes in government regulations can affect the availability, formulation, and marketing of specialty food products.

How unique are the company's products?

Unique merchandise helps specialty food retailers differentiate from competition and justify premium pricing.

What role does the Internet play in the company's business?

Internet retailing offers specialty food stores ways to reach more customers and sell a broader range of products.

Web Links

Food Marketing Institute

News, trends, statistics, government and regulatory issues for the food industry.
www.fmi.org

Gourmet Retailer

News and trends for specialty food and housewares industries.
www.gourmetretailer.com

Progressive Grocer

News, trends, statistics for grocery retail industry.
www.progressivegrocer.com

Specialty Food.com

News, trends, and annual survey from National Association for the Specialty Food Trade.
www.specialtyfood.com/do/Home

The Natural Foods Merchandiser

News and trends for the natural foods market.
www.naturalfoodsmerchandiser.com

Whole Foods

Leading organic/natural foods retailer.
www.wholefoods.com

Glossary of Acronyms

CPSC — Consumer Products Safety Commission
POS — point-of-sale
NASFT — National Association for the Specialty Food Trade
UPC — Universal Product Code

HOOVER'S TOP COMPANIES

Largest Employers	Employees
Whole Foods Market, Inc.	52,900
TAWA Supermarket, Inc.	1,300
Dean & DeLuca	765
Citarella	600
Earth Fare, Inc.	350
Tastefully Simple, Inc.	300
Hickory Farms, Inc.	250
Grace's Marketplace	160
Great Harvest Franchising, Inc.	30

SOURCE: HOOVER'S, INC., DATABASE

Sporting Goods Manufacturing

THIS INDUSTRY INCLUDES:

SIC CODES
3949   Sporting and Athletic Goods

NAICS CODES
339920   Sporting and Athletic Goods Manufacturing

About 2,000 US sporting goods manufacturing companies operate in the US, with combined sales of about $14 billion. Large companies include Callaway Golf Company; Easton-Bell Sports; Russell Corporation; Wilson Sporting Goods (a subsidiary of Finland-based Amer Sports); and Rawlings Sporting Goods (a subsidiary of Jarden Corporation). The industry is fragmented: the 10 largest sporting goods companies account for only about 35 percent of industry revenue.

Competitive Landscape

The primary demand drivers for sporting goods are consumer income and demographic trends. The profitability of individual companies is determined by efficient manufacturing and effective marketing. Large companies enjoy advantages in economies of scale and brand recognition, and often offer a wide range of products. Small companies can compete effectively by offering specialized or unique products that interest enthusiasts. Average annual revenue per employee is about $250,000.

Products, Operations & Technology

Major products include golf (excluding apparel and shoes), gym and exercise, playground, and fishing tackle and equipment, and other sporting and athletic goods. General sporting and athletic goods include equipment used to play racket sports such as tennis, badminton, and squash; and team sports including baseball, basketball, football, soccer, and hockey. General sporting and athletic goods and golf equipment each account for about 25 percent of industry revenue; gym and exercise equipment for about 20 percent.

Products are used generally for recreation and fitness. Some products, primarily those for team sports, are also sold to collegiate, amateur, and interscholastic organizations. Specific com-

BUSINESS CHALLENGES

» Dependence on Discretionary Spending

The sporting goods industry relies heavily on consumer disposable income. The industry depends on the general health of the US economy and the economies of key export markets in Europe and Asia. Factors, including unemployment levels, energy costs, interest rates, and inflation, strongly affect demand for sporting goods.

» Short Product Life Cycles

Due to shifting consumer interests and desire for increased innovation, sporting goods product life cycles can be quite short, often less than two years. A company's design and R&D departments are constantly challenged to predict consumer preferences and effectively deliver desirable products that address those preferences. New products must meet consumer expectations, and be priced at levels that increase revenue relative to the product they replaced.

» Competition from Imports

US companies face intense competition from imported sporting goods. Japan produces high-quality, premium sporting goods such as fishing lures and golf equipment. Developing countries including China, Thailand, and Vietnam can offer competitive prices due to low wage costs.

panies may also supply products to professional sports leagues.

A wide variety of manufacturing processes are used to produce various types of sporting goods including metal, plastic, and woodworking operations and tooling; assembly; packaging; supply chain coordination; and shipping. Although much sporting goods manufacture is automated, some processes, such as golf club assembly, can be fairly labor-intensive. Most manufacturing operations have fewer than 200 employees.

Raw materials include wood, steel, aluminum, plastics and resins, fiberglass, textiles, and packaging. Products are generally shipped directly to retailers and sporting goods distributors. Third-party warehouses and logistics providers are often used to bring products to market.

Products often are designed and manufactured using CAD and computer-aided manufacturing (CAM) software. R&D can be important in creating product innovation that can be used to market products as offering a competitive advantage. Companies typically spend about 1 to 3 percent of revenue on R&D. Supply chain management systems electronically link suppliers and customers with manufacturing and assembly facilities. Technology is also used to implement just-in-time strategies that reduce inventory needs while shortening product delivery times.

Sales & Marketing

Sporting goods manufacturers typically sell products through sporting goods retailers, off- and on-course golf equipment retailers, department stores, mass merchandisers, and third-party distributors. Certain manufacturers may also sell directly to consumers via company websites. Large customers for sporting goods include Wal-Mart, Target, Kmart, Dick's Sporting Goods, and The Sports Authority. Sales forces are usually organized geographically.

Companies often have recognized brand names that are commonly promoted using endorsement tie-ins with professional sports leagues and teams, and individual professional athletes. Some manufacturers advertise their products in magazines, and on TV and the Internet, targeting enthusiasts of particular sports, namely golf. Others, such as makers of ping pong tables and playground equipment, work with retailers on product promotion and don't directly advertise to consumers.

Prices for sporting goods vary considerably due to the wide variety of specific products. Prices for specific products can also vary significantly, depending on quality and brand. A set of golf clubs can cost from just over $100 to nearly $1,000. A basketball may cost less than $20, but a basketball goal can cost as much as $1,000. Large manufacturers tend to offer a number of different models of a specific product across a spectrum of prices to accommodate various budgets and skill levels.

Human Resources

Generally, workers in the sporting goods manufacturing industry aren't highly skilled, and earn slightly less than the average for all

US production workers. While union participation is typically minimal, some sporting goods workers may be represented by labor unions, which periodically engage in collective bargaining for wages and benefits.

The injury rate in the sporting goods manufacturing industry is about the same as manufacturing in general, about six annually per 100 employees.

Industry Employment Growth

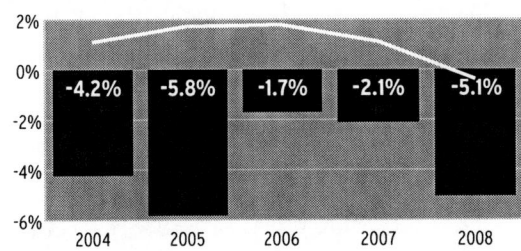

Average Hourly Earnings

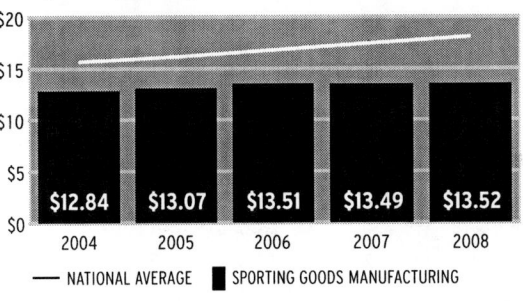

SOURCE: BUREAU OF LABOR STATISTICS

Call Preparation Questions

What trend is the company seeing in demand?

The sporting goods industry relies heavily on consumer disposable income.

How long are the company's product life cycles?

Due to shifting consumer interests and desire for increased innovation, sporting goods product life cycles can be quite short, often less than two years.

How much competition does the company face from imported sporting goods?

US companies face intense competition from imported sporting goods.

What opportunities does the company see in emerging markets like China?

As more people in developing nations such as China and India enter the middle class, demand for sporting goods is likely to increase.

How has growth in sales of used sporting goods affected the company's business?

Pre-owned sporting goods purchases have become a $1 billion per year business, according to the National Sporting Goods Association (NSGA).

Web Links

Callaway Golf Company

Manufacturer of golf equipment.
www.callawaygolf.com

National Sporting Goods Association

Trade association for sporting goods retailers.
www.nsga.org

Rawlings Sporting Goods Company

Manufacturer of team sports equipment.
www.rawlings.com

Sporting Goods Intelligence

News, analysis, and information about the sporting
goods market.
www.sginews.com/sginews

Sporting Goods Manufacturers Association

Trade association for sporting goods manufacturers.
www.sgma.com

Sporting Goods Newswire

Sporting goods company and industry news.
www.sportinggoodsnewswire.com

Sports One Source

Sporting goods industry information.
www.sportsonesource.com

Wilson Sporting Goods Company

Manufacturer of sporting goods.
www.wilson.com/wilson/home

Glossary of Acronyms

CAD — computer-aided design
NSGA — National Sporting Goods Association
PHIT — The Personal Health and Investment Act
SGMA — Sporting Goods Manufacturers Association

HOOVER'S TOP COMPANIES

Largest Companies by Sales	($ mil.)
Jarden Corporation (Rawlings Sporting Goods)	5,383.3
Callaway Golf Company	1,117.2
Easton-Bell Sports, Inc.	724.6
Russell Corporation	561.8
Wilson Sporting Goods Co.	556.8
Acushnet Company	481.3
Johnson Outdoors Inc.	420.8
Volcom, Inc.	334.3
Bauer NIKE Hockey Inc.	215.7
TaylorMade-adidas Golf	—

Largest Employers	Employees
Jarden Corporation (Rawlings Sporting Goods)	25,000
Russell Corporation	7,000
Acushnet Company	4,600
Callaway Golf Company	3,000
Wilson Sporting Goods Co.	2,440
Easton-Bell Sports, Inc.	2,248
Johnson Outdoors Inc.	1,400
Bauer NIKE Hockey Inc.	950
True Temper Sports, Inc.	807
PlayCore, Inc.	700

Fastest Growing* by Five-Year Sales Growth	(%)
Jarden Corporation (Rawlings Sporting Goods)	55.7
Volcom, Inc.	34.4
Easton-Bell Sports, Inc.	29.4
Adams Golf, Inc.	12.4
Aldila, Inc.	7.2
Callaway Golf Company	6.5
Johnson Outdoors Inc.	5.9
Escalade, Incorporated	3.6
True Temper Sports, Inc.	1.6

Fastest Growing* by Five-Year Employee Growth	(%)
Easton-Bell Sports, Inc.	30.2
Volcom, Inc.	25.1
Jarden Corporation (Rawlings Sporting Goods)	19.5
Escalade, Incorporated	9.0
True Temper Sports, Inc.	7.5
Johnson Outdoors Inc.	2.5

Top Public Companies by Market Value	($ mil.)
Jarden Corporation (Rawlings Sporting Goods)	869.4
Callaway Golf Company	599.3
Volcom, Inc.	265.7
Escalade, Incorporated	117.2
Johnson Outdoors Inc.	99.3

* These rates are compounded annualized increases and may
have resulted from acquisitions or one time gains. If less
than 6 years of data are available, growth is for the years
available.

SOURCE: HOOVER'S, INC., DATABASE

Sporting Goods Retailers

THIS INDUSTRY INCLUDES:

SIC CODES

5941   Sporting Goods Stores and Bicycle Shops

NAICS CODES

45111   Sporting Goods Stores

The retail sporting goods industry in the US includes about 20,000 companies with combined annual revenue of $25 billion. Large chain operators include The Sports Authority, REI, and Hibbett Sports. The industry is highly fragmented: the 50 largest companies hold less than 50 percent of the market. Only about 150 companies have more than five stores. A typical store has $5 million of annual sales.

Competitive Landscape

Demand is driven by population demographics and consumer income. The profitability of individual companies depends on merchandising and marketing skills. Large chains have an advantage in stocking a wide variety of goods. Small companies can compete successfully by carrying a deeper product line in specialized sports, or by serving a local market. The industry is fairly labor-intensive: average annual revenue per employee is about $130,000.

Products, Operations & Technology

Major products are outdoor clothing and shoes, firearms, golf equipment, and bicycles. Clothing and shoes together account for about 25 percent of industry revenue, firearms 10 percent, bicycles and golf equipment 8 percent each. Other products include exercise, camping, and ski equipment; fishing tackle; and team sports equipment.

Sporting goods stores vary according to format and merchandise. Most chains operate stores of a single type. Large-format stores are from 20,000 to 100,000 square feet, stock a large number of items, and are typically found as anchor stores in strip malls or in stand-alone locations. Traditional sporting goods retail stores vary in size from 5,000 to 20,000 square feet, carry a more limited number of items, and are typically found in strip or enclosed malls. Specialty stores have a wide selection of items for just one or two sports, such as golf, tennis,

BUSINESS CHALLENGES

» Dependence on Consumer Income

The revenue of sporting goods stores is sensitive to the health of the economy, as most sports are a leisure activity. Spending on sporting goods correlates strongly with gains in consumer income. During the last recession, for example, sporting goods sales were flat, following years of 7 percent growth.

» Slower Growth of Athlete Population

Demographics play a big part in sporting goods sales, since population growth and age groups affect sport participation. The number of Americans 5 to 19, the most athletically active segment of the population, will increase just 1 percent from 2000 to 2010. The more affluent and still active group, 20 to 45, will have virtually no growth.

» Competition from Mass Merchants

Large discounters like Wal-Mart with big sports departments have rapidly expanded in recent years. Wal-Mart now sells almost $10 billion of sporting goods and toys.

skiing, camping, etc.; are typically 1,000 to 10,000 square feet; and located in enclosed and strip malls. Large-format stores typically have more than $5 million in annual revenue and more than 50 employees. Specialty stores have less than $1 million in annual revenue and fewer than ten employees. Sporting goods are also sold by mass merchandisers like Wal-Mart, Kmart, and Target, and by catalog and Internet retailers like Cabela's and LL Bean.

Although large chains can sell a broad range of merchandise at lower prices, small local stores can successfully compete by offering better service or specializing in a particular sport. Because the equipment for many sports is very technical, knowledgeable salespeople are a strong competitive factor. The operations of sporting goods stores are fairly straightforward:

companies acquire merchandise, determine store layout, train employees, advertise goods, provide services, sell goods, and manage inventory.

Product is acquired from manufacturers and about 1,000 wholesale distributors. Manufacturers regularly introduce new models, which often have only minor changes from older models. Trade shows are an important way of finding out about new products. The type of merchandise purchased varies according to the season and regional and local preferences. Large-format stores may carry up to 100,000 separate items (stock keeping units — SKUs). Sports Authority stores usually carry 40,000 SKUs, with a range of brands in about 30 different sports categories. Sports Authority buys from 750 vendors. Specialty stores carry significantly fewer items. In addition to equipment, most retailers sell sports apparel and shoes. Nike, mainly a manufacturer of shoes and sports clothing, is one of the biggest vendors to Sports Authority, accounting for more than 10 percent of its merchandise.

Store layouts and merchandise presentation are often changed, especially in large-format stores that try to maintain the atmosphere of a collection of specialty departments. Layout and presentation may be designed with the help of special software from companies like Marketmax. Because much sports equipment is highly specialized, employees must be trained to understand and explain differences. Companies typically try to recruit employees who are avid sports participants. Many companies rely on part-time employees for 50 percent or more of their workforce.

Inventory management is a major concern for all sporting goods retailers because of the large numbers of items they sell and the short selling season for many sports. Chains usually supply their stores from a central distribution facility, with weekly resupply based on sales. Hibbett Sports supplies 280 stores from a single 200,000 square foot distribution facility. Many companies use highly sophisticated computerized inventory management systems that include point-of-sale (POS) terminals, scanners, and handheld radio frequency terminals to record merchandise receipts, print pricing labels, monitor inventory levels, facilitate automatic inventory replenishment, and identify popular items.

Sales & Marketing

Marketing is typically through a combination of advertising and promotional events. Advertising is most often through newspaper ads,

inserts, direct mailings, and billboards. Stores often have special sales associated with seasonal sports, like skiing. Many companies sponsor local sports events or competitions and host store appearances by sports celebrities. Stores provide technical services, such as racquet stringing, skate sharpening, ski adjustments, bike overhauls, etc. to build customer loyalty. Some stores feature "participation areas," like basketball hoops and climbing walls. In addition to selling individual items, many stores specialize in selling team uniforms and equipment to local schools and clubs. To promote products, many manufacturers provide cooperative marketing funds to retailers.

Human Resources

Employees in retail operations are involved mostly in stocking shelves, operating cash registers, and answering customer questions. This largely unskilled work pays low wages. Companies try to get and keep employees with special technical knowledge about sports and sports equipment, particularly in specialty stores. Employee turnover in retail sales is typically high, around 30 to 50 percent annually.

Like other retailers, sporting goods companies rely heavily on part-timers because of uneven customer traffic during the day, week, and year. Since part-time workers usually receive only minimal benefits, the total cost of benefits is small relative to payroll expense. The indirect benefits given to workers are discounts of 15 to 25 percent on what they buy.

Industry Employment Growth

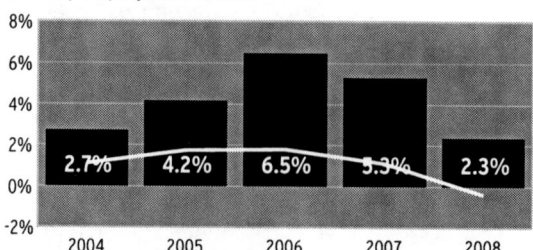

Average Hourly Earnings

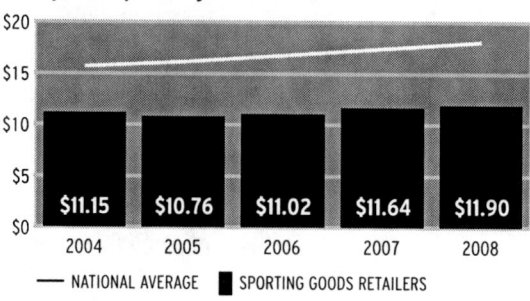

— NATIONAL AVERAGE ■ SPORTING GOODS RETAILERS

SOURCE: BUREAU OF LABOR STATISTICS

Call Preparation Questions

How does the company manage changes in demand during an economic slowdown?

The revenue of sporting goods stores is sensitive to the health of the economy, as most sports are a leisure activity.

How does the company encourage greater sports participation?

Demographics play a big part in sporting goods sales, since population growth and age groups affect sport participation.

How does the company address rising competition from mass merchants?

Large discounters like Wal-Mart with big sports departments have rapidly expanded in recent years.

How does the company capture sales from affluent older athletes?

Even though sports participation drops as people age, older athletes have more money to spend on sporting goods.

Web Links

American Sports Data

Market research company.
www.americansportsdata.com

National Association of Sporting Goods Wholesalers

Mainly hunting and fishing.
www.nasgw.org

National Sporting Goods Association

Industry statistics. Trade show calendar. Issues.
www.nsga.org/i4a/pages/index.cfm?pageid=1

Sporting Goods Manufacturers Association

News. Industry research.
www.sgma.com

SportsOneSource

News on the industry.
www.sportsonesource.com

Glossary of Acronyms

NSGA — National Sporting Goods Association
POS — point-of-sale
SGMA — Sporting Goods Manufacturers Association
SGMAI — Sporting Goods Manufacturers Association International

HOOVER'S TOP COMPANIES

Largest Companies by Sales	($ mil.)
Dick's Sporting Goods, Inc.	3,888.4
The Sports Authority, Inc.	2,980.0
Bass Pro Shops, Inc.	2,650.0
Cabela's Incorporated	2,552.7
Academy Sports & Outdoors, Ltd.	2,100.0
Recreational Equipment, Inc.	1,342.0
Gander Mountain Company	969.4
Big 5 Sporting Goods Corporation	864.7
Affinity Group, Inc.	562.2
Hibbett Sports, Inc.	520.7

Largest Employers	Employees
Dick's Sporting Goods, Inc.	26,400
The Sports Authority, Inc.	15,825
Cabela's Incorporated	15,000
Bass Pro Shops, Inc.	14,000
Academy Sports & Outdoors, Ltd.	13,000
Recreational Equipment, Inc.	10,000
Big 5 Sporting Goods Corporation	8,900
Gander Mountain Company	6,238
Hibbett Sports, Inc.	5,400
Sport Chalet, Inc.	4,300

Fastest Growing* by Five-Year Sales Growth	(%)
Sport Supply Group, Inc.	64.1
Dick's Sporting Goods, Inc.	25.0
The Sports Authority, Inc.	23.2
Gander Mountain Company	22.1
Dover Saddlery, Inc.	13.8
Bass Pro Shops, Inc.	13.6
Hibbett Sports, Inc.	13.3
Cabela's Incorporated	12.9
Recreational Equipment, Inc.	12.8
Sport Chalet, Inc.	11.1

Fastest Growing* by Five-Year Employee Growth	(%)
Dover Saddlery, Inc.	43.0
Cabela's Incorporated	21.9
Dick's Sporting Goods, Inc.	21.7
The Sports Authority, Inc.	17.4
Sport Supply Group, Inc.	16.7
Recreational Equipment, Inc.	15.4
Sport Chalet, Inc.	13.6
Hibbett Sports, Inc.	12.8
Golfsmith International Holdings, Inc.	11.9
Big 5 Sporting Goods Corporation	4.6

Top Public Companies by Market Value	($ mil.)
Dick's Sporting Goods, Inc.	2,793.7
Hibbett Sports, Inc.	561.4
Cabela's Incorporated	434.4
Sport Supply Group, Inc.	127.0
Big 5 Sporting Goods Corporation	114.7

* These rates are compounded annualized increases and may have resulted from acquisitions or one time gains. If less than 6 years of data are available, growth is for the years available.

SOURCE: HOOVER'S, INC., DATABASE

Steel Distribution

In the US, about 10,000 companies distribute steel and other metals, with combined annual revenue of $110 billion. Large companies include Ryerson, Metals USA, Reliance Steel & Aluminum, and ThyssenKrupp Steel. The industry is fragmented: the 50 largest companies only hold about 50 percent of the market. A typical large distributor has annual sales of $50 million and around 35 employees.

Competitive Landscape

The health of the manufacturing and construction industries drives demand for steel. A distributor's sales volume determines profitability because many costs are fixed. Large distributors benefit from economies of scale in purchasing, processing, and distribution. Small companies can compete by specializing in particular products or offering special processing services.

Products, Operations & Technology

Steel products are made from carbon or alloy, stainless or specialty steels, and come in the form of sheets, plates, bars, rods, tubes, and structural items like rails and I-beams. In addition to selling steel mill products, distributors sell various processing services that customize products for particular customers. Because of the large number of steel products, most distributors specialize in the types of steel they carry and types of processing operations they perform. Different grades of metal and the varying thicknesses and sizes of materials result in a large variety of products. A large distributor may handle 85,000 products.

Although several large companies have grown by acquisition in the past decade, most distributors have just one facility and a very local customer base. Distributors handle about 25 percent of steel products in the US, including two-thirds of all stainless steel.

BUSINESS CHALLENGES

» Profits Tied to Manufacturing

The volume of steel demand depends on US manufacturing levels, which are cyclical. Since steel distributors operate with fairly low gross margins, they need high sales volume to be profitable. During the last recession, when US manufacturing activity declined 5 percent, production of primary metals dropped 17 percent.

» Volatile Prices Affect Inventory Values

Because distributors may hold substantial inventories, they're exposed to changes in the price of steel products. Although most distributors use the "last in first out" (LIFO) method of inventory accounting, in which the most recently acquired items are assumed to be the first sold, future profitability can be affected if prices are volatile. Steel prices can change more than 10 percent per year.

» Pre-Delivery Processing Raises Fixed Costs

The decision by many distributors to add manufacturing capabilities (pre-delivery processing) has increased fixed costs. While this strategy works well when manufacturing activity is high, it also exposes distributors to lower profitability when volume falls.

The two types of distribution operations are pure distributors and steel service centers. Pure distributors buy standard grades of metal in bulk from producers and resell them in smaller quantity to local end-users, mainly providing an inventory service. Steel service centers also buy in bulk and resell products in smaller quantities, but provide additional processing services that make the products more suitable for subsequent handling by the end-user. Such services include cut-to-length; leveling (cutting wide coils of steel into sheet lengths); slitting (cutting coils into a narrower width); coating; bending; blanking; cutting, pickling (using acid to remove surface corrosion); welding; and a large variety of other fairly simple manufacturing processes. At service centers that provide inventory management services and just-in-time (JIT) delivery services, 50 percent or more of orders typically involve some type of processing.

Suppliers include local steel mills and foreign suppliers that distributors often have long-term relationships with. Service centers are the single largest customer group of the US steel industry and serve about 300,000 customers. Long-term supply contracts are usually sought only if a distributor has long-term sales contracts to cover. Local suppliers are favored because of transportation costs. The lower cost of foreign steel sometimes makes it an attractive source for US distributors.

Inventory management is important for all steel distributors, especially those that provide inventory and JIT delivery. Many large distributors use sophisticated inventory/distribution information systems developed specifically for the metals service industry. These systems use bar coding on products, take electronic orders, and can link directly into a customer or supplier's computer system.

Sales & Marketing

Customers typically are in the machinery, metal products, auto parts, or construction industries. Most customers make small, frequent purchases. Prices can be volatile. Delivered price is the major competitive factor for sales of what are essentially commodity products, although reliability and the ability to provide quality processing are major factors. Most distributors have an in-house sales staff that gets new business by visiting prospective customers.

Distributors sell mainly to midsized companies that don't have sufficient demand to buy directly from steel producers. Big distributors also sell to smaller distributors. Most distributors have a large number of customers who make frequent, small purchases. Sales often depend on bidding for a piece of business following a request for quote (RFQ). Long-term contracts are rare, although long-term relationships with customers are the rule. Customers are usually located within about 250 miles of the distributor. Most distributors operate a fleet of delivery trucks.

Steel producers compete with distributors for large end-users that need basic products regularly and periodically, can directly feed them into their manufacturing process, and can tolerate long delivery times. Distributors serve customers who don't buy in quantity, buy irregularly, or can't wait for long delivery times.

Human Resources

Average wages for metals distribution workers are slightly higher than the national average. Annual personnel turnover in wholesaling is 29 percent.

Industry Employment Growth

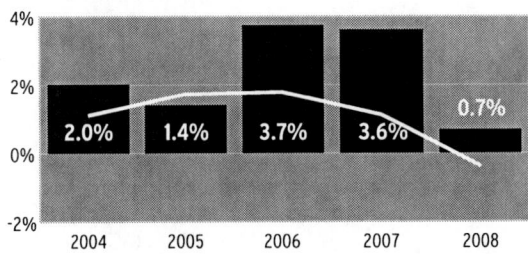

Average Hourly Earnings

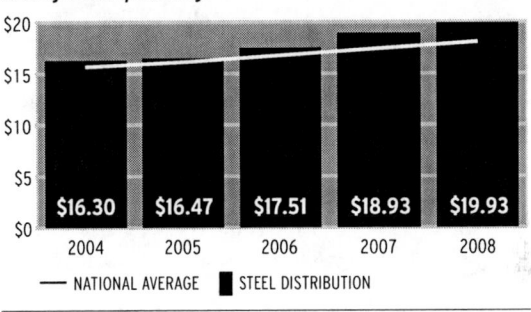

NATIONAL AVERAGE   ■ STEEL DISTRIBUTION

SOURCE: BUREAU OF LABOR STATISTICS

Call Preparation Questions

How does the company compensate for cyclical changes in demand?

The volume of steel demand depends on US manufacturing levels, which are cyclical.

How does the company protect itself against steel price changes?

Because distributors may hold substantial inventories, they're exposed to changes in the price of steel products.

What challenges does the company see in offering pre-processing capabilities?

The decision by many distributors to add manufacturing capabilities (pre-delivery processing) has increased fixed costs.

What plans does the company have to provide additional value-added services to customers?

Distributors provide a greater range of value-added services, as more customers outsource materials and supply chain functions in recent years.

To what extent does the company use e-commerce to extend its supply network?

Internet commerce has more potential on the supply side than on the customer side for distributors.

Web Links

American Iron and Steel Institute

Industry news, statistics, links.
www.steel.org

American Metal Market

Extensive industry news (subscription) and issues.
www.amm.com

Metal Center News

Industry news.
www.metalcenternews.com

Metals Service Center Institute

Government news.
www.msci.org

Steel.com

International news portal.
www.steel.com

SteelLinks.com

Search engine dedicated to the steel industry.
www.steellinks.com

The Association of Steel Distributors (ASD)

www.steeldistributors.org

The World Steel Association

World news.
www.worldsteel.org

Glossary of Acronyms

AISI — American Iron and Steel Institute
ASD — Association of Steel Distributors
ITC — International Trade Commission
JIT — just-in-time
LME — London Metal Exchange
MMT — million metric tons
MSCI — Metals Service Center Institute
RFQ — request for quote

HOOVER'S TOP COMPANIES

Largest Companies by Sales	($ mil.)
Reliance Steel & Aluminum Co.	8,718.8
Schnitzer Steel Industries, Inc.	3,641.6
Worthington Industries, Inc.	3,067.2
O'Neal Steel, Inc.	2,440.0
McJunkin Red Man Holding Corporation	2,267.5
Metals USA Holdings Corp.	1,845.3
Tang Industries, Inc.	1,650.0
Marubeni-Itochu Steel America Inc.	—
Ryerson Inc.	—
ThyssenKrupp Materials NA, Inc.	—

Largest Employers	Employees
Reliance Steel & Aluminum Co.	8,600
Worthington Industries, Inc.	6,900
Ryerson Inc.	5,700
O'Neal Steel, Inc.	4,400
Schnitzer Steel Industries, Inc.	3,669
Tang Industries, Inc.	3,600
McJunkin Red Man Holding Corporation	3,484
Metals USA Holdings Corp.	2,700
A. M. Castle & Co.	1,945
ThyssenKrupp Materials NA, Inc.	1,900

Fastest Growing* by Five-Year Sales Growth	(%)
Schnitzer Steel Industries, Inc.	48.9
Reliance Steel & Aluminum Co.	35.8
Blue Tee Corp.	29.7
McJunkin Red Man Holding Corporation	25.2
Empire Resources, Inc.	24.5
O'Neal Steel, Inc.	23.5
A. M. Castle & Co.	21.4
Olympic Steel, Inc.	21.0
Metals USA Holdings Corp.	14.4
Worthington Industries, Inc.	6.7

Fastest Growing* by Five-Year Employee Growth	(%)
McJunkin Red Man Holding Corporation	55.8
Reliance Steel & Aluminum Co.	53.6
Empire Resources, Inc.	30.7
Schnitzer Steel Industries, Inc.	26.8
O'Neal Steel, Inc.	9.0
Olympic Steel, Inc.	7.0
Tang Industries, Inc.	6.1
A. M. Castle & Co.	5.3
Blue Tee Corp.	3.8
Metals USA Holdings Corp.	1.8

Top Public Companies by Market Value	($ mil.)
Worthington Industries, Inc.	1,581.4
Schnitzer Steel Industries, Inc.	1,477.1
Reliance Steel & Aluminum Co.	1,461.9
A. M. Castle & Co.	600.8
Olympic Steel, Inc.	223.3

* These rates are compounded annualized increases and may have resulted from acquisitions or one time gains. If less than 6 years of data are available, growth is for the years available.

SOURCE: HOOVER'S, INC., DATABASE

Structural Metals Manufacture

The US structural metals manufacturing industry consists of 13,000 companies with combined annual revenue of $60 billion. Major companies include units of integrated metal producers, such as Alcoa, Nucor Steel, and US Steel, as well as large metal fabricators, such as NCI Building Systems and Dietrich Industries. The industry is highly fragmented: the 50 largest companies have only about 25 percent of industry sales.

Competitive Landscape

Demand depends primarily on the level of construction activity, particularly non-residential. Large companies have advantages in efficiency of operations and economies of scale. Smaller producers compete by focusing on specialized product offerings and responsive customer service to local markets. Revenue per employee averages about $160,000.

Structural metals compete with other building materials, primarily wood, for many uses in construction projects.

Products, Operations & Technology

Major product types are structural steel (joists and concrete reinforcing bars); sheet metal (ductwork, metal enclosures); metal windows and doors; and prefabricated metal buildings. Structural steel components comprise 35 percent of US shipments, followed by sheet metal work (25 percent), and metal windows and doors (20 percent). Other products include ornamental building components, such as metal staircases and fire escapes.

Basic raw materials are primarily steel (carbon, alloy, and stainless) or aluminum. Raw materials are bought in semi-finished form (slabs, billets, and blooms) or finished form (plates, coils, sheets, wire, bars, rails, and beams). Companies buy either directly from primary metal producers, such as Nucor Steel or Alcoa, or from metals distributors, known as

BUSINESS CHALLENGES

» Demand Depends on Construction Activity

Demand for structural metals depends on the level of construction activity, particularly nonresidential, which rises and falls with the economy and interest rates. Nonresidential construction can rise or fall more than 5 percent per year.

» Volatile Raw Material Prices

Raw materials consist primarily of various forms of steel and aluminum, prices for which can vary widely from year to year. The US imposes tariffs on imported steel occasionally to protect jobs in the domestic steel industry. Prices for iron, steel, and aluminum can rise more than 20 percent within 12 months.

» Supplier Concentration

In recent years, bankruptcies and acquisitions in the steel industry have reduced the number of raw material suppliers to the structural metals industry. Many companies now depend on a few suppliers for the majority of their raw material needs. Sufficient raw materials to meet production demands could be at risk if these suppliers go out of business or have production problems.

metals service centers. About 70 percent of all structural steel for the US market comes through service centers.

The manufacturing process varies depending on the product type, but generally involves fabrication, preparation, and finishing. Fabrication includes processes like punching, cutting, bending, welding, coil processing, roll forming, laser cutting, and stamping. Machining, a fabrication method, uses a variety of machine tools to cut or form material to precise specifications. Preparation includes cleaning and surfacing materials with chemicals. Finishing includes plating, polishing, coloring, and coating.

Products include both standard components built to stock and custom systems engineered to order. Engineered building systems are designed to meet a specific project's requirements and are shipped to the construction site complete and ready for assembly with no additional field welding necessary.

Companies use CAD systems to develop new products and custom orders. A variety of machines are used to automate steps in the production process, including presses, punches, saws, grinders, and welders. These operations may be automated using computer numeric control (CNC) systems. During fabrication, raw materials and steel pieces are moved by cranes, jibs, carts, and automated conveyor systems.

Sales & Marketing

Customers are primarily builders and contractors for commercial and industrial buildings. Architects and engineering design firms are important for many products since they specify components in project designs. Some products, such as metal windows and doors, are sold to homeowners through home improvement retailers like Home Depot and Lowe's.

Products are sold through direct sales forces and authorized resellers. Relationships with local builders, architects, and contractors are critical for sales. Companies publish product catalogs that include specifications and suggested list prices for standard products; they may also be available via the Internet. Custom orders usually involve competitive bids that are awarded based on both price and delivery schedules.

Human Resources

Structural metals manufacturing requires moderate skills, as reflected in average wages compared to other manufacturing industries. Hourly wages of production workers averaged $15 in 2005, up 3 percent over the previous year. Fringe benefits average 21 percent of payroll. Workers at larger companies may be unionized.

The production process involves cutting and welding metal components and operating high-speed machinery, resulting in an annual injury rate of nine cases per 100 workers, 50 percent higher than the average for all US manufacturing industries.

Industry Employment Growth

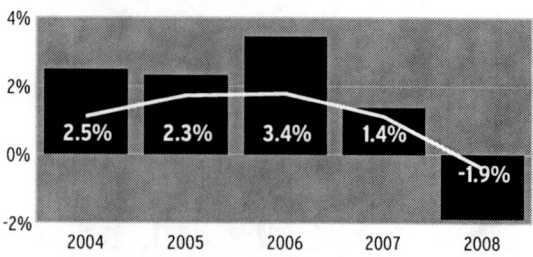

Average Hourly Earnings

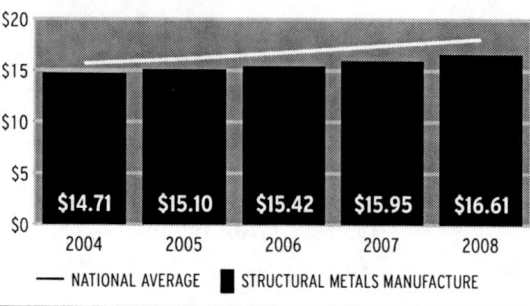

— NATIONAL AVERAGE ■ STRUCTURAL METALS MANUFACTURE

SOURCE: BUREAU OF LABOR STATISTICS

Call Preparation Questions

What trends is the company seeing in product sales?

Demand for structural metals depends on the level of construction activity, particularly nonresidential, which rises and falls with the economy and interest rates.

How have raw material prices affected the company's costs?

Raw materials consist primarily of various forms of steel and aluminum, prices for which can vary widely from year to year.

How have the company's supplier relationships been affected by consolidation in the steel industry?

In recent years, bankruptcies and acquisitions in the steel industry have reduced the number of raw material suppliers to the structural metals industry.

What opportunities does the company see to grow sales in the residential market?

Increasing the use of steel in home construction is a large growth opportunity for structural metal manufacturers.

How is the company taking advantage of the "green building" movement?

Growing interest in environmentally friendly construction, or "green building," could spur an increase in steel components in new construction.

Web Links

American Institute of Steel Construction

News and articles on use of structural steel in construction.
www.aisc.org

American Iron and Steel Institute

News, statistics, and issues for the steel industry.
www.steel.org

American Metal Market

News on the metals industry.
www.amm.com

Metal Construction News

Industry news and contractor profiles.
www.metalhomedigest.com/Default.aspx?
PublicationID=2

Steel Framing Alliance

Trade association promoting use of steel framing in construction.
www.steelframingalliance.com/mc/page.do

Glossary of Acronyms

AISC — American Institute of Steel Construction
AMM — American Metal Market
CAD — computer-aided design
CERCLA — Comprehensive Environmental Response, Compensation, and Liability Act
CNC — computer numeric control
RCRA — Resource Conservation and Recovery Act

HOOVER'S TOP COMPANIES

Largest Companies by Sales	($ mil.)
Alcoa Inc.	26,901.0
United States Steel Corporation	23,754.0
Nucor Corporation	23,663.3
Worthington Industries (Dietrich Metal Framing)	3,067.2
Valmont Industries, Inc.	1,907.3
NCI Building Systems, Inc.	1,764.2
Euramax International, Inc.	1,300.0
Quanex Building Products Corporation	868.9
Atrium Companies, Inc.	700.0

Largest Employers	Employees
Alcoa Inc.	87,000
United States Steel Corporation	28,000
Nucor Corporation	18,000
Worthington Industries (Dietrich Metal Framing)	6,900
Valmont Industries, Inc.	6,029
NCI Building Systems, Inc.	6,010
Atrium Companies, Inc.	5,100
Butler Manufacturing Company	4,298
Drew Industries Incorporated	3,690
Euramax International, Inc.	3,471

Fastest Growing* by Five-Year Sales Growth	(%)
Nucor Corporation	30.4
Chart Industries, Inc.	22.9
North American Galvanizing & Coatings, Inc.	21.0
United States Steel Corporation	20.2
Metwood, Inc.	17.6
Drew Industries Incorporated	15.5
Euramax International, Inc.	15.3
NCI Building Systems, Inc.	14.5
L. B. Foster Company	14.2
Global Power Equipment Group Inc.	12.9

Fastest Growing* by Five-Year Employee Growth	(%)
American Technologies Group, Inc.	130.5
NCI Building Systems, Inc.	58.2
Nucor Corporation	26.2
Chart Industries, Inc.	15.9
Euramax International, Inc.	8.5
Drew Industries Incorporated	7.1
Valmont Industries, Inc.	6.3
Atrium Companies, Inc.	2.9
Worthington Industries (Dietrich Metal Framing)	0.6

Top Public Companies by Market Value	($ mil.)
Nucor Corporation	14,505.7
Alcoa Inc.	9,011.6
United States Steel Corporation	4,322.6
Worthington Industries (Dietrich Metal Framing)	1,581.4
Valmont Industries, Inc.	1,531.1

* These rates are compounded annualized increases and may have resulted from acquisitions or one time gains. If less than 6 years of data are available, growth is for the years available.

SOURCE: HOOVER'S, INC., DATABASE

Sugar Manufacturing

The US sugar manufacturing industry consists of 52 companies with combined annual revenue of $7 billion. Large companies include American Crystal Sugar, Imperial Sugar, Amalgamated Sugar, and Florida Crystals. The industry is highly concentrated: the 50 largest companies account for nearly 100 percent of industry revenue.

Competitive Landscape

Demand is driven by domestic sugar consumption and government controls on imports and pricing. The profitability of individual companies depends on efficient operations and cost controls. Large companies have economies of scale in production and distribution. Small companies can compete effectively by serving local markets. The industry is highly automated: average annual revenue per worker is over $400,000.

US sugar consumption fell in the last two decades as domestic food manufacturers switched from sugar to lower cost sweeteners, such as high fructose corn syrup. Candy and pastry makers continue to use refined cane sugar.

Products, Operations & Technology

The major product of sugar manufacturers is refined sugar (sucrose) for industrial and consumer use. Sugar is produced in various forms, including granulated, powdered, liquid, brown, and molasses. The basic production method is to dissolve sucrose out of those plants that concentrate it naturally in their stem or roots, and then remove impurities and water. Sugar cane and sugar beets are the major plants used. Sugar cane grows mainly in subtropical and tropical regions, sugar beets in colder climates.

Sugar cane is crushed in sugar mills, producing a syrup that is concentrated to raw sugar by evaporators and centrifuges. The raw sugar is processed further in refineries, using

BUSINESS CHALLENGES

» Dependence on Government Support

The sugar manufacturing industry depends on price supports from the federal government, which keeps the US sugar price about twice as high as the world price. Without price supports, many US producers couldn't continue in business.

» Increasing Use of Alternative Sweeteners

High fructose corn syrup, which is cheaper than sugar, has replaced sugar in numerous processed foods, notably sodas. Corn sweeteners have experienced 5 percent annual market growth, but demand for refined sugar has been flat.

» Global Manufacture of Products Containing Sugar

More companies that buy sugar manufacture their products outside the US to use sugar at lower world prices. Candy and hard candy are the primary products being re-exported into the US. Candy imports have increased more than 50 percent in the last four years. As more products are manufactured outside the US, domestic demand for sugar continues to fall.

various chemical methods to precipitate out the remaining impurities. The final products are refined white sugar, brown sugar, and molasses. Processing from sugar beets is similar, with stages for soaking sucrose out of sliced beets, chemical removal of impurities, and concentration and drying of the final product using evaporation and centrifuges.

Large sugar cane mills can process 20,000 tons of cane per day. Large beet processing installations can process 15,000 tons of beets per day. Bagasse, the fibrous material left behind after sucrose is separated from the cane, is used as fuel. Sugar beet waste is used as animal feed, or can be burned to provide energy.

While some sugar refiners buy raw material from independent farmers, some also own agricultural operations that produce a portion of their needs. Sugar cane refiners typically buy raw cane sugar from a number of suppliers. Supply contracts specify quantities but prices are typically tied to market prices, which can vary substantially. Since sugar refining is energy-intensive, manufacturers have supply contracts for natural gas, fuel oil, or coal if they need more energy than they can produce from burning waste.

Sales & Marketing

Major customers are industrial food manufacturers, supermarket chains, and food service distributors. Products are sold by an internal sales force and independent brokers.

Federal programs keep the price of US refined sugar higher than world market prices, sometimes twice as high. Raw sugar is generally purchased under annual or spot contracts from sugar mills. Raw cane sugar prices can change as much as 15 percent in a year.

Human Resources

The average hourly pay for production workers is slightly below the national average. The industry injury rate is twice as high as the national average because of slippery surfaces, incorrect use of equipment, and contact with sharp edges on equipment.

Average Hourly Earnings

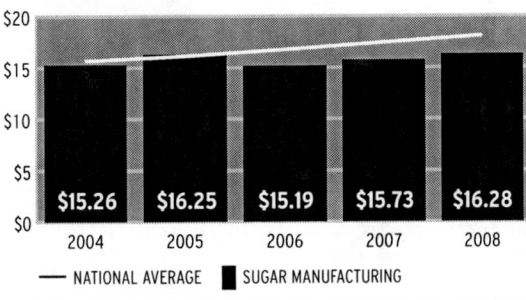

	2004	2005	2006	2007	2008
SUGAR MANUFACTURING	$15.26	$16.25	$15.19	$15.73	$16.28

— NATIONAL AVERAGE ■ SUGAR MANUFACTURING

SOURCE: BUREAU OF LABOR STATISTICS

Call Preparation Questions

How critical is government price support to the company's operations?

The sugar manufacturing industry depends on price supports from the federal government, which keeps the US sugar price about twice as high as the world price.

How has the company's business been affected by increasing use of corn syrup in food manufacture?

High fructose corn syrup, which is cheaper than sugar, has replaced sugar in numerous processed foods, notably sodas.

How has the global oversupply of sugar affected the company?

More companies that buy sugar manufacture their products outside the US to use sugar at lower world prices.

Has the company considered developing new packaging?

Although sugar is seen as a commodity, manufacturers can develop value-added, innovative packaging for use by consumers and food manufacturers.

Has the company explored using bagasse as a source of paper fiber?

Waste products from sugar manufacturing can be converted into animal feed and paper-making materials.

Web Links

American Sugarbeet Growers Association

National coalition of sugar cane and sugar beet farmers, processors, refiners, and suppliers.
www.americansugarbeet.org

Canadian Sugar Institute

Facts about Canadian sugar industry.
www.sugar.ca/english

Sugar Association

Information on sugar and nutrition from sugar producers and growers.
www.sugar.org

Sugaronline

Worldwide trade, news, and price information.
www.sugaronline.com

USDA Sugar Briefing Room

Trade, market outlook, and policy information.
www.ers.usda.gov/briefing/sugar

Glossary of Acronyms

CAFTA — Central American Free Trade Agreement
CWT — hundredweight
HFCS — high fructose corn syrup
WTO — World Trade Organization

HOOVER'S TOP COMPANIES

Largest Employers	Employees
Florida Crystals Corporation	2,000
U. S. Sugar Corporation	1,500
Amalgamated Sugar Company LLC	1,500
American Crystal Sugar Company	1,380
Imperial Sugar Company	759
The Western Sugar Cooperative, Inc.	750
Southern Minnesota Beet Sugar Cooperative	610
Michigan Sugar Company	430
M A Patout & Son Limited	413
Minn-Dak Farmers Cooperative	307

SOURCE: HOOVER'S, INC., DATABASE

Talent and Modeling Agencies

The talent and modeling agency industry includes more than 30,000 companies with combined annual revenue of about $5 billion. Major companies include Creative Artists Agency (CAA); William Morris; International Creative Management (ICM); and IMG. The industry is fragmented: the top 50 companies account for less than 45 percent of industry revenue. The industry is characterized by many sole proprietorships with no paid employees.

The industry includes agents and personal managers who represent or manage actors and entertainers, models, sports figures, and other public figures. Agents focus on finding clients work; personal managers generally find sponsorships and endorsements for clients.

Competitive Landscape

Demand is driven by the performing arts, sports entertainment, and advertising industries. The profitability of individual agencies depends on the success of agents' talent in winning auditions, leading to a steady stream of contracts. Large agencies have advantages in relationships with major studios, fashion designers, and cosmetic companies. Small agencies can compete successfully by specializing in a particular medium or location and developing niche customer relationships. Talent and modeling agencies are labor-intensive: while average annual revenue per worker for agencies with employees exceeds $200,000, single agent businesses average less than $40,000 in annual revenue.

Products, Operations & Technology

Major services are finding auditions for clients and negotiating contracts. Additional services include finding photographers, arranging acting teachers, satisfying other support needs, and securing endorsement deals.

Agents promote their talent and models to buyers based on required gender, age, race,

BUSINESS CHALLENGES

» Agent Defections

Most entertainment talent is loyal to their talent agent; agents who leave one firm for another often take their clients with them, causing negative publicity and impacting revenue of the jilted agency. ICM lost several Hollywood superstars when a long-time agent left the company. Top regional or local talent often leave for opportunities in larger cities. Major agencies have been formed by defections of high-profile agents: CAA was formed when several agents defected from William Morris.

» Dependence on Consumer Spending

Demand for creative and modeling talent is somewhat a function of the public's willingness to spend for entertainment, leisure, and fashion. In economic downturns, consumers reduce discretionary spending, which affects hiring entertainment at trade shows, civic events, and local entertainment, decreasing the need for talent.

» Cultivating, Maintaining Relationships

Having special relationships with both talent and buying clients is important in retaining business and getting referrals. As pressure to reign in star salaries strains even the best relationships, knowing the idiosyncrasies of star talent and buyers' needs is key to winning future projects. Agency revenue is a function of clients successfully winning auditions, so agents have to find suitable auditions to ensure client loyalty. Having good relations with major studios, cosmetic companies, and fashion designers ensures agents learn of potential projects for their talent/models.

looks, and talent the buyer needs for a project. Agents submit the talent's head shot, composite card, or portfolio to arrange for an audition or, in the case of modeling agencies, "look-sees." Successful auditions lead to bookings. Modeling agencies also have open calls where they advertise for potential talent to interview on a particular day; hundreds of candidates may attend open calls.

Modeling agencies generally sign models to exclusive contracts that vary in length depending on the model's status and experience. Modeling agencies stage fashion weeks in major cities, where multiple fashion designers showcase their work and participate in cosmetic campaigns. Talent agents generally have exclusive contracts with talent in certain territories.

Agents operate across the country, representing local talent, as well as better known Hollywood stars and New York fashion models. Local agents provide talent for events such as birthday parties, trade shows, and civic events.

Some agencies use the Internet to promote their clients. Modeling agencies have begun emailing portfolios to potential buyers, which speeds the booking process and reduces costs.

Sales & Marketing

Typical customers include TV and movie studios, fashion magazines, and cosmetic companies for national agencies; local agencies service companies, civic organizations, and private functions, such as birthday parties.

Agencies market themselves on the Internet, advertise in trade publications, conduct open viewings/auditions, and entertain potential clients. Advertising in the Yellow Pages is common for agencies serving a local market.

Agents typically receive 10 to 20 percent of the project fee; union contracts, such as with the Screen Actors Guild (SAG) or American Federation of Television and Radio Artists (AFTRA), pay agents 20 percent. Modeling agent commissions range between 10 and 20 percent for each modeling job. Modeling agents also typically bill the buyer a 20 percent service charge.

Human Resources

No special skills are required to become agents and company setup costs are minimal, so almost anyone can become a talent or modeling agent. Large agencies employ support staff and agents. Average wages for talent and modeling agents are much higher than the national norm. The industry injury rate is minimal.

Call Preparation Questions

What challenges has the agency faced from defections to other agencies?

Most entertainment talent is loyal to their talent agent; agents who leave one firm for another often take their clients with them, causing negative publicity and impacting revenue of the jilted agency.

How sensitive is the agency's business to changes in consumer spending on entertainment?

Demand for creative and modeling talent is somewhat a function of the public's willingness to spend for entertainment, leisure, and fashion.

What is key to the agency's success in retaining business?

Having special relationships with both talent and buying clients is important in retaining business and getting referrals.

What opportunities does the agency see in new technologies and media outlets?

As new media outlets emerge and new technologies change consumer entertainment habits, opportunities arise for agents to specialize and find new bookings for their talent.

How important are seniors to the agency's business?

As the population ages, more ad money is directed at older Americans, creating increased roles for seniors, both in modeling and acting.

Web Links

Alliance of Motion Picture and Television Producers

News, organizational proposals.
www.amptp.org

American Federation of Television and Radio Artists

Links, TV and radio news, legislation.
www.aftra.com

Association of Talent Agents

Industry and legal news, job openings.
www.agentassociation.com

Creative Artists Agency (CAA)

The largest US talent agency.
www.caa.com

Model Lifestyle

Information on becoming a model, jobs, tips.
www.modellifestyle.com

Model Network.com

Industry and agency news, model profiles.
www.modelnetwork.com

Motion Picture Association of America

Industry news and statistics, news of major studios.
www.mpaa.org

Screen Actors Guild (SAG)

Acting news and issues, press releases.
www.sag.org

Variety

Entertainment news.
www.variety.com

Glossary of Acronyms

AFTRA — American Federation of Television and Radio Artists

CAA — Creative Artists Agency

ICM — International Creative Management

SAG — Screen Actors Guild

HOOVER'S TOP COMPANIES

Largest Employers	Employees
IMG	3,000
William Morris Agency, Inc.	500
International Creative Management, Inc.	500
Creative Artists Agency, Inc.	500
Brillstein Entertainment Partners, LLC	290
The Endeavor Agency, LLC.	190
United Talent Agency, Inc.	175
The Gersh Agency	130
Ford Models, Inc.	100
Wilhelmina Models, Inc.	62

SOURCE: HOOVER'S, INC., DATABASE

Taxi and Limousine Services

Taxi and limousine services generate about $4 billion in annual revenue for 5,000 companies that operate in the US, half in the taxi segment and half in the limousine segment. The industry has no publicly held companies. The limousine segment is particularly fragmented. The average taxi or limousine company has nine employees and $600,000 per year in revenue.

Competitive Landscape

Taxi and limousine revenue is driven by business and leisure travel. The profitability of individual companies depends on good marketing. Small companies can effectively compete with large ones because there are few economies of scale in operations. Average annual revenue per employee is only about $60,000 for both large and small companies.

Products, Operations & Technology

Both taxis and limousines transport passengers after being dispatched per customer request or reservation. Taxi cabs also pick up passengers that hail them while driving on city streets or at taxi stands. Limousines can pick up customers only by telephone request. Limousine companies may lease vehicles with a driver by the hour, or may operate for-hire vehicles (FHV) that charge flat rates for specific trips, in competition with taxis. Companies typically have a central dispatching office, own a fleet of vehicles, may own fuel tanks and pumps, and may operate a maintenance and repair shop.

Drivers and fuel are major operating costs. Because prices for taxi service are usually fixed by local commissions, companies increase profitability by hiring the cheapest labor available; therefore, many drivers are part-time employees. Drivers may be paid a flat wage or a percentage of revenue; some are hired as independent contractors (so-called lease drivers), paying for fuel themselves and paying the

BUSINESS CHALLENGES

» Revenue Linked to Cyclical Business, Leisure Travel

Taxi and limo revenues are linked to business and tourist travel; industry jobs dropped 8 percent during the last recession. Because vehicle and medallion (for taxis) costs are high and fixed, operators can't easily adjust to lower revenue.

» Gas Prices Volatile

Gas is a significant operating cost for taxi and limo companies. During periods of high gas prices, many local commissions allow fuel surcharges, but customers often reduce tips by the cost of the surcharge, leaving revenue unchanged. Gas prices can move rapidly, sometimes more than 25 percent in six months.

» Dependence on Regulatory Commissions

The profitability of both taxi and limousine companies is directly affected by the actions of local regulatory commissions, which can set fares, restrict competition, and dictate operating practices and equipment. Local commissions must account for politics and consumer interests, which can work against industry profits.

taxi company a fixed amount per day or week; some may own their own cab.

In addition to providing transportation, taxis also sell advertising on the outside and inside of their cabs in multi-media form including banners, voice, and video ads. Ad type, amount, and locations are regulated by local commissions. Companies like Medallion Financial broker taxicab advertisements across the US.

Sales & Marketing

Taxi and limousine companies serve both retail consumers and business accounts. Taxi companies have more retail business; limousine companies more corporate business.

Limousine companies with 20 or more vehicles get up to 75 percent of their revenue from business accounts. Companies with three or fewer vehicles do most of their business for weddings, proms, nights on the town, and tours, according to Limousine and Chauffeured Transportation. Hotel and resort contracts for limousine companies account for less than 10 percent of annual revenue.

Companies advertise to attract new customers. Yellow Pages' advertising is very important. Most companies have promotional Internet websites and some companies take online reservations, and many subscribe to Internet portals that drive traffic to their websites. Both taxi and limousine companies also contract with businesses, restaurants, hotels and airports, which give them preferred or exclusive access to passengers.

Fares for limousine companies are determined by market demand. Contracts with business customers and airport authorities often provide for discounted fares. Fares vary from $30 per hour for an ordinary sedan to $150 an hour or more for a customized stretch limo. Many companies have a 3 hour minimum for a limo rental.

Taxi fares are typically regulated by local taxi commissions and vary substantially nationwide. Because fuel is such a large cost, fuel surcharges are usually allowed when fuel prices are high.

Human Resources

Getting and keeping qualified drivers are among the biggest challenges facing companies because of the low pay. This challenge increases in good economic times as better paying employment opportunities emerge.

The average wage for a taxi and limousine driver is about 30 percent lower than that of the average US worker.

Industry Employment Growth

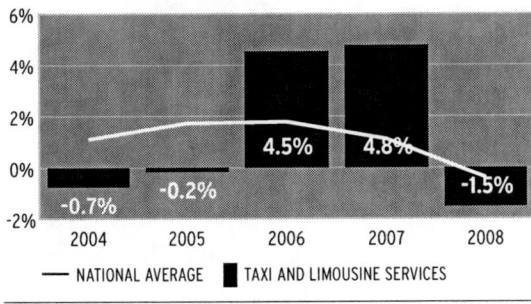

SOURCE: BUREAU OF LABOR STATISTICS

Call Preparation Questions

How does the company manage fluctuations in business and leisure travel demand?

Taxi and limo revenues are linked to business and tourist travel; industry jobs dropped 8 percent during the last recession.

How does the company protect against gas price hikes?

Gas is a significant operating cost for taxi and limo companies.

What regulations affect the company the most?

The profitability of both taxi and limousine companies is directly affected by the actions of local regulatory commissions, which can set fares, restrict competition, and dictate operating practices and equipment.

How beneficial is the company's website in growing business?

Some limousine and taxi companies allow customers to make reservations over the Internet.

If adopting new technologies, what advantages does the company expect to gain?

Using improved technology is expanding rapidly across the industry.

Web Links

Limousine & Chauffeured Transportation Magazine

News and articles.
www.lctmag.com

Medallion Financial Group

Provides services to taxi companies.
www.medallionfinancial.com

Metro Cars

Representative limousine company.
www.metrocars.com

National Limousine Association

Legislative news.
www.limo.org

New York City Taxi & Limousine Commission

www.nyc.gov/html/tlc/html/home/home.shtml

San Francisco Taxi Commission

www.ci.sf.ca.us/site/taxicommission_index.asp

Taxicab, Limousine & Paratransit Association

Lobbying organization.
www.tlpa.org

Travel Industry Association of America

News about business and tourist travel.
www.tia.org

Glossary of Acronyms

FHV — for-hire vehicle
TIAA — Travel Industry Association of America
TLC — New York City Taxi & Limousine Commission
TLPA — Taxicab, Limousine & Paratransit Association

HOOVER'S TOP COMPANIES

Largest Employers	Employees
BostonCoach	1,260
SuperShuttle International, Inc.	1,000
Carey International, Inc.	700
American Airport Limousine, Inc.	104

SOURCE: HOOVER'S, INC., DATABASE

Technology Sector

The technology sector in the US consists of more than 140,000 companies with combined annual revenue of about $900 billion. Major companies include AT&T, IBM, Intel, and Microsoft. Industry concentration is high in many subsectors: the largest 50 participants often hold more than 60 percent of the market.

The technology sector includes telecommunications, IT services, semiconductor manufacturing, software, Internet services, biotechnology, and scientific research, including aerospace research. Not included, for purposes of this profile, are related industries such as aerospace, computer hardware, pharmaceuticals, and telecommunications equipment manufacturing.

Competitive Landscape

Demand often depends on the income of consumers or the profitability of business customers, because many technology products and services are expensive. The profitability of individual companies is driven by their ability to develop and market new products. Large companies often have advantages in access to capital and marketing. Small companies can compete successfully if they have expertise in a particular field of knowledge. The industry is capital-intensive: average annual revenue per worker is nearly $300,000.

Products, Operations & Technology

Companies in the technology sector take advantage of scientific discoveries and turn them into marketable products. Of the several distinct fields within the technology sector, most are based on computer technology. Even biotech and aerospace rely heavily on computers.

The key scientific discoveries and developments that underlie many of today's technology companies were made more than 50 years ago: the transistor, the laser, the computer, the integrated circuit, and the structure of DNA. The

BUSINESS CHALLENGES

» High R&D Investment Required

To develop new products and improve old ones, tech companies must continually invest in R&D. Big companies like Intel, Cisco, and Amgen typically spend between 10 and 25 percent of revenues on R&D. Smaller tech companies often have more limited access to R&D funding.

» Dependence on Consumer, Business Spending

Demand for technology products and services depends on the state of the economy. Because many tech products are improved versions of older products, their purchase can be deferred during difficult economic times. Spending on information techonology is particularly vulnerable to corporate budget cuts.

» Dependence on Highly Skilled Workers

The highly technical and specialized nature of much of the work at technology companies requires specialized education and training. The rapid growth of the US technology sector in the past decade has outstripped the supply of qualified workers, and many US companies have made up the difference by hiring workers who have been trained abroad, or who have come to the US for training. More than 40 percent of US doctorates in engineering and computer sciences are currently awarded to foreigners.

technology sector of the US economy was built through large financial investments committed to developing these discoveries once they were sufficiently well understood to promise practical products. Newer scientific discoveries like nanotechnology, superconductivity, and carbon nano-tubes have yet to receive similar levels of investment, because the pathways to practical applications are not yet clear.

Tech companies are driven by continuing advances in knowledge, which produce a stream of improved products. The product cycle at technology companies is often short; a new version of their products is often being developed.

In addition to developing their own technology, many companies acquire it from other companies, either through licenses or by buying entire companies. A strong link between industry and academic research institutions exists, including a flow of personnel between them. Technology companies employ large numbers of engineers and scientists, invest heavily in expensive research equipment, and have R&D expenses that often exceed 10 percent of revenues. Companies hold patents that protect their products and are frequently embroiled in patent disputes.

Companies depend on the increasing power and decreasing cost of computing capabilities resulting from the miniaturization of computing elements. New technologies first applied to telecommunications, like fiber optics and wireless communication, have migrated into the broader computer area. Increases in computing power have made advances in aerospace and biotech research possible.

Sales & Marketing

Typical customers are commercial and industrial companies, governments, educational institutions, and consumers located across the globe. Sales are often made through a direct sales force, distributors, dealers, value-added resellers, and original equipment manufacturers.

Technology companies use combinations of direct marketing and co-marketing to advertise their products or services. Television, print and Web-based ads, and trade shows are among the most popular marketing media. Marketing usually involves lengthy testing and extensive product evaluation by a customer's technical staff. Once a customer buys a product, close and frequent communication between technical personnel is the rule: strong technical support is essential. Large technology companies often have marketing resources and expertise that smaller companies cannot duplicate. Consequently, small companies often sell or license their products to large companies, or form marketing partnerships with them.

The Internet has become a key sales medium for technology companies in recent years, accounting for as much as 40 percent of a firm's overall revenue. Web sales can be handled through a company's own proprietary site or through resellers.

The prices technology companies charge vary widely and depend on the type of product or service sold. Pricing pressure is common among rivals that have comparable offerings. Because many technology companies face global competition, cost control can be critical to success. Large players are able to invest in the development of differentiated, premium products that are more profitable.

Human Resources

Compensation is well above average, due to the technical expertise required of many technology workers. Technology workers are often found among college graduates with degrees in computer science, mathematics, and engineering. The rapid pace of innovation often requires continuing training and education. Shortages of specialist workers are common. Foreign technology professionals are often brought to the US through visas under the H-1B program, which can allow them to work in the US for up to six years.

Call Preparation Questions

How does the company measure the success of its R&D efforts?

To develop new products and improve old ones, tech companies must continually invest in R&D.

How does the company adapt to cyclical consumer and business spending on technology-driven products?

Demand for technology products and services depends on the state of the economy.

What challenges or obstacles has the company had hiring scientists, engineers, and other highly trained employees?

The highly technical and specialized nature of much of the work at technology companies requires specialized education and training.

What opportunities or challenges does the company expect in government contracting?

High-resolution sensing and satellite communications will benefit from additional government spending on defense.

Does the company expect to benefit from increased spending on homeland security?

Federal, state, and local governments and private industry face huge demands to increase security.

Web Links

Association of University Technology Managers

Research issues. Annual survey on technology licensing activities.
www.autm.net

Computerworld

News, white papers, industry resources.
www.computerworld.com

Defense Advanced Research Projects Agency

New technologies.
www.darpa.mil

Forrester Research

Industry research and news.
www.forrester.com

Gartner

Industry research and news.
www.gartner.com

IEEE Spectrum Online

Technology news.
www.spectrum.ieee.org

Information Technology Association of America

Public policy issues.
www.itaa.org

InformationWeek

Industry news, research, and archives.
www.informationweek.com

National Institutes of Health

Areas of biomedical research.
www.nih.gov

National Science Foundation

R&D statistics.
www.nsf.gov

National Venture Capital Association

Venture capital events, industry news, statistics.
www.nvca.org

Office of Science & Technology Policy

Policy issues.
www.ostp.gov

Technology Review

New technologies.
www.techreview.com

TechWeb

News and technology on segments of electronic industry, like networks, wireless, and e-business.
www.techweb.com

US Patent and Trademark Office

Information on patent and trademark laws.
www.uspto.gov

Glossary of Acronyms

GMO — genetically modified organism
POS — point-of-sale
VC — venture capital

HOOVER'S TOP COMPANIES

Largest Companies by Sales	($ mil.)
AT&T Inc.	124,028.0
International Business Machines Corporation	103,630.0
Verizon Communications Inc.	97,354.0
Microsoft Corporation	60,420.0
Intel Corporation	37,586.0
Sprint Nextel Corporation	35,635.0
Motorola, Inc.	30,146.0
Avnet, Inc.	17,952.7
Arrow Electronics, Inc.	16,761.0
Amgen Inc.	15,003.0

Largest Employers	Employees
International Business Machines Corporation	426,969
AT&T Inc.	310,000
Verizon Communications Inc.	235,000
Tyco Electronics Ltd.	96,000
Microsoft Corporation	91,000
Intel Corporation	83,900
Motorola, Inc.	66,000
L-3 Communications Holdings, Inc.	65,000
Jabil Circuit, Inc.	61,000
Sprint Nextel Corporation	60,000

Fastest Growing* by Five-Year Sales Growth	(%)
Tercica, Inc.	1,966.7
Solera Holdings, Inc.	1,292.3
Hughes Communications, Inc.	1,109.0
Global Telecom & Technology, Inc.	448.6
Infinera Corporation	442.4
The Orchard Enterprises, Inc.	408.9
Collexis Holdings, Inc.	355.6
Halozyme Therapeutics, Inc.	344.8
Entropic Communications, Inc.	337.1
Samaritan Pharmaceuticals, Inc.	295.8

Fastest Growing* by Five-Year Employee Growth	(%)
InfoLogix, Inc.	800.0
IA Global, Inc.	208.7
Wireless Ronin Technologies, Inc.	197.2
FiberTower Corporation	176.1
IHS Inc.	142.9
CV Therapeutics, Inc.	136.6
Silverstar Holdings, Ltd.	131.7
eGain Communications Corporation	121.2
First Solar, Inc.	120.8
Etelos, Inc.	112.5

Top Public Companies by Market Value	($ mil.)
Microsoft Corporation	251,744.0
AT&T Inc.	167,950.8
International Business Machines Corporation	112,698.3
Verizon Communications Inc.	100,602.0
Genentech, Inc.	87,304.2

* These rates are compounded annualized increases and may have resulted from acquisitions or one time gains. If less than 6 years of data are available, growth is for the years available.

SOURCE: HOOVER'S, INC., DATABASE

Telecommunication Services

In the US, about 11,000 companies provide telecommunication services, with total annual revenue over $400 billion. Large companies include AT&T, Verizon Communications, and Comcast. The industry includes 3,000 wireline carriers (annual revenues about $240 billion); 3,000 wireless companies ($100 billion); 2,000 cable companies ($60 billion); and satellite companies and telecommunication resellers. The industry is highly concentrated: the 50 largest companies hold 90 percent of the market.

Competitive Landscape

Demand is driven by technological innovation and by growth in business activity. The profitability of individual companies depends on efficient operations and good marketing. Large companies have big economies of scale in providing a highly automated service to large numbers of customers, and have the financial resources required to build and maintain a large network. Smaller companies can compete effectively only in small markets or by providing specialty services. Because of the large degree of automation, average revenue per employee is a high $300,000.

Products, Operations & Technology

The industry provides mainly telephone, TV distribution, and data transmission services (such as the Internet). Companies provide these services through networks of wires, computers, transmitters, and receivers. In the voice and data segments, companies merely provide a channel over which customers transmit their own information. In the TV distribution segment, companies also supply the content transmitted to the customer.

The operations of telecom service providers revolve around building, maintaining, and operating networks to reach customers. Networks can be built by physically laying wires, building transmission towers, and interconnecting

BUSINESS CHALLENGES

» Industry Depends Highly on Regulatory Decisions

The FCC regulates the interstate activities of telecom providers, including pricing and operations, while state public utility commissions (PUCs) regulate similar matters at the state level. Regulations affect most strategic decisions of telecom companies. Although the industry is moving toward deregulation and greater competition, pricing is likely to remain regulated.

» Demand Affected by Economic Growth

Demand for telecom services is affected by economic conditions, mainly because business customers provide a large portion of industry revenue. Consumers are also income-sensitive to the expensive new services providers offer. As a result, large phone companies had flat revenue during the last recession.

» Large Required Capital Investments

Companies in all segments of the telecommunication industry need to periodically invest in equipment. Large phone companies regularly make annual capital investments equal to 25 percent of revenue. Depreciation is often 25 percent of total expenses. Because of the large amount of investment required, telecommunication providers frequently carry a high level of debt, leaving them vulnerable to interest rate changes.

switching centers. Networks can also be assembled by buying existing facilities or leasing capacity on another company's network. Computers are the heart of all telecom facilities. Equipment is bought from large manufacturers like Cisco, Lucent, Motorola, and Nortel. Daily operations consist mainly of field maintenance work and tending interconnected computer systems.

Wireline Telephone

The modern US telephone industry is an outgrowth of the monopoly Bell telephone system. Rapid changes followed the 1982 AT&T

Divestiture Decree, which broke the AT&T monopoly into regional bell operating companies (RBOCs), manufacturing operations, and a long-distance service. A number of the RBOCs created then have since consolidated into large regional companies.

The wireline (as opposed to wireless) telephone network in the US consists of wires and switches that carry and route signals to the correct receiver, and gateways that allow wireless services to connect to the wireline network. Most local telephone traffic is still sent via a process called circuit-switching, which requires that an end-to-end communications channel be opened and used for the duration of each telephone call. Data traffic (including Internet traffic) and many long distance calls are sent via more-efficient packet-switching, which cuts a stream of information into little pieces, commingles it with other traffic sent over the same channel, and reassembles it at the receiving end.

The telephone industry uses a large and sometimes confusing variety of signaling systems and communication conventions ("protocols"). The current signaling system used to set up a phone call is called Signaling System 7 (SS7). Integrated systems digital network (ISDN) and digital subscriber loop (xDSL) are protocols that allow high-speed communication over local access wires. Asynchronous transfer mode (ATM) can send mixed voice, data, and video information. Frame relay switching is often used for sending data between users.

Wireless Telephone

Wireless phone networks consist of handsets (cell phones, which are radio transmitters/receivers), a network of radio antennas and base stations that can send and receive signals within a local area (a cell), and a network of switching stations that connect the cells with each other and with the wireline telephone network. Computers monitor the signal from a caller and "hand-off" the call from one cell to an adjacent cell as a caller moves.

Wireless providers sell customized phones and operate networks of antennas, base stations, and switching centers. Each wireless network operates in a particular wavelength frequency range (the "spectrum"). Licenses to use spectrum are issued by the government and can be bought and sold by holders. Phones that operate at a higher frequency have greater signal capacity (needed to transmit high-quality sound, photos, or data) but lower signal strength, and therefore require a more concentrated network of antennas. Wireless companies use one of several incompatible signal processing systems. The most common wireless signal processing technologies are TDMA, CDMA, and GSM. Most wireless companies operate regionally but interconnect with other companies that use the same technology, allowing customers to have roaming service outside their local area.

Cable Systems

Unlike wireline or wireless telephone companies that can send only a fairly small amount of information through their copper wires and phones, cable companies can send a large amount of information through the special coaxial cable wires that make up their networks. First formed to transmit regular TV signals outside regular broadcast areas, cable companies have made large investments in facilities and equipment in recent years to provide additional services. They now use their high-capacity wires to simultaneously transmit hundreds of TV and radio channels, Internet access, telephone, HDTV, and on-demand movies.

In addition to operating a network that carries signals, cable companies provide TV and movie "content." Companies acquire content from large media companies like Disney, Fox, and Viacom or from independent producers, much in the same way that local TV stations operate. Cable companies may buy transmission rights to entire cable channels like MTV, CNN, HBO, and ESPN, or to individual productions. Many cable companies also produce some of their own content. Large content providers may require that cable companies take an entire package of channels.

Other Systems

Paging systems basically consist of one-way radio transmitters that receive an activation signal from the wireline phone system and signal a mobile receiving unit. The handsets for satellite systems must be able to communicate with a system of satellites, requiring greater power than cell phones. Satellite TV and radio systems send one-way signals from satellites in "geo-synchronous" orbit (they stay over the same spot).

The Internet is a computer-to-computer communication system that uses many of the same structural elements as the telephone system, such as local cable or phone access lines, but uses packet-switching signal processing and special computer switches called routers. Its signaling system is called TCP/IP or Internet Protocol.

Technology

Computers and computer chips are at the center of all telecom systems. To route traffic, wireline telephone companies use special computers called Class 5 switches; Internet networks use computers called routers. Wireless phones use special computer chips for transmitting and receiving signals. Wireline operators largely use high-capacity fiber optic cable for long distance transmission and are starting to bring fiber optic cable directly to customer locations. All telecom providers use computers to monitor traffic and provide detailed billing statements to customers.

Sales & Marketing

About 50 percent of telephone services are bought by consumers and 50 percent by businesses and government. Consumers account for almost all cable services. The majority of revenue from Internet access comes from businesses, but since centralized records aren't kept, the exact percentage is unknown.

Because the cost of one individual communication over a telephone, cable, or data network is so small compared to the cost of establishing the network, companies sell mainly fixed-price subscriptions that give users access to their network. Telephone companies still base some charges on usage, but this practice is rapidly disappearing as the cost of monitoring and billing for individual communications is higher than the cost of usage. Most telephone and data service companies offer a range of fixed-price plans that have broad usage restrictions. Cable companies charge for access to specific channels but not for usage.

Marketing is confined to the area within which a company offers service. Most companies use heavy TV, radio, and direct mail advertising to reach consumers and small businesses, and a direct sales force to reach large businesses. Wireless companies also sell their services through mass merchants.

Human Resources

Production workers in the phone industry are technically skilled, and therefore earn above-average wages. The industry has rapidly automated, eliminating large numbers of operators. Workers mainly operate computers or are specialists in equipment installation and maintenance. To retain skilled workers, companies often offer fairly generous fringe benefits.

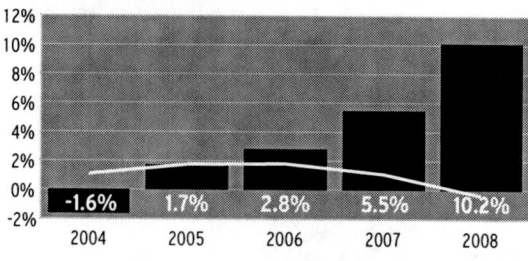

Industry Employment Growth

Year	Growth
2004	-1.6%
2005	1.7%
2006	2.8%
2007	5.5%
2008	10.2%

SOURCE: BUREAU OF LABOR STATISTICS

Call Preparation Questions

What government regulations are impacting the company's strategies?

The FCC regulates the interstate activities of telecom providers, including pricing and operations, while state public utility commissions (PUCs) regulate similar matters at the state level.

How does the company manage swings in revenue?

Demand for telecom services is affected by economic conditions, mainly because business customers provide a large portion of industry revenue.

What large capital investments is the company planning?

Companies in all segments of the telecommunication industry need to periodically invest in equipment.

How rapidly is fiber optic deployment to consumers occurring?

Although most non-local telephone transmission runs over high-speed fiber optic lines, a large majority of the "last mile" connection to customers still consists of copper wires, as does "in-house" wiring.

How is the company positioned to take advantage of growing foreign telecom markets?

Communication systems in North America, the EU, and Japan are well developed, in the sense that most of the population has inexpensive access, but systems in much of the rest of the world are more rudimentary.

Web Links

cellular-news

News.
www.cellular-news.com

CTIA – The Wireless Association

News.
www.ctia.org

Federal Communications Commission (FCC)

Releases, updates, and resources.
www.fcc.gov

International Telecommunication Union (ITU)

United Nations Agency.
itu.int

National Telecommunications and Information Administration (NTIA)

Press, publications, and policy.
www.ntia.doc.gov

PCIA – The Wireless Infrastructure Association

Wireless news and research.
pcia.com

TechWeb

Recent telecom news, analysis, magazines, links, and research tools.
www.techweb.com/tech/mobile

Telecommunications Industry Association (TIA)

Facts, statistics, technology, press releases, publications, international affairs, and resources.
www.tiaonline.org

Telephony Online

News magazine.
www.internettelephony.com

United States Telecom Association (USTelecom)

Association of local phone companies.
usta.org

Glossary of Acronyms

AMPS — advanced mobile phone system
ATM — asynchronous transfer mode
CDMA — code division multiple access
CLEC — competitive local exchange carrier
ILEC — incumbent local exchange carrier
LATA — local access and transport area
LEC — local exchange company
PCS — personal communications system
PSTN — public switched telephone network
PTT — push-to-talk
RBOCS — Regional Bell operating companies
TDMA — Time division multiple access
VOIP — Voice over Internet Protocol

HOOVER'S TOP COMPANIES

Largest Companies by Sales	($ mil.)
AT&T Inc.	124,028.0
Verizon Communications Inc.	97,354.0
Time Warner Inc.	46,984.0
Sprint Nextel Corporation	35,635.0
Comcast Corporation	34,256.0
The DIRECTV Group, Inc.	19,693.0
Viacom Inc.	14,625.0
Qwest Communications International Inc.	13,475.0
DISH Network Corporation	11,617.2
T-Mobile USA, Inc.	—

Largest Employers	Employees
AT&T Inc.	310,000
Verizon Communications Inc.	235,000
Comcast Corporation	100,000
Time Warner Inc.	86,400
Sprint Nextel Corporation	60,000
Qwest Communications International Inc.	32,937
T-Mobile USA, Inc.	29,000
DISH Network Corporation	23,000
Cablevision Systems Corporation	22,935
Cox Communications, Inc.	22,530

Fastest Growing* by Five-Year Sales Growth	(%)
Hughes Communications, Inc.	1,109.0
FiberTower Corporation	245.5
IA Global, Inc.	135.7
New World Brands, Inc.	124.5
SkyTerra Communications, Inc.	118.0
Vonage Holdings Corp.	83.3
GeoEye, Inc.	81.0
Cinedigm Digital Cinema Corp.	80.7
Windstream Corporation	58.1
MetroPCS Communications, Inc.	43.0

Fastest Growing* by Five-Year Employee Growth	(%)
IA Global, Inc.	208.7
FiberTower Corporation	176.1
iPCS, Inc.	66.2
Cinedigm Digital Cinema Corp.	50.5
Rackspace Hosting, Inc.	45.6
GeoEye, Inc.	45.5
MetroPCS Communications, Inc.	34.7
CapRock Communications, Inc.	32.6
NeuStar, Inc.	32.5
GoAmerica, Inc.	31.0

Top Public Companies by Market Value	($ mil.)
AT&T Inc.	167,950.8
Verizon Communications Inc.	100,602.0
Time Warner Inc.	36,095.3
Comcast Corporation	34,789.4
Sprint Nextel Corporation	5,228.3

* These rates are compounded annualized increases and may have resulted from acquisitions or one time gains. If less than 6 years of data are available, growth is for the years available.

SOURCE: HOOVER'S, INC., DATABASE

Telecommunications Equipment Manufacturers

The US telecommunication industry comprises about 2,000 companies with combined annual revenue of $65 billion. Major US companies include Cisco Systems, 3Com, and Motorola. Large foreign competitors in the US market include Nortel Networks, Nokia, NEC, Alcatel-Lucent, and Siemens. The industry is highly concentrated: the 50 largest companies hold 75 percent of the market.

Competitive Landscape

The industry depends on purchases from businesses, telephone companies, cable companies, data communications providers, and TV and radio broadcasters. Profitability for individual companies is linked to technical innovation and the ability to secure high-volume contracts from large customers. Small companies can be successful if they make highly specialized products. There are large economies of scale in manufacturing standard products, but many products are specialized and produced in small manufacturing plants. Annual revenue per employee in a large plant varies from $500,000 to $1 million.

The US telecom industry is entering a transition phase where the current telephone system is converted to VoIP technology and the TV broadcast industry is migrating to HDTV technology. These changeovers will require replacing a substantial portion of the equipment in use today, presenting an opportunity for all vendors.

The industry is recovering from a major boom and bust that saw revenue fall 50 percent between 2000 and 2002, after climbing 40 percent in previous years.

Products, Operations & Technology

The industry produces transmitters and receivers (including satellites); signal boosters; signal processors; connecting devices; power supplies; switches; and phones. About half of in-

BUSINESS CHALLENGES

» Revenues Tied to Cyclical Business, Consumer Demand

Although manufacturers sell mainly to telecom service providers, demand for services depends on the economic situation of businesses and consumers. Small changes in demand largely affect manufacturers: during the last recession, when corporate profits fell 5 percent and personal income growth was low, telecom equipment manufacture fell 25 percent.

» Telecom Service Providers Subject to Regulation

Demand for new telecom equipment depends partly on the types of services various providers can offer per federal regulations. The FCC and state regulators greatly affect the structure and operations of the telecom services industry. Because of rapid advances in technology, these regulators and the courts are often required to make decisions that affect demand for new equipment.

» Obsolescence Risk: Rapidly Evolving Technology

Because of rapid advances in technology, equipment manufacturers run a large risk of making outdated products. To keep up with advances, companies must spend large amounts on R&D, the costs of which typically equal 15 to 25 percent of revenue. Many high-tech products are routinely replaced every two to three years.

dustry revenue comes from equipment for wireless communications (including radio and TV) and half from equipment for line-based communications. Telephone handsets (wired and wireless) account for about a third of industry sales.

The industry makes a large variety of products that are used by the different communications networks currently installed in the US, including radio and TV broadcasting, microwave communications, remote alarm systems, wireless telephone, cable TV, cable data, and telephony communications (including the Internet), and the "wireline" telephone system.

The number of products is very large because communications' signals can be sent in different forms (electrical, optical, electromagnetic); at different frequencies, in different modulations (AM or FM); different modes (digital or analog); and signals can be composed and processed in many different ways (CDMA, TDMA, GSM, ATM, circuit-switching, packet-switching, etc.) Products range from $10 telephones to $5 million room-sized Class 5 switches that are the backbone of the wireline telephone system. With leading-edge technology content, equipment is often expensive.

Because of the large number of possible products, most companies concentrate efforts in a particular segment with the objective of dominating that segment. Motorola specializes in wireless telephone, Cisco in Internet infrastructure, Lucent in wireline infrastructure.

Many telecom products are electronic devices assembled from standard components (such as computer chips and circuit boards) that are customized for a particular application. Production facilities are often highly automated. Systems are designed to be highly modular, consisting of cabinets, shelves, boards, etc. Large, expensive pieces of equipment may be assembled by hand from pre-built components. Parts are bought from a large number of electronic component suppliers, many of which are located abroad.

Outsourcing has become pervasive in telecommunications manufacturing. Specialized chips may be shipped to companies fabricating circuit boards and then shipped to other vendors doing the final assembly and test. Many large manufacturers, including Lucent and Motorola, outsource some or all of the actual manufacturing to contract manufacturers like Flextronics and Solectron that operate factories in low-cost countries. Computer chips, the core of most products, are sometimes in tight supply. Individual product testing is usually required to ensure that the internal electronics of finished products work properly. Software is a significant part of finished systems and can be a significant contributor to profit margins. Manufacturers hold the code as highly proprietary.

The technology of telecommunications is rapidly changing. Companies constantly introduce advanced versions of their products and spend heavily on R&D. From being passive devices that perform a single function, many products have evolved into programmable computer-controlled devices that can adapt to different needs. For many manufacturers, R&D

spending is greater than 10 percent of revenue; for some, more than 20 percent.

Sales & Marketing

Products are sold mostly to companies that provide telecom services, such as phone companies, radio and TV stations, cable systems, data communication companies, and ISPs. Most companies use an internal sales force with strong technical knowledge. Because of the complexity of technical issues involved, sales are typically "engineer-to-engineer." Equipment is sold based on technical specifications and performance as well as price. Sales proposals are often in response to requests for bids from large customers. Negotiations on large multi-year sales contracts can be lengthy.

Pricing is often unrelated to production costs. With the rapid pace of technological change in the industry, manufacturers must recoup development and production costs as rapidly as possible before a product is obsolete. As in the computer industry, for many years prices have been falling relative to performance.

Trade shows are an important marketing tool for manufacturers. Many large companies in the industry have alliances with smaller ones to stay abreast of technological developments. Co- or re-branding of smaller company equipment is common, with the large company warranting and servicing the smaller company's equipment.

Human Resources

Telecom manufacturers depend heavily on a workforce of highly educated and well-paid engineers to design products, manage the manufacturing process, and help with sales. Technicians who assemble complicated products like phone switches also require special training and have high earnings. Overall, industry wages are 15 percent above the national average.

The number of US workers in the industry has declined sharply in recent years, both because production volume fell 25 percent during the recession and because more production moved to low-cost countries.

Industry Employment Growth

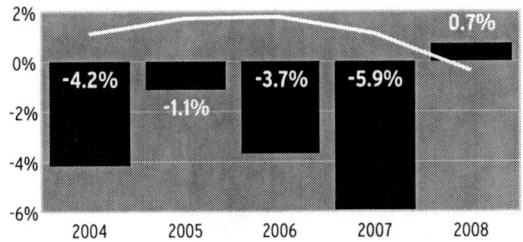

Average Hourly Earnings

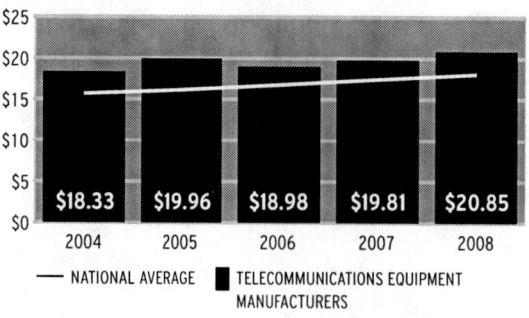

	2004	2005	2006	2007	2008
	$18.33	$19.96	$18.98	$19.81	$20.85

— NATIONAL AVERAGE ■ TELECOMMUNICATIONS EQUIPMENT MANUFACTURERS

SOURCE: BUREAU OF LABOR STATISTICS

Call Preparation Questions

How does the company adjust to changes in demand?

Although manufacturers sell mainly to telecom service providers, demand for services depends on the economic situation of businesses and consumers.

Does the company expect that continuing deregulation will increase technological innovation?

Demand for new telecom equipment depends partly on the types of services various providers can offer per federal regulations.

How does the company plan to keep up with advances in technology?

Because of rapid advances in technology, equipment manufacturers run a large risk of making outdated products.

Will the company profit from the switch to a national VoIP phone system?

While the traditional telephone system dedicates a single open line to each phone call, the packet-switching technology used by the Internet can send small pieces of many calls along one line, reassembling them at the end.

Is the company developing products for the digital TV market?

With prodding from the federal government, which has granted TV broadcasters extra spectrum and set various deadlines, the US TV system is converting from analog to digital signals.

Web Links

Broadcast Net

Good industry and manufacturer links.
www.broadcast.net

BusinessWeek Online – Technology

Industry news.
www.businessweek.com/technology

Cellular-News

News.
www.cellular-news.com

CTIA – The Wireless Association

Industry news and issues.
www.ctia.org

Federal Communications Commission FCC

Regulatory actions and policy.
www.fcc.gov

National Association of Broadcasters

Industry issues.
www.nab.org

National Cable & Telecommunications Association

Good industry overview, industry issues.
www.ncta.com

Telecommunications Industry Association

Industry statistics, policy issues.
www.tiaonline.org

Telephony Online

Industry news.
telephonyonline.com

United States Telecom Association (USTelecom)

Industry issues.
www.usta.org

Glossary of Acronyms

3G — third generation
AMPS — advanced mobile phone system
ATM — asynchronous transfer mode
CDMA — code-division multiple access
CLEC — competitive local exchange carrier
FTTP — fiber-to-premises
GSM — global system for mobile communications
ILEC — incumbent local exchange carrier
ISDN — integrated services digital network
NEBS — network equipment building standards
PCS — personal communications system
PSTN — public switched telephone network
PUC — Public utility commission
RBOC — Regional Bell operating company
TDMA — time-division multiple access
VOIP — Voice over Internet Protocol

HOOVER'S TOP COMPANIES

Largest Companies by Sales	($ mil.)
Cisco Systems, Inc.	39,540.0
Motorola, Inc.	30,146.0
Harris Corporation	5,311.0
Juniper Networks, Inc.	3,572.4
EchoStar Corporation	2,150.5
Tellabs, Inc.	1,729.0
UTStarcom, Inc.	1,640.4
ADC Telecommunications, Inc.	1,456.4
3Com Corporation	1,294.9
ARRIS Group, Inc.	1,144.6

Largest Employers	Employees
Cisco Systems, Inc.	66,129
Motorola, Inc.	66,000
Harris Corporation	16,500
ADC Telecommunications, Inc.	9,050
Juniper Networks, Inc.	5,879
3Com Corporation	5,572
UTStarcom, Inc.	5,100
Plantronics, Inc.	5,000
Tellabs, Inc.	3,716
Polycom, Inc.	2,478

Fastest Growing* by Five-Year Sales Growth	(%)
Franklin Wireless Corp.	387.2
Proxim Wireless Corporation	266.7
Telkonet, Inc.	244.6
Ambient Corporation	239.1
Airvana, Inc.	148.9
Acme Packet, Inc.	103.9
Occam Networks, Inc.	65.5
Starent Networks Corporation	64.9
ShoreTel, Inc.	61.8
Novatel Wireless, Inc.	56.9

Fastest Growing* by Five-Year Employee Growth	(%)
3Com Corporation	201.2
PCTEL, Inc.	61.2
ShoreTel, Inc.	45.7
Blue Coat Systems, Inc.	39.6
Starent Networks Corporation	38.3
Novatel Wireless, Inc.	32.3
Optelecom-NKF, Inc.	30.5
Acme Packet, Inc.	30.4
F5 Networks, Inc.	27.3
Juniper Networks, Inc.	19.1

Top Public Companies by Market Value	($ mil.)
Cisco Systems, Inc.	132,180.0
Motorola, Inc.	10,084.9
Juniper Networks, Inc.	9,223.4
Harris Corporation	6,837.4
Tellabs, Inc.	1,661.8

* These rates are compounded annualized increases and may have resulted from acquisitions or one time gains. If less than 6 years of data are available, growth is for the years available.

SOURCE: HOOVER'S, INC., DATABASE

Telemarketing Services

THIS INDUSTRY INCLUDES:

SIC CODES
7389   Business Services

NAICS CODES
56142   Telephone Call Centers

The US telemarketing industry includes 5,000 companies with combined annual revenue of about $15 billion. Large companies include Convergys, Teletech, West, and Sitel. The industry is concentrated at the top: the 50 largest companies hold about 60 percent of the market. Despite the dominance of big companies, most firms are small, with annual revenue less than $1 million and fewer than 20 employees.

Competitive Landscape

Demand is largely driven by consumer spending and business activity. The profitability of individual companies depends on efficiency of operations. Big companies have the scale to provide services to large corporate customers. Small companies can compete successfully for small and midsized customers because there are few economies of scale. The industry is very labor-intensive: average annual revenue per employee is just $35,000.

The industry has been sharply affected in recent years by regulatory controls on telemarketing practices and strong competition from offshore operators.

Products, Operations & Technology

Major services are telemarketing sales, customer care, technical support, and call answering. Smaller companies generally specialize in one of these services. Telemarketing sales — also called "customer acquisition" — consists mainly of making outbound phone calls to sell products or services to new customers. Customer care and technical support consist primarily of taking inbound phone calls from existing customers or from new customers placing orders. Technical support helps customers figure out how to use a product, such as a computer or computer program. Customer care can involve passive activities such as taking orders and answering billing or technical

BUSINESS CHALLENGES

» Revenue Tied to Consumer Spending
Because much telemarketing involves selling consumer products or helping consumers who've bought a product, the volume of activity can drop sharply during an economic slowdown. The revenue of many large telemarketing companies fell sharply during the last recession, and industry employment fell 15 percent. To counteract vulnerability to economic cycles, some companies have expanded into other services.

» Competition from Foreign Call Centers
US telemarketing companies face increasing competition from call centers in low-wage countries. Countries like India and the Philippines have an educated, English-speaking workforce that can be paid much less than US workers. Because annual revenue per worker for the industry is under $40,000, labor costs are important in determining profitability.

» Heavy Industry Regulation
The operations of telemarketing companies are strongly affected by state and federal regulations, including restrictions on contact hours and sales practices, and do-not-call registries. Existing and possible future restrictions concern the collection, use, and protection of information about consumers, and how personal health information is handled. Companies that make credit collections or sell insurance, investments, or loans are subject to additional regulations.

support questions, or active initiatives such as follow-up calls to customers and cross- or up-selling. Answering services include automated voicemail systems and live operators, and are often used to provide information to callers outside of regular business hours, especially for critical businesses like doctor offices.

Some companies also provide credit collections services and employee or member care services, such as explaining health care benefits to customer employees or members of managed health care plans.

Telemarketing companies operate call centers, also called "customer management centers" (CMCs), where employees (sometimes called "agents" or "seats") sit at computer workstations and either answer incoming telephone calls or make outgoing calls. For sales calls, computer systems, called "predictive dialers," initiate calls using a call list, screen busy signals and answering machines, and route answered calls to an employee along with a marketing script. Call lists may be acquired from client companies or brokers, or through the firm's own research. For customer care and technical support, computers route incoming calls to an agent who has the information the customer needs, and may provide detailed information about both the product and the caller. Large call centers may hold 500 workstations.

Because computer systems and labor are expensive, telemarketing firms closely monitor capacity utilization and try to maximize the efficiency of their operations. With phone traffic uneven during the day and week, companies may use a large number of part-time employees. Incoming customer service traffic is heaviest during business hours, while outgoing marketing activity is heaviest in the early evening hours. To use labor and computers most efficiently, some companies operate "blended" call centers that handle both customer care and sales.

Computer and telecommunication systems are important aspects of call center operations. Computer systems typically monitor efficiency such as call volume, the average time to answer a call, the average call length, abandoned calls, and call success rate ("contact conversion rate"). The integration of call center activity with customer computer systems ("computer-telephony integration," or CTI) allows call centers to operate as extensions of customers' own phone and information systems.

Sales & Marketing

Telemarketing companies sell services to corporate customers that don't want to handle these functions internally. Most telemarketing is still done internally, but the industry has grown rapidly in the past decade because outsourcing this function is often less costly for customers. Sales are handled by a direct sales force that emphasizes the lower cost of outsourcing.

Major clients are in customer-intensive industries like telecommunication; financial services; publishing (magazine subscriptions); fundraising; cable TV advertising; and computer technology.

Contracts usually last for several years, and may contain a variety of revenue schedules that are typically linked to various performance metrics. Revenues may be based on the time employees are in touch with customers, measured by the hour or minute, success rates for marketing calls, or other performance measures. Base fees, coupled with performance incentives, are common. Sometimes companies work as subcontractors to larger telemarketing companies, or have contracts to handle only the overflow from customers or other operators.

Prices vary widely, depending on contract length, business volume, and the specific performance metrics involved, but some companies quote retail prices for outgoing calls of $400 for 10 hours or $250 for 1,000 calls.

Human Resources

Employee staffing, training, and supervision are major operating activities, especially because employee pay is low and personnel turnover often very high. Average hourly pay for US call centers is 35 percent lower than the average for all US workers. Employee training is especially important for companies that provide technical support for complicated products like computers or software.

Industry Employment Growth

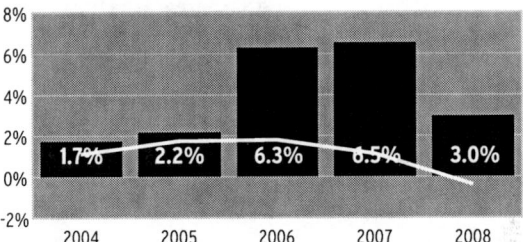

	2004	2005	2006	2007	2008
	1.7%	2.2%	6.3%	6.5%	3.0%

Average Hourly Earnings

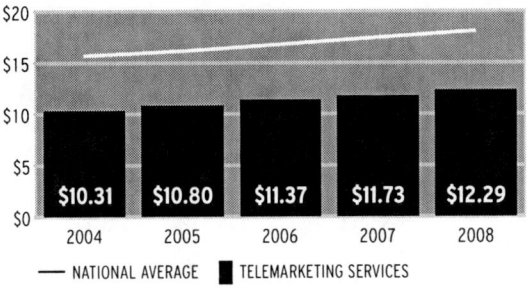

	2004	2005	2006	2007	2008
	$10.31	$10.80	$11.37	$11.73	$12.29

— NATIONAL AVERAGE   ■ TELEMARKETING SERVICES

SOURCE: BUREAU OF LABOR STATISTICS

Call Preparation Questions

How much flexibility does the company have to cut expenses during an economic slowdown?

Because much telemarketing involves selling consumer products or helping consumers who've bought a product, the volume of activity can drop sharply during an economic slowdown.

How are low-cost foreign call centers affecting the company's business?

US telemarketing companies face increasing competition from call centers in low-wage countries.

Does the company expect more government regulation of the industry?

The operations of telemarketing companies are strongly affected by state and federal regulations, including restrictions on contact hours and sales practices, and do-not-call registries.

What new services is the company developing?

As outbound sales calls and inbound customer care have become commodity products, telemarketers have evolved other services that use the same call center infrastructure.

Does the company expect to offer more international services?

The expansion of international trade provides telemarketers the opportunity to support companies with international operations.

Web Links

American Teleservices Association

Good information on legislative/legal developments.
www.ataconnect.org

Canadian Marketing Association

Telemarketing regulatory affairs.
www.the-cma.org/regulatory/telemarketing.cfm

Direct Marketing Association

Industry positions on various regulatory issues.
www.the-dma.org

Federal Trade Commission

Details of the Telemarketing Sales Rule.
www.ftc.gov/bcp/rulemaking/tsr

International Customer Management Institute

Some call center performance statistics. Glossary. Associations.
www.incoming.com/knowledge

Glossary of Acronyms

CMC — customer management centers

CTI — computer-telephony integration

TCFAPA — Telemarketing Consumer Fraud and Abuse Protection Act

TCPA — Telephone Consumer Protections Act

TSR — Telemarketing Sales Rule

HOOVER'S TOP COMPANIES

Largest Companies by Sales	($ mil.)
Convergys Corporation	2,785.8
West Corporation	2,099.5
Sitel Corporation	1,700.0
TeleTech Holdings, Inc.	1,400.2
Protocol Integrated Direct Marketing	1,238.1
Sykes Enterprises, Incorporated	819.2
Sutherland Global Services, Inc.	761.3
ICT Group, Inc.	453.6

Largest Employers	Employees
Convergys Corporation	75,000
Sitel Corporation	66,000
TeleTech Holdings, Inc.	47,000
West Corporation	42,000
Sykes Enterprises, Incorporated	29,560
ICT Group, Inc.	19,006
Teleperformance USA	11,900
Sutherland Global Services, Inc.	10,715
PRC, LLC	10,000
Americall Group, Inc.	10,000

Fastest Growing* by Five-Year Sales Growth	(%)
IA Global, Inc.	135.7
PeopleSupport, Inc.	48.0
Sitel Corporation	33.6
West Corporation	20.7
Rainmaker Systems, Inc.	13.3
Sykes Enterprises, Incorporated	11.3
ICT Group, Inc.	8.7
TeleTech Holdings, Inc.	6.9
Convergys Corporation	4.0

Fastest Growing* by Five-Year Employee Growth	(%)
IA Global, Inc.	208.7
Rainmaker Systems, Inc.	71.8
PeopleSupport, Inc.	42.7
Sitel Corporation	42.1
Convergys Corporation	14.2
Sykes Enterprises, Incorporated	13.5
TeleTech Holdings, Inc.	12.5
West Corporation	11.8
ICT Group, Inc.	11.2

Top Public Companies by Market Value	($ mil.)
Convergys Corporation	1,171.7
Sykes Enterprises, Incorporated	787.3
TeleTech Holdings, Inc.	532.9
PeopleSupport, Inc.	295.5
Stream Global Services, Inc.	216.7

* These rates are compounded annualized increases and may have resulted from acquisitions or one time gains. If less than 6 years of data are available, growth is for the years available.

SOURCE: HOOVER'S, INC., DATABASE

Testing Laboratories

About 6,000 testing laboratories in the US are in operation, with combined annual revenue of around $9 billion. Major companies include National Technical Systems, and subsidiaries of major corporations such as Pratt & Whitney and Hexagon Metrology. The industry is fragmented: the top 50 firms account for only 35 percent of industry revenue. Most labs have about 10 employees; the largest have more than 1,000.

Testing labs provide a variety of engineering, quality control, and certification services by performing physical and chemical tests on products and processes. Companies perform these tests either in a lab or at the customer's site. The industry doesn't include medical or pharmaceutical testing.

Competitive Landscape

Demand is driven largely by industry and government spending on R&D to improve the efficiency of operations and develop new products and services. The profitability of individual companies depends on technical expertise and the ability to accurately predict project costs. Large labs have advantages in providing a larger breadth of service through multiple locations; some have strategic partnerships with major corporations. Small labs compete effectively by specializing in particular types of service. The industry is labor-intensive: average revenue per worker is less than $100,000. Testing labs compete with internal labs of major corporations and government entities.

Products, Operations & Technology

Major testing lab services include chemical, nondestructive, mechanical, and electrical testing. Chemical testing accounts for about 36 percent of industry revenue; nondestructive testing (testing that doesn't destroy the test object) for about 19 percent; mechanical testing, 9 percent; and electrical testing, 8 percent. Other

BUSINESS CHALLENGES

» Reliance on Cyclical Customer Industries

The auto, telecom, aerospace, and high-tech industries, major users of testing labs, are sensitive to economic cycles. During economic downturns, these industries often cut new product development. Increases in US market share by imported products also reduce domestic demand for testing labs. Testing labs that rely on the auto industry have experienced declining gross margins since 2005.

» Dependence on Government Spending

The US Department of Defense (DoD) and the Department of Homeland Security are major customers of independent testing labs. Some labs rely on the DoD for all their work. Testing labs certify innovations in weapons systems and homeland security equipment. Fluctuations in authorized government spending or changes in program priorities can greatly affect testing lab revenue.

» Customer Concentration

Many testing laboratories rely on just a few key clients. The loss of any large client, due to government cutbacks or company budget cuts, can significantly impact the testing lab. Since many labs specialize in narrow fields, finding new clients or expanding into new areas is difficult in the short-term.

services include calibration testing, thermal testing, and assaying.

Testing laboratories have facilities or warehouses specifically constructed to perform tests, simulating various environments according to temperature, altitude, humidity, sunshine, dust, or explosive atmosphere. Items tested include high-technology products, electrical components, hazardous materials, automotive parts, and military items. Testing labs test products for safety; provide product and electrical certifications; and provide compatibility, stress/performance functionality, and compliance testing.

Testing often involves measuring the flow of fluids, chemicals, water, steam, and propellants.

Most tests require special equipment such as electromagnetic interference (EMI) chambers; seismic simulators; environmental, fire, and gas flow chambers; and munitions testing equipment. The cost of such equipment can be substantial, with individual equipment prices ranging from $15,000 to more than $400,000.

Testing labs need to stay abreast of advancing technology and may develop new technologies. They frequently install state-of-the-art equipment to perform tests for clients. Computer systems and proprietary software are used in many testing applications.

Sales & Marketing

Typical customers are companies in the automotive, aerospace, telecommunications, transportation, electronics, and manufacturing industries, along with government agencies. Large labs can have several hundred customers over a variety of industries. Small labs generally specialize in a service area and a particular industry or government agency. Most companies sell their services through direct sales organizations; large labs may also use distributor arrangements for sales overseas.

Many labs rely on just a few customers for repeat business, especially the federal government. Referrals are an important source of new business as labs rely on their professional reputation to generate additional business. Labs may advertise in trade magazines for their target industries, such as automotive or telecommunication journals. Many projects are awarded after a bidding process where the labs demonstrate their capabilities and technical expertise.

Contracts are negotiated with clients and include professional hours, materials, and equipment use. Contract prices vary considerably depending on the types of tests and length of the contract, but can be in the millions. Contracts may call for an initial payment and then progress payments throughout the contract's term.

Human Resources

A large percentage of testing laboratory employees is engineers or scientists with special technical skills, and consequently is well paid. Average earnings for production workers are well above the national average. Companies may hire temporary or part-time workers to meet peaks in project workloads or to acquire

specific technical skills. The industry injury rate is less than a third of the national average.

Industry Employment Growth

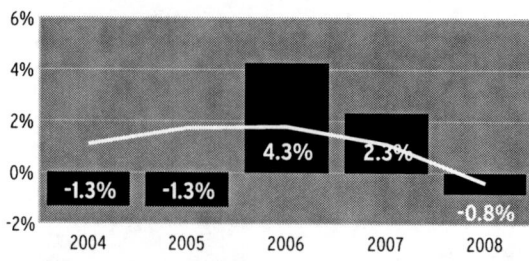

Average Hourly Earnings

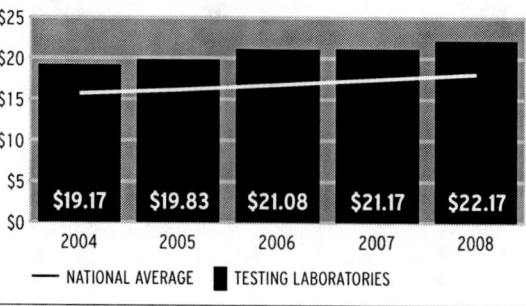

— NATIONAL AVERAGE ▪ TESTING LABORATORIES

SOURCE: BUREAU OF LABOR STATISTICS

Call Preparation Questions

How cyclical is demand for the company's services?

The auto, telecom, aerospace, and high-tech industries, major users of testing labs, are sensitive to economic cycles.

How reliant is the company on federal spending for defense and homeland security?

The US Department of Defense (DoD) and the Department of Homeland Security are major customers of independent testing labs.

What percentage of revenue comes from the company's top five customers?

Many testing laboratories rely on just a few key clients.

What new technology areas is the company pursuing?

Many testing labs are growing by expanding into new technology areas to better service existing customers, and are investing in new equipment to enhance capacity and capabilities.

What opportunities does the company see in the expected growth of wireless communications?

New generation communication systems will require telecommunication companies to update their systems and equipment.

Web Links

American Council of Independent Laboratories

Position papers, publications.
www.acil.org

American Society for Quality

Quality concepts, news, events, links.
www.asq.org

ASM International

Industry news, materials information, events.
www.asminternational.org

ASTM International

Standards, news, workshop listings.
www.astm.org

eCalibration

Events, news, company directories.
www.ecalibration.com

National Institute of Standards & Technology

News, government programs.
www.nist.gov

Quality Magazine

Articles, industry and association links.
www.qualitymag.com

Glossary of Acronyms

ASQ — American Society for Quality
CAB — conformity assessment body
ISO — International Standards Organization
ITL — independent test laboratory
NEBS — network equipment building specifications
NIST — National Institute of Standards & Technology
QSU — quality systems update
RFP — request for proposal

HOOVER'S TOP COMPANIES

Largest Companies by Sales	($ mil.)
Wyle Laboratories, Inc.	800.0
National Technical Systems, Inc.	122.4
TestAmerica Laboratories, Inc.	112.1
SGS North America Inc.	91.0
Lancaster Laboratories, Inc.	76.0
Silliker, Inc.	50.0
Luna Innovations Incorporated	36.9
Professional Service Industries, Inc.	—
Underwriters Laboratories Inc.	—

Largest Employers	Employees
Underwriters Laboratories Inc.	6,023
SGS North America Inc.	4,500
Wyle Laboratories, Inc.	4,200
Professional Service Industries, Inc.	3,000
TestAmerica Laboratories, Inc.	2,150
National Technical Systems, Inc.	874
Lancaster Laboratories, Inc.	800
Silliker, Inc.	635
EMLab P&K	200
Quality Inspection Services, Inc.	140

Top Public Companies by Market Value	($ mil.)
National Technical Systems, Inc.	54.0
Senesco Technologies, Inc.	34.0
Luna Innovations Incorporated	21.4
Genelink, Inc.	8.0

SOURCE: HOOVER'S, INC., DATABASE

Textile Manufacturing

The US textile industry includes about 10,000 companies with combined annual sales of $65 billion. Large companies include Burlington Industries and Unifi. The industry has become concentrated: the 50 largest companies hold more than 60 percent of the market. About 100 companies have annual sales over $100 million.

Competitive Landscape

Demand is driven by the domestic apparel industry and consumer demand for home furnishings like carpets, furniture, and curtains. The profitability of individual companies depends on efficient operations. Large companies have economies of scale in production for high-production items. Small companies can compete successfully by producing specialized textiles. The industry has become more automated but is still labor-intensive: average annual revenue per employee is under $170,000.

Products, Operations & Technology

Major products are yarns and threads, fabrics, carpets, and curtains. The industry produces yarns and threads out of natural (wool and cotton) and synthetic (plastics) materials, uses yarns and threads to produce fabrics that are woven or knit, finishes fabrics by dyeing or coating them, and makes fabrics into simple finished consumer products like rugs, carpets, curtains, linens, and textile bags. Fabrics account for about 40 percent of industry revenue, carpets 20 percent, yarns and threads 20 percent.

Textiles are made in factories (still called mills because they were among the earliest industrial users of water power) using highly specialized, automated machinery, mainly yarn spinning machines, knitting machines, and various looms. The combination of a large number of possible yarns and a large number of knitting and weaving techniques produces a gigantic

BUSINESS CHALLENGES

» Declining Domestic Demand
US textile production has steadily decreased as demand from US apparel makers has dropped. Textile production decreased 30 percent in the last five years, as US apparel manufacture dropped almost 50 percent.

» Import Competition
Imports hold about 25 percent of the US textile market. In the last five years, imports of finished textile mill products doubled. Textile imports from China have increased at an annual rate of 30 to 40 percent.

» Dependence on Trade Regulations
To support stronger international trade, the US has lowered its protection of the US textile and apparel industry. US quotas on apparel and textiles will be lifted; tariffs will remain, but imports are expected to increase.

number of possible textiles in a wide array of colors. Larger textile firms tend to be vertically integrated, often converting raw material into yarn, then using the yarn to produce fabric, which they also dye and finish. Small companies tend to concentrate on niches, and usually aren't involved in all phases of production. Many firms manufacture "greige goods": raw fabric that is dyed and processed by customers.

Textile manufacturers buy raw material for production from various sources. Cellulosic, or natural, fibers, such as cotton, silk, or wool are typically purchased from commodity brokers and farm cooperatives. Synthetic fibers, such as olefin, polyester, acrylic, or nylon, are usually bought from chemical manufacturers like DuPont. Nylon, polyester, and silk are called filaments. Companies manufacture yarns to have various characteristics depending on the intended end-use. A loom runs filaments or yarn threads in various patterns called weaves. The type of thread used and the type of weave pattern applied to it determine the type of fabric produced. Weaves are categorized according to the manufacturing method used, such as plain or satin. The major categories of fabrics are broadloom and knit.

The technology used in textile production is well-known. Most machines are computer controlled. Fabrics are designed using special software programs that can send designs directly to production equipment.

Sales & Marketing

Textile firms sell to apparel manufacturers, furniture manufacturers, other textile companies, and various retailers. The end-uses of US textiles (in pounds) are apparel (35 percent); floor coverings (25 percent); industrial (23 percent); and home furnishings (16 percent). Marketing is often through personal connections, but also sales representatives and trade shows. Given the many possible products, companies often sell their ability to manufacture products to customer specifications. Textile mills usually sell through supply or contract agreements. Some niche companies are vulnerable to customer concentrations.

Human Resources

Many jobs in the industry involve tending automated textile machines, work that requires only modest technical skills and is accordingly paid at below-average rates. The industry has been losing jobs for many years as textile manufacturers have followed their customers, apparel manufacturers, to low-wage countries.

Industry Employment Growth

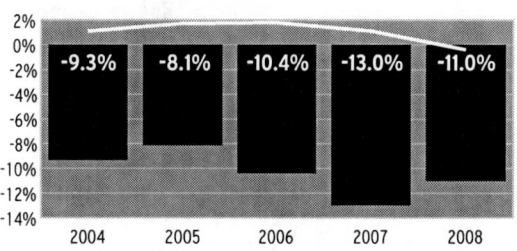

Average Hourly Earnings

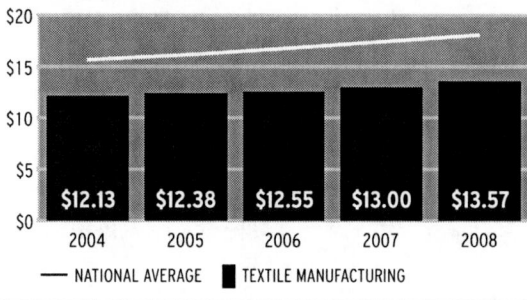

—— NATIONAL AVERAGE ▮ TEXTILE MANUFACTURING

SOURCE: BUREAU OF LABOR STATISTICS

Call Preparation Questions

How might trends in US textile production affect the company in the coming year?

US textile production has steadily decreased as demand from US apparel makers has dropped.

How has the company adapted to competition from imports?

Imports hold about 25 percent of the US textile market. In the last five years, imports of finished textile mill products doubled.

How reliant is the company on trade regulations, like quotas and tariffs?

To support stronger international trade, the US has lowered its protection of the US textile and apparel industry.

What opportunities or challenges does the company see in export markets?

Expansion into Mexico and Caribbean markets has become a new opportunity for US mills.

How much is the company involved in developing new fibers or fabrics?

The use of bio-based products continues to increase.

Web Links

American Association of Textile Chemists and Colorists (AATCC)

Foundation that provides links, magazines, test methods, FAQs, and events.
www.aatcc.org

Fibersource

Statistical publications, news, economic bureau, bookstore, links, and facts.
www.fibersource.com

Industrial Fabrics Association International

International trade association with a resource center, magazines, events, and news.
www.ifai.com

Office of Textiles and Apparel (OTEXA)

Trade data for US textile and apparel imports and exports.
www.otexa.ita.doc.gov

Textile Institute

International organization provides industry news, publications and more.
www.textileinstitute.org

Textile World

Online business information; includes Textile World magazine.
www.textileworld.com

TextileWeb.com

Editorials, financial and industrial news, articles, search engines, and trend spotting.
www.textileweb.com/content/hubs/dir.asp?hub=news

UNITE HERE

Union issues, political action.
www.uniteunion.org

Glossary of Acronyms

ATMI — American Textile Manufacturers Institute
ATA — Agreement on Textiles and Apparel
CBI — Caribbean Basin Initiative
CAD — computer-aided design
EDI — electronic data interchange
JIT — just-in-time
MFA — Multi Fiber Arrangement
PNTR — Permanent Normal Trade Relations
WTO — World Trade Organization

HOOVER'S TOP COMPANIES

Largest Companies by Sales	($ mil.)
Mohawk Industries, Inc.	6,826.4
Milliken & Company	2,270.0
Beaulieu Group, L.L.C.	1,100.0
Albany International Corp.	1,086.5
Interface, Inc.	1,082.3
Polymer Group, Inc.	1,059.7
Springs Global US, Inc.	338.1
Shaw Industries, Inc.	—

Largest Employers	Employees
Mohawk Industries, Inc.	36,200
Shaw Industries, Inc.	30,000
Springs Global US, Inc.	20,000
WestPoint Home, Inc.	15,337
International Textile Group, Inc.	11,900
Milliken & Company	10,000
Albany International Corp.	6,100
Beaulieu Group, L.L.C.	5,850
Interface, Inc.	3,838

Fastest Growing* by Five-Year Sales Growth	(%)
International Textile Group, Inc.	32.8
Polymer Group, Inc.	7.0
The Hallwood Group Incorporated	7.0
Mohawk Industries, Inc.	6.4
Albany International Corp.	4.6
Decorator Industries, Inc.	3.6
Interface, Inc.	3.2
Xerium Technologies, Inc.	3.1

Fastest Growing* by Five-Year Employee Growth	(%)
International Textile Group, Inc.	36.8
Decorator Industries, Inc.	8.0

Top Public Companies by Market Value	($ mil.)
Mohawk Industries, Inc.	2,940.1
Albany International Corp.	343.1
Interface, Inc.	286.1
Xerium Technologies, Inc.	30.5

* These rates are compounded annualized increases and may have resulted from acquisitions or one time gains. If less than 6 years of data are available, growth is for the years available.

SOURCE: HOOVER'S, INC., DATABASE

Timber Operations

The $30 billion US timber industry includes about 300 companies that are involved mainly in timber management, and close to 12,000 firms involved in logging operations. Large companies include Weyerhaeuser, Plum Creek Timber, and Potlatch. The industry is highly fragmented. A large number of companies and individuals are passive owners of timberlands. Some large companies have vertically integrated operations that may combine land ownership, land management, logging, sawmills, and the production of wood or paper products.

Competitive Landscape

Timber is harvested to make paper or wood products (mainly lumber and plywood). Residential construction and repair/remodeling account for nearly 70 percent of all lumber used in the US. Demand for paper is driven partly by the general health of the economy, which influences demand for office papers, cardboard boxes, newspapers, magazines, and tissue papers. Large logging companies can have a cost advantage over smaller ones through the use of more efficient (and more expensive) machinery, but logging is a very local activity, often without significant economies of scale.

Products, Operations & Technology

The US contains about 750 million acres of forest land, including 500 million acres of timberlands. About 180 million acres are considered highly productive, of which half are located in the South and a quarter in the Pacific Northwest. Timberlands in the South contain softwoods like loblolly-shortleaf pines and longleaf-slash pines. Timberlands in the West contain mainly Douglas-fir, fir-spruce, and ponderosa pine. Hardwood timberlands are located mainly in the East and contain mainly oak-hickory or maple-beech-birch. The timber inventory on a piece of land is measured in terms of "cunits" — 100 cubic feet of solid wood.

BUSINESS CHALLENGES

» Competition from Canadian Imports

Because of its large forests, Canada can export large quantities of value-added timber products to the US at competitive prices, despite significant transportation costs. In recent years, Canadian lumber products accounted for about a third of US lumber consumption. The US and Canada frequently have trade disputes over timber products, with US producers charging that Canadian stumpage fees are artificially low.

» Heavy Dependence on Residential Real Estate Construction

Demand for lumber is strongly affected by the residential real estate construction industry, and demand for new residential buildings can change rapidly, depending on the economy and interest rates. Residential construction accounts for nearly 70 percent of all lumber used in the US.

» High Variable Cash Flow

Owners of timberland may have uneven revenue from year to year. Logging operators typically have highly seasonal cash flow.

The federal government, through the USDA Forest Service, is the largest owner of timberland in the US, holding about 30 percent of the total. Major wood products companies own about 10 percent, states and other government bodies own 10 percent, and private owners hold the rest, about 50 percent. Timber companies may own or lease timberland or hold licenses for logging rights on private or public lands. Recently, Weyerhaeuser, for example, owned 6 million acres of land and held long-term licenses on 33 million acres of land in Canada.

Timber operations can be divided into forestry operations and logging operations. Forestry involves the care of growing forests, including planting and tending trees (silviculture); controlling erosion; creating fire breaks; surveying; removing diseased or damaged trees;

and marking trees for logging. Logging involves felling trees; removing branches and top; cutting into lengths ("bucking"); hauling the logs out of the forest; sorting logs by type; loading logs onto trucks; and trucking to sawmills or other destinations. Logging operations are usually handled by crews of four to eight. While felling, branch removal, and bucking are still done with chainsaws in smaller operations, many operators now use mechanized harvesters, that can fell, trim, and cut a tree in one operation. Logging a tract of forest may consist of the removal of selected trees or of all trees (clear-cutting). Clear-cutting is more common on tree farms, where all the trees in a tract are of the same age and size. To be able to remove logs from a forest, operators often must first build access roads. Timber operations may also enter into management contracts with independent logging companies that harvest the timber; management then sells the timber to brokers or at market.

Merchantable timber inventory is an estimate of standing timber available for harvesting. Timber managers consider site indexes, which measure a forest's quality according to timber height growth in a particular location. Timber companies that cultivate their own trees stagger maturation cycles, the age distribution of merchantable timber on their lands.

Sales & Marketing

Larger diameter trees are typically classified as high-value sawtimber, which can be processed into lumber and plywood. Smaller diameter trees are often classified as pulpwood that is used to make paper and cardboard. Advanced technology and management allows the use of every part of the tree to make products. In addition to lumber and paper produced from the tree trunk, products are made from bark, tree resins, cellulose, chips, scraps, and even sawdust.

Standing timber is sold through a variety of contractual arrangements. Buyers are local or regional mills, either independent or owned by integrated wood products companies. Owners sell timber through stumpage sales or timber auctions. These contracts give buyers the right to harvest a specified amount of timber over a certain time period (usually 12 to 24 months). The seller usually receives a 20 percent deposit fee or performance bond, with the balance paid before or as trees are harvested. The buyer usually bears risks associated with changes in market prices. Local prices are influenced by property location; proximity to mills; accessibility (roads); logging conditions; tree size and

quality and species; and the amount of timber per acre. Logs may be sold directly to sawmills or to brokers.

Stumpage prices (prices for standing timber) are usually quoted as dollar per ton or as dollar per thousand board feet (mbf). In 2006, typical Texas stumpage prices were $38 per ton for pine sawtimber ($295/mbf); $15 per ton for hardwood sawtimber; and $5 per ton for pulpwood.

Human Resources

Wages in the timber industry vary from minimum wage for new workers to 50 percent higher than the national average for experienced foresters. About one-third of timber workers are self-employed.

Timber workers are moderately skilled to operate heavy equipment, such as harvesters, loaders, and chainsaws. Timber managers acquire specialized forestry knowledge, and often have college degrees and industry certification.

Due to the hazards of felling trees and operating heavy equipment, the injury rate is 35 percent higher than the national average. The industry's illness rate is double the national average, due largely to workers' exposure to the weather.

Industry Employment Growth

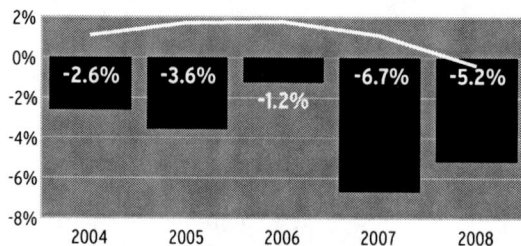

Average Hourly Earnings

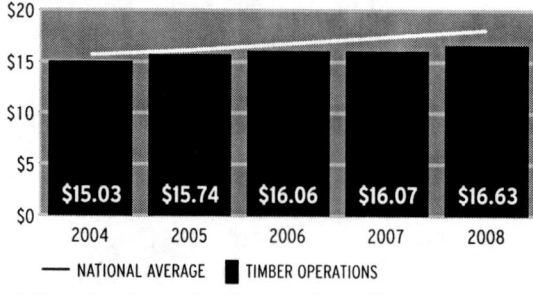

SOURCE: BUREAU OF LABOR STATISTICS

Call Preparation Questions

How is the company affected by timber imports from Canada?

Because of its large forests, Canada can export large quantities of value-added timber products to the US at competitive prices, despite significant transportation costs.

How does the company protect itself from changes in construction demand for wood products?

Demand for lumber is strongly affected by the residential real estate construction industry, and demand for new residential buildings can change rapidly, depending on the economy and interest rates.

If a landowner, what opportunities does the company see in real estate development?

Due to their land's proximity to populated areas, some timber landholders have entered into joint ventures or partnerships with real estate developers to ensure the most profitable and best use of their property.

Web Links

American Forest & Paper Association

Forest products industry news.
http://www.afandpa.org

CME Lumber Futures Ticker

Lumber future prices updated every 10 minutes.
www.cme.com/html.wrap/wrappedpages/end_of_day/daily_settlement_prices/lb.html

Forest Protection Portal

Environmental point of view.
www.forests.org

International Wood Products Association

International programs, industry news, market information, and publications.
www.iwpawood.org

pulpandpaper.net

International features and news.
www.pulpandpaper.net

Random Lengths

Wood and timber prices, market analyses, and more.
www.randomlengths.com

Society of American Foresters

Policy, media, forestry facts, education, publications, and market news.
www.safnet.org

Softwood Export Council

News, information, sources, pricing, and links on exporting softwoods.
www.softwood.org

TimberSource.com

Timber, land, and log sales, stumpage/log pricing, products, and equipment.
www.timbersource.com

US Forest Service

Vast information on forest resources and management.
www.fs.fed.us

Glossary of Acronyms

AF&PA — American Forest & Paper Association
AFRC — American Forest Resource Council
EIA — Energy Information Administration
GM — genetically modified
ITC — International Trade Commission
MBF — thousand board feet
MMSF — million square feet
NIFC — National Interagency Fire Center
SLA — US/Canada Softwood Lumber Agreement
TIMO — timber investment management organization
TMDL — total maximum daily load
WTO — World Trade Organization
WWPA — Western Wood Products Association

HOOVER'S TOP COMPANIES

Largest Companies by Sales	($ mil.)
Weyerhaeuser Company	8,018.0
Louisiana-Pacific Corporation	1,376.2
Plum Creek Timber Company, Inc.	1,614.0
Potlatch Corporation	440.0
Sealaska Corporation	203.2
Pope Resources	51.9
The Westervelt Company	29.3
Vanport International, Inc.	7.4

Largest Employers	Employees
Weyerhaeuser Company	37,900
Louisiana-Pacific Corporation	5,100
Potlatch Corporation	3,800
The Westervelt Company	2,000
Plum Creek Timber Company, Inc.	1,740
Pope Resources, A Delaware Limited Partnership	81
Vanport International, Inc.	31

Top Public Companies by Market Value	($ mil.)
Weyerhaeuser Company	6,467.6
Plum Creek Timber Company, Inc.	5,766.8
Potlatch Corporation	1,033.7
Pope Resources	198.1
Louisiana-Pacific Corporation	161.1

SOURCE: HOOVER'S, INC., DATABASE

Tire Dealers

THIS INDUSTRY INCLUDES:

SIC CODES

5014 Tires and Tubes

5531 Auto and Home
      Supply Stores

NAICS CODES

44132 Tire Dealers

The US tire dealer industry includes about 11,000 firms with combined annual revenue of $22 billion. Large companies include TBC Corporation, Discount Tire, Les Schwab Tire Centers, and retail units of manufacturers Goodyear and Bridgestone. The industry is fairly fragmented: the 50 largest companies hold about 45 percent of the market. A typical dealer store has annual revenue of $1.5 million.

Competitive Landscape

Demand for replacement tires is tied to vehicle usage, which in turn depends on economic activity. The profitability of individual companies depends on marketing, since the product is largely a commodity. Large companies benefit from economies of scale in purchasing and advertising. Small firms can compete effectively by specializing (such as in tires for high-end cars or farm equipment) or by joining purchasing/distribution networks. The average annual revenue per employee is about $140,000.

Products, Operations & Technology

Dealers sell replacement tires for passenger cars (55 percent of the market) and commercial vehicles (25 percent). The industry includes tire-specific stores, automotive parts stores, tire departments of mass retailers, and a variety of automobile service centers. The majority of dealerships are independently owned, though many are franchises or owned by tire manufacturers.

Most tires are made predominantly from natural or synthetic rubber, and may also include steel, rubber-like elastomer polymers, carbon black and other compounds, and processing oils and waxes. An average sized steel-belted radial tire for passenger cars weighs approximately 20 pounds, 16 pounds of which is rubber. A medium truck tire weighs about 117 pounds, 47 pounds of which is rubber. Increases in the cost of rubber triggers price increases

BUSINESS CHALLENGES

» Demand Tied to Car Sales, Economic Cycles

Demand for replacement tires is closely tied to vehicle use and longevity, which are directly affected by the economy. During a recession, consumers tend to keep the cars they have and replace tires less frequently. New car production can drop 5 to 10 percent during a recession, and car traffic decreases. US tire production dropped 13 percent during the last recession.

» Imports Affect Pricing

Competition from imports, which comprise about 20 percent of the US tire market, has kept tire prices down. Among the top five sources of tire imports are low-cost producers China, Korea, and Taiwan. In recent years, tire imports rose 10 percent, while consumer prices were almost flat.

» Cost Pressures Squeeze Supply Chain

Tire retailers are less likely than manufacturers or wholesalers to be able to pass cost increases to price-sensitive customers. A per-tire price difference of $10 to $15 is enough to result in product switching. During periods of increasing wholesale costs, tire dealers may have to accept lower profit margins.

throughout the tire supply chain, from manufacturers to wholesalers to retailers.

Dealers carry inventory, which most buy from wholesalers and distributors. The largest retailers, such as national chains, buy directly under contract from tire manufacturers. Large dealers have the resources to customize inventory for specific stores based on market research that identifies the quantity and types of cars registered in the respective regions. Tire dealers may sell national or private label brands, although some specialize in one or the other; private label tires often are cheaper. Consumers tend to have brand loyalty, but are price-sensitive.

Technology related to inventory management and sales systems are widely used. Point-of-sale data are transmitted to the inventory systems, which can trigger a purchase notice if supplies dip below a specified level. The most integrated systems link purchase orders directly to suppliers' systems. Suppliers often provide retailers with desktop or free-standing computer display systems called kiosks, which dealer salespeople or customers can use to read tire specifications and see pictures of various tire sizes and styles.

Sales & Marketing

Dealers depend heavily on manufacturer advertising to create demand and brand recognition. Established trademarks have a market advantage, particularly over new, imported brands. Large dealers may contribute to cooperative advertising campaigns that manufacturers manage. Newspapers are a major advertising medium. Dealers benefit from manufacturers' use of cooperative TV advertising with automakers, and from their sponsorship of racing cars and events that feature company tires. Dealers offer credit cards, coupons, frequent purchaser incentives, and special sales they promote via direct mail and websites.

Large commercial customers may have contracts in which they receive discounts in exchange for committing to purchase a specific number of tires or spend a certain amount of money in a specified time. Dealers may also contract with large companies, such as truck fleets or taxi companies, to manage their tire replacement programs, including tires, installation, and service.

Prices for new tires range from $40 to hundreds of dollars, whereas used tires can cost less than $10 each. The majority of business is retail, though dealers typically offer wholesale prices to commercial customers who buy frequently or in large quantities. The market is highly price-sensitive: imports of cheap tires have kept consumer prices low for a decade. From 2000 through 2006, consumer prices rose 11 percent.

Human Resources

Workers in tire dealerships include salespeople and installers. Because the work requires only modest training and skills, wages are typically 15 percent lower than for the average US worker. The average annual personnel turnover rate in the retail sector as a whole is close to 50 percent.

Industry Employment Growth

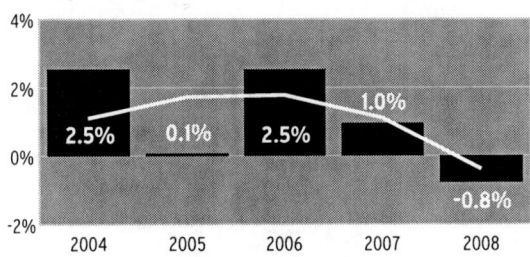

Average Hourly Earnings

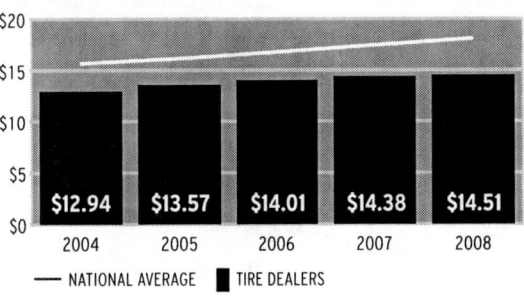

— NATIONAL AVERAGE ■ TIRE DEALERS

SOURCE: BUREAU OF LABOR STATISTICS

Call Preparation Questions

How has the economy affected the company's business the past few years?

Demand for replacement tires is closely tied to vehicle use and longevity, which are directly affected by the economy.

How are low-cost imports impacting the company?

Competition from imports, which comprise about 20 percent of the US tire market, has kept tire prices down.

What percentage of cost increases can the company pass to customers?

Tire retailers are less likely than manufacturers or wholesalers to be able to pass cost increases to price-sensitive customers.

How important to the company is improving its product mix?

To reduce dependence on a single supplier and improve revenues, many dealers offer a merchandising mix of low-cost imports, high-demand performance tires, and wheel accessories.

How would the company benefit if it introduced or expanded services?

Some dealers offer auto maintenance or fleet maintenance services in addition to tire sales.

Web Links

Modern Tire Dealer

Industry news.
www.mtdealer.com

National Highway Traffic Safety Administration

Regulatory issues about tire safety.
www.nhtsa.gov

National Retail Federation

Retail news, information and resources.
www.nrf.com

Retail Benchmarking Association

Specific data related to retail performance and
benchmarking.
www.rbabenchmarking.com

Rubber Manufacturers Association

Manufacturing news and technical information.
www.rma.org

Rubber.com

Information about rubber and tires, plus directory of
tire retailers.
www.rubber.com

TBC Corporation

Industry leader in private brands with wholesale and
retail tire operations.
www.tbccorp.com

Tire Business

Industry news.
www.tirebusiness.com

Tire Industry Association

News, events and government issues concerning the
industry.
www.tireindustry.org

Tire Review

Annual survey of dealers. Some industry news.
www.tirereview.com

Glossary of Acronyms

NHTSA — National Highway Traffic Safety
Administration
RFID — radio frequency identification
TPMS — tire pressure monitoring system
TREAD — Transportation Recall Enhancement,
Accountability and Documentation Act of 2000

HOOVER'S TOP COMPANIES

Largest Companies by Sales	($ mil.)
The Goodyear Tire & Rubber Company	19,488.0
Discount Tire Co. Inc.	2,310.0
American Tire Distributors Holdings, Inc.	1,877.5
TBC Corporation	1,779.4
Les Schwab Tire Centers	1,480.0
Bridgestone Americas, Inc.	—

Largest Employers	Employees
The Goodyear Tire & Rubber Company	74,700
Discount Tire Co. Inc.	11,630
TBC Corporation	9,400
Les Schwab Tire Centers	7,900
TCI Tire Centers, LLC	2,400
American Tire Distributors Holdings, Inc.	2,400

Fastest Growing* by Five-Year Sales Growth	(%)
American Tire Distributors Holdings, Inc.	12.1
Discount Tire Co. Inc.	10.3
Les Schwab Tire Centers	8.2
The Goodyear Tire & Rubber Company	5.2

Fastest Growing* by Five-Year Employee Growth	(%)
Les Schwab Tire Centers	5.7
Discount Tire Co. Inc.	5.4
American Tire Distributors Holdings, Inc.	4.6

Top Public Companies by Market Value	($ mil.)
The Goodyear Tire & Rubber Company	1,440.5

* These rates are compounded annualized increases and may
have resulted from acquisitions or one time gains. If less
than 6 years of data are available, growth is for the years
available.

SOURCE: HOOVER'S, INC., DATABASE

Tire Manufacturers

The US tire manufacturing industry consists of about 100 companies that operate 160 plants with combined annual revenue of $13 billion. Large companies include Goodyear, Bridgestone, Michelin, and Cooper. The industry is highly concentrated: the top four companies hold more than 75 percent of the market. About 35 plants have annual revenue over $100 million.

Competitive Landscape

Demand is driven by sales of new vehicles and the need for replacement tires. Because tires are largely a commodity, profitability depends on cost-efficient operations. Small companies can compete by producing tires or tire-related products for niche markets, such as bicycles or farm equipment. Large companies can afford the research to develop tires from new, technologically advanced materials, and can invest in improving production efficiency. The industry is capital-intensive: average annual revenue per employee is over $200,000.

Products, Operations & Technology

Companies in the tire industry manufacture new tires, inner tubes, and materials for tire repair and retreading, primarily from synthetic and natural rubber. Tire manufacturers may specialize by type of vehicle or size of tire, such as for cars, trucks, airplanes, farm equipment, or children's vehicles. They may also specialize by type of tire: pneumatic (inflatable); solid; or semi-pneumatic, and may make tire repair and retreading materials.

The top revenue-producing products are tires for passenger cars (55 percent of industry revenue); trucks and buses (30 percent); and tractor, farm and industrial vehicles (5 percent). About 300 million tires are produced in the US each year.

A major tire manufacturer may design, manufacture, and sell thousands of different products for a wide range of vehicles and sizes.

BUSINESS CHALLENGES

» Demand Closely Tied to Auto Sales, Economic Cycles

Demand for tires depends on new car sales and highway-miles of driving, both which are affected by economic slowdowns. New car production can drop 5 to 10 percent in one year during a recession, as car and truck traffic flattens. US tire production dropped 13 percent during the last recession.

» Competition from Low-Cost Imports

Tire imports from low-cost countries have kept retail prices flat, despite higher costs for US producers. Foreign producers can use low-cost labor to assemble tires by hand. In the last five years, tire imports from China doubled. Imported tires hold about 30 percent of the US market.

» Varying Raw Material Prices

Synthetic rubber and carbon black, which together account for almost half of the material in a tire, are manufactured from petroleum. Synthetic rubber prices can rise rapidly in response to higher crude oil prices; natural rubber prices rise primarily due to supply and demand. Materials account for about half the total cost to make a tire.

Bridgestone has over 8,000 different types and sizes of tires: the largest is a 13-foot-tall giant radial tire for earthmoving equipment; the smallest is a 10-inch-high kart tire.

The basic tire-making process consists of mixing rubber and various additives in a large mixer called a Banbury machine, then cooling the mixture, rolling it flat, and cutting it into strips. Tires are assembled as layers of rubber strips along with reinforcing materials and adhesives on a tire-building machine to produce a "green" (uncured) tire. The tire is then heated in a curing press at a high temperature, which "vulcanizes" the rubber and produces the final shape. The process is capital-intensive, uses a fair amount of energy, and produces polluting vapors.

The primary raw materials used are synthetic rubber; carbon black (for traction); natural rubber; various chemicals; and reinforcing components such as steel wire, steel cord, and polyester. Both synthetic rubber and carbon black are derived from petroleum or natural gas. Other components used in manufacturing synthetic rubber are styrene and butadiene. Natural rubber is collected as sap from rubber trees on large plantations in Indonesia, Malaysia, Thailand, and Brazil.

A wide variety of compounds are used in various types of tires. The compounds in passenger tires differ from those in truck tires. Traditionally tires are made from rubber, but newer compositions include chemical compounds called elastomer polymers, which are elastic, rubber-like substances. Some tires are made from new types of polyurethane foam, used for wheelchairs, golf carts, and other "low-cycle" purposes. Companies often use proprietary chemical engineering processes and different ingredients to compound their tires.

Non-tire products include tread rubber, accessories like mud flaps, and repair materials. Tread rubber, also called camelback, is the patterned rubber bonded to worn tires. In 2003, Goodyear and Bandag had about 70 percent of the tread rubber market segment. Products that compete with new US-made tires include retreads (treads bonded to existing casings) and imports from Asia and South America.

Designing and building a new tire model can be costly. Advanced processes use state-of-the-art "virtual" technology that simulates three dimensions and the sense of touch, so that design engineers can modify the tire without building a non-production model.

The industry depends on technology for competitive advantage in design, development, and manufacture. Designers use CAD systems to create visual models and drawings of tires that an engineer has specified in a design-specification document. Production plants use computer-aided manufacturing (CAM) systems to pinpoint exactly where to put each compound on the tire. Manufacture of low-volume products, however, often isn't automated. Some companies produce low-volume products, such as motorcycle tires, in addition to high-volume products.

Sales & Marketing

Sales channels include vehicle manufacturers, tire dealers, wholesalers, and retail chains, and in some cases, direct sales to end-users through company-owned retail stores, such as those owned by Bridgestone and Goodyear. The industry sells to car and truck manufacturers, such as Ford and GM (OEMs) that need tires for new vehicles. The largest segment of the market, about 80 percent, is for replacement tires. Large fleet truck operators and consumers are key end-users of replacement tires.

Since the replacement market is highly competitive, account managers pay careful attention to distribution channels and dealers. Value-added programs, such as warranty, credit, and training programs, are important to the channels. For many manufacturers, large regional and national tire retailers are becoming increasingly important customers.

Tire manufacturers vary in their use of sales channels. Cooper, for instance, doesn't sell to OEMs. Some large tire manufacturers sell directly to national and large accounts and use distributors to sell to automotive chains and other retail stores. Manufacturers such as Goodyear and Bridgestone have retail store divisions that sell directly to consumers.

Pricing varies greatly by tire type and size and vehicle type. Competitive pricing pressures are high in the passenger car segment, particularly from low-priced imports. Some companies introduce new tire products to encourage a sense of changing style, so to speak, and a reason for higher prices, as seen with the spoke-type tires on recent new cars. Truck tires, however unstylish, tend to have higher profit margins.

Tire manufacturers may sell multiple brand names. Michelin, for example, owns the BF Goodrich, Uniroyal, and Cavalier brands. Bridgestone also makes the Firestone and Dayton brands. Goodyear sells Dunlop through a Japanese alliance. Many tire manufacturers also produce products under private label.

TV, magazines, and newspapers are key advertising media. Racecar usage of a brand's tires and a tire manufacturer's sponsorship of a racecar can reap huge amounts of public relations and media coverage.

Human Resources

Tire production workers require special skills and earn 35 percent more than the average US worker. The industry injury rate is 50 percent higher than average; a third of injuries are serious enough to result in more then 30 days missed from work.

Special technical knowledge comes from designers who use CAD systems, chemical engineers who compound the substances that go into the tires, manufacturing plant managers, and waste and environmental specialists who manage recycling manufacturing byproducts.

Industry Employment Growth

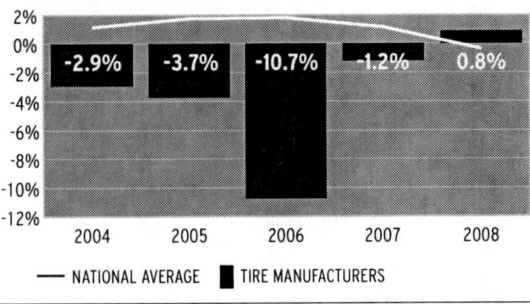

SOURCE: BUREAU OF LABOR STATISTICS

Call Preparation Questions

How are imports from low-cost countries like China impacting the company?

Tire imports from low-cost countries have kept retail prices flat, despite higher costs for US producers.

How do higher oil prices impact company expenses?

Synthetic rubber and carbon black, which together account for almost half of the material in a tire, are manufactured from petroleum.

How are new technologies like tire pressure sensors impacting demand for replacement tires?

"Run-flat" tires meet consumer demand to eliminate blowouts and tire-changing on the side of the road.

What monitoring system does the company use to detect defective tires in the field?

Accidents and product recalls cost lives and money, so companies seek new ways to proactively address potential problems.

Web Links

Modern Tire Dealer

Industry news. Excellent statistics.
www.mtdealer.com

National Highway Traffic Safety Administration

Regulator of tires.
www.nhtsa.dot.gov

Rubber Association of Canada

Excellent Canadian market information.
www.rubberassociation.ca

Rubber Manufacturers Association

www.rma.org

Rubber News

www.rubbernews.com

Tire Business

Industry news.
www.tirebusiness.com

Tire Industry Association

Calendar of trade shows.
www.tireindustry.org

Tire Retread Information Bureau

Retread industry facts.
www.retread.org

Tire Review

Industry news.
www.tirereview.com

Glossary of Acronyms

CAD — computer-aided design system

CAM — computer-aided manufacturing system

FMVSS109 — The Federal Motor Vehicle Safety Standard 109

ISO — International Organization for Standardization

ISO 9000 — ISO's standard for quality management of business processes and operations

ISO 14000 — ISO's standard for environmental management

NTSB — National Transportation Safety Board

OEM — original equipment manufacturer

TREAD — Transportation Recall Enhancement, Accountability and Documentation Act

HOOVER'S TOP COMPANIES

Largest Companies by Sales	($ mil.)
The Goodyear Tire & Rubber Company	19,488.0
Cooper Tire & Rubber Company	2,881.8
Carlisle Tire & Wheel Company	290.1
Falken Tire Corporation	17.6
Amerityre Corporation	2.9
Bridgestone Americas, Inc.	—
Michelin North America, Inc.	—

Largest Employers	Employees
The Goodyear Tire & Rubber Company	74,700
Michelin North America, Inc.	23,453
Cooper Tire & Rubber Company	13,355
Carlisle Tire & Wheel Company	2,800
Falken Tire Corporation	50
Amerityre Corporation	28

Top Public Companies by Market Value	($ mil.)
The Goodyear Tire & Rubber Company	1,440.5
Cooper Tire & Rubber Company	362.9
Amerityre Corporation	31.4

SOURCE: HOOVER'S, INC., DATABASE

Tire Wholesalers

The US tire and tube wholesaler industry includes about 2,000 companies with combined annual revenue of $17 billion. Major companies include American Tire Distributors and TBC Corporation. The industry is highly concentrated: the 50 largest companies hold about 70 percent the market. Most companies are small, with a dozen employees and less than $5 million in annual revenue. A large wholesaler may have $200 million in annual revenue and a network of 10 sales centers.

Competitive Landscape

Demand depends on consumer income and driving volume. The profitability of individual companies is linked to merchandising and good marketing. Small companies can compete by specializing in types of tires or applications (such as for farm equipment or motorcycles) or offering superior service and support. Large wholesalers have economies of scale in distribution, support of national accounts, and advertising and promotion. Annual revenue per employee is close to $600,000.

Products, Operations & Technology

Tire wholesalers sell new replacement automobile tires (50 percent of revenue); new replacement truck, bus, and industrial tires (40 percent); and used or retreaded tires (less than 10 percent). (Original tires for new cars are sold directly to car companies, called OEMs, by tire manufacturers.) Some wholesalers also sell wheels and associated parts. About 75 percent of consumer tire sales are "flag" brands (premium manufacturer brands); 10 percent are "associate" brands (economy manufacturer); and 15 percent are private-label.

Product is bought from manufacturers like Goodyear, Bridgestone, and Cooper Tire, and is also imported from foreign producers. Supply contracts with manufacturers are typically ne-

BUSINESS CHALLENGES

» Dependence on Large Suppliers

Most wholesalers depend highly on a few large suppliers. Because of industry consolidation in the past decade, the four largest manufacturers account for 75 percent of US production. Consequently, wholesalers have reduced power to negotiate favorable prices and are vulnerable to their suppliers' financial situation. American Tire Distributors, the largest US wholesaler, buys close to 80 percent of its tires from just three suppliers.

» Vulnerable to Higher Fuel Costs

Because they distribute a heavy product with a fairly low profit margin, tire wholesalers are vulnerable to increases in fuel costs, as prices for gas or diesel can increase 50 percent within a year. If higher delivery costs are passed to customers, the effective sales radius around a distribution center is reduced.

» Large Retailers Bypass Wholesalers

Large tire retailers, like Sears and Wal-Mart, and buyers clubs, like Costco, are big enough to buy product directly from tire manufacturers. The growth of retail tire chains in the past decade has also resulted in companies able to bypass wholesalers. Independent dealers, the major customers of wholesalers, now hold only about 60 percent of the market.

gotiated annually and include quantities and prices.

Wholesaler operations consist of warehouse operations and sales. Large wholesalers operate a network of warehouses and sales offices. Warehouses may receive product from the 160 tire manufacturing plants in the US; large wholesalers buy product from a number of manufacturers.

Warehouse operations and inventory management can be complicated, because of the large number of tire products. Bridgestone, for example, produces 8,000 types and sizes of tires. In addition to serving as a warehouse for customers, wholesalers may also handle orders for customers, arranging to have product shipped directly ("drop-shipped") from the manufacturer to the customer.

Computer systems are essential for efficient inventory management. Wholesalers' systems track sales and orders and match them against inventory. When inventory for a particular item drops below a specified number, supply chain automation systems trigger an order to the supplier, which may be another wholesaler or the manufacturer. Most companies link to their suppliers and customers to share product specifications and availability, shipping, and pricing information. Wholesalers use the Web for sales and customer support to businesses.

Sales & Marketing

Wholesalers sell mainly to independent tire dealers, but also national chains, repair shops, auto parts stores, and other wholesalers. Wholesalers may compete with dealers for small customers and tire manufacturers for large customers. Manufacturers' sales branches handle about $5 billion in annual business and are major competitors for national accounts.

Large wholesalers typically use telemarketing and have a field sales force; some advertise in industry magazines.

Large wholesale distributors provide retail dealers with computerized tools, such as software that allows them to show customers how a specific tire and wheel "fitment" will look on a customer's car. Online marketplaces, where sellers and buyers post "wanted" or "for sale" notices, are used especially by those wholesalers who focus on selling older product lines, used tires, and exports to developing countries.

Human Resources

Jobs in tire wholesaling require few special skills and therefore have wages close to the national average. Warehouse material handling and trucking jobs typically pay slightly more. Salespeople make up about 30 percent of staff, for whom training is important, as they must be familiar with tire materials and construction.

Call Preparation Questions

How sharply would the company be affected if it lost its main supplier?

Most wholesalers depend highly on a few large suppliers.

How does the company protect itself from higher fuel costs?

Because they distribute a heavy product with a fairly low profit margin, tire wholesalers are vulnerable to increases in fuel costs, as prices for gas or diesel can increase 50 percent within a year.

How do retailers like Sears, Wal-Mart, and other big chains impact competition in the company's market?

Large tire retailers, like Sears and Wal-Mart, and buyers clubs, like Costco, are big enough to buy product directly from tire manufacturers.

Does the company plan to sell more private-label tires?

Some distributors sell their own brands, typically manufactured by one of the major tire companies.

What types of non-tire products or services could increase revenues?

Some tire wholesalers are expanding their product line by selling associated products like wheels, tire mounting equipment; and by offering training, advertising, and other services.

Web Links

American Tire Distributors

"Retailer Home" button shows services provided to retailers.
www.americantiredistributors.com

Modern Tire Dealer

Breaking news and industry resources.
www.mtdealer.com

National Association of Wholesaler-Distributors

A lobbying group that promotes issues of the wholesaler-distributor industry.
www.naw.org

Rubber Association of Canada

Excellent Canadian market information.
www.rubberassociation.ca

Rubber Manufacturers Association

News, data and publications about the tire industry.
www.rma.org

Rubber.com

Includes directories of tire manufacturers, wholesalers, distributors and retailers.
www.rubber.com

Tire Business

Tire industry news.
www.tirebusiness.com

Tire Industry Association

Calendar of trade shows.
www.tireindustry.org

Glossary of Acronyms

OEM — original equipment manufacturer
TREAD — Transportation Recall Enhancement, Accountability and Documentation Act

HOOVER'S TOP COMPANIES

Largest Companies by Sales	($ mil.)
Discount Tire Co. Inc.	2,310.0
American Tire Distributors Holdings, Inc.	1,877.5
TBC Corporation	1,779.4
Les Schwab Tire Centers	1,480.0

Largest Employers	Employees
Discount Tire Co. Inc.	11,630
TBC Corporation	9,400
Les Schwab Tire Centers	7,900
TCI Tire Centers, LLC	2,400
American Tire Distributors Holdings, Inc.	2,400

Fastest Growing* by Five-Year Sales Growth	(%)
American Tire Distributors Holdings, Inc.	12.1
Discount Tire Co. Inc.	10.3
Les Schwab Tire Centers	8.2

Fastest Growing* by Five-Year Employee Growth	(%)
Les Schwab Tire Centers	5.7
Discount Tire Co. Inc.	5.4
American Tire Distributors Holdings, Inc.	4.6

* These rates are compounded annualized increases and may have resulted from acquisitions or one time gains. If less than 6 years of data are available, growth is for the years available.

SOURCE: HOOVER'S, INC., DATABASE

Title Insurance Services

THIS INDUSTRY INCLUDES:

SIC CODES
6361   Title Insurance

NAICS CODES
524127   Direct Title
         Insurance Carriers

Slightly more than 100 licensed title insurance carriers operate in the US, with combined revenue of $12 billion. Large companies include Fidelity National Financial, First American Title Insurance, Old Republic International, and Stewart Information Services. The industry is highly concentrated.

Competitive Landscape

Home sales and mortgage refinancing are the primary drivers of demand for the title insurance industry. The profitability of individual companies depends on efficient operations because of the large volume of transactions. Large companies benefit from economies of scale in access to large accumulated databases of property records. Small companies can mainly compete by specializing in non-standard titles or in geographical regions that the large companies don't cover.

Products, Operations & Technology

The two types of title insurance policies are for owners and lenders, and may be issued for either residential or commercial properties. Most title companies get the majority of their revenue from the residential real estate market. Although commercial real estate transactions are generally larger, about 80 percent of insurance volume is from residential properties (although accurate data are unavailable). Both home sales and mortgage refinancing trigger the need for a title search and an insurance policy.

Title insurance is issued after a search of various public records to establish who owns the title to a property and to uncover any existing liens, use restrictions, or ownership interest held by any other party. Owner policies protect the owner against defects in the title that existed at the time a property was purchased. Lender policies protect a lender against title defects that existed at the time a loan was made

BUSINESS CHALLENGES

» Highly Dependent on Mortgage Originations

Industry revenue is tied to the volume of residential mortgage originations, which can swing widely from year to year. The number of home sales depends on the strength of the economy, and rising and falling mortgage rates affect the volume of mortgage refinancing activity. The total volume of mortgage originations can fluctuate more than 50 percent in a single year.

» Competition from Other Insurance Products

Due to the high cost of title insurance, other types of insurance coverage have been proposed. "Lien protection" insurance would protect pools of mortgages against lien claims, at lower cost. State regulators continue to focus on whether lien protection can be defined as mortgage guarantee or title insurance.

» Competition from Government

The title insurance industry essentially has a monopoly, which Iowa has upset by undercutting industry rates by about 80 percent. Iowa issues its own title guarantees based on title opinions from 2,000 participating lawyers. Private companies can't easily compete in the state, because the premium for government-issued title insurance is so low. The state charges 0.1 percent of the amount insured compared to an average of 0.5 percent private title companies charge. Critics of the title insurance industry point to the Iowa program as a lower-cost alternative.

on a property. Owner policies remain in force until a property is sold, lender policies until a loan has been repaid. In a typical residential real estate transaction, the mortgage lender requires that the home buyer pay for title insurance to cover the lender in the amount of the mortgage. The home owner may buy an owner policy as well, but the bulk of policies sold in the residential market are lender policies.

Title insurance is different from other types of insurance in that it indemnifies a holder against past, rather than future, events. Because of this key distinction, insurers can minimize losses by thoroughly searching public records, maps, and other documents. The main expense for title insurance companies is not insurance losses, but the expense of searching records. In recent years, insurance losses amounted to only about 5 percent at national companies. Insurance losses arise through research errors that fail to notice title defects and through "hidden defects" such as fraud and forgery.

Title searches are conducted through local branch offices, approved lawyers, and independent insurance agents. Although public records offices are the focus of title research, in many cases, searches are aided by the establishment of local "title plants" that are repositories of copies of public and other documents, indexed by individual property. The information in these plants is updated daily or weekly by arrangement with public records offices and other sources of information. Title plants are often highly automated and allow searches to be made at low cost, as the need for an examiner to visit public records' offices for each search is eliminated. Local plants may be operated by a single title insurer or shared with other title companies.

Sales & Marketing

Title companies get business through local contacts with real estate attorneys, real estate brokers, developers, home builders, mortgage originators, mortgage brokers, and escrow agents. In addition to local sources, business comes from large regional or national mortgage originators. Large originators are often interested in a title company that can provide one-stop shopping for a variety of real estate services. Most title insurance is sold through agents. If agents or approved attorneys conduct a title search, they retain much of the title insurance premium. Independent agents may choose among several title companies, depending on the split of fees. To keep more of the premium, title insurers may use their own agents. Fidelity National has a network of 7,000 agents.

Pricing is not the major point of competition, partly because state insurance commissioners often fix rates, and partly because the home owner, rather than the lender, pays the premium. Title insurance premiums are linked to property values, which generally appreciate over time. Customers pay the premium in one lump sum, usually at the real estate closing. Prices are often around 0.5 percent of the insured amount. In addition to the cost of the title insurance, many customers also pay fees for other services that support real estate transactions, such as escrow and closing services, property appraisals, document preparation, recordings, and credit reporting. For a typical $200,000 mortgage, fees for such related services may total $750, while the title insurance costs $1,000.

Human Resources

Wages are high, personnel turnover is low, and the safety record is good for title industry employees. People who conduct title searches and underwrite insurance are highly skilled in real estate research, finance, and insurance. They earn average hourly wages over $22, well above the national average of $15. The annual personnel turnover rate in finance and insurance is about half the national average for private industry.

Due to swings in transaction volume that can vary greatly throughout the year and from year to year, companies have varying needs for labor. Some companies use a significant number of part-time employees. Maintaining high-quality title searches with part-time workers can be a problem.

Industry Employment Growth

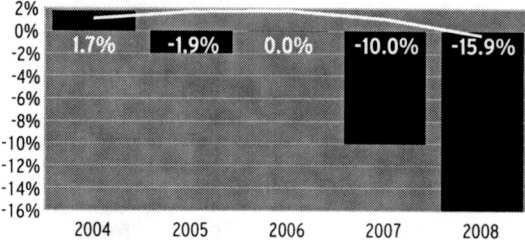

Average Hourly Earnings

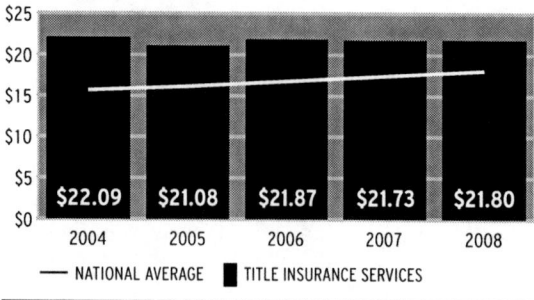

NATIONAL AVERAGE ■ TITLE INSURANCE SERVICES

SOURCE: BUREAU OF LABOR STATISTICS

Call Preparation Questions

What strategies does the company use to deal with fluctuating mortgage demand?

Industry revenue is tied to the volume of residential mortgage originations, which can swing widely from year to year.

What impact could competing insurance products have on the company?

Due to the high cost of title insurance, other types of insurance coverage have been proposed.

How concerned is the company that states will follow Iowa in offering government-sponsored title insurance?

The title insurance industry essentially has a monopoly, which Iowa has upset by undercutting industry rates by about 80 percent.

How does the company benefit from selling fee-based products (in contrast to mortgage-based titles)? What plans does it have to add more?

While title insurance revenue is based on the size of a mortgage, revenue from other types of services related to real estate is in the form of flat fees.

How have lenders' increasing demands for one-stop shopping affected the company?

Mortgage industry consolidation has concentrated more lending in fewer hands and increased demand for one-stop shopping for real estate-related services.

Web Links

American Land Title Association

News. Industry association.
www.alta.org

Mortgage Bankers Association

www.mortgagebankers.org

National Association of Insurance Commissioners

www.naic.org

National Association of Realtors

Housing market information.
www.realtor.org

National Mortgage News

News.
www.nationalmortgagenews.com

US Department of Housing and Urban Development

www.hud.gov

Glossary of Acronyms

ALTA — American Land Title Association
FNF — Fidelity National Financial
MBA — Mortgage Bankers Association
RESPA — Real Estate Settlement Procedures Act

HOOVER'S TOP COMPANIES

Largest Companies by Sales	($ mil.)
The First American Corporation	6,213.8
Fidelity National Financial, Inc.	4,329.1
LandAmerica Financial Group, Inc.	3,705.8
Stewart Information Services Corporation	2,106.7
Old Republic Title Holding Company, Inc	185.7
Attorneys' Title Insurance Fund, Inc.	143.6
Investors Title Company	71.1
North American Title Group, Inc.	62.6
Heritage Title Company of Austin, Inc.	24.9

Largest Employers	Employees
The First American Corporation	37,354
Fidelity National Financial, Inc.	15,500
LandAmerica Financial Group, Inc.	11,050
Stewart Information Services Corporation	8,500
North American Title Group, Inc.	1,002
Attorneys' Title Insurance Fund, Inc.	819
Old Republic Title Holding Company, Inc	600
Heritage Title Company of Austin, Inc.	83

Fastest Growing* by Five-Year Sales Growth	(%)
Heritage Title Company of Austin, Inc.	21.0
LandAmerica Financial Group, Inc.	7.5
Stewart Information Services Corporation	3.4
Attorneys' Title Insurance Fund, Inc.	1.5

Fastest Growing* by Five-Year Employee Growth	(%)
Heritage Title Company of Austin, Inc.	5.9
The First American Corporation	2.7
LandAmerica Financial Group, Inc.	1.9
Stewart Information Services Corporation	1.6

Top Public Companies by Market Value	($ mil.)
Fidelity National Financial, Inc.	3,814.5
The First American Corporation	2,685.7
Stewart Information Services Corporation	451.7
Investors Title Company	85.7

* These rates are compounded annualized increases and may have resulted from acquisitions or one time gains. If less than 6 years of data are available, growth is for the years available.

SOURCE: HOOVER'S, INC., DATABASE

Tobacco Manufacture

The tobacco manufacturing industry includes about 100 companies with combined annual revenue of nearly $40 billion. Major companies include Philip Morris USA, Reynolds American, Lorillard, and Vector Group. The industry is highly concentrated: the 50 largest companies hold nearly 100 percent of the market.

Competitive Landscape

Demand is driven by discretionary consumer spending and awareness of the health effects of smoking. The profitability of individual companies depends on effective marketing. Large companies have advantages in economies of scale in manufacturing and product loyalty. Small companies can compete effectively through heavy discounting, clever branding and packaging, and by exploiting niche categories such as pipe tobacco and additive-free cigarettes. The industry is highly capital-intensive: average annual revenue per worker for a typical company is $1.5 million.

Products, Operations & Technology

Major consumer tobacco products include cigarettes, chewing tobacco and snuff, and cigars. Cigarettes account for 90 percent of all US-produced tobacco products, chewing tobacco and snuff for 6 percent, and cigars for 2 percent. Tobacco processing, an initial step in the production process, is a $1 billion industry.

Tobacco is an annual plant with leaves that are hand- or machine-cut and then cured. Curing removes all moisture from the leaf and enhances flavor. Flue-curing takes about a week; air-curing takes two months. Cured tobacco is cleaned and sorted in tobacco processing plants, where stems are removed in a process called threshing. The tobacco is then re-dried, compressed into boxes or wooden vats, and aged in a warehouse for up to two years.

BUSINESS CHALLENGES

» Government Regulation

Government oversight of the tobacco industry significantly impacts the profitability of individual companies. Federal regulation of tobacco advertising, state and local excise taxes, restrictions on public and workplace smoking, and the 1998 Master Settlement Agreement (MSA) have led to significant declines in tobacco production and smoking rates. FDA regulation of tobacco products and additional federal restrictions are possible.

» Litigation Poses Ongoing Threat

While the MSA effectively ended state lawsuits against the tobacco industry, major cigarette manufacturers still face hundreds of individual and class action lawsuits. Philip Morris USA has nearly 200 lawsuits pending regarding individual smoking and health, and another 20 claiming misuse of the terms "light" and "ultra light." A loss in any one could cost a cigarette maker billions.

» Shrinking US Market Demand

US production of tobacco products fell 30 percent in the past decade and industry employment fell 40 percent. The national smoking rate is over 65 percent lower than its peak in 1963. Cigarette companies are legally constrained in how they can attract new smokers.

At the cigarette manufacturing facility, workers blend processed tobacco of various types to establish a uniform quality. Major types of tobacco are Virginia, Burley, and Oriental. Blended tobacco is moistened, flavored with casing agents, cut into thin strands, dried, and cooled. To make cigarettes, cut tobacco is molded into a circular form. Machines then add paper and filters before the final product is glued and packed. This highly automated and capital-intensive process is capable of producing up to 16,000 cigarettes per minute.

A farmer typically sells tobacco directly to a tobacco processor through a pre-sold contract arrangement. In turn, the processor sells blended tobacco to cigarette manufacturers under multi-year contracts. Farmer cooperatives are increasingly bypassing processors by supplying cured and cut tobacco directly to cigarette manufacturers.

Technology centers on product innovation to reduce carcinogens and new products like self-extinguishing, fireproof cigarettes.

Sales & Marketing

Major customers are licensed wholesalers, large chain retailers, warehouse clubs, and the armed services. Companies rely on their own sales force. Because of regulatory restrictions on TV and radio advertising, marketing focuses on advertising in print media and on billboards, and on event sponsorships. Most promotions are in the form of price discounts to cigarette retailers and wholesalers. Manufacturers also promote cigarette brands through "buy one get one free" offers, coupons, and point-of-sale advertising.

Due to a wide range in state excise taxes, the retail price of a pack of cigarettes can range from $3 to $6.50.

Human Resources

Production and assembly line work requires familiarity and skill with complex machinery. Wages are 20 percent higher than the US average. The injury rate in cigarette manufacturing is 25 percent higher than the national average, with machinery-based injuries to the hands accounting for a large percentage of on-site accidents.

Industry Employment Growth

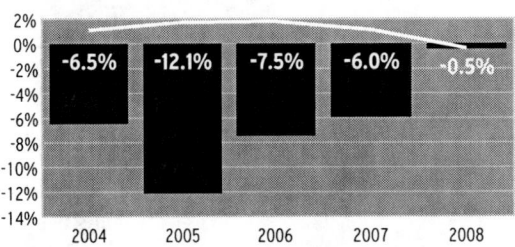

Average Hourly Earnings

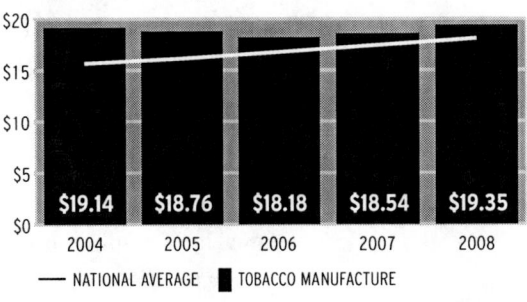

— NATIONAL AVERAGE ■ TOBACCO MANUFACTURE

SOURCE: BUREAU OF LABOR STATISTICS

Call Preparation Questions

What does the company believe the government's role should be in regulating tobacco?

Government oversight of the tobacco industry significantly impacts the profitability of individual companies.

How vulnerable is the company to pending litigation?

While the MSA effectively ended state lawsuits against the tobacco industry, major cigarette manufacturers still face hundreds of individual and class action lawsuits.

How can the company attract new consumers in light of the decreasing US smoking rate?

US production of tobacco products fell 30 percent in the past decade and industry employment fell 40 percent.

Does the company believe in the potential of a "safe," non-carcinogenic cigarette?

The tobacco industry dreams of a "safe cigarette" that reduces or eliminates carcinogens.

In which international markets is the company experiencing high growth?

Cigarette manufacturers are benefiting from growth in international markets such as Russia, China, India, and developing countries.

Web Links

Campaign for Tobacco-Free Kids

News from anti-smoking lobbying group.
tobaccofreekids.org

The Tobacco Institute Document Site

Access to documents produced by the Tobacco Institute.
www.tobaccoinstitute.com

Tobacco Merchants Association

Industry news.
www.tma.org/tmalive/FrmMain

Tobacco.org

News on tobacco and smoking issues.
www.tobacco.org

USDA Economic Research Service: Tobacco Briefing Room

Comprehensive overview on smoking rates and US tobacco production.
www.ers.usda.gov/Briefing/tobacco

Glossary of Acronyms

MSA — Master Settlement Agreement
NRT — nicotine replacement therapy
RYO — roll-your-own (unfiltered cigarettes)

HOOVER'S TOP COMPANIES

Largest Companies by Sales	($ mil.)
Altria Group, Inc. (Philip Morris USA)	19,356.0
Reynolds American Inc.	8,845.0
Lorillard, Inc.	892.1
Vector Group Ltd.	565.2
Commonwealth Brands, Inc.	200.0
Swisher International, Inc.	89.8
General Cigar Holdings, Inc.	—
Vibo Corporation	—

Largest Employers	Employees
Altria Group, Inc. (Philip Morris USA)	84,000
Reynolds American Inc.	7,300
General Cigar Holdings, Inc.	5,000
Lorillard, Inc.	3,100
Swisher International, Inc.	1,600
Commonwealth Brands, Inc.	800
Vector Group Ltd.	450
S&M Brands, Inc.	170
Nat Sherman, Inc.	105
Smokin Joes	100
Vibo Corporation	80

Top Public Companies by Market Value	($ mil.)
Altria Group, Inc. (Philip Morris USA)	31,044.3
Reynolds American Inc.	11,748.4
Star Scientific, Inc.	353.3

SOURCE: HOOVER'S, INC., DATABASE

Toy and Hobby Stores

THIS INDUSTRY INCLUDES:

SIC CODES
5945　Hobby, Toy, and
　　　Game Shops

NAICS CODES
451120　Hobby, Toy, and
　　　　Game Stores

The toy and hobby store industry includes about 12,000 stores with combined annual revenue of almost $20 billion. Major companies include Toys "R" Us, Michaels Stores, and A.C. Moore Arts & Crafts. The industry is highly concentrated: the top 50 companies hold 85 percent of the market.

Competitive Landscape

Consumer spending is a key driver of demand for toy and hobby stores. In addition, population growth among young children (under 12) drives demand for toy stores, and population growth among women 35 and older drives demand for hobby stores. The profitability of individual companies depends on the ability to generate store traffic and effective merchandising. Large companies offer wide selections and deep discounts. Small companies can compete effectively by offering specialized products, providing superior customer service, or serving a local market. Average annual revenue per employee is $160,000.

Toy and hobby stores compete with mass merchandisers. Toy retailers also compete with consumer electronics stores, due to the increasing popularity of electronic toys and video games. Hobby stores compete with fabric and sewing goods stores in select market segments.

Products, Operations & Technology

Major products include toys, games, hobby goods, craft supplies, and decorative accessories. Toys account for 25 percent of sales, games for 20 percent, and hobby goods and craft supplies for 20 percent. Other products include furniture, artist supplies, and artificial flowers, plants, and trees. Toy stores may provide assembly or delivery services. Hobby stores may offer classes, known as "how-to" seminars, and picture framing or floral arrangement.

Toy and hobby stores include national chains, regional chains, and independent retail-

BUSINESS CHALLENGES

» Dependence on Consumer Income and Expenditures

Most consumers classify toys and hobby products as leisure purchases, and sales depend on personal income, consumer confidence, and economic health. During the last recession, growth of personal consumer expenditures in toy, game, and hobby stores slowed considerably. Consumers typically cut leisure purchases and holiday spending during difficult economic times.

» Competition from Alternative Retailers

Toy and hobby stores face strong competition from mass merchandisers like Wal-Mart and Target. In 2005, mass merchandisers represented over half of all retail toy sales, according to the Toy Industry Association. In addition, toy stores must compete with consumer electronics retailers, like Best Buy and Circuit City, for sales of electronic toys and video games. By expanding craft and seasonal merchandise sections, fabric and sewing supply stores, such as Joann Stores, give hobby stores additional competition.

» Seasonal Sales

Toy and hobby stores depend highly on sales of traditional and seasonal merchandise during the winter holidays, as some retailers generate over half of operating income during fourth quarter. Companies may require financing to build inventory to prepare for holiday sales. In addition, inaccurate forecasting for seasonal items, like Christmas products and Halloween costumes, can cause massive inventory write-offs.

ers. National and regional chains operate in large strip malls or stand-alone locations, and stores range from 18,000 to 45,000 square feet. Chains may operate midsized stores, ranging from 3,000 to 5,000 square feet, in indoor shopping malls. Independent retailers typically operate much smaller stores, often as small as 1,500 square feet. Chains consider proximity to distribution centers when opening new stores.

Large toy stores generate up to $9 million annually and average $240 per square foot.

Large hobby stores generate between $4 and $5 million annually and average between $200 and $240 per square foot.

Inventory assortment depends on store size and product specialization. Large toy stores offer between 8,000 and 24,000 stock-keeping units (SKUs), while a specialty toy store may only carry 500. Large hobby stores carry up to 45,000 SKUs, while a specialty hobby store may offer 6,000. Most retailers must accommodate seasonal inventory, as demand for toys and hobby goods increases during holidays like Easter and Christmas. Inaccurate forecasting is a frequent problem and most retailers rely on end-of-season sales to clear merchandise. Some retailers use automated merchandise replenishment systems to minimize out-of-stocks and allocate products across stores. Stores receive inventory directly from suppliers or from off-site distribution centers. Large stores may receive shipments several times a week.

Toy and hobby stores buy products from manufacturers, importers, or distributors. Both retailers may offer unique private label products, which generate higher margins. Toy stores may depend greatly on major toy manufacturers due to the popularity of branded products like Barbie and Hot Wheels. Imports are a high percentage of toy and hobby products, and retailers may place orders up to six months in advance. Due to the importance of the winter holiday season, major toy retailers may place positional orders over a year in advance. Retailers attend trade shows (like the American International Toy Fair for toy stores) or craft fairs to help decide on merchandise.

Due to the large number of SKUs, companies rely on computerized inventory management systems to manage products at stores and distribution centers. Handheld radio frequency (RF) guns track in-store inventory. Companies may use electronic data interchange (EDI) to optimize purchasing. In addition, companies may use Internet-based transportation management systems to track merchandise shipments through the supply chain.

Sales & Marketing

The typical customer for toy stores is a parent or grandparent; the typical customer for hobby stores is a married, relatively affluent, educated woman 35 or older. Children under 12 receive the majority of toys.

Marketing and promotional vehicles include newspaper, TV, print, and radio advertising, direct mail, and in-store programs. Seasonal events, especially Christmas promotions, are extremely important. Toy stores may start marketing efforts as early as October, and increase activity around Thanksgiving. Hobby stores may begin holiday promotions as early as late summer due to time required for customers to complete Christmas crafts. Some toy stores offer registries or wish lists to aid in gift giving.

Toy stores may have interactive play areas where children can try products. Hobby stores may hold in-store demonstrations to promote a craft project.

Most toy and hobby stores have Internet websites that provide store and product information, and both use customer e-mail lists to communicate in-store events and promotions. Hobby store websites offer project ideas, instructions, and supply lists. Toy stores may operate retail websites internally or partner with an Internet retailer. Highly specialized retailers depend on the Internet to reach customers beyond physical locations. After an initial boom in the late 1990s, strictly Internet toy retailers, like eToys and Toys.com, went through numerous mergers and acquisitions, eventually ending in bankruptcy proceedings.

Branded toys (like Barbie and Hot Wheels) retail for under $10, media-licensed toys for under $8, and all other toys for just over $5, according to NPD Group. Toy stores may price popular toys at a loss during peak selling periods to drive store traffic and compete with mass merchandisers. Hobby stores may heavily discount end-of-season items or offer to match or beat competitors' pricing.

Human Resources

Most jobs in toy and hobby stores require minimum skills, and workers are paid accordingly. The average wage is almost 40 percent below that of all US workers, and personnel turnover in retailing is high. The industry relies highly on part-time workers, especially during the winter holidays. Hobby stores try to recruit craft enthusiasts to provide better customer service and act as project demonstrators or class leaders.

The industry injury rate is higher than the average for all workers, mainly due to falls and injuries from handling large containers of goods.

Industry Employment Growth

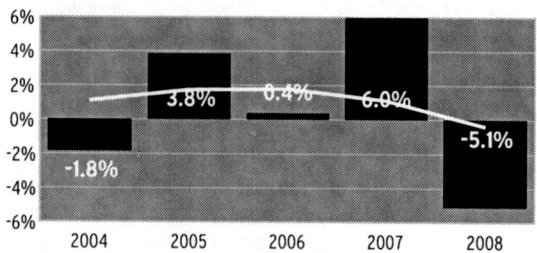

Average Hourly Earnings

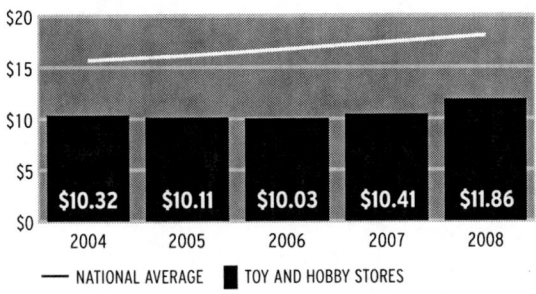

	2004	2005	2006	2007	2008
TOY AND HOBBY STORES	$10.32	$10.11	$10.03	$10.41	$11.86

— NATIONAL AVERAGE ■ TOY AND HOBBY STORES

SOURCE: BUREAU OF LABOR STATISTICS

Call Preparation Questions

How do changes in consumer spending affect the company's business?

Most consumers classify toys and hobby products as leisure purchases, and sales depend on personal income, consumer confidence, and economic health.

How does the company compete with mass merchandisers?

Toy and hobby stores face strong competition from mass merchandisers like Wal-Mart and Target.

What advantages do specialty products offer the company?

By focusing on depth of selection versus breadth, specialty toy and hobby retailers have a competitive advantage over mass merchandisers.

Web Links

American Specialty Toy Retailing Association

Specialty toy retailing trade association providing industry news.
www.astratoy.org

NPD Group – Toys

Market research website for toy statistics and research on children.
www.npd.com/corpServlet?
nextpage=toys-categories_s.html

Playthings

Trade association — good source of industry news.
www.playthings.com

Toy Industry Association

Toy industry trade association — good source for statistics and news.
www.toy-tia.org/Content/NavigationMenu/
Press_Room/Press_Room.htm

Glossary of Acronyms

CHA — Craft and Hobby Association
CPSC — Consumer Product Safety Commission
DIY — Do-It-Yourself Network
EDI — electronic data interchange
HGTV — Home and Garden Television

HIA — Hobby Industry Association (now part of Craft and Hobby Association)
RF — radio frequency
SKU — stock-keeping unit
TIA — Toy Industry Association

HOOVER'S TOP COMPANIES

Largest Companies by Sales	($ mil.)
Toys "R" Us, Inc.	13,794.0
GameStop Corp.	7,094.0
Michaels Stores, Inc.	3,862.0
Jo-Ann Stores, Inc.	1,878.8
Hobby Lobby Stores, Inc.	1,800.0
A.C. Moore Arts & Crafts, Inc.	559.7
Build-A-Bear Workshop, Inc.	474.4
Hancock Fabrics, Inc.	276.3

Largest Employers	Employees
Toys "R" Us, Inc.	72,000
GameStop Corp.	43,000
Michaels Stores, Inc.	42,000
Jo-Ann Stores, Inc.	21,707
Hobby Lobby Stores, Inc.	18,000
Build-A-Bear Workshop, Inc.	6,900
A.C. Moore Arts & Crafts, Inc.	5,459
Hancock Fabrics, Inc.	5,200
Lakeshore Learning Materials	1,200

Fastest Growing* by Five-Year Sales Growth	(%)
GameStop Corp.	39.3
Build-A-Bear Workshop, Inc.	22.9
Hobby Lobby Stores, Inc.	9.1
A.C. Moore Arts & Crafts, Inc.	7.3
Michaels Stores, Inc.	6.2
Toys "R" Us, Inc.	4.1
Jo-Ann Stores, Inc.	2.2

Fastest Growing* by Five-Year Employee Growth	(%)
GameStop Corp.	26.1
Hobby Lobby Stores, Inc.	5.9
Build-A-Bear Workshop, Inc.	4.2
A.C. Moore Arts & Crafts, Inc.	3.3
Michaels Stores, Inc.	1.8
Jo-Ann Stores, Inc.	0.5

Top Public Companies by Market Value	($ mil.)
GameStop Corp.	8,456.1
Jo-Ann Stores, Inc.	313.9
Build-A-Bear Workshop, Inc.	300.2
A.C. Moore Arts & Crafts, Inc.	279.1

* These rates are compounded annualized increases and may have resulted from acquisitions or one time gains. If less than 6 years of data are available, growth is for the years available.

SOURCE: HOOVER'S, INC., DATABASE

Toy Manufacture

The toy manufacturing industry includes about 900 companies with combined annual revenue of $5 billion. Major companies include Mattel, Hasbro, and JAKKS Pacific. The industry is highly concentrated: the top 50 companies hold 75 percent of the market.

This profile doesn't include manufacturers of video games or computer game software.

Competitive Landscape

Population growth of young children (ages 12 and younger) drives demand. The profitability of individual companies depends on identifying market trends and marketing effectively. Large companies can offer a wide selection of toys, and have scale advantages in purchasing, manufacturing, distributing, selling, and marketing. Small companies compete effectively by specializing in a product segment, like educational toys, or responding faster to market trends. Average annual revenue per US worker is $220,000, although doll and stuffed toy manufacturing averages $140,000.

Toy manufacturers face increasing competition from electronic entertainment for children, including video games, the Internet, TV, and other consumer electronics.

Products, Operations & Technology

Major product segments for toys produced in the US include non-electronic toys (transportation toys and sets); electronic toys and games (video game consoles, excluding game cartridges and software); children's vehicles (scooters, wagons, excluding bikes); model and collector sets; and non-electronic games and puzzles. Non-electronic toys account for 35 percent of revenue; electronic games and toys, 20; and children's vehicles, 15. Other products include dolls; stuffed animals (also known as "plush"); action figures; and doll clothing, accessories, and playsets.

BUSINESS CHALLENGES

» Reliance on Foreign Manufacture

Companies depend greatly on Chinese contract manufacturers, which produce the majority of the world's toys. Imports are almost 95 percent of the US doll and stuffed toy market, and almost 80 percent of the toy, game, and children's vehicle market. China's low labor costs have driven decreases in the number of US doll and stuffed toy manufacturers, and in total US toy manufacturing employment. Reliance on foreign manufacture exposes companies to political, economic, foreign exchange, and shipping risks.

» Competition from Electronic Entertainment

As part of the phenomenon "Kids Getting Older Younger," children are maturing faster and switching from traditional toys to consumer electronics and video games. Between 2005 and 2006, ownership of digital cameras and MP3 players among children under 14 doubled and ownership of cell phones increased 50 percent, according to NPD Group. Toy manufacturers also compete with the increasing time children spend watching TV and using the Internet.

» Demand Tied to Demographics

Changes in the population of young children greatly affect demand for toys. Population "bubbles," like the baby boom, drive significant increases in births followed by drops, resulting in uneven demand. Population shifts can also affect demand for products designed for specific age groups, like preschool toys. Although the total population for children is projected to grow through 2050, the trend toward families having fewer children may limit future growth.

US production doesn't reflect the total US toy market, since most manufacturers produce toys in China. Including imports, major product segments include infant/preschool toys, outdoor and sports toys, dolls, games and puzzles, and arts and crafts sets. In 2005, each major segment exceeded $2 billion in retail sales, according to the NPD Group.

The manufacturing process for toys differs depending on the type of toy. Blow- or injection-molding uses air or pressure to force heated plastic into shapes, like dolls and action figures. Die-casting molds heated metal into shapes, like cars and trains. Spray painting adds color to toys and components. Companies use various printing processes to produce game boards and game components. Producing toys like dolls and stuffed animals is labor-intensive, and may require sewing, stuffing, or hand painting. Companies may source toy components from multiple third party manufacturers, and assemble a toy at a separate facility. For example, a company may buy a doll's body parts from a vendor, then assemble, paint, dress, and package the doll at a separate facility.

Most companies produce toys through third party contract manufacturers in the Far East, primarily China, due to low production and labor costs. Mattel, the largest US toy company, owns production facilities in the Far East and Mexico. Due to lengthy transport time, most companies must produce toys well in advance of when customers take delivery. Some large retailers place positional orders over a year in advance. Companies use customer estimates, historical trends, and market conditions to schedule production. Actual shipments can vary greatly from forecasts, resulting in inventory excesses or shortages. While most companies use warehouses to store inventory, many deliver large shipments directly to major retailers.

Major raw materials include toy components, plastic, resins, paperboard, fabricated metal, zinc alloy, fabric, and electronic components. Depending on the toy, companies may be sensitive to price fluctuations in the plastic and oil-based resin markets. Some companies source almost all components from third parties. Large companies may have contracts for key toy parts.

Technology has greatly influenced demand for electronic toys and toys that respond to and interact with children. As children gravitate toward video games and consumer electronics at younger ages, toy manufacturers have integrated computers into traditional toys to improve play value and remain competitive. For example, sensors and computers allow robotic dogs to move and respond to commands. Traditional games like "Candyland" and "Twister" have DVD versions. And some companies offer children's versions of popular consumer electronics like digital cameras and DVD players.

Toy designers may use CAD to model prototypes. Companies may use computer-integrated manufacturing (CIM) to automate certain assembly processes.

Sales & Marketing

Typical customers include major toy retailers, mass merchandisers, specialty toy stores, department stores, warehouse clubs, food and drug stores, wholesalers, distributors, and Internet retailers. Large manufacturers may sell major brands, like LEGO and American Girl, directly to consumers through a few flagship stores. Children ages 5 and under are responsible for about half of retail toy sales, according to the Toy Industry Association (TIA). As children mature, interest in traditional toys begins to decline.

Marketing and promotional vehicles include TV, magazine, radio, and newspaper advertising, in-store displays, sweepstakes, and joint events with companies with complementary products. Brand names, like Barbie, Hot Wheels, and LEGO, are extremely important. Most large companies use a direct sales force. Small companies may use manufacturer rep firms to cover accounts. Trade shows, like the American International Toy Fair, are an important sales vehicle and forecasting tool, where manufacturers can get feedback from retailers for the upcoming selling season.

Licensing is extremely important, and allows companies to use the likeness of well-known children's characters from TV, movies, or books. Well-known licenses include Winnie-the-Pooh, Sesame Street, and Batman. Companies may also license product concepts or designs from independent toy and game designers. In addition, companies may license characters developed in-house to other companies for promotions, like using Hot Wheels for McDonald's Happy Meal toys.

Some companies have Internet-based retail operations that allow consumers to buy products directly. Companies may offer specialty or limited edition products that may not meet the volume or pricing requirements of large retailers. Companies use websites to offer accessories or replacement parts, and to communicate product recall information or safety issues.

Branded toys (like Barbie and Hot Wheels) typically retail for under $10, media-licensed toys for under $8, and all other toys for just over $5, according to the NPD Group.

Human Resources

Toy production can be labor-intensive, and most jobs require very basic skills. US wages in the doll and stuffed toy segment are almost 40 percent lower than average, and wages in the toy and game segment are 10 percent lower than average. Fringe benefits are between 15 and 20 percent of payroll costs.

The average injury rate is about equal to the US average for all industries.

Call Preparation Questions

How has the company been challenged dealing with foreign contract manufacturers?

Companies depend greatly on Chinese contract manufacturers, which produce the majority of the world's toys.

How does the company address growing competition from electronic entertainment?

As part of the phenomenon "Kids Getting Older Younger," children are maturing faster and switching from traditional toys to consumer electronics and video games.

How important are educational toys to the company's business?

Educational toys tend to have longer life cycles, and can justify higher pricing than trend-driven toys.

Web Links

International Council of Toy Industries

Trade association — good source for safety and foreign labor issues.
www.toy-icti.org

NPD Group

Market research website for toy statistics and research on children.
www.npd.com/corpServlet?
nextpage=toys-categories_s.html

Playthings

Trade association — good source of industry news.
www.playthings.com

Toy Directory Monthly

Trade magazine — statistics, news, trends.
www.toydirectory.com/monthly

Toy Industry Association

Trade association for manufacturers and importers.
www.toyassociation.org

Glossary of Acronyms

CAD — computer-aided design
CIM — computer-integrated manufacturing
CPSC — Consumer Product Safety Commission
ICTI — International Council of Toy Industries
RFID — radio frequency identification
TIA — Toy Industry Association

HOOVER'S TOP COMPANIES

Largest Companies by Sales	($ mil.)
Mattel, Inc.	5,918.0
Hasbro, Inc.	4,021.5
MGA Entertainment, Inc.	1,000.0
JAKKS Pacific, Inc.	903.4
LeapFrog Enterprises, Inc.	459.1
RC2 Corporation	437.0
Ty Inc.	—

Largest Employers	Employees
Mattel, Inc.	31,000
Hasbro, Inc.	5,900
MGA Entertainment, Inc.	1,600
The Step2 Company, LLC	900
LeapFrog Enterprises, Inc.	844
Imperial Toy, LLC	800
Ty Inc.	600
JAKKS Pacific, Inc.	598
American Plastic Toys, Inc.	400
Playworld Systems Incorporated	300

Fastest Growing* by Five-Year Sales Growth	(%)
JAKKS Pacific, Inc.	23.4
RC2 Corporation	7.0
Hasbro, Inc.	5.1
Mattel, Inc.	3.6

Fastest Growing* by Five-Year Employee Growth	(%)
MGA Entertainment, Inc.	60.0
Action Products International, Inc.	9.3
Mattel, Inc.	5.5
LeapFrog Enterprises, Inc.	0.4

Top Public Companies by Market Value	($ mil.)
Mattel, Inc.	5,736.0
Hasbro, Inc.	4,043.2
JAKKS Pacific, Inc.	567.8
RC2 Corporation	184.0
LeapFrog Enterprises, Inc.	128.2

* These rates are compounded annualized increases and may have resulted from acquisitions or one time gains. If less than 6 years of data are available, growth is for the years available.

SOURCE: HOOVER'S, INC., DATABASE

Trade Show and Event Planning

The trade show and event planning industry includes about 4,000 companies with combined annual revenue of over $8 billion. Major companies include GES, Freeman, and Champion Exposition Services; the industry is composed primarily of privately held companies. The industry is fragmented: the top 50 companies have about 45 percent of the market. A typical trade show company has $1.8 million in annual revenue and fewer than 20 employees.

The industry is comprised of meeting planners and suppliers who organize, design, promote, and manage business and consumer trade shows, conferences, and meetings, and doesn't include those who organize performing arts or sports events.

Competitive Landscape

Demand is driven by overall economic activity and corporate profits. The profitability of individual companies depends on managing costs, marketing shows effectively, and retaining valuable staff. Large companies have advantages of multiple locations and economies of scale in negotiating labor, transportation, and supply contracts. Small companies compete successfully by delivering superior customer service that drives repeat business. The industry is labor intensive: average annual revenue per employee is about $100,000.

Products, Operations & Technology

The primary industry service is producing and managing conventions, association meetings, trade shows, and company meetings. Events typically include presentations and workshops; an exhibition area for vendors to promote their products and services; and entertainment activities, such as meals, receptions, and local sightseeing tours. In addition to planning and staging events, some companies also design, build, ship, and set up trade show booths for individual exhibitors.

BUSINESS CHALLENGES

» Dependence on US Economy

Spending on trade shows and events is highly sensitive to fluctuations in the general economy, and is often seen as a discretionary expense that can be cut when corporate profits fall. Various industries cut or increase shows based on their economic viability. The number and size of shows generally falls during economic downturns.

» Retaining Qualified Staff

Trade show and event planning companies' success depends on the close relationships between meeting planners and clients. Planning companies rely on repeat business from clients, particularly for annual trade shows and conferences. Successful meeting planners develop knowledge of client goals and strategies, and build relationships with client executives, industry speakers, meeting venue managers, and event service suppliers. Planners who leave a company generally take clients with them.

» Internet Competition

The availability of information on the Internet has lessened the role of trade shows and conferences in keeping people current on industry trends and new products. New product announcements and demonstrations are still a mainstay of trade shows, but the Internet provides a convenient alternative to research and compare products from multiple vendors. While trade shows continue to be a way to network and see firsthand what's new, meeting planners must ensure that the value derived by attendees exceeds the cost of admission and travel.

Most shows and events are one to three days long. Resort locations are generally favored for company meetings, hotels in major cities are chosen for trade shows, and conference centers and university locations are favored by government agencies. Once a location is selected, planners work with the host facility to set up meeting rooms, exhibit halls, demonstration areas, and storage facilities. Planners also arrange for logistics support, such as electrical connections, transportation, booth carpeting, and construction of signage and exhibit halls. Labor may be provided by the host facility, the planner, or local contractors, and is often subject to labor union work rules.

Planning companies generally send an exhibitor manual to each exhibitor detailing available services. Conference materials, speaker reception areas, and publicity are also services that may be provided. Planning companies typically contract with independent transport companies to send exhibits to and from meetings. Large firms have storage facilities for exhibits and booths.

Technological innovation has expanded the use of multimedia presentations for shows and events. The Internet has become a major advertising medium, both by show organizers and customers who advertise show details on their company website. Webcasts are a more frequent feature of meetings, both as a way to increase attendance and to attract speakers unable to travel. Shows often have a room devoted to providing computer and Internet access to allow attendees to communicate with their offices. Software systems streamline show registration, name badge creation, attendee feedback, and pre- and post-event marketing.

Sales & Marketing

Typical customers are associations, government agencies, and private companies. Most planning companies use a dedicated sales force to reach customers, supplemented by senior officers, industry publications, and the Internet.

Trade show and event planning suppliers generally receive a request for proposal (RFP) to conduct a show. Planners put together a show design, layout, incorporate a theme, and provide cost estimates and timelines. Besides cost, experience successfully staging similar events and relationships with customer executives are critical to winning competitive bids.

The Internet has become a key sales channel for meeting planners to advertise their capabilities, and for clients to market upcoming shows to potential attendees. Associations also mail brochures of upcoming shows to members.

Most events have operating budgets of about $50,000; large trade show budgets can approach $2.5 million. Registration fees for attendees are generally less than $500, but can be higher for large shows lasting multiple days.

Human Resources

The major asset of trade show and event planning firms is their staff. Retaining accomplished meeting planners is critical for success, as much business is relationship-driven. Wages are above the national norm and account for about half of revenue. Some companies have unionized labor, and all companies must follow local union rules when using contract labor at shows. The industry injury rate is minimal.

Industry Employment Growth

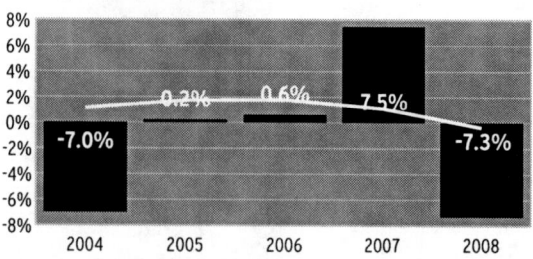

Average Hourly Earnings

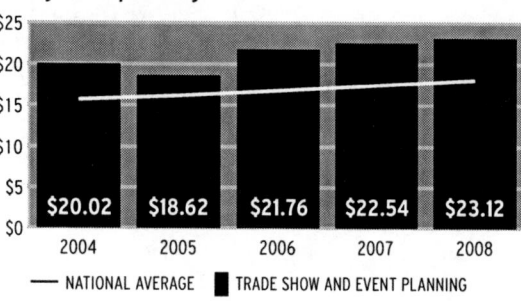

— NATIONAL AVERAGE   ■ TRADE SHOW AND EVENT PLANNING

SOURCE: BUREAU OF LABOR STATISTICS

Call Preparation Questions

How does the company maintain profits during economic downturns?

Spending on trade shows and events is highly sensitive to fluctuations in the general economy, and is often seen as a discretionary expense that can be cut when corporate profits fall.

How successfully is the company retaining key employees?

Trade show and event planning companies' success depends on the close relationships between meeting planners and clients.

How is the Internet affecting attendance at trade shows and conferences?

The availability of information on the Internet has lessened the role of trade shows and conferences in keeping people current on industry trends and new products.

How involved is the company in helping clients with meeting strategies?

The strategic purpose of regularly held meetings is emerging as an area where planners can get involved.

What opportunities does the company see in using webcasts?

Webcasts can be used to enhance attendees' experience at meetings and shows.

Web Links

Advertising Specialty Institute

News, publications, events.
www.asicentral.com

American Society of Association Executives

News (under advocacy and outreach button), education, events, resources.
www.asaecenter.org

Event Marketing Institute

White papers, help with industry metrics.
www.eventmarketing.com

Exhibitor Online

Learning events, news tips, programs.
www.exhibitoronline.com

Meeting Professionals International

News, events, member blog, links.
www.mpiweb.org

MeetingsNet

News, events, programs.
www.meetingsnet.com

Trade Show Executive

News, people, links.
www.tradeshowexecutive.com

Trade Show Week

News, meeting announcements.
www.tradeshoweek.com

Glossary of Acronyms

ASAE — American Society of Association Executives
RFP — request for proposal

HOOVER'S TOP COMPANIES

Largest Employers	Employees
Freeman Decorating Services, Inc.	32,200
GES Exposition Services, Inc.	2,160
George P. Johnson Company	1,000
Diversified Communications	412
Sparks Marketing Group, Inc.	313
TBA Global Events, LLC	223
Pierce Promotions & Event Management	200
Hargrove, Inc.	185
M|C Communications, LLC	160
Nth Degree, Inc.	130

SOURCE: HOOVER'S, INC., DATABASE

Travel Agencies and Services

The US travel service industry includes about 20,000 companies with combined annual revenue of $25 billion. Large companies include the travel agency operations of American Express, and Carlson Wagonlit Travel; Travelocity.com; and Expedia. The industry is fragmented: the 50 largest companies account for about 50 percent of industry revenue. A typical traditional agency office has 12 employees and $1 million of annual revenue.

Travel agencies frequently mention their sales volume or "bookings," the value of the tickets they purchase for customers, a figure much higher than the actual revenue they receive in commissions.

Competitive Landscape

Demand is driven by business and tourist travel, which depends on the economy. The profitability of individual companies depends on marketing. Large companies have an advantage in being able to provide a wider range of services, especially to corporate customers, and to afford sophisticated websites. Small companies can compete effectively by providing service to a few large customers or by serving a local market. Despite automation, the industry remains labor-intensive; average annual revenue per employee at traditional travel agencies is just $75,000.

Two major factors have shaped the industry in recent years: sophisticated pricing schemes developed by the airlines to maximize profitability, and the emergence of the Internet as a widely available information and booking tool.

Products, Operations & Technology

Major services are reservations or tickets for airline flights, tours, hotels, and entertainment. Airline reservations account for about 25 percent of industry revenue, tours and cruises 15 percent, hotel reservations 10 percent, and event tickets 7 percent. Other services include

BUSINESS CHALLENGES

» Travel Sharply Affected by Economy, Terrorism Fears

Air travel is closely connected to the strength of the US economy, partly because of business travel and partly because personal travel (which accounts for about 75 percent of air travel) depends heavily on income. Terrorism or natural disaster fears can easily prompt tourists to cancel vacation plans.

» Competition from Internet Agencies

Travelers can dispense with traditional travel agents by booking flights directly at airline websites and using travel websites like Travelocity and Expedia. Even travel websites face competition directly from the originators of travel services such as Orbitz, a travel website owned by airlines. Online travel bookings have been growing by double-digits in recent years.

» Falling Ticket Commissions

The increasing efficiency of selling plane tickets has prompted airlines to progressively lower the commissions they pay travel agents. From the traditional level of 10 percent of the fare, commissions have come down to a flat $10 per one-way ticket and many airlines have eliminated them altogether. Southwest, for example, sells the majority of its tickets through its own website.

time-share exchange services, automobile clubs, convention and sightseeing services, and car rental reservations.

The basic business of travel agencies is simple: helping travelers choose flights, accommodations, and rental cars they need for a pleasure or business trip (or a package that combines these elements at a lower total cost), and selling them the tickets and reservations they need.

The industry includes three types of companies, with considerable overlap: retail travel agencies, business travel management companies, and tour operators (including distributors of specialized travel products). In the retail business there are traditional agencies and a large number of independent agents. In the business travel segment there are fewer than 500 competitors of significant size.

Retail agencies typically operate just a few offices. Most of their business comes from tourist or small-business travel. Operations are simple, requiring office space, computers, and access to the large reservations systems run by Sabre, Galileo/Apollo, and Worldspan.

Business travel management companies usually work with corporate customers who have annual travel budgets of $1 million or more. They typically have onsite offices (at their customers' locations) and use sophisticated computer programs to provide lowest-cost travel reservations, centralized accounting, and detailed management reporting. Size is an important asset for travel management companies as it allows them to negotiate larger discounts with hotels and rental car companies. Navigant, one of the largest companies, operates 140 branch offices and 500 onsite locations.

Tour operators are intermediaries between travel agencies and the service providers like cruise lines, hotel chains, and airlines. They secure access to blocks of cabins, rooms, and airline seats at discounted prices and then re-market them to travel agents, and sometimes directly to travelers through their own Internet sites.

Computer systems have long been used to manage airplane reservations. For decades, the most important assets of travel agencies were computer terminals connected to reservation systems, like Sabre, that had been developed by the airlines (initially to manage their own reservations but then also to allow reservations on other air carriers). The wide availability of the Internet in recent years has allowed an easy transition of these older computerized reservations systems to the Internet, where they are used by travel agencies and also directly by travelers. Customized Internet versions of reservation systems are licensed to traditional travel agents and to travel websites like Travelocity and Expedia. Used primarily for airplane reservations and tickets, travel websites also provide reservations for hotels, rental cars, cruises and package tours, and have become virtual travel agencies. Travelocity, the largest Internet travel site, is a direct outgrowth of the older Sabre reservation system. Other major computer reservation systems in addition to Sabre are Galileo/Apollo and Worldspan. Galileo/Apollo connects 45,000 worldwide travel agencies with 500 airlines, 50 rental car companies, and 50,000 hotels.

Sales & Marketing

Major customers are business and leisure travelers (tourists). Travel management companies sell their services through a sales force and at industry conventions. Most small retail travel agencies depend heavily on walk-in traffic. Other retail marketing is through newspaper ads and radio. TV ads are less common because they're not sufficiently localized.

Most travel agencies still derive most of their revenue from commissions from the sale of tickets and reservations. For many years, commissions were 10 percent of the price of plane tickets. But commissions on airplane tickets have eroded in recent years, first to 5 percent, then to fixed fees of $10 per one-way ticket, and then to zero at some airlines. Commissions on hotel reservations and car rentals remain at 5 to 10 percent, and commissions on tour packages and cruises can go as high as 20. In addition to traditional commissions, agencies can earn significant override commissions from travel suppliers based on the volume of business they do. Both retail and business travel agencies may also charge service fees. Business travel management companies may receive commissions on sales, management fees from their corporate customers, or both.

Following deregulation of the airline industry in 1978, airlines developed intricate pricing schemes that provide incentives for travelers to buy airplane tickets at different times, on different terms, and at different prices. By using these very complicated pricing systems, airlines are able to sell the maximum number of seats on flights at the best possible price. The complexity of these pricing systems has enlarged the role of travel agents to help retail travelers decide among the many pricing options, and has created opportunities for business travel companies to manage the large travel budgets of corporate customers.

Human Resources

Because much of the work at travel agencies involves computer skills and requires some special knowledge, agents are paid a moderate amount — close to the average for all US workers. With pay only average, the annual personnel turnover rate is also likely to be average.

Industry Employment Growth

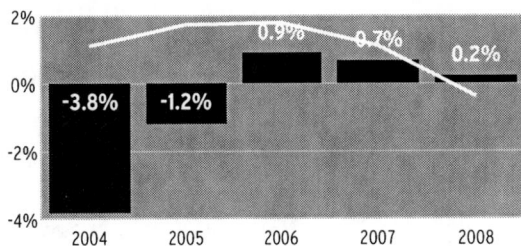

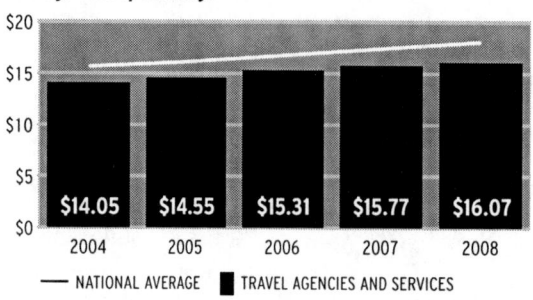

Average Hourly Earnings

Year	Travel Agencies and Services
2004	$14.05
2005	$14.55
2006	$15.31
2007	$15.77
2008	$16.07

— NATIONAL AVERAGE ■ TRAVEL AGENCIES AND SERVICES

SOURCE: BUREAU OF LABOR STATISTICS

Call Preparation Questions

How has the company managed fluctuations in business and leisure travel?

Air travel is closely connected to the strength of the US economy, partly because of business travel and partly because personal travel (which accounts for about 75 percent of air travel) depends heavily on income.

How is the agency addressing increased online competition?

Travelers can dispense with traditional travel agents by booking flights directly at airline websites and using travel websites like Travelocity and Expedia.

How has the agency adapted to the loss of air ticket commissions?

The increasing efficiency of selling plane tickets has prompted airlines to progressively lower the commissions they pay travel agents.

What opportunities does the company see in developing specialized tour services?

As airline tickets become commodities, many agencies are shifting focus to providing packaged tours.

Web Links

Business Travel News Online

News.
www.btnmag.com/businesstravelnews

National Business Travel Association

News.
www.nbta.org

Travel Industry Association of America

Publications and research.
www.tia.org

Travel Weekly

News.
www.travelweekly.com

Glossary of Acronyms

ASTA — American Society of Travel Agents
BTS — Bureau of Transportation Statistics

IATA — International Air Transport Association
NATA — National Association of Travel Agents
TIAA — Travel Industry Association of America
TSA — Transportation Security Administration
WTTC — World Travel & Tourism Council

HOOVER'S TOP COMPANIES

Largest Companies by Sales	($ mil.)
American Express Company	31,920.0
Carnival Corporation	14,646.0
Royal Caribbean Cruises Ltd.	6,532.5
Sabre Holdings (Travelocity.com)	3,000.0
Expedia, Inc.	2,937.0
Travelport Limited	2,527.0
priceline.com Incorporated	1,884.8
Orbitz Worldwide, Inc.	870.0
Omega World Travel	279.1

Largest Employers	Employees
Carnival Corporation	81,200
American Express Company	66,000
Sabre Holdings (Travelocity.com)	9,000
Expedia, Inc.	7,150
Travelport Limited	5,500
Royal Caribbean Cruises Ltd.	5,068
ResortQuest International, Inc.	5,000
Cunard Line	3,500
Grand Circle Corporation	3,000
The Mark Travel Corporation	2,311

Fastest Growing* by Five-Year Sales Growth	(%)
YTB International, Inc.	127.9
Ambassadors International, Inc.	81.2
Online Vacation Center Holdings Corp.	42.2
Orbitz Worldwide, Inc.	37.4
Ambassadors Group, Inc.	21.0
priceline.com Incorporated	16.9
Royal Caribbean Cruises Ltd.	11.5
Sabre Holdings (Travelocity.com)	7.8
Expedia, Inc.	4.7

Fastest Growing* by Five-Year Employee Growth	(%)
Ambassadors International, Inc.	47.8
priceline.com Incorporated	30.8
Expedia, Inc.	17.6
Ambassadors Group, Inc.	8.6
Sabre Holdings (Travelocity.com)	7.4

Top Public Companies by Market Value	($ mil.)
priceline.com Incorporated	3,018.2
Royal Caribbean Cruises Ltd.	2,926.3
Expedia, Inc.	2,153.7
Orbitz Worldwide, Inc.	323.4
Ambassadors Group, Inc.	173.2

* These rates are compounded annualized increases and may have resulted from acquisitions or one time gains. If less than 6 years of data are available, growth is for the years available.

SOURCE: HOOVER'S, INC., DATABASE

Truck and Bus Manufacturing

**THIS INDUSTRY
INCLUDES:**

SIC CODES
3711   Motor Vehicles
        and Passenger Car
        Bodies

NAICS CODES
336120 Heavy Duty Truck
        Manufacturing

US heavy truck and bus manufacturers include about 80 companies with combined annual revenue of about $25 billion. Major companies include PACCAR (Peterbilt and Kenworth); Navistar International; Daimler Trucks North America (Freightliner); Volvo Trucks North America; and Blue Bird. The industry is highly concentrated: the top five manufacturers have about 70 percent market share; the top 20 have 97 percent. Many companies are parts suppliers to assembly plants.

Competitive Landscape

Heavy truck demand is driven by growth in the agriculture, manufacturing, construction, and retail sectors. Bus demand is driven by growth in the number of school-aged children and investment in public transportation systems. The profitability of individual companies depends on volume and sales of high-margin options. Small manufacturers compete by supplying parts to other assemblers or by offering highly customized products. The industry is capital-intensive: annual sales per employee averages about $750,000.

The industry competes with other forms of transportation, namely trains and planes, which also move freight and people over long distances. Reconditioned and used vehicles also compete with newly manufactured products, since equipment may have a useful life in excess of 1 million miles.

Products, Operations & Technology

Heavy trucks and buses are classified by Gross Vehicle Weight Rating (GVWR), a measure of the total allowable weight of the truck when fully loaded. Class 6 (GVWR of 19,001 to 26,000 pounds); Class 7 (GVWR of 26,001 to 33,000 pounds); and Class 8 (GVWR of 33,000 pounds and over) vehicles make up the majority of heavy trucks on US highways. Class 6 represents about 15 percent of total US unit sales,

BUSINESS CHALLENGES

» Cyclical Truck Demand

The heavy truck industry is subject to volatile demand swings as economic conditions change. Over the last 10 years, Class 8 unit sales have fluctuated as much as 40 percent in a single year. Changes in environmental regulations can drive spikes in purchases prior to new restrictions taking effect. Manufacturers want to smooth the demand curve so that resource planning can be more efficient and profitable, but economic factors and changing regulations continue to drive cyclical demand.

» High Material Costs

Purchased materials and parts are about 85 percent of sales revenue. Changes prices for aluminum, steel, plastic, rubber, coatings, and other petroleum-related products can substantially impact profitability. Entering long-term pricing agreements can be especially difficult for truck and bus manufacturers due to the cyclical demand for their products.

» Emissions Compliance

Environmental compliance issues for heavy trucks and buses are complex. A tighter set of regulations became effective January 1, 2007, requiring all new diesel engines to operate on ultra low sulfur diesel fuel (ULSD). The goal is a reduction of up to 90 percent in nitrogen oxide emissions, a major pollutant. Starting in 2010, all diesel fuel sold in the US will be required to be ULSD. Sales are affected by these changing regulations as vehicle buyers evaluate how the cost of compliance will affect purchase prices and operating expenses.

Class 7 about 20 percent, and Class 8 about 65 percent. In addition to new units, aftermarket sale of parts represents about 10 percent of industry revenues.

Buses and local delivery trucks generally are rated Class 6 and Class 7. Most heavy trucks, called tractors, which pull detachable trailers, are Class 8. Tractors are equipped with a fifth wheel, the coupling that connects the trailer to the back of the tractor for towing. These rigs are frequently known as 18-wheelers due to the combined number of wheels on the tractor and trailer.

Heavy trucks and buses are typically produced on assembly lines, much like auto manufacturing. Parts are received from outside sources (either third parties or other corporate-owned plants), usually on a just-in-time basis. Beginning with the assembly of the basic frame of two steel beams with cross-members for support, the product proceeds from station to station where components are added to complete the finished chassis. Axles, a suspension system, an engine, a drive train, and a transmission are part of the completed chassis. Fuel tanks, fans, coupling, and hoses are connected to the chassis. The truck cab, hood, and sleeper compartment are assembled separately and lowered onto the chassis assembly after painting. Final components are attached and the truck is tested using a dynamometer, an instrument that measures engine power while the truck wheels spin on rollers. Additional quality control checks are performed before the truck is driven off the assembly line for a test drive.

Plant capacities vary by size and capital investment, but a typical facility may be several hundred thousand square feet. A recently opened 200,000 square foot assembly plant has an annual production capacity of 2,500 heavy-duty trucks. Some manufacturers provide chassis to other assemblers that outfit the completed rig.

Almost all heavy duty trucks have diesel engines, which are bought from suppliers like Cummins and Detroit Diesel. Raw materials include steel, aluminum, plastics, glass, and rubber. Metal parts are a combination of forgings, extrusions, and sheet products. Aluminum and plastics lessen vehicle weights and improve fuel consumption. Material costs represent about 85 percent of revenues.

The heavy truck and bus industry uses computer modeling extensively to optimize raw materials, engine performance, and aerodynamics, all which affect cost and fuel efficiency. Technology-enabled safety equipment is available to help reduce heavy-duty vehicle accidents on the nation's highways. Suppliers offer systems that include collision warning, lane departure warning, vehicle stability, and brake monitoring. Vehicles can be equipped with wireless computers and GPS to help navigate and communicate with drivers.

Sales & Marketing

Typical customers are freight haulers, construction companies, school districts, and municipal transit authorities. The primary sales channel consists of about 2,500 dealers located throughout the US. Some dealerships are company-owned, but most are independent, and sell new and used equipment across multiple makes and models. Companies have sales offices in countries with fast growing economies, such as China.

Major marketing programs include trade shows, dealer showroom promotions, print advertising in trade magazines, and corporate websites providing performance, price, availability, and warranty information.

Prices for new Class 8 tractors range from $75,000 to $250,000, and from $65,000 to $110,000 for school buses; some municipal transit buses cost as much as $250,000. Estimates put the number of Class 8 vehicles on US roadways at more than 2 million. Since many diesel truck engines are built to exceed 1 million miles, used trucks are significant competition for new truck sales.

Human Resources

Manufacturers require engineering talent in addition to production employees. Some companies spend up to 3 percent of revenues on R&D. Recruiting is on college campuses and through programs designed to lure engineering talent from other industries.

Production workers, who are skilled in welding, machining, and assembly work, earn about 25 percent more than the average US production worker. Due to automated assembly lines, production wages are less than 5 percent of revenues. Most large company work forces are unionized.

The industry's injury rate is about double the average manufacturing industry rate.

Industry Employment Growth

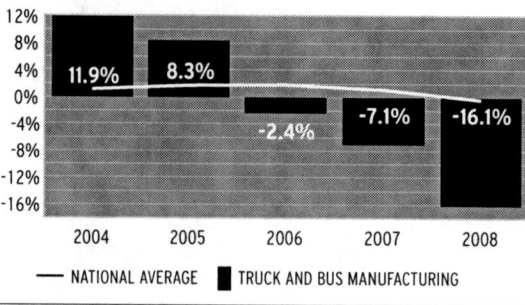

11.9%   8.3%   -2.4%   -7.1%   -16.1%

2004   2005   2006   2007   2008

— NATIONAL AVERAGE   ■ TRUCK AND BUS MANUFACTURING

SOURCE: BUREAU OF LABOR STATISTICS

Call Preparation Questions

How is the company affected by the cyclical nature of the industry?

The heavy truck industry is subject to volatile demand swings as economic conditions change.

How does the company manage material costs?

Purchased materials and parts are about 85 percent of sales revenue.

How will the company ensure environmental compliance on its future models?

Environmental compliance issues for heavy trucks and buses are complex.

What aftermarket offerings does the company provide?

Manufacturers offer services to fleet owners, owner-operators, and independent drivers that include extended warranties, roadside service, call centers, computerized maintenance logs, and other record keeping.

What options to reduce engine idling during rest stops is the company providing?

Long distance haulers with sleeper cabs typically idle the engines to provide driver comfort during rest.

Web Links

American Trucking Association

News of legislative, regulatory, and priority issues of the industry.
www.truckline.com

ETrucker.com

News and site for fleet owners, independent truckers, and dealers.
www.etrucker.com

Fleet Owner

News of the trucking industry from fleet owner's perspective.
www.fleetowner.com

Heavy Duty Manufacturers Association

News of industry suppliers and manufacturers.
www.hdma.org

The Trucker.Com

Headlines and news related to manufacturers, dealers, purchasers, and drivers.
www.thetrucker.com

Truck Manufacturers Association

Sales statistics, regulatory issue updates, news, and events of the industry.
www.truckmanufacturersassociation.org

Glossary of Acronyms

AASHTO — American Association of State Highway and Transportation Officials
APU — auxiliary power unit
EGR — exhaust gas recirculating
GVWR — Gross Vehicle Weight Rating
TMA — Truck Manufacturers Association
ULSD — ultra low sulfur diesel
VMT — vehicle miles traveled

HOOVER'S TOP COMPANIES

Largest Companies by Sales	($ mil.)
PACCAR Inc	14,972.5
Navistar International	14,724.0
Oshkosh Corporation	7,138.3
Daimler Trucks North America LLC	2,799.4
Spartan Motors, Inc.	681.9
Mack Trucks, Inc.	628.8
Volvo Trucks North America	383.2
Blue Bird Corporation	271.7
Mitsubishi Fuso Truck of America, Inc.	250.0

Largest Employers	Employees
PACCAR Inc	21,800
Daimler Trucks North America LLC	20,000
Navistar International	17,800
Oshkosh Corporation	14,000
Mack Trucks, Inc.	4,500
Volvo Trucks North America	3,700
Blue Bird Corporation	1,950
Spartan Motors, Inc.	1,855
Mitsubishi Fuso Truck of America, Inc.	100

Fastest Growing* by Five-Year Sales Growth	(%)
Oshkosh Corporation	30.0
Spartan Motors, Inc.	21.3
PACCAR Inc	12.7

Fastest Growing* by Five-Year Employee Growth	(%)
Spartan Motors, Inc.	20.0
Oshkosh Corporation	18.1

Top Public Companies by Market Value	($ mil.)
PACCAR Inc	10,238.8
Navistar International	2,147.6
Oshkosh Corporation	979.5
Spartan Motors, Inc.	247.2

* These rates are compounded annualized increases and may have resulted from acquisitions or one time gains. If less than 6 years of data are available, growth is for the years available.

SOURCE: HOOVER'S, INC., DATABASE

Trucking

The trucking industry includes about 110,000 for-hire carriers and 350,000 independent owner-operators with combined annual revenue of nearly $200 billion. Major companies include YRC Worldwide, Schneider National, JB Hunt, and Con-Way. The industry is fragmented: the 50 largest companies account for less than 30 percent of the market.

The industry is comprised of carriers that transport commodities for shippers using a commercial motor vehicle (CMV). The industry doesn't include the US Postal Service (USPS); couriers; or private carriers (a company that transports its own products and raw materials).

Competitive Landscape

Demand is driven by consumer spending and manufacturing output. The profitability of individual companies depends on efficient operations. Large companies have advantages in account relationships, bulk fuel purchasing, fleet size, and access to drivers. Small operations can compete effectively by providing quick turnaround, serving a local market, or transporting unusually sized goods. Average annual revenue per employee is $135,000.

Trucking competes with other forms of cargo transportation, including rail, air, and water. However, the shift toward intermodal transportation means that these modes of delivery are often more complementary than competitive.

Products, Operations & Technology

Major services include long-distance trucking (70 percent of industry revenue) and local trucking (30 percent). The industry hauls over 10 billion tons of goods annually, representing 60 percent of the total volume and 70 percent of value of all US commercial freight activity. Including private carriers, the US truck fleet is comprised of nearly 6 million single-unit trucks and 2 million tractor-trailers.

BUSINESS CHALLENGES

» Demand Tied to Economic Cycles

Profitability in the trucking industry is closely tied to the overall health of the national economy, which varies from year to year. Drops in construction spending, consumer confidence, and industrial production can negatively impact trucking profits. During the last recession, US manufacturing production dropped 5 percent and imports of manufactured goods fell 4 percent.

» Vulnerable to Fuel Prices

Fuel costs are rivaling labor as the trucking industry's highest operating cost. Diesel fuel typically accounts for 20 to 25 percent of revenues. Some companies buy fuel in bulk, hedge on fuel prices, or charge shippers fuel surcharges. JB Hunt, a large truck load carrier, relies on contracts for 80 percent of its fuel purchases. Carriers can sometimes get locked into expensive contracts when the price of fuel drops.

» High Personnel Turnover

Most trucking companies have high driver turnover; annual turnover in the TL sector can sometimes exceed 100 percent. Driver costs are the largest expense in the highly competitive long-haul trucking industry, so firms have little leeway to raise salaries. Fleet operators spend around $5,000 to $8,000 to recruit and train a new driver, yet fewer people want to join an industry with a demanding lifestyle and little chance for career progression. Turnover in the LTL and local trucking industry is much lower, around 15 percent.

Within the long-distance trucking market, 80 percent of revenue comes from general merchandise, typically moved on pallets loaded on tractor-trailers; 20 percent comes from specialized trucks transporting liquid chemicals, autos, and oversized or fragile goods over long distances.

In the local trucking market (within 50 miles from origination to destination), general merchandise shipping accounts for 40 percent of revenue. Specialized freight trucking (household movers, cement mixers, dump trucks) accounts for 60 percent of the local truck transportation industry. The type of operation a trucker runs depends on the type of shipments handled. Some truckers handle only truckload (TL) shipments that dedicate trailers to a single shipper's cargo. Others specialize in less-than-truckload (LTL) shipments, which transport the consolidated cargo of several shippers on one truck, dropping goods off at multiple delivery points.

At nearly $100 billion in annual revenue, TL shipments of general merchandise are the largest part of the market. A trucking customer typically loads a trailer full (or nearly full), the trucker transports the container, and a receiver unloads the contents. Shipments are usually delivered within one or two days, depending on the distance.

LTL shipments (under 10,000 pounds) are a smaller but fast-growing part of the market. Locally, LTL truckers may collect loads from several customers and deliver them directly to local destinations, or may operate a local terminal that receives loads and transfers them to small delivery trucks. Long-distance LTL truckers typically operate a network of terminals connected by long-distance routes. Because most shipments involve transfers at terminals, delivery times for LTL shipments average two to five days. To lower delivery costs, LTL trucking companies often work with logistics companies to arrange, consolidate, time, and monitor shipments.

Common transported goods include mixed freight, food products, autos, tools and equipment, courier products and mail under contract with the USPS, and chemicals. Trucks with empty trailers account for 20 percent of all vehicle traffic miles (VTM).

Major inputs and expenses include drivers, diesel fuel, and repairs. Commercial trucks represent 3 percent of all US highway vehicles but account for 20 percent of all highway fuel consumption. The average US power unit (truck tractor) travels 65,000 miles each year and typically accrues more than 500,000 miles before being replaced. Large companies generally perform their own truck maintenance; small ones may outsource this function.

Recent technological advances include on-truck communications between driver and dispatcher; improved entertainment offerings for drivers (satellite TV and radio); and sophisticated GPS scheduling systems that track and direct truck fleets and individual truck operations. On-board advancements include computer systems that monitor speed, maximize fuel consumption, and determine maintenance schedules. These technical advancements have increased productivity, with fewer empty miles and less waiting time between loads.

Sales & Marketing

A carrier's major customer is a shipper: a company seeking to have its goods transported by truck. A key link between carrier and shipper are third-party intermediaries like freight forwarders, freight brokers, and logistics providers. Freight brokers connect shippers and carriers without handling any goods. A freight forwarder typically takes possession of the goods, consolidates smaller shipments into one large shipment, and arranges transportation of the large shipment. Logistics providers manage the flow of goods to ensure sufficient warehousing and efficient distribution of goods.

Major types of marketing include face-to-face visits with potential customers, referrals, and Internet advertising. Truckers pursue long-term relationships with large customers through "dedicated" contracts.

Internet sales are increasingly standard in the trucking industry. Large carriers maintain sophisticated software that allow shippers to request a quote online, fill out a bill of lading, and track cargo. Smaller carriers are typically limited to promoting services online.

Prices depend on the type of good shipped, the route taken, and the total distance traveled. Freight rates are different for truck load (TL) and less-than-truckload (LTL) shipments: TL shipments are quoted in dollar per mile ($2 per mile might be typical for furniture), while LTL freight rates are calculated based on weight, distance, and type of freight. Pricing is relatively stable in the long-distance LTL segment of the market. Because barriers to entry are lower for local trucking services, prices tend to be more volatile in local markets.

When diesel prices rise, trucking companies may try to impose fuel surcharges. However, the highly competitive nature of the trucking industry forces companies to keep fuel surcharges to a minimum. Some shippers refuse to pay fuel surcharges, or simply take their business elsewhere.

Human Resources

Wages average $18 an hour, comparable to the national average. Trucking is a semiskilled occupation that requires some initial training and continued education. Deregulation has allowed easy entry into the industry by companies using nonunion, lower-paid drivers, which has kept wage increases low in recent years. Of all truck drivers, 90 percent are men.

For some companies, annual turnover of drivers can exceed 100 percent, meaning that more drivers quit or are terminated than are hired. Many drivers belong to the Teamsters

Union, which negotiates a National Master Freight Agreement that sets wages and work rules for many unionized truckers. Companies hire their own drivers but also contract with independent owner-operators who drive their own tractors, typically pay all their own expenses, and are often paid on a rate-per-mile basis.

The annual injury rate in the trucking industry is more than twice the national average. Long-distance trucking has a much higher incidence rate than local truck transportation. Most injuries involve sprains, strains, fractures, and bruises from handling containers and vehicle accidents. Out of 8 million registered trucks, about 100,000 are involved in injury crashes each year and 4,000 truck drivers are killed. Studies by AAA and Virginia Tech agree that around 80 percent of all truck accidents were caused by car drivers.

The American Trucking Association (ATA) says that large truck fatal crash rates have declined, despite a climb in total trucking miles: in 1975, the industry had 4.5 fatal crashes per 100 million truck vehicle miles, a rate that's now fewer than two per 100 million.

The legal blood alcohol limit for truck drivers is .04, compared to .08 for the general public. Companies routinely and randomly test drivers for illegal substances.

Industry Employment Growth

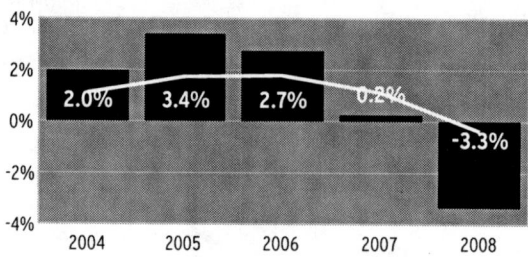

Average Hourly Earnings

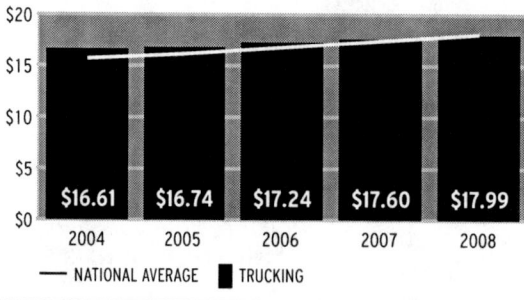

— NATIONAL AVERAGE ■ TRUCKING

SOURCE: BUREAU OF LABOR STATISTICS

Call Preparation Questions

How does the company manage fluctuations in demand for shipping?

Profitability in the trucking industry is closely tied to the overall health of the national economy, which varies from year to year.

How does the company deal with changing fuel costs?

Fuel costs are rivaling labor as the trucking industry's highest operating cost.

How successfully have the company's recruitment and retention efforts reduced driver turnover?

Most trucking companies have high driver turnover; annual turnover in the TL sector can sometimes exceed 100 percent.

How has the company increased fuel efficiency?

Carriers and owner-operators can maximize profits by managing fuel consumption.

Does the company plan to use longer combination vehicles (LCV) on long-haul trips?

Carriers can increase efficiency and save on labor costs by using longer trucks.

Web Links

American Trucking Associations

General information, news, and a useful search engine.
www.truckline.com

Commercial Vehicle Safety Alliance

News highlights, events, publications, information on inspections and safety.
www.cvsa.org

eTrucker.com

A wealth of recent trucking news.
www.etrucker.com

Federal Motor Carrier Safety Administration (FMCSA)

Safety regulations for trucks, safety statistics.
www.fmcsa.dot.gov

International Brotherhood of Teamsters

Information on the most important labor union in the trucking industry.

www.teamster.org

Owner-Operator Independent Drivers Association

Industry news. Industry issues.

www.ooida.com

Traffic World

Industry news and issues.

www.trafficworld.com

Transport Topics News

Excellent news, a chart of the top 100 trucking companies, and more.

www.ttnews.com

Truck.net

Industry news.

www.truck.net

Trucker.com

Industry news, trade shows, associations, manufacturers links, buy and sell trailers and trucks.

www.trucker.com

Trucking Info

Latest news, information, research, product and services guides, diesel prices, road conditions, industry links.

www.truckinginfo.com

Glossary of Acronyms

ATA — American Trucking Association
CDL — commercial driver's license
CMV — commercial motor vehicle
FMCSA — Federal Motor Carrier Safety Administration
HOS — hours-of-service
LCV — longer combination vehicles
LTL — less-than-truckload; a load of less than 10,000 pounds
TL — truck load
VTM — vehicle traffic miles

HOOVER'S TOP COMPANIES

Largest Companies by Sales	($ mil.)
YRC Worldwide Inc.	8,940.4
Con-way Inc.	5,036.8
SIRVA, Inc.	3,969.9
J.B. Hunt Transport Services, Inc.	3,731.9
Schneider National, Inc.	3,400.0
Swift Transportation Co., Inc.	3,270.0
Landstar System, Inc.	2,643.1
UniGroup, Inc.	2,200.0
Werner Enterprises, Inc.	2,165.6
Arkansas Best Corporation	1,833.1

Largest Employers	Employees
YRC Worldwide Inc.	63,000
Con-way Inc.	27,100
Schneider National, Inc.	22,216
Swift Transportation Co., Inc.	21,900
J.B. Hunt Transport Services, Inc.	15,795
Werner Enterprises, Inc.	13,608
Estes Express Lines, Inc.	12,374
Arkansas Best Corporation	10,968
U.S. Xpress Enterprises, Inc.	10,885
Saia, Inc.	8,200

Fastest Growing* by Five-Year Sales Growth	(%)
Express-1 Expedited Solutions, Inc.	39.5
Roadrunner Transportation Services Holdings, Inc.	35.2
YRC Worldwide Inc.	23.8
Universal Truckload Services, Inc.	22.3
Knight Transportation, Inc.	20.1
Old Dominion Freight Line, Inc.	18.2
SIRVA, Inc.	12.7
Marten Transport, Ltd.	12.6
USA Truck, Inc.	12.4
Milan Express Co., Inc.	12.0

Fastest Growing* by Five-Year Employee Growth	(%)
Quality Distribution, Inc.	128.6
Smart Move, Inc.	46.8
USA Truck, Inc.	14.5
Universal Truckload Services, Inc.	14.0
Knight Transportation, Inc.	9.7
U.S. Xpress Enterprises, Inc.	6.3
Estes Express Lines, Inc.	6.2
YRC Worldwide Inc.	5.9
Patriot Transportation Holding, Inc.	4.8
Marten Transport, Ltd.	3.7

Top Public Companies by Market Value	($ mil.)
J.B. Hunt Transport Services, Inc.	3,311.7
Landstar System, Inc.	1,856.0
Heartland Express, Inc.	1,485.0
Knight Transportation, Inc.	1,284.0
Con-way Inc.	1,219.8

* These rates are compounded annualized increases and may have resulted from acquisitions or one time gains. If less than 6 years of data are available, growth is for the years available.

SOURCE: HOOVER'S, INC., DATABASE

TV Cable, Pay and Broadcast Networks

The TV cable, pay, and broadcast network industry ("TV broadcasting") in the US includes about 2,600 networks and stations with combined annual revenue of $57 billion. Major broadcast TV networks are ABC, CBS, FOX, and NBC; major TV cable networks are Discovery Channel, ESPN, CNN, and TNT. Large nonnetwork station groups include Sinclair Broadcast Group, Hearst-Argyle Television, and Clear Channel TV. The industry is highly concentrated: the top 50 companies account for over 80 percent of industry revenue. Annual revenue for an independent midsized TV station is under $5 million.

The industry includes almost 2,000 broadcast TV firms and over 600 cable/subscription firms; broadcast TV accounts for slightly over half of industry revenue and cable TV, for slightly less than half. The industry doesn't include companies that broadcast primarily on the Internet, produce and sell taped TV programs, distribute cable and other TV programs, or use TV as a retail outlet.

Competitive Landscape

Business advertising, program popularity, and consumer demographics drive demand. The profitability of individual companies depends on advertising volume, programming mix, and efficient operations. Large companies have advantages of market dominance, often owning the only TV stations in a geography. Small companies can compete effectively with special programming that attracts a targeted audience. Average annual industry revenue per employee is $350,000: broadcast TV averages $257,000 per worker and cable TV about $651,000.

Products, Operations & Technology

Major industry product lines are broadcasts (air time) and programming, production, and post-production services. Other products include program rights, merchandise sales, and

BUSINESS CHALLENGES

» Dependence on Ad Revenue

Broadcast TV stations depend heavily on advertisers for revenue, because delivery is usually free to users, and cable stations need ads to supplement subscription fees. Ads account for 70 percent of US TV broadcasting industry revenue. Ad spending, however, is closely tied to the health of the national economy, as reflected in corporate profits and the GDP. The TV broadcasting industry competes for advertiser dollars with a variety of other media, including radio, outdoor display, newspapers, magazines, direct mail, and Internet sites.

» Increased Competition for Audience

TV broadcasting competes for audiences with many forms of media transmission, in addition to radio and movies, the traditional competitors. Competitors include the Internet, especially video-sharing websites; DVDs; portable video device makers' content services; electronic games; and satellite radio. Although TV broadcasters also use some of these media, the growth in broadband, wireless, and satellite transmission may threaten conventional broadcasting as the primary media delivery system. Ad revenue at TV networks and stations depends on market share, which competing outlets can erode.

» Dependence on Federal Regulations

TV networks and stations are subject to government regulation mainly through the FCC, which grants and renews licenses and limits on ownership concentration in local markets. The license renewal process is mandatory on a prescribed schedule, but a station can lose its license for failing to adhere to requirements. FCC regulatory changes can significantly affect the industry, as in 1996 when limits on ownership concentration eased, fueling consolidation.

sales of website advertising space. In the for-free broadcast TV segment, air time provides about 90 percent of revenue: national and regional advertising accounts for over 55 percent; local ads, over 30 percent; and network compensation, 4 percent. Programming services account for 4 percent and other services, less than 2 percent.

In the fee-based cable/subscription segment, air time provides only 60 percent of revenue: national and regional advertising accounts for 45 percent; network compensation, 14 percent; and local ads, 1 percent. Fees from cable and satellite systems (wholesale programming fees) bring 28 percent of segment revenue. Additional revenue sources include sales of program rights, merchandise, and other services.

TV stations comprise the majority of industry firms. A national network may own dozens of TV stations and have hundreds of affiliate stations that use the network's branding and primarily buy its programming. A large independent broadcast group (non-network-owned) often owns multiple TV stations and, like a national network, achieves advantages of scale in negotiating advertising and programming contracts and in centralizing backoffice operations. Broadcast companies are small compared to firms in other industries. Most large independent groups have annual revenue less than $1 billion.

Industry companies produce or acquire TV programs and/or operate TV broadcasting studios and transmission facilities. TV networks and stations provide a variety of programs and sell advertising time ("inventory") to businesses and organizations. Ad sales and audience size are major industry metrics. Stations attract advertisers' targeted audiences by airing programs that appeal to them. A station earns a reputation for the type of programs ("format") it typically broadcasts. TV stations sell air time directly to advertisers or to brokers under Time Brokerage Agreements. The broker finds programming and sells advertising slots. Ad rates generally depend on the size of a station's audience, as measured by ratings firm Nielsen. Funding for public TV stations comes mainly from the Corporation for Public Broadcasting and donations from foundations, companies, and individuals, but many stations also run subtle advertising.

Program sources include local productions and syndicated and network shows. Stations often produce local news, sports, "talk," and local-interest programs, but may also buy shows from local sources. Stations buy syndicated programs from owners or independent producers or through brokers. TV networks often produce their own shows for distribution to stations they own and for syndication to affiliates or other stations. Syndicated shows are available for cash or for "cash-plus-barter,"

which includes commercials the syndicator sells.

Cable TV programming typically is "narrowcast," with a limited format, such as mostly news, sports, or education, or a narrowly targeted audience, such as youth, Latinos, or women. Cable programming generally goes to third-party cable systems or direct-to-home satellite systems for transmission to consumers. In addition to programming, TV personalities are a major draw for stations, especially during early evening ("prime time"), when the largest number of viewers is watching.

A TV station becomes an affiliate of a national network by signing an exclusive agreement that grants the station the right to air network programs, and allows the network to sell a significant amount of advertising to appear with its programs. The network pays network compensation fees to the TV station for broadcasting network programs and advertising; the station pays an affiliate fee. Affiliation agreements typically cover five to 10 years initially and are eligible for renewal every three to five years. Unaffiliated stations may incur higher relative costs to acquire current programs, but don't have to relinquish ad revenue to a network.

Technology and equipment are changing rapidly, enabling TV networks and stations to convert from analog to digital production and broadcasting by 2009 to meet US government mandates. Analog TV signals historically transmitted at either very high frequency (VHF) for wider coverage or ultra high frequency (UHF) for shorter distance, but the categories have blurred and even HDTV uses UHF in most US cities. Digital signals are higher quality, easier to edit and to enhance with special effects, and use less broadcast spectrum (frequency bandwidth) than do analog signals. The major categories of digital resolution, in order of increasing clarity, are standard, enhanced, and high definition. The conversion to digital broadcasting makes available more spectrum, which is a public resource the government manages and auctions to raise revenue.

Sales & Marketing

Typical customers are businesses and organizations that advertise and subscribers who pay a service fee. The ultimate end-users are consumers who watch TV for information or entertainment; 98 percent of US households have TVs. Major sales channels are advertising brokers, a direct sales force for large accounts, and internal sales staff for telemarketing and incoming orders. Companies in the beauty and household products, auto, pharmaceutical, and telecommunication industries are among the top national advertisers on TV. Auto dealers, telecom companies, restaurants, and furniture stores are top local advertisers. Ads are available "upfront" — well before a program airs — or on a "spot" basis. Fees for upfront ads are often lower than for spot. Media representatives like Katz Media sell ad time, primarily to national advertisers.

Major types of marketing include advertising on the network's or station's own broadcasts and in other media, including newspapers, magazines, and trade publications. Event sponsorship is a common promotional strategy. Cross-promoting is common among stations owned by the same group. Internet sales are increasingly important, because many media buyers prefer to buy air time ads electronically.

Prices for TV ad time vary greatly, from hundreds to thousands per minute, depending on the station, locale, audience demographics and size, time of day, and other factors. A 30-second spot ad during a top prime time show can cost over $500,000 and during the Super Bowl can average almost $3 million, reaching over 90 million viewers. Complex formulas produce a cost per rating point (CPP) or cost per thousand impressions (CPM). Ratings by firms like Nielsen affect rate formulas, but ad prices are highly volatile. Ads generally are 15, 30, or 60 seconds long. TV broadcasting companies compete with other media, including Internet ads, for advertiser dollars.

Human Resources

Much of the work at TV networks and stations requires highly technical skills, reporting, or on-air broadcasting experience; accordingly, industry wages are 45 percent above the national average. Most jobs are in ad sales, program production, and broadcasting, which require very different skills. Turnover can be high, especially at small stations, which often serve as low-paying entry jobs for broadcasters who plan to move to larger markets to advance their careers. Strong competition for top employees exists in large metropolitan areas. Unions are influential, especially in negotiating contracts with networks and stations on behalf of members, and can keep members from working at companies without valid contracts. Industry injury rates are low, at less than half the national average.

Industry Employment Growth

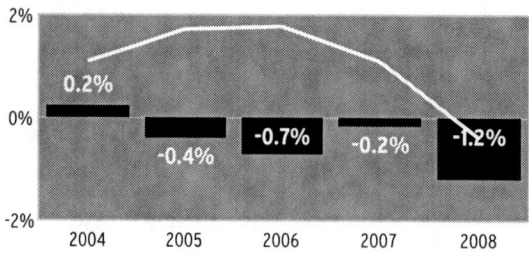

Average Hourly Earnings

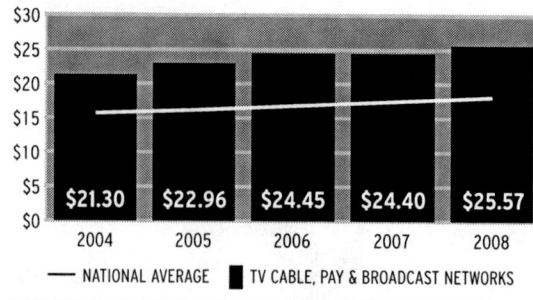

SOURCE: BUREAU OF LABOR STATISTICS

Call Preparation Questions

How important is advertising to the company's total revenue?

Broadcast TV stations depend heavily on advertisers for revenue, because delivery is usually free to users, and cable stations need ads to supplement subscription fees.

What media are the company's biggest competitors for audiences?

TV broadcasting competes for audiences with many forms of media transmission, in addition to radio and movies, the traditional competitors.

How do government regulations affect the company's operations?

TV networks and stations are subject to government regulation mainly through the FCC, which grants and renews licenses and limits on ownership concentration in local markets.

How might the company be advantaged by converting to digital broadcast technology?

Converting to digital technology improves production, broadcast operations, and reception.

How could the company increase revenue through various digital media, like websites and mobile devices?

A variety of digital platforms provides the TV broadcasting industry with new distribution channels and revenue sources.

Web Links

American Federation of Television & Radio Artists

Labor union news, contract negotiation, stop-work orders.
www.aftra.com/aftra/aftra.htm

Corporation for Public Broadcasting

Public TV grants, press releases.
www.cpb.org/pressroom

Federal Communications Commission (FCC)

Federal regulations for broadcasting.
www.fcc.gov

I Want Media

Media news, resources.
www.iwantmedia.com

Media Buyer Planner

News.
www.mediabuyerplanner.com

National Association of Broadcasters

Industry lobbying news, positions.
www.nab.org

Nielsen Media Research

News about TV program ratings, audience size, markets.
www.nielsenmedia.com/nc/portal/site/Public

Radio & Television Business Report

Industry news and analysis by subscription.
www.rbr.com

Society of Broadcast Engineers

Trade association certification programs.
www.sbe.org

Television Bureau of Advertising

News, statistics about advertising on local broadcast TV.
www.tvb.org/nav/build_frameset.asp

Glossary of Acronyms

CPP — cost per rating point
CPM — cost per thousand impressions
HDTV — high-definition TV
NAB — National Association of Broadcasters

HOOVER'S TOP COMPANIES

Largest Companies by Sales	($ mil.)
Time Warner Inc.	46,984.0
The Walt Disney Company (ABC, ESPN)	37,843.0
NBC Universal, Inc.	15,416.0
Viacom Inc.	14,625.0
CBS Corporation	13,950.4
Liberty Media Corporation	10,084.0
CSC Holdings, Inc.	6,484.5
Discovery Communications, Inc.	3,443.0
FOX Broadcasting Company	2,624.0
Univision Communications Inc.	2,072.8

Largest Employers	Employees
The Walt Disney Company (ABC, ESPN)	137,000
Time Warner Inc.	86,400
CBS Corporation	23,970
Viacom Inc.	11,500
Belo Corp.	7,100
Univision Communications Inc.	4,282
Hearst-Argyle Television, Inc.	3,312
Sinclair Broadcast Group, Inc.	2,786
Scripps Networks Interactive, Inc.	2,300
Nexstar Broadcasting Group, Inc.	2,265

Fastest Growing* by Five-Year Sales Growth	(%)
Local TV, LLC	69.3
Current Media, Inc.	61.7
Equity Media Holdings Corporation	45.4
BET Holdings, Inc.	25.9
Scripps Networks Interactive, Inc.	24.3
Univision Communications Inc.	13.7
Nexstar Broadcasting Group, Inc.	11.6
Outdoor Channel Holdings, Inc.	11.3
Gray Television, Inc.	9.1
Crown Media Holdings, Inc.	6.3

Fastest Growing* by Five-Year Employee Growth	(%)
Scripps Networks Interactive, Inc.	16.3
Univision Communications Inc.	7.4
The Walt Disney Company (ABC, ESPN)	3.0
Nexstar Broadcasting Group, Inc.	2.3

Top Public Companies by Market Value	($ mil.)
The Walt Disney Company (ABC, ESPN)	59,700.0
Time Warner Inc.	36,095.3
CBS Corporation	5,021.3
Discovery Communications, Inc.	1,897.4
Viacom Inc.	1,154.9

* These rates are compounded annualized increases and may have resulted from acquisitions or one time gains. If less than 6 years of data are available, growth is for the years available.

SOURCE: HOOVER'S, INC., DATABASE

TV Program Production and Distribution

The US TV program production and distribution industry includes about 500 companies with combined annual revenue of $13 billion. Major companies are NBC Universal, CBS Paramount, Disney-ABC, Fox Television Studios, Warner Bros Television Group, and Sony Pictures Television. Companies that mainly produce and distribute movies derive on average about 30 percent of revenue from TV programs, dominating this industry. As a result, the industry is highly concentrated: the 50 largest companies account for about 80 percent of industry revenue. Most firms, however, are small, privately held production companies.

This industry doesn't include broadcasting or the production and distribution of TV sets.

Competitive Landscape

Consumer leisure activity and the general economy drive demand. The profitability of individual companies depends on the marketability of products, mainly their potential to attract advertising revenue for TV networks. Large companies have advantages in financing, distribution, on-staff creative and technical talent, and multiple-year contracts with key performers and directors of popular programs. Small companies can compete successfully by focusing on special topics, niche audiences, or nonmainstream TV channels. Production work is labor-intensive: average annual industry revenue is about $200,000 per employee, although a typical small company earns about $70,000 per worker.

Products, Operations & Technology

Major products and services are the production and distribution of TV programs, commercials, and related products, like DVDs. Program production types (genres) include TV movies; dramas; situational comedies (sitcoms); reality, game, and talk shows; and documentaries, children's, art, sports, and news programs. Most programs are scripted, though some genres are largely unscripted, including talk and reality shows. First-run programs typically earn less than subsequent releases for reruns ("repeats"); long off-network runs (syndication); and other media like DVD.

BUSINESS CHALLENGES

» High Production Costs

Producing TV programs is expensive and costs occur well in advance of revenue. An hour-long network show can cost from $1 to $2 million to produce. Pilots for series are especially risky, as financial backing can cease at multiple stages before, during, and after program development or after one or more episodes airs. In addition to production costs, studios and networks often have financial commitments to key actors, directors, and producers.

» High Failure Rate

Despite the larger number of exhibition outlets for TV programs, many productions are financial failures. The major networks combined accept fewer than 25 percent of TV pilots, a large percentage of which never air or run a complete season, due to low ratings by viewers or failure to attract advertisers. Major studios and networks spend large amounts on market research and forecasting models, but the industry has poor ability to predict public acceptance of any TV product.

» Competition for New Media Market

The Internet, broadband, and mobile technologies provide new distribution outlets for TV products – and lead to confusion and competition among industries and companies vying for the market. Many traditional TV production and distribution companies see new media as a threat, while leading networks and studios are trying new business models to accommodate change. New media involves convergence of broadcast TV, telecommunications, and information technology, resulting in each industry promoting its own technology and competing for content, audiences, and advertisers.

Revenue mix from major outlets differs for producers and sole distributors. Distribution to TV networks and stations comprises about 65 percent of production companies' collective revenue; to cable and direct broadcast satellite, 15 percent; to independent distributors and syndicates, 15 percent; and to DVD and other video media, 5 percent. For TV sole distributors, DVD and non-TV media are significantly more important. Distributors' business with TV networks and stations accounts for 45 percent of collective revenue; cable and direct broadcast satellite, 15 percent; independent distributors and syndicates, 20 percent; and DVD and other video media, 20 percent.

Creation of a TV program, series, commercial, or other product goes through four phases: development, pre-production, production, and post-production. Large studios and networks often prefer to create on a proprietary basis and own the product. Other producers develop a program concept or a sample episode (pilot) to pitch to studios, networks, cable operators, or other potential sources of funding. For a potential series, funding may be only for one or a few episodes.

After receiving financing, the program goes into pre-production. The producer secures director, cinematographer, and lead actor contracts; finalizes most details of the script; hires a production crew; ensures development of a detailed schedule that identifies timing and need for cast, costumes, equipment, and other production elements; and monitors rehearsals. The production phase is the actual filming and making of the program. Filming ("principal photography") for a commercial may take a day, but a show may require a few days to several weeks, depending on the length and number of episodes.

Once shooting is complete, the program goes into post-production, which includes in-studio processes and tasks such as editing, music scoring, audiovisual synchronization, special effects, and titles. Post-production finalizes content for the intended broadcasting time, typically a 30- or 60-minute time slot for a show. For a "30-minute" show, the finished product is actually about 22 minutes, allowing time for commercials. The result of the cumulative post-production work is a master negative that will serve as the original source for any subsequent releases or copies.

Few programs and pilots make it to the screen. Backers can kill products at any stage, even after completion, or put them on hiatus for potential future use. After a pilot for a series

airs on TV, if the audience is large enough and their reaction is favorable — according to ratings by market research companies like AC Nielsen — the network or station will commit to "pick up" a certain number of episodes. A series pickup is usually for six or 13 episodes. Few aired pilots succeed in becoming an ongoing series. Pilots that don't launch a series may undergo editing and later appear as a TV movie, a special, or in other media where revenue from advertising or license fees can help recover production costs.

A major production company may have from three to 17 shows actively in production and numerous products under license for short-term repeats or long-term syndication. A small company may do only commercials or short spots, while others may produce from one to a few programs a year. A variety of industry media and organizations track the success of TV producers and individual shows, using metrics such as number of shows in production, on hiatus, canceled, or picked up, and a show's audience size and advertising revenue. A key demographic metric is viewers 18 through 49.

Distribution of first-run shows includes marketing to networks, stations, and other broadcasters that rent ("license") programs; obtaining license contracts; advertising; and providing short promotional "clips" and copies of the show. Networks typically specify that broadcasters air a certain amount of network-provided content and commercials. Broadcast stations have more flexibility with non-network content and may contract with producers to shorten the licensed show to run more local advertising, which is more profitable for them on a per-minute basis.

The industry uses advanced technology for business forecasts and production. Computer forecasting models help predict success of projects and decision-support tools help determine marketing and distribution strategy. Many crews use digital cameras to film and specialized computer software for editing. Many productions combine film from shoots on location and in the studio with special effects that are mainly computer-generated imagery (CGI). Digital files enable electronic distribution to customers. With the increase in digital processes, companies use special digital media and distribution management software to manage content internally and with distributors and customers.

Sales & Marketing

Typical customers are TV studios; broadcast networks and stations; cable and satellite companies; syndicates, which are agencies that sell groups of programs directly to stations; and the Public Broadcasting System (PBS). With the exception of syndicates, these firms may also develop their own programs. Over 1,300

FAST FACTS

» The US TV program production and distribution industry includes about 500 companies with combined annual revenue of $13 billion.

» Major companies are NBC Universal, CBS Paramount, Disney-ABC, Fox Television Studios, Warner Bros Television Group, and Sony Pictures Television.

» Major products and services are the production and distribution of TV programs, commercials, and related products, like DVDs.

» Typical customers are TV studios; broadcast networks and stations; cable and satellite companies; syndicates, which are agencies that sell groups of programs directly to stations; and the Public Broadcasting System (PBS).

» Cash flow from producing TV shows is highly uneven, because costs typically occur in advance of revenue.

commercial TV stations, 350 public TV stations, and 200 cable program networks operate in the US. The ultimate end-users are viewers in the 111 million US households that have TVs, representing about 98 percent of the nation's total households.

Major types of marketing include executive relationships to obtain funding and distribution through studios, networks, and large chains of stations, and a sales force to secure independent distributors, stations, and syndicates. Concept presentations, preview clips, and individual pilots are means of promoting programs and series to funding sources; single- or multi-episode pilots are important ways to introduce new series to customers. The industry relies heavily on professional relationships among production companies, distributors, and customers, and on public relations coverage. Variety magazine is the industry's main outlet for information about shows receiving funding, under commission, and in production; pilot pickups; and news of actor commitments and executive changes.

Product prices are actually license fees for the right to broadcast programs or produce them on media other than for TV. Customers determine the value of a show based on its potential to attract targeted audiences and advertisers; most networks have key advertisers to whom they want to deliver specific types of viewers. Prices for first-run shows typically do not cover development costs, so production companies and distributors depend on licenses from short-term repeats; long-term syndication; additional media, like DVDs or computer games; and formats for other countries and languages. License agreements for TV shows usually specify a fee, the number of episodes, a time limit, and the geographical area for exhibition, such as a US locale or an international region. The major networks and PBS also commission production companies to develop shows.

Human Resources

Industry employees are highly skilled specialists, many performing jobs unique to TV production, and accordingly receive pay 50 percent higher than the average national wage. Employment levels of full-time workers vary as much as 8 percent yearly and do not follow national trends. Annual personnel turnover is high, due to competitive hiring. Actors and production crews occasionally sustain injuries while filming.

Production companies manage relationships with many talent agencies and unions. Talent agencies represent creative personnel, including actors and directors, in finding roles and production opportunities. A variety of unions represents actors, writers, directors, and production personnel for most TV work. Many production personnel, including actors, work on a project basis and may be unemployed for parts of the year. Companies manage large numbers of temporary workers, in addition to permanent staff.

Industry Employment Growth

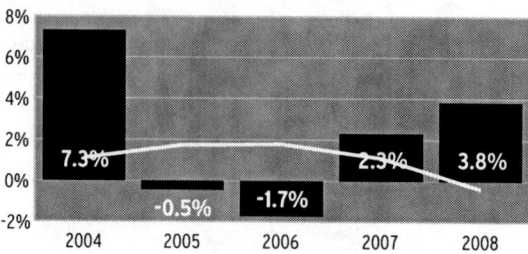

Average Hourly Earnings

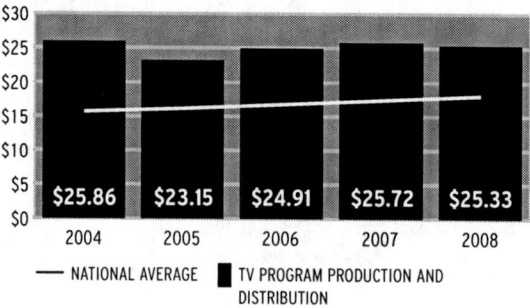

— NATIONAL AVERAGE ■ TV PROGRAM PRODUCTION AND DISTRIBUTION

SOURCE: BUREAU OF LABOR STATISTICS

Call Preparation Questions

How is the company challenged by the high cost to finance TV programs?

Producing TV programs is expensive and costs occur well in advance of revenue.

How does the company determine the potential success of a TV program, series, commercial, or other product?

Despite the larger number of exhibition outlets for TV programs, many productions are financial failures.

What potential does the company see in new media, like broadband and mobile technologies, as distribution outlets for TV programs?

The Internet, broadband, and mobile technologies provide new distribution outlets for TV products — and lead to confusion and competition among industries and companies vying for the market.

What opportunities does the company see in producing TV programs for a variety of media platforms?

Demand is increasing for more entertainment products on a variety of platforms.

What plans does the company have to target the US Spanish-speaking audience?

Advertisers want to reach Latinos, the US' fastest-growing population segment, and spend heavily when programs attract this target audience.

Web Links

Alliance of Motion Picture and Television Producers (AMPTP)

Collective bargaining issues.
www.amptp.org

Directors Guild of America (DGA)

Monthly news related to directing.
www.dga.org/index2.php3

National Association of Television Program Executives (NATPE)

TV programming trends in the news; issues of interest to executives.
www.natpe.org

Screen Actors Guild (SAG)

News and issues related to acting.
www.sag.org

The Canadian Film and Television Production Association

Industry news and production statistics.
www.cftpa.ca

Variety

TV industry news, production charts, pilot pickups.
www.variety.com

Writers Guild of America, West

Industry news.
www.wga.org

Glossary of Acronyms

AMPTP — Alliance of Motion Picture & Television Producers
SAG — Screen Actors Guild
SVOD — subscription video-on-demand
UGC — user-generated content
VOD — video-on-demand

HOOVER'S TOP COMPANIES

Largest Companies by Sales	($ mil.)
CBS Corporation	13,950.4
Liberty Capital Group (Starz Media)	10,084.0
The Walt Disney Studios	7,587.0
Paramount Pictures Corporation	5,205.6
Fox Entertainment Group, Inc.	2,413.5
Universal Studios, Inc.	2,147.5
Warner Bros. Entertainment Inc.	1,408.3
Lions Gate Entertainment Corp.	1,361.0
Sony Pictures Entertainment Inc.	809.1
Warner Bros. Television Production Inc.	773.83

Largest Employers	Employees
CBS Corporation	23,970
Universal Studios, Inc.	15,000
Fox Entertainment Group, Inc.	12,500
Warner Bros. Entertainment Inc.	7,300
Sony Pictures Entertainment Inc.	4,200
Ascent Media Corporation	4,000
Twentieth Century Fox Film Corporation	2,000
Paramount Pictures Corporation	1,900
Metro-Goldwyn-Mayer Inc.	1,440
WGBH Educational Foundation	1,100

Top Public Companies by Market Value	($ mil.)
CBS Corporation	5,021.3
Lions Gate Entertainment Corp.	1,157.0
Liberty Capital Group (Starz Media)	424.1

SOURCE: HOOVER'S, INC., DATABASE

Used Merchandise Stores

THIS INDUSTRY INCLUDES:

SIC CODES
5932   Used Merchandise
Stores

NAICS CODES
453310   Used Merchandise
Stores

The used merchandise store industry includes about 20,000 stores with combined annual revenue of $8 billion. Major companies include Goodwill, The Salvation Army, Winmark, and Cash America. The industry is highly fragmented: the 50 largest companies hold just 20 percent of industry sales.

The industry includes resale shops, consignment shops, thrift shops, antique stores, and pawn shops. Excluded are stores reselling cars, boats, trailers, and mobile homes.

Competitive Landscape

Population demographics, consumer income, and consumer tastes drive demand. The profitability of individual companies depends on efficient procurement and effective merchandising. Large companies have advantages in marketing and finance. Small companies can compete effectively by offering specialty products, serving a local market, or providing superior customer service. The industry is labor-intensive: average annual revenue per worker is under $70,000.

Used merchandise stores compete with retailers offering new merchandise. Companies also compete with individuals selling used merchandise privately or through websites, such as eBay.

Products, Operations & Technology

Major products include used clothing (25 percent of sales); antiques (15 percent); used furniture and collectibles (10 percent each); used books and kitchenware (5 percent each). Companies may also sell used jewelry; music (CDs, records, or tapes); or footwear. Pawn shops may offer check-cashing services or short-term cash advances.

Resale shops buy merchandise directly from owners. Consignment shops accept merchandise and pay owners a percentage of sales (typically 40 to 60 percent) when the item is sold.

BUSINESS CHALLENGES

» Competition from New Goods Retailers, Internet

Companies compete with traditional retailers offering inexpensive, new merchandise and Internet sites directly linking buyers and sellers of used goods. By offering a wide range of new merchandise at value prices, mass merchants, warehouse clubs, and discount stores have lowered the price differential between new and used items. While websites like eBay have made the used merchandise trade more mainstream, the Internet allows sellers to eliminate stores from the retail equation and reach buyers directly.

» Dependence on Consumer Income

Contrary to popular belief, used merchandise retailers suffer when consumer spending decreases. During the early 2000s recession, employment in used merchandise stores was flat. Companies specializing in used goods in luxury categories, such as antiques, struggle when consumers cut unnecessary items. During tough economic times, pawn shops suffer because more customers default on pawn loans.

» Variable Supply

Suppliers of used goods usually lack a set schedule, and merchandise can vary significantly in quality and type with each delivery. As a result, getting a steady supply of high-quality used merchandise can be difficult. While retailers of new merchandise enjoy reasonable guarantees of supply from manufacturers and distributors, used merchandise stores typically count on less reliable sources, including donations and individual sellers.

Thrift stores are nonprofit organizations that resell donated items and raise money for charity. Pawn shops hold goods from customers as collateral on loans, often referred to as "pawn loans." If the customer fails to pay off the loan, the pawn shop can sell the goods.

Stores range from between 2,000 and 5,000 square feet. Annual sales are between $150,000 and $400,000. Sales per square foot range from

$40 to $100 and are very low compared to most retailers. Common locations include strip malls and stand-alone buildings. Used merchandise retailers are rarely located in traditional shopping malls.

Companies may specialize in a category (such as women's apparel) or a price range within a category (designer women's apparel). Antique stores typically specialize in either a low, middle, or high price/quality tier. Most companies look for "gently used" items in good condition; however, retailers may repair or refurbish items. Many used merchandise retailers offer new goods to complement their inventory of used products.

Companies acquire used goods from individuals, wholesalers, dealers, nonprofit organizations, Internet sites, or other used merchandise retailers. Antique stores may buy merchandise from flea markets, salvage companies, or pickers (specialized wholesalers). Thrift stores may use donation bins or have pick-up routes. Companies may buy large amounts of donated goods from nonprofits at a bulk rate. Sometimes, up to half of donated items aren't suitable for resale, requiring companies to sort through donations. Leftover merchandise may ship to developing countries or recycling organizations.

Catalogs, "blue books," price guides, newspapers, the Internet, and employee experience help companies assess the value of used items. Estimating value for expensive goods, such as jewelry and antiques, can be especially difficult and may require a professional appraisal.

Companies may use integrated computer systems to manage point-of-sale (POS); inventory; and customer information. Large companies may have proprietary software using standardized pricing information to help stores estimate merchandise value and facilitate buying or consigning used merchandise. Customer databases, including sellers and buyers, help companies execute targeted marketing programs.

Sales & Marketing

While the typical customer varies by merchandise type, bargain shoppers, collectors, wholesalers, dealers, and Internet retailers are common buyers for used goods. Repeat customers are extremely important to used merchandise retailers. Used merchandise retailers consider buyers and sellers as customers.

Marketing and promotional vehicles include local TV, radio, print, and newspaper advertising; direct mail; and instore signage. Companies may shift advertising focus between buying

and selling used merchandise depending on inventory levels. Franchises typically pay a fee or percentage of sales toward a corporate ad budget and may be required to participate in regional cooperative marketing programs.

Internet retailing and online auctions have become popular ways to sell used merchandise. Companies may operate retail websites or link to existing sites, such as eBay. For inexpensive categories, such as used children's clothing, retail Internet sales can be time- and cost-prohibitive since selection can change rapidly and absolute margins are low.

Prices in used merchandise stores may range from 60 to 75 percent below retail prices. Prices in pawn shops are between 30 and 50 percent off retail prices, according to the National Pawnbrokers Association (NPA). Antique stores base pricing on a "grade level" ranging from 1 to 10, with 10 being of highest quality.

Human Resources

Many jobs in used merchandise stores require few skills and pay is low. Wages are 45 percent lower than the average for all US workers. Some nonprofits rely on volunteers to staff stores. Computer systems have replaced some of the human expertise required to set retail prices and calculate acquisition costs for used merchandise. Companies specializing in high-end or unique merchandise, such as antiques or rare coins, hire workers with in-depth category knowledge.

The industry injury rate is 20 percent higher than the average for all US workers. Jobs involving lifting and moving large objects, such as used furniture and bulk donated goods, contribute to a higher rate of strains, sprains, and bruises.

Industry Employment Growth

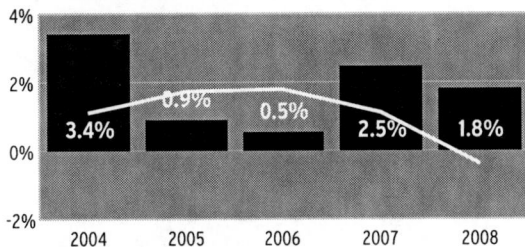

Average Hourly Earnings

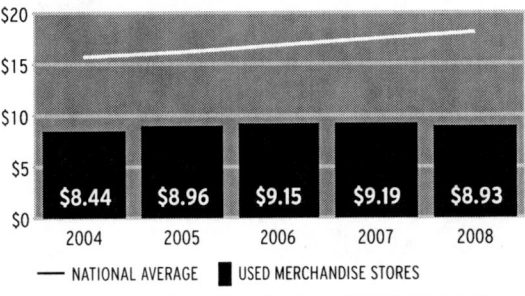

SOURCE: BUREAU OF LABOR STATISTICS

Call Preparation Questions

What is the company's biggest competitive threat?

Companies compete with traditional retailers offering inexpensive, new merchandise and Internet sites directly linking buyers and sellers of used goods.

How does economic change affect the company's sales?

Contrary to popular belief, used merchandise retailers suffer when consumer spending decreases.

How does the company deal with a constantly changing selection of merchandise?

Suppliers of used goods usually lack a set schedule, and merchandise can vary significantly in quality and type with each delivery.

What types of merchandise are the company's specialty?

Focusing on a particular category can help used merchandise retailers acquire better inventory and differentiate from other retailers.

How has the Internet changed the used merchandise market?

Companies can use web retailing to participate in the rapidly growing online used merchandise market.

Web Links

Consumer Products Safety Commission

Product safety and recall information.
www.cpsc.gov

Goodwill

Major nonprofit thrift store chain.
www.goodwill.org

Journal of Antiques and Collectibles

News, trends, operational information.
www.journalofantiques.com

National Association of Resale and Thrift Shops

News, trends, statistics available for purchase from industry trade association.
www.narts.com

National Pawnbrokers Association

News, trends, legislation, state specific information.
www.nationalpawnbrokers.org

Glossary of Acronyms

NARTS — National Association of Resale and Thrift Shops
NPA — National Pawnbrokers Association
POS — point-of-sale

HOOVER'S TOP COMPANIES

Largest Companies by Sales	($ mil.)
Goodwill Industries International, Inc.	3,163.5
Cash America International, Inc.	1,030.8
EZCORP, Inc.	457.4
The Salvation Army	113.0
Winmark Corporation	31.2

Largest Employers	Employees
Goodwill Industries International, Inc.	87,444
The Salvation Army	59,651
Cash America International, Inc.	5,501
EZCORP, Inc.	3,300
Value Financial Services, Inc.	530
Winmark Corporation	102
M&M Merchandisers, Inc.	81

Fastest Growing* by Five-Year Sales Growth	(%)
Cash America International, Inc.	18.7
EZCORP, Inc.	17.3

Fastest Growing* by Five-Year Employee Growth	(%)
Cash America International, Inc.	9.5
EZCORP, Inc.	6.9

Top Public Companies by Market Value	($ mil.)
Cash America International, Inc.	804.5
EZCORP, Inc.	724.8
Winmark Corporation	113.8

* These rates are compounded annualized increases and may have resulted from acquisitions or one time gains. If less than 6 years of data are available, growth is for the years available.

SOURCE: HOOVER'S, INC., DATABASE

Vegetable and Melon Farming

The vegetable and melon farming industry includes about 35,000 farms with combined annual revenue of $19 billion. Major US companies include Dole Food Company, Fresh Del Monte Produce, and Chiquita. Average total annual revenue per farm is $375,000, which may include some non-vegetable and non-melon revenue. The industry is concentrated: the top 10 percent of farms generate two-thirds of total industry revenue.

Vegetable and melon farming includes about 50 types of produce, including lettuce, dried beans, carrots, sweet corn, potatoes, tomatoes, broccoli, watermelon, honeydew, and cantaloupe.

Competitive Landscape

Demand is driven by population growth, consumer interest in healthy eating, and government programs promoting fresh produce. The profitability of individual companies depends on maximizing crop yield and minimizing loss from disease, insects, or unfavorable weather. Large companies have advantages in diversified crop production and access to labor. Small companies can compete effectively by specializing in organic, heirloom, or specialty crops. The industry is highly labor-intensive: average annual revenue per employee is less than $40,000.

The vegetable and melon industry competes with grain, oilseed, fruit, and tree nut farming for cropland and acreage, as farmers tend to grow crops with the highest yield and payout.

Products, Operations & Technology

Major products include potatoes (20 percent of the market); fresh tomatoes (10 percent); and lettuce (10 percent). Other key products include onions, mushrooms, sweet corn, watermelon, cantaloupe, and tomatoes grown for processing.

BUSINESS CHALLENGES

» Volatile Yields, Prices

Vegetable and melon yields and prices fluctuate sharply due to demand, acres planted, weather conditions, and inventory. Some years can produce bumper crops; other times, a major freeze, storm, or drought can wipe out an entire crop. Prices received for vegetables and melons swing widely, not only from year-to-year, but also month-to-month. Some farm operators can offset this risk by storing bulbs, tubers, and root vegetables. Storage isn't an option for tender vegetables, which account for 15 of the top 20 revenue-generating crops.

» Dependence on Seasonal Labor

Vegetable and melon farming are highly labor-intensive. Around 50 to 70 percent of all vegetable and melon farm workers are migrant laborers, mostly from Mexico. Tough working conditions and low pay have led to labor shortages. Vegetables often rot in the field, unpicked due to a lack of seasonal labor. Some farms have increased wages, reduced acreage to better match crop yield with available labor, or switched to mechanically harvested crops like corn. Changes in border enforcement practices or crackdowns on falsely documented workers could further limit labor availability.

» Weather, Disease

Vegetable and melon crops are highly susceptible to damage from hurricanes, high winds, drought, and disease. Weather, as with almost all agricultural crops, is a constant challenge. The USDA manages crop insurance and crop disaster assistance programs for farmers facing natural disasters and disease outbreaks. However, federal crop insurance programs favor grain farming, as total payouts are lower than for the vegetable and melon industry.

Vegetables are farmed according to two primary end-uses: fresh or processed. Processing is the canning, freezing, or dehydrating of vegetables. Melons are a fresh market crop. The US harvests around 80 billion pounds of vegetables and melons annually. Vegetable processing accounts for 40 percent of this total industry volume and 20 percent of industry revenue.

Vegetable and melon farms are typically small, family-run operations. Of farms, 70 percent harvest less than 50 acres. However, the largest vegetable and melon farms are large, devoting thousands of acres to a single crop. Almost all vegetables intended for processing are grown on farms larger than 2,000 acres.

Fresh market and processed crops require distinct seed stock and growing methods. For example, a potato farmer selects tuber sets specifically engineered to be sold and consumed fresh or as a processed product (French fries, potato chips, dehydrated potato flakes).

A plant's transplant-to-harvest growing season can range from 40 (herbs and lettuce) to 120 days (peppers and tomatoes). Slow-growing vegetables and melons are almost always warm weather crops. Farm operators start the growing season by raising seeds in greenhouses or covering seedlings under plastic row covers. Temperature control is important during the growing season and at harvest. For example, many tomato plants are grown on long poles and picked daily to encourage continued upright growth and an extended harvest.

Harvesting methods vary from crop to crop. Tender plants, melons, and soft-skinned fruits like tomatoes are hand-harvested by field workers. Most processed vegetable, root, and tuber crops are harvested mechanically. Hand-harvested crops are typically field-packed into boxes and kept cool prior to marketing. Cantaloupes and watermelons are often force-air-cooled to remove field heat, which maximizes shelf life. Root and tuber crops such as carrots, onions, and sweet potatoes often require long-term storage and/or short-term curing to heal scrapes and cuts.

Common inputs include seed, plants, and vines; chemicals to control weeds, disease, and insects; fertilizer to condition the soil; and machinery and supplies. Depending on the crop and weather conditions, irrigation can be a costly input. Operator and hired farm labor is a significant input, although one-third of all vegetable and melon farms are run by an operator whose primary profession isn't farming.

Recent technological advances include hybridized plants; crop irrigation; mechanical harvesters; GPS; geographic information systems (GIS); and yield monitors. Automated drip irrigation provides consistent moisture for vegetables and melons. Mechanical harvesters can improve a farm's yield, reducing dependence on seasonal labor. Tractors and mechanical harvesters can be equipped with GPS to direct their production or harvesting. GIS satellite imagery can detect insect damage, soil differences, and moisture content to protect and enhance production.

Sales & Marketing

A vegetable and melon farm's primary customers are packaging companies, food distributors, and processors. The farm's target customer depends on the type of crop and the extent of the farm's vertical integration. Farms that grow in bulk usually sell to packaging companies, while farms that develop branded products typically sell to distributors or retailers, but may also sell to specialty stores, restaurants, and direct-sale consumers.

Small farms have minimal sales and marketing needs, focusing on word-of-mouth, magazine, or newspaper advertising. Some farmers participate in cooperatives to pool funds for collective marketing. Larger companies advertise using TV, radio, national newspapers, and magazines. Many large companies market via rebates, promotions, merchandise, trademark licensing, and partnerships with industry and consumer groups.

Farms may be required by law to pay an assessment to a state commission based on production levels. State commissions, such as the Idaho Potato Commission, promote, educate, and develop the state's potato market. National "checkoff" programs for potato, mushroom, and watermelon farmers require contributions to a national checkoff board for research and promotion.

Internet sales are rare due to high shipping costs, limited freshness, and produce fragility. A few organic and specialty vegetable farmers specialize in Web-based sales; 50 percent of all vegetable and melon farmers have Internet access.

Prices received by farmers are highly volatile and vary based on the type of produce, where it's grown, and the market in which it's sold. Prices drop by more than half at peak harvest times but can double the following month. Prices for fresh market produce are measured per hundredweight (cwt), and for vegetables for processing are expressed as price per ton. Fresh potatoes can range from $7/cwt in fall to $25/cwt in winter. Lettuce prices are steady year-round, with iceberg typically priced at $15/cwt and leaf lettuce at $35/cwt. Fresh tomatoes range from $40 to $100/cwt depending on the time of year. Processed tomatoes are steady at around $60/ton.

The grower-packer return (the difference between the retail price and marketing spread for wholesalers, brokers, and retailers) ranges from 15 to 25 percent for fresh vegetables and melons. The spread is slightly lower for processed vegetables, around 10 to 20 percent.

Human Resources

Vegetable and melon farming wages average slightly less than $400 per week, nearly 50 percent lower than the national average. The industry is highly seasonal and labor-intensive. Demand for labor is highest in fall and spring for cool weather crops. Warm weather crops require additional labor in summer and fall.

Of all farms, 60 percent rely on farm labor, hiring an average of 20 farmhands. Three-quarters of this labor is through direct hiring; one-quarter is through farm labor contractors. Farm workers average only 35 weeks of work a year. About 20 percent of farms provide free worker housing to recruit migrant workers. Operators must pay all workers — migrant or not — at least the federal or state minimum wage, whichever is higher. Enforcing this regulation is difficult: despite a federal H-2A guest worker program, the Department of Labor estimates that around 90 percent of all farm laborers are not authorized to work in the US.

Vegetable and melon farming requires mechanical, horticultural, technical, and managerial skills. The average vegetable and melon operator is nearly 55 years old. The annual injury rate in vegetable and melon farming is 35 percent higher than the national average. Most injuries involve sprains, strains, and fractures resulting from falls, overexertion, and equipment use.

Call Preparation Questions

How does the farm handle the volatility of crop prices?

Vegetable and melon yields and prices fluctuate sharply due to demand, acres planted, weather conditions, and inventory.

How can machinery improvements reduce the farm's dependence on labor?

Some farms are investing in modified or refurbished farm machinery to lower dependence on seasonal labor.

What opportunities does the farm see in ready-to-eat or value-added produce?

Consumers are increasingly demanding convenience and are willing to pay for it.

Web Links

Specialty Farm Crop Bill Alliance

Ninety-member alliance of vegetable and fruit commissions, associations, and councils.
www.competitiveagriculture.org

The Vegetable Growers News

Excellent resource for vegetable farming trends and policy news.
www.vegetablegrowersnews.com

UC Vegetable Research and Information Center

Well-written overviews of specific crops and farming issues.
vric.ucdavis.edu/veginfo/veginfor.htm

USDA Vegetable and Melons Outlook

USDA bimonthly newsletter and annual yearbooks.
www.ers.usda.gov/Publications/VGS

Glossary of Acronyms

APHIS — Animal and Plant Health Inspection Service
CCC — Community Credit Corporation
CSA — community-supported agriculture
CWT — hundredweight (a unit of measurement)
GM — genetic modification; genetically modified
MPSA — Migrant and Seasonal Agricultural Worker Protection Act
PACA — Perishable Agricultural Commodities Act
RTE — ready-to-eat

HOOVER'S TOP COMPANIES

Largest Companies by Sales	($ mil.)
Dole Food Company, Inc.	6,931.0
Chiquita Brands International, Inc.	4,662.8
Del Monte Foods Company	3,736.8

Largest Employers	Employees
Dole Food Company, Inc.	45,000
Chiquita Brands International, Inc.	24,000
Del Monte Foods Company	18,100
Sun World International, LLC	2,500
A. Duda & Sons, Inc.	1,600
D'Arrigo Bros. Company	935
Salyer American Fresh Foods	900
Larsen Farms	687
Growers Express, LLC	300
Six L's Packing Company, Inc.	290

Fastest Growing* by Five-Year Sales Growth	(%)
Chiquita Brands International, Inc.	18.6
Del Monte Foods Company	11.5
Dole Food Company, Inc.	9.8

Top Public Companies by Market Value	($ mil.)
Del Monte Foods Company	1,734.1
Chiquita Brands International, Inc.	786.0

* These rates are compounded annualized increases and may have resulted from acquisitions or one time gains. If less than 6 years of data are available, growth is for the years available.

SOURCE: HOOVER'S, INC., DATABASE

Vending Machine Operators

The vending machine operator industry includes about 5,000 companies with combined annual revenue of about $6 billion. Major companies include divisions of Coca-Cola, Compass Group, ARAMARK, and Sodexo. The industry is fragmented: the top 50 companies are about 40 percent of industry sales.

Competitive Landscape

Consumer spending and business growth drive demand, since many vending machines are located in workplaces. The profitability of individual companies depends on effective merchandising, reliable service and maintenance, and securing prime locations. Large companies can offer a wide product selection, service large accounts, and enjoy scale advantages in purchasing, finance, and distribution. Small companies can compete effectively by serving a local market, providing superior customer service, or offering unique products. The industry is labor-intensive: average annual sales per employee are about $100,000.

Vending machine operators compete with companies providing food and beverages, including restaurants, grocery stores, convenience stores, and coffee shops.

Products, Operations & Technology

Major products sold include cold beverages (40 percent of industry sales) and candy and snacks (30 percent). Other products include hot beverages, hot and cold meal products, ice cream, and cigarettes. The majority of cold beverages sold are soft drinks in cans, bottles, or cups. Candy includes chocolate, gum, and mints. Snacks include salty snacks (potato chips and pretzels); baked goods (cookies and cakes); crackers, nuts, and seeds; and nutritious bars. Companies may also offer office coffee services (OCS) and provide brewing machines, sweeteners, and cream. With bulk vending, ma-

BUSINESS CHALLENGES

» Competition from Alternative Food Service Outlets

As the typical workplace evolves, vending machine operators face increasing competition from alternative food service outlets. Vending machine sales grew just 7 percent between 2003 and 2006, while total food service sales increased more than 15 percent. Increased autonomy in the workplace leaves workers free to leave worksites for snacks and meals. Restaurants, which typically have better quality food and more choices, have lured customers from vending sites with drive-thru windows and take-out.

» Evolving Workplace

The shrinking manufacturing sector, the vending industry's top customer, and smaller workplaces have hurt vending operator performance. Weakness in the auto industry, a sector where vending sales are typically strong, has especially harmed operators. Blue collar workplaces generate 20 to 50 percent more sales than white collar, according to Automatic Merchandiser. With most US workplaces employing fewer than 100, vending operators face a smaller number of financially viable sites.

» Volatile Gas Prices Affect Profitability

Significant gas price increases affect both operating and product costs and can hurt vending margins. On average, vending operators spend more on transportation expenses than they make in operating profits, according to Automatic Merchandiser. When gas prices rise, inventory costs often increase due to higher wholesale prices and fuel surcharges. Because vending products are already premium priced, most operators hesitate to raise consumer prices to cover the effects of higher fuel costs.

chines randomly dispense candies, nuts, gumballs, or capsules containing novelty items.

Most operators manage groups of vending machines in multiple locations known as a route. Drivers travel to each location and record sales, rotate and restock products, collect money, and service machines. The average route covers between 18 and 25 machines per day and generates $6,500 weekly, according to Automatic Merchandiser. Three-fourths of vending machine operators make less than $1 million annually.

Vending machines vary by merchandise type. Cold vending machines dispense items requiring refrigeration, including soft drinks, ice cream, and sandwiches. Some machines can store frozen items or reheat/cook foods. Cup drink machines with mixing capabilities can produce multiple beverages, such as coffee and hot chocolate. Glassfront machines can hold different types of products and allow customers to see products prior to purchase. Machines typically accept payment by coin or bill, with a small percentage accepting credit/debit cards. Some soft drink manufacturers offer free vending machines if an operator agrees to sell the manufacturer's brands exclusively. A new beverage/snack machine costs from $2,900 to $4,300; cold food machines from $7,000 to $8,500. Companies may also buy used or refurbished machines at discounted prices.

Companies rent space for vending machines in workplaces or high-traffic areas. While manufacturing facilities and office buildings are the most common locations, vending machines can also be found in retail centers, hotels, hospitals, and schools. To secure key sites, companies typically pay customer locations commissions based on sales. Contracts may contain exclusivity clauses, which prevent machines with competitive brands.

Companies buy inventory from a variety of sources depending on the size of operations. Large companies typically purchase directly from manufacturers, while small companies rely on distributors and retailers. The vending industry relies on well-recognized brand name products to drive sales. Because the markup on vend products is high, small operators can often buy merchandise at retail and still make a profit. Establishing the right product mix is critical to maximizing sales: many large vending companies have location-specific plan-o-grams, or product layouts.

Open technology and data standardization can help vending companies operate more efficiently. The Data EXchange (DEX) protocol provides an electronic standard for recording vending product movement, inventory, and sales information. The multi-drop bus (MDB) standard ensures payment devices can interface with any vending machine, regardless of manufacturer. DEX- and MDB-compatible devices, such as handheld scanners, improve the speed

and accuracy of data collection. Through the Internet, remote monitoring systems help operators identify product shortages and machine malfunctions and schedule routes more effectively.

While cashless vending technology using credit/debit cards exists, many vending operators have resisted due to the incremental cost of installing card systems and transaction fees. Some operators are testing cashless payment using cards containing radio frequency identification (RFID) tags, similar to the "EZ passes" used at toll booths.

Sales & Marketing

Customers include workers in manufacturing plants and office buildings, retail shoppers, and students. Historically, the typical vending machine customer was a white, blue-collar male; however, the evolving workplace has resulted in a more diverse demographic.

Most companies rely on referrals and personal contacts to secure new accounts because traditional advertising has limited effectiveness in the vending business. Responsive route drivers can help companies develop long-term customer relationships. Drivers who handle machine malfunctions promptly, minimize product shortages, and issue refunds for unsatisfactory product help operators retain business. While glassfront machines and machines with colorful graphics can help promote sales, companies typically rely on manufacturer advertising to generate consumer pull for products.

Average retail prices for vend soft drinks are 67 cents per can and $1.08 per bottle, according to Automatic Merchandiser. Retail prices for vend candy and snacks range from 70 to 80 cents. Prices for prepared and shelf stable foods range from $1.30 to $2. Coffee and other hot beverages range from 50 to 60 cents.

Human Resources

Wages for vending route drivers are about 15 percent lower than the average for all US workers. The industry injury rate is 30 percent higher than average due to heavy lifting-related injuries while restocking machines. Low wages and strenuous working conditions have resulted in high turnover.

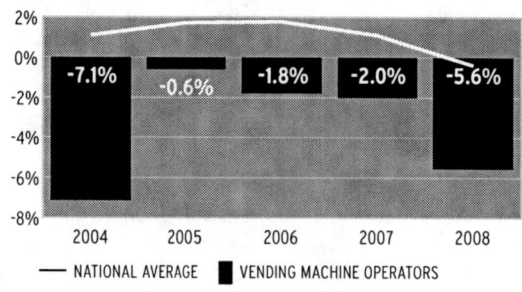

Industry Employment Growth

-7.1% (2004)
-0.6% (2005)
-1.8% (2006)
-2.0% (2007)
-5.6% (2008)

— NATIONAL AVERAGE ■ VENDING MACHINE OPERATORS

SOURCE: BUREAU OF LABOR STATISTICS

Call Preparation Questions

What is the company's biggest competitive threat?

As the typical workplace evolves, vending machine operators face increasing competition from alternative food service outlets.

How have changes in the US workforce affected the company?

The shrinking manufacturing sector, the vending industry's top customer, and smaller workplaces have hurt vending operator performance.

How do transportation cost increases affect the company's profitability?

Significant gas price increases affect both operating and product costs and can hurt vending margins.

How have advances in technology benefited or challenged the company?

Technology can help vending operators improve operating efficiency and customer satisfaction.

How has the vending market for coffee changed over the last decade?

Office coffee systems (OCS), which provide brewed coffee and associated condiments, are a small but growing segment of the vending industry.

Web Links

All About Vending

News, statistics, and trends from Management Science Associates.
www.allaboutvending.com

Automatic Merchandiser

News, statistics, annual State of the Vending Industry report.
www.amonline.com

National Automatic Merchandising Association

News, trends, and legislative information from trade association.
www.vending.org

National Bulk Vendors Association

Background information, safety issues from trade association.
www.nbva.org

Vending Times

News and trends.
www.vendingtimes.com

Glossary of Acronyms

MDB — multi-drop bus

NAMA — National Automatic Merchandising Association

NBVA — National Bulk Vending Association

OCS — office coffee services

HOOVER'S TOP COMPANIES

Largest Employers	Employees
ARAMARK Refreshment Services, Inc.	4,500
Compass Group USA, Inc.	4,200
Five Star Food Service, Inc.	1,400
Universal Sodexho USA	1,100

SOURCE: HOOVER'S, INC., DATABASE

Venture Capital

THIS INDUSTRY INCLUDES:

SIC CODES
6799   Investors

NAICS CODES
523910   Miscellaneous
            Intermediation

The US venture capital industry includes about 900 companies with combined annual investments of about $26 billion and over $250 billion of investments under management. Major companies include Kleiner Perkins Caufield and Byers, New Enterprise Associates, and Technology Crossover Ventures. The industry is concentrated: the top 50 companies invest about two-thirds of venture capital dollars.

Competitive Landscape

Demand is driven primarily by the pace of technological innovation and the number of companies created to commercialize new technologies. The profitability of individual companies depends on successfully choosing and managing a portfolio of investments. Large companies have advantages in attracting investors, developing expertise in multiple technology markets, and funding large deals. Small companies can compete effectively by concentrating on specific market sectors or geographic areas. The average venture capital investment is about $8 million.

Individual, or angel, investors, and large companies with strategic interests in early stage companies are also sources of new venture funding.

Products, Operations & Technology

Venture capital companies provide money to young, rapidly growing companies with promising new products or services in exchange for ownership in the company. Major market sectors for venture capital investments include software; life sciences (including biotechnology and medical devices); telecommunications; media and entertainment; and clean tech (energy and environmental technologies).

Venture capitalists (VCs) create pools of money, or funds, by raising capital from pension funds, endowments, foundations, corporations, foreign investors, insurance companies,

BUSINESS CHALLENGES

» Dependence on Stock Market Performance

The venture capital industry depends highly on stock market performance. Technological innovation is driven, in part, by available risk capital from market performance. Investors are frequently entities or individuals who have registered big gains on stock market investments and have discretionary capital to invest in more risky venture capital investments. Venture capitalists drive portfolio companies toward exit strategies that include IPOs. A positive stock market environment is essential to raise money through IPOs.

» Pace of Technology Innovation

Emerging technologies drive most venture capital investment opportunities. The pace of innovation is driven, in large part, by university research funded by the federal government. In 2006, the federal government allocated about $20 billion to university research in the life sciences, engineering, environmental, computer science, and math fields. More than 80 percent of venture capital investments are made in companies dependent on technology from these fields. The rapid pace of innovation in these fields creates numerous opportunities for start-up companies, but also makes predicting which companies and technologies will be successful more difficult for venture capital firms.

» Selecting Investments

Selecting companies for investment is one of the most critical aspects of running a venture capital fund. Venture capitalists invest in a very small percentage of companies they review. Start-ups or early stage companies have an unproven business model, strategy, and management team; many won't be successful. VC firms must accurately assess new technologies, market potential, and the management talent of prospective companies.

and high net worth individuals. A firm may operate several funds simultaneously.

Venture capital firms are organized as limited partnerships, limited liability partnerships

(LLP), or limited liability companies (LLC). The most common form is the limited partnership, where the firm serves as the general partner and investors are limited partners. General partners operate the business on a daily basis, performing both fundraising and investment activities. General partners are paid a management fee for operating the fund, as well as a share of profits from the fund's investment activities, known as "carried interest." The terms and conditions of general partner compensation are spelled out in the fund's prospectus.

The firm sets a target fund size and begins fundraising, which may range from weeks to several months. Once the target fund level is raised, the fund is closed and investment activity begins. Limited partners, the fund's investors, may range from a few to less than 100, as a more restrictive set of regulations govern fundraising efforts when more than 100 investors are involved. General partners may also be limited partners in company funds. Capital calls, requests for investment dollars based on partner commitments, occur over the life of the fund's investment activity, either as-needed or on a predetermined time frame.

VCs invest funds into companies using a portfolio approach. Recognizing the risky nature of venture capital investing, VCs anticipate high rates of return from their investments, knowing that not all portfolio companies will give them the expected return. VCs look for a portfolio company to have a liquidity event, such as an initial public offering (IPO), merger, or sale, within a three to seven year time horizon. Expected returns from this event are typically targeted at 10 times or more. Pre-money valuations, the value of a portfolio company before receiving venture capital, are determined by a combination of factors, including negotiations between company management and the VCs.

Venture capital investments are categorized in three stages: early stage or start-up funding, growth funding, and late stage funding, sometimes called mezzanine financing. A venture capital fund may participate in any or all, although most concentrate in a particular stage. The advantage to early stage investing is the lower valuation upon which the investment is based, providing the opportunity for a higher return. The advantage of later stage investing is the shorter time to a liquidity event and greater certainty of the company's performance. If a venture capital company invests in an early round, it typically reserves funds to invest in later rounds. Fund sizes range from as little as

$15 to $25 million for early stage funds to late stage funds of more than $500 million.

A venture capital firm may invest alone or may co-invest with other venture firms in a syndicated deal. Syndications are used when a company needs a large amount of capital or to bring in the market or technical expertise of other venture firms. Venture firms are actively involved in portfolio companies, and usually receive one or more seats on the company's board of directors to protect and advance their investment.

Venture capital operations normally consist of general partners, partners, associates, entrepreneurs in residence, interns, and administrative personnel. Partners, unlike general partners, benefit only from the success of the specific portfolio companies they're involved with. Research and due diligence are critical components of the investment process. Many company business plans are reviewed by the operations staff, but only a very small percentage of reviewed companies are chosen for investment.

Sales & Marketing

Limited partners are a venture capital firm's customers. Limited partners can include pension funds, endowments, foundations, corporations, foreign investors, insurance companies, and high net worth individuals. The process for soliciting limited partners varies based on the historical success of a firm. New or very young venture capital companies must convince limited partners to participate with no track record of performance. These newer ventures usually market the previous success of the general partners in the entrepreneurial world or rely on contacts from previous business experience to build a fund. Older, more established firms with proven track records can call on the same limited partners for participation in the next fund.

Venture capital companies market primarily by networking, word-of-mouth, and individual contacts. Venture capital trade associations, along with local and regional entrepreneurial development associations, host symposiums and conferences where venture capital companies, current and prospective limited partners, and emerging growth companies gather to exchange information. A typical conference will include presentations by industry experts and selected companies seeking venture capital. Networking is a critical element of success for both venture capital firms and businesses seeking venture capital.

General partners receive a management fee, which is typically about 2 percent of the fund size. In addition, general partners' carried interest typically ranges from about 20 to 30 percent of the profits generated from the fund's investments. Many variations of management fees and carried interest agreements exist.

Human Resources

Venture capital companies vary greatly in size, ranging from $15 to $25 million early stage funds with fewer than five employees, to mature companies with funds of several hundred million and 50 or more employees.

Venture capital companies are staffed by employees who have graduate engineering, business, and finance degrees. Most general partners have extensive business experience, usually in industry sectors that match the firm's investment focus. As associates grow in experience and performance, they become partners, then general partners in the firm.

Industry Employment Growth

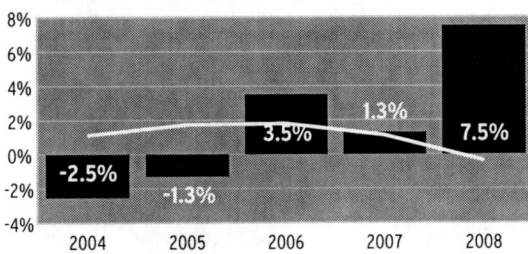

Average Hourly Earnings

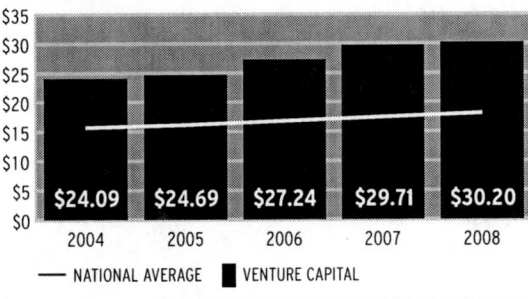

— NATIONAL AVERAGE ■ VENTURE CAPITAL

SOURCE: BUREAU OF LABOR STATISTICS

Call Preparation Questions

What external factors influence the company's strategy for fundraising and investment?

The venture capital industry depends highly on stock market performance.

What technologies does the firm focus on for investments?

Emerging technologies drive most venture capital investment opportunities.

How does the company select which companies to invest in?

Selecting companies for investment is one of the most critical aspects of running a venture capital fund.

What is the company doing to build relationships with universities?

Investment opportunities for venture capital firms often arise from university research.

What opportunities does the company see in developing clean technology?

Investments in technology companies with an energy or environmental focus increased $1 billion in 2006, rising to over 7 percent of total venture capital investment.

Web Links

American Venture Magazine

Online magazine with articles related to venture capital industry.
www.americanventuremagazine.com

Canada's Venture Capital & Private Equity Association

News on venture capital in Canada.
www.cvca.ca

National Venture Capital Association

Statistics, press releases, and other industry information.
www.nvca.org

PricewaterhouseCoopers MoneyTree Report

Quarterly information on investments and fundraising.
www.pwcmoneytree.com/MTPublic/ns

Glossary of Acronyms

CVCA — Canada's Venture Capital and Private Equity Association
DJIA — Dow Jones Industrial Average
ERISA — Employee Retirement Income Security Act
IPO — initial public offering
LLC — Limited Liability Company
LLP — Limited Liability Partnership
NVCA — National Venture Capital Association
VC — venture capitalist

Warehouse Clubs and Superstores

The warehouse club and superstore industry (warehouse clubs) includes about 3,000 stores with combined annual revenue of almost $200 billion. Major companies include Sam's Club (Wal-Mart); Costco Wholesale; BJ's Wholesale Club; and Meijer. The industry is highly concentrated: the top four companies own 85 percent of stores and hold over 90 percent of sales.

Competitive Landscape

Demographics and small business growth drive demand, and spending in warehouse clubs generally resists economic cycles. The profitability of individual companies depends on high volume sales, low-cost purchasing, and efficient distribution. Large chains dominate the market due to advantages in purchasing, distribution, and finance. Average annual revenue per employee is about $230,000.

Warehouse clubs differ from superstores in that clubs require a membership to shop. Superstores typically offer a wide range of products within each merchandise category, while warehouse clubs offer a limited selection. Both types of retailers offer products across many retail categories, and competition includes grocery stores, mass merchandisers, department stores, specialty retailers, and wholesalers.

Products, Operations & Technology

Major products sold by warehouse clubs are groceries (35 percent of revenue); drug, health, and beauty aids (10 percent); apparel (8 percent); electronics (5 percent); and membership fees (2 percent). Other products include cleaning products, toys, and appliances. Most products are available only in large sizes or bulk quantity. Warehouse clubs may also have onsite gas stations, pharmacies, optical centers, or food courts.

Warehouse clubs offer multiple types of membership plans, including programs for both

BUSINESS CHALLENGES

» Low Margins Drive Dependence on High Volume

To be profitable, companies must compensate for low margins through extremely high-volume sales. The business model for a warehouse club depends on volume, and soft sales due to slow store traffic reduce efficiency and increase operating costs. Because companies stock only a few products in each category, merchandising errors can disastrously affect sales. Companies typically carry gross margins between 8 and 12 percent, versus 25 to 35 percent for grocery and general merchandise stores.

» Competition from Alternative Retailers

Because warehouse clubs offer products in numerous categories, companies compete with many types of retailers. The market response to a new club can be intense, and deep discounts by competitors on key products can make warehouse clubs appear less attractive. Grocery stores and mass merchandisers offer wider selections and tend to be in more convenient locations. In addition, food retailers carry similar large sizes previously available only in warehouse clubs. Specialty retailers can provide an extremely broad selection within a product category, and typically provide much better customer service.

» Keeping Operating Costs Low

With thin margins, warehouse clubs depend on extremely efficient operations to keep costs low. Companies rely on direct manufacturer shipments and cross-docking facilities to reduce distribution and storage costs. At the same time, warehouse clubs rely on high volume sales and can't afford stock-outs. Companies must strike the proper balance between low inventory costs and potential lost sales.

consumers and businesses. Fees range from $35 to $50 for a standard membership to $80 to $100 for a premium membership. Renewals are important; the renewal rate for Costco members is over 85 percent.

Warehouse clubs are able to provide deep discounts by offering no-frills, self-service operations where the customer experience is secondary to operational efficiency. Companies design floor plans to maximize selling space and optimize merchandise handling and inventory control. Warehouse clubs typically display merchandise on pallets and store extra inventory on overhead racks.

Because customers are willing to drive long distances to enjoy low prices, companies may build retail stores on remote sites, and locations can be far from major shopping areas. Over 40 percent of warehouse club customers drive more than 11 miles to shop, according to ACNielsen. Warehouse clubs need lots of real estate; most retail locations range from 110,000 to 140,000 square feet. A typical BJ's, including parking, requires about 14 acres of land. Annual sales for a single warehouse club range from $50 to $130 million.

Warehouse clubs buy most merchandise directly from manufacturers or importers, typically in full truckloads. Volume purchasing allows companies to receive substantial discounts, resulting in savings to customers. Frequently, companies work directly with manufacturers to develop special sizes or packaging to reduce handling costs and provide the best possible consumer value. Because of the sizable sales opportunity, competition for club business among manufacturers is fierce and most warehouse clubs enjoy favorable purchasing terms. `

Warehouse clubs offer a limited selection of products in a wide range of merchandise categories. Rapid inventory turns are critical, and most companies limit product offerings to the fastest selling styles, sizes, flavors, or colors. Inventory is generally limited to the top brand names in each category and private label goods. Warehouse clubs typically offer between 4,000 and 8,000 stock-keeping units (SKUs), much lower than the 30,000 to 60,000 SKUs carried by grocery stores and mass merchandisers. Because companies target volume purchasers, most products are available in institutional sizes, bulk packaging, cases, or multiple packs. Some companies offer commercial grade appliances and equipment. Unlike most retail operations, inventory shrinkage is low, primarily due to membership requirements and tightly controlled entrances and exits.

By eliminating the traditional multi-level distribution channel, companies save on distributor commissions and storage costs. Retail locations receive shipments either directly from manufacturers or through cross-docking facilities, where workers unload and reallocate truckloads of merchandise for individual stores. Direct and cross-dock shipments minimize stored inventory and reduce receiving costs. Most companies try to turn around merchandise at cross-docking facilities in less than 24 hours.

Warehouse clubs use bar code scanners and computerized point-of-sale (POS) systems at the check out. Inventory management systems track shrinkage and replenishment needs. Some warehouse clubs require manufacturers to tag merchandise with radio frequency identification (RFID) tags to monitor inventory as it moves through the supply chain.

Sales & Marketing

Typical customers include women in large households (five or more members) with income of $50,000 or more, and small businesses. Warehouse clubs tend to be popular with Asian and Hispanic ethnic groups. A typical customer visits a warehouse club between eight and 11 times a year.

Most warehouse clubs rely on targeted direct mailings to attract new members and advertise promotions to existing members. TV and radio advertising is infrequent, and typically funded in part by manufacturers. Companies may offer free trial memberships or one-day memberships to attract new customers. Word-of-mouth is important, and many enthusiastic club customers encourage friends to join. In conjunction with new store openings, companies may dedicate sales staff to group sales or local businesses. Consistent with a low-cost strategy, marketing and promotional spending is much lower than that of other retailers.

Most companies have retail Internet sites that provide basic store, membership, and product information. Companies may offer special products or discounts for online shoppers. In addition, most warehouse clubs allow customers to purchase or renew memberships online.

Warehouse clubs sell in quantity, and retail prices per serving or unit can be significantly lower than prices in grocery stores and mass merchandisers. Because some companies consistently sell products at prices below the manufacturer suggested retail price, certain manufacturers refuse to sell to warehouse clubs. The average "ring," or total purchase, at a warehouse club is $83, according to AC Nielsen. Most companies watch competitive prices carefully, as periodic promotions by other retailers can reduce the effective discount at a warehouse club.

Human Resources

Workers in warehouse clubs require few skills, and wages are 40 percent lower than the US average. Most companies rely on part-time workers. The industry injury rate is about 15 percent higher than the US average, primarily due to sprain, strains, and bruises from moving merchandise. Some Costco employees belong to unions.

Industry Employment Growth

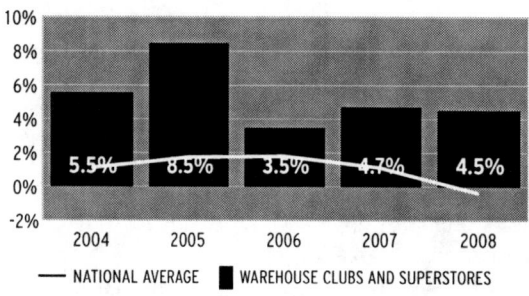

SOURCE: BUREAU OF LABOR STATISTICS

Call Preparation Questions

How sensitive are the company's profits to changes in sales volume?

To be profitable, companies must compensate for low margins through extremely high-volume sales.

How does the company develop a competitive strategy that addresses different types of retailers?

Because warehouse clubs offer products in numerous categories, companies compete with many types of retailers.

What ongoing programs does the company have to improve operational efficiency?

With thin margins, warehouse clubs depend on extremely efficient operations to keep costs low.

What trends has the company seen in demand for high-end merchandise?

By offering more expensive products, companies can attract affluent customers who tend to spend more.

How does the company generate customer excitement?

By searching out unique, hard-to-find items and pricing them low, warehouse clubs can create a "treasure hunt" experience and increase customer enthusiasm.

Web Links

AC Nielsen

Retail market research website — statistics and trends.
us.acnielsen.com

BJ's

Warehouse club retailer.
www.bjs.com

Costco

Warehouse club retailer.
www.costco.com

Sam's Clubs

Warehouse club retailer.
www.samsclub.com

Warehouse Club Focus

Industry news, statistics, pricing studies.
www.warehouseclubfocus.com/
warehouse_club_focus.php

Glossary of Acronyms

EDLP — every day low price
POS — point-of-sale
RFID — radio frequency identification
SKU — stock-keeping unit

HOOVER'S TOP COMPANIES

Largest Companies by Sales	($ mil.)
Costco Wholesale Corporation	72,483.0
BJ's Wholesale Club, Inc.	9,005.0
Meijer, Inc.	4,247.1
Fred Meyer Stores, Inc.	3,254.8
Smart & Final Inc.	2,300.0
PriceSmart, Inc.	1,119.9
Bi-Mart Corporation	720.0
SAM'S CLUB	—

Largest Employers	Employees
Costco Wholesale Corporation	137,000
Meijer, Inc.	67,000
Fred Meyer Stores, Inc.	28,000
BJ's Wholesale Club, Inc.	20,800
Smart & Final Inc.	6,200
PriceSmart, Inc.	4,200
Bi-Mart Corporation	3,000
Cost-U-Less, Inc.	600

Fastest Growing* by Five-Year Sales Growth	(%)
Costco Wholesale Corporation	11.2
PriceSmart, Inc.	11.1
BJ's Wholesale Club, Inc.	9.0
Smart & Final Inc.	2.7

Fastest Growing* by Five-Year Employee Growth	(%)
PriceSmart, Inc.	12.4
Costco Wholesale Corporation	5.1
BJ's Wholesale Club, Inc.	1.2
Smart & Final Inc.	1.0

Top Public Companies by Market Value	($ mil.)
Costco Wholesale Corporation	29,004.3
BJ's Wholesale Club, Inc.	2,018.0
PriceSmart, Inc.	629.3

* These rates are compounded annualized increases and may have resulted from acquisitions or one time gains. If less than 6 years of data are available, growth is for the years available.

SOURCE: HOOVER'S, INC., DATABASE

Warehousing and Storage

The public warehousing and storage industry is handled by about 4,500 companies in the US, with combined annual revenue of $20 billion. Large companies include Iron Mountain (records storage); Public Storage (self-storage); and units of DHL and CEVA Logistics. The industry is highly fragmented: the 20 largest companies control less than 30 percent of the market. Typically, warehousing companies operate a single facility of 200,000 square feet and have annual revenue of about $1 million.

Competitive Landscape

The flow of goods through the domestic economy drives demand in the warehousing business. The profitability of individual companies depends on good marketing, as operations are fairly simple. Although there are economies of scale in operating larger warehouses, there are few economies in owning multiple warehouses. Small companies can compete effectively with larger ones in local markets. The industry is highly labor-intensive: average annual revenue per employee is under $30,000.

Products, Operations & Technology

Services include general warehousing, refrigerated warehousing, records storage, farm products storage, and self-storage. Passive real estate owners, such as AMB Property, lease warehouse space to others, but aren't active operators. General warehousing accounts for about 55 percent of industry revenue; refrigerated warehousing for 15 percent. Companies with national warehousing needs usually operate their own facilities. So-called "public" warehousing serves mainly local and regional companies without sufficient volume to justify operating their own warehousing facilities.

The operations of all warehousing and storage operations are essentially similar: operators provide a protected space where customers can leave items for varying periods. The space is

BUSINESS CHALLENGES

» Demand Depends Highly on Flow of Goods

Economic slowdowns greatly impact the industry, as many business customers use public and contract warehousing mainly to handle peak demand. Industrial production, import volume, and office vacancy rates are indicators of demand for warehousing.

» Energy Costs

Cold storage and temperature-controlled facilities have high energy requirements, contributing significantly to operating costs. Increased volatility in energy costs over the past few years resulted in a dramatic rise in cooling and heating costs. In times of rising costs, facility managers investigate new, more affordable technologies to reduce consumption. Electricity costs can comprise over 25 percent of a cold storage building's ongoing operating costs.

» Vulnerability from Specialization

Some warehouses serve only one large customer or one specific industry, specializing their equipment and distribution system for particular needs. While specialization creates longer-term contracts and higher profits, greater customer exposure exists for these warehouses if the customer or the industry suffers a downturn. Diversification across several markets and customers might be important to mitigate this risk.

usually protected against fire and theft, and may be climate-controlled or refrigerated for special items like documents, clothing, and food. In addition to basic storage service, operators may provide services such as pickup and delivery, materials handling, computerized inventory control, order processing, report generation and shipping. Operators must hire and train guards and other personnel, operate security systems, and carry sufficient insurance. While the norm is for operators to handle warehousing needs for many customers, some also handle "contract" warehousing operations: running an entire warehouse operation for a single large customer. Prices vary widely and depend on market location and services. Annual leasing costs for large warehouses average around $5 per square foot.

The records storage segment of the industry has special characteristics. Virtually all large companies use offsite storage for records that are either vital to current operations (such as backups of computerized data bases) or that are inactive, but must be kept for legal reasons. Consolidation has been strong in this market segment because large customers prefer to contract with a single storage provider that can service locations around the country. Most records that companies store are paper, but a growing share consists of backup computer tapes and other electronic media.

The self-storage segment provides consumers and small businesses with personal storage space leased monthly. Public Storage and Storage USA (owned by GE), the largest companies in this segment, own and operate hundreds of local facilities. Unlike public warehouses, such companies usually offer no ancillary services, except the sale of insurance. They're often organized as REITs. An average facility has 700 units, sometimes called lockers, and covers 70,000 square feet. Average annual rent per square foot is typically around $10, while direct operating expenses are close to $2 per square foot. Occupancy rates for mature sites may be 80 to 90 percent.

Warehouse operators use a variety of technologies to handle inventory and respond to customer requests to move contents. Operators may use pick-and-pack systems to help fill customers' requests for retrieving and shipping stored inventory. To correctly track items, some operators are assessing the effectiveness of radio frequency identification (RFID) tags that automatically communicate with a local computer. The cost of such devices has fallen rapidly, encouraging their use. With such tags, operators and customers can know the exact location of stored goods.

Sales & Marketing

Typical local and regional warehouse operators advertise in the Yellow Pages and newspapers. Large companies may advertise in trade journals that focus on transportation, logistics, and supply chain services, and moving companies that serve the business market. Sales are via representatives who call on businesses, and in-house salespeople who handle inquires and responses to ads.

Human Resources

Some warehousing jobs involve operating materials handling equipment. Some operations also involve trucking services. The skills required are fairly modest, as reflected in the below-average earnings. Benefits are relatively low, as the pool of available workers has usually been large. Turnover is likely to be above average. The number of jobs available increased rapidly in the late 1990s, as companies used more public warehousing services rather than build their own facilities.

Because materials handling can be dangerous, safety and training are major concerns for warehouse employers. The industry's safety performance has increased sharply in the past decade: the annual rate of illness and injury per 100 workers is about eight cases, equal to the rate for manufacturing workers.

Industry Employment Growth

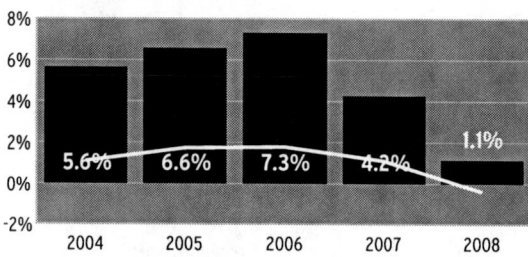

Average Hourly Earnings

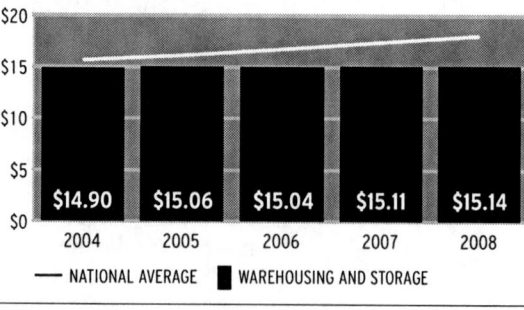

— NATIONAL AVERAGE ■ WAREHOUSING AND STORAGE

SOURCE: BUREAU OF LABOR STATISTICS

Call Preparation Questions

How does the company manage slowdowns in warehousing demand due to the economy?

Economic slowdowns greatly impact the industry, as many business customers use public and contract warehousing mainly to handle peak demand.

What strategies does the facility use to control fuel costs, especially if climate-controlled?

Cold storage and temperature-controlled facilities have high energy requirements, contributing significantly to operating costs.

What are the risks or benefits of becoming a dedicated service for one customer or industry?

Some warehouses serve only one large customer or one specific industry, specializing their equipment and distribution system for particular needs.

What opportunities does the company have to provide outsourced services, such as logistics, inventory management, and shipping?

Recognizing the importance of efficient storage and distribution functions, more companies are outsourcing to logistics specialists.

What benefits can the company derive from offering container services?

A relatively new service is providing self-storage containers that customers fill and store on their own site or the operator's.

Web Links

Industrial Truck Association

Represents lift truck manufacturers.
www.indtrk.org

Inside Self Storage Magazine

www.insideselfstorage.com

International Warehouse Logistics Association

Industry news. Links.
www.iwla.com/press.aspx

Material Handling Industry of America

Material handling and logistics association.
www.mhia.org

Modern Materials Handling

Articles.
www.mmh.com

Self Storage Association

Self Storage trade organization.
www.selfstorage.org

Glossary of Acronyms

3PL — third-party logistics provider
DC — distribution center
DOD — Department of Defense
HTD — high throughput distribution (facility)
IWLA — International Warehouse Logistics Association
LM — logistics management
MHCS — material handling control systems
MHE — material handling equipment
PRW — public refrigerated warehouse
RFDC — radio frequency data communication
RFID — radio frequency identification
SSF — self-storage facility
WMS — warehouse management systems

HOOVER'S TOP COMPANIES

Largest Companies by Sales	($ mil.)
Iron Mountain Incorporated	3,055.1
AMERCO	2,049.2
Public Storage	1,745.6
Pitney Bowes Management Services, Inc.	1,135.0
Emdeon Inc.	808.5
AmeriCold Logistics, LLC	314.7
Burris Logistics	284.0
Menlo Worldwide, LLC	209.0

Largest Employers	Employees
Iron Mountain Incorporated	20,100
AMERCO	18,500
AmeriCold Logistics, LLC	5,900
Public Storage	5,700
UTi Integrated Logistics Inc.	4,000
Recall Corporation	4,000
Emdeon Inc.	2,250
Menlo Worldwide, LLC	2,205
Extra Space Storage Inc.	1,853
Sovran Self Storage, Inc.	1,057

Fastest Growing* by Five-Year Sales Growth	(%)
VillageEDOCS	54.8
Auxilio, Inc.	52.2
Extra Space Storage Inc.	49.7
Iron Mountain Incorporated	15.3
Public Storage	14.8
Sovran Self Storage, Inc.	12.4
Emdeon Inc.	8.2
Pitney Bowes Management Services, Inc.	3.1

Fastest Growing* by Five-Year Employee Growth	(%)
Iron Mountain Incorporated	86.2
Extra Space Storage Inc.	48.9
Public Storage	18.9
Sovran Self Storage, Inc.	10.4
AMERCO	2.8

Top Public Companies by Market Value	($ mil.)
Public Storage	13,378.2
Iron Mountain Incorporated	4,993.8
AMERCO	1,120.8
Extra Space Storage Inc.	885.4
Sovran Self Storage, Inc.	792.6

* These rates are compounded annualized increases and may have resulted from acquisitions or one time gains. If less than 6 years of data are available, growth is for the years available.

SOURCE: HOOVER'S, INC., DATABASE

Waste Management

The private waste management industry in the US includes over 10,000 companies with combined annual revenue of $50 billion. Two national companies, Waste Management and Republic Services, together handle more than half the solid waste generated in the US. Other top companies include BFI Canada, which handles solid waste in Canada and the US. Beyond the top companies, the industry is highly fragmented: a midsized company has $10 million in annual revenue.

Competitive Landscape

Demand depends on the volume of waste generated, which depends on the level of economic activity and consumer spending. The profitability of individual companies depends on efficient operations, because the service is a commodity sold based on price. Big companies have large efficiencies of scale in operations. Small companies can compete successfully by offering specialized services or serving local markets. Annual revenue per employee is $200,000 at large companies, $125,000 at smaller.

Products, Operations & Technology

Major services are waste collection, waste treatment and disposal, remediation, and recycling. Waste collection accounts for about 55 percent of industry revenue, treatment and disposal for 20 percent, and remediation for 15 percent. Small companies usually operate in only one of these segments. Larger companies often have vertically integrated operations that include all of these components.

Waste management involves primarily the collection, transfer, and disposal in landfills of non-hazardous, solid waste. Companies may also handle and treat hazardous, low-level radioactive, and liquid wastes. The business is conceptually simple: trash is collected from businesses, industrial sites, and residences, and

BUSINESS CHALLENGES

» Dependence on Government Regulations

The waste disposal industry, and landfill operations in particular, are subject to rigorous EPA, state, and local regulations, especially regarding possible groundwater pollution. Because landfills are considered undesirable, some states and cities try to restrict their expansion and forbid waste imports from other states. Many state and local governments claim the right to direct the flow of waste collected in their jurisdiction to specific facilities for processing and disposal, so-called "flow-control."

» Customer Concentration

Although waste collectors often have a diversified customer base, some hold contracts with commercial, industrial, or municipal customers that account for a large portion of business. Changes in population, amount of trash produced, and cost to collect can affect profitability of customer bases; waste management companies may also gain or lose contracts with customer segments depending on municipal involvement and area competition.

» Unknown Future Environmental Liabilities

Although operators estimate the future costs of decommissioning landfills, the time and unclear technical issues that may be involved (especially for hazardous wastes), may subject them to much higher final costs than currently anticipated. In common with past liability assignments from Superfund waste sites, waste collectors might be held financially liable for hazardous materials found at landfills they used.

is buried. Growing public awareness of possible environmental dangers of this simple approach have complicated the business, making it more technologically demanding. US homes, businesses, and institutions produce more than 200 million tons of solid waste per year, approximately 4.4 pounds of waste per person per day. About 30 percent of waste is recycled or composted, 15 percent is incinerated, and the remaining 55 percent is disposed of in landfills.

Trash is usually collected from commercial sites using either small (1 to 8 cubic yard) steel containers (dumpsters) that are mechanically emptied into collection trucks, or large (20 to 40 cubic yard) "roll-off" containers that are loaded onto a special truck and hauled away. Residential collection is mainly done with back-end loading trucks.

Recycling and material recovery are a major part of waste management. Recycling is collection and disposal of commodity items like paper, cardboard, newspaper, glass, plastic, and metal cans that have been sorted out of the wastestream. Materials' recovery involves separating recyclable items from collected waste, usually by manually picking through a wastestream on a conveyor belt. Recycling collection is frequently part of commercial and residential waste collection, but may be charged for separately. Recyclables are sold to purchasers at prices that can fluctuate wildly, depending on demand.

Because landfills are now often located at a significant distance from many cities, companies operate transfer stations, where waste is received from various trash collectors, compacted, and hauled to landfills in special trailers. Operators charge fees based on the type and volume of trash received and the distance to the landfill. Recycling and materials' recovery operations are often located alongside transfer stations.

Modern landfills are technologically very different from the town dumps that used to exist in every city. Landfills usually have a clay liner on the bottom and sides to prevent waste from leaching into the local water table. Wastes are spread, compacted, and covered with earth daily. Monitoring devices detect leakage, and piping systems vent the methane gas created by organic decomposition. Full landfills are capped and may eventually be used for other purposes such as parks. For hazardous material landfills, the design, operation, and post-closure requirements are more stringent. Landfill operators usually own the landfill, but sometimes operate them for a municipal owner for a fee. The eventual closure costs of a non-hazardous landfill involve monitoring and possible repair for up to 30 years, while monitoring responsibilities for hazardous and radioactive sites last much longer.

Handling and disposing of hazardous (usually liquid chemicals); low-level radioactive (high-level radioactive wastes are handled by the federal government); and other liquid wastes are technologically complex and expensive, often involving chemical treatment to separate the toxic components. In some cases, treated hazardous wastes are injected into deep wells that are geologically isolated from the water table. The growing need for remediation services — the cleaning up of crude oil spills and ground contamination, asbestos and lead paint removal, and restoration of strip-mined areas — is allowing small companies with sophisticated technology to enter the field. While much of the work is technologically driven, it also usually involves disposal of materials in a hazardous material landfill.

Sales & Marketing

Major customers are individual businesses and households and entire municipalities. Fees for commercial services depend on collection frequency, container size, waste type, distance to a disposal site, and disposal cost. Residential trash pickup may be on an individual monthly-contract basis, or, more frequently, through a municipal contract that gives the collector exclusive rights to service homes in all or a part of the municipality. Municipal contracts generally last one to five years (sometimes longer); frequently have automatic renewal options; and are often obtained through sealed bidding. Landfill operators charge tipping fees that vary according to waste type and volume.

Human Resources

Waste collection and landfill jobs mainly involve operating trucks and other large pieces of equipment, and wages are accordingly somewhat above the average of all US workers. Recovery and recycling operations use large numbers of workers who are paid low wages, and may therefore have high personnel turnover. The injury rate for the industry is 60 percent higher than for all US workers.

Industry Employment Growth

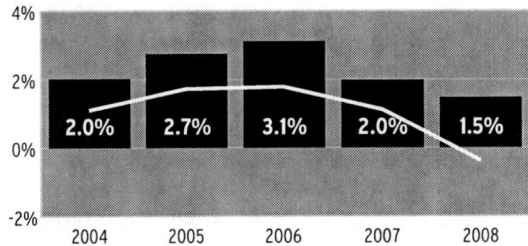

	2004	2005	2006	2007	2008
	2.0%	2.7%	3.1%	2.0%	1.5%

Average Hourly Earnings

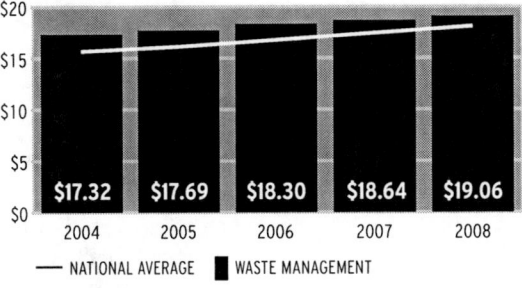

	2004	2005	2006	2007	2008
	$17.32	$17.69	$18.30	$18.64	$19.06

— NATIONAL AVERAGE ■ WASTE MANAGEMENT

SOURCE: BUREAU OF LABOR STATISTICS

Call Preparation Questions

How have company operations been affected by regulatory bans, incentives, or environmental issues?

The waste disposal industry, and landfill operations in particular, are subject to rigorous EPA, state, and local regulations, especially regarding possible groundwater pollution.

How reliant is the company on a top few contracts?

Although waste collectors often have a diversified customer base, some hold contracts with commercial, industrial, or municipal customers that account for a large portion of business.

For what future liabilities is the company preparing or considering?

Although operators estimate the future costs of decommissioning landfills, the time and unclear technical issues that may be involved (especially for hazardous wastes), may subject them to much higher final costs than currently anticipated.

Web Links

Association of State & Territorial Solid Waste Management Officials

Professional organization.
www.astswmo.org

EPA Office of Solid Waste

National statistics on solid waste generated, recycled, landfilled, etc.
www.epa.gov/osw

Municipal Waste Management Association

Political/legislative affiliate of the US Conference of Mayors. Waste management issues.
www.usmayors.org/mwma/main.htm

Recycler's World

Plastic and rubber recycling.
www.recycle.net

Solid Waste Association of North America

Educational and legislative advocacy organization.
www.swana.org

Waste Age

News, links, events.
www.wasteage.com

Glossary of Acronyms

CERCLA — Comprehensive Environmental Response, Compensation and Liability Act
HAP — hazardous air pollutant
HDPE — high-density polyethylene
PET — polyethylene terephthalate
PAYT — pay-as-you-throw
TDF — tire-derived fuel

HOOVER'S TOP COMPANIES

Largest Companies by Sales	($ mil.)
Waste Management, Inc.	13,388.0
Republic Services, Inc.	3,176.2
EnergySolutions, Inc.	1,791.6
Brand Energy, Inc.	1,089.7
Stericycle, Inc.	1,083.7
Waste Connections, Inc.	1,049.6
Clean Harbors, Inc.	1,030.7
Casella Waste Systems, Inc.	579.5
TRC Companies, Inc.	475.1
Shaw Environmental & Infrastructure, Inc.	—

Largest Employers	Employees
Waste Management, Inc.	45,900
Republic Services, Inc.	13,000
Brand Energy, Inc.	12,300
Stericycle, Inc.	6,342
Waste Connections, Inc.	4,978
Clean Harbors, Inc.	4,769
Casella Waste Systems, Inc.	2,800
TRC Companies, Inc.	2,600
Norcal Waste Systems, Inc.	2,100
Rumpke Consolidated Companies, Inc.	2,000

Fastest Growing* by Five-Year Sales Growth	(%)
EnergySolutions, Inc.	67.7
GS CleanTech Corporation	49.6
Brand Energy, Inc.	29.0
WCA Waste Corporation	26.5
American Ecology Corporation	25.3
Stericycle, Inc.	19.0
PDG Environmental, Inc.	18.9
Amanasu Environment Corporation	18.3
OP-TECH Environmental Services, Inc.	16.6
Clean Harbors, Inc.	11.0

Fastest Growing* by Five-Year Employee Growth	(%)
Brand Energy, Inc.	123.8
WCA Waste Corporation	30.5
Stericycle, Inc.	21.8
Ecology and Environment, Inc.	12.6
Clean Harbors, Inc.	10.6
Waste Connections, Inc.	10.1
American Ecology Corporation	5.7
TRC Companies, Inc.	4.0
Perma-Fix Environmental Services, Inc.	1.3
Republic Services, Inc.	0.5

Top Public Companies by Market Value	($ mil.)
Waste Management, Inc.	16,263.0
Republic Services, Inc.	5,753.9
Stericycle, Inc.	4,440.0
Waste Connections, Inc.	2,520.6
EnergySolutions, Inc.	498.9

* These rates are compounded annualized increases and may have resulted from acquisitions or one time gains. If less than 6 years of data are available, growth is for the years available.

SOURCE: HOOVER'S, INC., DATABASE

Water and Sewer Utilities

The US commercial water and sewer industry includes about 5,000 companies with combined annual revenue of $7 billion. Large companies include American Water, Aqua America, and California Water Service. The industry is fairly concentrated: the 50 largest companies account for 65 percent of industry revenue. The commercial industry is small compared to the $55 billion spent annually on water and sewer services by regional and local governments that operate their own systems.

Competitive Landscape

Demand depends on commercial and residential water needs, which are partly related to population growth and partly to the level of economic activity. The profitability of individual companies depends on efficiency of operations, because prices are fixed by public utility commissions (PUCs). Large companies have economies of scale in operations and the ability to raise capital for infrastructure improvements. Small companies can compete successfully through superior engineering or by serving smaller local markets. The industry is capital-intensive: average annual revenue per employee at the large companies is $250,000.

Products, Operations & Technology

Major services are operating water supply systems and operating sewage removal systems. Water services account for 85 percent of industry revenue, sewer services for 15 percent. The operations of small or large water and sewer systems and commercial or municipal utilities are identical. Water and sewer operations are local monopolies, mainly because of the large infrastructure of reservoirs, pipes, and treatment facilities needed. Competition exists only in determining who operates a system. Commercial companies may own a local system, or operate a system on behalf of a local government ("contract operations"), or may own parts of a system, such as water wells or a reservoir.

BUSINESS CHALLENGES

» Required Capital Investments

Deteriorating sewage collection and water distribution pipes and pumps requires large periodic capital investments. Federally mandated water and sewer improvements to fix outdated sewer systems are expensive, with little federal money available. Annual spending to maintain and expand water and sewage systems lags tens of billions what's needed to keep up with population growth and tighter health and pollution standards, according to the EPA, which confirms studies by private groups. About 450,000 of the 1.2 million miles of water and sewer pipes in the US need repair or replacement, and by 2020, about 45 percent of the nation's sewer pipes will. Spending requirements in the commercial end of the industry are smaller but just as urgent. Utilities sometimes defer needed repairs and upgrades because of the short-term impact on profitability.

» Profitability Tied to Unpredictable Water Consumption

The revenue of water utilities depends on the volume of water consumed, which in turn depends on weather conditions. Residential water use increases in hot, dry weather and decreases during cool, rainy periods. During dry periods, municipalities may also restrict water use to conserve depleted supplies; consequently, profitability can vary highly throughout the year.

» Vulnerability to "Condemnation" Proceedings

Most municipalities and other local governments have the legal authority to acquire commercially run utilities against their will ("condemnation") through eminent domain proceedings, compensating the owners. Commercial water and sewer utilities run the risk of being condemned if they're run ineffectively or if the rates they charge are perceived as being too high.

California Water Services, for example, operates the water system of Hawthorne, California, under a 15-year lease.

A water system consists of a water source, a system of storage reservoirs, a water treatment facility, and a pipe distribution system. The water source may be surface (lakes or rivers) or ground water (springs and wells). Washington, DC, for example, uses about 180 million gallons of water per day from the Potomac River. While water from lakes or rivers is sometimes free, companies must often pay wholesale fees for water owned by private owners or local or regional public water authorities. Typical long-term wholesale water prices in California are $500 to $600 per acre foot. Water from wells is often cheaper than surface water.

To ensure that water is available during periods of peak use (which often coincide with periods of low accumulation, like the summer months), utilities may operate various types of reservoirs, including tanks, artificial lakes, and covered ground reservoirs. Water treatment consists of various steps to remove contaminants. A coagulant like alum (aluminum sulfate) may be added to the water to attract and clump suspended particles, which settle to the bottom in sedimentation basins. Water is then filtered through sand and gravel beds, and disinfected with chlorine to kill bacteria and viruses. Fluoride is usually added (as hydrofluorosilicic acid) to help prevent tooth decay, and lime (calcium hydroxide) is added to adjust the water's acidity and prevent corrosion of distribution pipes. Treated water runs through meters before flowing through distribution pipes to final customers. Water is periodically tested for quality at various stages in the system.

A sewer system works much the same as a water system, but in reverse. Wastewater is collected through a system of pipes from residential and industrial customers and rain sewers, and is processed in a treatment plant before being discharged. Primary treatment consists of settling out solids from the waste stream and separating the sludge from the water. In secondary treatment, oxygen is added to encourage the growth of bacteria that consume much of the rest of the waste. The remaining water is then disinfected and discharged into rivers, lakes, or the ocean. Sludge is treated with heat to kill bacteria and may be dried for use as fertilizer or placed in landfills.

The operation of both water and sewer systems is highly automated and requires mainly monitoring. The average local water or sewer utility has fewer than a dozen employees. Maintenance and capital costs are often higher than operating costs, because of the large network of pipes, valves, pumps, reservoirs, and treatment facilities that make up a complete system. Pipe maintenance or replacement is especially expensive, as pipes are usually located under roadways.

Computer systems have become important to some water or sewer systems to monitor flow and quality at many points of the large networks of pipes and valves. Many older systems operate with only rudimentary monitoring.

Sales & Marketing

Customers are businesses, individuals, and municipalities. Typical rates are $30 per month for residential customers, but can be much higher for older systems that must make large investments for repair and upgrading. Large commercial customers pay lower rates than residential customers. Rates are set by state Public Utility Commissions (PUCs). The rate setting mechanism of most PUCs is complicated and slow, sometimes stretching out for years. Consequently, the managers of utilities are constantly involved in rate-setting procedures.

Human Resources

Employees in commercial water and sewer utilities generally have special technical or engineering skills that command above-average earnings, just under $18 an hour. Commercial companies generally have to pay the same wages as their public sector counterparts. The industry injury rate of 5.9 injuries per 100 workers is slightly above the national average of 4.5, as of 2004.

Industry Employment Growth

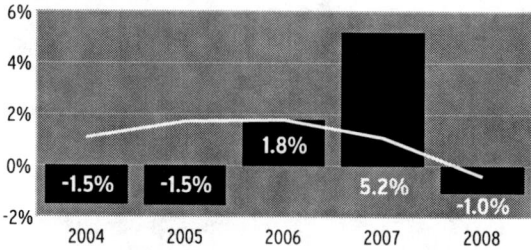

Average Hourly Earnings

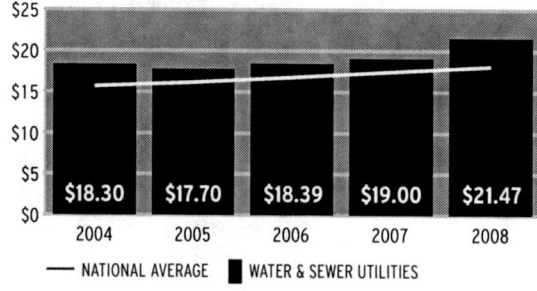

SOURCE: BUREAU OF LABOR STATISTICS

Call Preparation Questions

How does the company plan to fund construction and repair of the US water and sewer infrastructure?

Deteriorating sewage collection and water distribution pipes and pumps requires large periodic capital investments.

If the company has management contracts, how long will they last, and what is the likelihood of renewal?

Municipalities may sell their water and sewer systems to private companies, which are expected to operate them more effectively.

What non-regulated income sources does the company benefit from?

Utilities often engage in non-regulated activities: they may provide laboratory services for smaller operators, or, as owners of large amounts of land, they are often in a position to lease antenna sites to cell phone companies, a growing business in recent years.

Web Links

American Water Works Association

News. Listing and links to water utilities, public and private.

www.awwa.org

National Association of Clean Water Agencies

News and information about clean water issues.

www.nacwa.org

National Rural Water Association

www.nrwa.org

US EPA – Drinking Water Systems

Facts and regulations.

www.epa.gov/ebtpages/watedrinkingwater.html

US EPA – Office of Wastewater Management

Good descriptions of municipal technologies.

www.epa.gov/owm

Water and Wastewater Equipment Manufacturers Association

www.wwema.org

Water Infrastructure Network

Political association in favor of federal funding for infrastructure upgrades.

www.win-water.org

Glossary of Acronyms

CSO — combined sewage overflow
PUC — Public Utility Commission
SRF — state revolving fund
SDWA — Safe Drinking Water Act
WEF — Water Environment Federation

HOOVER'S TOP COMPANIES

Largest Companies by Sales	($ mil.)
American Water Works Company, Inc.	2,336.9
Aqua America, Inc.	627.0
United Water Inc.	163.9
California Water Service Group	410.3
Pennsylvania-American Water Company	442.4
Severn Trent Services	308.1
American States Water Company	301.4
Southwest Water Company	217.4
SJW Corp.	206.6
Gundle/SLT Environmental, Inc.	—

Largest Employers	Employees
American Water Works Company, Inc.	7,000
Severn Trent Services	3,000
United Water Inc.	2,200
Aqua America, Inc.	1,638
Veolia Water North America Operating Services	1,600
Southwest Water Company	1,600
Pennsylvania-American Water Company	1,000
Gundle/SLT Environmental, Inc.	928
Utilities, Inc.	530
SJW Corp.	364

Fastest Growing* by Five-Year Sales Growth	(%)
ThermoEnergy Corporation	41.4
Global Water Resources, Inc.	41.4
Aqua America, Inc.	11.3
Southwest Water Company	10.7
The York Water Company	9.4
Artesian Resources Corporation	8.7
Pure Cycle Corporation	8.4
California Water Service Group	8.2
American States Water Company	7.6
SJW Corp.	7.2

Fastest Growing* by Five-Year Employee Growth	(%)
Southwest Water Company	10.1
The York Water Company	9.3
Middlesex Water Company	8.0
Aqua America, Inc.	5.4
American Water Works Company, Inc.	5.2
SJW Corp.	3.9
Artesian Resources Corporation	0.9

Top Public Companies by Market Value	($ mil.)
Aqua America, Inc.	2,787.3
California Water Service Group	962.2
American States Water Company	649.3
SJW Corp.	636.6
Southwest Water Company	303.8

* These rates are compounded annualized increases and may have resulted from acquisitions or one time gains. If less than 6 years of data are available, growth is for the years available.

SOURCE: HOOVER'S, INC., DATABASE

Weight Reduction Services

THIS INDUSTRY INCLUDES:

SIC CODES

7299   Miscellaneous
      Personal Services

NAICS CODES

812191   Diet and Weight
        Reducing Centers

The US weight reduction services industry includes about 1,300 companies with combined annual revenue of almost $2 billion. Major companies include Weight Watchers, Nestlé, Jenny Craig, NutriSystem, and the online-only eDiets. The industry is highly concentrated: the 50 largest companies account for 80 percent of industry revenue and the four largest, for 60 percent. A typical company is small, with one location, fewer than 10 employees, and annual revenue less than $500,000.

The industry doesn't include companies that provide primarily medical or surgical weight reduction, or that operate physical fitness facilities, health resorts, or spas.

Competitive Landscape

Consumers' excess weight, personal income, and leisure time drive demand. The profitability of individual companies depends on effective marketing, customer acquisition and retention, and efficient operations. Large companies have advantages of scale in marketing, infrastructure, and partnerships. Small companies can compete effectively by offering individualized services or upscale facilities. The industry is labor-intensive: average annual revenue per worker is under $50,000.

Products, Operations & Technology

Major product lines are program fees, food supplements, and other merchandise sales related to diet and weight reduction. Fees account for almost 60 percent of industry revenue, and food and other merchandise sales for about 40 percent. Products include DVDs, CDs, food scales, journals and other record-keeping materials, cookbooks, and motivational and self-help guides. Specialty products include exercise accessories, magazines, and packaged food, often available for home delivery. Weight Watchers' branded magazine had about 7 million US read-

BUSINESS CHALLENGES

» Competition from Other Weight Loss Methods

Weight loss services compete with a variety of weight loss methods, programs, and products, with price a differentiating factor for many consumers. During difficult economic times, consumers may be less willing to commit to the monthly fees and cost of meals that many programs require. Competing approaches include do-it-yourself (DIY) diet and exercise, celebrity and mass media diets, diet foods, meal replacement drinks and bars, appetite suppressants and diet pills, medically supervised programs, and surgery. Competitors also include fitness centers, low-cost or free services from nonprofit groups and government agencies, and free online diet information.

» Maintaining Credibility

Weight reduction services firms struggle to maintain credibility with the public and enrolled customers. Despite an industry history of deceptive advertising and practices, coupled with government oversight, companies continue to promote atypical success stories to attract new clients. High customer dropout rates indicate that many customers don't meet their goals, raising the issue of effectiveness. Industry credibility is also affected by unsubstantiated claims and aggressive marketing by competing weight loss products, such as diet pills, health supplements, and exercise devices.

» Market Domination by Large Companies

Although most weight reduction services firms are small, the top four companies hold about 60 percent of industry revenue and the top 50 hold about 80 percent, presenting stiff competition and risk for smaller and new companies. Weight Watchers has established a strong market presence with over 4,400 North American locations. Many of the largest companies have grown through acquisitions, and some from being acquired by corporate giants outside the industry, which contributes to industry concentration.

ers per copy in a recent year, according to MediaMark.

Industry operations consist of providing customers with diet and weight management plans, advice, and monitoring. Companies provide a meeting place, meeting leader, and administrative staff. Staff evaluate a customer's weight against age and height guidelines and develop an individualized diet plan. Staff weigh and record the customer's progress relative to individual goals, usually at weekly meetings. Typical meetings include personal weigh-in, a lecture by the meeting leader, and group discussion and sharing of diet and exercise hints, weight-loss problems, and possible solutions. Many companies emphasize in-person participation and group support, which they say help customers' success, and offer online tools to supplement handouts. Some companies offer full online programs as an alternative to in-person events, but other firms operate solely via websites.

The industry is subject to seasonal demand, which peaks during the post-holiday "winter diet season" in January and lasts through the "spring diet season," as consumers prepare for summertime. Most industry companies are small: about 95 percent are single-unit operations and only about 15 firms have 10 or more facilities. Industry metrics include customer acquisition cost, fees and product sales per customer, and customer renewal rates. For online services, additional metrics include click-through and conversion-to-customer rates. NutriSystem reported that average acquisition costs for new meal program customers varied from $147 to $156 per person over a recent three-year period.

Industry companies either fund nutritional studies and develop proprietary diet programs based on the results, license programs from other organizations, or function as a franchisee. Weight reduction services companies often sell private-label or co-branded products. For interaction with customers, companies hire employees who are highly personable, motivational, and sensitive to weight issues. Sales skills are important for staff who work on commission to recruit and enroll new members and sell products.

The industry uses websites for marketing, sales, and online operations. Websites provide program details, self-management tools, recipes, support groups, articles, products for sale, and payment capability. Opt-in e-mail newsletters help companies stay in touch with customers. By moving more marketing and program functions to the Internet, companies reach larger numbers of consumers, service more customers, and reduce cost-per-customer for acquisition and retention. The largest companies have extensive consumer databases that are a considerable asset and marketing advantage. Large companies use advanced data modeling software with consumer and operational data to help determine the content and timing of sales promotions. Most firms use third-party technology providers.

Sales & Marketing

Typical customers are women (about 75 to 80 percent), although more men are using weight reduction services in recent years. Major industry sales channels are websites and internal and external salespeople. Websites often have different sections tailored to men, women, or specific ethnic groups. Internal salespeople register and renew memberships or subscriptions. External salespeople call on companies and organizations to establish diet groups at those facilities.

Major types of marketing include direct mail and ads in magazines and newspapers and on TV and websites. Large companies with significant customer databases use mass marketing; smaller companies often use local coupon promotions. Companies prize referrals and often offer product or service incentives for a customer who makes a successful referral. Sales promotions are common and typically offer free registration or discounted membership for a specific number of weeks or months.

The largest companies have numerous licensing agreements in which they or their business partners license one another's brand. Licensing partners include restaurants, food manufacturers and distributors, and diet- or exercise-related consumer products and programs.

The industry's Internet sales have grown as a direct result of increased web marketing. The Internet is a relatively low-cost way to collect fees and sell products. Because Web-based registration and program participation are mainly self-directed, online membership follows a subscription model, rather than the service model of in-person meetings. Easy-to-use and effective websites have become significant contributors to a company's brand. Firms also sell advertising space on their websites.

Typical prices for participation in a weight reduction service range from $20 to $60 monthly, with the base price of online-only programs usually costing less than an in-person or combination service. Some firms charge a single inclusive program fee, while others price options a la carte. An initial enrollment fee typically equals about one month's service fee. Special promotions waive the enrollment fee or offer a reduced per-month fee. Specials generally require the customer to prepay or preauthorize credit card or bank deductions for multiple months. Prices of prepackaged, delivered meals start at about $80 to $100 weekly.

Human Resources

Companies provide in-house and on-the-job training for employees who interact with customers, such as meeting leaders, weight-and-measurement takers, and counselors. Meeting-related employees typically work part-time and are former clients who have succeeded on the company's weight loss program, maintain their goal weight, and inspire clients. Many meeting personnel earn commission for enrollments and product sales, as do many employees who interact with consumers online and by phone. Online and phone counselors generally work full-time and may have backgrounds in nutrition, psychology, or other health-related fields. Industry wages are higher than the national average and injury rates are negligible.

Call Preparation Questions

What types of weight loss methods does the company see as its biggest competitors?

Weight loss services compete with a variety of weight loss methods, programs, and products, with price a differentiating factor for many consumers.

What challenges does the company face maintaining credibility with customers?

Weight reduction services firms struggle to maintain credibility with the public and enrolled customers.

How dependent is the company on third-party firms, either as providers or sales channels?

Although most weight reduction services firms are small, the top four companies hold about 60 percent of industry revenue and the top 50 hold about 80 percent, presenting stiff competition and risk for smaller and new companies.

How is the company focusing on men as a potential growth opportunity?

Although the industry's major customer segment is adult women, focusing on men increases their participation.

How important is the aging population to the company's plans?

As the large baby boomer generation retires and the national population ages, older consumers provide a growth opportunity for weight reduction companies.

Web Links

Centers for Disease Control and Prevention

Overweight and obesity information, trends, FAQs.
www.cdc.gov/nccdphp/dnpa/obesity

eDiets

Diet plans, weight loss programs, meal delivery.
www.ediets.com

Shape Up America!

Obesity facts; prevention and weight management information.
www.shapeup.org

The Calorie Control Council

Calorie information, sponsored by low-calorie food industry.
www.caloriecontrol.org

Glossary of Acronyms

BMI — body mass index
CDC — Centers for Disease Control and Prevention

HOOVER'S TOP COMPANIES

Largest Companies by Sales	($ mil.)
Weight Watchers International, Inc.	1,535.8
NutriSystem, Inc.	687.7
eDiets.com, Inc.	29.7
Dr. Tattoff, Inc.	0.7
Jenny Craig, Inc.	—

Largest Employers	Employees
Weight Watchers International, Inc.	49,000
Jenny Craig, Inc.	3,000
NutriSystem, Inc.	602
eDiets.com, Inc.	108
Dr. Tattoff, Inc.	14

Fastest Growing* by Five-Year Sales Growth	(%)
NutriSystem, Inc.	98.0
Weight Watchers International, Inc.	10.2
eDiets.com, Inc.	0.1

Fastest Growing* by Five-Year Employee Growth	(%)
Weight Watchers International, Inc.	3.2
NutriSystem, Inc.	1.1

Top Public Companies by Market Value	($ mil.)
Weight Watchers International, Inc.	2,239.2
NutriSystem, Inc.	449.2
eDiets.com, Inc.	147.4

* These rates are compounded annualized increases and may have resulted from acquisitions or one time gains. If less than 6 years of data are available, growth is for the years available.

SOURCE: HOOVER'S, INC., DATABASE

Wholesale Sector

THIS INDUSTRY INCLUDES:

SIC CODES
50   Wholesale Trade –
     Durable Goods
51   Wholesale Trade –
     Nondurable Goods

NAICS CODES
42   Wholesale Trade

The wholesale distribution industry in the US includes about 300,000 companies with combined annual sales of $4.8 trillion. Large distributors include SYSCO (foods); McKesson (drugs); and Avnet (electronics). Only about 3,000 companies have annual revenue over $100 million, but these large companies account for 70 percent of industry revenue. A typical midsized distributor has 30 employees and annual sales of $15 million.

Distributors specialize by product. Within product segments, concentration is often moderately high. In many segments, the 50 largest distributors hold between 40 and 60 percent of the market.

Competitive Landscape

For most distributors, demand is closely linked to local economic activity. The profitability of individual companies depends on efficient inventory management and order fulfillment operations. Large companies can supply customers with a wider range of goods and in more markets, but smaller distributors can compete successfully by carrying specialty products or providing add-on services. The industry is highly automated: average annual revenue per worker is over $1 million for large distributors, about $500,000 for smaller ones.

Computer and communications technology have had a major effect on the industry by improving the efficiency of warehouse and distribution operations. Because of automation, industry labor productivity improved more than 40 percent in the past 10 years.

Supply chain efficiencies allow some manufacturers and retailers to bypass independent distributors. Manufacturers account for 32 percent of wholesale trade in the US, up from 22 percent 10 years ago. And large retailers like Wal-Mart operate their own distribution systems, taking products directly from producers.

BUSINESS CHALLENGES

» Inventory Carrying Costs Are Sensitive to Interest Rates

Because many distributors finance their inventories, they're sensitive to interest rates. On average, distributors hold inventory equal to 45 days sales, but machinery distributors may hold 90 days. Grocery and petroleum product distributors hold the lowest inventories, 20 days and 10 days sales, respectively. Because industry profit margins are low, financing costs have a large impact on profits. Inventory financing is often tied to the prime lending rate.

» Large Retailers By-Pass Distributors

Big retailers like Wal-Mart, Home Depot, and Costco buy much of their merchandise directly from manufacturers, bypassing distributors. Because they buy in large quantity and operate their own warehouse systems, these retailers don't need distributors. Superstores and warehouse clubs now account for 50 percent of sales of general merchandise stores, up from just 25 percent 10 years ago.

» Distribution Costs Sensitive to Energy Prices

Distributors that operate delivery fleets are sensitive to energy costs. Most vulnerable are distributors that make multiple deliveries per day to many customers, such as supermarkets or car repair shops. Energy costs can be 1 percent of revenue, a significant cost when industry profit margins are often less than 5 percent.

Products, Operations & Technology

The major segments of the wholesale sector are wholesale merchants of durable goods (42 percent of revenues); wholesale merchants of nondurable goods (46 percent); and business to business electronic markets, agents, and brokers (12 percent). The largest durable goods segments are professional and commercial equipment, motor vehicles and parts, machinery, and electrical goods. The largest nondurable goods segments are groceries, petroleum products, and drugs. Electronic market agents and brokers arrange sales for a commission and generally don't handle or take possession of goods.

Operations typically consist of merchandising decisions, purchasing from manufacturers and other suppliers, warehouse inventory management, product transportation and distribution, and providing various types of customer services. Operations vary widely according to the type of product. For example, food distributors not only deliver products to individual customer stores, but also arrange them on store shelves; steel distributors often have fabrication operations to make semifinished goods for their customers; some auto parts distributors also operate retail stores.

Deciding what merchandise to carry determines the types of customers a distributor can sell to. Many distributors carry a broad range of goods to satisfy all of their customers' needs. A distributor of fasteners may stock some 100,000 items (stockkeeping units, or SKUs) bought from 1,000 manufacturers. Customers often ask distributors to carry new products. Trade shows are a major source of new products.

Distributors may have contractual arrangements with manufacturers or may order products as needed. Large distributors frequently have annual supply contracts with manufacturers, under which they commit to taking a certain volume of product in exchange for a discounted price. In some segments — especially those with a few large manufacturers, such as beer — distributors may hold exclusive sales territories as long as they meet volume requirements. Distributors may also have "authorized distributor" agreements with manufacturers, which typically require that they maintain a certain level of service to customers. Some distributors receive some or all of their product as imports, and may have exclusive distribution rights.

Big distributors may operate a network of warehouses, but the majority operate a single warehouse. For many products, warehouse operations consist of receiving products at a loading dock, storing them on shelving systems, and assembling loads to be delivered to customers. Warehouses may cover hundreds of thousands of square feet. Managing inventory is a major activity. Incoming product is typically moved on pallets by forklift trucks.

The complexity of warehouse and order fulfillment operations depends greatly on the type of product. In general, the smaller and more numerous the product, the more complicated the operations. Distributors of farming machin-

ery, for example, can park an inventory of tractors in a lot, see each item from the office window, and drive one off on a trailer when an order comes in. Distributors of electrical supplies, on the other hand, may stock tens of thousands of different items, of which a customer may need only a dozen; quickly finding those items requires a sophisticated location and retrieval system.

Another general rule about warehouse operations is that the faster the inventory must move, the fewer the items that can be stocked. Distributors of fresh foods, for example, typically specialize in just a limited line of goods, whereas distributors of canned or frozen foods carry a wider selection.

Distributors may own or lease a fleet of delivery trucks. In many cases, special trucks are required — such as for gas, beverages, or refrigerated foods. Some distributors contract with transportation companies to deliver their products. The operation and maintenance of a delivery fleet can be costly. Depending on the product, distributors may make deliveries to customers several times per day. Fuel costs are a major concern. Many distributors have a sales territory that extends several hundred miles from their warehouse.

The additional services that distributors most often provide are spare parts, repairs, maintenance, and training. Some distributors provide logistics to customers, including inventory management and just-in-time delivery. In many cases, customers rely heavily on distributors to advise them on how to use existing products and information about new products.

Most distributors operate transaction-oriented systems that maintain an inventory database as goods are received from suppliers and dispatched to customers. Small distributors may maintain an inventory database on a standalone PC and update it overnight using receiving and shipping data. Large distributors have fully automated supply chain systems tying together suppliers, shippers, warehouse management systems (WMS), and customers. The goals of both types of systems are to minimize inventory of slow-moving items, increase inventory turns, reduce warehouse staff, and reduce inventory shrinkage.

A WMS tracks the physical location of inventory throughout the warehouse, typically by scanning bar codes on the merchandise. These systems may include automated materials handling systems used to convey the inventory and place it automatically in bins for later retrieval. The WMS also tracks inventory by age and, for certain perishables, by environmental conditions. WMS systems schedule dock personnel for loading and unloading according to anticipated traffic volumes. For distributors operating multiple warehouses, inventory systems are linked, allowing materials to be shipped between warehouses as demand requires.

Radio frequency identification (RFID) devices are coming into widespread use, replacing the bar codes on merchandise and pallets. Wal-Mart, Home Depot, the Department of Defense, the FDA, and others have implemented programs requiring RFIDs. These devices allow tracking of the location and movement of merchandise automatically. As the prices for these devices drop, and more vendors have experience with them, they'll eventually become the dominant method of merchandise tagging.

Some distributors have online interfaces with customers and suppliers. Customers may be able to place orders online, receive confirmations and shipping information, and track shipments. As orders are received and fulfilled, distributor systems automatically generate orders to suppliers to replenish inventory. Financial systems capture order information and automatically generate accounts receivable and payable entries. The customer systems include online catalogs, product configurators, order entry, and order tracking, all of which are available 24/7. Systems also allow customers to schedule delivery and access help desks to get support for orders.

Distributors that operate their own delivery fleets have logistics applications that optimize loading and delivery routes. Many distributors have GPS in their vehicles that allow them to track the vehicles and reroute them as required.

Sales & Marketing

Distributors sell to retailers, other distributors, and industrial and commercial customers. About 35 percent of industry sales go to retailers, 30 percent to other distributors, 10 percent to industrial customers, and 10 percent to commercial businesses, but the distribution of customers varies widely depending on the type of product. For example, 75 percent of computer sales go to retailers.

Depending on the product, sales are often handled through an internal sales force. Trade shows are an important source of new customers. Many distributors advertise in trade publications and Yellow Pages, and use direct mail. In some industry segments, distributors are directly involved in retail advertising or promotional programs, and may coordinate advertising with manufacturers.

Because of improving distribution methods, many distributors face competition both from manufacturers that operate their own distribution systems and from large retailers that buy directly from manufacturers. The Internet has made buying from distant distributors easier.

Prices are usually based on the manufacturer's price. Price markups tend to be relatively modest because of competition from other distributors.

Human Resources

About 25 percent of distributor jobs involve selling, while most of the rest are clerical, customer service, or involve warehouse operations. Because of the special knowledge that many workers must have about company products, wages are about 15 percent higher than the average wage for all US workers. Overall, the industry injury rate is about equal to the US average rate, although there are more lifting and transportation injuries. Injuries in warehouse operations often are serious.

Industry Employment Growth

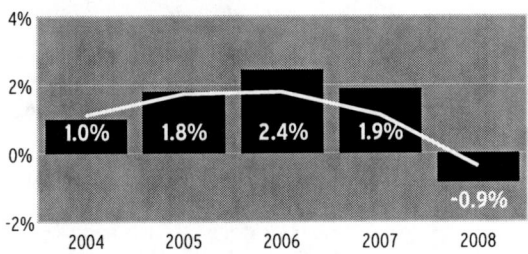

Average Hourly Earnings

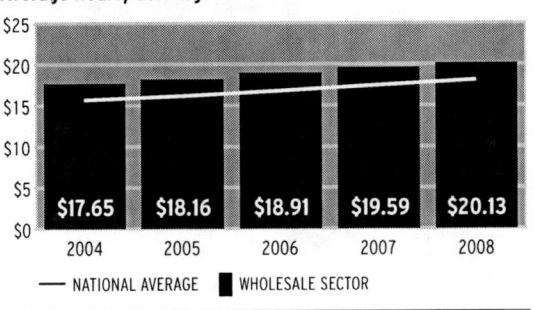

SOURCE: BUREAU OF LABOR STATISTICS

Call Preparation Questions

How do changes in interest rates affect the company's profits?

Because many distributors finance their inventories, they're sensitive to interest rates.

How much business has the company lost due to retailers buying directly from manufacturers?

Big retailers like Wal-Mart, Home Depot, and Costco buy much of their merchandise directly from manufacturers, bypassing distributors.

How do volatile energy prices affect the company?

Distributors that operate delivery fleets are sensitive to energy costs.

What opportunities does the company see in using the Internet to reach new markets?

Because they already stock a large inventory of products, distributors are in a strong position to sell products beyond their traditional market.

What additional services is the company providing customers?

Distributors can provide inventory management, just-in-time delivery, and order fulfillment services to customers.

Web Links

American Supply Association

Plumbing, heating, cooling, and piping distributor news.
www.asa.net

Association of Steel Distributors

Steel distributor news.
www.steeldistributors.org

Health Industry Distributors Association

Medical devices and supplies distributor news.
www.hida.org/am/template.cfm?section=home

Modern Distribution Management

Articles and industry news.
www.mdm.com

National Association of Chemical Distributors

Chemical distributor news.
www.nacd.com

National Association of Wholesaler-Distributors

Industry news, analysis, and policy positions.
www.naw.org

National Electronic Distributors Association

Electronics distributor news.
www.nedassoc.org

National Lumber and Building Material Dealers Association

Building material distributor news.
www.dealer.org

Office Products Wholesalers Association

Office products distributor news.
www.opwa.org

Petroleum Marketers Association of America

Petroleum marketing and distribution news.
www.pmaa.org

Glossary of Acronyms

GPS — global positioning system
NAW — National Association of Wholesaler-Distributors
RFID — radio frequency identification
SKU — stock-keeping unit
WMS — warehouse management system

HOOVER'S TOP COMPANIES

Largest Companies by Sales	($ mil.)
McKesson Corporation	101,703.0
Cardinal Health, Inc.	91,091.4
AmerisourceBergen Corporation	70,189.7
Medco Health Solutions, Inc.	51,258.0
SYSCO Corporation	37,522.1
Express Scripts, Inc.	21,978.0
U.S. Foodservice, Inc.	20,200.0
World Fuel Services Corporation	18,509.4
Avnet, Inc.	17,952.7
Arrow Electronics, Inc.	16,761.0

Largest Employers	Employees
SYSCO Corporation	50,000
Cardinal Health, Inc.	43,500
McKesson Corporation	32,900
U.S. Foodservice, Inc.	27,160
Universal Corporation	25,000
Medco Health Solutions, Inc.	20,800
General Parts, Inc.	18,000
Omnicare, Inc.	17,800
Pro-Build Holdings Inc.	17,000
Keystone Foods LLC	13,000

Fastest Growing* by Five-Year Sales Growth	(%)
Titan Global Holdings, Inc.	110.2
Sport Supply Group, Inc.	64.1
Oxbow Corporation	61.7
Mansfield Oil Company	55.8
Delek US Holdings, Inc.	52.3
Allion Healthcare, Inc.	51.6
Source Interlink Companies, Inc.	50.6
Schnitzer Steel Industries, Inc.	48.9
World Fuel Services Corporation	47.4
Catalyst Health Solutions, Inc.	45.9

Fastest Growing* by Five-Year Employee Growth	(%)
The Grocers Supply Co., Inc.	111.0
InfoSonics Corporation	85.7
Decorize, Inc.	61.7
Brightstar Corp.	55.8
McJunkin Red Man Holding Corporation	55.8
Source Interlink Companies, Inc.	45.6
Catalyst Health Solutions, Inc.	40.5
LKQ Corporation	38.3
China Huaren Organic Products, Inc.	38.0
Empire Resources, Inc.	30.7

Top Public Companies by Market Value	($ mil.)
Medco Health Solutions, Inc.	20,857.8
Cardinal Health, Inc.	18,419.2
SYSCO Corporation	16,966.8
McKesson Corporation	14,506.5
Express Scripts, Inc.	13,615.7

* These rates are compounded annualized increases and may have resulted from acquisitions or one time gains. If less than 6 years of data are available, growth is for the years available.

SOURCE: HOOVER'S, INC., DATABASE

Wineries

The US wineries industry includes about 1,000 companies with combined annual revenue of $8 billion. Large companies include E&J Gallo, Constellation Brands, and The Wine Group. Almost half of wineries are small, with fewer than five employees. The industry is highly concentrated: the 50 largest companies hold more than 80 percent of the market. The large wine companies typically own several wineries and may also be major importers.

Competitive Landscape

Demand for wine is driven by the restaurant and hotel industries, the level of business entertainment spending, and consumer income. A winery's profitability depends on production volume and sales price, both of which can vary from year to year. Large companies have stronger distribution channels. There are large economies of scale in production. Small wineries can compete with big-volume producers by making higher-quality wines that sell at a premium price.

Products, Operations & Technology

Wineries manufacture wine and brandies through fermentation of grapes and other fruit. Grapevines are tended in spring and summer and grapes harvested in early fall. After being crushed, the grapes (skins, pulp and liquid, called the "must") are fermented in large vats for several weeks. Fermentation is caused by the yeast Saccharomyces, found naturally on grape skins, that transforms the sugar of the grape into alcohol. After fermentation, the wine is pressed out and aged in metal vats for several months before being filtered and bottled. Some companies blend several different wines before bottling and may buy blending wine from other producers. Higher-quality wine is aged in oak casks for up to two years before bottling. White wines are produced by removing the grape skins at the crushing stage. Wine may be stored and shipped in tanks, barrels, and bottle case

BUSINESS CHALLENGES

» Competition from Imports
Imported wines, mainly from France, Italy, and Australia, hold about a third of the US market. The higher-end market segments are most affected by imports. Chronic oversupply of wine in France and Italy, due to government policies, has depressed US prices. In the past 10 years, US wholesale wine prices increased just 14 percent.

» Dependence on Consumer Spending
A high correlation exists between levels of consumer income and the amount spent on wine. The volume of wine produced in the US dropped almost 20 percent during the last recession, and imports were flat.

» Vulnerability to Growing Conditions
Grapes are susceptible to adverse weather, such as frost and drought, and to harmful pests and plant disease. Growing conditions affect the quality and quantity of a grape harvest and the cost and profitability of the resultant wine. When a vineyard needs to be replanted, for example, it can take three to five years for new vines to produce useful grapes.

lots. Annual production for small wineries is under 50,000 12-bottle cases per year. A large winery may produce more than 500,000 cases.

The type of grape determines the taste of the wine, as do soil and weather conditions during the year. Many wineries grow their own grapes, but some (especially the large ones) also buy grapes from contract growers. A large winery could own more than 8,000 acres of land. High-volume wineries may buy most of their grape supply from independent growers. In 2003, Robert Mondavi bought 90 percent of its grape needs from 200 contract growers.

Contracts with growers may extend over several years, or may be for a one-year ("spot market") period. The cost of grapes can fluctuate substantially from year to year, depending on quality and yield. Many contracts for future purchase of grapes or bulk wine stipulate that market conditions will determine price, but other contracts have minimum price requirements.

Despite having contracts, wineries don't know the final costs until after harvest, because of contract variables such as grape quality, vineyard yield, and market conditions. The average cost for California wine grapes in 2003 was $520 per ton.

Red and white wines each comprise about 40 percent of the US market, blush wines about 20 percent. Leading varietals (wines named after the grape they are made from) are Chardonnay, Pinot Noir, Merlot, White Zinfandel, Cabernet Sauvignon, Pinot Grigio, Syrah, and Sauvignon Blanc.

Sales & Marketing

The market for wine is defined by price categories. The three general categories are premium table wines (more than $3 a bottle); super-value and "jug" wines (under $3); and a variety of wine products, including flavored, sparkling, and fortified wines, and wine coolers.

Within the premium wine category, the four sub-categories are Luxury (over $25); ultra-premium ($14 to $25); super-premium ($7 to $14); and popular-premium ($3 to $7).

Wineries sell to about 1,000 independent distributors, who in turn sell to retailers such as restaurants, hotels, clubs, supermarkets, and liquor stores. In most states, all wine sales must pass through licensed distributors. A large winery may sell to more than 100 distributors. International sales typically go through brokers. A large winery may have hundreds of sales representatives who maintain relationships with distributors and large end-use buyers such as hotel and supermarket chains.

Large wineries may sell as much as 65 percent of revenue through their top 15 distributors, with as much as one-third of revenue coming from the top distributor. A small winery may sell to just a handful or one distributor. Distributors usually sell wine from competitors and may also handle beer and liquor.

Wine companies develop brand recognition via advertising and promotion. Small wineries depend heavily on their distributors for promotional support. Label design plays an important role in appealing to various segments of wine consumers: winery owners often spend relatively large amounts of money developing logos and labels. Consumer advertising, mainly in magazines, is an ongoing expense for large companies and increases in times of lower consumer demand or market oversupply. In those situations, the cost of sales incentives often increases. Smaller wineries that make premium wines promote themselves through trade shows, local tastings and competitions, wine magazines, and wine experts.

Wine competes with other alcoholic and non-alcoholic beverages for retailer shelf space, restaurant presence, and distributor attention and promotions.

Human Resources

Employees range from the highly paid and sought-after "winemaker" experts who plan and oversee the vineyards and winemaking, to relatively unskilled field labor. Field labor may include union and contract workers. Wineries typically have full-time production employees, plus part-time and seasonal field workers. Many smaller wineries are family-owned and operated.

Average wages for winery production workers are slightly above the US average. Fringe benefits comprise a little more than 25 percent of payroll costs. The industry injury rate is 70 percent higher than the average US rate.

Call Preparation Questions

How much competition do the company's wines get from imports?

Imported wines, mainly from France, Italy, and Australia, hold about a third of the US market.

How much are the company's prices affected during an economic slowdown?

A high correlation exists between levels of consumer income and the amount spent on wine.

How much have growing conditions affected the company's wine quality in recent years?

Grapes are susceptible to adverse weather, such as frost and drought, and to harmful pests and plant disease.

What benefits or challenges does the company see in exporting products?

Industry associations and individual wineries show commitment to expanding exports through advertising and promotion abroad.

What new packaging options is the company considering?

New types of packaging, such as small bottles, cartons, and six-packs may help wineries expand the accessibility of their products.

Web Links

Alcohol and Tobacco Tax and Trade Bureau

Monthly production and inventory levels, but several years old. Excise tax rates.
www.ttb.treas.gov

Free The Grapes

Winery and Retailer Advocacy Group.
www.freethegrapes.org

Specialty Wine Retailers Association

Wine retailers who support direct shipping, open trade.
www.specialtywineretailers.org

The Wine Guide

List of wineries by state.
www.travelenvoy.com/wine/USA.htm

Vineyard & Winery Management

Industry magazine, directories, trade events and competitions.
www.vwm-online.com

Wine & Spirits Wholesalers of America

Lobbying organization.
www.wswa.org

Wine Business

News and information for wine industry professionals.
www.winebusiness.com

Wine Institute

California statewide industry association.
www.wineinstitute.org

Wine Market Council

Consumer statistics. Excellent industry links.
www.winemarketcouncil.com

Wine Spectator

News and features that appeal to wine consumers.
www.winespectator.com

WineAmerica, The National Association of American Wineries

Good discussion of direct shipment legislation and policy.
wineamerica.org

Glossary of Acronyms

DPI — disposable personal income
TTB — The Federal Alcohol and Tobacco Tax and Trade Bureau

HOOVER'S TOP COMPANIES

Largest Companies by Sales	($ mil.)
Constellation Brands, Inc.	3,773.0
E. & J. Gallo Winery	3,150.0

Largest Employers	Employees
Constellation Brands, Inc.	8,200
E. & J. Gallo Winery	5,000
Kendall-Jackson Wine Estates, Ltd.	1,200
Trinchero Family Estates	520
F. Korbel & Bros. Inc.	500
Winebow, Inc.	299
The Terlato Wine Group	291
Banfi Vintners	145
Willamette Valley Vineyards, Inc.	102
Scheid Vineyards Inc.	100

Top Public Companies by Market Value	($ mil.)
Constellation Brands, Inc.	3,693.6
Willamette Valley Vineyards, Inc.	31.2

SOURCE: HOOVER'S, INC., DATABASE

Wired Telecommunications Carriers

THIS INDUSTRY INCLUDES:

SIC CODES
7372   Prepackaged
        Software

NAICS CODES
51711   Wired
        Telecommunications
        Carriers

In the US, about 5,000 companies provide wired telecommunication services, with total annual revenue over $200 billion. Large companies include AT&T, Verizon Communications, and Qwest Communications. The industry is highly concentrated: the 50 largest companies hold 90 percent of the market.

The industry includes local service carriers (annual revenues about $130 billion); long distance carriers (about $70 billion); pay phone operators; pre-paid card providers; and telecom resellers.

Competitive Landscape

Demand is driven by new services and growth in business activity. The profitability of individual companies depends on efficient operations and effective marketing. Large companies have economies of scale in providing a highly automated service to large numbers of customers, and the financial resources required to build and maintain a large network. Smaller companies can compete effectively in small markets or by providing specialty services. Because of the large degree of automation, average revenue per employee is about $200,000.

Products, Operations & Technology

Major services are local calling, network access services, long-distance calling, calling features such as caller ID and voice mail, and broadband services. Local calling accounts for about 40 percent of industry revenue, network access 25 percent, long distance 20 percent, calling features and Internet connectivity less than 10 percent each. Other services include data transmission, private networks, installation, and equipment sales. Network access charges are levied against other carriers, mainly long-distance and wireless service providers, that need access to local wired phone systems.

Telephone systems consist of wires, connections, and switches. From a demarc (demarca-

BUSINESS CHALLENGES

» Stagnant Revenue from Basic Phone Service

The US volume of wireline phone calls has steadily decreased as cell phones are used instead. Wired phone volume peaked in 2000, but declined 30 percent over the next five years. Despite regular price increases, the average monthly bill for basic phone service continues to decline.

» Dependence on Regulators

Because they're essential utilities, wireline phone companies are regulated at the state and federal levels. Price schedules must be approved by state regulatory commissions. The FCC and federal legislation affect new services such as video and broadband.

» Large Required Capital Investments

Because of technological changes, wireline phone companies must make large investments in new equipment. In addition to routine spending to upgrade infrastructure like poles and conduits, companies must invest in equipment that supports the new Internet protocol way of sending calls. Many companies also invest in fiber optic technology to deliver broadband to homes and businesses.

tion) box located at a customer's address, wires are strung on poles or underground to a local facility called a central office. Here, the wires are connected to a main distribution frame (MDF) that in turn is connected to a class 5 switch, basically a large computer. The entire collection of equipment and wires leading up to a central office is called the outside plant.

Local central offices are connected with each other in what is called the public switched telephone network (PSTN). Companies may own and operate different pieces of this network, either local connections or regional and national "backbone" systems. The common technical language that allows all switches in the network to communicate with each other is called signaling system 7 (SS7). Companies use customized operational and business support systems (B/OSS) to manage their parts of the network and to supply services.

To provide data and Internet services, phone companies may use existing wires or may string special cables such as fiber optic cable to a customer's location. Connections among central offices and between cities are usually sent over fiber optic cable.

Most companies are replacing older equipment that dedicated an entire path for a single phone call with equipment that allows many digital signals to use a path at the same time, through a method called Internet protocol (IP).

Sales & Marketing

Typical customers for wired telecom services are residences, businesses, and other phone service providers. Residential users produce more revenue than business.

Most phone company advertising features packages of service, basic phone service bundled with TV, video and high-speed Internet access. Direct mail, TV, and print advertising are used heavily.

Typical prices for a single phone line are $20 to $30 per month; Internet access charges may be an additional $30. Packages that combine phone service, Internet access, and TV and video services can cost less than $100 per month.

Human Resources

Most industry jobs are related to either computer operations or involve technical field work, and are accordingly well-paid, almost 50 percent above the average for all US workers. Because most jobs are office jobs, the overall injury rate is well below the US average, although the rate of falls (field workers) is higher than average.

Industry Employment Growth

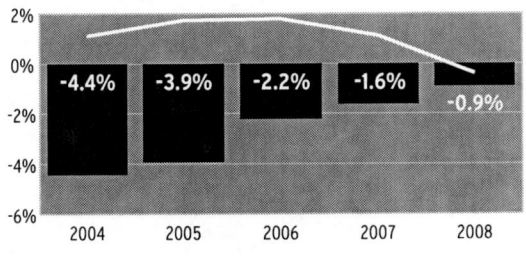

Average Hourly Earnings

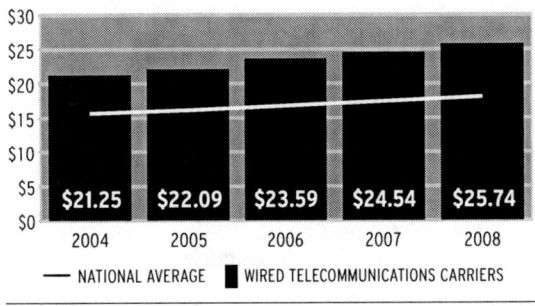

SOURCE: BUREAU OF LABOR STATISTICS

Call Preparation Questions

How will the company offset declines in basic wireline phone use?

The US volume of wireline phone calls has steadily decreased as cell phones are used instead.

How much deregulation does the company expect?

Because they're essential utilities, wireline phone companies are regulated at the state and federal levels.

Does the company expect continuing investments in new equipment?

Because of technological changes, wireline phone companies must make large investments in new equipment.

How might the company benefit from a simplified technical standard for future services?

Switching and routing systems and subscriber equipment for cable, wireless data, and new generation wired communications are being developed to industry standards and can be mixed to provide advanced services.

To what extent has the company switched to IP for phone service?

The industry is converting to Internet protocol (IP) telephony.

Web Links

Conformity Magazine

News about regulatory compliance issues. www.conformity.com

FCC

Regulatory issues. www.fcc.gov

National Exchange Carrier Association

Industry news. www.neca.org

National Telecommunications Cooperative Association

Industry news.
www.ntca.org

Privateline.com

Telecom tutorial.
www.privateline.com/manual/threeA.html

TelecomWeb

News, analysis, and newsletters.
www.telecomweb.com

Telephony Magazine

News, analysis, newsletters, and commentary.
telephonyonline.com

US Telecom Association

Industry news.
www.ustelecom.org

Glossary of Acronyms

B/OSS — business and operational support system
CLEC — competitive local exchange carrier
IP — Internet Protocol
MDF — main distribution frame
PSTN — public switched telephone network
VOIP — Voice over Internet Protocol

HOOVER'S TOP COMPANIES

Largest Companies by Sales	($ mil.)
AT&T Inc.	124,028.0
Verizon Communications Inc.	97,354.0
Qwest Communications International Inc.	13,475.0
Embarq Corporation	6,124.0
Level 3 Communications, Inc.	4,301.0
Windstream Corporation	3,171.5
CenturyTel, Inc.	2,656.2
Frontier Communications Corporation	2,237.0
IDT Corporation	1,878.0
XO Holdings, Inc.	1,428.7

Largest Employers	Employees
AT&T Inc.	310,000
Verizon Communications Inc.	235,000
Qwest Communications International Inc.	32,937
Embarq Corporation	18,000
Windstream Corporation	7,570
Level 3 Communications, Inc.	6,680
CenturyTel, Inc.	6,600
Frontier Communications Corporation	5,900
Cincinnati Bell Inc.	3,100
IDT Corporation	1,850

Fastest Growing* by Five-Year Sales Growth	(%)
Vonage Holdings Corp.	83.3
Terremark Worldwide, Inc.	66.4
Windstream Corporation	58.1
Hungarian Telephone and Cable Corp.	49.1
ATSI Communications, Inc.	43.5
iBasis, Inc.	41.6
Cbeyond, Inc.	39.8
Consolidated Communications Holdings, Inc.	25.9
AT&T Inc.	24.9
inContact, Inc.	4.7

Fastest Growing* by Five-Year Employee Growth	(%)
AT&T Inc.	28.1
Cbeyond, Inc.	26.5
ATSI Communications, Inc.	24.6
Terremark Worldwide, Inc.	23.6
Hungarian Telephone and Cable Corp.	18.6
iBasis, Inc.	13.3
Knology, Inc.	10.3
FairPoint Communications, Inc.	9.9
Deltathree, Inc.	9.0
inContact, Inc.	8.1

Top Public Companies by Market Value	($ mil.)
AT&T Inc.	167,950.8
Verizon Communications Inc.	100,602.0
Qwest Communications International Inc.	6,212.6
Embarq Corporation	5,120.7
Windstream Corporation	4,042.5

* These rates are compounded annualized increases and may have resulted from acquisitions or one time gains. If less than 6 years of data are available, growth is for the years available.

SOURCE: HOOVER'S, INC., DATABASE

Wireless Telecommunications Services

The wireless telecommunications services industry includes about 600 companies with combined annual revenue of over $110 billion. Major companies include the four national wireless carriers: AT&T, Verizon, Sprint Nextel, and T-Mobile USA. The industry is highly concentrated: the four national carriers earn about 85 percent of industry revenue.

Competitive Landscape

Demand for wireless services is driven by consumer income. The profitability of individual companies depends on marketing and technological skill. Large companies have advantages in marketing and in delivering a comprehensive array of services nationally. Small companies can compete effectively by delivering economically attractive service packages tailored to niche groups regionally. The industry is capital intensive: average annual revenue per employee is about $350,000.

Products, Operations & Technology

Major services provided include voice telephony (ordinary cell phone service); messaging (voice, text, image, and video); Internet access; music and video distribution; and ring tone distribution. Voice telephony accounts for about 80 percent of industry revenue, with the remaining 20 percent coming mainly from message and roaming charges.

Cellular communications networks consist of a series of low power base transceiver stations (BTS) interconnected through a regional base station controller (BSC) to a mobile switching center (MSC). The BTS, or cellular tower, consists of a set of antennae mounted on a tall structure or tower with a large two-way radio. The BTS communicates with mobile phones and devices in its geographic area, or cell. The BSC, which controls communications with up to several hundred cellular towers in a geographic area, allocates radio channels to in-

BUSINESS CHALLENGES

» Dependence on Consumer Income

Demand for high-end services, such as video distribution and interactive GPS mapping programs, depends on growth in US personal income. These high-end services are key to profitability for many wireless operators. As personal income stagnates or declines, consumers tend to forgo high-end services and revert to basic voice and text message services.

» Market Saturation

With about 85 percent of the US population already subscribing to wireless services, companies must attract subscribers from other carriers to sustain revenue growth. Competition for subscribers is intense, as nearly all US consumers have at least three wireless carriers to choose from. Companies invest heavily in advertising and promotions to convince consumers to switch to their service and to counter competitive attacks on their own customer base.

» High Expense of Spectrum Auctions

Several blocks of spectrum in the 700 MHz frequency will be auctioned by the FCC for use once UHF stations have converted to digital broadcasts on other frequencies. This spectrum offers superior penetration of buildings and other obstacles, and can cover wider areas than the 1900 to 2400 MHz frequencies currently used. New capabilities and services will encourage competition with existing service providers, particularly since the FCC is setting conditions to encourage small bidders.

dividual mobile phones and controls handovers from one cellular tower to another. The mobile switching center connects calls between network users and is also connected to the wired phone system, the Public Switched Telephone Network (PSTN).

The two main cellular standards in the US are Global System for Mobile (GSM) and Code Division Multiple Access (CDMA). GSM is the standard in Europe. CDMA is slightly more efficient in spectrum usage and has a more advanced methodology for hand-offs between cellular towers. Some older legacy analog systems are being gradually phased out.

Companies with their own cellular communication networks are known as premise-based operators. Companies typically have roaming arrangements with other operators, which permit their customers to use other networks for a fee. Some operators also have wholesale arrangements with non-premise based operators, who resell under their own brand name.

Users of cell services demand high quality services (no dropped calls, no crosstalk between calls); accurate billing; and responsive customer service. To meet these needs, cellular operators frequently survey their operating areas, gaging signal strength and number of users. New base stations are added as needed to maintain operations quality. Most operators have centralized computer systems to collect call records and process billing.

Sales & Marketing

About 95 percent of wireless services sales are directly to end-users and 5 percent to resellers. With about 85 percent of the population subscribing to cell phone services, the market of new subscribers is diminishing rapidly. Companies make heavy use of TV and print advertising, and sell through their own stores or through counters in chains like Best Buy, Wal-Mart, and Radio Shack.

To sustain revenue growth, cellular operators try to attract subscribers from other operators, identify underserved niches in the population, or increase the average revenue per subscriber. Subscriber movement between cellular carriers, called churn, averages about 1.5 to 3 percent of subscribers per month.

The average revenue per user (ARPU) is about $50 per month, and has declined slightly with the addition of family plans and prepaid users. Increasing the average revenue per user depends on offering new fee-based services. Many users upgrade from basic voice to services like Internet access, music and video on-demand, and GPS.

Human Resources

Production workers in the phone industry are technically skilled, and therefore earn above-average wages. Despite substantial revenue growth in the cellular industry, productivity gains and outsourcing have kept employment growth low. The industry has rapidly automated, eliminating large numbers of

operators; workers mainly operate computers or are specialists in equipment installation and maintenance. Some companies outsource operator functions and some customer service to third parties.

Illness and injury rates for the telecommunication industry are less than half the rates for private industry as a whole.

Industry Employment Growth

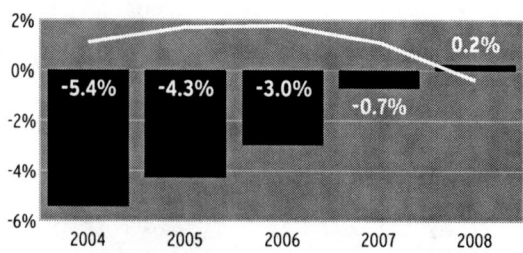

Average Hourly Earnings

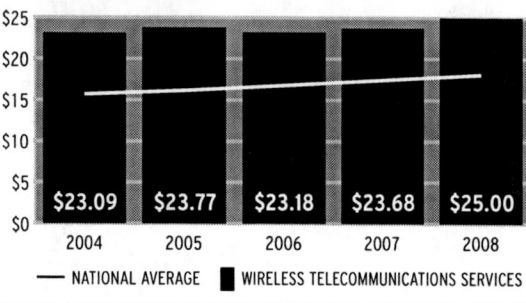

— NATIONAL AVERAGE   ■ WIRELESS TELECOMMUNICATIONS SERVICES

SOURCE: BUREAU OF LABOR STATISTICS

Call Preparation Questions

Is the company seeing an overall increase in demand for high-end services?

Demand for high-end services, such as video distribution and interactive GPS mapping programs, depends on growth in US personal income.

What market segment does the company anticipate will supply future subscriber growth?

With about 85 percent of the US population already subscribing to wireless services, companies must attract subscribers from other carriers to sustain revenue growth.

Will the company be bidding in the 700 MHz spectrum auction?

Several blocks of spectrum in the 700 MHz frequency will be auctioned by the FCC for use once UHF stations have converted to digital broadcasts on other frequencies.

What opportunity does the company see for advertising on mobile devices?

The mobile phone has become the "third screen," after TV and computers.

How is the company reducing customer churn?

Customer turnover (churn) represents a substantial cost for operators.

Web Links

3GNewsroom.com

Third generation telecom technology news.
3gnewsroom.com

CTIA – The Wireless Association

Statistics from wireless telecommunications trade association.
www.ctia.org

FCC Wireless Telecommunications Bureau

Statistics and news about the industry and regulatory matters.
wireless.fcc.gov

TelecomWeb

Wireless Telecom news.
telecomweb.com

Total Telecom

Wireless Telecom news and events.
www.totaltele.com

Unstrung

Online magazine featuring daily news and analysis of wireless technology and events.
www.unstrung.com

Wireless Week

Trade magazine with daily news of the wireless industry.
www.wirelessweek.com

Glossary of Acronyms

ARPU — average revenue per user
BSC — base station controller
BTS — base transceiver station
CDMA — code division multiple access
CMA — cellular market area
GSM — global system for mobile
MSA — metropolitan statistical area
MSC — mobile switching center
OSS — operational support subsystem
PSTN — public switched telephone network
RSA — rural statistical area

HOOVER'S TOP COMPANIES

Largest Companies by Sales	($ mil.)
AT&T Inc.	124,028.0
Cellco Partnership (Verizon Wireless)	43,900.0
Sprint Nextel Corporation	35,635.0
Alltel Corporation	8,803.1
Telephone and Data Systems, Inc.	4,829.0
NII Holdings, Inc.	4,269.4
United States Cellular Corporation	4,243.2
MetroPCS Communications, Inc.	2,751.5
Leap Wireless International, Inc.	1,958.9
T-Mobile USA, Inc.	—

Largest Employers	Employees
AT&T Inc.	310,000
Cellco Partnership (Verizon Wireless)	69,000
Sprint Nextel Corporation	56.000
T-Mobile USA, Inc.	29,000
Alltel Corporation	16,104
Telephone and Data Systems, Inc.	11,800
NII Holdings, Inc.	9,873
United States Cellular Corporation	8,400
Centennial Communications Corp.	3,100
MetroPCS Communications, Inc.	2,498

Fastest Growing* by Five-Year Sales Growth	(%)
FiberTower Corporation	245.5
FTS Group, Inc.	189.3
MetroPCS Communications, Inc.	43.0
NII Holdings, Inc.	35.4
AT&T Inc.	24.9
iPCS, Inc.	21.2
Leap Wireless International, Inc.	21.1
Atlantic Tele-Network, Inc.	20.1
Cellco Partnership (Verizon Wireless)	17.9
Virgin Mobile USA, Inc.	17.7

Fastest Growing* by Five-Year Employee Growth	(%)
FiberTower Corporation	176.1
iPCS, Inc.	66.2
MetroPCS Communications, Inc.	34.7
GoAmerica, Inc.	31.0
NII Holdings, Inc.	28.1
AT&T Inc.	28.1
Leap Wireless International, Inc.	26.9
Teletouch Communications, Inc.	25.0
Syniverse Holdings, Inc.	19.0

Top Public Companies by Market Value	($ mil.)
AT&T Inc.	167,950.8
Sprint Nextel Corporation	5,228.3
MetroPCS Communications, Inc.	5,211.1
NII Holdings, Inc.	3,013.9
United States Cellular Corporation	2,346.8

* These rates are compounded annualized increases and may have resulted from acquisitions or one time gains. If less than 6 years of data are available, growth is for the years available.

SOURCE: HOOVER'S, INC., DATABASE

Wood Flooring Manufacture

The US hardwood flooring industry includes fewer than 100 manufacturers, with combined annual revenue of about $1.5 billion. Flooring is still dominated by small independents, but the industry continues to consolidate. There are thousands of distributors and installers. Annual production varies considerably, but is on the order of 500 million board feet (mmbf).

Competitive Landscape

Demand for wood flooring is closely tied to residential real estate construction, both new and remodeling. The industry is highly competitive because the product is largely a commodity. Small manufacturers typically sell their product within a local region. Competition comes from other manufacturers and competing flooring products like carpeting, linoleum, tiles, etc.

Products, Operations & Technology

Wood flooring is milled from hardwoods, principally oak (which accounts for about 70 percent of the market) but also maple, ash, beech, birch, pecan, walnut, hickory, and others. Most flooring is used in residential and commercial buildings, but about 10 percent of production (mainly glued, laminated material) is used in truck trailers and railroad cars. Wood flooring comes in three main shapes: strips, planks, and parquet. Strips account for 80 percent of the market; vary in thickness from 3/8 inch to 3/4 inch; in width from 1 1/2 to 3 1/2 inches; and are 2 to 3 feet long. Planks are 3/4 inches thick and 3 to 8 inches wide. Strips, planks, and parquet are milled so that one side has a tongue, the other a groove, allowing a tight fit when installed.

The production process involves drying boards of wood in kilns until the wood's moisture content (MC) is reduced to a range of 6 to 9 percent. Pieces are then cut from boards and the sides milled to produce the tongue and groove.

BUSINESS CHALLENGES

» Changing Lumber Prices

Prices for hardwood lumber and finished wood flooring, a minimally processed product, don't move in tandem. Manufacturers often can't pass lumber price increases to consumers because alternative flooring is readily available. Hardwood lumber prices can change 10 percent within a year.

» Demand Linked to Residential Construction

Since most wood flooring is installed in residential buildings, demand depends almost entirely on the volume of new home construction and renovation. Hardwood Floors reports that 70 percent of flooring demand is due to remodeling, 30 percent to new construction.

» Competition from Alternative Products

Rather than spend $15 per square foot to install traditional oak flooring, consumers can install vinyl flooring with a wood pattern for $2 per square foot. Engineered wood floors cost from $7 to $11 per square foot unfinished; prefinished versions cost about $1 more. Laminate flooring, a plastic substitute that can be "floated" over a concrete floor on a thin foam pad, costs from $8 to $15 per square foot.

The angle of cut partly determines the wood's final appearance: "plainsawn" (the most common); "quartersawn;" or "riftsawn." After the wood is cut, it's given one of four grades for appearance: for oak, "clear," "select," "No. 1 common," and "No. 2 common," which describe the amount of variation produced by knots and color differences; for maple, beech, birch, and most other woods, "first," "second," and "third." After manufacture, the wood is sorted, packed in ready-to-sell bundles, and shipped in pallet loads of about 1,000 board feet.

A typical manufacturer is a sawmill operator who also operates a dry kiln facility and flooring manufacturing plant. Some manufacturers buy rough lumber on the open market. Because of the simple nature of the manufacturing process, most production is highly automated.

Most flooring leaves the manufacturer unfinished, to be sanded and coated with a finish after installation, but some is also prefinished at the factory. Finishes include penetrating stains and waxes that soak into the wood, and surface finishes, blends of synthetic resins (usually urethanes and polyurethanes). Installing hardwood floors requires preparing a subsurface (usually plywood or closely spaced joists). As strips or planks are fitted together, they are nailed to the subsurface with special nail guns. After the flooring is laid, it is lightly sanded and coated with several layers of finish.

Engineered laminated flooring consists of thin layers of wood glued together, with alternating grain direction. The top layer is a finishing veneer. Engineered flooring is kiln-dried to a MC of 5 to 11 percent and produced as both unfinished and prefinished. Acrylic impregnated flooring is produced in various colors and finishes by forcing acrylic into the pores of the wood at high pressure to produce a very hard surface suitable for heavily used commercial areas.

Sales & Marketing

Manufacturers sell to distributors or directly to independent lumber yards, construction companies, and national chains like Home Depot. Marketing is mainly through personal contact with potential buyers; sales are largely based on price. Producers generally hold large inventories, partly because wood must be kiln-dried before processing and the finished product is essentially a commodity that can be stockpiled for later sale. Warehouses must be climate-controlled to maintain proper humidity.

Oak is the most popular wood flooring due to it hardness, low cost, appearance, and wide availability. Hardwood Floors reports that red oak accounts for about half of distributor sales, white oak a fifth, and maple a tenth.

Human Resources

Wood flooring manufacturing jobs don't require special skills, and accordingly are low paid. The average wood flooring manufacturing job pays just under $13 an hour, compared to the approximately $17 hourly wage of all other manufacturing employees. The injury rate among wood flooring manufacturing employees is almost double the national average.

Call Preparation Questions

How does the company manage fluctuations in raw material prices?

Prices for hardwood lumber and finished wood flooring, a minimally processed product, don't move in tandem.

How does the company protect itself from changes in construction demand for wood products?

Since most wood flooring is installed in residential buildings, demand depends almost entirely on the volume of new home construction and renovation.

How does the company address competition from alternative floor coverings?

Rather than spend $15 per square foot to install traditional oak flooring, consumers can install vinyl flooring with a wood pattern for $2 per square foot.

How has the company's market changed due to new wood flooring products?

Engineered wood flooring and more durable surfaces, like acrylic impregnated wood, have extended the uses of wood flooring, both for residential applications that were impossible with solid wood products, and commercial applications where heavy traffic formerly precluded the use of wood.

How do home fashion trends affect the company's product offerings and sales?

Combining exotic woods, like maple, cherry, and birch, to make custom borders is gaining popularity, with more than a dozen manufacturers producing them.

Web Links

Hardwood Floors Magazine

News and resources.
www.nwfa.org/member/mag.aspx

Maple Flooring Manufacturers Association

Source of technical and general information on
maple sports flooring with a membership of
manufacturing mills, installation contractors,
distributors, and allied product manufacturers.
www.maplefloor.org

National Floor Trends

Industry news.
www.ntlfloortrends.com

National Hardwood Lumber Association

Technical literature.
www.natlhardwood.org

National Wood Flooring Association

Technical information. Good links.
www.woodfloors.org

The Hardwood Council

FAQs, species guide, and links.
www.hardwoodcouncil.com

The Wood Flooring Manufacturers Association

Grading standards. Technical information.
www.nofma.org

Wood Floors Online

Directories, links, and listings.
www.woodfloorsonline.com

Glossary of Acronyms

ACAH — American Consumers for Affordable Homes
ENR — Engineering News-Record
MBF — thousand board feet
MMBF — million board feet
MC — moisture content
NALFA — North American Laminate Flooring
Association
RMI — Remodeling Market Index
WFMA — Wood Flooring Manufacturers Association
WWPA — Western Wood Products Association

Handbook of
Industry Profiles 2009

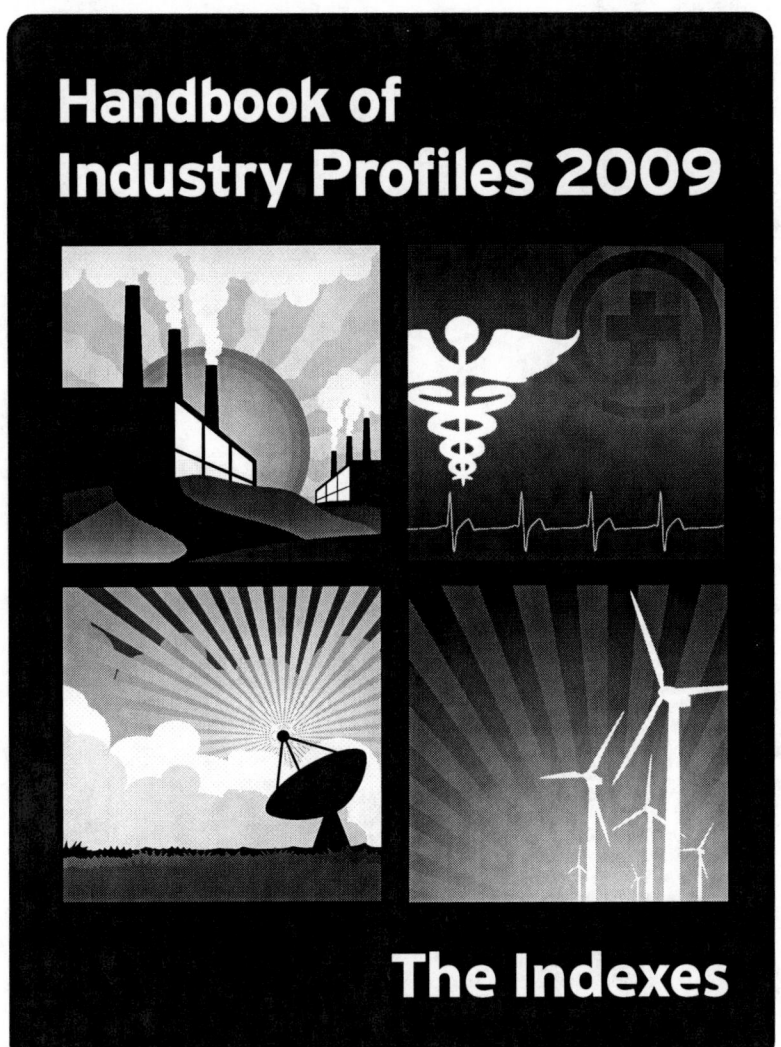

The Indexes

Index of Industries by Sector

Index of Hoover's Top Companies